THE MOTION PICTURE ANNUAL

S0-ACM-342

1990

CineBooks

This book is available at special quantity discounts for bulk purchases for sales promotions, premiums or fund-raising. Special books or excerpts can also be created to fit specific needs. Write: Sales Department, CineBooks, 990 Grove Street, Evanston, Illinois 60201.

Published by CineBooks, a division of News America Publishing Incorporated

Editorial & Sales Offices
CINEBOOKS
990 Grove Street
Evanston, Illinois 60201

Copyright 1990, News America Publishing Incorporated

All rights reserved; no part of this book or subsequent volumes of THE MOTION PICTURE GUIDE may be reproduced or utilized in any form or means, electronic or mechanical, including photocopying, recording, or by any information retrieval system, without permission in writing from CINEBOOKS, 990 Grove Street, Evanston, Illinois 60201.

ISBN: 0-933997-28-0

Printed in the United States

First Edition

1   2   3   4   5   6   7   8   9   10

TABLE OF CONTENTS

INTRODUCTION

The 1990 Motion Picture Annual is the third review of the US film year produced by CineBooks. This Annual includes entries on 330 films released theatrically or straight-to-video in the US in 1989. In addition, the volume features profiles of 16 rising stars in the industry, obituaries for 80 industry veterans who passed away in 1989, a listing of the major film awards presented to last year's releases.

In response to reader requests, we have attempted to make the annual more graphically appealing. We have increased the size of the type as well as the size of the photos. In addition, we have added a "Review Attribution" section identifying the authors of each review.

With *The 1990 Motion Picture Annual*, it is CineBooks' goal to provide an extensive survey of the 1989 film year in the United States. In chronicling nearly every picture released in the US this past year (as well as scores of straight-to-video releases), we have attempted to provide a valuable reference source covering the films of 1989. While every effort has been made to provide as much information about each film as possible, sources listing cast and credits, running times, and other information often conflict. CineBooks has made a concerted effort to assure the reliability of our information. Mistakes inevitably will be made, and we apologize for any that may have slipped past us.

As always, we welcome your comments about the Annual.

The Year in Review

It could have been dubbed The Year of the Bat. BATMAN, which grossed over $250 million, led the pack of box office hits in a recordbreaking year. For the first time in history, domestic box office reached the incredible mark of $5 billion, and eight movies passed or neared the $100 million gross mark. Financially, if not artistically, it was truly an amazing year at the movies.

In addition to BATMAN (which broke opening weekend records and dominated the summer box office for months), there were other blockbusters that more than held their own. Sequels were once again prevalent with the successful showings of INDIANA JONES AND THE LAST CRUSADE (the year's second biggest hit), LETHAL WEAPON 2, BACK TO THE FUTURE, PART II (which also scored big over its opening three days), GHOSTBUSTERS II (which opened strong but dropped off considerably), and NATIONAL LAMPOON'S CHRISTMAS VACATION. But for every successful sequel, there were five unsuccessful ones, and in most cases it was for good reason. Titles such as THE FLY II, THE KARATE KID PART III, FLETCH LIVES and FRIGHT NIGHT II did fair to poor business. Even the normally reliable series-films had their share of problems, with tepid showings from NIGHTMARE ON ELM STREET 5: THE DREAM CHILD, FRIDAY THE 13th PART VIII: JASON TAKES MANHATTAN, HALLOWEEN 5 and STAR TREK 5: THE FINAL FRONTIER (which was mercilessly lambasted by most critics).

Generally films aimed at the family or those offering "sweet" messages did very well in 1989. Walt Disney's HONEY I SHRUNK THE KIDS was the year's surprise big hit while THE BEAR and LOOK WHO'S TALKING also scored well. FIELD OF DREAMS (which was notorious for turning strong men into blubbering babies) did extremely well both financially and

critically. Rounding out this category of sweetness were PARENTHOOD, UNCLE BUCK, STEEL MAGNOLIAS and the Academy Award winning DRIVING MISS DAISY, all of which made major profits. At the other end of the spectrum were several dark comedies which were much less successful. These included films such as THE WAR OF THE ROSES, PENN AND TELLER GET KILLED, THE 'BURBS, WEEKEND AT BERNIE'S and the terrific HEATHERS.

As dark and unusual as some of these movies were, they weren't (with the exception of PENN AND TELLER GET KILLED and HEATHERS) as brave as the work of the independent filmmakers of 1989. Spike Lee made what was easily the most important film of the year in DO THE RIGHT THING. The film stirred controversy as some thought it was the best film of the year, while others thought it was a whitewashed version of reality that promoted violence. But whatever the opinion, it remains the boldest film of the year (and of course it was snubbed by the Academy Awards). Other independent films worth mentioning are Gus Van Zant's fantastic DRUGSTORE COWBOY, Steven Soderbergh's SEX,LIES AND VIDEOTAPE and the most impressive independent film in years, John McNaughton's stunning HENRY, PORTRAIT OF A SERIAL KILLER.

There were also a number of comebacks in 1989. John Travolta came back strong in LOOK WHO'S TALKING, Al Pacino hit gold with SEA OF LOVE, Richard Pryor and Gene Wilder made good in SEE NO EVIL, HEAR NO EVIL and, to some extent, Sylvester Stallone came back by starring in a film that actually made a profit—TANGO AND CASH. There were also a share of surprise bombs, the highly touted GREAT BALLS OF FIRE became Dennis Quaid's latest flop and Patrick Swayze followed his phenomenal success in DIRTY DANCING with a rabid exercise in machismo called ROADHOUSE. Eddie Murphy's misogynist ego trip, HARLEM NIGHTS proved he too can make an unsuccessful film. Paul Newman struck out twice in 1989 with FAT MAN AND LITTLE BOY and BLAZE, as did Tom Selleck with AN INNOCENT MAN and HER ALIBI. Another two-time loser was director Susan Siedelman, whose COOKIE and SHE-DEVIL combined didn't reach the $7 million mark. Steven Spielberg didn't crack any box office records with ALWAYS, though many felt it was his best film in years. Although critically acclaimed, Terry Gilliam's THE ADVENTURES OF BARON MUNCHAUSEN also flopped.

Of course the end of 1989 brought serious films such as BORN ON THE FOURTH OF JULY (which earned Oliver Stone his second Best Director Oscar), GLORY, and ENEMIES: A LOVE STORY and MY LEFT FOOT, all of which scored well with critics.

On the international scene, in addition to THE BEAR, the French film CAMILLE CLAUDEL did reasonably well, while the revival of the British film industry continued as that country offered notable films such as DISTANT VOICES, STILL LIVES, SCANDAL, HENRY V and HIGH HOPES. One of the most impressive international releases, however, was from Australia—Jane Campion's SWEETIE.

With box office records, blockbuster hits, a little controversy, and whole bunch of sequels, 1989 was fairly typical of the 1980s, and perhaps a strong indication of what the 1990s will bring.

THE MOTION PICTURE ANNUAL

1990

The Year's Best

♥DO THE RIGHT THING

120m 40 Acres And A Mule
Filmworks/UNIV c

CAST:
Danny Aiello *(Sal)*, Ossie Davis *(Da Mayor)*, Ruby Dee *(Mother Sister)*, Richard Edson *(Vito)*, Giancarlo Esposito *(Buggin Out)*, Spike Lee *(Mookie)*, Bill Nunn *(Radio Raheem)*, John Turturro *(Pino)*, Paul Benjamin *(ML)*, Frankie Faison *(Coconut Sid)*, Robin Harris *(Sweet Dick Willie)*, Joie Lee *(Jade)*, Miguel Sandoval *(Officer Ponte)*, Rick Aiello *(Officer Long)*, John Savage *(Clifton)*, Sam Jackson *(Mister Senor Love Daddy)*, Rosie Perez *(Tina)*, Roger Guenveur Smith *(Smiley)*, Steve White *(Ahmad)*, Martin Lawrence *(Cee)*, Leonard Thomas *(Punchy)*, Christa Rivers *(Ella)*, Frank Vincent *(Charlie)*, Luis Ramos *(Stevie)*, Richard Habersham *(Eddie)*, Gwen McGee *(Louise)*, Steve Park *(Sonny)*, Ginny Yang *(Kim)*, Sherwin Park *(Korean Child)*, Shawn Elliott *(Puerto Rican Ice Man)*, Diva Osorio *(Carmen)*.

PRODUCTION CREDITS:
p, Spike Lee and Monty Ross; d, Spike Lee; w, Spike Lee; ph, Ernest Dickerson Duart Color; ed, Barry Alexander Brown; m, Bill Lee; prod d, Wynn Thomas; set d, Steve Rosse; spec eff, Steve Kirshoff; cos, Ruth Carter; chor, Rosie Perez; stunts, Eddie Smith; makeup, Matiki Anoff.

BATMAN may have cornered the market on hype, GHOSTBUSTERS II may have made more money, but the thinking person's must-see movie in the summer of 1989 was Spike Lee's DO THE RIGHT THING. Released nationwide in June, but debated for weeks in advance, DO THE RIGHT THING was variously hailed as the most insightful view of race relations ever to hit US screens or condemned as dangerous agitprop, but its timeliness and ability to strike nerves were never in question.

The story is set in Brooklyn's predominantly black and Latino Bedford-Stuyvesant. The local eatery, Sal's Famous Pizzeria, is owned and managed by the Italian American Sal (Aiello), and his sons, Vito (Edson) and Pino (Turturro). Also working at Sal's is Mookie (writer-director Lee), the deliveryman, who lives with and mooches off his sister, Jade (Joie Lee, the director's real-life sister). As the hottest day of the year gets underway at Sal's, local activist Buggin Out (Esposito) stops in for a slice of pizza, and unhappily notices that there aren't any black faces on Sal's "Wall of Fame" (which has photos of Robert De Niro, Al Pacino, Frank Sinatra, etc.). This apparently trivial incident eventually sparks the explosion with which DO THE RIGHT THING ends. Buggin Out spends the rest of the day trying to organize a local

Spike Lee and Danny Aiello in DO THE RIGHT THING (©Universal).

boycott of the pizzeria. Meanwhile, the film presents a rich and colorful variety of local figures, mostly by following Mookie around on his deliveries. Buggin Out is joined in his crusade by the retarded Smiley (Smith), and Radio Raheem (Nunn), a *big* man with a *big* boom box with which he roams the area, blasting Public Enemy's "Fight the Power." As Sal's is about to close for the night, Radio Raheem shows up in confrontational mood, blasting Public Enemy, and demanding service. Sal, at the end of his rope, calls Raheem a "nigger" and smashes his radio. A fight breaks out, and the police arrive, accidentally killing Raheem, and beating Buggin Out in the back of the squad car. From the enraged crowd surrounding Raheem's body, Mookie steps forward and throws a garbage can through Sal's window, setting off a riot in which Sal's is trashed, looted, and set on fire. The following day, Mookie returns to the scene to pick up his pay. Sal tosses the money on the ground in anger at what he views as Mookie's betrayal. Before the credits roll, Lee offers two quotations: the first from Martin Luther King, preaching nonviolence, the second from Malcolm X, arguing that violence may be an oppressed people's only form of self-defense.

Writer-director-producer Lee's film is marked by a dialectical approach, both in content and style, representing a giant step forward from his first two films, SHE'S GOTTA HAVE IT and SCHOOL DAZE. DO THE RIGHT THING presents a society in crisis, a crisis both immediate and historical in nature. To Buggin Out, Sal's wall represents a historical distortion: the lie that black people's contributions to our society don't rate commemoration. Lee's structure also reflects the disjunction between the historical and the immediate moment: the "episodic" plot reveals the nature of its construction only at the end,

when it becomes clear how inexorably all the apparently minor incidents in Lee's script have led to the concluding violent impasse. As the film proceeds, random events accrete with the weight of history, forcing characters to react, and making the definition of the right thing all the more grave and perplexing.

Caught in the middle of all this is Mookie, a young black man in a dead-end job, who can't begin to support his infant son and apparently doesn't care. He's also intelligent, easy-going, and (with Jade) the black character who comes closest to bridging the gap between black and white. Sal and Mookie are both basically well meaning, although their differing notions of what constitutes the right thing finally makes dialog between them impossible.

Dedicated to the families of six blacks who died under controversial circumstances recently in New York (including Michael Griffith, whose death in Howard Beach is said to have inspired Lee's script) and released by Lee with the admitted intention of affecting the New York City mayor's race, DO THE RIGHT THING couldn't be more timely. Because its view of race relations strikes such a sensitive nerve, focuses on such a critical issue, and has directed so much attention to the crisis it depicts without sacrificing aesthetic complexity, DO THE RIGHT THING can fairly be labelled—for now—the most important American film of 1989. Whether it retains this status in 2009 seems almost beside the point. Songs include: "Fight the Power" (Carlton Ridenhour, Hank Shocklee, Eric Sadler, Keith Shocklee, performed by Public Enemy), "Don't Shoot Me" (Spike Lee, Mervyn Warren, Claude McKnight, David Thomas, performed by Take 6), "Can't Stand It" (David Hines, performed by Steel Pulse), "Tu Y Yo" (Ruben Blades, performed by Blades), "Why Don't We Try"

(Raymond Jones, Larry DeCarmine, Vincent Morris, performed by Keith John), "Hard to Say" (Jones, performed by Lorri Perry and Gerald Alston), "Party Hearty" (William "Ju Ju" House, Kent Wood, performed by EU), "Prove to Me" (Jones, Sami McKinney, performed by Perri), "Feel So Good" (McKinney, Perry, Michael O'Hara, performed by Perri), "My Fantasy" (Teddy Riley, performed by Riley and Guy), "Never Explain Love" (Jones, Cathy Block, performed by Al Jarreau), "We Love Radio Jingles" (performed by Take 6), "Lift Every Voice and Sing" (James Weldon Johnson, John Rosemond Johnson, performed by the Natural Spiritual Orchestra). *(Violence, excessive profanity, sexual situations, adult situations, nudity, substance abuse.)*

Comedy/Drama   (PR:O MPAA:R)

DRIVING MISS DAISY

99m Zanuck/WB c

CAST:

Jessica Tandy *(Miss Daisy Werthan)*, Morgan Freeman *(Hoke Colburn)*, Dan Aykroyd *(Boolie Werthan)*, Patti LuPone *(Florine Werthan)*, Esther Rolle *(Idella)*, Joann Havrilla *(Miss McClatchey)*, William Hall Jr. *(Oscar)*, Alvin M. Sugarman *(Dr. Weil)*, Clarice F. Geigerman *(Nonie)*, Muriel Moore *(Miriam)*, Sylvia Kaler *(Beulah)*, Carolyn Gold *(Neighbor Lady)*, Crystal R. Fox *(Katie Bell)*, Bob Hannah *(Red Mitchell)*, Ray McKinnon, Ashley Josey *(Troopers)*, Jack Rousso *(Slick)*, Fred Faser *(Insurance Agent)*, Indra A. Thomas *(Soloist)*.

PRODUCTION CREDITS:

p, Richard D. Zanuck and Lili Fini Zanuck; d, Bruce Beresford; w, Alfred Uhry based on his play; ph, Peter James; ed, Mark Warner; m, Hans Zimmer; prod d, Bruno Rubeo; art d, Victor Kempster; set d, Crispian Sallis; spec eff, Bob Shelley; cos, Elizabeth McBride; makeup, Manlio Rocchetti.

In DRIVING MISS DAISY, Australian director Bruce Beresford (BREAKER MORANT; TENDER MERCIES) successfully translates playwright-screenwriter Alfred Uhry's loosely autobiographical, Pulitzer Prize-winning play of the same name to the screen. The simple but compelling story opens in 1948, when Miss Daisy (Tandy), a wealthy, 72-year-old southern Jewish matron who lives in quiet dignity, accidentally backs her Packard into her neighbor's prized garden. Miss Daisy's already frustrated son, Boolie (Aykroyd), insists that his mother hire a chauffeur. Reluctantly, she accepts the services of the African-American Hoke (Freeman), thus beginning a friendship that blossoms over the next quarter century until, in her mid-90s, after many years of really getting to know and appreciate Hoke, the eccentric Miss Daisy at last concedes that the respectful yet forceful driver is indeed her very best friend.

Set in a small community near Atlanta, DRIVING MISS DAISY covers 25 years (1948-73) in a changing South, and the manner in which the momentous and turbulent events of the civil rights movement affect Hoke and Daisy personally is the film's true subject. Directed and written with unique simplicity and clarity (and with a refreshing lack of soundtrack noise, violence, and sexual titillation), DRIVING MISS DAISY is clearly a labor of love: a simple (but never simplistic), straightforward, honest, and dignified depiction of decent human beings who must live their everyday lives amid the turmoil of recent historical events. DRIVING MISS DAISY conveys a memorable integrity, not only in the well-realized characters and relationships provided by the script, but in the sensitivity with which Beresford and his players invest each thoughtfully presented scene.

Chief among the film's rewards are its trio of stars, Morgan Freeman, Jessica Tandy, and Dan Aykroyd. Freeman, delivering yet another faultless performance, gives Hoke just the right proportions of sincerity, toughness, humility, sense of irony, and innate dignity. Tandy is equally brilliant as the title character, who never fully comprehends the racial intolerance behind the bombing of the Jewish Temple in Atlanta or other expressions of anti-Semitism (unlike Hoke, who has come to grips with his victimization by racism). As played by Freeman and Tandy, Hoke and Miss Daisy make a fascinating and touching odd couple.

Aykroyd, hitherto a specialist in cinematic sight gags, one-liners, and comic caricatures, reveals himself to be a fine actor in the role of Daisy's son, giving depth and compassion to the exasperated Boolie. Lending fine support are Broadway star Patti LuPone (as Aykroyd's nouveau riche, social-climbing wife, conscious only of the latest fads and how best to keep up with the Joneses) and Esther Rolle (the matriarch in TV's "Good Times") as Idella, Miss Daisy's sharp-tongued but devoted housekeeper. Also deserving of high praise are Elizabeth McBride's costume design, Peter James' cinematography, Bruno Rubeo's production design, Mark Warner's editing, and Hans Zimmer's heartfelt score. Musical selections include: "After the Ball" (Charles K. Harris), "I Love You (for Sentimental Reasons)" (Deek Watson, Derek Best, performed by Ella Fitzgerald), "Jingle Bells" (performed by Les Peel), "Kiss of Fire" (Lester Allen, Robert Hill, performed by Louis Armstrong), "Santa Baby" (Tony Springer, Phil Spring, Joann Jarvitz, performed by Eartha Kitt), "Song to the Moon," from *Rusalka* (Antonin Dvorak, performed by Gabriel Benackova and the Czech Philharmonic), "What a Friend We Have in Jesus" (performed by the Little Friendship Missionary Baptist Church Choir). *(Profanity, adult situations.)*

Jessica Tandy and Morgan Freeman in DRIVING MISS DAISY (©Warner Bros.).

Comedy/Drama   (PR:A MPAA:PG)

DRUGSTORE COWBOY

100m Avenue c

CAST:
Matt Dillon *(Bob)*, Kelly Lynch *(Dianne)*, James Le Gros *(Rick)*, Heather Graham *(Nadine)*, James Remar *(Gentry)*, William S. Burroughs *(Tom the Priest)*, Grace Zabriskie *(Bob's Mother)*, Max Perlich *(David)*, Beah Richards *(Drug Counselor)*.

PRODUCTION CREDITS:
p, Nick Wechsler and Karen Murphy; d, Gus Van Sant Jr.; w, Gus Van Sant Jr. and Daniel Yost based on a novel by James Fogle; ph, Robert Yeoman Alpha Cine, Deluxe Color; ed, Curtiss Clayton; m, Elliot Goldenthal; prod d, David Brisbin; art d, Eve Cauley; cos, Beatrix Aruna Pasztor.

A darkly funny, stylish, and realistic look at the world of drug addiction in 1971, DRUGSTORE COWBOY stars Dillon as the leader of a bedraggled quartet of addicts who get what they need by robbing drugstore pharmacy departments in the Pacific Northwest. His crew consists of his wife, Lynch, and their "kids": Dillon's sluggish lieutenant, Le Gros, and Le Gros' underage girl friend, Graham. After one particularly fruitful heist, Dillon devises a scheme whereby they can all stay constantly high, at least for a while, by sending their stash of drugs ahead of them via Greyhound bus as they migrate through the region, fleeing Remar, a cop bent on nailing Dillon. Exasperated, Dillon takes an elaborately cruel revenge on the cops that provides the film's comic showpiece, but his euphoria is shattered when Graham dies from an overdose. Beset by the law and wearied by his endless efforts to stay high, Dillon decides to go straight—a resolution met with horrified incomprehension by Lynch—and becomes, in his own words, "a regular guy, with a regular room and a regular job (as a drill press operator)." Temptation is still present, however; a defrocked, junkie priest (Burroughs) lives in Dillon's boarding house, and Lynch turns up again with a cache of drugs. Dillon's rehabilitation is especially tested on one particularly harrowing, life-threatening night, but by the end of the film one feels that he will somehow pull through.

Gus Van Sant's previous (and first) feature, MALA NOCHE, won the Los Angeles Critics Award for best independent film of 1987, and his direction here is supremely confident, fusing witty camerawork, neat editing, and a jazz-oriented score to make DRUGSTORE COWBOY an exhilaratingly bumpy ride. Written by Van Sant and Daniel Yost and based on an unpublished novel by James Fogle (who is presently serving a prison sentence for pharmaceutical robberies),

DRUGSTORE COWBOY presents a rare insider's view of the drug lifestyle that is all the more refreshing for its lack of facile moralizing or apologies. Starting from the premise that drug abuse occurs because people *like* getting high, a rather radical stance in these times of "war on drugs," it's a true comedy of desperation. Struck by how droll and affecting these lost characters are, one doesn't question their motivation·so much as immerse oneself in the grungy, lovingly detailed process of their quest for the ultimate altered state.

After many photogenic but empty roles, Matt Dillon is a wonder here, portraying his antihero with an empathy that recalls Cagney, Brando, Dean, and DeNiro. Dillon's Bob is a born hustler, with a quick, ingenuous smile for the old ladies and a charisma that makes him a natural leader of his band of outsiders. Few actors—or films—have been so good at expressing the state of being high: Dillon handles tricky, opiated lines like "the whole world sympathized, and took on a soft, lofty affability" with a beatific ease, while cinematographer Robert Yeoman's beautifully subjective, hallucinogenic images complement his euphoric observations. Dillon gets across Bob's glee in inventing strategies to procure drugs or thwart his adversaries, as well as the deadpan, TV-trained wit that invests his "Honey, I'm home" after a strenuous, bloody attempt to take down an entire hospital. In later scenes, Dillon manages to convey an effectively opaque, resolute sincerity and the detached control common to enforced sobriety, and his timing is uncannily right when, in the picture's best line, he tells a counselor that people use drugs to relieve the pressures of their everyday life—"like having to tie their shoes."

Dillon is ably supported by the tall, lithe Kelly Lynch, who makes a very elegant, unrepentant junkie. Clad in the appalling fashions of the period, with a copy of *Love Story* never far from reach, she's both amusing and compelling as she recounts the portentous tale of her dog or tries to entice her drugged-out husband with Jackie DeShannon's "Put a Little Love in Your Heart" playing in the background. (The film's score is extremely savvy.) James Le Gros makes his Rick a touchingly doltish stooge for Dillon's Bob, while Heather Graham is appropriately juicy as an eager member of the "Just Say Yes" generation. James Remar, Max Perlich, and Grace Zabriskie (as Bob's jaded mother) are all just right in their roles, while William Burroughs—as much of an icon for a hip generation as Dillon—provides the film's final elegiac note when he predicts that "in the near future" the right wing will "demonize" and "scapegoat" drugs and users to set

up a police state, because "the idea that anyone can use drugs and escape a horrible fate is anathema" to them.

Burroughs wrote those lines for his role, keeping in step with DRUGSTORE COWBOY's refusal to condemn its characters for their drug use, an unpopular approach in Hollywood these days. In fact, the film's producers at Avenue Pictures (which picked up Van Sant's film after it had been rejected by some 50 backers) anticipated that DRUGSTORE COWBOY might receive an X rating for its explicit depiction of drug paraphernalia and use. Luckily, their fears proved wrong, allowing this honest, genuinely independent film to reach the broad audience it deserves. *(Violence, profanity, substance abuse, adult situations.)*

Drama   **(PR:O   MPAA:R)**

Matt Dillon in DRUGSTORE COWBOY (ⒸAvenue).

GLORY

Denzel Washington and Morgan Freeman in GLORY (©Tri-Star).

122m Tri-Star c

CAST:

Matthew Broderick *(Col. Robert Gould Shaw)*, Denzel Washington *(Trip)*, Cary Elwes *(Cabot Forbes)*, Morgan Freeman *(John Rawlins)*, Jihmi Kennedy *(Sharts)*, Andre Braugher *(Searles)*, John Finn *(Sgt. Mulcahy)*, Donovan Leitch *(Morse)*, John David Cullum *(Russell)*, Alan North *(Gov. Andrew)*, Bob Gunton *(Gen. Harker)*, Cliff DeYoung *(Col. Montgomery)*, Christian Baskous *(Pierce)*, RonReaco Lee *(Mute Drummer Boy)*, Jay O. Sanders *(Gen. Strong)*, Raymond St. Jacques *(Frederick Douglass)*, Jane Alexander *(Shaw's Mother)*, Richard Riehle *(Quartermaster)*, Daniel Jenkins *("A" Company Officer)*, Michael Smith Guess, Abdul Salaam El Razzac *("A" Company Soldiers)*, Peter Michael Goetz *(Francis Shaw)*, Pete Munro *(Surgeon)*, Benji Wilhoite *(Young Soldier)*, Ethan Phillips *(Hospital Steward)*, Mark A. Levy *(Bigoted Soldier)*, Randell Haynes *(Paymaster)*, Afemo Omilami *(Tall Contraband)*, Keith Noble *(Short Contraband)*, Dan Biggers *(Minister)*, Marc Gowan *(Dr. Rogers)*, Raymond Godshall Jr. *(Dr. Thorpe)*, Bob Minor *(Contraband Soldier)*, Joan Riordan *(White Woman)*, Saundra Franks *(Black Woman)*, Mark A. Jones *(54th Soldier)*, Peter Grandfirld, Mark Margolis, Paul Desmond, Tom Barrington, Michael Fowler, Kevin Jarre, Richard Wright *(10th Conn. Soldiers)*.

PRODUCTION CREDITS:

p, Freddie Fields; d, Edward Zwick; w, Kevin Jarre based on the books *Lay This Laurel* by Lincoln Kirstein, *One Gallant Rush* by Peter Burchard and the letters of Robert Gould Shaw; ph, Freddie Francis Technicolor; ed, Steven Rosenblum; m, James Horner; prod d, Norman Garwood; art d, Keith Pain and Dan Webster; set d, Garrett Lewis; spec eff, Phil Cory; cos, Francine Jamison-Tanchuck; stunts, Bob Minor; makeup, Carl Fullerton.

Mercifully unsentimental but deeply moving, GLORY tells the true (and hitherto shamefully uncelebrated) story of a Union regiment of black soldiers in the Civil War. In the process, the film provides what is undoubtedly the most authentic portrayal of the conflict that killed 700,000 Americans (more than 37,000 of them black), comprising more than half the total American dead in all US wars.

GLORY focuses on the 54th Regiment of Massachusetts Volunteer Infantry, the first unit of black troops raised by the Union, which fought under the command of Col. Robert Shaw. As the film opens, Shaw (Broderick), the son of abolitionist Boston Brahmins, is a wounded Union Army veteran of 25 who volunteers to lead the first regiment of blacks against the Confederacy. A ragtag assemblage of freedmen and runaway slaves, some of them shoeless, follow him to boot camp, hoping to become fighting men. There the troops, who are for the most part unworldly and illiterate, endure not only relentless training by Mulcahy (Finn), a brutal Irish drill sergeant, but also the racism of the white enlistees and officers. The blacks are denied shoes and uniforms, and only reluctantly issued rifles—after all, opines one white officer, "they are little monkey children" who will probably bolt at the first shot. The Confederacy lets it be known that it will re-enslave all captured blacks and summarily execute those in uniform. Nonetheless, when the men of the 54th are offered immediate discharges, none of them accept. Among the mixed bag of would-be soldiers are Rawlins (Freeman), a gravedigger who is the regiment's anchor of strength and voice of reason, and Trip (Washington), an embittered runaway slave who is something of a bully but also

tough as steel. Others include a bespectacled Emerson scholar (Braugher) who is the weakest member of the troop, a mute drummer (Lee), and a shy, stuttering former field slave who is an expert marksman (Kennedy). Trip is the most rebellious soldier, and is subjected to a brutal military whipping as punishment after he goes AWOL to find some desperately needed boots. Eventually, tenaciously, the soldiers of the 54th draw together and weather their training to become a crack regiment, albeit untested in battle—only to be rewarded with the news that they will receive a salary of $10 a month, instead of the $13 given to whites. The men revolt, and Shaw pledges that he and his officers will also protest this treatment by refusing to accept their own pay. His determination wins his unit boots, uniforms, and a grudging respect. Also gaining respect is Rawlins, who rises to the rank of sergeant major, becoming one of America's first black noncommissioned officers. Finally, the regiment anxiously marches south, ready for combat. Instead, they are assigned to do menial work and foraging—the mindless looting of civilian villages, which they resist—befitting their perceived inferior status as soldiers. Shaw relentlessly badgers his superiors to respect his men and allow them to go into battle, and eventually resorts to blackmailing a general who has been profiting by trading in contraband and army equipment. Finally, the 54th is thrown against a sizable rebel assault. Standing in ranks, shoulder to shoulder, loading and reloading, they acquit themselves heroically, their intensive training coming to the fore. The men are anxious to prove their competence further, and the opportunity quickly arises in the form of a suicide mission against an impregnable harbor fortification, South Carolina's Fort Wagner. Defended by more than 1,000 Confederate soldiers and stockpiled with powerful ordnance, it is an impossible target. Nonetheless, the 54th volunteers to make the first hellish assault, advancing through sand, marsh, and bristling pickets. Vastly outgunned and outnumbered, the regiment—led on foot by Shaw, a detail that is for once historical fact, not war-movie cliche—storms the battlements again and again, but is horribly decimated. Defeated, the black troops and the white officers are buried in a common grave on the beach by the Confederates. Half of the regiment is dead; the fort is never taken.

Based on the real Robert Gould Shaw's letters (archived at Harvard) and on the books *Lay This Laurel* by Lincoln Kirstein and *One Gallant Rush* by Peter Burchard, GLORY is remarkable in its fidelity to history, especially since its protagonists' deeds have been virtually unheralded.

Though blacks made up nearly 10 percent of the Union Army, their contribution has been treated cursorily at best in history textbooks, and the story of the 54th—which in addition to Shaw included two of Frederick Douglass' sons and the brother of William and Henry James—has been just one of many unsung instances of black soldiers' valor during the war. In more cinematic terms, GLORY is one of surprisingly few creditable Civil War films; moreover, even the other good films concerning the War Between the States (including BIRTH OF A NATION; THE GENERAL; and GONE WITH THE WIND) have been most frequently presented from the southern point of view. Working in this traditionally uncommercial genre, GLORY's production team, advisors, and director (Edward Zwick), re-create the period with accuracy and an intent to rectify past oversights, both in the observation of small details (shoes were issued under the assumption that the soldiers would wear them into left and right shapes) and in the truly harrowing battle scenes, which show the devastation caused by the deadly combination of advanced technology and outmoded techniques.

Zwick's previous credits include the 1986 feature ABOUT LAST NIGHT and the creation of TV's "thirtysomething," neither of which demanded the kind of large-scale treatment he handles so successfully here. Zwick *has* already shown his skill in meshing numerous characters and subplots, however, as well as a talent for directing actors. Both traits are again in evidence in this lucidly structured, well-acted film. Though GLORY is essentially an ensemble piece, it contains especially compelling performances by Matthew Broderick, Denzel Washington, and Morgan Freeman that particularize and heighten its already impressive display of heroism in battle. (Freeman, with his roles here and in DRIVING MISS DAISY, has given two of 1989's most memorable performances. After redeeming bad parts and films throughout the decade, he is finally getting the major roles he deserved all along.) Freeman and Washington play against each other brilliantly, and Broderick movingly conveys the young Shaw's mix of sensitivity, spirit, and confusion.

In addition to Zwick, the cast, and writer Kevin Jarre, GLORY's production designer (Norman Garwood) and composer (James Horner) are to be highly commended. So too is veteran cinematographer Freddie Francis, whose photography of the battle scenes lends the film considerable power. Thick with fascinating detail and spectacle, richly plotted, alternately inspiring and horrifying (the film's realistic scenes of violence gained it an R rating), GLORY is an extraordinary film, an enlightening, entertaining, and inspiring tribute to heroes too long forgotten. *(Graphic violence, profanity.)*

Historical/War (PR:C MPAA:R)

HENRY V

(Brit.) 138m
BBC-Curzon-Renaissance/Goldwyn c

CAST:
Kenneth Branagh *(King Henry V)*, Derek Jacobi *(Chorus)*, Simon Shepherd *(Duke of Gloucester)*, James Larkin *(Bedford)*, Brian Blessed *(Duke of Exeter)*, James Simmons *(York)*, Paul Gregory *(Earl of Westmoreland)*, Charles Kay *(Archbishop of Canterbury)*, Alec McCowen *(Bishop of Ely)*, Fabian Cartwright *(Cambridge)*, Stephen Simms *(Scroop)*, Jay Villiers *(Grey)*, Edward Jewesbury *(Sir Thomas Erpingham)*, Ian Holm *(Fluellen)*, Daniel Webb *(Capt. Gower)*, Jimmy Yuill *(Jamy)*, John Sessions *(Capt. MacMorris)*, Shaun Prendergast *(Bates)*, Pat Doyle *(Court)*, Michael Williams *(Williams)*, Richard Briers *(Lt. Bardolph)*, Geoffrey Hutchins *(Cpl. Nym)*, Robert Stephens *(Ancient Pistol)*, Robbie Coltrane *(Sir John Falstaff)*, Christian Bale *(Falstaff's Boy)*, Judi Dench *(Mistress Quickly)*, Paul Scofield *(French King)*, Michael Maloney *(Dauphin)*, Richard Innocent *(Duke of Burgundy)*, Richard Clifford *(Duke of Orleans)*, Colin Hurley *(Grandpre)*, Richard Easton *(Constable of France)*, Christopher Ravenscroft *(Mountjoy)*, Emma Thompson *(Princess Katherine)*, Geraldine McEwan *(Alice)*, David Lloyd Meredith *(Governor of Harfleur)*, David Parfitt *(Messenger)*, Nicholas Ferguson *(Warwick)*, Tom Whitehouse *(Talbot)*, Nigel Greaves *(Duke of Berri)*, Julian Gartside *(Bretagne)*, Mark Inman, Chris Armstrong *(Soldiers)*, Calum Yuill *(Child)*.

PRODUCTION CREDITS:
p, Bruce Sharman; d, Kenneth Branagh; w, Kenneth Branagh; ph, Kenneth MacMillan Eastmancolor; ed, Mike Bradsell; m, Pat Doyle; md, Simon Rattle; prod d, Tim Harvey; art d, Norman Dorme; spec eff, Ian Wingrove; cos, Phyllis Dalton; stunts, Vic Armstrong; makeup, Peter Frampton.

Shakespeare—and sexy to boot! The Bard has been updated; and the late, great Laurence Olivier notwithstanding, a young interloper has redefined the essence of this historical play and made it more germane to 20th-century sensibilities. But don't be tempted to take sides. Kenneth Branagh's spellbinding version of Shakespeare's "Henry" isn't superior to Olivier's, it's different from it and complements it. The 28-year-old Branagh's virtuoso achievement (Olivier was 38) as the film's star-director-adapter makes for a stunning debut. In this era of BATMAN, he set out to prove he could make a popular film to hold audiences and, while severely pruning the text of the 400-year-old play, "satisfy both Shakespearean scholars as well as those who like CROCODILE DUNDEE." He has.

Branagh's version opens on a bare, contemporary movie soundstage. Jacobi (the Chorus), in all-black modern dress, somberly sets the tone for the scenes to follow; then, dramatically thrusting open enormous double doors, both he and the 20th century disappear into the 15th as, simultaneously, Branagh struts through those same doors in 1413 to appear before his royal council. It's an impressive on-screen introduction to the newly-crowned king, who's had to face a sudden change of lifestyle following the death of his father, Henry IV, the usurper of the throne of England. Here, and throughout the film, using brief flashbacks (excerpted from the earlier "Henry IV" plays to help clarify events), Branagh shows the young Crown Prince Hal sowing his wild oats (and barley malt) at the Boar's Head Tavern. Clearly, he's led a less than exemplary life for a future king, slumming and carousing with his drinking buddies Falstaff, Bardolph, Nym, Pistol and Nell Quickly. With his drunken years now behind him, the untried monarch faces two immediate concerns: to live down his reckless reputation, and to act on politically motivated advice (questionable at best) that he has legal claim to the French throne. But the arrogant Dauphin (Maloney), eldest son of the French King, considers that demand ridiculous, and looks upon Henry as an irresponsible hothead. To show his contempt, Maloney insultingly gifts him with tennis balls, causing the enraged Branagh to threaten war and, with his captain Fluellen (Holm) and meager troops, set sail to invade France. Maloney has dismissed the warning; and when Branagh's small army lays siege to Harfleur, the Dauphin does nothing to help defend the city from attack. Branagh's soldiers are inspired by his rousing speech encouraging them not to give up, but to go "Once more, unto the breach," and the battle is won by the English almost before it begins. With no reinforcements, the French governor

Simon Shepherd, Kenneth Brannagh, and James Larkin in HENRY V (©Samuel Goldwyn).

surrenders. The troops continue into France, elated by their triumph, but saddened by the death of Bardolph (Briers), hung, on the king's orders, for pillaging. (A hard decision for Branagh's Henry; but though Bardolph was an old friend, the king can't show favoritism.) At the French court, everyone except the French king (Scofield) is alarmed by Branagh's rapid progress through their country. The French king's daughter Katherine (Thompson), thinking it expedient to learn English, has her bilingual lady-in-waiting (McEwan) tutor her in vocabulary. In a delightful comic interlude, McEwan gently guides the beautiful young princess through the mysteries of such unfamiliar words as *hand, finger, neck, chin* and *elbow* (which comes out "de bilbow"). Scofield, meanwhile, is unperturbed and, thinking the win at Harfleur was a fluke, sends his herald Mountjoy (Ravenscroft, in a small but sensitively delivered role) to demand that Branagh pay a ransom to the French, give himself up, and have his soldiers return home. But Branagh, filled with confidence, returns the message that if the king wants him, he should come and get him. Continuing to Agincourt, Branagh and his men prepare to face a full complement of French forces that outnumber the English five to one. The night before what promises to be a bloody massacre, the English soldiers, underdogs on unfamiliar soil and plagued with illness, are understandably disheartened. Branagh, disguised in a borrowed cloak, circulates among them, and to raise morale, says that if he were the king, he wouldn't want to be anywhere else except where he was, in battle with his troops. But privately, he thinks of all his regal responsibilities, and concludes that only in ceremony—in itself an empty thing—does he differ from his men. His dismal thoughts, turning on the horror of the English blood that will be shed within a few hours, greatly differ from those of the

confident French. With their superior forces, they have no doubt they will easily defeat their enemy, and in a brazen show of confidence, they again send the herald to give the English one last chance to surrender. The offer is refused, and Branagh, in one of the most brilliant, inspirational examples of patriotic rhetoric in all of literature, delivers what has become known as "The St. Crispin's Day Speech." In it, he grants those who want to leave permission to do so. But for those who decide to stay on and fight, he tells them, "From this day to the ending of the world . . . we in it shall be remembered—We few, we happy few, we band of brothers." In the morning's battle, the English, more mobile with their longbows, outmaneuver their heavily armored opponent in bloody combat on the field at Agincourt. When the French herald later approaches the war-weary king, humbly requesting a truce to bury the dead Frenchmen, Branagh poignantly says, "I tell thee truly, herald, I know not if the day be ours or no"; to which Ravenscroft softly replies, "The day is yours." Incredibly, the French have conceded defeat. More unbelievable is the final tally (one of Shakespeare's famous liberties with verisimilitude): the French lost 10,000 men, the English only 29. The English victory is tempered by sorrow when all the young English boys—the camp's servants—are found ruthlessly massacred by the French. With a deep sense of despair over the deaths, Branagh orders his men to sing "Non nobis domine." More like a dirge than a psalm, the music continues for four minutes (in one of the longest tracking shots in memory) as Branagh silently carries the body of Falstaff's boy (Bale, of EMPIRE OF THE SUN) through the bloodied, body-strewn battlefield—a quietly intense journey that speaks volumes about the futility of war. All that remains for Branagh is to meet with Scofield to discuss terms of peace, the

chief condition of which is alliance between the two countries through Branagh's marriage to the French princess. While Branagh's aides settle the details of surrender, the young royals meet for the first time. Though each has scant knowledge of the other's language, through charm and chemistry, the English king successfully woos and wins her. (A reflection of real life: Branagh married Thompson in August 1989.)

Until now, Olivier's 1944 Oscar-winning epic had been considered definitive, a standard for others to follow. The idea of Branagh, a young, little-known actor (A MONTH IN THE COUNTRY) who never before directed a film, taking on that classic was certainly audacious, if not foolhardy. Yet the Irish-born, English-reared Branagh felt that after nearly 50 years, the film was ripe for reinterpretation, noting, "It happens all the time in the theatre. This time we did it on film."

The two versions differ vastly in approach. Branagh's, the more intimate, filmed mostly in medium and close-up shots, discards the pageantry of Olivier's grand spectacle. Olivier's jingoistic (and almost bloodless) vision, filmed as a paean to England's greatness, was a morale-builder for his countrymen embroiled in a world war. But where he glorified battle, Branagh's far bloodier HENRY V is strongly antiwar, focusing on its carnage, its casualties, and the lamentable price of imperialism. Branagh's is also the more lusty, a visceral coming-of-age film with a hero as familiar to moviegoers as, say, Tom Cruise in COCKTAIL en route to maturity. His Henry is a boozer, a young playboy prince forced to grow up quickly and to become the leader of his rather scruffy band—a far cry from Olivier's lordly monarch and knights in shining armor. Branagh's men sweat. They have warts and bad teeth. Doubt and fear are written all over their pockmarked faces. Where Olivier offers romance and grandiose rhetoric, Branagh provides an elegant simplicity of style. He's created a passionate Everyman torn by war and the sudden responsibility of command.

During the film's early stages, when Branagh was trying to get a handle on his character, he realized he didn't have an inkling as to how a person would feel if, like Henry, he were suddenly made king. He took the problem to Britain's Prince Charles, the one person who could offer him insight, and a planned short meeting turned into a three-hour conversation. The Prince gave his enthusiastic support to both the film and to Branagh's innovative Renaissance Theatre Company, from which most of the roles for HENRY V were cast. Along with Stephen Evans, his executive producer, Branagh, the neophyte filmmaker, brought this $7.5 million production—a real cheapie by today's standards—in under budget and ahead of schedule in only seven weeks.

Like most Shakespearean stage-to-screen translations, this film didn't attain blockbuster status. But chances are it will endure, and if Branagh does nothing else in his career, his HENRY V safely assures his place in the pantheon of cinema classics. The film has such tremendous style and passion, and is presented in such a thrilling, entertaining manner, it should cause—as did Olivier's film—a new generation to look upon the works of Shakespeare as entirely approachable and rewarding. (Violence.)

Drama/Historical   (PR:A MPAA:PG)

MONSIEUR HIRE

(Fr.) 81m
Cinea-Hachette-FR3/UGC-Orion c
(AKA: M. HIRE)

CAST:
Michel Blanc *(M. Hire)*, Sandrine Bonnaire *(Alice)*, Luc Thuillier *(Emile)*, Andre Wilms *(Inspector)*.

PRODUCTION CREDITS:
p, Philippe Carcassonne and Rene Cleitman; d, Patrice Leconte; w, Patrice Leconte and Patrick Dewolf based on the novel *Les Fiancailles de Monsieur Hire* by Georges Simenon; ph, Denis Lenoir; ed, Joelle Hache; m, Michael Nyman; art d, Yvan Maussion.

A superb thriller containing the ugliest portrait of French provincialism since Henri-Georges Clouzot's LE CORBEAU (1943), Patrice Leconte's MONSIEUR HIRE is set in a Parisian suburb in which conformity reigns supreme, and anyone who doesn't behave like everyone else is apt to be viewed suspiciously. Based on *Les Fiancailles de Monsieur Hire*, the Georges Simenon novel that also inspired Julien Duvivier's PANIQUE (1946), MONSIEUR HIRE is a penetrating psychological portrait of a warped, love-starved outsider who, by the film's end, arouses the audience's protective instincts. When a lovely young girl is murdered, a dogged police investigator (Wilms) immediately suspects Blanc, a loner distrusted and hated by his neighbors. Tormented by children who play vicious pranks and singled out for suspicion by his neighbors, Blanc is hounded mercilessly by the detective. Blanc resembles his tormenter in that he is an ever-vigilant soul, if in a less acceptable form—for the outcast is a voyeur who spies on Bonnaire, the country-fresh girl who has moved in across the way, when he is not toiling away joylessly at his tailor's shop. Watching Bonnaire—whose innocent look recalls that of the murdered girl—as she undresses or as she makes love to her handsome, ne'er-do-well boy friend (Thuillier), Blanc becomes infatuated with her. Eventually, she spots her secret admirer and, surprisingly, pays him a visit rather than reporting him to the police. An uninhibited free spirit, she is drawn to Blanc and allows him to share the simple pleasures of his life with her. Despite continual harassment from Wilms, Blanc even makes plans to move to Switzerland with Bonnaire—who, despite her apparent attraction to the rabbitlike Blanc, remains loyal to Thuillier, no matter how much he may take her for granted or what he may have done. It would destroy the film's suspenseful climax to reveal further plot developments, but the denouement provides a heart-rending exploration of duplicity and betrayal, with a particularly effective freeze-frame halting the action just before it flows into the twist ending.

Rather than jazz up the suspense through the conventional device of cross-cutting, director Leconte works within the frame to create a sense of inexorable doom. MONSIEUR HIRE doesn't move at a fast clip; instead, it involves the viewer in a downward spiral by making us covoyeurs with the title character, whose life has been a study in self-protective detachment. The audience is implicated in this point of view, eyeing Bonnaire hungrily through her window as Leconte's camera pulls back to an over-the-shoulder shot of Blanc doing the same. In another dazzling, sexually provocative sequence that puts the same motif to very different purposes, the film cuts from an over-the-shoulder shot of Bonnaire watching Thuillier as he enjoys a brutal boxing match to a shot of Blanc fondling her sensually—connecting Blanc and Bonnaire at last, and irrevocably.

Anchored by a haunting performance from Michel Blanc (Gerard Depardieu's diminutive lover in Bertrand Blier's MENAGE [1986]) as the Peeping Tom who throws years of self-control to the winds, MONSIEUR BLANC is a study of blindness on two levels: that of prejudice and that of love. As a result of this blindness, both the deceiver and the deceived become victims of fate in this icily compelling film. *(Violence, sexual situations, adult situations.)*

Thriller   (PR:O)

Michel Blanc and Sandrine Bonnaire in MONSIEUR HIRE (©Orion).

MY LEFT FOOT

(Brit.) 98m Granada/Miramax c

CAST:
Daniel Day-Lewis *(Christy Brown)*, Ray McAnally *(Mr. Brown)*, Brenda Fricker *(Mrs. Brown)*, Ruth McCabe *(Mary Carr)*, Fiona Shaw *(Dr. Eileen Cole)*, Eanna MacLiam *(Old Benny)*, Alison Whelan *(Old Sheila)*, Declan Croghan *(Old Tom)*, Hugh O'Conor *(Young Christy)*, Cyril Cusack *(Lord Castlewelland)*, Owen Sharp *(Young Tom)*, Darren McHugh *(Young Benny)*, Keith O'Conor *(Young Brian)*, Marie Conmee *(Sadie)*, Adrian Dunbar *(Peter)*, Kirsten Sheridan *(Young Sharon)*, Jacinta Whyte *(Jenny)*, Julie Hale *(Rachel)*, Tom Hickey *(Priest)*.

PRODUCTION CREDITS:
p, Noel Pearson; d, Jim Sheridan; w, Shane Connaughton and Jim Sheridan based on the book by Christy Brown; ph, Jack Conroy Technicolor; ed, J. Patrick Duffner; m, Elmer Bernstein; md, Elmer Bernstein.

Stories about people overcoming devastating handicaps have long been grist for the filmmaker's mill, running the gamut from TV's disease-of-the-week tearjerkers to more memorable features such as ELEPHANT MAN; THE MIRACLE WORKER; and MASK. To the latter group can now be added this screen adaptation of Christy Brown's best-selling autobiography. Its title, MY LEFT FOOT, refers to the only limb over which Brown, crippled since birth by a severe case of cerebral palsy, ever had any control. (Even his speech was adversely affected; only after rigorous practice could he be understood by others.)

Daniel Day-Lewis plays the acclaimed Irish-born artist and author, as the film intercuts flashbacks of his formative years with scenes at the stately Dublin home of Lord Castlewelland (Cusack) in 1959. There, the wheelchair-bound Brown, guest of honor at a benefit dinner for a cerebral palsy foundation, first meets Mary (McCabe), a young nurse assigned to care for him that evening. It's her job to see that her 27-year-old charge, noted for his volatile behavior and heavy drinking, stays sane and sober for his speech. Not surprisingly, she has her hands full. To pass the time, Brown sips whiskey through a straw from a flask hidden in his tuxedo jacket. Presented with a copy of Brown's book, Mary leafs through its pages, and the author's life is re-created on the screen, beginning with his early years as the ninth of 13 surviving children (out of 22) in a close-knit, working-class Irish Catholic family. After his birth, the doctor tells Brown's desperately poor parents that in all probability he is retarded and should be "put away." That option is firmly rejected by his jovial, hard-drinking father (McAnally, in his penultimate role before his untimely death in

Daniel Day-Lewis in MY LEFT FOOT (©Miramax).

1989), an often unemployed mason. Equally unwilling is Brown's continually pregnant mother (Fricker), the family linchpin, who remains devoted to her nearly immobile son and to the arduous personal care he requires. In a very funny scene, the young Brown (played by O'Conor) gets hauled off to church by his deeply religious mother after she finds a girlie magazine his brothers have hidden under his "chariot" (a hand-made wheelbarrow, his only source of locomotion). There, the naive, uncomprehending boy is subjected to a long sermon by the priest on the evils of the flesh and the horrors of eternal damnation. More frequently, however, young Brown's mental state is simply ignored. Sequestered under the staircase, he's treated like a family pet. Even when he summons help for his mother when she falls down the stairs, he's given no credit for his wits; because he's not able to communicate verbally, Brown is considered a moron. Finally, in a poignant, unforgettable moment, he is able to demonstrate his intelligence to his family: while his ever-growing clan of sisters and brothers do homework in the family parlor, Brown edges along the floor with extreme difficulty, picks up a piece of chalk with the especially prehensile toes of his left foot, and, to everyone's astonishment, writes the word "mother" on a slate. His elated father lifts up the boy, carries him into his local pub, and proudly introduces his son to his drinking buddies as "Christy Brown, genius." Thereafter, there's no holding back Brown's eagerness to learn and experience life as fully as he can despite his limitations. Feeling the first pangs of teenage love, he develops a crush on a pretty neighborhood girl, but is rejected when he sends her an illustrated love note. His next emotional attachment is to a woman doctor (Shaw), a specialist in the treatment and education of cerebral palsy victims, who takes the now 19-year-old Brown, a talented artist, under her wing. Through therapy, she helps him make remarkable

progress with his speech and painting, unleashing his romantic spirit when she introduces him to the works of Shakespeare. In the process, he falls madly in love with her. After she arranges a public exhibition of his art, Brown is devastated to learn that the doctor is engaged to the gallery owner and creates an embarrassing scene when he reveals his feelings. With biting sarcasm he drunkenly toasts the doctor: "Con-gra-tu-la-tions to you and Peter. I'm glad you taught me how to speak so I can say that." Disconsolate, Brown unsuccessfully attempts suicide (leaving a note that reads, "All is nothing, therefore nothing must end"). Although Brown has seemingly given up, his stalwart mother hasn't, and, recognizing his needs as an adult, she persuades her husband to build their son his own little house adjacent to theirs. ("Well Christy, that's the nearest he'll ever come to saying I love you," she says of her husband's efforts.) When his father dies of a heart attack, Brown loses confidence in his ability as a painter and begins work on his autobiography, the sensitive tale of his struggle to be accepted despite his handicap. After it becomes an international best-seller, he is invited to read from the book at the fund-raising dinner that opens the film and at which Mary is struck by the passion of his writing and charmed by his wicked sense of humor. As the film closes, the pair stay out until dawn. A closing title then informs us that they married in 1972 and lived together until Brown's death in 1981.

That MY LEFT FOOT succeeds as well as it does is in large part due to a superb supporting cast and the virtuoso performances of Hugh O'Conor and Daniel Day-Lewis (THE UNBEARABLE LIGHTNESS OF BEING; A ROOM WITH A VIEW), who play Brown as child and adult, respectively. In these most difficult roles, both actors masterfully convey Brown's intelligence and determination to function normally, without resorting to the sentimentalized histrionics often found in films of this type. Despite the physical constraints imposed by the role, both O'Conor and Day-Lewis radiate a fierce intensity with their realistic portrayals of Brown.

MY LEFT FOOT begs comparison with GABY, A TRUE STORY, the depiction of another cerebral palsy victim (who, coincidentally, could also move only her left foot). Indeed, the films are like two sides of the same coin. While the less satisfying GABY focuses on the dour aspects of its subject's plight, the better-scripted, more entertaining MY LEFT FOOT is filled with wit and unself-conscious humor. A rich cinematic experience, this uplifting British production will leave you in awe of the extraordinary Christy Brown. *(Adult situations.)*

Biography   **(PR:A MPAA:R)**

♥QUEEN OF HEARTS

(Brit.) 112m
Enterprise-TVS-Nelson/Cinecom c

CAST:
Vittorio Duse (*Nonno*), Joseph Long (*Danilo*), Anita Zagaria (*Rosa*), Eileen Way (*Mama Sibilla*), Vittorio Amandola (*Barbariccia*), Roberto Scateni (*Falco*), Stefano Spagnoli (*Young Eddie*), Alec Bregonzi (*Headwaiter*), Ronan Vivert (*Man in Pig Scene*), Matilda Thorpe (*Woman in Pig Scene*), Anthony Manzoni (*Doorman*), Sydney Kean (*Pepe*), Ray Marioni (*Mario*), Sarah Hadaway (*Teresa*), Anna Pernicci (*Angelica*), Ian Hawkes (*Eddie*).

PRODUCTION CREDITS:
p, John Hardy; d, Jon Amiel; w, Tony Grisoni; ph, Mike Southon; ed, Peter Boyle; m, Michael Convertino; prod d, Jim Clay; art d, Philip Elton; cos, Lindy Hemming; stunts, Gareth Milne; makeup, Magdalen Gaffney.

Like Ruy Guerra's ERENDIRA (1984), the far better QUEEN OF HEARTS is a slightly mystical romantic fable that leaves you smiling, as much in wonder as in delight at the story's simple pleasures. An engagingly wrought jewel of a film from director Jon Amiel, whose award-winning "The Singing Detective" transformed Dennis Potter's script into a feast for the eyes and ears, QUEEN OF HEARTS is a tale of love and revenge, seen through the imaginative eyes of a child. Now grown, Hawkes, the film's narrator, looks back on the previous 20 years in the charmed life of his close-knit Italian family, who emigrated to England after WW II. A whimsical, stage-setting montage depicts the elopement of Hawkes' parents in a small village near Florence. Against her will, the beautiful Zagaria is betrothed to Amandola, the proud, overbearing son of the local butcher. Her heart, however, belongs to another—the oafish, but wellmeaning, Long—and the two are prepared to die rather than face life apart. Miraculously surviving a 120-foot leap from a tower onto a moving hay wagon (the stunt performed by members of a well-known Italian circus family), the pair flees to Britain and settles in London, desperately happy, but desperately poor. One day, after receiving a five-pound tip, Long, who works as a waiter, has a vision of a fanciful talking pig: "Only if you trust the coins will you become a man of property; only then will you be happy. But beware the king of swords," warns the pig. And therein lies the key to the story that follows. Long gambles the money, and, heeding the pig's advice, wins enough to buy the Lucky Cafe and support his ever-growing family of six: his wife, four children, and quarrelsome, unsmiling mother-in-law Way (seven if you

include Hawkes' best friend, Whalley, an electronics buff, whose father runs a betting parlor next door and of whom Hawkes says: "Beetle [Whalley] didn't really have a family, so we lent him ours"). The constantly complaining grandmother has never quite forgiven Long for taking her daughter away from the rich Amandola; in fact, she never gives up, even confessing for him at church because "he's a Casanova, an animal, a beatnik." Loyal Zagaria will have none of this, however. She's the glue that binds the whole family together, and, gently but firmly, she keeps her mother in line by asking her if she wants go to an old people's home "like an English granny?" Their household situation is further complicated when Long's father, Duse, comes from Italy to live with them. Everyone except Way loves the old geezer, who arrives with only a hearing aid and his few worldly belongings, including a mysterious black box he says "will make everything right" and which he never lets out of his sight. Then Amandola, the villain of the piece, shows up. Bent on revenge, the spurned suitor has followed the family to London, where he has become the prosperous owner of three gambling houses. To taunt the family, he hires its eldest son, Lambert, to repossess Whalley's father's betting parlor and The Lucky Cafe's cappuccino machine. Furious, Long visits his former rival, intending to win back everything at cards. Instead, he loses *everything*: his cafe, his apartment above the shop, and, most pitifully, his wedding ring. In the meantime, Duse dies and Long opens the mysterious black box, but though it turns out to contain a gun, Long can't bring himself to kill his nemesis. Instead, with Whalley's help, he devises a "sting" operation to recoup his losses and simultaneously ruin Amandola. The scam, strikingly similar to the one Robert Red-

ford and Paul Newman pull off in THE STING, involves placing sure-fire bets on dog races in Amandola's newest gambling parlor. Before the results are announced in the parlor, Spagnoli (who plays the narrator as a boy) receives the names of the winners through his grandfather's old hearing aid—which Whalley has adjusted to pick up radio broadcast of the races. Long then places the bets and in no time parlays his winnings into a fortune, getting back his shop, home, and wife's ring, and as in all such fanciful stories, living happily ever after. And that goes for Duse's Nonno, too. Throughout the film, in his dreams, he's symbolically trapped in limbo as a solitary specter on a mountaintop. But in the film's finale, the shrouded figure becomes Nonno the child, and he's last seen rushing into the welcoming arms of his mother. As Hawkes observes at the end, thinking about his beloved grandfather, "Heaven must be like coming home."

There may be a few Italian Immigrant Family cliches along the way, but the characters in QUEEN OF HEARTS are treated sensitively, with much humor and warmth—never patronized. Much credit has to go to the film's wonderful cast, handpicked by director Amiel from what he called "a treasure trove" of relative unknowns—a small pool of Italian or half-Italian actors living in Britain who, until their roles in QUEEN OF HEARTS, "played only Italian waiters or the occasional Arab." They're practically flawless in their interpretation of immigrants adjusting to their new environment, and lend credibility to Tony Grisoni's altogether charming script.

The low-budget QUEEN OF HEARTS, filmed in London in just nine weeks, debuted to great acclaim at the 1989 Cannes Film Festival.

Comedy/Romance   (PR:A MPAA:PG)

Anita Zagaria and Joseph Long in QUEEN OF HEARTS (©Cinecom).

ⱽSAY ANYTHING

John Cusack and Ione Skye in SAY ANYTHING (©20th Century Fox).

100m Gracie-Cameron Crowe/FOX c

CAST:

John Cusack *(Lloyd Dobler)*, Ione Skye *(Diane Court)*, John Mahoney *(James Court)*, Lili Taylor *(Corey)*, Amy Brooks *(D.C.)*, Pamela Segall *(Rebecca)*, Jason Gould *(Mike Cameron)*, Loren Dean *(Joe)*, Glenn Walker Harris Jr. *(Jason)*, Charles Walker *(Principal)*, Russel Lunday *(Parent)*, Polly Platt *(Mrs. Flood)*, Gloria Cromwell *(Ruth)*, Jeremy Piven *(Mark)*, Patrick O'Neill *(Denny)*, Gregory Sporleder *(Howard)*, John Green Jr. *(Luke)*, Bebe Neuwirth *(Mrs. Evans)*, Eric Stoltz *(Vahlere)*, Kim Walker *(Sheila)*, Chynna Phillips *(Mimi)*, Allison Roth *(Tammy)*, Lisanne Falk *(Sandra)*, Jonathan Chapin, Donald Willis, Arlan Feiles, Christopher Ziesmer, John Bruner *(Guys)*, Jim Ladd *(D.J.)*, Montrose Hagins *(Bess)*, Kathryn Fuller *(Eva)*, Lenore Woodward *(Sabina)*, Edward A. Wright *(Mr. Taylor)*, Joanna Frank *(Mrs. Kerwin)*, Jay R. Goldenberg *(Al Kerwin)*, Richard Portnow *(Agent Stewart)*, Stephen Shortridge *(Ray)*, Kathleen Layman *(Saleswoman)*, Tom Lawrence *(Shop Customer)*, Annie Waterman *(IRS Secretary)*, Philip Baker Hall *(IRS Boss)*, Jerry Ziesmer *(U.S. Attorney)*, John Hillner *(Court's Attorney)*, Don "The Dragon" Wilson *(Sparring Parnter)*, Nicholas Kallsen *(Nose-Setter)*, Thomas Payne *(Man in Kickboxing Doorway)*, Joan Cusack *(Constance)*.

PRODUCTION CREDITS:

p, Polly Platt; d, Cameron Crowe; w, Cameron Crowe; ph, Laszlo Kovacs Deluxe Color; ed, Richard Marks; m, Richard Gibbs, Anne Dudley, and Nancy Wilson; md, Danny Bramson; prod d, Mark Mansbridge; set d, Joe Mitchell; cos, Jane Ruhm; makeup, Cheri Minns.

A far cry from the standard Hollywood teen romance, SAY ANYTHING is the extraordinary directorial debut of Cameron Crowe (who adapted his own novel for the hilariously inventive FAST TIMES AT RIDGEMONT HIGH). Set in Seattle, Crowe's wonderfully nuanced screenplay develops a complex triangular relationship involving a gifted high-school graduate, her doting father, and the likable, underachieving classmate who falls for her. Class valedictorian Diane Court (Skye) is brilliant, beautiful, and the recipient of a prestigious fellowship to study in England, much to the delight of her divorced father, James (Mahoney), a kindhearted nursing home operator with whom she shares a special closeness and to whom she can "say anything." Their relationship is tested that summer, however, when Diane is wooed by Lloyd Dobler (John Cusack), an Army brat who lives with his unmarried sister (real-life sibling Joan Cusack) and her young son (Harris) while their parents finish a European tour of duty. Daunted by her brains and beauty, few of Diane's classmates have dared to ask her out, and after striving so to achieve the goals she and her father have set for her, Diane wants to experience some of the fun and friendship she's missed out on. Fast-talking, funny Lloyd's academic record is checkered at best, and unlike Diane he has no real plans, notwithstanding his vague notions about becoming a professional kick boxer (and his desire to spend as much time with Diane as possible). His best friends are girls—Corey (Taylor), whose unrequited love for a classmate has led her to attempt suicide and write 63 songs for him, and level-headed D.C.

(Brooks). Although no one else can imagine Lloyd with Diane, Corey and D.C. know just how sensitive, creative, and loving he is. Diane, too, is eventually won over by Lloyd's quirky generosity of spirit, but her father, who wants nothing to stand in the way of Diane's success, is upset by his daughter's growing involvement with Lloyd, especially after she tells him she's slept with Lloyd. Pressured by her father, Diane breaks up with Lloyd, who can't comprehend her actions and, heartbroken, tries everything to win her back (endless unanswered phone calls, standing outside her house with a boombox blaring Peter Gabriel's "In Your Eyes," etc.). Meanwhile, James, whose lifestyle subtly belies the altruism of his profession, comes under investigation by the IRS. As the film moves to its emotional conclusion, Diane learns that her father isn't everything that she thought he was, and that Lloyd is.

Seldom has such complexity, emotional depth, honesty, and realism been invested in what is ostensibly a teen love story; even the best of John Hughes' genre-defining films pale in comparison with SAY ANYTHING. Crowe's script is full of careful observations not only of contemporary teenage rituals, but of human interaction, and his unobtrusive camera allows viewers to make the most of all the well-crafted details available to them, from the spot-on production design to the witty but believable dialog, and especially the outstanding performances by Ione Skye (costar of RIVER'S EDGE and A NIGHT IN THE LIFE OF JIMMY REARDON, daughter of 60s folk rocker Donovan), John Mahoney (MOONSTRUCK; SUSPECT; BETRAYAL), and John Cusack, who gives an incredibly winning portrayal of Lloyd Dobler. Cusack's energized, wholly convincing, feminist Lloyd is one of the most memorable characters in recent film history—a stereotype-busting alternative male role model, the teenage equivalent of Alan Bates' Saul in AN UNMARRIED WOMAN. To appreciate the 22-year-old Cusack's artistry, one need only look so far as his portrayal of an immensely different character, dishonored third baseman Buck Weaver, in EIGHT MEN OUT (1988), John Sayles' film about the 1919 Black Sox scandal.

The chemistry is excellent between Mahoney, who brings deft shading to his "father who loves too much" (all of his misdeeds have been done in the name of his daughter's future), and Skye, whose first-love confusion and loss of faith are believable and moving; but from the outset Cusack takes charge of the film, while still managing to give a very generous performance. (Significantly, Cusack, anxious to put behind him forever the teen roles with which he had made his reputation, initially showed little interest in the part; however, Mahoney, who was working with him on EIGHT MEN OUT at the time, convinced him that the script was an excellent one.) In supporting roles, Lili Taylor (MYSTIC PIZZA), as the morose but humorously caustic Corey, and Amy Brooks, as the reliable D.C., are wonderful foils for Cusack, just the sort of friends Lloyd would have. And Cusack's Oscar-nominated sister, Joan (WORKING GIRL), delivers a fine cameo as his hard-used but supportive screen sister. In keeping with the film's family-affair approach, Crowe's rock-star wife, Heart's Nancy Wilson, contributed to the score and sings "All for Love."

That SAY ANYTHING transcends the usual expectations for a teen film is at least partly due to the genesis of its screenplay. During a meeting, Academy Award-winning producer-director James L. Brooks (TERMS OF ENDEARMENT; BROADCAST NEWS) told Crowe about a simple scene he'd witnessed in New York City: A man guided his beautiful young daughter across a street with a light touch on her elbow, and the look that passed between them was "inspiring." Brooks, however,

wondered how their relationship would be changed if the man were a criminal. Crowe liked the idea, and under Brooks advisement used it in a 90-page novella that would eventually become SAY ANYTHING. Thus, the story started with a father-daughter relationship and moved towards a teen romance, rather than the other way around. Brooks became the project's executive producer; Polly Platt, who was nominated for an Oscar for the production design of BROADCAST NEWS, took on the producing chores; and when they began considering first-time directors, Crowe seemed an appropriate choice.

A *wunderkind* journalist, Crowe began writing about rock'n'roll at age 15 and, a year later, became a *Rolling Stone* staffer, interviewing some of popular music's biggest names in the course of his 10 years with the magazine. Later, to write the best-selling *Fast Times at Ridgemont High*, the youthful-looking Crowe actually returned to high school in 1979 as a student. In addition to his screen adaptation of that novel, Crowe also wrote the screenplay for another teen-centered film, 1984's THE WILD LIFE. At only 31, with a film as artful as SAY ANYTHING under his belt

as a director, it seems certain that Crowe, like Cusack, will be a force to be reckoned with for a long time to come.

The film's nicely employed rock soundtrack includes: "All for Love" (John Bettis, Martin Page, performed by Nancy Wilson), "Cult of Personality" (Vernon Reid, Corey Glover, Muzz Skillings, William Calhoun, performed by Living Colour), "One Big Rush" (Joe Satriani, performed by Satriani), "You Want It" (Robin Zander, Tom Petersson, performed by Cheap Trick), "Taste the Pain" (Anthony Kiedis, Mike Balzary, John Frusciante, performed by the Red Hot Chili Peppers), "In Your Eyes" (Peter Gabriel, performed by Gabriel), "Stripped" (Martin Gore, performed by Depeche Mode), "Skankin to the Beat" (K.R. Jones, W.A. Kibby II, performed by Fishbone), "Within Your Reach" (Paul Westerberg, performed by the Replacements), "Keeping the Dream Alive" (Stefan Zauner, Aron Strobel, Timothy Touchton, Curtis Briggs, performed by Freiheit), "Rikki Don't Lose That Number" (Walter Becker, Donald Fagen, performed by Ste Masser, Linda Creed). *(Profanity, adult situations, sexual situations.)*

Comedy/Drama (PR:A-C MPAA:PG-13)

•

WAR OF THE ROSES, THE

116m Gracie/FOX c

CAST:
Michael Douglas *(Oliver Rose)*, Kathleen Turner *(Barbara Rose)*, Danny DeVito *(Gavin D'Amato)*, Marianne Sagebrecht *(Susan)*, Sean Astin *(Josh, Age 17)*, Heather Fairfield *(Carolyn, Age 17)*, G.D. Spradlin *(Harry Thurmont)*, Trenton Teigen *(Josh, Age 10)*, Bethany McKinney *(Carolyn, Age 10)*, Peter Donat *(Larrabee)*, Dan Castellaneta *(Man in Chair)*, Gloria Cromwell *(Mrs. Marshall)*, Harlan Arnold *(Mr. Dell)*, Mary Fogarty *(Mrs. Dell)*, Rika Hofmann *(Elke)*, Patricia Allison *(Maureen)*, Peter Brocco *(Elderly Mourner)*, Philip Perlman *(Bidder at Auction)*, Susan Isaacs *(Auctioneer's Assistant)*, Shirley Mitchell *(Mrs. Dewitt)*, Ellen Crawford, Lisa Howard *(Nurses)*, Michael Adler *(Dr. Hillerman)*, Jeff Thomas *(Orderly)*, Jacqueline Cassell *(Gavin's Secretary)*, Vickilyn Reynolds *(Nancy, Oliver's Secretary)*, Eunice Suarez *(Latin Woman)*, Julia Elliott *(Latin Assistant)*, Tony Crane *(Teenage Boy)*, Ryan Wickers, Shaun Wickers *(Josh, Age 3)*, Catherine Donohue, Mary Donohue *(Carolyn, Age 3)*, Sue Palka *(Anchorwoman)*, Morris Jones *(Anchorman)*, Popeye the Dog *(Bennie)*, Tyler the Cat *(Kitty Kitty)*, Roy Brocksmith *(Mr. Fisk)*, Peter Hansen *(Mr. Marshall)*, Robert Harper *(Heath)*, Prince Hughes *(Bleeding Man)*,

Danitra Vance *(Manicurist Trainee)*, David Wohl *(Dr. Gordon)*.

PRODUCTION CREDITS:
p, James L. Brooks and Arnon Milchan; d, Danny DeVito; w, Michael Leeson based on the novel by Warren Adler; ph, Stephen H. Burum Deluxe Color; ed, Lynzee Klingman and Nicholas C. Smith; m, David Newman; prod d, Ida Random; art d, Mark Mansbridge; set d, Stan Tropp, Mark Fabus, and Perry Gray; spec eff, John Frazier; cos, Gloria Gresham; stunts, Mike Runyard; makeup, Stephen Abrums.

Few things are sadder, sillier, or scarier than what can happen between a long-married couple when love dies. In THE WAR OF THE ROSES, director Danny DeVito and writer Michael Leeson (adapting a novel by Warren Adler) have captured just such a fiasco in its full ingloriousness, making their film the smartest, most sophisticated, and funniest American comedy of 1989. After 17 years of wedlock, the love Barbara Rose (Turner) once felt for her husband, Oliver (Douglas), has curdled into hate. She hates his phony laugh. She hates the way he patronizes her when she decides to start a catering business. She hates his dog (she's a cat person). She just hates him. He still loves her—as much as he can love anybody—but he loves their big, beautiful,

antique-filled house more. And therein lies the cautionary tale, told by Gavin D'Amato (director DeVito himself), a divorce lawyer and associate in Oliver's firm who begins to recount the story (to a prospective client) in the film's prolog. Gavin has decided to represent Oliver in the divorce action; Barbara's attorney is Harry Thurmont. (He's played by G.D. Spradlin, whom viewers may remember as the military commander who sent Martin Sheen on his mission to terminate Marlon Brando in APOCALYPSE NOW. If you think the casting here is arbitrary, take note of the helicopter that begins buzzing by Gavin's office window as his tale gets progressively crazier.) Barbara wants no money, only the house. Oliver is ready to give up anything but the house. To help Oliver assert his claim and protect his assets, Gavin finds an obscure legal precedent that allows his client to remain in the house with Barbara until final deposition of assets is made. Stuck in legally binding close proximity—a dark reversal of their legally binding marriage—the Roses escalate tensions until the hostilities erupt into the full-scale war of the title. And no prisoners are taken. Barbara nails the door to Oliver's basement sauna shut while he is inside. Oliver saws the heels off all of Barbara's shoes. He destroys the dinner party she throws to entertain and impress

Kathleen Turner and Michael Douglas in WAR OF THE ROSES (©20th Century Fox).

her catering clients. She destroys his vintage Morgan sports car. And then there's the chandelier . . .

Director DeVito tells this tale with what seems a fiendish, unhealthy gusto, yet he refuses to sneer over the decline of the Roses. THE WAR OF THE ROSES has the exaggeration of an anti-fairy tale—in fact, we can't be sure that DeVito's Gavin hasn't made the story up out of a composite of every ugly divorce case he has handled. Making it all work are the psychological realism and the meticulous attention to a horribly inexorable logic in the plotting, which serve both to bolster Gavin's credibility as someone who knows whereof he speaks and, more important, to prevent viewers from becoming completely disengaged from the Roses—even as their acts escalate from the outlandish to the surreal. THE WAR OF THE ROSES is at once horrific and hilarious, because the film has no villains, just a vaguely sad sense of how the magic of love can be worn to nothing under the slow assault of day-to-day life. Once the first punch is thrown (by Barbara—for Oliver to do so would be too true to life, and therefore too depressing to watch), there is no turning back. And DeVito doesn't turn back either—although, through his ingenious framing narrative, he does manage to turn THE WAR OF THE ROSES into a staunchly (if oddly) pro-family film, during a time when *family* is the buzzword for Hollywood suc-

cess. Nonetheless, there is only one logical ending for THE WAR OF THE ROSES, and DeVito doesn't shrink from the conclusion.

Boiled down to its basic elements, THE WAR OF THE ROSES is little more than a campfire horror story mounted on a mammoth scale and conveyed in legal terms. It's a tale told with such satisfying care and craft, however, that it provides not only nasty, chuckling delight in its plot, but also the more refined pleasures of cinematic art. As in ROMANCING THE STONE (1984) and its 1985 sequel, JEWEL OF THE NILE (both of which costarred DeVito), Kathleen Turner and Michael Douglas prove to be the quintessential anti-romantic screen couple for an anti-romantic decade. As Turner's Barbara throws the full, fearsome force of her considerable womanhood into asserting her too-long-suppressed independence, Douglas' Oliver can only cower and be reduced to sputtering impotence. But he simultaneously makes his indomitable love for Barbara a countering force, however stifled and battered it may be. In a neat departure from convention, Turner gives THE WAR OF THE ROSES its bite (literally, in one scene) while Douglas gives the film its odd poignancy.

But that poignancy doesn't detract from the fun. The loving venom with which the Roses hurl their darts, distilled by their 17 years together, has to be seen and heard to

be believed and savored. As a director, DeVito continues to build on the promise he showed in his equally dark and funny feature debut, THROW MOMMA FROM THE TRAIN. Here, in what is essentially a film about control, DeVito exerts a control behind the camera that is otherwise almost nonexistent in contemporary American film comedy. A filmmaker who is masterfully able to deflate the shoddiness of some American dreams without at the same time deflating American dreamers, DeVito bears favorable comparison to Preston Sturges, and brings a sharpness and wit to the screen that recalls such Sturges films as HAIL THE CONQUERING HERO (1944) and SULLIVAN'S TRAVELS (1941). Just when it seemed time to write the American movie comedy's obituary—1989 having been a year of debacles like WORTH WINNING and LET IT RIDE—the noisy little guy from "Taxi" is turning moviegoers into true believers once again. Songs include: "Only You (and You Alone)" (Buck Ram, Ande Rand, performed by the Platters), "We Wish You a Merry Christmas" (Traditional, arranged by Sam Pottle, performed by the "Sesame Street" cast), "Pretty Lady, Lovely Lady" (Nicky Addeo, performed by Addeo). *(Adult situations, profanity, violence.)*

Comedy   **(PR:O MPAA:R)**

THE MOTION PICTURE ANNUAL

1990

Film Reviews

A

ⓋABYSS, THE**
140m FOX c
Ed Harris *(Bud Brigman)*, Mary Elizabeth Mastrantonio *(Lindsey Brigman)*, Michael Biehn *(Lt. Coffey)*, George Robert Klek *(Wilhite)*, John Bedford Lloyd *("Jammer" Willis)*, Christopher Murphy *(Seal Schoenick)*, Adam Nelson *(Ensign Monk)*, J.C. Quinn *("Sonny" Dawson)*, Kimberly Scott *(Lisa "One Night" Standing)*, Capt. Kidd Brewer Jr. *(Lew Finler)*, Leo Burmester *("Catfish" De Vries)*, Todd Graff *(Alan "Hippy" Carnes)*, Richard Warlock *(Dwight Perry)*, Jimmie Ray Weeks *(Leland McBride)*, J. Kenneth Campbell *(DeMarco)*, Ken Jenkins *(Gerard Kirkhill)*, Chris Elliot *(Bendix)*, Peter Ratray *(Captain)*, Michael Beach *(Barnes)*, Brad Sullivan *(Executive)*, Frank Lloyd *(Navigator)*, Joe Farago *(Anchorman)*, William Wisher *(Bill Tyler)*, Phillip Darlington, Joseph Nemec III *(Crew Members)*.

Picture the opening scene of JAWS, except that in THE ABYSS, it's not a great white shark but an underwater UFO, travelling an unheard-of 130 knots and climbing, that propels the movie into its plot. Spotted on sonar by a US nuclear submarine on patrol some 80 miles off the coast of Cuba, the still-unseen "thing" is eerily tracked below deck, where, with absence of malice, it creates a disaster because of the crew's ensuing panic. The sub sinks 2,000 feet onto the ledge of an abyss, and a team of roughneck oil riggers working nearby on "Deepcore," a manned submersible drilling habitat, is pressed into a seek-and-save rescue mission. The seven-man civilian crew, led by rig foreman Harris, is joined by Mastrantonio, Deepcore's project-design engineer, who also happens to be Harris' soon-to-be ex-wife. (She's also the only female in the film.) Last to come aboard is a do-or-die group of US navy SEAL underwater experts headed by Biehn, whose top-secret priority is to oversee the 150 nuclear warheads located within the sub's bowels—each containing "five times the explosive power of Hiroshima." For the rest of the movie's two-and-a-quarter-hour running time, this team's mission impossible is to retrieve the sub from the brink of a precipice on the floor of the Atlantic, the Cayman Trough, extending straight down for more than 2.5 miles. This task, already complicated by internal strife, takes on a wholly new character when the extra-terrestrial force makes its presence known. When the alien first appears, it's a benign, tiny Tinker Bell-like creature; later, through special effects wizardry, it converts into an amazing "pseudopod," a luminous, giant, eel-shaped creature made of sea water that can

assume human facial characteristics (in a remarkable special-effects innovation that defies description; it *must* be seen). Though she intuitively senses that this alien is no bug-eyed monster, Mastrantonio has a hard time persuading the others that it means no harm, especially Biehn and his men, who believe the alien is all part of a Soviet plot. (In one of the film's funniest bits—and there are a few—Mastrantonio confronts the cynical SEALs with the demand, "Raise your hand if you think it was a Russian water tentacle.") Crazed by a water pressure-induced psychosis, the paranoid Biehn commandeers the rescue ship, threatening to blow it (and everyone else) up in his attempt to activate one of the nuclear devices. He's stopped in hand-to-hand combat with Harris, who then bravely volunteers to bravely drop into the abyss, and apparent certain death, to trash the warheads. Harris, encased in a diving suit containing a special fluorocarbon mixture that permits him to breathe underwater (the substance actually exists), sinks over 25,000 feet, further than any man has ever gone before. "A record!" says Mastrantonio, in voice contact with Harris. "Call Guinness," he answers, right before he encounters a vastly superior alien civilization. Holding hands with an underwater E.T. (a la Lois Lane flying with Superman), he's given a quick tour of their underwater kingdom (as in the finale of CLOSE ENCOUNTERS OF THE THIRD KIND) and is magically returned to the safety of the surface, an intact crew and craft, and the loving arms of his no-longer-estranged wife.

A disquieting sense of deja vu pervades almost every frame of this waterlogged science-fiction adventure. We've been here many times before; despite the fact that most of the action occurs below sea level instead of in outer space, THE ABYSS merely recycles elements of the stellar blockbusters whose success it tries so hard to emulate (CLOSE ENCOUNTERS; E.T.; and director James Cameron's own ALIENS among them), substituting diving suits for space suits and aquanauts for astronauts. The similarities aren't all that surprising, considering THE ABYSS came from the same team (Cameron and producer Gale Anne Hurd) that put together both ALIENS and the 1984 hit THE TERMINATOR, and the film does have spectacle to spare. Unfortunately, however, it lacks the stirring emotional impact and suspense of its predecessors, despite the reported $60 million spent to make this underwater fantasy. What ultimately saves THE ABYSS from becoming an abysmal also-ran has less to do with its plot, dialog, and direction—which for the most part are heavy-handed and stilted—than with its extraordinary sets and phenomenal special effects, all from the drawing board of Industrial Light & Magic, the people who

have contributed so mightily to the Spielberg-Lucas epics of the last decade.

THE ABYSS is also a love story, pairing Harris' blue-collar, laid-back character with Mastrantonio's high-tech and deadly earnest Deepcore designer in the unlikely style of the old Hepburn and Tracy movies. Harris and Mastrantonio work well together, despite being hampered by some excessively melodramatic dialog. Like Robert Duvall, the balding Harris is one of the few actors who can appear sexy without cosmetic appeal; while Mastrantonio is cast in the same mold as Sigourney Weaver in ALIENS: a smart, shrewd, no-nonsense type of scientist with classic good looks, part of the new generation of Hollywood heroines who couldn't give a hoot about rings around the collar. In a dialogical aside, her character is said to have given "four years to designing Deepcore, and only three years to her marriage," a remark that brings to mind the working relationship between the formerly wed Cameron and Hurd. Writer-director Cameron, who wrote the treatment for THE ABYSS more than four years ago (working from a short story he wrote in high school) calls the similarity "life coincidentally imitating art."

About 40 percent of this ambitious effort was filmed entirely underwater in the murky depths of two mammoth tanks

THE ABYSS (©20th Century Fox).

located at the never-completed Cherokee Nuclear Power Station outside Gaffney, South Carolina. To lend the action an even greater sense of reality, no stunt divers were used in place of the actors. 20th Century Fox, which gambled a huge bankroll (and their reputation) on this epic, was concerned that a considerable segment of the population didn't know who the lead actors were or what the title THE ABYSS meant (a restriction that didn't hinder APOCALYPSE NOW or POLTERGEIST), and that audiences might be accordingly limited. Unfortunately, there are other, more serious problems to worry about in this plodding picture. Despite all out efforts from a fine, talented cast, THE ABYSS doesn't seem to go anywhere much except down. *(Nudity, profanity.)*

p, Gale Anne Hurd; d, James Cameron; w, James Cameron; ph, Mikael Salomon and Dennis Skotak (DuArt Color); ed, Joel Goodman; m, Alan Silvestri; prod d, Leslie Dilley; art d, Peter Childs; set d, Andrew Precht, Tom Wilkins, and Gershon Ginsburg; spec eff, Joe Unsinn and Joseph Viskocil; cos, Deborah Everton; stunts, Richard Warlock; makeup, Kathryn Miles Kelly.

Science Fiction   (PR:C MPAA:PG-13)

⊙ADVENTURES OF BARON MUNCHAUSEN, THE***
(Brit./Ger.) 126m Prominent Features-Laura-Allied/COL-Tri-Star c

John Neville *(Baron Munchausen)*, Eric Idle *(Desmond/Berthold)*, Sarah Polley *(Sally Salt)*, Oliver Reed *(Vulcan)*, Charles McKeown *(Rupert/Adolphus)*, Winston Dennis *(Bill Albrecht)*, Jack Purvis *(Jeremy/Gustavus)*, Valentina Cortese *(Queen Ariadne/Violet)*, Jonathan Pryce *(Horatio Jackson)*, Bill Paterson *(Henry Salt)*, Peter Jeffrey *(The Sultan)*, Uma Thurman *(Venus/Rose)*, Alison Steadman *(Daisy)*, Ray Cooper *(Functionary)*, Don Henderson *(Commander)*, Andrew Maclachlan *(Colonel)*, Mohamed Badrsalem *(Executioner)*, Kiran Shah *(Executioner's Assistant)*, Ettore Martini *(First General)*, Sting *(Heroic Officer)*, Jose Lifante *(Dr. Death)*, Robin Williams *(King of the Moon)*, Franco Adducci *(Treasurer)*.

Terry Gilliam's THE ADVENTURES OF BARON VON MUNCHAUSEN adapts the fables concerning Karl Friedrich Hieronymous von Munchausen (1720-97), the German soldier and nobleman whose tall tales were the basis of stories by Rudolf Erich Raspe and, in turn, the focus of numerous European popular legends. The film begins in a walled city whose denizens suffer under a siege by the army of the Ottoman Empire and under the government of the evil Horatio Jackson (Pryce, star of Gilliam's BRAZIL). Within the town's heavily shelled walls, a theater troupe stages their rendition of the

THE ADVENTURES OF BARON MUNCHAUSEN (©Columbia).

Munchausen saga. Impresario Henry Salt (Paterson) plays the Baron; three players (Idle, McKeown, and Purvis) essay the roles of the Baron's famous servants Berthold (the fastest man alive), Adolphus (an expert marksman with amazing powers of vision), and Gustavus (a dwarf with gale-force lung capacity). They are interrupted from the audience by the aged Neville, who announces that the play is all wrong, and that he should know, because he's the *real* Baron. What's more, only he can lift the siege, because he's responsible for it in the first place. A flashback shows that the war originated as the result of a younger Neville's winning a bet with the Turkish sultan, after which he, with the help of Berthold, Adolphus, and Gustavus (played again, and for the rest of the film, by Idle, McKeown, and Purvis), along with the fantastically strong Albrecht (Dennis), carried off the sultan's treasury. Back in the theater, however, no one believes Neville's story, except Polley, Paterson's little daughter—especially after she sees his flight via cannonball beyond the city walls and back. Eventually, Neville convinces the rest of the town that only he can save them, and departs in a makeshift balloon, searching for his superhumanly gifted aides.

En route to his first stop—the moon—he discovers stowaway Polley, who tries to keep Neville from getting too distracted by their wild adventures. These include a confrontation with the lunatic Moon King (Williams, uncredited) who jails Neville and Polley in a cage with the aged, no-longer-speedy Idle, whom Neville left to his lunar fate years before. After a narrow escape from the moon, Neville, Polley, and

Idle wind up in Mount Etna, where Vulcan (Reed) is busy making nuclear weapons. Among his minions is Dennis, who has renounced his old powers in favor of gentleness and a maid's uniform. Also making an appearance is Vulcan's wife, Venus (gorgeous, semi-nude Thurman). Neville and company are tossed into a whirlpool and swallowed by a giant whale in whose belly they encounter the blind McKeown and the deaf, wheezy Purvis. Eventually, all are disgorged back into the sea and drift ashore near the besieged city, where, urged on by Polley, the decrepit ex-companions set out to save the city in a fantastic battle whose dazzling elements include hordes of extras, elephants, and Idle's special-effects race with a bullet. Re-entering the city, Neville is shot by Pryce (who, it turns out, has had a secret pact with the enemy all along), and would seem to have indulged in his last exploit. Through the magic of storytelling, however, the Angel of Death is banished once more, the city opens its gate to find the enemy gone for good, and Neville rides off to further adventures.

A much beleaguered production, Gilliam's film ended up costing an estimated $40-45 million, about twice its original budget. As costs escalated, Gilliam found himself battling to retain control of the project, wary of his experience with BRAZIL, which was almost released in a bastardized, upbeat form. Investors tried to force the director to cut the moon sequence, causing Sean Connery to quit his role as the Moon King. Further complications arose with the ouster of David Puttnam as head of Columbia.

If the end result is not the poetic masterpiece Gilliam envisioned, neither is it the debacle others predicted. While the verbal suffers badly in contrast to the visual, the visuals are often quite impressive. The scenes in Vulcan's lair, for example, charm with the witty, wonderful entrance of Venus and her splendid special-effects midair dance with the Baron, but grate with the simplistic, perfunctory business of Vulcan's nuclear arms-building industry. Similarly, the lunar scenes are an imaginative *visual* triumph—the effects at once fantastic, delicate, and surprising—but Robin Williams' manic performance seems forced and distracting.

A serious dramatic problem with the film is its failure to develop Jonathan Pryce's character and the danger he represents. One never cares much whether the town is saved, because the sense of peril is never made tangible. Fine actor though he is, Pryce is hampered by the script's weaknesses and manages to do merely serviceable work. The same can be said for Neville and Polley. Williams manages to be sporadically funny and certainly stands out, but Oliver Reed is more *fun*, while Eric Idle, Uma Thurman, Valentina Cortese, and Charles McKeown do well in roles that mainly require them to look their parts. Luckily, the pyrotechnics make for very worthwhile viewing, for which credit must go to Gilliam, special-effects supervisor Richard Conway, production designer Dante Ferretti, and cinematographer Giuseppe Rotunno. *(Comic violence, brief nudity, sexual situations.)*

p, Thomas Schuhly and Ray Cooper; d, Terry Gilliam; w, Charles McKeown and Terry Gilliam (based on the stories by Rudolph Erich Raspe); ph, Giuseppe Rotunno (Eastmancolor); ed, Peter Hollywood; m, Michael Kamen; prod d, Dante Ferretti; art d, Massimo Razzi and Teresa Barbasso; set d, Francesca Lo Schiavo; spec eff, Richard Conway; cos, Gabriella Pescucci; chor, Pino Penesse; stunts, Tony Smart; makeup, Maggie Westeon.

Fantasy   (PR:A-C MPAA:PG)

ⓥADVENTURES OF MILO AND OTIS, THE***
(Jap.) 76m Fuji Television Network/COL c
(KONEKO MONOGATARI; AKA: THE ADVENTURES OF CHATRAN), Dudley Moore *(Narrator).*

Of all the buddy movies ever made, MILO AND OTIS has one of the most unlikely pairs of friends—a cat and dog that befriend each other on a farm and eventually wander out into the not-so-friendly world. Not a single human being appears on-screen in this delightful live-action offering from Japan that was five years in the making.

It all starts when the kitten, Milo, decides to take a trip down the river in a box, with his faithful canine chum Otis following behind. But soon Otis loses track of his friend who, by nightfall, is way downstream. The next morning, Otis, still in hot pursuit, finds the empty box. Meanwhile, Milo ventures to some hot springs, meets a fox, and gets caught in a rainstorm at the beach. Figuring his luck can't get any worse, Milo follows some railroad tracks into a meadow where he meets an owl that lets him sleep in his "dreaming nest". Longing for the good old days, Milo dreams of life on the farm and playing with his pal Otis. Later that evening, Milo rescues a little piglet from a hawk, and is taken in by a family of pigs who treat Milo as one of their own. Soon, however, the intrepid feline adventurer leaves his adoptive family, only to be attacked by sea gulls and harassed by an unrelenting bear. About this time Otis finally catches up with his furry friend, and the two have a joyful reunion before heading back to the farm. En route, Milo meets the feline fatale of his dreams, Joyce, who makes the duo a trio until Otis, feeling neglected and slightly jealous, goes his own way. In no time, though, Otis has his own love interest, a pretty puppy named Sandra. Winter falls before either couple can make it back home, so they hole up for the long cold months. During this time Joyce and Sandra both give birth to a litter, and the two families eventually meet up at the farm in the springtime.

Based on a charming screenplay by Mark Saltzman, this clever children's film contains beautiful nature photography and moments of humor along with many impressive animal stunts (over 20 trainers worked on this film). Surely it was no small feat to get bears and dogs, chickens and cats, pigs and cows to work together onscreen. Shot from the animals' point of view and narrated by Dudley Moore, MILO AND OTIS also contains some important messages about friendship and responsibility. Despite the fact that Milo and Otis are a cat and dog (and therefore "natural" enemies) they manage to form a close friendship that endures many hardships. Responsibility is addressed near the beginning of the film, when our heroes are given the task of taking care of a chicken's egg. And later, Otis is faced with the problem of finding enough food to get his family through the winter. The only drawback to MILO AND OTIS is that it tends to drag in spots, but the animal "performances" and the nature scenes are enough to hold anyone's interest, especially animal lovers.

p, Masaru Kakutani and Satoru Ogata; d, Masanori Hata; w, Mark Saltzman (based on a story by Masanori Hata); ph, Hideo Fujii and Shinji Tomita; ed, Chizuko Osada; m, Michael Boddicker.

Children's   (PR:AA MPAA:G)

AFTER MIDNIGHT*
90m High Bar/MGM-UA c
Jillian McWhirter *(Allison)*, Pamela Segall *(Cheryl)*, Ramy Zeda *(Prof. Derek)*, Nadine van der Velde *(Joan)*, Marc McClure *(Kevin)*, Marg Helgenberger *(Alex)*, Billy Ray Sharkey *(Ray).*

Although anthology horror films have acquired a bad reputation, this spotty subgenre has produced a few successful films, TALES FROM THE CRYPT and VAULT OF HORROR among them. More often, though, horror anthologies, like NIGHTMARES and TWILIGHT ZONE—THE MOVIE, have failed. AFTER MIDNIGHT can be added to the latter category. Oddly constructed, AFTER MIDNIGHT doesn't get to its first story until some 20 minutes have passed. The film begins as two college girls (one of whom is overcome by a weird sense of dread) go to their new class, "The Psychology of Fear," taught by Zeda. This is no normal class, and Zeda is not a normal instructor. Instead of books he uses guns (routinely threatening to shoot his students, causing them to wet their pants) to enforce his motto: "In order to understand fear, you must experience it." One of the girls in the class (McWhirter) is weary of the whole experience and especially of Zeda. After the dean forces Zeda to change his teaching techniques, the professor invites his more adventurous students to his home for private lessons. There, the group tells stories that touch upon primal fears. Zeda goes first, recounting the story of a married couple and their experiences in a haunted house. The tale ends with a twist as the husband (McClure) mistakenly beheads his wife. The second story, told by a student, depicts the consequences four teenage girls face when they attempt to sneak into an adult bar. The girls run out of gas, are attacked by a psycho, and are eaten by wild dogs. Easily the worst of the film's installments, this sick, suspenseless segment leaves a bad aftertaste. The third, and best, tale (edited by a different unit) tells the story of an all-night answering service operator (Helgenberger) who is threatened and eventually attacked by a maniac who telephones her throughout the night. Though owing much to BLACK CHRISTMAS and REAR WINDOW, this segment succeeds mostly by virtue of Helgenberger's natural performance and strong pacing (it's the only story that's not way too long).

Poorly paced and handled, AFTER MIDNIGHT is absolutely stultifying. The stories range from predictable to offensive and the connecting element, the psychology class, comes off as ridiculous. Directors Ken and Jim Wheat, the men behind the TV movie "Ewoks: The Battle for Endor," try desperately to create a mood (in the first tale there are enough creepy vines and luminous fog to fill at least 10 haunted house movies), but despite their efforts the bulk of the film remains boring. Each story is supposed to end with a twist, but nothing in this movie comes as a surprise, and most of the "twists" can be seen from a mile away. AFTER MIDNIGHT might be dismissed as a brainless horror flick were it not for its second tale, in which the Wheat brothers attack the teenage girls—nasty genre stereotypes—with disconcerting vigor, the camera dwelling on shots of wild dogs gnawing on the girls' limbs or gruesomely depicting their terror as a psychopath nearly rapes them. A demented display of purposeless violence presented without style, this second story pushes AFTER MIDNIGHT into the realm of the offensive. The one saving grace of the movie is Marg Helgenberger, who brings a sense of conviction to her serviceable performance in the final episode. Although quicker paced and easier to watch than the rest of the film, the last story is still predictable and dumb, and when it's all over, it's obvious that Helgenberger has wasted her time. AFTER MIDNIGHT does nothing to improve the awful reputation of anthology horror films. (*Profanity, graphic violence, adult situations.*)

p, Ken Wheat and Jim Wheat; d, Ken Wheat and Jim Wheat; w, Ken Wheat and Jim Wheat; ph, Phedon Papamichael (Foto-Kem Color); ed, Phillip Linson and Quinnie Martin Jr.; m, Marc Donahue; art d, Chris Henry.

Horror   **(PR:O MPAA:R)**

ⓥAFTER SCHOOL*
89m Hugh Parks/Moviestore c
Sam Bottoms (*Father Michael McCarren*), Renee Coleman (*September Lane*), Edward Binns (*Monsignor Barrett*), James Farkas (*First Leader*), Page Hannah (*Annie*), Don Harvey (*Nathan*), Robert Lansing (*C.A. Thomas*), Dick Cavett (*Himself*).

A strange but uninvolving mix of subjects and styles, AFTER SCHOOL attempts to combine the theories of evolution and creation with a story line involving a priest's sexual temptation. The film begins in prehistoric times, when cavemen and women play in a stream, then flashes forward to the present day, as hip priest Bottoms rides his motorcycle to the college where he teaches. The intercutting between time frames continues without apparent pattern and reason throughout the film, while the story follows Bottoms as he prepares to defend the Catholic Church on "The Dick Cavett Show" (Cavett himself does a cameo), having been asked by his monsignor (Binns) to appear on the show and rebut Perkins, an ex-priest who has written a book questioning the existence of God. While preparing for the show, however, Bottoms begins to have doubts of his own, precipitated by his feelings for his smartest student, Coleman.

It seems Coleman doesn't believe in God and, to make matters worse, is sexually attracted to Bottoms. Meanwhile, back in the Stone Age, the cavepeople hunt, perform rituals, and discover a large, hollowed tree that particularly fascinates group leader Farkas. (Is it God or some other supernatural power? No, it's just a lame ripoff of 2001: A SPACE ODYSSEY.) These Neanderthal sequences are loosely parallel to the situation between Coleman and Bottoms; a scene involving prehistoric sex is preceded by Bottoms' near-seduction. As the contemporary pair's relationship develops, Bottoms' crisis of faith worsens. Coleman won't let him rest—in one scene she phones him from a bathtub while eating a symbolic apple—and her old boy friend has misleading photographs of her and the priest that he threatens to make public if they don't stop seeing each other. Nothing ever comes of the threat, however, and the relationship proceeds apace until the day of the Cavett show debate. Meanwhile, caveman Farkas is struck by lightning, leaving a cut over the left side of his rib cage. Perhaps a rib is missing? In the subsequent sequence combining evolution and the Genesis story, a naked woman (not a Neanderthal) appears, a snake emerges from a tree, and an apple is eaten . . . Back on the Cavett show, Bottoms is swayed by Perkins' argument, leaves the set abruptly, and walks off with Coleman into the woods. The movie ends with the image of the caveman/Adam extending his arm skyward.

What does all of this mean? Who knows. Director-coproducer William Olsen's film raises more questions than it answers. The narrative structure is both uninteresting and hard to follow, the prehistoric sequences are ridiculously acted and cliched beyond belief, and the story of the priest's temptation is so stiffly performed (Renee Coleman is particularly bad) and blandly directed that the supposed heat and suspense of the situation is nowhere to be found. You never believe for a minute that Bottoms can't control himself, or that Coleman is in love with him. (*Nudity, profanity, sexual situations, mild violence, adult situations.*)

p, Hugh Parks and William Olsen; d, William Olsen; w, Hugh Parks, John Linde, Rod McBrien, and Joe Tankersley; ph, Austin McKinney (TVC Color); ed, John David Allen; m, David C. Williams; art d, David Meo.

Drama   **(PR:O MPAA:R)**

ⓥALEXA*½
80m Hydra-Platinum-B Tru c
Christine Moore (*Alexa Avery*), Kirk Baily (*Tony*), Ruth Collins (*Marshall Newhouse*), Joseph P. Giardina (*Jan*), Tom Voth (*Tommy*), Adam Michenner (*March*), Thomas Walker, Sarah Halley,

Trula Hoosier, Leslie Lowe, Mary Round, Joseph Haddock, Sharon Kane, Sheri St. Claire.

While it is not hard to guess the target audience (dirty old men) for the sensationally titled ALEXA: A PROSTITUTE'S OWN STORY, the film should come with a warning: "Tamer than you would expect." Despite their sexy subject matter, soft-core skin flicks are not always erotic, and this movie's appeal to the prurient is limited. Those looking for vicarious thrills will likely feel that there's not enough sleazy sex, not enough heat generated by the leading players, and not enough gratuitous nudity. Viewing ALEXA is about as sexually stimulating as watching kindergartners play "doctor."

As the eponymous prostitute, the alluring Moore has made sure that wealthy men have "kept" her in grand style. But although spending a few hours a week on her back has proved to be a lucrative profession for Moore, her general unhappiness is all too transparent. Weary of the powerful men who avail themselves of her services, Moore is headed for a breakdown when best friend Collins introduces her to Baily, a sexy, Adonis-like playwright who wants to do research on her for a work-in-progress. Baring her soul but not her body, Moore reveals the sordid secrets of the skin trade to Baily. Unaware of the time required to complete a project like the one Baily has undertaken, Moore demands to see the fruit of the writer's labor and accuses him of being as exploitative as her clients. At the same time, she finds herself attracted to him. For his part, Baily admits that he, too, has prostituted himself—though it's never clear whether he means literal hustling or literary hustling. When her pimp, Giardina, refuses to take her career malaise seriously, Moore petulantly toys with the idea of a job change while alternately pursuing and rejecting Baily. Jealous of the other call girls that Baily interviews, Moore begins to come apart at the seams. Imploring Baily to make her the sole subject of his masterpiece, Moore commits the cardinal sin of her trade and falls in love with him. After tossing out her see-through panties and assorted S&M toys, she visits her happily domesticated sister, confesses her sins, and then denounces her sibling as a married whore. Free of all ties to her living relatives, and honest but unemployed, Moore abandons herself to Baily, proving her devotion by enduring *all* of his writer's cliches, like "Prostitution isn't just spreading your legs." But tragedy rears its predictable head when a low-life pimp shows up at a theater party and kills Baily, who dies defending Moore's honor. Nevertheless, Baily has bequeathed Moore a new lease on life and a "can't miss" play about her past. What more could a reformed prostitute ask for?

Meandering along teasingly, ALEXA promises much but delivers little; its love scenes lack sensuality and its portrait of two lost souls who find each other in the neon jungle is passionless. On the surface, director Sean Delgado's film is reminiscent of DARLING; PUZZLE OF A DOWN-FALL CHILD, and other glossy looks at beautiful, bored women who've sold their souls for a dollar. But without magnetic stars to flesh out these superficial *Confession* magazine concepts, the film emerges as a distaff CITIZEN KANE filtered through a massage parlor mentality. ALEXA attempts to probe an enigmatic soul whose beauty and suffering are both skin-deep. Although she looks great in a stunning array of clothes for the contemporary "working girl," the beautiful Christine Moore does not have the modulated voice of a trained actress. When she is called upon to deliver soul-baring pronouncements, Moore's shrieks are so grating that one feels the need to check the projector's decibel level. Somewhat less forced, Kirk Baily's performance is marginally better; however, he is never believable in the role of a produced playwright. Instead, he reminds one of an aerobics instructor who calls himself a writer because he's written an exercise pamphlet. The rest of the cast are without the distraction of physical charms to recommend them. Notably, Ruth Collins is a Marilyn Monroe impersonator who's gone off the deep end. *(Nudity, profanity, violence, sexual situations.)*

p, Peggy Bruen; d, Sean Delgado; w, Peggy Bruen and Sean Delgado; ph, Joey Forsyte; ed, James Davalos; m, Gregory Alper; art d, Liz Deutsch.

Drama　　　　　**(PR:O　MPAA:R)**

ALL DOGS GO TO HEAVEN*
87m Sullivan Bluth-Goldcrest/UA c
VOICES OF: Burt Reynolds *(Charlie)*, Dom DeLuise *(Itchy)*, Vic Tayback *(Carface)*, Melba Moore *(Whippet Angel)*, Judith Barsi *(Anne-Marie)*, Charles Nelson Reilly *(Killer)*, Loni Anderson *(Flo)*, Candy Devine *(Vera)*, Ken Page *(King Gator)*.

A G-rated children's cartoon with a scheming antihero, fistfights, a descent into hell, and death? That's what Don Bluth presents in his latest animated feature, ALL DOGS GO TO HEAVEN, an entertaining but surprisingly adult musical adventure that features the voices of Burt Reynolds, Loni Anderson, Dom DeLuise, and Vic Tayback (perhaps they just brought a microphone to the set of TV's "Win, Lose or Draw"). Set in Louisiana in 1939, ALL DOGS GO TO HEAVEN tells the story of Charlie (Reynolds), a mangy canine convict who escapes from the slammer with the help of his friend Itchy (DeLuise). He then reappears at the casino and rat-racing

establishment he co-owns with the evil Carface (Tayback), hoping to get back to business. Carface has other plans, however; wanting the business all to himself, he decides to kill his partner. One night, after getting Charlie drunk and leaving him on a pier, Carface runs over him with an automobile. Immediately, Charlie is transported to the cloudy, golden world of heaven, where he is greeted by an angel (Moore), told that he is dead, and given wings and a halo. Even though he is informed that he can never return to heaven if he leaves, Charlie goes back to earth (by winding backwards a watch that represents his life) to seek revenge on Carface. Back on earth, Charlie reunites with Itchy. Together, they discover that Carface has kidnaped Anne-Marie, a little orphan girl (Barsi) who has the ability to talk with animals, and is exploiting her special talent to learn which rat racers are sure things. Charlie and Itchy steal the girl from Carface, nickname her Squeaker, and use her power to put Carface out of business. Charlie then promises to find some loving parents for Squeaker but instead uses her gift to enrich himself. Eventually, Carface comes after them (at one point with a raygun), but the trio always manages to elude him. As the film progresses, Charlie, who is haunted by nightmares of hell (no doubt brought about by his guilty conscience), makes friends with a giant, soulful alligator; Itchy is beaten up by Carface and his gang; and Squeaker becomes very sick. The climax comprises a huge fight between Charlie and Carface.

The subject matter of ALL DOGS GO TO HEAVEN (death, hell, gambling, and drinking all figure prominently) has rarely been dealt with so bluntly in an animated children's film. Indeed, Bluth seems to be going for an older crowd (as the choice of

the actors who provide the voices further suggests), and some scenes in the movie may frighten or confuse more impressionable children. Closer in spirit to the films of Ralph Bakshi than to those of Walt Disney, ALL DOGS GO TO HEAVEN is, nonetheless, never offensive and perfectly suitable for most children (though many may be bored by it). As with all of Bluth's films, the animation here is exceptional, full of wonderfully realized alternative worlds (heaven is interesting, hell is astounding) and rich, fluid character movements. Bluth is a splendid technician and the film is always a joy to watch. Equally entertaining is the use of Reynolds' voice (in one of his best comedic roles in years), and Reynolds' and DeLuise's familiar screen shtick transfers perfectly to their animated counterparts. *(Violence, adult situations, substance abuse.)*

p, Don Bluth, Gary Goldman, and John Pomeroy; d, Gary Goldman, Dan Kuenster, and Don Bluth; w, David Weiss (based on a story by Weiss, Don Bluth, Ken Cromar, Gary Goldman, Larry Leker, Linda Miller, Monica Parker, John Pomeroy, Guy Schulman, David Steinberg); ed, John K. Carr; m, Ralph Burns; prod d, Don Bluth and Larry Leker.

Animated/Children's　(PR:A　MPAA:G)

ALWAYS½
121m UNIV-UA/UNIV c
Richard Dreyfuss *(Pete Sandich)*, Holly Hunter *(Dorinda Durston)*, Brad Johnson *(Ted Baker)*, John Goodman *(Al Yackey)*, Audrey Hepburn *(Hap)*, Roberts Blossom *(Dave)*, Keith David *(Powerhouse)*, Ed Van Nuys *(Nails)*, Marg Helgenberger *(Rachel)*, Dale Dye *(Fire Boss)*, Brian

Holly Hunter and Richard Dreyfuss in ALWAYS (©Universal).

Haley *(Alex)*, James Lashly *(Charlie)*, Michael Steve Jones *(Grey)*, Kim Robillard *(Air Traffic Controller)*, Jim Sparkman *(Dispatcher)*, Doug McGrath *(Bus Driver)*, Joseph McCrossin *(Mechanic)*, J.D. Souther *(Singer)*, Gerry Rothschild *(Carl the Barkeep)*, Loren Smothers *(Bartender)*, Taleena Ottwell *(Bar Girl)*.

Old habits die hard, and sometimes not at all. If ALWAYS is director Steven Spielberg's breakthrough to maturity—as many an erstwhile Spielberg-basher has insisted it is—it's a maturity rooted in the callow habits of his past: the fantasy escapism of E.T. and CLOSE ENCOUNTERS OF THE THIRD KIND, the self-announcing sentiment of THE COLOR PURPLE and EMPIRE OF THE SUN (Look Ma, I'm feeling!), the anxious overreaching of the Indiana Jones films, in which life-size is never quite enough. The child was never more father to the man than in Spielberg's latest, a would-be grown-up bauble. But it's the child in ALWAYS—straining for cosmic (read: parental) reassurance and underlining every small effect—that causes all the problems, making Spielberg's close encounter with adulthood look more like a case of arrested development.

The film begins with a gratuitous bit of business: Two anglers, a small open boat, a quiet lake. Suddenly a monster airplane looms behind the anglers, bearing down on their tiny craft. The plane buzzes, the anglers dive, the scene abruptly ends. (Moral: Mere stories must be consistent, but "high" art needn't be. Or maybe it's just an homage to the shark in JAWS?) Shift now to the main locus of the tale, an airfield in the Northwest, where air controller Hunter frets over the fate of Dreyfuss, a fire-fighting ace known for taking chances on the job. It's the 21st day of a raging blaze and Dreyfuss is in trouble. His plane's engines having conked out, he's gliding in on a wing and a prayer (Hawks' ONLY ANGELS HAVE WINGS isn't far to seek in this prop-driven low-tech scenario). At a critical moment, a young stunt flier (Johnson) buzzes the landing strip (he's been hired by Dreyfuss to deliver a birthday gift to Hunter), inadvertently creating an updraft that allows Dreyfuss to land safely (no coincidence is too improbable for this film). Hunter is angry over the prank but glad to have Dreyfuss back on the ground. At the birthday celebration that follows, she dons the white dress and pumps Dreyfuss has bought for her, little realizing that deliveryman Johnson has been smitten with her charms. Later, Hunter professes her love for Dreyfuss and urges him to give up his risky profession (she has a premonition of what's to come), and Dreyfuss' best friend in the squadron (Goodman) suggests the same, but Dreyfuss decides to go out on one last fire-fight-

ing run. The decision proves to be fatal when his plane catches fire and explodes in midair. While others mourn his death, Dreyfuss is surprised to find that he's apparently still alive. It's only after he meets an angel in a forest clearing (Hepburn, who gives him his first afterlife haircut) that he realizes he isn't. Hepburn assigns him to pass on his earthly knowledge to a would-be firefighter pilot. The pilot turns out to be Johnson, of course, and Dreyfuss—invisible to all save the audience—soon proves an erratic teacher, especially after finding out that the novice has a crush on Hunter. But Hunter hasn't recovered from Dreyfuss' death, and it's only after an emotional harangue from Goodman (who, not coincidentally, runs the flight school where Johnson is a student) that she decides to get on with her life. The fates soon conspire to bring Hunter and Johnson together. The two meet when a driverless utility cart plows into Hunter's house, and are soon in love; meanwhile, Dreyfuss stews invisibly in the wings. ("That's my girl, pal," he mutters at his hunky rival.) But Hunter still dreams of her former beau. The white birthday dress comes out again as Hunter dances with her memories and Dreyfuss whispers endearments in her ear, but angel Hepburn soon reminds Dreyfuss that his time is past and that Hunter can't live again unless he lets her go. This he eventually does, but not before Hunter has (a) flown into the heart of a blazing forest to test her fire-fighting mettle, with Dreyfuss barking instructions at her side, (b) soared up and out into the starry night with her ghostly hanger-on, and (c) plunged to the murky bottom of a lake when her disabled plane crashes. It's up to Dreyfuss to save her, and he does, floating with Hunter towards light and a necessary parting. Life wins out again, new love supplants old, and it's Kleenex all around.

Supposedly a remake of A GUY NAMED JOE, an MGM weeper of the 40s starring Spencer Tracy and Irene Dunne, ALWAYS manages to recycle bits and pieces of at least a half-dozen other movies as well, from Howard Hawks' classics to THE HELLFIGHTERS, to RED SKIES OF MONTANA, and to the films of Spielberg's past (the bicycle from E.T., the airfield from EMPIRE OF THE SUN, etc.). This piling up of references makes for a certain density, but it's a density that simply sits onscreen, doing nothing. ALWAYS has no real dramatic conflict, because Spielberg doesn't want it. Instead of making messes, he'd rather reassure, tidying up emotions and sending his characters off to bed with a cookie and a kiss. Authority is still protective in this world of counterfeit adulthood—ironically, a world that inverts the Hawksian meanings it tries so hard to achieve. (In Hawks, overlapping dialog crackles because it has to, because

the characters speaking it have different points of view. In ALWAYS, overlap is simply overlap, sounding more like static than emotional give-and-take.)

The performances are more than adequate given the story's sentimental thrust, although associations with other movies are what really determine the characterizations. This holds especially true for newcomer Brad Johnson's pilot: Johnson's DAWN PATROL bomber togs, Rock Hudson-like good looks, and haphazard stabs at impersonating John Wayne turn him into a medley of old-movie memories and allusions. But all the warmed-over texture in the world can't make up for the film's lack of tension. Overbusy and out of scale, with every random detail a self-conscious event, ALWAYS is a minor work played grandiosely in a major key. Songs include: "Smoke Gets in Your Eyes" (Jerome Kern, Otto Harbach, performed by J.D. Souther and by the Platters), "Nick of Time" (Bonnie Raitt, performed by Raitt), "Boomerang Love" (Jimmy Buffett, performed by Buffett), "Give Me Your Heart" (Phil Marshall, performed by Denette Hoover, Sherwood Ball), "Matzoh Balls" (Slim Gaillard, performed by Gaillard), "Cowboy Man" (Lyle Lovett, performed by Lovett), "A Fool in Love" (Michael Smotherman, performed by Smotherman), "Yakety Yak" (Jerry Leiber, Mike Stoller, performed by the Coasters), "Crazy Love" (Van Morrison, performed by Morrison). *(Adult situations, profanity.)*

p, Steven Spielberg, Frank Marshall, and Kathleen Kennedy; d, Steven Spielberg; w, Jerry Belson (based on the screenplay "A Guy Named Joe" by Dalton Trumbo, from a story by Frederick Hazlitt Brennan, Chandler Sprague, David Boehm); ph, Mikael Salomon (Deluxe Color); ed, Michael Kahn; m, John Williams; prod d, James Bissell; art d, Chris Burian-Mohr; set d, Carl Stensel; spec eff, Mike Wood and Industrial Light & Magic; cos, Ellen Mirojnick; chor, Bob Banas; stunts, Steve Lambert; makeup, James McCoy.

Fantasy/Romance

(PR:A-C MPAA:PG)

Ⓥ**AMERICAN NINJA 3: BLOOD HUNT***
93m Breton/Cannon c
David Bradley *(Sean)*, Steve James *(Curtis Jackson)*, Marjoe Gortner *(Cobra)*, Michele Chan *(Chan Lee)*, Yehuda Efroni *(Andreas)*, Calvin Jung *(Izumo)*, Adrienne Pearce *(Minister's Secretary)*, Evan J. Klisser *(Dexter)*, Grant Preston *(Minister of Interior)*, Mike Huff *(Hodges)*, Alan Swerdlow *(Police Captain)*, Thapelo Mofokeng *(Police Sergeant)*, Ekard Rabi *(Sean's Father)*, Stephen Webber *(Young Sean)*.

There are three "blood hunts" in AMERICAN NINJA 3, in which karate champ

David Bradley takes over for series' star Michael Dudikoff. Blood Hunt No. 1 involves the murder of Bradley's father, which Bradley witnesses as a boy. Bent on avenging Dad's death, Bradley heads to Japan, where he becomes a ninja. After making himself into a fighting machine, he is invited to the karate world championship in Port San Luco, Triana—somewhere in the Caribbean. But the championship is really only a front for Blood Hunt No. 2: bad guys Gortner and Efroni, the very folks responsible for the death of Bradley's father, are holding the contest to find the toughest man in the world so that they can test Gortner's new lab-produced disease on him. If the strain proves as potent as they hope, Gortner and Efroni expect to have terrorists knocking down their door to buy the stuff. Deciding that Bradley is their man, the evil duo lures him to the East Bay Labs by staging a mock abduction of Chan, who is impersonating Bradley's ninja master. Bradley takes the bait and, along with countrymen James and Klisser, fights dozens of ninjas en route to the Labs. However, Bradley is caught and administered the dreaded disease. Blood Hunt No. 3 occurs when James, Klisser, and Chan (who has seen the light) come to the rescue. Of course, they have to fight an awful lot of ninjas along the way. Klisser and Chan die heroically, and James finds the antidote for the disease, but Bradley doesn't need it anyway. Having exerted "mind and soul over body" even before his friend shows up, Bradley dispatches several more ninjas before destroying the evil Gortner.

AMERICAN NINJA 3 is a comic book of a movie that goes too far to be a satisfying adventure and not far enough to be an entertaining parody. Believe it or not, when characters in this movie talk of *hitsu jitsu*, the art of impersonation, or *nisu jitsu*, the practice of mind games, they appear to be serious. Bradley is too stone-faced to have fun with material that begs to be treated with tongue in cheek, and Evan J. Klisser, as a doe-eyed California innocent, is so cartoonlike that it's surprising to see him bleed when he dies. Only Steve James, a holdover from the first two films in the series, and Marjoe Gortner, making a "special appearance," seem well-suited for their roles. James contributes some very welcome comic relief, and Gortner keeps a straight face when uttering the unforgettable line, "Alert the ninjas: I think we'll be having company." Speaking of ninjas, the ones in this film are more or less Keystone Kops in black masks, their inept fighting consisting of striking poses that make them easy targets for counterpunches from the good guys. When they attack in groups against a single fighter, they practice *solo jitsu*, the ancient ninja art of politeness—taking a number and waiting their turn. Still, the problem with AMERICAN

NINJA 3 isn't that it's bad; it's that it isn't bad enough. A little self-conscious silliness would have gone a long way here. Instead, AMERICAN NINJA 3: BLOOD HUNT takes itself entirely too seriously. *(Violence, adult situations.)*

p, Harry Alan Towers; d, Cedric Sundstrom; w, Cedric Sundstrom (based on a story by Gary Conway and characters created by Avi Kleinberger, Gideon Amir); ph, George Bartels (Rank Color); ed, Michael J. Duthie; m, George S. Clinton; prod d, Ruth Strimling; chor, Mike Stone.

Action   **(PR:C MPAA:R)**

Ⓥ**APARTMENT ZERO*****
125m Summit/Skouras c
Hart Bochner *(Jack Carney)*, Colin Firth *(Adrian LeDuc)*, Dora Bryan *(Margaret McKinney)*, Liz Smith *(Mary Louise McKinney)*, Fabrizio Bentivoglio *(Carlos Sanchez-Verne)*, James Telfer *(Vanessa)*, Mirella D'Angelo *(Laura Werpachowsky)*, Juan Vitali *(Alberto Werpachowsky)*, Cipe Lincovsky *(Mrs. Treniev)*, Francesca d'Aloja *(Claudia)*, Miguel Ligero *(Mr. Palma)*, Elvia Andreoli *(Adrian's Mother)*, Marikena Monti *(Tango Singer)*, Luis Romero *(Projectionist)*, Oca Spirito, Micky Chapman *(Women in Cinema)*, Claudia Rosenblat, Sandra Calderon *(Nurses)*, Max Berliner, Mane Arauz, Maria Jose Catino *(Prospective Tenants)*, Debora Bianco *(Girl in Cafe)*, Federico D'Elia *(Boy in Cafe)*, Veronica Gambini *(Girl with Carlos in Building)*, Rosario Varela *(Girl with Carlos at Tango)*, Raul Florido *(Jack's Argentine Contact)*, Claudio Ciacci *(Young Man in Cinema)*, Gabriel Posniak *(Dead Man)*, Guillermo Willart, Javier Balina *(Paramedics)*, Darwin Sanchez *(Police Inspector)*, Daniel Queirolo *(Young Cop)*, Miguel Angel Porro *(Taxi Driver)*, Ezequiel Donovan, Eduardo Peralta Ramos, John Kamps, Goran Johansson *(Foreign Elements)*, Lisanne Cole, German Palacios, Horacio Erman, Ines Estevez, Robert Baldi, Sebastian De Nico, Ruth Jasiuk, Marina Zemma, Pablo Lena, Juan Jose Gato *(Political Groups in Cinema)*, Daniel Astesano *(Immigration Officer)*, Alfredo Quesada *(Speaker at Group Meeting)*, Stephen Cole *(Strange-looking Man in Airport)*, Nicolas Pereyra *(Doctor at Institution)*, Gabriel Corrado *(Victim in Hotel Room)*, Jorge Caseres *(Young Man with Vanessa)*.

With APARTMENT ZERO director-cowriter Martin Donovan uses a thriller format to fashion a clever diatribe against the oppressive Argentine military regime that was responsible for countless brutal "disappearances." Set in the post-junta era, this rococo suspense film hinges on a disturbing question: If democracy is in full swing, why are mercenary-style executions still happening?

Colin Firth (ANOTHER COUNTRY; A MONTH IN THE COUNTRY) plays a fastidious, paranoid Argentine who pretends to be British so he can remain an outsider in his homeland. For him nothing matters but the repertory cinema he owns and operates. Old movies are his raison d'etre; his only friend is the theater cashier. Apart from the visions of Montgomery Clift that dance in his head, Firth occupies himself with visits to his terminally ill mother and with avoiding his neighbors, who he fears will invade his cocoonlike existence. Politically neutral and socially self-exiled, Firth lives an uneventful life until financial needs force him to seek a roommate. Like a reincarnation of eternal movie rebel and sex symbol James Dean, Bochner enters Firth's life—a film fantasy come true. For Firth, Bochner is the trustworthy companion for whom he has so desperately longed, but the mysterious stranger also proves to be all things to all people in the apartment building: gallant gentleman to two nosy English biddies, father figure to a lonely married woman, the object of a bisexual man's "teenage" crush, and lover/protector of a transvestite. Jealous of Bochner's many involvements, Firth discovers his roommate has been lying about working for an American computer company and becomes suspicious about Bochner's real identity. Their psychological gamesmanship is intercut with news reports of a serial killer whose methods recall the paid assassins once employed by the military government and now the subject of a propaganda film shown in the theater by Firth's cashier friend. Devastated by his mother's death, Firth reaches out to his soulmate, unaware that Bochner has other plans involving foreign travel. As has been all too apparent, Bochner is the mystery killer. Once the military decides it can dispense with him, Bochner murders a man he resembles in order to obtain his passport. Refusing to believe that Bochner has suddenly gone away on a trip, the busybody apartment dwellers suspect that Firth is the killer and that he has eliminated his roommate. After they accidentally push Firth off a hall landing, Bochner returns providentially and nurses his roommate back to health. Unfortunately, the theater cashier recognizes Bochner, and she, too, is killed. So enamored of Bochner is Firth that he actually helps him dispose of the corpse before memories of his dead friend shock him to his senses. The overwrought surprise ending (which owes something to PSYCHO) almost defies description and blunts the impact of the tense psychological study by replacing disturbing headline-inspired horror with less effective funhouse fright.

For much of its running time, APARTMENT ZERO makes fascinating use of its engrossing subtext of lonely misfits and social outcasts, presenting a world where a contract killer is able to find temporary happiness with a mama's boy. The escapist backdrop of the repertory cinema is a perfect counterpoint to the real-life terror encircling the characters; like a movie hero, Bochner looms large in the lives of the others who live in the apartment building, offering them a dream of salvation. Regrettably, director Donovan doesn't trust the strengths of the screenplay he cowrote with 26-year-old whiz kid David Koepp, and the film grows ludicrous as the apartment dwellers become clownlike Furies. In the final reel, the black humor that has been subtly woven into the film is undermined by Donovan's suddenly heavy hand. Moreover, APARTMENT ZERO might have been a stronger psychodrama if there were more doubt as to Bochner's identity and if the homoerotic undertones of his relationship with Firth had been spelled out. Still, the film's intriguing perversity compensates for the excesses of its plot and presentation.

With his matinee idol looks, Hart Bochner is ideally cast as the gung ho, heartless killer. Firth, a fine stage actor who seldom seems truly at ease on-screen, is more in his element here; his nervousness is well-suited to this role—a character who's a cross between a Kafka protagonist and Myron Breckinridge. The beautifully acted duel of wills between these two actors makes this otherwise flawed film riveting. *(Extreme violence, nudity, profanity, adult situations.)*

p, Martin Donovan and David Koepp; d, Martin Donovan; w, Martin Donovan and David Koepp (based on the story by Donovan); ph, Miguel Rodriguez (CFI Color); ed, Conrad M. Gonzalez; m, Elia Cmiral; prod d, Miguel Angel Lumaldo; cos, Angelica Fuentes; makeup, Mirta Blanco.

Thriller   **(PR:O MPAA:NR)**

B

BABAR: THE MOVIE**½
70m Nelvana-Ellipse-Clifford Ross/New Line c
VOICES OF: Gordon Pinsent *(King Babar)*, Gavin Magrath *(Boy Babar)*, Elizabeth Hanna *(Queen Celeste)*, Sarah Polley *(Young Celeste)*, Chris Wiggins *(Cornelius)*, Stephen Ouimette *(Pompadour)*, John Stocker *(Zephir)*, Charles Kerr *(Rataxes)*, Lisa Yamanaka *(Isabelle)*, Marsha Moreau *(Flora)*, Bobby Becken *(Pom)*, Amos Crawley *(Alexander)*.

Babar the Elephant has captivated young children for 50 years, since Jean de Brunhoff published the first book in his series of gentle, whimsical elephant adventures in Paris. After his death, his son, Laurent, continued to produce Babar stories, and also created a television series starring the lovable pachyderm. Now Babar has made it to the big screen in BABAR: THE MOVIE, an animated feature that will undoubtedly charm most younger viewers, but may leave their parents yawning.

The movie takes the form of a bedtime story told by the adult King Babar to his children. Explaining the origin of the Celesteville Victory Parade, he recounts his triumphant youthful defense of Elephantland against a marauding rhino army led by the rapacious Lord Rataxes. Babar, the boy-king, has just been crowned when his sweetheart, Celeste, begs the court to help her village, which is suffering under the rhino attacks. Babar's advisors can't seem to get their minds around the urgency of the problem, however, and putter about shuffling papers and being bureaucrats. It's left up to Babar and Celeste to save the day, so they set out through the dark, mysterious jungle to see what they can do. Along the way, they befriend a crocodile (who gives them sage advice about how to get along) and encounter a group of cheery monkeys (for whom Babar does a good turn). Finally they arrive at Celeste's village, which is being devastated. The rhinos have abducted the adult elephants and forced them into slavery, leaving the babies helpless in the burning town. Celeste's mother is being held prisoner, and soon Babar and Celeste are also captured by the rhinos. Only Babar's courage and resourcefulness can save them.

The film's strength, of course, is that little Babar overcomes both fear and great adversity by relying on his own wits. The elephants have other charms, too—they're drawn in comforting pastel colors; they have gentle, intelligent, humorous faces; and they do almost everything with their trunks. Stouthearted Babar also embodies some unexceptional ethical standards, dealing with others in a spirit of generosity and cooperation.

BABAR: THE MOVIE has some shortcomings, however. Because it retains the visual simplicity of the Babar books, the film's animation is a little flat; the mild colors, so winning on the page, tend to look washed-out on the screen. As in Disney's BAMBI, the film contains scenes of tearful, abandoned babies that may upset very young or sensitive children, and young female viewers will be disappointed to find that Celeste is a wimp—entirely dependent on Babar's strength, courage, and intelligence. Overall, however, the implicit values and the artistic treatment of the story are very acceptable, and the film is a salutary and amusing entertainment.

p, Patrick Loubert, Michael Hirsh, and Clive A. Smith; d, Alan Bunce; w, Peter Sauder, J.D. Smith, John De Klein, Raymond Jaffelice, and Alan Bunce (based on a story by Peter Sauder, Patrick Loubert, Michael Hirsh and characters created by Jean de Brunhoff, Laurent de Brunhoff); ed, Evan Landis; m, Milan Kymlicka; prod d, Ted Bastien; art d, Clive Powsey and Carol Bradbury; anim, John Laurence Collins.

Animated/Children's   (PR:A   MPAA:G)

BACK TO THE FUTURE PART II***½
105m Amblin/UNIV c
Michael J. Fox *(Marty McFly/Marty McFly, Jr./Marlene McFly)*, Christopher Lloyd *(Dr. Emmett Brown)*, Lea Thompson *(Lorraine)*, Thomas F. Wilson *(Biff Tannen/Griff)*, Harry Waters Jr. *(Marvin Berry)*, Charles Fleischer *(Terry)*, Joe Flaherty *(Western Union Man)*, Flea *(Needles)*, Elizabeth Shue *(Jennifer)*, James Tolkan *(Strickland)*, Jeffrey Weissman *(George McFly)*, Casey Siemaszko *(3-D)*, Billy Zane *(Match)*, J.J. Cohen *(Skinhead)*, 2015: E. Casanova Evans *(Michael Jackson)*, Jay Koch *(Ronald Reagan)*, Charles Gherardi *(Ayatollah Khomeini)*, Ricky Dean Logan *(Data)*, Darlene Vogel *(Spike)*, Jason Scott Lee *(Whitey)*, Elijah Wood, John Thornton *(Video Game Boys)*, Theo Schwartz, Lindsey Barry *(Hoverboard Girls)*, Judy Ovitz *(Anitque Store Saleswoman)*, Stephanie E. Williams *(Officer Foley)*, Marty Levy *(Cab Driver)*, James Ishida *(Fujitsu)*, 1985: Nikki Birdsong *(Loretta)*, Al White *(Dad)*, Junior Fann *(Mom)*, Shaun Hunter *(Harold)*, Buck Flower *(Bum)*, Neil Ross *(Museum Narrator)*, Tamara Carrera, Tracy D'Aldia *(Jacuzzi Girls)*, 1955: Jennifer Brown, Irina Cashen, Angela Greenblatt, Cameron Moore, Justin Mosley Spink *(Baseball Kids)*, Lisa Freeman *(Babs)*, John Erwin *(Radio Sportscaster)*, David Harold Brown, Tommy Thomas, Lloyd L. Tolbert, Granville "Danny" Young *(Starlighters)*, Wesley Mann *(CPR Kid)*, Freddie *(Einstein)*, Kevin Holloway *(Marty Photo Double)*, Charles F. Fitzsimons *(Biff Photo Double)*, Crispin Glover *(George McFly in footage from BACK TO THE FUTURE)*.

When BACK TO THE FUTURE was released for home video a few years ago, a title appeared at the end that wasn't in the original top-grossing 1985 theatrical release: "To Be Continued." Certainly, if any movie of the 80s seemed ripe for a sequel, it was this enormously popular time-travel fantasy from the directing-writing partnership of Robert Zemekis and Bob Gale. In fact, BACK TO THE FUTURE's creators were so confident of the original's formula and of the bankability of its stars (Michael J. Fox and Christopher Lloyd) that they shot *two* sequels back to back, the third being slated for release in the summer of 1990. Do Zemekis and Gale (and executive producer Steven Spielberg) have a time machine of their own by which they can predict future cinematic success? Perhaps, but only if the moviegoing public is capable of suspending disbelief and following the mind-boggling pretzel logic that accompanies the traversal of the fourth dimension.

BACK TO THE FUTURE PART II picks up where the original story left off. All's well in the new and improved McFly household, and teenager Marty (Fox)—barely recovered from his exhilarating sojourn to 1955—and his sweetheart, Shue, are about to resume a normal life when Lloyd arrives in the DeLorean time machine. The wigged-out scientist tells Fox and Shue that they are urgently needed in the future, and soon all three are propelled forward to the year 2015, where Fox must prevent a crime involving his teenage son that would bring disgrace to the future McFly family. Unaware of the previous adventure and of the details laid out in the original BACK TO THE FUTURE, Shue is put into a state of suspended animation. Fox (playing multiple roles) assumes his son's identity to rebuff the hectoring of Griff, the chip-off-the-old-block grandson of the original's bully, Biff (Wilson). Fox outwits the punkish Wilson and his gang, eluding them via a Mattel hoverboard when they give chase, and thereby saving the McFly name. Before returning to 1985, however, Fox picks up a sports almanac, figuring he'll have 15 years' worth of sure bets. An offended Lloyd throws the book away, but not before the elderly Biff (Wilson again) overhears the idea. Meanwhile, the cops have picked up the unconscious Shue and, through computer fingerprint identification, dump her off at the McFly residence. When Fox and Lloyd attempt to retrieve her, old man Wilson borrows the DeLorean and, with the sports almanac in hand, heads back to 1955. The car returns and, unaware of its misuse, Fox, Shue, and

BACK TO THE FUTURE II (©Universal).

Lloyd head back to 1985—only to find a much different world. Fox's sedate hometown, Hill Valley, now resembles Las Vegas at its worst. Greed and depravity are rife, and presiding over all this altered reality is Biff's Pleasure Palace, a casino and hotel. Fox discovers that all the work he accomplished in the original film has been perverted by the mean-spirited lout: Wilson's time-travel distortions have resulted in Fox's father having been murdered in 1973, while his mother (Thompson) is now married to fat cat Wilson and has become a floozy alcoholic. All Wilson's riches, of course, have been accumulated as a result of his infallible sports betting. To reverse *this* reality, Fox and Lloyd must travel back (as they did in the first BACK TO THE FUTURE) to the point when this time tangent was skewed—to 1955, where the elderly Wilson is to deliver the almanac to himself as a teen. Hill Valley and its inhabitants are just as they were in the original version, but Fox fails to intercept the almanac exchange and must shadow Wilson to the Enchantment Under the Sea dance without confronting his former self of Part I *or* upsetting that same former self's plan to ensure his parents' marriage. When his father punches out Wilson for assaulting Thompson (a reprise of Part I's action), Fox makes off with the almanac; how-

ever—after much intercutting with the replicated dance and music scenes of the original—Fox again loses the book to Wilson. A dramatic chase ensues, ending with Fox's retrieval of the almanac and Wilson's crashing into a manure truck. Meanwhile Lloyd, preparing for the return trip to the restored 1985, is struck by lightning. Confused and alone in the rain, Fox is approached by Flaherty, a Western Union man with instructions to deliver a 70-year old letter. The letter is from Lloyd, reporting that he is alive and well and living in the wild west of the 1880s. Fox heads back into town to rejoin Lloyd's 1955 self, and the second installment of the trilogy closes with a preview of Part III.

Pondering the vagaries of time travel has been a source of fascination for artists and authors since . . . well, since time immemorial. The permutations of cause and effect have served as a story premise for many a movie, with success generally measured by how neatly events fall into place by journey's end, or whether some moral purpose has been served by the device (as in IT'S A WONDERFUL LIFE). In both BACK TO THE FUTURE and BACK TO THE FUTURE PART II, however, these are not appropriate measures. True, the sequel is ever-aware of the need to explain the complications of geometric time and

space travel, and attempts to do so chiefly through Lloyd's frenetic ramblings and often-unintelligible discourses. Nonetheless, the film works best through its magnificent technical achievements and the inherent charm of Fox, Lloyd, and especially the delightfully menacing Thomas F. Wilson (who, like most of the major players, reprises his role from the original). In light of the comically rich performance turned in by this deceptively facile actor, perhaps the alternate title for BACK TO THE FUTURE PART II should have been BIFF'S STORY.

Except for Lloyd, whose role is the least changed, all of the main actors are given opportunities to exploit the 50-year range of physical possibilities for their characters. Eternal *wunderkind* Fox not only ages, but does triple duty, his roles including that of Marty McFly's 2015 teenage daughter. Lea Thompson, though less prominently featured here than in the original, undergoes a respectable transformation as the silicone-lifted lush in the surrealistically skewed Pleasure Palace sequence. Absent from the nearly intact original ensemble, however, is Crispin Glover, whose character (George McFly) is conspicuously relegated to rumor and shadow.

If present movie trends are any indication, BACK TO THE FUTURE PART II itself accurately conveys the future in its incessant merchandising of products. Pepsi and Nike shoes are ubiquitous and, not surprisingly, the Mattel toy company has been deluged with inquiries as to the availability of its flying hoverboards, prominently identified here. Evidently Zemeckis and Spielberg (who also collaborated on WHO FRAMED ROGER RABBIT) have not overestimated the gullibility of today's young moviegoers.

If nothing else, BACK TO THE THE FUTURE PART II is one of the most visually impressive films of the past year. Credit for bringing this fantastic vision to its remarkable technical level should go to several longtime Spielberg associates, including Zemeckis; production designer Rick Carter (THE ADVENTURES OF BUCKEROO BANZAI; THREE FUGITIVES), who successfully took the town of Hill Valley through its various incarnations; cinematographer Dean Cundey (BACK TO THE FUTURE; ROGER RABBIT); and the film's editors, Arthur Schmidt (an Academy Award-winner for ROGER RABBIT) and Harry Keramidas (BACK TO THE FUTURE). *(Violence, profanity.)*

p, Neil Canton and Bob Gale; d, Robert Zemeckis; w, Bob Gale (based on a story by Robert Zemeckis, Bob Gale); ph, Dean Cundey (Deluxe Color); ed, Arthur Schmidt and Harry Keramidas; m, Alan Silvestri; prod d, Rick Carter; art d, Margie Stone McShirley; set d, Linda De Scenna; spec eff, Michael Lantieri; cos, Joanna Johnston; chor, Brad Jeffries; anim, Wes Takahashi; stunts, Walter Scott; makeup, Ken Chase.

Adventure/Fantasy   (PR:A MPAA:PG)

ⓥ**BACKFIRE****
90m ITC/Vidmark c
Karen Allen *(Mara),* Keith Carradine *(Reed),* Jeff Fahey *(Donnie),* Bernie Casey *(Clint),* Dean Paul Martin *(Jake),* Dinah Manoff *(Jill),* Virginia Capers *(Maxine),* Philip Sterling *(Dr. Creason),* Frances Flanagan *(Claire),* Anthony Holland *(Judge Hardin),* Dwight Ross *(Deputy "Buzz"),* Gordon McIntosh *(Big George),* Wendy Van Riesen *(Alice),* Eric Schneider *(Dr. Cooper),* Enid Saunders *(Aunt Elizabeth),* Jay Banzeau *(Junior),* Leslie Ewen *(Dispatcher),* Dwight McFee, Kim Kondrashoff *(Searchers),* Brian Linds *(Bob),* Robert Metcalfe *(Deputy No. 2),* Tom McBeath *(Man in Bar).*

That old tried-and-true movie plot in which a spouse and his or her lover attempt to drive the adulterous party's wealthy mate over the edge, hoping to get their greedy hands on the victim's big bucks, has worked well for screenwriters and provided many actors with juicy roles over the years. Movies like DIABOLIQUE; GASLIGHT; SLEEP, MY LOVE; and even the unforget-tably silly STRAIGHTJACKET! have proved that, despite the material's transparently generic nature, it can result in some very entertaining films. BACKFIRE, the most recent example of this hardy subgenre, deftly triumphs over its lackluster direction with a few clever plot twists here and there, but gets its greatest boost from the unlikely but eminently successful casting of Karen Allen in the role of the greedy, murderous wife.

Everyone on Washington's St. James Island envies Fahey and his wife, Allen. They're rich, young, and attractive; their beautiful mansion on vast, manicured grounds overlooking the sea is the showpiece of the community. What most people don't know is that Vietnam vet Fahey is suffering from an extreme case of Post-traumatic Stress Syndrome that manifests itself in a recurring nightmare. In the dream, Fahey struggles to save a nearly eviscerated buddy, then, slogging though the mud and carnage of battle, stumbles upon the rest of his platoon—all dead and mutilated, their eyes mounted on nearby stakes in the ground. Allen appears concerned and sympathetic, seeking advice from the family doctor and putting up a brave front with her friends. But one night, while Allen is away nursing a sick girl friend, Fahey finds himself covered in blood that rushes out of the showerhead while he bathes. Next, he discovers his service revolver handily nearby and his bed covered with blood and eyeballs. When Allen returns home the next morning, she coolly fixes the showerhead, takes a tape of battle sounds from the cassette player, and cleans up the gross mess on the bed. Expecting to find Fahey dead from a self-inflicted gunshot, she is shocked to discover that he is alive, though catatonic. To make matters worse, it seems that Fahey—whose family history of insanity has engendered his fear of being institutionalized—has had a legal document drawn up that grants Allen power of attorney in the event of his incapacitation, but only if she personally nurses him at home. It turns out Fahey's loyal, close-mouthed sister (Manoff) has been holding the document since his marriage. To complete Allen's run of bad luck, Martin, her lover and coconspirator, is so disappointed with their scheme's failure that he decides to leave town.

Allen's response to all this disheartening news is to pour herself into a tight red dress and slither off to her favorite lounge. There she meets and picks up Carradine, a drifter whose worldly goods are secured in a locker at the bus station. Allen wastes no time in moving Carradine into the mansion, telling him about her wrong-side-of-the-tracks background and her determination to get rid of the vegetating Fahey and wind up with all his loot. Soon the town sheriff reports that Martin and $100,000 he has apparently stolen from his employer are missing, but Allen has too many problems of her own to pay the news much attention. She's now having nightly bad dreams, and—although she keeps putting it back where it belongs—Fahey's gun keeps popping up in her bedside table drawer. Deciding that Fahey must be faking his catatonia, she asks Carradine to murder him. When Carradine refuses, she steals the key to his locker, threatening to use it to frame him for Fahey's death anyway if he doesn't kill her husband that night. Forced to comply, Carradine tells her to go visit a girl friend and establish an alibi; when she returns to the house, the deed will have been done.

Meanwhile, the sheriff's men find Martin's car in the river and discover his headless body buried nearby. When Allen returns to the mansion late that night, she finds Carradine's nearly eviscerated corpse, along with the severed head of Martin on the bureau. Hysterical, she grabs Fahey's gun, runs into his room, points and shoots, leading up to some surprising final revelations as to who is and who is not dead and why.

Well-shot by top cinematographer Tak Fujimoto on beautiful Canadian locations, BACKFIRE is benefitted by an adequate budget, a serviceable script brightened by some pithy dialog, and a game cast. Unfortunately, the direction and editing are not as good. Gilbert Cates' work is competent, but his direction seems distanced and by-the-numbers, shepherding the viewer from one plot twist to the next without displaying the sharp and witty point-of-view that so distinguished Joseph Ruben's THE STEPFATHER, for example. Similarly, Melvin Shapiro's editing lacks the urgency and pace necessary to keep the audience guessing, without much time to think—an indispensable quality in this kind of film. Too many unnecessary shots, held for too long, permit the viewer to guess the next turn of events in BACK-FIRE.

By far the most entertaining aspect of BACKFIRE is Allen's acting, which pulls out all stops. Although hampered by Anna Hill Johnstone's unfortunate costumes (the supposedly provocative tight red dress is startlingly unflattering), Allen (STARMAN; RAIDERS OF THE LOST ARK) nonetheless seems to relish the opportunity to play a thoroughly despicable character after having been cast in so many nice-girl parts. Playing against type as the murderous and foul-mouthed adulteress here, Allen uses her sensitive face and doe eyes with palpable impact. Keith Carradine, as the film's wild-card drifter, is stuck with a character who is more plot mechanism than recognizable human being, but comes through with his customary aplomb; Jeff Fahey (SILVERADO) is suitably wild-eyed in the cliched part of the

Vietnam vet; and Dinah Manoff (BLOODHOUNDS OF BROADWAY; STAYING TOGETHER) wisely underplays her woefully underwritten role as the stalwart sister. All things considered, BACKFIRE provides a reasonably diverting hour and a half of greed, lust, and mayhem, due in large measure to the energy pumped into it by the redoubtable Allen. Songs include: "Building Heartaches" (Willie Nelson), "Nashville Just Wrote Another Cheatin' Song" (Ed Molyski). *(Graphic violence, profanity, sexual situations, adult situations.)*

p, Danton Rissner; d, Gilbert Cates; w, Larry Brand and Rebecca Reynolds; ph, Tak Fujimoto; ed, Melvin Shapiro; m, David Shire; prod d, Daniel Lomino; set d, Sandy Arthur; spec eff, Roy Arbogast; cos, Anna Hill Johnstone; stunts, Jacob Rupp; makeup, John Inzerella.

Mystery/Thriller   (PR:O MPAA:R)

ⓥBATMAN**½
126m WB c
Michael Keaton *(Batman/Bruce Wayne)*, Jack Nicholson *(Joker/Jack Napier)*, Kim Basinger *(Vicki Vale)*, Robert Wuhl *(Alexander Knox)*, Pat Hingle *(Commissioner Gordon)*, Billy Dee Williams *(District Attorney Harvey Dent)*, Michael Gough *(Alfred, Wayne Butler)*, Jack Palance *(Carl Grissom)*, Jerry Hall *(Alicia)*, Lee Wallace *(Mayor)*, Tracey Walter *(Bob The Goon)*, William Hootkins.

You've got the T-shirt, the key chain, the mug, the auto sun shield, the boxer shorts, the lunchpail, the handcuffs (!), and the Prince LP; have you seen the movie? Just in case you haven't, here's some of what goes on in the mega-grossing BATMAN. Gotham City is the scene of your worst dreams, a crime-ridden, debris-strewn, sunless, architecturally incoherent metropolis in distorted perspective—futuristic, retro, and contemporary all at once. As the film opens, a man attempts to shepherd his wife and son through this claustrophobic Babylon, but is mugged and beaten in an alley while his family looks on. The muggers retire to count their loot and discuss the rumor that a mysterious, giant vigilante bat has been plaguing the criminal community, knocking evildoers off rooftops to their deaths and so on. Almost before one can say, "Holy pop-cultural icon" (or words to that effect), a figure dressed in black cowl, cape, and bulletproof, musculature-enhancing black suit emerges silently from the shadows to beat up the bad guys, stopping short of killing them so that they'll spread the message that a new crime-fighting force is in town. "I'm Batman," advises the Caped Crusader, for it is indeed he. Gotham is desperately in need of such a savior; for the city (New York in all but name) is in the corrupting grip of crime boss Grissom (Palance), and

Michael Keaton and Kim Basinger in BATMAN (©Warner Bros.)

the mayor (Ed Koch look-alike Wallace), police commissioner (Hingle), and district attorney (Williams) seem powerless to break Grissom's hold. Meanwhile, investigative reporter Alex (Wuhl) looks into the vigilante bat sightings, to the bemusement of all his colleagues save gorgeous ace photographer Vicki Vale (Basinger). When Vicki and Alex attend a party at the mansion of enigmatic millionaire Bruce Wayne (Keaton), Wayne is quite taken with the lovely Vicki, but distracted by the police commissioner's hasty exit from the bash. Meanwhile, Grissom's top henchman, Jack Napier (Nicholson), attempts a heist with his goons at a chemical plant. It turns out the whole thing is a set-up, however; Grissom, angered by Napier's affair with his moll (Hall), has tipped off his police contacts. The cops arrive, setting off a chase through the plant. Napier is about to escape, but Batman—who, of course, is really Bruce Wayne's alter ego—arrives on the scene and dumps him into a vat of toxic waste. Batman/Bruce now takes time out to woo Vicki, and the two spend a blissful night together. Meanwhile, Napier literally resurfaces as the Joker, his face distorted in a hideous grin and his mind warped beyond redemption by chemicals. Sporting white skin, green hair, ruby leer, and a

purple and green outfit, the Joker kills Grissom, takes over his crime empire, and unleashes fear throughout the city, especially when he floods stores with chemically altered cosmetics that, in certain combinations, cause their users to die a horrible, grinning death. Bruce/Batman keeps track of the Joker's moves, tracked himself by Vicki, who is intrigued and peeved by her millionaire lover's inexplicable ways. The Joker, meanwhile, develops his own interest in Vicki, and tries to kidnap her at Gotham's art museum after he and his goons gleefully deface the world's greatest art treasures. Batman foils the scheme, rescuing Vicki from the Joker's clutches and zooming off with her in his Batmobile, pursued in green and purple cars by the Joker's men. With Batman and the Joker having targeted each other as nemeses, the film girds for their showdown, along the way disclosing Bruce's bat-identity to Vicki and revealing the traumatic source of his bizarre behavior (he saw his parents' killing—by Napier—as a boy) to the audience. Eventually, the Joker organizes a devious parade, riding on a float trailing huge balloons and luring Gothamites into the streets by throwing money, then releasing lethal gas from the balloons. Batman flies through the city in his Batwing, removing all the balloons (save one) before they can do their genocidal work, but is shot down by the Joker. The Joker nabs Vicki, dragging her up to the top of Gotham cathedral and setting the stage for the big fight between Batman and his arch-enemy in the belfry, which, after a last cliff-hanger, frees Bruce and Vicki to pursue their romance—allowing time out for Bruce's continuing bat-antics, of course.

Perhaps it was inevitable, considering all the hype preceding and surrounding its release, that BATMAN would fall a bit flat once it finally reached the screen. Despite its interesting, moody tone and undeniably striking visuals from director Tim Burton and production designer Anton Furst, the film fails to synthesize its strengths into a compelling whole. Although Burton, a former animator, was regarded by many as Hollywood's most original, visually inventive young director on the strength of his surprise hits PEE-WEE'S BIG ADVENTURE (1985) and BEETLEJUICE (1988), both those films were made for under $15 million, and Warner Bros. was reportedly uneasy about trusting Burton with BATMAN's $35 million budget. Perhaps anxiety over the amount of money, talent, and word of mouth invested in the film—not to mention the fact that "Batmania" had already kicked off in the UK and the US, ensuring a merchandising bonanza if the film did well—caused Burton and the producers to restrain their wilder impulses. BATMAN is dark, moody, and stylish—but wants to be more so. It's possible that too many cooks diluted its broth.

Key to the film's tone is the reinterpretation of the character himself. BATMAN was conceived as a faithful representation of the original DC Comics character created by Bob Kane (who served as a consultant on the film) and Bill Finger. A dark, driven, mysterious, non-superhuman figure, the original Batman went through many transformations that lightened the character, including his campy 60s TV incarnation in the figure of Adam West. After the huge success of Frank Miller's serial novel *Batman: The Dark Knight Returns* in 1986, however, Batman was restored with renewed popularity to the comic book shadows, and it's this brooding mystique (minus Miller's graphic violence) that inspires Batman/Bruce Wayne's characterization here.

As conceived by Michael Keaton, Burton, and writers Sam Hamm and Warren Skaaren, BATMAN's central character is a disturbed sort. As Bruce Wayne, he's both re- and depressed, giving off a sense of buried anger and confusion over his identity—and no wonder, considering he's devoted his secret life to honing vigilante skills and likes to dress up in a fetishistic black outfit. Burton's choice of Keaton

(star of BEETLEJUICE) for the role outraged many aficionados of the DC character, who viewed Keaton as a lightweight, clownish performer. Keaton has brought a certain neurotic edge to his comedy since his debut in NIGHT SHIFT, however, and proved he could play a driven, dislikable character in 1988's CLEAN AND SOBER. In BATMAN, he manages to suggest both Bruce Wayne's nice guy, little-boy-lost quality and his moody, withdrawn qualities, and when he puts on Batman's cowl, his eyes go to work to suggest the anger Wayne represses.

Since BATMAN gets distracted over the issue of what makes Bruce Wayne tick, its obvious intention to parallel the Joker and Batman as two psychotics, one promoting Good and the other Evil, doesn't come through with as much impact as it should. As the Joker, Jack Nicholson gives the kind of over-the-top turn everyone expected, but one can't help feeling he could do the role in his sleep. Nicholson gets most of the good lines and delivers them with glee, but the Joker's homicidally sadistic side is undermined by his comic book trappings. Buried under all his makeup, prosthetic leer, and purple and green surroundings, Nicholson loses the element of risky exposure that partly redeemed his outlandish performances in THE WITCHES OF EASTWICK and THE SHINING, making the Joker—dare we say it, considering the TV show's bad rep?—almost campy. When the Joker goes prancing and babbling about, defacing paintings and riding parade floats to the accompaniment of Prince's songs (which, in keeping with so much of BATMAN, are really rather tame contributions from the Purple King), he seems maniacal, all right, but hardly as sinister as the silent Batman with his unmistakably human face beneath that bizarre cowl, or the city of Gotham itself.

Production designer Furst's Gotham City (actually a huge soundstage in London) is one of BATMAN's most fully realized—if not fully original—aspects. Recalling such dystopic visions as Fritz Lang's expressionist METROPOLIS, Ridley Scott's BLADE RUNNER, and Terry Gilliam's BRAZIL, it successfully distorts scale and jumbles design styles and periods to give a sense of urban disorientation, without being disorienting in itself. Batman's gadgets, courtesy of Derek Meddings' special-effects crew, are also fun, especially the Batmobile and the Batwing. Burton, who is generally at his best in the action sequences, makes Batman and Vicki's high-speed drive in the Batmobile and Batman's STAR WARS-like flight over Gotham in the Batwing particularly exciting. Danny Elfman's booming score (within which Prince's music is buried, notwithstanding Warner Bros.' release of his latest as the BATMAN "Motion Picture Soundtrack") enhances

the moody atmosphere, as does Roger Pratt's (BRAZIL) cinematography.

BATMAN, as everyone knows and expected, set new standards at the box-office and in merchandizing, and made huge amounts of money for everyone involved in its making. But as for the movie itself, director Burton's own lukewarm assessment of the film, quoted in *Time*, seems to sum it up well: "Given the scale, the number of people involved, and how quickly we did it, it still has a personality, which big movies often lose. It doesn't feel like a cardboard clone." Given all its potential, it's a shame BATMAN wasn't more. *(Violence, sexual situations, profanity.)*

p, Jon Peters, Peter Guber, and Chris Kenney; d, Tim Burton; w, Sam Hamm and Warren Skaaren (based on a story by Sam Hamm and characters created by Bob Kane); ph, Roger Pratt (Eastmancolor); ed, Ray Lovejoy; m, Danny Elfman; prod d, Anton Furst; art d, Les Tomkins, Terry Ackland-Snow, and Nigel Phelps; set d, Peter Young; spec eff, Derek Meddings; cos, Bob Ringwood; stunts, Eddie Stacey; makeup, Paul Engelen.

Fantasy   (PR:A-C   MPAA:PG-13)

BEAR, THE**
(Fr.) 93m Price Ent.-Renn/Tri Star c
Jack Wallace *(Bill)*, Tcheky Karyo *(Tom)*, Andre Lacombe *(The Dog Handler)*, Bart the Bear *(Kaar)*, Douce the Bear *(Youk)*.

This deceptively simple wilderness tale began production in 1982 with a four-line synopsis—"A big solitary bear. An orphan bear cub. Two hunters in the forest. The animals' point of view"—and went on to cost $25 million, earn numerous Cesar nominations, and take in over $100 million *before* its US release, edging out WHO FRAMED ROGER RABBIT during its Paris opening. The practically nonexistent plot focuses on a bear cub and a pair of hunters—a calm, calculating veteran (played by Chicago stage actor Jack Wallace) and his young, overeager friend (French-Turkish actor Tcheky Karyo). Set in British Columbia in 1885 (with Northern Italy and the Austrian Tyrol doubling for the once-virgin BC locales), much of the action centers on the curious, mischievous young cub, showing its playful antics in the pastoral wilderness, its confrontations with other animals, its flirtations with danger, and even its dream world. Early in the film, the cub's mother is killed by a rock slide. Alone in the wilderness, the cub tries to befriend an adult male bear who rejects his overtures and snaps at him. Later the 2000-pound male is shot by Karyo and wounded in the shoulder. As the bear tries to recover in a mountain stream, the cub approaches and licks the wound, thus sealing a bond between the two. Meanwhile, determined to chase the wounded animal to its death, Wallace travels upriver to the nearest outpost and fetches a scout and team of tracking dogs. Upon his return, the hunters trace the bear and its cub to a rocky mountain pass. There, the bear wins a violent battle with the dog pack but, in the process, is separated from the cub—the quivering little animal captured by much larger and braver Wallace. The hunters are amused by the playful cub, and have no intention of killing it, their sights still set on the big male. Scouting the region, Karyo finally comes face to face with the bear on a hazardous precipice. Unarmed and taken by surprise, the hunter collapses in tears and begs for mercy as the huge creature shows its razor-sharp teeth and emits a low, angry growl from the depths of its bulk. Instead of killing the hunter, however, the bear turns its back on the defenseless, pathetic Karyo without harming him. A short time later the bear is seen again, this time in the sights of Wallace's gun. But Karyo silently forces down the barrel of his partner's rifle, showing mercy, in turn, to the bear who spared him.

A far cry from the sweet nature adventures that Disney popularized, THE BEAR is a sublime, graceful tale of nature told from the perspective of the animals. Employing the long-forgotten cinema techniques of such film geniuses as D.W. Griffith and Robert Flaherty, director Jean-Jacques Annaud (whose films include BLACK AND WHITE IN COLOR, an Oscar winner for Best Foreign Film of 1976; QUEST FOR FIRE [1981]; and THE NAME OF THE ROSE [1986]) tells his story almost exclusively through visuals, using a minimum of dialog and a soundtrack elegantly constructed from the "language" of the bears. Bridging cinema history, Annaud also makes excellent use of many of the most modern film techniques, including bear Animatrons (computerized, remote-controlled puppets) designed by Jim Henson.

To describe THE BEAR as "quite unlike anything yet seen on the screen" may sound like hyperbole, but one cannot help but be struck by the extraordinary "acting" of the bears. The creative success of this entirely fictive film is almost wholly dependent on the audience's ability to perceive the bears as creatures with discernible (*i.e.*, human) emotions. While in the past such animal emotions have been depicted on the screen through trickery (creative editing, manipulative music), here the animals (all tame creatures trained to appear wild) actually display human characteristics in their interactions with one another and their human costars.

With preproduction on THE BEAR beginning as far back as November 1981 (just after Annaud completed QUEST FOR FIRE), the filmmaking team, which included producer Claude Berri (JEAN

THE BEAR (©Tri-Star).

DE FLORETTE; MANON OF THE SPRING), had ample opportunity to organize the production. Casting on the film began with the adult male bear, Bart, a nine-foot-tall Kodiak who then weighed a slender 1,800 pounds. Carefully trained over the next few years, Bart eventually learned how to catch fish, and how to pretend to be partially crippled when the script called for him to be wounded by a gunshot. With the success of QUEST FOR FIRE (a prehistoric adventure that grossed more than $130 million theatrically), Annaud, fearing that he would be pigeonholed as a "back-to-nature" director, chose to put THE BEAR on hold and instead direct his adaptation of Umberto Eco's gothic thriller *The Name of the Rose*. With that film's box-office tally also rising above the $100 million mark, Annaud had little trouble persuading producer Berri to loosen his purse strings to the tune of $25 million for THE BEAR. By early 1987, Annaud was still casting, choosing 12 personable cubs to audition as the young animal star. One of them, Douce (French for *gentle* or *soft*), proved a born actor and won the lead role.

After four months of shooting and more than one million feet of film, THE BEAR was released in France in October 1988 and was an immediate smash hit. Notwithstanding the fact that it was in various stages of production for some seven years and took a team of over 200 to bring to the screen, it is a beautifully simple picture that seems to have been captured effortlessly by the cameras. Presenting myriad human emotions despite its animal characters, THE BEAR, like so many great, otherwise dissimilar films, speaks a universal message of humanism and morality in every frame. In English.

p, Claude Berri; d, Jean-Jacques Annaud; w, Gerard Brach (based on the novel *The Grizzly King* by James Oliver Curwood); ph, Philippe Rousselot; ed, Noelle Boisson; m, Philippe Sarde; prod d, Toni Ludi; art d, Heidi Ludi, Antony Greengrow, and George Dietz; spec eff, Willy Neuner, Uli Nefzer, and Johann Fickel; cos, Corinne Jorry; anim, Bretislav Pojar; makeup, Hans-Jurgen Schmelzle.

Adventure   (PR:A-C MPAA:PG)

ⓥ**BERT RIGBY, YOU'RE A FOOL***
94m Lorimar-Clear/WB c

Robert Lindsay *(Bert Rigby)*, Cathryn Bradshaw *(Laurel Pennington)*, Robbie Coltrane *(Sid Trample)*, Anne Bancroft *(Meredith Perlestein)*, Corbin Bernsen *(Jim Shirley)*, Jackie Gayle *(I.I. Perlestein)*, Liberty Mounten *(Elvis Impersonator)*, Bruno Kirby *(Kyle De Forrest)*, Liz Smith, Lila Kaye, Fanny Carby.

Since the dawn of sound in motion pictures there have been performers, such as Fred Astaire, with a natural affinity for the camera, their every move accomplished without any seeming effort by the entertainer to coax a laugh from a pratfall or dazzle with the execution of an intricate dance routine. Then there are others who, though they may be extremely gifted theatrical performers, lose something in the transition to film—their well-projected stage persona perhaps overwhelming the camera's intimate eye. Judging from BERT RIGBY, YOU'RE A FOOL, Tony Award-winner Robert Lindsay's first major American film outing, it would seem that Lindsay belongs in the latter class. His antics, wildly funny onstage in "Me and My Girl," seem unduly labored on the screen, and might profitably have been toned down by the film's writer-director,

Carl Reiner. As it is, Lindsay's Bert Rigby, a happy-go-lucky striking Cockney coal miner with a penchant for mimicking Astaire, Gene Kelly, and Buster Keaton, comes off more as a farcical cartoon than as a simple man who loves to sing and dance.

The slight, trite plot follows Lindsay's antic and amorous adventures though England and eventually to Hollywood, where he winds up as the butler of a Hollywood superstar (Bernsen) and becomes entangled with a movie mogul's sexually uninhibited wife (Bancroft). Bancroft takes a stab at spoofing her Mrs. Robinson character from THE GRADUATE, but the scenes devoted to her seduction of Lindsay largely misfire. The raspy-voiced Lindsay's goal is to launch a career as a movie song-and-dance man, but that kind of entertainer has long been "out" in Hollywood, as Lindsay soon discovers, and the good-natured innocent loses his bid for stardom, returning home to England a sadder but wiser fellow. Along the way, Lindsay does have one shining moment, in which he does a first-rate impersonation of Keaton for a TV commercial, but another sequence obviously intended to spotlight the actor's talents—in which he tries to impress his girl friend by performing ultra-condensed versions of all the major numbers from SINGING IN THE RAIN—backfires. No doubt it looked great on paper, but on film the sequence dissolves into a dismal example of the kind of miscalculated homage best left on the cutting-room floor.

Considering that Reiner intentionally fashioned this picture as an unabashed tribute to the "golden era" Hollywood musicals of the 30s and 40s, it's a shame he didn't achieve something more original and inspired and, above all, closer to the realm of a G rating. What did these musicals have going for them, if not their irresistible charm, inherent decency, and fun-loving, sweet and simple boy-meets-girl plots? BERT RIGBY, by contrast, is an R-rated endeavor that incorporates generous doses of profanity, sexual innuendo, toilet humor, and a variety of other vulgarities that hardly relate to its supposed musical prototypes. To claim to honor this unique art form through such material is neither consistent with, nor does it capture the spirit of, the high standard set during that glorious period that stretched roughly from 42ND STREET (1933) to GIGI (1958). *(Adult situations, sexual situations, profanity.)*

p, George Shapiro; d, Carl Reiner; w, Carl Reiner; ph, Jan de Bont (Metrocolor); ed, Bud Molin; m, Ralph Burns; prod d, Terrence Marsh; art d, Dianne Wager; set d, John Franco Jr.; cos, Ruth Myers; chor, Larry Hyman.

Comedy/Musical   (PR:O MPAA:R)

❤BEST OF THE BEST**
95m SVS-The Movie Group/Taurus c
Eric Roberts *(Alex Grady)*, James Earl Jones *(Coach Couzo)*, Sally Kirkland *(Catherine Wade)*, Phillip Rhee *(Tommy Lee)*, Christopher Penn *(Travis Brickley)*, John Dye *(Virgil Keller)*, David Agresta *(Sonny Grasso)*, Simon Rhee *(Dae Han)*, Tom Everett *(Don Peterson)*, Louise Fletcher *(Mrs. Grady)*, John P. Ryan *(Jennings)*, Edan Gross *(Walter Grady)*, Ahmad Rashad *(Himself)*, Master Hee Il Cho *(Korean Coach)*, James Lew *(Sae Jin Kwon)*, Ken Nagayama *(Yung Kim)*, Ho Sik Pak *(Han Cho)*, Dae Kyu Chang *(Tung Sung Moon)*, Samantha Scully *(Carol Ann)*, Adrienne Sachs *(Kelly)*, Kane Hodder *(Burt)*, Diane Mizrahi *(Nurse)*, Cal Bartlett *(Dr. Weisman)*, Edward Bunker *(Stan)*, Helen Funai *(Tommy's Mother)*, Eugene Choe *(Little Tommy)*, R. Lee Telford, Ricky Barnard, Danny Gibson, Greg Williams *(Referees)*, David Rody *(Announcer at Try Outs)*, Melanie Kinnaman *(Woman)*, Steve Hulin *(Buzz Cut)*, Pete Antico, William H. Burton, Steve Santosusso *(Townies)*, Orion Masters *(Gate Attendant)*, Miriam Ezra *(Tommy's Secretary)*, Jonathan Strauss, Jeffery Jagger *(Boys)*, David Park *(Tommy's Older Brother)*, Chang Park Kim *(Referee)*, Kwang Jae Lee *(Announcer)*.

Why Eric Roberts, whose work in STAR 80 is among the best performances of the decade, decided to do BEST OF THE BEST is a giant mystery. The thoroughly predictable, blandly directed action film tells the story of the members of a US karate team as they prepare for their battle against a Korean team. Roberts plays Alex, the quiet, sensitive one, who had given up fighting because of a bad shoulder. His domestic life is unrewarding; his wife is dead, and he lives with his mother (Fletcher) and his son. He longs to fight again, and joining the US team is a dream come true for him. His teammates are Rhee, an Asian karate instructor whose brother was killed by the same opponent he will face in the contest; Penn, a pugnacious southerner; Dye, a meditating Buddhist; and Agresta, a proud Italian ladies' man. The team is coached by Jones, a ruthlessly strict trainer who wants his team to be the "best of the best." The film is constructed in the predictable style that so many macho sports movies since ROCKY have followed. Once the team is chosen, they must overcome their personal problems, pull together as a team, and finally fight for victory. A barroom brawl is thrown in—presumably for the sole purpose of showing stuntmen flying through windows, since it doesn't relate much to plot or character. The training sequences are full of sweaty, painful shots of actors doing push-ups and lifting weights, while a blasting rock score pulsates on the soundtrack.

The team members and the coach finally overcome their personal problems, which include Roberts' son being hit by a car, Rhee holding back his true strength in fear of seriously hurting someone, Penn overcoming his bad attitude, and Jones using some underhanded coaching techniques, and head off to give it their all in Korea. Roberts' and Rhee's matches become crucial for US victory; late in the contest, with the US trailing, Roberts continues to fight with his shoulder dislocated, bringing the point-spread to a winnable level, and Rhee, in the grip of his deadly lust for revenge, takes over to try and score the much-needed points. After a grueling and difficult match, Rhee has inflicted major damage on his opponent and is one point away from victory as the film reaches its climax.

Despite a shamelessly predictable story and familiar characters, BEST OF THE BEST is still watchable, thanks mainly to the performers. Roberts, who is always interesting, creates an odd character with shoulder-length hair and eccentric mannerisms, and Jones has a fine time playing the "hard coach" with a fervor seldom seen in low-budget exploitation films. Unfortunately, BEST OF THE BEST offers little more than good performances; Bob Radler, in his feature directorial debut, messes up the fight scenes with lots of unnecessary slow-motion shots, and the film overall follows its formula mechanically, leaving no room for surprise or visual flourishes (the camera, except for a few zoom close-ups, seldom moves). Sportscaster Ahmad Rashad give a gratingly annoying play-by-play description of the fights. At one point, he tells the audience exactly how to feel after describing something in detail that was perfectly clear from the visuals. Apart from these lapses, for a viewer who's in the mood for predictable "underdog" nonsense, BEST OF THE BEST is a perfectly serviceable action yarn. Musical selections include: "Tales of Power" (Jim Capaldi, Carlos Santana, Walker, Thompson, Vilato, performed by Capaldi), "Something So Strong" (Capaldi, Vale, Waters, performed by Capaldi), "Back Roads," "Someday I'm Gonna Ride in a Cadillac" (Charlie Major, performed by Major), "Radar Love—Live," "The Devil Made Me Do It" (George Kooymans, Barry Hay, performed by Golden Earring), "Best of the Best" (Ike Stubblefield, performed by Stubblefield, Tony Hall), "American Hotel" (Kirsten Nash), "Enemy" (Paul Airey, performed by David Steele, Sue Leonard), "La Donna e Mobile" from "Rigoletto" (Giuseppe Verdi). *(Graphic violence, adult situations, profanity.)*

p, Phillip Rhee and Peter E. Strauss; d, Bob Radler; w, Paul Levine (based on a story by Phillip Rhee and Levine); ph, Doug Ryan (CFI Color); ed, William Hoy;

m, Paul Gilman; prod d, Kim Rees; art d, Maxine Shepard; spec eff, Peggy Teague; cos, Cynthia Bergstrom; stunts, Simon Rhee; makeup, Peggy Teague.

Action   (PR:C MPAA:PG-13)

BEVERLY HILLS BRATS*
91m Terry Moore-Jerry Rivers/Taurus c
Burt Young *(Clive)*, Martin Sheen *(Jeffrey Miller)*, Terry Moore *(Veronica Miller)*, Peter Billingsley *(Scooter)*, Ramon Sheen *(Sterling)*, Cathy Podewell *(Tiffany)*.

For most people, making a home movie entails getting out the video recorder and driving your relatives nuts at major family functions with hot lights and directions to act as if they're having fun. The result is usually an apparently endless, amateurish effort. On the evidence of BEVERLY HILLS BRATS, it would seem that for the folks in Beverly Hills home moviemaking involves hiring a professional cast and crew to ensure a better-looking product—but the result is just as dull. As in humbler homes, family ties usually play a key role in Hollywood home movies. In this case, the family name is Sheen. BEVERLY HILLS BRATS stars Martin Sheen, without whose participation this relentlessly unfunny comedy that wastes the talents of some of Hollywood's better character actors probably would not have seen the light of day. Also in the cast is Ramon Sheen, who plays his real-life father's movie son, while Janet Sheen is credited as an associate producer. The elder Sheen plays Jeffrey Miller, a Beverly Hills plastic surgeon whose specialty, breasts and buttocks, provides the film's excuse to indulge in a numbing string of forgettable one-liners, double entendres, and dreadful PG-13 sight gags. While Jeffrey spends his evenings making intimate, "follow-up" house calls on former patients, his wife (Terry Moore) amuses herself by cavorting with a Latino artist living in the Millers' guest house. Meanwhile, son Sterling (Ramon Sheen) fences stolen goods for a Chicano burglary ring and daughter Tiffany (Cathy Podewell) indulges in some heavy petting with a wealthy East Indian heir. Sensitive youngest child Scooter (Peter Billingsley), however, spends his time alone with his computer feeling neglected—for BEVERLY HILLS BRATS is a story about how the rich need love too. Accordingly, the film goes to work on Scooter's problem by having a soft-hearted burglar, Clive (Burt Young), stumble into the Miller homestead one night. Scooter and Clive concoct a phony kidnaping designed to make the latter rich and the former's family more attentive, and the only (slight) diversion that follows in this terribly predictable film occurs when a pair of more hardened crooks threaten to make the kidnaping real. Martin Sheen is reported to have said that he got involved with BEVERLY

HILLS BRATS mainly to prove that he could do comedy, and—though the film itself is a comedy in *intent* only—neither he nor his son Ramon does a bad job here. Sheen the elder manages to wring what laughs can be gotten from his woeful lines, while Ramon, though he lacks the charisma of his famous brothers Charlie Sheen and Emilio Estevez, is nevertheless likable and easygoing in his role. The supporting cast also does what it can to bring some energy to the proceedings, but they are finally done in by a feeble script and by director Dimitri Sotirakis' laboring under the impression that close-ups of vanity license plates are enough to put anyone into stitches. When not cloyingly cute, BEVERLY HILLS BRATS exhibits a predilection for stale racist and sexist humor—making the involvement of the Sheens, a family noted for their political activism, all the more baffling. Beyond the nepotism revealed in its credits, what really makes BEVERLY HILLS BRATS a home movie is its point of view. The film has the ingredients to become a sharp, corrosive farce—along the intermittently successful lines of Paul Bartel's SCENES FROM THE CLASS STRUGGLE IN BEVERLY HILLS, for example—but to do so, it also needed a sharp, corrosive sensibility behind the camera. Instead, BEVERLY HILLS BRATS is merely a movie made in Beverly Hills for people who live in Beverly Hills. Equating Rodeo Drive with Main Street, USA, it's the kind of movie only Zsa Zsa Gabor could love. *(Adult situations, brief nudity, profanity.)*

p, Terry Moore and Jerry Rivers; d, Dimitri Sotirakis; w, Linda Silverthorn (based on a story by Rivers, Terry Moore); ph, Harry Mathias (Technicolor); ed, Jerry Frizell; m, Barry Goldberg; prod d, George Costello; art d, Jay Burkhardt; set d, Maria Caso.

Comedy   (PR:C MPAA:PG-13)

BIG BLUE, THE*
100m Angelika/Angelika-ZDF c
David Brisbin *(Jack Kidd)*, Taunie VreNon *(Carmen)*, John Erdman *(Max)*, Jim Neu *(Howard Monroe)*, Sheila McLaughlin *(Myrna Monroe)*, Bill Rice *(Arthur Murray)*, Jose Rafael Arango *(Ramone)*, Soozie Tyrell *(Doreen)*, John Nesci *(Tony)*, Frank Conversano *(Frankie)*, Roberta Levine, Dan Corzier *(Adulterous Couple)*, Ruth Peyser *(Gloria)*, Mike Sappol *(Gloria's Husband)*, Muriel Castanis *(Mrs. Murray)*, Kirsten Bates *(Voice of Marlene)*, Jacob Burkhardt *(Counterman)*, Terry O'Reilly *(Voiceovers)*, Amy Hill *(Computer Operator)*, Diane Jeep Ries *(Sex Club Hostess)*, Amit Ben Yehuda *(Bartender)*, Ted Castle *(Man in Steamroom)*, Ezra Teitelbaum, Jonah Teitelbaum, Wyatt Knaster *(Arthur's Grandchildren)*, Marisa Powers *(Wait-*

Taunie Vrenon in THE BIG BLUE (©Angelika).

ress), Nick Edwards *(Man at Bar)*, Eliza Stuhler *(Kid in Museum)*.

With plotting that lends itself to convoluted cleverness, with glamorous and bizarre characters, and with its heavily stylized atmosphere, *film noir* has a timeless appeal for moviemakers. The best *films noir* all share wickedly savvy scripts, hypnotically masterful direction, and memorable performances that loom vividly in Neo-Expressionistic shadows. THE BIG BLUE, on the other hand, offers interminable stylization and little else. Visually sophisticated in the exaggerated, cheap mode of pulp detective-novel jackets, it also offers many shots that have an almost Edward Hopper-like look to them. Jim Neu's dialog has a purposely stilted quality that presumably is a parody of the dry terseness of 40s *film noir* classics. Typical exchanges include: "You're cute when you're cute." "And I'm bad when I'm bad, right?" "You're even cute when you're bad, sometimes." A few minutes of this chatter is more than sufficient, but when one realizes that this is the only way in which the characters will communicate, sheer torpor sets in. The film continually flashes back to songstress Soozie Tyrell, wailing on a TV screen about them mean ole "Big Blues." She and the song are nothing special, but they are, at least, some form of recognizable life.

The obscure, inwardly spiralling plot concerns a private detective, Brisbin, who is hired by McLaughlin to tail her cop husband, Neu, whom she suspects of adultery. With the aid of an arsenal of electronic devices, Brisbin discovers that Neu's shadiness really involves a drug deal he is setting up with Erdman. When Erdman's girl friend, VreNon, becomes aware of Brisbin, they hop into the sack, and the confusion really begins. The requisite number of betrayals and counter-betrayals ensue before the climactic shootout between Brisbin and Erdman.

David Brisbin, who spends a good deal of the film sipping coffee in a diner as he recalls the story, is a studiously offbeat choice for the film's meta-Philip Marlowe. His ultra-nerd persona is reminiscent of Buck Henry or a less eccentric Woody Allen. It's a long way from Bogart's homburg and trenchcoat to the plaid shirts and computerized myopia of this 80s private eye, and it is impossible to warm to Brisbin's performance. There's a modicum of humor in the exchanges between John Erdman and Jim Neu, who often sound like some long and unhappily married couple, but the device becomes as overworked as everything else in this creatively deficient effort. Bill Rice plays a retired cop with patented downtown-Manhattan wryness and has a funny moment when he instructs a telephone caller to refer to his wife by her first name, because it will make her feel younger. Taunie VreNon is a total unalluring blank as Carmen, which makes her an apt partner for Brisbin. Traditionally, *noir* heroines have provided the beating heart (however duplicitous) amid all the murky machinations; VreNon, like THE BIG BLUE, is strictly DOA. The climax of all this—wildly angled shots of various characters intoning their portentous, meaningless lines, presumably intended to wrap up the film in a neat finish—manages to pile on yet more irritation. One leaves the film with a sense of relief at having outlived it. Songs include: "The Big Blue" (Lenny Pickett, Jim Neu, performed by Soozie Tyrell). *(Violence, adult situations, sexual situations.)*

p, Yoram Mandel; d, Andrew Horn; w, Jim Neu (based on a story by Andrew Horn); ph, Carl Teitelbaum; ed, Ila von Hasperg; m, Jill Jaffe; art d, Ann Stuhler; cos, Susan Young; makeup, Rick Rodier.

Crime/Mystery   (PR:C MPAA:NR)

Ⓥ**BIG PICTURE, THE***
99m Aspen Film Society/COL c
Kevin Bacon *(Nick Chapman)*, Emily Longstreth *(Susan Rawlings)*, J.T. Walsh *(Allen Habel)*, Jennifer Jason Leigh *(Lydia Johnson)*, Martin Short *(Neil Sussman)*, Michael McKean *(Emmett Sumner)*, Kim Miyori *(Jenny Sumner)*, Teri Hatcher *(Gretchen)*, Dan Schneider *(Jonathan Tristan-Bennet)*, Jason Gould *(Carl Manknik)*, Tracy Brooks Swope *(Lori Pressman)*, Don Franklin *(Todd Marvin)*, Fran Drescher *(Polo Habel)*, Suzy Cote *(Mindy Habel)*, Eddie Albert *(M.C.)*, June Lockhart *(Janet Kingsley)*, Stephen Collins *(Attorney)*, Roddy McDowall *(Judge)*, Gary Kroeger *(Mark)*, Alice Hirson *(Mrs. Chapman)*, Grant Owens *(Mr. Chapman)*, Robert Bauer *(Wounded Soldier)*, Vladimir Skomarovsky *(Man in Nick's Movie)*, C.W. Hemingway *(Joey)*, Holly Fields *(Daughter)*, Yvonne Peattie *(Mrs. Feldzar)*, Stan Ivar *(Charlie)*, David Hayward *(George)*, Caitlin Clarke *(Sharon)*, Nancy Valen *(Young Sharon)*, Wesley

Pfenning *(Woman in Cabin)*, Richard Blake *(Abe Lincoln)*, Walter Olkewicz *(Babe Ruth)*, T. Scott Coffey *(Waiter)*, John Cleese *(Bartender)*, Bruce Kirby *(Businessman)*, Richard Belzer *(Video Show Host)*, Tom Maier *(Building Manager)*, Scott Williamson *(Restaurant Manager)*, Victor Steinbach *(Andres Vargiak)*, Arlene Lorre *(Cleopatra)*, George Rogan *(Security Guard/Nazi)*, Perla Walter *(Housekeeper)*, Pamela Morris *(Cheryl)*, Lulie Newcomb *(Receptionist)*, Patty Horweth *(Woman with Fridge)*, Matthew Eichler *(Piano Player)*, Nadine Lenore Patterson *(Twin)*, Elliott Gould.

Like its equally dreary kissin' cousin MOVERS AND SHAKERS, THE BIG PICTURE is a failed attempt to spoof the wheelers and dealers behind the scenes in Hollywood. Christopher Guest (a THIS IS SPINAL TAP cowriter-actor), who directed and cowrote this diatribe against the inanities of the studio system, has created what amounts to no more than a series of sketches that would probably work better on television than in this prolonged, belabored movie. A comical cautionary tale, THE BIG PICTURE follows the rise and fall of a tyro director (Bacon) who is only too eager to compromise his ideals and relationships on his way to the top, a process that begins after he wins first prize for his student film at a national awards banquet. Now everyone in the business wants him, and Bacon soon acquires an eccentric, insincere agent (Martin Short, uncredited in this role). Short, in turn, feeds him to a smarmy studio production chief (Walsh) who signs him up to make his movie. At an altogether daffy story conference, Walsh and his cronies (including a studio head whose characterization prefigures the advent of Dawn Steel) pervert Bacon's original concept in every conceivable way. His idea for a black-and-white movie without music, set in a cabin in midwinter and featuring a lovers' triangle among one woman and two men who are all over 40, is blithely changed by the blithering group to center around a beach house *menage* with two girls and a guy, ages 14 to 24, with about 15 or 20 pop songs thrown in and shot in color—since "they're going to colorize it anyway." En route to success, Bacon also attends what the film's writers would have you believe are typical showbiz house parties. Everyone makes out with everyone else's wife or date, and the only topic of interest is who's the hot new guy in town. For the moment, it's Bacon. Everyone wants to hang on to his coattails (including a lusciously ribald starlet who vamps herself into a role in his picture), turning his head, and before you can say "Porsche" he leases one, breaks up with his live-in architect girl friend (Longstreth), becomes estranged from his cinematographer best friend (Michael McKean, another SPINAL TAP cowriter-actor), and

rents a plush home that once belonged to Chuck Barris. But all good things must come to an end, and the end comes for Bacon when he's rudely jolted by a *Variety* headline, "Allen Habel Gets the Hook," referring to Bacon's producer and signifying that his project is dead. No one wants him anymore, and he's down and out in Beverly Hills. Reduced to doing odd jobs to make ends meet, Bacon runs into Leigh, a runner-up at the awards dinner who now gathers shopping carts at supermarkets. On the side, she moonlights with a rock group, and enlists Bacon to come up with a clever concept for marketing them. He dresses them up like candy dispensers, dubs them the PEZ People, and directs a music video that catches the approving eyes of the Powers That Be. He's out with Longstreth and not returning his calls, however, so within minutes—in a parody of Hollywood paranoia ("From what I hear, he's probably booked for the next two years")—word passes along the grapevine that he's again the hottest property in town. But Bacon has learned his lesson by this time. With a new deal to direct on his own terms, Longstreth looking on, and his old pals back on his film crew, he finally makes his big picture his way.

If Bacon's way is like that of the Guest-Michael Varhol-McKean triumvirate that created this film, however, it's probably way off base. Their attempt to satirize the Hollywood infrastructure fails on almost all counts, hampered by poor pacing, sophomoric parodying, and for the most part lackluster performances by leads Kevin Bacon and Emily Longstreth. THE BIG PICTURE sat on the shelf for more than a year before being released, and could easily have stayed there. Though it begins well enough—the opening sketch showing the student films, with Roddy McDowall, Elliott Gould, June Lockhart and Stephen Collins in cameos (John Cleese is also seen later on as a bartender), is both funny and clever—the wit doesn't last. Except for the all-too-few appearances by Short, who steals the show in electrifying fashion as the glibly moronic agent, and by Jennifer Jason Leigh, who gives a wonderfully inspired performance as a kooky young avant-garde filmmaker, THE BIG PICTURE is barely worth even the rental cost at the video stores in which it's destined to expire.

p, Michael Varhol; d, Christopher Guest; w, Michael Varhol, Christopher Guest, and Michael McKean (based on a story by Michael Varhol, Christopher Guest); ph, Jeff Jur (Deluxe Color); ed, Martin Nicholson; m, David Nichtern; prod d, Joseph T. Garrity; art d, Patrick Tagliaferro; set d, Jerie Kelter; spec eff, Gary P. D'Amico; cos, Karen Patch; makeup, Lizbeth Williamson.

Comedy   (PR:C MPAA:PG-13)

Dan Shor, Tony Steedman, Alex Winter, and Keanu Reeves in BILL & TED'S EXCELLENT ADVENTURE (©Orion).

Ⓥ BILL & TED'S EXCELLENT ADVENTURE**½
90m
Nelson-Interscope-Soisson-Murphey/ Orion c
Keanu Reeves (Ted "Theodore" Logan), Alex Winter (Bill S. Preston), George Carlin (Rufus), Terry Camilleri (Napoleon), Dan Shor (Billy the Kid), Tony Steedman (Socrates), Rod Loomis (Sigmund Freud), Al Leong (Genghis Khan), Jane Wiedlin (Joan of Arc), Robert V. Barron (Abraham Lincoln), Clifford David (Ludwig van Beethoven), Hal Landon Jr. (Capt. Logan), Bernie Casey (Mr. Ryan), Amy Stock-Poynton (Missy/Mom), J. Patrick McNamara (Mr. Preston), Frazier Bain (Deacon), Diane Franklin (Princess Joanna), Kimberley LaBelle (Princess Elizabeth), Will Robbins (Ox), Steve Shepherd (Randolf), Anne Machette (Buffy), Traci Dawn Davis (Jody), Duncan McLeod (Bartender), John Clure (Tatooed Cowboy), Jim Cody Williams (Bearded Cowboy), Dusty O'Dee (Old West Ugly Dude), Heather Pittman (Kerry), Ruth Pittman (Daphne), Dick Alexander (Bowling Alley Manager), James Bowbitch (John the Serf), John Karlsen (Evil Duke), Jeff S. Goodrich (Music Store Salesman), Marjean Holden (Student Speaker), Claudia Templeton (Aerobic Saleswoman), Carol Gossler (Aerobic Instructor), Steve Rotblatt (Police Psychiatrist), Ed Solomon (Stupid Waiter), Chris Matheson (Ugly Waiter), Mark Ogden, Tom Dugan (Neanderthals), Ron R. Althoff (Security Guard), Martha Davis, Clarence Clemons, Fee Waybill ("The Three Most Important People In The World").

An undeniably stupid film, BILL & TED'S EXCELLENT ADVENTURE is, however, goofy enough in its own boneheaded way to be consistently funny through the machinations of its somewhat anemic plot line. Set in the southern California community of San Dimas, the film introduces us to Bill (Winter) and Ted (Reeves), a pair of rather dimwitted best friends and aspiring heavy metal rock'n'roll stars. The boys communicate with the usual overuse of such words as "excellent," "awesome," "totally," and "dude"—speech that would make Sean Penn's Jeff Spicoli from 1982's FAST TIMES AT RIDGEMONT HIGH feel right at home. In the final weeks of their senior year of high school, Winter and Reeves are informed by their exasperated history teacher, Casey, that if they do not pass an upcoming oral exam (requiring them to explain how a significant historical figure might react to modern-day San Dimas) they will not be allowed to graduate, or, as Reeves puts it, they are "in danger of flunking most heinously." The boys are desperate to pass the class, because if they don't, Reeves' dad will enroll him in a military school and their plans to start a rock band will be shattered. Amazingly, help arrives in the form of Carlin, an emissary from the future who has been sent to help Winter and Reeves pass their history exam. It seems that in the future, a new and progressive society has been based on Winter and Reeves' rock music. If the boys don't pass the test, they'll never form their band, and the future will be in doubt (or some such nonsense). Therefore, the future's "Three Most Important People in the World" (rock stars Davis, Clemons, and Waybill) have sent Carlin back in time

to assist Winter and Reeves. Carlin presents the stunned teens with a phone booth in which one can zoom through time by simply dialing the proper code (a phone book detailing which numbers apply to which years is also provided). Winter and Reeves climb inside the booth and zip into the past, waylaying various significant historical figures (Billy the Kid, Socrates, Beethoven, Joan of Arc, Genghis Khan, Sigmund Freud, Napoleon, and Abraham Lincoln) and bringing them back to modern-day San Dimas so that they can speak for themselves during the oral exam. To give the prestigious historical personages a taste of San Dimas, Winter and Reeves take them on a field trip to the local mall, where, of course, they get into trouble (especially Genghis Khan, who trashes a sporting goods store) and are arrested. Desperate to retrieve history's most significant figures from the hoosegow, Winter and Reeves break them out of jail. Lincoln, Socrates, and the others are then spirited to San Dimas High, where their oral presentation is the hit of the class. Winter and Reeves pass the class with flying colors, thus saving the future and ensuring their own success as rock stars.

Believe it or not, BILL & TED'S EXCELLENT ADVENTURE was the hot script in Hollywood back in 1986. Fresh from UCLA film school, screenwriters Chris Matheson and Ed Solomon took their script to the powerful Creative Artists Agency, where it was snapped up and sold in a matter of three days. Of course, shortly thereafter the flavor of the month changed, and it took three years and several different studios to finally get BILL & TED produced and released. The film was to be released by DEG in March 1988, but when the studio went belly-up, the film sat on the shelf for nearly a year with no takers until Orion finally picked it up for distribution. Although many predicted dismal box-office returns, BILL & TED was the surprise hit of the first quarter of 1989, grossing nearly $40 million by midsummer—an especially surprising success considering that the script is essentially a one-joke gag stretched to feature length, that the direction by Stephen Herek (CRITTERS) is rather flat, and that there are no big stars in the cast.

What the naysayers didn't take into account, however, is that BILL & TED has an intangibly charming goofiness about it that is irresistible and endearing. While it certainly isn't as powerful, funny, or insightful as Amy Heckerling's excellent FAST TIMES AS RIDGEMONT HIGH, BILL & TED shares some of that film's main elements and basically takes FAST TIMES' most popular character, perpetually wacked-out surfer Jeff Spicoli, and gives him his own movie. Since most of the comedy scenes are unimaginatively written and poorly staged, one must cling to the one-liners and, luckily, they do not disappoint. The mass appeal of BILL & TED comes from its eminently quotable dialog, which was enthusiastically repeated throughout every high school in the land, ad nauseum. Examples: When Reeves is asked, "Who was Joan of Arc?" by his history teacher, the dunderheaded teen confidently responds, "Noah's wife." When Reeves comments to Winter on the huge age difference between Winter's father and stepmother, saying, "Remember when we were freshmen and she was a senior?" Winter responds with an annoyed, "Shut up, dude." And at the climax, when introducing the various historical personages, the boys present in their best rock-concert fashion "That most excellent Mongol, Genghis Khan!"

What is most remarkable about the success of BILL & TED is that for once, here is a movie about teenagers that contains no excessive profanity, no drug references, and no explicit sexual activity. The film actually promotes—in its own warped way—education, although it makes no serious effort to actually *be* educational. Indeed, the only remotely accurate historical reference occurs midway through the film after Napoleon, one of the first figures captured, is left with Reeves' younger brother and some friends for safekeeping while Winter and Reeves go off to fetch more historical "dudes." The kids take Napoleon bowling, but grow so tired of the smug little dictator that they ditch him. Napoleon is later discovered at the local water slide, where he causes a stir by pushing small children out of the way so that he can get to the front of the line. When Reeves confronts his brother about ditching "one of history's great personages," the kid responds with all frankness, "He was a dick." In this year of unabashed celebration of the French Revolution, the kid's ruthless assessment of Napoleon's contribution to world history kind of puts things in its proper perspective. Songs include: "I Can't Break Away" (Mitch Bottler, Gary Zekley, performed by Big Pig), "In Time" (Bob Marlette, Sue Shifrin, performed by Robbie Robb), "Dancing with a Gypsy" (Anthony Corder, Keith Douglas, Patrick Francis, John Patterson, performed by Tora Tora), "Dangerous" (Richard Czemy, Spencer Sercombe, Kevin Kreis, performed by Shark Island), "No Right to Do Me Wrong" (Lee Ving, David Wills, Michael Ballew, performed by Range War), "Not So Far Away" (Tom Cochrane, performed by Glen Burtnick), "The Boys and Girls Are Doing It" (Frankie Miller, Jeff Barry, performed by Vital Signs), "Party Up" (Michael Wells, Rori, performed by Rori), "Walk Away" (Brian Bricklin, Scott Bricklin, Jake Meyer, Ian Cross, James Goetz, Eddie Bader, performed by Bricklin), "Father Time" (Czerny, Sercombe, performed by Shark Island), "Play with

Me" (Nuno Bettencourt, Gary Cherone, performed by Extreme), "Bad Guitar" (Stevie "No Wonder" Salas, performed by Salas), "Carlin's Solo" (Salas, performed by Salas), "Two Heads Are Better Than One" (Matthew Nelson, Gunnar Nelson, Dweezil Zappa, performed by Power Too). *(Mild profanity.)*

p, Scott Kroopf, Michael S. Murphey, and Joel Soisson; d, Stephen Herek; w, Chris Matheson and Ed Solomon; ph, Timothy Suhrstedt (Technicolor); ed, Larry Bock and Patrick Rand; m, David Newman; prod d, Roy Forge Smith; art d, Gordon White; set d, Jennifer Williams; spec eff, Barry Nolan; cos, Jill Ohanneson; chor, Brad Jeffries; stunts, Dan Bradley; makeup, Daniel Marc.

Comedy　　　　　**(PR:A MPAA:PG)**

BLACK RAIN**½
125m Jaffe-Lansing/PAR c
Michael Douglas *(Nick Conklin)*, Andy Garcia *(Charlie Vincent)*, Ken Takakura *(Masahiro Matsumoto)*, Kate Capshaw *(Joyce Kingsley)*, Yusaku Matsuda *(Sato)*, Tomisaburo Wakayama *(Sugai)*, Shigeru Koyama *(Ohashi)*, Yuya Uchida *(Nashida)*, Miyuki Ono *(Miyuki)*.

BLACK RAIN is a police thriller with plenty of police but far too few thrills. Despite an honest attempt to make a film at once thoroughly original and thoroughly commercial, director Ridley Scott (BLADE RUNNER; ALIEN; SOMEONE TO WATCH OVER ME) is finally lost at sea with a script that bites off far more than

formance, dripping with imperial arrogance, nearly steals the film), to get close enough to Sato to arrest him.

In attempting to capture the mass audience, BLACK RAIN throws in every "high-concept" element imaginable, from maverick cops to male bonding to harrowing chases, with the addition of the ever-it can ever comfortably digest. As an attempt at intelligent filmmaking in a genre in which intelligence too often translates into boredom, BLACK RAIN is a great-looking movie with more than its share of lugubrious lulls.

A rather haggard Michael Douglas stars as Nick Conklin, a New York vice detective accused of skimming confiscated drug money in the wake of an expensive divorce and under the burden of an expensive lifestyle. During a break from being interrogated by Internal Affairs—the despised "suits," as Nick calls them—Nick and his partner, Charlie (Garcia), stumble into a gun battle between rival Japanese yakuza criminal groups. Nick collars one of the Japanese, Sato (Matsuda), who turns out to be the upstart head of a gang that has come to New York to disrupt a rival's counterfeiting coventure with the American mafia. Assigned to transport Sato back to Japan, Nick and Charlie land in Osaka and immediately lose their prisoner to his henchmen, who con them into believing they are police. In his quest to recapture Sato, Nick manages to arouse the ire of both Japanese and American authorities and is finally forced to strike a deal with one of Sato's rivals, Sugai (Tomisaburo Wakayama), whose guttural, growling per-

Michael Douglas and Andy Garcia in BLACK RAIN (©Paramount).

popular fish-out-of-water premise. The effect is to make much of BLACK RAIN seem as tired and worn as its star looks. On a thematic level, the film is just plain confused. Nick's plug-in tendency to bend the rules to the breaking point, which too predictably causes him to become a bull in a china shop when confronted with the bureaucratic Japanese style of law enforcement, is belabored to the point of boredom. Meanwhile, the far more interesting angle developed at the film's beginning—that of a corrupt cop's trying to redeem himself through a trial by fire—gets lost somewhere along the way. It's given lip service by Nick's Japanese police liaison, Masahiro Matsumoto (Japanese superstar Ken Takakura), whose tradition-bound code of conduct is offended by Nick's sometimes sleazy situational ethics. But Nick's need for redemption never has much bearing either on the plot or on the character. Further muddying the mix is the old-versus-new yakuza subplot and the baffling appearances of Kate Capshaw as Joyce, a nightclub hostess who drops into the film from time to time to keep Nick well supplied with clues. Apparently meant to provide Nick with a love interest and to move along a plot that desperately needs all the help it can get (not to mention jolting male audience members back to attention in outfits that wear her rather than vice versa), the character makes a welcome diversion, but no sense.

Scott's visual gifts are still evident in BLACK RAIN. His New York is full of beautiful architecture and dark, menacing corners; Osaka appears as a giant, smoke-belching industrial machine in which its people are cogs; and the Japanese countryside, where the climactic confrontation takes place, has an eerie, ruined visual grandeur. But with little more than a retread plot and characters, and only a few underdeveloped themes upon which to pin them, Scott's stylistic flourishes become just another form of bric a brac in a film that is cluttered enough as it is. Treading a unsteady line between intelligent artistry and box-office excess, BLACK RAIN finally does neither very well, and winds up as a film with something to disappoint just about everybody. (Violence, profanity.)

p, Stanley R. Jaffe and Sherry Lansing; d, Ridley Scott; w, Craig Bolotin and Warren Lewis; ph, Jan Debont; ed, Tom Rolf; m, Hans Zimmer; prod d, Norris Spencer; cos, Ellen Mirojnick.

Crime/Thriller   (PR:C MPAA:R)

ⓥBLACK ROSES*
83m Rayvan/Shapiro Glickenhaus c
John Martin (Matthew Moorhouse), Ken Swofford (Mayor Farnsworth), Sal Viviano (Damian), Julia Adams (Mrs. Miller), Frank Dietz (Johnny), Carla Ferrigno (Priscilla Farnsworth), Carmine

Appice (Vinny Apache), Anthony C. Bua (Tony Ames), Karen Planden (Julie).

BLACK ROSES is a sloppy little horror film that is either one of the worst or one of the funniest movies in a long time, although the on-screen evidence suggests that the first is the strongest possibility. The story concerns the arrival of a heavy metal band, Black Roses, in the small town of Mill Basin, pitting the teenagers there against their strict fathers and wildly overprotective mothers. It seems the only person in Mill Basin who understands the kids is their English teacher (Martin). The teens have never seen a rock concert before, and their parents are, predictably, in an uproar over Black Roses. During a town meeting, one woman claims that the band members, led by lead singer Damian (Viviano), are "disciples of the Devil" and want to brainwash the children; nonetheless, the mayor (Swofford) okays the band's upcoming gigs. With the adults in attendance, the band begins its first concert in a relatively tame fashion, but once the parents leave it turns into "black leather and praise Satan" stuff. Before long, the kids have become zombielike and unresponsive in Martin's class; after the second concert, when the kids start beating each other in the street and attacking people, Martin decides something strange is going on and starts reading up on black magic. Meanwhile, the kids run amok, turning into monsters, killing their parents, and—worst of all—neglecting their schoolwork. After countless murders and scenes of teens transforming into hideous creatures, Martin walks in on the fourth and final concert armed with a gallon of gas and road flares. After a fight with the now-monsterlike Black Roses, he sets the stage on fire, which apparently frees the teenagers from their enslavement. The kids run from the burning band, screaming for their parents; Martin escapes; and the hall burns down while Swofford utters lines like "This is a nightmare." The last scene shows a news report that Black Roses has sold out five nights at Madison Square Garden, where they will play to more people than ever—how they escaped the fire and what has happened to the kids of Mill Basin is left a mystery—and the film ends with a devious laugh from singer Viviano.

Hysterically over the top, BLACK ROSES is to heavy metal what REEFER MADNESS was to marijuana. That the teenagers turn so wildly rebellious and nasty after one concert is already amusing; once they transform into fanged demons the film is flat out hilarious. In one particularly funny scene, Martin is attacked in his home by a love-struck student (Planden) who changes into a monster; he defends himself by stuffing tennis balls into her mouth and whacking her with a tennis racquet. Another funny sequence involves a monster coming out of a stereo

speaker (an idea lifted from a much better heavy-metal horror film, TRICK OR TREAT) to attack an adult. Overlong and full of laughably cheap and plastic-looking special effects, the sequence ends, appropriately enough, with a belch. The performances are uniformly bad, particularly that of John Martin, who strains in his hopeless role of "The Cool Teacher." (We know we're supposed to approve of him because he "understands" the kids and unwinds at home to Mozart.) Martin's one-note, stale performance and his ridiculous heroic theme music only add to our dislike of the character.

Director John Fasano seems very confused as to just what he thinks of heavy metal. It's never quite clear whether BLACK ROSES is a hysterical send-up of Tipper Gore-style paranoia or if it's meant to be a sincere warning about the music's potential for harm. BLACK ROSES is played so straight that it appears to be the latter, however (notwithstanding the cameo by real-life heavy metal drummer Carmine Appice, who looks totally bored, as Black Roses' drummer). The easiest answer is that no one, including Fasano and Appice, either knew or cared what BLACK ROSES was supposed to be, and just threw together an inept and careless movie, hoping to take advantage of the popularity of heavy metal. If that indeed was their intention, they did a terrific job. (Violence, nudity, adult situations, sexual situations, profanity.)

p, John Fasano and Ray Van Doorn; d, John Fasano; w, Cindy Sorrell; ph, Paul Mitchnick (Medallion Color); ed, John Fasano, Ray Van Doorn, and James K. Ruxin; m, Elliot Solomon; art d, Nick White; spec eff, Richard Alonzo, Anthony C. Bua, and Arnold Gargiulo II.

Horror   (PR:O MPAA:R)

BLAZE½**
120m A&M-Touchstone-Silver Screen Partners IV/BV c
Paul Newman (Gov. Earl K. Long), Lolita Davidovich (Blaze Starr), Jerry Hardin (Thibodeaux), Gailard Sartain (LaGrange), Jeffrey DeMunn (Tuck), Garland Bunting (Doc Ferriday), Richard Jenkins (Times-Picayune Reporter), Brandon Smith (Arvin Deeter), Robert Wuhl (Red Snyder), Michael Brockman (Bobby), Eloy Casados (Antoine), James Harper (Willie Rainach), Teresa Gilmore Capps (Tamara Knight), Dianne Brill (Delilah Dough), Blaze Starr (Lily), Gilbert Lewis (Rev. Marquez), Gary Sturgis (Marquez's Son), Louanne Stephens (Lora Fleming), Emily Warfield (Debbie Fleming), Ben Cook (Younger Brother), John Fertitta (Hospital Director), Harlan Jordan (Dr. Cheeseborough), Rod Masterson, Bill Dunleavy (Town Talk Reporters), King Cotton (Jimmie Davis),

Mike Baer *(Secretary of Legislature)*, Bob Cherry, Sid Lacey, Harold G. Herthum *(Earl's Cronies)*, Frederick F. Lewis *(Heckling Reporter)*, Al Robinson *(Magnolia Local)*, Dick Person *(General Store Owner)*, Brooks Read *(Reporter in Store)*, Bill Mesman *(Rep. Davis)*, John A. Barber *(Rep. Hebert)*, Patrik Baldauff *(Rep. Kennon)*, Carey Rauhman Holliday *(Rep. Alexander)*, Robert Earle *(Rep. Elfin)*, Thomas Radcliffe Atkins *(Rep. Johnson)*, Thomas C. Smith-Alden *(Asylum Spokesman)*, Donald J. Lee Jr. *(Donut Shop Man)*, Pat Snow *(Johnnie Mae)*, George Wyatt, Deano Thornton *(Drunken Officers)*, David R. Conly *(Drunken Sailor)*, Janet Shea, Glynn Rubin *(Crony Wives)*, Michael O'Neal, Michael Brooks, Stanley Hughes, Kevin Graham, Wendell Raybon *(Motorcycle Troopers)*, Brad Leland *(Dufee)*.

Despite its steamy premise, BLAZE is about the most clean-minded movie about whoring since THE BEST LITTLE WHOREHOUSE IN TEXAS. Paul Newman stars as three-term Louisiana governor (and younger brother of the legendary Huey Long) Earl K. Long in this sanitized and Hollywoodized romance adapted by writer-director Ron Shelton (BULL DURHAM) from the autobiography of Blaze Starr, the Bourbon Street stripper who is supposed to have stolen Long's heart. The movie starts with a bit of background on Starr (Davidovich). An aspiring singer, she left her backwoods home to make it in the big city. Working as a waitress in a Washington, DC, diner, she is "discovered" by an oily club owner (Wuhl) who promises her an opportunity to sing but instead calls on her to disrobe—and more—before Davidovich makes a hasty exit out the club's back window. She heads to New Orleans, expecting that city's French-derived culture to be enlightened. In montage, Davidovich becomes the burlesque star of Bourbon Street, where Newman hands out fur coats to strippers in return for their favors. When he first lays eyes on Davidovich, Newman is immediately smitten, and his appetite is whetted when she proudly refuses the usual fur-coat fee for services rendered. Newman begins courting Davidovich by taking her along on his political appearances. (In reality Long had a wife, who is conveniently absent from the film, as is any mention of the messy divorce Starr was going through at the time she met Long.) Davidovich begins to soften, but it's only when Newman brings her to his own backwoods home that she tumbles for him. Momentarily impotent, Newman becomes a raging bull when Davidovich strums her out-of-tune guitar and sings for him. Meanwhile, in the state legislature, Newman is trying to push through a then-revolutionary law granting voting rights to blacks. When he reneges on a deal to keep

Paul Newman and Lolita Davidovich in BLAZE (©Buena Vista).

silent while the bill dies on the legislature floor, his political machine turns against him. His former cronies plot to have him committed to a mental hospital and rig an election so that he will be ousted from office. Though she temporarily leaves Newman when she becomes a campaign issue, Davidovich returns to stick nobly by him as he noisily endures his forced retirement, and later, when he runs successfully for Congress. However, Newman (like the historical Long) dies before assuming his new post.

Notwithstanding its hot mix of characters, setting, and story, BLAZE emerges as a rather tepid affair, due in no small part to Shelton's failure to find any dramatic focus, as well as to the odd decision to purge the Starr-Long relationship of any hint of lust after their randy first meeting. The film has a scattershot structure, jumping back and forth between Long and Starr's romance and Long's political crises without doing either justice. The only strong thread that runs through the entire film is Long's (and presumably Shelton's) contempt for the press, which is singled out as the real culprit in Long's downfall. Though she has the appropriate looks and build (having gained 20 pounds for the part), Davidovich, a relative newcomer to film acting, never really convinces as the queen of Bourbon Street. In fact, she was a late replacement in the role for Melanie Griffith, who dropped out when she became pregnant. One can only wonder what Griffith, who has made a career out of torching the libidos of her male costars, would have done with a role so seemingly up her alley.

Alas, we can only report on the film as is. After the tart sexiness, sharp wit, and insight of BULL DURHAM, BLAZE is a disappointment from writer-director Shelton. It's as if, overnight, he was transformed from a clever craftsman into a Director with Something to Say. What Shelton seems intent on saying in BLAZE is that machine politics are okay as long as they champion liberal causes, and that the press *should not* report the news. Had Shel-

ton really delivered the lowdown goods on the Long-Starr affair rather than engage in this skewed didacticism, he might have arrived at a more savory film. As it is, BLAZE is gruff, off-putting pomposity—indecipherable much of the time because Shelton evidently encouraged his stars to mumble much of their dialog—masquerading as titillating entertainment. *(Adult situations, nudity, profanity.)*

p, Gil Friesen and Dale Pollock; d, Ron Shelton; w, Ron Shelton (based on the book *Blaze Starr: My Life as Told to Huey Perry* by Blaze Starr and Huey Perry); ph, Haskell Wexler (DuArt Color); ed, Robert Leighton; m, Bennie Wallace and Wayne Peet; md, David Anderle; prod d, Armin Ganz; art d, Edward Richardson; set d, Harold Fuhrman; cos, Ruth Myers; makeup, Monty Westmore.

Biography   **(PR:O MPAA:R)**

ⓥBLOODFIST*
85m Concorde/New Horizons c
Joe Marie Avellana *(Kwong)*, Michael Shaner *(Baby)*, Riley Bowman *(Nancy)*, Rob Kaman *(Raton)*, Billy Blanks *(Black Rose)*, Kris Aguilar *(Chin Woo)*, Vic Diaz *(Detective)*, Don "The Dragon" Wilson *(Jake)*.

BLOODFIST is a tragically misguided attempt to introduce a new martial arts star to the public. Real-life kickboxing champion, Don "The Dragon" Wilson, stars as a kickboxing instructor who goes to Manila to investigate his brother's murder. He stumbles upon a secret organization called the Red Fist, which is holding a kickboxing tournament surrounded by crooked betting and greedy criminals. As soon as Wilson arrives in Manila, he meets Avellana, a mysterious artist who knows the secrets of this style of fighting. Wilson wants to infiltrate the contest and find his brother's killer, and Avellana decides to teach him some techniques that will help him win the contest. Wilson also meets an American fighter, Kaman, and his sister, and stays with them while he's in Manila. Through several fight scenes intercut with training sequences, as well as moments of hi-jinx among the American friends, Wilson continues to move up in the tournament and discover more clues concerning his brother's death. At one point, he sees an old man, walking on the street with his brother's baseball cap on. He catches the old man, who tells him that a "snake" killed his brother. Then his American friend is murdered in the ring, giving him more reasons than ever to fight and make it to the final match, which he does, of course, and wins. He finally discovers that Avellana is really his brother's murderer (his nickname is "Snake") and the movie climaxes in a bloody battle between Avellana and Wilson. If all of that sounds familiar, it should, the screenplay being recycled from at least five other kung fu films (BLOODSPORT and KICKBOXER most notably) with nothing new added. The stars of the film may be world-champion kickboxers, but they are not actors. Wilson is an extremely stiff, lobotomized-seeming version of Bruce Lee; even his martial arts technique is bland so that the fight sequences lack the punch and spark needed to make them work. Director Terence Winkless handles his action sequences ineptly, framing his actors' movements for the least amount of visual impact. The restraints of the budget are apparent in every scene (a lot of "stock" footage is used, a trademark of producer Roger Corman's Concorde Pictures), the photography is grainy and dull, and the sound is wretchedly poor (at times the actors are simply inaudible). But even within a low budget it's possible to make a decent action/fight film—it just takes talent and energy, traits not much in evidence in BLOODFIST. *(Graphic violence, profanity, nudity, adult situations.)*

p, Roger Corman; d, Terence H. Winkless; w, Robert King; ph, Ricardo Jacques Gale; ed, Karen Horn; m, Sasha Matson.

Action **(PR:O MPAA:R)**

ⓥBLOODHOUNDS OF BROADWAY**
101m American Playhouse/COL c
Julie Hagerty *(Harriet MacKyle)*, Randy Quaid *(Feet Samuels)*, Madonna *(Hortense Hathaway)*, Esai Morales *(Handsome Jack Maddigan)*, Ethan Phillips *(Basil Valentine)*, Matt Dillon *(Regret)*, Jennifer Grey *(Lovey Lou)*, Josef Sommer *(Waldo Winchester)*, Anita Morris *(Missouri Martin)*, Rutger Hauer *(The Brain)*, Tony Azito *(Waiter)*, Tony Longo *(Crunch Sweeney)*, Stephen McHattie *(Red Henry)*, Alan Ruck *(John Wangle)*, Dinah Manoff *(Maud Milligan)*, David Youse *(Busboy)*, Louis Zorich *(Mindy)*, Fisher Stevens *(Hotfoot Harry)*, Richard Edson *(Johnny Crackow)*, Howard Brookner *(Daffy Jack)*, John Rothman *(Marvin Clay)*, Mark Nelson *(Sam the*

Skate), Madeleine Potter *(Widow Mary)*, Stellar Bennett *(Thelma)*, Nicole Burdette *(Woman on Corner)*, Colman deKay *(Nosmo)*, Gerry Bamman *(Inspector McNamara)*, Jane Brucker *(Charlotte)*, Googy Gress *(McGinty)*, Robert Donley *(Doc Bodeeker)*, Grant Forsberg *(Cab Driver)*, Shelly Abend *(Long George)*, Veryle Rupp *(Whitey)*, Helmar Augustus Cooper *(Brother Divine)*, George Ede *(Judge Witherspoon)*, William Burroughs *(Butler)*, Michael Wincott *(Soupy Mike)*, Herschel Sparber *(Big Shelley)*, Black Eyed Susan *(Minnie the Shrimp)*, Steve Buscemi *(Whining Willie)*, Patrick Garner *(Rodent Ralph)*, Tobin Wheeler *(Fleming Meeks)*, Jean Brookner *(Woman)*, Tamara Tunie *(Cynthia Harris)*, Cathryn De Prume *(Showgirl)*, Katherine Monick *(Bobby Baker)*, Sara Driver *(Yvette)*, William Murray Weiss *(Joey the Toothpick)*, Leonard Termo *(Goodtime Nate Fishkin)*, Graham Brown *(Doc Frischer)*, Ed Zang *(Hymie Weisberger)*, Vince Giordano and the Nighthawks *("300 Club" Musicians)*, Linda Beausoleil, Cynthia Friberg, Lorien House, Dana Pinchera, Lynette Tompkins *(Showgirls)*.

For fans of the old films based on the characters created by Damon Runyon, this attempt to re-create four Runyon stories is almost sure to be a major disappointment. BLOODHOUNDS OF BROADWAY bears absolutely no resemblance to the unique blend of wit, pathos, sentiment, and sly humor that marked such films as the Bob Hope-Mary Jane Saunders romp SORROWFUL JONES (one of many remakes of Runyon's classic "Little Miss Marker") and Samuel Goldwyn's GUYS AND DOLLS. The innate charm of Runyon's delightful assortment of street hoods, showgirls, self-proclaimed gangsters, and petty crooks is glaringly absent here. In its place are actors with hip, sophisticated 1980s sensibilities who fail to grasp the authentic motivations of the lovable, naive-yet-streetwise, hoods Runyon captured so ably on paper.

Rather than presenting a single story, the film weaves together four subplots, including a tale involving Madonna and Quaid as a nightclub singer and a down-on-his-luck gambler. (This is the film's most accomplished segment, mainly because of the fine performances of Madonna and Quaid, both of whom demonstrate an appreciation for Runyon that is lacking in the rest of the cast.) To pay off heavy gambling debts, Quaid has agreed to sell his extremely large feet to a mad doctor. However, once he realizes Madonna has fallen in love with him, the idea of being killed no longer appeals to him. In another subplot, Hagerty is a socialite whose party spirit is dampened by the arbitrary shooting of her pet parrot by a swarthy thug. The third story give us another unlucky gambler (Dillon), who becomes a murder suspect,

though he remains preoccupied with his romance with Grey, Madonna's singing partner. Finally, the least interesting of the quartet of subplots involves Hauer as "the Brain"; stabbed during the opening reel, he is whisked all over town by cronies who try to find one among his ex-girl friends who is willing to take Hauer in and try to save his life.

BLOODHOUNDS OF BROADWAY is the feature debut of the late Howard Brookner, who produced, directed, and cowrote with Colman deKay. In style, subdued lighting effects, and production design, Brookner's film is closer to Francis Ford Coppola's THE COTTON CLUB than it is to the 1930s, 40s, and 50s film adaptations of Runyon's work. Judged as a cinematic interpretation of Runyon, BLOODHOUNDS OF BROADWAY comes up wanting. If one divorces BLOODHOUNDS OF BROADWAY from Runyon's writing and evaluates it strictly as a 1980s look at "the way we were" in New York on New Year's Eve, 1928, the film fares better; however, even when looked at in this light, BLOODHOUNDS OF BROADWAY still leaves much to be desired. To begin with, there are the project's frustrating television ("American Playhouse") origins, which are made painfully obvious by the constant, monotonous use of small-screen-style super close-ups. Just when the various Runyon characters most need the freedom to do their thing, the claustrophobic camerawork stifles them. The film desperately wants to be opened up to some sense of excitement. Although the soundtrack incorporates original music that is more or less written in the style of the 1920s, both the soundtrack and the film's emotions badly need an infusion of toe-tapping 20s rhythms. Columbia Pictures, the distributor for this independent production, made one clever addition to Brookner's film, adding some Walter Winchell-like narration by Josef Sommer. As a newscaster, Sommer helps the viewer make sense of the proceedings, which are often bogged down by a lingering camera that works against plot structure and character development.

One of BLOODHOUNDS OF BROADWAY's highlights is Madonna and Jennifer Grey's duet on "I Surrender, Dear." More musical numbers like this would have helped the film tremendously. Moreover, had Brookner's film been made with a broad sense of satire and fun, instead of such seriousness, it might have been a gem. Songs include: "Big Bucks" (Horace Henderson, Lorraine Feather), "I Surrender, Dear" (Gordon Clifford, Harry Barris), "The Mooch" (Duke Ellington, Irving Mills), "The Man from Harlem" (Will Hudson). *(Adult situations, violence.)*

p, Howard Brookner; d, Howard Brookner; w, Howard Brookner and Colman deKay (based on the short stories "The Bloodhounds of Broadway," "A Very Honorable Guy," "Social Error," and "The Brain Goes Home" by Damon Runyon); ph, Elliot Davis (Duart Film Color); ed, Camilla Toniolo; m, Jonathan Sheffer; md, Jonathan Sheffer; prod d, Linda Conaway-Parsloe; art d, Jefferson Sage; set d, Ruth Ammon; spec eff, David Scott Gagnon and Arthur Lorenz; cos, Beatrix Aruna Pasztor; chor, Diane Martel; stunts, Jery Hewitt; makeup, Nina Port.

Comedy/Drama   **(PR:C MPAA:PG)**

ⓥ**B.O.R.N.***
92m Movie Outfit c
Ross Hagen *(Buck Cassidy)*, P.J. Soles *(Liz)*, Hoke Howell *(Charlie)*, William Smith *(Dr. Farley)*, Russ Tamblyn *(Hugh)*, Amanda Blake *(Rosie)*, Rance Howard, Clint Howard, Claire Hagen, Wendy Cooke, Debra Lamb, Kelly Mullis, Corine Cook, Louie Elias, Aspa Nakapoulou, Greg Cummins, Debra Burger, Dawn Wildsmith.

Following in the footsteps of Michael Crichton's adaptation of Robin Cook's *Coma*, B.O.R.N. is not the first film to be concerned with the macabre concept of black-market organs. However, this Ross Hagen-directed effort takes a slightly different and less tasteful look at shopping for human body parts than its predecessor did. The film opens with an idyllic scene of a young couple on the beach—the first and last pleasant moment of the movie. The girl suddenly drops into the ocean, is rushed to the hospital, and faces certain death unless she receives an immediate heart transplant. For a few hundred thousand dollars, a healthy heart can be delivered and implanted within a matter of hours, provided the girl's family agrees to the conditions of the operation. They do, and the search is on for a suitable "donor." A group of thugs in a phony ambulance go hunting for an appropriate subject and nab three young women. The women's foster father (director Hagen, who also cowrote the film) witnesses the abduction and tries to stop it, but the ambulance drivers are too quick and too tough. Alas, this is the first time the thugs have left a witness, and after getting the girls to the operating room, the bad news bunch undertakes a search-and-destroy mission with Hagen as their quarry. Meanwhile, Hagen is busy trying to track down the thugs and his girls. The adversaries spend the rest of the movie trying to find each other, and in the process Hagen's wife and son are killed by a psychopathic henchman. By the time Hagen finds his foster daughters, one of them has already been sacrificed for her lucrative heart.

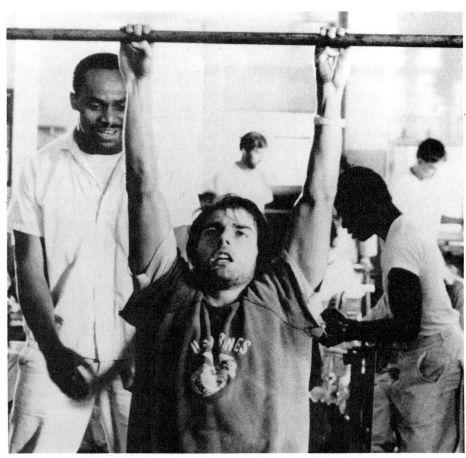

Rocky Carroll and Tom Cruise in BORN ON THE FOURTH OF JULY (©Universal).

Featuring lots of gratuitous blood and guts, and some disturbing offbeat scenes, B.O.R.N. is even less pleasant than the subject matter suggests it might be. Among the film's cast of off-putting creeps are a corpse-fondling surgeon and a maniacal gunman who shoots down anyone who gets in his way, then laments his father's insistence that boys never cry. Too long and offering little besides aggravation, confusion, and violence, B.O.R.N. is not a film for the weak of heart, or for many other people. *(Violence, profanity, nudity, adult situations, sexual situations.)*

p, Claire Hagen; d, Ross Hagen; w, Hoke Howell and Ross Hagen; ph, Gary Graver (Foto-Kem Color); ed, Diana Friedberg; m, William Belote; art d, Shirley Thompson; stunts, Louie Elias.

Horror   **(PR:O MPAA:R)**

BORN ON THE FOURTH OF JULY***
140m Fourth of July/UNIV c
Tom Cruise *(Ron Kovic)*, Bryan Larkin *(Young Ron)*, Raymond J. Barry *(Mr. Kovic)*, Caroline Kava *(Mrs. Kovic)*, Josh Evans *(Tommy Kovic)*, Seth Allen *(Young Tommy)*, Jamie Talisman *(Jimmy Kovic)*, Sean Stone *(Young Jimmy)*, Anne Bobby *(Susanne Kovic)*, Jenna von Oy *(Young Susanne)*, Samantha Larkin *(Patty Kovic)*, Erika Geminder *(Young Patty)*, Amanda Davis *(Baby Patty)*, Kevin Harvey Morse *(Jackie Kovic)*, MASSAPEQUA: Kyra Sedgwick *(Donna)*, Jessica Prunell *(Young Donna)*, Frank Whaley *(Timmy)*, Jason Klein *(Young Timmy)*, Jerry Levine *(Steve Boyer)*, Lane R. Davis *(Young Steve)*, Richard Panebianco *(Joey Walsh)*, John Pinto *(Young Joey)*, Robert Camilletti *(Tommy Finnelli)*, J.R. Nutt *(Young Tommy)*, Stephen Baldwin *(Billy Vorsovich)*, Philip Amelio *(Young Billy)*, Michael McTighe *(Danny Fantozzi)*, Cody Beard *(Young Danny)*, Ryan Beadle *(Ballplayer)*, Harold Woloschin *(Umpire)*, Richard Grusin *(Coach)*, Tom Berenger, Richard Haus *(Recruiting Sergeants)*, Mel Allen *(Mel Allen)*, Ed Lauter *(Legion Commander)*, Liz Moore *(Fat Lady at Parade)*, Sean McGraw *(Young Donna's Father)*, Oliver Stone *(News Reporter)*, Dyle Dye *(Infantry Colonel)*, Norma Moore *(Massapequa Mom)*, Stacey Moseley *(Young Donna's Friend)*, Mike Miller, Ellen Pasternack, Joy Zapata *(Neighbors)*, Bob Tillotson *(Truck Driver)*, VIETNAM: John Getz *(Marine Major)*, David Warshofsky *(Lieutenant)*, Jason Gedrick *(Martinez)*, Michael Compotaro *(Wilson)*, Paul Abbott, Bill Allen, William Baldwin, Claude Brooks, Michael Smith

Guess, James LeGros, William R. Mapother, Christopher W. Mills, Byron Minns, Ben Wright *(Platoon)*, Markus Flanagan *(Doctor)*, R.D. Call *(Chaplain)*, John Falch, Dan Furnad, Fred Geise, Greg Hackbarth, Don Wilson *(Corpsmen)*, VETERANS HOSPITAL: Corkey Ford *(Marvin)*, Rocky Carroll *(Willie)*, SaMi Chester, Chris Pedersen, Chris Walker *(Aides)*, Willie Minor *(Eddie)*, David Herman, Bruce MacVittie, Damien Leake, David Neidorf, Paul Sanchez, Richard Lubin, Norm Wilson, Peter Benson, Sergio Scognamiglio *(Patients)*, Billie Neal *(Nurse Washington)*, Richard Poe *(Frankie)*, Bob Gunton, Mark Moses *(Doctors)*, Vivica Fox *(Hooker)*, SYRACUSE: Abbie Hoffman *(Strike Organizer)*, Jake Weber *(Donna's Boy Friend)*, Reg E. Cathey *(Speaker)*, Edie Brickell *(Folksinger)*, Keri Roebuck *(Loudspeaker)*, Geoff Garza *(Young Radical)*, Joseph Reidy *(Student Organizer)*, ARTHUR'S BAR: Holly Marie Combs *(Jenny)*, Mike Starr, Beau Starr, Rick Masters *(Men)*, John Del Regno, Gale Mayron, Lisa Barnes *(Friends)*, Melinda Ramos Renna *(Bar Maid)*, VILLA DULCE: Willem Dafoe *(Charlie)*, Tom Sizemore, Andrew Lauer, Michael Wincott *(Vets)*, Ivan Kane, Ed Jupp Jr., Michael Sulsona *(Villa Vets)*, Cordelia Gonzalez *(Maria Elena)*, Karen Newman *(Whore)*, Begonia Plaza *(Charlie's Whore)*, Edith Diaz *(Madam)*, Anthony Pena *(Bartender)*, Eduardo Ricardo *(Cab Driver)*, GEORGIA: Tony Frank *(Mr. Wilson)*, Jayne Haynes *(Mrs. Wilson)*, Lili Taylor *(Jamie Wilson)*, Elbert Lewis *(Cab Driver)*, MIAMI: Peter Crombie *(Undercover Vet)*, Kevin McGuire, Ken Osborne, Alan Toy *(Paraplegics)*, Chuck Pfeiffer *(Secret Service Agent)*, Frank Girardeau, William Wallace *(Agents)*, Chip Moody *(TV Anchor)*, Eagle Eye Cherry, Brian Tarantina, Frank Cavestani, Jimmy L. Parker *(Vets)*, William Knight *(Chief Cop)*, David Carriere *(Miami Hippie)*, John Galt *(Fat Republican)*, DEMOCRATIC CONVENTION: Jack McGee *(Democratic Delegate)*, Keri Roebuck, Kristel Otney, Pamela S. Neill *(Women)*, Jodi Long, Michelle Hurst *(Reporters)*, John C. McGinley, Wayne Knight *(Officials)*, Elizabeth Hoffman, Lucinda Jenney, Lorraine Morin-Torre, Annie McEnroe *(Passersby)*, Daniel Baldwin, Real Andrews *(Vets)*.

Oliver Stone (PLATOON) returns to the Vietnam War but covers different territory in BORN ON THE FOURTH OF JULY, starring Tom Cruise as a disillusioned Vietnam veteran. Running almost two-and-a-half hours, BORN ON THE FOURTH OF JULY tells the true story of Ron Kovic (Cruise), a young Marine who went patriotically and proudly off to Vietnam and came back in a wheelchair, paralyzed from mid-chest down. As the film begins, Kovic is a child playing war games with his friends in Massapequa, New York, during the 1950s. A fiercely patriotic boy, he is in awe of soldiers and hopes to be a hero himself one day. After watching President Kennedy on TV, Kovic's mother (Kava) informs him that she has had a dream in which Ron was at a podium, speaking to a large group of people. They were all listening intently and he was an important man. The film then jumps forward to Kovic's adolescence. An all-American teen full of determination and macho pride, an intense athlete, good student, and God-fearing young man, Kovic is clearly loved by his family. His parents (who favor him over his brother) have wildly high expectations of him—expectations that his mother's dream will come true. Kovic is shattered, however, when he is defeated in a wrestling match. Having done everything he was supposed to do—trained tirelessly, prayed, listened to his parents—he cannot understand how he could lose. After Marine recruiters visit his high school, Kovic tries to regain his pride and fulfill his patriotic passion by joining up; like his father and grandfather before him, he will proudly go into battle and defend his country. After receiving reluctant approval from his parents, declaring his love to his longtime sweetheart (Sedgwick), and, of course, praying, Kovic goes to Vietnam. There, during a firefight, he becomes frightened and disoriented, mistakenly shooting one of his own men. After confessing to the killing—telling a major (Getz), who suggests that he forget it and keep his mouth shut—Kovic becomes increasingly confused and frustrated, haunted by the memories of what happened, and eventually takes two bullets himself. With a shattered spinal cord that leaves him paralyzed, he spends months in a dirty, rat-infested veteran's hospital. Unable to accept his condition at first, he finally realizes that he will never walk again. He has gone from a strong, healthy warrior (the perfect example of a "real man") to a wheelchair-bound veteran dependent on others and without the use of his legs or genitals (the ultimate emasculation). After coming home to a rather cold reception from his mother and brother—the latter now a war protestor—Kovic eventually degenerates into a drunken, pathetically self-pitying, embittered hippie. Following a loud confrontation with his mother that brings his suppressed emotions and sense of failure painfully into the open, he travels to Mexico and, over time, confronts the things he has chosen not to deal with—including his feelings about sex, politics, and America itself—then returns to the States with the intent of fixing his life. As a first stage in the healing, he travels to Georgia to confess to the parents of the soldier he killed. (Recounting the event, he breaks down, and is forgiven by the parents.) Kovic's experiences have so changed his views that he now becomes an antiwar activist, recovering his self-respect in the process. At the end of the film, Kovic—who has become a successful author and the leader of many antiwar organizations—is wheeled to a podium to speak at the 1976 Democratic convention. His manhood has been destroyed, his hopes shattered, and his view of life forever changed, but for the first time he fits in, and his mother's dream has come true.

A Vietnam veteran himself, Stone has adapted the real Ron Kovic's autobiography with powerful but mixed results. In attempting to cover so much ground, Stone dilutes the power of his main themes, and pads his film with unnecessary subplots, all-too-familiar situations, and redundant scenes—all of which detract from the script's real focus, which is Kovic's changing idea of manhood. Despite its many problems, however, BORN ON THE FOURTH OF JULY remains a surprisingly powerful film. Most of the credit should go to Cruise, whose impassioned performance as Kovic is a revelation. A talented actor, Cruise should finally get the respect he deserves after his work here and in RAIN MAN. His finest moments, and the film's strongest section, are the harrowing scenes in the VA hospital, when Cruise forsakes all movie-star glamor to show Kovic's physical degradation. Although Stone seems determined to undermine his best work—during one of Cruise's most emotional moments, Stone cuts to a completely unnecessary and distracting flashback—Cruise keeps his head above it all.

In fact, Cruise's pivotal scene—the devastating confrontation with his mother—is the most ineptly directed sequence in the film. Using the wild camera style he employed in WALL STREET and framing his actors in unflattering close-ups, Stone nearly sinks the scene. Cruise saves it, however, with a flawlessly delivered speech and a pathetic cry for help as he tears a catheter from his body and sits helplessly in his own urine. It is a scene of visceral dramatic intensity, and one of the most thematically telling. Overall, however, Stone—who usually overstates his points—eschews the hammering dramatic intensity that has become a trademark of his style. With nice work from PLATOON star Willem Dafoe (who has an intense but purposeless fight scene with Cruise), Caroline Kava, and Kyra Sedgwick in support of Cruise, BORN ON THE FOURTH OF JULY is the first Oliver Stone movie that is acted more intensely than it is directed. Still, BORN ON THE FOURTH OF JULY is never boring, with some undeniably effective commentary on the myth of manhood and the power of pride. It is also Tom Cruise's breakthrough movie, and it's about time. Songs include: "Rock Around the Clock" (Jimmy De Knight, Max Freeman, performed by Rodney Lay and the Wild West), "Venus" (Ed Marshall, performed by Frankie Avalon), "Soldier Boy" (Luther Dixon, Florence Green, performed by the Shirelles), "The Times They Are A-Changin" (Bob Dylan), "Moon River" (Johnny Mercer, Henry Mancini), "My Girl" (William Robinson, Ronald White, performed by the Temptations), "Brown-Eyed Girl" (Van Morrison, performed by Morrison), "American Pie" (Don McLean, performed by McLean), "Love Is Blue" (Pierre Cour, Andre Charles Popp, performed by 101 Strings), "San Francisco (Be Sure to Wear Flowers in Your Hair)" (John Phillips, performed by 101 Strings), "Up, Up, and Away" (Jimmy Webb, performed by the Fifth Dimension), "A Hard Rain's A-Gonna Fall" (Dylan, performed by Edie Brickell), "We Don't Need Arms" (James Palmer, performed by Palmer), "Born on the Bayou" (John C. Fogerty, performed by the Broken Homes), "Hace Un Ano" (F. Valdes Leal, performed by Luis Alberto Del Parana and His Trio Los Paraguayos), "Que Voy a Hacer" (Gustavo Pimentel, performed by Pimentel), "Maleguena" (Ramirez, Galindo, performed by Luis Alberto Del Parana and His Trio Los Paraguayos), "Cielito Lindo" (Traditional, performed by Trini Lopez), "Rebecca" (Wello Rivas, performed by Perez Prado), "You're a Grand Old Flag" (George M. Cohan, performed by Catalina Strings). *(Violence, excessive profanity, substance abuse, sexual situations, nudity.)*

p, A. Kitman Ho and Oliver Stone; d, Oliver Stone; w, Oliver Stone and Ron Kovic (based on his autobiography); ph, Rob Richardson (Deluxe Color); ed, David Brenner; m, John Williams; prod d, Bruno Rubeo; art d, Victor Kempster and Richard L. Johnson; set d, Derek R. Hill; spec eff, William A. Purcell; cos, Judy Ruskin; makeup, Sharon Ilson.

Drama/War   (PR:O   MPAA:R)

ⓥBREAKING IN**½
91m Act III/Goldwyn c
Burt Reynolds *(Ernie Mullins)*, Casey Siemaszko *(Mike Lefebb)*, Sheila Kelley *(Carrie)*, Lorraine Toussaint *(Delphine)*, Albert Salmi *(Johnny Scat)*, Harry Carey Jr. *(Shoes)*, Maury Chaykin *(Tucci)*, Stephen Tobolowsky *(District Attorney)*, Richard Key Jones *(Lou)*, Tom Laswell *(Bud)*, Frank A. Damiani *(Waiter)*, David Frishberg *(Nightclub Singer)*, John Baldwin *(Sam the Apostle)*, Eddie Driscoll *(Paul the Apostle)*, Melanie Moseley *(Young Woman Apostle)*, Galen B. Schrick *(Choir Master)*, Duggan L. Wendeborn *(Faith House Member)*, K. Gordan Scott *(Counterman)*, Clifford Nelson, Roy McGillivray *(Old Men)*, Kim Singer *(Anchorwoman)*, Charles E. Compton *(Real Estate Agent)*, Earle Taylor *(Mr.*

Withrow), Julianne R. Johnson *(Cashier)*, Rod Long *(Garbage Truck Driver)*, Daryl Olson, George Catalano *(Security Guards)*, Aaron Cooley *(Teenage Boy On Skates)*, John R. Knotts, Alan Fudge, Russ Fast *(Detectives)*, Eddie Gove *(Scavenger)*, Joseph Burke *(Ted)*, Gene Dynarski *(Brock)*, Ted Bryant *(Newscaster)*, Garcia Phelps *(Gerry Hacker)*, Douglas Mace, Stephan Adam Szymel *(Prison Guards)*, Jack Esformes *(Mike's Prison Buddy)*, Charles Bernard *(Judge)*.

Pairing writer-directors John Sayles (THE RETURN OF THE SECAUCUS SEVEN; THE BROTHER FROM ANOTHER PLANET) and Bill Forsyth (LOCAL HERO; GREGORY'S GIRL) is the kind of idea that must have sounded great in pitch meetings; however, the product of their collaboration, BREAKING IN, fails to live up to the kind of expectations that presumably led to Burt Reynolds' involvement in the project. Sayles actually wrote the screenplay some 10 years ago, but, reluctant to direct it himself and particular about who he was going to allow to have a crack at it, he sold the script only after learning that Forsyth had been lined up to direct the film. It is all the more surprising, then, that Sayles' serviceable but lackluster script has left Forsyth so utterly at sea.

Reynolds plays an aging professional burglar who takes budding young breaking-and-entering specialist Siemaszko under his wing. The two meet when Reynolds, having broken into a house on the ground floor, bumps into Siemaszko, who has come in through the second floor, not

to steal, but to eat, watch a little TV, and read the mail. At first, the fastidious Reynolds is put off by Siemaszko's goofy carelessness, but after a practice job, he allows Siemaszko to join him in an assortment of heists—a grocery store, the headquarters of a religious organization, and the big score, an amusement park. Siemaszko quickly absorbs the techniques of successful larceny as taught by the seasoned Reynolds, but he never learns much about how to live as a thief. Letting himself get fired from his daytime job, Siemaszko becomes, as Reynolds presciently puts it, a bum with too much money who attracts the unwanted attention of the authorities. Siemaszko compounds his mistake by living high off the loot in a luxury apartment and driving around in a flashy car. In time, Siemaszko pays the price for carelessness, prompting us to wonder just how wily Reynolds really is. But, then, that's the point of the film. At heart, Reynolds is just an old softie, while Siemaszko, representing the younger generation, reveals himself to be mostly crass, cold, and acquisitive.

It's a little strange to find these old-fogy sentiments in a script by Sayles, writer-director of the left-leaning MATEWAN and EIGHT MEN OUT; Sayles' script here is elegant and expressive as far as it goes, but it's also clearly a labor of lucre, more craftsmanlike than heartfelt. Still, good films, like THE HOWLING and ALLIGATOR, have been made from Sayles' self-described hackwork. The problem is that while Sayles is a master of theme and character, the tightly knit narrative has never been his strong suit. Forsyth's best

Casey Siemaszko and Burt Reynolds in BREAKING IN (©Samuel Goldwyn).

Bruce Dern, Tom Hanks, and Rick Ducommun in THE 'BURBS (© Universal).

films also have mood, character, and atmosphere to spare. But what gives them their snap and drive are the well-crafted, almost insanely complex plots at their cores. BREAKING IN has virtually no plot, however, and Forsyth demonstrates little empathy for his two leads, who seem to be acting in different movies. Reynolds' idea of serious acting here seems to consist of swallowing his lines and wearing too much makeup. Casey Siemaszko (BILOXI BLUES; THREE O'CLOCK HIGH) fares somewhat better with the showier of the two roles, but neither character really comes to life.

Seemingly unable to find much at the center of the film to engage his interest, Forsyth instead concentrates on the fringe characters who wander into and out of the main plot and wind up providing the movie's best moments. The best single scene—in which Sheila Kelley, as a likable, offbeat prostitute, reads a self-penned ode to Siemaszko's private parts—wasn't even written by Sayles, as the credits take pains to point out. Other supporting scene stealers include Lorraine Toussaint, as Kelley's roommate and professional mentor, and Maury Chaykin and Steve Tobolowsky as the wacky, self-absorbed defense lawyer and district attorney, respectively, who bicker amusingly over Siemaszko's fate late in the film. It's only in these throwaway scenes that one sees flashes of the Forsyth

comic genius at work. But a few flashes aren't enough to light a fire. BREAKING IN suggests that perhaps the only writer good enough to write a Bill Forsyth film is Bill Forsyth. (Adult situations, profanity.)

p, Harry Gittes; d, Bill Forsyth; w, John Sayles; ph, Michael Coulter (Medallion Color); ed, Michael Ellis; m, Michael Gibbs; prod d, Adrienne Atkinson and John Willett; set d, Woody Crocker; spec eff, Larry L. Fuentes; cos, Louise Frogley; makeup, Manlio Rocchetti.

Comedy   (PR:C MPAA:R)

Ⓥ'BURBS, THE**½
102m
Rollins-Morra-Brezner-Imagine/UNIV c
Tom Hanks (Ray Peterson), Bruce Dern (Mark Rumsfield), Carrie Fisher (Carol Peterson), Rick Ducommun (Art Weingartner), Corey Feldman (Ricky Butler), Wendy Schaal (Bonnie Rumsfield), Henry Gibson (Dr. Werner Klopek), Brother Theodore (Uncle Reuben Klopek), Courtney Gains (Hans Klopek), Gale Gordon (Walter), Dick Miller, Robert Picardo (Garbagemen), Cory Danziger (Dave Peterson), Franklyn Ajaye, Rance Howard (Detectives), Heather Haase (Ricky's Girl Friend), Nick Katt (Steve Kuntz), Bill Stevenson, Gary Hays (Ricky's Friends), Kevin Gage, Dana

Olsen (Cops), Brenda Benner (Walter's Daughter), Patrika Darbo (Art's Wife).

A terribly uneven effort from GREMLINS (1984) director Joe Dante, this black comedy begins with an impressive first hour, then disintegrates rapidly, climaxing with a twist ending that violates everything that has come before it. The film opens as Dante's camera moves in on the familiar Universal planet-Earth logo and descends through the clouds, surveying various landscapes until it comes to rest in a quiet Midwestern suburb (although the set is obviously Universal's familiar backlot with the Hollywood Hills visible in the background). We then meet Hanks, a happy family man· with a perfect wife, child, dog, and home. He's taken a week off from work to recharge his batteries and has no plans other than to sleep late, drink beer, and tinker around the house. Things change, however, when his chubby neighbor, Ducommun, begins piquing Hanks' curiosity about their new neighbors, the Klopeks (Gibson, Theodore, and Gains). A strange-looking bunch of Eastern Europeans, the Klopeks rarely come out of their dilapidated house, and at night, strange lights and sounds emanate from the basement. The newcomers have also been seen digging holes in their backyard in the middle of the night, and teenager Gains has been spotted removing large garbage bags from the trunk of their car. Ducommun is convinced that the Klopeks are satanists, but Hanks dismisses this notion as nonsense until an elderly neighbor (Gordon) disappears and Hanks' dog finds a human femur bone buried in the Klopeks' backyard. Sucked into Ducommun's obsession with the Klopeks, Hanks and gung-ho Vietnam vet Dern join their corpulent pal in spying on the neighbors. All of this activity strikes Hanks' wife, Fisher, and Dern's wife, Schaal, as absurd, and suddenly they find themselves treating their husbands like unruly children, much to the delight of local teenager Feldman, who sets up chairs on his front porch and invites friends over to watch the action unfold as if it were a drive-in movie. After much circumstantial evidence is uncovered, even Fisher and Schaal are forced to admit that something strange is definitely occurring. The women, however, are more mature than their spouses and decide to confront the Klopeks directly by inviting themselves into their house under the pretense of welcoming them to the neighborhood. The meeting is odd and uncomfortable for all concerned, with Fisher, Schaal, and the men all trying to snoop while scientist Gibson, his hostile uncle, Theodore, and the bizarre-looking Gains all act very suspiciously. In time the suburbanites' obsession with the mysterious Klopeks becomes so all-consuming that a full-scale invasion of their neighbors' home is planned, with Dern poised as lookout on his roof and Hanks and Ducommun assigned to actually break in and explore the basement. Things get out of hand, however, and the paranoid neighbors wind up accidentally destroying the house. Still convinced that the Klopeks are up to no good, Hanks, Ducommun, and Dern are shocked to discover that their missing neighbor, Gordon, was simply away at his daughter's house. As fire engines and emergency personnel crowd around the burning house, Hanks is finally overwhelmed with embarrassment and shame at having victimized the Klopeks and rebukes Ducommun and Dern. While Theodore is enraged by their intrusion, Gibson, a doctor, tends to the burned Hanks and is seemingly genial and understanding—that is, until he tries to kill Hanks. A spectacular chase ensues, during which it is revealed that the neighbors were right after all: the Klopeks' car is full of rotting corpses and they *are* unspeakable monsters. Although Hanks is still uncomfortable with the means he and his neighbors have employed in exposing the Klopeks, in the end, it all seems justified.

During the first 60 minutes or so of THE 'BURBS, director Dante presents a delightfully complicated portrait of suburban voyeurism wherein everyone spies on everyone else. From the rather innocent suburban ritual of comparing lawns to a local teen's fascination with a buxom housewife's cleavage, Dante sees the suburbs as a place where the favorite pastimes are keeping tabs on the neighbors and gossiping. Taking this notion to its most absurd extreme, he then introduces "foreign" elements into the environment and, like a scientist looking into a microscope, watches his xenophobic characters attack the intruder. During this phase the film is a devastating satire of suburban values, rendered confidently by Dante, whose always mobile camera forces the viewer to see things from several different perspectives. Unfortunately, when the neighbors actually come face-to-face with the dreaded Klopeks, the film jettisons its narrative complexity in favor of mundane audience-pleasing thrills and the ending—reportedly conceived and shot after the production wrapped—undercuts what begins as an impassioned plea for tolerance. Instead, Dante hedges his bets at the last minute and comes up with a feel-good ending that vindicates the nosy neighbors. While some have contended that Dante has provided several different points of view and left the filmgoer to interpret events, it can also be argued that this not-so-clever approach is actually a cop-out, that he has simply avoided taking a decisive directorial point of view. An even more cynical reading—and one that may be closer to the truth—is that Dante actually intended his dark satire of the suburbs to be a plea for tolerance, but in pursuing large box-office returns, was willing to violate his point of view by tacking on the dramatically inconsistent conclusion.

While this twist ending throws the whole film out of kilter, THE 'BURBS does have its enjoyable moments, most of which stem from Dante's gleeful use of cinematic technique. In addition to some stunning camerawork, the film is filled with amusing visual references to other movies—some as elaborate as an impeccably staged Sergio Leone homage, others as simple as a box of "Gremlins" cereal on the breakfast table. There are also some inspired comic performances from the excellent ensemble. Tom Hanks, fresh from his triumph in BIG, contributes a nicely modulated performance, deftly capturing his character's repressed boredom with his "perfect" life (the real reason for his obsessive pursuit of the Klopeks) as well as his inherent decency, the catalyst of his ambivalence toward the whole sordid affair. Also excellent are Carrie Fisher as the wife forced to become her husband's mother, Corey Feldman as the bored teenager who thinks that his neighbors' antics are "better than television," Henry Gibson as the mysterious head of the Klopek clan, and Bruce Dern, who comes close to stealing the movie with his hilariously gung-ho performance. Unfortunately, all this good work is negated by an ending that cheapens the sincerity of the performances. Songs include: "Machine" (Alex Mitchell, Ricky Beck Mahler, Gary Sunshine, performed by Circus of Power), "Bloodstone" (Mickey Finn, Fernie Rod, Billy Rowe, Mark Radice, performed by Jetboy), "Questa O Quella" (excerpt from Giuseppe Verdi's "Rigoletto," performed by Enrico Caruso), "Locked in a Cage" (Finn, Rod, Rowe, Sam Yaffa, performed by Jetboy), "Make Some Noise" (Finn, Rod, Rowe, Yaffa, Ron Tostenson, performed by Jetboy). *(Violence.)*

p, Michael Finnell, Larry Brezner, and Dana Olsen; d, Joe Dante; w, Dana Olsen; ph, Robert Stevens (Deluxe Color); ed, Marshall Harvey; m, Jerry Goldsmith; prod d, James Spencer; art d, Charles L. Hughes; set d, John Anderson; spec eff, Ken Pepiot; cos, Rosanna Norton; stunts, Jeff Smolek; makeup, Michael Germain.

Comedy   **(PR:A-C MPAA:PG)**

Ⓥ**BUY & CELL***
91m Altar/Empire c

Malcolm McDowell *(Warden Tennant)*, Robert Carradine *(Herbie Altman)*, Michael Winslow *(Sly)*, Randall "Tex" Cobb *(Wolf)*, Ben Vereen *(Shaka)*, Lise Cutter *(Dr. Ellen Scott)*, Fred Travalena, Imogene Coca, Rowdy Roddy Piper, Tony Plana, Michael Goodwin.

As a comedic indictment of Wall Street greed and corruption in the US prison system, BUY & CELL earns enough petty laughs to warrant a Standard & Poors rating of barely poor. Partially graduating from his role as the head nerd in REVENGE OF THE NERDS and REVENGE OF THE NERDS II, Carradine here essays the part of a bright but naive investment broker who is unwittingly framed by Goodwin, the senior partner of his firm, for embezzlement and insider trading violations. Carradine's swift conviction carries with it a 13-year prison sentence and a whopping $200 million fine. Upon arriving at prison, he confronts the first of several ethical tests when he is offered special accommodations in exchange for advising warden McDowell in his stock market dealings. Unable even to pronounce the word "investment" without sneezing, Carradine declines the offer and is immediately dispatched to a cell block simmering with stock characters—thieves, thugs, and Bowery Boys retreads of various ethnic stereotypes. Thrown in their midst, Carradine must finesse his survival against quick-tempered Plana, boneheaded cowboy Piper, Zuluesque straw boss Vereen, schizoid Travalena, and menacing guard Cobb. At first, Carradine's only allies are Winslow, a cellmate with a three-card monte mouth, and Cutter, the rosy-cheeked prison psychologist. Although McDowell has fostered a penal environment ripe for a breakout, Carradine instead persuades his ragtag comrades to break *into* the world of high finance. With Cutter as courier, the prisoners parlay their meager savings into a tidy profit, enabling them to move (financially at least) from the big house onto the big board, as Con Inc. A crash course in computers and high finance is matched with ongoing lessons in ethics, and eventually, by trading through Carradine's former firm, Con Inc. is able to earn enough to buy out the prison and exact payback for Goodwin's and McDowell's dirty dealings, and when these two convene at the climax they are greeted by every law enforcement agency from the SEC to the state police.

Carradine is cleared and his coinvestors have each earned a nice little nest egg with which to build a rehabilitated life.

In addition to telling a timely moral tale, BUY & CELL has to its credit enough characters and contrasting worlds to rally the kind of audience approval that REVENGE OF THE NERDS inspired. But the film's script depends too heavily on prison movie cliches, and the "convicts" themselves seem to be serving out sentences with time off for bad behavior. Fred Travalena and Michael Winslow, in particular, are allowed every license but escape, yet even their frenetic energies can't sustain

the go-for-broke script; it's especially painful to watch Malcolm McDowell's great talents go to waste under Robert Boris' direction; and Robert Carradine, on whom the film rests, has done this sort of thing too many times already. Notwithstanding its well-intentioned themes, BUY & CELL must ultimately be judged guilty of second-degree farce. *(Profanity, brief nudity.)*

p, Frank Yablans; d, Robert Boris; w, Neal Israel and Larry Siegel; ph, Daniele Nannuzzi; ed, Gert Glatstein; m, Mark Shreeve; prod d, Giovanni Natalucci.

Comedy   **(PR:C MPAA:R)**

C

CAGE*

101m Lang Elliott/New Century-Vista c

Lou Ferrigno *(Billy)*, Reb Brown *(Scott)*, Michael Dante *(Lucky)*, Mike Moroff *(Dominic)*, James Shigeta *(Tim Lum Yin)*, Marilyn Tokuda *(Morgan Garrett)*, Al Leong *(Tiger Joe)*, Branscombe Richmond *(Diablo)*, Tiger Chung Lee *(Chang)*, Al Ruscio *(Costello)*, Daniel Martine *(Mono)*.

CAGE is a crazy hybrid of many genres. It's part war movie, part martial arts film, part gang movie, part action-adventure entertainment—even part domestic drama—and it fails on nearly all these levels. The film opens in 1969 in Vietnam, where Ferrigno and Brown are in the midst of a heavy firefight. Ferrigno catches a bullet in the head, but he survives and is eventually nursed back to health, learning to walk and read all over again. Brown (whose life Ferrigno saved in the course of getting shot) sticks with him through thick and thin, teaching him, helping him, and in general being his best friend. The film then moves forward to the present day. Brown now owns a bar, the mentally impaired Ferrigno lives with him, and life goes pretty well for the buddies until two sleazy mobsters happen to see them defending their bar against a troublemaking gang of hoodlums. Impressed by the friends' fighting abilities (especially Ferrigno's), the mobsters try to recruit them to battle in a secret "cage" tournament. Cage, it turns out, is a brutal sport in which two hulking maniacs are locked in a huge cage so they can beat each other to a pulp. The winner is the one left standing, and audiences bet on the outcome. The tournament is run by a Chinese mafioso whose undefeated fighter has made him piles of money. The two mobsters owe this don $10,000, and view Ferrigno as their way out of debt. Brown and Ferrigno want no part of this, however, so the mobsters have the bar burned down and kidnap Ferrigno. Meanwhile, two undercover cops infiltrate the cage games and try to break up the underground tournament. Told by the mobsters that Brown wants him to fight in the cage in order to raise money to rebuild the bar, the unwitting Ferrigno agrees to fight, winning his first match, a bloody battle that gets the mobsters their money back. Brown tears up half the city looking for his friend, while the two cops are caught by the cage insiders, and eventually everyone joins forces to fight the Chinese don and get even with the mobsters. Brown and Ferrigno are both forced to appear in the cage and fight brutal matches, but things are finally resolved for the happy ending, in which the friends receive enough confiscated betting money to rebuild their bar.

If you can get past some of the ridiculous ethnic stereotypes in CAGE you may have a fun time watching it, because it's one of those movies that's so bad it's good. Full of ridiculous dialog, outlandish situations, and laughably wretched acting, CAGE is an uncommonly funny movie. Lou Ferrigno plays the brain-damaged Billy as if he were a cute dog, Reb Brown is just plain awful, and the film's title could easily be changed to "Rain Man Meets Bloodsport." The fight sequences, though extremely violent and brutal, have no visceral impact thanks to the boring style of Lang Elliott, under whose direction the action lacks punch (so vital to the success of this kind of film) and the pacing is erratic. The subplot concerning the undercover cops is so ineptly handled that it's almost an hour into the film before one of them utters a single line of dialog and it becomes apparent what she's up to (until then, she's just a woman in a trenchcoat secretly snapping photos for an unknown reason), and the film's schizophrenic style begins to annoy when it jumps from an offensive sequence involving a Mexican gang to a "serious" scene concerning the Ferrigno character's unfortunate difficulties. The portrayal of a brain-damaged Vietnam vet has no place in utter nonsense like this anyway, and though CAGE's many moments of unintentional humor make it very entertaining at times, serious fans of the action genre will be bored and possibly even offended by this lame entry. *(Graphic violence, profanity, adult situations.)*

p, Lang Elliott; d, Lang Elliott; w, Hugh Kelley; ph, Jacques Haitkin (Deluxe Color); ed, Mark Westmore; m, Michael Wetherwax; prod d, Joseph M. Altadonna.

Action   (PR:O MPAA:R)

⊙CAMERON'S CLOSET*

86m Smart Egg/SVS c

Cotter Smith *(Det. Sam Talliaferro)*, Mel Harris *(Nora Haley)*, Scott Curtis *(Cameron Lansing)*, Chuck McCann *(Ben Majors)*, Leigh McCloskey *(Det. Pete Groom)*, Kim Lankford *(Dory Lansing)*, Gary Hudson *(Bob Froelich)*, Tab Hunter *(Owen Lansing)*, Dort Donald Clark *(Alan Wilson)*, David Estruardo *(Capt. Navarro)*, Wilson Smith *(Joe Crespy)*, Kerry Nakagawa *(Policeman)*, Raymond Patterson *(Physician)*.

Yet another in the string of "nightmare" horror films, CAMERON'S CLOSET borrows liberally from the 1984 Dennis Quaid vehicle DREAMSCAPE. Ten-year-old Cameron Lansing (Curtis), the product of a broken marriage, lives with his parapsychologist father (Hunter). For years, Curtis has been the subject of experiments conducted by Hunter and his research partner McCann, with the result that he now possesses remarkable psychic powers. After Hunter dies in a grisly "accident," Curtis is

sent to live with his mother and her creep live-in lover (Hudson), who shows nothing but contempt for the boy. Paralleling this story is that of a police detective (Smith) who is suffering from horrifying nightmares. The strain is starting to affect Smith's job performance and his superiors order him to get treatment from a psychiatrist (Smith's real-life wife, Harris, of TV's "thirtysomething"). The two stories come together after Hudson, investigating a noise in Curtis' closet, is confronted by a demon who burns out his eyeballs, then sends him hurtling across the room and through a second-story window. Smith is assigned to the case and Harris is brought in to counsel Curtis, who witnessed the death. Smith and Curtis immediately sense a kinship, and soon the boy begins appearing in Smith's nightmares. Through her meetings with Curtis, Harris learns of his psychic abilities and of the experiments conducted by his father and McCann. She and Smith visit McCann and find him a deeply troubled man, mumbling about how things went "too far." He gives Harris a videotape that depicts some of Curtis' training sessions, and reveals that he inadvertently used his image projection abilities to unleash a murderous demon. After some more bloodshed—both in Smith's nightmares and in the waking world—Smith and Harris find Curtis alone and seemingly in a trance in his room. The detective enters the bedroom closet and is transported to a huge cavern, where he is confronted by the demon. While man and monster struggle, Harris calmly holds Curtis and encourages him to find the strength to control the demon. Finally, Curtis appears in the cavern and banishes the demon back to perdition.

Undoubtedly the biggest "star" connected with this project was Academy Award-winning special effects wizard Carlo Rambaldi (ALIEN; E.T. THE EXTRATERRESTRIAL; KING KONG), and gorehounds are likely to be pleased with the several renditions of the demon he provides, not to mention the half-dozen gruesome deaths. The story, however, based on a novel by Gary Brandner, author of *The Howling*, is confusing and illogical. Notably, through half the film it's indicated that the only way to destroy the demon is to kill the boy, but by the movie's end the plot holds that if the boy dies there will be no control on the demon (though the rising body count indicates the kid doesn't have a big future in demon control). Basics such as pace, logic, and character motivation are pretty much ignored in favor of pyrotechnics. Not that it matters much, but the cast is adequate, though they're so low-key one sometimes wonders if they know they're in a horror film. *(Excessive violence, gore effects, profanity.)*

p, Luigi Cingolani; d, Armand Mastroianni; w, Gary Brandner (based on his novel); ph, Russell Carpenter (United Color); m, Harry Manfredini; set d, Sarah Burdick; spec eff, Carlo Rambaldi and Greg Landerer; cos, Constance Buck; stunts, Spiro Razatos; makeup, Rose Librizzi.

Horror   (PR:O MPAA:R)

CAMILLE CLAUDEL½
(Fr.) 149m Films Christian
Fechner-Lilith-Gaumont-A2 T.V.
France-Films A2-D.D./Gaumont c
Isabelle Adjani *(Camille Claudel)*, Gerard Depardieu *(Auguste Rodin)*, Laurent Grevill *(Paul Claudel)*, Alain Cuny *(Louis-Prosper Claudel)*, Madeleine Robinson *(Louise-Athanaise Claudel)*, Katrine Boorman *(Jessie Lipscomb)*, Daniele Lebrun *(Rose Beuret)*, Aurelle Doazan *(Louise Claudel)*, Madeleine Marie *(Victoire)*, Maxime Leroux *(Claude Debussy)*, Philippe Clevenot *(Eugene Blot)*, Roger Planchon *(Morhardt)*, Flaminio Corcos *(Schwob)*, Roch Leibovici *(Louis)*, Gerard Darier *(Marcel)*, Jean-Pierre Sentier *(Limet)*, Benoit Vergne *(Auguste Beuret)*, Philippe Paimblanc *(Giganti)*, Hester Wilcox *(Adele)*, Ariane Kah *(Model)*, Patrick Palmero *(Photographer)*, Anne-Marie Pisani *(Opera Singer)*, Francois Berleand *(Dr. Michaux)*, Martin Berleand *(Robert)*, Claudine Delvaux *(Concierge)*, Lison Bonfils *(Hostel Manager)*, Eric Lorvoire *(Ferdinand de Massary)*, Dany Simon *(Mme. Morhardt)*, Michel Beroff *(Orchestra Conductor)*, Francois Revillard *(Bailiff)*.

Isabelle Adjani (who coproduced and plays the title role) and director Bruno Nuytten have made a film about the life of the artist Camille Claudel that is as dark, twisted, and unwieldy as one of its subject's sculptures. Since little is actually known about Claudel and very few of her works remain, Adjani and Nuytten labored under a real difficulty. Born into a bourgeois French family in 1864, Camille demonstrated artistic promise at an early age. At 20, she encountered Auguste Rodin (played here by Depardieu), who took her into his tutelage and eventually became her lover. Their liaison lasted about 12 years and was an artistically fertile time for Camille; however, their break-up was disastrous. Rodin's fame and prestige outweighed every other consideration. Added to this was the fact that he refused to break off with his long-time mistress, Rose Beuret (Lebrun), the mother of his illegitimate son. These occurrences had a devastating effect on Camille's high-strung nature, and she began to deteriorate emotionally. Uppermost in her mind seems to have been a paranoia regarding Rodin and his supposed conspiracy against her. Camille

became a recluse and was beset with financial problems. To make matters worse, an exhibition of her work organized by her supporter, Eugene Blot (Clevenot), was not a success. On March 10, 1913, a few days after the death of her father (Cuny), the news of which was kept from her, Camille was forcibly taken from her studio and placed in a psychiatric hospital. Her mother (Robinson) and brother, the famous poet Paul Claudel (Grevill), signed the papers which committed her. She remained interned in various asylums for the next 30 years, until her death in 1943.

Based on a biography of the artist written by her grand-niece, Reine-Marie Paris, CAMILLE CLAUDEL is an admiring, but sketchy, account of the life of an enigma. Camille's dark fate seems to have imposed forgetfulness and evasiveness upon those who knew her best; conjecture and chronological gaps (especially in regard to her confinement) abound. As a result Adjani and her collaborators have been left to imagine a tale of towering romantic passion and destruction for her. It begins briskly enough, with the young Camille's first meeting and early antagonisms with the renowned Rodin. The plot motivation becomes murky, however, with the demise of their relationship. Rose Beuret is facilely portrayed as a bourgeois slob, a thorn in everyone's side. Easy points are scored off her at a seemingly endless lunch, during which she gorges herself and makes asinine conversation. Later, compelled by jealousy, she scurries through shadows, spying on the lovers, and even has water pitched at her (shades of wicked witch Margaret Hamilton) when she attacks Camille. Rodin's decision to remain with her seems senseless and weak. (It is also at this point that his character evaporates almost totally on the screen.) Adjani then indulges in aria after aria of unrequited torment. She makes moaning physical love to hunks of clay in her atelier, gets photogenically dirtied, assails governmental art officials, proclaiming, "I AM CAMILLE CLAUDEL!" and, like Brando's Stanley Kowalski (she gets to be Blanche DuBois, too, in the final scene), calls out for Rodin on the street where he lives. These protracted emotional fireworks diminish the effectiveness of her performance; less would have been more. As if to compensate for her bundled-up, half-hidden appearance in ISHTAR, Adjani has given herself as many admiring closeups as were ever lavished on Garbo, or on Streisand, at least, in A STAR IS BORN. She remains, of course, one of the pre-eminent beauties of our time, and many of these shots are, indeed, breathtaking. In Dominique Borg's lovely *fin-de-siecle* gowns, Adjani looks as if she's stepped off a Renoir canvas and one could bask in those star-sapphire eyes forever.

Regrettably, *forever* seems to be about the length of CAMILLE CLAUDEL, and

after beginning as a powerful film it dissipates into something of a vanity production. The ravages of poverty and drink are soft-pedalled on Adjani's physiognomy, preventing her garish entrance at her final exhibit from becoming the shocker it is intended to be. While the real Camille Claudel was 48 years old at the time of her incarceration, Adjani appears to be hardly older in the committal scene than at the beginning of the film—a conceit that seems a holdover from THE STORY OF ADELE H. (There are other, somewhat discomfiting referrals to that previous triumph about a romantically obsessed woman—an emphasis for instance on the importance of Victor Hugo on the artists, and Camille's snapping on of a pair of eccentric glasses.)

Although portrayals of "great" artists are always tricky, Gerard Depardieu is amazingly successful as Rodin. He is wholly convincing as a man of importance and celebrity, and his hands, when molding stone, are indeed those of an artist. Depardieu is even able to overcome such awful dialog as "Sensual pleasures are everywhere," which he exclaims while holding up a head of lettuce (the earthiness in the man, you see). Likewise, he survives whispering Rodin's innermost doubts to one of Camille's busts. In his final confrontation with Camille, he displays an authentic weary resignation that is almost a balm for the imprecations that have preceded it. Madeleine Robinson brings an impressive, leather-lunged voice to her performance as Camille's mother. Alain Cuny is both forceful and touching as her doting father. Laurent Grevill plays Paul in a prissy, humorless manner that some might find appropriate for a poet. (When in doubt, Nuytten's and Marilyn Goldin's script falls back on readings from Paul's works and from those of Rimbaud.)

Nuytten has been a marvelous cinematographer for Bertrand Blier, Andre Techine, Claude Berri, Jean-Luc Godard, and a host of others. CAMILLE CLAUDEL is filled with memorable images: the first dizzying overhead shot of Camille, possessed of "the madness of mud," scraping up her findings in a ditch at night; Rodin's gorgeously airy and light-filled workshop; and Camille in yellow, framed in a window seat like a flower. Nuytten's inexperience as a first-time director shows, however, in the film's uncertain pacing and lack of dramatic cohesiveness (though the inadequate script is no help). At the beginning, as if to convey youthful fervor, Nuytten repeatedly sends Camille spinning through the streets at breakneck speed. Later, too many of the scenes are not sufficiently shaped and seem to linger desultorily—a drunken Camille being lectured by Blot, endless "creation montages" showing her busy at work and closing with a pristine shot of the finished, often none-too-impressive product. (Claudel's artistic genius is presented here as a given; the viewer may have his doubts.) Moreover, the use of a watchful, solemn little boy and a menagerie of cats as Camille self-destructs feels gimmicky. Debussy's music on the soundtrack is in the right brooding mode but unfortunately only emphasizes the muffled, uncertainly veering tone of the film. *(Nudity, substance abuse, adult situations.)*

p, Christian Fechner; d, Bruno Nuytten; w, Bruno Nuytten and Marilyn Goldin (based on the biography by Reine-Marie Paris); ph, Pierre Lhomme (Eastmancolor, Fujicolor); ed, Joelle Hache and Jeanne Kef; m, Gabriel Yared; art d, Bernard Vezat; cos, Dominique Borg; makeup, Thi Loan N'Guyen.

Biography   (PR:O MPAA:R)

ⓋCARPENTER, THE*
(Can.) 87m Goldgems
Canada/Cinepix/Capstone c
Wings Hauser *(Ed)*, Lynne Adams *(Alice)*, Pierre Lenoir *(Martin)*, Barbara Jones *(Rachel)*.

THE CARPENTER, a slow-paced, low-budget entry from Canada, focuses on a young couple (Adams and Lenoir) who move into a new home in a strange suburban neighborhood, only to be visited by the ghost of the previous resident, a carpenter who was executed for murder. Needless to say, he is not an especially nice guy. After a stay in a mental ward, Adams returns to her professor husband and their new house, parts of which are still being constructed. Things go well for her until she hears odd noises coming from the basement one night. Investigating, she finds a carpenter (Hauser, the previous resident) still working. They talk briefly and Adams goes back to bed. The next evening, another carpenter, from the day shift, comes to the house and attacks Adams. Hauser, who has been toiling away downstairs as usual, rescues her by killing the would-be rapist with a drill. Meanwhile, Lenoir is conveniently absent—off having sex with one of his female students. When he returns home, there is no dead body, and Adams says nothing about the murder. However, like many sequences in this movie, it isn't clear what has actually happened. Has there really been a killing or has Adams just imagined it? To complicate matters further, Adams' sister (Jones) shows up and manages to get her unbalanced sibling a job at a paint store. The narrative then jumps back to Adams' house, where she and the weird sheriff (who stops by for no apparent reason) discuss the house's dark past, foreshadowing more murders to come. Next on the casualty list are two more carpenters. Disgruntled and out for revenge after they are fired, the two attempt to burglarize Adams'

home. Not surprisingly, they run into Hauser, who tries out a chainsaw on them. These killings are followed by another ridiculous conversation between Hauser and Adams, and again it isn't clear which events are real and which have been hallucinated. What is certain is that Lenoir is oblivious to all the violence. As the film moves toward its conclusion, an exchange takes place between Adams and her husband's mistress, who, like Lenoir, ends up dead. Finally, Adams confronts Hauser. "You're sick, you're filthy, and you smell bad," she says, among other memorable lines of dialog. Then, out of the blue, Jones shows up to rescue her sister. During the struggle with the carpenter that follows, the house catches fire, Hauser disappears, and Jones and Adams escape alive.

Though it features some surprisingly good production values, THE CARPENTER fails both as a simple horror film and as a black comedy—its tragedy and violence neither exaggerated enough nor given the farcical spin necessary to suggest the dark humor of such films as MURDER BY DEATH or EATING RAOUL. Moreover, too many occurrences in the film are never adequately explained. Notably, we don't learn what brought about Adams' mental instability in the first place; the cause of her illness is only alluded to during an unlikely conversation she has with her would-be employer. More important, we never find out which incidents are real and which Adams has manufactured. Doug Taylor's weak script and David Wellington's unfocused direction leave us with a frustrating, unbelievable film—a black comedy that isn't funny and a horror tale without suspense. *(Violence, profanity, sexual situations.)*

p, Pierre Grise; d, David Wellington; w, Doug Taylor; ph, David Franco; ed, Roland Pollack; m, Pierre Bundock; set d, Sylvain Gendron.

Comedy/Horror   (PR:O MPAA:R)

CASUALTIES OF WAR***½
120m COL c
Michael J. Fox *(Pfc. Eriksson)*, Sean Penn *(Sgt. Meserve)*, Don Harvey *(Clark)*, John C. Reilly *(Hatcher)*, John Leguizamo *(Diaz)*, Thuy Thu Le *(Oahn)*, Erik King *(Brown, Radio Man)*, Jack Gwaltney *(Rowan)*, Ving Rhames *(Lt. Reilly)*, Dan Martin *(Hawthorne)*, Dale Dye *(Capt. Hill)*, Steve Larson, John Linton *(Agents)*, Vyto Ruginis *(Prosecutor)*, Al Shannon *(Wilkins)*, Wendell Pierce *(MacIntire)*, Sam Robards *(Chaplain Kirk)*, Maris Valainis *(Streibig)*, Darren E. Burrows *(Cherry)*, Sherman Howard *(Court Martial President)*, J.J. *(M.P.)*, Holt McCallany *(Lt. Kramer)*, Kady Tran *(Yen, Oahn's Sister)*, Scott Gregory, Ennalls Berl *(Soldier Charlies)*, Vinh Tran *(V.C. Interpreter)*, Somsak *(ARVN Interpreter)*,

Michael J. Fox, Don Harvey, and Sean Penn in CASUALTIES OF WAR (©Columbia).

Hataya Sarmount (Girl Villager), Ba Thuan T. Le (Oahn's Mother), Nootch, Kwan (Children Villagers), J. Chalerm (Villager Old Man Farmer), Sigma (Villager Woman), Po Powpi (Villager Old Man), Shaun Shea, Kristopher Dunn, Donal Gibson, Shkane Kerwin (Soldiers), Niran (V.C. in Tunnel).

With CASUALTIES OF WAR, Brian DePalma joins the ranks of Francis Ford Coppola, Oliver Stone, and Stanley Kubrick, major directors who have brought their personal visions and styles to bear on the Vietnam War. Based on a true story, DePalma's film is in many ways a scaled-down PLATOON: the war is encapsulated and viewed through the existential conflict between two factions in a small unit of fighting men.

Fox plays Eriksson, a recent enlistee who, as the film opens, is ambushed with his squad in the jungle. In the hellish crossfire that ensues, Fox finds himself waist deep in an underground Viet Cong tunnel. As he screams for help, we see an enemy guerilla, knife in mouth, slither through the tunnel, approaching his dangling legs. Just as the guerilla lunges, Sgt. Meserve (Penn) pulls the new man up and out of danger. But Penn is no guardian angel; although he was probably hardened on the streets before he was toughened by combat, the war has pushed him to something verging on sadism, and his leadership owes less to brains or nerve than to a perverse aggression. Fox, by contrast, seems anything but made for combat: A sensitive enlistee, he is an altar boy with an M-16. Fox is appalled when Penn and his charges terrorize a hamlet, suspecting Viet Cong sympathizers everywhere. Afterwards, while the squad takes some brief R and R at the village, Fox is shown up to his ankles in a rice paddy, helping an elderly farmer as if he were doing a stint in the Peace Corps. This idyll is interrupted, however, when the squad is ambushed and Brown (King), Penn's closest friend, is fatally shot. Penn is visibly distraught; later, after the squad arrives at a checkpoint en route to a night on the town and are turned back by the sentry, he's pushed past the breaking point. In what at first appears to be a momentary fit of pique, Penn vows to "requisition" a Vietnamese girl from one of the villages, and his men soon find he means business. In the middle of the night, they drag a young woman (Thuy Thu Le) off, then take her through the jungle to an abandoned hut, where they rape her. Fox protests and refuses to take part, although he can do nothing to help her. Later, as the rest of the squad poises to ambush some Viet Cong, Fox tries to console the bruised and mortified girl. He is about to set her free, but one of the other squad members (sent by Penn) intervenes and brings them back to the bluff where the squad lies in wait for the enemy. The girl coughs, putting their

position in jeopardy, and Penn orders Fox to kill her, but he refuses, and the task goes to the reluctant Diaz (Leguizamo). Before he kills her, however, fighting breaks out and the men take cover. The girl staggers away, but one of the men stabs her. As they scramble along a railroad bridge, the girl, covered in blood, teeters along the rail as the squad looks on in horror. Penn gives the order to shoot, and she falls spectacularly to the ground below. Later, when the squad reaches camp, Fox goes through the chain of command in his attempt to report the atrocity, but to no avail. By the time an attempt is made on his life, he has given up; however, after Fox tells the story to an Army chaplain, four squad members are tried in a military court and sentenced. The movie then comes full circle to its first scene, in which Fox spied a college-aged Vietnamese girl while on a bus in southern California, an event that triggered the memory recounted in the film. In the closing scene, he awakens, suggesting that while for some Vietnam may have *been* a bad dream—in period parlance, a bad trip—to Fox and others it *is* and will remain a recurring nightmare.

Although CASUALTIES OF WAR has a seductive beauty that at times undermines the moral and physical ugliness of the events depicted, the visuals by and large pay substantial dividends. Blood-red skies clash with wide-angle shots of lush, rolling countryside, underscoring the merciless machinery of war and its effect on the pristine landscape. DePalma's oft-criticized penchant for showy directorial gimmicks and didactic homages (most recently, the POTEMKIN reference in THE UNTOUCHABLES) don't get in the way of the story here.

As Meserve, Sean Penn's tightly coiled physicality, fierce scowl, and hair-trigger temper make for a well-defined, economical performance. Michael J. Fox, on the other hand, never measures up to the moral dilemma of his character. His pixieish face has limited emotional range, and is incapable of conveying the full spectrum of his character's horror. Too light to pose as a moral counterweight to Penn's perverted Meserve, Fox winds up not a symbol of a nation's tortured soul—as he was intended to be—but as a mere flyspeck tossed about in a violent whorl of confusion. (*Violence, adult situations, sexual situations, profanity.*)

p, Art Linson and Fred Caruso; d, Brian DePalma; w, David Rabe (based on the book by Daniel Lang); ph, Stephen H. Burum (Panavision, Deluxe Color); ed, Bill Pankow; m, Ennio Morricone; prod d, Wolf Kroeger; art d, Bernard Hydes; set d, Peter Hancock and Hugh Scaife; spec eff, Kit West; cos, Richard Bruno; tech, Art Smith, Jr.; stunts, Jeff Jensen; makeup, Paul Engelen.

War   (PR:C MPAA:R)

CHAIR, THE*
94m Urban/Angelika c
(AKA: HOT SEAT)

James Coco (Dr. Harold Woodhouse Langer), Trini Alvarado (Lisa Titus), Paul Benedict (Warden Edward Dwyer), John Bentley (Warden Callahan), Clark Morgan (Power Inspector), Jack Betts (Detective), Richard Edson (Riot Leader), Jerry Lott (Real Estate Developer), Gary McCleery (Rick Donner), Stephen Geoffreys (Roach), Ron Taylor (Tiny), Calvin Levels (Wilma), Mark Von Holstein (Mazzini), Antonio Aponte (Romeo), Paul Calderon (Pizza), Brad Greenquist (Mushmouth), Jihmi Kennedy (Walkman), Mike Starr (Wilson), Jaime Tirelli (Luis), Daryl Edwards (Bob), Willie Carpenter (Al).

James Coco stars in THE CHAIR as a psychiatrist who sets up a "psychosupport" unit in a prison haunted by inmates who died during an uprising in the 60s. Although warden Benedict thinks Coco is a dreamer and worse, the psychiatrist attempts to help the prisoners with primal scream and group therapy, aided by his assistant, Alvarado. Electrocuted during the fateful uprising, the previous warden, Bentley, now haunts his successor; Benedict is troubled by visions of his former boss' eyes in light bulbs and in the electric chair, which still sits in an unused wing of the prison.

It takes a long time to realize the significance of these ghostly phenomena, however, because the film's characterization is particularly poor and its flashbacks are badly timed. The underdeveloped script is not helped by gratuitous scenes that attempt to add dimension to Paul Benedict's Warden Dwyer. In one of these scenes, Dwyer cuts off the fans that provide fresh air for the toiling prisoners; in another, he offers one inmate (McCleery) a milder sentence if he "cooperates." Benedict is convincingly neurotic, but he doesn't have the presence to be really evil and conniving. It's as though screenwriter Carolyn Swartz, wife of THE CHAIR's director, Waldemar Korzeniowsky, couldn't decide what Warden Dwyer should be, and Benedict is unable to fill in the gaps. On the other hand, Coco brings much added dimension to the underwritten Dr. Langer. Coco's Langer is a genuinely in-touch individual who never allows the prisoners' pranks to get in the way of his doctoring. Despite being terribly miscast, Coco triumphs over the material and will delight viewers with his flawless comic timing. (Regrettably, he died shortly after most of the photography on THE CHAIR was completed in 1986.) Even more detrimental than the film's weak characterization is THE CHAIR's lack of cohesiveness. Director Korzeniowsky—a Polish documentarian who emigrated to the US in the early 1970s and who makes his feature debut with this film—tries very hard to deliver a black comedy, but THE CHAIR lacks the clarity of vision required by that cinematic approach. Had Swartz's screenplay traded more in stereotypes and drawn clearer distinctions between Warden Dwyer's and Dr. Langer's characters, the resulting tension could have been the source of both drama and comedy. What's more, the plot has too many loose ends and lacks resolution; the final scenes are particularly unsatisfying. Some of this may be due to the problems created by Coco's death. Filming on the project, which was shot in the shuttered Essex County Jail in Newark, New Jersey, had to be halted before the film was finished. When cast and crew returned to finish THE CHAIR a year later, the plot was altered to accommodate Coco's absence. Still, the film's problems generally seem to be the result of a lack of professional polish, from less-than-fluid editing by Swartz to Eddie Reyes' intrusive, inappropriate score. Despite some funny scenes—like the appearance of a Valley Power Authority representative during a primal scream session—THE CHAIR is a would-be black comedy that never really gets off the ground. *(Violence.)*

p, Anthony Jones; d, Waldemar Korzeniowsky; w, Carolyn Swartz; ph, Steven Ross; ed, Carolyn Swartz; m, Eddie Reyes; prod d, Robert Pusilo; art d, Gary Levinson; cos, Sheila Kehoe; chor, Fern Feller; stunts, Cliff Cudney; makeup, Laurie Flaquer.

Prison   **(PR:O MPAA:NR)**

Ⓥ**CHANCES ARE*****
108m Lobell/Bergman/Tri-Star c
Cybill Shepherd *(Corinne Jeffries)*, Robert Downey Jr. *(Alex Finch)*, Ryan O'Neal *(Philip Train)*, Mary Stuart Masterson *(Miranda Jeffries)*, Christopher McDonald *(Louie Jeffries)*, Josef Sommer *(Judge Fenwick)*, Joe Grifasi *(Omar)*, Henderson Forsythe *(Ben Bradlee)*, Susan Ruttan *(Woman in Bookstore)*, Lester Lanin *(Conductor)*, Richard DeAngelis *(Hot Dog Vendor)*, Franchelle Dorn *(Receptionist)*, Jacquelyn Drake *(Bradlee's Secretary)*, Don Richards *(Bonino's Defense Attorney)*, June Thorne *(Clerk of the Court)*, Nat Benchley, Cliff McMullen *(Marshals)*, Carey Hauser, Laura Lee Stetzel *(Paramedics)*, Max Trumpower, Dennis Mancini *(Ministers)*, Fran Ryan *(Mavis Talmadge)*, James Noble *(Dr. Bailey)*, Marc McClure *(Richard)*, Mimi Kennedy *(Sally)*, Kathleen Freeman *(Mrs. Handy)*, Dennis Patrick *(Archibald Blair)*, Martin Garner *(Mr. Zellerbach)*, Gianni Russo *(Anthony Bonino)*, Channing Chase *(Aide at Smithsonian)*.

An enjoyable, lighthearted romantic comedy with some cute incestuous undertones, CHANCES ARE isn't nearly as intelligent

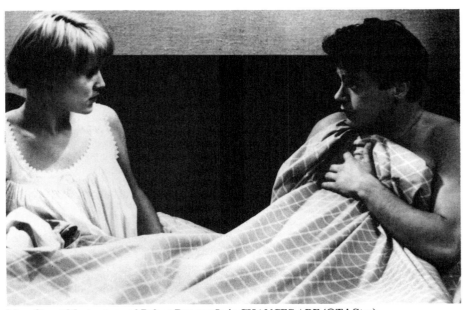

Mary Stuart Masterston and Robert Downey Jr. in CHANCES ARE (©Tri-Star).

as it ought to be, despite the fact that everyone involved seems to be treating it as if it were. A HEAVEN CAN WAIT with mass appeal, CHANCES ARE (taking its title from the Johnny Mathis tune and thereby apparently wooing an older audience) is among the best of the body-switch films that have cluttered the nation's movie screens in the latter half of the 1980s. The film opens in the mid-1960s with the wedding of Shepherd and her lawyer sweetheart, McDonald. Their best man is O'Neal, a devoted best friend if ever there was one. The three of them lead a blissful, problem-free life in Washington, DC, where the threat of Vietnam War-era strife apparently does not exist, nor do counterculture insurgencies or civil rights marches. This is the nation's capital as Hollywood remembers it. A year after the wedding, Shepherd learns that she is pregnant, McDonald documents the corruption of a high-ranking judge, and O'Neal is still as devoted to his friends as ever. Tragedy strikes, however, when McDonald is struck down and killed by a speeding car. He is sent to heaven (the stereotypical comic heaven of clouds and dopey celestial attendants), where he protests his demise. He is told that he, along with everybody else, will be reincarnated and returned to Earth. Excitedly, he runs off to be reborn in Cleveland, exiting heaven before he can receive the standard injection that will make him forget his previous life on Earth. In the meantime, the widowed Shepherd has had some difficulty adjusting to life without hubby. She refuses to forget him, and to keep his memory alive leaves photographs strategically placed throughout her home. She even makes his favorite dinners and leaves sweets for him on their nightstand. Shepherd and O'Neal remain best friends, albeit platonically, and O'Neal

becomes a surrogate father to Masterson, her daughter. Enter Downey as the reincarnated McDonald, a Yale grad pounding the Washington pavement in search of a newspaper job. He is befriended, rather inexplicably (they do not yet know they were best friends in another life), by O'Neal, who takes the rookie reporter home for dinner to meet his friend Shepherd and her daughter, Masterson. In bits and pieces, Downey's memory comes back, but not until after he finds himself sexually attracted to Masterson. Eventually, he realizes that Masterson is the daughter who was born after he (McDonald) died. As he represses his feelings for Masterson, his romantic spark for Shepherd is rekindled. She, however, is still too in love with her "dead" husband to pay Downey any attention, until Downey is able to prove that he really is her departed spouse reincarnated in another's body. While their romance is renewed, Masterson grows distressed over Downey's habit of treating her like his daughter, and persuades O'Neal to finally make a move on Shepherd. Before any of these romantic entanglements can be consummated, however, aspiring lawyer Masterson must try her first case, presided over by the same judge whom Downey/McDonald nearly exposed before his untimely death (or was it murder?). Downey accuses the judge of wrongdoing and, in an ensuing chase through the courthouse halls, tumbles down a flight of stairs and is knocked unconscious. In the hospital room, he is injected with that same heavenly memory drug whose benefits he missed when last in the clouds. Surprise, surprise—Downey doesn't remember a thing and, as a result, is free to love Masterson. Likewise, Shepherd is free to love O'Neal.

Something less than believable, CHANCES ARE is a serving of light entertainment with enough substance to thrill critics eager to read between the lines. Much can be made of Downey's affection for his daughter, or Masterson's Electra complex, but Emile Ardolino's daft direction surely doesn't warrant such energy. (In that respect, CHANCES ARE is much like DIRTY DANCING, Ardolino's previous feature.) The script (by sisters Perry and Randy Howze, of MAID TO ORDER and MYSTIC PIZZA fame) is thoughtful, the characters relatively complex, and the performances entirely likable, but that's about it. Subtext notwithstanding, Ardolino's direction suggests he's no rocket scientist; more often than not, he opts for the easy way out or the cute one-liner, instead of really getting to the heart of the film—the psychological need, bordering on insanity, that some people feel after losing a loved one. Shepherd's character is deeply distressed in CHANCES ARE. Actually, she's a complete nut case, but her madness is legitimized by the appearance of her dead husband. She loves him so much, and so deeply believes that he (or his soul) is still near her, that he actually does appear. The real strength of CHANCES ARE is the script that provides this focus and, as hard as Ardolino tries, he cannot ruin it with his silly direction. Adding to Ardolino's damage are the ugly photography by William Fraker (he also lensed HEAVEN CAN WAIT), the sappy score by Maurice Jarre, and a pathetic final theme, "After All (Love Theme from CHANCES ARE)," sung by Cher and Peter Cetera and written by Tom Snow and Dean Pitchford. Also included are "Chances Are" (Robert Allen, Al Stillman, performed by Johnny Mathis), "Wonderful, Wonderful" (Sherman Edwards, Ben Raleigh, performed by Mathis), "Forever Young" (Rod Stewart, James Cregan, Kevin Savigar, performed by Stewart), "Can't Get over You" (Billy Burnette, David Malloy, performed by Gregg Allman), "Nuestro Adios" (Ruben Blades, performed by Blades), "If You Wanna Be Happy" (Frank J. Guida, Carmela Guida, Joseph Royster, performed by Jimmy Soul), "Happy Couple" (Michael Hedges, performed by Hedges), and orchestral arrangements conducted by Lester Lanin of "It's Impossible" (Sid Wayne, Armando Manzanero), "Strangers in the Night (Charles Singleton, Eddie Snyder, Bert Kaempfert), and "Whole Lotta Shakin' Goin' On" (Curly Williams, Sonny David), and "Fascination" (F.D. Marchetti). (Sexual situations.)

p, Mike Lobell; d, Emile Ardolino; w, Perry Howze and Randy Howze; ph, William A. Fraker (Metrocolor); ed, Harry Keramidas; m, Maurice Jarre; prod d, Dennis Washington; set d, Robert R. Benton; spec eff, Stan Parks; cos, Albert Wolsky; chor, Miranda Garrison; stunts, John Moio; makeup, Cheri Minns.

Comedy/Fantasy/Romance
(PR:A MPAA:PG)

Ⓥ**CHASING DREAMS zero**
94m Nascent c
David G. Brown *(Gavin)*, John Fife *(Parks)*, Jim Shane *(Father)*, Matthew Clark *(Ben)*, Lisa Kingston *(Sue)*, Claudia Carroll *(Mother)*, Cecilia Bennett, Kelly McCarthy, Don Margolin, Marc Brandes, Dan Waldman, Kevin Costner.

Young Brown, the hero of CHASING DREAMS, has problems. He just doesn't fit in. Girls aren't interested in him. At school, he sleeps through lectures on Hemingway's *The Old Man and the Sea.* His father, Shane, never sees eye to eye with him on anything, and his loving little brother, Clark, is confined to a wheelchair. Just when it seems time for Brown to pack it all in and become another teenage suicide statistic, however, fate steps in in the form of his school's baseball coach, Fife. This wise, lonely old codger sees a natural batting talent—largely the result of Brown's experiences chopping wood on the family farm—in the troubled boy, and soon, thanks to America's favorite pastime, Brown's life begins to come together. His abilities even begin to attract the attentions of some big-league scouts, as well as a sweetheart (Kingston). Shane, however, just can't seem to grasp the notion that playing ball might be more fulfilling (not to say more profitable) than working one's own land with one's own hands, and the conflict between father and son causes everything to fall apart. Eventually, on his way back from a promising meet with the scouts, Brown learns that his little brother has died. He loses it and becomes a walking catatonic. A happy ending is provided, however, as the beauty of life and baseball pierces through his depressed fog, he hits the winning homer, and the family goes home together, presumably to inhale apple pie.

Filmed in 1981, CHASING DREAMS is every bit as treacly and derivative as the synopsis above would imply. Its myriad faults are even more glaring when compared with the best baseball film ever made, BULL DURHAM, whose richly humorous, satirical, and informed script; sexy and witty performances; and immaculately timed direction are totally absent from this pathetic effort. (BULL DURHAM and FIELD OF DREAMS star Kevin Costner *does* make an appearance here, which may be presumed a major reason for the film's belated video release, but his role is basically a cameo.) Since it was obviously made on a shoestring and perhaps even "with love," one might hesitate to criticize a film like CHASING DREAMS too heavily were it not so

unforgivably amateurish. As it is, however, David G. Brown must bear most of the blame, for he is not only the film's star, but its coproducer and writer as well. Onscreen, his scarecrow physique and lack of grace make him the most unconvincing athlete since Anthony Perkins played Jimmy Piersall in FEAR STRIKES OUT, and his acting is so inexpressive that the change barely registers when his character suffers an emotional breakdown. The baseball scenes are also unconvincing, clumsily staged and edited for full falsifying effect—all choppy takes—with none of the cerebral quality, free-flowing grace, movement, and strategic intrigue that define the sport at its best. The addition of a ROCKY-style inspirational musical theme only worsens matters, while the use of the younger brother's handicap as a plot device to jerk tears is offensive.

p, David G. Brown, Therese Conte, and Marc Schwartz; d, Sean Roche and Therese Conte; w, David G. Brown; ph, Connie Holt (CFI Color); ed, Jerry Weldon and Robert Sinise; m, Gregory Conte; prod d, Bobbi Peterson Himber; stunts, Scott Cook.

Drama
(PR:A MPAA:PG)

Ⓥ**CHECKING OUT****
93m HandMade/WB c
Jeff Daniels *(Ray Macklin)*, Melanie Mayron *(Jenny Macklin)*, Michael Tucker *(Harry Lardner)*, Kathleen York *(Diana)*, Ann Magnuson *(Connie Hagen)*, Allan Havey *(Pat Hagen)*, Jo Harvey Allen *(Barbara)*, Felton Perry *(Dr. Duffin)*, Ian Wolfe *(Mr. D'Amato)*, John Durbin *(Spencer Gittinger)*, Billy Beck *(Fr. Carmody)*, Adelle Lutz *(Dr. Helmsley)*, Trudi Dochtermann *(Val)*, Allan Rich *(Dr. Haskell)*, Danton Stone *(Dr. Wolfe)*, Stephen Tobolowsky *(Pharmacist)*, Matthew Hurley *(Joey Macklin)*, Courtney Sonne *(Mo Macklin)*, Joe Gosha *(Andrews)*, Mark Lowenthal *(Phillips)*, Randy Pelish *(Spencer's Driver)*, Dean Abston *(Security Guard)*, Ruth Manning *(Dr. Duffin's Receptionist)*, William Kerr *(Policeman)*, Dan Leegant *(Drunk)*, Douglas Koth *(Workman)*, David Byrne *(Bartender)*, Joe Unger *(Joe)*, Kristen Trucksess *(Stewardess)*, Martin Doyne *(Surgeon)*, Robert Goyette *(Doctor)*, Benjamin Wendel *(Young Ray)*, Kevin Mockrin *(Young Pat)*, Jimi Wisner *(Pat Hagen, Jr.)*, Denis Wisner *(Denis Hagen)*, Lydia Nielson *(Mrs. Feldman)*, John Cherrod *(Coffin Truck Driver)*, Beth Barish, Neal Fugate, Janet Jeffries, Adam Karwowsky, Andrea Walker *(Heaven Singers)*.

Though hypochondria has provided many a funny movie moment—most notably in the work of Woody Allen—CHECKING OUT is too messy a film to maintain viewer interest in the subject. Daniels works for childhood buddy Havey doing advertising and promotion for a minor airline. When Havey dies of a heart attack at a company barbecue—after setting up one of his frequent tasteless jokes ("Why don't Italians have barbecues?")—Daniels is so horrified that he wakes up the next morning a raging hypochondriac, convinced his own heart is about to fail. Visiting a top cardiologist, he is subjected to a variety of sophisticated tests that show him to be perfectly healthy, but he refuses to accept the results. Taking over Havey's job, Daniels grows even more uncomfortable when he moves into his late friend's office. He is further upset by the dismissal of his chubby, competent secretary (Allen), fired because company president Tucker thinks she makes "lousy coffee." Daniels becomes obsessed with discovering the answer to the Italian barbecue question, as if it were the antidote to death. Still convinced he is on his last legs, Daniels is sent to yet another specialist. When he realizes that this new doctor is a psychiatrist, Daniels bolts, then seeks advice from Durbin, a wealthy super-hypochondriac he has met in the shrink's waiting room. Durbin, a junk-food junkie, claims to have been "terminally ill for the last eight years." His stretch limo is stocked with a mammoth collection of arcane medical self-help literature and a lifetime supply of tongue depressors. After witnessing Durbin's bizarre behavior, Daniels decides his own health is fine and becomes his old self again; that is, until it is discovered that he has a prolapsed valve in his heart. Sent into a tailspin by his fear of this minor disorder, Daniels buys heart-monitoring equipment and gives up sleeping with his wife (Mayron). Thinking Daniels is having an affair with his new, sexy secretary, Mayron throws her husband out of the house. Daniels goes on a binge, gets beaten up, and is almost killed by a truck. When Allen finds him, battered and exhausted, in his car in the company parking lot, she has her way with him. Daniels is then fired for sexual harassment, but rehired to calm the press after one of the airline's planes crashes. However, when he has to jet to a press conference, Daniels' fear of flying gets the better of him; panicking, he prevents takeoff by announcing that there is a bomb on board. Fired again, he collapses on the runway and is rushed to the hospital with a real attack of appendicitis. During the operation, Daniels dies, and Havey shows up to escort him to heaven, which turns out to be pretty dreary. There, Daniels is assigned a nondescript motel room, shared with a fat, uncommunicative roommate. After learning that nothing much happens in heaven (a lot of time is spent sitting around a swimming pool, singing "Dixie"), Daniels finally arrives at the answer to the Italian barbecue question that has so perplexed him. Of course, the whole affair turns out to have been a dream, and when he awak-

ens, Daniels is able to resume his happy life.

Weakly scripted by Joe Eszterhas (MUSIC BOX) and sloppily directed by David Leland (whose eclectic mix of cinematic styles was much more successfully applied in WISH YOU WERE HERE than it is here), CHECKING OUT looks as if it was written as it was shot. Like Havey's one-liners, the film is little more than a string of comic vignettes and jokes that never quite work. Devoid of likable characters—with Daniels' Ray Macklin being the biggest jerk of all—the film fails to provide the viewer with anyone to care about. Still, despite the awful roles with which they have been saddled, the actors turn in generally good performances. Cut to an hour, CHECKING OUT might have worked better as a made-for-TV production; as is, it is disappointing and frequently in bad taste. Songs include: "End of the Line" (The Travelling Wilburys, performed by The Travelling Wilburys), "Only the Lonely" (Roy Orbison). *(Sexual situations, adult situations.)*

p, Ben Myron and Garth Thomas; d, David Leland; w, Joe Eszterhas; ph, Ian Wilson (Technicolor); ed, Lee Percy; m, Carter Burwell; prod d, Barbara Ling; art d, Richard Hoover; set d, Nancy Haigh; spec eff, Robbie Knott; cos, Adelle Lutz; stunts, Ray Lykins; makeup, Valli O'Reilly.

Comedy   **(PR:O MPAA:R)**

CHEETAH***
84m Walt Disney-Silver Screen Partners III/BV c
Keith Coogan *(Ted Johnson)*, Lucy Deakins *(Susan Johnson)*, Collin Mothupi *(Morogo)*, Timothy Landfield *(Earl Johnson)*, Breon Gorman *(Jean Johnson)*, Ka Vundla *(Kipoin)*, Lydia Kigada *(Lani)*, Kuldeep Bhakoo *(Patel)*, Paul Onsongo *(Abdullah)*, Anthony Baird *(Nigel)*, Rory McGuinness *(Larry)*, Rod Jacobsen *(David)*, David Adido *(Mwangi)*, Konga Mbandu *(Police Captain)*, Martin Okello *(Friendly Policeman)*, Allaudin Qureshi *(Patel's Cousin)*, William Tsuma *(Cabbie)*, Waigwa Wachira *(Racetrack Policeman)*, James Ward *(Announcer)*, Jan Maccoy *(Stewardess)*, Evalyne Kamau *(Nyambura)*, Jane Gelardi *(Announcer's Girl Friend)*, "J.J." Joseph Otieno Adamson, David Otieno, Wally Amalemba, Tony Evans Kalanzi, Kelly Harry Ngetsa *(Band at the Blue Duka)*, Thomas Akare, Denis Doughty, Siddik Ebrahim, Lee Harvin *(Bettors)*, Aloysius Lazarus, Njorogue M. Ngoima, Frank Turner *(Greyhound Owners)*, Richard Clarke *(Voice of Announcer)*, Michael Rogers *(Voice of Racetrack Policeman)*.

Keith Coogan in CHEETAH (©Walt Disney).

Based on Alan Caillou's book *The Cheetahs*, this Disney film presents the heartwarming story of the Johnsons, a contemporary American family conducting research in Kenya, and their eventual involvement with a wild cat named Duma. While Landfield and wife Gorman immerse themselves in their work, their teenage children, Coogan and Deakins, become restless and yearn to explore the beautiful wilds of Africa. Then one afternoon while taking photographs, the youngsters befriend a native boy (Mothupi), who introduces them to African culture and wilderness survival. After several days of exploring with Mothupi, the kids come upon an abandoned baby cheetah that they instantly adopt (with reluctant parental approval). But six months later, Duma, an animal they once held in their arms, is now a full grown cat. It's just about this time when the Johnsons learn they are to be transferred back to the US and therefore must return Duma to her natural environment. Despite the family's attachment to the cheetah, they "undomesticate" her and teach the animal hunting skills. It isn't long, however, before Duma is kidnaped by a greedy and unscrupulous store owner who plans to exploit the cheetah at the East African dog races. With the school year in America rapidly approaching, Landfield and Gorman send the children on ahead to the US. Or do they? Just as they are about to board an airplane, Coogan remembers the strange conversation he had with the store owner concerning Duma's future.

Fearful for the cheetah's well-being, the kids decide to remain in Kenya to find Duma on their own. After a few days of wandering aimlessly through the wilderness, they are reunited with Mothupi and, with his help, manage to track down the poachers and rescue Duma on the day of the big race.

Even though the friendship between the young Kenyan and the Johnson children isn't explored in depth, some interesting contrasts are made between African and Western cultures. For instance, Mothupi's Morogo teaches his new friends a game played with pebbles, and later the three are seen at the Johnson home playing Pacman. Moreover, the subtitles during African dialog and the captivating photography of wildlife and landscape by Tom Burstyn help to create a good sense of atmosphere.

CHEETAH is a wholesome adventure movie with a sense of humor. Keith Coogan, Lucy Deakins, and Collin Mothupi deliver fine performances, as do Timothy Landfield and Breon Gorman (despite the limitation of their rather two-dimensional characters). Although the film is geared toward children, the screenplay by Erik Tarloff, John Cotter, and Griff Du Rhone, and direction by Jeff Blyth are solid enough to make this movie interesting and enjoyable for adults as well. More important, the relationship between the Johnson kids and Morogo is a good example of interracial and intercultural friendship and cooperation.

p, Robert Halmi; d, Jeff Blyth; w, Erik Tarloff, John Cotter, and Griff Du Rhone (based on the book *The Cheetahs* by Alan Caillou); ph, Tom Burstyn (TVC Color); ed, Eric Albertson; m, Bruce Rowland; prod d, Jane Cavedon; cos, Elizabeth Ryrie; makeup, Norma Hill.

Children's/Adventure

(PR:AA   MPAA:G)

Ⓥ**CHORUS OF DISAPPROVAL, A*** **
(Brit.) 92m South Gate/J&M c
Jeremy Irons (*Guy Jones*), Anthony Hopkins (*Dafydd Ap Llewellyn*), Prunella Scales (*Hannah Ap Llewellyn*), Jenny Seagrove (*Fay Hubbard*), Sylvia Syms (*Rebecca Huntley-Pike*), Gareth Hunt (*Ian Hubbard*), Lionel Jeffries (*Jarvis Huntley-Pike*), Alexandra Pigg (*Bridget Baines*), Patsy Kensit (*Linda Washbrook*), Richard Briers (*Ted Washbrook*), Barbara Ferris (*Enid Washbrook*), Pete Lee-Wilson (*Crispin Usher*), David King (*Mr. Ames*), Audrey Trotter (*Mrs. Bawden*), Dinah May (*Girl at Work*), Amanda Mainard (*Woman in Theater*), Anne Priestley (*Hilda Shaw*).

Like Michael Frayn's "Noises Off," this screen adaptation of popular British playwright Alan Ayckbourn's "A Chorus of Disapproval" uses an onstage-offstage structure to take a humorous, offbeat look at an English theater company—in this case a community theater group in Yorkshire. Jeremy Irons stars as a shy, recent widower whose company transfers him to the seaside town of Scarborough. There he joins the Pendon Amateur Light Operatic Society (PALOS) in hopes of making some friends, and ends up as the local lothario. The film begins with Irons nervously auditioning for Hopkins, the eccentric Welsh solicitor who directs PALOS' productions. Impressed by Irons' talent, Hopkins casts him on the spot in the company's production of "The Beggar's Opera," then brings Irons home to meet his wife (skillfully played by Scales, of British TV's "Fawlty Towers"). Among other topics discussed during Irons' visit are the couple's giant doll, referred to as "Daddy Doll," and their children, "the twins," who are never actually seen. Although Scales seems a bit odd, Irons is nevertheless attracted to her, as she is to him. As opening night approaches, Hopkins becomes increasingly disenchanted with the company; incompetence, infighting, and personal relationships continually disrupt the production. Scales and Irons, meanwhile, grow closer and closer and eventually begin an affair, though they never consummate it. It's a very different story, however, when Irons is seduced by Seagrove, another married member of the company. The attentions of these two women do much to boost Irons' confidence, which continues to grow as the male members of the company also become chummy with him when they learn he has inside information on a big upcoming real-estate deal. In no time, Irons finds himself given a bigger role in the play, as the onstage goings-on begin to parallel the real-life experiences of the actors.

A CHORUS OF DISAPPROVAL drags in spots and certain plot elements never become entirely clear. Moreover, director Michael Winner—best known for his work in Charles Bronson's "Death Wish" films—doesn't quite create the atmosphere of total lunacy for which he seems to be striving. However, the film's talented and likable cast (including the much-respected Anthony Hopkins as the blustering director) does contribute some very funny moments, not the least of which is Irons' visit to the home of Seagrove and husband Hunt, who've invited him for "a bit of fun." Naively thinking it's going to be a standard dinner party, Irons invites an elderly friend to join them, only to learn that this is hardly the foursome the married swingers had in mind. There are also some very amusing rehearsal scenes that accurately depict the awkwardness of amateur theater. Though one need not have been involved in a theatrical production to enjoy A CHORUS OF DISAPPROVAL, those who have should surely appreciate the film.

After seeing the National Theatre's production of Ayckbourn's play in 1985, Winner bought the film rights to it. When the adaptations of two screenwriters failed to satisfy him, Winner took on the screenplay himself. Later, he turned to Ayckbourn for help, and the final script employs a structure that was mostly contributed by the director, while the words remain almost exclusively Ayckbourn's. With a budget of $3 million, the film was then shot on location in Scarborough, where Ayckbourn lives and runs a theater. (*Adult situations, profanity.*)

p, Michael Winner; d, Michael Winner; w, Michael Winner and Alan Ayckbourn (based on the play by Alan Ayckbourn); ph, Alan Jones (Rank Color); ed, Chris Barnes and Arnold Crust; m, John Du Prez, De Wolfe, and Boosey Hawkes; art d, Peter Young; chor, Sandra Blair; makeup, Dickie Mills.

Comedy/Drama   (PR:A-C MPAA:PG)

Ⓥ**C.H.U.D. II: BUD THE C.H.U.D.*** *
84m MCEG-Lightning/Vestron C
Brian Robbins (*Steve*), Bill Calvert (*Kevin*), Tricia Leigh Fisher (*Katie*), Gerrit Graham (*Bud the Chud*), Robert Vaughn (*Masters*), Larry Cedar (*Graves*), Bianca Jagger, Larry Linville, Judd Omen, Jack Riley, Sandra Kerns, Norman Fell, June Lockhart, Clive Revill, Priscilla Pointer, Rich Hall.

There must have been at least 30 or 40 people waiting breathlessly for this sequel to the 1984 schlock-horror classic C.H.U.D.—memorable mostly because John Heard, Daniel Stern, and Kim Greist consented to be menaced by slobbering guys in rubber suits, on cheap sets. The original was a bona fide bad-movie howler, though an unintentional one, a guilty pleasure for people who will watch just about anything. The big mistake made by the makers of C.H.U.D. II was aspiring to intentional humor. The results are only intermittently amusing and, in the only genuine way the sequel matches the original, virtually devoid of suspense. For those unfamiliar with the premise, C.H.U.D. is shorthand for Cannibalistic Humanoid Underground Dwellers. In the first film they lived in the sewers of New York, coming up through manholes at night to munch on U.A.U.D.'s (Unsuspecting Aboveground Urban Dwellers). It was left to the hapless Heard, Stern, and Greist to uncover and vanquish a standard-issue deranged military experiment that had gone horribly out of control, creating indestructible supersoldiers. In touching homage to THE BLOB, it was discovered that a good blast of cold air rendered the C.H.U.D.'s immobile. As the sequel opens, the last existing C.H.U.D., nicknamed Bud (Graham), is being put into permanent cold storage, the experiment having been terminated for lack of funds. Down but not out, wacky, scenery-chewing general Vaughn has Bud shipped to an out-of-the-way suburban government facility for safekeeping until he can cajole Congress into appropriating funds to continue the C.H.U.D. project. Enter a trio of zany teenagers (Robbins, Calvert, and Fisher) who steal Bud (for reasons too tedious to recount here) and bring him back to life. The revived Bud turns out to be something of a party animal, gathering a merry crew (in homage to NIGHT OF THE LIVING DEAD, anybody bitten by a C.H.U.D. becomes a C.H.U.D.) to join him in a climactic flesh feast at the town's annual Halloween dance. Will those spunky teenagers recover Bud before they get grounded by their parents? Will Vaughn recover Bud from the teenagers before blowing the town back to the Stone Age? Has Vaughn brought enough CO2 fire extinguishers with him to cool the ghouls before they turn the dance into a body-part buffet? Will the C.H.U.D. epidemic become a national phenomenon? Is there no limit to Hollywood's capacity for churning out boring B movies that nobody wants to see?

But we're getting ahead of ourselves. In the annals of B movies there are few genres more failure-prone than the horror spoof. Roger Corman's LITTLE SHOP OF HORRORS is as good a model as any on the plus side, but he had plenty of practice. Corman's output in the 1950s and 60s includes many straight-faced efforts that are just as funny as LITTLE SHOP, some even funnier. (We're still waiting for someone to mount a stage musical based on ATTACK OF THE CRAB MONSTERS, and who could forget Vaughn himself as TEENAGE CAVEMAN?) But well-done horror spoofs require more wit and conviction than are displayed by the makers of C.H.U.D. II. Director David Irving (brother of Amy, son of Priscilla Pointer, who pops up in a cameo role) tries to bring some visual style and inventive humor to the proceedings, but he's hobbled by Ed Naha's script, with its lackluster plotting, and by dialog that provokes more groans than giggles. Though the lead acting is uninspired, Gerrit Graham has some funny moments as Bud, and comedian Rich Hall drops in to contribute a humorous minute of his own before getting the C.H.U.D. treatment. However, the film as a whole is neither a great horror movie nor a great comedy, and it's not nearly inept enough to pretend to the camp-classic status of the original. Instead, C.H.U.D. II is a classic exercise in B-movie tedium. The soundtrack includes instantly forgettable selections by Wall of Voodoo, minus one-time vocalist Stan Ridgeway. (Violence, profanity.)

p, Jonathan D. Krane and Simon R. Lewis; d, David Irving; w, Ed Naha; ph, Arnie Sirlin; ed, Barbara Pokras; m, Nich-olas Pike; prod d, Randy Moore; art d, Don Day; stunts, Hubie Kerns.

Comedy/Horror   (PR:C MPAA:R)

⊙CODE NAME VENGEANCE*½
96m Killmasters/Action c
Robert Ginty (Monroe Bieler), Shannon Tweed (Sam), Cameron Mitchell (Dutch), Don Gordon (Harry Applegate), Kevin Brophy (Chuck), James Ryan (Tabrak).

At the beginning of CODE NAME VENGEANCE, a terrorist (Ryan), attempting to force the government of an Middle Eastern monarchy to withdraw from an unfavorable disarmament agreement with the West, raids the kingdom's palace and kidnaps the queen and prince. Pressured by the king to rescue the royal family, the Americans assign their head of covert activities (Gordon) to coerce an imprisoned commando (Ginty) into staging the rescue. Ginty—whom the Americans have allowed to languish in a loathsome prison because they want to cover up the failure of an earlier anti-terrorist mission—resists Gordon's solicitations until he learns that his release will afford him the opportunity to avenge his imprisonment by killing Ryan. Soon, Ginty is swept out of captivity and seduced by his American rescuer (Tweed); meanwhile, Ryan slaughters his way through the countryside and foments anti-American sentiment. Ginty embarks upon his quest for Ryan, but becomes suspicious when he is unexpectedly assigned an American agent (Brophy) as a partner. Mitchell, an old ally Ginty has recruited for the mission, immediately determines that Brophy is untrustworthy and should be eliminated, but Ginty ignores the advice. The terrorist camp is quickly located, a siege is successfully laid, and Ginty lines Ryan up in his gunsights; but Brophy "accidentally" trips at a strategic moment, sending Ginty's bullet astray and allowing Ryan to retreat in the mountains. Hot in pursuit, Ginty and his men survive an ambush and assault Ryan's camp a second time. After gravely wounding Ryan in a mine shaft, Ginty is shocked to learn that Gordon orchestrated not only the kidnapping of the queen and prince, but his own 12-year imprisonment as well. Brophy, sensing his opportunity, blows up the mine shaft before Ginty can escape, shoots Mitchell in the back, and whisks the royal family into a clearing where Tweed, his partner, waits in a helicopter. But Ginty, who survives the explosion, quickly overpowers Brophy and convinces the vacillating Tweed that her loyalties are misplaced. While she transports the royal family to a joyful reunion with the king, Ginty enters the American compound and visits swift and violent revenge upon Gordon. Despite the heavy assault from American troops that follows, Ginty and Tweed escape in the helicopter, en route to a long and anxiously awaited romance.

Though the genre is notable for its narrative implausibilities and perfunctory characters, the made-for-video action-adventure film nevertheless fills an ever-growing demand for cinematic revenge fantasies. The battle against personal injustice is also the driving force behind CODE NAME VENGEANCE, but the film's heroic theme is quickly obscured by its many preposterous and pedestrian action scenes. When an impetuous Brophy delivers his unwitting compatriots into a massive terrorist ambush, for example, the commandos extricate themselves from a barrage of bullets and shells simply by standing up and running out of frame. The lack of credible action sequences is exceeded only by the characters' ignorance of their physical circumstances: when the commandos conduct a nighttime raid on Ryan's camp, the enemy's vigilant guards fail to notice the attackers' booming voices and thundering footsteps until the battle has actually begun. The casting of the feeble Cameron Mitchell as a rugged commando is particularly suspect given the difficulty of the terrain his character must cover, and the arbitrary nature of his role is further highlighted by his repetitive dialog. After Mitchell makes his quick and apparently instinctive assertion that Brophy is not to be trusted, he wheezes his way across the desert breathlessly repeating his discovery whenever Ginty moves into earshot. Despite its flaws, however, CODE NAME VENGEANCE is notable in its sympathetic portrayal of its Third World ruler's predicament, a rarity in this sort of film. (Violence, profanity, adult situations.)

p, David Winters; d, David Winters; w, Anthony Palmer; ph, Keith Dunkley (Irene Color); ed, Brian G. Frost; m, Tim James, Steve McClintock, and Mark Mancina.

Action/Adventure   (PR:C MPAA:R)

⊙COHEN AND TATE***½
85m Nelson/Tri-Star c
Roy Scheider (Cohen), Adam Baldwin (Tate), Harley Cross (Travis Knight), Cooper Huckabee, Suzanne Savoy.

Some of the finest films of the past few years fall into a category of American movie-making that might be called subversive cinema. Influenced principally by B movies, subversive cinema combines a focus on nasty people who do nasty things in nasty places with a strong moral message, disturbing subtext, and haunting imagery. Examples include such films as BLUE VELVET; Brian DePalma's SCARFACE; AT CLOSE RANGE; NEAR DARK; and THE HITCHER. The last two features were scripted by Eric Red, who makes his directorial debut with COHEN

& TATE, a fine example of subversive cinema and a remarkably assured first film.

COHEN & TATE begins at a farm in Oklahoma, where nine-year-old Travis Knight (Cross) and his family are hiding under FBI protection as a result of Cross' having witnessed a mob hit. When Cohen (Scheider) and Tate (Baldwin) show up, the two hit men kill Cross' family and kidnap the child, planning to take him to their mob bosses in Houston. Scheider is the older and more professional of the two; complete with trench coat and hearing aid, he wants to get the job done. Baldwin, by contrast, is a young, psychotic hothead who eats wooden matches and caresses his pump shotgun with trigger-happy abandon. As the journey to Houston begins, it is revealed that Scheider has worked alone for 30 years and hates Baldwin. Cross observes this enmity, and gradually works their antagonistic relationship to his advantage, eventually convincing Scheider that Baldwin wants to kill him and that Schieder must kill him first. After meeting roadblocks, losing maps, changing cars, and battling road fatigue, the two men are near the breaking point. Baldwin attempts to kill Cross and Scheider blows him out of the car with his gun, putting the body in the trunk and driving on with the intent of finishing his job. After a tire blowout, however, Baldwin jumps from the trunk and attacks Scheider, then stalks the escaping Cross across oil fields. After another climactic confrontation between Scheider and Baldwin that leaves Cross' life hanging in the balance, the half-dead victor continues the drive to Houston, with helicopters and troopers on his tail. Eventually surrounded by cops, the film ends abruptly as the dying hit man speaks his last line, which proves ironically funny and terribly tragic at the same time.

COHEN & TATE works because of its unapologetic B-movie style, including its underlying themes. Baldwin and Scheider sarcastically refer to each other as "Mr. Cohen" and "Mr. Tate," and the ideals of family values and responsibility are present throughout the movie. The performances are terrific. Cross offers an interesting performance, making his character seem both sweet and annoying and handling Red's strange dialog with ease. Adam Baldwin is completely over the top as Tate, while Roy Scheider (who turns in his best performance in years) provides a perfect counterbalance in Cohen.

Although more than half the film's action takes place in a car, COHEN & TATE is never boring, thanks to Red's crackling dialog and interesting visual style. Set against the desolate highways and lonely truckstops of America (not unlike THE HITCHER), the film has an interestingly empty look. The movie has one notable technical flaw, however, namely the strange dubbing of some of Baldwin's dia-

log in which, for no apparent reason, some of his profane remarks are poorly looped. Aside from that, COHEN & TATE is a suspenseful, funny, and insightful thriller that should please people with a taste for something different, something subversive. *(Graphic violence, excessive profanity, adult situations.)*

p, Antony Rufus Isaacs and Jeff Young; d, Eric Red; w, Eric Red; ph, Victor J. Kemper (Eastmancolor); ed, Ed Abroms; m, Bill Conti; prod d, Davis Haber.

Action/Thriller   (PR:O MPAA:R)

ⓥ**COMMUNION***½
109m Pheasantry-Allied Vision-The Picture Property/New Line c
Christopher Walken *(Whitley Strieber)*, Lindsay Crouse *(Anne Strieber)*, Joel Carlson *(Andrew Strieber)*, Frances Sternhagen *(Dr. Janet Duffy)*, Andreas Katsulas *(Alex)*, Terri Hanauer *(Sara)*, Basil Hoffman *(Dr. Friedman)*, John Dennis Johnston *(Fireman)*, Dee Dee Rescher *(Mrs. Greenberg)*, Aileen Fitzpatrick *(Mother)*, R.J. Miller *(Father)*, Holly Fields *(Praying Mantis Girl)*, Paula Shaw *(Woman from Apartment)*, Juliet Sorcey *(Second-grade Girl)*, Kate Stern *(Woman on Bus)*, Johnny Dark *(Lab Technician)*, Irene Forrest *(Sally)*, Vince McKewin *(Bob)*, Sally Kemp *(Laurie)*, Maggie Egan *(Nancy)*, Paul Clemens *(Patrick)*, Andrew Magarian *(Man in Hallway)*, Madeleine Mora *(Baby Girl)*.

COMMUNION is a limp propaganda piece for the already converted. Adapted by Whitley Strieber from his autobiographical best-seller about his close encounters with extra-terrestrial beings, this interminable exploration of one

writer's reluctance to believe the unbelievable fails as a thriller, as a psychological drama, and even as unintentional self-parody. If any alien visitors have been worried that American pop culture might blow their cover with a Hollywood blockbuster, they can rest assured that few moviegoers will bother attending COMMUNION.

Walken is blessed with an attractive wife, a precocious son, and a thriving literary career that has been temporarily derailed by writer's block. Trying to unwind with friends at his country cabin, he's understandably perplexed when the retreat is flooded with blazing white lights and things start to go bump in the night. After his frightened pals persuade him to hightail it back home to New York City, Walken begins to withdraw from his impatient spouse and to behave in a highly paranoid fashion. His increasingly weird actions even incur his neighbor's wrath when he freaks out during a child's Halloween prank. What could have happened in the brightly lit boondocks? A convention of football-field floodlight manufacturers? No, indeed, for during Walken's next country getaway it is revealed that itsy-bitsy aliens clad in robes have been carrying the writer off to their mobile space lab for scientific experimentation and testing—he is one of those chosen few whom we read about in the *National Enquirer*. For the sake of concealing the aliens' true identities (and for the sake of plot convenience), these abductions are such that neither Walken nor his wife (Crouse) remember anything about them. Failing to convince himself he's merely the victim of nightmares, Walken visits supportive psychiatrist Sternhagen, and the full extent of his trauma is revealed while he is under

Christopher Walken in COMMUNION (©New Line).

hypnosis. It seems the excessively curious interplanetary visitors have given him the ultimate cosmic physical check-up, culminating in a rectal exam! In therapy with Sternhagen, Walken experiences flashbacks to his childhood and realizes he's met the little doctors from outer space repeatedly over the years. After sharing this secret shame with an encounter group of fellow abductees, Walken is able to shake off the heebie-jeebies, save his shaky marriage, and even defeat his writer's block. Moreover—although Blue Cross/Blue Shield would probably frown on these free extra-terrestrial medical consultations—Walken returns to the country and embraces his spacemates whole-heartedly. Later, as they stare up at the heavens, Crouse tells Walken, "They've given you a gift; use it." As we know, he does—he writes a whopping, surprise international best-seller called *Communion*.

Critical objections to this "science-fact" movie needn't begin by rejecting the idea that alien creatures might pop down to Earth and use human beings as guinea pigs for interplanetary research. No, subject matter aside, COMMUNION is simply an ill-conceived and -constructed film that lacks the thrills of, say, INVASION OF THE BODY SNATCHERS or the wonder of CLOSE ENCOUNTERS OF THE THIRD KIND. Despite its glossy visuals, COMMUNION plays like an extended segment of TV's "A Current Affair"; it's a by-the-numbers presentation of tabloid material that fails to deliver surprise, suspense, or even rudimentary dramatic punch. Yes, it's possible to make a dull film about a man who's been given a rectal probe by internists from the Great Beyond. The film's failure to generate thrills is all the more surprising given that screenwriter Strieber and director Philippe Mora, friends who teamed to bring this $7-million independent production to the screen, are hardly newcomers to genre artistry. Strieber's novels include *The Hunger* and *The Wolfen*, both of which were adapted for the screen; Mora's credits include the horror films THE BEAST WITHIN; THE HOWLING II; and THE HOWLING III, as well as the political thriller DEATH OF A SOLDIER.

COMMUNION disappoints even on the technical level. The sound recording has a hollow, echoing quality (considering the insipid dialog, this may be a blessing), and although the white-hot light effects are convincing, the make-up and costuming of the aliens are laughable. It's no wonder these intruders from space don't want to reveal themselves—they look like munchkin versions of the cast of THE PLANET OF THE APES.

Worse than the shoddy five-and-dime Halloween costuming is the film's depiction of the modern urban family. Everyone speaks in support-group cliches, and the

jargonized lines only become more annoying when over-lapping dialog and repetition of phrases are employed to give them a spontaneous quality. COMMUNION strives hard to ground its bizarre story in realistic detail, but only succeeds in revealing its desperation. Lindsay Crouse and Christopher Walken demonstrate every actor's trick in the book, and the result isn't a naturalistic background for this flight of fantasy, but a mannered approximation of reality in which the leading players are given free rein to pause pointedly and cry calculatedly on cue. Walken (looking haggard, with spiky hair and cold fish-eyes) is particularly unsympathetic, and without a hero audiences can root for, this implausible sci-fact film falls apart.

Boring and shapeless, COMMUNION is like a self-help film that suggests outer space trolls as both cause and cure for neuroticism. Did those aliens really travel all that way just to break Whitley Strieber's writer's block? *(Violence, profanity, adult situations.)*

p, Philippe Mora, Whitley Strieber, Dan Allingham, and Edward Simons; d, Philippe Mora; w, Whitley Strieber (based on his book); ph, Louis Irving (Deluxe Color); ed, Lee Smith; m, Eric Clapton and Allan Zavod; prod d, Linda Pearl; art d, Dena Roth; spec eff, Michael McCracken, Michael McCracken Jr., Jim MacPherson, Steve Frakes, and Paul Stewart; cos, Melissa Daniel; anim, Hal Milnes; makeup, Michelle Buhler.

Science Fiction   (PR:C MPAA:R)

COOKIE**
93m Lorimar/WB c
Peter Falk *(Dominick "Dino" Capisco)*, Dianne Wiest *(Lenore)*, Emily Lloyd *(Carmella "Cookie" Voltecki)*, Michael V. Gazzo *(Carmine Taratino)*, Brenda Vaccaro *(Bunny Capisco)*, Adrian Pasdar *(Vito)*, Lionel Stander *(Enzo Della Testa)*, Jerry Lewis *(Arnold Ross)*, Bob Gunton *(Richard Segretto)*, Ben Rayson *(Henry Solomon)*, Ricki Lake *(Pia)*, Joe Mantello *(Dominick)*, Thomas Quinn *(Vinnie)*, David Wohl *(Alvin Diamond)*, Joy Behar *(Dottie)*, Frank Gio *(Frankie)*, Mario Todisco *(Sloppy Louie)*, Tony LaFortezza *(Angelo)*, Rockets Redglare, Anthony Powers, Tony Sirico *(Carmine's Wiseguys)*, Frank Aquilino, Clem Caserta, Barry Squitieri, Mike Marino, Jim Mauro, Guido Innacelli *(Dino's Wiseguys)*, F.X. Vitolo *(Motorcycle Cop)*, Ira Flitter *(State Trooper)*, Joe Pentangelo, David K. Reilly *(Feds)*, William Jay Marshall *(Frank Pearl)*, George Bartenieff *(Andy O'Brien)*, Ed Setrakian *(Mike Fusco)*, Paul Slimak *(Priest)*, Sydney Sheriff *(Vendor)*, Mark Boone Jr. *(Transit Cop)*, Arto Lindsay *(Court Clerk)*, Ralph Monaco *(Judge)*, Evan Bell *(Court Guard)*, Kim Chan *(Hong Kong Tailor)*,

Marshall Anker *(Parole Board Member)*, Aida Linares *(Carmen)*, Delphi Harrington *(Rosa Tarantino)*, Margaret Knopf *(Recipe Woman)*, Crystal Field *(Angela)*, J.D. DeKranis *(Cookie's Friend)*, Alfred de la Fuente *(Maitre d')*, Lynn White *(TV Reporter)*, Teresa Bellettieri *(Vito's Girl Friend)*, Isabell Monk *(Matron)*, Richard Caselnove *(Driver)*, Tony Devon *(Bodyguard)*, Steve DeLuca *(Bomb Squad Man)*, Ben Spell *(Justice of the Peace)*, Jerry Blavat *(DJ at Chateau Mer)*, Bob Martana *(Ritz Truck Driver)*, Marv Albert *(Voice of the New York Knicks)*.

Throughout COOKIE, one has the uncomfortable feeling that director Susan Seidelman couldn't decide which direction to take the story, concerning the budding relationship between Brooklyn-born mobster Falk, just released from a 13-year stint in prison, and his hot-tempered, illegitimate daughter (Lloyd), whose punkish lifestyle clashes disconcertingly with Falk's way of looking at things. When Falk is not subduing his volatile daughter, he's trying to appease Wiest, who is his mistress and Lloyd's fading beauty-queen mother, or his shrewish wife (Vaccaro). And if all that weren't enough, he's got to worry about the deadly intentions of his ex-partner in crime, Gazzo. Falk wants what he feels is due him from Gazzo, whereas Gazzo is thinking more in terms of giving Falk a permanent parcel of ground, six feet deep in a Brooklyn cemetery.

It's a shame that Seidelman didn't see fit to mix her COOKIE with very different ingredients. Particularly in light of its terrific cast of leading players (Peter Falk, Emily Lloyd, Dianne Wiest) and veteran supporting character actors (Jerry Lewis, Michael V. Gazzo, Lionel Stander, Brenda Vaccaro), the film cries out for the deft, warm, sentimental hand of Frank Capra. It's quite clear that the screenplay by Nora Ephron (WHEN HARRY MET SALLY) and Alice Arlen contains all the elements of a wryly humorous, Damon Runyanesque story, with (potentially) amusing hoods and other assorted oddball characters of the sort that Capra handled with aplomb. In COOKIE, however, Seidelman attempts to fuse what would have been better left a comical gangster farce with her own ultrahip, DESPERATELY SEEKING SUSAN filmmaking style, and the end result just doesn't work. If it weren't for the crackerjack performances turned in by Falk, Lloyd, and Wiest, the feature would offer almost nothing in the way of entertainment.

The unique talents of Gazzo, Lewis, Stander, Ricki Lake, and Vaccaro are among the elements badly wasted here. COOKIE has the potential to be a really first-rate, hilarious comedy, with glib, tongue-in-cheek humor, salty one-liners, and funny situations (as well as some serious undertones), but most of the funny lines are thrown away as actors swallow, mumble, or otherwise garble their lines. Where the film ought to soar, it remains earthbound and lackluster, and where the highly gifted cast ought to have been allowed to play their roles with no holds barred, they are inexplicably held back. The story often lacks focus, and the fun promised by the film's opening never materializes, leaving the rest of COOKIE dull and sluggish, muddled by bad enunciation and a general failure to achieve continuity or clarity. Fortunately, Oliver Stapleton's cinematography is effective and, along with the infectious performances of the leading players, helps somewhat to carry the film. *(Violence, adult situations, excessive profanity.)*

p, Laurence Mark and Jennifer Ogden; d, Susan Seidelman; w, Nora Ephron and Alice Arlen; ph, Oliver Stapleton (DuArt Color); ed, Andrew Mondshein; m, Thomas Newman; prod d, Michael Haller; art d, Bill Groom; set d, Les Bloom; spec eff, Connie Brink; cos, Albert Wolsky; stunts, Jery Hewitt; makeup, Richard Dean.

Comedy/Crime   (PR:C MPAA:R)

ⓥCOUSINS***
110m PAR c

Ted Danson *(Larry Kozinski)*, Isabella Rossellini *(Maria Hardy)*, Sean Young *(Tish Kozinski)*, William Petersen *(Tom Hardy)*, Lloyd Bridges *(Vince Kozinski)*, Norma Aleandro *(Edie Costello)*, Keith Coogan *(Mitch Kozinski)*, Gina de Angelis *(Aunt Sofia)*, George Coe *(Phil Kozinski)*, Katie Murray *(Chloe Hardy)*, Alex Bruhanski *(Herbie)*, Stephen E. Miller *(Stan)*, Gerry Bean *(Kevin Costello)*, Gordon Currie *(Dean Kozinski)*, Saffron Henderson *(Terri Costello)*, Michele Goodger *(Claudia)*, Andrea Mann *(Rosanna)*, Mark Frank *(Arnie Slevins)*, Leroy Schultz *(Cousin Harry)*, Gloria Harris *(Terri's Mother)*, John Civitarese *(Terri's Father)*, Kate Danson *(Wedding Killer Listener)*, David Hurwitz, John Hurwitz *(Twins)*, Babs Chula *(Mrs. Davidow)*, Bernadette Leonard *(Bernadette)*, Denalda Williams *(Olga)*, Margot Pinvidic *(Natalie)*, Tom McBeath *(Mr. Dionne)*, Dolores Drake *(Mrs. Dionne)*, Michael Naxos *(Mr. Bregman)*, Lorraine Butler *(Mrs. Greenblatt)*, Ann Leong *(Chinese Fish Saleswoman)*, Harold MacDonald *(Priest at Funeral)*, Lorena Gale *(Cosmetic Demonstrator)*, Monica Marko *(Cosmetic Customer)*, Wes Tritter *(Waiter)*, David W. Rose *(Maitre d')*, Sharon Wahl *(Weddingland Hostess)*, George Goodman *(Jewish Father of Bride)*, Gary Pembroke Allen *(Oil Painting Teacher)*, Antony Holland *(Wedding Priest)*, Cathy Bayer *(Cathy)*, John Paterson *(Magician)*, Michele Moyier *(Magician's Assistant)*.

Ted Danson, Isabella Rossellini, and William Peterson in COUSINS (©Paramount).

What better way to show appreciation for two of France's more popular films than to remake them? The charming THREE MEN AND A BABY easily surpassed TROIS HOMMES ET UN COUFFIN (THREE MEN AND A CRADLE), a not particularly distinctive film that was nonetheless nominated for an Oscar as Best Foreign-Language Film in 1986; COUSINS, however, was presented with a more difficult task in trying to better COUSIN COUSINE (1976), one of the most delightful and enduring French romps. But while it doesn't measure up to Jean-Charles Tacchella's original (lacking its pathos and light touch), COUSINS does acquit itself surprisingly well. As in the original, the story develops against a backdrop of several weddings (and one funeral) during which a host of relationships are played out in capsule form: families are joined, romances bud, affairs develop, fights erupt. During the wedding of Rossellini's middle-aged mother (Aleandro) to Danson's uncle, the film's central relationships emerge. Petersen, Rossellini's womanizing car-salesman husband, prevails upon Young, Danson's wife, to take a "test drive" in his Subaru. As the band leaves at the end of the celebration, Danson and Rossellini strike up a casual conversation while they wait for their spouses to return. But when Petersen and Young come back, it's obvious that he has shown her more than just what's beneath his hood. Initially, Danson and Rossellini are discreet about their spouses' infidelity: Rossellini is inured to her husband's philandering, and Danson, a forgiving husband in a liberal marriage, pretends to be

unfazed. Only when Rossellini suspects Petersen is having an affair and asks Danson whether her suspicions are justified, do the cousins (by marriage) acknowledge their mutual attraction. Danson and Rossellini then begin a series of platonic rendezvous that are at least partly intended to get back at their unfaithful spouses. In time, however, their "affair" escalates into the real thing, and Danson, Rossellini, Young, and Petersen all realize they have married the wrong person. The narcissistic, career-driven Young seems made for the like-minded Petersen, while warm and zany Danson ("a failure at everything but life") meshes with the caring, sensitive Rossellini. Nevertheless sobriety ultimately prevails, and the two couples decide to patch things up and return to normalcy. But destiny is stubborn; it can be deferred, but not denied. Danson and Rossellini's feelings for each other resurface at a wedding, Aleandro's second of the film, this time to Danson's father (Bridges). After a brief verbal skirmish between Danson and the pugnacious Petersen, the soundtrack swells as Danson and Rossellini happily yield to their fate.

Although the script reflects no small degree of demographic calculation (the principals span three loveable generations, providing someone for everyone to identify with), it is generally spirited and winning. And after the breathless opening shots, director Joel Schumacher (THE LOST BOYS; ST. ELMO'S FIRE) settles in and escorts us through a breezy, if occasionally heavy-handed, romantic comedy. Ted Danson (TV's "Cheers," THREE MEN AND A BABY), an engaging presence, imbues Larry with a quirky charm and develops an easy, although sometimes shaky, chemistry with Isabella Rossellini, who is fine as the demure Maria (notwithstanding some of the clunky lines with which she is encumbered). William Petersen (TO LIVE AND DIE IN L.A.), however, is unconvincing as the perpetually contentious womanizer, while the beautiful Sean Young is most believable when she "affects" boredom, which, unfortunately, is most of the time. In lesser, albeit pungent, roles, the versatile Norma Aleandro (THE OFFICIAL STORY) is colorful as Maria's spunky mother, Lloyd Bridges is predictably workmanlike as Larry's ribald dad, and young Keith Coogan (grandson of actor Jackie Coogan) contributes an unaffected turn as Larry's camera-toting, somewhat cliched, teenage son. Songs include: "The Brady Bunch" (Sherwood Schwartz, Frank De Vol), "The Bunny Hop" (Ray Anthony, Leonard Auletti), "Guantanamera" (Jose Marti, Pete Seeger, Hector Angulo, performed by the Jean-Marc Dompierre Orchestra), "Happy Days" (Charles Fox, Norman Gimbel, performed by Kirk Thatcher, David Russo, Joan E. Jones, Duane Clark), "I Love You for Today" (Angelo Badalamenti, performed by Pearl Huang), "Isn't It Romantic" (Richard Rodgers, Lorenz Hart), "The Long and Winding Road" (John Lennon, Paul McCartney), "Love Man" (Otis Redding, performed by Redding), "Speak Softly Love" (Nino Rota, Larry Kusik), "Tangerine" (Johnny Mercer, Victor Schertzinger), "A Time for Us" (Rota, Kusik, Eddie Snyder), "Time to Dance the Bamba" (Luis Valentino), "With or Without You" (U2). (Adult situations, sexual situations.)

p, William Allyn; d, Joel Schumacher; w, Stephen Metcalfe (based on the film COUSINE, COUSINE written by Jean-Charles Tacchella); ph, Ralf D. Bode (Alpha Cine Color); ed, Robert Brown; m, Angelo Badalamenti; prod d, Mark S. Freeborn; set d, Linda Vipond; spec eff, William H. Orr; cos, Michael Kaplan; makeup, Fern Buchner.

Comedy/Romance

(PR:A MPAA:PG-13)

CRACK HOUSE zero
90m Silverman/21st Century c
Jim Brown (Steadman), Anthony Geary (Dockett), Richard Roundtree (Lt. Johnson), Cheryl Kay (Melissa), Gregg Gomez Thomsen (Rick Morales), Angel Tompkins (Mother), Clyde R. Jones (B.T.), Albert Michel Jr. (Chico), Heidi Thomas (Annie), Kenneth Edwards (Tripper), Joey Green (Buzz), Jon Greene (Officer Baylor), T. Rodgers (Jammer), Louis Rivera (Jesus), Willie Hernandez (Lou), Jacob Vargas (Danny), Michael Matthews (Teddy), Derek Googe (David), Maria Kelly (Hooker), Thomas Morgan (Lookout), Bert Brown, Gerald Hunter, James Cornelius, Donny Ray, Donavan Haylock, Chris Pearson (Rock House Workers), George Cuezos, Nikoli Mendoza, Joey D'Attilli, Daniel Street, Anthony Escabor, Richard Torpey, Jeffrey Garcia, Wilbur Urbina, Artemio Guiterez, Tony Zarte (Pochos), Roseanna Rios, Mariann Solano (Pocho Girls), Gary Gray, George King, George Shaperson, Sheldon Barker, Marlin Holt, Jesse Hudson Rivers, Antonie Jordan (Grays), George Alderson, Jim Quinlan, Sam Arase, Greg DeSoto, William Bowen, Scott DeGarmo, Derek Brandon, Michael Harrington, Mason Burroughs, Gary Milligan, George Sanders, Jay Taylor, Michael Tyus, Curtis Woodle (Police), Floyd Henry.

This lurid, leering, and inept COLORS-ripoff is maybe as loathsome a movie as ever came out of the generally loathsome exploitation genre. Cashing in on the crack epidemic, CRACK HOUSE begins by paying lip service to exploring the roots of the nationwide drug crisis. However, this serves merely as a pretext for an offensive peep-show exercise in misogynistic violence. Utterly incoherent by any conventional standards—seemingly a Cannon trademark—CRACK HOUSE revolves around two overaged students, Thomsen and Kay, trying to graduate from their Los Angeles ghetto high school and enter mainstream society without falling prey to gang and drug violence. Of course, if they succeeded there wouldn't be much of a movie; so, after getting engaged to Kay, Thomsen is sucked into gang violence when his cousin is killed in a drive-by shooting. Arrested during a revenge attack, he is sent to jail, where he spends much of the remainder of the film. Thomsen breaks off his engagement to Kay, who almost immediately takes up with small-time crack dealer Jones and begins a quick downward spiral into addiction and degradation. The gang subplot is abruptly dropped once white-girl Kay takes up with the black Jones, who does some fast talking to save her from being gang raped by her chicano neighbors. She ends up becoming the personal prostitute and punching bag for the sadistic Brown. Imprisoned in Brown's crack house as partial payment for a debt owed by Jones to Brown, Kay gets smacked around occasionally by the drug baron and is forced to witness the gang rape of one of Brown's other women, who gets turned over to the crack house employees as a party toy once Brown has gotten tired of her. The rape victim later commits suicide in the crack house bathtub, the camera leeringly caressing her naked body. Hearing of Kay's plight, Thomsen cooperates with the police to help bust Brown and his wholesale supplier, and get Kay back.
CRACK HOUSE isn't so much a crime drama as a collection of cliches tossed into a cinematic cuisinart, spiked with blood-pellet violence, racist pandering, and sicko sex. Despite a few well-staged confrontation scenes early in the film, the issue of gang violence is given only cursory treatment. The feuding chicanos and blacks are depicted as subhumans. The blacks spend much of the film hollering and shooting at each other, weighing bags of drugs, and beating up and raping white women. The chicanos fare only slightly better, perhaps because the hero is chicano. But stereotypes still abound, with much dialog and action devoted to machismo strutting, swearing revenge, and, again, raping white women. Thomsen's and Kay's characters are themselves conceived in two-dimensional stereotyped terms. Thomsen, the chicano man, is tough, stand-up, and stoic. Kay, meanwhile, who lives with her alcoholic mother, Tompkins, is a reactionary feminine stereotype, weak and easily influenced, going from a bright, talented, straight-A student to sniveling drug slut in record time. What is most baffling about CRACK HOUSE is the level of talent involved. As a cop who takes a personal interest in Thomsen's rehabilitation, Richard Roundtree deserves the benefit of some doubt for not being involved in any of the film's more stomach-turning sequences. There can be no excuses, however, for either Jim Brown or Anthony Geary, both of whom contribute to the film's general, mean-spirited mood of misogynist mayhem. Songs include: "Drop the Bomb," "Move Somethin'" (L. Campbell, C. Wong-Won, D. Hobbs, M. Ross, performed by 2 Live Crew), "Shake It" (P. Jones, performed by MC Shy D), "Slippin' into Darkness" (S. Allen, H.R. Brown, M. Dickerson, L. Jordan, C.W. Miller, L. Oskar, H. Scott, performed by War), "Egypt, Egypt" (the Egyptian Lover, performed by the Egyptian Lover), "Nosedive" (K. Howard, performed by Jambalaya), "Talk Is Cheap" (B. Boyle, performed by D.B. Night), "I Swear" (Boyle, D. Darnell, performed by Night), "Rush It Baby-O (Beam Me Up Scotty)" (B. Reed, A. Reed, P. Simmons, performed by Bus Stop Creepers), "Viva La Ganga" (L. Aielli, Pancho D. Rock, performed by Rock), "Anna Marie" "You Take Me Higher" (Joe Lamont, Aielli, performed by Lamont), "Don't Rely on Me" (Aielli, J. Hargis, performed by Channel One), "XTC" (Aielli, Hargis, performed by Veronica), "Ethiopian Girl" (S. Hood, performed by Zack). (Violence, profanity, nudity, substance abuse.)

p, Jim Silverman and Joan Weidman; d, Michael Fischa; w, Blake Schaefer (based on a story by Jack Silverman); ph, Arledge Armenaki (Foto-Kem Color); ed, Claudia Finkle; m, Michael Piccirillo; md, David Chackler; prod d, Keith Barrett.

Crime   (PR:O MPAA:R)

CRIME ZONE**
93m Concorde-New
Horizons/Concorde c
David Carradine *(Jason)*, Peter Nelson *(Bone)*, Sherilyn Fenn *(Helen)*, Michael Shaner *(Creon)*, Orlando Sacha *(Alexi)*, Don Manor *(J.D.)*, Alfredo Calder *(Cruz)*, Jorgo Bustamante *(Hector)*.

Intermittently entertaining but doggedly uninspired, CRIME ZONE is a futuristic action thriller that borrows liberally from other sci-fi sources without adding anything very new to the mix. The film is set in the totalitarian future society Soleil, where Nelson—recently fired from his job for appearing disgruntled—meets Fenn, a state-sanctioned prostitute who bolts from her bordello after seeing Nelson in a pool hall. Nelson and Fenn are "supergrades," who are forbidden many things, including consensual sex, which makes them criminals once they begin climbing all over each other. Yearning for the freedom to frolic, the outlaw lovers accept a dubious proposition from a mysterious bigwig (Carradine). If the supergrade pair will steal a computer disk from a well-guarded justice facility for him, Carradine will secure their escape to Froidan, with which Soleil is continuously at war. Nelson and Fenn pull off the heist and deliver the disk as promised, but the escape plan develops snags, and Carradine suggests that the couple might as well rob a bank while they wait to make their getaway. Nelson and Fenn do the second job, only to discover that (surprise, surprise) Carradine is with the government, and has launched the lovers' criminal career as a bit of theater for state-run television in order to keep money flowing to the police and defense budgets, which Carradine controls. After some running around, a few gunfights, and a car chase or two, Nelson and Fenn—with the help of an old friend, retired pilot Sacha—steal a helicopter and make good their escape to Froidan. But guess what doesn't really exist? And guess what's waiting for them when they discover the answer to the first question? Not to worry, though. The last-minute twist-that-can-be-spotted-10-minutes-ahead doesn't prevent the film from ending with a shot of Fenn and Nelson strolling unmolested along a shore. Sure, they're stranded in a nuclear-ravaged wasteland with no food or drinkable water. But they're young and in love and they've got each other.

As down-and-dirty B-budget action thrillers go, CRIME ZONE is better than average. Director Luis Llosa stages most of the action at night, which makes the video transfer a mite on the murky side. But it also serves the higher purpose of covering up for the film's bargain-basement budget, and allows for a bit of visual style in scenes bathed in garish neon and contoured by menacing shadows. The cast isn't half-bad, either. Peter Nelson is competent (if not especially charismatic) as the hero, and Sherilyn Fenn is cool, tough, and sexy as his partner in love and crime, who sports a Madonna-ish punk peroxide haircut to match her hardboiled attitude. David Carradine, well-padded and chomping a cigar, looks as though his own action-hero days are safely in the past, but he's just fine here as the government operative. Standing out in support are Michael Shaner in the role of Nelson's best friend, who betrays him when the chips are down, and the balletic Don Manor as J.D., another of Nelson's friends, who's not quite playing with a full deck and who does back flips when he's happy.

CRIME ZONE does suffer from over-ambitiousness. As bellicose futuristic epics go, it aspires too much after the literary models of *1984* or *Brave New World* and not enough after the pulpier, more appropriate, style of such films as RUNNING MAN and ROBOCOP. Llosa keeps the action moving along at a crisp pace, but the script, by Daryl Haney, is as padded as Carradine's girth—full of speeches and superfluous subplots that tend to belabor the obvious and underscore the film's lack of originality. The effect is to throw off the pacing, making CRIME ZONE seem oddly slow and cumbersome even when events are moving along at lightning speed. With a little less weight and a little more wit, CRIME ZONE could have zinged, not sagged. *(Violence, profanity, adult situations, nudity.)*

p, Luis Llosa; d, Luis Llosa; w, Daryl Haney; ph, Cusi Barrio; ed, William Flicker; m, Rick Conrad; art d, Angel Valdez, Jose Troncojo, Susana Aragon, and Adrian Arias; spec eff, Fernando Vasquez de Velasce; cos, Patricia Maguill.

Action/Science Fiction

(PR:O   MPAA:R)

CRIMES AND MISDEMEANORS**
107m Orion c
Caroline Aaron *(Barbara)*, Alan Alda *(Lester)*, Woody Allen *(Cliff Stern)*, Claire Bloom *(Miriam Rosenthal)*, Mia Farrow *(Halley Reed)*, Joanna Gleason *(Wendy Stern)*, Anjelica Huston *(Dolores Paley)*, Martin Landau *(Judah Rosenthal)*, Jenny Nichols *(Jenny)*, Jerry Orbach *(Jack Rosenthal)*, Sam Waterston *(Ben)*, Bill Bernstein *(Testimonial Speaker)*, Stephanie Roth *(Sharon Rosenthal)*, Gregg Edelman *(Chris)*, George Manos *(Photographer)*, Zina Jasper *(Carol)*, Dolores Sutton *(Judah's Secretary)*, Joel S. Fogel, Donna Castellano, Thomas P. Crow *(TV Producers)*, Martin Bergmann *(Prof. Louis Levy)*, Kenny Vance *(Murray)*, Jerry Zaks *(Man on Campus)*, Barry Finkel, Steve Maidment *(TV Writers)*, Nadia Sanford *(Alva)*, Chester Malinowski *(Hit Man)*, Stanley Reichman *(Chris' Father)*, Rebecca Schull *(Chris' Mother)*, David S. Howard *(Sol Rosenthal)*, Garrett Simowitz *(Young Judah)*, Frances Conroy *(House Owner)*, Anna Berger *(Aunt May)*, Sol Frieder, Justin Zaremby, Marvin Terban, Hy Anzell, Sylvia Kauders *(Seder Guests)*, Victor Argo *(Detective)*, Lenore Loveman, Nora Ephron, Sunny Keyser, Merv Bloch, Nancy Arden, Thomas L. Bolster, Myla Pitt, Robin Bartlett *(Wedding Guests)*, Grace Zimmerman *(Bride)*, Randy Aaron Fink *(Groom)*, Rabbi Joel Zion *(Rabbi)*, Mayor Halley Jr., Walter Levinsky, George Masso, Charles Miles, Derek Smith, Warren Vache *(Jazz Band)*, Pete Antell, Anthony Gorruso, Gary Allen Meyers, Lee Musiker, Tony Sotos, Tony Tedeasco *(Wedding Band)*.

Proceeding as if he were Fyodor Dostoevsky, Woody Allen has made a film tackling the morality of murder—an exploration not so much of the act itself as of responsibility for its occurrence. It is an issue that has long haunted Allen's creative output, whether in the genocidal form of the Holocaust (which, his characters would argue, was a crime committed by all humanity, not just the Nazis), or the almost effortless murder of an unwanted lover that occurs in CRIMES AND MISDEMEANORS. In a world in which morality has been tossed by the wayside, CRIMES AND MISDEMEANORS departs from the Dostoevskian act and consequence in *Crime and Punishment* by removing the latter from the narrative.

Allen (whose creative voice seems heightened only when borrowing from other artists) opens his film in a Hitchcockian mode. A renowned ophthalmologist (Landau) is being honored for his distinguished career at a gala affair in the presence of his family, friends, and colleagues. Intercut with this ceremonious scene are vignettes revealing the good doctor's secret life. Landau has just intercepted an incriminating letter that his mistress (Huston) sent to his wife (Bloom), and prevented the latter from learning of his guilt by burning the letter in the fireplace of his rich, cozy home. In an effort by Allen to combine his "funny" side with his "serious" side, a peripheral, more comic story is introduced in which Allen plays an ethically frustrated documentary filmmaker. Although he has plans for a serious-minded documentary (we see posters for Richard Leacock and Jean-Luc Godard films on the walls of his editing suite), the financially strapped Allen is reduced to accepting the job of filming a documentary portrait of his phenomenally egotistical brother-in-law (Alda), a highly successful director of TV sitcoms whom Allen loathes. While Allen—working for money, rather than in the service of art or enlightenment—battles his artistic conscience, he falls in love with a television producer. Farrow, whose company is producing the Alda documentary. Although she is intellectually stimulated by Allen's work-in-progress, a portrait of a Jewish philosophy professor (Bergmann), she is stimulated in more carnal ways by Alda (who can also help her professionally). As Allen's extramarital romance (he is wed to Gleason) becomes increasingly tangled, Landau's completely unravels. Instead of behaving "reasonably," the unstable Huston becomes hysterically insistent that Landau fulfill his past "promises" to leave Bloom and marry her, implying that she may use her knowledge of some embezzling Landau has done as ammunition in her attempt to supplant Bloom. Frightened and confused, Landau turns to his brother, Orbach, a mafia type who suggests that, for an affordable sum, Huston "can be gotten rid of." Without lifting a finger himself, Landau can put a permanent end to his involvement with Huston; all Orbach needs to do is make one phone call and a hitman will appear at Huston's doorstep. Tortured by thoughts of moral damnation, Landau the infidel considers one of his heady talks with Waterston, a rabbi friend whom Landau is treating for imminent blindness (and who is Allen's other brother-in-law, linking the storylines). Refusing to believe in a higher power ("God is a luxury I cannot afford," he tells Waterston), Landau finally gives Orbach the okay to deep-six his troublesome mistress. Later, seeing Huston's corpse when he goes to her apartment to retrieve incriminating evidence of their affair, Landau nearly goes blood simple, but keeps his head and tries to forget about the incident. Unlike Raskolnikov, Landau seems unlikely ever to be brought to justice; our world is no longer Dostoevsky's. Meanwhile, Allen is forced to live with bitter knowledge and a broken heart when he learns that Farrow is marrying Alda. It is only in the final scene of the film that Landau and Allen—two characters with a gift (or curse) for seeing the world as it is (as reflected in their work as opthamologist and documentarist)—meet for the first time, both struggling with the concepts of good and evil, morality and immorality, crimes and misdemeanors.

As is now to be expected of Allen, CRIMES AND MISDEMEANORS is not so important on its own as it is within the body of work of an *auteur*. But Allen is an *auteur* whose artistic vision cannot be defined without reference to those who have come before him, a kind of cinematic parasite, feeding on the movies of such artists as Ingmar Bergman and Alfred Hitchcock (the latter a relatively new source for Allen) in order to nourish his own body of work. While this comparison is meant to define Allen more than criticize him, it is still difficult for an educated film viewer to take Allen's creative intent on good faith. While some in the audience are being charmed, like naively trusting lovers,

Woody Allen and Mia Farrow in CRIMES AND MISDEMEANORS (©Orion).

by Allen's film art, others will discover that Allen has been hiding something from them as he raids the work of geniuses and deposits the booty in his own productions (which legions of fans and critical advocates accept as "Allenesque" in theme and style). Those knowledgeable viewers will not only recognize Hitchcock's stamp on the opening scene of CRIMES AND MISDEMEANORS and Allen's reference to Hitchcock's only comedy, MR. AND MRS. SMITH, they will also recognize the ophthalmologist's visit to the house where he grew up as a restaging of Uncle Isak's return to his childhood home in Bergman's WILD STRAWBERRIES—which Allen lifts nearly *shot for shot*, in a dubious act of homage. Though clearly very talented, Allen should be recognized not as the master he is often considered, but as the skillful student he is. No wonder Godard, in his KING LEAR (1986), cast Woody Allen as "Mr. Alien," a filmmaker (wearing a Picasso t-shirt) who thinks he is creating art but is actually playing the Fool. Allen, like CRIMES AND MISDEMEANORS' lionized doctor, is not quite the great man he is cracked up to be, though he still possesses much skill and charm. Unfortunately for the filmmaker, it's harder to burn the negatives of WILD STRAWBERRIES than a mistress' incriminating letter.

Easy as it is to spot Allen's creative Achilles' heel, it is not possible to attack the deftness with which he fashions his films. Allen's latest is, as usual, blessed with stunning ensemble acting (Martin Landau proves that his Oscar-nominated performance in TUCKER was no scratch hit); with inspiring composition, lighting, and set design (compliments of Bergman's former cinematographer Sven Nykvist and production designer Santo Loquasto); with intelligent writing; and with a cheery musical score. Like the early Bernardo Bertolucci—who, throughout the 1960s, was unable to make a film that did not owe a heavy debt to Godard—Allen is a filmmaker of undeniable skill, who has (with the inclusion of his NEW YORK STORIES segment) delivered 20 films in

the last 23 years. However, unlike Bertolucci (who successfully managed to shake free of his creative phantoms), Allen has yet to prove that he can shed his Bergmania and finally find his own voice as a serious film artist.

Musical selections include: "Rosalie" (Cole Porter), excerpt from the soundtrack of MR. AND MRS. SMITH (Edward Ward), "Dancing on the Ceiling" (Richard Rodgers, Lorenz Hart, performed by Bernie Leighton), "Taking a Chance on Love" (Vernon Duke, John LaTouche, Ted Fetter), "I Know That You Know" (Vincent Youmans, Anne Caldwell O'Dea, Otto A. Harbach, performed by Leighton), English Suite No. 2 in A Minor (Johann Sebastian Bach, performed by Alicia De Larrocha), "Homecooking" (Hilton Ruiz, performed by the Hilton Ruiz Quartet), "Happy Birthday to You" (Mildred J. Hill, Patty S. Hill), "Sweet Georgia Brown" (Ben Bernie, Maceo Pinkard, Kenneth Casey, performed by Coleman Hawkins and his All-Star Jam Band), "I've Got You," from the soundtrack of THIS GUN FOR HIRE (Frank Loesser, Jacques Press), "This Year's Kisses" (Irving Berlin, performed by Ozzie Nelson and His Orchestra), "All I Do Is Dream of You," from the soundtrack of SINGIN' IN THE RAIN (Nacio Herb Brown, Arthur Freed), "Quartet No. 15 in G Major, Op. 161, D.887 (Franz Schubert, performed by the Juilliard Quartet), "Murder He Says," from the soundtrack of HAPPY GO LUCKY (Loesser, Jimmy McHugh, performed by Betty Hutton), "Beautiful Love" (Victor Young, Wayne King, Egbert Van Alstyne, Haven Gillespie), "Great Day" (Youmans, William Rose, Edward Eliscu, performed by Leighton), "Star Eyes" (Don Raye, Gene DePaul, performed by Lee Musiker), "Because" (Guy D'Hardelot, Edward Teschmacher, performed by Musiker), "Crazy Rhythm" (Irving Caesar, R. Wolfe Kahn, Joseph Meyer), "I'll See You Again" (Noel Coward), "Cuban Mambo" (Xavier Cugat, Rafael Angulo, Jack Wiseman), "Polkadots and Moonbeams" (Jimmy Van Heusen, Johnny Burke), "I'll Be Seeing

You" (Sammy Fain, Irving Kahal, performed by Liberace). (Adult situations.)

p, Robert Greenhut; d, Woody Allen; w, Woody Allen; ph, Sven Nykvist (DuArt Color); ed, Susan E. Morse; prod d, Santo Loquasto; art d, Speed Hopkins; set d, Susan Bode; cos, Jeffrey Kurland; makeup, Fern Buchner.

Drama   (PR:A-C MPAA:PG-13)

ⓋCRIMINAL LAW***

112m Hemdale-Northwood/Tri-Star c
Gary Oldman (Ben Chase), Kevin Bacon (Martin Thiel), Karen Young (Ellen Faulkner), Joe Don Baker (Detective Mesel), Tess Harper (Detective Stillwell), Ron Lea (Gary Hull), Karen Woolridge (Claudia Curwen), Elizabeth Sheppard (Dr. Sybil Thiel), Michael Sinelnicoff (Prof. Clemens).

CRIMINAL LAW covers essentially the same territory as Norman Jewison's . . . AND JUSTICE FOR ALL (1979), telling the story of a defense attorney who must come to terms with the realities and responsibilities of his job. Gary Oldman plays Ben Chase, a hard-playing, affluent, and self-satisfied criminal lawyer who gains acquittal for Martin Thiel (Kevin Bacon) in a murder trial. Accused of raping and murdering a woman, Bacon is found not guilty thanks to Oldman's slick defense. Days later, after celebrating his victory, Oldman hears about another murder that sounds very similar to the one of which Bacon was accused. After receiving a phone call from Bacon, Oldman agrees to meet him late at night, in a park, to discuss continuing as his lawyer. Oldman arrives, but instead of meeting with Bacon, he discovers a woman's charred corpse. After confronting the police, led by detectives Mesel (Joe Don Baker) and Stillwell (Tess Harper), Oldman becomes convinced that Bacon is a murderer and devises a plan to catch him. Attorney and client begin a bizarre relationship, almost a partnership, in which Bacon tests the limits of Oldman's will power, while Oldman looks for ways to legally set up Bacon. The situation (a lawyer, who is also a witness, betraying the confidence of his client) is complicated by Baker's incessant desire to nail both Bacon and Oldman, and by Oldman's affair with Ellen (Karen Young), the roommate of the most recent murder victim. After several false leads, Oldman finally discovers the real reason for Bacon's murderous sprees: it seems Bacon has an unstable relationship with his mother, a doctor who specializes in abortions. As a child he witnessed his mother performing an abortion and, with his mind forever changed, Bacon now sees himself as an "avenger" of lost souls. All of Bacon's victims have had abortions, and his twisted logic justifies the murder of these women as fair punishment for the

murder of their babies. Having put his total trust in Oldman, Bacon soon realizes that his lawyer is scheming to put him away. After unsuccessfully trying to kill Young, Bacon murders his mother and calls Oldman for a final meeting. Begging Oldman to come alone, Bacon requests that they meet in the park to discuss the death of his mother and the other women. Oldman immediately goes to the courthouse to cut a deal with Baker and Harper: he will lead them to Bacon as long as they take part in the arrest. For Oldman this is the only way to right the wrongs he has made possible, to ease his conscience, and to come to terms with the power of his job. The police agree to Oldman's terms, but as he leaves the courtroom, Oldman is ambushed by Bacon, who forces him at gunpoint into the same courtroom in which Oldman had originally defended the murderer. Bacon makes Oldman confront his darkest inclinations and act upon his gut instincts, forcing the lawyer to become an "avenger." Giving Oldman his gun, Bacon tells him to do what he feels is necessary. Face to face with Bacon, Oldman pulls the trigger only to discover that the gun is loaded with blanks. Bacon begins to cry as Oldman, shaken and confused, begins to walk away. Grabbing a glass pitcher and breaking it, Bacon then attacks Oldman, but is shot by Harper. Oldman looks at Bacon's body and walks out of the courtroom. Having confronted the malevolence in his heart (essentially becoming as twisted as Bacon), he leaves the courthouse a different man.

Loaded with cliches, CRIMINAL LAW can be nit-picked to death. It begins on a pretentious note with a quote from Nietzsche that basically explains everything the screenplay has to say in two minutes. Some characters are unexplained or unnecessary (Michael Sinelnicoff plays a professor whose two scenes with Oldman are intense but completely purposeless and totally distracting), and some of the dialog is extremely weak (at one point Baker says, "If there is one thing I can tell you, it's that a crazy killer is crazy and he will kill you"). Moreover, the message is hammered home with a heavy hand (although the use of water as a leitmotif is nicely handled), and there are one too many phony "shock" cuts.

Still, these are minor complaints. CRIMINAL LAW is an undeniably entertaining thriller with a few interesting insights into the law and some astounding performances. Although director Martin Campbell handles the suspense sequences in a disappointing go-for-the-throat style—with a pounding Jerry Goldsmith score (which, at times, sounds suspiciously like Peter Gabriel's score for BIRDY) and cheap "jump" scares—he appears to be much more adept at working with actors. Oldman is brilliant as the smug attorney, and the film works best when he is center

stage (the fear he conveys when he discovers the murdered woman is some of the most convincing emotion seen in films in years). His intensity and attention-grabbing energy alone are enough to keep the picture moving, and his American accent is flawless. Equally mesmerizing is Bacon, who makes a surprisingly convincing psycho. There is also strong work from the supporting players, particularly from Harper and Ron Lea, in a small but memorable role.

The moral responsibilities of a defense attorney are treated seriously and provide the most interesting aspects of Mark Kasdan's otherwise lackluster script. However, Campbell manages to keep things moving, and the picture is never boring. What's more, the ending—sold by Oldman's and Bacon's extraordinary performances—is surprising and powerful. CRIMINAL LAW is a flawed but effective little thriller that shouldn't be dismissed. (Violence, profanity, brief nudity, sexual situations, adult situations, substance abuse.)

p, Robert MacLean and Hilary Heath; d, Martin Campbell; w, Mark Kasdan; ph, Phil Meheux; ed, Christopher Wimble; m, Jerry Goldsmith; prod d, Curtis A. Schnell.

Thriller   (PR:O MPAA:R)

ⓋCRUSOE**

95m Island c
Aidan Quinn (Crusoe), Ade Sapara (Warrior), Elvis Payne (Runaway Slave), Richard Sharp (Colcol), Colin Bruce (Clerk), William Hootkins (Auctioneer), Shane Rimmer (Mr. Mather), Jimmy Nail (Tarik), Patrick Monkton (Cook), Chris Pitt (Kitchen Lad), James Kennedy (Capt. Harding), Tim Spall (Rev. Milne), Warren Clarke (Capt. Lee), Hepburn Graham (Lucky), Michael Higgins (Dr. Martin).

This revisionist adaptation of Daniel Defoe's 1719 novel Robinson Crusoe is not without merit, but its attempt to mix an anti-racism message with travelog footage distracts from the film's socially conscious content. Cinematographer-turned-director Caleb Deschanel seems more concerned with painting pretty pictures than with illuminating character and theme through active imagery.

Updated and transplanted, the story begins early in the 19th century with Crusoe (Quinn), a heartless Virginia slave trader, en route to West Africa. After a terrible storm destroys the ship, Quinn finds himself and the ship's dog, Scamp, the sole survivors of the wreck. Washed ashore on a tiny uninhabited island, Quinn constructs a shelter from items culled from the ship's wreckage and survives by hunting, gardening, and eating the eggs of wild geese he corrals. Seemingly in high spirits, he busies himself gathering food and exploring, and even attempts to build a small boat, only to have it destroyed when it hits a huge rock on its maiden voyage. Despite this setback, Quinn remains optimistic about his survival and eventual rescue; that is, until Scamp takes ill and dies. For the first time since the shipwreck, Quinn is struck by how truly alone he is, and the notion tears at his sanity. His isolation is disrupted some weeks later, however, by a small group of natives who canoe to the island to conduct a weird funeral rite. Armed with a rifle, Quinn trails them into the jungle and watches as they prepare to sacrifice two male servants by cutting their throats. Horrified by the murder of the first man, Quinn fires a shot before the second, Graham, suffers the same fate. The noise frightens the natives and they scatter, including Graham, whom Quinn manages to capture, taking him back to his hut, fully intending to make "Lucky," as he calls him, his slave. That evening, Quinn tries to give Graham a quick European education, teaching him a few English phrases and making him eat "politely." Before retiring, Quinn manacles Graham, but the next morning he is gone. While searching the jungle, Quinn is disgusted to discover Graham's head impaled on a pike next to the other unfortunate sacrificial victim. It seems one of the natives (Sapara) has remained behind to complete the job, and though Quinn spots him and gives chase, it is the slaver who is snared in a booby-trap set by the proud warrior. Eventually Sapara releases Quinn, but the native proves to be his equal in every way, and resists Quinn's attempts to domesticate him. Indeed, Sapara has the run of the island and even steals Quinn's geese, eating them with impunity. When Quinn attempts to teach Sapara English, the warrior refuses and instead prompts Quinn to learn his language. An uneasy truce exists between the two, who begin to respect and understand each other; however, their fortunes change when a ship, apparently on a scientific expedition, appears on the horizon. Quinn is finally saved, but the scientists capture Sapara and intend to take him back to America to exhibit. Although delighted to be going home, Quinn is troubled by the treatment of Sapara (who is kept in a cage on the deck). Enlightened by his contact with the black man, Quinn cannot stand to see the noble warrior caged like an animal, so the once-ruthless slave trader risks enraging his rescuers, frees Sapara, and helps him escape.

While CRUSOE has its redeeming moments, it is a curiously lifeless film as a result of Deschanel's emphasis on the simply picturesque over a more engaged directorial perspective. It is almost as if the director chose the material purely for its visual potential and left screenwriter Walon Green (THE WILD BUNCH) to worry about meaning. Regrettably, this filmmaking approach has delivered a movie so detached that the performers are left to flounder while Deschanel concentrates on capturing the "right light" for a perfectly composed sunset. While some may find the storytelling in CRUSOE refreshingly sparse and unforced, it is really a matter of too little story given too much screentime. Indeed, the natives don't even make their appearance until almost an hour has lapsed. Although this certainly runs the risk of boring the audience, it nonetheless provides ample time for the camera to linger lovingly on extreme close-ups of flora, fauna, and other painterly pursuits. Perhaps this facile method of filmmaking wouldn't be so annoying if the picture didn't also aspire to be an important statement on racism and, by inference, apartheid. But by presenting this vital message as just another element in his overall visual scheme, Deschanel fatally undermines the purpose of his film—to enlighten modern audiences to the horrors of racial oppression by putting a new spin on a familiar tale. *(Violence.)*

p, Andrew Braunsberg; d, Caleb Deschanel; w, Christopher Logue and Walon Green (based on the novel *Life and Adventures of Robinson Crusoe* by Daniel Defoe); ph, Tom Pinter (Technicolor); ed, Humphrey Dixon; m, Michael Kamen; prod d, Velco Despotovic; art d, Nemanja Petrovic, Vlastimir Gavrik, and Andrew Sanders; set d, Vladislav Tomanovic and Ivan Ujevic; spec eff, John Evans; cos, Nada Perovic; stunts, Eddie Stacey; makeup, Radmila Ivatovic.

Drama   (PR:C MPAA:PG-13)

ⓥCURFEW*
84m York Image/NW c
Kyle Richards *(Stephanie Davenport)*, Wendell Wellman *(Ray Perkins)*, John Putch *(Bob Perkins)*, Jean Brooks *(Megan Davenport)*, Frank Miller *(Walter Davenport)*, Peter Nelson, Nori Morgan, Bert Remsen, Christopher Knight, Niels Mueller, Bob Romanus.

CURFEW, a low-budget thriller containing few thrills, stars the striking Kyle Richards as a teenage girl whose late-night carousing has forced her parents to impose a 10 P.M. curfew on her. At the same time, two vicious brothers (Wellman and Putch) have escaped from prison and are seeking revenge on the people who put them there. They kill a psychiatrist and a judge, then head for the home of the district attorney who prosecuted them, who happens to be Miller, Richards' father. When they arrive, Richards is out—past curfew, of course. The psychotic Wellman and the oafish Putch take Miller and his wife (Brooks) prisoner and begin torturing the couple. Several people stop by, including three of Richards' friends and a policeman, and all are murdered by the brothers, but when Richards herself finally shows up Putch immediately swoons over her. His desire to protect her from harm leads to a violent fight with his brother, which ends when Wellman kills Putch with a power drill. During the struggle, however, Richards manages to get hold of a gun and, just as Wellman is about to electrocute her parents, kills him. The next day, Richards is leaving for school and is horrified to find Putch waiting for her in the car . . . but wait, it's only a dream.

CURFEW has a few interesting ideas that seem to get lost in all of the cheap gore and shock effects. The relationship between the killer brothers is rich with possibilities but is never developed. Among the actors, Wendell Wellman is actually pretty good, and Richards has a strong screen presence, but they are stuck in a muddled and cheaply made film, badly directed by Gary Winick. Winick's blunt style begins to wear the viewer out after a while: The players all act at a fever pitch (especially Frank Miller, who is awful) and the generally brutal murder sequences are ham-handedly accompanied by noisy music or sound effects. The underlying theme—of the Richards character's sexual awakening and her punishment therefor—is glossed over to concentrate solely on the torture and murder of other characters. *(Graphic violence, profanity, substance abuse, adult situations, brief nudity.)*

p, Julie Philips, Gregory Choa, and Gregory Cundiff; d, Gary Winick; w, Kevin Kennedy; ph, Makoto Watanabe (CFI Color); ed, Carole Kravetz; m, Cengiz Yaltkaya; stunts, Chuck Borden.

Thriller   (PR:O MPAA:R)

ⓥCUTTING CLASS*½
91m April/Gower Street c
Donovan Leitch *(Brian Woods)*, Jill Schoelen *(Paula Carson)*, Brad Pitt *(Dwight Ingalls)*, Roddy McDowall *(Mr. Dante)*, Martin Mull *(William Carson III)*, Brenda Lynn Klemme *(Colleen)*, Mark Barnet *(Gary)*, Robert Glaudini *(Shultz)*, Tom Ligon *(Mr. Ingalls)*, Eric Boles *(Mr. Glynn)*, Nancy Fish *(Mrs. Knocht)*, Robert Machray *(Mr. Conklin)*, Dirk Blocker *(Coach Harris)*.

Barely meriting a grade of "D," this schooldays slasher-send-up is a retread of HEATHERS with generous borrowing from FAST TIMES AT RIDGEMONT HIGH; PRETTY POISON; and MASSACRE AT CENTRAL HIGH tossed in. Before hunting enthusiast Mull leaves for a duck shoot, he warns his daughter, Schoelen, not to cut class. Newspaper headlines inform us that Leitch, a teen who killed his father (in a case prosecuted by Mull), has been released from a mental institution. Will Leitch still be up to his old tricks or was he unjustly accused in the past? In the first reel, Mull is shot with a bow and arrow in a duck blind; in a running gag, he stumbles through the rest of the film trying to get help. Meanwhile, back at school, troubled teen Leitch is being bullied by his former pal, Pitt, who's Schoelen's main squeeze. Horny Pitt tries to get Schoelen to go all the way, but she holds out, saying, "Not until your grades improve!" (What a role model for teenage girls!) When the school's art teacher is "kilned" by being pushed into a hot oven, the film focuses our suspicions on seedy school janitor Glaudini, lascivious principal McDowall, and Pitt, who seems like a junior-league sadist. For kicks, Pitt persuades Schoelen to give him the key to the school records so they and their pals can peruse Leitch's files. Unaware that the sweet-faced Leitch is watching them, the pranksters rifle his files and poke fun at him. The next day, they spread word about his shock treatments around school. Then Pitt gets into a fight while playing basketball, upsetting his father and a visiting athletic scout. At the same time, underneath the bleachers full of cheering crowds, Pitt's rambunctious friends Klemme and Barnet are brutally murdered. Shortly after this, the vice-principal, Fish, gets bashed to death on a photocopying machine, and Pitt runs around the school accusing his ex-pal of this latest killing. Soon, the entire student body and the police are hunting down Leitch. At home, Schoelen investigates her father's records and discovers that Pitt had an indirect connection with the slaying of Leitch's father. Sneaking into Schoelen's home, the much-persecuted Leitch proclaims his innocence and offers her proof of Pitt's guilt. After Pitt argues with his gym teacher, Blocker, another murder occurs, Blocker being buggered to death with the American flag. While searching for Pitt so she can persuade him to turn himself in, Schoelen finds her dead pals, Barnet and Klemme, and then encounters her math teacher at the school. Before the confused Schoelen can figure out her next move, Leitch pops up and kills the math teacher. Too late, Schoelen realizes that the mentally ill have a low recovery rate. She hooks up with Pitt, and the two lovers are chased by Leitch through the chem lab and into the student auto garage. When Leitch sticks Pitt in a vice, Schoelen pretends to neck with Leitch and then hammers and electrocutes him. As she and Pitt drive away, they nearly run over Mull. Leitch had fixed their brakes.

Strictly in the remedial class as a black comedy, this slasher spoof fails to establish any audience rapport with its characters. Sloppily directed and indifferently written, CUTTING CLASS is so concerned with throwing us off the track as to the killer's identity, it doesn't have any energy left over to create sympathetic characters, or at least deliciously nasty ones. Unlike slicker slasher movies, this film doesn't discrimi-

nate between obnoxious characters, who deserve to be sliced and diced, and those we'd like to see spared. Spoofing horror films on the most superficial level, it lacks the cinematic polish and spitefully inventive writing that a black comedy needs. Memorable dialog is scarce, the story structure is wobbly, the direction doesn't register any comic menace, and the film's tone is uncertain. Admittedly, CUTTING CLASS does manage to conceal the maniac's true identity even as it leaves behind a trail of clues pointing to his guilt. It's a neat double cross. And Jill Schoelen is appealing even in this dunce-cap comedy. Unfortunately, the adult roles are all cast-offs from the John Hughes all-grown-ups-are-jerks school, and the adolescent characters are cruel enough to make Carrie's classmates seem like teen humanitarians. Even a movie as dark as HEATHERS allows redemptive glimmers in some of its characters; this unsophisticated put-on merely parodies films about maniac teenagers in a sophomoric manner. Because the teen behavior depicted seems forced and artificial, CUTTING CLASS can never hope to move us to fear or laughter, let alone manage to provoke the two emotions in us simultaneously. *(Profanity, excessive violence, alcohol abuse, adult situations.)*

p, Rudy Cohen and Donald R. Beck; d, Rospo Pallenberg; w, Steve Slavkin; ph, Avi Karpick; ed, Natan Zahavi and Bill Butler; m, Jill Fraser; prod d, Richard Sherman.

Comedy/Horror   (PR:O MPAA:R)

⊙CYBORG*
86m Golan-Globus/Cannon c
Jean-Claude Van Damme *(Gibson Rickenbacker)*, Deborah Richter *(Nady Simmons)*, Vincent Klyn *(Fender Tremolo)*, Alex Daniels *(Marshall Strat)*, Dayle Haddon *(Pearl Prophet)*, Blaise Loong *(Furman Vox)*, Rolf Muller *(Brick Bardo)*, Haley Peterson *(Haley)*, Terrie Batson *(Mary)*, Jackson "Rock" Pinckney *(Tytus)*, Janice Graser *(Vorg)*, Robert Pentz *(Base)*, Sharon K. Tew *(Prather)*, Chuck Allen *(Vondo)*, Stefanos Miltsakakis *(Xylo)*, Kristina Sebastian *(Young Haley)*, Thomas Barley *(Willy)*, Dale Frye *(Sather)*, Jophery Brown *(Saloon Owner)*, Jim Creech *(Roland Pick)*.

Jean-Claude Van Damme, one of the new challengers for the market dominated by Arnold Schwarzenegger and Sylvester Stallone, stars in this actioner set in the future. Van Damme's first feature, BLOODSPORT, became a popular video rental and in this, his second film, his acting skills are much improved, although he has a long way to go to catch his competition. The film begins with the camera panning the smoldering ruins of a bombed-out city; a voice explains that a plague has decimated the population and that anar-

chy and evil prevail—which is just the way the narrator likes it. We learn later that the voice belongs to Klyn, the brutal leader of the Flesh Pirates, a cannibalistic gang that roams the city, pillaging and killing. Caught in this madness is Haddon, a cyborg—part computer, part human being —who, with the aid of her guard (Daniels) is trying to escape to Atlanta (the Center for Disease Control?) with information vital for the development of a serum to combat the plague. When the Pirates kill Daniels, Haddon is rescued by Van Damme, only to be kidnaped by Klyn, who plans to take her to Atlanta himself to acquire the crucial information for his own use. A chase ensues with Van Damme following Klyn and his band of musclebound henchmen (through flashbacks we learn that Van Damme has a personal stake in destroying Klyn; the villain and his band of goons killed Van Damme's lover and her family). Along the way, Van Damme picks up a sidekick (Richter) who is determined to tag along to help save the cyborg. The road they travel from the Brooklyn Bridge to Atlanta is left littered with bodies—victims of one balletic fight sequence after another (Van Damme has five years of classical ballet training under his black belt). Klyn's inevitable trouncing concludes the series of violent encounters, during which the audience has been subjected to interminable head shots of inexpressive faces, a script that consists primarily of monosyllables, and one of the longest crucifixion scenes on film. Van Damme successfully delivers Haddon to her destination, thereby assuring civilization a future. In the process, Richter's life is sacrificed but her spot is filled by Peterson, Van Damme's long-lost adopted daughter, and they go off together into the sunset.

Simply put, director Albert Pyun has attempted a melange of the styles of such films as ROAD WARRIOR and BLADE RUNNER and come up short. Martial arts fans will find plenty of action to hold their interest here, but those in search of plot and character are advised to look elsewhere. Should you find yourself looking for something to occupy your mind while watching CYBORG, you might want to try figure out why the major characters have names that are related to electric guitar equipment and techniques. Then again, you might just want to find something else to do. *(Excessive violence, nudity, adult situations.)*

p, Menahem Golan and Yoram Globus; d, Albert Pyun; w, Kitty Chalmers; ph, Philip Alan Waters; ed, Rozanne Zingale and Scott Stevenson; m, Kevin Bassinson; md, Joachim H. Hansch; prod d, Douglas Leonard; set d, Yvonne Hegney; spec eff, Joey DiGaetano and R.J. Hohman; cos, Heidi Kaczenski; stunts, Tom Elliott; makeup, Greg Cannom.

Action   (PR:O MPAA:R)

D

DAD*

117m Amblin/UNIV c

Jack Lemmon *(Jake Tremont)*, Ted Danson *(John Tremont)*, Olympia Dukakis *(Bette Tremont)*, Kathy Baker *(Annie Tremont)*, Kevin Spacey *(Mario)*, Ethan Hawke *(Billy Tremont)*, Zakes Mokae *(Dr. Chad)*, J.T. Walsh *(Dr. Santana)*, Peter Michael Goetz *(Dr. Ethridge)*, John Apicella *(Dr. Delibro)*, Richard McGonagle *(Victor Walton)*, Bill Morey *(Hal McCarthy)*, Mary Fogarty *(Gloria McCarthy)*, Art Frankel *(DMV Instructor)*, Ray Girardin *(Butcher)*, Vickilyn Reynolds *(CCU Nurse)*, Jimmy Higa *(Chris)*, Edith Fields, Takayo Fischer, Andi Chapman *(Jake's Nurses)*, Emily Kuroda *(Vicki)*, Gregory Itzin *(Ralph Kramer)*, Richard Fiske *(Bingo Caller)*, Tony Kienitz *(Bank Executive)*, Terry Wills *(Dry Cleaner)*, Patti Arpaia *(Receptionist)*, Donna Porter *(Surprised Neighbor)*, Chris Lemmon *(Young Jake)*, Gina Raymond *(Young Bette)*, Justin Petersen *(Young John)*, Sprague Grayden *(Young Annie)*, Lucas Hall *(Hank)*, Katie Kissell *(Lizbeth)*.

Jack Lemmon and Ted Danson in DAD (©Universal).

Tinkle, tinkle, tinkle. From the opening seconds of DAD, the music gets down to work, telling the audience what to think and feel about the images on-screen. Tinkle, tinkle, tinkle—think sensitive, everybody, it's time to adjust your attitude. And it's a good thing DAD has that tinkle, tinkle, tinkle, since without it the resentment that passes as affection, the manipulation that masquerades as caring, the condescension that pretends concern—in short, the pathologies that underlie its characters' relationships—would be laid bare for all to see. DAD is more concerned with covering things up than with revealing them. We know its people well because, alas, they are us—or would be, were it not for DAD's gooey sentiment and warm glow of self-deception.

Lemmon is the title dad, once an active father and still the semblance of a husband, but now old and increasingly feeble. He's dominated by his resentful wife (Dukakis), whose chronic sourness and frustration are meant to be seen as crusty lovableness (tinkle, tinkle, tinkle). Dukakis whiles away the hours by treating Lemmon like the helpless infant he's become, but when she suffers a heart attack while shopping in a supermarket (in the dairy section, with doddering Dad in tow), Lemmon is suddenly left to fend for himself. Into the picture comes son Danson, a successful Wall Street high roller whose exploits previously left him little time for his aging parents, his sister and brother-in-law (Baker and Spacey), his ex-wife, or his own son (Hawke). Danson decides to take Lemmon

under his wing (becoming a parent to his parent, every child's revenge fantasy—tinkle, tinkle), teaching him to brush his teeth, dress himself, and prepare his own meals. By the time Dukakis comes home from the hospital, Lemmon is able to do all these things and more, and mother and son are soon at odds as to who can manipulate Dad the best—for his own good, of course. Fate intervenes, however, when Lemmon undergoes some minor surgery and a traumatic hospitalization. Incensed by the doctor's treatment of his father, Danson literally carries Lemmon out of the hospital to care for him at home (a grotesque, theatrical gesture, though the music insists it's noble). The strain of tending to his dad soon proves too much for Danson, however, and Lemmon continues to deteriorate. Danson brings him back to the hospital, where a new, upbeat doctor (Mokae) is put on the case, and things start to improve. In no time, Lemmon is up on his feet and back home (thanks to the loving attention of his family, the medical pros declare), wearing funny clothes and party hats and playing innocuous cutup to a captive domestic audience. Alas, another illness looms, and this time it's terminal cancer. Lemmon slips into fantasy as he slides out of life, and his family plays along with his dream world (Dukakis initially objects to this pretense, but—tinkle, tinkle, tinkle—is soon marching in patronizing step with everyone else). When Dad finally dies, it's almost a blessing in dis-

guise, since Danson, Dukakis, and the rest of the family are now closer than they've ever been. Death is the family tonic, the therapy of last resort.

DAD is supposedly based on William Wharton's novel of the same name, but writer-director Gary David Goldberg (creator of TV's "Family Ties") and executive producer Steven Spielberg have somehow managed to stand Wharton's best-seller on its head. Everything honest and hard-hitting in the book has been tastefully subverted: a suffocating marriage becomes a sustaining one; the contemptuous lies that save the deceiver from his or her own discomfort become the white lies that spare a loved one pain; the unruly power of sexual release (in the novel it's Dad's affair with an African-American nurse, not the treacly ministrations of family, that puts pep back in his step) becomes the cuddly manageability of spirit tamed. Traditional "family" values are anathema in Wharton, but Goldberg and Spielberg push them as a cure-all.

The performances are scaled to meet the script's tiny demands. Jack Lemmon is a purely superficial codger, doddering and twinkling with an eye to the Academy Award applause meter. Ted Danson (TV's "Cheers," THREE MEN AND A BABY; COUSINS) would settle for as much (or as little) and tries very hard to match Lemmon's sentiment, but his TV acting style keeps getting in the way. There's no center to his performance, no basis for his character's emotions (when Danson rails at Lemmon's doctors, he might just as well be complaining that a garbage truck had side-swiped his Porsche). Given one sour note by the script, Dukakis (MOONSTRUCK; STEEL MAGNOLIAS) plays it well, but becomes tiresome as she plays it over and over again. And Zakes Mokae, who was so good in A DRY WHITE SEASON, has nothing to do here but fill the racial void left by the deletion of the novel's redemptive nurse—a thankless task in a compromised film. Race, sex, and death are DAD's dirty secrets—the problem is, they're also the core of what DAD's supposedly about. *(Adult situations.)*

p, Joseph Stern and Gary David Goldberg; d, Gary David Goldberg; w, Gary David Goldberg (based on the novel *Dad* by William Wharton); ph, Jan Kiesser (Deluxe Color); ed, Eric Sears; m, James Horner; prod d, Jack DeGovia; art d, John R. Jensen and Paul W. Gorfine; set d, Thomas L. Roysden; spec eff, Gary Zink; cos, Dan Bronson; makeup, Ken Diaz.

Drama **(PR:C MPAA:PG)**

◐DANCE OF THE DAMNED*

83m New Classics/Concorde c

Starr Andreeff *(Jodi Hurtz)*, Cyril O'Reilly *(Vampire)*, Deborah Ann Nassar *(La Donna)*, Maria Ford *(Teacher)*, Athena Worthy *(Ray Gun Girl)*, Tom Ruben *(Cabby)*.

Husband-and-wife movie-making team Andy and Katt Shea Ruben seem to have a thing for go-go bars. STRIPPED TO KILL and its sequel, LIVE GIRLS: STRIPPED TO KILL II, both Ruben productions, revolved around strip clubs, and now comes DANCE OF THE DAMNED, cowritten by Andy (who produced) and Katt (who directed). Astute B-movie viewers will spot LIVE GIRLS leading lady Maria Ford as one of the dancers at DANCE OF THE DAMNED's strip venue, the Paradise Cafe, and LIVE GIRLS' costar Tom Ruben plays a cabbie here. What's more, those in the know might even observe that the Paradise looks suspiciously similar to LIVE GIRLS' Paragon Club. But even if you fail to note any of these commonalities, you shouldn't have any difficulty noticing what a dud of movie DANCE OF THE DAMNED is. Indeed, it might be a good idea for the Rubens to give go-go the heave-ho for awhile.

A vampire thriller minus the thrills, DANCE starts with the ominous-looking O'Reilly stopping in at the seedy Paradise just as lithe dancer Andreeff is flinging herself around the stage to climax her act. Offstage, Andreeff is a rather sad case; forced to work, she has missed her son's birthday and, in the process, provided her ex-husband with further grounds to win complete custody of the youngster. These

developments and Andreeff's later suicide attempt in the Paradise dressing room are all overheard by O'Reilly, who has supernatural sensory powers. Left to lock up the club after closing time, Andreeff bumps into O'Reilly, who has lingered behind and offers the stripper $1,000 and a proposition—if she will spend the night with him, just to talk, he will "relieve" her pain. Against her better judgement, Andreeff agrees. Later, however, she learns that O'Reilly is none other than (ta da!) a vampire and that she (uh oh!) is to be his main course.

DANCE OF THE DAMNED has the makings of a good pursuit drama—perhaps a fanged variation on THE TERMINATOR—unfortunately, the Rubens have a loftier purpose in mind as they attempt to present a cross-species romance. Along the way, there are bits of violence and dashes of sex to keep the grind-house crowd from going comatose, and a brief tender visit with Andreeff's son plucks a few heartstrings. But generally, DANCE OF THE DAMNED is the worst type of picture to undertake with a B-movie budget and cast—a terrifying two-headed talkathon. Even under the best conditions, movies of this sort are tricky to pull off—Louis Malle's two-character MY DINNER WITH ANDRE and Robert Altman's one-character SECRET HONOR being notable exceptions—and to put it kindly, DANCE falls far short of the mark.

Notwithstanding his glazed-over blue eyes and barbarian haircut, Cyril O'Reilly has neither the force nor the charisma to stand beside such classic bloodsuckers as Bela Lugosi or Christopher Lee. It doesn't help much either that his dialog is mostly warmed-over vampire schlock from countless other, mostly better, genre efforts. Indeed, it seems likely he'll bore Andreeff to death before he can ever get his fangs into her. Although Andreeff fares only a little better as a frail lady who has led a tough, bitter life, the Rubens have, over the course of their stripper trilogy, shown a knack for drawing knowing, sympathetic portraits of ladies in the fantasy skin trade. If they can find the confidence and a producer willing to let them leave out the slashers and vampires, they may someday even make a satisfying drama dealing with this little-understood demimonde. But in the meantime, DANCE OF THE DAMNED just ain't it. *(Nudity, violence.)*

p, Andy Ruben; d, Katt Shea Ruben; w, Andy Ruben and Katt Shea Ruben; ph, Phedon Papamichael (Foto-Kem Color); ed, Carole Kravetz; m, Gary Stockdale; prod d, Stephen Greenberg; spec eff, Steve Neill; chor, Ted Lin.

Horror **(PR:O MPAA:R)**

◐DANGER ZONE II: REAPER'S REVENGE*

95m Jason Williams-Tom Friedman/Skouras c

Jason Williams *(Wade Olson)*, Robert Random *(Reaper)*, Jane Higginson *(Donna)*, Alisha Das *(Francine)*, Walter Cox *(Doug)*, Barne Wms. Subkoski *(Rainmaker)*.

With the major Hollywood studios reportedly set to unleash a wave of big-budget biker action-adventures (Eddie Murphy and Nick Nolte reportedly will take on an outlaw biker gang in the upcoming 48 HRS. sequel, for example), DANGER ZONE II may be said to be ahead of its time. An ultraviolent—and ultrasexist—biker epic set for the most part in the Arizona desert, it's steeped in biker lore and southwestern mysticism, giving it the eccentricity that seems to be the exclusive province of B movies these days. (Meanwhile, their bland, bigger-budgeted cousins strive for the widest possible audience appeal.) Unfortunately, DANGER ZONE II's virtues, both as a genuinely offbeat adventure and as a well-crafted action thriller, are negated by the film's emphasis on sexual violence and the underdeveloped, curiously uninvolving conflict at its core.

Briefly to recap the first DANGER ZONE (which helps to fill out the sequel's sketchier aspects): A drug-pushing motorcycle gang led by a character named Reaper kidnaped a busload of beauty pageant contestants, setting off the conflict between Reaper and Wade Olson, the undercover cop who brought him to justice. As DANGER ZONE II begins, Reaper (Random) is being freed from prison on one of those all-purpose revenge-movie legal technicalities. Meanwhile, Wade (Williams) is doing his best to win the war on drugs singlehandedly and struggling at home in the battle of the sexes—since his live-in girl friend, Donna (Higginson), is pressuring him to make their arrangement legal. After arguing with Donna, Wade stomps off to bust more pushers. Donna, a physical swim therapist, goes off to work and conveniently lingers in the pool after closing time, making her easy pickings for Reaper and his boys. The gang kidnaps Donna, carrying her off to their desert hideout to lure Wade into a confrontation. To keep him motivated, they leave lurid, compromising photos of Donna and various members of the gang at key points on Wade's route of pursuit. Along the way, Wade picks up an unlikely trio of allies comprising Reaper's business manager (Cox), a rain-making mystic (Subkoski), and the bad-guy biker's ex-girl friend (Das).

The only character lacking motivation is Reaper himself, which tends to make DANGER ZONE II gratuitously nonsensical, even for an action film. Despite Robert Random's best efforts to portray the character as a sort of MAD MAX-style, evil-incarnate villain, it finally makes too little sense that Reaper, freed on appeal, would endanger his highly profitable drug operation (which distributes cocaine around the country through other biker gangs) by indulging himself in the violent sexual humiliation of his most fanatical enemy's girl friend.

Such quibbles are often pointless in assessing a movie of this type; normally, one would switch one's brain off the second the VCR was switched on. But DANGER ZONE II comes so close to being a solidly engaging action-adventure on its own terms that its push-button porno violence seems not just ugly and stupid, but incongruous. The sexism is particularly disappointing because there are flashes of genuine wit in both the writing and direction, while the cast provides a number of sharp, well-turned performances. (Jason Williams alone fails to make much of an impression, perhaps because he was distracted by his many off-screen duties, which included coproducing, cowriting the story, and second-unit direction.) Even Daniel Yarussi's cinematography is noteworthy, expressively using the Arizona desert locations to frame the film's elemental conflicts. It's that much more regrettable, therefore, that DANGER ZONE II, which values guts so highly, didn't have enough guts itself to leave the sleaze off-screen. (Violence, sexual situations, nudity, profanity.)

p, Jason Williams and Tom Friedman; d, Geoffrey G. Bowers; w, Dulany Ross Clements (based on a story by Jason Williams, Tom Friedman); ph, Daniel Yarussi (Foto-Kem Color); ed, Susan Medaglia; m, Robert Etoll; art d, Richard Wirsich; stunts, Mike Tino.

Action/Adventure   (PR:O MPAA:R)

Ⓥ**DARK TOWER***
91m Sandy Howard/Spectrafilm c
Michael Moriarty (Dennis Randall), Jenny Agutter (Carolyn Page), Carol Lynley (Tilly Ambrose), Theodore Bikel (Dr. Max Gold), Anne Lockhart (Elaine), Kevin McCarthy (Sergie), Patch Mackenzie (Maria), Robert Sherman (Williams), Rick Azulay (Charlie), Radmiro Oliveros (Joseph).

A seasoned cast and the beauty of Barcelona go to waste in this dull, talky, and incoherent haunted-skyscraper suspense thriller. As gorgeous as ever, Jenny Agutter (AN AMERICAN WEREWOLF IN LONDON; WALKABOUT) plays a chilly architect whose just-completed high-rise project is the site of some strange goings-on. The weird events begin when a peeping window washer is hurled to his death by that familiar ghost-movie gimmick The Powerful Unseen Force. The mayhem con-

tinues when a security guard is torn to pieces in an elevator—also presumably by The Force. Then a building security executive goes bananas and commits mass murder in the building's lobby after seeing something in the elevator. Called back from his vacation, another security official (Moriarty) investigates and begins having strange dreams about Agutter that combine sexual fantasy with ominous fear and loathing. The violent occurrences continue, but the Barcelona police fail to take any action. Moriarty's growing bafflement leads him to seek the assistance of parapsychologist Bikel—a descendant of Sigmund Freud—and his wacky, boozing psychic friend (McCarthy). Moriarty's investigation of Agutter reveals a shady past and an abusive husband who died mysteriously and may be tormenting her from beyond the grave.

Much of the above is necessarily speculation, since DARK TOWER's plot is exceedingly opaque. We're never sure, for example, just who Moriarty is; but because he doesn't work for the police, it seems reasonable to assume that he's supposed to be some sort of corporate gumshoe. The only way we know for sure that the film is even set in Barcelona is because the producers thank that city's officials in the movie's end titles. Most important, it's never clear what Agutter did to deserve all of this special-effects torment in the first place. Granted, she's neurotic and a tad aloof, but she never appears to be mysterious or evil. In place of informative exposition, we get such tension builders as endless shots of the elevator-from-hell going up and down. Instead of character development, we're treated to McCarthy shuffling around in a stupor, never once displaying the psychic powers Bikel insists he possesses; or we are shown Bikel wandering around the building and talking to himself while trying to flush the evil spirits out into the open. Even the nature of the spirits is glossed over.

Some explanation for the movie's sorry state may be found in the removal of British director Freddie Francis' real name from the credits in favor of a pseudonym—always a sure sign of a troubled production. A veteran cinematographer and the director of THE DOCTOR AND THE DEVILS; DRACULA HAS RISEN FROM THE GRAVE; THE CREEPING FLESH, and other solid horror entries, Francis has proved that he knows how to put together a good yarn. Unfortunately, DARK TOWER doesn't begin to approach the high standards of his previous work. This boring mishmash is all the more annoying because its potentially intriguing premise and visual elegance betray a deft directorial hand that may not have been around for the final cut.

Agutter contributes a particularly solid performance, but the rest of the cast is

spotty, though, under the circumstances, it's a little hard to tell whether this is the performers' fault. Michael Moriarty relies on his usual array of hammy outbursts and facial contortions in lieu of a performance; Theodore Bikel and Kevin McCarthy are oddly superfluous to the main action—what there is of it. Among the women, Carol Lynley shows up long enough to be recognized as Agutter's earnest, dutiful assistant; and, in the role of Moriarty's girl friend, Anne Lockhart goes though the film looking inexplicably pensive and biting her lower lip a lot. To an extent, Lockhart's performance is understandable: Wouldn't you be nervous if you had to face Moriarty across your breakfast table every morning? Except for a few well-orchestrated horror set pieces and a sensational—though utterly bewildering—climax, DARK TOWER has little to offer either genre fans or casual observers. Only admirers of Agutter and those who wish to pay a movie visit to Barcelona may want to check out DARK TOWER, which was released straight to video in the US after a two-year theatrical release abroad. (Violence, profanity, adult situations.)

p, John R. Bowey and David M. Witz; d, Freddie Francis; w, Robert J. Avrech, Ken Wiederhorn, and Ken Blackwell (based on a story by Avrech); ph, Gordon Hayman; ed, Tom Merchant; m, Stacy Widelitz; art d, Jose Maria Espada; makeup, Steve Neill.

Horror   (PR:C MPAA:R)

Ⓥ**DEAD-BANG***
105m Lorimar/WB c
Don Johnson (Jerry Beck), Penelope Ann Miller (Linda), William Forsythe (Arthur Kressler), Bob Balaban (Elliot Webly), Frank Military (Bobby Burns), Tate Donovan (John Burns), Tim Reid (Chief Dixon), Antoni Stutz (Ray), Mickey Jones (Sleepy), Ron Campbell (Crossfield), William Taylor (Elton Tremmel), Hy Anzell (Capt. Waxman), Michael Jeter (Dr. Krantz), James B. Douglas (Agent Gilroy), Brad Sullivan (Chief Hillard), Phyllis Guerrini (Louisa), Darwyn Swalve, David H. "Hutch" Van Dalsem, Ron Jeremy Hyatt (Bikers), Sam Scarber (Detective Bilson), Mic Rodgers (Sgt. Kimble), Tiger Haynes (Edwin Gates), Garwin Sanford, Lon Katzman (Officers), Daniel Quinn (James "Hard Rock" Ellis), Jarion Monroe (LAPD Officer), Ricardo Ascencio (Ponchito), William Taylor (Officer Franklin), Trudy Forbes (Female Officer), Michael Higgins (Rev. Gebhardt), Evans Evans (Mrs. Gebhardt), Stephen E. Miller (Bogan, Oklahoma Officer), Dawn Mortensen (Daughter), Frank C. Turner (Cottonwood Officer), Lennard Camarillo (Juancho), Jerome Beck (Detective John), Valerie Pearson (Helpful Person), Billy Boyle (Priest), Justin Stillwell (Mark

Beck), Christine Cable *(Karen Beck)*, Maureen Thomas *(Teacher)*, Ron Carothers, Ernie Jackson *(Dixon's Men)*, Juliana Carter *(Dixon's Wife)*.

As cartoonish action movies go, DEAD-BANG is a solid example of Hollywood professionalism. Technically accomplished, well-directed, and well-constructed, the film zips along at an appropriately breathless clip and provides its lead, Don Johnson, with a proper vehicle for a successful transition from television to big-screen stardom. Though the plot entails a potentially explosive issue, the filmmakers have wisely elected not to take its social implications too seriously, concentrating instead on fulfilling genre expectations and creating a movie filled with thrills and goofy humor.

Johnson, a Los Angeles Sheriff's Office homicide detective, finds his life in a shambles. His divorce has left him broke, his ex-wife has obtained a restraining order preventing him from seeing his children, his apartment is a mess, he can't hold his liquor, and his grooming habits leave a lot to be desired. All he has going for him is his iron will to see the cases on which he works through to the end. When an African-American storekeeper is shot in a robbery and a policeman looking for suspects is gunned down just minutes later, Johnson's empty Christmas Eve is suddenly filled with activity. Searching computer records, he comes upon a picture of Military, who fits the storekeeper's description of the suspect to a T. The next morning, after Johnson and Military's parole officer, Balaban, have looked through Military's file, Johnson tricks Balaban into accompanying him to the house Military shares with his straight-arrow college student brother (Donovan), his mother, her "old man," and a collection of biker types. It seems that Johnson may enter the premises only if accompanied by the suspect's parole officer, and though Balaban is outraged by Johnson's tactics, the tenacious cop won't take no for an answer. As Donovan pleads ignorance of Military's whereabouts, a biker scoots out the back door. Pursued and caught by the cops, he refuses to talk until Johnson, suffering the effects of the previous night's drinking, throws up on him. This proves an unexpectedly effective interrogative approach, and the horrified biker immediately tells Johnson that Military left with three men the night before. When a Mexican bar in Arizona is robbed and its occupants murdered by assailants matching Military and company's description, Johnson arrives on the scene and makes a startling discovery: Not only are Military and his cohorts part of a white supremacy group, they are headed to a big meeting in Colorado planned to unite a large number of such groups into one powerful, well-funded organization. Johnson shares this revelation with Forsythe, an

FBI agent sent in to investigate, but the impeccably groomed, arrogant Fed refuses to take him seriously. Trailing Military, Johnson uncovers the activities of Higgins, the head of the Aryan Nation Church, near Oklahoma City, but just as Johnson feels he is making real progress, he is called back to LA to answer complaints filed by Balaban, Forsythe (who is offended by his foul language), and others, and told he won't be put back on the case unless given a clean bill of health by police psychiatrist Jeter. Realizing that the pretentious Jeter is not on his side, Johnson gets a positive report after threatening the shrink's life, then storms the Colorado meeting with Forsythe and a group of volunteer black police officers led by Reid. A search of the camp reveals Nazi artifacts and goons in fatigues, but not Johnson's suspects. Higgins' threat of a lawsuit puts more heat on Johnson, who refuses to give up and finally discovers the fugitives' hiding place. After a raging gun battle, the dying Military swears he is not the man who killed the storekeeper and the cop, giving Forsythe an opportunity to rail further at Johnson. The mystery is solved after Donovan unexpectedly turns up, and the film ends with an FBI press conference where a modest Forsythe takes all the credit for solving the case.

John Frankenheimer's first new film since 1986's 52 PICK-UP is hardly innovative work from the veteran director of BIRDMAN OF ALCATRAZ; THE TRAIN; SEVEN DAYS IN MAY; and the recently re-released MANCHURIAN CANDIDATE, but DEAD-BANG solidly delivers the goods for the sizable audience that enjoys fast, well-told action films laced with humor. Leaving a serious examination of the white supremacy movement to other films (such as Costa-Gavras' BETRAYED) and using the ugly phenomenon simply to make its heavies especially hateful, DEAD-BANG instead focuses squarely on its action sequences and on Johnson's obsessive character, and the decision pays off. Johnson gives an adept, amusing, colorful star performance here, displaying considerable acting skills that have been somewhat obscured by his stylized "Miami Vice" persona. Robert Foster's caricature-ish but lively script also offers Frank Military, William Forsythe, and Bob Balaban impressive supporting turns, and veteran British cinematographer Gerry Fisher contributes his usual top-level work.

Often silly, more than a bit gross, and played with tongue firmly in cheek, DEAD-BANG is a good-looking, well-paced genre piece. Audiences may hunger for more substantial fare an hour after seeing it, but the movie is fun while it lasts. *(Violence, profanity, substance abuse, adult situations.)*

p, Steve Roth; d, John Frankenheimer; w, Robert Foster; ph, Gerry Fisher (Alpha Cine Color); ed, Robert F. Shugrue; m, Gary Chang and Michael Kamen; prod d, Ken Adam; art d, Richard Hudolin and Alan Manzer; set d, Art Parker; spec eff, Clifford P. Wenger; cos, Jodie Tillen; stunts, Mic Rodgers; makeup, John Inzerella.

Crime   (PR:O MPAA:R)

▼DEAD CALM*½
(Aus.) 96m Kennedy Miller/WB c
Sam Neill *(John Ingram)*, Nicole Kidman *(Rae Ingram)*, Billy Zane *(Hughie Warriner)*, Rod Mullinar *(Russell Bellows)*, Joshua Tilden *(Danny)*, George Shevtsov *(Doctor)*, Michael Long *(Specialist Doctor)*.

Lately, it's become all too common for film publicists to promote their latest thriller as being "in the grand tradition of Alfred Hitchcock," or some variation of that description. For the most part, films advertised in this way fall far short of Hitchcock's movies, but DEAD CALM is an exception. Though it lacks Hitchcock's wry and macabre sense of humor, DEAD CALM is a cracklingly good, cold-blooded film that never lets up in its truly Hitchcockian suspense. Under the gripping direction of Phillip Noyce (NEWSFRONT; HEAT WAVE), the film sustains tension and power beautifully, right through to its startling conclusion.

Middle-aged Australian surgeon Neill and his wife, Kidman, embark on an extended yachting trip after the gruesome death of their little son in a car accident. The tragedy has left Kidman in an emotionally fragile state—she suffers from recurring nightmares in which she sees her child's mangled body—and Neill has taken her sailing as a therapeutic measure. The therapy seems to be working, and things go well until the couple rescues the sole survivor (Zane) from a sinking schooner near the Great Barrier Reef. A strange young man, Zane claims his sailing companions died as a result of food poisoning, but Neill suspects foul play and rows to the schooner to investigate, leaving Kidman alone with the sleeping Zane on the yacht. Neill's worst fears are confirmed when he reaches the ill-fated boat: it's obvious the dead were victims of a maniacal killer, and only Zane could be responsible for the gruesome murders. Neill jumps back into his rowboat and frantically paddles back to his own yacht—but too late. Having awakened during Neill's absence, the murderous "survivor" has taken off with Kidman and the yacht, leaving Neill far behind. The film now concentrates on a spine-tingling cat-and-mouse game of survival between Kidman and Zane.

Sam Neill (A CRY IN THE DARK; PLENTY) and Billy Zane both turn in excellent performances, but Nicole Kidman (a relative newcomer to films, as is Zane) does the most interesting and demanding work as the wife who must snap out of her melancholy distraction to outwit her vile captor. During the film's last half, Kidman convincingly transforms from a vulnerable, distraught housewife to a ferocious battler—and it's an electrifying metamorphosis.

Coproduced by George Miller (director of the "Mad Max" films and THE WITCHES OF EASTWICK) and scripted by Terry Hayes (who wrote Miller's ROAD WARRIOR and MAD MAX BEYOND THUNDERDOME and who coproduced with Miller and Doug Mitchell here), DEAD CALM is an adaptation of Charles Williams' novel of the same name, published in 1963. Williams' mystery was also the basis of Orson Welles' unfinished movie THE DEEP (also known as DEAD RECKONING), which Welles adapted and began filming in 1968, casting himself and Jeanne Moreau as the couple and Laurence Harvey as the psychotic survivor. Reportedly, a copy of Welles' script and an unreleased print are held by the Welles estate, which owned the rights to *Dead Calm*, but Noyce, Miller, and Hayes avoided looking at Welles' material after obtaining the property. Instead, they concentrated on deepening the psychological emphasis of Williams' story, most notably by adding the death of the couple's son.

The taut editing and Noyce's direction are splendid, augmenting Hayes' sharp (though somewhat predictable) script. The cinematography by Dean Semler is also fine, as is the score by Graeme Revell. Songs include: "Who Stole the Isopropyl Alcohol," "New York Turnpike," "No-Mad" (Tim O'Connor, performed by O'Connor), "The Lion Sleeps Tonight" (Hugo Peretti, Luigi Creatore, George

Weiss, Albert Stanton [from a traditional African song], performed by the Tokens), and "Wired for Sound" (Graeme Revell, performed by SPK). *(Graphic violence, profanity, adult situations, brief nudity.)*

p, Terry Hayes, Doug Mitchell, and George Miller; d, Phillip Noyce; w, Terry Hayes (based on the novel by Charles Williams); ph, Dean Semler (Panavision, Eastmancolor); ed, Richard Francis-Bruce; m, Graeme Revell; prod d, Graham "Grace" Walker; art d, Kim Hilder; spec eff, Brian Cox; cos, Norma Moriceau; stunts, Glen Boswell; makeup, Noriko Spencer.

Horror/Thriller　　　　(PR:O　MPAA:R)

ⓥ**DEAD POETS SOCIETY***½
128m Touchstone-Silver Screen Partners IV/BV c
Robin Williams *(John Keating)*, Robert Sean Leonard *(Neil Perry)*, Ethan Hawke *(Todd Anderson)*, Josh Charles *(Knox Overstreet)*, Gale Hansen *(Charlie Dalton)*, Dylan Kussman *(Richard Cameron)*, Allelon Ruggiero *(Steven Meeks)*, James Waterson *(Gerard Pitts)*, Norman Lloyd *(Mr. Nolan)*, Kurtwood Smith *(Mr. Perry)*, Carla Belver *(Mrs. Perry)*, Leon Pownall *(McAllister)*.

Making a definitive change in his screen persona, comedian-actor Robin Williams plays it fairly straight as a dedicated teacher at an elite Vermont prep school in THE DEAD POETS SOCIETY. The attention-getting title of this compelling film refers to a secret club to which English teacher John Keating (Williams) belonged when he himself was a student at Welton Academy, where he is now a faculty member. The year is 1959, a time of staid national leadership by President Eisenhower and strict adherence to educational goals and teaching methods at Welton, under the no-

nonsense stewardship of headmaster Lloyd. The academic apple cart teeters, however, and is finally upset, when Williams is engaged to teach a class of bright and impressionable young men. An inspirational, brilliant mentor, Williams ignores conventional teaching procedures and offers his students access to a world of culture, ideas, and creativity that changes their lives. The story turns on how the boys are affected by the counsel of the educator (whom they call "Captain," after Walt Whitman's elegy of Abraham Lincoln), focusing on seven of the students: Hawke, a hopeful writer; his roommate, Leonard, who longs to be an actor but is intimidated by his disapproving father (Smith); the intellectual Ruggiero; the lovesick Charles; the flip Hansen; the maverick Waterson; and the pragmatic Kussman. Leonard boldly defies his father—with Williams' encouragement—in taking a role in a school play, resulting in a tragic aftermath. Leading up to the story's climax are the newly revived Dead Poets Society's secret meetings in a cave, where the students address their hopes and fantasies, fueled by the prodding of their English teacher to dream big dreams and make their lives extraordinary. "Carpe diem" ("Seize the day"), he tells them—quoting the epigraph attributed to Horace and exhorting them to lead full and creative lives. The discovery of the clandestine activities of the Dead Poets Society and the unorthodox teaching methods of Williams, who disdains almost every aspect of conventional academia, lead to his dismissal by the headmaster. In a poignant departure from the school, while his former class is in session under the stern tutelage of Lloyd, a concerted movement by the boys convinces the ousted teacher that his work has not been in vain.

The role of Keating is a plum assignment for the talented Williams, who brings to his portrayal the passion and empathy that is pivotal to the character and—without resorting to shtick—additionally injects the role with a credible and sympathetic blend of warmth and humor. The students are also delineated with the necessary conviction, with especially notable work from Robert Sean Leonard, Kurtwood Smith as the misunderstanding father, and Norman Lloyd as the headmaster. Peter Weir directs Tom Schulman's fine screenplay with an excellent eye for detail, underscoring the story's rising complications; and John Seale's photography is evocative, especially his snowy winter scenes. *(Adult situations, profanity.)*

p, Steven Haft, Paul Junger Witt, and Tony Thomas; d, Peter Weir; w, Tom Schulman; ph, John Seale (Duart Color); m, Maurice Jarre; prod d, Wendy Stites; art d, Sandy Veneziano; set d, John Anderson; cos, Marilyn Matthews.

Drama　　　　(PR:A　MPAA:PG)

Robin Williams in DEAD POETS SOCIETY (©Buena Vista).

⊙DEADLY OBSESSION*
95m Distant Horizon c
Jeffrey R. Iorio *(Dino Andretti)*, Joe Paradise *(John Doe)*, Darnell Martin *(Denise)*, Martin Haber *(Lt. Walsh)*, William F.X. Klein *(President Brickley)*, Monica Breckenridge *(Pamela)*.

Shot on the campus of Columbia University, this thriller revolves around a standard-issue madman (Paradise) who uses the threat of product tampering in an extortion plot. A maintenance man for Gotham University, Paradise lives in the bowels of the school's administration building. The university owns a dairy and in a call to the school's president (Klein), Paradise says he'll contaminate hundreds of containers of the company's product unless he gets $1 million. To show he's not bluffing, he places an ice cream container injected with rat poison in a cooler of a dorm convenience store, and reveals the location of the container to Klein when he calls him from a pay phone in the dorm. His threat conveyed, Paradise returns to the cooler to check on the ice cream, and is stunned to find it missing. A clerk tells him that a dorm resident (Martin) has purchased the deadly dessert, and Paradise heads for her room, breaks in, and finds the coed, who has already eaten some of the ice cream, collapsed and semiconscious on the bathroom floor. Summoned by Klein, police arrive at the dorm, and Paradise makes a quick exit, though he's worried that Martin may have been conscious enough to recognize him. Martin is rushed to the hospital, where her life is saved, and a week later she returns to school, with wise-cracking rookie cop Iorio assigned to stay with her day and night. Paradise, who is still attempting to pull off his extortion caper, makes repeated efforts to get to Martin and finish her off, but is thwarted by the presence of Iorio. One night, while Iorio is asleep, Martin is asked by her roommate (Breckenridge) for her psychology notes, only to learn that she has left them in her gym locker. Without disturbing Iorio, the two sneak off to the gym. It's closed for the night, but the enterprising coeds enter through an open window. Although the gym is only barely illuminated by lights from outside, the girls decide to take advantage of the facilities, Martin shooting baskets while Breckenridge heads for the weight room. Naturally, Paradise lurks nearby and promptly dispatches Breckenridge, then begins pursuing Martin through the gym, threatening her with a huge syringe filled with poison. It's Iorio to the rescue once again, though, as the cop awakens to find Martin missing and learns her whereabouts from a dorm security man. Paradise has had enough messing around, and he makes one more call to Klein, telling the president he has two days to come up with the $1 million and that he wants Martin to hand it over to him in the

school's administration building. Haber, the crusty veteran cop who's Iorio's supervisor, goes along with the plan, but has police strategically placed inside and outside the building as Martin waits to deliver the money. However, Paradise breaks into Klein's apartment, which is in the administration building, and forces him to call Haber and tell him to get all his men out of the building. As Haber reluctantly complies, Paradise injects Klein with a lethal dose of poison, then heads off to meet Martin and collect the booty, hauling her down into the maze of tunnels that runs beneath the school, pursued by Iorio and a dozen more cops. A lengthy struggle between Martin and Paradise follows, before Martin fatally shoots the loony and is then reunited with Iorio at the fade-out.

DEADLY OBSESSION producer Anant Singh achieved some critical acclaim with such South Africa-shot films as CITY OF BLOOD and PLACE OF WEEPING. There's little of quality, though, in this straight-to-video thriller, his first US production. Joe Paradise is properly vile and quirky as the demented extortionist, Darnell Martin is adequate as the shy student in danger, and Monica Breckenridge is appealing as her more adventurous roommate. As the terminally horny Andretti, who comes on to any female within earshot, Jeffrey R. Iorio is at times a little too cute, but does manage to convey a genuine concern for Martin. Far too much of the movie is devoted to struggles between Martin and Paradise in barely lit surroundings, however. The endless cycle of escape and capture, as depicted in the extended scene in the gymnasium and the lengthy climax in the network of tunnels under the Gotham campus, becomes unbearably monotonous. It's damn near impossible to sustain a high level of tension for periods as long as director-writer Jeno Hodi shoots for here, and a little more dialog would have helped make her moments of danger more effective. *(Gore effects, nudity, profanity, sexual situations, substance abuse.)*

p, Anant Singh; d, Jeno Hodi; w, Jeno Hodi, Paul Wolansky, and Brian Cox (based on a story by Hodi, Wolansky); ph, Zoltan David (Technicolor); ed, Paul Wolansky; m, Marty Dunayer; prod d, Kimberly von Brandenstein; stunts, Jeffrey R. Iorio.

Thriller   (PR:O MPAA:R)

⊙DEADLY POSSESSION zero
99m Craig Lahiff/Vestron c
Penny Cook *(Katie Martin)*, Arna-Maria Winchester *(Dr. Steiner)*, Liddy Clark *(Sally)*, Olivia Hamnett *(Ms. Turner)*, Patrick Frost *(Katie's Ex-Husband)*.

DEADLY POSSESSION takes place at a conservatory, and begins with the murder of a student named Anna who is "obsessed

with music." The film's opening shots are disorienting and dark: Two women arrive in a car, and one emerges after what appears to be an impassioned good-bye (because of the way the scene is shot we can't be sure). Eventually Anna returns to her apartment, where she answers a knock at the door and is suddenly accosted by an intruder, who, we are led to believe, is the man shown skulking in the bushes earlier. Cook, a fellow student who arrives as Anna is being put into an ambulance, doesn't appear to be too upset about her neighbor's imminent demise. However, when Cook's ex-husband is charged with the murder, she begins her own investigation, aided by another neighbor (Clark). Cook's ex has been charged because he was seen running from the crime scene, but in fact he was only there because he saw Anna pushed from her window and came to her aid. When he reached the dying young woman, he found an unusual key in her hand. Thinking this significant, Cook later notices a similar key in the possession of Winchester, one of the instructors at the conservatory. But the key proves to be of no significance—at least none that is discernable to the viewer—as the film winds toward its odd resolution.

At the end of DEADLY POSSESSION, director-cowriter Craig Lahiff offers a 1950s-vintage Freudian explanation of psychopathic behavior, and this ridiculous coda would be laughable were it not the only interpretation presented. Lahiff's script (written with Terry Jennings) is awful, his direction is nonexistent, and the viewer is left with the impression that the maker of DEADLY POSSESSION has stayed up too many nights watching PSYCHO without ever twigging Hitchcock's intent. Hitchcock realized that the psychotic's ability to function normally at times is far more interesting than psychosis itself—a concept that has completely eluded Lahiff. The distance Hitchcock maintains from his characters allows us to see a process and a resolution; Lahiff, on the other hand, lacks perspective, and as a result, has made an empty, lifeless chop-'em-up film. Moreover, given Lahiff's inability to create rounded female characters and the repugnant way in which Winchester's mad Dr. Steiner is presented, one must also question the director's view of women.

To put it kindly, the acting in DEADLY POSSESSION is undistinguished. Arna-Maria Winchester appears to believe that a vapid expression and unnatural posture are all that is necessary to communicate the abnormalities of her psychopathic music teacher; as the sleuthing ex-wife, Penny Cook looks confused throughout the film and displays little emotion; and Olivia Hamnett, playing the policewoman in charge of the murder investigation, delivers all of her lines in the same lifeless monotone. The film's lighting, or lack thereof, is even worse. Cinematographer David Foreman apparently believes that the best way to create a dramatic situation is to shoot in darkness, and he does so again and again. Little planning seems to have gone into the camera placement here, but that is relatively consistent with the rest of the film, which appears to have been conceived and created on the fly. *(Violence, adult situations.)*

p, Terry Jennings; d, Craig Lahiff; w, Craig Lahiff and Terry Jennings; ph, David Foreman; ed, Catherine Murphy; m, Frank Strangio; prod d, Anni Browning.

Thriller   **(PR:O MPAA:NR)**

ⓥDEALERS*
(Brit.) 95m Euston/Rank c
Paul McGann *(Daniel Pascoe)*, Rebecca DeMornay *(Anna Schuman)*, Derrick O'Connor *(Robby Barrell)*, John Castle *(Frank Mallory)*, Paul Guilfoyle *(Lee Peters)*, Rosalind Bennett *(Bonnie)*, Adrian Dunbar *(Lennox Mayhew)*, Nicholas Hewetson *(Jamie Dunbar)*, Sara Sugarman *(Elana)*, Dikran Tulaine *(Wolfgang)*, Douglas Hodge *(Patrick Skill)*, Annabel Brooks *(Lucy)*, Simon Slater *(Tony Eisner)*, Rohan McCollough *(Carla Mallory)*, Richenda Carey *(Mallory's Secretary)*, Paul Atkinson *(Whitney Paine Guard)*, Paul Stacey *(Private Eye)*, Willie Ross *(Anna's Doorman)*, Choy Ling Man *(Riki)*, Beverley Hills *(Tape-Room Girl)*, Andrew Baker *(Barman)*, Irene Marot *(Taxi Passenger)*, Barry Ewart *(Commissionaire)*, Kit Hollerbach *(Newscaster)*, Georgia Byng *(Bar Girl)*, Amanda Dickinson *(Whitney Paine Clerk)*, Marissa Dunlop *(Little Girl)*, Paul Archard, Rupert Blackburn, Andrew Drummond, Zoe Grace, David Hancock, Charles Meyrick, Louise Morgan, Andrew Penn, Josh Robertson, Sabastion Robertson *(Dealers)*.

The London branch of Whitney Paine, an American bank, has been rocked to its foundations. One of its traders (Slater) has blown his brains out at the boardroom table because of a $100 million loss. The firm's star trader, McGann, fully expects to take over Slater's spot, but is chagrined when the higher-ups bring in a shapely comer from America (DeMornay) instead. Hotshot McGann already has a full load of woes: his girl friend has dumped him in disgust at his careerism ("Can't you see what happened? A man kills himself. What for?!"), and his best friend, O'Connor, has been fired by Whitney Paine. McGann at first sets about trying to undo DeMornay by hiring a paparazzo to snap pictures of her after-hours networking activities with various bosses in cars, but—as inevitably as the morning bell rings to start the day's commerce—McGann and his professional adversary soon begin a wary

Paul McGann, Nicholas Hewetson, and Rebecca DeMornay in DEALERS (©Rank).

romance. McGann woos DeMornay with dinners at his little castle in Kent and rides in his private seaplane, and takes O'Connor under his wing as well, trying to help his friend kick the coke and booze that caused his downfall. This proves to be a lost cause, however, and O'Connor goes to the big investment firm in the sky. McGann follows in his daredevil footsteps by doubling the risks in trading treasury bills, and as the film reaches its climax, McGann's anxious fellow traders huddle around doom-saying computer screens, with $200 million and McGann's job hanging in the balance. Eventually, McGann's daring pays off, but only after he makes the self-transforming discovery that a yuppie's soulless life is not all it's cracked up to be.

Why should we care? With the exception of the somewhat sympathetic O'Connor (who gets to hurl a computer through a glass office wall), the characters in this ultraslick and empty film are all avaricious, career-crazed ciphers. Director Colin Bucksey and screenwriter Andrew MacLear have tried to concoct a businessman's martini of a movie, dry and acerbic, but the results are wholly lacking in the bracing rewards of that libation, with any number of stale, flat lines. (A typical exchange between one character and his discontented inamorata: "We've put a lot

into this." "What have we got?" "We've been to Uruguay." And then there's DeMornay's supposedly irresistible rallying cry: "Let's make money.") Works like WALL STREET; WORKING GIRL; and Caryl Churchill's play "Serious Money" have just about exhausted whatever potential for excitement lay in the spectacle of high-finance chicanery anyway, and DEALERS reinvestigates the territory with such formulaic and deadening solemnity that any further opportunities for satire or genuine insight are lost. Especially frustrating (and dull) is the film's cliche-plagued ending, with its last-minute change of heart by the hero—surely the most exhausted dramatic ploy imaginable.

Rebecca DeMornay's character in DEALERS sets the screen image of the modern American professional woman back decades, an image for which Katharine Hepburn with apparent effortlessness provided the archetype. In place of intelligence, DeMornay (RISKY BUSINESS; the remake of AND GOD CREATED WOMAN) brings a rapid-fire facility to her meaningless lines; in place of sexiness, she gives us obviousness—in scene after scene. DEALERS achieves some kind of high point in laughableness when DeMornay, charmed by McGann's having festooned her apartment with balloons (a trick lifted from the Joel McCrea-Constance Bennett romance in George Cukor's ROCKABYE [1932]), gives herself to him on the hallway's floor. It's a sad commentary on how little women's film roles have progressed that DeMornay enacts these sorts of high-jinks with far more ease and ability than she does the brainier aspects of the part. As DeMornay writhes in her obligatory black detachable lingerie, one can only conclude that DEALERS is really more concerned with such frisky business than with business ethics.

Etruscan-profiled Paul McGann, who proved his talent in WITHNAIL AND I, cannot overcome the repellent quality in his character here. He's all too easy to withstand as a hero; in place of the suave wit and solidity embodied by Hepburn's male counterparts Cary Grant and Spencer Tracy, McGann can only manage a shrill intensity in delivering lines like "This market has to turn! I hate this market!" Have movies reached the 1990s only to hold career success as the highest of romantic attributes?

The rest of the cast is wasted in cookie-cutter, corporate-stereotype roles—with the unfortunate exception of Sara Sugarman, who, as a punky, loudmouth trader, comes across as an inferior British version of Julie Kavner. Songs include: "Corporate World," "Where Is Your Love" (Gail Ann Dorsey, performed by Dorsey), "Doing the Creepers" (Richard Hartley, Chass D.C. Scarlett, performed by Scarlett). *(Profanity, substance abuse, adult situations, sexual situations.)*

p, William P. Cartlidge; d, Colin Bucksey; w, Andrew MacLear; ph, Peter Sinclair (Rank Color); ed, Jon Costelloe; m, Richard Hartley; prod d, Peter J. Hampton; art d, Ken Wheatley; set d, Stephanie McMillan; cos, Dizzy Downs; makeup, Beryl Lerman.

Drama   **(PR:O MPAA:R)**

⊘DEATHSTALKER AND THE WARRIORS FROM HELL*½
86m Triana-New Classics/Concorde c
John Allen Nelson *(Deathstalker)*, Carla Herd *(Princess Carissa/Princess Elezena)*, Terri Treas *(Camisarde)*, Thom Christopher *(Troxartas)*, Aaron Hernan *(Nicias)*, Roger Cudney *(Inares)*, Agustin Salvat *(Makut)*, Claudia Inchaurregui *(Marinda)*.

Deathstalker continues his free-wheeling adventures (begun in 1984's THE DEATHSTALKER and continued in 1988's DEATHSTALKER II) in this inconsequential odyssey, involving some occult mumbo-jumbo by which unlimited powers are granted to the owner of three magical stones joined together. Naturally, everyone wandering through the film's mythical landscape—including Nelson, who plays the eponymous Deathstalker—

is trying to get their hands on the three talismans. At a fair, Nelson observes the carnival's star attraction, Hernan, a whimsical wizard who can predict the future. Herd, a mysterious princess, insists that Hernan has the twin stone to her fabled amulet, but their conversation is cut short by troops of bad guys who storm the peaceful fair. In the melee, Hernan magically blows himself up (for the time being). Nelson rescues Herd, who confides in him and tells him about her royal quest to find a Treasure City with enough riches to feed her nomadic people. The princess is subsequently killed, but not before she gives Nelson her supernatural stone. Years later, Nelson spots a woman who's a dead ringer for the late lamented princess. In fact, she's the princess' twin, but unlike her dead sibling, the sister-princess (also played by Herd) is a selfish airhead. She's en route to marry Christopher, who covets the magical amulets and whose plans for world conquest include raising the dead. After a brush with Christopher's soldiers, Nelson is befriended by a forest-dwelling amazon and her daughter, Inchaurregui. The latter beds our hero and enables him to elude capture once more, but Nelson abandons his deflowered forest cutie and meets up again with Herd. Meanwhile, back at his palace, Christopher rants and raves to his mistress (Treas) about his mission to collect all the magic gems. In fact, he only means to marry Herd because he wants a talisman he thinks is in her possession (but which her twin, in fact, gave Nelson long ago.) Later, Nelson discovers that one of Christopher's henchmen is a warrior Nelson once slew, and hence a prime exhibit of Christopher's talent for raising the dead. While Christopher encounters some hitches in his plan to retrieve all the land's magical talismans, Herd prepares for her wedding, refusing to believe Nelson when he tells her that the groom-to-be killed her twin sister. Treas subsequently captures Nelson and tortures him, but he cleverly escapes. Meanwhile, Christopher tries to retrieve the missing stone from Hernan, the magician having been summoned through Christopher's resuscitative powers. Scouting the castle, Nelson bumps into tag-along Inchaurregui and encounters an array of Living Dead resurrected soldiers, whom he recruits to his cause by promising to return their souls to them. Before long, Nelson manages to get his hands on two of the talismans and a major battle ensues. During the fray (in which Nelson is aided by rebellious peasants and the Living Dead troops), Nelson accidentally grabs the third magical stone, nearly gets killed, and slays Christopher (though only after the loyal Inchaurregui has sacrificed her life for her seducer). Putting all three stones together, Hernan summons up the Treasure City for the new, mature, chastised Herd. Perennial bachelor Nelson departs

without succumbing to the lures of Herd or of riches, presumably to prepare for another "Deathstalker" sequel.

Movies like this generally succeed as undemanding diversions or as unintentionally hilarious camp; only a handful of mythical adventure films (JASON AND THE ARGONAUTS or the Kirk Douglas ULYSSES are two examples) can be rated as serious action-film escapism. Despite its tongue-in-cheek tone and incessant sexual innuendos, however, DEATHSTALKER AND THE WARRIORS FROM HELL doesn't have the imagination to succeed as a spoof, and it's too run-of-the-mill in other respects to work as camp. Having failed as both deliberate parody and as campfest, DEATHSTALKER AND THE WARRIORS FROM HELL emerges as just another arrow-whizzing, sword-clanging adventure film, but it's still below par, weakened by a wholly derivative storyline.

Of the large and mediocre cast, only Terri Treas demonstrates any panache. Carla Herd, in the dual-princess role, exhibits the range of a beauty contestant placing last in the talent competition. Handsome, wiry John Allen Nelson seems more like a slimmer, younger brother of Steve Reeves than a true beefcake star; only if DEATHSTALKER AND THE WARRIORS FROM HELL took place on a southern California beach overrun by villainous surfers could the sun-kissed Nelson be considered a heroic presence. The film takes its cue from its star—inoffensive and insubstantial, DEATHSTALKER AND THE WARRIORS FROM HELL figuratively and literally lacks the muscle required for gladiatorial action flicks. If you must see the film, think of it as "Andy Hardy Dresses Up as Hercules" or "Gold's Gym Neophyte Goes Mythical." *(Violence, nudity, sexual situations.)*

p, Alfonso Corona and Antonio De Noriega; d, Alfonso Corona; w, Howard R. Cohen; ph, Xavier Cruz; m, Israel Torres and Alejandro Rulfo; art d, Francisco Magallon.

Adventure/Fantasy   **(PR:C MPAA:R)**

⊘DEEPSTAR SIX**
100m Carolco/Tri-Star c
Taurean Blacque *(Laidlaw)*, Nancy Everhard *(Joyce Collins)*, Greg Evigan *(McBride)*, Miguel Ferrer *(Snyder)*, Nia Peeples *(Scarpelli)*, Matt McCoy *(Richardson)*, Cindy Pickett *(Diane Norris)*, Marius Weyers *(Van Gelder)*, Elya Baskin *(Burciaga)*, Thom Bray *(Hodges)*, Ronn Carroll *(Osborne)*.

Produced and directed by Sean S. Cunningham, creator of the sequel-spawning FRIDAY THE 13TH and "House" film series, DEEPSTAR SIX is set in the not-too-distant future against a backdrop of advanced undersea technology. In a submarine laboratory many miles below the

Marius Weyers in DEEPSTAR SIX
(© Tri-Star).

surface, a team of scientists and Naval personnel is nearing the end of a six-month project to install the first underwater missile base, as well as study the feasibility of an undersea colony. The dozen men and women, already suffering from their claustrophobic living and working conditions, are subjected to further pressure when they learn that their military funding will be cut off if the missiles are not placed in their submerged silos within a week. When it is discovered that the storage site is actually a thin layer of ocean floor, below which lies a cavern of unknown depth and size, project head Weyers dispenses with caution and orders the thin layer destroyed by explosives. Although Peeples, a skeptical scientist, cites a long list of strange sonar soundings and unexplained disappearances in the vicinity dating back hundreds of years, Weyers insists that the demolition proceed immediately. From the depths of the cavern emerges a huge, fast-moving, deadly sea monster. After quickly dispatching the two demolition men in their mini-sub, the behemoth heads straight for the submarine lab and its unwary occupants, proceeding to do away with them one by one. Within the sub, the cabin fever affecting the team has taken its most devastating toll on radioman-technician Ferrer. When ordered to follow procedure in protecting the sub from the monster's attacks, he misreads the handbook and

mistakenly fires a 50-megaton missile, effectively crippling the vessel. Paranoid and panicky, he accidentally kills Weyers and, without benefit of a trip to the decompression chamber, takes off in one of the two remaining mini-subs, in which he virtually implodes minutes later. The eventual survivors are laid-back Navy honcho Evigan and super-scientist Everhard, whose love story is woven through the action.

About 10 minutes into DEEPSTAR SIX, it becomes clear that the film is yet another uninspired variation of ALIEN. The mechanical screenplay and flat direction fail to build suspense, and the characters are routinely drawn. While the technical work, relying heavily on miniatures, is competent, the rendering of the monster—which does not appear until the middle of the film and is seen only in quick glimpses thereafter—is hardly worth the wait. An amorphous, elephant-skinned creature with tusks lining its two huge front flaps, it is seen only head on and never in a long shot.

If ALIEN was indeed this film's model, screenwriters Lewis Abernathy and Geof Miller would have been wise to follow its lead in eschewing romantic interludes between action scenes. That the lovers are to be the sole survivors (Everhard is pregnant) is obvious early on, exacerbating an already predictable story line. With the exceptions of Miguel Ferrer, who transforms his Snyder from a hassled technician into an hysterical psychotic with admirable style, and Cindy Pickett, quietly effective as a no-nonsense scientist, the acting is strictly standard. As derivative as it is, the idea of DEEPSTAR SIX had the potential to generate a fair amount of suspense and surprise, but the by-the-numbers storytelling and unimaginative production place it squarely in the realm of the mediocre. Cunningham's track record notwithstanding, a DEEPSTAR SIX II seems highly unlikely. *(Violence, profanity, brief nudity.)*

p, Sean S. Cunningham and Patrick Markey; d, Sean S. Cunningham; w, Lewis Abernathy and Geof Miller (based on a story by Lewis Abernathy); ph, Mac Ahlberg (Metrocolor); ed, David Handman; m, Harry Manfredini; prod d, John Reinhart; art d, Larry Fulton and Don Diers; set d, Scott Herbertson; spec eff, Mark Shostrom; cos, Amy Endries; stunts, Kane Hodder.

Horror/Science Fiction

(PR:C   MPAA:R)

ⓥDISORGANIZED CRIME*½
99m Touchstone-Silver Screen Partners IV/BV c

Hoyt Axton *(Sheriff Henault)*, Corbin Bernsen *(Frank Salazar)*, Ruben Blades *(Carlos Barrios)*, Fred Gwynne *(Max Green)*, Ed O'Neill *(George Denver)*, Lou

Diamond Phillips *(Ray Forgy)*, Daniel Roebuck *(Bill Lonigan)*, William Russ *(Nick Bartkowski)*, Marie Butler Kouf *(Wanda Brem)*, Gregory Wurster *(Deputy Greg)*, Patrick Collins *(Deputy Monroe)*, Mitch Carter *(Deputy Larry)*, Dean Norris *(Deputy Joe)*, Thomas Schellenberg *(Deputy Jim)*, Robert Feldmann *(Dispatcher)*, David Hart *(Proprietor)*, Jeff Duus *(Stock Truck Driver)*, Noah Keen *(Farmer)*, Marie Stelin *(Farmer's Wife)*, Dena Dietrich *(Judge D. Greenwalt)*, Monica Rapalli *(Young Girl (Gina))*, John Oblinger *(Store Owner)*.

More tedious fluff from Touchstone, DISORGANIZED CRIME is a banal, wholly forgettable caper movie that attempts to be an entertaining blend of crime and comedy, but is crippled by a stupefying lack of originality. Squandering a likable cast, the film is set in Montana and introduces us to Bernsen, a small-time hood planning the robbery of the local bank. After casing the joint and jotting down a plan of attack, Bernsen sends letters to a number of cohorts telling them where and when to gather. Shortly thereafter, he is arrested by two bumbling New Jersey cops (O'Neill and Roebuck), who plan to extradite him to the Garden State. Bernsen outwits his dim captors, however, and manages to escape, only to face a long walk through the wilderness to his hideout. Meanwhile, the gang arrives. Gwynne, the oldest of the bunch, is an explosives expert; Blades a vain and stylish thief; Russ a rather unbalanced safecracker; and Phillips a young getaway driver. When they arrive at Bernsen's remote shack, they find him missing, and while they wait for his return, rivalries erupt among the gang members, leading the nervous Russ to split with the getaway car. An infuriated Blades gives chase on foot, only to find that Russ has crashed the car and been arrested. In the meantime, Gwynne discovers Bernsen's plans for the heist and decides that they can do the job without him but not without Russ, so they rob a few local stores to raise his bail. With the gang intact, the heist is carried out as planned, though both local sheriff Axton and the bumbling Jersey cops—who think the robbery is being committed by Bernsen—are hot on the trail. At the same time, Bernsen is still stumbling through the woods toward his shack. Overcoming the usual tension-filled obstacles, the gang gets the loot and beats the cops to the hideout, where they change cars and zoom off. Unbeknownst to them, the exhausted Bernsen has finally made it back to the hideout and fallen asleep inside. When the cops arrive, they find Bernsen and arrest the confused fugitive for a robbery he didn't commit. When Bernsen's comrades learn that he has been nabbed for their robbery, they nobly decide to return to the town and use their newly acquired loot to post bail for their pal.

Originally titled "Waiting for Salazar" but burdened with a bland generic moniker by the Touchstone marketing people, the script by director Jim Kouf, author of STAKEOUT, certainly had potential, but it doesn't appear as if it was developed past the "concept" stage. The situation is routine, the characters are stereotypes, the action is dull, and the jokes stale. Perhaps if the script had been directed by someone who knew how to infuse familiar material with at least a spark of vitality, the project might have been salvaged. Unfortunately, as a director Kouf is clueless when it comes to pacing, timing, rhythm, and developing characters—either comedic or action-oriented. As a result we are subjected to a hackneyed concept presented as efficiently as possible with absolutely no personality. Nonetheless, one might expect that the competent cast assembled here would at least provide a little inspired mugging; instead we are presented with several dull performances (by Bernsen, Russ, Gwynne, and Phillips), a somewhat energetic one (Blades), and two that are awful, numbing, and over-the-top (O'Neill and Roebuck). Worse yet, the film disintegrates into a series of decrepit sight gags designed to evoke cheap laughs, including O'Neill running around in his underwear, and the crooks sliding around in a truckbed full of pig dung (this *joke* is used several times). Touchstone has been grinding out this sort of cheap, inane, sub made-for-television junk for years and has been turning a handsome profit doing it. DISORGANIZED CRIME, however, bombed at the box office and perhaps the powers that be at Touchstone may see this as a signal to stop churning out vapid formulaic movies and concentrate on material a little more innovative and adult. On second thought, they probably won't. *(Violence, profanity.)*

p, Lynn Bigelow; d, Jim Kouf; w, Jim Kouf; ph, Ron Garcia (Metrocolor); ed, Frank Morriss and Dallas Puett; m, David Newman; prod d, Waldemar Kalinowski; art d, David Lubin; set d, Florence Fellman; spec eff, Burt Dalton; cos, Stephanie Maslansky; stunts, Dan Bradley; makeup, Joann Wabisca.

Comedy/Crime   (PR:C   MPAA:R)

⊙DISTANT VOICES, STILL LIVES***½
(Brit.) 85m BFI-Film Four International-Channel Four-ZDF c
Freda Dowie *(Mother)*, Pete Postlethwaite *(Father)*, Angela Walsh *(Eileen)*, Lorraine Ashbourne *(Maisie)*, Dean Williams *(Tony)*, Sally Davies *(Eileen as a child)*, Nathan Walsh *(Tony as a child)*, Susan Flanagan *(Maisie as a Child)*, Michael Starke *(Dave)*, Vincent MaGuire *(George)*, Antonia Mallen *(Rose)*, Debi Jones *(Micky)*, Chris Darwin *(Red)*, Marie Jelliman *(Jingles)*, Andrew Schofield *(Les)*, Anny Dyson *(Granny)*, Jean Boht *(Aunty Nell)*, Alan Bird *(Baptismal Priest)*, Pauline Quirke *(Doreen)*, Matthew Long *(Mr. Spaull)*, Frances Dell *(Margie)*, Carl Chase *(Uncle Ted)*, Roy Ford *(Wedding Priest)*, Terry Melia *(Military Policemen)*, John Carr *(Registrar)*, John Michie *(Soldier)*, Jeanette Moseley *(Barmaid)*, Ina Clough *(Licensee)*, Chris Benson, Judith Barker, Tom Williamson, Lorraine Michaels *(Rose's Family)*.

Part nostalgia, part nightmare, the autobiographical DISTANT VOICES, STILL LIVES is writer-director Terence Davies' bittersweet look back at his working-class upbringing in postwar Liverpool. His past is an interesting place to visit, but you wouldn't want to live there.

To set the mood, no primary colors are used on-screen. Like a canvas gradually modulated with somber brown hues, dusky images emerge at random to reveal a stark, haunting picture of the England of the have-nots. But while it's beautifully photographed, Davies' portrait of a house divided by a near-psychotic father—loving one moment, brutal the next—is not a pretty sight. All of the familial warts and blemishes are visible; Davies avoids romanticizing the past in any way. In this highly stylized, cinematic portrait of his family, there are no enhancements. No glitz. Not even much of a plot. Rather, Davies leaves us with a series of impressions, presented non-chronologically, that evoke memories of his basically repressive Catholic childhood in the 1950s.

Father (Postlethwaite) is an abusive tyrant. "Why did you marry him, Mum?" a daughter asks after one of his typical, inexplicably violent outbursts. "He was a good dancer," she replies matter-of-factly. Dowie, the ever-accepting mother, never considers challenging her husband's irrational actions. But his often brutal behavior alienates the three children, resulting in a running love-hate relationship that continues long after his death. Told in flashback, the film begins and ends with family weddings held several years apart. On the morning of the first, elder daughter Walsh wishes her dad were there. This in turn triggers the children's memories of him, and of his mostly negative influence upon their lives. Walsh remembers him slapping her face when she was late getting to the air raid shelter, then forcing her to sing "Roll out the Barrel" as an act of contrition. Her sister (Ashbourne) remembers a beating he gave her when she needed money to go to a dance. And their brother (Williams) recalls Postlethwaite's lack of affection for him through the years: his callousness and indifference when Williams joined the army; his locking his young son out of the house, forcing him to stay on the streets overnight. Vignettes like these, wisps of memory—some painful, some not—continue throughout the film. As the children and their nucleus of friends get older, marry, and have kids of their own, their lives come full circle. They are seen replicating the same dreary patterns, the same male-dominant, unsatisfactory relationships that typified traditional working-class upbringing during the postwar years.

Theirs is an often dour, Dickensian world updated to the mid-20th century. But through it all, the family keeps a proverbial stiff upper lip and their sense of humor intact. Their pleasures, simple as they may be, are found in downing a pint at the local pub, or gleefully belting out the tunes of the day at the slightest provocation. It's as if people could actually sing away their woe when they feel rotten, just as it says in the lyric from "Bye Bye Blackbird," one of many popular songs of the era interspersed throughout the film. Despite Davies' often harsh, brutal focus, this is no gloom-and-doom period piece. Remarkably, all his sensitively drawn, subtle observations coalesce, forming an emotionally compelling whole that visually and vividly recalls a traditional way of life that, for the most part, is long gone.

DISTANT VOICES, STILL LIVES is a strangely appealing film; it's also a strangely constructed one that began as a British Film Institute-financed 45-minute short. Although the powers that be at the BFI were delighted with that film, DISTANT VOICES, and determined that it be expanded to feature length, they were unable to provide additional financing, so Davies turned instead to British (Channel 4) and West German (ZDF) television for funding. It then took him nearly two years to write his minutely detailed screenplay for STILL LIVES, the second half of the film, shot with the same actors, whose noticeably older, and in some cases chunkier, appearances add verisimilitude to the time that passes between the film's two distinctly divided sections. Significantly, the characters they play are nevertheless none the wiser, as Davies seemingly strives to recapture the essence of his family's unchanging ways, to preserve for posterity their still lives.

Davies has said of the film that it's "not what happens next—it's what happens next emotionally that's important." Static as their lives may be, his people are never dull. In this very personal portrait, Davies, the artist, has re-created universal experiences—familiar passions and needs—that draw us to his family's humanity. *(Adult situations, violence.)*

p, Jennifer Howarth; d, Terence Davies; w, Terence Davies; ph, William Diver and Patrick Duval; ed, William Diver; art d, Miki van Zwanenberg and Jocelyn James; spec eff, Richard Roberts; cos, Monica Howe; stunts, Alf Joint.

Drama   (PR:C   MPAA:PG-13)

DO THE RIGHT THING
(See THE YEAR'S BEST)

Ⓥ**DR. ALIEN** zero
87m Phantom c
Billy Jacoby *(Wesley Littlejohn)*, Judy Landers *(Ms. Xenobia)*, Olivia Barash *(Leeanne)*, Stuart Fratkin *(Marvin)*, Raymond O'Connor *(Drax)*, Arlene Golonka *(Mom)*, Jim Hackett *(Dad)*, Bobby Jacoby *(Bradford Littlejohn)*, Julie Gray *(Karla)*, Scott Morris *(Dirk)*, Troy Donahue *(Dr. Ackerman)*, Tom De Franco, Linnea Quigley, Michelle Bauer, Edy Williams, Elizabeth Kaitan.

Wesley Littlejohn (Jacoby) is such a good boy. He wears ties and vests to school, parts his hair neatly on the side, does all his homework, and never goes out with girls. In other words, Wesley is a nerd. One day, a gorgeous substitute teacher walks into his biology class clad in tight clothes and high heels. While the rest of the students drool in awe, Wesley is unimpressed—until, that is, Ms. Xenobia (Landers) selects him for some extra-credit research after school. Wesley goes to Ms. Xenobia's lab; her assistant, Drax (O'Connor), jabs a needle into his rear; and Wesley is a changed boy. A kind of seizure overcomes him, after which a fleshy antenna emerges from the top of his head, causing Ms. Xenobia, suddenly overcome with passion, to jump on Wesley and introduce him to manhood. This scenario repeats itself several times over the next couple of weeks, but Ms. Xenobia is not the only victim of the amorous appendage. Unbeknownst to its bearer, it shows itself to a number of pretty girls and, once they catch a glimpse of the strange growth, watch out Wesley! He becomes temporarily irresistible to any woman except the one he really cares for, Leeanne (Barash). And not only is Wesley hot as a pistol sexually, he also loses his goody-two-shoes image. He now dresses and acts cool, and becomes the singer in a rock'n'roll band, the Sex Mutants—none of which impresses sweet Leeanne, who just wants someone to be nice to her. Eventually, the truth about Ms. Xenobia is revealed when she removes her head, showing herself to be an ET-like alien who has come to Earth to test a serum designed to perpetuate her dying species. Wesley just happened to be her lucky guinea pig.

For all its gratuitous soft-core sex, DR. ALIEN is for the most part dull. Much of the film is merely an excuse for displaying Judy Landers and several other attractive women in sexy lingerie, but the effect falls flat because of Dave DeCoteau's meandering direction. Though apparently striving for tongue-in-cheek humor, DR. ALIEN's mix of science fiction and teen sex comedy is simply and consistently boring. *(Nudity, adult situations, sexual situations.)*

p, Dave DeCoteau and John Schouweiler; d, Dave DeCoteau; w, Kenneth J. Hall; ph, Nicholas Von Sternberg; ed, Tony Malanowski; m, Reg Purcell and Sam Winans; prod d, Royce Mathew; makeup, Greg Cannom Creations.

Comedy/Science Fiction

                                    (PR:O   MPAA:R)

Ⓥ**DR. HACKENSTEIN***½
88m Feifer-Miller/Vista Street c
David Muir *(Dr. Elliot Hackenstein)*, Stacey Travis *(Melanie Victor)*, Catherine Davis Cox *(Leslie)*, Dyanne DiRosario *(Wendy)*, John Alexis *(Alex)*, Catherine Cahn *(Yolanda)*, Sylvia Lee Baker *(Dr. Hackenstein's Wife)*, Anne Ramsey, Logan Ramsey *(Graverobbers)*, William Schreiner, Jeff Rector, Phyllis Diller, Michael Ensign.

The producers of DR. HACKENSTEIN aspired to bring another YOUNG FRANKENSTEIN to the screen but lacked the imagination and actors to come up with anything nearly as enjoyable as Mel Brooks' spoof of the Frankenstein legend. In this version, set in 1912, the mad doctor (Muir) is searching for a way to bring his beloved wife back to life. He has already succeeded in reviving a rat, and as he works to adapt the process for a human subject, he realizes that his wife's remains—namely her head, which speaks to him—are disintegrating rapidly. He vows to find the necessary body parts for her soon, but receives no assistance from the grave-robbing duo (Anne and Logan Ramsey) he employs, since they bring him a man's body. However, potential limbs do appear in the form of three young women whose car breaks down near the doctor's home. He invites them to spend the night. Two of the women, DiRosario and Cox, awaken separately during the night to prowl the house, and end up victims of the doctor's hacksaw. Using DiRosario's legs and Cox's hands, Muir reconstructs his wife. Later, after trapping the third woman (Travis) in his lab, he tries to remove her eyes—the last piece missing from his wife's anatomy. As Muir and Travis struggle, a detective—hired to look for the young women—breaks into the lab and poisons the doctor. As Muir lies dying, his eyeless wife (Baker) awakens and runs off into a nearby field. The doctor then leaps out of the window and chases after her. The two disappear forever.

DR. HACKENSTEIN could be a lot worse, considering that it is part slasher film and part teen sex comedy—two genres that tend to run low on taste and brains. It's an unfunny comedy and a not particularly scary horror film, but that's pretty much the worst you can say about it. Unfortunately, you also can't say anything better about it. The late Anne Ramsey, an Oscar nominee for 1987's THROW

MOMMA FROM THE TRAIN, and TV stalwart Phyllis Diller were the best the filmmakers could come up with for "big-name" comediennes. But then DR. HACKENSTEIN is low-budget all around —from the writing, to the acting, to the sets—so what do you expect? The gore in the film is nearly nonexistent; Dr. Hackenstein fervidly saws away at his female victim, but only he and little spurts of blood are shown. Later the stitched-together bodies are shown, which will startle only those who are repulsed by scars.

The running gag in DR. HACKENSTEIN revolves around Catherine Cahn, who plays the deaf-mute maid. Her ignorance of the fight between the doctor and one of the girls, which takes place steps away from the servant, is probably the only thing in the movie that may force a smile. Basically, DR. HACKENSTEIN just chugs along to its convoluted ending, which could come about an hour earlier— had the doctor just taken all the necessary body parts from his first victim. Why does he need three different women? That says it all for DR. HACKENSTEIN; the entire story progresses from a lapse in logic. *(Nudity, adult situations.)*

p, Reza Mizbani and Megan Barnett; d, Richard Clark; w, Richard Clark; ph, Jens Sturup; ed, Tony Miller; m, Randy Miller; prod d, Leon King; art d, Craig Voigt.

Comedy/Horror   **(PR:C   MPAA:R)**

Ⓥ**DOIN' TIME ON PLANET EARTH****
85m Golan-Globus/Cannon c
Nicholas Strouse *(Ryan Richmond)*, Hugh Gillin *(Fred Richmond)*, Gloria Henry *(Mary Richmond)*, Hugh O'Brian *(Richard Camalier)*, Martha Scott *(Virginia Camalier)*, Timothy Patrick Murphy *(Jeff Richmond)*, Isabelle Walker *(Jenny Camalier)*, Paula Irvine *(Marilyn Richmond)*, Andrea Thompson *(Lisa Winston)*, Adam West *(Charles Pinaky)*, Candice Azzara *(Edna Pinaky)*.

A shaggy space comedy that never quite hits the heights of hilarity, DOIN' TIME ON PLANET EARTH stars Strouse as its teenage hero, to whose strangeness a procession of friends, relatives, and acquaintances testify during the opening credit sequence. Although the testimonials give the impression he's seriously eccentric, Strouse turns out to be an offbeat teenage dreamer who's only slightly out of step with the rest of the small, decidedly strange, community of Sunnyvale, Arizona (touted as the "Prune Capital of the World"). The town's centerpiece is a high-tech Holiday Inn, owned by Strouse's dad (Gillin), that boasts a revolving rooftop restaurant. As the film opens, Strouse's brother (Murphy) is about to marry Walker, the daughter of a defeated presidential candidate (O'Brian). Though he lacks a date for the wedding, Strouse shuns the girls at his high school (who are none too fond of him, either), pining instead for Thompson, the spectacularly untalented singer who performs regularly (constantly, actually) at his dad's rooftop lounge. But she won't give him the time of day, much less a date. With the wedding day fast approaching and Thompson showing no signs of defrosting, Strouse turns for help to a computer dating service accessed through his home PC. After Strouse answers some increasingly weird questions on the service application, the service informs him that he is actually an extra-terrestrial stranded on Earth. Responding to Strouse's completed "application" are West and Azzara, an ET couple who roam the countryside in a vintage bus. According to this alien twosome, the Holiday Inn's revolving restaurant is actually their space vehicle, and Strouse is destined to be its navigator. West and Azzara believe that the information to guide them home is stored in a DNA packet implanted in Strouse's brain, though this information can only be released, or "exploded," by some kind of trauma. After punching out a tormenting jock and clipping the ponytail of the girl who sits in front of him in class fail to do this trick, Strouse resorts to visiting Thompson, whose estimation of him has risen because of his association with West and Azzara—who really *are* seriously eccentric. Strouse tells Thompson that only by losing his virginity to her can he make his DNA packet explode, and though Thompson doesn't really buy it, she appreciates the novelty of his seductive approach. Sure enough, the DNA packet explodes while the pair are making love, and Strouse at once envisions the space destination. Having finally gained the attentions of his beloved Thompson, however, Strouse begins to feel that life on Earth isn't so bad after all.

At first glance, DOIN' TIME ON PLANET EARTH has the marks of a Hollywood vanity production. Debuting director Charles Matthau dutifully thanks his parents (Mr. and Mrs. Walter Matthau) in the credits, along with Elliott Gould and other screen notables. Folks like Maureen Stapleton and Roddy McDowall drop in for brief, uncredited cameos, while Hugh O'Brian and Adam ("Batman") West figure more prominently in the low-budget ($3 million) proceedings. Yet DOIN' TIME is neither as amateurish nor as self-indulgent as show-biz family affairs often tend to be. It's a reasonably entertaining, breezily paced (if unevenly scripted) confection for the eye and ear whose main flaw is that its makers neglected to place its characters and situations in a crisp comic focus, and worked to establish an other-worldly mood and spacy tone instead. As a result, DOIN' TIME too closely recalls too many other ultrahip, surreal satires of

recent years, ranging from the works of David Lynch and David Byrne (TRUE STORIES) to Julien Temple's strikingly similar EARTH GIRLS ARE EASY.

Still, the cast is attractive, capable, and spirited under Matthau's direction— which, though derivative, betrays enough talent and flair to bode well for his future, if not on the big screen, then certainly in television. As time-passers go, there are infinitely worse films lurking on video store shelves than DOIN' TIME ON PLANET EARTH. *(Adult situations, profanity.)*

p, Menahem Golan and Yoram Globus; d, Charles Matthau; w, Darren Star (based on a story by Darren Star, Andrew Licht, Jeffrey A. Mueller); ph, Timothy Suhrstedt (TVC Color); ed, Alan Balsam and Sharyn L. Ross; m, Dana Kaproff; prod d, Curtis A. Schnell; art d, Colin D. Irwin; set d, Douglas A. Mowat; spec eff, Bill Millar; cos, Reve Richards.

Comedy **(PR:C MPAA:PG)**

DOWN TWISTED*½
97m Golan-Globus/Cannon c

Carey Lowell *(Maxine)*, Charles Rocket *(Reno)*, Trudi Dochtermann *(Michelle)*, Thom Mathews *(Damalas)*, Norbert Weisser *(Deltoid)*, Linda Kerridge *(Soames)*, Nicholas Guest *(Brady)*, Gaylyn Gorg *(Blake)*.

Caper movies rely on star performances (or at least on actors who have magnetic presences) to help them coast over improbabilities in their storylines. When unsuitably cast, a run-of-the-mill suspense movie leaves viewers questioning the actors' every move. DOWN TWISTED gives rise to many questions and little entertainment.

Weisser, a business tycoon and unscrupulous art collector, plots the perfect theft of a priceless religious artifact from San Lucas, a hotbed of intrigue in Central or South America. Unfortunately, a few of the thieves he's hired to replace the real religious crucible with a flawlessly executed duplicate plan a double cross. When Guest, the pilot, holds out on his pals, they send him sailing through a window. Wandering innocently into this maze of dishonor among thieves is Lowell, a wide-eyed lass from southern California who makes the near-fatal mistake of helping her neurotically selfish roommate, Dochtermann, the girl friend of the defenestrated crook. When Lowell accompanies her high-strung friend on a supposed drug deal, she watches in horror as Dochtermann is killed in a car explosion. In an indoor garage, Rocket, a bystander, gets involved when Weisser's cut-throat band (Mathews, Kerridge, and Gorg) pursues Lowell. Eventually, apprehended and drugged, Lowell wakes up on a slow boat to San Lucas with the shifty

Rocket, who insists she give the criminals the information they so desperately want. Protesting her ignorance of the missing artifact, she escapes with Rocket and swims to the mainland. As Weisser frets about being caught by the local government because the famous crucible will be prominently displayed during an imminent religious festival, Rocket and Lowell keep one step ahead of the three relic-robbers. When Mathews, a sadistic albino, catches up with them, Lowell learns that Rocket is really a gang member who was supposed to gain her confidence. To increase his share of the take, Mathews calmly murders Gorg; he and Rocket then trail Lowell. During a chase through a religious procession, Rocket is forced to kill Mathews and predictably realizes he's fallen for Lowell, who keeps whining about getting back to LA. Back at corporate headquarters, Weisser cuts a new deal with Kerridge, who vows to make Lowell spill her guts. To everyone's surprise, Dochtermann, having faked the car explosion, shows up and tells Rocket that Guest swallowed the sought-after key to the locker where the holy cache is hidden. After performing a makeshift autopsy, Rocket meets everyone at a terminal where Weisser pays millions for his stolen treasure, Dochtermann is seized, Kerridge is gunned down in a shootout, Rocket is arrested, and Lowell gets away with the cash. One final twist awaits Weisser before Lowell uses some of the ill-gotten gains to bribe guards to free Rocket, and the reunited lovers sail off into the sunset.

Despite the new wave look of the art direction and the new wave sound of the musical score, DOWN TWISTED is fairly old wave at heart. Director Albert Pyun brings no sense of urgency to the muddled double crosses, although he does have a talent for depicting violence. When a screenplay has this many twists in it, moviemakers have to make sure that audiences can keep track of later developments in order to insure a payoff; if not, a viewer is less likely to be surprised than to shrug and say, "Oh, I forgot about that!" In general, DOWN TWISTED disappoints: it fails to capitalize on the lush local color, and its editing lacks the razor-sharp precision required in a thriller. Where DOWN TWISTED really goes down for the count, however, is in the acting department. Not since BLUE CITY, in which Judd Nelson and Ally Sheedy do the sleuthing, has there been such a sorry display of unseasoned young performers playing genre dress-up games. To be blunt, you can't send Nancy Drew and one of the Hardy boys to do a grown-up's job.

If this weren't the kind of light thriller (like 39 STEPS or CHARADE) that depends on acting charisma, nitpicking wouldn't be in order. However, DOWN TWISTED needs all the zing a top-flight cast could provide. Instead, one gets the smugly self-satisfied Rocket, who can't even manage the lovable klutz part of his role, and who acts as if he were saving his energy for a better project. He's bad enough to make one long for Chevy Chase! Although much more appealing, Lowell demonstrates a slightly smirky technique that might have been learned at the Ali MacGraw Modeling School of Acting; the emotion she expresses is as thin as her voice. The reappearance of Trudi Dochtermann's Michelle is the one genuine surprise in DOWN TWISTED that's effective, but by the time she returns, the endless, enervating chase scenes and Rocket's narcissistic manner have worn down one's goodwill. As DOWN TWISTED twists and turns and twists some more, viewers may slump in their seats, check their watches, or half-heartedly recast the film in their heads. *(Graphic violence, profanity.)*

p, Menahem Golan and Yoram Globus; d, Albert Pyun; w, Gene O'Neill and Noreen Tobin (based on a story by Albert Pyun); ph, Walt Lloyd (TVC Color); ed, Dennis O'Connor; m, Berlin Game; prod d, Chester Kaczenski; art d, Richard Hummell and Douglas H. Leonard; cos, Renee Johnston.

Action/Thriller   (PR:O MPAA:R)

ⓥDREAM A LITTLE DREAM**
99m Vestron c
Corey Feldman *(Bobby Keller)*, Meredith Salenger *(Lainie Diamond)*, Jason Robards Jr. *(Coleman Ettinger)*, Piper Laurie *(Gene Ettinger)*, Harry Dean Stanton *(Ike Baker)*, William McNamara *(Joel)*, Corey Haim *(Dinger)*, Alex Rocco *(Gus Keller)*, Victoria Jackson *(Kit Keller)*, Susan Blakely *(Mrs. Diamond)*.

DREAM A LITTLE DREAM is the third in a string of two-Corey movies (Corey Feldman and Corey Haim also costarred in THE LOST BOYS and LICENSE TO DRIVE) and the umpteenth in a string of body-switching films (BIG; VICE VERSA; 18 AGAIN; LIKE FATHER, LIKE SON). This time around, Feldman and Robards constitute the unlikely pair of generational enemies who are reconciled by a personality transfusion. Robards plays Coleman Ettinger, a small-town eccentric who practices meditation and martial arts to ward off the direr consequences of aging. He passes the time quietly with his loving wife (Laurie) and looks for a psychic means to preserve their souls in more durable forms. His peace is disrupted by the unruly teenagers, including best friends Feldman and Haim, who make a habit of traipsing through his yard on their way to high school. One evening, Feldman and his dream girl, Salenger, are involved in a bicycle accident on Robards' lawn while Robards and Laurie are doing tai chi in the

moonlight. Finding he has a sudden liking for Frank Sinatra, "Feldman" discovers Robards' mind has entered his body and believes Salenger has undergone a similar transference vis a vis Laurie. The situation allows Feldman/Robards to spend a lot of time with his beloved Salenger/Laurie, but incurs disapproval from her mother and violence from her jealous boy friend. The problems are all resolved and the personality swap reversed during one long and eventful night.

For a romantic comedy, DREAM A LITTLE DREAM has few laughs and little tenderness, and mainly evokes confusion. The muddled storyline and inept execution raise questions like: What is the point of the mind-switching? Why doesn't Feldman act like he is older when Robards moves into his body? What endears Salenger to Feldman? Why is Harry Dean Stanton in this film? (He plays a neighbor who is always ready to lend an ear or give advice but never says anything important.) Why does Feldman stop washing his hair after the first half-hour? Who is this picture meant for? The plot of DREAM A LITTLE DREAM revolves too much around "old people" to interest teenagers and the teen characters are too unsightly to interest adults. (Thanks to ridiculous dye jobs and recycled clothing, Feldman's and Haim's looks here may put their teen-idol status in jeopardy.) The teens' parents are even more unlikable. Blakely, as Salenger's divorced mother, is insensitive to her daughter's concerns about sex and conspires with a boy friend to slip Salenger a sleeping pill when the girl wants to stay awake. Haim suffers a broken foot when his mother runs over it with her car; Jackson and Rocco, as Feldman's parents, are insulting caricatures—she's always in curlers, he's constantly eating.

DREAM A LITTLE DREAM was cowritten, produced, and directed by 25-year-old Marc Rocco, obviously a member of the MTV generation. A relentless soundtrack beats throughout the film, and the scenes cut quickly from one location to another in an attempt at "clever" editing that merely adds to the confused feel of the movie. However, the novice filmmakers behind DREAM A LITTLE DREAM did do one thing right in relying on the catchy title song (Gus Kahn, Wilbur Schwandt, Fabian Andre), the only memorable part of the movie, heard repeatedly as rendered by Mel Torme and in rock versions. Feldman dances to the tune in a meaningless scene midway through the film, then teams with Robards for a soft-shoe duet during the closing credits. The latter routine is the only entertaining part of DREAM A LITTLE DREAM, occurring much too late to make this convoluted affair worth watching. *(Profanity, substance abuse.)*

p, D.E. Eisenberg and Marc Rocco; d, Marc Rocco; w, Daniel Jay Franklin, Marc Rocco, and D.E. Eisenberg; ph, King Baggot (Foto-Kem Color); ed, Russell Livingstone; m, John William Dexter; prod d, Matthew Jacobs; cos, Kristine Brown.

Comedy   (PR:C MPAA:PG-13)

ⓥDREAM TEAM, THE***
113m Imagine/UNIV c
Michael Keaton *(Billy Caulfield)*, Christopher Lloyd *(Henry Sikorsky)*, Peter Boyle *(Jack McDermott)*, Stephen Furst *(Albert Ianuzzi)*, Dennis Boutsikaris *(Dr. Weitzman)*, Lorraine Bracco *(Riley)*, Milo O'Shea *(Dr. Newald)*, Philip Bosco *(O'Malley)*, James Remar *(Gianelli)*, Jack Gilpin *(Dr. Talmer)*, MacIntyre Dixon *(Dr. Verboven)*, Michael Lembeck *(Ed)*, Marilyn Peppiatt, Myra Fried *(Floor*

Michael Keaton, Stephen Furst, Christopher Lloyd, and Peter Boyle in THE DREAM TEAM (©Universal).

Nurses), J.R. Zimmerman *(Hospital Guard)*, Maxine Miller *(Newald's Secretary)*, Pat Idlette *(Woman at Police Station)*, Max Haines, Henry Gomez *(Guards)*, Ellen Maguire *(Canning's Secretary)*, Al Therrien, Don Saunders *(Security Guards)*, John Liddle *(Cop)*, Dwayne MacLean *(Old Gent)*, Kay Hawtrey, Patricia Carol Brown *(Nurses)*, Chick Roberts *(Old Guard)*, Nicholas Pasco *(Man Out Window)*, Jack Duffy *(Bernie)*, Brad Sullivan *(Sgt. Vincente)*, Larry Pine *(Canning)*, Harold Surratt *(Pastor Lester)*, The Frierson Family Singers *(Gospel Group)*, Kenneth Raybourne, Alphonsus E. Platt *(Gospel Musicians)*, Robert Weil *(Caesar)*, Janet Feindel *(Senior Nurce)*, Tico Wells *(Station Attendant)*, Barry Flatman *(Arrogant Yuppie)*, Ted Simonett, Bruce Hunter *(Yuppies)*, John Stocker *(Murray)*, Lizbeth MacKay *(Henry's Wife)*, Olivia Horton *(Henry's Daughter)*, Richard Fitzpatrick *(Dr. Bauer)*, Jack Jessop *(Dr. Meekum)*, Ron James *(Dwight)*, Dennis Parlato, Freda Foh Shen *(TV Newscasters)*, Donna Hanover, Greg Beresford *(Field Reporters)*, Wayne Tippit *(Capt. Lewitt)*, Eric Fink *(Priest)*, A. Frank Ruffo *(Relative)*, Michael Copeman *(Con Man Ed)*, Victor Ertmanis *(Man in Mets Jersey)*, Cynthia Belliveau *(Nurse)*.

The message in this unusual comedy from independent producer Christopher W. Knight and director Howard Zieff is that the genuine road to recovery winds through the heart and not necessarily through the mind. In this case, the travelers are the mentally dysfunctional. However, it requires an adroit hand to balance a story of recovery with a satire on mental health care, a crime-solving odyssey, and a study of four distinctively deranged characters. To that end, writers Jon Connolly and David Loucka have fashioned a script that works largely because of the efforts of the four capable and credible actors who comprise The Dream Team.

The story begins with an amusing and telling exposition of character in a series of psychosis-revealing scenes set at the Cedarbrook Psychiatric Hospital in Trenton, New Jersey. So get your scorecards and pencils ready; here is The Dream Team lineup: Lloyd is a former postal worker and anal-retentive priss whose operative delusion is that he's a doctor. Furst, the youngest, or at least most infantile, member of the team, communicates only with a television set, or in TV cliches, and serves mainly as a passive convenience for several plot turns. Boyle, in some measure the broadest character, is a former ad agency vice-president crucified by his colleagues. Now he regards himself as a transfigured Christ with a penchant for preaching at the drop of . . . well, his trousers. And batting cleanup is Keaton. A writer beset with a low threshold of tolerance and a high degree of self-grandeur, he is at once the

most destructive member of the team, and the most capable as its leader. He has reluctantly accepted accommodation at Cedarbrook as a result of his assault on a referee at a New York Rangers' hockey game. The therapist to this none-too-cooperative team, Boutsikaris, convinces the hospital's administrators that a field trip to a Yankee day game would be just the ticket to raise the spirits of his group. While chauffeuring his charges through midtown Manhattan en route to the game, he stops to allow Furst to relieve himself in an alley. There the doctor stumbles across a murder in progress. Unaware that Boutsikaris has been knocked cold by the two assassins (Bosco and Remar) and whisked away by an ambulance, the team waits obediently in the van until nightfall. One by one they head off in search of help, with each confronting the various insanities of the nocturnal urban jungle. Keaton wanders into a yuppie restaurant where he roughs up a customer who is harassing Bracco, a waitress who also happens to be Keaton's former girl friend. Boyle stumbles upon a black gospel congregation and joins them in baring testimony and practically everything else. And Lloyd takes on a mission of his own by gathering litter and admonishing others for their flagrant disregard of civic duty. Meanwhile, Bosco and Remar turn out to be cops, and the murder Boutsikaris witnessed was that of another cop who was about to turn the two in for shakedown payoffs. Resolved to eliminate the only witness, they set off for Mercy Hospital to snuff out Boutsikaris, who is listed only as a John Doe. The team huddles and sets aside its internal bickering long enough to determine the good doctor's whereabouts. Unaware of the life-threatening situation, they arrive just in time to foil Bosco and Remar. The two crooked cops flee, but the plot twists, with the team wrongly accused of attempting to kill their therapist. Now they're faced with keeping their doctor safe from another attack and mustering enough wit to avoid their own capture. Keaton leads the team to Bracco's home, where she lives with straight arrow boy friend Lembeck, who calls 911, leading to Keaton and Furst's capture, while Boyle and Lloyd manage to escape. As Boyle futilely attempts to enlist help from his old agency cronies, Lloyd has a touching reunion with the wife and daughter he has not seen in three years. Boyle and Lloyd ultimately turn themselves in to join their comrades in jail. Bracco, the only one who believes their story, visits Keaton to help him galvanize the group. The team now truly becomes a team, accepting their therapist's faith in their ability to recover. While being transferred to East Side Psychiatric, they engineer an escape. Posing as doctors, Keaton, Lloyd, and Boyle return to Mercy in time to help Bracco save the now-conscious

Boutsikaris. Bosco and Remar are captured after some derring-do by Keaton, the team is exonerated, and, with an "all's well that ends well" spirit, the four acknowledge a heightened sense of self-determination and mutual respect. Together they decide that an unescorted trip to the cheap seats at Yankee Stadium is just what the doctor should order.

THE DREAM TEAM is the kind of story in which the players must work hard against themselves and one another for the movie to succeed as a whole. And in large part it does. It's impossible not to recall the inmate outing in ONE FLEW OVER THE CUCKOO'S NEST when considering the comic core of THE DREAM TEAM, but credit is due Michael Keaton, Christopher Lloyd, Peter Boyle, and to a lesser degree Stephen Furst, for this fresh and innovative approach. A synergistic quality is evident in the ensemble scenes, and yet each member is accorded enough solo moments to evoke our sympathy and hope for his recovery. This is particularly true with Lloyd and Boyle. As far as poking fun at the mentally ill, Zieff has taken particular care to elicit only the kinds of laughs that remind us of our own fragile existence. Only in Keaton's early scenes does the humor seem cruel, but that cruelty is easily understood as the defensive product of his own denial. Like disaster jokes that abound after real tragedies, Keaton's behavior is, in its most benign interpretation, a way to reconcile the senseless twists of fate heaped upon the innocent. Those moments of lucidity and harmony that come together for the team when the dramatic stakes go up suggest that it's possible for the mentally infirm to face their fear of chaos only when they can turn to their love for and commitment to one another or, in this case, to the psychiatrist who believes in them. For the seriously mentally ill, THE DREAM TEAM method of self-recovery is wholly inappropriate, akin to a coach's exhortation to keep running in spite of the agony and limitations of a severe injury. But the effort of the four members of The Dream Team to rally support for one another is careful not to exceed their functional capacities as individuals. And this is where the performances of Keaton, Lloyd, and Boyle are best served. Even if one has a tough time cheering for the damn Yankees, it's easy to applaud these guys who "gotta have heart" to win their game. *(Profanity.)*

p, Christopher W. Knight; d, Howard Zieff; w, Jon Connolly and David Loucka; ph, Adam Holender (Deluxe Color); ed, C. Timothy O'Meara; m, David McHugh; prod d, Todd Hallowell; art d, Christopher Nowak and Gregory Keen; set d, John Alan Hicks; spec eff, Neil N. Trifunovich; cos, Ruth Morley; stunts, Danny Aiello III; makeup, Alan Weisinger.

Comedy (PR:C MPAA:PG-13)

DRIVING MISS DAISY
(See THE YEAR'S BEST)

DRUGSTORE COWBOY
(See THE YEAR'S BEST)

DRY WHITE SEASON, A***
97m MGM/MGM-UA c
Donald Sutherland *(Ben du Toit)*, Winston Ntshona *(Gordon Ngubene)*, Susan Sarandon *(Melanie Bruwer)*, Janet Suzman *(Susan du Toit)*, Marlon Brando *(Ian McKenzie)*, Zakes Mokae *(Stanley)*, Jurgen Prochnow *(Capt. Stolz)*, Thoko Ntshinga *(Emily Ngubene)*, Susannah Harker *(Suzette du Toit)*, Leonard Maguire *(Mr. Bruwer)*, Rowen Elmes *(Johan du Toit)*, Gerard Thoolin *(Col. Viljoen)*, Stella Dickin *(Susan's Mother)*, David de Keyser *(Susan's Father)*, Andrew Whaley *(Chris)*, John Kani *(Julius)*, Sophie Mgcina *(Margaret)*, Bekhithemba Mpofu *(Jonathan)*, Tinashe Makoni *(Robert)*, Precious Thiri *(Wellington)*, Richard Wilson *(Cicete)*, Derek Hanekom *(Viviers)*, Michael Gambon *(Magistrate)*, Paul Brooke *(Dr. Herzog)*, Ronald Pickup *(Louw)*, Ernest Ndlovu *(Archibald Mabaso)*, Stephen Hanly *(Sgt. Van Zyl)*, Andre Proctor *(Jaimie)*, Kevin Johnson *(Gert)*, Grant Davidson *(Lt. Venter)*, Ndu Gumede *(Douma)*, Sello Maake *(Johnson Seroke)*, Charles Pillai *(Dr. Hassiem)*, Rosemary Martin *(Mrs. Beachley)*, Willie Zweni *(Aubrey Kunene)*, Mercia Davids *(Sadie)*, Mannie De Villiers *(Police Commandant)*, Anna Manimanzi *(Soweto Girl)*.

Don't be misled by the stellar cast featuring Donald Sutherland, Susan Sarandon, Janet Suzman, Jurgen Prochnow, and (especially) Marlon Brando. A DRY WHITE SEASON is not an "entertainment" in the usual sense. It's a polemic against South African apartheid, and while it may not meet the criteria for "great" filmmaking, Euzhan Palcy's film, with its intent and potential to reach mass audiences—and, ironically, its racially representative story and personnel—succeeds in being significant.

History teacher Sutherland, an Afrikaner, lives a comfortable middle-class existence with wife Suzman and their three children in Johannesburg in the 1970s. Though he's basically a decent man, he's also lived with blinders on, unable to see the injustices and hardships of life under apartheid. Sutherland finds all of his personal and political ties thrown into question, however, following the event that sparked the Soweto uprising of 1976, when a peaceful protest march (vividly re-created here) by black schoolchildren demanding better education was put down in a bloody massacre in which 58 died and 700 were injured in one day. When the

Marlon Brando and Donald Sutherland in A DRY WHITE SEASON (©MGM-UA).

young son of his long-time gardener (Ntshona) is taken into custody during the protest and killed by the police, Sutherland, though sympathetic, says there isn't anything he can do. He believes in what he considers the orderly process of South African law. But when Ntshona, in the process of trying to recover his son's body, is himself arrested, then brutally tortured and murdered by the police's paramilitary Special Branch, Sutherland's liberal consciousness is raised. Unable to believe the official contention that his gardener committed suicide and incensed for the first time in his life, Sutherland seeks justice, particularly after Mokae, a black cab driver, hides him in the back of his cab and sneaks him into a Soweto funeral parlor to view Ntshona's horribly tortured remains. Sutherland enlists the help of human rights legal activist Brando to bring criminal charges against the police, but Brando doesn't hold out much hope, telling Sutherland that every time he wins a case, the government simply changes the law. Brando takes on the case, "if only to prove that justice in South Africa is misapplied when it concerns the question of race," but, true to his prophecy and despite overwhelming evidence to the contrary, his charge that Ntshona was murdered is dismissed. Sutherland, determined to have the case retried in civil court, arranges with Mokae and liberal journalist Sarandon (in a minor, undeveloped role) to help him get affidavits from witnesses to the crime. Meanwhile, the white community ostracizes him. He's fired by the school; his

daughter demands that things return to "just the way they were"; and Suzman, leaves him after a melodramatic confrontation in which she argues that "you have to choose your own people," to which Sutherland counters, "You have to choose the truth." Only his young son (convincingly played by South African schoolboy Elmes in his first screen role) fully supports Sutherland in his fight, but life becomes dangerous for the dissident father and son. Once it's learned that they're seeking proof of the murder, the two are harassed by vicious Special Branch captain Prochnow, who has their garage blown up in an effort to destroy evidence, and finally runs Sutherland over in his car (Prochnow, in turn, is shot dead by Mokae, who has been tailing him). Sutherland does not die in vain, however: The film ends on a hopeful note, ending with the newspaper headline "Special Branch Brutality Exposed"and a dedication to the victims of the Soweto uprising and to those who have given their lives to the struggle against apartheid since a state of emergency was declared in 1986.

The accents and attempted accents here take a little getting used to; both Donald Sutherland and Susan Sarandon sound as if they've swallowed marbles, and the black actors' laboriously articulated English gives it a plodding and pedagogic quality. Sutherland's character, moreover, must be taken somewhat on faith, because it's hard to believe he could have been so ill-informed and in such political limbo for so long. If it's sometimes difficult to suspend one's disbelief in watching the film, however, A DRY WHITE SEASON is none-theless worth watching for the (sometimes painful) force of its truths and its perspec-tive. Unlike CRY FREEDOM and A WORLD APART (or even MISSISSIPPI BURNING, for that matter), all films seen through the eyes of white people, A DRY WHITE SEASON shows the effects of rac-ism from both white *and* black stand-points, balancing points of view. For the first time in a major production with Hol-lywood studio backing, blacks are given more than token representation, as Palcy (a black filmmaker from Martinique) cuts back and forth between the white charac-ters in Johannesburg and their fully-real-ized black counterparts, only six miles—but also a world—away in Soweto.

Lending credibility to these scenes is the fine acting of the black South African actors in leading roles, including Winston Ntshona and John Kani, who both received Tony Awards for their perfor-mances in the plays "Sizwe Banzi Is Dead" and "The Island," which they also cowrote. Zakes Mokae (CRY FREEDOM), now liv-ing in exile in the United States, is consid-ered a hero in his country as the first black to overcome official prejudice and earn a living there as an actor. (With Ntshona and Kani, he joined playwright Athol Fugard in the small theater group the Serpent Play-ers, later a world-renowned company.) Also impressive is white South African Janet Suzman (who is the niece of Helen Suzman, a liberal member of the South African parliament and leading white opponent of apartheid), as the Sutherland character's wife. Shooting primarily in Zimbabwe, Palcy used nonprofessionals from the local citizenry in walk-on parts, and 2,000 students, many of whom were children of South African exiles, were given three days' leave from school to appear in the realistic demonstration scenes.

Based on the novel by white South Afri-can Andre Brink, A DRY WHITE SEA-SON is the first full-length feature to be directed by a black woman for a major US studio. Adding to this already significant achievement, Palcy (SUGAR CANE ALLEY), in what amounts to the casting coup of the year, enlisted the reclusive Brando to make his brief but memorably cameo appearance—his first film role since 1980—for union scale. (Brando reportedly offered to do it for nothing as an expression of his anti-apartheid views, but Screen Actors Guild regulations precluded it.) And what a performance he gives. There's so much more of him now, in his early 60s, that he resembles Sidney Greenstreet (or the middle-aged Orson Welles) more than he does the Brando of A STREETCAR NAMED DESIRE or even LAST TANGO IN PARIS. But though when he first appears one marvels simply at his girth, by the time he is seen arguing his hopeless case before an blatantly racist judge in a sobering courtroom scene, Brando mesmerizes simply with the stat-ure of his acting. The pounds and inches melt away, and, great actor that he is, his performance alone is worth the price of admission to this earnest, somewhat pre-dictable, but moving and significant film. *(Graphic violence, adult situations.)*

p, Paula Weinstein; d, Euzhan Palcy; w, Euzhan Palcy and Colin Welland (based on the novel by Andre Brink); ph, Kelvin Pike and Pierre-William Glenn (Deluxe Color); ed, Sam O'Steen and Glenn Cun-ningham; m, Dave Grusin; prod d, John Fenner; art d, Alan Tomkins and Mike Phillips; set d, Peter James; spec eff, David Harris; tech, Lionel Ngakane; stunts, Marc Boyle; makeup, Tommie Manderson.

Drama   (PR:C MPAA:R)

E

Ⓥ**EARTH GIRLS ARE EASY****½
100m Vestron c
Geena Davis *(Valerie Dale)*, Jeff Goldblum *(Mac)*, Julie Brown *(Candy Pink)*, Jim Carrey *(Wiploc)*, Damon Wayans *(Zeebo)*, Charles Rocket *(Dr. Ted Gallagher)*, Michael McKean *(Woody, Pool Boy)*, Larry Linville *(Dr. Bob)*, Rick Overton *(Dr. Rick)*.

Of late, Hollywood has been unsuccessful in its attempts to better the "mildly amusing" formula that's been used to send up science-fiction films. Mel Brooks' SPACEBALLS was aggressive and gross; MY STEPMOTHER IS AN ALIEN was cute but lame. The most recent attempt, Julien Temple's EARTH GIRLS ARE EASY, is silly, sexy, and filled with music.

In Los Angeles, Davis is about to be married to housemate Rocket, a physician who is also a kinky, compulsive cheater (he likes to "do it" wearing a surgical mask, stethoscope, and handcuffs). Ditzy Valley Girl Davis is a manicurist whose idea of high culture is attending cuticle conventions. She catches Rocket trying to ravish an overstuffed, ditzy nurse (this film is full of ditzy characters) in their bed and throws him out. Meanwhile, three furry, pastel-colored space aliens crash-land their UFO in Davis' pool. In a panic, she almost drowns, and Goldblum, the alien captain, saves her. She, in turn, helps conceal the aliens' identities until they can repair their spaceship and escape. Goldblum and his buddies, Wayans and Carrey, quickly learn English from the worst TV shows and satiate their hunger with junk food—Twinkies, Oreos, spray-on cheese, and Pop-tarts, not to mention phonograph records and anything colorful they find swimming in the fish tank. What to do? Davis hauls them off for a consultation with her (you guessed it) ditzy coworker, Brown, a cosmetician. With the aid of plenty of Nair, Brown defoliates the trio and turns them into La-La-Land-style hunks. She then leads the bunch to a disco—after all, ditzes and aliens just wanna have fun. There the movie rolls out the first of several lackluster MTV musical send-ups. Naturally, the space guys outdance the earth guys, and, naturally, all the disco ditzes lust after the alien Adonises. "But they're bald!" exclaims Wayans. "Who cares?" says Carrey. "They're round and bouncy." And, oh, are they ever bouncy in their heels and skimpy, come-hither clothes. Not too surprisingly, Davis and Goldblum get cozy and wind up in the sack and in love. In the morning, McKean, the spaced-out surfer poolman, shows up to empty the pool, but instead takes Wayans and Carrey on a trip to the beach. The field trip turns into a Buster Keaton-like adventure, with the aliens inadvertently holding up a convenience store, then driving backwards on a busy freeway, and winding up in a hospital. There, the aliens are treated by Rocket, who learns they have two hearts and imagines this discovery putting him on the cover of *Time*. Goldblum and Davis arrive, thwart Rocket's efforts to exploit the aliens, and get Wayans and Carrey back to the repaired spaceship. Rocket arrives as they are blasting off, and Davis almost accepts his new bid for marriage. But, realizing he's still a creep, she elects to take off for outer space with Goldblum, though not before pressing him with some vital Valley Girl questions: "Is driving a UFO good work? Do you own or rent?"

In trying to satisfy too many different audiences, director Temple is left with a film that fails to completely satisfy any of them. The Valley Girls and Boys who are so central to EARTH GIRLS ARE EASY may find much to amuse them here, but Temple doesn't go far enough in his attempt to satirize the shallowness of the Valley lifestyle. Indeed, he goes about his lampooning so timidly that the film seems to glorify the ditzy life. Likewise, his attempt to send up the MTV aesthetic lacks punch, primarily because the film's songs are entirely forgettable. Temple's failure in this arena is particularly disappointing, given the innovative work he's done as the director of such music videos as the Rolling Stones' "Undercover of the Night" and David Bowie's "Jazzin' for Blue Jean," not to mention his brilliant staging of the ultrahip ABSOLUTE BEGINNERS. Hoping to titillate with sex, while staying within the bounds of a PG rating, Temple opts for tantalizing talk and the constant display of bra-busting females in stiletto heels. But all this display without

Jeff Goldblum, Damon Wayans, and Jim Carrey in EARTH GIRLS ARE EASY (©Vestron).

delivery on its prurient promises is obscene in its own odd way.

The acting here is respectable, but doesn't rise beyond the film's unexceptional script and the direction. Geena Davis (cast by Temple before her Oscar-winning performance in THE ACCIDENTAL TOURIST made her a star) is appropriately wide-eyed and naive as Valerie, though the role is hardly one that will inspire the admiration of feminists. Davis' real-life husband, Jeff Goldblum, gives the pleasant performance that his role calls for, and Julie Brown shows herself to be a versatile talent. Born and raised in the Valley, Brown had plenty of experience on which to draw when she coauthored EARTH GIRLS' script with husband Terrence McNally, Charlie Coffey, and Temple. A pop singer with two albums to her credit, she also collaborated on the writing of three of the film's songs. Of the supporting characters, Michael McKean's "wasted" poolman is the most memorable, though Cheech and Chong abandoned the druggy clown prototype a decade ago.

Temple has pointed to filmmaker Frank Tashlin as a major influence on his work, and Tashlin's THE GIRL CAN'T HELP IT clearly provided the English director with at least some of the inspiration for his approach to EARTH GIRLS ARE EASY; unfortunately, Temple's film never approaches the greatness of Tashlin's camp classic. *(Adult situations, sexual situations.)*

p, Tony Garnett; d, Julien Temple; w, Julie Brown, Charlie Coffey, and Terrence E. McNally; ph, Oliver Stapleton; ed, Richard Halsey; m, Nile Rodgers; prod d, Dennis Gassner; art d, Dina Danielsen; set d, Nancy Haigh; chor, Sarah Elgart.

Comedy/Science Fiction

(PR:C MPAA:PG)

Ⓥ**EASY WHEELS***
90m New Star Ent./Fries Dist. c
Paul Le Mat *(Biker Bruce)*, Eileen Davidson *(She-Wolf)*, Marjorie Bransfield *(Wendy)*, Jon Menick *(Prof)*, Mark Holton *(Animal)*, Karen Russell *(Candy)*, Jami Richards *(Merilee)*, Roberta Vasquez *(Tondaleyo)*, Theresa Randal *(Allie)*, Barry Livingston *(Reporter)*, Stevie Sterling *(Fascination)*, Carlos Campean *(Paco)*, Mike Leinert *(Meatball)*, Lisa Nelson *(Becky Sue)*, Robert Miano *(Nick)*, Robert Traviano *(Domingo)*, Joe Shea *(Schollstrom)*, Rebecca York *(Marian)*, Danny Hicks *(Joe)*, Kevin Brophy *(Tony Wolf)*, Louan Gideon *(Molly Wolf)*, Barry Doe *(Sheriff)*, Annie O'Donnell *(Enid)*, Ben Stein *(Preacher)*, Joleen Lutz *(Novice Nun)*, Ivan Naranjo *(Navajo Indian)*, Gary Ballard, R.J. Walker *(Hunters)*, Dimitri Villard *(Police Captain)*, Theodore Raimi, George Plimpton.

As a shoestring-budgeted send-up of the motorcycle gang B-movies of the early 1970s, this film leaves much to be desired. As a serious piece of filmmaking, forget it! Scripted by Ivan Raimi, Celia Abrams, and David O'Malley (who also directed), EASY WHEELS concerns itself with a lowbrow battle-of-the-sexes between a wildcat female gang led by She Wolf (Eileen Davidson) and a macho male gang overseen by the philosophical Biker Bruce (Paul LeMat). Orphaned and raised by wolves, Davidson leads her gang of ultra-Amazons on a quest for girl babies, who they intend to kidnap and turn over to wolves for feral upbringing. The idea is to provide the next generation with a group of totally fearless females tough enough to subdue the entire male population. Davidson envisions a race of super women who, presumably, will treat men as slaves, much as men have treated women through the centuries—with verbal and physical abuse, and a variety of other more unspeakable humiliations. In order to insure that this new world order will come about, Davidson has sworn to remain celibate. LeMat, however, causes a crack in her determination. Davidson resists her urges for a time, but in an interlude between the beer guzzling and barroom brawls she and LeMat engage in roadside sex. The film's explosive climax then occurs shortly after the She Wolf gang raids a home for unwed mothers. At this point, the gang's one reasonably sane and compassionate member separates herself from her crueler comrades and takes sides with LeMat and the boys in the slam-bang showdown with the women.

There is an audience for films such as EASY WHEELS, but one won't find it at institutes of higher learning. Rather this is a film for folks who prefer their men *and* women unshaven, uncouth, and unwholesome. If the film has a comedy "highlight," it is the bad-taste, high-pitched rendition of "Rock of Ages" by the Biker Bruce gang while incarcerated in an Iowa jail cell. (The story takes place on and around the main highway connecting Des Moines and Dubuque.) LeMat and Davidson contribute some fairly convincing, though hardly distinguished, thesping, and the rest of the performances are generally okay. The production values are standard for the genre; the humor is strictly from-the-gutter shtick, and the violence is of the wham-bang comic-strip variety. *(Violence, profanity, substance abuse, adult situations, sexual situations.)*

p, Dmitri Villard, Robby Wald, and Jake Jacobson; d, David O'Malley; w, David O'Malley, Celia Abrams, and Ivan Raimi; ph, James Lemmo (Technicolor); ed, John Currin; m, John Ross; prod d, Helen Dersjam; set d, Gary Shartsis; spec eff, Neil Smith; cos, Sarah Bardo; stunts, Jack Gill; makeup, Bill Miller-Jones.

Action/Comedy   (PR:O MPAA:NR)

Ⓥ**ECHOES IN PARADISE****
89m Laughing Kookaburra/Quartet c
Wendy Hughes *(Maria)*, John Lone *(Raka)*, Steven Jacobs *(George)*, Peta Toppano *(Judy)*, Rod Mullinar *(Terry)*, Gillian Jones *(Mitty)*, Claudia Karvan *(Julie)*, Matthew Taylor *(Simon)*, Lynda Stoner *(Beth Mason)*.

This oddball exotica poses a question not often asked these days: "Can a long-suffering, middle-aged Australian woman recover from her husband's infidelities and regain her self-respect in the arms of a Balinese folk dancer who's lost the desire to dance?" After overcoming her grief over her father's death and discovering that Jacobs, her staid husband, has been dallying with a mutual friend, Hughes agrees to vacation with her pal, Toppano, on scenic Phuket Island, Thailand. There, Hughes feels at one with nature and in tune with the mysteries of the Orient, particularly those embodied in Lone, a young dancer. Befriended by Mullinar, a charming homosexual hotelier with a yen for Lone, Hughes finds it increasingly difficult to abandon tranquil Thailand for her stormy domestic situation. Deciding not to return home with her friend, Hughes encounters the lithe and beautiful Lone in a forest and at a Buddhist temple. Reluctant to become just a holiday romance and one more notch in Lone's belt, the frustrated matron plays hard-to-get, but finally accepts his invitation to a local bar. While the two make eyes at each other, Lone expresses his anguish over his waning interest in his art. At one time, dance was like a religion for Lone, but the Parisian high life has left him dissipated and uninspired (like Hughes, he's nursing his wounds in Thailand). Later that evening, a sensual massage leads to unbridled passion. Smitten with Hughes, Lone even puts on a private dance exhibition for her, but there's soon trouble in paradise. First, Jacobs flies in to play on Hughes' guilt about her neglected children, and to assure her his affair "didn't mean anything." Unmoved, Hughes sends him packing and keeps her new job as a waitress. Soon, her friends prove to be jealous of her searing passion for Lone. The possessive Mullinar plans an evening out at a disco in the hope of spoiling the lovers' idealized views of each other. Dropping liberal hints that Lone has bartered his favors to keep a thatched roof over his head, Mullinar and Lone's former mistress (Jones) provoke an argument between the starry-eyed Hughes and Lone. The row fails to shatter their emotional involvement, but their eyes are opened to reality. Unlike the other drifters who avoid facing their problems, Lone and Hughes have gained strength from their affair: He has acquired the courage to shake off indolence and return to his dancing; she has found peace of mind and the resolve to resume her role as loving mother, whatever the eventual fate of her marriage. And they'll always have Thailand.

Movie soap operas have to be a little larger than life to realize their function as bon-bon-munching escapism. To refashion a tearjerker in realistic terms is self-defeating. In ECHOES IN PARADISE, there's not enough contrast between the heroine's mundane existence and the way in which her fantasy options are presented. Despite the fancy trappings and the quotes from Buddha, the emotions expressed and the way in which everyone's life-crisis is facilely resolved come straight from the realm of daytime TV soaps. Moreover, ECHOES hesitates between two worlds. While the filmmakers seem determined to delve earnestly into a married woman's mid-life angst, their methods are lifted from old-fashioned Hollywood melodramas. Yet they don't have the courage to provide the full-throttle romanticism this approach requires. A sort of "Brief Encounter Down Among the Sheltering Palms," ECHOES seems intent on scaling down its drama when it ought to be investing its characters with the grand passions that might have allowed this bittersweet interlude to tug at our heart-strings.

ECHOES does have its virtues. The Thai locations are picture-postcard pretty, and the film has the cynical good sense to incorporate the jealousies of spurned lovers Jones and Mullinar into the storyline. While the movie obviously strives for the languorous aura it achieves, it would have benefitted from snappier pacing. A few tangy anti-climaxes along the way might have brewed a more potent Oriental tempest in a teapot. As it stands, there's too much travelog and not enough dramatic excitement. The film also risks losing audience sympathy when Hughes rather petulantly refuses to return to her children. No one begrudges a woman a little time for soul-searching, but Hughes' behavior seems more like simple drifting than a firm decision to rethink her priorities, and vacillation doesn't make for compelling melodrama. Regrettably, ECHOES' two versatile stars, Wendy Hughes and John Lone, aren't seen to good advantage. Hughes (WARM NIGHTS ON A SLOW MOVING TRAIN) coasts attractively through the film but brings none of her accustomed brittleness to her character. In the tricky role of the exotic stud, Lone (THE LAST EMPEROR; THE MODERNS) is sensual but effete; he mistakenly plays the part with a bizarre speech pattern that accents the last syllable of every word. As is generally the case in this love story, the emphasis is never where it should be. *(Sexual situations, nudity, profanity.)*

d, Phillip Noyce; w, Jan Sharp and Anne Brooksbank; ph, Peter James; ed, Frans Vandenburg; m, William Motzing; prod d, Judith Russell; cos, Clarrissa Patterson.

Romance   **(PR:C MPAA:R)**

⊙EDDIE AND THE CRUISERS II: EDDIE LIVES!**
100m Les Productions Alliance-Aurora/Scotti c
Michael Pare *(Eddie Wilson/Joe West)*, Marina Orsini *(Diane Armani)*, Bernie Coulson *(Rick DeSal)*, Matthew Laurance *(Sal Amato)*, Michael Rhoades *(Dave Pagent)*, Anthony Sherwood *(Hilton Overstreet)*, Mark Holmes *(Quinn Quinley)*, David Matheson *(Stewart Fairbanks)*, Paul Markle *(Charlie Tansey)*, Kate Lynch *(Lyndsay)*, Harvey Atkin *(Lew Eisen)*, Vlasta Vrana *(Frank)*, Larry King *(T.V. Talk Show Host)*, Bo Diddley *(Legendary Guitarist)*, Martha Quinn *(Music Video Hostess)*, Merrill Shindler *(Musicologist)*, Sunny Joe White *(Radio Disc Jockey)*, James Rae *(Tom)*, Michael "Tunes" Antunes *(Wendall Newton)*, Ulla Moreland *(Art Critic)*, Bruno Verdoni *(Rick's Keyboard Player)*, Phil Mattera *(Rick's Bass Player)*, Kim Lombard *(Rick's Drummer)*.

Fans of EDDIE AND THE CRUISERS (yes, both of you)—the wait is over! Six years after the release of the original film, Michael Pare returns in the role he made famous. Why? Film fans with good memories may remember the lackluster original, not from their neighborhood movie theaters (where it performed poorly) but from cable TV, where the film managed to find a following. Avid radio listeners may even remember the theme song from the 1983 original, performed by John Cafferty and the Beaver Brown Band, a group whose lead singer not only sounds like Bruce Springsteen but whose songs are nearly note-for-note imitations. This time out, Pare again plays New Jersey rock 'n' roller Eddie Wilson, whose dreams of superstardom were cut short by a ruthless record producer. In the early 1960s, Pare, unable to handle the dejection, dropped out of sight after an apparently fatal car wreck. When his car was dragged out of the river into which it plunged, no corpse was found, and the police assumed it was washed away. Die-hard fans continued to believe that Eddie was still alive, however. Years later, Pare has assumed a new name and a new identity (as a construction worker in Montreal), and the record album he recorded way back when has found a new life on the charts. Eddie Wilson is finally a star, albeit a dead one. Tortured by his memories, Pare flirts with the idea of forming a new band, sparking the interest of a black sax man (played by Sherwood, whose character Springsteen fans will recognize as the film's Clarence Clemons) and an eager young guitarist (Coulson). However, Pare decides against forming the band, thus sparing himself another round of record company abuse. At a hockey game one night with some buddies, Pare meets an attractive painter (Orsini) who expresses a strong desire to paint his por-

trait. Pare refuses, but the woman insists. Before long, Pare is immortalized on canvas, is in love with the painter, *and* is touring on the road with his new band. Meanwhile Eddie-mania is sweeping the nation. His record company is pulling a promotional scam involving some unreleased Eddie Wilson recordings with a "mystery" backup band. (Later we learn from Bo Diddley, in a surprising cameo, that Bo was one of the session players.) There is also a nationwide talent search under way to find an Eddie Wilson lookalike. A video program reports all the latest Eddie news (with MTV vidjock Martha Quinn contributing a cameo). Even Larry King makes a guest appearance, hosting a special program on the Eddie Wilson phenomenon, which has shades of those Elvis-sighting reports. Naturally, "Joe West," as Pare calls himself, must face the Eddie Wilson legacy, and he does so with the help of his former best friend and bandmate, Laurance. Although he hasn't seen Laurance in years, Pare seeks out his old pal. At the film's climax, Eddie and his new Cruisers get their big break at a music festival, where Pare admits to a crowd of cheering thousands that he is really Eddie Wilson. As the band kicks into another number, chants of "Ed-die, Ed-die" fill the stadium.

Plagued by a miserable script and countless improbabilities (for instance, why does only one of his fellow band members notice that Joe is really Eddie, especially since he looks and sounds just like the superstar *and* since the whole country is swept by rumors that Eddie lives?), EDDIE AND THE CRUISERS II is just barely entertaining. The only point in the film's favor is its interesting concept (a "dead" rock star who may still be alive, like the Doors' Jim Morrison)—which, coincidentally, was the only point in the original's favor. Otherwise, the new EDDIE is marred by mediocre acting (none of the actors is really bad, but they don't have a script they can work with), a nondescript style, and a definite overabundance of musical numbers. The last half of the film consists of one song after another, with an occasional line of dialog tossed in to break up the monotony. If you liked the original, you'll probably like this one, but odds are you don't even remember the original.

p, Stephane Reichel; d, Jean-Claude Lord; w, Charles Zev Cohen and Rick Doehring (based on characters created by P.F. Kluge); ph, Rene Verzier; ed, Jean-Guy Montpetite; m, Marty Simon and Leon Aronson; art d, Dominic Ricard; set d, Gilles Aird; cos, Ginnette Magny; makeup, Jocelyne Bellemare.

Drama   **(PR:A MPAA:PG-13)**

ⓥEDGE OF SANITY*

86m Millimeter-Allied/Allied Vision c
Anthony Perkins *(Dr. Jekyll/Mr. Hyde)*, Glynis Barber *(Elisabeth Jekyll)*, Sarah Maur-Thorp *(Susannah)*, David Lodge *(Underwood)*, Ben Cole *(Johnny, the Pimp)*, Ray Jewers *(Newcomen)*, Jill Melford *(Flora)*, Lisa Davis *(Maria)*, Noel Coleman *(Egglestone)*, Briony McRoberts *(Ann Underwood)*, Mark Elliot *(Lanyon)*, Harry Landis *(Coroner)*, Jill Pearson *(Mrs. Egglestone)*, Basil Hoskins *(Mr. Bottingham)*, Ruth Burnett *(Margo)*, Carolyn Cortez *(Maggie)*, Cathy Murphy *(Cockney Prostitute)*, Claudia Udy *(Liza)*.

Is Norman Bates alive and well and living in England? PSYCHO's Anthony Perkins, once again capitalizing on his Hitchcock persona of a schizoid homicidal maniac, appears in dual roles as Dr. Jekyll and Mr. Hyde in EDGE OF SANITY, yet another reworking of Robert Louis Stevenson's Victorian classic of murder, mayhem, and split personality. Havoc (and crack) is created when a laboratory monkey knocks over a corrosive liquid into cocaine Jekyll had been testing for use as an anaesthesic. The dedicated doctor inhales the noxious fumes and turns into Jack Hyde, a Jack the Ripper type who stalks and kills prostitutes in 19th-century London. Hyde's MO is to turn a deadly trick on tarts unwittingly going about their business, fatally slicing them with a scalpel after apparently soliciting their services. It seems no wanton woman is immune from his serial killings, which put the city in a panic and the police on overdrive. In fact, Scotland Yard enlists the good Dr. Jekyll's expertise to help track down the culprit, whom they suspect to be a medical man because, as the coroner says of one corpse, his victims are cut "clean as a codfish from Billingsgate Alley." During Perkins' all-too-frequent nights out as the sociopathic Hyde, he frequents Madam Flora's, a brothel that boasts "a little bit of something for everyone." There he takes a lascivious liking to both Maur-Thorp and her pimp. Maur-Thorp, it seems, bears an uncanny resemblance to a promiscuous woman Perkins' recollects from a traumatic childhood experience—the apparent psychological key to his aberrant behavior. (The film opens with the young Jekyll as voyeur, observing a nightmarish, bloody roll in the hay between Maur-Thorp's lookalike and an unidentified man, perhaps his father.) In the meantime, Perkins' patient wife (Barber), who does volunteer work in a shelter for tarts in London's East End, begins to suspect her husband of philandering. Finally, she realizes that he might be the mad slasher (she recognizes his scarf, found beside a victim) and, burning with curiosity, tracks him to Maur-Thorp's apartment, where he is engaged in a sadistic, drug-ridden menage a trois with Maur-Thorp and her pimp. The last two are brutally massacred during an opium-induced orgy, and the horrified Barber is silenced when Perkins follows her home and permanently puts an end to her snooping. The movie ends as Perkins—doing a cross between Norman Bates and Jack Nicholson in THE SHINING—leers out his window, still very much alive and no doubt preparing to return, if the movie makes enough money to warrant a sequel.

It shouldn't. It's all pseudo-psychosexual and just plain silly. Occasionally attempting high camp, EDGE OF SANITY obviously isn't meant to be taken seriously, despite its expensive production values and surrealistic photography—both surprisingly good. With only a few lapses, the film's "look" is quite appealing, in the tradition of THE CABINET OF DR. CALIGARI and FRANKENSTEIN or, more recently, David Cronenberg's starkly surreal DEAD RINGERS. But the rest of EDGE OF SANITY (shot mostly in Budapest with some English exteriors) doesn't measure up to its technical proficiency, working neither as horror nor camp. As for Perkins, the years haven't been too kind to the once perennial juvenile, who seems unable to break away from repeated self-parody in the PSYCHOpathic mode that brought him fame in 1960. Rolling his eyes and grimacing as if he were sucking a bitter olive, Perkins seems insane even when he shouldn't, while Glynis Barber's namby-pamby portrayal of his wife is living proof that virtue isn't necessarily its own reward. Gorehounds should get their money's worth—blood flows freely—and there's enough gratuitous nudity (of both sexes) to appeal to prepubescent prurient interests, but the Jekyll-and-Hyde story, in its various incarnations, has been done far better elsewhere. EDGE OF SANITY does contain some incidental humor, as when Perkins introduces himself to a whore (before killing her), prompting her response: "Mr. Hyde? Maybe I should be Miss Seek. I used to play that game when I was a girl." The lady—and the audience—should have been forewarned. *(Violence, nudity, adult situations, sexual situations.)*

p, Edward Simons and Harry Alan Towers; d, Gerard Kikoine; w, J.P. Felix and Ron Raley; ph, Tony Spratling (Eastmancolor); ed, Malcolm Cooke; m, Fredric Talgorn; prod d, Jean Charles Dedieu; art d, Fred Carter and Tivadar Bertalan; cos, Valerie Lanee; makeup, Gordon Kaye.

Horror   **(PR:O MPAA:R)**

ⓥ84 CHARLIE MOPIC***½

95m Charlie Mopic/New Century-Vista c

Jonathan Emerson *(LT)*, Nicholas Cascone *(Easy)*, Jason Tomlins *(Pretty Boy)*, Christopher Burgard *(Hammer)*, Glenn Morshower *(Cracker)*, Richard Brooks *(OD)*, Byron Thames *(Mopic)*, Russ Thurman, Joseph Hieu, Don Schiff.

The vast majority of Vietnam War films have attempted to analyze the political and moral aspects of the conflict while still providing both the emotional pull and violent spectacle associated with the genre. Recently this broad approach has been replaced by a more old-fashioned one in films like HAMBURGER HILL (1987) that show the day-to-day reality of men in war. Virtually plotless and featuring unknown actors playing faceless "grunts," these films attempt to be more intimate than their predecessors and relate the harsh experiences of men in battle without moralizing on the cause of the conflict. The purest expression of this approach yet, 84 CHARLIE MOPIC presents the events surrounding a single reconnaissance mission by a six-man team as seen through the eyes of an Army Motion Picture (MoPic) unit cameraman shooting footage for a documentary that will introduce recruits to the realities of combat. Shot entirely in hand-held documentary style (an experiment previously undertaken in the Vietnam segment of the now-forgotten MORE AMERICAN GRAFFITI, 1979), the film follows the close-knit group of soldiers as they "hump" through the brush in the Central Highlands, led by their taciturn black sergeant (Brooks). Along on the mission are the inexperienced lieutenant in charge of the documentary project (Emerson) and the cameraman (Thames), known only as Mopic, a young soldier who is almost never seen, though his voice is heard asking questions from behind the camera. The very presence of strangers rankles the no-nonsense Brooks, especially that of the arrogant lieutenant, who tries to pull rank on him. During the first part of the film the camera records the soldiers making their way through the jungle, capturing the dos and don'ts of combat survival, shattering the myth that soldiers chain-smoked in the brush (not only can smoke be smelled from hundreds of yards away, but the enemy is also able to identify American brands). During breaks in the march, Emerson encourages the men to relate their personal histories to the camera. The radioman, Cascone, a nervy wise-guy who constantly puns and cracks jokes, has recently begun fearing that he will be killed before his discharge. Tomlins, nicknamed "Pretty Boy" because of his good looks, is a southern California screw-up; Burgard is a gung-ho blue-collar kid who got himself into legal trouble and was given the choice of serving in the Army or going to prison; Morshower is a dour white southerner whose closest friend is the black sergeant. As for Brooks, he simply refuses to reveal anything about himself, stating that his personal life is none of the Army's business. On the other hand, the ambitious and cynical Emerson momentarily opens up, admitting he sees a Vietnam stint as vital if one plans to succeed in the corporation known as the Army. When the soldiers playfully grab Thames' camera and catch him urinating, we learn that he has worked behind the lines editing footage shot by other combat photographers and that he has volunteered for the mission because of his curiosity about footage retrieved from a cameraman killed in combat. In time, the soldiers spot an encampment of North Vietnamese and call in an air strike. The mission is a success, but on their return trip the squad is ambushed several times and Tomlins, Morshower, and Burgard are killed, while Brooks is badly wounded. The survivors finally make their way to a destroyed Vietnamese village, where they await a helicopter to take them back to their base. The landing zone is extremely "hot," however, and when the chopper arrives, the area receives heavy fire. The camera makes it to the helicopter, but, seeing the wounded Brooks struggling, Thames leaves his "eyes" on board and runs back to help. Brooks is saved, but Thames is killed in the process, as yet another Army cameraman doesn't live to see his footage processed.

After years of trying to convince producers that a Vietnam film could be made *without* a cast of brat-packers or a nonstop rock'n'roll soundtrack, writer-director Patrick Duncan—a Vietnam veteran who served as an infantryman for 13 months during 1968-69—finally landed a $1 million budget (minuscule by Hollywood standards) and shot the film in the hills outside Los Angeles, using Super 16mm film stock, later blown up to 35mm for theatrical release. The gimmick here—an entire movie seen through the eyes of an Army cameraman—works better than it has any right to. While other mainstream movies have experimented with extensive use of subjective camera—most notably in Robert Montgomery's THE LADY IN THE LAKE (1947)—the approach usually comes off as forced or simply silly. In 84 CHARLIE MOPIC, however, the gimmick works, partly because most American viewers witnessed the Vietnam War through the eyes of television cameramen. Furthermore, as a result of the current glut of "reality" TV programming (shows such as "Cops," in which a cameraman rides with real-life policemen), viewers are more used to seeing the camera as participant in the action. By creating a viable situation for use of the subjective camera, director Duncan further reduces audience reluctance to accept the device, drawing us into his vision of Vietnam through long takes in which the camera changes focus, pans, or zooms to follow the action. Keeping editing to a bare minimum, he cuts from the action only when Mopic shuts the camera off or when the film runs out. This method is fraught with peril for both the director and the actors, but when it works, the sense of realism—characters seemingly caught

Richard Brooks and Jonathan Emerson in 84 CHARLIE MOPIC (©Columbia).

off-guard, their meaningful glances and muffled comments captured—lends an air of spontaneity and excitement to familiar material. While some may find the first half of the film boring, 84 CHARLIE MOPIC presents a fascinating account of the day-to-day existence of the common infantryman. From jungle rot and booby traps to chewing gum wrappers buried so the enemy won't find them, the film offers a wealth of heretofore unrevealed details from the life of the foot-soldier in Vietnam. Using this method, Duncan establishes a sense of intimacy with his soldiers that few other war films have ever achieved. Indeed, the most effective passages of the film come when the emotional sergeant carefully prepares the bodies of dead soldiers for transport out of the jungle.

While Duncan provides an insider's view of men at war, he nonetheless strays from

his technical conceit on occasion, especially when dramatically advantageous. Although seemingly obsessed with authenticity and detail, he missteps at times: notably, the lighting of the nighttime scenes is far too good to be realistic; the soldiers would certainly have demanded Mopic shut off the camera during the execution of a prisoner and when the sergeant puts a fatally wounded GI out of his misery; and there are simply too many screenwriterly character-revealing monologs. When Duncan avoids traditional narrative filmmaking, his movie succeeds beautifully, but when he strays into standard storytelling, he reveals a rather blunt hand. Tellingly, he strives too hard for irony when he sets up the death of Mopic by having him both scared by and curious about the cans of film sent back by dead cameramen. Despite its flaws, however, 84 CHARLIE

MOPIC is one of the most unique and affecting of all Vietnam films. *(Violence, excessive profanity.)*

p, Michael Nolin and Jill Griffith; d, Patrick Duncan; w, Patrick Duncan; ph, Alan Caso (Duart Color); ed, Stephen Purvis; m, Donovan; art d, Douglas Dick; spec eff, Eric Rylander; cos, Lyn Paolo; tech, Capt. Russ "Gunny" Thurman; makeup, Ron Wild.

War   **(PR:O MPAA:R)**

ENEMIES, A LOVE STORY**½
119m Morgan Creek/FOX c

Anjelica Huston *(Tamara)*, Ron Silver *(Herman)*, Margaret Sophie Stein *(Yadwiga)*, Lena Olin *(Masha)*, Alan King *(Rabbi Lembeck)*, Judith Malina *(Masha's Mother)*, Rita Karin *(Mrs. Schreier)*, Phil Leeds *(Pesheles)*, Elya Baskin *(Yasha Kotik)*, Paul Mazursky *(Leon Tortshiner)*, I.J. Dollinger *(Reb Nissen Yaroslaver)*, Zypora Spaisman *(Sheva Haddas)*, Arthur Grosser *(Doctor)*, Burney Lieberman *(Yom Kippur Cantor)*, Nathaniel Katzman *(Wedding Cantor)*, Gayle Garfinkle *(Mrs. Lembeck)*, Shelley Goldstein *(Mrs. Regal)*, Henry Bronchtein *(Benny)*, Howard Rushpan *(Onlooker)*, Doris Gramovot *(Yadwiga's Neighbor)*, Vera Miller *(Masha's Neighbor)*, Shimon Aviel *(Windbag)*, Jacob Greenbaum *(Rabbi at Catskills)*, Rhona Shekter *(Rabbi's Wife)*, Bobby Pierson *(Rhumba Instructor)*, Edward Sebic *(Fitness Instructor)*, Shirley Merovitz, Robin Bronfman *(Catskill Women)*, Tyrone Benskin *(Cabbie)*, Rummy Bishop *(Waiter at Dairy Restaurant)*, Brian Dooley *(Man on Ladder)*, Kevin Fenlon *(Desk Clerk)*, Manal Hassib *(Hooker)*, Libby Owen *(Cashier)*, Sam Sperber *(Violinist)*, Tommy Canary *(Cotton Candy Man)*, Terry Clark *(Beach Acrobat)*, Wally Roberts *(Barker)*, Mark Robinson *(Snowcone Vendor)*, Joe Viviani *(Newsstand Vendor)*, Michael Dunetz *(Customer)*, Mick Muldoon *(Doorman)*, Marie-Adele Lemieux *(Baby Masha)*.

An adaptation of Isaac Bashevis Singer's novel, ENEMIES, A LOVE STORY was directed and cowritten by Paul Mazursky (WILLIE AND PHIL; MOSCOW ON THE HUDSON; DOWN AND OUT IN BEVERLY HILLS) and stars Silver as a Jew who survived the Holocaust because his family's Catholic Polish servant, Stein, helped him hide from the Nazis. Believing his own wife to have died in the Holocaust, Silver marries Stein out of gratitude when the couple emigrates to the US and settles in Coney Island after the war. Although he works as a ghost writer for a rabbi (King), Silver tells his wife that he is a traveling book salesman; thus he explains the time he spends away from home with his mistress, Olin, another Holocaust survivor.

When Olin becomes pregnant, he impulsively marries her—since Stein is a Gentile, her marriage to Silver is not recognized by his religion—but does not divorce Stein. Life becomes even more complicated for Silver when his first wife, Huston, arrives on the scene. Left for dead after being shot by the Nazis, she escaped to Russia and made her way to America to be reunited with her husband. Silver thus finds himself married to three women simultaneously, and unable to leave any of them. Owing Stein his life, he can't bear to abandon her, but is clearly bound to her by duty rather than passion. Passion is precisely what he gets from Olin, as well as the bond of shared religion and experience. Huston, however, knows him best—better than he knows himself—and Silver gives himself over to Huston, who volunteers to be his "manager," getting him a job with her uncle and advising him on his marriage to Stein. Olin drops out of the picture when she becomes fed up with Silver's inability to leave his other wives, but returns to bring about the film's climax, in which Silver decides to leave his now-stable domestic life to run away with her. In the end, he literally disappears, having failed all three of the women in his life.

Though hobbled by their Hollywood-European accents, Ron Silver and Anjelica Huston nevertheless etch strong, memorable characters, as do Swedish actress Lena Olin (who played another mistress in THE UNBEARABLE LIGHTNESS OF BEING) and Polish actress Margaret Sophie Stein (DANTON). The capable supporting cast is highlighted by Alan King and by director Mazursky himself, who plays the husband Olin divorces to marry Silver. The production is flawless, meticulously and richly recreating the New York City of 1949. Despite these strengths, however, ENEMIES, A LOVE STORY remains a frustrating, inaccessible film. In bringing Singer's story of how a group of Holocaust survivors succeed or fail in living with their pasts, Mazursky and his coscripter, Roger L. Simon (creator of the Jewish detective-novel sleuth Moses Wine) show a great deal of care and respect for their literary source, as well as reverence for its historical background. But, as is too often the case with self-consciously serious Hollywood films, the results are more admirable than they are enjoyable or engrossing, an exercise in artistic restraint rather than affirmation. ENEMIES remains remote, chiefly because of Mazursky's surprisingly colorless direction and the meandering script. The filmmakers squash the story's comedy and downplay the drama almost to the point of incoherence, presumably to avoid the charge of manipulation. But movie audiences *want* to be manipulated (at least to a point), to be made to laugh or cry, to give themselves over to the moviegoing experi-

Anjelica Huston and Ron Silver in ENEMIES: A LOVE STORY (©20th Century Fox).

ence. As an experience, ENEMIES is more likely to engender respect for its source and subject than to earn respect on its own. Songs include: "Sunny Side of the Street" (Dorothy Fields, Jimmy McHugh, performed by Tommy Dorsey and His Orchestra), "Love Is Here to Stay" (Ira Gershwin, George Gershwin, performed by Billie Holiday), "Joseph! Joseph!" (Sammy Cahn, Saul Chaplin, Nellie Casma, Samuel Steinberg, performed by the Andrews Sisters), "Happy Talk" (Oscar Hammerstein II, Richard Rodgers, performed by Juanita Hall), "Leap Frog" (Joe Garland, Les Brown, performed by Les Brown and His Band of Reknown), "Mona Lisa" (Jay Livingston, Ray Evans, performed by Leo Parker), "Palestina (Lena from Palesteena)" (Con Conrad, J. Russel Robinson, performed by the Klezmer Conservatory Band), "Di Zilberne Khasene" (performed by the Klezmorim), "Kol Nidre" (performed by Cantor Burny Lieberman), "Hashem Molokh" (performed by Cantor Gershon Sirota), "Song of Songs" (performed by Cantor Nathaniel Katzman). *(Sexual situations, adult situations, nudity, violence.)*

p, Paul Mazursky, Pato Guzman, and Irby Smith; d, Paul Mazursky; w, Roger L. Simon and Paul Mazursky (based on the novel by Isaac Bashevis Singer); ph, Fred Murphy (Deluxe Color); ed, Stuart Pappe; m, Maurice Jarre; prod d, Pato Guzman; art d, Steven J. Jordan; spec eff, Jacques Godbout; cos, Albert Wolsky; makeup, David Craig Forrest.

Comedy/Drama   (PR:C MPAA:R)

ERIK THE VIKING**
(Brit.) 103m John Goldstone-Prominent Features-Svensk/Orion c
Tim Robbins *(Erik)*, Gary Cady *(Keitel Blacksmith)*, Mickey Rooney *(Erik's Grandfather)*, Eartha Kitt *(Freya)*, Imogen Stubbs *(Princess Aud)*, John Cleese *(Halfdan the Black)*, Antony Sher *(Loki)*, John Gordon Sinclair *(Ivar the Boneless)*, Samantha Bond *(Helga)*, Tim McInnerny *(Sven the Berserk)*, Richard Ridings *(Thorfinn Skullsplitter)*, Freddie Jones *(Harald the Missionary)*, Charles McKeown *(Sven's Dad)*, Danny Schiller *(Snorri the Miserable)*, Tsutomu Sekine *(Slavemaster)*, Terry Jones *(King Arnulf)*, Jim Broadbent *(Ernest the Viking, a Rapist)*, Jim Carter *(Jennifer the Viking, another Rapist)*, Matyelok Gibbs *(Erik's Mum)*, Tilly Vosburgh *(Unn-the-Thrown-at)*, Jay Simpson *(Leif the Lucky)*, John Scott Martin *(Ingemund the Old)*, Sian Thomas *(Thorhild the Sarcastic)*, Sarah Crowden *(Grimhild Housewife)*, Bernard Padden *(Mordfiddle the Cook)*, Bernard Latham *(Ulf the Unmemorable)*, Julia McCarthy *(Thorfinn's Mum)*, Allan Surtees *(Thorfinn's Dad)*, Sandra Voe *(Ivar's Mum)*, Angela Connolly *(Thorkatla the*

Indiscreet), Sally Jones *(Leif's Pregnant Girlfriend)*, Andrew Maclachlan *(Ornulf/Chamberlain/Dog Soldier)*, Tim Killick *(Bjarni/Halfdan's Guard/Musician)*, Graham McTavish *(Thangbrand/Citizen/Dog Soldier)*, Cyril Shaps *(Gisli the Chiseller)*, Peter Geeves *(Eilif the Mongol Horde/Musician)*, Paddy Joyce, Colin Harper, Harry Jones, Barry McCarthy, Gary Roost *(Prisoners)*, Neil Innes *(Hy Brasilian)*, Simon Evans *(Odin)*, Matthew Baker *(Thor)*, Dave Duffy *(Horribly Slain Warrior)*, Frank Bednash *(Even More Horribly Slain Warrior)*.

Probably the only genuine bit of Nordic mythology in ERIK THE VIKING is Erik's visit to Valhalla, where those who have perished in battle join Odin in an eternal round of feasts and combat. The rest of this film is mythology according to writer-director Terry Jones, who based ERIK THE VIKING on stories he wrote for his seven-year-old son (though, according to the film's production notes, these stories were much changed during the scriptwriting process). Jones' eponymous Erik (Robbins) is a very unhappy Viking, tired of raping and pillaging. Accordingly, he visits the soothsayer Freya (Kitt) and asks her how to stop the destruction of his times—the dark, war-plagued Age of Ragnarok. She sends him on a quest to the Atlantis-like Hy-Brasil to find the Horn Resounding, which he must sound three times in order to wake the gods. Then the long winter of Ragnarok will give way to the sun—and, of course, to a new, golden age.

It's a nice idea that doesn't quite work. Jones has said he conceived the film as an adventure, but ERIK THE VIKING lacks that genre's edge-of-the-seat pace and tension. Instead, ERIK THE VIKING is a fantasy that—like most of the Monty Python alumni's films—plays more as a collection of extended comedy bits than as a full-length feature. Not that ERIK THE VIKING is always funny—it's not—but it also lacks the depth that would allow viewers to identify with its characters. As a result, we are unable to feel that Erik is a hero, or to revel in his quest to save his race from destruction through virtuous deeds. Moreover, if the script leaves much to be desired, the dialog is at times indecipherable—what with all the noise of battles, floods, and other natural and unnatural disasters that occur.

There are, however, some unforgettable performances, including a delightful turn by director Jones himself. As King Arnulf of Hy-Brasil, Jones has by far the best scene in the film when, after the Vikings land on Hy-Brasil, he insists on singing for the visitors. John Cleese is also marvelous, dispensing his own rare form of "justice" as the villainous Halfdan the Black. Unfortunately, Tim Robbins (BULL DURHAM) looks terribly confused in the lead, and Mickey Rooney is also badly miscast in a

cameo as Erik's grandfather. The women (not surprisingly, in a Python adventure) are forgettable; as Erik's love interest, Imogen Stubbs evidently thinks she's doing Shakespeare, and Eartha Kitt isn't onscreen for more than five minutes. Only Samantha Bond, as the girl who inspires Erik's heroism, has any spark.

Despite its many flaws, children will probably love ERIK THE VIKING, especially the film's strongest element: the beautiful production design by John Beard (who studied Viking ships in Norway to create the custom-built vessel used here). Special-effects man Richard Conway (ALIEN; INDIANA JONES AND THE TEMPLE OF DOOM) also contributes fine work, especially the marvelous Dragon of the North Sea and the magical images of the Rainbow Bridge and Valhalla.

ERIK THE VIKING isn't an exciting movie, but it's fairly entertaining, especially for children. All the Age of Ragnarok's Nordic violence remains offscreen, and the memorable character acting—something Hollywood has all but forgotten—will add to the fun for older viewers.

p, John Goldstone; d, Terry Jones; w, Terry Jones; ph, Ian Wilson (Fujicolor); ed, George Akers; m, Neil Innes; md, Neil Innes; prod d, John Beard; art d, Gavin Bocquet and Roger Cain; set d, Joan Woollard; spec eff, Richard Conway; cos, Pam Tait; stunts, Martin Grace; makeup, Jenny Shircore.

Fantasy   (PR:AA MPAA:PG-13)

Ⓥ**EXPERTS, THE***
83m James Keach/PAR c
John Travolta *(Travis)*, Arye Gross *(Wendell)*, Kelly Preston *(Bonnie)*, Deborah Foreman *(Jill)*, James Keach *(Yuri)*, Charles Martin Smith *(Cameron Smith)*, Jan Rubes, Brian Doyle Murray, Mimi Maynard, Eve Brent, Rick Docommun, Steve Levitt, Tony Edwards.

John Travolta, whose career has cooled considerably since SATURDAY NIGHT FEVER, stars in this comedy that holds some promise but fails to deliver on it. Deep in the heart of the Soviet Union lies the KGB's most guarded spy-training outpost—a replicated Hometown USA where future spies are literally raised as Americans. Their conception of American culture, however, is woefully behind the times. Smith, a KGB middle-management type closer to the cutting edge, convinces his superiors to allow him to give the town a modern makeover by duping a couple of real American "experts" to act as advisers. On a trip through the trendy night club district of New York City, Smith manages to recruit down-on-his-luck Travolta and partner Gross to open a hip night club in the sleepy little hamlet of Indian Springs,

Nebraska. After being drugged en route, the two wake up to find themselves in a world that's somewhere between "Happy Days" and "Twilight Zone." Their impact on the local denizens is immediate, as they transform a cliched Polynesian bar into a modern disco, where Travolta, not surprisingly, is allowed to reactivate his pelvis for the enjoyment of Preston, a fetching Soviet spy who soon falls for the expert's all-American lovemaking know-how. She finds herself in a quandary, though, because she's been assigned to undermine Smith's operation by Murray, a rival KGB official determined to see the makeover fail. The townsfolk are totally enamored of the new changes and Smith further excites their newfound taste for the au courant by importing the latest in electronic toys and modern creature comforts. When the goods arrive Smith has Keach, the plane's Latvian pilot, jailed for pilfering condoms. In a matter of weeks the town is totally hip, much to the delight of Smith and the chagrin of Murray. When the Fourth of July rolls around, Travolta and Gross conduct their entourage to a lake outside of the confines of the compound. After the brewski runs out, the two volunteer to drive back to restock. Narrowly escaping an attempt on their lives by Murray's hit

men, they soon learn the real nature of their mission and are captured and jailed. Offered the choice of death or defection, the two opt instead to rally the locals by reminding them that they are more American than Russian. A frenzied escape follows with Travolta, Gross, and Keach spiriting the converts to freedom in Keach's cargo plane. Landing in New York, the townsfolk find themselves poorly served by their newly adopted land, but a Greyhound bus is chartered and off they go to Nebraska to set up a more wholesome life.

THE EXPERTS is at best what used to be called an "okay drive-in flick," meaning it's well-suited for today's less judgmental home video market. Seemingly responding to the ever-increasing dents being made in the Iron Curtain, the film has at its heart the wistful supposition that the Russian people would be just like us given the chance. But the real joke here is not so much a poke at the naive Russians as it is a parody of American television—hardly new, hardly funny. That Travolta and Gross come off clumsily, however, is due more to a weak script than to an awkward premise; their eternal bickering is particularly annoying and adds conspicuously to the burden they must bear. Travolta, the senior

partner, struggles through one uneven scene after another as if he is already aware of the box-office indifference that would greet the film upon its limited theatrical release. For his part, Arye Gross fashions his approach to the material as if his only acting lesson were learned at the Gene Wilder School of Hyperbolic Reaction. Even the dance scene between Travolta and Kelly Preston is not particularly well choreographed and inappropriately salacious for its moment in the story. Moreover, director Dave Thomas, the funny SCTV alum, should be embarrassed by his obvious attempt to enliven this flimsy comedy with a rollicking madcap ending reminiscent of the pace of the last 10 minutes of any episode of TV's "Moonlighting." The only slightly relevant touch of irony provided by this paean to American patriotism is that the movie was filmed entirely in Canada. *(Sexual situations, profanity.)*

p, James Keach; d, Dave Thomas; w, Nick Thile, Steven Greene, and Eric Alter (based on a story by Steven Greene, Eric Alter); ph, Ronnie Taylor (Alpha Cine Color); ed, Bud Molin and Eric Strand; m, Marvin Hamlisch; prod d, David Fischer; set d, Kim MacKenzie; spec eff, George Erschbamer.

Comedy   (PR:C   MPAA:PG-13)

F

FABULOUS BAKER BOYS, THE**½
114m Gladden-Mirage/FOX c

Jeff Bridges *(Jack Baker)*, Beau Bridges *(Frank Baker)*, Michelle Pfeiffer *(Susie Diamond)*, Ellie Raab *(Nina)*, Xander Berkeley *(Lloyd)*, Dakin Matthews *(Charlie)*, Ken Lerner *(Ray)*, Albert Hall *(Henry)*, Terri Treas *(Girl in Bed)*, Gregory Itzin *(Vince Nancy)*, Bradford English *(Earl)*, David Coburn *(Kid in Veterinarian's Office)*, Todd Jeffries *(Theo)*, Jeffrey J. Nowinski *(Hotel Masseuse)*, Nancy Fish *(Laughing Bar Patron)*, Beege Barkette *(Waitress)*, Del Zamora *(Man with Cleaver)*, Howard Matthew Johnson *(Bathroom Attendant)*, Stuart Nisbet *(Veterinarian)*, Robert Henry *(Doorman)*, Drake the Dog *(Eddie)*, Martina Finch, Winifred Freedman, Wendy Goldman, Karen Hartman, D.D. Howard, Lisa Raggio, Vickilyn Reynolds, Krisie Spear, Carol Ita White *(Bad Singers)*, Steve Alterman, Bach August, Greg Finley, J.D. Hall, Doris Hess, Rosanna Huffman, John La Fayette, Tina Lifford, Arlin Miller, Paige Nan Pollack, David J. Randolph, Stephani Ryan *(Background Voices)*, Jennifer Tilly *(Monica Moran)*.

Jeff Bridges' long-standing affinity for fringe characters has resulted in memorable portrayals in such diverse movies as THUNDERBOLT AND LIGHTFOOT (1974); 8 MILLION WAYS TO DIE (1986); FAT CITY (1972); and STARMAN (1984). The trend continues with THE FABULOUS BAKER BOYS, which, unfortunately, raises the question of whether playing handsome but seedy outsiders has reached a point of diminishing returns for the twice Oscar-nominated actor. Though full of atmosphere, mood, and attitude, THE FABULOUS BAKER BOYS is all dressed up with no place to go.

Jeff plays Jack Baker; real-life sibling Beau Bridges plays Jack's brother, Frank. Once musical prodigies, the boys are now looking a little hard around the arteries, chasing one cheap date after another through the sleazy cocktail lounges of Seattle. The Fabulous Baker Boys' act consists of playing dueling piano arrangements of every bad lounge song you've ever heard, from "Little Green Apples" to the immortal "Feelings," but when an unctuous club owner actually pays the boys *not* to show up for the second half of a two-night stand, Frank (the older, more responsible brother who serves as their manager) decides it's time to shake up the act by bringing in a female singer. After numerous singers clomp and bellow their way through an audition from hell, the nod finally goes to Susie Diamond (Michelle Pfeiffer), whose professional experience has been limited to an extended engagement with an "escort" service. The film never provides an adequate explanation for Susie's polished vocal talents, but to say she knows how to sell a song is an understatement. After raising the temperature in a number of rooms with her sultry renditions of lounge-lizard standards, Susie is still second-billed, but her picture and name loom larger on the billboard than do those of the Bakers. Tensions rise when womanizing Jack fails to heed Frank's unsolicited advice to "stick to cocktail waitresses" and embarks on a professionally dangerous liaison with Susie.

In its early going, THE FABULOUS BAKER BOYS crackles with smart talk and clever moves from writer-director Steve Kloves, who makes his directing debut here and who wrote the equally off-center RACING WITH THE MOON (1984). Later in the film, Pfeiffer continues to captivate, and more—her writhing turn atop a piano while performing "Makin' Whoopee" will not soon be forgotten by connoisseurs of mainstream film eroticism. When it comes to plot and characters, however, THE FABULOUS BAKER BOYS is purely superficial, and the three principals become less interesting as the action grinds on. In an attempt to intensify the drama, Kloves focuses on moody Jack, the least intriguing of the trio, and his internal struggle over whether to pursue the bucks as a Baker Boy or to pursue art as a jazz pianist (as if cabaret acts like the Baker Boys were completely lacking in aesthetic credibility and "serious" jazz musicians had no use for money). Not only has this sort of thing been done before—and better—in other films, but it becomes frustrating as Kloves ignores Frank and Susie in order to examine Jack's boring pseudo-crisis. What is it like for Frank, a well-padded family man and straight arrow with a house in the suburbs, to spend 300 nights a year on the road in seedy motel rooms surrounded by watery booze, cheap women, and cheating men? We're barely given a clue. It's a measure of the movie's supreme lack of interest in Frank that we never even see his wife or kids—and we know even less about what Susie does when she's not performing with the Bakers.

Though the Bridges boys give typically solid performances, it's Pfeiffer who

Beau Bridges, Michelle Pfeiffer, and Jeff Bridges in THE FABULOUS BAKER BOYS (©20th Century Fox).

deserves the most credit for keeping THE FABULOUS BAKER BOYS interesting long after it's run out of gas, and not just because of her form-fitting outfits. Throughout the film, she keeps her Susie from becoming just another cliched, road-worn torch singer or hooker with a heart of gold. Instead, Susie is an original—smart, hard-headed, and thoroughly unsentimental, she knows exactly what she's got and how to use it, but Pfeiffer makes her as humane as she is seductive. Pfeiffer worked hard at the role, getting her singing voice (last heard on film in GREASE 2 [1982]) in shape and working for months before filming began to develop a chanteuse's vocal style. Her efforts pay off as well as they can, considering the thinness of her character as written.

Photographed by the gifted Michael Ballhaus, THE FABULOUS BAKER BOYS is all atmosphere and offbeat tone. Unfortunately, like many another "unconventional" Hollywood effort, it fails to base its evocative style on real substance, and thus fails to emerge from the run of the mill. Songs include: "People" (Jule Styne, Bob Merrill, performed by Dave Grusin, John Hammond), "Jingle Bells" (performed by Ellie Raab), "The Girl from Ipanema" (Antonio Carlos Jobim, Norman Gimbel, Vinicius de Moraes, performed by Grusin, Hammond), "The Candy Man" (Leslie Bricusse, Anthony Newley, performed by Jennifer Tilly), "My Way" (Paul Anka, Gillis Thibault, Claude Francois, Jacques Revaux, performed by Lisa Raggio), "Up-Up and Away" (Jimmy Webb, performed by D.D. Howard), "Tiny Bubbles" (Leon Pober, performed by Carole Ita White), "I Go to Rio" (Peter Allen, Adrienne Anderson, performed by Wendy Goldman), "Feelings" (Louis Gaste, Morris Albert, performed by Winifred Freedman, Michelle Pfeiffer), "I'm So Excited" (Anita Pointer, June Pointer, Ruth Pointer, Trevor Lawrence, performed by Krisie Spear, Martina Finch, Vickilyn Reynolds, Karen Hartman), "More Than You Know" (Edward Eliscu, Billy Rose, Vincent Youmans, performed by Pfeiffer), "Bluebird" (A. Hawkshaw), "Ten Cents a Dance" (Richard Rodgers, Lorenz Hart, performed by Pfeiffer, Jeff Bridges, Beau Bridges), "Can't Take My Eyes off of You" (Bob Crewe, Bob Gaudio, performed by Pfeiffer), "Lullaby of Birdland" (George Shearing, performed by Louis Spears, Kenny Dennis, Joel Scott), "Perdido" (Juan Tizol, performed by the Duke Ellington Orchestra), "The Look of Love" (Burt Bacharach, Hal David, performed by Pfeiffer), "Prelude to a Kiss" (Edward Kennedy [Duke] Ellington, Irving Gordon, Irving Mills, performed by the Duke Ellington Orchestra), "Moonglow" (Will Hudson, Eddie de Lange, Irving Mills, performed by the Benny Goodman Quartet), "Do Nothin' Till You Hear from Me"

(Ellington, Bob Russell, performed by the Duke Ellington Orchestra), "Makin' Whoopee (Walter Donaldson, Gus Kahn, performed by Pfeiffer), "Solitude" (Ellington, de Lange, Mills, performed by Tony Bennett), "You're Sixteen, You're Beautiful and You're Mine" (Robert Sherman, Richard Sherman, performed by Jeff Bridges, Beau Bridges), "The Pea Song" (Steve Kloves, Pfeiffer, performed by Pfeiffer), "My Funny Valentine" (Rodgers, Hart, performed by Pfeiffer). (Adult situations, profanity.)

p, Paula Weinstein, Mark Rosenberg, and Bill Finnegan; d, Steve Kloves; w, Steve Kloves; ph, Michael Ballhaus (Deluxe Color); ed, William Steinkamp; m, Dave Grusin; prod d, Jeffrey Townsend; set d, Don Gibbin Jr.; spec eff, Robert E. Worthington; cos, Lisa Jensen; chor, Peggy Holmes; stunts, John Pochron; makeup, Ronnie Spector.

Comedy/Drama   (PR:C-O MPAA:R)

FAMILY BUSINESS*½

114m Tri-Star-Regency-Gordon/ Tri-Star c

Sean Connery (*Jessie McMullen*), Dustin Hoffman (*Vito McMullen*), Matthew Broderick (*Adam McMullen*), Rosana DeSoto (*Elaine McMullen*), Janet Carroll (*Margie*), Victoria Jackson (*Christine*), Bill McCutcheon (*Doheny*), B.D. Wong (*Jimmy Chiu*), Deborah Rush (*Michele Dempsey*), Marilyn Cooper (*Rose*), Salem Ludwig (*Nat*), Rex Everhart (*Ray Garvey*), Marilyn Sokol (*Marie*), Thomas A. Carlin (*Neary*), Tony DiBenedetto (*Phil*), James S. Tolkan (*Judges*), Isabell Monk (*Judges*), Wendell Pierce (*Prosecutor*), James Carruthers (*Court Clerk*), Jack O'Connell (*Police Lieutenant*), John C. Capodice (*Tommy*), Luis Guzman (*Torres*), Dermot A. McNamara (*Casket Mourner*), William Preston (*Flask Mourner*), John P. Connell (*Wake "Suit" Cop*), Raymond H. Bazemore (*"Caper" Guard*), Conrad Fowkes (*"Caper" Detective*), Willie Carpenter (*"Caper" Cop*), Hal Lehrman (*Assistant D.A.*), Nick Discenza (*Detective*), Ed Crowley (*Charlie*), Arthur Pierce (*Convict*), Elizabeth A. Reilly (*Phil's Girl Friend*), Karen Needle (*Denise*), Susan Korn (*Margo*), Aideen O'Kelly (*Widow Doheny*), George Kodisch (*Wake Cop*).

FAMILY BUSINESS tells the story of the McMullen clan, a New York family consisting of Jessie (Connery), a 65-year-old thief with a vibrant personality and devious ideas; his son Vito (Hoffman), a one-time crook who now runs a meat-packing business; and Vito's son Adam (Broderick), a Westinghouse scholar with a bright, totally legal future. After leaving graduate school, with only three months left for his master's degree, Broderick hooks up with his grandfather and tells him about a heist he would like to attempt.

Seeking revenge against his company, a disgruntled employee of a laboratory has presented Broderick with a plan calling for the theft of test tubes full of experimental gene-splicing plasmas that will revolutionize science. It's a sure thing: easy access, simple work, and a million dollars cash upon completion of the job. Broderick and Connery approach Hoffman with the idea; however, he holds a grudge against Connery for raising him with only illegal aspirations (as a child he even helped Connery steal Christmas trees and train sets). Hoffman has higher hopes for his own son, whom he doesn't want to be a thief. But after an initial meeting and a few arguments, Hoffman reluctantly agrees to participate in the heist. The McMullens plan and prepare for the job carefully, buying tools and renting hotel rooms. Everything goes smoothly, except for a little trouble with Hoffman's ski mask, and they break in and out of the lab safely. Broderick forgets some important documents, however, and must go back inside to retrieve them. On the way out he trips an alarm, bringing the police, who arrest him. Meanwhile, Hoffman and Connery get away with the plasma and the documents. In time, Hoffman confesses to the crime both to his wife and to the authorities, telling the police everything in order to save Broderick. Connery and Hoffman are arrested and the whole family is brought to trial. Hoffman and son receive light probationary sentences, but Connery is given a 25-year prison term. As the months go by, Broderick (who has stopped speaking to Hoffman because he "ratted" on his own father) visits the now sick and old-looking Connery in prison. They discuss their relationship and what the job meant to them, and, finally, Connery dies. Hoffman and Broderick reunite, forgive and forget, and the film ends with father and son scattering Connery's ashes on a rooftop in Brooklyn.

FAMILY BUSINESS has all the makings of a good film: the cast is exceptional, director Sidney Lumet is a Hollywood favorite, and the screenplay is by acclaimed author Vincent Patrick (*The Pope of Greenwich Village*). So why does this movie stink? The answer lies with Patrick's ridiculous screenplay. Full of ethnic stereotypes and surprisingly offensive dialog (Wop, Polack, Chink, Mick, and many other racial and ethnic slurs are heard with regularity), the script is an exercise in repulsive cliche. Moreover, the story is predictable to the point of boredom, and Lumet's wildly meandering direction doesn't help. The film is paced in sporadic bursts, with the first hour (covering the initial meetings and the caper itself) moving like lightning, and the final 50 minutes crawling along lifelessly.

The actors seem lost in this mess, especially Dustin Hoffman, who gives a weirdly sadistic performance. Only Sean

Matthew Broderick, Sean Connery, and Dustin Hoffman in FAMILY BUSINESS (©Tri-Star).

Connery's flamboyant Jessie has any personality. The strange casting only adds to the film's bizarre ethnic overtones. Jewish actors play Italians, Spanish actors play Jews, Italians play Irishmen, and so on, as if Lumet actually believes in the existence of the plot's gene-splicing plasmas. The emotion is shallow, the relationships are unbelievable (it isn't for an instant credible that the three leads are related), and the father-son conflict between Jessie and Vito is never explored. Character traits are also insufficiently explained. Vito beats up one of his employees for stealing meat, and Jessie slaps around an off-duty policeman, but this violent behavior is never discussed (except for one brief mention in a confrontation between Vito and Jessie). Not surprisingly, the result of this absence of adequate motivation is viewer frustration. Credit should be given to Matthew Broderick, though, for holding his own against two heavyweights like Hoffman and Connery. An actor whom some have found annoying in the past, Broderick keeps his smug mannerisms (unbearable in FERRIS BEULLER'S DAY OFF) to a minimum and tries to bring his character to life. Although he doesn't succeed (thanks to Lumet's and Patrick's dismal contributions), it's a valiant effort. Hoffman follows his Oscar-winning turn in RAIN MAN with an aloof and sometimes painfully overdone performance; Connery is watchable, but seems to be coasting, relying on his own likable personality to carry him through the dreck.

FAMILY BUSINESS is a totally confused picture. Written like a caper film, directed like a comedy (the awful score is probably the funniest thing about the film), and acted like a drama, it simply never gels. If viewers are not totally uninterested, they likely will be offended by the film's unnecessary ethnic jokes (at one point Connery says living with a Sicilian is like "cooking pasta and pissing olive oil 24 hours a day"). One thing is certain, no one is going to rush off to buy the Patrick novel on which the film is based. Songs include: "Danny Boy" (Frederick E. Weatherly), "The Tenement Symphony" (Hal Borne, Sid Kuller), "Almost Like Being in Love" (Alan Jay Lerner, Frederick Loewe), "Red Roses for a Blue Lady" (Roy C. Bennett, Sid Tepper). *(Profanity, violence, substance abuse, adult situations.)*

p, Lawrence Gordon; d, Sidney Lumet; w, Vincent Patrick (based on his novel); ph, Andrzej Bartkowiak (Technicolor); ed, Andrew Mondshein; m, Cy Coleman; md, Sonny Kompanek; prod d, Philip Rosenberg; art d, Robert Guerra; set d, Gary Brink; cos, Ann Roth; makeup, Joseph Cranzano.

Comedy/Drama   (PR:C MPAA:R)

ⓥFAR FROM HOME**
86m Lightning/Vestron c
Matt Frewer *(Charlie Cross)*, Drew Barrymore *(Joleen Cross)*, Richard Masur *(Duckett)*, Karen Austin *(Louise)*, Susan Tyrrell *(Agnes Reed)*, Anthony Rapp *(Pinky Sears)*, Jennifer Tilly *(Amy)*, Andras Jones *(Jimmy Reed)*, Dick Miller *(Sheriff Bill Childers)*, Connie Sawyer *(Viney Hunt)*, Stephanie Walski *(Sissy Reed)*, Teri Weigel *(Girl in Trailer)*.

Stop us if you've heard this one before: A divorced father (Matt Frewer, of "Max Headroom" fame) and his rapidly maturing young daughter (Drew Barrymore, *People* magazine cover girl) are traveling through the desert when they run out of gas, wind up in a sleazy trailer park, and battle a steadicam psycho. FAR FROM HOME is one of those movies you feel you've seen before, even if you haven't. Though not as bad as it might have been, it easily could have been much better, especially given the film's promising mix of ingredients. Frewer and Barrymore are less-than-inspired choices for the leads, but Susan Tyrrell is well-cast as the hilarious trailer-park owner. Equally well-suited for their roles are Richard Masur, as a Vietnam vet who's likable, though a little the worse for wear; Jennifer Tilly and Karen Austin, whose lack of gasoline has also trapped them in the trailer park; and Dick Miller as the sheriff. Former *Playboy* Playmate Teri Weigel, who has become a pulchritudinous icon of 80s B movies, even shows up—appropriately enough—for the film's sole nude scene. Bringing this amusingly motley bunch together in the godforsaken oasis of a trailer park in Banco, Nevada, is a script by Tommy Lee Wallace, the John Carpenter crony who directed HALLOWEEN III.

Yet, the resulting film has little in the way of humor and even less genuine suspense. Wallace's script tries for a degree of psychological subtlety in its central relationship between a daughter perched precariously between childhood and maturity (Barrymore) and her divorced father (Frewer). A free-lance writer, he tries awkwardly to reach out to his daughter by bringing her along on an assignment involving America's national parks. The ill-fated exercise in father-daughter bonding is coming to a disastrous close when the two are brought closer together by a blood-soaked fight for survival at Tyrrell's trailer park of terror. Wallace's script even attempts to draw a parallel between a daughter who takes her father for granted and a son who has been left to fend for himself after his mother dies. Whether Wallace's script lacked the depth to follow through on its premise, or whether director Meiert Avis simply decided to drop any pretense of subtlety and go for the jugular, FAR FROM HOME soon abandons any interest in its characters to become just another PSYCHO clone. While stranded in the trailer park, Barrymore becomes the object of the affections of both Tyrrell's rude but ruggedly handsome offspring (Jones) and the nerdish-but-sweet son (Rapp) of an invalid mother. The film then hinges on discovering which of the two is the insane killer bumping off the trailer-park denizens in a spectacularly grisly fashion. But the killer's identity is bound to be blatantly obvious to anyone who has ever seen a slasher film.

Of course, originality has never been a hallmark of the psycho-killer subgenre. What counts is a compelling hero and/or heroine, and FAR FROM HOME has neither. To be charitable, Barrymore is no Jamie Lee Curtis, and Frewer is bland and uninvolving as the dad, though the script and direction provide them with little help (for a film revolving around a father-daughter relationship, FAR FROM HOME inexplicably separates its father and daughter for most of the action). Among the supporting performers, Miller has little to do but stand around and look serious as the sheriff, and Tyrrell chews the scenery with her usual shrill abandon, but Masur is low-keyed and funny as the vet who has come to the desert to get away from it all, and Tilly manages to draw a few chuckles as Austin's dimwitted pal.

What pleasures there are to be had from FAR FROM HOME are purely incidental. Production designer Victoria Paul's trailer park is a masterpiece of sunbaked sordidness, and Paul Elliott's cinematography makes good use of the otherworldly Nevada desert setting. But being neither offbeat enough to be interesting, nor well-crafted enough to qualify as a serviceable genre piece, FAR FROM HOME is simply another routine low-budget slasher picture. *(Violence, adult situations, brief nudity, profanity.)*

p, Donald P. Borchers; d, Meiert Avis; w, Tommy Lee Wallace (based on a story by Ted Gershun); ph, Paul Elliott (CFI Color); ed, Marc Grossman; m, Jonathan Elias; prod d, Victoria Paul; cos, Donna Linson.

Horror   (PR:O MPAA:R)

◉FAREWELL TO THE KING**
117m Vestron/Orion c

Nick Nolte *(Learoyd)*, Nigel Havers *(Capt. Fairbourne)*, Frank McRae *(Sgt. Tenga)*, Gerry Lopez *(Gwai)*, Marilyn Tokuda *(Yoo)*, Choy Chang Wing *(Lian)*, Aki Aleong *(Col. Mitamura)*, Marius Weyers *(Sgt. Conklin)*, William Wise *(Dynamite Dave)*, Wayne Pygram *(Bren Armstrong)*, Richard Morgan *(Stretch Lewis)*, Elan Oberon *(Vivienne)*, James Fox *(Col. Ferguson)*, Michael Nissman *(Gen. Sutherland)*, John Bennett Perry *(Gen. MacArthur)*.

Once again writer-director John Milius attempts to re-create the sort of epic romantic adventure typical of 19th-century literature, only to fail miserably due to his basic ineptness as a writer and filmmaker. While he strives to emulate Conrad and Kipling, his work is really much closer to the daydreams of a lonely 10-year-old—and about as insightful. Milius' wistfulness for a time and place where white men could penetrate the deep

jungle in search of the heart of darkness may be repulsive in the 1990s, but a film derived from it might at least offer some good old-fashioned mindless fun at the movies. Unfortunately, though Milius is not a particularly good writer, he is an even worse director.

FAREWELL TO THE KING opens with the desertion of several Allied soldiers, attempting to escape both their own army and the Japanese. Washed ashore on Japanese-controlled Borneo, one soldier (Nolte) abandons his comrades, saying, "I've had enough! Bataan! Corregidor! We're free now, free to go our own way!" then runs into the jungle, only to witness the slaughter of his companions by the brutal Japanese. Unable to bring himself to kill the Japanese commander who sits astride a white horse nearby, Nolte crawls deep into the jungle. Two years later, British officer Havers and his African-born sergeant, McRae, parachute into Borneo to enlist the aid of Nolte, who has become king of a tribe of Dayak headhunters. Impressed by his blue eyes and chest-tattoo, the Dayaks have accepted Nolte as their leader (these events related in a clumsy flashback narrated by Nolte). Although moved by Nolte's obvious passion for the Dayaks and their culture, Havers presses the "king" for his assistance in battling the Japanese. At first Nolte refuses, but after much talk of the inevitability of history, Nolte agrees to help, with the stipulation that he receive a contract signed by Gen. Douglas MacArthur that recognizes Nolte's sovereignty and the Dayak's right to remain autonomous upon the defeat of the Japanese. Havers returns to his base camp only to be scoffed at by his cynical commander (Fox), who ominously intones, "You do know that one fine day you'll have to betray your king." Be that as it may, Havers meets with MacArthur and the treaty is signed. Back in Borneo, Nolte assembles a group of warriors to fight the Japanese alongside a small contingent of crack Allied commandos. After many battles, the Japanese are whittled down to one small force led by the mysterious general on the white horse. Although they have long ago run out of rations, the Japanese soldiers seem well fed, and McRae suddenly realizes that the enemy are cannibalizing their victims to survive. Tragically, Nolte's idyllic village is destroyed by the Japanese and most of his people slaughtered. With his blood lust high, Nolte leads his men onward and traps the remaining Japanese in a gully, slaughtering them, much to Havers' horror. Once again the general escapes, only to nobly surrender to Nolte, who vows never to raise his hand against another man and brings his enemy into the fold. Later, Havers does indeed have to betray Nolte. The treaty is rescinded and a detachment of Australians cuts off Nolte's supply of precious salt, thus

forcing the king's small band of soldiers—including McRae, the Japanese general, and one of the commandos—to surrender. Whereupon Nolte is arrested as a deserter and put aboard a ship to be transported to a court martial. When the ship hits a coral reef, however, Havers uses the confusion to help Nolte escape, and the king returns to his people.

Often accused of being Hollywood's reigning blatantly right-wing filmmaker, writer-director Milius does little to dispel that notion, preferring to be categorized as a "Zen fascist," whatever that means. Insisting that he is anti-establishment, Milius claims to believe strongly in personal freedom—a phrase given mantric weight in FAREWELL TO THE KING. Apparently, Milius fails to see the difference in his averred political stance and the actual product of his imagination; for one who calls himself an "anti-government anarchist," he certainly pines for the good old days when white men were able to test their manhood in strange lands among exotic dark-skinned people of less "civilized" cultures. The very notion that a caucasian could ascend to leadership of an indigenous people merely by virtue of his blue eyes smacks more of imperialism and white man's burden than any anti-establishment sentiment Milius seeks to espouse. Moreover, how can a man claim to support the rejection of empire while at the same time idolizing the likes of Douglas MacArthur?

Muddled and pernicious politics aside, FAREWELL TO THE KING simply isn't a very good movie, even if you shut off your mind. As was the case with CONAN THE BARBARIAN and RED DAWN, FAREWELL TO THE KING boasts a scenario bursting with opportunities to showcase stunning action sequences, only to have that potential squandered by a director who really doesn't know how to stage them. For a man as enamored of military tactics as Milius is, he doesn't seem to have a clue how to convey violent action on-screen. As much as Milius purports to admire director David Lean, he hasn't learned a thing from his films, or from Sam Peckinpah, or even his contemporary Walter Hill. Consequently, his scenes of men in conflict are unengaging and disappointingly dull. Even worse are his basic narrative skills. Stitched together with such unwieldy cinematic devices as poorly deployed flashbacks and awkward narration, the film lurches along like a car with a busted clutch. Finally, Milius' dialog is horribly contrived—imagine Nolte solemnly intoning, "From this day forward, I will raise my hand against no man," or better yet, "You will love the velvet texture of her thighs." With lines like these only the British actors stand a chance. What we are left with, then, is some gorgeous Bornean scenery and a remarkably physical performance from Nick Nolte, who toughs it out and is fairly memorable in a role fraught with potentially humiliating pitfalls. (Violence, sexual situations, profanity.)

p, Albert S. Ruddy and Andre Morgan; d, John Milius; w, John Milius (based on the novel L'Adieu Au Roi by Pierre Schoendoerffer); ph, Dean Semler (Deluxe Color); ed, Anne V. Coates and C. Timothy O'Meara; m, Basil Poledouris; prod d, Gil Parrondo; art d, Bernard Hides; set d, Virginia Bieneman; spec eff, Gene Griggs; cos, David Rowe; chor, Anne Semler; stunts, Terry Leonard; makeup, Jose Perez.

War   (PR:C MPAA:PG-13)

◉FAST FOOD*
92m Double Helix/Fries c
Clark Brandon (Auggie), Randal Patrick (Drew), Tracy Griffith (Samantha), Michael J. Pollard (Bud), Lanny Horn (Calvin), Jim Varney (Wrangler Bob Bundy), Blake Clark (E.G. McCormick), Traci Lords (Dixie Love), Pamela Springsteen (Mary Beth Bensen), Randi Layne (Alexandra Lowell), Kevin McCarthy (Judge Reinholt), Don Ferguson.

According to the box of this straight-to-video release, FAST FOOD offers "No nutritional value." What the box doesn't say is that the film also offers no entertainment value. After a particularly confused opening, it becomes little more than a humorless "comedy" about a war between fast-food establishments. Clark Brandon (who cowrote the screenplay with Lanny Horn and Randal Patrick) plays an opportunistic college senior and member of Kappa Kappa Fraternity at Hopkins University. Like the heroes of so many other lowbrow comedies pitched at teenagers, Brandon and cohort Patrick brag about their ability to fix grades, sell term papers, and keep photographs of their sexual conquests in a bedroom hall of fame, in full view of potential inductees. After being caught scamming other students with a rigged casino party, Brandon and Patrick are unexpectedly graduated from the college they've attended for more than eight years. Wondering what to do next, they spend an afternoon antagonizing their pretty friend Griffith, who runs a filling station with the help of Pollard. Meanwhile, "Wrangler Bob" (Varney), the vicious owner of a successful chain of hamburger joints, has determined that Griffith's gas station would make a perfect spot for another of his popular hangouts. Although Varney has made several offers to Griffith, she's been reluctant to sell. It seems the gas station was her father's dream, and as Griffith says, "You can't sell your dreams." The imaginative Brandon, who once dated Griffith but is now despised by her, sets about winning back her love by coming up with a scheme to

save the station. Planning on turning 'Pop's Place' into an independently operated burger joint, Brandon goes to a bank and, without Griffith's knowledge, secures a loan by putting up the station as collateral. Were Griffith to find out, Brandon would be in big trouble, and it is the threat of this discovery that infuses FAST FOOD with what tension it manages to deliver.

Along the way (and a very long way it sometimes seems), FAST FOOD throws in unrelated elements that are clearly meant to enchance its box-office appeal: wet T-shirt contests, a secret sauce laced with a powerful aphrodisiac, and an on-again, off-again romance. Even former porn star Traci Lords makes an appearance as a spy working for Varney. Indeed, the only thing missing is a fast-food fight. Without providing a single laugh in the film's entire 92-minute running time, the lame screenplay fails to capture the sort of tastelessness that proved so successful for PORKY'S and POLICE ACADEMY. Likewise, the acting in the film is neither capable nor camp; even the presence of TV pitchman-actor Jim Varney (ERNEST GOES TO CAMP; ERNEST SAVES CHRISTMAS) is not much help. With indoor thermometers rising during the lovemaking scenes and other hackneyed jokes, FAST FOOD is as unexciting and unsatisfying as the title burgers themselves, which are shown over and over again, devoid of lettuce, tomato, bacon, or pickle. Though the film is remarkably well photographed by Bill Mills, and John D. Allen's editing is also assured, there isn't much else to recommend in FAST FOOD. (Profanity, adult situations.)

p, Stan Wakefield and Michael A. Simpson; d, Michael A. Simpson; w, Clark Brandon, Randal Patrick, and Lanny Horn (based on a story by Scott B. Sowers, Jim Bastille); ph, Bill Mills; ed, John David Allen; m, Iris Gillon; art d, Shad Leach; set d, Julie Malm.

Comedy   (PR:C MPAA:PG-13)

FAT MAN AND LITTLE BOY**
126m Lightmotive/PAR c
Paul Newman (Gen. Leslie R. Groves), Dwight Schultz (J. Robert Oppenheimer), Bonnie Bedelia (Kitty Oppenheimer), John Cusack (Michael Merriman), Laura Dern (Kathleen Robinson), Ron Frazier (Peer de Silva), John C. McGinley (Richard Schoenfield), Natasha Richardson (Jean Tatlock), Ron Vawter (Jamie Latrobe), Michael Brockman (William "Deke" Parsons), Del Close (Dr. Kenneth Whiteside), John Considine (Robert Tuckson), Alan Corduner (Franz Goethe), Joseph d'Angerio (Seth Neddermeyer), Jon De Vries (Johnny Mount), James Eckhouse (Norbert Harper), Todd Field (Robert Wilson), Mary Pat Gleason (Dora Welsh), Clark Gregg (Douglas Panton),

Peter Halasz (George Kistiakowsky), Gerald Hiken (Leo Szilard), Arthur Holden (Oakridge Doctor), Ed Lauter (Whitney Ashbridge), Donald Mackechnie (James Tuck), Madison Mason (Boris Pash), Christopher Pieczynski (Otto Frisch), Don Pugsley (Bronson), Logan Ramsey (Gen. Brehon Somervell), Fred Dalton Thompson (Melrose Hayden Barry), Jim True (Donald Hornig), Barry Yourgrau (Edward Teller), Steven Baigelman (Dr. Avenell), Frank Benettieri Jr. (Messenger), David Brainard (Samuel Allison), Roger Cubicciotti (Frank Oppenheimer), Franco Cutietta (Enrico Fermi), Robert Peter Gale (Dr. Louis Hempelmann), Wesley Harrison, Brent Harrison (Peter Oppenheimer), Marek Alboszta, Tom McFarlane (Scientists), David C. Parnes (Raincoat Man), Allen Poirson (Howard McDonald), David Politzer (Robert Serber), Bill Rubenstein (Times Reporter), Ken Strausbaugh (Observation Officer), Walter Sullivan (Henry Stimson), Brian Wandell (Dennis Talmudge), John Williams (Mack Stoddard), VOICES OF: Walker Edmiston, Matthew Faison, Stanley Jones, Alan Oppenheimer.

On paper, this slightly fictionalized account of the Manhattan Project appears to have everything going for it, including a cast headed by Paul Newman and featuring Bonnie Bedelia, Laura Dern, Natasha Richardson, and John Cusack. Moreover, it was directed by Roland Joffe, the Academy Award-nominated director of THE KILLING FIELDS (1984), and cowritten by Joffe and Bruce Robinson, whose script for THE KILLING FIELDS also earned an Oscar nomination, and who went on to direct WITHNAIL AND I (1987) and HOW TO GET AHEAD IN ADVERTISING (1989). Yet, despite the considerable talents of those involved, FAT MAN AND LITTLE BOY is slow, stilted, and stultifying.

Newman plays Gen. Leslie Groves, the tough-minded career soldier who oversees the Manhattan Project, which has brought some of the world's most eminent scientists to Los Alamos, in the New Mexico desert, to create the atomic bomb that will bring a speedy end to WW II and forever change the world. The liaison between the scientists and the military is physicist J. Robert Oppenheimer (Dwight Schultz), best-known for his continuing role as H.M. Murdock on TV's "The A-Team"), whose left-leaning political past and affair with radical Jean Tatlock (Richardson) have brought him under constant government scrutiny. Ironically, Groves, a died-in-the-wool patriot, finds himself in the position of defending Oppenheimer from his detractors, despite Groves' personal distrust of the scientist, of his politics, and even of his wife (Bedelia, who weaves through the turgid drama, martini glass in hand, and gives the film's only wholly

Peter Halasz, Joseph d'Angerio, and John Cusack in FAT MAN AND LITTLE BOY (©Paramount).

million was spent on an exacting re-creation of them in Mexico. As was the case in THE KILLING FIELDS and Joffe's second film, THE MISSION, some of the actors in FAT MAN AND LITTLE BOY are nonprofessionals, including real-life scientists. (Most notably, Dr. Robert Peter Gale, a cancer specialist who aided victims of the Chernobyl disaster, plays a small role in addition to having served as the film's technical advisor.) Unfortunately, this film isn't nearly as satisfying as Joffe's previous efforts. (*Profanity, adult situations.*)

p, Tony Garnett; d, Roland Joffe; w, Bruce Robinson and Roland Joffe (based on a story by Robinson); ph, Vilmos Zsigmond (Technicolor); ed, Francoise Bonnot; m, Ennio Morricone; prod d, Gregg Fonseca; art d, Peter Landsdown Smith and Larry Fulton; set d, Dorree Cooper; spec eff, Fred Cramer; cos, Nic Ede; chor, Marilyn Corwin; tech, Robert Peter Gale; stunts, Warren Stevens; makeup, Monty Westmore.

Historical   (PR:C MPAA:PG-13)

❶FEAR*
95m Cinetel c
Cliff DeYoung (*Don Haden*), Kay Lenz (*Sharon Haden*), Robert Factor (*Jack Gracie*), Scott Schwartz (*Brian Haden*), Geri Betzler (*Jennifer Haden*), Frank Stallone (*Robert Armitage*), Charles Meshack (*Cy Canelle*), Michael Watson (*Mitch Barnett*), Eddit Banker (*Lenny*).

As FEAR opens, a Californian couple and their two bickering teenagers are on their way to a remote mountain cabin to spend some time together ironing out family tensions. Husband DeYoung has trouble expressing love, while wife Lenz is dissatisfied with her life and has been offered a job in another city. Traveling the same rural road is a bus full of prison inmates being transferred to the state penitentiary. When a fight erupts on board, the guard and the driver are hurt and the bus pitches over a cliff into a lake. Five prisoners survive, one of whom suggests they turn themselves in, leading the other four to promptly kill him. Heading for freedom, the convicts encounter DeYoung and family at a roadside rest area and take them hostage aboard the family's van. Heading for the cabin, the criminals insist upon stopping at a country store to find decent clothes, where a Korean war vet taunts Factor, an ex-Green Beret imprisoned after a murderous rampage against his sister and her family. Factor responds by slaughtering four innocent bystanders and one of his prisonmates, foul-mouthed bully Stallone. Once the group reaches the cabin, the family is tied up by their captors. Factor begins to argue with fellow escapees Meshack and Watson, who realizes he is a psycho, but play along with his crazed plans in order to escape alive. A snoopy police officer arrives, only

believable performance). Besides the uneasy relationship between Groves and Oppenheimer, there are conflicting factions among the scientists, as there are bound to be whenever too many brilliant people are put into too small a space. The most dramatic of these conflicts comes to the fore when a group of the scientists advocate disbanding the project after the Allied victory in Europe (the project had been initiated in the belief that the Germans were working on their own atomic bomb).

Despite the dramatic potential of his material, director Joffe fails to find a single engaging personality among the cast of characters, and, as a result, little real interest is generated. Newman manages to make his Gen. Groves at least periodically interesting through his gruff, knowing performance; however, Schultz's Oppenheimer is so bland that he's boring. Regrettably, so are most of the rest of the cast. Other than Bedelia, Richardson (star of PATTY HEARST, daughter of Vanessa Redgrave and director Tony Richardson) comes closest to creating any sparks with her portrayal of Oppenheimer's mistress, whom Groves orders the physicist to stop seeing, with tragic results. Mainly the cast is done in by the script, which alternates some of the most insipid dialog to be found outside of a bad TV miniseries with an endless stream of soapbox speeches. Surely the most grating example of the latter is Groves' lecture to Mrs. Oppenheimer about the virtues of being a good wife

(Groves' own wife hasn't made the trip to Los Alamos).

As if admitting their inability to make one of the most important events in history exciting, writers Joffe and Robinson resort to a fictional subplot in the film's latter stages: an affair between a young scientist (Cusack) and a nurse (Dern) that is left unconsummated because of the scientist's accidental exposure to a high dose of radiation. A typically eerie Dern performance almost saves the episode from becoming too cloying, but ultimately their story derails in the graphic depiction of the scientist's slow death, which doesn't so much prick one's conscience as take the film on an unwanted detour into Freddy Krueger territory, with a heavy emphasis on horrific makeup and special effects. This episode exemplifies the oppressively heavy hand Joffe and Robinson have brought to the entire story. When the film's payoff—the explosion of the first test bomb—finally comes, it's too late to save what has become a pompous, overloaded epic. The unintentionally silly sight of Schultz's cheeks puffing out from the force of the blast serves as a symbolic reminder of just how much hot air some films are capable of producing. In the case of FAT MAN AND LITTLE BOY, that hot air didn't come cheaply, as the film cost $20-25 million to make, despite the fact that a number of the actors reportedly worked for less than their normal fees because of their dedication to the film's theme. Because the facilities at Los Alamos had become too modern to be used for filming, some $2 to be killed; and during this diversion the family members untie themselves and flee into the woods. DeYoung blows up the police car, killing Meshack; Lenz and the kids flee to a deserted boat house, where they must fend off Watson, a "pretty boy" who really doesn't want to kill anyone but needs to prove his manhood through rape. The daughter defends herself with a perfectly placed rat trap she finds nearby, and Lenz beats the attacker to death with a wooden beam. Now the battle is one-on-one, as Factor and DeYoung, who is also a Vietnam veteran, stalk each other through the dark woods. DeYoung ambushes Factor and leaves him for dead, but after the family's joyful reunion at the boat house, Factor reappears for one more climactic battle.

Sincere performances by Kay Lenz and Cliff DeYoung, and credible portrayals in difficult roles from Robert Factor, Charles Meshack and Eddit Banker, the last as an old prison pro, keep FEAR afloat. The most interesting (if potentially offensive and stereotypical) story element is that of two Vietnam vets, one left crazed by the war and one who has put it all behind him, drawing on their wartime guerrilla skills to defeat each other. But this twist gets only minimal screen time, while director and story originator Robert Ferretti instead lingers over the rigors of prison life, which, besides being only marginally relevant here, have been portrayed better on many other occasions. *(Violence, excessive profanity, adult situations.)*

p, Lisa M. Hansen; d, Robert A. Ferretti; w, Rick Scarry and Kathryn Connell (based on a story by Robert A. Ferretti); ph, Dana Christiaansen (Foto-Kem Color); ed, Michael Eliot; m, Alfi Kabiljo; art d, Fernando Altschul; set d, Trevor Norris; cos, Jan Rowton.

Action   **(PR:O MPAA:R)**

FEAR, ANXIETY AND DEPRESSION**

85m Propaganda/Goldwyn c

Todd Solondz *(Ira)*, Max Cantor *(Jack)*, Alexandra Gersten *(Janice)*, Jane Hamper *(Junk)*, Jill Wisloff *(Sharon)*, Stanley Tucci *(Donny)*.

A sporadically amusing but slow-paced, Woody Allenesque movie lacking real comedic bite, FEAR, ANXIETY AND DEPRESSION features director Todd Solondz in its lead role as a struggling, neurotic, and inept New York playwright searching for love and success. The film opens with the off-off Broadway premiere of an avant-garde play called "Despair." Unfortunately, and much to the despair of the play's author (Solondz), audiences don't understand the piece and the critics pan it. Distraught over this theatrical disaster, he tries to kill himself—unsuccessfully, of course. Only one person appreciates Solondz's masterpiece, namely Wisloff, a small, wallflower-like fast-food worker who loves the playwright and believes in his talent completely. Running short of cash, Solondz appeals for help to his parents (who, in a rather amusing dinner scene, try to talk him out of a show-biz career and offer their son a day job). He also breaks up with Wisloff, and becomes interested in Hamper, a bizarre performance artist. After meeting Hamper at a nightclub (the Palladium) and again at a copy store, Solondz manages to get a date with her; unfortunately, Solondz's friend Cantor tags along. The three go to another club (the Cairo), where Hamper declares, "I'm a performance artist, not an actress. I hate actresses." By the end of the evening, she dumps Solondz for Cantor, a hip, attractive minimalist painter. Rejected again, Solondz goes over to Wisloff's place, only to find his ex in the midst of a suicide attempt. Wisloff is saved after Solondz rushes her to the hospital, and the couple reunites briefly before breaking up again. To complicate matters even more, Cantor's girl friend (Gersten) has a fling with Solondz, and Wisloff gets involved with another of Solondz's friends, the successful but obnoxious Tucci. After Gersten gets a job singing in a bank as a "Show Tuner"—an Andrews Sisters-type act—she discovers Cantor's involvement with Hamper, quits her job, and moves back to Indiana. In the meantime, Solondz visits the shallow, wealthy Tucci in an attempt to get his latest work produced. As Solondz's luck would have it, however, he not only doesn't get backing for his play, but finds Wisloff living with Tucci. As the film ends, Cantor heads for Los Angeles and Solondz labors at a day job.

Written and directed by Solondz, FEAR, ANXIETY AND DEPRESSION features some good performances and offers some amusing scenes of the New York art world. The premiere of "Despair" effectively spoofs avant-garde theater; another funny bit features Solondz in a gallery, surrounded by giant pieces of standard-issue "art." Despite its fairly sure evocation of the artist's milieu, however, the film places too much emphasis on the various romantic pairings and breakups, without offering real insight into the characters' lives. Solondz's conception of his playwright is highly derivative of Woody Allen, and the overall lack of originality slows the story down. *(Profanity.)*

p, Stanley Wlodowski, Steve Golin, and Joni Sighvatsson; d, Todd Solondz; w, Todd Solondz; ph, Stefan Czapsky (Foto-Kem Color); ed, Peter Austin, Emily Paine, and Barry Rubinow; m, Karyn Rachtman, Joe Romano, and Moogy Klingman; prod d, Marek Dobrowolski; art d, Susan Block; cos, Susan Lyall.

Comedy   **(PR:C MPAA:R)**

FEW DAYS WITH ME, A***½

(Fr.) 131m Sara-Cinea-Films A2/ Galaxy c

Daniel Auteuil *(Martial)*, Sandrine Bonnaire *(Francine)*, Jean-Pierre Marielle *(Fonfrin)*, Dominique Lavanant *(Mme. Fonfrin)*, Vincent Lindon *(Fernand)*, Danielle Darrieux *(Mme. Pasquier)*, Therese Liotard *(Regine)*, Gerard Ismael *(Rocky)*, Tanya Lopert *(Mme. Maillotte)*, Philippe Laudenbach *(Maillotte)*, Dominique Blanc *(Georgette)*, Jean-Pierre Castaldi *(Max)*, Elisa Servier *(Lucie)*, Xavier Saint-Macary *(Paul)*, Jean-Louis Richard *(Dr. Appert)*, Francois Chaumette *(Bassompierre)*, Alain Doutey *(Police Chief)*.

In this superbly acted, crafted, scripted, paced, and directed entertainment, veteran French director Claude Sautet leaves his bourgeois characters (CHARLIE AND ROSALIE; A SIMPLE STORY) behind in favor of a more youthful and invigorating tale. Auteuil (JEAN DE FLORETTE; MANON OF THE SPRING) stars as the heir to a chain of supermarkets who has just ended a stay in an asylum after battling his chronic indifference to his wife, family, and friends. His mother, Darrieux, runs the grocery empire with a closely knit team of supporters. Trying to bring her son back into the fold, Darrieux agrees to let him visit the several out-of-town stores that are losing money. His first stop is Limoges, where he meets with store manager Marielle and spends the day examining the books. Auteuil is at first all business, ignoring Marielle's phony friendliness and declining his invitation to have dinner as a guest of Marielle and his wife (Lavanant). On his way to the airport, however, Auteuil abruptly changes his mind and accepts the offer. At the dinner, after quietly listening to Marielle and his guests spout bourgeois political cliches, Auteuil politely attacks the party. They are all shocked at his candor, but can't kick him out, since he is technically their employer. The following morning, rather than continuing to the next town on his itinerary, Auteuil rents a flat with the intent of spending some time in Limoges, much to Marielle and Lavanant's chagrin. Auteuil imagines that it is here that he can once again communicate with others, where he can find people that he cares for and who will care for him. He therefore asks Marielle's maid, Bonnaire, to come to his barren apartment and serve at a dinner party. Unknown to the maid, the dinner party guests are just two—Auteuil and Bonnaire. The initially insulted Bonnaire agrees to stay, gets drunk, and takes a liking to Auteuil. The following morning, he invites her to move in and redecorate, and to quit her job as Marielle's housemaid. The free-and-easy Bonnaire accepts his offer and the pair spend a few idyllic days together. Auteuil is introduced into Bonnaire's circle, and even develops a friendship with Lindon, the complacent young man who loves Bonnaire. Auteuil is not jealous of Lindon, and Lindon feels no threat from Auteuil. Things change, however, when Auteuil receives an emergency phone call to return to Paris to attend to his ailing mother. Although the call turns out to be a ruse to get him back where he belongs, Auteuil accepts his responsibility as the supermarket heir and dives headlong into an examination of the company books, discovering that his mother's closest and most trusted friend has embezzled some $500,000 in funds. Auteuil announces at a board meeting that he is surrendering his interest in the company—in all stores except Limoges, to which he returns only to find that Bonnaire has left both him and Lindon and moved in with a sleazy club owner (Ismael). Auteuil makes every effort to convince Bonnaire to return to him, an offer she would accept were it not for her fear of her present lover. Fate intervenes when the despondent Lindon stabs Ismael and Auteuil takes the blame, paving the way for Lindon and Bonnaire to start anew. Their relationship fails, however, and Lindon leaves town permanently. Auteuil is sent back to the confines of an asylum, where Bonnaire, realizing just how much she loves him, comes to visit—for more than just a few days.

Sautet's first film since 1983's Yves Montand starrer GARCON!, A FEW DAYS WITH ME was met with a lukewarm reception when it opened in Paris in August 1988, despite the box-office appeal of Sandrine Bonnaire and Daniel Auteuil. Running a lengthy (but not overlong) 131 minutes, the film is a wonderfully warm and romantic character comedy that exists, not as a piece of great cinema or intellectual stimulation, but as a well-made entertainment. Although the film is technically top-notch, it is the acting that makes A FEW DAYS WITH ME such a

joy. Everyone in the cast, from leads Bonnaire and Auteuil to a collection of colorful minor characters, delivers an excellent performance. The film revolves, however, around Auteuil, the character whose armor of indifference towards the world must be penetrated. After spending the first few days with Bonnaire, he begins to feel again, taking a liking to her friends, and they to him. He learns that he does have a place in the world—not among the corporate board rooms and back-stabbing employees of his Parisian company, but in Limoges. A FEW DAYS WITH ME is filled with memorable scenes, especially a dinner party thrown by Bonnaire and Auteuil at the newly decorated flat. Auteuil, dressed in a bathrobe, surprises his first guests—the formally dressed Marielle and Lavanant—when he pretends that they've come on the wrong night. The guests that follow are as diverse as can be, including one couple who arrive dressed as Robin Hood and Little Bo Peep, misled by Auteuil into believing that they were to attend a costume party. Excess is the word of the night, and after much drink and dance, a bond is formed that erases the class differences that marked the party's start. Shown in the US as a competing entry in the Chicago International Film Festival. (In French; English subtitles.) *(Nudity, profanity, adult situations.)*

d, Claude Sautet; w, Claude Sautet, Jacques Fieschi, and Jerome Tonnerre (based on the novel by Jean-Francois Josselin); ph, Jean-Francois Robin; ed, Jacqueline Thiedot; m, Philippe Sarde; set d, Carlos Conti; cos, Olga Berlutti.

Drama   (PR:C MPAA:PG-13)

FIELD OF DREAMS*½
107m Gordon/UNIV c
Kevin Costner *(Ray Kinsella)*, Amy Madigan *(Annie Kinsella)*, Gaby Hoffman

(Karin Kinsella), Ray Liotta *(Shoeless Joe Jackson)*, Timothy Busfield *(Mark)*, James Earl Jones *(Terence Mann)*, Burt Lancaster *(Dr. "Moonlight" Graham)*, Frank Whaley *(Archie Graham)*, Dwier Brown *(John Kinsella)*, James Andelin *(Feed Store Farmer)*, Mary Anne Kean *(Feed Store Lady)*, Fern Persons *(Annie's Mother)*, Kelly Coffield *(Dee, Mark's Wife)*, Michael Milhoan *(Buck Weaver (3B))*, Steve Eastin *(Eddie Cicotte (P))*, Charles Hoyes *(Swede Risberg (C))*, Art LaFleur *(Chick Gandil (1B))*, Lee Garlington *(Beulah, Angry PTA Mother)*, Mike Nussbaum *(Principal)*, Larry Brandenburg, Mary McDonald Gershon, Robert Kurcz *(PTA Hecklers)*, Don John Ross *(Boston Butcher)*, Bea Fredman *(Boston Yenta)*, Geoffrey Nauffts *(Boston Pump Jockey)*, Anne Seymour *(Chisolm Newspaper Publisher)*, C. George Baisi, Howard Sherf, Joseph Ryan *(Men in Bar)*, Joe Glasberg *(Costumer)*, Brian Frankish *(Clean-shaven Umpire)*, Jeffrey Neal Silverman *(Clean-shaven Center Fielder)*.

One of 1989's biggest movies, Phil Alden Robinson's charming FIELD OF DREAMS firmly fixed Kevin Costner's position in the Hollywood firmament. A baseball movie about much more than baseball, Robinson's film, based on W.P. Kinsella's novel *Shoeless Joe*, is more than a little manipulative, carefully pitched at male baby boomers, and continually threatens to become just so much sweet corn, yet its skillful blend of myth, dreams, and emotion steers clear of the saccharine and obvious, making a beeline for the heart but refusing to ignore the head along the way.

Costner is Ray Kinsella, a 36-year-old, Berkeley-educated Iowa farmer with a smart wife (Madigan), an extraordinarily cute daughter (Hoffman), and an underlying idealism rooted in the 60s. When he begins hearing a voice in his cornfield ("If you build it, he will come"), Costner questions his sanity, then his way of life. Terrified of becoming old and staid before his time like his father—a onetime minor league baseball player who gave up the game to take a mundane job and raise a family—Costner comes to believe that if he carves a baseball field out of his cornfield, his late father's hero, long-dead baseball great Shoeless Joe Jackson, whose reputation was forever tarnished by the 1919 "Black Sox" World Series scandal, will return to play. Supported by Madigan, he embraces what he believes may be his last chance to do something really different, plows under his family's livelihood, and constructs a gorgeous baseball field complete with lights. The community and Madigan's real estate investor brother, Busfield (TV's "thirtysomething"), think Costner is crazy, but in time Jackson (Liotta) does indeed come, later bringing with him not just his disgraced White Sox

Kevin Kostner, Amy Madigan, Gaby Hoffman, and Dwier Brown in FIELD OF DREAMS (©Universal).

teammates but an incredible assemblage of ghosts of all-stars past. While Costner and family delight in the presence of these baseball greats, however, their spirited games are invisible to everyone else. With his farm threatened by bankruptcy, Costner is advised by the voice to "ease [his] pain," a cryptic message that leads Costner to Boston, where he feels it is his mission to take Terence Mann (Jones), the "Voice of the 60s," a former activist and writer who has withdrawn from public life, to a Red Sox game. Reluctantly, the "kidnaped" Jones goes to Fenway Park, where he and Costner (and no one else) hear the voice ("Go the distance") and see, flashed on the scoreboard, the name of an obscure baseball player whose major league career was limited to one inning in 1922. Together, Jones and Costner venture to the small Minnesota town that was the home of Archibald "Moonlight" Graham, and learn that he gave up baseball to become a doctor and bedrock of decency in the little community. Mysteriously transported back to 1972, the year of Doc Graham's death, Costner talks with the kindly physician (Lancaster), though he still isn't sure what all this adds up to. The meaning becomes clearer as Costner and Jones return to Iowa, picking up a young baseball-playing hitchhiker who turns out to be one Archie Graham (Whaley) along the way. Back at Costner's field of dreams, now about to be taken over by creditors, Whaley finally gets his chance to prove himself against big-league competition. Then miraculous events occur in rapid succession, as Hoffman, who has taken a bad fall, is rescued from death; Costner suddenly finds himself face to face with his dead father, who has come to the diamond as the young ball player he once was; and farm and field are saved.

Favorable comparisons between contemporary films and those of Frank Capra have become commonplace of late, but if any recent movie deserves to be called Capraesque it is FIELD OF DREAMS. A mixture of fantasy and reality, comedy and romance, home truths and ideology, this life-affirming celebration of idealism and family may indeed be, as some critics have suggested, the 1980s' IT'S A WONDERFUL LIFE. It took writer-director Robinson (IN THE MOOD), seven years to convince moviedom's powers that be to give him a chance to bring Kinsella's novel (an expansion of his short story "Shoeless Joe Jackson Comes to Iowa") to the screen, but his determination has resulted in an entertaining, deeply moving film. In addition to creating 60s guru Terence Mann especially for Jones (the parallel character in Kinsella's novel, real-life writer J.D. Salinger, wasn't happy with being included as a character in the book), the 39-year-old Robinson has given his screen adaptation a distinctly 60s slant. But while FIELD OF

DREAMS pays much lip service to the idealism of Robinson's generation—to the importance of dreams, individualism, and freedom of expression—it is also a film whose reverence for traditional family values is firmly grounded in the myths and symbols of the Reagan era. Twice Costner is asked if his baseball field and farm are heaven, and twice he replies, "No, this Iowa"—the implication being that here, in the heartland that includes his family, he has found heaven on earth. Robinson gives this domestic bliss a hip spin, however: Warhol prints hang on the farmhouse walls, a peace symbol adorns the window of Costner's VW van, and the Allman Brothers Band and the Doobie Brothers provide the film's traveling music (careful selections that nostalgically transport boomers back to their youth).

It seems undeniable that FIELD OF DREAMS has been meticulously crafted to appeal to its target audience, but to dismiss Robinson's fusion of "The Prairie Home Companion" and "thirtysomething" as merely manipulative, as some critics have done, or to belittle his deft emotional button-pushing shortchanges the sincerity and gentleness at the film's core. Using the familiar iconography of the national pastime as symbolic shorthand, Robinson creates a world that is both fantastic and grounded in reality, and it's difficult not to get caught up in it. On the other hand, while FIELD OF DREAMS is not exclusively a male fantasy, some of its symbolism will probably resonate more for men than women. Notably, Ray's game of catch with his father, an integral part of many American boyhoods, provides a magical resolution to all the hurt that has passed between father and son and to all that has gone unspoken.

One doesn't have to be male or a baseball fan to enjoy FIELD OF DREAMS or appreciate its message, however. To his credit, Robinson has attempted to present Amy Madigan's Annie as something more than a supportive wife. Even if she doesn't accompany Ray on his journey, philosophically she is a fellow traveler, and in her big scene at a town meeting she becomes a kind of latter-day Jefferson Smith (hero of Capra's MR. SMITH GOES TO WASHINGTON), boldly castigating her neighbors for considering banning books. Ultimately, however, Madigan (whose performance is occasionally strained) is a supporting player: This is Costner's movie, and he milks the Gary Cooper-Jimmy Stewart school sincerity that has become the cornerstone of his screen persona for all it's worth. Like Cooper and Stewart, Costner (who landed on the cover of *Time* in the wake of the film's success) is not afraid to allow himself endearing moments of ineffectuality, making his character all the more real. In support, James Earl Jones contributes his usual assured performance

as the bitter, tired activist in whose well-hidden heart burns an eternal flame of hope; Burt Lancaster, in a small but memorable appearance, conveys the sort of grizzled decency that has become his forte as a mature actor; and Ray Liotta (SOMETHING WILD) plays his southern-accentless Joe Jackson as a ballplayer with a poet's appreciation of minutiae in the game he plays so brilliantly.

Serendipity also played an important role is the film's magical realism. In a scene calling for Jackson to line Ray's curve back at him, Liotta managed to actually hit the ball right at the pitcher's mound, forcing Costner to scramble for *real*. Likewise, fog fortuitously rolled in for one shot calling for Liotta to exit into the netherworld beyond the cornfield. Filmed on location in Iowa, FIELD OF DREAMS is neither a political treatise nor an attempt to get at the truth behind the Black Sox (see John Sayles' EIGHT MEN OUT for the latter), but an uplifting, heart-tugging paean to the redemptive power of love, hope, forgiveness, and—most of all—dreams. Songs include: "Daydream" (John Sebastian, performed by the Lovin' Spoonful), "Jessica" (Dickie Betts, performed by the Allman Brothers Band), "China Grove" (Tom Johnston, performed by the Doobie Brothers), "Lotus Blossom" (Billy Strayhorn, performed by Duke Ellington).

p, Lawrence Gordon and Charles Gordon; d, Phil Alden Robinson; w, Phil Alden Robinson (based on the book *Shoeless Joe* by W.P. Kinsella); ph, John Lindley (Deluxe Color); ed, Ian Crafford; m, James Horner; prod d, Dennis Gassner; art d, Leslie McDonald; set d, Nancy Haigh; cos, Linda Bass; makeup, Richard Arrington.

Sports   **(PR:A MPAA:PG)**

ⓥFIST FIGHTER*
100m Izaro-Eagle-Esme/Taurus c
George Rivero *(C.J. Thunderbird)*, Edward Albert *(Harry "Punchy" Moses)*, Mike Connors *(Billy Vance)*, Brenda Bakke *(Ellen)*, Matthias Hues *(Rhino Reinhart)*, Simon Andreu *(Moreno)*, Billy Graham *(Ruby)*, Gus Rethwisch *(The Beast)*, Jimmy Nickerson *(King Belitnakov)*, Tony Isbert.

FIST FIGHTER, starring George Rivero and Edward Albert, is an unengaging story about the corrupt and often dangerous world of bare-knuckle boxing in Mexico. The film opens in Arizona with Rivero beating a blond behemoth in an arm-wrestling match, prompting the Hulk Hogan look-alike to challenge his opponent to a fistfight that Rivero, of course, wins. After receiving a telegram from a friend about the fight circuit in Mexico, Rivero heads south. Once in Mexico, he attracts plenty of attention after defeating the local favorite in a knock-down-drag-out confrontation. Impressed with Rivero's fancy footwork, fight promoter Connors offers to manage the battler, but Rivero turns him down flat. Instead, Rivero decides to form a partnership with former boxer Albert. Determined to bring Rivero down a peg, Connors arranges a match between Rivero and the local champ. After it becomes evident that Rivero will win, the police burst into the bar, the lights suddenly go out, and the prize money disappears. Later, Albert and Rivero have a futile confrontation with Connors over the "mysterious" disappearance of the fight purse. As they leave Connors' mansion, the promoter's girl friend (Bakke) gives them the money due them, but while they are counting it, Albert and Rivero are arrested. Albert is eventually released, but Rivero remains behind in jail, abused by the sadistic prison warden (Andreu), who also wants to manage the talented fistfighter. Just when things look hopeless for Rivero, he manages to escape, only to be recaptured. Meanwhile, on the outside, another confrontation with Connors results in Albert's being beaten to a pulp. Eventually Rivero accepts Andreu's challenge to battle the warden's "beast," and after a long, especially violent contest, Rivero wins his freedom. After visiting the dying Albert, Rivero exacts revenge from Connors, frees Bakke from the promoter's clutches, and is given one more shot at the local champ.

Written by Max Bloom, FIST FIGHTER is an overlong story with little character development. Provided with no history for Rivero's fighter, the viewer can't even begin to guess what has drawn the character to his violent profession. Moreover, Brenda Bakke's Ellen, virtually the only female in the movie, is strictly there for decoration. The most baffling aspect of the film, however, is the nature of the warden's "beast." Where did this thing come from? More important, just exactly what the hell is it? Director Frank Zuniga elicits less-than-impressive performances from his actors (Rivero is extremely stiff; Albert slides in and out of his Mexican accent), but the photography by Hans Burman and the sets by Francisco Magallon and Seth Santacruz are quite good. Clearly too much time was spent on the technical aspects of the film and not enough on the story and direction. *(Graphic violence, profanity, sexual situations.)*

p, Carlos Vasallo; d, Frank Zuniga; w, Max Bloom (based on a story by Carlos Vasallo); ph, Hans Burman (Kodak Color); ed, Drake Silliman; m, Emilio Kauderer; set d, Francisco Magallon and Seth Santacruz; spec eff, Rosi Duprat; chor, Jimmy Nickerson; stunts, Jimmy Nickerson.

Action (PR:O MPAA:R)

⊙FLETCH LIVES**

95m Douglas-Greisman/UNIV c

Chevy Chase *(Irwin Maurice "Fletch" Fletcher)*, Hal Holbrook *(Hamilton "Ham" Johnson)*, Julianne Phillips *(Becky Ann Culpepper)*, Cleavon Little *(Calculus)*, R. Lee Ermey *(Jimmy Lee Farnsworth)*, Patricia Kalember *(Amanda Ray Ross)*, Richard Libertini *(Frank Walker)*, Randall "Tex" Cobb *(Ben Dover)*, George Wyner *(Gillet)*, Geoffrey Lewis *(KKK Leader)*, Richard Belzer *(Phil)*, Phil Hartman *(Bly Manager)*, Titos Vandis *(Uncle Kakakis)*, Don Hood *(Tom Barbour)*, Dennis Burkley *(Joe Jack)*, Noelle Beck *(Betty Dilworth)*, William Traylor *(Mr. Underhill)*, Barney D. Arceneaux *(Party Guest)*, Roy Babich *(Klansman)*, Mary Battilana *(Bly Assistant)*, Don Brockett *(Sheriff)*, Walter Charles *(Tony)*, Robert M. Dawson *(Tour Guide)*, Darren Dublin *(Ancient Copy Boy)*, R. Bruce Elliott *(Info Technician)*, Patrick Farrelly *(O'Reilly)*, Grace Gaynor *(Mrs. Underhill)*, Richmond Harrison *(T'Boo Ted)*, Catherine Hearne *(Lyda Perl)*, Christian Kauffmann *(Bruce)*, Matthew Kimbrough *(Bly Guard)*, Clarence M. Landry *(Damon Feather)*, Marcella Lowery *(Selma)*, Jordan Lund *(Deputy Sheriff)*, Thom McCleister *(Klansman)*, Patricia G. McConnell *(Deputy's Wife)*, Dick McGarvin *(Announcer)*, Louis M. Rapaport *(Walter Bob Buggem)*, Constance Shulman *(Cindy Mae)*, Robert Silver *(Kakakis Brother)*, Ebbe Roe Smith *(Jim Bob)*, R. David Smith *(Gordon Joe)*, John Wylie *(Accountant)*.

Since the release of the original FLETCH in 1985, star Chevy Chase and director Michael Ritchie have had four years to get a running start on this sequel, which starts out with promising energy, then stumbles. Reprising his role as I.M. ("Don't Call Me Irwin") Fletcher, an LA investigative reporter originally created by novelist Gregory McDonald, Chase again dons the Lakers' jersey and high-top sneakers that complement his character's casual irreverence so well. Long overdue for a vacation from the gritty city, his nagging editor, and alimony obligations, Chase heads for that other LA—Louisiana—after he inherits Belle Isle, the antebellum mansion of his long-forgotten aunt. En route, he slips into a fantasy of life as a wealthy plantation owner: surrounded by thousands of southern belles and gents, domestic servants and field hands, Chase conducts a grandiose rendition of "Zip-a-Dee-Doo-Dah" complete with animated dancing critters—in a spoof of the 1947 Disney classic SONG OF THE SOUTH. But reality falls far short of this vision when Chase arrives at his 80-acre estate, crowned by a dilapidated, moss-covered mansion tended by Little, its Stepin Fetchit-styled caretaker. Chase's disappointment is eased by a dinner invitation from Kalember, the sexy lawyer han-

dling the estate probate, who informs him that an anonymous bidder has offered a quarter of a million dollars for Belle Isle. He decides to sleep on the offer—with Kalember, who dies during the night as the result of a lethal injection administered by an unseen, rubber-gloved intruder. Naturally, the local sheriff, who doesn't cotton to Chase's wiseacre routine, dispatches Chase to the pokey, where he is menaced by cellmate Cobb. Aided by the intercession of Holbrook, a local attorney and power broker, Chase is released and—ignoring Holbrook's admonitions that his presence is unwelcome in town—launches his own investigation, during which he trots out a number of local yokel-mocking disguises. In between denture changes, Chase pursues Phillips, a real estate broker representing the anonymous bidder for Belle Isle, and begins to suspect that Ermey, a slick cable TV minister, is the source of all his troubles. But Chase's troubles are just beginning. His mansion is torched, and when a few sympathetic townsfolk try to cheer him up by taking him out on a nocturnal coon hunt, he is nearly blown away by Cobb. Moreover, he finds himself literally up to his ankles in toxic waste on his newly acquired property. Meanwhile, a background check on Ermey reveals that the tele-evangelist, who also operates the "Bibleland" theme park, has a past more checkered than a used-car salesman's sportscoat, *and* he is Phillips' father. Putting aside his feelings for her, Chase goes back into his bag of disguises, this time passing himself off as a guest faith healer on Ermey's show, and manages to sneak into the control room to wreak madcap havoc against the charlatan's pocket-picking operation. In a sudden change of heart, however, Chase dismisses Ermey as the major player in all his recent travails, for, with Phillips' help, he now has gathered enough evidence to connect Holbrook to the illegal toxic waste dumping. After an unholy chase through Bibleland, Holbrook is captured on the set during a live broadcast of Ermey's show. Chase returns to LA with Phillips and a hefty fire insurance settlement, his final triumph occurring when he manages to palm off half of his polluted estate on his ex-wife's unsuspecting, greedy lawyer.

Not unlike the clunker Cadillac Chase inherits along with his run-down estate, the comedy of FLETCH LIVES seems to be fueled by cheap, high-knocking gasoline. Chase should be credited for his ambition—he appears in virtually every scene, either as Fletch or as Fletch-in-disguise, and does the *film noir*ish voice-over that patches the story together—and his assorted disguises do keep the film from becoming a total bore, not because they are particularly funny, but because they create a mild diversion from the main character's general insouciance. However, Chase delivers a rather one-note performance, consisting mainly of predictable comebacks and salacious leers reminiscent of the old Bob Hope, while the characters who become the targets of his witty rejoinders are weak and silly stereotypes, lampooning themselves with such ease that they don't require a formidable foil. Screenwriter Leon Capetanos (DOWN AND OUT IN BEVERLY HILLS) hails from the South, but most of his Louisiana characters are cliches, and the script has other problems—most notably the abrupt switch in focus from self-serving TV ministers to the menace of illegal waste disposal. Another weak link is the pairing of Chase and Julianne Phillips. In spite of the promotional ads' depiction of their romance as that of a modern-day Rhett Butler and Scarlett O'Hara, the two never really catch fire. FLETCH LIVES is a custom-built Chevy Chase vehicle throughout; the other performers are only along for the ride. Songs include "Ain't No Use, Baby," "Buckwheat's Special," "1-4 Zydeco," "Bim Bam Thank You Ma'am," "Hard Times," "Uptown Zydeco," and "Zydeco Rock," all written by Stanley Dural and performed by Buckwheat Zydeco. (Profanity, sexual situations.)

p, Alan Greisman and Peter Douglas; d, Michael Ritchie; w, Leon Capetanos (based on characters created by Gregory McDonald); ph, John McPherson (Deluxe color); ed, Richard A. Harris; m, Harold Faltermeyer; art d, Cameron Birnie, Jimmie Bly, W. Steven Graham, and Donald B. Woodruff; set d, Garry Fettis and Susan Bode; spec eff, Clifford P. Wenger; cos, Anna Hill Johnstone; chor, Michael Smuin; stunts, Chuck Waters; makeup, Tom Miller.

Comedy   (PR:C   MPAA:PG)

●FLY II, THE*½
105m Brooksfilms/FOX c
Eric Stoltz (Martin Brundle), Daphne Zuniga (Beth Logan), Lee Richardson (Anton Bartok), John Getz (Stathis Borans), Frank Turner (Dr. Shepard), Ann Marie Lee (Dr. Jainway), Gary Chalk (Scorby), Saffron Henderson (Ronnie), Harley Cross (10-Year Old Martin), Matthew Moore (4-Year Old Martin), Rob Roy (Wiley), Andrew Rhodes (Hargis), Pat Bermel (Mackenzie), William Taylor (Dr. Trimble), Jerry Wasserman (Simms), Duncan Fraser (Obstetrician), Janet Hodgkinson (Nurse), Sean O'Byrne (Perinatologist), Mike Winlaw (Neonatologist), Kimely Anne Warren (Marla), Ken Camroux (Linder), Bruce Harwood (Technician), Lorena Gale (Woman), David Mylrea (Flywalker), Robert Metcalfe, Garwin Sanford (Observers), Tom Heaton (Manager), Cecilia Warren (Anchorwoman), Andrea Mann (Cute Girl).

Like the pair of sequels that sprang from the original THE FLY (1958), this sequel to David Cronenberg's masterful 1986 remake is uninspired, uninvolving, and wholly unnecessary. The directing chores this time out were handled by first-time director Chris Walas, the Oscar-winning special-effects whiz who created the various viscera for the 1986 remake. Not surprisingly, Walas is no Cronenberg and his film is merely an excuse to indulge in a surfeit of special-effects sequences while letting the narrative suffer like a neglected stepchild. Beginning a few months after the events of the first film, the movie opens as Veronica, lover of the late Seth Brundle (played by Jeff Goldblum in the previous effort) and mother of his child, gives nightmarish birth to a writhing larva. Veronica (not played by Geena Davis; indeed, the actress' face is purposely obscured through most of the scene) dies in childbirth before the larva splits open to reveal a beautiful, normal-looking, baby boy. Adopted and raised by Richardson, the head of an ominous mega-corporation, the boy, named Martin, is housed at the company's massive research facility and every moment of his life is monitored and analyzed, and for good reason, because the boy matures five years for every calender year. By the time he is five years old, Martin (Stoltz) appears to be a young adult and is well on his way to becoming a brilliant scientist. Richardson is thrilled by Stoltz's rapid progress and impressive intellect, for he intends to resurrect Stoltz's father's project—the telepods—by persuading the boy to perfect the matter-transmitting machines. Stoltz accepts the assignment and begins to tinker with the telepods with the help of Zuniga, a bright young computer operator with whom Stoltz has fallen in love. While undertaking his research, however, Stoltz begins to notice disturbing changes in his body. Like his father, he is metamorphosing into a fly—another aspect of his development Richardson has counted on and intends to exploit commercially. What Richardson didn't expect, however, is the man-sized fly's rebellion and the havoc he wreaks on the corporation. The huge insect takes on a small army of gun-toting security personnel and whips them singlehandedly. Then, with Zuniga's help, the fly captures Richardson and forces him into one of the telepods. It seems that before becoming a fly, Stoltz learned—as did his father—that the fly metamorphosis can be reversed if the victim enters the telepod with a healthy person. When the teleportation process that is to transfer genetic impurities from one body to the other is completed, a disgusting amalgamation of Richardson, Stoltz, and housefly comes writhing out of the second telepod. Although at first it appears that the experiment is a failure, close examination of the grotesque creation reveals a womblike sack

containing a miraculously restored Stoltz. In the end, the young lovers are reunited and, in a postscript, Richardson, the evil industrialist, is forced to spend the rest of his life as a grotesque, sluglike freak of science, left forgotten in a dank holding cell.

Wholly derivative, not only of its predecessor, but of a variety of other—better—horror and science-fiction films, THE FLY II is a complete misfire. The movie borrows its opening from IT'S ALIVE (1974), degenerates into ALIEN (1979), and then ends with a quote from the 1932 classic FREAKS, with nothing particularly creative or interesting taking place in between. Whereas Cronenberg took a mediocre old science-fiction film and elevated it to classic status by combining gutwrenching gruesomeness with a powerful, thought-provoking narrative that transcended simple genre conventions and explored the very nature of humanity, THE FLY II offers nothing but special effects. Made from a shooting script that reportedly went through at least three drafts, THE FLY II contains no humor, irony, nuance, ambiguity, or psychological complexity, and no greater meaning—none of the elements that gave Cronenberg's film its incredible power and resonance. Instead what we have is a juvenile version of the same film in which essential components such as thematics and character development are hinted at rather than explored. As a director, Walas hasn't the foggiest notion of how to lift the film beyond its pulp origins, thus transforming it into something more than a gore-soaked roller-coaster ride. As one might expect from a special-effects expert, the film is filled with bravura effects sequences possessed of little emotion, intellect, or visual style. But while the effects are impressive in a tactical sort of way, they aren't contextually engaging and simply become redundant and boring well before the climax. In fact, actor Eric Stoltz disappears two-thirds of the way into the film and is replaced by a series of articulated puppets constructed out of metal and foam rubber. As a visual stylist, Walas is merely efficient, his camera set-ups dictated by the various requirements of the special-effects, handcuffing any true cinematic creativity. While effects hounds may be pleased with THE FLY II, anyone with any interest at all in story and character will come away disappointed.

Walas also seems to have let his actors fend for themselves here, for there is little in the way of inspired thesping. Stoltz, no stranger to heavy make-up (MASK), struggles mightily to inject some nuance into his underwritten role, but fails. The wholly unnecessary romance between him and Daphne Zuniga—a holdover approach from the first film—is so unconvincing and uninvolving that it merely serves to

Lee Richardson in THE FLY II (©20th Century Fox).

remind just how great the Goldblum-Davis chemistry was in Cronenberg's film. The totally ludicrous happy ending, unthinkable in the first film, is such an obvious pandering to the teenage audience that Cronenberg fans will be stunned by its cloying no muss, no fuss wrap-up. In the first film, shy, insecure, lovestruck Seth Brundle tampers in areas he shouldn't and is slowly turned into a monstrous fly for his trouble. He maims a few people and kills no one, but dies in the end at the hands of his lover. His son, however, grows up in five years, is relatively well-adjusted, falls in love with a swell girl, turns into a fly-monster, kills at least a dozen people, gets revenge on the man who betrayed him, returns to normal, and gets the girl in the end! If the sins of the father are visited upon the son, maybe it's really not that bad a deal after all. *(Violence, gore effects, sexual situations, profanity.)*

p, Steven-Charles Jaffe; d, Chris Walas; w, Mick Garris, Jim Wheat, Ken Wheat, and Frank Darabont (based on a story by Mick Garris); ph, Robin Vidgeon (Deluxe color); ed, Sean Barton; m, Christopher Young; prod d, Michael S. Bolton; art d, Sandy Cochrane; set d, Rose Marie McSherry; spec eff, John Thomas and Jon Berg; cos, Christopher Ryan; stunts, John Wardlow; makeup, Jayne Dancose.

Horror/Science Fiction

(PR:O   MPAA:R)

FOR QUEEN AND COUNTRY**
(Brit.) 105m Working
Title-Zenith/Atlantic c
Denzel Washington *(Reuben James)*, Craig Fairbrass *(Challoner)*, Dorian Healey *(Fish)*, Amanda Redman *(Stacey)*, George Baker *(Kilcoyne)*, Bruce Payne *(Colin)*, Sean Chapman *(Bob Harper)*, Geff Francis *(Lynford)*, Stella Gonet *(Debbie)*, Michael Bray *(Bryant)*, Lisa O'Connor *(Hayley)*, Anselm Peters *(Oscar)*, Colin Thomas *(Feargal)*, James Harkishin *(Sadiq)*, Carlton Dixon *(Stylee)*, Jo Martin *(Pearl)*, Frank Harper *(Mickey)*, Titiana Strauss, Valerie Chassigneaux *(French Girls)*, Suzette Llewellyn *(Girl with Bull Terrier)*, Debbie Killingback, Judith Conyers *(Girls)*, Ken Stott *(Civil Servant)*, Brian McDermott *(Harry)*, Chris Pitt *(Chris)*, Mike Smart *(Peelhead)*, Paul McKenzie *(Sean)*, Peter McNamara *(Pete)*, Dan Armour *(Drunken Man)*, Charlie Appleby *(Fairground Stallholder)*, Stewart Harwood *(Cab Office Onwer)*, Peter Spraggon *(Landlord)*, James Warrior *(LEB Man)*, Joginder Singh Lal *(Sikh Minder)*, Graham McTavish *(Lieutenant)*, Beverly Michaels, Shaheen Khan, Alison Rowley *(Party Girls)*.

Racism, Thatcher-era despair, and the disillusionment of a returning vet are at the heart of screenwriter Martin Stellman's well-intentioned but overreaching directorial debut. Academy Award nominee Denzel Washington (CRY FREEDOM) stars as a much-decorated paratrooper who leaves the British army after a nine-year hitch that has taken him from Northern Ireland to the Falklands. Returning to a council estate in his native South London, he finds his have-not neighbors engaged in their own battle. Old women rush about clutching purses, racist police brutally harass people of color, and poverty and hopelessness are everywhere. Washington also discovers, when it comes time to look for work, that his service record means less than the color of his skin. His old friends have already been forced to find their own ways of coping with the situation: Francis, who is also black, has turned to crime, though not nearly so successfully as Payne, a drug dealer who offers Washington a piece of the action. Washington's best friend is Healey, another former soldier who saved his life during an ambush in Northern Ireland, but who is now paraplegic and unemployed. As his marriage and life go to hell, Healey becomes increasingly bitter even as Washington tries to prop him up; meanwhile, Washington becomes involved with Redman, the mother of a teenager he caught burgling his apartment. Tensions between the police and the estate residents reach the boiling point after a popular local bobby is killed, and Washington, who has witnessed the killing, suddenly finds himself caught between his loyalty to his neighbors and his inclination to side with the forces of law and order. To complicate his life further, Washington learns that, according to the 1981 British Nationality Act, he is no longer a citizen because he was born on the Commonwealth island of St. Lucia. After making some quick money on a drug run with Payne, Washington prepares to return to St. Lucia, but before he can, the estate erupts in a violent riot.

Like several other contemporary British filmmakers, Stellman has made a commendable attempt to depict the desperation of those Britons whose lives have only gotten worse under Thatcher, and his hyperrealistic picture of the nightmarish council estate and the rebellion that grows there—literally underground—is believable and disturbing. As Stephen Frears did in MY BEAUTIFUL LAUNDRETTE and SAMMY AND ROSIE GET LAID, Stellman also addresses the issue of Britain's growing racial problems. But in structuring what is essentially a social-problem film along the lines of the cycle of Hollywood movies dealing with returning Vietnam veterans, Stellman has bitten off more than he can chew. His political message is delivered with a heavy hand, while his narrative is compromised by its dependence on coincidence.

Stellman has called FOR QUEEN AND COUNTRY an "urban western" and explained that he used that time-tested genre as a model in the same way that

FIRST BLOOD did, but that doesn't excuse his screenplay's continual placement of Washington's Reuben at the right place at the right time. Whenever something of significance to the plot is going down, Reuben is there—whether it's the theft that leads to his meeting with Amanda Redman's Stacey or his exiting an elevator just as his best friend is being confronted by trigger-happy police. Similarly, Reuben's encounters with police racism have, for the most part, a staged quality, as if Stellman were afraid that a more naturalistic presentation would fail to convey the obvious injustice already at work in these situations. Further, his script offers little insight into the origins of this racism or the poverty of hope that grips his beaten characters. (Yes, Thatcherism is surely at the root of all this, but how has it remained ascendant?) There is an important film contained somewhere in Stellman's script, but it isn't the one that made it to the screen.

Stellman and cowriter Trix Worrell found the inspiration for their story in the real-life experiences of a mutual friend, a black Falklands vet who did indeed return to Britain to find out that he was no longer a citizen. Believing that his screenplay for DEFENCE OF THE REALM had been botched in the filming, Stellman was determined to direct FOR QUEEN AND COUNTRY himself. And producers Sarah Radclyffe and Tim Bevan, whose company, Working Title, was responsible for such films as MY BEAUTIFUL LAUNDRETTE and A WORLD APART, gave Stellman the opportunity that David Puttnam (then in charge at Enigma) had denied him with DEFENCE OF THE REALM. Under Stellman's guidance the film was made for roughly $3.25 million, and shot in some of London's most depressed neighborhoods.

Despite the shortcomings of the script, the performances are generally capable, and Washington (clearly the star attraction here) once again demonstrates his incredible screen presence—though he is again cast in a role that mainly calls for him to demonstrate the sort of quiet dignity that long characterized Sidney Poitier's career and that doesn't begin to tap the range of his talent. As in CRY FREEDOM and THE MIGHTY QUINN, the American actor is again required to perform a foreign accent, and again he responds flawlessly. Some 50 black British actors were auditioned for the role of Reuben before it was decided that Washington would be right and add some needed prestige to the picture. If only he had been given more to work with. Songs include: "A Matter of Time" (J. Vincent), "School Days" (M. Dread, performed by Singers and Players), "Stay with Me," "Disaster," "Do You Wanna Be," (I'm Talking, performed by I'm Talking), "Under the Apple Tree" (I.

Jones, performed by Jah Warriors). (Violence, profanity, adult situations, sexual situations.)

p, Tim Bevan; d, Martin Stellman; w, Martin Stellman and Trix Worrell; ph, Richard Greatrex (Eastmancolor); ed, Stephen Singleton; m, Michael Kamen, Geoff MacCormack, and Simon Goldenberg; prod d, Andrew McAlpine; art d, Charmian Adams; spec eff, Arthur Beavis; cos, Sandy Powell; stunts, Gareth Milne; makeup, Morag Ross.

Drama   **(PR:O MPAA:R)**

⊘FORBIDDEN SUN*½
(Brit.) 88m Filmscreen c
Lauren Hutton *(Francine Lake)*, Cliff De Young *(Prof. Charles Lake)*, Renee Estevez *(Elaine)*, Robert Beltran *(Jack, Coach)*, Viveka Davis *(Jane)*, Samantha Mathis *(Paula)*, Christine Harnos *(Steph)*, Svetislav Goncic *(Ulysses)*, Renee Props *(Betsey)*, Enver Petrovci *(Lt. Ionnides)*.

At the American School on Crete, nubile young female gymnasts soak up sun, work out, dream about romance, and study ancient Greek culture. While that isn't a bad curriculum, this Greek isle is not the paradise it appears to be. Behind its picturesque facade, sexual repression lurks. Among those toning their bodies and exercising their teenage angst are Mathis, a promising athlete who catches the eye of De Young, a fatherly but sexually frustrated professor; Estevez, who's having an affair with a British rock musician-artist; and Davis, the troubled ward of De Young and his wife, Hutton. By day, Hutton regales the girls with the legend of the Minotaur, which the ancient Greeks celebrated with a death-defying ritual in which a dancer vaulted over a bull. By night, the wholesome role-model abstains from sex with her husband so she can dally with coach Beltran, with whom Davis is obsessed. Davis persuades the other girls to do somersaults on a high parapet and talks Estevez into getting her boy friend to design a Minotaur mask so the young gymnasts can perform the bull dance as an end-of-term surprise. However, tension mounts under the hot Greek sun. While participating in the daily communal jog through the woods, Mathis falls behind and is sexually assaulted. Everyone accuses Goncic, the school's janitor and resident peeping Tom. Always one to put her lessons to good use, Davis leads her classmates in a revenge plot. The girls lure the unsuspecting Goncic to the gym, trick him into donning the Minotaur mask, and then torment him, nearly killing him in the process. When the cops come looking for the missing handyman, the girls are surprised to learn that the man they have just stuffed into a box has an air-tight alibi. After spotting Hutton making love with the dreamboat coach, Davis takes her cue from yet

another myth, this time looking to the Furies for her inspiration. Conning Beltran into trying on the Minotaur mask in the gym, she locks the door, rips her clothing strategically, and cries rape. Amidst the annual folk festival, hordes of teenage girls chase Beltran, until Davis finally pushes him off a cliff. But even taking this bull by the horns isn't enough to satisfy Davis. She tries setting fire to Hutton's home, but is intercepted by her pals, who begin to realize that Davis is slightly deranged. Racing to the bull ring, Davis is saved from death by De Young, who steps into the charging bull's path. Out of nowhere, Beltran returns with his arm in a sling. Then, in full view of her school chums and the happy villagers, the severely disturbed Davis somersaults over the bull, keeping her promise to provide an end-of-term surprise that no one will forget.

While the makers of this film were obviously attempting to create a distaff version of LORD OF THE FLIES, FORBIDDEN SUN is too diffuse and indifferently directed to disturb or enthrall. Its plot is undeniably offbeat, but tony allusions to mythology don't disguise this psychodrama's rampant silliness. Significantly, the movie fails to generate suspense, with the identity of the rapist becoming apparent much too early. The direction is pedestrian, offering an overabundance of shots of teens exercising and sunbathing, and wastes far too much time on travelog footage. Instead of creating an idyllic atmosphere that is rippling with undercurrents of sexual tension, FORBIDDEN SUN turns into an instructional film for female athletes abroad. Moreover, its poorly written characters are neither sympathetic nor interesting, and the young actresses who portray them never make credible vigilantes. In a key role, the phlegmatic Viveka Davis seems less the embodiment of the vengeful spirit of Greek legends than a prom queen who's miffed because she hasn't been elected student council president. Regrettably, the film's mature performers register no more strongly. Reminiscent of some of the wrongheaded projects made during David Puttnam's tenure at Columbia Pictures (most notably ROCKET GIBRALTAR), this ambitious effort fails to make clear its meaning. Perhaps it would take a genius to make a viable drama out of a yarn about an adolescent girl who talks her classmates into reenacting the Minotaur fable. Clearly, the task has proved too much for director Zelda Barron. It's hard not to laugh when a man in a bull mask stumbles around like the front end of a dancing cow act, while naughty gymnasts kick him as if they were in a martial arts film. Did Barron and the screenwriters think that drawing a parallel between their story's simplistic psychological premise and mythology would compensate for a lack of pacing?

Nowhere is this wishy-washy film's lack of resolve more evident than in the mystifying finale. How does Beltran survive falling off a cliff? Why does the involvement of the other teens in the destructive shenanigans go unpunished? Will Davis find happiness at a prison rodeo? The film's climax encapsulates everything that is wrong with this ill-conceived drama—its sparsity of logic, its surfeit of ludicrousness, and its pretentious overreliance on cultural references. *(Adult situations, nudity, profanity, sexual situations.)*

p, Peter Watson-Wood; d, Zelda Barron; w, Robin Hardy (based on his story); ph, Richard Greatrex (Technicolor); ed, George Akers and Dennis McTaggart; m, Hard Rain; prod d, Miljan Kljakovic; cos, Siobhan Barron; stunts, Bill Weston.

Drama   **(PR:C MPAA:R)**

Ⓥ**FREEWAY MANIAC, THE zero**
93m Cannon Intl.-Wintertree/Cannon Group c
Loren Winters *(Linda Kenney)*, James Courtney *(Arthur)*, Shepard Sanders *(Burt Overman)*, Donald Hotton *(Steven Day)*, Jeff Morris *(Ray)*, Robert Bruce *(Terry)*, Frank Jasper *(Mannie)*.

A young boy brutally stabs his mother and her boy friend when he finds them making love on her kitchen table. Flash forward: Years later, the now-grown young man (Courtney) overpowers his unsuspecting guards and escapes from his cell in a maximum-security asylum. At the same time, a would-be actress (Winters) drives aimlessly through the desert, trying to calm down after discovering her lover's (Jasper) infidelity. Her car breaks down and she seeks help in a deserted gas station, but quickly finds herself under attack from a pair of lecherous truck drivers. In what seems a stroke of good luck, another car pulls in and she seeks help from the driver —who, however, turns out to be Courtney. He tries to throttle her, but she manages to escape by running over him with his own vehicle, and Courtney is caught by the police. In the days that follow, Winters is praised in the local press for her part in returning Courtney to confinement, and she lands a part in a cheap science-fiction/ horror film when the producer (Sanders) decides to capitalize on her recent publicity. Unfortunately, Courtney, enraged and humiliated over his capture, escapes a second time and heads towards the film's set to avenge himself, leaving a trail of dead bodies in his wake. The personnel on the film's location learn that Courtney has escaped, but hide the news from Winters to keep her from leaving the production. When Courtney arrives on the scene, he adds some of the crew to his toll of victims, then strangles the lecherous Sanders. Wearing an alien costume found on the set, he manages to abduct Winters, but his

escape is blocked by a contrite Jasper. Courtney climbs atop the burning set where the film's climax is being shot, Jasper follows him, and a battle ensues that frees Winters. Courtney topples into a cloud of smoke and apparently to his death —but (surprise) his body is never found.

Notwithstanding the chainsaw imagery on the video rental box, THE FREEWAY MANIAC pays only a token nod to the slasher genre and concentrates instead on satirizing the making of low-budget horror films. Encumbered with an insipid script and an infinitesimal budget, however, THE FREEWAY MANIAC soon sinks to the level of its target. Suspense is negated by the insufficient footage and sloppy editing, whose ragged, hurried rhythms frequently confuse the narrative. In the climactic battle atop the burning space station set, the combatants are so obscured by orange smoke and a gliding camera boom that it becomes next to impossible to determine their identities or fates.

The actors can shed no light on the situation, and give apathetic performances in their ill-written roles. James Courtney is especially lost in a part that requires him to be a symbol of evil without personality. The cast is further victimized by the monotonous dubbing and by the pounding rock score that all but drowns out their characters' dialog. While the idea of using the horror genre to spoof the perils of low-budget Hollywood filmmaking may have seemed interesting at the outset, the premise is botched by the poor execution. *(Violence, profanity, adult situations, sexual situations.)*

p, Paul Winters and Loren Winters; d, Paul Winters; w, Paul Winters and Gahan Wilson; ph, Ronald Vidor (United Color); ed, David Marsh; m, Greg Stewart.

Comedy/Horror   **(PR:C MPAA:R)**

Ⓥ**FRIDAY THE 13TH PART VIII— JASON TAKES MANHATTAN zero**
100m PAR c
Jensen Daggett *(Rennie Wickham)*, Scott Reeves *(Sean Robertson)*, Peter Mark Richman *(Charles McCulloch)*, Barbara Bingham *(Colleen Van Deusen)*, Kane Hodder *(Jason)*, V.C. Dupree *(Julius Gaw)*.

VIII. Eight. 8. Did anyone think that this series would last this long? What exactly is the appeal here? Not only are these films boneheaded and offensive, each sequel is duller than the last—basically the *same movie* eight times! Judging from its trailers and television commercials showing the hockey-masked killer Jason Voorhees stomping through a New York City subway and stalking Times Square, this one—*part eight*—at least seemed to hold some promise. At last the series seemed to have moved beyond the generic woods of Camp Crystal Lake onto new, fertile terrain, with Man-

Kane Hodder in FRIDAY THE 13TH PART VII—JASON TAKES MANHATTAN (©Paramount).

hattan offering seemingly dozens of opportunities for Jason—not just for kills—but for some black comedy and social satire. Well, no such luck. FRIDAY THE 13TH PART VIII—JASON TAKES MANHATTAN has the most deceptive title and ad campaign of the entire series, in that Jason doesn't even set foot in Manhattan until the last 15 minutes of what is yet another plodding entry in the stalk-and-slash genre. Indeed, the film should have been titled "Jason Takes an Ocean Liner Docked in Vancouver, British Columbia" for that's where the vast majority of the action was filmed.

The plot, such as it is, sees Jason—previously entombed at the bottom of Crystal Lake—brought back to life when the anchor from a pleasure boat severs an electrical cable and jolts his inert body with a zillion volts. Naturally, Jason makes quick work of the boat's two teenage passengers. He then drifts into a harbor where a ship full of seniors from Crystal Lake High is preparing to depart on a class trip to Manhattan, boards the ship, and kills off most of the teens and the crew. Only three students and two adult chaperons manage to escape in a life boat, winding up in Manhattan. Jason, still in hot pursuit, surfaces in New York long enough to terrorize some street people, burst into a diner, stomp through a subway, and frighten gang members in Times Square (the only scene actually shot in Manhattan) before the two surviving teens dispose of him in the sewer system, where he is dissolved by toxic waste.

During all of this tediously staged action, writer-director Rob Hedden attempts to introduce some NIGHTMARE ON ELM STREET-type thrills by having the virginal female heroine (Daggett) suffer from visions and nightmares of the young Jason Voorhees, who has haunted her ever since her mean uncle tried to teach her how to swim by dumping her in Crystal Lake (fans of the series will recall that Jason, as a child, drowned in Crystal Lake). As legend has it, drownings in the lake are caused by the vengeful Jason pulling the kids under, which is exactly what happened to Daggett, though she escaped, growing into young adulthood with a morbid fear of water. Not surprisingly, the hallucination scenes—which feel as if they belong in another movie—are among the most effective in the film, a welcome distraction from the mundane mechanics of the rest of this predictable effort. Maybe the inevitable Part IX will actually take place in Manhattan; more likely the dissolved Jason will drift from NYC's sewer system back to Crystal Lake, where he will somehow be reborn and . . . (Violence, gore effects, sexual situations, substance abuse, profanity.)

p, Randolph Cheveldave; d, Rob Hedden; w, Rob Hedden; ph, Byron England; ed, Steven Mirkovich; m, Fred Mollin; prod d, David Fischer.

Horror   (PR:O MPAA:R)

Ⓥ**FRIENDS, LOVERS AND LUNATICS***½
(Can.) 87m SC/Fries c
Daniel Stern, Sheila McCarthy, Damir Andrei, Deborah Foreman (Annie), Page Fletcher (Buddy), Elias Koteas.

Romance may not be dead, but it certainly suffers a severe maiming at the hands of this bumbling, boring Canadian production, which features cute, perky Yuppie characters who babble tiresomely about their relationships while they fall in and out of love. Among them is Stern, the stereotypical Free-spirited Artist Who Just Can't Live by the Rules (in other words, he's annoying as hell). Fired from his job and dumped by his live-in girl friend (McCarthy) on the same day, Stern retaliates with an infantile barrage of artsy terrorist gags directed against McCarthy and her new beau, the stereotypical Stuffy Academic (Andrei)—pranks which, in a slightly different context, might have been the stuff of an interesting thriller. Instead, the film sets about pondering the question of how on earth McCarthy could ever have split from such a lovably irritating fellow as Stern, and sends Andrei and McCarthy on a romantic weekend to the country with Stern in "zany" hot pursuit (consisting of endless, tedious footage of Stern zipping up and down country roads). Along the way, the three cross paths with a comical biker/sociopath (Fletcher); his kooky, hip-

pie girl friend (Foreman); and a moronic hick farmer (Koteas). While McCarthy and Andrei shack up in their country cabin—discovering, predictably, how little they have in common—Stern obtains Fletcher's motorcycle from Foreman (who has tossed Stern's car keys into a wishing well). Discovering Stern's abandoned auto, Fletcher concludes that Andrei has absconded with both the bike and Foreman—since Stern has cleverly replaced his own expired license plate with one stolen from Andrei's all-terrain Yupmobile (an event that raises the unanswered question, for those who have not been bored to sleep already, of how Andrei was able to drive all the way to the country in a plate-less vehicle unmolested by police). All these laboriously wacky complications lead to the cabin and a shrill, extended confrontation involving Fletcher, Koteas, Andrei, and McCarthy that ends when Stern mercifully shows up to set the story straight and put the picture out of its misery. Stern and McCarthy are reunited, as are Fletcher and his bike. It's hard to decide which of the two reunions is more touching.

It's also hard to figure out how so many talented people could have been persuaded to appear in such a dumb movie. An accomplished comedic actor whose credits include BREAKING AWAY; DINER; and HANNAH AND HER SISTERS, Daniel Stern is currently charming TV audiences as the offscreen narrator of TV's "The Wonder Years." McCarthy beguiled critics and arthouse audiences alike as the star of the Canadian film I'VE HEARD THE MERMAIDS SINGING; Koteas has lent amusing support in John Hughes' SOME KIND OF WONDERFUL and other movies. Even Page Fletcher (familiar to HBO viewers from THE HITCHER) and chipmunk-cheeked B-movie queen Deborah Foreman (VALLEY GIRL) have drawn deserved attention for their work in the past. Because the cast is so promising, FRIENDS, LOVERS & LUNATICS becomes one of those movies you find yourself desperately rooting for long after you know it's run out of gas, which makes the film's failure all the more dispiriting.

Indeed, the performers (especially Koteas) do as much as they can with their roles, but in the end all are ignominiously defeated by the writer-director team of Michael Taav and Stephen Withrow. Taav's script displays a blithe disregard for anything resembling plot structure, and his characters (who are never more than stale romantic comedy cliches) don't so much interact as bump into one another. Withrow, meanwhile, provides a surfeit of slack, uninspired direction—of the type that attempts to elicit belly laughs by having the actors scream their lines and that uses slapstick to cover up the plot's lack of invention.

If nothing else, FRIENDS, LOVERS & LUNATICS may deserve some kind of truth-in-advertising award for billing itself as "The Comedy Surprise of the Year." Unfortunately, the "comedy surprise" is that a concoction of such dullness could have resulted from so many promising ingredients. (Adult situations, profanity.)

p, Nicolas Stiliadis; d, Stephen Withrow; w, Michael Taav.

Comedy/Romance   (PR:C MPAA:R)

Ⓥ**FRIGHT NIGHT—PART 2****
101m Vista/New Century-Vista c
Roddy McDowall (Peter Vincent), William Ragsdale (Charley Brewster), Traci Lin (Alex), Julie Carmen (Regine), Russell Clark (Belle), Brian Thompson (Bozworth), Jonathan Gries (Louie), Ernie Sabella (Dr. Harrison), Merritt Butrick (Ritchie), Matt Landers (Mel), Josh Richman (Fritzy), Karen Andrews (Mrs. Stern), Rochelle Ashana (Art Major), Blair Tefkin (Beatrice), Alexander Folk (Sergeant), Scanlon Gail (Watch Captain), Grant Owens (Jailer), John LaFayette (Bartender), Gary Allen (Mr. Newberry), Brad Kepnick (Hip Young Guy), Neith Hunter (Young Admirer), Ed Quinlan (Newscaster), Jennifer Joan Taylor (Secretary-Receptionist), Jill Augustine (Coed), Gar Campbell (Director), Ed Corbett, Robert Jenkins (Stagehands), David Efron (Orderly).

The nominal stars of this extremely weak horror film are William Ragsdale, Roddy McDowall, Traci Lin, and Julie Carmen, but the real stars are the grisly melting flesh, and the convincing werewolf makeup and special effects. Strictly for avid fans of the vampire subgenre, this gory, uninspired sequel to FRIGHT NIGHT offers neither the fascinating plot twists nor the startlingly horrific gimmicks employed so well by director Tom Holland in the original. FRIGHT NIGHT—PART 2 picks up right where its 1987 predecessor left off. The story once again concerns the adventures of young Ragsdale, who presumably killed the creature that struck terror into the hearts of all concerned in the original. Although Ragsdale is certain that he polished off a genuine vampire, his therapist is bent on convincing him that it was a serial killer, not a vampire, that he killed. In any event, Ragsdale's hope of resuming a normal collegiate existence with his girl friend (Lin) soon vanishes. Ragsdale makes the mistake of visiting McDowall, a self-proclaimed vampire killer and well-known host of a weekly horror film series. While at McDowall's gothic-style apartment building, Ragsdale spots three strange boxes being deposited. As the story unfolds, it is revealed that the vampire Ragsdale disposed of in the first film (Chris Sarandon) had an equally hateful sister (Carmen, THE MILAGRO BEANFIELD

WAR), who, along with several confederates, is determined to make Ragsdale suffer for what he did to her brother. With great glee she visualizes how she is going to transform Ragsdale into one of the undead. As is to be expected in a film like this, just when things are looking bleakest for Ragsdale, his fortunes are reversed and the vampires get their comeuppance, rotting before the audience's eyes. One problem with FRIGHT NIGHT—PART 2 is that the viewer never knows when the filmmakers are trying to scare the pants off fans of grisliness or when they are parodying such efforts. Notably, the scene in which a psychologist-turned-vampire spouts pseudopsychological drivel while dying can be read as a put-on; but to the uninitiated observer, the scene is more nauseatingly horrific than funny. Just where one's sympathies are to lie in a film like this is difficult to determine. The direction by John Carpenter protege Tommy Lee Wallace (HALLOWEEN III—SEASON OF THE WITCH), acting, script, editing, camerawork, and score are all predictable but adequate. Songs include: "Come to Me" (Brad Fiedel, performed by Deborah Holland), "Louie, Louie" (Richard Berry, performed by Berry), "Marvel Age" (Ross Levinson, performed by Levinson), "You Could Look It Up" (T Bone Burnett, performed by Burnett), "Dressed in Red" (Van Dyke Parks, Todd Hayen, performed by Leslie Lewis), "In the Midnight Hour" (Steve Cropper, Wilson Pickett, performed by Pickett). *(Graphic violence, profanity, adult situations, sexual situations.)*

p, Herb Jaffe and Mort Engelberg; d, Tommy Lee Wallace; w, Tim Metcalfe, Miguel Tejada-Flores, and Tommy Lee Wallace (based on characters created by Tom Holland); ph, Mark Irwin (Panavision, Deluxe Color); ed, Jay Lash Cassidy; m, Brad Fiedel; prod d, Dean Tschetter; art d, Randy Moore; set d, Eric Compton and Thomas Wilkins; spec eff, Rick Josephson; cos, Joseph Porro; chor, Russell Clark; stunts, Edward James Ulrich; makeup, Lilly Benyair.

Comedy/Horror   (PR:O MPAA:R)

FROM HOLLYWOOD TO DEADWOOD**½
102m Nightfilm c

Scott Paulin *(Raymond Savage)*, Jim Haynie *(Jack Haines)*, Barbara Shock *(Lana Dark)*, Jurgen Doeres *(Steve Reese)*, Chris Mulkey *(Nick Detroit)*, Mike Genovese *(Ernie November)*, Norbert Weisser *(Peter Mueller)*, Tom Dahlgren *(Ted Field)*, Campbell Scott *(Bobby)*.

A private-eye tale with some deadpan, tongue-in-cheek humor, FROM HOLLYWOOD TO DEADWOOD centers around a pair of gumshoes (Paulin and Haynie) who are hired by a Hollywood film studio to track down an actress (Shock) whose disappearance has halted a movie production. Shock, who has a reputation for "difficult" behavior, can't be found anywhere in Los Angeles, and all signs point to her departure by car. Paulin and Haynie pursue her to the Black Hills of South Dakota, where the three collide after a lengthy chase in the little town of Deadwood, famous as the site of Wild Bill Hickok's murder. In Deadwood, Paulin becomes infatuated with Shock and throws professional ethics (along with the studio's reward money) to the wind in his attempts to romance her. She resists his advances, but Paulin won't leave her alone until he finds out why she felt she had to leave LA. With great effort, he finally manages to gain enough of her confidence to learn that the studio actually *suggested* that she take off, in light of the uninspired performance she was giving in the movie being filmed. The insurance, they claimed, would cover the loss only if an investigation took place. But it would really be in their best financial interests if the actress turned up dead, allowing them to be reimbursed for the total cost of the unusable film . . . A wry throwback to the Raymond Chandler-style mysteries of the 1940s and 50s, FROM HOLLYWOOD TO DEADWOOD has a certain brash style, and is technically accomplished for its budget of less than $1 million. Unfortunately, writer-director Rex Pickett (making his feature debut) lets the story drag in spots—it takes far too long for the two detectives to catch up to their quarry, for example—and the perfunctory development of the relationship between Shock and Paulin's characters is one of several shaky stretches in the narrative. The script's means of getting the detectives from one locale to the next as they pursue the actress to Deadwood seem particularly arbitrary, and once they arrive in town, even the beautiful South Dakota scenery isn't distracting enough to compensate for the implausible goings-on. As the mysterious Lana Dark, Barbara Shock (the filmmaker's wife) recalls the reclusive Greta Garbo and the young Ingrid Bergman; still, she's a little *too* icy to fire detective Paulin's desires to the extent posited by Pickett's screenplay. What does work in FROM HOLLYWOOD TO DEADWOOD is the unique rapport between Paulin and Haynie's characters. Underneath their Philip Marlowesque trappings, Pickett's detectives turn out to be a would-be novelist and a crass but sympathetic ex-actor whose relationship and career make for a fascinating mix of toughness and vulnerability, well played by Scott Paulin (TEEN WOLF) and Jim Haynie (JACK'S BACK; PRETTY IN PINK). Chris Mulkey, Mike Genovese, and Campbell Scott provide able acting support, while Peter Deming's cinematography should earn him plenty of better budgeted jobs down the line. *(Profanity, adult situations.)*

p, Jo Peterson; d, Rex Pickett; w, Rex Pickett; ph, Peter Deming (Duart Color); ed, Steven Adrianson and Robert Erickson; m, Alex Gibson and Gregory Kuehn; cos, Meg Goodwin.

Mystery   (PR:C MPAA:R)

Traci Lynn, William Ragsdale, and Roddy McDowall in FRIGHT NIGHT—PART 2 (©New Century).

G

GANG OF FOUR, THE***

(Fr.) 150m Pierre Grise/Metropolis c
Bulle Ogier *(Constance)*, Benoit Regent *(Thomas)*, Laurence Cote *(Claude)*, Fejria Deliba *(Anna)*, Bernadette Giraud *(Joyce)*, Ines de Medeiros-D'Almeida *(Lucia)*, Nathalie Richard *(Cecile)*.

Jacques Rivette's THE GANG OF FOUR is an intriguing, if somewhat overextended, melodrama that delves into Pirandellian questions of real versus theatrical life, and considers the nature of deception and fate. Rivette sets his story (cowritten with Pascal Bonitzer and Christine Laurent) in a specifically theatrical milieu and allows the audience to draw many of its own conclusions.

Ogier is a celebrated drama teacher who has chosen to work only with women. In her very exclusive class are Deliba, Giraud, Cote, and de Medeiros-D'Almeida. Under Ogier's rigorous tutelage, they rehearse various plays together, in particular Marivaux's "Double Infidelities." The four girls also live together in a small suburban house. Portuguese de Medeiros-D'Almeida is the newest roommate, having recently replaced Richard, another acting student who has moved in with her new, secret lover. One night, while leaving an art exhibition, Deliba is attacked by two men. A mysterious man (Regent) rushes to her aid and, while driving her home, informs Deliba that Richard's lover has embroiled her old roommate in a shady affair that could prove harmful to Richard. This information seems to explain Richard's increasingly distraught behavior during class. Deliba and Giraud try to draw her out, but she rebuffs them and runs away; meanwhile, Regent begins to infiltrate the four actresses' household, seducing the hitherto lesbian Cote. It seems the house harbors a secret related to the Richard affair and Regent is determined to discover it. Unknown to anyone, de Medeiros-D'Almeida holds the key to the mystery. The happy little sisterhood begins to disintegrate under the pressure of the intrigue, but the four young women finally resolve to settle their differences and help Richard; however, the price they must pay to do so proves devastating.

Rivette (CELINE AND JULIE GO BOATING) maintains virtuoso control over his material, and the film unfolds in a leisurely but penetrating manner. He opens the film with a bravura stroke, taking Deliba from a cafe, through the streets of Paris, and into a room, where she strikes up a conversation with another woman—rehearsal having begun with a mysterious seamlessness worthy of Hitchcock. The rest of the film is similarly elegant in technique. The camera rests lovingly on the women, who, luckily, have sufficient presence and talent to emerge as real individuals (numerous rehearsal scenes reveal all of these relative newcomers to be fine actresses). On the other hand, Rivette has given short shrift to the film's suspense elements, and the ending is unsatisfyingly perplexing.

With its theatrical atmosphere and intensely feminine focus, THE GANG OF FOUR recalls Gregory LaCava's scintillating STAGE DOOR (1937) and Mervyn LeRoy's intriguing, neglected DRAMATIC SCHOOL (1938), best remembered for its fascinating, diverse cast (Luise Rainer, Paulette Goddard, Lana Turner, Gale Sondergaard, Genevieve Tobin). As Lucia, Ines de Medeiros-D'Almeida conveys a dark, spooky beauty and eerie self-possession reminiscent of Rainer; Sondergaard's ambivalent attitude toward her students has its echoes here in Bulle Ogier's Constance; and both films are suggestive in their presentation of dissimilar beings thrown together and bound by artistic dedication. Fejria Deliba has the lush, tropical looks of a Lonette McKee or Jasmine Guy, and the confidence of Paulette Goddard. Laurence Cote aptly captures the androgyny and messy emotionalism of Claude; Bernadette Giraud is humorously self-effacing as Joyce; and Nathalie Richard's hysterics are well suited to the role of Cecile. Unfortunately, Benoit Regent—who is better as the kind of unimaginative, four-square character he plays in Alain Tanner's FLAME IN MY HEART—lacks the requisite charisma to be convincing as an irresistible Lothario. *(Nudity, adult situations.)*

p, Pierre Grise; d, Jacques Rivette; w, Jacques Rivette, Pascal Bonitzer, and Christine Laurent; ph, Caroline Champetier; ed, Catherine Quesemand.

Drama   (PR:C   MPAA:NR)

ⓥGATOR BAIT II: CAJUN JUSTICE
zero
94m Sebastian Intl./PAR c
Jan MacKenzie *(Angelique)*, Tray Loren *(Big T)*, Paul Muzzcat *(Leroy)*, Brad Kepnick *(Luke)*, Jerry Armstrong *(Joe Boy)*, Ben Sebastian *(Elick)*, Reyn Hubbard *(Geke)*.

GATOR BAIT II: CAJUN JUSTICE is the ultra-low-budget sequel to the 1976 B movie GATOR BAIT, which starred *Playboy* Playmate Claudia Jennings as a sexy southern woman pursued by a gang of drooling Cajun maniacs. If you haven't already guessed, GATOR BAIT wasn't a particularly pleasant moviegoing experience. In a real twist, GATOR BAIT II: CAJUN JUSTICE stars Jan MacKenzie as a sexy southern woman pursued by a gang of drooling Cajun maniacs. It too is not a pleasant film to watch.

The movie opens with the Cajun wedding of MacKenzie and Loren, during which a group of backwoodsmen, led by the crazy Muzzcat, crash the party and cause a huge fight. It seems that, after a confrontation some years earlier, Muzzcat was left for dead by Loren, and now he wants revenge. The battle breaks up, however, when Loren and MacKenzie head off in their speedboat to spend their honeymoon in Loren's swamp shack. There they pass several days frolicking in the woods and floating through the bayou, with Loren teaching city girl MacKenzie swamp survival. Fishing, hunting, and fighting are included in her curriculum—naturally, MacKenzie will have to use these newfound skills to survive later in the film. One day, Loren goes fishing, leaving MacKenzie alone. Muzzcat and his gang arrive at the shack just in time to watch MacKenzie take a bath. Forcing their way into the house, they proceed to terrorize her (pawing her and compelling her to strip and put on sexy undergarments) until Loren comes home. Muzzcat shoots Loren and ties him to a tree in the swamp, leaving his victim for dead the way he himself was left years earlier. The backwoods thugs then take MacKenzie to their camp, where they take turns raping her, until a sympathetic member of the gang (Kepnick) sets her free. Returning to the shack, she finds Loren's body missing. As the gang pursues MacKenzie through the swamp by boat, she calls on her new survival skills and begins eliminating the Cajun creeps one by one. What's more, it is soon revealed that Loren is alive (an old swamper having saved him and nursed him back to health), and he comes to the rescue when MacKenzie is attacked by Muzzcat—who is blown away by Loren just before the newlyweds are tearfully reunited.

Virtually plotless and full of nasty situations, GATOR BAIT II: CAJUN JUSTICE is grade-Z nonsense. Hoping to get viewers riled, producer-directors Ferd and Beverly Sebastian rely heavily on the "revenge" factor (a staple in B-movie plotting), but instead of arousing audience anger, the Sebastians present endlessly tedious scenes of morons running around the swamp. Apparently this mindless activity is the filmmakers' idea of character development and plot set-up. In addition to having virtually no plot, shallow characters, and boring chase scenes, GATOR BAIT II is also an unusually nasty picture, full of misogynist dialog and degrading peek-a-boo nudity. Indeed, the camera stalks MacKenzie's body in movie-psycho fashion. The technical flaws of the film only add to its ugly tone. Bad lighting, bad editing, and awful shot composition dog every scene, and, at times, the dialog is barely audible (actually a blessing). GATOR BAIT II (and its predecessor) owes a lot to DELIVERANCE in terms of desired effect, but while DELIVERANCE has three-dimensional characters (not to mention brilliant suspense and interesting subtext), GATOR BAIT II offers drivel-spouting stereotypes. Starting off terribly and becoming progressively worse, the film hits rock bottom when it virtually repeats a scene from I SPIT ON YOUR GRAVE (involving a man and an outboard motor). There is always a place for a *good* grade-B revenge film (VICE SQUAD and WHITE LINE FEVER are two excellent examples), but this tasteless waste of celluloid is pure torture. *(Nudity, violence, profanity, adult situations, substance abuse.)*

p, Ferd Sebastian and Beverly Sebastian; d, Ferd Sebastian and Beverly Sebastian; w, Ferd Sebastian and Beverly Sebastian; ph, Ferd Sebastian; m, George H. Hamilton, Ferd Sebastian, Julius Adams, and Vernon Rodrique; prod d, Beverly Sebastian; cos, Martha Marcantel.

Action   (PR:O MPAA:R)

ⓥGETTING IT RIGHT***
102m Management Company
Entertainment Group c
Jesse Birdsall *(Gavin Lamb)*, Helena Bonham Carter *(Lady Minerva Munday)*, Peter Cook *(Mr. Adrian)*, John Gielgud *(Sir Gordon Munday)*, Shirley Anne Field *(Anne)*, Jane Horrocks *(Jenny)*, Judy Parfitt *(Lady Stella Munday)*, Lynn Redgrave *(Joan)*, Richard Huw *(Harry)*, Pat Heywood *(Mrs. Lamb)*, Bryan Pringle *(Mr. Lamb)*, Kevin Drinkwater *(Winthrop)*, Nan Munro *(Lady Blackwater)*, Ian Redford *(Bill)*, Ben Miles *(Spiro)*, Cyril Conway *(Manservant)*, Noriko Aida *(Maid)*, Richard Strange *(Sheila's Friend)*, Irene Marot *(Sheila)*, Janet Amsden *(Mrs. Blake)*, Aimee Delamain *(Mrs. Arbuthnot)*, Rupert Holliday Evans *(Peter)*, June Ellis *(Mrs. Wagstaffe)*, Pauline Quirke *(Muriel Sutton)*, Anne-Marie Owens, Vivian Tierney, John Cashmore *(Opera Singers)*, Richard MacDonald *(Man at Opera)*, Lula Ioannou, Sarah Morgan *(Salon Juniors)*, Elizabeth Jane Howard *(Woman at Party)*, Cut Double *(Rock Band)*.

American director Randal Kleiser (GREASE; BIG TOP PEE-WEE) journeyed to England to film this gentle comedy based on a novel by Elizabeth Jane Howard. Birdsall stars as Gavin Lamb, a 31-year-old West End hairdresser who lives with his passive father (Pringle) and a mother (Heywood) who's constantly inflicting culinary catastrophes upon his family. Birdsall is still a virgin and tends to be frightened of people, especially women, as he tells us in voice-over. He soon is involved with various members of the "frightening" sex, however, beginning with a party at a posh apartment on the Thames. He's there at the invitation of his best friend (Huw), a gay makeup artist

Jesse Birdsall and Helena Bonham Carter in GETTING IT RIGHT (©MCEG).

whose lover, the boorish Winthrop (Drinkwater), is friendly with the hostess (Redgrave). At the party, an obviously uncomfortable Birdsall is spotted by Redgrave, who makes a successful effort to put him at ease. He then encounters the very naked and thoroughly neurotic Carter, who, though she has all the markings of a tramp, introduces herself as Lady Minerva Munday. When the party breaks up, she follows Birdsall to his parents' home and pleads with him to put her up for the night. Ever the gentleman, Birdsall consents (which sets up a very funny scene the next morning, when his mother is thrilled to have a "lady" for breakfast). A few nights later, Birdsall runs into Redgrave at the opera. She invites him back to her place and, with her husband away (as is usually the case), seduces him. He spends the night with her and seems to have genuinely deep feelings for her, but his repeated attempts to call Redgrave after the evening's dalliance are rebuffed. In the meantime, Carter reenters his life, phoning his mother and arranging for Birdsall to have lunch at her home. Birdsall reluctantly goes through with the meeting and is surprised to see that Carter lives in a palatial estate owned by her stepfather (Gielgud), a wealthy manufacturer. When Birdsall finds out that Carter has told Gielgud she is pregnant by and engaged to him, he bolts from the house. It's about this time that Birdsall takes notice of Horrocks, the shy young woman who has been his assistant for nearly two years. He learns that she was impregnated by a sailor while on holiday in France when she was 16, and now has a two-and-a-half-year-old son whom she leaves in the care of her widowed mother when she's working. Birdsall takes

a liking to Horrocks, and she is soon spending evenings at his home, where he teaches her about "art." His idyll is shattered, however, by a series of crises, beginning with his discovery of the bulimic Carter gorging herself in the basement of her sister's flat. He has her rushed to the hospital, and she phones a few days later to say that she's married and that her stepfather has given her new husband a good job and a car. Next, a distraught Huw informs Birdsall that Drinkwater is leaving him to go to the US with Redgrave, who has been dumped by her husband. Birdsall confronts Redgrave, urging her not to come between Huw and Drinkwater, but to no avail. Despondent, he then discovers that Horrocks is planning to move to Germany with her mother, who is marrying a serviceman stationed there. Overwhelmed by the thought of losing her, Birdsall confesses his love and asks Horrocks to marry him. She consents, and the blissfully wed pair head off on their honeymoon at the fade-out.

At its heart, GETTING IT RIGHT harbors a sentimentality no different from any number of mundane television programs. Yet Howard's screenplay is so fresh and is so well handled under Kleiser's deft direction that the film rises above its potentially melodramatic nature. Of course, the main character is so perfect in every way he strains credibility. He's so sensitive, responsible, compassionate, moral, and cultured he would have to rank as the world's most desirable bachelor; moreover, his charm and thoughtfulness toward all the women who cross his path in the film belie its contention that he is painfully uncomfortable around the opposite sex. If the hero is too perfect, however, at least GETTING IT RIGHT provides him with a worthy beneficiary for his goodness. As portrayed by Jane Horrocks, Jenny is a sweet young lady who stoically bears her lot in life, but whose looks, voice, and walk betray a painful vulnerability. Surely she deserves a better fate, and Jesse Birdsall's Gavin is just the man to provide it for her. Though the scenes in which he teaches her about Mozart, Chopin, and Degas are rather banal, the two do have some genuinely tender moments together, as do Birdsall and Redgrave, who is quite effective as the wealthy sophisticate with a vulnerability of her own.

While there is a sincere warmth to GETTING IT RIGHT, it also has its share of humor. Sir John Gielgud, who is wonderful in his brief appearance, has a very funny scene in which he initially mistakes Birdsall for a fortune hunter, then, recognizing his error, slowly escalates the amount he's willing to pay to marry off his stepdaughter. Pat Heywood is also very amusing as the hero's mother, and her recipe for Spanish chicken mole (which she pronounces like the animal rather than the Spanish mo-LAY) is a gem. Helena Bonham Carter gets a lot out of her quirky, airheaded character, and if her efforts to turn Minerva into something of a tragic figure are less successful, that's more a fault in the script than in her acting. Peter Cook also does a nice turn as Birdsall's pompous boss with a bad toupee.

GETTING IT RIGHT represents a change of pace for Kleiser, who had been interested in filming the story for seven years before being given the chance to do so by Management Company Entertainment Group, a company founded by Blake Edwards' former partner Jonathan D. Krane. Coming from a director who had previously helmed primarily big-star, big-budget projects, this was definitely something new, and the shift in scale seems to suit Kleiser well. Unfortunately, in the absence of a big star or big budget, the movie did little box-office business in the US, despite favorable reviews. It's nevertheless worth seeing. Musical selections include: "Getting It Right" (Colin Towns, Stephanie Tyrell, Steve Tyrell, performed by Dusty Springfield), "Ye Ke Ye Ke" (performed by Mory Kante), "Love Take Over" (Ashton Liburd, Paul Gold, performed by Cut Double); extracts from "Aida" (Giuseppe Verdi, performed by the Chorus and Orchestra of the Sofia National Opera), "Les Sylphides" (Frederic Chopin, performed by the Sofia Philharmonic Orchestra), Piano Concerto No. 14 in E-flat Major, K. 449 (Wolfgang Amadeus Mozart, performed by the Czech Chamber Orchestra), "Piano Concerto No. 24 in C Minor, K. 491 (Mozart, performed by the Czech Philharmonic Orchestra). (Brief nudity, profanity, sexual situations.)

p, Randal Kleiser, Jonathan D. Krane, and Gregory Hinton; d, Randal Kleiser; w,

Elizabeth Jane Howard (based on her novel); ph, Clive Tickner (Fuji Color); ed, Chris Kelly; m, Colin Towns and Steve Tyrell; prod d, Caroline Amies; art d, Frank Walsh; cos, Hazel Pethig; makeup, Sue Black.

Comedy/Drama   (PR:O MPAA:R)

ⓥ**GHETTOBLASTER****
86m Prism c
Richard Hatch *(Travis)*, R.G. Armstrong *(Curtis)*, Rosemarie *(Helen)*, Courtney Gebhart *(Lisa)*, Del Zamora *(Jesus)*, Diane Moser *(Gina)*, Keymar Reyes *(Chato)*, Marco Hernandez *(Hector)*, Harry Caesar *(Mr. Dobson)*, Rick Telles *(Luis)*, Richard Jaeckel *(Mike Henry)*.

Just when you thought it was safe to go into the barrio, those nasty inner-city punks have taken over the turf again. Inspired by COLORS and descended from 1970s revenge fantasies like DEATH WISH and VIGILANTE FORCE, GHETTO-BLASTER is a totally unnecessary action flick about one man's battle to redeem his ungentrified neighborhood.

Opening with a montage of gang violence that is meant to terrify us, GHETTOBLASTER wastes no time in establishing its "life is cheap in the ghetto" ethos. When not gunning down innocent bystanders, African-American and Chicano thugs use each other for target practice. Accompanied by daughter Gebhart, Hatch visits his parents in the neighborhood where he grew up and discovers it has become a war zone. Failing to persuade his father (Armstrong) to throw in the towel, Hatch helps out in the family grocery store, butts heads with evil teens, and, foolishly, is polite to Moser, an attractive miss much admired by Zamora, leader of the Hammer gang. While working in the back of the store, Hatch hears gunshots; his father has been murdered by the Hammers. Naturally, Hatch is mighty riled, but policeman Jaeckel warns him that no one can triumph over the gangs. Hatch's only allies in his attempt to do just that are Caesar, an elderly cat-fancier, and Moser, whose brother, Reyes, is Zamora's right-hand man. After Vietnam vet Hatch punishes some of his adversaries in his store, he finds himself surrounded and menaced by Hammers. Caesar comes to his rescue, and the gang vows revenge. After the Hammers gut Caesar's cat and set fire to the old man, Hatch becomes a one-man vigilante force—mad as hell, he (1) paints over unsightly graffiti, (2) foils muggings, (3) booby-traps stolen merchandise, and (4) murders a few Hammers. When he receives a mysterious tip about a drug deal, Hatch suspects a trap and manages to rip off Zamora by masquerading as a clown and escaping on a motorbike. The Hammers retaliate by kidnaping Hatch's daughter; however, in the climactic con-

frontation, Hatch easily dispatches most of the street scum. Surprisingly, it turns out that Hatch's informant is Reyes, who hopes to take over and reform the gang, thereby making the neighborhood safe for his beloved sister. When Reyes is shot, it looks as if Hatch will be next, but daughter Gebhart gets into the vigilante spirit and blasts Zamora—like father, like daughter. Although Jaeckel publicly takes credit for eliminating the Hammers, it's clear that modest citizens like Hatch are the ones who've really made the neighborhood safe. All that was required was a multiracial block patrol led by a demolitions expert.

Watchable on a mindless level, this passable avenger film never rises above its limited aspirations. Exploiting all-too-real inner-city calamities, GHETTO-BLASTER eschews plot logic and concentrates on cheap thrills while cashing in on "vigilante chic." No one in the cast even tries to act; they just coast through the familiar plot developments in a daze. But then, why bother, when the storyline has been recycled from old Charles Bronson movies and revved up with 1980s special effects-laden violence? Even such nasty scenes as the burning of Caesar and an attempted rape have little impact. Richard Hatch, a boyish leading man only a few years ago, looks too tired for the nonstop killing duties he's been assigned here. But if Hatch fans (assuming there are any) will be disappointed, those who follow the career of Rosemarie will be glad to learn that the actress is still working, though her role as Hatch's mother is a long way from "The Dick Van Dyke Show" and "Hollywood Squares."

In the final analysis, GHETTO-BLASTER offers enough explosions and shoot-em-ups to keep viewers awake, and enough cliched writing and flaccid direction to make them wonder why they bothered watching. Unless you're interested in seeing street punks flushed down city sewers by a honky-gringo savior, skip this one. *(Graphic violence, nudity, profanity, adult situations, sexual situations, substance abuse.)*

p, David Decoteau and John Schouweiler; d, Alan L. Stewart; w, Clay McBride; ph, Thomas Callaway; ed, Tony Malanowski; m, Reg Powell and Sam Winans; prod d, Royce Mathew.

Action   (PR:O MPAA:R)

ⓥ**GHOSTBUSTERS II*½**
108m COL c
Bill Murray *(Dr. Peter Venkman)*, Dan Aykroyd *(Dr. Raymond Stantz)*, Sigourney Weaver *(Dana Barrett)*, Harold Ramis *(Dr. Egon Spengler)*, Rick Moranis *(Louis Tully)*, Ernie Hudson *(Winston Zeddemore)*, Annie Potts *(Janine Melnitz)*, Peter MacNicol *(Janosz Poha)*, Harris Yulin *(The Judge)*, David

Sigourney Weaver, Bill Murray, Harold Ramis, and Dan Aykroyd in GHOSTBUSTERS II (©Columbia).

Margulies *(The Mayor of New York)*, Kurt Fuller *(Hardemeyer)*, Janet Margolin *(The Prosecutor)*, Wilhelm Von Homburg *(Vigo)*, William T. Deutschendorf, Henry J. Deutschendorf II *(Baby Oscar)*, Michael P. Moran *(Frank, the Doorman)*, Olivia Ward *(Meter Maid)*, Mordecai Lawner *(Man with a Ticket)*, Susan Boehm *(Young Woman on Crutches)*, Mary Ellen Trainor *(Brownstone Mother)*, Christopher Villasenor, Jason Reitman *(Brownstone Boys)*, Aaron Lustig *(Norman, the Producer)*, Page Leong *(Spengler's Assistant)*, Mark Schneider, Valery Pappas *(Arguing Couple)*, Catherine Reitman *(Girl with Puppy)*, Dave Florek *(lst Cop)*, Richard Foronjy *(Con Ed Supervisor)*, George Wilbur *(Bailiff)*, Sharon Kramer *(Stenographer)*, Walter Flanagan *(Rudy, the Museum Guard)*, Bobby Baresford Brown *(Mayor's Doorman)*, Christopher Neame *(Maitre d')*, Judy Ovitz *(Slimed Restaurant Patron)*, Tom Dugan, Angelo Di Mascio *(Restaurant Cops)*, Robert Alan Beuth *(Store Manager)*, Ralph Monaco *(Police Sergeant)*, Ron Cummins *(Police Lieutenant)*, Cheech Marin *(Dock Supervisor)*, Yvette Cruise *(Maria, Dana's Maid)*, John Hammil, Ray Glanzmann, Alex Zimmerman *(Detectives)*, Brian Doyle Murray *(Psychiatrist)*, Louise Troy *(Woman with Fur Coat)*, Douglas Seale *(Plaza Hotel Man)*, Ben Stein *(Public Works Official)*, Erik Holland *(Fire Commissioner)*, Philip Baker Hall *(Police Commissioner)*.

Perhaps the most eagerly anticipated sequel of the summer, GHOSTBUSTERS II was a terrible disappointment. After five years of wrangling, wooing, planning, and hoping, Columbia Pictures, director Ivan

Reitman, and writers Harold Ramis and Dan Aykroyd delivered a shockingly self-satisfied and unforgivably slapdash sequel to the phenomenally popular 1984 comedy GHOSTBUSTERS. Bereft of originality, GHOSTBUSTERS II is content merely to parrot the highlights of the first film while borrowing elements from other successful recent films, such as THREE MEN AND A BABY (1987).

Wholly monotonous whenever Bill Murray isn't on-screen, the film begins as Weaver, Murray's flame from the first film, wheels her eight-month-old baby down a Manhattan street in a carriage (Weaver has married, had a baby, and conveniently divorced during the five-year interim between films). Unbeknownst to Weaver, she rolls the buggy over some slime that has oozed up from the sidewalk, and the carriage suddenly has a mind of its own, zooming through the streets of Manhattan pursued by the harried mother. When her baby is finally safe and sound, Weaver comes to believe that the incident was paranormal and calls her old friends, the Ghostbusters. Although they saved New York from certain doom five years previously, the Ghostbusters have fallen on hard times due to a series of lawsuits brought by the city. Aykroyd and Hudson make ends meet by entertaining at children's birthday parties, Ramis has returned to academia, and Murray hosts a cheesy cable-access show dealing with psychic phenomena. Weaver's predicament, however, brings the boys back together and they invade her home with their outlandish gizmos to check the baby and his nursery for evidence of paranormal activity. This also brings Murray and Weaver back together, and the glib Ghostbuster

attempts to get back into the single mother's good graces, while having plenty of time, to engage in cutesy-pie shtick with her baby. For reasons never satisfactorily explained, Weaver has given up her concert cello seat to do restoration work at a Manhattan art museum under the tutelage of MacNicol, a wacky Eastern European immigrant with a funny accent. MacNicol, it seems, is possessed by an old painting of an evil Carpathian despot named Vigo, who informs him that a male baby must be brought to him on New Year's Eve so that he can return to life through the child and terrorize the world once again. Meanwhile, the Ghostbusters discover a huge river of pink slime running through an abandoned old subway tunnel, their investigation of the stuff revealing that it is created by all of the city's negative energy—the more tension that exists among the citizenry, the more powerful the slime becomes. Everything comes to a head on New Year's Eve, when MacNicol kidnaps Weaver's baby and takes him to the museum for sacrifice. Protected by a huge layer of slime that prevents anyone from entering the building, Vigo begins the ceremony. Knowing that the slime will subside if they can get New Yorkers to feel good about themselves and each other, the Ghostbusters scramble for something (a symbol perhaps?) that will unite the populace. The boys head for the Statue of Liberty and, using some "positively charged" slime, coat the inside of the statue and bring it to life. Positioned in the monument's crown, the Ghostbusters guide it through the streets of Manhattan to the art museum while huge crowds cheer them on. With the help of Lady Liberty, the Ghostbusters are then able to break into the museum and put a stop to the evil

Vigo—saving the baby, Weaver, the basically innocent MacNicol, and, once again, the people of New York from certain doom.

Within the last 10 years, movie sequels have ceased to be merely films, and have been turned into major American cultural *events*. These purely mercenary, highly profitable projects (conventional wisdom maintains that the first sequel to a hit movie is certain to gross 60 percent of its progenitor's take) are rarely justified artistically; their stories and characters—with few exceptions—simply do not warrant continuation. Sequels exist, then, to spoon-feed an undiscriminating public the same laughs and thrills that made the original film a hit. Studios do not want a sequel that improves or expands on the first film, they want the *same film* made over and over again until the public tires of it.

GHOSTBUSTERS II is such a lazy effort that the formula machinery is laid bare for all to see. One can imagine the story conference where the powers-that-be discussed the elements that *must* be included if the sequel were to be successful: "What was the biggest laugh in the first film? Why, the giant Stay-Puff marshmallow man! Now how can we repeat that? Hmmm . . . what other large object can we bring to life to walk the streets of Manhattan? I've got it! Why not the Statue of Liberty?! Okay, BEVERLY HILLS COP grossed hundreds of millions of dollars. It got laughs from a foreigner with a funny accent. Let's put one in! What else? THREE MEN AND A BABY was a smash! Of course! Why don't we give Sigourney a baby for the Ghostbusters to play with!"

There is certainly nothing wrong with trying to incorporate a few proven crowd-pleasing elements into a narrative to give it some punch, but the writing of GHOSTBUSTERS II is so obvious, sloppy, and unimaginative one can only conclude that the filmmakers have nothing but contempt for the paying customer. Secure in the knowledge that the old audience will turn out to see the sequel at least once, regardless of its quality, they simply regurgitate old ideas. Why work hard if you're virtually guaranteed an audience? Instead, writers Ramis and Aykroyd come up with a premise—a painting of an evil despot brought to life—and then try to force the characters they created in the first film to fit it, even if they have to warp them a bit. Never mind that Sigourney Weaver is a concert cellist in the first film; Ramis and Aykroyd merely insert a throwaway line expressing Weaver's desire to return to the orchestra and then show her doing delicate restoration work in the museum—as if such exacting work could be done as a hobby! Worse yet is the handling of Rick Moranis' character. In the original he is a nerdy accountant; here, because a court-room scene is included, he has become a lawyer, *explained* by another throwaway gag line about studying law in night school!

Most of the film's problems arise from the fact that though the producers were able to reunite the entire cast of the original, they haven't the foggiest notion of what to do with them. Moranis and Annie Potts are thrown together for some predictable romance (their characters lingering in scenes long after they should leave—the result of "We paid 'em, leave 'em on screen!" logic), and poor Ernie Hudson, who has ruefully joked on television talk shows about his status as the token black, is barely in the movie. Ramis and Aykroyd are so cavalier in their treatment of Hudson's character they even subject him to a thoughtless and offensive sight gag wherein he is the only Ghostbuster whose hat flies off, hair sticks up, and eyes bug out at the sight of a ghost-train (one half expects to hear, "Feets, do your duty!"). Indeed, the most frightening ghosts in the entire movie are the spirits of Mantan Moreland and Stepin Fetchit, resurrected in this scene. The most amazing aspect of this sorry sequel is the overwhelming aura of self-congratulation that permeates it. There must be at least four or five moments when the Ghostbusters line up four abreast across director Reitman's wide-screen frame and announce themselves as conquering heroes to adoring cheers. Apparently we, the audience, should be *grateful* that Murray (*especially* Murray), Aykroyd, Ramis, and Reitman deemed to honor us with their presence one more time. But quite frankly, if this is the best they can come up with, who needs it? Songs include: "Ghostbusters" (Ray Parker, Jr., performed by Parker and Run-D.M.C.), "On Our Own" (L.A. Reid, Babyface, Daryl Simmons, performed by Bobby Brown), "Flip City" (Glenn Frey, Hawk Wolinski, performed by Frey), "Higher and Higher" (Gary Jackson, Carl Smith, Raynard Miner, performed by Jackie Wilson), "Spirit" (Doug E. Fresh, Bernard Wright, performed by Doug E. Fresh and the Get Fresh Crew), "Flesh 'n Blood" (Danny Elfman, performed by Oingo Boingo), "We're Back" (Bobby Brown, Dennis Austin, Larry White, Kirk Crumpler, performed by Brown). (*Violence.*)

p, Ivan Reitman; d, Ivan Reitman; w, Harold Ramis and Dan Aykroyd; ph, Michael Chapman (Deluxe Color); ed, Sheldon Kahn and Donn Cambern; m, Randy Edelman; prod d, Bo Welch; art d, Tom Duffield; set d, Cheryl Carasik; spec eff, Dennis Muren, Chuck Gaspar, Joe Day, and Dick Wood; cos, Gloria Gresham; anim, Jammie Friday; stunts, Joel Kramer; makeup, Stephen Abrums.

Comedy/Horror   (PR:A   MPAA:PG)

GIRL IN A SWING, THE*½
(Brit./US) 117m Panorama/J&M c

Meg Tilly (*Karin Foster*), Rupert Frazer (*Alan*), Nicholas Le Prevost (*The Vicar*), Elspet Gray (*Mrs. Dresland*), Lorna Heilbron (*Flick*), Claire Shepherd (*Angela*), Jean Both (*Mrs. Taswell*), Sophie Thursfield (*Deidre*), Lynsey Baxter (*Barbara*), Klaus Pagh, Hanne Borchsenius, Axel Strolye, Ebbe Langberg, Jan Petersen, Helen Cherry, Patrick Godfrey, June Ellis, Hilary Minster, Leonard McCuire, Oliver Ford Davis.

Fans of author Richard Adams (*Watership Down*) who have read the novel upon which this film is based may find reason to praise, pity, or damn the results. But they'll certainly have to explain this flat attempt at suspenseful surrealism to their friends who haven't read Adams book and who are sure to leave THE GIRL IN A SWING baffled.

Alan (Frazer) is a very reserved British dealer in antique ceramics—so reserved that when a sexy, blonde family friend offers herself to him with no strings attached, he turns her down, citing the sanctity of love and marriage. Although he's clearly a chap who slept through the sexual revolution alone, Frazer's passions soon come to a boil in sexy, swinging Copenhagen, where, on a business trip, he becomes instantly smitten with German secretary Karin (Tilly). It's only a matter of days before he is proposing marriage, despite the fact that he knows virtually nothing about Tilly, whose behavior is as mysterious as her background. At first enticing, then indifferent, then downright off-putting, she finally breaks down and confesses her love for Frazer only after he tells her he will return to England without her in despair. Tilly's acceptance of his proposal leaves Frazer in a state of bliss, although he's been having troubling nightmares in which he dives underwater to discover a decomposing female corpse. Tilly also has some strange phobias—of churches, for example, and she insists that their marriage not take place before an altar—and there is also some unexplained panic surrounding a vanishing pillow. After the wedding, life only gets more mysterious for the couple, while the film only gets more confusing for the audience. After seemingly overbidding at an auction on a box of old pots and pans, Tilly finds at the bottom of the box a rare figurine—the title's "Girl in a Swing"—whose value Sotheby's assesses at a sum large enough to set the couple up for life. Their troubles aren't over, however. Just as Tilly announces that she believes herself to be pregnant, Frazer begins to hear the cries of a child. He finds this disturbing; she finds it terrifying, and insists that Frazer lock all the doors and windows against the wailing, then that he take her away from the house immediately. She also begins fighting her church phobia, only to swoon during Communion.

"I understand," Frazer tells Tilly. But we don't. It all seems to have something to do with her character's prior, tragic experience with motherhood—but there is also something more, something that seems to be unspeakably malevolent, in her past, the revelation of which should form the crux of the movie. Sadly, THE GIRL ON A SWING'S ending is more likely to prompt a "Whaaaa?" than an "Aha!" from the viewer.

Writer-director Gordon Hessler, a veteran British filmmaker whose works include the dark, witty Vincent Price horror vehicle SCREAM AND SCREAM AGAIN, seems to have succumbed to a "Masterpiece Theatre" tastefulness here. Where an unbridled surrealist like Luis Bunuel would undoubtedly have had a field day with the volatile collision between Frazer's repressed, religious character and the mercurial mixture of nurturing kindness, casual cruelty, and sometimes startling carnality in Tilly's secretary. Alas, Hessler has taken an oddly sedate approach in tackling the intriguing story, pulling all his punches when he should be pulling out all stops. The final effect is rather like watching a very stately version of an old Hammer horror film, bereft of all the cheap, gloppy thrills that make such movies entertaining.

In fact, while Rupert Frazer (EMPIRE OF THE SUN) gives a serviceable performance, THE GIRL IN A SWING would be an exercise in pure creeping catatonia without the beautiful, sloe-eyed Meg Tilly. Her Karin is a bedeviling (if not downright Bunuelian) child-woman, a swirling pool of deep, probably bitter secrets. If only we could figure out what they were. *(Nudity, sexual situations.)*

p, Just Betzer and Benni Korzen; d, Gordon Hessler; w, Gordon Hessler (based on the novel by Richard Adams); ph, Claus Loof (Eastmancolor); ed, Robert Gordon; m, Carl Davis; prod d, Rob Schilling; cos, Betina Betzer.

Thriller   **(PR:O MPAA:R)**

⊙**GLEAMING THE CUBE*****
105m Gladden Entertainment/FOX c
Christian Slater *(Brian Kelly)*, Steven Bauer *(Al Lucero)*, Richard Herd *(Ed Lawndale)*, Le Tuan *(Col. Trac)*, Min Luong *(Tina Trac)*, Art Chudabala *(Vinh Kelly)*, Ed Lauter *(Mr. Kelly)*, Nicole Mercurio *(Mrs. Kelly)*, Peter Kwong *(Bobby Nguyen)*, Charles Cyphers *(Harvey McGill)*, Max Perlich *(Yabbo)*, Tony Hawk *(Buddy)*, Tommy Guerrero *(Sam)*, Christian Jacobs *(Gremic)*, Joe Gosha *(Nick Oliver)*, Andy Nguyen *(Tran Thanh)*, Kieu Chinh *(Mme. Trac)*, Joshua Ravetch *(Student Pilot)*, Jack Riley *(Homeowner)*, Angela Moya *(Housekeeper)*, F. William Parker *(Motel Manager)*, J. Jay Saunders *(Medical Examiner)*.

In GLEAMING THE CUBE, Christian Slater plays Brian Kelly, an Orange County high schooler alienated from his parents because he doesn't live up to their ideal—while their adopted Vietnamese refugee son, Chudabala, does. As a result, Slater's only joy in life is skateboarding. He's wrapped up in it to the point that, as a fellow boarder tells him, he's achieved a Zen-like state of skateboarding power called "gleaming the cube" (reaching the ultimate, the point at which he's so good he doesn't even know how good he is). While Slater skates, Chudabala does part-time jobs, including work with a Vietnamese relief organization. One day at work, he discovers a discrepancy in a shipment of medical supplies, brings it to his boss's attention, and is fired for his trouble. Stunned, Chudabala begins trying to find out what the discrepancy means. He breaks into the warehouse where the supplies are stored and is caught by the owner (Herd), who, along with a Vietnamese accomplice, tortures the youth to find out what he knows and accidentally kills him. Although Chudabala's death is made to look like a suicide, Slater doesn't believe it and sets out to discover the truth. Finding no answers in Orange County's tightly knit Vietnamese community, Slater begins tracking a suspicious refugee on his skateboard and, after witnessing the man's murder, reluctantly calls in savvy local detective Bauer. The young cop, however, proves of little help to Slater, who again pursues the case on his own. Becoming suspicious of Chudabala's girl friend's (Min Luong) father, Le Tuan, Slater ingratiates his way into her house, then, having linked Le Tuan and Herd in a gun-running scheme, begins to follow Herd. After Slater's life is threatened, Bauer begins to believe his story and continues the investigation; meanwhile, Slater gets his fellow skaters to assist him in catching Herd. Bauer, Slater, and the skaters all descend on Herd as he tries to escape, and after a magnificent chase, Herd is captured and Chudabala's death is ruled a homicide.

GLEAMING THE CUBE's plot is not the most original, but its deficiencies are largely overcome by the skateboarding. The sequences in which the boarders perform are exhilarating (and at times vertigo inducing) and, when integrated into the plot, as in the closing chase or the one between Slater and three motorcyclists bent on killing him, add a great deal of excitement to otherwise routine material. The focus on the skaters' milieu, and especially Slater's initial involvement and later rejection of its punkish juvenile nihilism, strengthens the story—when Slater begins to see there are some things worth caring about (even if he's not quite sure what they are), that's quite a step forward for a character whose strongest previous motivation was to find empty swimming pools in which to do his tricks. Unfortunately, GLEAMING THE CUBE's portrait of the southern Californian culture that gave rise to the skaters' subculture is thinly sketched, as are the teen characters. Slater, however, does a good job in his more substantial role, while the others—including skateboard whizzes Tommy Guerrero, Tony Hawk, Rodney Mullen, Mark "Gator" Rogowski, and Mike McGill, who doubles for Slater—demonstrate their talents with verve. Technical advisor and second-unit director Stacy Peralta, a former world champion, puts his skating skills to use as well, shooting some scenes atop a board with a hand-held camera. Songs include: "Gleaming the Cube" (Robbin Thompson, Carlos Chafin, Eric Heiberg, performed by James House), "Brother to Brother" (Bob Crewe, Jerry Corbetta, Bob Gaudio, performed by Billy Burnette), "Stukas over Disneyland" (Leonard Phillips, Stan Lee, Billy Club, Steve Hufsteter, performed by the Dickies), "Nowhere to Run" (Brian Holland, Lamont Dozier, Eddie Holland, performed by Khanh Ha in a Vietnamese translation by Jean-Pierre Nguyen), "Never Can Say Goodbye" (Clifton Davis, performed by Khanh Ha in a Vietnamese translation by Nguyen), "Right Now" (Jay Ferguson, Rob Fitzgerald, performed by Johnny Rad), "Saigon Angel" (La Van Lien, performed by the AVT Trio). *(Violence, profanity.)*

p, Lawrence Turman and David Foster; d, Graeme Clifford; w, Michael Tolkin; ph, Reed Smoot (Deluxe Color); ed, John Wright; m, Jay Ferguson; prod d, John Muto; art d, Dan Webster; set d, Susan Emshwiller; spec eff, Phil Cory; cos, Ann Somers Major; stunts, Buddy Joe Hooker; makeup, Annie D'Angelo.

Action/Adventure

(PR:C MPAA:PG-13)

Christian Slater in GLEAMING THE CUBE (©20th Century Fox).

Ⓥ GLITCH zero
90m Omega c

Will Egan *(Todd)*, Steve Donmyer *(Bo)*, Julia Nickson *(Michelle)*, Dick Gautier *(Julius Lazar)*, Ted Lange *(DuBois)*, Teri Weigel *(Lydia)*, Dan Speaker *(Brucie)*, Dallas Cole, Ji-Tu Cumbuka, Fernando Carzon, John Kreng, Lindsay Carr, Susan Youngbluth, Bunty Bailey, Joy Rinaldi, Lisa Erickson, Caroldean Ross, Penny Wiggins, Christina Cardan, Kahlena Marie, Laura Albert, Debra Lamb, Bridget Boland.

Destined to become a hit with those who will sit through just about anything, GLITCH is a self-described "sexy comedy" with precious little sexiness or comedy. Instead, writer-director-producer-coeditor Nico Mastorakis (THE WIND) plunges us back into cinema's late and unlamented PORKY'S era of babes popping out of their bikini tops to the pop-eyed delight of a troupe of laboriously zany, no-name actors and imaginary audiences everywhere. Mastorakis' one—marginal—distinction here is that the scene is Hollywood the company town rather than Hollywood High, and apparently the director doesn't care too much for the movie business. GLITCH revels in taking satirical shots at the industry, all within the context of a rather cynical film, but somebody should have told Mastorakis that Blake Edwards did it better in S.O.B.

Egan and Donmyer play zany California dudes Todd and Bo, bumbling would-be burglars who break into the Hollywood estate of producer Gautier just after he heads off to Hawaii. While ripping off Gautier's homestead, the dudes discover that a scheduling snafu has resulted in a mob of the aforementioned bikinied babes turning up at the estate to audition for the producer's latest epic. After popping his eyeballs back into his head, Egan pretends to be Gautier and Donmyer becomes a director. Together they put the full-figured gals through their paces for parts in the film, which will be "X-rated, of course." Making for some theoretically sidesplitting complications are an ethnically stereotyped Mexican-Japanese team of burglars also intent on robbing the estate and a mob collector (Lange, whose career has evidently fallen on hard times since the demise of "The Love Boat") who shows up looking for the money Gautier has supposedly laundered in the budget of one of his spectaculars, the helicopter action-adventure "Pink Thunder."

Even fans of feminine pulchritude will be sorely disappointed by GLITCH. Nudity is confined to occasional quick cutaways, probably meant to be easily excisable for—God help us!—television showings. The "100—count 'em, 100—beautiful models" touted on the home video packaging (no, we didn't count 'em) spend most of the film hanging out on the lawn munching hors d'oeuvres and occasionally taking off their tops to hop into the pool. Thankfully, despite repeated threats, Mastorakis mostly spares us any sexual activity.

Otherwise, Will Egan and Steve Donmyer—forget those names—are about as hilarious as a bad headache, which matches them well with Mastorakis' ham-handed script. Of the real-life actors on hand, Ted Lange and Dick Gautier trudge through the sludge with professional aplomb. Perhaps in order to add to her resume reel, Julia Nickson (of RAMBO fame) actually attempts to give a performance as one of the auditioners. She was probably able to draw on real-life inspiration, since her character is angry at her agent for sending her there.

The saddest thing about GLITCH is that Mastorakis actually shows signs that he knows something about making movies here. There are a few funny lines and, as the trades put it, the "tech credits are okay"—meaning that the film doesn't look as though it were culled from someone's amateur soft-core home video collection, as does much other PORKY'S spawn. But what little good there is in GLITCH is negated in that Mastorakis seems on the whole to be *proud* of it. In fact, the film's full title is the possessory NICO MASTORAKIS' GLITCH. As far as we're concerned, he can have it. *(Nudity, profanity, adult situations, sexual situations.)*

p, Nico Mastorakis; d, Nico Mastorakis; w, Nico Mastorakis; ph, Peter Jensen (CFI Color); ed, Nico Mastorakis and George Rosenberg; m, Tom Marolda; prod d, Gary New.

Comedy   **(PR:O MPAA:R)**

GLORY

(See THE YEAR'S BEST)

Ⓥ GNAW: FOOD OF THE GODS II**
(Can.) 91m Rose & Ruby/Concorde-Centauri
(AKA: FOOD OF THE GODS II)

Paul Coufos *(Prof. Neil Hamilton)*, Lisa Schrage *(Alex Reed)*, Colin Fox *(Edmund Delhurst)*, Frank Moore *(Jacques)*, Real Andrews *(Mark)*, Jackie Burroughs *(Dr. Treger)*, Stuart Hughes *(Al)*.

"Imagine it, big cows! Big fish! Big pigs! It's the food of the gods!" exclaims an excited scientist in GNAW: FOOD OF THE GODS II. Of course we never get to see how those animals react to Methadone 192, the new growth formula that works better than anyone expected. Instead, we get rats—"Big rats!" the doctor might have said, had he lived to say it. Besides being six feet in length, these extraordinary rats are mean *and* they are hungry.

Coufos, a botanist working at a university in New York City, is summoned to the lab of a fellow scientist who desperately needs his help. When he arrives, she shows him the shocking result of her experiments with Methadone 192: a relatively normal 10-year-old boy has been transformed into a 15-foot-tall giant and is meaner than a rattlesnake. Returning to his own lab, Coufos tries to concoct an antidote for the boy's growth surge. An assistant hears about the new growth formula and encourages Coufos to inject a few lab rats, just to see what happens. Curiosity gets the best of the botanist and he sticks it to the rats. That night, animal-rights protestors break into the lab only to come face to face with the newly gigantic rodents, which eat the protesters' leader. Naturally, the authorities start asking questions, and Coufos panics. The cops don't believe his or the students' story, and the dean, worried about the effect the rumors might have on the university's financial well-being, doesn't *want* to believe any of it. Coufos, his entourage, and the two remaining protestors then begin separate hunts for the rats. Eventually, the gigantic creatures are found in the sewers beneath the school, but before they can be trapped and killed, the rats crawl up the drainage system into the school's new swimming pool, where a grand opening is being held. The crowd in the stands is horrified, but not nearly as shocked as the team of synchronized swimmers performing in the water! One by one, they are eaten in grand JAWS style. As the rats pursue the fleeing spectators, they are met by a squad of policemen who open fire and destroy the monster rodents. Coufos is relieved that the nightmare is over, but before he can say "Thank God," he receives a call from his scientist friend informing him that the big, bad boy from the beginning of the film has gotten out of control.

Working from a script that borrows generously from Steven Spielberg's Big Fish movie, JAWS, director Damian Lee has fashioned a predictable nature-gone-awry film that never rises above its B-movie trappings. A sequel in title only (no reference to the original film is ever made), GNAW: FOOD OF THE GODS II is low on suspense and high on gore—the norm these days—but despite its many downfalls, GNAW has a surprising number of enjoyable moments, and one cannot help being amused by the film's campy elements. Faced with the task of creating six-foot rats, the filmmakers placed normal-sized rats in scaled-down sets, and the sight of a monster rat scampering madly through a miniature library is especially funny. The film's high point, though, is the pool sequence in which the synchronized swimmers meet their doom. Bloody and disturbing, the scene conveys the perfect tone for this type of film. Unfortunately, these moments are few and far between, and the acting is serviceable at best. GNAW: FOOD OF THE GODS II won't win any awards, but if you're in the mood for a campy, bloody B-movie, this is your slice of cheese. *(Violence, profanity, nudity.)*

p, David Mitchell and Damian Lee; d, Damian Lee; w, Richard Bennett and E. Kim Brewster (based on a story by Richard Bennett); ph, Curtis Petersen; ed, David Mitchell; m, Parsons/Haines; spec eff, Ted Rae.

Horror   (PR:O MPAA:R)

Ⓥ**GOING UNDERCOVER***½
(Brit.) 88m Jefferson
Colgate-Stone-Norfolk/Miramax c
Chris Lemmon *(Henry Brilliant)*, Jean Simmons *(Maxine De La Hunt)*, Lea Thompson *(Marigold De La Hunt)*, Mills Watson *(Billy O'Shea)*, Viveca Lindfors *(Mrs. Bellinger)*, Nancy Cartwright *(Stephanie)*, Joe Michael Terry *(Gary)*, Jewel Shepard *(Peaches)*.

An unsubtle spoof of detective films, GOING UNDERCOVER features a protagonist who combines the dubious attributes of a junior-league James Bond and son of Inspector Clouseau. Lemmon plays a handsome blueblood who turns his back on high society and struggles mightily to make a living as a hard-boiled private eye, then lands his biggest case when wealthy Simmons offers him a tidy sum to shepherd her high-spirited stepdaughter (Thompson) on a European tour because the girl's father (a renowned meteorologist) is concerned that she might be kidnaped. Unfortunately, Thompson, a party girl who doesn't like being tailed, continually gives her shadow the slip, clings to a copy of the book *The Sophisticated Traveler*, and makes Lemmon's life a living hell. Eventually, Thompson is indeed kidnaped and Lemmon winds up in the hospital. When he finally pursues the abductors, he's captured by stock Germanic villains and dumped onto a yacht, where he's reunited with Thompson. Simmons now pops up unexpected to reveal that she hired Lemmon because of his ineptitude. What the sinister stepmother really wants is the copy of *The Sophisticated Traveler*, which contains her husband's secret formula for controlling the weather. Her plan to eliminate Thompson and Lemmon after obtaining the document is foiled, however, when Lemmon cleverly engineers an explosion on board. In hot pursuit during the climactic amusement-park chase scene, Simmons and her henchman fail to take basic roller-coaster safety precautions and fall to their deaths, saving the free world from arch-fiends.

Aimed at the Brat Packer audience, GOING UNDERCOVER clumsily grafts elements of a college sex comedy onto the private eye genre. The result is bound to

bore audiences of all ages. Establishing the proper combination of thrills and laughter for a lighthearted suspense film is tricky, because the scenes of peril must never be presented so literally that the film's sense of fun is crushed. GOING UNDERCOVER fails to achieve the difficult balance that distinguished FOUL PLAY or CHARADE, for example, and emerges as neither suspenseful nor amusing. The screenplay is so poorly structured, the direction by writer-helmer James Kenelm Clarke is so heavy-handed, and Lea Thompson's character is so excessively nasty that the audience ceases to care about the overly complicated plot.

Of the cast, only the veteran Jean Simmons, as the dragon stepmother, lends any finesse to these second-rate spy shenanigans. Making Snow White's stepmom look like Mother Walton, Simmons sneers deliciously and spits out her lines with the requisite venom. Chris Lemmon is more conventionally handsome than his famous dad Jack, but his similar comedic timing and exasperated mannerisms, while sufficient for the role, reveal no unique personality of his own. *(Violence, substance abuse, adult situations, profanity.)*

p, John D. Schofield and Jefferson Colgate-Stone; d, James Kenelm Clarke; w, James Kenelm Clarke; ph, John Coquillon (Technicolor); ed, Eric Boyd-Perkins and Danny Retz; m, Alan Hawkshaw; art d, Jim Dultz; cos, Moss Mabry.

Thriller/Comedy (PR:C MPAA:PG-13)

Ⓥ**GOR***½
94m Cannon c
Urbano Barberini *(Tarl Cabot)*, Rebecca Ferratti *(Talena)*, Paul L. Smith *(Surbus)*, Oliver Reed *(Sarm)*, Jack Palance *(Xenos)*, Larry Taylor *(King Marlenus)*, Donna Denton *(Queen Lara)*, Graham Clarke, Janine Denison, Jennifer Oltmann.

For nondiscriminating action fans who like their sword-and-sandal flicks laced with a dose of science fiction, GOR may prove a mildly entertaining if derivative adventure in another world. Echoes of STAR WARS; MAD MAX; STEEL DAWN; DUNE; and those 1960s Italian-made pasta-and-pectoral extravaganzas starring Steve Reeves or Mark Forest reverberate throughout. Barberini stars as an absent-minded college professor who, en route to a peaceful but solitary vacation in the country, has an automobile accident. When he regains consciousness, he's neither recuperating at a hospital nor vacationing at a Ramada Inn, but wandering through the desolate wastelands of a bizarre land known as Gor. Although his students had earlier scoffed at his tales of a family heirloom with magical properties, Barberini's magical ring has gained him access to Gor, a counterworld that exists alongside our own in a simultaneous pres-

ent. (Thus, even as you read this review, the embattled inhabitants of Gor are probably parading around in skimpy costumes left over from a biblical epic and fighting tyrants bent on enslaving them.) Although he's a milquetoast on Earth, Barberini is a new man on Gor. Transforming himself a la the bespectacled ingenue Ruby Keeler in an old musical, he whips off his glasses, takes a crash course in archery, and turns into the long-awaited savior of Gor. And not a moment too soon: former high priest Reed has been raiding villages, forcing survivors into prison or slavery, and stealing their "homestones" (big, bubblelike versions of the gem in Barberini's ring). Accompanied by the daughter (Ferratti) of Gor's captured king, two sidekicks (one old and sage, one young and headstrong), and a plucky dwarf, Barberini battles nomads and bandits as the determined group proceeds on its mission to rescue the king and save mankind. Along the way, they encounter a counterworldly, primitive form of female wrestling; assorted cave-dwelling lepers, desert muggers, and Reed's brutal soldiers; a fiery pit; and an orgy in which the dancers do the latest steps from a topless revue at Caesar's Palace, demonstrating that some cultural cross over from Earth to Gor has transpired. Despite a fling with Ferratti, Barberini gets homesick after setting things right in Gor. Using his magical ring, he returns to civilization and his campus, where he reveals his new macho side by punching out a student who'd been putting him down (and where a female assistant who previously ignored him now pursues him). Meanwhile, Palance sets the stage for GOR's sequel (OUTLAW OF GOR) by popping up in a cameo near the fade-out as still another evil, homestone-collecting high priest.

If you can put up with the aimless milling about of the extras during the allegedly exciting battle scenes, GOR's mindless, nonstop action provides campy fun of a comic book variety. The stirring whoops and hollers of the victorious and the cries and moans of the oppressed are ludicrously over-dubbed (the sound effects seem to be coming from everywhere, as if the Mormon Tabernacle Choir had been hired to dub the voices of a few singers), none of the actors are convincing (the overall effect is of watching grown-ups play gladiatorial dress-up), the John Williams-inspired score blares insistently throughout, but there is a blessed absence of gore and gruesome violence as the attractive cast parades around in jock straps and G-strings. Chintzy-looking and woefully unoriginal, GOR doesn't offer enough thrills to provide "quality entertainment," but its mongrel, inept appeal may prove agreeable for sword-and-sorcery buffs of all ages. *(Brief nudity, violence.)*

p, Harry Alan Towers and Avi Lerner; d, Fritz Kiersch; w, Rick Marx and Harry Alan Towers (based on the novel *Tarnsman of Gor* by John Norman); ph, Hans Khule (Rank Color); ed, Max Lemon and Ken Bornstein; stunts, Reo Ruiters.

Action/Fantasy   (PR:C MPAA:PG)

⊙GRANDMOTHER'S HOUSE*
89m Omega c
Eric Foster *(David)*, Kim Valentine *(Lynn)*, Brinke Stevens *(Woman)*, Ida Lee *(Grandmother)*, Len Lesser *(Grandfather)*, David Donham, Michael Robinson, Craig Yerman, Joan-Carol Bensen, Furley Lumpkin.

After their father dies, teenaged Valentine and her little brother, Foster, come to live with their grandmother and grandfather (Lee and Lesser) on the old people's farm. There they are watched from afar by a mysterious figure in a long dress and shawl (Stevens), and Foster dreams that his grandfather has brutally murdered the enigmatic woman. Later, he sees his grandparents dragging Stevens' body about the house in real life, and finally stuffing her into a refrigerator in the basement. (Meanwhile, in a rather stiff attempt at comic relief, some guests enjoy a holiday barbecue—it's not clear what day is being celebrated—outside.) Eventually, a sheriff's deputy explains to Valentine and Foster what the audience guessed long ago: Stevens is actually their crazy mother, who was institutionalized years before and whom they believed to be long dead. Moreover, it turns out that Lee and Lesser have not killed but merely drugged Stevens, whom the kids find handcuffed to the steering wheel of a truck in the garage. They free her, then watch in horror as she stabs the deputy and kills him. Now Stevens chases her children, who must flee for their lives in the truck, lurching through their grandparents' orange groves as they try to work the vehicle's stick shift. They retreat to the house, where Foster appears to go a bit crazy himself while smearing blood on his face and setting off fireworks to destroy his insane mother. He also fires a rifle to ward off an invader at the door—who unfortunately turns out not to be his mother, but his sister's boy friend (Robinson). At last help arrives, everyone is carted off to the hospital, and the film appears to be over. No such luck—a bandaged Foster wakes up in the hospital, peers out the window, observes Lesser sneaking away from the building, and follows the old man back to the farm. There, with a vague and somewhat illogical plot twist, the story finally ends in earnest—and rather abruptly.

Apart from its stylish photography by Peter Jensen (who also wrote the inadequate script), GRANDMOTHER'S HOUSE is a botched job. The dialog is generally sketchy and uninformative, so that the exact location of the farm and even the identity of the grandparents, or such plot points as whether Lee's character is dead at the end of the film, are never fully made clear. (Other aspects of the story, such as the true identity of the "mysterious" Stevens, are obvious by virtue of their being cliches.) Also working against this gothic horror tale, filmed in the California citrus belt, is its sunny setting. To compensate, the filmmakers unload an arsenal of ominous sound effects—creaking doors, howling winds, ticking clocks—at every opportunity. But a disconcertingly cheery atmosphere still prevails around the macabre action.

The acting is similarly uneven, the young performers being particularly ill-served by Peter Rader's poor direction. Rarely seen in close-up, Kim Valentine and Eric Foster seem more confused than terrified and vulnerable as the menaced kids, while Michael Robinson, as the teenaged boy friend, is gratingly inept. Only craggy-faced Len Lesser, though forced to lurk about sinisterly as the evil grandfather, gives a creditable performance—a tribute to his restraint as an actor. *(Violence.)*

p, Nico Mastorakis; d, Peter Rader; w, Peter Jensen (based on a story by Gayle Jensen, Peter Jensen); ph, Peter Jensen (CFI Color); ed, Barry Zetlin; m, Nigel Holton and Clive Wright; art d, Steven Michael Casey; set d, Janet Laick.

Horror   (PR:O MPAA:R)

⊙GREAT BALLS OF FIRE**
108m Adam Fields/Orion c
Dennis Quaid *(Jerry Lee Lewis)*, Winona Ryder *(Myra Gail Lewis)*, Alec Baldwin *(Jimmy Lee Swaggart)*, John Doe *(J. W. Brown)*, Stephen Tobolowsky *(John Phillips)*, Trey Wilson *(Sam Phillips)*, Steve Allen *(Himself)*, Lisa Blount *(Lois Brown)*, Joshua Sheffield *(Rusty Brown)*, Mojo Nixon *(James Van Eaton)*, Jimmie Vaughn *(Roland James)*, David Ferguson *(Jack Clement)*, Robert Lesser *(Alan Freed)*, Lisa Jane Persky *(Babe)*, Paula Person *(Marilyn)*, Valerie Wellington *(Big Maybelle)*, Booker T. Laury *(Piano Slim)*, Michael St. Gerard *(Elvis)*, Carol Russell *(Mamie Lewis)*, Crystal Robbins *(Frankie Jean)*, Tav Falco *(New Bass Player)*, Ryan Rushton *(Young Jimmy)*, Bert Dedman *(Young Jerry)*, Bruce Stuart *(Bank Teller)*, W.W. Painter *(Onlooker)*, Mark Johnson *(Sheriff)*, Jody Lynne *(Party Doll)*, Joseph Woodward Jr. *(Wedding Preacher)*, Linn Sitler *(Realty Agent)*, Ashley Paige Cook *(Mona)*, Sara Van Horn *(Minnie Belle)*, Juliette Claire Spirson *(Lewis Infant)*, John Mulrooney *(Talk Show Host)*, Peter Cook, Kim Smith, David Sibley *(English Reporters)*, Susan Lonergan, Bonnie Beutler, Chris Solari, Snowy Winters *(Rebel Room Dancers)*, Priscilla Harris *(Honky-Tonk Angel)*, Joe Bob Briggs *(Dewey "Daddy-O" Phillips)*.

This disappointing film biography of rock 'n' roller Jerry Lee Lewis virtually ignores Lewis' much-publicized dark side, instead adopting a sanitized, light-hearted comedic approach that is both unenlightening and uninvolving. As cowritten and directed by Jim McBride (THE BIG EASY), GREAT BALLS OF FIRE is an attempt to recapture the wild, high energy of such early rock 'n' roll films as ROCK, ROCK, ROCK! (1956); DON'T KNOCK THE ROCK (1957); THE BIG BEAT (1957); and Frank Tashlin's magnificent THE GIRL CAN'T HELP IT (1956). Unfortunately, the approach simply doesn't work when applied to as complex and controversial a character as Lewis.

Concerned mainly with Lewis' rapid rise and fall during the years 1956-58, the film begins with a brief glimpse of his childhood in Ferriday, Louisiana, as Lewis and his cousin Jimmy Lee Swaggart literally cross over to the other side of the railroad tracks and sneak a peak at the raunchy goings-on inside a local black boogie-woogie joint. While the moral and upright young Swaggart grows increasingly uncomfortable around the blacks and their raucous music ("It's the devil's music, I can feel it!"), Jerry Lee is completely captivated by the sights and sounds. The film then jumps ahead to 1956, as the twice-married and -divorced Jerry Lee (Quaid) arrives in Memphis to live with his cousin J.W. Brown (Doe) and his family while trying to score a record deal at Sun Records, the label that launched Elvis Presley. Quaid is immediately taken with his cousin's 13-year-old daughter Myra (Winona Ryder), and she with him. After several attempts, Quaid finally manages to impress Sun Records head Sam Phillips (Wilson), who signs him on. After his first record, "Crazy Arms," does well, Quaid records a scorching and suggestive cover version of the old R&B tune "Whole Lotta Shakin' Goin' On." This is followed by a wild appearance on television with Steve Allen, and the record rapidly climbs the charts. Quaid finds himself earning $10,000 a performance, and since Doe plays bass in the band and has a 50-50 salary split with Quaid, he puts up with his cousin's presence in his home, but begins to worry about Quaid's close relationship with Ryder. These fears are justified when Quaid spirits the 13-year-old girl across the state line and marries her. His friends, family, and business associates are horrified by the marriage and try to keep it quiet, but when the singer insists on bringing his child bride with him on his first concert tour of England, word gets out and the ensuing scandal forces the cancellation of the tour. Things aren't any better for Quaid back in the States, where his latest record, "High School Confidential," takes a nose-

Dennis Quaid in GREAT BALLS OF FIRE (©Orion).

dive on the charts and his concert bookings dry up. With his marriage ruining his chance to depose the recently drafted Presley as the king of rock 'n' roll, Quaid becomes bitter and restless, drinking heavily and abusing Ryder, who is now pregnant. Eventually Quaid goes to church, where the pastor is none other than Swaggart (Baldwin). After hearing his cousin's fire-and-brimstone sermon condemning the "devil's music," a disgusted Quaid walks out and declares that if he's going to go to hell, he'll do it playing the piano.

So much about this production is right (including the casting and the shooting on some of the actual Memphis locations) that McBride's insistence on presenting everything in a distorted and campy manner is infuriating to anyone who knows anything about Lewis' life and the vibrant musical scene in Memphis in the 1950s. In addition to being extremely limited in insight, McBride's giddy presentation seems contemptuous of the personalities involved and of the milieu that spawned them: he turns everyone into a redneck caricature. As misguided as this approach is, one would think that at least McBride could convey the wild and uninhibited sense of fun captured by the early rock 'n' roll films, but he botches even this so badly that the film's many self-conscious moments (old-fashioned montages showing Lewis songs charted in *Billboard* magazine, Elvis interrupting his foreplay with a female fan in order to sneer at Lewis on television, extras playing directly to the camera, etc.) come off as forced. The kitschy garishness of the Frank Tashlin-influenced production design seems more appropriate to the winking postmodernism of "Pee-Wee's Playhouse" than to Memphis circa 1958, and one comes away from GREAT BALLS OF FIRE with the unfortunate feeling that McBride has been having a good time snickering at the fashion sense of these ignorant *nouveau-riche* rednecks. These distancing techniques give off such an air of directorial condescension that one has to call into question McBride's motives for making the film. Although McBride pays lip service to rock 'n' roll history by shooting the film in Memphis, his broadly comic bent leaves no room for reflection on the town or the time that made the music (a few references to the H-bomb and "Leave It to Beaver" are unconvincing).

What is most disappointing about the film, however, is its near-total refusal to delve into Lewis' psyche. One of the most fascinating figures in American music, Lewis is a man tormented by his conflicting love for the music and his belief (at least at the beginning of his career) that he is possessed by the devil and will go to hell for playing the "devil's music." Although McBride touches on "the Killer's" drinking, propensity for violence, and generally self-destructive behavior, his treatment of these dark elements is very superficial and melodramatic. Especially frustrating is McBride's almost flip examination of Lewis' relationship with his cousin Swaggart, the future televangelist who would himself become notorious, and of whom McBride is content to present a cliched and sketchy portrait. Knowing full well that the audience has in mind the very recent scandalous revelations concerning Swaggart, McBride lets viewers' hindsight do the work for him. This stacks the deck when it comes to Lewis' struggle between his faith, represented by Swaggart, and his music: since we all know Swaggart is a hypocrite, rock 'n' roll is the right choice. Whereas the real-life Lewis seems to be suffering under the burden of a contradictory and ambivalent faith, McBride's presentation of Lewis' inner conflict is summed up in Quaid's unambiguous, defiant rock 'n' roll posturing.

Dennis Quaid, an actor who is capable of more than just duplicating Lewis' man-

nerisms, gives a gratingly one-note performance here, boldly sauntering his way into every scene and contorting his face into a grotesque parody of the Killer. Alec Baldwin (WORKING GIRL, MARRIED TO THE MOB), an interesting actor in other films, is woefully miscast as Swaggart. The late Trey Wilson (BULL DURHAM, RAISING ARIZONA) perfectly cast as rock 'n' roll pioneer Sam Phillips, is wasted by a script that depicts Phillips as nothing more than a fretting penny-pincher. Lisa Blount is also misused as Myra's mother, characterized here as a greedy woman willing to sacrifice her daughter for the promise of wealth. Luckily, two cast members do manage to stand out: Winona Ryder (BETTLEJUICE, LUCAS) as Myra and John Doe as her father. Proving again that she's one of America's most promising young actresses, Ryder brings a delightful mixture of innocence and savvy to her role and makes one see what Jerry Lee saw in this 13-year-old. Doe does a nice job subverting McBride's goonish direction by underplaying his role, lending some dignity to the bass player who is torn between financial necessity and paternal concern.

McBride does succeed in his staging of the musical sequences, which are entertaining and energetic. After much debate, it was decided that Quaid (who wanted to sing the songs himself) would lip-sync to newly recorded versions of Lewis' old hits. The new recordings find the Killer in fine form, although his update of the classic "Breathless" is much more subdued than the raucous original. Unfortunately, the music alone isn't enough to save GREAT BALLS OF FIRE. A great movie could have been made about Jerry Lee Lewis. This isn't it. *(Adult situations, sexual situations.)*

p, Adam Fields; d, Jim McBride; w, Jim McBride and Jack Baran (based on the book by Myra Lewis, Murray Silver, Jr.); ph, Alfonso Beato (Deluxe color); ed, Lisa Day, Pembroke Herring, and Bert Lovitt; m, Jack Baran and Jim McBride; prod d, David Nichols; art d, Jon Spirson; set d, Kathleen McKernin and Lauren Polizzi; spec eff, Phil Corey; cos, Tracy Tynan; chor, Bill Landrum; tech, Jerry Schilling; stunts, Steve Davison; makeup, Richard Arrington.

Biography/Musical

(PR:C MPAA:PG-13)

GROSS ANATOMY**
107m Silver Screen Partners IV-Hill-Rosenman-Touchstone/BV c
Matthew Modine *(Joe Slovak)*, Daphne Zuniga *(Laurie Rorbach)*, Christine Lahti *(Dr. Rachel Woodruff)*, Todd Field *(David Schreiner)*, John Scott Clough *(Miles Reed)*, Alice Carter *(Kim McCauley)*, Robert Desiderio *(Dr. Banks)*, Zakes Mokae *(Dr. Banumbra)*, J.C. Quinn *(Papa*

Slovak), Clyde Kusatsu, John Petlock, J. Patrick McNamara, Jan Munroe *(Interviewing Professors)*, Michael Flanagan, Don Perry, Kay E. Kuter *(Lecturing Professors)*, Rutanya Alda *(Mama Slovak)*, Brandis Kemp *(Aunt Rose)*, Ryan Cash *(Frankie Slovak)*, Angus MacInnes *(Dean Torrence)*, Lisa Zane *(Luann)*, Alison Taylor *(Cynthia Wilkes)*, Michael Stoyanov *(Joel Cleaver)*, Max Perlich *(Ethan Cleaver)*, Bruce Beatty *(Kelly)*, John Short *(Resident)*, Steven Culp *(Jerry Fanning Forrester)*, Scott Allan Campbell *(Ed McCauley)*, Elizabeth Gilliam *(Nina)*, Gordon Clapp *(Doctor)*, Jack Murdock *(Old Patient)*, Kimberly Scott *(Nurse Louise)*, Diane Robin *(Waitress)*, Rick Goldman *(Truck Driver)*, Tom Kurlander, Susanne Goldstein *(Students)*, Beth Hogan *(Marie)*, O. LaRon Clark *(Food Server)*, Russell Bobbitt *(Gunshot Victim)*, Frank Torres *(Gang Member)*, Bill E. Rogers, Frank Foti Jr. *(Cops)*, Pola Del Mar *(Gang Member's Mother)*, Jesse Anthony Gonzalez *(Gang Member's Brother)*.

Doctors and lawyers: the symbolic twins of American upward mobility. They're what every blue-collar parent wants his or her kid to be, despite statistics that show that professionals tend to beget professionals. Yet the myth of class mobility lingers on, and nowhere more than in Hollywood films, wherein every refrigerator repairman's son has what it takes to make the grade in law school or med school, as long as his working-class heart is in the right place. So PAPER CHASE meet GROSS ANATOMY. You're made for each other. In fact, change torts to tourniquets and lawyers' tweeds to doctors' smocks and you *are* each other, identical twins to the undemystified core.

Modine is the working-class exemplar here, an all-around regular guy apparently intent on wisecracking his way through his first year at the Chandler School of Medicine. Surrounded by the sons and daughters of privilege, he's a fish out of water and behaves accordingly, walking in late on his classes, bouncing a basketball down school hallways, and treating his studies with cavalier disregard. Tough anatomy prof Lahti doesn't take kindly to his attitude, though one of the members of his cadaver-dissecting team (Zuniga) finds his brash-prole routine intriguing, first from a safe, ironic distance and later at romantic close range. Meanwhile, Modine proves to be the wonderful, caring guy we knew he was all along (the egalitarian *us* as opposed to the elitist, moneyed *them*), showing social-workerlike concern for his uptight, speed-freak roommate and working in his spare time as a bottom-of-the-pole hospital attendant (he even gets a foot in the face from an unhappy emergency-room patient: who says med school isn't like boot camp?). Lahti senses the potential behind the provocative swagger and badgers Modine to

apply himself more diligently, but problems with Zuniga (her old boy friend drops in for a visit) and anger at the school's treatment of his roommate (he's forced to leave after cheating on a test) cause him to have second thoughts about continuing his studies. Lahti tries to rally him with a tear-jerking emotional appeal—"I want you to be better than you want yourself to be"—made all the more pointed (and contrived) by the fact that she's suffering from a fatal disease and hasn't got long to live. Modine snaps out of his blue funk just in time to crash the books for his finals, help deliver a baby at a roadside diner while rushing back to class, and pass his anatomy exam with flying colors in spite of the news that Lahti has died. With operatic twists and turns like these, it's a miracle doctors get through med school at all.

For all the righteous ranting about excellence and being true to your potential, the watchword here is mediocrity. Mediocrity for Matthew Modine, who's reverted to brash-boy posing after the grown-up ambitions of FULL METAL JACKET and MARRIED TO THE MOB. Mediocrity for Daphne Zuniga, once more a functional space-filler after the early promise she demonstrated in THE SURE THING and the otherwise forgettable SPACEBALLS. Mediocrity for Christine Lahti, who's making a career out of reviving the soap-opera assumptions of the '40s: that the strong woman is a woman without a man, that female independence breeds neurosis and social isolation (HOUSE-KEEPING), that a woman's nobility is conferred by sickness, suffering, and death. And, finally, mediocrity for director Thom Eberhardt (NIGHT OF THE COMET; WITHOUT A CLUE), for whom it is a step up. Characterization has never been Eberhardt's strong suit, though here at least he manages to sustain an even, semi-naturalistic tone, which is more than can be said of his other films. On the other hand, the small personal touches he brought to NIGHT OF THE COMET—a taste for odd camera angles and colorful detail—have been whittled down to nothing. GROSS ANATOMY is slick, anonymous, and bland in the Disney Touchstone manner. Everything in it seems borrowed from somewhere else, and THE PAPER CHASE hangs over plot and characters like the domineering Professor Kingsfield himself. For this kind of cribbing they throw you out of med school. Unfortunately, in Hollywood it never gets less than a passing grade. Songs include: "Burnin" (Larry Hester, Terry Quinn, performed by Rebel Faction), Overture from "Marriage of Figaro" (Wolfgang Amadeus Mozart, arranged and performed by Lee Ashley), "Piano with Rhythm" (Les Peel, performed by Peel), "She Drives Me Crazy" (David Steele, Roland Gift, performed by Fine Young Cannibals), "White Flag"

(Michael Sherwood, David Young, performed by Sherwood), "Blue Moon Revisited (Song for Elvis)" (Margo Timmims, Michael Timmins, Richard Rodgers, Lorenz Hart, performed by the Cowboy Junkies), Flute Quartet 2, K.298, Minuet (Mozart, arranged and performed by Les Peel), "David's Theme" (Todd Field), "Take a Better Look at Yourself" (Kevin Dever, Dale Chadwick, performed by Roadwork), "Jingle Bell Rock" (Joseph Beal, James Boothe, performed by Bobby Helms), "It Won't Be Love 'Til We Make It" (written and performed by Sam Hogin, Byron Gallimore), "If I Give My Heart to You" (Jimmie Crane, Al Jacobs, Jimmy Brewster, performed by Doris Day), "I'll Be There" (Mickey Thomas, Craig Chaquico, Steven Diamond, performed by Starship). *(Adult situations.)*

p, Howard Rosenman and Debra Hill; d, Thom Eberhardt; w, Ron Nyswaner and Mark Spragg (based on a story by Mark Spragg, Howard Rosenman, Alan Jay Glueckman, Stanley Isaacs); ph, Steve Yaconelli (Technicolor); ed, Bud Smith and Scott Smith; m, David Newman; prod d, William F. Matthews; art d, P. Michael Johnston; set d, Catherine Mann and Lauren Polizzi; spec eff, Calvin Joe Acord; cos, Gale Parker; makeup, Edouard F. Henriques III.

Comedy/Drama   (PR:C MPAA:PG-13)

Ⓥ**GUNRUNNER, THE*½**
(Can.) 84m NW-Video Voice c
Kevin Costner *(Ted Beaubien)*, Sara Botsford *(Maude)*, Paul Soles *(Lochman)*, Gerard Parkes *(Wilson)*, Ron Lea *(George)*, Mitch Martin *(Rosalyn)*, Larry Lewis *(Robert)*, Daniel Nalbach *(Max)*.

Filmed long before Kevin Costner became famous, and released on video in 1989 to capitalize on his current stardom, THE GUNRUNNER is a feeble actioner set in the world of illegal arms sales in 1926 Montreal. Returning home from China, where he has just made a gun-running deal, Costner finds himself drawn into the current underworld rage: speakeasies. One such emporium is run by Botsford, to whom Costner is increasingly attracted, even as he discovers that he can trust no one. Though Costner's brother, Lea, tries to set up a weapons purchase, he lacks the financing to see it through. Lea—who also has his eye on Martin, the daughter of a well-to-do financier—is eventually killed while trying to set up a meeting with some arms dealers, leaving Costner alone to volunteer to deliver the ransom money when Martin's brother, Lewis, is kidnaped. It all leads to some complicated revelations involving Lewis' inheritance, Botsford's duplicity, and Costner's motivations.

Considering the then-unknown Costner's involvement, it's not surprising that THE GUNRUNNER has turned up on video now, some six years after it was made. What is surprising is that this pointless film was made in the first place. Character motivations are so completely arbitrary that as little as five minutes into the film it's impossible to care what anyone does or says. And don't look for action scenes to relieve the boredom and bewilderment, because the action is almost as nonexistent as the plot. The film's opening sequences are particularly confusing (perhaps because viewers are still paying attention at this point), and the rest is simply a series of scenes and plot ideas that play like an extended trailer—very little of which actually pertains to the weapons trade, the title notwithstanding. Moreover, it's a good thing that THE GUNRUNNER's adver-

tising tells us the film is set in 1926, since—apart from the few rented antique cars that repeatedly roll by in the background—there's little indication of this. The architecture and dialog belie the period setting throughout; even some of the costumes (especially Costner's) look more like modern-day clothes with a few "vintage" touches than the genuine article.

Arnie Gelbart's screenplay is filled with such banalities as "Every time there's trouble, I find you" and "It's difficult to decide whether you're a hunter or a predator" (figure that one out). Nor is THE GUN-RUNNER assisted by Rex Taylor Smith's atrocious score, which proves that slow cocktail jazz is not cinematically foolproof. Judging from his frequent use of fade-outs, director Nardo Castillo may

have intended the film for television, though he neglects to give several lead performers as much as a single close-up. And as for the film's *raison d'etre*, the young Costner (for those interested, he's shirtless in one scene), he seems to do little but sulk. THE GUNRUNNER can't even come up to the relatively low standard for arms-dealing movies set in 1983, when William Friedkin's long-forgotten DEAL OF THE CENTURY hit the screen. *(Profanity, violence, adult situations.)*

p, Richard Sadler and Robert J. Langevin; d, Nardo Castillo; w, Arnie Gelbart; ph, Alain Dostie (Foto-Kem Color); ed, Diane Fingado and Andre Corriveau; m, Rex Taylor Smith; prod d, Wendell Dennis.

Action   **(PR:C MPAA:NR)**

H

Ⓥ**HALLOWEEN 5:**
THE REVENGE OF MICHAEL
MYERS zero
96m Ramsey Thomas/Galaxy c
Donald L. Shanks *(Michael Myers)*, Dan-
ielle Harris *(Jamie)*, Donald Pleasence
(Detective Loomis).

Frustrating, inept, confusing, loud, offensive—all of these words apply to this horribly bad sequel, a film that not only
continues to ruin the story line and characters created by a brilliant filmmaker
(John Carpenter), but sets a new standard
of stupidity. In 1978, Carpenter unleashed
HALLOWEEN; a triumph of suspense, it
told the simple story of a group of
babysitters terrorized by a madman named
Michael Myers. Universal demanded a
sequel, and, in 1981, HALLOWEEN II—
directed, with a heavy emphasis on gore, by
Rick Rosenthal—was released. In the
wake of that film's financial success came
the campy, enjoyable HALLOWEEN III:
SEASON OF THE WITCH. Unrelated to
the saga of Michael Myers, it was made in
the hope of ending the sequels before they
became just another stupid slasher series.
This was not to be the case, however, as
1988's HALLOWEEN IV: THE
RETURN OF MICHAEL MYERS, an
inept attempt to repeat Carpenter's style,
reduced a masterful premise to bland
slasher nonsense. But at least HALLOW-
EEN IV, as bad as it is, can be categorized.
The latest sequel, HALLOWEEN 5, is so
confused and awkward it's difficult to figure out exactly what it is. Is it a slasher film?
(It certainly has elements of that genre.) Is
it a psychological thriller? (There are two
really disturbed characters in it.) Or is it a
comedy? (It introduces a strange new character armed with a new subplot and no
explanation.) The only thing certain is that
HALLOWEEN 5 is a big mess.

The first 10 minutes of the film are
enough to confuse just about anybody, and
not surprisingly it's virtually impossible to
summarize the plot. The story concerns
Michael Myers' return to Haddonfield
after surviving a shootout and living with
an old man for a year. He has come back
to kill (for no apparent reason) a little girl
with whom he is psychically linked. Of
course, the indestructible Dr. Loomis
(Donald Pleasence) pops in and out hoping to catch Michael before he gets to the
girl. There are teenagers having parties,
couples having sex (naturally, the promiscuous ones are dealt with appropriately),
and girls giggling and exchanging fashion
tips. All the while, Loomis runs rampant,
warning the police that Michael is ready to
kill again, while the little girl shakes uncon-
trollably whenever Michael is near. However, there is no explanation of her psychic

episodes, or even of why Loomis is still
around. As a matter of fact, there is little or
no explanation of anything. Especially
confusing is the introduction of a mysterious cloaked figure with steel-toed boots,
who wanders Haddonfield carrying a briefcase. His (or her) face is never shown; who
he is and the reason for his appearance are
never explained. Of course, there are a few
murders with a variety of weapons: one kid
has a pitchfork slammed through his chest;
another is beheaded with a sickle. Yet the
murders are so matter-of-factly handled
that even the most dedicated slasher fan
will be bored. After killing several people,
but failing to get the little girl, Michael is
thrown in jail, where he sits wearing his
famous white mask (was his mug-shot
taken like this?) until he is busted out by
the mysterious figure in the steel-toed
boots. The film then abruptly ends right
there, with no explanation, leaving the
viewer angry, confused, and offended.

Directed with no sense of pace or style
by Dominique Othenin-Girard, HAL-
LOWEEN 5 isn't suspenseful, scary, or the
least bit interesting. Characters run in and
out of the scenes without rhyme or reason,
leaving the viewer with such questions as:
Who is that? Why is he doing that? Where
did he come from? Or, simply, What the
hell is going on? There is little concern with
craftsmanship and Othenin-Girard's self-
indulgent camera style is awkward and
annoying. As for the acting, Pleasence is
completely wacko in this one, his performance so blatantly over-the-top that it is
almost worth seeing. Ranting and raving,
he adds life to the completely dead atmosphere. The film, however, never builds to
a climax, and large-scale "suspense"
sequences are thrown in without creating a
sense of anticipation. Notably, a sequence
in which Myers, at the wheel of a car, chases
his running victims through a field is handled as if it were the climactic battle, but
proves to be only another attempt on the
girl's life.

The dialog is pathetic, the characters are
sketchy at best, and the story is nonsense.
HALLOWEEN 5 is a terrible movie, but
what makes it even more disappointing is
that Michael Myers (an effectively stark
representation of pure evil in HALLOW-
EEN), like Norman Bates in the PSYCHO
sequels, has been reduced to just another
faceless slasher who could easily pass for
Jason's brother. The premise and style of
HALLOWEEN have been stomped on by
money-hungry producers and uninspired
filmmakers. John Carpenter should be
steamed. *(Graphic violence, profanity,
adult situation, sexual situations.)*

p, Ramsey Thomas; d, Dominique
Othenin-Girard; w, Michael Jacobs, Dominique Othenin-Girard, and Shem Bitter-
man; ph, Robert Draper; ed, Charles Tetoni;
m, Alan Howarth; prod d, Brenton Swift.

Horror   **(PR:O MPAA:R)**

Ⓥ**HARDCASE AND FIST****½
92m United c
Ted Prior *(Bud McCall)*, Carter Wong
(Eddy Lee), Christina Lunde *(Sharon)*,
Maureen Lavette *(Nora)*, Tony Zarindast
(Tony Marino), Vincent Barbi *(Vincent)*,
Tony Bova, Beano, Stacy Nemour, Bill
Summers, Debra Lamb, Angelyne.

At the beginning of HARDCASE AND
FIST, undercover detective Prior arrives in
Folsom Prison and is introduced to the
prison lifestyle by his cellmate, Wong.
Prior, supposedly doing time for cocaine
dealing, has actually been assigned to infiltrate the cellblock and to prevent a prisoner
with syndicate connections from testifying
in defense of underworld chieftain Barbi.
Barbi, on trial for racketeering, senses that
his conviction is imminent after Prior
removes his prison-dwelling alibi. When
he is unable to intimidate the federal judge
who is trying his case, an infuriated Barbi
instructs an assistant (played by producer-
director-cowriter Tony Zarindast) to visit
Prior inside the prison and make arrangements for the cop's elimination. In fact,
Zarindast owes much to Prior (who heroically saved his life in Vietnam), but now
despises his old war buddy for becoming a
policeman. Inside the prison, Prior is brutally attacked by a contingent of Barbi's
henchmen, and is saved when Wong fends
the assailants off with his martial-arts
expertise. Barbi's plans seem further
imperiled when Zarindast expresses mis-
givings about his orders, so Barbi kidnaps
Zarindast's girl friend (Lunde) to guaran-
tee that the scheme will be carried out.
While Prior and Wong are being transferred to a maximum security prison,
Zarindast fakes an automobile accident in
an effort to capture them. During the
attempt, however, Zarindast changes his
mind and helps Prior and Wong escape the
clutches of Barbi's men. They are subsequently captured by a crippled Vietnam
veteran whose car they've attempted to
steal, but he offers them refuge on his farm
once he learns that they also served in the
war. The next morning, Barbi sends his
malevolent lieutenant, Bova, and a sizable
contingent of men to pound the farmhouse
with heavy artillery. During the grueling
siege, Zarindast and his host are killed by
an exploding grenade, though not before
Zarindast learns that Lunde is being held
captive on Barbi's ranch. As the farmhouse
is splintered apart by exploding shells,
Prior and Wong scurry through a cloud of
smoke and flee. Afterwards Wong, in a rare
contemplative moment, decides to resume
his relationship with his estranged wife, but
his quest only leads him to a squalid strip
joint, where a crowd of leering bikers are
transfixed by his ex's lewd dancing. Prior
manages to get Wong out of the place
before the martial-arts expert's annihilation of the bikers and devastation of the
premises is complete, then transports his

former cellmate to Bova's hideout, where they mount a surprise attack and rescue the beleaguered Lunde.

The first half of Zarindast's nihilistic martial-arts drama is tautly confined to the volatile world of organized crime, where the search for tranquility is as elusive as it is dangerous. Zarindast's steady, gliding camera continually shifts the characters' relationship to their surroundings, keeping them in a constant state of imbalance in an otherwise coldly symmetrical environment. When his characters finally achieve their moments of relative quiet, these periods quickly end in a jarring eruption of violence. The single moment of lasting repose is bestowed upon the gravely wounded Tony Marino (the character played by Zarindast himself) as he sits amidst a raging battle moments before his death. But Zarindast's carefully constructed tale comes apart in the second half of HARDCASE AND FIST, when attention shifts to Carter Wong's Eddy Lee and his absurd displays of martial-arts wizardry. While this expertise comes in handy when Bova unleashes a kung-fu battalion upon the escaped prisoners during the artillery bombardment at the farmhouse, it also serves to undermine both the scene's credibility and the credibility of the filmmaker, who had hitherto seemed committed to an engaging narrative. Moreover, Wong's garbled pronunciation and grunting intonation are matched in their egregiousness only by his flaring nostrils and bulging eyes, making for an unceasingly rabid characterization. Filmmaker Zarindast clearly shows a gift for evocative storytelling in HARDCASE AND FIST, but his casting and scripting leave room for considerable improvement. *(Violence, profanity, nudity.)*

p, Tony Zarindast; d, Tony Zarindast; w, Bud Fleischer and Tony Zarindast (based on a story by Tony Zarindast); ph, Robert Hayes (Foto-Kem Color); ed, Bill Cunningham; m, Tom Tucciarone and Matthew Tucciarone; prod d, Alan Scott.

Action   **(PR:C   MPAA:R)**

HARLEM NIGHTS**
115m Eddie Murphy/PAR c

Eddie Murphy *(Quick)*, Richard Pryor *(Sugar Ray)*, Redd Foxx *(Bennie Wilson)*, Danny Aiello *(Phil Cantone)*, Michael Lerner *(Bugsy Calhoune)*, Della Reese *(Vera)*, Berlinda Tolbert *(Annie)*, Stan Shaw *(Jack Jenkins)*, Jasmine Guy *(Dominique La Rue)*, Vic Polizos *(Richie Vento)*, Lela Rochon *(Sunshine)*, Arsenio Hall *(Crying Man)*, Uncle Ray *(Willie)*, Robin Harris *(Jerome)*, Charles Q. Murphy *(Jimmy)*, Tommy Ford *(Tommy Smalls)*, Michael Goldfinger *(Max)*, Joe Pecoraro *(Joe Leoni)*, Miguel Nunez *(Man with Broken Nose)*, Desi Arnez Hines II *(Young Quick)*, Reynaldo Rey *(Gambler)*, Howard "Sandman" Sims *(Crapshooter)*, Prince C. Spencer *(Himself)*, Roberto Duran *(Bouncer)*.

Nineteen-thirties Harlem is a state of mind, a place where forbidden fantasies intersect (actually twenties Harlem is more to the point, but history has never been Hollywood's strong suit). For whites it's the promise of illicit pleasure, for blacks the promise of illicit power, and each promise feeds on the other, a supply-and-demand parody of integration. We're all criminals, the characters in HARLEM NIGHTS keep reminding each other, and that's part of the fantasy, too. Sex, power, fancy clothes, fancier cars, and a world where all the rules are permanently warped: these are the makings of an adolescent dream of life on the edge, and writer-director (executive producer-star) Murphy buys into this vision wholeheartedly. The problem is he's not an adolescent anymore, and these particular fantasies (all commonplace, all regressive) have been around the Hollywood block more times than anyone can count.

The story opens with a young Harlem orphan (Hines) returning from an errand with cigarettes for Mr. Sugar Ray (Pryor), the proprietor of a seedy after-hours joint in the back of a candy shop. One of the back-room gamblers is having a run of bad luck and curses Pryor (everybody curses everybody in this film) for letting young Hines stick around to watch. Matters escalate, violence is threatened, and Pryor is about to be knifed when young Hines shoots the irate gambler in the head, whereupon Pryor decides that the kid will make a fine companion and takes him home as his ward. Flash forward 20 years to late 1930s Harlem, where Hines has grown into Murphy, and Pryor's old gambling den has been transformed into the fashionable Club Sugar Ray. Murphy provides the muscle at the club, which he and Pryor co-own, and which has become the main competition for the even more paradisiacal establishment run by Lerner, a Capone-like mobster. Lerner dispatches a pair of goons to check out Pryor's place, and they're accompanied by the mobster's siren girl friend (Guy), who inevitably catches Murphy's eye. The tough madam at the Club Sugar Ray (Reese) also catches Murphy . . . in the eye, jaw, and solar plexus when he suggests that her girls have been skimming the club's profits. Murphy retaliates by shooting Reese in the foot (a little gratuitous misogyny masquerading as equal treatment for the uppity sex). Meanwhile, Pryor gets a call from a corrupt cop in Lerner's employ (Aiello) who applies the protection squeeze but comes up empty-handed. Lerner tries squeezing even harder by offering Murphy a job at his own lavish club, but Murphy, prince that he is, indignantly declines. The mobster then decides to get rid of Murphy for good, using Guy as the deadly bait; however, Murphy sees through the seductive ruse, and after a short frolic in the sack, shoots Guy in the head. Lerner, of course, is furious and gets his revenge through Aiello, who leads a police raid on Club Sugar Ray and ultimately trashes the place. Pryor and company decide to relocate in New Jersey, but not before settling a few scores. They

Eddie Murphy and Richard Pryor in HARLEM NIGHTS (©Paramount).

relieve Lerner's mob of a significant amount of cash (unfixing a fixed fight and waylaying a mob flunky on his collection rounds), trap Aiello in a bank vault, and finally blow away Lerner and his honchos in Pryor's own booby-trapped mansion. Safely across the Hudson, Murphy and Pryor look back on the city they've left behind. Hoboken may not be Harlem, but the nights there are better for your health.

If HARLEM NIGHTS isn't the embarrassing vanity production it might have been, there's still not a lot to be said for it. As a first-time director, Murphy has his fantasies to play with—his own peculiar idea of the hip and the cool, but at this point in his filmmaking career he lacks the craft to make much of them. The film's technical execution is adequate to awful; aside from Lawrence G. Paull's sleekly designed sets, there's no body to HARLEM NIGHTS at all. The cast, on the other hand, is varied and substantial, ranging from raw ingenues (Jasmine Guy, Lela Rochon) to dues-paying veterans and show-business icons (Redd Foxx as a near-sighted croupier). Unfortunately, writer Murphy's undernourished script doesn't give anyone much to work with—Richard Pryor mainly coasts, and actor Murphy defers to everyone else. Nevertheless, Michael Lerner makes the most of his melancholy mobster, and Arsenio Hall's cameo braying as a bereaved mob hitman gives the film a delirious, giddy kick. But HARLEM NIGHTS is finally done in by its own fantasies of consumption: everything is subservient to Murphy's ego; everything becomes a lavish toy for him, from women in slinky dresses to fancy cars and the ambiguous, exploitable legend of Harlem itself. There's no soul to be had in this city of appearances. Musical selections include: "Drop Me off in Harlem" (Duke Ellington, Nick Kenny, performed by Louis Armstrong), "It Don't Mean a Thing (If It Ain't Got That Swing)," "Sophisticated Lady," "Mood Indigo," "The Gal from Joe's," "Black Beauty" (Ellington). *(Violence, excessive profanity, adult situations.)*

p, Mark Lipsky and Robert D. Wachs; d, Eddie Murphy; w, Eddie Murphy; ph, Woody Omens; ed, George Bowers; m, Herbie Hancock; prod d, Lawrence G. Paull; cos, Joe I. Tompkins.

Action/Comedy   (PR:O MPAA:R)

🅥**HEART OF DIXIE****½
101m Orion c
Ally Sheedy *(Maggie)*, Virginia Madsen *(Delia)*, Phoebe Cates *(Aiken)*, Don Michael Paul *(Boots)*, Treat Williams *(Hoyt)*, Dyle Secor *(Tuck)*, Francesca Roberts *(Keefi)*, Peter Berg *(Jenks)*, Jenny Robertson *(Sister)*, Kurtwood Smith, Richard Bradford.

HEART OF DIXIE is one of those good news-bad news films. The good news is that

director Martin Davidson has drawn solid performances from his three lead actresses and done a good job of re-creating the genteel, racist South of 1957, when the civil rights movement was still in its early stages. The bad news is that audiences are likely to come away from DIXIE wondering what the point of it was.

Sheedy, Madsen, and Cates respectively play Maggie, Delia and Aiken, sorority sisters at an Alabama college during a time when the rumblings of the civil rights movement were still largely unheard. Maggie, a budding journalist working for the campus newspaper, senses the winds of racial change and becomes tentatively active in the drive toward desegregation. She has problems accommodating both her progressive social beliefs and Southern womanhood's traditional submission to male authority, however, and her political stance is made even more difficult in that she has been "pinned"—a commitment tantamount to a wedding engagement—by Boots (Paul), the most eligible frat brother on campus. Standing on either side of Maggie are Delia, a quintessential Southern belle who compensates for her second-rate social status by leading men on unmercifully, and Aiken, a budding beatnik in black leotards who harbors ambitions of moving to Greenwich Village and becoming a full-time bohemian. Helping to steer Maggie in Aiken's direction is hunky, liberal Hoyt (Williams), an AP photographer covering the growing racial unrest in the South.

More than a look at changing racial politics, HEART OF DIXIE intends no less than to make a sweeping indictment of the whole patriarchal power structure of 1950s Southern culture by revealing the iron fist beneath the velvet glove of courtly gentility. Delia is brutally beaten by her boy friend after dancing with another man; another sorority sister endures a date rape in order to lose what was considered to be the far worse stigma of being the only senior-classwoman who has yet to be pinned. In one scene involving the college president and another with Boots' father, condescending Southern chivalry gives way to sputtering obscenities and ominous threats when Maggie persists in questioning male authority.

What is remarkable about HEART OF DIXIE is how rarely it descends to easy rhetoric to make these points. If anything, Davidson (who directed the memorable HBO baseball comedy LONG GONE, also featuring Virginia Madsen) goes out of his way to show the seductive charm of a culture steeped in ritual and a comfortable sense of order. In doing so, he also shows how much Maggie stands to lose by taking a moral stand against a world that has supported and nurtured her and that further promises her a life of leisurely adult comfort as Boots' bride.

Unfortunately, HEART OF DIXIE is fatally distracted and diffuse on a dramatic level, gaining neither focus nor momentum as it goes on. Instead, it only gets more confusing. The editing is choppy, as if the film were cut from a considerably longer running time, so that actors like Kurtwood Smith and Barbara Babcock appear in single scenes and then vanish for the remainder of the film. Of the principals, Treat Williams and Phoebe Cates come and go in the film without much rhyme or reason. Similarly, the script, adapted by Tom McCown from Anne Rivers Siddons' novel *Heartbreak Hotel*, rushes from one burning issue to the next, as if it were more interested in being comprehensive than in being coherent.

HEART OF DIXIE is partially redeemed by its performances and Davidson's rich rendering of the story's time, place, and mood. But in ambitiously mixing history, politics, sociology, and drama, it winds up doing a little bit of everything without doing much of anything effectively, biting off far more than it can chew. This may make it a noble failure, but it's a failure nonetheless. *(Profanity, adult situations.)*

p, Steve Tisch and Paul Kurta; d, Martin Davidson; w, Tom McCown (based on the novel *Heartbreak Hotel* by Anne Rivers Siddons); ph, Robert Elswit; ed, Bonnie Koehler; m, Kenny Vance; prod d, Glenda Ganis.

Drama   (PR:C MPAA:PG)

🅥**HEART OF MIDNIGHT****
105m AG/Goldwyn c
Jennifer Jason Leigh *(Carol Rivers)*, Peter Coyote *("Lt. Sharpe"/Larry)*, Gale Mayron *(Sonny)*, James Rebhorn *(Richard)*, Sam Schacht *(Uncle Fletcher)*, Denise Dummont *(Mariana)*, Frank Stallone *(Ledray)*, Brenda Vaccaro *(Betty Rivers)*, James Geallis *(Lt. Sharpe)*, Jack Hallett *(Lawyer)*, Nick Love *(Tom)*, Tico Wells *(Henry)*, Nina Lora *(Carol as a Child)*, Steve Buscemi *(Eddy)*, Ken Moser *(Ledray's Sidekick)*, Nicholas Cimino, Drew Taylor *(Boys with Kittens)*, Trey Greene *(Sonny as a Boy)*, Carolyn Torlay *(Apple Lady)*.

In his 1984 film STRANGERS KISS, director Matthew Chapman paid tribute to Stanley Kubrick by casting Peter Coyote as a coolly manipulative director making a low-budget film patterned after Kubrick's own ultra-cheap debut, KILLER'S KISS. Filmed in 1987, HEART OF MIDNIGHT reunites Chapman, Coyote, and the spirit of Kubrick, this time in an atmospheric homage to Kubrick's Stephen King adaptation THE SHINING. HEART OF MIDNIGHT might have been a better film, however, had Chapman also followed Kubrick's lead in trimming his story to its bare minimum and trusting his characters to carry the drama.

Jennifer Jason Leigh, a good actress who rarely seems to get good roles, plays a woman who, while recovering from a nervous breakdown, inherits the Midnight, a rundown nightclub in Charleston, South Carolina, from her recently deceased uncle. Against the advice of her mother (Vaccaro), Leigh decides not to sell the place, but to go ahead with her uncle's plans to renovate and re-open the club. As it turns out, however, Leigh would have done well to heed Vaccaro's warnings. Moving into an apartment over the club, she discovers that there was far more to her uncle's business than the usual night-life drinking and dancing. The place holds a series of rooms decorated to suit every imaginable sexual taste and fetish, from hardcore sadomasochism to an indoor beach setting, complete with sand, that appears to have been designed for fans of FROM HERE TO ETERNITY. And that's only the beginning, since, like THE SHINING's Overlook Hotel, the Midnight seems to have a grim, ghastly life of its own —mumbling, groaning, and subjecting its already unhinged new inhabitant to bizarre hallucinations. Not unlike Jack Nicholson's character in Kubrick's film, Leigh starts talking to people who aren't there, and begins parading around in selections from a closetful of bordello outfits. Chapman displays a mastery of Kubrickian film language through these early sections, using a combination of soundtrack manipulation, eerie camerawork, and flashy cutting—in concert with Leigh's finely tuned performance—to suggest how the nightclub seems to absorb the woman's personality and transform her into one of its aberrant past patrons. It's when the Midnight literally opens its doors, beckoning to a trio of thugs who enter and brutally rape Leigh, that the film both swings into high narrative gear and begins to slip from its moorings. Sent to investigate, police lieutenant Coyote takes an immediate liking to Leigh—or so it seems. Coyote, it emerges, isn't wrapped too tightly himself, and begins badgering Leigh, then cooks her dinner in order to drug her so he can search the premises. The plot further thickens when a second man claiming to be the real police lieutenant (played by James Geallis, the film's supervising producer) appears at the club, only to be turned away by Leigh, who mistakes him for Coyote over her apartment intercom.

It's not long before Leigh is caught up in a dazzling array of violence and perversion —including, but not limited to, voyeurism, pedophilia, recreational torture, and murder. However, in providing a catalog of lurid explanations for why everybody in the film is acting so strangely, Chapman, who also wrote the script, winds up raising more questions than he answers. More importantly, he also loses track of his main character, whose interior struggle to regain

her sanity gets lost in cumbersome plot mechanics. Chapman may deserve the benefit of some doubt—although originally released at 105 minutes, the video version reviewed here clocks in at 93, indicating some postproduction tampering. But it's hard to imagine the missing minutes doing much to alter what starts out as a serviceable nerve-jangler, with a nod to Roman Polanski's REPULSION as well as THE SHINING, only to bog down into turgid, Southern Gothic melodramatics. Songs include: "Baby, What Else Can I Do" (G. Marks, W. Hirsch, performed by Ethel Waters), "(Mama) He Treats Your Daughter Mean" (Johnny Wallace, Herbert J. Lance, performed by Ruth Brown), "So Long" (Russ Morgan, Irving Melsher, Remus Harris), "She's My Guiding Light" (Frank Stallone, performed by Stallone).*(Sexual situations, profanity, violence.)*

p, Andrew Gaty; d, Matthew Chapman; w, Matthew Chapman (based on a story by Chapman, Everett De Roche); ph, Ray Rivas (TVC Color); ed, Penelope Shaw; m, Yanni; prod d, Gene Rudolf; art d, Christa Munro; set d, Stephanie Waldron; spec eff, Guy H. Tuttle; cos, Linda Fisher; makeup, Hiram Ortiz.

Thriller   (PR:O MPAA:R)

ⓥHEATHERS***½
102m Cinemarque/NW c
Winona Ryder *(Veronica Sawyer)*, Christian Slater *(J.D.)*, Shannen Doherty *(Heather Duke)*, Lisanne Falk *(Heather McNamara)*, Kim Walker *(Heather Chandler)*, Penelope Milford *(Pauline Fleming)*, Glenn Shadix *(Fr. Ripper)*, Lance Fenton *(Kurt Kelly)*, Patrick Labyorteaux *(Ram)*, Jeremy Applegate *(Peter Dawson)*, Jon Matthews *(Rodney)*, Carrie Lynn *(Martha Dunnstock/Dumptruck)*.

The near-surreal world of high-school *popularity* is imaginatively probed in this black comedy revolving around, of all things, teenage suicide. Morally reprehensible, with scenes and dialog sure to offend many, HEATHERS is, nevertheless, a film of startling originality and verve. Fictitious Westerburg High in Sherwood, Ohio, provides the backdrop for the star triumvirate of princesses, the eponymous Heathers, who comprise the most exclusive clique in school. Heather Chandler (Walker) is the leader of this petulantly pubescent pack, and a mighty witch is she. Her disciples, Heather Duke (Doherty) and Heather McNamara (Falk), let her pulverize them at the croquet games that symbolize the Heathers' power structure, drop insufficiently cool friends, and humiliate poor Martha "Dumptruck" Dunnstock (Lynn) in the cafeteria. Only Veronica (Ryder), a relatively recent addition to their clique, evinces any guilt over her friends' rapacious behavior. Her first attempt at independence comes when she takes up with

J.D. (Slater), a misfit who doesn't fit the beer-guzzling jock mold favored by her clique. Predictably, the Heathers ridicule her infatuation, thereby provoking homicidal tendencies in Slater and, accessorily, Ryder. Soon, three of the school's most popular, albeit piggish, students are found dead, with heartrending suicide notes attached to their persons that provide some startling revelations: Doherty reveals herself in death to have been a deeply sensitive, misunderstood being; and two football players are discovered to have been driven to their demise by a love that dare not speak its name. But what begins as a lark for Ryder becomes a nightmare as she realizes that her mischievous fantasies are diabolical realities for the increasingly psychotic Slater.

HEATHERS might have been a moronic teen gross-out film were it not for the immediacy and careful observation of the surprisingly rich script by Daniel Waters. His uncanny ear for the glib, casually obscene, and at times startlingly literate way teenagers speak results in a dazzling mix of references to corn nuts, chain saws, "convenience-store speak," Sylvia Plath, "crucial" yearbook layouts, and, of course, any number of bright euphemisms for sex. Director Michael Lehmann is likewise attuned to the milieu, and his film has a messy, try-anything-once charm to it that is perfectly suited to the material. The cast is all one could desire. Christian Slater contributes an effectively creepy Jack Nicholson imitation (raspy vocal delivery, eyebrows working like apostrophes); 16-year-old Winona Ryder has the etched, surefire prettiness of a Gene Tierney or Gail Russell and invests her difficult, ambivalent part with real likability and complexity. Watching her holed up in her bedroom wearing a monocle and furiously scribbling out her frustrations in her diary, one gets a true sense of adolescent anguish. Moreover, her timing is flawless in scenes like the wittily repetitive conversations she has with her blandly upmarket parents, and she clearly enjoys getting messed up, whether it's vomiting on herself at a fraternity party or being splashed with mud at a cow-tipping scene. Indeed, at the film's apocalyptic conclusion, she resembles the Queen of Gore herself, Barbara Steele, as she fatalistically ascends the school's front steps. The Heathers themselves are an impressive array of pulchritude, with Kim Walker a standout as the embodiment of every heartless high-school beauty.

Despite the film's modest budget, the specificity of its art direction and costumes stand out, capturing the full woozy range of 1980s bourgeois appurtenances. Dark, cynical, but deliciously funny, HEATHERS is a fascinating look not just at high school, but at the way we look at high school. *(Sexual situations, adult situations, violence, profanity.)*

p, Denise Di Novi; d, Michael Lehmann; w, Daniel Waters; ph, Francis Kenney (Deluxe Color); ed, Norman Hollyn; m, David Newman; prod d, Jon Hutman; art d, Kara Lindstrom; cos, Rudy Dillon.

Comedy/Fantasy   (PR:O MPAA:R)

❶HELL HIGH***
79m DGS-Grossman-Steinman/JGM c
Christopher Stryker *(Dickens)*, Maureen Mooney *(Brooke Storm)*, Christopher Cousins *(Jon Jon)*, Millie Prezioso *(Queenie)*, Jason Brill *(Smiler)*, Kathy Rossetter, J.R. Horne, Daniel Beer, Karen Russell, Webster Whinery.

This teen horror offering has the standard ingredients of murder, mayhem, terrified females, rape threats, and nudity (female, of course), but is a cut above the average genre dreck in that it creates relatively plausible motivation for its psycho killer, and features a hero who gets involved in the killings but is torn apart by remorse.

In a prolog, we are shown a young high-school biology teacher (Mooney) as she becomes the terrified witness to the murder of two teenagers at a swamp near the school. Eighteen years later, the horrifying scene has left her with permanent psychological scars, and the event has passed into local folklore. One of her students (Stryker) masterminds a vicious prank in which a group of teens, masked and disguised as swamp monsters, terrorize Mooney. The prank degenerates from vicious to criminal when they try to rape her; in desperation, she falls through a window and is apparently killed. But she comes back, loaded for bear, and draws the hero (Cousins) into a gory series of revenge murders. Blame for the killings is pinned on innocent football player Beer, though Cousins nearly goes insane with guilt by the time the film reaches its tricky ending.

The performances range from adequate to good, with Christopher Stryker serving up a rewardingly mean-minded, rotten brat, and Maureen Mooney handling the shift from terrorized female to marauding killer with persuasive flair. Technically, HELL HIGH invites few complaints. Steven Fierberg's photography is craftsmanlike, the pacing and editing are assured, and the score does a nice job of hyping the action. The terror level is not going to make cinematic history, however, and gorehounds will find more—and more grisly—effects elsewhere. *(Nudity, profanity, sexual situations, violence.)*

p, David Steinman and Douglas Grossman; d, Douglas Grossman; w, Leo Evans and Douglas Grossman; ph, Steven Fierberg (Precision Color); ed, Claire Simpson-Crozier and Greg Sheldon; m, Rich Macar and Christopher Hyans-Hart; art d, William Bilowit and Joan Brockschmidt.

Horror   (PR:O MPAA:R)

HENRY: PORTRAIT OF A SERIAL KILLER***
83m Maljack c
Michael Rooker *(Henry)*, Tom Towles *(Otis)*, Tracy Arnold.

HENRY: PORTRAIT OF A SERIAL KILLER surely ranks as one of the most frightening and disturbing films ever made. An angry and raw independent feature that received limited release after becoming a cult favorite in Chicago (where it was filmed), and three years after its 1986 completion, HENRY begins with a creepy montage of shots of dead bodies. The corpses are the victims of Henry (Rooker), a low-life drifter who looks for victims while driving around in his green Impala. Rooker murders with knives, guns, rope, even his hands—he has no preferred method or pattern. Rooker lives with Towles, a degenerate he met while in prison (for killing his mother) and who now works in a gas station and sells drugs on the side. When Towles' sister (Arnold) comes to Chicago, she stays with Towles and Rooker while she looks for a job; meanwhile, Rooker, who works as a bug sprayer, continues to kill. Arnold becomes interested in him, and (after hearing a few things from Towles) asks some very personal questions, including "Did you really kill your momma?" Rooker proceeds to tell her how his mother would force him to watch her have sex with strangers and sometimes made him wear a dress. He says he killed his mother on his 14th birthday, although he's not sure how (after so many murders you lose track of individual details). None of this seems to shock Arnold (a victim of paternal incest herself), who still seems interested in Rooker. Towles takes no notice; he wants to seduce her himself. (At one point, Towles grabs Arnold and kisses her, whereupon Rooker threatens him, saying, "It's not right; she's your sister.") One night, Towles and Rooker pick up a couple of hookers and park their car in an alley. Moments later, Rooker snaps the women's necks and dumps the bodies—an action that at first shocks Towles, but once he and Rooker get something to eat he seems fine. Soon, Towles joins Rooker in his killing spree. When he and Rooker visit a fat, sleazy TV repairman who operates out of a garage, Rooker stabs the repairman, smashes a TV over his head, and instructs Towles to plug the set in. Though he has become a murderer, Towles feels no remorse, having gotten a video camera out of the deal. Afterwards, they go home and have fun with the camera, filming Rooker and Arnold as they dance and Towles as he jumps around. The next day, Towles reports to his parole officer, a shockingly quick and meaningless meeting. He continues to sell marijuana—to teenage boys, coming on to them while he's at it and saying offhandedly, after one of the kids punches him, that he'd like to kill someone. Replies Rooker, "Let's me and you take a ride," and the two wind up on the shoulder of Chicago's Lower Wacker Drive, where they pop their car's hood and flag down a car. When a driver stops to see if they need help, Rooker laughs, Towles shoots the man dead, and they get back in the car and drive off, both feeling much better.

Michael Rooker in HENRY: PORTRAIT OF A SERIAL KILLER (©Maljack).

Towles and Rooker continue to murder people at random, videotaping every detail, until they start to get on each other's nerves. When Rooker can no longer stand Towles' stupidity and sloppiness, the two argue; meanwhile, Arnold quits her job in a hair salon and asks Rooker to move away with her. After Arnold and Rooker go out for dinner one night, they return home to find Towles (who likes to watch the videotaped murders, viewing them repeatedly and in slow motion) passed out on the couch. Arnold brings Rooker into the bedroom, but Towles wakes up and interrupts them. Feeling uncomfortable, Rooker goes out for cigarettes and—after passing up an opportunity to kill another person—returns home to find Towles raping his sister. Towles and Rooker fight, Arnold stabs her brother in the eye, and Rooker finishes him off with a screwdriver in the stomach. Arnold is hysterical; Rooker calmly chops his ex-roommate into pieces, which he deposits in garbage bags. After packing their suitcases, Rooker and Arnold drive to a bridge, from which Rooker drops the garbage bags. He and Arnold then declare their love, talk of a future together, and drive to a motel. The next day, Rooker departs alone in his car. Stopping, he opens the trunk, removes a large, heavy suitcase, and drops it by the side of the road. Having left Arnold's body behind, Rooker drives off, free to continue murdering.

A stunning feature debut from director John McNaughton, HENRY tells its horrible story with chilling straightforwardness. Presenting his sick characters nonjudgmentally and without shrinking from gory details, McNaughton creates a world in which there is no good to counterbalance evil, where incest and rape are permitted and murder is an acceptable way to relieve tension. Providing no "good" characters to identify with—not even a cop to offer us hope—and ending on a bitter, ugly note, HENRY leaves viewers emotionally drained and deeply, deeply disturbed. Mainstream audiences are so used to faceless killers who get their comeuppance in the end (or are at least temporarily defeated) that HENRY may simply be too much for most to take. (The film's distributors rejected an X rating from the MPAA.) McNaughton succeeds in showing just how vulnerable anyone can be to someone like Henry, a frightening reality few will want to contemplate. HENRY forces one to think about such things, however.

In addition to its brave, raw screenplay by McNaughton and Richard Fire, HENRY benefits from some extraordinary performances. Michael Rooker is absolutely chilling as Henry, a deeply deranged character who—unlike the killers in most horror films—is a multifaceted man with a bizarre set of "morals."

Although never a sympathetic character, he is not an evil stereotype either, but ultimately both sick and sad. Tom Towles is brilliant in his role, making Otis a monster who is, at times, even more frightening than Henry (as when he gleefully snaps the neck of one woman and attempts to rape her corpse). There is not one false note in his terrifying performance.

HENRY even benefits from the constraints of its $120,000 budget, which lends the film a moody edge. McNaughton uses his Chicago locations impeccably, creating a dark, at times surrealistic atmosphere (some Chicagoans may want to move after seeing this picture). The film is well-paced and intelligently constructed: it begins quietly, then builds in perversity and intensity until it reaches its shattering climax.

No film in recent memory has tapped into primal, visceral fear like HENRY does, with its vision of a depraved world that seems at once too horrible to exist and too realistic to be denied. Hard to watch (though at times it's bizarrely and blackly funny) and definitely not for the squeamish, HENRY will prove unforgettable for the brave souls who do see it. A major achievement in independent filmmaking, HENRY: PORTRAIT OF A SERIAL KILLER is a horror masterpiece. *(Graphic violence, nudity, adult situations, profanity, sexual situations.)*

p, Lisa Dedmond and Steven A. Jones; d, John McNaughton; w, Richard Fire and John McNaughton; ph, Charlie Lieberman; ed, Elena Maganini; md, Robert McNaughton; art d, Rick Paul; spec eff, Jefferey Lyle Segal; makeup, Berndt Rantscheff.

Crime/Horror   (PR:O MPAA:NR)

HENRY V
(See THE YEAR'S BEST)

⊙HER ALIBI*
94m WB c

Tom Selleck *(Phil Blackwood)*, Paulina Porizkova *(Nina Ionescu)*, William Daniels *(Sam)*, James Farentino *(Frank Polito)*, Hurd Hatfield *(Troppa)*, Ronald Guttman *("Lucy" Comanescu)*, Victor Argo *(Avram)*, Patrick Wayne *(Gary Blackwood)*, Tess Harper *(Sally Blackwood)*, Joan Copeland *(Audrey)*, Bill Smitrovich *(Lt. Farrell)*, Bobo Lewis *(Rose)*, Jane Welch *(Millie)*, Austin Hay *(Oliver)*, W. Benson Terry *(FX)*, Liliana Komorowska *(Laura)*, Alan Mixon *(Nina's Father)*, Barbara Caruso *(Nina's Mother)*, Marlene Bryan *(Laurie)*, William Aylward *(Greg)*, Sara E. Pfaff *(Heather Blackwood)*, Trevor Soponis *(Tony Blackwood)*, David S. Chandler *(Eugene Mason)*, Bill Grimmett, Ted Sutton, Brian Costantini *(Cops)*, Norman Fitz *(Judge)*, Nat Benchley *(Prosecutor)*,

T.J. Edwards, John Badila *(Defenders)*, Leonard Auclair *(Jack the Author)*, Dick Harrington *(Henry the Neighbor)*, Corazon Adams *(Consuela)*, Lisa Nicholas *(Waitress)*, Hank deLuca *(Ian the Editor)*, Joann Havrilla *(Woman at Lecture)*, Pankaj Talwar *(Dr. Singh)*, Dick Rizzo *(Knife Clerk)*, Joseph Eubanks *(Cocktail Man)*.

In HER ALIBI, Selleck plays a best-selling author of pulp detective novels suffering from writer's block. Looking for inspiration, he goes to the courthouse, where a gorgeous, mysterious, Romanian defendant in a murder case, Porizkova, is brought out to be arraigned. Smitten, Selleck decides to continue his novel-in-progress with Porizkova as its center. As he delivers his mystery's tortured prose in voice-over, it's obvious that Selleck perceives himself as the novel's suave, debonair hero, Peter Swift, whose sophisticated actions and reactions provide what is meant to be a humorous counterpoint to the often bumbling author. In "real life," Selleck poses as a priest in order to visit Porizkova in jail, offering to give her an alibi. Naturally, she takes him up on the offer. Selleck gets his agent to back up their story, which posits a long-term affair between Porizkova and the writer (Selleck claims they were together at the time of the murder in question), and drives her out to his country home in Connecticut. All is not well, however; Farentino, the DA prosecuting Porizkova, doesn't believe Selleck's story, and the KGB is lurking about with an interest in making off with the mysterious Eastern European. Moreover, as Farentino reminds him, if Selleck dies, Porizkova's alibi would hold up forever, leaving Selleck to wonder (in a lax sort of way) whether the enigmatic beauty might be planning to murder *him*. Love, however, pushes these thoughts aside—even though, just after they make love for the first time, Porizkova conveniently decides to take a dip in the pool just when the house blows up. Selleck, who stood at the door to watch her, doesn't take the possibility of her wanting to kill him any more seriously than before, although later, during a dinner party at his brother's house, a dead cat and a missing Porizkova lead him to suspect that the food has been poisoned and set up a tediously directed trip to the emergency room, for what is supposed to be a humorous stomach-pumping. As it turns out, Porizkova's parents are trying to obtain political asylum, bringing everyone—including Selleck, his agent, the KGB, and Farentino—to the climactic scene at a clown convention, where Porizkova is to rendezvous with her circus acrobat folks. This gives the filmmakers an opportunity to present a pie-in-the-face fight that no one but the participants knows is real as a device to wind up the action, whereupon, not surprisingly, the Romanian beauty's name is cleared.

HER ALIBI veers with little purpose from bland drama to heavy-handed slapstick, with rhythm, characterization, and plotting better suited to television than the movies. Selleck's novelistic voice-over, meant to juxtapose humorously with developments in his writer character's actual predicament, requires both a finer touch from the actor and more skillful work from the director (who, surprisingly, is Bruce Beresford, helmer of BREAKER MORANT; TENDER MERCIES; and CRIMES OF THE HEART). Tom Selleck and supermodel Paulina Porizkova are certainly attractive, but the large screen exposes their reliance on poses and lackluster acting. The patriotic platitudes are heavy-handed and offensive. (When Selleck drives Porizkova to his Connecticut home, he uses the phone in his sports car en route, then remarks that she must not see phones in cars back home in Romania. She admits that they don't even have phones in their houses. Arriving at his home, they have another such exchange. Porizkova: "You must be rich." Selleck: "Not really—I do okay." Quite "okay," really, considering he has an apartment in the city, a country house with pool, a sports car, and a recreational truck.) Moreover, the holes in the plot are inexcusably large —the denouement, for example, takes place in the same house that supposedly was blown up a couple of days previously.

In HER ALIBI, Selleck is the only character who is not aware that his books are pedestrian, predictable potboilers. It would be nice if a similar innocence could be ascribed to the actors, director, and writers of the film. (*Adult situations, sexual situations, violence.*)

p, Keith Barish; d, Bruce Beresford; w, Charlie Peters; ph, Freddie Francis (Technicolor); ed, Anne Goursaud; m, Georges Delerue; prod d, Henry Bumstead; art d, Steve Walker; set d, James W. Payne; cos, Ann Roth; stunts, Ron Rondell; makeup, Marietta Carter.

Comedy/Mystery   (PR:C MPAA:PG)

●HIGH HOPES****
(Brit.) 110m Portman-Film
Four/Skouras c
Philip Davis (*Cyril Bender*), Ruth Sheen (*Shirley*), Edna Dore (*Mrs. Bender*), Philip Jackson (*Martin Burke*), Heather Tobias (*Valerie Burke*), Lesley Manville (*Laetitia Boothe-Braine*), David Bamber (*Rupert Boothe-Braine*), Jason Watkins (*Wayne*), Judith Scott (*Suzi*), Cheryl Prime (*Martin's Girl Friend*), Diane-Louise Jordan (*Chemist-shop Assistant*), Linda Beckett (*Receptionist*), Ali (*Baby*).

Some may bristle at the notion that Margaret Thatcher—and not Stephen Frears, Hugh Hudson, or Alex Cox—has had the greatest impact on British cinema in the last decade, but in dismantling the welfare state and remolding British society, the Prime Minister has provoked impassioned, inventive cinematic responses from a generation of morally outraged UK filmmakers. Mike Leigh's funny and deeply touching HIGH HOPES, another film with its sensibility undeniably grounded in the realities of Thatcher's Britain, is an important addition to this growing body of work. Employing an episodic structure and the semi-improvisational approach that he perfected working in theater and television, Leigh presents three couples and an elderly woman as a microcosm of modern-day Britain. Davis, a 35-year-old, bearded motorcycle messenger, and Sheen, his companion of 10 years, a green-thumbed laborer, live contentedly in a cramped council flat near London's Kings Cross. Children of the working class, they have embraced a countercultural lifestyle that has long included acceptance of revolutionary ideology, but recently their Marxism has had less to do with taking to the streets than with sitting on their duffs. Moreover, Sheen is growing increasingly aware of her biological clock and would like to have a baby, but though she and Davis are still affectionate lovers, he refuses to bring another child into the all-too-unjust world. They do, however, perform their share of parenting: first for Watkins, a thick-skulled provincial lad who comes to London looking for his sister and a job; and second for Davis' increasingly senile mother, Dore, who lives in the last council-owned house on her gentrified street. Her yuppie neighbors, the Booth-Braines (Manville and Bamber), manage to ignore her until she locks herself out and seeks their help. Then, reluctantly, they allow her into their home, though Manville is less than willing to let Dore use their bathroom. Summoned by Manville, Dore's shrill, nouveau riche daughter (Tobias) appears, using the opportunity to reconnoiter *chez* Booth-Braines, but forgetting the key to her mother's house. Eventually, Davis and Sheen arrive and get Dore back into her home, but not before confronting Bamber, who snootily observes that what *was* great about Britain was that "there was a place for everyone, and everyone knew his place." Later, Sheen and Davis attend a surprise birthday party for Dore at the impossibly garish suburban home of Tobias and her philandering used-car-salesman husband, Jackson. As Dore sinks deeper into melancholy confusion, her children and their mates row, clashing over conflicting values. That night, the befuddled Dore stays at Sheen and Davis' apartment, musing sadly over her past. In the spare room, after a tender discussion, Sheen and Davis decide to make contraceptiveless love. "What would you rather have . . . a boy or girl?" Sheen asks.

"I'd rather have a hot poker up my arse," replies Davis, though it's clear he's come around. The next morning they take Dore up on the roof of their building, from which Kings Cross, St. Paul's, and a gasworks are visible, prompting Dore to observe, "It's the top of the world"— unwittingly offering tribute to Jimmy Cagney in WHITE HEAT.

Alternately silly, serious, and poignant, HIGH HOPES—Leigh's second feature film, following his auspicious 1971 debut, BLEAK MOMENTS—uses its players as political symbols, without subordinating character to the demands of allegory . . . at least, almost. Admittedly, the Booth-Braines are little more than cartoons of upper-class twitism, cold-heartedly *yaah*ing their way through life and turning a blissful blind eye to Dore's pitiful existence. Likewise, Tobias' Valerie and Jackson's Martin are less well-rounded characters than representations of the misguided aspirations of those who have embraced Thatcher's entrepreneurial spirit and lifted themselves out of the working class, only to find hollow lives that will never be the equal of (or at least as tasteful as) those of their "betters." On the other hand, the characters writer-director Leigh is most concerned with—Davis' Cyril, Sheen's Shirley, and Dore's Mrs. Bender— are all naturally and complexly rendered. Because of the care Leigh takes to show these three lives, HIGH HOPES is not just an indictment of Thatcher-engendered inequity and unconcern, it is also a survival primer for those who have lost faith in the Left's traditional grand solutions yet refused to succumb to "compassion fatigue." Davis and Sheen, who make a pilgrimage to Marx's grave in Highgate Cemetery, may no longer believe in the inevitability of revolution, but they continue to live for humanity, offering comfort to the wayward and the infirm. And by the film's end, Davis, who earlier decried the family as obsolete, is not only committed to easing his mother's burden, but ready to start his own family. Like George Orwell's *Keep the Aspidistra Flying*, HIGH HOPES allows its protagonists to let go of their most obstinate rebelliousness without relinquishing the fundamental decency of their idealism.

It should not be forgotten, however, that this is also a very funny movie, offering several big laughs and lots of small ones. Though the cruelty of the Booth-Braines is undeniably repulsive, Lesley Manville and David Bamber's portrayal of the effete, self-satisfied yuppie couple is frequently hilarious, and never more funny than when they engage in their ridiculous "Mr. Sausage" verbal foreplay. Sex (or the lack thereof) between the couples is one of HIGH HOPES' leitmotifs, and the scene in which Heather Tobias' pathetic parvenu and her yobbish husband, played by Philip

Jackson, argue over who will make the first move ("You be Michael Douglas and I'll be a virgin") is one of the film's comedic highlights. Despite his brief screen time, Jason Watkins also provides some of HIGH HOPES' most amusing moments as the dim-witted provincial lad, making the most of a goofy walk and a look of unremitting incomprehension. Some nicely underplayed comedy is also incorporated into the intimate conversations between Philip Davis and Ruth Sheen, but it is the sincerity and vulnerability of these scenes that are most memorable and that give HIGH HOPES its power. The chemistry between Davis and Sheen is excellent and both turn in fine performances, but it is the buck-toothed Sheen whose work stands out. Although not conventionally pretty, she creates a character whose wondrous inner beauty lends her a beatific aura. Speaking volumes with her silence, Edna Dore also contributes a fine portrayal of the Tory-voting pensioner who has been left out in the cold.

After the fashion of John Cassavetes, Leigh rehearsed his actors for 15 weeks, and the film's final script grew out of these improvisations. Using an abundance of extreme closeups and gritty photography, the director and his cinematographer, Roger Pratt, lend HIGH HOPES a documentary-like immediacy perfectly suited to the emotional honesty at the film's core, and while little really happens in the film and it proceeds at a slow pace, the viewer's attention is always engaged. Ultimately, Leigh doesn't offer a very rosy picture of life under the Iron Lady, but, in small ways, he does provide his characters and audience with a measure of hope. Songs include: "Poor Man's Prison" (Henderson, Colley), "Lonely Street" (Blue, Fowder, Stevenson, performed by Gene Vincent), "Brown-eyed Handsome Man" (Chuck Berry, performed by Berry). *(Sexual situations, adult situations, profanity.)*

p, Simon Channing-Williams and Victor Glynn; d, Mike Leigh; w, Mike Leigh; ph, Roger Pratt (Eastmancolor); ed, Jon Gregory; m, Andrew Dixon; prod d, Diana Charnley; art d, Andrew Rothschild; cos, Lindy Hemming; makeup, Morag Ross.

Comedy/Drama   (PR:C MPAA:PG)

ⓥHIGH STAKES***
102m Vidmark c
Sally Kirkland *(Melanie "Bambi" Rose)*, Robert LuPone *(John Stratton)*, Richard Lynch *(Slim)*, Sarah Gellar *(Karen)*, Kathy Bates *(Jill)*, W.T. Martin *(Bob)*, Eddie Earl Hatch *(Earl)*, Betty Miller *(Mother)*, Maia Danziger *(Veronica)*.

HIGH STAKES is built on three well-worn plot devices: the whore with a heart of gold; Scrooge sees the light; and boy meets girl, boy loses girl, boy gets girl. Oddly enough, writer-producer-director Amos Kollek

makes the combination work reasonably well. Kirkland is a sexy, albeit aging, New York prostitute who is at the mercy of Lynch, a vicious racketeer pimp. A victim who frequently "gets thrown out of cars without her clothes on," Kirkland is too tired and not quite bright enough to get her life in order. On Wall Street, where "only a real scumbag makes it to the top," bachelor LuPone prospers. Like WALL STREET's Gordon Gekko, he risks millions on a falling market with nary a white knuckle. When his partner becomes depressed over his wife's infidelity and kills himself, LuPone eschews his limo, wanders Times Square, and is promptly mugged outside Kirkland's ratty apartment building. She offers to call the police, but LuPone asks only for some water and a chance to clean up. Reluctantly, Kirkland takes him upstairs and soon spills her tale of woe. Widowed by a car accident that she barely survived, Kirkland is the single mother of an 8-year-old who lives with the hooker's mother. Though Lynch "helps" her, Kirkland is barely able to support herself. Just as she and LuPone are about to kiss, one of Lynch's henchmen enters and brutally beats both of them. However, the spunky Kirkland manages to relieve the thug of his gun and $4,000. The game now becomes getting the kid and leaving town before, well, you know. To return Kirkland's favor, LuPone goes to the suburbs to help her collect her daughter, but the bad guys get there first. At Lynch's hellish hangout, Kirkland almost gets gang raped and LuPone, whose compulsive gambling comes to the fore, becomes involved in a game of Russian Roulette. Playing for the stolen money and the child's freedom, he braves three pulls of the trigger and survives. Nonetheless, he and Kirkland have to fight their way out. They drive to a beach in Brooklyn, but are followed by Lynch and one of his henchmen. LuPone puts a bullet through Lynch's thug, but takes a serious wound himself. The pimp then aims a shotgun at the couple, but decides to walk away. (Is he really in love with the blowzy blonde?) Kirkland takes LuPone to an underworld hospital and uses their hard-earned cash to pay for his treatment. "You're the only man who ever stood up for me," she says. Gratefully, he rewards her with a check for $100,000 that she reluctantly accepts. Kirkland takes a job as a waitress and finds a decent apartment to share with her daughter, and LuPone gets back to the business of making money, but neither is very happy. They both care for each other, but when one is ready to make a move, the other isn't. Ultimately, however, they overcome the differences in their lifestyles, and get together on the sidewalk outside LuPone's office, where Kirkland almost tears his clothes off as she delivers the big punch line: "Everybody gets screwed on Wall Street."

If you can accept some small lapses in credibility, this is not a bad film, particularly if you're a fan of the kind of sentimental plot turns one finds in films like STELLA DALLAS. Somehow Kollek makes the whole affair not only acceptable but engaging. He also generates plenty of tension and elicits profound concern for his characters. Sally Kirkland's portrayal of a woman who can hot-wire cars but can't resist exploitative men is touching and believable, though at times she becomes a bit too kittenish. About five years too young to be an appropriate love match for Kirkland and a bit callow for the role of a financial wizard, Robert LuPone nevertheless acquits himself well as the profit-hungry heavy hitter who discovers that there is more to life than outwitting the ticker tape. As the silver-haired pimp, Richard Lynch is chilling, kinky, and intriguingly vicious. His splendid performance is less about what he shows than what he doesn't show—Jack Nicholson's forte. Despite its lack of big names, this low-budget production is worth viewing. *(Graphic violence, sexual situations, adult situations.)*

p, Amos Kollek; d, Amos Kollek; w, Amos Kollek; ph, Marc Hirschfeld; ed, Robert Reitano; m, Mira J. Spektor; prod d, Joan Herder.

Thriller/Romance   (PR:O MPAA:R)

ⓥHOMEBOY**
116m J&M/FOX c
Mickey Rourke *(Johnny Walker)*, Christopher Walken *(Wesley Pendergrass)*, Debra Feuer *(Ruby)*, Thomas Quinn *(Lou)*, Kevin Conway *(Grazziano)*, Antony Alda *(Ray)*, Jon Polito *(Moe Fingers)*, Bill Slayton *(Bill)*, David Taylor *(Cannonball)*, Joseph Ragno *(Cotten's Trainer)*, Matthew Lewis *(Cotten)*, Willy Deville *(Moe's Bodyguard)*, Ruben Blades *(Doctor)*, Sam Gray *(Barber)*, Dondre Whitfield, Teddy Abner, Anthony Means *(Street Toughs)*, Jimmy Dupree *(Hurricane)*, Michael Buffer *(Ring Announcer)*, Marty Denkin, Larry Hazzard Sr. *(Referees)*, Morty Storm *(MC)*, Gianna Rains *(Phyllis)*, Jeanne Daly *(Melanie)*, Jonathan Freeman *(Hotel Room Man)*, Liz Trepel *(Hotel Room Woman)*, Gloria Irizarry *(Hotel Maid)*, Jack Lotz, Jimmy Archer, Al Braverman *(Coffee Shop Customers)*, Stu Black *(Commentator)*, Sheila Gray *(Luna Park Assistant)*, Sol Frieder *(Hassidic Diamond Dealer)*, Lenny Mancini, Charles Prior *(Cornermen)*, Jose Morales *(Cuban Boxer)*, Cordelia Gonzalez *(Cuban Boxer's Wife)*, Gavin J. O'Conner *(Rookie Cop)*, Nick Ballo, Stephen Baldwin *(Luna Park Drunks)*, Lydia Hannibal *(Cameo Bar Woman)*, Patience Moore *(Moe's Girlfriend)*, Julie Janney *(Waitress)*, Iran Barkley *(Roscoe)*, Carmen Grazziano *(Roscoe's Trainer)*, Nicholas De Cegli *(Pimp)*, Thomas Patti

(Franzatti), Angel Sindo, Buster Drayton *(Sparring Partners)*, Van Holmes, James Walsh *(Fighters)*, Guido Innacelli *(Fat Heckler)*, Lenny LaPaglia *(Fight Second)*, Michael Sessa *(Crowd Bigmouth)*.

Just as HOMEBOY is nothing more than a hodgepodge of cliches, its central character, played by Rourke, is a composite of nearly all the down-and-out, golden-hearted pugs ever put on screen. The film's awkwardly patched together opening establishes Rourke as an innocent abroad, a simple cowboy cum club boxer adrift in the alien demimonde of the burnt-out seaside Jersey town (Asbury Park) where he has been invited to fight by promoter Polito. Hobbled with a limp that seems left over from BARFLY, Rourke enters a bar, runs the suspicious gauntlet of its all-African-American clientele, casually orders a whiskey, and is soon dancing atop the bar with another patron, bottle in hand. After this prefight regimen, Rourke sits in the locker room "preparing" for his bout. In saunters flamboyant hustler and ex-con Walken, who announces his "interest" in fighters and the "fight game," then makes an exit equal in flash to his entrance. One of the more uninspiringly choreographed and performed boxing sequences in recent memory follows, with Rourke dully plodding about the ring and pawing his opponent. In between the lackluster rounds, he peers out over the crowd—which we view through his punch-drunk perspective, in which faces are blurred and noises drone lethargically like a record played too slow. Finally, however, he manages to knock out his opponent (who almost literally walks into one of his punches). Afterwards, Walken whisks Rourke off to the club and performs a blithely inept singing act. A few minutes of this is all Rourke can take, so he picks up his weathered cowboy hat and roams the desolate streets, winding up at a run-down beachside arcade and coming to the rescue of its comely proprietress, Feuer, when she is set upon by some roughhousing teens. So begins the inevitable relationship between the uncommunicative -but-surprisingly-sensitive pug and the lonely-woman-with-a-troubled-past who gradually discovers the caring soul lurking beneath his coarse exterior. Each time Rourke returns to Feuer's arcade after one of his local bouts, the film draws a parallel between their psychological states (alienated) and between their limited existences (as he struggles through round after round, she attempts to restore a broken-down carousel). More alike than they seem, the two manage to revive each other's deadened spirits. Meanwhile, Walken wins Rourke's confidence and makes him an unwitting lookout during a jewelry heist. He also takes Rourke (at Rourke's request) to a doctor for an exam, but though the physician tells Walken in confidence that Rourke may be only a couple of blows away

from fatal injury, Walken doesn't pass this information on to Rourke, since he needs the fighter's fists to carry out a new scheme. Rourke is then lined up for a big fight offering a substantial purse and, with the help of trainer Quinn and for the first time in his mediocre career, devotes himself to preparing seriously for the bout. While Rourke undergoes his new regimen, Walken tells him of his plan to rob a heavily guarded jewelry store. Rourke pledges his support, but when the day of the heist is moved up to coincide with the date of his big fight, Rourke wavers, inspiring Walken finally to inform Rourke of the risks he takes in stepping into the ring. Nonetheless, when the day arrives, Rourke opts for the ring and is battered from pillar to post while Walken carries out the robbery with his sidekick, Alda. Emerging from the store with a bag of diamonds in hand, Walken discovers he's been betrayed to the police by Alda. Meanwhile, Rourke continues to take a pounding. Just as Walken is gunned down at the beach, Rourke crumbles to his knees, his face a bloody mess, a weird, sad smile lingering on his lips. In the last sequence, Feuer sits in the rain at the cusp of the restored, illuminated carousel. In a wholly arbitrary, symbol-laden ending, the camera pulls back and, using an overhead crane shot, reveals a resurrected Rourke, framed in the carousel's glow.

It's no wonder Mickey Rourke—charging he was neither paid nor given the creative approval rights he contracted for—sued to stop the release of HOMEBOY, for which he is credited with writing the original story. The film is a dismal, pretentious melange of boxing-film cliches, its only flashes of originality provided by Christopher Walken's parodying antics as the vain, posturing Wesley. However, in choosing to highlight the comic aspects of his sociopath, Walken undermines the sense of danger his character is meant to provide as the story unfolds. Rourke, playing another in his line of laconic, self-absorbed antiheroes, curiously endows his boxer with a hunched, tortuous gait that comes closer to suggesting the torments of Quasimodo than the bearing of a martyred club fighter, and tends to slip in and out of his southern-accented mumble. (The cast also features cameos by real-life boxer Buster Drayton, singer Willy DeVille, and salsa star Ruben Blades.) Like a boxer fighting out of his weight class, HOMEBOY is also encumbered with heavy-handed, clanging "artistic" touches that attempt to elevate its dreary, familiar story into something vastly more significant. The result is a ponderous, pointless film, as pitiful as a battle between two over-the-hill and flabby heavyweights. *(Violence, adult situations.)*

p, Alan Marshall and Elliott Kastner; d, Michael Seresin; w, Eddie Cook (based on a story by Mickey Rourke); ph, Gail Tattersall (Technicolor); ed, Ray Lovejoy; m,

Eric Clapton and Michael Kamen; prod d, Brian Morris; art d, Wynn Thomas; set d, Ted Glass; spec eff, Russell Berg; cos, Richard Shissler; stunts, Webster Whinery; makeup, Ken Diaz.

Sports   **(PR:C MPAA:R)**

⊙HONEY, I SHRUNK THE KIDS***
86m Walt Disney/BV c
Rick Moranis *(Wayne Szalinski)*, Matt Frewer *(Big Russ Thompson)*, Marcia Strassman *(Diane Szalinski)*, Kristine Sutherland *(Mae Thompson)*, Thomas Brown *(Little Russ Thompson)*, Jared Rushton *(Ron Thompson)*, Amy O'Neill *(Amy Szalinski)*, Robert Oliveri *(Nick Szalinski)*, Carl Steven *(Tommy Pervis)*, Mark L. Taylor *(Don Forrester)*, Lou Cutell *(Dr. Brainard)*, Laura Waterbury *(Female Cop)*, Trevor Galtress *(Male Cop)*, Martin Aylett *(Harold Boorstein)*, Janet Sunderland *(Lauren Boorstein)*, Kimmy Robertson *(Gloria Forrester)*.

The most pleasant surprise of the megahit summer of '89 was HONEY, I SHRUNK THE KIDS, which successfully evokes earlier Disney live-action classics like THE ABSENT-MINDED PROFESSOR (1961) and SON OF FLUBBER (1963). Set in a quiet southern Californian suburb (although the film was shot entirely at Churubusco Studios in Mexico City), the film introduces us to Prof. Wayne Szalinski (Moranis), a nutty inventor who is trying to build a machine that will shrink living things. Since Moranis spends all his time in the attic tinkering with his machine, it is up to his wife (Strassman) to run the household, as well as to bring home the brunt of the income as a real estate agent. With their dad's eccentricities the talk of the neighborhood, teenager O'Neill and her bespectacled little brother (Oliveri) find themselves having to deal with stares, gossip, and scorn—especially from their next-door neighbor, macho-man Big Russ Thompson (Frewer). Thinking himself a man's man, Frewer openly mocks the intellectual Moranis and there is not much neighborliness between the families, although Frewer's wife (Sutherland) is sympathetic and teenage son "Little" Russ (Brown) is attracted to O'Neill. While Strassman is at work and Moranis is at a science conference trying to generate interest in his still-imperfect machine (it tends to blow up objects it's supposed to shrink), Brown's younger brother (Rushton), accidentally hits a baseball into Moranis' attic window. It hits the shrinking machine and lodges in the mechanism, causing the machine to come to life and actually *work* (something to do with the laser beam's shooting through the baseball). When Brown forces his little brother to go next door and confess, all four kids go upstairs to fetch the ball, are hit by the laser, and shrunk to a quarter-inch size. To make

Marcia Strassman and Rick Moranis in HONEY I SHRUNK THE KIDS (©Walt Disney).

matters worse, Moranis returns home and, seeing the shattered glass on the attic floor, sweeps up the shards *and* the kids. Unaware of what he has done, Moranis places the bag of garbage in the alley. The kids manage to escape before the garbageman comes, but they must make a long and difficult trek through the backyard—which looks like a jungle to them—in order to get back to the porch, where they might be seen and rescued. Like Lewis and Clark, the kids make their way through the wilderness of seemingly huge blades of grass. At one point, Oliveri is attacked by a bee and when Brown tries to rescue him, both end up taking a wild ride through the neighborhood on the creature's back (later, the kids befriend a baby ant that eventually defends them against a dangerous scorpion). Meanwhile, Moranis has realized what happened to the kids and has set up a trapeze-like device enabling him to hover over his backyard and peer into the grass with a magnifying glass. He is later assisted by Strassman, and Frewer, who is himself trying to find his missing kids, thinks they're both crazy. Sensing Frewer and Sutherland's anguish over their missing sons, Moranis finally tells them that the machine he invented shrunk their children, though an incredulous Frewer refuses to believe the nutty inventor. Eventually the kids make it to the porch and are rescued by the family dog. Walking across the dog's nose, the kids jump onto the kitchen table, where Moranis is eating a bowl of cereal. Because they are so small,

however, the kids fail to get Moranis' attention until Oliveri is knocked into his father's breakfast and manages to scream loud enough for Moranis to hear—just before eating a spoonful of cereal containing his son. With Frewer and Sutherland present, Moranis reverses the process and returns the kids to normal size.

A nice blend of thrills, character, and humor—enough of each to keep both children and adults charmed and engaged throughout—HONEY, I SHRUNK THE KIDS came as a complete surprise to industry insiders who thought that the film would get blown away by BATMAN, which opened on the same day. Amazingly, HONEY, I SHRUNK THE KIDS came in second for the weekend, beating such established blockbusters as INDIANA JONES AND THE LAST CRUSADE and GHOSTBUSTERS II. Blessed with a great title and an enticing trailer and television commercial, the film drew those unable to get in to see BATMAN and the family audience looking for something lighter than the brooding Caped Crusader or the violent Indiana Jones. Based on a story by Stuart Gordon (RE-ANIMATOR), Brian Yuzna, and Ed Naha, HONEY, I SHRUNK THE KIDS was to have been directed by Gordon (an odd occurrence, considering Gordon's previous work in ultra-gory horror films), but, after conflicts with the studio, Gordon left the project and was replaced by special-effects man Joe Johnston, making his directorial debut. Although the last-minute changes

seemed to spell doom for the project (special-effects men do not good directors make—see THE FLY II), Johnston acquitted himself admirably and turned in a wholly enjoyable film.

Recalling Disney's past in more than just concept, HONEY, I SHRUNK THE KIDS espouses values of decency between its action sequences, showing characters who dislike and mistrust each other overcoming their differences to pull together in a time of crisis and reach a new understanding. The characters—both children and parents—are forced to confront their preconceptions and prejudices and come to the realization that, deep down, they're all good people despite their individual eccentricities and foibles. Surprisingly, children's films illustrating such simple lessons seem to have become scarce in recent years, modern youth-oriented films having become much more cynical than in the past. Children in the 1980s have consistently been shown to be infinitely smarter and more clever than the screwed-up adults: it's up to the kids either to take charge (last year's THE RESCUE) or actually to *fix* their parents so that they are more to their liking (as in BACK TO THE FUTURE). While some may find the "message" of HONEY, I SHRUNK THE KIDS cliched and corny, at least it's *positive*, encouraging dialog and understanding.

Messages aside, the film is also a rollicking good adventure, with enough bravura effects sequences to keep the most hyperactive youngster interested. From the scene in which the kids try to outrun a broom, through the battle with the scorpion, to the desperate swim among the Cheerios, HONEY, I SHRUNK THE KIDS is consistently exciting, inventive, and fun. Filmed on a relatively low budget, some of the special effects are a bit spotty, but the movie's lack of ultraslickness is charming and endearing in the same way that low-budget science-fiction films of the 1950s are. The performances director Johnston elicits from his small cast are fine, with every character—even Frewer's hard-nosed neighbor—coming across as multidimensional and likable.

Fittingly, Buena Vista's best release since WHO FRAMED ROGER RABBIT was coupled with a brand new Roger Rabbit cartoon short. Entitled TUMMY TROUBLE, this "Maroon Cartoon"—the first animated short produced by the Disney studio in over 25 years—continues the Tex Avery-inspired zaniness established in the opening of WHO FRAMED ROGER RABBIT. While strictly traditional cell animation throughout the vast majority of its seven and one-half minutes of running time, the incredible combination of animation and live action that marked WHO FRAMED ROGER RABBIT is reprised in TUMMY TROUBLE's hilarious coda.

The clever one-two punch of TUMMY TROUBLE and HONEY, I SHRUNK THE KIDS on the same bill not only drew surprisingly sizable audiences, but also provided one of the most enjoyable family outings of the summer.

p, Penney Finkelman Cox, Brian Yuzna, and Jon Landau; d, Joe Johnston; w, Ed Naha and Tom Schulman (based on a story by Stuart Gordon, Brian Yuzna, Ed Naha); ph, Hiro Narita (Metrocolor); ed, Michael A. Stevenson; m, James Horner; prod d, Gregg Fonseca; art d, John Iacovelli and Dorree Cooper; spec eff, Frank Welker; cos, Carol Brolaski; stunts, Mike Cassidy; makeup, Del Armstrong.

Children's/Science Fiction
                                                                         (PR:A   MPAA:PG)

ⓥHORROR SHOW, THE*
94m UA/MGM-UA c
Lance Henriksen *(Lucas McCarthy)*, Brion James *(Max Jenke)*, Rita Taggart *(Donna McCarthy)*, Deedee Pfeiffer *(Bonnie McCarthy)*, Aron Eisenberg *(Scott McCarthy)*, Thom Bray *(Peter Campbell)*, Matt Clark *(Dr. Tower)*, David Oliver *(Vinnie)*, Lewis Arquette *(Lt. Miller)*, Terry Alexander *(Casey)*, Lawrence Tierney, Alvy Moore.

Having captured one of the most heinous mass murderers in the history of mankind (James), a veteran police detective, Henriksen, finds himself suffering from post-psycho-killer stress syndrome at the beginning of THE HORROR SHOW. Forced to take a leave of absence from his job because of his terrible nightmares and hallucinations relating to James and his crimes, Henriksen sees a psychiatrist (Clark) regularly and eagerly awaits the day of James' execution, which he believes will cure him of his nightmares. When the big day arrives, the detective gets himself a front-row seat at the execution and is not intimidated when the killer spots him— not too difficult, considering the 30 or so spectators are seated in folding chairs five feet away from the electric chair, with no barrier between them and the prisoner. Snarling and cackling, James threatens to come back from the dead and kill Henriksen's entire family. After the killer is strapped into the electric chair, a priest gives him communion, only to have the masticated Host spit back at him (this guy is *bad*). The executioner throws the switch and the killer slumps over, apparently dead; however, when the doctor walks up to check for vital signs, James' eyes snap open and he begins yowling. The executioner reapplies the juice, but James seems to thrive on it, breaking his bonds and stumbling forward. As the horrified spectators run for the exits, the executioner turns up the voltage at the warden's command. Skin blistering and bursting, clothes aflame, the killer attacks a few guards but

finally falls face-down on the floor—this time dead for sure. In the morgue, Bray, a nerdy-looking professor, checks the body for signs of electricity. Suddenly a small electrical storm crackles around the body and the evil spirit of James zooms out of the room with a high-pitched laugh, heading straight for Henriksen's house and taking up residence in the basement furnace. From there the evil James begins to torment Henriksen, causing hallucinations so terrible that his family begins to think him insane. Compelled to learn more about the killer, Henriksen goes to James' seedy apartment and finds Bray, who points out a home-made electric chair and tells him that James actually practiced being electrocuted, so that he could turn his pure evil into electromagnetic energy (giving new meaning to the term "mean-spirited"). To kill the killer once and for all, he must be reelectrocuted—which will turn him back to human form—and then shot. Meanwhile, James kills Henriksen's daughter's boy friend, framing Henriksen for the crime. Henriksen is interrogated by Internal Affairs; at the same time, his family is terrorized by the psycho killer's spirit. Breaking out of jail, Henriksen rushes home to find his boy dead, his daughter raped and instantly nine months pregnant (with the adult-sized face of James pushing against her belly to get out), and his wife missing; next, he traces the killer back to the power plant where he was initially captured and tries to rescue his wife. Baiting James to attack him with his trademark cleaver, Henriksen steps aside in a manner that causes the killer to sever an electrical cord. With juice surging through his body, Henriksen pins James against the current with a wooden beam, instructing his brave wife to press the other end of the severed cable against James' body. As the electricity reaches its peak, James and Henriksen are magically catapulted back to James' seedy apartment, where Henriksen grabs his pistol and unloads a whole clip of bullets into the killer, who is now flesh and blood. With James really, finally dead this time, Henriksen and family sell their house and move away.

With a ruthless, seemingly indestructible villain who delights in murderous mayhem, able to invade his victims' consciousness and cause terrible hallucinations, THE HORROR SHOW obviously intends to create yet another Freddy (A NIGHTMARE ON ELM STREET) Krueger-inspired horror movie character. Unfortunately, this movie is indeed a horror show—for the wrong reasons. Blessed with an impressive cast of veteran character actors, THE HORROR SHOW attempts to scare the wits out of its viewers with a barrage of bizarre and violent shocks, but the script (partially credited to "Alan Smithee," the perennial Hollywood pseudonym for writers and directors who

want their names taken off the project) is so absurd and the direction so disjointed that this exercise in horror winds up as simply horrible, and often laughable. Some of this failure can be attributed to the picture's turbulent production, including the dismissal of the film's first director, Australian David Blythe (DEATH WARMED UP) in midshoot. Reportedly, Blythe was kept on long enough to handle the dialog scenes and then fired, making way for special-effects man James Isaac to be brought in to direct the effects scenes. While any movie that suffers a director switch so late in the game is bound to be disjointed, yet another monkey wrench was thrown into the works when the MPAA forced the filmmakers to trim much of the gore—as a result of which some scenes have a terribly perfunctory and abrupt feel. These setbacks, combined with a script that might have been written by a 13-year-old boy—with its ludicrous premise (the electromagnetic evil mumbo-jumbo is silly even for a horror movie), an incongruous subplot (Henriksen's son writes to food companies, complaining that their products are contaminated, in order to get free supplies of the stuff), and some of the worst dialog of the year—make THE HORROR SHOW very nearly intolerable viewing. Loaded with cliched "suspense" scenes, the very first being the long and pointless sequence in which Henriksen creeps around his own home in the dead of night to investigate a noise that turns out to have been made by the family cat, the film is mostly dull, when it's not unintentionally funny. (A huge framed photo of Freud hangs prominently in the office of the psychiatrist; Henriksen's wife cooks an entire turkey, with all the trimmings, for *lunch*.) The only thing going for it is the fine cast, whose efforts are largely wasted due to the cripplingly bad dialog, although veteran character actor Brion James (SOUTHERN COMFORT; BLADE RUNNER) is allowed to have a really good time as the maniacal meat-cleaver-wielding killer. Unfortunately, as a whole THE HORROR SHOW is too disjointed and stupid to be much fun. *(Violence, gore effects, nudity, excessive profanity, sexual situations.)*

p, Sean S. Cunningham; d, James Isaac; w, Allyn Warner and Leslie Bohem; ph, Mac Ahlberg (Metrocolor); ed, Edward Anton; m, Harry Manfredini; spec eff, Peter Kuran; stunts, Kane Hodder.

Horror   **(PR:O   MPAA:R)**

ⓥHOW I GOT INTO COLLEGE**
87m FOX c
Anthony Edwards *(Kip Hammet)*, Corey Parker *(Marlon Browne)*, Lara Flynn Boyle *(Jessica Kailo)*, Finn Carter *(Nina Saatchi)*, Charles Rocket *(Leo Whitman)*, Christopher Rydell *(Oliver)*, Gary Owens *(Sports Announcer)*, Brian Doyle-Murray

Lara Flynn Boyle in HOW I GOT INTO COLLEGE (©20th Century Fox).

(Coach), Tichina Arnold *(Vera Cook)*, Bill Raymond *(Flutter)*, Philip Baker Hall *(Dean Patterson)*, Nicolas Coster *(Jellinek, Sr.)*, Nicole Mercurio *(Betty Kailo)*, Robert Ridgely *(George Kailo)*, Richard Jenkins *(Bill Browne)*, Bill Henderson *(High-School Coach)*, Helen Lloyd Breed *(Chancellor Holbrooke)*, Nora Dunn *(Bauer)*, Phil Hartman *(Benedek)*, Bob Eubanks *(Himself)*, Susan Krebs *(Mrs. Wyler)*, O-Lan Jones *(Sally)*, Maya Lebenzon *(Amy)*, Annie Oringer *(Kelly)*, Queen Kong *(Female Wrestler)*, Diane Franklin *(Sharon Browne)*, Bruce Wagner *("A")*, Tom Kenny *("B")*, Taylor Negron *(Mailman)*, Fran Bennett *(Mrs. Cook)*, Duane Davis *(Ronny Paulson)*, Adam Silbar *(Jellinek, Jr.)*, Marlene Warfield *(Librarian)*, Edward Mehler *(Anxious Boy)*, Daniel William Carter, Marisa DeSimone, Greg Binkley *(Eggheads)*, Lawrence C. Spinak *(Startled Boy)*, Willie Smith *(Willie)*, Phill Lewis *(Earnest Boy)*, Stella E. Hall *(Woman with Lasso)*, Morris Wilkes Jr. *(Smart Aleck)*, Leon Fan *(Asian Student)*, Emily Munson, Sara Munson *(Twins)*, Richard S. Horvitz *(Young Enterpriser)*, Vernetta R. Jenkins *(Cassandra)*, James McIntire *(Army Recruiter)*, Jim Painter *(Lonestar State Recruiter)*, Tara Vessels *(Waitress)*, Ashleigh Harris, Juliet Sorcey *(Kiddie Korral Girls)*, Davyd McCoy *(McDonald's Employee)*, Hope Marie Carlton, Rebecca Ferratti, Lisa Fuller *(Game Show Hostesses)*, Dale E. House *(Helicopter Pilot)*.

HOW I GOT INTO COLLEGE is a film with a good idea; sadly, it also is a film that doesn't make the most of its good idea. After reading a series of *New York Times* articles about the admissions system at Wesleyan College, Scott Rudin, formerly president of production for 20th Century

Fox (which released this film), hit upon making a movie about the difficulties encountered by young people struggling to maintain high grade-point averages in order to get into the college of their choice. He then presented this concept to Terrel Seltzer, who wrote the screenplay for HOW I GOT INTO COLLEGE. Directed with self-assurance (though without much originality) by 29-year-old Savage Steve Holland, the film offers a talented cast of young players—notably, Corey Parker, Lara Flynn Boyle, Anthony Edwards, and Finn Carter—but not much else. Where it should be hilarious, it tends to be just plain silly. The characters remain underdeveloped and the plot, while straightforward, lacks focus. Moreover, the picture is wholly without subtlety. While the film's premise offers Holland ample opportunity to be funny, original, and offbeat, he fails to make the most of his material, and the result is another often (though not always) dumb, low-budget teen comedy. This is a pity, for if HOW I GOT INTO COLLEGE had been fashioned along the lines of, say, PAPER CHASE, or presented as a youth-oriented variation of HOW TO SUCCEED IN BUSINESS WITHOUT REALLY TRYING, it might have been delightful entertainment. As is, the picture is an easily forgettable B movie shaped in an all-too-familiar mold.

The plot is simple. Parker plays a young man with very low grades who nevertheless yearns to attend elite Ramsey College. Unfortunately for Parker, Rocket, the head of the institution's admissions committee, is determined to limit admission to individuals with a grade-point average of 3.5 or better. Equally desperate to attend Ramsey is Boyle, the attractive, popular president of their Michigan high school's student government. Although she has everything going for her, Boyle also finds the competition for entrance to Ramsey's hallowed halls super-stiff. Parker has had little luck gaining Boyle's attention in the past, but a bond grows between them as they both struggle to make the grade. Luckily, Parker has an imaginative streak, *and* a lot of ready cash. With the help of an agency whose business it is to help (for an exorbitant fee) aspiring college students enter the institution of their choice, Parker "markets" himself with a videotape of his fiery juggling act. Two members of the admissions committee (Edwards and Carter) are impressed by Parker's performance video, but it makes no impression on Rocket. He remains determined to keep Ramsey dunce-free. The situation looks bleak for both Parker and Boyle, but this is a very predictable movie, and, thanks in part to a baby elephant with a high IQ, our heroes' dreams come true.

Despite its oversimplified plot and thin characterizations, HOW I GOT INTO COLLEGE does have a certain charm—in

large part because the film is well cast and all its leading players are attractive and very watchable. The core problem is that the actors aren't given enough solid material with which to work: no clever lines, no out-and-out funny situations, and, most important, no developed characters in which to sink their creative teeth. In short, this film has the right idea and the right players but the wrong screenplay and the wrong director. The MPAA's PG-13 rating is strictly for language; without the "naughty" words, HOW I GOT INTO COLLEGE could easily be a G-rated picture.

Songs include: "Young" (Joseph Vitarelli, Jason Scheff, Edgy Lee, Savage Steve Holland, performed by Scheff), "Get Ready" (William Robinson, performed by Rare Earth), "Words of a Freestyle" (Shawn Moltke, Marlon Williams, performed by M.C. Shan), "What I Like About You" (Jimmy Marinos, Wally Palmar, Mike Skill, performed by Michael Morales), "Tobacco Road" (John D. Loudermilk, performed by David Lee Roth), "In the Name of Love" (Steve Dorff, Philip Allen Brown), "Love Like We Do" (Edie Brickell, performed by Edie Brickell and New Bohemians), "Love Changes Everything" (Simon Climie, Rob Fisher, Jennis Morgan, performed by Climie Fisher), "Hail to the Matadors" (Richard S. Kaufman). *(Profanity.)*

p, Michael Shamberg and Elizabeth Cantillon; d, Savage Steve Holland; w, Terrel Seltzer; ph, Robert Elswit (Deluxe Color); ed, Sonya Sones Tramer and Kaja Fehr; m, Joseph Vitarelli; prod d, Ida Random; art d, Richard Reynolds; set d, Kathe Klopp; spec eff, Louis Cooper; cos, Taryn DeChellis; makeup, Ken Chase.

Comedy   (PR:C MPAA:PG-13)

⊽HOW TO GET AHEAD IN ADVERTISING**
(Brit.) 95m Handmade/WB c
Richard E. Grant *(Dennis Bagley)*, Rachel Ward *(Julia Bagley)*, Richard Wilson *(Bristol)*, Jacqueline Tong *(Penny Wheelstock)*, John Shrapnel *(Psychiatrist)*, Susan Wooldridge *(Monica)*, Mick Ford *(Richard)*, Jacqueline Pearce *(Maud)*, Roddy Maude-Roxby *(Dr. Gatty)*, Pauline Melville *(Mrs. Wallace)*, Rachel Fielding *(Jennifer)*, Tony Slattery *(Basil)*, Pip Torrens *(Jonathan)*, Donald Hoath, John Levitt *(Businessmen)*, Gordon Gostelow *(Priest)*, Sean Bean *(Larry Frisk)*, Hugh Armstrong *(Harry Wax)*, Francesca Longrigg *(Nurse)*, Tanveer Ghani *(Hospital Doctor)*, Joanna Mays *(Phillis Blokey)*, Vivienne McKone *(Receptionist)*, Victor Lucas *(Tweedy Man)*, Dawn Keeler *(Tweedy Woman)*, Kerryann White *(Girl in Elevator)*, Christopher Simon, Gino Melvazzi *(Waiters)*.

More satire than comedy, and aimed at a sophisticated audience that can appreciate its barbs at the pragmatic world of advertising, HOW TO GET AHEAD IN ADVERTISING is a movie of extremes, both in plot and characterizations. The protagonist is Dennis Bagley (Grant), a veteran advertising executive who has all the perks of success: attractive wife (Ward), country home, expensive car, and a stable of purebred horses. What Grant doesn't have is peace of mind. The ad agency he works for is about to launch a campaign for a new pimple cream, and creative input is needed to sell the product. Grant, however, is suffering from inspirational block. The creator of countless advisory antidotes to bad breath, underarm odor, and multiple other social horrors, he's in a fallow mode. Dispirited and cynical, he informs his boss (Wilson) that he is quitting to embark on an *anti-advertising* campaign. Soon thereafter, Grant becomes acutely aware of a boil on the side of his neck, and becomes obsessed with it as it continues to grow. Eventually, the pustule assumes a mocking personality that dominates its victim's mind and body—and becomes a metaphor for advertising. As the boil assumes a human visage, complete with pencil-thin mustache, Grant develops a physical and mental fixation. He rants, he raves, and Ward puts up with his whims and tantrums, realizing her husband is under diabolical pressure. Suddenly, however, Grant experiences a sudden change of heart and direction, and the erstwhile anti-advertising champion turns into a proponent of the pristine business-as-usual adman in action. He has a purple pimple cream to sell, and he's gung ho about reaching the masses with his magic elixir.

There is a moral question to be resolved here. Which is the real Dennis Bagley—the advocate of free trade advertising and its exploitation of the naively hopeful, or the anti-advertising knight in shining armor whose slogan is *caveat emptor*? It is pushing the limits of suspension of disbelief to accept the character's sudden conversion to the cause of honesty in advertising because he cannot dream up a campaign to sell a client's pimple cream. He's a man whose creative flair has brought him the good things in life, and who has no reason to turn his back on a career that has brought him all the symbols of success, and there is no *peripeteia*—no moment of truth—in the screenplay that would account for his turnabout.

Bruce Robinson, who wrote the screenplay and directed, gives Grant (costar of Robinson's 1987 film WITHNAIL AND I) a loose hand in interpreting his eccentric character. The actor pushes Dennis Bagley to his outer limits—storming, bashing, and soapbox crusading at every opportunity. He makes life miserable for himself and for everyone unfortunate enough to be within earshot. Some subtlety or quiet introspection might have lent a measure of credibility to the role. Rachel Ward doesn't have much to do except react to Grant's tantrums as the bedeviled husband, a predicament shared by rest of the cast. George Kaufman's well-known axiom that "Satire is what closes Saturday night" remains relevant in the case of HOW TO GET AHEAD IN ADVERTISING. *(Excessive profanity, sexual situations, adult situations.)*

p, David Wimbury and Ray Cooper; d, Bruce Robinson; w, Bruce Robinson; ph, Peter Hannan (Fujicolor); ed, Alan Strachan; m, David Dundas and Rick Wentworth; prod d, Michael Pickwoad; art d, Henry Harris; set d, Robyn Hamilton-Doney; cos, Andrea Galer; chor, David Toguri; makeup, Peter Frampton.

Comedy   (PR:C MPAA:R)

☑**HOWLING 5:**
THE REBIRTH, THE*½
99m Allied Vision-Lane Pringle c
Ben Cole *(David)*, William Shockley *(Richard)*, Mark Sivertsen *(Jonathan)*, Stephanie Faulkner *(Gail)*, Mary Stavin *(Anna)*, Clive Turner *(Ray)*, Jill Pearson *(Eleanor)*, Nigel Treffitt *(Professor)*, Joszef Madaras *(Peter)*, Renata Szatler *(Susan)*, Philip Davis *(The Count)*, Elizabeth She *(Marylou Summers)*, Victoria Catlin *(Dr. Catherine Peake)*.

HOWLING 5: THE REBIRTH begins with a prolog set in Central Europe in the Middle Ages. All the residents of the local castle have committed suicide in order to stamp out the bloodline of a werewolf. As the last two people expire, a baby's cry is heard; one little lycanthrope lives. Flashing forward to present-day Budapest, the film introduces some travelers who've been selected for a fun-filled weekend at a 15th-century castle. These vacationers include a movie star (Stavin), a dumb blonde (She), a tennis pro (Sivertsen), a writer (Faulkner), a professor (Treffitt), a rock star (Turner), a photographer (Cole), a doctor (Catlin), the doctor's adulterous lover (Shockley), and the not altogether trustworthy count (Davis) who acts as the host. Needless to say, the real reason for this surprise European getaway is left unexplained. Snowbound in the castle, which hasn't been open to the public for five centuries, the visitors soon discover they are pawns in a deadly game with origins in the mass suicide depicted in the prolog. Snooping through the castle's passageways, Treffitt is the first to be chomped to death. After the inquisitive Faulkner expresses her fear of a set-up, Turner finds a secret door and, hidden from sight, watches in horror as Faulkner is slaughtered by a werewolf. Falling down a staircase, Turner discovers the professor's body and wanders outside into a snowstorm, in which he becomes lost. While exploring an escape route with Davis, Cole and Sivertsen discover Turner's bloodied watch. Splitting into search parties, the terrified guests scour the castle for their fellow vacationers. After being separated from She, Sivertsen is the next to get it. While Catlin and Shockley argue about Davis' culpability, Stavin shoots someone or something before encountering Cole. The hair-raising plot thickens as Davis refuses to be medically examined by Catlin, and Shockley and Stavin point out that all of the guests are orphans and have similar birthmarks. As the corpses pile up, Davis reveals that one of them is a bona fide werewolf that can only be put to rest for good by a "blood" relative. It seems the count has brought the visitors to Budapest in an attempt to weed out the real werewolf. Before the mystery is finally solved, Davis and Cole accuse each other of being the sought-after lycanthrope, Stavin and Catlin are killed, and She shoots the butler and rescues Cole by killing Davis.

Is there a more lugubrious horror film in existence? Although fans of werewolf films may welcome this movie's earnestness, HOWLING 5 plods along with all the urgency of an appearance in traffic court. Eschewing the tongue-in-cheek spirit of the previous entries in the "Howling" series, HOWLING 5: THE REBIRTH is more faithful to the myths that inspired the Gary Brandner books on which the films are based. Fidelity to werewolf legends doesn't breed excitement in this case, however. Overly talky, sluggishly paced, and hampered by a large, undistinguished cast playing cliched characters, the film quickly becomes tiresome. Agatha Christie's "Ten Little Indians" formula is revamped with fur and fangs but to little avail; one loses interest in this werewolf-and-mouse game almost from the outset. On the plus side, the score provides a few shudders, and the identity of the werewolf is genuinely surprising. But even with this surprise ending the film is almost wholly devoid of suspense. Moreover, for all the visual thrills on display, HOWLING 5 may as well have been a radio play. Few will be satisfied by this lackluster effort: mystery buffs won't find enough surprises, gorehounds won't see enough blood and guts, and werewolf film lovers will encounter few variations on their favorite furry motifs. The next "Howling" installment will fare better if it adds some humor to the mix and unreels with more visual daring and much less weighty exposition. *(Graphic violence, sexual situations, nudity.)*

p, Clive Turner; d, Neal Sundstrom; w, Clive Turner and Freddie Rowe (based on the books *Howling 1*, *Howling 2*, and *Howling 3* by Gray Brandner); ph, Arledge Armenaki; m, The Factory.

Horror   (PR:C MPAA:R)

HUNGARIAN FAIRY TALE, A***½
(Hung.) 97m MD Wax/Courier b&w
(HOL VOLT, HOL NEM VOLT)
David Vermes *(Andris)*, Maria Varga
(Maria), Frantisek Husak *(Antal Orban)*,
Pal Hetenyi *(Hungarian Voice)*, Eszter
Csakanyi *(Young Woman)*, Peter Trokan
(Teacher), Szilvia Toth *(Tunde)*, Judit
Pogany *(Tunde's Mother)*, Geza Balkay
(Tunde's Stepfather), Gabor Reviczky
(Tunde's Father), Jolan Jaszai *(Old
Woman)*, Laszlo Polgar *(Greyhaired Man/
Sarastro)*, Gyozo Mihalyo *(Tamino)*, Bar-
bara Hegyi *(Pamina)*, Anna Feher, Olivia
Velez, Adel Kovats *(Handmaidens)*,
VOICES OF: Gabor Vaghelyi *(Holy
Father)*, Jutta Bokor, Eva Jablonkay,
Gulyas *(Denes)*, Maria Sudlik, Julia
Paszthy.

For most American viewers, Eastern European filmmaking (at least prior to the
recent wave of reform in the Communist
bloc) presents a paradox. On the one hand,
it's insistently political, obsessed with the
individual's relation to the state, or at least
to the bureaucracy that represents the
state. On the other hand, its politics are
deliberately obscured, since any perceived
challenge to official ideology invites censorship. To be political without seeming to
be political is the Eastern European
filmmaker's primary task, and indirection
is a primary instrument to that end. Impas-
sivity translates as resistance, an innocuous children's tale as an allegory of
oppression. It's a discipline that feeds on
the interpretive paranoia of the viewer, in
which "Seek and ye shall find" becomes
the creed that makes revolutionaries of us
all. A HUNGARIAN FAIRY TALE purports to be an allegory, a child's story (but
for adults, director Gyula Gazdag insists)
that implies more than its literal surface
can reveal—though whether the depth of

its implication can be appreciated by a
non-Hungarian viewer depends on the
viewer's approaching the film in a spirit of
openness and interpretive flexibility.

The story centers around a quest. While
attending a performance of Mozart's *The
Magic Flute* (already a fantasy analogue of
what's to come), a young woman (Varga) is
smitten by a handsome stranger, leading to
sudden and fleeting romance. A child is
born of this quicksilver affair, but Varga,
knowing neither the identity nor the
whereabouts of the boy's father, can't get
the government to certify that her son actually exists. A kindly bureaucrat (Husak)
solves the problem by entering a false name
on official records, providing an imaginary
father to verify the existence of a real son.
But the boy (Vermes) is soon left an
orphan, a providential pigeon having
knocked loose a brick that hits Varga on the
head (in an airy, lyrical sequence worthy of
Vincente Minnelli). Though all he knows
about the father of his dreams is that he
lives somewhere on "Freedom Street"
(another fabrication, and also an overloaded symbol), the boy sets out to find
him. In the course of his travels he meets
an unhappy family (whose dead-end misery seems to mock his idealism), a glum
group of junior marksmen and their mar-
tinet teacher, and a lonely nurse who
becomes a kind of substitute mother to
him. Meanwhile, Husak has left his paper-
pushing job behind and set out on his own
to track down the wandering Vermes. After
a number of near misses he finds him, as
well as the nurse, and together they form a
makeshift family whose union is based on
hope and shared need, rather than biology.
In a finale that recalls MIRACLE IN
MILAN (and which is marred by some
shoddy matting that's not without a certain
charm), the three are borne aloft by a huge

stone eagle that soars over Budapest, across
the Danube, and out into a fairy-tale
future. It's an ambiguous close: is Hungary
a land where hope can soar, or one where
hope can only be impossible fantasy? The
film leaves the question hanging along with
its trio of seekers.

A HUNGARIAN FAIRY TALE marks
a change of pace for writer-director
Gazdag, whose antibureaucratic
documentaries and satires (THE RESO-
LUTION; SINGING ON THE TREAD-
MILL) have won him an international
following. Gazdag's FAIRY TALE is also
antibureaucratic, but lighter in tone and
more direct in its emotional appeal than
most of his previous work. State paternal-
ism is Gazdag's enemy, though at times his
subversive intentions appear a bit confused here. Freedom and its absence seem
less the issue in A HUNGARIAN FAIRY
TALE than government incompetence
and lethargy, and if socialist bureaucracy is
oppressive . . . well, so is the IRS, and
when's the last time anyone made a film
about that? On the other hand, the film is
beautifully put together, a deft combination of old Hollywood texture and lumi-
nosity (Elemer Ragalyi's black-and-white
cinematography is superb), 60s New Wave
freedom, and surreal fantasy atmospher-
ics. The satire may have already lost its
topical bite, but the structure underlying it
—the simple myth at the complex heart of
things—is made to last. *(Adult situations.)*

d, Gyula Gazdag; w, Gyula Gazdag,
Miklos Gyorffy, and Kata Tolmar; ph, Ele-
mer Ragalyi; ed, Julia Sivo; m, Istvan
Martha; md, Peter Peterdi; prod d, Jozsef
Romvari; set d, Miklos Fabian and Gyula
Toth; spec eff, Andras Szobrasz; cos,
Zsuzsa Stenger.

Fantasy/Political   (PR:A MPAA:NR)

I

◉I, MADMAN*½
89m Sarlui-Diamant/Trans World c
Jenny Wright *(Virginia/Anna)*, Clayton
Rohner *(Richard)*, Randall William Cook
(Malcolm Brand), Steven Memel *(Lenny)*,
Stephanie Hodge *(Mona)*, Michelle Jor-
dan *(Colette)*, Vance Valencia *(St.
Navarro)*, Bruce Wagner *(Pianist)*.

One might expect the worst of a film called
I, MADMAN, but Tibor Takacs' film is
wonderful, a beautifully shot and terrifi-
cally acted film that harkens back to classic
horror movies. I, MADMAN tells the story
of a bookstore employee, Virginia
(Wright), who is currently reading (and
almost obsessed with) a book called *I,
Madman* by a mysterious author named
Malcolm Brand. After reading a chapter,
Wright begins to notice that objects in the
book (a rose, a cup of tea) are beginning to
pop up in reality, and it's not too long
before the title madman (Cook), a strange,
lovesick doctor patterned after his author,
also escapes into the actual. Murders that
follow the book precisely begin to occur,
but though Wright's police detective boyfriend (Rohner) is assigned to investigate
the killings, he has a difficult time believing
her contention that the killer is a fictional
maniac come to life. Meanwhile—turnabout being fair play—the madman mistakes Wright for a character in the book, an
actress who rejects him because of his
appearance, but whom he loves so desperately that he cuts off his facial features—
nose, lips, ears, and so on—and kills to
replace them with more attractive ones.
After several murders, he acquires an
entirely new face, and is now ready to kill
Wright. After a failed stakeout, Wright ends
up back at her bookstore to save the life of
his next victim, but arrives too late and is
attacked by Cook. Rohner arrives on the
scene and shoots the madman—but that's
not the end of the madman, of course, and
the final confrontation involves elements
from yet another of Malcolm Brand's
books. Borrowing from PHANTOM OF
THE OPERA; HOUSE OF WAX; and
FRANKENSTEIN, I, MADMAN is a loving salute to the days when movie monsters
had hearts. With the current trend in faceless, Jason-style killers, it's great to see this
madman with passion. Cook's character
has a clear motive for his murders, one that
inspires sympathy along with disgust; he's
a descendant of the classic horror films'
"misunderstood monster," worthy of our
attention and fear.

Also refreshing is Takacs' lively, sharp
direction and the high technical quality
overall. Photographed and lit with great
style (some sequences recall the work of
Italian horror master Dario Argento), I,
MADMAN looks more expensive than it

really was. One particularly effective
sequence involves the killer's quest for a
scalp and hair. He follows a redhead to her
building, breaks in, and chases her to her
apartment, where he injects her with something to make her lose consciousness and
scalps her. It sounds like a typically revolting horror sequence, but it plays like visual
poetry, Takacs giving great attention to the
nightmare images and spicing up the scene
with an energetic zoom shot (apparently
inspired by Sam Raimi's EVIL DEAD
films) of a man at the end of a hall. In fact,
many of the images in I, MADMAN
remain in the mind long after it is over. A
lot of care went into the movie's making,
and it shows.

That the performers seem to be enjoying
themselves makes I, MADMAN all the
more entertaining. Jenny Wright, in particular, appears to relish her role, and Clayton
Rohner (who was very good in the teen
comedy MODERN GIRLS) manages to
give a watchable performance even in the
thankless cop/boyfriend part. As the title
madman, Randall William Cook stalks
and poses in the classic manner. A makeup
artist (he created all the makeup effects for
the film), Cook makes an impressive acting
debut here, creating a memorable and passionate monster.

Takacs' only previous feature was the
silly (but extremely well made) THE
GATE. He surpasses the quality of that
film within the first five minutes of I,
MADMAN, and goes on to create one of
the finest horror movies in a long time. It's
also a lot of fun. *(Violence, adult situations,
profanity.)*

p, Rafael Eisenman; d, Tibor Takacs; w,
David Chaskin; ph, Bryan England; ed,
Marcus Manton; m, Michael Hoenig;
prod d, Ron Wilson and Matthew Jacobs;
spec eff, Randall William Cook.

Horror   (PR:C-O MPAA:R)

IMMEDIATE FAMILY***
95m Lawrence
Kasdan-Sanford-Pillsbury/COL c
Glenn Close *(Linda Spector)*, James
Woods *(Michael Spector)*, Mary Stuart
Masterson *(Lucy Moore)*, Kevin Dillon
(Sam), Linda Darlow *(Susan Drew)*, Jane
Greer *(Michael's Mother)*, Jessica James
(Bessie), Mimi Kennedy *(Eli's Mom)*,
Charles Levin *(Eli's Dad)*, Harrison Mohr
(Eli), Matthew Moore *(Jason)*, Kristin
Sanderson *(Kristin "Picasso")*, Merrilyn
Gann *(Kristin's Mom)*, Wendy Van Riesen
(Pregnant Woman), Ashlee MacMilliam,
Nora Kletter *(Girls at Puppet Show)*,
Alisha Bell, Tony Dakota, Jennifer
Sedman, Chelsea Hooper *(Kids on Blan-
ket)*, Katie Murray *(Birthday Girl)*, Babs
Chula *(Birthday Girl's Mom)*, Ben Reeder
(Paul), Thor Derksen *(Paper Boy)*, Jona-
than Sedman *(Kid with Football)*, Jeff
Stanford *(Lab Technician)*, Elinore Then

(Dr. Nathanson's Nurse), Walter Marsh
(Dr. Nathanson), Ken Lerner *(Josh)*,
Deryl Fell *(Father at Game)*, John
Kirkconnell *(Son at Game)*, Rebecca
Toolan *(Real Estate Woman)*, Donna
Peerless *(Linda's Client)*, Pamela Ludwig
(Anna), Deborah Offner *(Kathy)*, Lynn
Eastman *(Phone Operator)*, Janet Judd
(Woman on Bus), Freda Perry *(Lawyer's
Receptionist)*, Brenda Crichlow *(Doctor's
Receptionist)*, Celine Lockhart *(Rich
Mother)*, Anita Kam *(Rich Daughter)*, Bill
Croft *(Man on Phone)*, Veena Sood
(Admitting Nurse), Tess Brady *(Delivery
Doctor)*, Royce Wallace *(Nurse)*, Daniel
Roberds *(Baby William/Andrew)*, Benja-
min Altschul *(One-Year-Old William)*,
Nora Heflin *(Dr. Samuels)*, Richard
White, Darrell Roberds *(Anxious
Fathers)*, Gloria Reuben *(Maternity
Nurse)*, Blu Mankuma, Andrew Kavadas
(Crib Movers), Alma Beltran *(Spanish
Woman)*, Andrea Mann, Beatriz Pizano,
Venus Terzo *(Spanish Woman's Daugh-
ters)*, Jo-Anne Bates, Rob Roy *(Home
Buyers)*, Joyce Erickson *(Vet Reception-
ist)*, Simone Clelland *(Anne Marie)*,
Robyn Simons *(Girl in Vet's Office)*, Liam
Ramsey *(Lucy's Stepbrother)*, Maya
Saunders *(Lucy's Stepsister)*, Stephen E.
Miller *(Lucy's Stepfather)*, Jane Mortifee-
Birch *(Sam's Mother)*, Chuck Bennett
(Sportscaster), Colleen Darnell *(Salon
Employee)*, Christmas the Dog *(Ellen)*,
Toothpick the Clown *(Himself)*.

IMMEDIATE FAMILY is as commendable for what it doesn't do as for what it
does. A drama about modified surrogate
motherhood, it doesn't indulge in heart
rending or tear jerking. There are few misty
close-ups or glycerine tears. No big
speeches. No big moments.

What IMMEDIATE FAMILY does is
dare to be low key and realistic rather than
hyper-emotional. James Woods and Glenn
Close play an upscale couple that is ordinary in every way except that they are
unable to conceive a child. Mary Stuart
Masterson and Kevin Dillon play a struggling young working-class couple, exceptional only in that they have jumped the
matrimonial gun and found themselves
with a child on the way. Desperate to
become parents, Woods and Close arrange
a brokered adoption with Masterson, under
the terms of which they will care for
Masterson through her pregnancy and she
will turn over the baby after its birth. When
her maternal instinct takes over, Masterson
reneges, however, busing back to Ohio
from Seattle, the film's main setting, with
the infant in tow. Woods and Close, a bit
sadder, return to their lawyer to look at
portfolios of other women with babies for
adoption.

That's not quite the end of the story, but
IMMEDIATE FAMILY has been so eminently sensible up to this point that the
ending isn't too hard to imagine. Director

Jonathan Kaplan maintains an emotional detachment from the action, which simultaneously revolves around Woods and Close's eagerness and anxieties and Masterson and Dillon's tentative attempts to build better lives than their parents have known. But Kaplan's detachment is one of respectful distance rather than condescension or noninvolvement.

That respect extends to Kaplan's willingness to risk the lack of emotional punch at the fadeout. The script by Barbara Benedek (THE BIG CHILL) doesn't reduce its characters to speech-making caricatures or sobbing, oversensitive thirtysomethings. These are real, flesh-and-blood people who have grand hopes and dreams, but who also must live from day to day. The compelling, detailed depiction of middle-class lives here recalls executive producer (and director of THE BIG CHILL) Lawrence Kasdan's THE ACCIDENTAL TOURIST, one of the best films of 1988. What keeps IMMEDIATE FAMILY from being one of the best of 1989 is that Kaplan isn't quite able to convey the emotions of the childless Spectors. Despite solid performances by Woods and Close, Michael and Linda Spector remain remote, shadowy figures. With the film's younger couple, however, Kaplan is on more familiar turf. The director's strongest films—from WHITE LINE FEVER to HEART LIKE A WHEEL and THE ACCUSED—have been grounded in the same working-class milieu from which Masterson's and Dillon's characters come. For Kaplan, people on the way up are inherently more interesting than people who have already made it.

Still, Dillon's leather-clad graduate of the school of hard knocks is a little too good to be wholly believable as the supportive, nurturing boy friend. The real heart and soul of IMMEDIATE FAMILY is Masterson's performance, an emotionally rich, completely guileless combination of charm and grit that steals the film. Kaplan seems to have a way with actresses (Bonnie Bedelia's performance in HEART LIKE A WHEEL remains the best of her career, and Jodie Foster won an Oscar for her work in THE ACCUSED), and his ability to coax great performances from them is again evident here in Masterson's work. Her character is a little tentative, but she is also self-possessed and wise enough to know not to stand in the way of natural forces, whether motherhood or the survival instinct that leads her, without regret, to the decision that brings about IMMEDIATE FAMILY's climax.

Without Masterson, IMMEDIATE FAMILY might have been a solid TV movie (though perhaps not even that, as Kaplan's overuse of popular tunes to telegraph emotions in scene after scene becomes grating long before the film ends). With Masterson, and under Kaplan's

direction, IMMEDIATE FAMILY becomes more than the pedantic social-problem drama it might have been and acquires the poetic power of a modern myth. Musical selections include: "Creatures of Love" (David Byrne, Chris Frantz, Jerry Harrison, Tina Weymouth, performed by Talking Heads), "My City Was Gone" (Chrissie Hynde, performed by the Pretenders), "Salem Girls," "Full Moon" (Michael Caronia, performed by Dead On), "Sexual Graduation" (Robert "White" Johnson, Mark Gendel, performed by Johnson, Gendel), "Into the Mystic" (Van Morrison, performed by Morrison), "Crazy Mama" (J.J. Cale, performed by Cale), "Over the Edge" (Paul Barrere, performed by Little Feat), "Motherless Children" (Eric Clapton, Carl Radle, performed by Clapton), "Try a Little Tenderness" (Harry Woods, Jimmy Campbell, Reg Connelly, performed by Otis Redding), "I Can See Clearly Now" (Johnny Nash, performed by Nash), Trio in E-flat Major, Op. 3 (Ludwig Van Beethoven, performed by Mozart String Trio). *(Profanity, adult situations)*

p, Sarah Pillsbury and Midge Sanford; d, Jonathan Kaplan; w, Barbara Benedek; ph, John W. Lindley (Deluxe Color); ed, Jane Kurson; m, Brad Fiedel; prod d, Mark Freeborn; art d, David Willson; set d, Byron Lance King; spec eff, John Thomas; cos, April Ferry; makeup, Irene Kent.

Drama   (PR:C   MPAA:PG-13)

• IN COUNTRY✶✶½
120m WB c
Bruce Willis *(Emmett Smith)*, Emily Lloyd *(Samantha Hughes)*, Joan Allen *(Irene)*, Kevin Anderson *(Lonnie)*, John Terry *(Tom)*, Peggy Rea *(Mamaw)*, Judith Ivey *(Anita)*, Dan Jenkins *(Dwayne)*, Jim Beaver *(Earl)*, Richard Hamilton *(Grampaw)*, Heidi Swedberg, Ken Jenkins, Jonathan Hogan, Patricia Richardson, Kimberly Faith Jones.

Despite the craftsmanship and care that obviously went into its making, this adaptation of Bobbie Ann Mason's novel *In Country* fails to take flight. The problem begins at the outset, a heavy-handed opening scene in which soldiers are loaded into the bowels of a flying troop carrier to the accompaniment of bluntly militaristic rant delivered over a PA system by an unseen speaker. Director Norman Jewison's camera portentously records the scene as a funeral march into inevitable darkness, blood, and death. Bearing a too-striking resemblance to the ending of Milos Forman's film of the musical HAIR, this opening is marred by an emotional crudeness out of step with the subtlety of IN COUNTRY's plot. Unfortunately, it's not the last stumble the film makes. The action flashes forward to present-day Ken-

tucky, where a high-school clearly parallels the troop loading: Having themselves completed "training," the students are sent out to do battle with life. But now the blood-and-guts speech of the opening gives way to a principal's don't-worry-be-happy address in tune with the mood of the Reagan 80s. Most exuberant among the graduates is Lloyd, who lives with and takes care of her "mentally alienated" uncle, Willis, a Vietnam vet still traumatized by his war memories, and who is herself the daughter of a soldier who was killed in Vietnam before she was born. The small, weather-beaten house she shares with Willis is owned by her mother (Allen), who has moved to Lexington with her new husband and baby. Exploring the house one day, Lloyd comes upon a trunk filled with mementos of her dead father, including his letters home and his diary. Only at this point do we realize that her father was among the soldiers in the opening scene (without this knowledge, unwary fans may spend the prolog straining to spot Willis). Lloyd's curiosity is piqued by the letters, and she begins questioning Willis in an attempt to understand what happened in Vietnam. She even attends a veteran's dance and goes home with one of Willis' fellow vets, in an effort to breach the wall of silence the men maintain concerning the war. Eventually, Lloyd herself becomes "mentally alienated" as she discovers the horrors the silence is meant to hide. Rather too abruptly, however, she reconciles with the past and faces the future after an emotional scene at the Vietnam War memorial in Washington, where she, Willis, and her paternal grandmother (Rea) find her father's name carved in the black stone.

IN COUNTRY's weaknesses may have been compounded as a consequence of employing a Canadian director (Jewison, whose last film was MOONSTRUCK) and a British star (Emily Lloyd, of WISH YOU WERE HERE and 1989's COOKIE) to tell what would seem to be a quintessentially American story. Jewison is almost saved by his talented supporting cast, which, besides Bruce Willis, Joan Allen, and Peggy Rea, also includes sharp performances by Judith Ivey and Kevin Anderson. But many of the points the script (by Frank Pierson and Cynthia Cidre) makes about the war, its casualties, and its survivors have been made elsewhere, and the film never convinces that it has a good reason for making them again. Similarly, Lloyd—though technically adept, with the kind of electricity and offbeat good looks that make her a movie natural—never finds a way to get beneath her character's skin and convey her conflicting emotions.

Like Hollywood's other major 1989 Vietnam movie, Brian De Palma's CASUALTIES OF WAR, IN COUNTRY ends with a plea to forgive and forget. But the odd emotional hollowness at the core of both films would seem to indicate that, for too many, the healing process remains far from simple or complete. *(Profanity, adult situations.)*

p, Norman Jewison and Richard Roth; d, Norman Jewison; w, Frank Pierson and Cynthia Cidre (based on the novel by Bobbie Ann Mason); ph, Russell Boyd (Technicolor); ed, Anthony Gibbs and Lou Lombardo; m, James Horner; prod d, Jackson De Govia; art d, John R. Jensen; cos, Aggie Guerard Rodgers.

Drama   (PR:C MPAA:R)

⊙INDIANA JONES AND THE LAST CRUSADE**½
127m Lucasfilm Ltd./PAR c
Harrison Ford *(Indiana Jones)*, Sean Connery *(Dr. Henry Jones)*, Denholm Elliott *(Marcus Brody)*, Alison Doody *(Dr. Elsa Schneider)*, John Rhys-Davies *(Sallah)*, Julian Glover *(Walter Donovan)*, River Phoenix *(Young Indy)*, Michael Byrne *(Vogel)*, Kevork Malikyan *(Kazim)*, Robert Eddison *(Grail Knight)*, Richard Young *(Fedora)*, Alexei Sayle *(Sultan)*, Alex Hyde-White *(Young Henry)*, Paul Maxwell *(Panama Hat)*, Mrs. Glover *(Mrs. Donovan)*, Vernon Dobtcheff *(Butler)*, J.J. Hardy *(Herman)*, Bradley Gregg *(Roscoe)*, Jeff O'Haco *(Half Breed)*, Vince Deadrick *(Rough Rider)*, Marc Miles *(Sheriff)*, Ted Grossman *(Deputy Sheriff)*, Tim Hiser *(Young Panama Hat)*, Larry Sanders *(Scout Master)*, Will Miles, David Murray *(Scouts)*, Frederick Jaeger *(WW I Ace)*, Jerry Harte *(Prof. Stanton)*, Billy J. Mitchell *(Dr. Mulbray)*, Martin Gordon *(Man at Hitler Rally)*, Paul Humpoletz *(German Officer at Hitler Rally)*, Tom Branch *(Hatay Soldier in Temple)*, Graeme Crowther *(Zeppelin Crewman)*, Luke Hanson *(Principal SS Officer at Castle)*, Chris Jenkinson *(Officer at Castle)*, Nicola Scott *(Female Officer at Castle)*, Louis Sheldon *(Young Officer at Castle)*, Stefan Kalipha *(Hatay Tank Gunner)*, Peter Pacey *(Hatay Tank Driver)*, Pat Roach *(Gestapo)*.

Steven Spielberg and George Lucas aren't messing around in this, the third and final installment of the Indiana Jones series—they've given us the Holy Grail, Jesus Christ, *and* Adolf Hitler all in the same movie. The Indy Jones adventure series is about Quests, Good Guys, and Bad Guys, and as these things go, the Grail, Christ, and Hitler reign supreme in their respective categories. When going out, go out with a bang.

Aptly titled (for this is, all involved promise, indeed the *last* series entry), INDIANA JONES AND THE LAST CRUSADE opens in 1912, with the young Indy Jones played by Phoenix. A Boy Scout, Indy is exploring a cave with his troop when he runs across a gang who have just unearthed an ancient relic—an elaborate 16th-century gold cross. Outraged that the relic is not going to be donated to a museum, Indy steals it and leads his pursuers on a chase, first by horse and then on board a circus train (featuring some expected encounters—with snakes, alligators, a rhinoceros, a lion, and a collection of magic-show gadgets). The chase leads to Indy's modest home, where his father is embroiled in his research—a diligent study of the whereabouts of the Holy Grail, the chalice from which Christ is said to have drunk at the Last Supper. Before long the head villain arrives and takes back the cross, but, impressed by young Indy's courage and persistence, the bad guy (who more than resembles Ford) takes off his weather-worn fedora and places it on the youngster's brow, telling him, "You lost today, kid, but that doesn't mean you have to like it." The scene then shifts to 1938: Indy (Ford), now an archaeology professor, is summoned to the museum-like penthouse of a famous art collector (one of his university's top donors), the wealthy Glover, who informs him of an expedition to find the Holy Grail. Glover tells Ford that he has a portion of one important stone tablet but is missing some necessary information, such as the name of a certain city, and also reminds Ford of an ancient tale of three knights said to have found the Grail's resting place. Reportedly, one remained to guard the chalice; another is buried somewhere in Venice. Then Glover breaks the news that the most important member of his expedition to find the chalice has disappeared, captured by Nazis who want the relic because it is believed to bring eternal life. This missing archaeolo-

Sean Connery and Harrison Ford in INDIANA JONES AND THE LAST CRUSADE (©Paramount).

gist is Ford's father, Dr. Henry Jones (played with crotchety exuberance by Connery). Without further ado, Ford and museum curator Elliott travel to Venice to find Dad. An unbeliever, Ford has no interest in finding the Grail; his mission is solely to find his father. In the process, however, he gets caught up in Connery's findings, and in just a few short minutes he meets and falls in love with a pretty blonde German scientist (Doody) *and* locates the knight's tomb, where he uncovers the secret for which his father has been searching. (Connery had drawn a map detailing the path to the Grail, but it was a map of hills, rivers, and canyons without the names of any cities to help locate the area.) Now armed with the name of the city, Ford travels to Germany to find his father, who is being kept prisoner by the Nazis. After tackling a number of obstacles, he saves his father but is double-crossed by Doody, who is revealed to be a Nazi agent. The Nazis prepare to execute the Americans, but Connery and Ford escape, and the father and son, who have not spoken in some 20 years, now find to their surprise that they have more than the Grail in common: both Dad and Junior (as they call each other spitefully) have slept with the pretty Nazi Doody. ("I'm as human as the next man," Connery says in defense of his philandering; a shocked Ford retorts, "I *was* the next man!") As it turns out, the Nazis, in collaboration with turncoat collector Glover, have stolen Connery's book of notes on the Grail, and he and Ford must go back behind Nazi lines to retrieve it (meanwhile, Elliott is off somewhere, conveniently and temporarily removed from the plot). Ford and Connery find Doody at a massive Nazi rally and book-burning attended by none other than Hitler himself. Ford takes the book, is thrust into a crowd of Nazi autograph hounds while trying to flee, and—after a priceless face-to-face meeting between Spielberg and Lucas' rugged hero and this century's greatest evil-doer—Hitler signs his name to Connery's book in Ford's hand. Later, as coincidence would have it, Ford and gang arrive at a Middle East desert wasteland inhabited by Glover, Doody, and a small army of Nazis and tanks. After an extravagant horse/tank chase, all concerned wind up in the cavern where the Holy Grail lies, but there are three obstacles that prevent entry into the room that holds the Grail. Glover, knowing Ford and Connery are privy to the secret of how to bypass these obstacles, ruthlessly shoots Connery in the stomach, leaving Ford no choice but to recover the Grail (with its powers of eternal life) in order to save his father. By the finale, Glover has been duped into drinking from the wrong chalice and is instantly turned into dust; Doody, in her greed, falls to her death while reaching for the Grail; the Grail itself is lost in a bottomless crack in the earth; Ford and

Connery both drink from the holy chalice and are given eternal life; and the heroes ride off into the sunset.

While treading a path well worn by the series' previous entries, RAIDERS OF THE LOST ARK (1981) and INDIANA JONES AND THE TEMPLE OF DOOM (1984), this latest adventure proceeds with considerably less blood, energy, excitement, danger, or surprise. Apologizing for the "bloody heart" debacle of TEMPLE OF DOOM, Spielberg and Lucas have turned THE LAST CRUSADE back to its sources—the relatively innocuous weekly cliffhangers of days gone by. The film offers some shocks (a bloodless head rolling down some stairs) and chills (a vat of snakes and a sewer full of rats [some 7,000 of them]), but does so with such sanitized and lifeless filmcraft that it's difficult to get excited about them. As in the previous films, Spielberg and Lucas have filled the picture with spectacular chases—the two standouts here being the opening circus-train sequence and the scene of Ford on horseback pursuing a Nazi tank, the latter a 10-minute chase that reportedly cost $200,000 per day and took two weeks to shoot. There is also some splendid period art direction (a zeppelin ride, the Nazi rally, and a gorgeous art deco penthouse) that captures the era, glamorizing (in that Hollywood way) rather than documenting it. More than anything, THE LAST CRUSADE is a show of filmmaking technique, and there is virtuosity in every frame—but the virtuosity comes without surprise. As in its prototype adventure serials, everything in the Indy Jones series has become so familiar and predictable that the sense of danger disappears, and while THE LAST CRUSADE runs its obstacle course with perfection, no viewer will be surprised at the character's next leap.

Vowing to put the cliffhanger mentality and his unsettling love for audience manipulation behind him, Spielberg gave one final farewell with THE LAST CRUSADE, capping the trilogy and honoring a handshake agreement between Spielberg and Lucas to make three Indiana Jones adventures. The pair had announced, however, that they wouldn't shoot the third Indiana Jones installment until they were excited about the script. What thrilled them here was the father-son relationship between Indy and Dr. Henry Jones, which lends the series some subtext. (Spielberg and Lucas have both made much of their lack of paternal figures *and* have both become fathers in recent years, augmenting the story's psychoanalytic interest.) Then there's the stress placed on the Joseph Campbell-inspired spiritualism of Indy's quest for his father and inseparable search for the Holy Grail. By the film's end, not only has a father-son unity been achieved, but these much-loved characters have presumably achieved immortality—

which is apparently reassuring for their creative fathers, Spielberg and Lucas.

Enhancing all this rather shallow philosophizing is a collection of great stunts and an excellent cast. Harrison Ford gets to play off the great Sean Connery—who, we remember, once made a career of adventure in the James Bond series. Likewise, Connery gets a chance to act with the superb Denholm Elliott, although the latter's character gets in the way of the action and is temporarily dismissed mid-film by the filmmakers. River Phoenix gets to have some fun in the 16-minute prolog without even having to act (he does, however, expend a fair amount of energy getting chased). Then there's Alison Doody. Poor Alison Doody. Boys will be boys, and Spielberg and Lucas are no exception; their idea here of character complexity is to make their *femme fatale* a Nazi spy who tricks both the Joneses.

In our *1988 Motion Picture Annual* review of EMPIRE OF THE SUN, we cited that film as "a celebration of the spirit and an affirmation of Spielberg's passion for filmmaking—a passion all too rare in filmmaking today." Unfortunately, that passion is also all too rare in INDIANA JONES AND THE LAST CRUSADE. After EMPIRE OF THE SUN, Spielberg reassessed all his previous work, realizing that he had made his films to please audiences, not himself. With the release of THE LAST CRUSADE, he has once again gone through a period of reassessment ("I made [my films] without having to think," he told *Premiere* magazine). Considering Spielberg's recent "love 'em and leave 'em" attitude towards his films, one wonders how long it will take him to reassess THE LAST CRUSADE. What the film does prove, besides its makers' mastery of filmmaking craft, is the phenomenal popularity of the Indiana Jones series. INDIANA JONES AND THE LAST CRUSADE grossed more than $50 million in its opening week (on over 2,300 screens)—the first such occurrence in the history of movies. *(Violence.)*

p, Robert Watts; d, Steven Spielberg; w, Jeffrey Boam (based on a story by George Lucas, Menno Meyjes and characters created by Lucas, Philip Kaufman); ph, Douglas Slocombe, Paul Beeson, and Robert Stevens (Rank Color); ed, Michael Kahn; m, John Williams; prod d, Elliot Scott; art d, Fred Hole, Stephen Scott, Richard Berger, Benjamin Fernandez, and Guido Salsilli; set d, Alan Kaye; spec eff, Michael J. McAlister; cos, Anthony Powell; stunts, Vic Armstrong; makeup, Peter Robb-King.

Adventure/Historical

(PR:A-C MPAA:PG-13)

INNOCENT MAN, AN***
113m Touchstone-Silver Screen
Partners IV-Interscope/BV c

Tom Selleck (*Jimmie Rainwood*), F. Murray Abraham (*Virgil Cane*), Laila Robins (*Kate Rainwood*), David Rasche (*Mike Parnell*), Richard Young (*Danny Scalise*), Badja Djola (*John Fitzgerald*), Todd Graff (*Robby*), M.C. Gainey (*Malcolm*), Peter Van Norden (*Peter Feldman*), Bruce A. Young (*Jingles*), James T. Morris (*Junior*), Terry Golden (*Felix*), Dennis Burkley (*Butcher*), Thomas B. Kackert (*Dove*), Vito Peterson (*Handjob*), Charlie Landry (*Stevie*), Tobin Bell (*Zeke*), Scott Jaeck (*Albert*), Holly Fulger (*Yvonne*), Philip Baker Hall (*Judge Lavet*), J. Kenneth Campbell (*Lt. Freebery*), Jim Ortlieb (*Convict at Robby's Death*), Ralph O. Benton, Jim Staskel, Brian J. Williams (*Men on Tuna Boat*), Maggie Baird (*Stacy*), Alanniss Allddero (*Convict Torturer*), Bob Maroff (*Venucci*), Derek Anunciation (*Lester*), Ben Slack (*Woznick*), J.J. Johnston (*Joseph Donatelli*), Brian Brophy (*Nate Blitman*), Ben Rawnsley (*Cop at Jimmie's*), Dean Hill (*Mike*), Gary Matanky (*Mechanic at Hangar*), Jack R. Orend (*Officer at Bust*), Ernie Lively (*Donatelli's Dealer*), David Rhodes Brown (*Convict*), Larry Brothers (*Basketball Con*), Jeffrey Earl Young (*Guard*), Lt. Mike Budge (*Warden*), David Meligan (*Correctional Officer*), Dave Florek (*Court Clerk*), Gary Velasco, Robert E. Nichols (*Courthouse Guards*), Ron Collins (*Fritz*).

AN INNOCENT MAN's paranoid premise of renegade narcotics cops on a rampage may throw a monkey wrench into the US government's war on drugs, but this surprisingly nasty, tough little revenge melodrama from the House of the Mouse (Disney subsidiary Touchstone Pictures) has seemingly revived more careers than any other 1989 film. Start with Tom Selleck, who proves here he can carry a big-screen film without an infant costar (see THREE MEN AND A BABY . . . if you must). Here he stars as an airline mechanic whose life becomes a nightmare when a pair of narcs (Rasche and Young) get an address wrong, burst into his house to make a bust, mistake his hair dryer for a weapon, and shoot him. To clean up their mess, Rasche and Young switch a real gun for the dryer and plant cocaine in the house. Selleck wakes up in a hospital, accused of being a drug dealer and assaulting a cop. Things go from bad to worse for Selleck as the canny cops manage to get him convicted and sent to California's dungeonlike Oroville Prison. At first, Selleck proves woefully ill-equipped for the dog-eat-dog rigors of life in the yard, but a crafty old con (Abraham) takes him under his wing and shows him how to survive and prosper. After his release, Selleck draws on the survival skills he learned at Oroville and, with a little more help from Abraham,

who has also been victimized by Rasche and Young, sets out to get revenge on the corrupt cops.

The plot of AN INNOCENT MAN is almost as old as Hollywood itself, recalling movies from THEY MADE ME A CRIMINAL to Phil Karlson's FRAMED. Yet the film's ironic, skeptical tone gives the material a new spin. (Even the film's title is ironic, since Selleck's Rainwood loses his innocence in prison, where he's forced to kill a fellow inmate.) The film also conveys a strong sense of conviction, at least partly because of director Peter Yates' familiarity with the territory covered by its story. But while Yates has specialized in films about the hard-bitten denizens of the underside of the American dream—from THE FRIENDS OF EDDIE COYLE to SUSPECT and THE HOUSE ON CARROLL STREET—he hasn't made a film as compelling as AN INNOCENT MAN in quite some time.

Perhaps the script by Larry Brothers, who was also the film's associate producer, provided Yates with the inspiration that was lacking in the screenplays for the director's other recent efforts. Although working in a well-worn genre, Brothers invests his script with an insider's understanding of pecking orders and power, both inside and outside the prison gates. Tellingly, prison life is depicted as a more concentrated version of life in the straight world; all that changes is who is in charge—the toughest cons on the inside and the toughest, most ruthless cops on the outside. Also contributing to the film's success is a fine cast that makes the most of Brothers' well-crafted dialog and sharply etched characters. Besides Selleck, AMADEUS Oscar winner F. Murray Abraham, as the wily Virgil, shows he can do something more than make life miserable for Mozart. Like almost everything else in the film, Abraham's performance is deviously double-edged. His Virgil is suave, charming, and likable, but when he smiles, he looks like a death's head. It's a measure of how convincing Abraham is that his character never lifts a finger against a fellow con throughout the film, yet when he tells Rainwood that he is respected and feared by the prison population, we take his word for it. David Rasche, who last played ruthlessness for laughs in the sitcom spoof SLEDGE HAMMER, plays it for real here and nearly steals the picture. An actor who can make people nervous just by walking into a room, he punctuates his soft, reassuring TV pitchman's delivery with sudden, startling outbursts of violent energy. Indeed, there is hardly a sour note from the entire cast, from Todd Graff's short stint as an ill-fated con cuffed to Rainwood early on to Laila Robins as Rainwood's hard-nosed, determined wife. Together these ingredients make for a superior, if slightly discomforting, evening of

cynical, streetwise entertainment. (*Violence, profanity, adult situations.*)

p, Ted Field, Robert W. Cort, and Neil A. Machlis; d, Peter Yates; w, Larry Brothers; ph, William A. Fraker (Technicolor); ed, Stephen A. Rotter and William S. Scharf; m, Howard Shore; prod d, Stuart Wurtzel; art d, Frank Richwood; set d, Sig Tinglof; spec eff, William H. Schirmer; cos, Rita Ryack; tech, Joel Salce; stunts, John Moio; makeup, James Lee McCoy.

Crime   (PR:C MPAA:R)

ⓥIRON TRIANGLE, THE**½
91m Eurobrothers/Scotti Bros. c

Beau Bridges (*Capt. Keene*), Haing S. Ngor (*Capt. Tuong*), Johnny Hallyday (*Jacques*), Liem Whatley (*Ho*), James Ishida (*Khoi*), Ping Wu (*Pham*), Richard Weygint (*Swan*), Allan Moore (*Murphy*), Bobby McGee (*Joop*), Joe Seely (*Grover*), Iilana B'Tiste (*Khan Ly*), Francois Chau (*Capt. Duc*), Jack Ong (*Shen*), Sunny Trinidad (*Thuy*), Sophie Trang (*Lai*), Glen Chin (*Chau*).

THE IRON TRIANGLE is a modestly scaled Vietnam War film that, rather effectively, for once, attempts to show both sides of the conflict. US Army captain Bridges, a rugged veteran, struggles to do the right thing by his platoon in the throes of senseless jungle combat, only to be thwarted at every turn, not only by the "enemy," but by his own men. Warfare brings out the worst in certain of his comrades, especially when it comes to the treatment of prisoners, many of whom are summarily annihilated. During a fierce firefight, Bridges is captured by a 17-year-old Viet Cong soldier, Whatley, who wrestles with his conscience over the goals of the Communist Party and considers suicide. Moreover, the wanton brutality of his compatriots, especially Ishida, causes him to withdraw even further into himself. In time, he comes to take a proprietary view of his prisoner, and, to insure justice for Bridges, breaks away from his troop. Alone together, the two men are wary of each other, but it is evident that they share basic beliefs. Although Ishida manages to catch up with them, the ensuing confrontation proves deadly for him. Ultimately, Bridges rejoins his unit and participates in a savage battle to take Whatley's village, My Tang, during which the young Viet Cong displays great bravery and Bridges is given a chance to return the mercy shown him earlier by Whatley. Bridges' final words sum up their relationship: "I never saw him again, but I had come to understand that at the other end of the barrel of a gun was a man like me."

Like all films of its genre, THE IRON TRIANGLE is faced with the immensely difficult task of re-creating the devastation and complexity of war, an undertaking that is further complicated in this case by the filmmakers' attempt to do so realistically *and* objectively. Few indeed are the movies that have accomplished this without being exploitative, sentimental, or downright insulting. Within the limits of its budget and simplistic script (which has the Vietnamese characters speaking English to each other), THE IRON TRIANGLE more or less accomplishes what it sets out to do without too many groan-inducing moments. The location photography, intelligent editing, and explosive special effects are impressive, quite the equal of many larger productions. The battle of My Tang, in particular, is effectively depicted in a montage of violent images, marred only by some obvious ominously mounting muzak.

As for the performances, Beau Bridges demonstrates again that he has become one our most economically natural actors, effortlessly convincing in any part, how-

ever weakly written it might be. He eschews the easy, despotic histrionics often favored by actors in roles of military command, bringing instead a quiet, gruff resignation that marks him as a natural leader and soft pedals some of the clinker lines he is called upon to deliver. Liem Whatley is equally believable as Ho and, admirably, not a stereotype of any kind. Without grandstanding, he suggests moody depths and conflicts in his character, his cautious, rueful performance going a long way to put over the film's premise of the universality of man. To the film's credit the relationship between Keene and Ho is never cornily overdone as director Eric Weston allows both to maintain their dignity. In support, James Ishida's savage Khoi is too much of a one-note performance, his mien and accent jarringly wrong—too Japanese and too California, respectively. On the other

hand, Johnny Hallyday, with his spooky eyes, livens things up a bit in a colorful appearance as a French soldier of fortune. His companion, a comely Vietnamese would-be rabble-rouser, is played by Iilana B'Tiste in a fashion that could best be described as half Faye Dunaway, half Imelda Marcos. Careful viewers will also note the presence of Oscar-winner Haing S. Ngor (THE KILLING FIELDS) in a blink-and-you'll-miss-it role as the VC leader. *(Excessive violence, profanity, nudity.)*

p, Tony Scotti and Angela P. Schapiro; d, Eric Weston; w, Eric Weston, John Bushelman, Larry Hilbrand, and Marshall Drazen; ph, Irv Goodnoff (Metrocolor); ed, Roy Watts; m, Michael Lloyd, John D'Andrea, and Nick Strimple; prod d, Errol Kelly; spec eff, Yves De Bono.

War   (PR:O MPAA:R)

J

●JACKNIFE***
102m Kings
Road-Sandollar-Schaffel/Cineplex
Odeon c
Robert De Niro (Joseph "Megs" Megessey), Ed Harris (Dave), Kathy Baker (Martha), Charles Dutton (Jake), Loudon Wainwright III (Ferretti), Elizabeth Franz, Tom Isbell, Sloane Shelton, Walter Massey, Jordan Lund, Ivan Brogger, Michael Arkin, Kirk Taylor, Bruce Ramsey, Jessalyn Gilsig.

This modest but compelling drama was for the most part overlooked during its brief theatrical release, making it a must-see on video, especially for its three lead performances—which are among 1989's best. Robert De Niro stars as the title character, who received his nickname as a soldier in Vietnam because of his fondness for wrecking vehicles. Back in the States, with the war long over, De Niro is still not quite all there, but he's curbed his violent tendencies and confines himself to putting his fist through windows from time to time. He also tends to run off at the mouth, irritating his war buddy Harris—who would just as soon forget his Vietnam experiences, as well as De Niro. As the film begins, Harris and De Niro haven't seen each other for some time. Having decided to hop in his car and drive 2,500 miles to join Harris on a trout-fishing trip—for which Harris and De Niro had made tentative, but unconfirmed, plans months earlier—De Niro arrives at Harris' home to find his buddy sleeping off a weekend bender. Harris lives with his sister, Baker, who is at first bewildered and frightened by De Niro and his lunatic gift of gab. Eventually De Niro charms her into helping him rouse Harris, however, and she even joins the fishing expedition—catching the only fish. The day ends inauspiciously when De Niro accidentally dumps Baker in the river, leaving her soaked and furious throughout the long ride home; nevertheless, a spark has been struck between them. De Niro stays on in the area, taking a job as an auto mechanic in order to make some money and fix his car, which has barely survived the trip. Baker drops by his garage to ask him out on a lunch date, and their romance begins to blossom—to the growing resentment of Harris, who likes the idea of De Niro dating his sister even less than he likes De Niro himself. Harris, it turns out, is unable to purge his nightmarish memories of the war, especially those involving a friend's death—a tragedy which he has always blamed on De Niro—and has withdrawn from the world, struggling to keep his demons at bay while sharing the old family home with Baker, who cooks and cleans for him. De Niro,

who brings back those unwelcome war memories and threatens Harris' dependent relationship with his sister, has worked out his own conflicts about the war with a veterans' support group, and tries to nudge Harris into doing the same.

Despite its emphasis on psychology over action, JACKNIFE emerges as a surprisingly fresh and vital drama, directed with sensitive understatement by David Jones (BETRAYAL; 84 CHARING CROSS ROAD), and skillfully scripted by Stephen Metcalfe (from his own play "Strange Snow"). Unlike the higher-profiled IN COUNTRY, which covered much the same territory with considerably less effect but bigger box-office returns, JACKNIFE eschews melodrama and concentrates on characters who are more concerned with getting through the day than with wrestling Big Issues. This subtlety is significantly enhanced by the high caliber of the film's three leads. Playing a more "regular" type than most of his characters of late, De Niro is typically arresting, bringing a rough but likable humor to his Vietnam vet, and adding just enough tension to keep him continually unpredictable and riveting. As Martha, Kathy Baker continues to prove herself one of the best actresses on the big screen today, adding to the string of rich, memorable performances that have gained her notice in films like STREET SMART and CLEAN AND SOBER. Tempering tenderness with tough-mindedness, Baker's Martha blossoms under the influence of romance and seems to draw visible strength from her newfound sense of independence. Ed Harris also contributes typically solid work as Dave—perhaps the most difficult of the three lead roles because of the character's repressed, inarticulate nature. As Harris plays him, Dave seems almost to be hiding warily beneath his scraggly growth of beard and moustache, just as he hides from life. Together, the talents that put together JACKNIFE make it one of those rare "small" films that packs a big punch. (Profanity, adult situations.)

p, Robert Schaffel and Carol Baum; d, David Jones; w, Stephen Metcalfe (based on the play "Strange Snow" by Stephen Metcalfe); ph, Brian West (Technicolor); ed, John Bloom; m, Bruce Broughton; prod d, Edward Pisoni; stunts, Everett Creach.

Drama   **(PR:C MPAA:R)**

●JANUARY MAN, THE**
97m MGM/MGM-UA c
Kevin Kline (Nick Starkey), Susan Sarandon (Christine Starkey), Mary Elizabeth Mastrantonio (Bernadette Flynn), Harvey Keitel (Frank Starkey), Danny Aiello (Capt. Vincent Alcoa), Rod Steiger (Mayor Eamon Flynn), Alan Rickman (Ed), Faye Grant (Alison Hawkins), Ken

Walsh (Roger Culver), Jayne Haynes (Alma), Brian Tarantina (Cone), Bruce MacVittie (Rip), Bill Cobbs (Detective Reilly), Greg Walker (January Man), Tandy Cronyn (Lana), Gerard Parkes (Rev. Drew), Errol Slue (Chief Sunday), William Christian (Tim), Ann Talman (Sarah), Bill Cwikowski (Press Representative), Billie Neal (Gwen), Malachy McCourt (Hob), Paul Geier (Det. Muse), Richard Johnson, Elizabeth Karr, Jerry Rector, James Ryan, Grant Shaud (Newscasters/Reporters), Lazaro Perez (Ramon), Katherine E. Miller (Olympia), Jane Sanders (Mia), Colin Mochrie (Pat), Warren Davis (Bill), Joan Heney (Claire), Maida Rogerson (Mildred), James Mainprize (Harry), J.B. Waters (Police Officer).

How convenient that a film as lame as THE JANUARY MAN should have the good fortune to be titled after the month that traditionally serves as a dumping ground for product that has failed to gain studio confidence. Unsuspecting patrons must have thought that the film was released in January to capitalize on its post-New Year's setting; unfortunately, despite the participation of MOONSTRUCK screenwriter John Patrick Shanley, A FISH CALLED WANDA's Kevin Kline, BULL DURHAM's Susan Sarandon, and DIE HARD's Alan Rickman, this terribly disappointing effort belongs with the rest of the dreck that clutters American screens in the first month of the year.

Playing like something that had been buried at the bottom of Shanley's desk drawer since his days at NYU—indeed, many elements suggest a first draft of MOONSTRUCK—THE JANUARY MAN attempts to be an offbeat police thriller with a dash of romance and a quirky sense of humor. Following the murder of his daughter's best friend—the 11th serial killing in as many months—apoplectic New York City mayor Steiger demands that dour police commissioner Keitel assign his younger brother, Kline, to the case. It seems, however, that Keitel and Kline don't get along, and while Kline is apparently the most brilliant detective ever to set foot in Manhattan, he was made the scapegoat in a corruption scandal and kicked off the force. Reluctantly, Keitel tracks down his brother at the site of a fire and watches the cop-turned-firefighter rescue a small child. The eccentric Kline plays coy with Keitel and refuses to rejoin the police force unless he is allowed to cook dinner for Keitel's wife, Sarandon, with whom he was once in love. Kline tries to rekindle their passion over some carefully prepared octopus at his Greenwich Village apartment, but his attempt fails because his icy sister-in-law is interested only in climbing the Manhattan social ladder. Nonetheless, Kline throws himself into the murder case with his usual bravura—

Alan Rickman, Kevin Kline, and Mary Elizabeth Mastrantonio in THE JANUARY MAN (©MGM-UA).

much to the dismay of grouchy police chief Aiello, who thinks him a "beatnik." Upon meeting the mayor's 22-year-old daughter, Mastrantonio, Kline is smitten and the two indulge in a quick tryst in a downtown hotel. Together with Mastrantonio and his droll artist neighbor, Rickman, Kline sets about deducing when and where the next killing will take place—right down to the exact building and room number (his methods are too silly and complicated to detail here). A face-off with the killer follows, leading to a supposedly comic fight wherein Kline and the murderer stumble down several flights of stairs while beating the snot out of each other. In the end, the killer is revealed to be a nobody with a mother complex and Kline snubs the now-adoring Sarandon to stroll off with Mastrantonio.

Directed by Irishman Pat O'Connor (CAL; A MONTH IN THE COUNTRY; STARS AND BARS), THE JANUARY MAN is, simply put, a mess. Given the complexity of the relationships and the wild variance in mood as Shanley's script veers precariously from comedy to thriller to romance, O'Connor seems to have just dug in and shot the film as straight and efficiently as possible, instead of trying to sort out the narrative and highlight its strong points. Regrettably, this slick-but-detached approach merely calls attention to the flaws in Shanley's disjointed screenplay. O'Connor appears to have let his

actors coast as well. Kline's performance runs at the same manic pitch as his Oscar-winning work in A FISH CALLED WANDA; Sarandon is completely wasted in a role that, by her own admission, required nothing more than tossing her mink on the couch and acting like a bitch (though a significant portion of her role was left on the editing room floor); Rod Steiger's performance is indescribably over-the-top, as he literally yells his way through the film; while Harvey Keitel is sullen and remote to the point of catatonia. Only Mary Elizabeth Mastrantonio, Danny Aiello, and Rickman impress. Mastrantonio comes across as genuinely sweet, Aiello—in contrast to Steiger—knows just exactly how to play Shanley's often overwrought and profane dialog (indeed, he may be as sympathetic an interpreter of Shanley as Joe Mantegna is of David Mamet), and Rickman merely underplays the whole affair to brilliant effect. Shanley's screenplay contains plenty of leftovers from MOONSTRUCK as well, most notably the Kline-Keitel-Sarandon triangle, which mirrors the one involving Nicolas Cage, Aiello, and Cher in the earlier film, though it isn't as well developed. Moreover, MOONSTRUCK's big-laugh-inducing slapping scene is also reprised here, but it was far funnier the first time around. Shanley is an interesting screenwriter because he takes real chances with his narratives, shifting gears unpre-

dictably, combining grandiose romantic sentiment with the harsh reality of New York City street life. THE JANUARY MAN, however, finds both Shanley and director O'Connor particularly uninspired. (Violence, sexual situations, nudity, excessive profanity.)

p, Norman Jewison and Ezra Swerdlow; d, Pat O'Connor; w, John Patrick Shanley; ph, Jerzy Zielinski (Duart, Medallion Color); ed, Lou Lombardo; m, Marvin Hamlisch and Moe Koffman; prod d, Philip Rosenberg; art d, Dan Davies; set d, Gary Brink and Carol Lavoie; spec eff, Neil Trifunovich; cos, Ann Roth; chor, David Allan; tech, Ed Zigo; stunts, Greg Walker; makeup, Bernadette Mazur.

Comedy/Crime   (PR:O MPAA:R)

JOHNNY HANDSOME**½
109m Guber-Peters-Carolco/Tri Star c
Mickey Rourke (John Sedley), Ellen Barkin (Sunny Boyd), Elizabeth McGovern (Donna McCarty), Morgan Freeman (Lt. A.Z. Drones), Forest Whitaker (Dr. Steven Resher), Lance Henriksen (Rafe Garrett), Scott Wilson (Mikey Chalmette), David Schramm (Vic Dumask), Yvonne Bryceland (Sister Luke), Peter Jason (Mr. Bonet), J.W. Smith (Larry), Jeff Meek (Earl), Allan Graf (Bob Lemoyne), Ed Zang (Prestige Manager), John Fertitta (Prestige Salesman), Raynor Scheine (Gun Dealer), Ed Walsh (Judge), Jim Burk (Prison Guard), Ken Medlock (Shipyard Accountant), Gie-G Duncombe (Accounting Secretary), Dick Butler (Shipyard Security Guard), Blake Clark (Sheriff), Eugenia Ives (Nurse).

When it comes to dealing with themes of physical deformity, Hollywood hasn't exactly been an equal-opportunity employer. Lots of places in the horror department, a few prestige slots for problem dramas like MASK and THE ELEPHANT MAN, but beyond that no other genres have openings. Action director Walter Hill (48 HRS.; EXTREME PREJUDICE) tries to stretch those boundaries a bit in JOHNNY HANDSOME, testing the unexplored ground between conventional shock and conventional uplift in the use of the subject. Unfortunately, the effort comes across as tentative and as something less than a success.

Rourke is the ironically named title character, a severely deformed Louisiana down-and-outer who lives by his criminal wits. He and his only friend (Wilson) mastermind a daring daylight robbery of a New Orleans coin store, assisted by a trigger-happy psychotic (Henriksen) and his over-the-edge girl friend (Barkin). The robbery comes off as planned, but Barkin and Henriksen double-cross their accomplices and take off with the loot on their own, gunning down Wilson in the process and leaving Rourke to take the rap for the robbery. Sent up the (Mississippi) river to the state pen in Angola, Rourke is knifed by prison goons on Henriksen's orders from the outside, then taken to a prison hospital. There he becomes a bone of contention between an idealistic doctor (Whitaker), who thinks Rourke can be rehabilitated if given a new face and social personality, and a cynical lawman (Freeman), who believes that bad is bad (or, as Hill has put it, that "character is destiny") and that Rourke is beyond saving. Whitaker goes ahead with his plan, reconstructing Rourke's features until he looks like . . . well, Mickey Rourke. Meanwhile a kindly hospital nun takes him under her wing, teaching him to speak with his surgically implanted palate and providing him with the kind of emotional mothering and social direction he never had as a kid. Rourke is subsequently paroled from prison and into a new, improved life—but is that really the case? Freeman argues no, hovering in the background like a Cassandra with unwelcome predictions of doom while Rourke works at a New Orleans shipyard and even finds romance with a girl at the shipyard office (McGovern). But the pull of his old life is strong, and Rourke soon sets about getting revenge against the psychotic duo who killed his friend and abandoned him to the cops. Barkin takes a shine to the new Rourke, unaware that he's also the old Rourke, and with Henriksen they plan another robbery, this time of the payroll at Rourke's shipyard. Again the robbery comes off (improbably, given the gang's crude gate-crashing methods), but this time Rourke winds up with the money, after pulling a bait-and-switch on his demented accomplices. Rourke prepares a final confrontation—a late-night meeting in a graveyard—but Henriksen and Barkin, having by now found out Rourke's real identity, come to the meeting with McGovern in tow as a hostage. Guns go off, heads are cracked, and much blood is spilled before, inevitably, Freeman saunters in to survey the damage, retrieve the money, and deliver an epitaph on the fate of rotten apples.

The need to live up to his reputation as an action director seems to be weighing on Hill. The action scenes here are mechanical and tired, the obligatory pummelings, careening cars, and showers of shattered glass—as much as in Hill's RED HEAT, but with far less narrative excuse—all done up in cookie-cutter montage and run out as if by rote. On the other hand, the narrative exposition is superb—tight, noirish, and almost contemplative, a model of minimalist restraint in provocatively lurid circumstances. Hill also maintains his ability to push his actors in new directions here, with Elizabeth McGovern's streetwise cookie being the biggest surprise. Unfortunately, the strategy doesn't pay off in Mickey Rourke's case. His familiar Method tics are gone, but so is some of his acting personality; like Nick Nolte in EXTREME PREJUDICE, Rourke controls himself so tightly he nearly sinks out of sight. Not so with Ellen Barkin and Lance Henriksen, whose overscaled performances have nothing to do with realism and everything to do with nightmare color and mood. They're the midnight flotsam of Mardi Gras, a delirious counterweight to Rourke's laconic underplaying.

For all the fine work on view here, there's still a hollowness at the center of JOHNNY HANDSOME. The story peters out in genre predictability and the novelty of the theme finally seems little more than superficial, a bit of topical fallout in the aftermath of RAINMAN. Like his stoic action heroes, Hill believes in reining himself in; unfortunately, he lets this creative control substitute for creative ambition. Robert Bresson and Carl Dreyer may be his formal models, but the ineffable complexities their films achieve have been beyond Hill's reach. *(Violence, profanity, brief nudity, adult situations.)*

p, Charles Roven; d, Walter Hill; w, Ken Friedman (based on the novel *The Three Worlds of Johnny Handsome* by John Godey); ph, Matthew F. Leonetti (Technicolor); ed, Freeman Davies, Carmel Davies, and Donn Aron; m, Ry Cooder; prod d, Gene Rudolf; art d, Christa Munro; set d, Ernie Bishop; spec eff, Joseph Mercurio; cos, Dan Moore; stunts, Allan Graf; makeup, Michael Westmore.

Action/Crime   (PR:O MPAA:R)

K

Ⓥ K-9 **½
105m UNIV c

James Belushi *(Thomas Dooley)*, Mel Harris *(Tracy)*, Kevin Tighe *(Lyman)*, Ed O'Neill *(Lt. Brannigan)*, Jerry Lee *(K-9)*, James Handy *(Lt. Byers)*, Daniel Davis *(Halstead)*, Cotter Smith *(Gilliam)*, John Snyder *(Freddie)*, Pruitt Taylor Vince *(Benny the Mule)*, Sherman Howard *(Dillon)*, Jeff Allin *(Chad)*, Bob Ari *(Dr. Saunders)*, Alan Blumenfeld *(Rental Salesman)*, Bill Sadler *(Salesman, Don)*, Marjorie Bransfield *(Hostess)*, Mark Mooring *(Cop)*, Jerry Levine *(Ernie)*, Rick Cicetti *(Waiter)*, Dan Castellaneta *(Maitre D')*, Wendel Meldrum *(Pretty Girl with Dog)*, John Castellanos *(Man in Rolls Royce)*, Coleen Morris *(Woman in Rolls Royce)*, Mckeiver Jones III *(Sergeant)*, J.W. Smith *(Pimp)*, Dean Hill *(Butler)*, Gary Combs *(Sculley)*.

The old actor's adage that warns against costarring with kids or animals hasn't stopped stars as diverse as Clint Eastwood, Matthew Broderick, and Tony Danza from sharing the screen with simian thesps in recent years. And now it's the dogs' turn. Following in the footsteps of Chevy Chase and Benji (OH HEAVENLY DOG), James Belushi teams with a German shepherd named Jerry Lee in this tepid but generally inoffensive comedy crime thriller, in which he plays San Diego detective Dooley, a loner who's hot on the trail of a cocaine kingpin (Tighe). When Belushi gets word that Tighe is storing a shipment of coke in a warehouse, he prevails upon K-9 supervisor O'Neill (of TV's controversial "Married with Children") to lend him a dope-sniffing dog. Since Belushi is working strictly outside department guidelines, he doesn't exactly get the pick of the litter. Instead, he winds up with Jerry Lee, an ornery pooch with a fondness for three-alarm-chili. In the time-honored tradition of the buddy film, Belushi and Jerry are like oil and water at first: Jerry refuses to sit in the back seat of Belushi's car and later interferes with the cop's lovemaking with girl friend Harris (TV's "thirtysomething"). But the two misfits warm to each other after Jerry comes to Belushi's rescue during a tense barroom confrontation, handily clearing the room of heavies and holding the chief baddie at bay with well-placed bite. Jerry later becomes instrumental in cracking Belushi's case by sniffing out the means by which Tighe plans to deliver his cache of cocaine to a buyer.

Veteran TV director Rod Daniel keeps the proceedings light and lively, a good thing since, as is the case with so many comedy cop thrillers, the crime plot doesn't make a whole lot of sense. The detective's superiors continually try to pull him off the case, despite the fact that catching big-time coke dealers would certainly seem to fit his job description. Moreover, Tighe's character has surprisingly little difficulty maintaining his facade as a respected businessman in spite of staging several sensational attempts on Belushi's life, including the APOCALYPSE NOW-like helicopter attack on Belushi's car at the lover's lane stakeout that opens the film. Never mind. The core of the film is the growing friendship between the cop and his cantankerous canine partner, and Belushi does a fine job of relating to Jerry Lee as a multi-dimensional character. To be honest, Jerry Lee is no Benji when it comes to his acting talents, but he is likable and receives ample help from editor Lois Freeman-Fox and an extensively credited team of sound mixers and editors that help him to appear almost human. Dean Semler also helps the film along with his moody cinematography.

The film's major irritant, however, is its soundtrack, which is even less original than the plotting. "Iko Iko," of RAIN-MAN fame, is included, as is the severely overused "Oh Yeah," first heard in FERRIS BUELLER'S DAY OFF and reprised far too many times since. Director Daniel even stoops to dusting off the much too familiar JAWS theme to score one comic sequence. Since K-9, like JAWS, is a Universal release, the low copyright payments must have been attractive; still, another choice (damn near any other choice) would have been in order. Yet, for what it is, K-9 is amiable enough entertainment, neither exceptionally good nor abysmally bad. In fact, though it's almost instantly forgettable, the film is just funny and energetic enough to be engaging for casual viewers and its violence is no more severe than that of an average TV cop show. *(Profanity, adult situations.)*

p, Lawrence Gordon and Charles Gordon; d, Rod Daniel; w, Steven Siegel and Scott Myers; ph, Dean Semler (Deluxe color); ed, Lois Freeman-Fox; m, Miles Goodman; prod d, George Costello; art d, Jay Burkhardt; set d, Rance Barela; cos, Eileen Kennedy; stunts, Gary Combs; makeup, Charles Balazs.

Comedy/Crime   (PR:C MPAA:PG-13)

Ⓥ KARATE KID PART III, THE **½
111m Jerry Weintraub/COL c

Ralph Macchio *(Daniel La Russo)*, Noriyuki "Pat" Morita *(Mr. Miyagi)*, Robyn Lively *(Jessica Andrews)*, Thomas Ian Griffith *(Terry Silver)*, Martin L. Kove *(John Kreese)*, Sean Kanan *(Mike Barnes)*, Jonathan Avildsen *(Snake)*, Christopher Paul Ford *(Dennis)*, Randee Heller *(Lucille)*, Pat E. Johnson *(Referee)*, Rick Hurst *(Announcer)*, Frances Bay *(Mrs. Milo)*, Joseph V. Perry *(Uncle Louie)*, Jan Triska *(Milos)*, Diana Webster *(Margaret)*, Patrick Posada *(Man)*, C. Darnell Rose *(Delivery Man)*, Glenn Medeiros *(Himself)*, Gabe Jarret *(Rudy)*, Doc Duhame *(Security Guard)*, Randell Widner, Raymond S. Sua *(Sparring Partners)*, Helen Lin, Meilani Figalan *(Tahitian Girls)*, Garth Johnson, E. David Tetro *(Spectators)*.

During David Puttnam's brief tenure as head of Columbia Pictures, he aired his contempt for Hollywood's obsession with meaningless sequels, declaring that none would be produced at Columbia under his reign. Predictably, Puttnam was deposed quickly and replaced by Hollywood insider Dawn Steel. Rejecting everything Puttnam tried to do, Steel sabotaged her predecessor's projects by refusing to market them properly (even the Academy Award-winning THE LAST EMPEROR was given a less than enthusiastic post-Oscar promotion, leaving Spike Lee's low-budget SCHOOL DAZE as the studio's highest grossing film of the year, despite Columbia's indifference). In addition, feeling the need to rebuke Puttnam's agenda and to refill Columbia's corporate coffers, Steel immediately requested sequels to the studio's highest-grossing movies, GHOST-BUSTERS and THE KARATE KID. Unfortunately, the two films spawned by this action present some of the laziest work to come out of a major Hollywood studio in years. GHOSTBUSTERS II is a shockingly slapdash and self-satisfied affair, and THE KARATE KID PART III is half-hearted, uninspired, and terribly dull.

More a sequel to the original film than a continuation of the action from THE KARATE KID II (the main character's girl friend in the second film is dismissed immediately, with a line of dialog explaining their breakup), the film begins with a reprise of the climax of THE KARATE KID as Macchio wins the All Valley karate tournament, snatching victory from the evil Cobra Kai karate dojo, a martial arts institution run by the venal Kove, whose philosophy is to show "no mercy." Enraged that his students lost the tournament, Kove physically abuses his charges in the parking lot. Outraged by this behavior, Macchio's mentor, the wise old Morita, intervenes to stop the violence and is attacked by the much younger and bigger Kove. Morita effortlessly deflects him, leaving Kove with two broken and bloodied hands. The action then moves to the present. Since losing the tournament, Kove's Cobra Kai dojo has suffered a disastrous decline in enrollment, leaving its owner practically a bum. Things begin to turn around for Kove, however, when he calls on Griffith, an old army buddy from Vietnam. Now a phenomenally successful businessman who has made a fortune dumping toxic waste (the name of his corporation is Dynatox!), Griffith is also an expert in martial arts and has a mean streak wider than Kove's. Taking pity on his compadre, Griffith offers to franchise the Cobra Kai dojos nationwide and to help defeat Macchio in the upcoming All Valley karate tournament. To this end, he concocts an elaborate plot designed first to force the reluctant Macchio to defend his title and then to con the boy into rejecting Morita's teaching in favor of a much more painful and aggressive regimen, which will hurt and humiliate Macchio at the tournament. Meanwhile, Macchio and Morita have returned to Los Angeles after a trip to Okinawa, only to discover that the apartment building where Macchio lived and Morita worked has been razed to make room for condominiums. Realizing that the elderly Morita is faced with a forced retirement, Macchio gives up his first semester college tuition money to finance the lease on a dilapidated shop in which Morita can open a bonsai tree nursery. Together, the pair begin to renovate the shop and stock it with bonsai trees. Macchio even makes the acquaintance of Lively, an attractive young woman who works in the pottery shop across the street. Everything seems to be going well until Kanan, the "bad boy" of karate selected by Griffith to defeat Macchio, shows up with a pair of teenage goons to intimidate Macchio into signing up for the tournament (after much debate with Morita, who believes karate shouldn't be used to win trophies, Macchio had decided not to defend his title). After Macchio refuses to comply on several different occasions, the brutal boys destroy the shop and steal Morita's stock of expensive bonsai trees. Remembering that Morita once showed him a secluded cliffside location near the ocean where he had planted a real bonsai tree from Okinawa, Macchio decides to fetch the tree (worth several thousand dollars) from the wild and sell it to refinance the shop. Macchio needs to rappel down a cliff face to do so, but, luckily, Lively just happens to be an expert rappeller and accompanies him on his quest. They are followed by Kanan and his thugs, who threaten the vulnerable couple with death unless Macchio signs up for the tournament. Left with no choice, he complies, but Morita refuses to train him for the competition. Frustrated, desperate, and confused, Macchio turns to toxic waste king Griffith (who has already positioned himself as an alternative instructor by posing as a friendly and concerned regular-guy karate expert). Griffith, of course, teaches Macchio to fight with anger in his heart according to the "no mercy" philosophy, encouraging the kid to inflict not just pain, but damage. The training has a profound effect on Macchio's personality and he becomes harsh and violent, going so far as to break the nose of a teenager who hits on Lively (in an incident instigated by Grif-

fith). Shocked by his own brutality, Macchio smartens up and begs Morita to undo the damage by re-training him. Inexplicably, Morita reverses himself and agrees. At the tournament, Kove and Griffith instruct Kanan to make Macchio suffer throughout the match by legitimately scoring a point and then having the point taken away by fighting dirty, thus prolonging Macchio's agony. But after a number of excruciating exchanges, the battered and bruised Macchio once again manages to beat his tormentors, and the film ends with a freeze-frame close-up of the triumphant Macchio and his mentor, Morita.

When one considers that the original KARATE KID was released five years ago and that its young star, Ralph Macchio, is now in his late 20s, married, and a father, shouldn't the title of this film be "The Karate *Man* I?" The further adventures of Macchio and Morita are becoming absurd, especially since Macchio's character seems to be pretty dim, having learned nothing from Morita's endless lectures and lessons on spirituality, discipline, and honor. But, quite frankly, it's hard to blame the kid because, in this installment, Morita's pseudo-Confucian sayings ("You, like bonsai tree, have strong root!") are about as profound as the average Charlie Chan aphorism. Since the scenes between Macchio and Morita—the real appeal of the series—seem uninspired and forced this time around, one has to make do with the totally over-the-top villains—guys who always dress in black, are unbelievably sadistic, and enjoy tilting their heads back and laughing maniacally every three minutes or so. The dour Martin Kove is back for what amounts to a cameo performance

(he appears in the beginning, then disappears until the very end), but Thomas Ian Griffith, as the toxic waste king, is the one who really steals the show. Turning in a performance that makes Jack Nicholson's turn as the Joker in BATMAN look restrained, Griffith, with his hair slicked back and tied in a small ponytail, leers, scowls, bugs out his eyes, yells, sneers, snaps at the help, and indulges frequently in the aforementioned maniacal laughter. (The highlight occurs in a scene in which Griffith sits in a Jacuzzi, smoking a cigar. Barking into a cellular phone, he commands a lackey to dump some waste in a Third World country because the locals won't know the difference, ending the conversation with a harsh "Just do it! HAHAHAHAHAHAHAHA!" This guy is *bad*.) The rest of the villains are the usual bunch of young Aryans who have plagued the swarthy Macchio throughout the series and simply lack the fiendish panache of their older counterparts. It is a testament to the bland predictability of THE KARATE KID PART III that these cartoon bad guys manage to steal the film, representing the only signs of life in an otherwise brain-dead movie. Songs include: "Listen to Your Heart" (Tom Kelly, Billy Steinberg, performed by Little River Band), "Summer in the City" (John Sebastian, Steve Boone, Mark Sebastian, performed by the Pointer Sisters), "Under Any Moon" (Diane Warren, performed by Glenn Medeiros, Elizabeth Wolfgramm), "The First Impression" (Jude Cole, performed by Cole), "This Could Take All Night" (Warren, performed by Boys Club), "In a Trance" (Sverre Wiik, Harald Wiik, performed by Money Talks), "48 Hours"

Jessica Andrews, Ralph Macchio, and Pat Morita in THE KARATE KID III (©Columbia).

(Vinnie Chas, Kari Kane, Kristy Majors, Steve Summers, Mitch Stevens, performed by PBF), "Bed O'Nails" (Miklos Factor, performed by Factor), "I Can't Help Myself" (Alan Roy Scott, Richard Hahn, Steve Greenberg, performed by Glenn Medeiros), "High Wire" (Jeff Silbar, Chuck Wild, performed by Medeiros), "Out For the Count" (Kip Winger, Reb Beach, Brad Miskell, performed by Winger). *(Violence.)*

p, Jerry Weingraub and Karen Trudy Rosenfelt; d, John G. Avildsen; w, Robert Mark Kamen; ph, Steve Yaconelli (Deluxe color); ed, John Carter and John G. Avildsen; m, Bill Conti; prod d, William F. Matthews; art d, Chris Burian-Mohr; set d, Carl Stensel; spec eff, Bill Mesa; cos, Michael Chavez; chor, Paula Abdul; stunts, Pat E. Johnson; makeup, Del Acevedo.

Drama   (PR:A-C MPAA:PG)

Ⓥ**KICKBOXER**½**
105m Kings Road/Pathe c
Jean-Claude Van Damme *(Kurt Sloane)*, Dennis Alexio *(Eric Sloane)*, Dennis Chan *(Xian Chow)*, Tong Po *(Himself)*, Haskell Anderson *(Winston Taylor)*, Rochelle Ashana *(Mylee)*, Steve Lee *(Freddy Li)*, Richard Foo *(Tao Liu)*, Ricky Liu *(Big Thai Man)*, Sin Ho Ying, Tony Chan *(Huge Village Men)*, Brad Kerner, Dean Harrington *(US Announcers)*, Mark DiSalle, Richard Santoro, Louis Roth, Nickolas James *(US Reporters)*, John Ladalski *(US Referee)*, Mathew Cheung *(Surgeon)*, Zennie Reynolds *(US Fighter)*, Montri Vongbuter, Amnart Komolthorn *(Ancient Warriors)*, Pairat Lavilard *(Gym Officer)*, Kanthima Vutti *(Eric's Girl)*.

ROCKY IV meets THE KARATE KID meets Jean-Claude Van Damme's feet in this kick-socky saga set and filmed in Thailand. As the film begins, Van Damme is helping his brother (real-life kickboxing champ Alexio) compete in American kickboxing championships. After distinguishing himself in that competition, Alexio travels to Thailand to test his talents in the land where the sport originated. But in his very first match there, Alexio is paralyzed by the fearsome Tong Po. Vowing revenge, Van Damme becomes the pupil of Chan, a whimsical martial-arts master in the Pat Morita mold, who drops coconuts on Van Damme from a great height to strengthen his stomach and ties raw meat to his protege's leg so his dog will chase him, forcing Van Damme to become faster. Chan also has a conveniently attractive, unmarried niece (Ashana), who provides the movie's love interest. She and Van Damme meet when he wrecks her small food market while dispatching two extortionist toughs, who, it turns out, are connected to a crime lord who also happens to be the feared Tong Po's manager. Kicking

his way through some preliminary matches, Van Damme becomes known as the "white warrior" and soon challenges Tong Po. Their battle is staged in the "ancient manner," with the fighters wearing hemp wraps on their hands that have been dipped in resin and coated with broken glass. Then, as if Van Damme isn't having enough fun, the crime lord ups the ante by sending his thugs to kidnap both Ashana, who is raped by Tong Po, and Alexio, who is held captive to force Van Damme to throw the fight. What's more, the thugs stab Chan's dog. (Oh, Jeez.) If you can't guess Chan's next move and how this all ends, it's time to turn in your moviegoer's black belt.

KICKBOXER deviates little from genre formula in its presentation of a peace-loving martial artist who is pushed too far and goes on a maniacal rampage in the final reel. Nobody, however, goes to martial-arts movies for their comic-book plots, klutzy dialog, or hammy acting—all of which KICKBOXER has in abundance. They go for the action. And on that level, at least, KICKBOXER delivers the goods.

Van Damme, though hardly in line for an Oscar nomination, nevertheless manages to be less than awful most of the time. In his second outing for Cannon (home studio for action bruisers Charles Bronson and Chuck Norris), Van Damme even allows himself a few self-mocking, humorous moments, a la Arnold Schwarzenegger, proving himself a likable good sport. In the fights, where it counts, Van Damme is quick, graceful, and balletic. Moreover, the fights themselves, choreographed and directed by the star, are crisply staged and sharply edited.

In short, with KICKBOXER (codirected by Mark DiSalle and David Worth), what you see is what you get. It ain't Shakespeare, but it moves fast and lives up to its title. Despite the broken glass and mostly offscreen (though thoroughly gratuitous) rape, it's not even as grisly as the genre sometimes gets. But for those with no use for the genre who find themselves shanghaied into a screening, there is an added perk. The exotic Thai scenery gives a better performance than the actors much of the time. *(Violence, profanity, sexual situations.)*

p, Mark DiSalle; d, Mark DiSalle and David Worth; w, Glenn Bruce (based on a story by Mark DiSalle, Jean-Claude Van Damme); ph, Jon Kranhouse (Technicolor); ed, Wayne Wahrman; m, Paul Hertzog; md, David Chackler; prod d, Shay Austin; art d, Sita Yeung and Chaiyan Chunsuttiwat; spec eff, Tuffy Lau, Samrit Sripaitakkulvilai, Bang, and Daeng; chor, Jean-Claude Van Damme; stunts, John Cheung; makeup, Earl Ellis.

Action   (PR:C MPAA:R)

Ⓥ**KINJITE: FORBIDDEN SUBJECTS****
97m Golan-Globus/Cannon c
Charles Bronson *(Lt. Crowe)*, Perry Lopez *(Eddie Rios)*, Juan Fernandez *(Duke)*, Peggy Lipton *(Kathleen Crowe)*, James Pax *(Hiroshi Hada)*, Sy Richardson *(Lavonne)*, Marion Kodama Yue *(Mr. Kazuko Hada)*, Bill McKinney *(Father Burke)*, Gerald Castillo *(Captain Tovar)*, Nicole Eggert *(DeeDee)*, Amy Hathaway *(Rita Crowe)*, Kumiko Hayakawa *(Fumiko Hada)*, Michelle Wong *(Setsuko Hada)*, Sam Chew, Jr. *(McLane)*, Sumant *(Pakistani Hotel Clerk)*, Alex Hyde-White *(English Instructor)*, James Ishida *(Nakata)*, Jill Ito *(Japanese Hostess, Tokyo)*, Leila Hee Olsen *(Nobu-Chan)*, Richard Egan Jr. *(Vince)*, Deonca Brown *(Louise)*, Sheila Gale Kandlbinder *(Swimming Coach)*, Chris Bennett *(School Photographer)*, George Van Noy *(Race Starter)*, Helen Lin *(Tokyo Subway Girl)*, Richard E. Butler *(Joey, Deli Owner)*, James Ogawa *(Kokuden Representative)*, Bill Cho Lee *(Ota)*, Cynthia Gouw *(Japanese Hostess, L.A.)*, Veronica Carothers *(Blonde Hostess)*, Alonzo Brown Jr. *(Mugger)*, Michael Chong *(Lt. Lim)*, Yung Sun *(Grey Haired Japanese)*, Shaun Shimoda *(Japanese Calligraphy Teacher)*, Mindy Simon *(Schoolgirl)*, Samuel E. Woods *(Hot Dog Vendor)*, Rob Narita *(Japanese School Principal)*, Yuri Ogawa *(Mrs. Ota)*, Shelli Rae, Jessica Younger *(Duke's Girls)*, William Brochtrup *(Hairdresser)*, Laura Crosson *(Officer Petrini)*, Tom Morga *(Krieger)*, Kim Lee *(Porno Actress)*, Marilyn Dodds Frank *(Lesbian Pedophile)*, John F. McCarthy *(Porno Theater Manager)*.

KINJITE: FORBIDDEN SUBJECTS is yet another spin-off of DEATH WISH, and probably the most distasteful of them all. For the prurient, the film has just about everything: rape, lesbianism, sadomasochism, sodomy, and, worst of all, forced child prostitution as its prime subject—forbidden subjects indeed! Once again, Bronson plays a bleeding heart lusting for blood, a man who spends his days slogging through slime as a cop on the vice squad and his nights fretting about the morals of his proper teenage daughter, Hathaway. His long-standing nemesis is rich, subsleazy pimp Fernandez, who specializes in impressing children into the kinky sex trade through abduction and drug addiction. Naturally, Bronson is no "by-the-book" cop, and goes after his quarry through such unconventional means as forcing the pimp to swallow a watch, blowing up his car, and (off-screen, thankfully) sodomizing a john with a dildo "to show you how it feels!" As his frustrated superior (Castillo) says, "Justice isn't good enough. You gotta exact a biblical vengeance." Still, Fernandez doesn't get the message and unsuccessfully attempts to blow Bronson away with a grease gun. Meanwhile, in

Charles Bronson in KINJITE (©Pathe).

Tokyo, a Japanese businessman, Pax, and his family prepare to transfer to Los Angeles and the film treats us to a view, for no real reason, of Japanese executive after-work rituals, including heavy drinking and fooling around with bar girls. When Pax, taking his cue from an earlier incident on a Tokyo subway, gets Stateside and gropes Hathaway on a bus, Bronson turns abusively anti-Asian. Next, Fernandez spots Hayakawa, Pax's young daughter, in a park. He kidnaps, gang rapes, and addicts her to heroin, then, inexplicably, markets the child right under Bronson's nose, lining her up with a lesbian, a spanking freak, and others. Bronson finds her in record time and, in the process, discovers that the Japanese are, golly, really decent people, too. When safe at home, Hayakawa commits suicide with an overdose of heroin, leaving Bronson a haiku that provides a clue to Fernandez's whereabouts. Now comes the obligatory "biblical" havoc the film has been gearing up for, as Bronson tracks the pimp to a boat in a nearby harbor and it takes the gory killing of a cop, the decimation of an assortment of baddies, and the blowing up of an entire ship's dock before Bronson gets his man. Finally, in quiet satisfaction, he follows the miscreant to a jail cell where a massive brute of an inmate droolingly waits to sodomize the pimp. "Poetic justice," says Bronson with a puffy, stolid twinkle. "Revolting," the viewer is likely to reply.

In general, the cast is acceptable. Bronson does his standard violent-teddy-bear number believably, and the supporting cast does as well as it can with a formula script by Harold Nebenzal and meet-the-budget direction by J. Lee Thompson. Juan Fernandez plays the slimeball pimp with stomach-turning authenticity;

Kumiko Hayakawa barely registers the horror of being subjected to the ugliest abuses a child can endure, but the fault may be assigned to the casual direction and writing of her character. KINJITE (the Japanese word for *forbidden subjects*) is sheer exploitation that barely escapes an X rating, a hodgepodge of shallow—if not fake—"moral" issues intended to lend the film an air of righteousness as it lick its lips over the vilely tititllating crimes it claims to condemn. There is nothing to be learned here about racial phobias, sexual hangups and excesses, or the tragedy of child sex exploitation, though the film pretends to touch on all these problems. KINJITE: FORBIDDEN SUBJECTS has no real plot, just a string of provocative scenes whose sole purpose is to provide cheap voyeuristic thrills. *(Graphic violence, excessive profanity, nudity, substance abuse, sexual situations.)*

p, Pancho Kohner; d, J. Lee Thompson; w, Harold Nebenzal; ph, Gideon Porath (TVC color); ed, Peter Lee Thompson and Mary E. Jochem; m, Greg DeBelles; art d, W. Brooke Wheeler; set d, Margaret C. Fischer; spec eff, Burt C. Dalton; cos, Michael Hoffman; stunts, Ernie Orsatti; makeup, Carla Fabrizi.

Crime/Thriller   (PR:O   MPAA:R)

ⓥKUNG FU MASTER**
(Fr.) 80m Cine-Tamaris-Sept/Capital c (LE PETIT AMOUR)
Jane Birkin *(Mary-Jane)*, Mathieu Demy *(Julien)*, Charlotte Gainsbourg *(Lucy)*, Lou Doillon, Eva Simonet, Judy Campbell. ·

Directed by French filmmaker Agnes Varda (VAGABOND), KUNG FU MASTER opens with a divorced Parisian mother of two (Birkin) comforting her young daughter (Doillon) who's sick in bed, while her other, teenaged child (Birkin's real-life daughter, Gainsbourg) has a party in the courtyard. In the bathroom, Birkin finds a young guest who has had too much drink (Demy) and ministers to his discomfort. After scolding him, she goes back to sing a lullaby to Doillon. When she looks up to see Demy watching them, Birkin is intrigued. She feels that she must see him again, and she makes sure she does. Demy pays another visit, and Birkin takes him and Doillon to an arcade, where the 40-year-old woman watches the teenager concentrate on his favorite video game (which provides the film with its misleading title). In the course of events, Birkin runs into Demy in a hotel elevator, and, later, she learns that he and Gainsbourg have arranged for Demy to be a part of the family trip to visit Birkin's parents in England. At Easter, Demy finds Birkin hiding eggs in the yard, and the two kiss. However, they are interrupted by Gainsbourg, who is appalled. Birkin tells her mother that she has to get away (though it is never

clear what it is she is getting away from) and is offered the use of the family summer cottage, conveniently located on a private island. Surprisingly, in the next scene, she arrives on the island, accompanied by Doillon and Demy. Upon their return from this romp in the wild, the flourishing romance between Birkin and Demy scandalizes the neighborhood.Demy has to change schools, and Birkin loses custody of Gainsbourg—her reason for living. The lovelorn Birkin wanders, sighs, and misses Demy. He, on the other hand, seems to be able to get on with his life rather easily. Hanging out with the guys, he relates the story of the liaison as a "duty" he performed for the benefit of Birkin.

Has Demy's young lover lost his grand passion, or was he ever capable of such profound emotion in the first place? Is Birkin's Mary Jane ever going to get over her intense feelings for this younger man? Will audiences be able to figure out what she saw in him? It's the last question that is the most troubling. KUNG FU MASTER hinges on an unconventional handling of the familiar May-December romance. Instead of suggesting that this older woman is too old for this younger man—the usual "ageist" response to this cinematic situation—the film wonders if Demy's Mathieu is old enough—period. At 14, is Mathieu even physically mature enough to consummate this relationship? In scenes such as the one where Mary Jane and Mathieu zip their sleeping bags together it seems reasonable to conclude that the two are simply "sleeping" together. Even when Mary Jane says, "Kiss me or I will die," the boy is only able to respond with an ardent childlike kiss. But if their relationship isn't based on sex, it seems no more likely that it is the result of intellectual compatibility. Like Mathieu's video gamesmanship, his explanation of "Dungeons and Dragons" hardly seems the sort of thing that would engage a mature woman's interest for long. Moreover, his extreme youth invests the romance and the film as a whole with the chill of perversion, even as director Varda appears to be attempting to persuade the viewer of the normalcy of the situation.

The point? Considering the number of references to AIDS in the film, KUNG FU MASTER appears to offer a recipe for a successful AIDS-era relationship: reserve the dizzying anguish of romance for women, allow men a flip, independent attitude, stir lightly to obtain just the right level of froth, but prohibit all sexual contact. (In French; English subtitles.) *(Substance abuse, sexual situations, adult situations.)*

p, Agnes Varda; d, Agnes Varda; w, Agnes Varda (based on an idea by Jane Birkin); ph, Pierre-Laurent Chenieux; ed, Marie-Josee Audiard; m, Joanna Bruzdowicz.

Romance   (PR:O   MPAA:R)

L

ⓥL.A. BOUNTY*½
81m Adventuress/Noble-Alpine c
Sybil Danning (Ruger), Wings Hauser (Cavanaugh), Henry Darrow (Lt. Chandler), Lenore Kasdorf (Kelly Rhodes), Robert Hanley (Mike Rhodes), Van Quattro (Michaels), Bob Minor (Martin), Frank Doubleday (Rand), Maxine Wasa (Model), Robert Quarry (Jimmy), Blackie Dammett (James Maxwell), J. Christopher Sullivan.

Buxom B-movie queen Sybil Danning stars as an ex-cop-turned-bounty-hunter in this lifeless thriller. The film begins as a prominent Los Angeles mayoral candidate (Hanley) is kidnaped by a group of drug dealers led by an insane artist (Hauser). After nearly being killed, the candidate's wife (Kasdorf) joins up with Danning, as the bounty hunter pursues Hauser. It seems that Danning has a score to settle: her failure to arrest Hauser and his cohorts when she was a cop resulted in the death of her partner, and now she wants revenge. Following several chase scenes and shootouts, the kidnapers finally make their demands. Kasdorf is to come up with $500,000 and bring it to the middle of the desert. Closely followed by the police, Kasdorf drives to the designated spot and is met by the kidnapers. Both she and the money are snatched by the drug thugs, who explode a truck full of SWAT officers before heading to Hauser's warehouse. Meanwhile, Danning hunts down, questions, and eventually kills three of Hauser's old friends. Learning the location of the warehouse, she drives there in her big pick-up truck. It is soon revealed that candidate Hanley has planned this elaborate kidnaping scheme himself, hoping to boost his popularity in the polls. However, his wife, who knew nothing of the scheme, is now in the hands of the sadistic drug dealers. What's more, Hauser double-crosses Hanley and eventually kills him. Just as he is about to do away with Kasdorf, Danning appears, and a wild shootout ensues. Fascinated with games, Hauser uses flashing lights and a stuffed polar bear to confuse Danning, but she negotiates his strange obstacle course and, in the film's climax, comes face to face with madman Hauser, who holds Kasdorf at gun-point.

L.A. BOUNTY is a sloppily structured, poorly executed B movie with tedious "action" sequences and soporific set pieces. Danning, who can be quite entertaining, provides a stiff, unconvincing female alternative to Clint Eastwood. Limited to about six lines of dialog, she spends the entire film in a stone-faced stupor, waltzing into scenes carrying automatic weapons and leaving behind dead bodies. Many drive-in-movie lovers argue that

Danning's best asset as an actress is her chest, but these fans will be disappointed to learn that the pneumatic star wears a turtleneck and leather jacket for the entire film.

Technically, L.A. BOUNTY is a mess. Although it is nicely photographed, the story is so predictable, choppy, and badly directed, that the film is never entertaining. The few energetic moments the movie offers are provided by the usually reliable, almost-always psychotic Wings Hauser. Hauser (who played one of the scariest villains in B-movie history in Gary Sherman's VICE SQUAD) again goes over the top here, wringing plenty of bizarre laughs out of the lifeless dialog. His fits of rage and his conversations with God are undeniably entertaining and, occasionally, quite scary. He is especially effective when he sadistically disposes of a couple of his double-crossing henchmen. All of the energetic insanity that Hauser provides goes to waste, however; L.A. BOUNTY remains a tired action yarn bound to disappoint those looking for B-movie thrills. (Violence, profanity, nudity, adult situations, substance abuse.)

p, Sybil Danning and Michael W. Leighton; d, Worth Keeter; w, Michael W. Leighton (based on a story by Sybil Danning); ph, Gary Graver (Foto-Kem Color); ed, Stewart Schill; m, Howard Leese and Sterling; art d, Phil Brandes; stunts, Bob Bralver.

Action   (PR:O MPAA:NR)

ⓥL.A. HEAT½**
85m Pepin-Merhi/PM Entertainment c
Lawrence-Hilton Jacobs (Jon Chance), Jim Brown (Captain), Kevin Benton (Clarence), Myles Thoroughgood (Spyder), Pat Johnson (Jane), Jay Richardson (Boris), Raymond Martino, Robert Gallo, Joe Vance, Gretchen Becker, Jamie Baker, Pamela Dixon, Jacqueline Jade, Marisa Wade, Renny Stroud.

A reasonably entertaining low-budget crime thriller, L.A. HEAT stars Jacobs as Jon Chance, a Los Angeles cop having a bad day. It all starts with a drug stakeout that turns bloody when the suspect (Benton) kills Jacobs' partner and escapes. When Jacobs sets a second trap for Benton with an undercover drug buy, three more cops are killed and Benton escapes once again, getting away with both the police department's money and the drugs. Jacobs' captain (Brown) gives him a 72-hour deadline to bring Benton in, but the bloodshed escalates, embarrassing the department and leading to Jacobs' suspension. Working with Thoroughgood, a gang leader who has captured Benton, Jacobs makes a deal to turn over Benton's drug boss (who has also killed the gang leader's brother) in return for Benton, the drugs, and the money. But Benton—you guessed

it—escapes yet again, and this time heads straight for Jacobs' house, where the gang leader has hidden the drugs and where Jacobs' girl friend is waiting for him.

Whenever a character in a film has a name like Jon Chance, action movie fans tend to sit up and take notice, since John Chance was also the name of John Wayne's character in Howard Hawks' classic western RIO BRAVO. Lawrence-Hilton Jacobs, who in addition to starring in L.A. HEAT coproduced and -scripted the film (he also cowrote one of its songs), even sends up the Duke in a dream sequence wherein Jacobs and Kevin Benton, in western garb, meet for a high-noon showdown. L.A. HEAT also shares RIO BRAVO's leisurely pacing, which doesn't necessarily work in its favor—in spite of its complicated story, it feels slow-moving. But the film passes a more important test in that it doesn't make you wish you were watching RIO BRAVO instead. Jacobs, though not as wooden as Wayne, is similarly laid back. To be sure, he's not as imposing as the Duke, and keeps threatening to lay too far back and disappear into the scenery, but even that is preferable to *chewing* the scenery as too many other would-be action heroes do. Overall, Jacobs is both competent and engaging, an actor to watch.

The supporting cast proves a solid ensemble, which (to further extend the comparison to RIO BRAVO) is to say that there's not a Ricky Nelson among them. Benton is imposing as the cold-blooded killer, bringing a steely eye and menacing presence to the film, and Myles Thoroughgood is also convincing as the smart, streetwise gang leader. But the real surprise is Jim Brown, who brings some real personality to the standard gruff-but-tenderhearted precinct captain role.

On the genre level, however, L.A. HEAT is rather tepid. The plot is really too complicated for its own good, and the filmmakers would have done well to further follow RIO BRAVO's example in providing an uncluttered, elemental scenario. L.A. HEAT could get rid of fully a third of its characters—mainly the drug boss and his entourage—without losing anything of importance. Moreover, Joseph Merhi's direction seldom rises above the routine. The pacing is slack and, perhaps as a result of the modest production budget, characters spend entirely too much time standing around and talking to each other rather than generating action and suspense. Still, when all the pluses and minuses are tallied, L.A. HEAT ranks above average as low-budget action thrillers go, proving that, even in the netherland of the direct-to-video B-movie, a little sensitivity to nuances of character, mood, and performance—along with just a bit of intelligence—can go a long way. (Violence, profanity, adult situations.)

p, Joseph Merhi, Richard Pepin, Charla Driver, and Addison Randall; d, Joseph Merhi; w, Charles T. Kanganis and Lawrence-Hilton Jacobs; ph, Richard Pepin; ed, Paul Volk; m, John Gonzalez; makeup, Judy Yonemoto.

Crime   **(PR:C MPAA:NR)**

🅥**LA LECTRICE****½
(Fr.) 100m Elefilm-AAA Prods-TSF-Cine 5/Orion c
(Trans: The Reader)
Miou-Miou *(Constance/Marie)*, Christian Ruche *(Jean/Philippe)*, Maria Casares *(The General's Widow)*, Patrick Chesnais *(Company Director)*, Marianne Denicourt *(Bella)*, Pierre Dux *(Magistrate)*, Sylvie Laporte *(Francoise)*, Brigitte Catillon *(Eric's Mother/Jocelyne)*, Michel Raskine *(Man at Agency)*, Christian Blanc *(Marie's Tutor)*, Regis Royer *(Eric)*, Simon Eine *(Hospital Professor)*, Andre Wilms *(Man in Rue Saint-Landry)*, Clotilde de Bayser *(Coralie's Mother)*, Berangere Bonvoisin *(Joel's Mother/Hotel Waitress)*, Jean-Luc Boutte *(Police Inspector)*, Charlotte Farran *(Coralie)*, Leo Campion *(Eric's Grandfather)*, Hito Jaulmes *(Joel)*, Maria de Medeiros *(Silent Nurse)*, Isabelle Janier *(Talkative Nurse)*, Sylvie Jean *(Agency Secretary)*, Gabriel Barakian *(Jocelyne's Husband)*.

Probably best known in the US for his stylish but hollow thriller PERIL (1985), director Michel Deville returns with this adaptation of Raymond Jean's 1986 novel *La Lectrice*. Miou-Miou stars as Constance, a short-haired blonde with a sonorous voice who enjoys reading to her boy friend in bed. As the film opens, the novel she's reading aloud is Jean's *La Lectrice*, whose main character, Marie, is not unlike Constance. As Constance reads, Marie (also played by Miou-Miou) is seen deciding to place a newspaper ad offering her services as a "reader" of novels, poems, manuscripts, and other texts on a private, in-home basis. Her first client is a young paraplegic (Royer) who lives with his overprotective mother and eccentric grandfather. Miou-Miou reads him Baudelaire, but it's the sexually arousing sight of the top of her stockings that sends the young man into remission. Already, the reader is affecting her clients in ways she cannot control. The next person to purchase her services is an aged, blind general's widow (Casares) who hires Marie to read Marx and Lenin and whose strange maid (Denicourt) believes that spiders live under her skin. A much younger client follows when Marie is hired to read to the six-year-old daughter (Farran) of a working mother too busy to care for her child. Marie tries to hold the child's attention by reading her Lewis Carroll's *Alice's Adventures in Wonderland*, but the girl would prefer to play outside, and Marie, forgetting for a

moment that she is a reader, agrees to put the book down and take the girl to a nearby carnival, only to be charged with kidnaping later. The lines between reader and companion become further blurred when she is hired by a pathetic, overworked businessman (Chesnais) who is more interested in the reader than what she reads—*The Lover*, by Marguerite Duras. In order to hold her client's interest in the text, Marie mixes literature with his sexual gratification—undressing for him, letting him touch and eventually make love to her—while she reads Duras aloud. Marie's career as a reader ends, however, when she refuses to read the Marquis de Sade to a retired judge and his two friends. As the fictional Marie ends her career with the final pages of the novel *La Lectrice*, the real-life Constance, aroused by the character's life and power, finishes the novel and tells her boy friend that she is considering advertising her services as a reader.

Though intricately structured and innovatively staged, LA LECTRICE is an essentially one-note movie with very little content and even less personality or heart. Deville's film revolves around the intimate bond between writer and audience, and the mysterious, subconscious, insatiable paths that reading opens up in the latter. When a third person—the reader—is placed between writer and audience, the intimacies, fantasies, mysteries, and desires that have taken seed in the world of the book become misguided and projected. Marie, the innocent reader at the film's start, gradually discovers that what she does makes her an intimate friend of the person to whom she is reading—not because of who she is (she admits to being completely unimaginative), but because of what she reads. For the paraplegic boy, she becomes the object of blossoming Baudelairean desires; for the general's widow, she becomes a political comrade; for the young girl, she becomes the guide on a path to Wonderland; for the repressed businessman, she becomes the ultimate lover. Marie wisely leaves her profession before becoming a victim of the old judge's Sadean pleasures.

While the theme of LA LECTRICE is compelling, the film itself is not. Rather than creating a movie with life and imagination all its own, Deville has produced a cold thesis on readers and reading that says nothing at all about real human emotions or desires. LA LECTRICE is an exercise in film language and cinematic structure, but unlike the work of the greatest directors in this mode (Jean-Luc Godard, Alain Resnais, Raul Ruiz), Deville's exercise is empty. Fortunately, there are some pleasant performances to captivate even the most demanding viewer. Miou-Miou is excellent as Constance/Marie, adapting to the surroundings of her clients and deliv-

ering lovely readings of the very different prose of de Sade, Duras, Lenin, and Carroll. Equally remarkable is Maria Casares, who so memorably embodied Death in Jean Cocteau's classic ORPHEUS (1950), and who is wonderfully vibrant as the general's widow here. (In French; English subtitles.) *(Nudity, sexual situations, profanity.)*

p, Michel Deville and Rosalinde Deville; d, Michel Deville; w, Michel Deville and Rosalinde Deville (based on the books *La Lectrice* and *Un Fantasme de Bella B. et Autre Recits* by Raymond Jean); ph, Dominique Le Rigoleur (Eastmancolor); ed, Raymonde Guyot; m, Ludwig van Beethoven; prod d, Thierry Leproust; art d, Ysabelle van Wersch-cot; set d, Max Legardeur, Roseanna Sacco, and Marion Griffouliere; cos, Cecile Balme; makeup, Joel Lavau.

Comedy/Drama   **(PR:O MPAA:R)**

🅥**LAST WARRIOR, THE****
(Brit.) 94m ITC-Label/SVS c
(AKA: COASTWATCHER)
Gary Graham *(Jim Kemp)*, Maria Holvoe *(Katherine)*, Cary-Hiroyuki Tagawa *(Imperial Marine)*, John Carson *(Priest)*.

From HEAVEN KNOWS, MR. ALLISON to HELL IN THE PACIFIC to RAMBO: FIRST BLOOD, PART II, films pitting a lone American soldier against an oriental counterpart in a remote island setting have existed as a subgenre of the war film. Combining action and symbolism, these films not only provide opportunities for fast-paced, visceral excitement, but also allow capable filmmakers to juxtapose the divergent cultures represented by the adversaries, who—although pledged to fight to the death—wind up with grudging admiration for each other. Intended as a meditation on the clash between the Samurai tradition of the honorable warrior and Western survival-at-all-costs pragmatism, writer-director Martin Wragge's ambitious THE LAST WARRIOR emerges as a carefully crafted but self-consciously arty effort that sacrifices suspense and excitement for obtuse symbolism and self-defeating displays of cinematic technique.

Graham is the sole American soldier posted on an obscure island in the South Pacific during the final days of WW II. Assigned to watch the coast and maintain radio contact with the faraway Allied command, he is considered something of a pariah by the other Westerners on the island—a priest and several nuns, who fear that Graham's radio will attract the Japanese to their peaceful spot, which has thus far remained untouched by the war. Graham seems content to deal with his isolation by listening to classical music on his wind-up Victrola, playing with his pet monkeys, and consorting with sarong-clad native women, but his idyll comes to an abrupt end when a Japanese ship suddenly appears in the bay. In a short burst of brutality, the Japanese "depopulate" the island, with the notable exceptions of Graham and Holvoe, an attractive young Swedish novice who has managed to secure a hiding place. Together, they try to radio for help while eluding the three Imperial Marines who remain on the island. Thanks to a back-up radio Graham has hidden in a beached, long-abandoned ship, the fugitives contact the Americans, only to learn that no troops are available to rescue them and that the Japanese are planning to use the island's deep-water bay to repair a severely damaged battleship. Heading for a cave in the hills, Graham and Holvoe are spotted by the sword-wielding marines, and the hunt is on. Graham wastes little time dispatching his first two adversaries, but the third—an intense, honor-obsessed modern samurai (Tagawa)—is strong, resourceful, and seemingly unstoppable. Which of the two warriors will triumph is the question that dominates the remainder of the film.

Although there are occasional timeouts for palpable sexual tension between Graham and Holvoe, as they progress from mutual dislike to the suggestion of possible romance (conveniently, she has yet to take her vows), the film focuses on Graham and Tagawa. As the two combatants move toward their inevitable final confrontation, they stalk and capture each other, escape, and express both contempt and respect for each other, though neither speaks the other's language. Tagawa, who is so fierce he stares down a poisonous snake, has ample opportunity to kill Graham, but instead gives his captive martial arts lessons to make him a more worthy opponent. In one scene, the Imperial Marine asserts that only technology permits Westerners to stand up to warriors like himself. This statement proves to be prophetic in the film's final moments of do-or-die hand-to-hand combat, when Graham gets hold of a pistol and simply blows Tagawa away.

Like Francis Ford Coppola's most self-indulgent work—in which obtrusive cinematic technique becomes a barrier between the story and the audience—Wragge's direction consistently distances and distracts. The combat scenes are drained of impact by excessive use of slow motion and pretentious camera angles, and the narrative, instead of inexorably building, simply unravels. Gary Graham, Cary-Hiroyuki Tagawa, and Maria Holvoe are competent performers, but the cards are stacked against them.

Despite its many flaws, THE LAST WARRIOR is not, like so many films of this genre, mindless. The care with which it was made is obvious. Fred Tammes' camerawork and use of light are impressive and the locations are well-chosen and

entirely convincing. Shot on what must have been a low budget, the film is nonetheless handsome and visually arresting. Yet, for all of its visual sophistication and notwithstanding the physical intensity of its performances, THE LAST WARRIOR is ultimately static and stultifying, bound to make the action-oriented audience at which the film's ad campaign was aimed twitch impatiently in their seats. Wragge is not without promise as a filmmaker, but one hopes that his future efforts will be free of his "Look, Ma, no hands" approach and simply tell the story. *(Violence, adult situations, sexual situations.)*

p, Keith Watkins; d, Martin Wragge; w, Martin Wragge; ph, Fred Tammes (Technicolor); ed, Jacqueline Le Cordeur; m, Adrian Strijdom.

Action/War   (PR:C-O MPAA:R)

Ⓥ**LEAN ON ME****½
104m WB c

Morgan Freeman *(Joe Clark),* Robert Guillaume *(Dr. Frank Napier),* Beverly Todd *(Ms. Levias),* Lynne Thigpen *(Leona Barrett),* Jermaine Hopkins *(Thomas Sams),* Karen Malina White *(Kaneesha Carter),* Alan North *(Mayor Don Bottman),* Robin Bartlett *(Mrs. Elliott),* Michael Beach *(Mr. Darnell),* Ethan Phillips *(Mr. Rosenberg),* Regina Taylor *(Mrs. Carter),* Sandra Reaves-Phillips, Sloane Shelton, Karina Arroyave, Ivonne Coll, Michael P. Moran, John Ring, Tyrone Jackson, Alex Romaguera.

Based on the story of controversial high-school principal Joe Clark, LEAN ON ME, directed by John G. Avildsen, begins in the 1960s, as Clark (Freeman) conducts an energetic class of junior-high students at Eastside High in Paterson, New Jersey. The class—an early indication of the bravura style for which Clark will later become famous—is interrupted when a friend (Guillaume) takes Freeman down the hall, where he is informed that the school board is fed up with his abrasive approach and is transferring him. The film then flashes forward 20 years, to Eastside High in the 1980s, a graffiti-scrawled haven for drug dealers and unrepentant juvenile delinquents. A scene of student anarchy culminates in the brutal beating of a teacher, in the wake of which Guillaume, now school superintendent, lobbies to make his buddy Freeman the new Eastside principal. Under pressure, Paterson's mayor agrees. If Eastside's mean score on the basic skills test doesn't rise above a certain level, however, the state will take over the school. On his first day as the new principal, Freeman rounds up Eastside's worst "miscreants" and expels them before the assembled student body, then gives his faculty similarly rough disciplinary treatment, brooking no dissension and demanding absolute silence as he gives

them a tongue-lashing at their first meeting. Next, Freeman meets the community at a heated school board meeting, where he again shouts down his critics, one of whom, Thigpen, a black activist whose son was among those expelled earlier, becomes determined to overthrow Freeman. Eventually, Freeman changes the face of Eastside High, chaining the doors against drug dealers, painting over the graffiti, and hectoring students into shape through his famous bullhorn—though he also reveals his sensitivity, developing personal relationships with troubled underachievers. But while he connects with the students, he alienates his faculty, humiliating teachers in front of their classes; moreover, while Eastside prepares for the crucial basic skills test, Thigpen pressures the mayor into having the principal arrested for fire code violations (the padlocked doors are a fire hazard). With Freeman in jail, the school board (of which Thigpen is now a member) meets to discuss his case and plans to dismiss him. If the pending test scores exceed the acceptable minimum, however, they will be forced to keep Freeman on, so they move to act fast, before the scores are announced. The meeting is interrupted by a throng of students gathered in support of their principal. Freeman is asked to address them, and requests that they disperse, but just at that moment his assistant principal fights through the crowd, waving an envelope containing the results of the basic skills test. Freeman opens the envelope, the scores meet the mean, he is vindicated, and the students rejoice.

As in ROCKY and THE KARATE KID, director Avildsen manipulates his audience skillfully, exploiting the real-life Clark's crusading, anti-bureaucratic image to the hilt and justifying the principal's means through an effective and galvanizing, if formulaic, presentation of his ends, a cinematic version of the dieter's "before and after" pictures. But LEAN ON ME's manipulations justify Clark's drastic methods—the salutary effects of which are still being debated—only superficially, by trivializing legitimate questions regarding Clark's actions. For the most part, viewers are only allowed to contrast the nightmarish, wild-in-the-streets environment of Eastside High "before" with the sane, orderly, basic-skills-improved universe of Eastside High "after"—cheering crowds, uplifting music and all. Avildsen is aided in this task by Morgan Freeman, who turns in his usual fine work as Clark in a primarily sympathetic performance (though he hardly turns Clark into a martyr). Robert Guillaume lends able support, and the rest of the cast, especially the teenagers who play the students, is also strong. *(Violence, profanity.)*

p, Norman Twain; d, John G. Avildsen; w, Michael Schiffer; ph, Victor Hammer (Technicolor); ed, John Carter and John

G. Avildsen; m, Bill Conti; prod d, Doug Kraner; art d, Tim Galvin; set d, Caryl Heller; cos, Jennifer Von Mayrthauper.

Drama   (PR:C MPAA:PG-13)

LET IT RIDE*½
86m PAR c

Richard Dreyfuss *(Trotter)*, David Johansen *(Looney)*, Teri Garr *(Pam)*, Jennifer Tilly *(Vicki)*, Allen Garfield *(Greenberg)*, Ed Walsh *(Marty)*, Michelle Phillips, Mary Woronov, Robbie Coltrane, Richard Edson, Cynthia Nixon, Richard Dimitri, Tony Longo.

Making his movie debut with LET IT RIDE, Joe Pytka joins the already burgeoning ranks of television commercial directors who have made the move from the shorter form to feature-length filmmaking. A winner of many awards in the ad field, Pytka is also infamous as the man who was behind the camera when Michael Jackson's hair caught fire during the filming of a Pepsi commercial, and also helmed (for the same soft drink), Madonna's "Like a Prayer" ad, which outraged Catholics all over the world.

If only Pytka had taken similar chances on LET IT RIDE. Instead, he handicaps himself from the start by choosing a genre—racetrack comedy—that has already defeated many a more seasoned filmmaker, most recently Blake Edwards (A FINE MESS) and Paul Bartel (THE LONGSHOT, executive produced by no less than Mike Nichols). Indeed, it's hard to imagine why anyone makes these movies anymore—Stanley Kubrick's THE KILLING was the last outstanding movie set at a racetrack, and that was released in 1956. LET IT RIDE isn't any worse than Edwards' or Bartel's unmemorable efforts, only more annoying. Taxi driver Dreyfuss starts the movie by making a pledge to his long-suffering wife, Garr, that he will cut down on playing the ponies. But, naturally, the pledge is quickly forgotten when fellow cabbie Johansen gives Dreyfuss a hot tip on a long shot. At the track, one tip leads to another, until Dreyfuss is letting his accumulated winnings of $69,000 ride on the last race of the day.

The best thing that can be said about LET IT RIDE's script is that it doesn't contain any false moralizing or incongruous irony. Nor are there any strained attempts to turn horse racing or betting into metaphors for life, fate, or anything else that happens to be handy. Indeed, what is unusual about LET IT RIDE is that, for racing fans, it's 86 minutes of pure wish-fulfillment fantasy. Not only is the cabbie winning every race, he gets cheered everywhere he goes and attracts the lustful attentions of every unattached woman in sight (especially Tilly and Phillips). And LET IT RIDE *is* fun to watch from time to time: With so many funny people together in a

single film, you're bound to get a few laughs along the way. Besides the sterling comic players cast in the leads, Allen Garfield, Mary Woronov, Richard Edson, Robbie Coltrane, and Cynthia Nixon also have some good moments.

The major irritant is Pytka's hyperactive direction. Betraying his commercial roots, Pytka films each scene as if it were the last, with everybody in the frame strenuously choreographed and overly busy in order to keep the climaxes coming every three minutes. The effect is wearying rather than energizing; one keeps expecting "Tastes great!" "Less filling!" shouting matches to break out in the grandstand. Pytka's comedic touch is no less heavy-handed. He never teases a gag when he can sledgehammer it—you don't come out of LET IT RIDE feeling like you've seen a comedy, but like you've been worked over—and matters aren't helped in that Pytka tries to draw humor from things that just aren't very funny. Gambling addiction is no joke, and, as a wish-fulfillment comedy, LET IT RIDE almost functions as a feature-length commercial for the habit. We're also expected to laugh ourselves silly over the gambler's unfunny neglect of his wife, which leads her to drink herself into a stupor in an attempt to become an alcoholic.

"Runyonesque" is the word sometimes applied to movies like this. Often, and in the case of LET IT RIDE in particular, the application tends to give Damon Runyon a bad name. *(Profanity, adult situations.)*

p, David Giler, Ned Dowd, and Randy Ostrow; d, Joe Pytka; w, Nancy Dowd (based on the novel *Good Vibes* by Jay Cronley); ph, Curtis J. Wehr (Technicolor); ed, Dede Allen and Jim Miller; m, Giorgio Moroder; prod d, Wolf Kroeger; set d, William D. McLane.

Comedy   (PR:C MPAA:PG-13)

Mel Gibson and Danny Glover in LETHAL WEAPON 2 (©Warner Bros.)

ⓥLETHAL WEAPON 2***½
113m Silver/WB c

Mel Gibson *(Martin Riggs)*, Danny Glover *(Roger Murtaugh)*, Joe Pesci *(Leo Getz)*, Joss Ackland *(Arjen Rudd)*, Derrick O'Connor *(Pieter Vorstedt)*, Patsy Kensit *(Rika van den Haas)*, Darlene Love *(Trish Murtaugh)*, Traci Wolfe *(Rianne Murtaugh)*, Steve Kahan *(Capt. Murphy)*, Mark Rolston *(Hans)*, Jenette Goldstein *(Meagan Shapiro)*, Dean Norris *(Tim Cavanaugh)*, Juney Smith *(Tom Wyler)*, Nestor Serrano *(Eddie Esteban)*, Philip Suriano *(Joseph Ragucci)*, Grand L. Bush *(Jerry Collins)*, Tony Carreiro *(Marcelli)*, Damon Hines *(Nick Murtaugh)*, Ebonie Smith *(Carrie Murtaugh)*, Allan Dean Moore *(George)*, Jack McGee *(Carpenter)*, Paul Tuerpe, Philip Maurice Miller, Sherman Howard, Bruce Young, Guy Mack, Danny Wyanos, Pat Skipper *(Hit Men)*, Robert Fol *(Consulate Guard)*, Virginia Shannon *(Consulate Office Worker)*, Danny Ondrejko *(Consulate Clerk)*, Jim Piddock *(Consulate Envoy)*, Kenneth Tigar *(Bomb Squad Leader)*, Jim Birge, Patrick Cameron *(Bomb Squad Cops)*, Mary Ellen Trainor *(Police Psychiatrist)*, David Marciano, Tommy Hinkley *(Cops)*, Norm Wilson *(Detective in Squad Room)*, Jeanne McGuire, Catherine Guel *(Computer Operators)*, Lionel Douglass *(Officer Friesen)*, James Oliver *(Officer Moss)*, Salim Jaidi *(Policeman)*, Al Weber Jr., Edward J. Rosen, Jay Della, Marian Collier *(Poolside Card Players)*, Orlando Bonner *(Tow Truck Driver)*, Cynthia Burr *(Owner of Honda)*, Sam the Dog, Burbank the Cat.

A sequel that stands on its own, LETHAL WEAPON 2 is a well-crafted, rousingly fast-paced action thriller with a first-rate cast. Returning to their Los Angeles cop roles, Danny Glover and Mel Gibson are in hot pursuit of a red BMW in Glover's wife's station wagon as the film gets off to a fender-bending start. True to character from the earlier film, the conservative Glover is more worried about protecting the car than apprehending the criminal. Meanwhile Gibson, still drawing his law-enforcement inspiration from The Three Stooges, will let nothing stand in his way. At one point, without a second thought, he even begins pursuing the BMW on foot. After much property destruction, including several dents in the hapless station wagon, the cops capture the red car, but lose the driver. Glover's kick to the trunk of the BMW, however, causes a fortune in South African gold Krugerrands to spill out. Determined to keep the two hyperactive cops out of further high-priced mayhem, their superior puts them in charge of guarding a government witness in a drug-money laundering case. But when the witness, a noisy, nonstop kvetcher (Pesci), reveals he was laundering for South Africans, Gibson and Glover spring back into action. Pesci leads Gibson and Glover to a house by the beach, where they discover South African diplomats counting and bundling huge stacks of drug money. The trouble is, as diplomats, they are immune to conventional law enforcement. Gibson and Glover are sent ignobly on their way, but as any smart viewer will guess, not for long. Since they can't arrest the South Africans, Gibson and Glover decide instead to separate them from their ill-gotten cash before they can ship it out of the country. Irritated by the interference, the South Africans begin slaughtering Gibson and Glover's fellow cops, leaving the two with a heavy blood score to settle at the climax as well.

Those stopping to think about such things may find more than a few holes in LETHAL WEAPON 2's plot. But to question is to quibble in this case; LETHAL WEAPON 2's pluses easily outweigh its minuses. If anything, Gibson and Glover are even better here than they were the first time out, fast establishing themselves as a classic buddy pairing. Jeffrey Boam's script polishes and improves their characters. Most notably, Gibson no longer chews on gun barrels contemplating suicide as he did in the first film. Here, he's "merely" a crazy guy battling crime in a crazy world. And, since the villains are virulent racists, Glover gets to indulge in some craziness of his own. In one of the film's best, and funniest, scenes, he creates a diversion at the South African embassy by applying to emigrate so he can join the armed struggle against apartheid. In addition to Glover and Gibson, there is a virtually flawless supporting cast, also well supported by Boam's script. Joss Ackland and Derrick O'Connor are darkly menacing and thoroughly loathsome as the head villains, and Patsy Kensit is sweetly engaging as Gibson

ill-fated love interest—a departure from her earlier *femme fatale* in ABSOLUTE BEGINNERS. Rounding out the ensemble, Joe Pesci provides side-splitting comic relief as the babbling Leo.

For all the talent on hand in front of and behind the camera, the real straw stirring the drink is returning director Richard Donner, who seems to have smoothed over the few stylistic rough edges remaining from the earlier film to deliver two hours of pure, breathless, high-impact entertainment. Parents should be forewarned, however. LETHAL WEAPON 2 is entertainment strictly for adults. The violence, while not gratuitous for the genre, is truly gruesome at times; the language is as salty as any to be found in a hard-edged police drama, and the lovemaking scene between Gibson and Kensit is very steamy. *(Violence, profanity, sexual situations.)*

p, Richard Donner, Joel Silver, Steve Perry, and Jennie Lew Tugend; d, Richard Donner; w, Jeffrey Boam (based on a story by Shane Black, Warren Murphy and on the characters created by Shane Black); ph, Stephen Goldblatt (Panavision, Technicolor); ed, Stuart Baird; m, Michael Kamen, Eric Clapton, and David Sanborn; prod d, J. Michael Riva; art d, Virginia Randolph and Richard Berger; set d, Dianne Wager; spec eff, Matt Sweeney; cos, Barry Delaney; tech, Art Fransen; stunts, Charles Picerni; makeup, Scott Eddo.

Crime/Thriller   (PR:O MPAA:R)

ⓥLEVIATHAN½**
98m Gordon-MGM/MGM-UA c
Peter Weller *(Beck)*, Richard Crenna *(Doc)*, Amanda Pays *(Willie)*, Daniel Stern *(Sixpack)*, Ernie Hudson *(Jones)*, Michael Carmine *(DeJesus)*, Lisa Eilbacher *(Bowman)*, Hector Elizondo *(Cobb)*, Meg Foster *(Martin)*.

An oceanic mining crew has just a few days left in its mission; the man in charge (Weller), a geologist, reports to "the company." Sound familiar? It should; LEVIATHAN is a cheap imitation of ALIEN. Although the earlier film revolves around an outer-space mission, and LEVIATHAN transpires in the ocean, their set and creature designs are, nonetheless, disturbingly similar.

While exploring *Leviathan*, a sunken Russian freighter whose disappearance was never reported, crew member Stern discovers a black box and brings it back with him. The box proves to contain some vodka and the captain's log, which indicates that the crew perished from an unknown tropical disease. Crenna, the mission's skeptical doctor, doesn't know what to make of this information, but he's definitely curious. Mission leader Weller doesn't share Crenna's interest, but the physician convinces him that the vodka

should be hidden until the cause of the Russian crew's deaths can be pinned down. Of course, Stern and Eilbacher drink some of the vodka before anyone realizes just how dangerous this libation is. It turns out that the disease that claimed the freighter's crew wasn't really a disease at all but horrible genetic mutations that resulted from experiments conducted by the Russians. As LEVIATHAN progresses, it becomes clear that this particular evil force is still in the business of hideously transforming its victims. The creature that results is straight out of ALIEN, except that it retains some of the victims' pre-mutation characteristics.

Scene after scene in the latter part of the movie is reminiscent of ALIEN. Just as in the earlier film, the creature in LEVIATHAN emerges from one crew member's chest, grows, and then hides in what appears to be a boiler room. Even the ship in LEVIATHAN resembles the spacecraft in ALIEN; however, this pale imitation lacks the sense of claustrophobic enclosure so effectively conveyed by ALIEN's spaceship. Not only does the vessel in LEVIATHAN lack the complexity of its ALIEN model, but its layout is incomprehensible. Because we don't understand where the recreation areas, infirmary, and boiler room are in relation to one another, potentially exciting chase scenes lack tension and the overall dramatic effect of the film is lessened.

As for the performances, Peter Weller (ROBOCOP) and Richard Crenna are miscast, and Amanda Pays proves to be more of a model than an actress. On the other hand, Ernie Hudson (GHOST-BUSTERS), Michael Carmine, and Daniel Stern are more successful. Carmine is DeJesus, a Hispanic New Yorker who dreams of snowcapped Swiss mountains; Stern is a beer-drinking leech, and Hudson is the guy who's ready to face reality when the others aren't. Regrettably, the uneven script isn't up to the talents of these three actors. Indeed, none of the characters in the film are well developed, and, not surprisingly, we don't really care what happens to any of them. The direction, by George P. Cosmatos (RAMBO: FIRST BLOOD PART II), is capable but uninspired. Mildly diverting but superficial, good looking but imitative, LEVIATHAN is the cinematic equivalent of soft ice cream. While its Stan Winston-created creatures may be frightening enough to give kids a thrill, it's unlikely real sci-fans will find much to satisfy them here. *(Violence.)*

p, Luigi De Laurentiis and Aurelio De Laurentiis; d, George Pan Cosmatos; w, David Peoples and Jeb Stuart (based on a story by David Peoples); ph, Alex Thomson (J-D-C widescreen, Technicolor); ed, Roberto Silvi and John F. Burnett; m, Jerry Goldsmith; prod d, Ron Cobb; art d,

David Klassen and Franco Ceraolo; set d, Craig Edgar, Jim Teegarden, Maria Teresa Barbasso, Alessandro Alberti, and Daniela Giovannoni; spec eff, Stan Winston, Nick Allder, and Barry Nolan.

Science Fiction   (PR:C MPAA:R)

Ⓥ**LICENCE TO KILL*****½
133m Eon/MGM-UA c
Timothy Dalton *(James Bond)*, Carey Lowell *(Pam Bouvier)*, Robert Davi *(Franz Sanchez)*, Talisa Soto *(Lupe Lamora)*, Anthony Zerbe *(Milton Krest)*, Frank McRae *(Sharkey)*, Everett McGill *(Killifer)*, Wayne Newton *(Prof. Joe Butcher)*, Benicio del Toro *(Dario)*, Desmond Llewelyn *(Q)*, David Hedison *(Felix Leiter)*, Priscilla Barnes *(Della Churchill)*, Robert Brown *(M)*, Caroline Bliss *(Miss Moneypenny)*, Anthony Starke *(Truman-Lodge)*, Pedro Armendariz Jr. *(President Hector Lopez)*, Don Stroud *(Heller)*, Grand L. Bush *(Hawkins)*, Cary-Hiroyuki Tagawa *(Kwang)*, Alejandro Bracho *(Perez)*, Guy de Saint Cyr *(Braun)*, Rafer Johnson *(Mullens)*, Diana Lee-Hsu *(Loti)*, Christopher Neame *(Fallon)*, Jeannine Bisignano *(Stripper)*, Claudio Brook *(Montelongo)*, Cynthia Fallon *(Consuelo)*, Enrique Novi *(Rasmussen)*, Osami Kawawo *(Oriental)*, George Belanger *(Doctor)*, Roger Cudney *("Wavekrest" Captain)*, Honorato Magaloni *(Chief Chemist)*, Jorge Russek *(Pit Boss)*, Sergio Corona *(Bellboy)*, Stuart Kwan *(Ninja)*, Jose Abdala *(Tanker Driver)*, Teresa Blake *(Ticket Agent)*, Samuel Benjamin Lancaster *(Della's Uncle)*, Juan Peleaz *(Casino Manager)*, Mark Kelty *(Coast Guard Radio Operator)*, Umberto Elizondo *(Hotel Assistant Manager)*, Fidel Carriga *(Sanchez's Driver)*, Edna Bolkan *(Barrelhead Waitress)*, Eddie Enderfield *(Clive)*, Jeff Moldovan, Carl Ciarfalio *(Warehouse Guards)*.

Although James Bond purists will no doubt be dismayed by the drastic character change undergone by 007 in his 16th outing (not counting such rogue productions as CASINO ROYALE and NEVER SAY NEVER AGAIN), LICENCE TO KILL offers a fresh look at the superspy, a new set of villains, and some of the most spectacular action sequences yet seen in the series. Opening with the traditional precredits action sequence, the film finds Bond (Dalton), his CIA buddy Hedison, and mutual friend McRae all dressed in tuxedos and being chauffeured to Hedison's wedding in the Florida Keys. En route, however, an American Drug Enforcement Agency helicopter shows up and informs Hedison that a notorious Colombian drug dealer (Davi) has been cornered nearby. Momentarily postponing the nuptials, Hedison and Dalton are off to catch the drug dealer, while the dismayed McRae is assigned the unenviable task of informing the bride of the

Timothy Dalton and Carey Lowell in LICENCE TO KILL (©MGM-UA).

delay. After an intense shootout during which Dalton meets Davi's beautiful mistress (Soto), who, moments earlier, had been whipped by the drug kingpin for her infidelity, Davi manages to escape in a small plane. Determined to catch the drug dealer, Dalton and Hedison climb aboard the government helicopter and give chase. Lowered from the big copter by a winch, Dalton lassos the tail of the plane, causing its engine to sputter and die, leaving the villainous Davi trapped in the dangling plane. With the helicopter hovering over the church where Hedison's wedding party waits, Dalton and Hedison parachute onto the steps and the ceremony begins. That night, however, Davi escapes imprisonment with the help of a corrupt DEA agent (Zerbe), his drug connection in southern Florida. Seeking revenge, Davi dispatches his goons to Hedison's home, and after killing the bride, they bring Hedison to Zerbe's headquarters, where he is fed to a great white shark. When Dalton learns of Davi's escape, he immediately goes to Hedison's house only to find the bride dead and his friend badly mangled by the shark. Desperate for revenge, Dalton ignores his superior's orders to give up his personal vendetta and is subsequently stripped of his license to kill by M (Brown) himself. Operating beyond the law, the renegade Dalton eventually hooks up with a beautiful-but-tough female CIA pilot (Lowell), who flies him to Davi's headquarters somewhere in South America. Passing himself off as a hit man for hire, Dalton meets with Davi, who is impressed with the

obviously experienced killer. While negotiating to sell shares of his massive drug empire to foreign investors—an operation fronted by a televangelist-style church run by Newton—Davi sees a need for Dalton's help. That evening, however, Dalton attempts to assassinate Davi with a high-powered rifle, but fails. After convincing Davi that the attempt on his life was made by one of the potential investors with Zerbe's help, Dalton gains the kingpin's trust and becomes part of the organization (frequently assisted in this deception by Soto, who has fallen in love with him). The angry Davi eventually kills Zerbe, but on a trip to his massive drug compound, nestled within the walls of Newton's TV ministry, Dalton is recognized by one of Davi's most vicious lieutenants (a former Nicaraguan contra who is selling US-made Stinger missiles to the drug dealer) and his cover is blown. Setting the compound on fire, Dalton manages to escape certain doom with the help of Lowell and the elderly Q (Llewelyn)—who has taken a leave of absence to help 007—and a massive chase involving three tanker trucks laden with cocaine, a helicopter, and a small plane begins. After many amazing stunts—including a flaming car shooting off a cliff *above* a low-flying plane, and Dalton's driving of a tilted 18-wheel truck on only half its tires—the battered and bruised 007 engages in some brutal hand-to-hand combat with the equally damaged Davi. Doused with cocaine-laced gasoline and wielding a machete, Davi is about to split Dalton in two when the intrepid super agent interrupts him by asking if he wants to know "why" (referring to Dalton's apparently motivationless destruction of Davi's empire). The drug kingpin pauses while Dalton produces the lighter Hedison and his bride had given him as their best man. As Davi's eyes widen with understanding, Dalton flips on the lighter and sets the villain aflame. Looking more like Mel Gibson at the end of THE ROAD WARRIOR than the suave 007, the exhausted Dalton stumbles into the arms of the waiting Lowell.

In his second outing as James Bond, Timothy Dalton presents a more serious, harder-edged agent 007 than either the Roger Moore or Sean Connery incarnations. While many of the familiar Bond series conventions remain (the pre-credits sequence, the meetings with M and Q, the signature salutation, "My name is Bond. James Bond," etc.), most are so warped as to be almost unrecognizable, due primarily to Bond's overriding motivation in this installment, his obsessive need for revenge. Some loyal fans may be shocked to see such an "unprofessional" Bond, but this new spin lends some badly needed complexity to a character that has become increasingly cartoonish and predictable ever since Roger Moore took over the role. In addition to Bond's rage, the series also shifts its emphasis away from international espionage—unsuitable in the Gorbachev era—to the more topical and easy-to-despise realm of drug trafficking. Like Bond, the villain here, played superbly by character actor Robert Davi, is much more realistic and complex than the usual exaggerated Bond heavy. Although shown to be brutal and ruthless, Davi has a personal code of conduct he refuses to violate, and he seems to enjoy the thrill of battle (both business negotiations and actual combat) more than making billions of dollars. He is also practical and demonstrates a very dark sense of humor; most notably, when his greedy yuppie account begins whining about how much money they're losing because of Bond's interference, Davi simply says, "Well, I guess I'd better cut some of my overhead," and shoots the annoying underling.

Because the film has such strong and obsessive characters at its center, there is no need for a plethora of high-tech gadgets and science-fictionlike locales. Instead, the final confrontation is a gritty, good old-fashioned hand-to-hand combat scene worthy of classic revenge tales (Anthony Mann's westerns with Jimmy Stewart come to mind). Another area where the Bond series is making progress is its portrayal of women. While the casting still seems based on comeliness and not acting ability—some of the line readings are hopelessly inept and may give rise to unintentional laughter—Bond women, like the character played here by Carey Lowell, are

beginning to demonstrate some strength and independence. Although Lowell (who refused to participate in the traditional Bond spread for *Playboy*) falls into bed with 007 on their first meeting, she is intelligent, a pilot, wields a shotgun expertly, and rescues Bond more times than he saves her. While the series has hardly embraced feminism, it has progressed somewhat.

Also somewhat surprising is the subtle liberal bent to the script by Michael G. Wilson and Richard Maibaum, which depicts televangelism as hypocritical and corrupt, and makes an unmistakably clear connection between Ronald Reagan's beloved Nicaraguan contras and international drug trade. Hardcore Bond fans may be dismayed by some of the changes, but no one can deny that the action scenes staged by director John Glen, with the help of stunt coordinator Paul Weston, are some of the most spectacular of the entire series and well worth the price of admission. With Dalton's more intense and brooding 007 developing with each film, the best Bond may be yet to come. Songs include: "Licence to Kill" (Narada Michael Walden, Jeffrey Cohen, Walter Afanasieff, performed by Gladys Knight), "Wedding Party" (Jimmy Duncan, Phillip Brennan, performed by Ivory), "Dirty Love" (Steve Dubin, Jeff Pescetto, performed by Tim Feehan), "If You Asked Me To" (Diane Warren, performed by Patti LaBelle), "James Bond Theme" (Monty Norman). *(Violence, adult situations, sexual situations.)*

p, Albert R. Broccoli and Michael G. Wilson; d, John Glen; w, Richard Maibaum and Michael G. Wilson (based on the characters created by Ian Fleming); ph, Alec Mills (Panavision, Deluxe Color); ed, John Grover; m, Michael Kamen; prod d, Peter Lamont; art d, Michael Lamont; set d, Michael Ford; spec eff, John Richardson; cos, Jodie Tillen; stunts, Paul Weston; makeup, George Frost.

Spy   (PR:C-O   MPAA:PG-13)

LIFE AND NOTHING BUT*½
(Fr.) 135m Hachette Premiere-AB-Little Bear-Films A2/UGC c
(LA VIE EST RIEN D'AUTRE)
Philippe Noiret *(Maj. Dellaplane)*, Sabine Azema *(Irene de Courtil)*, Pascale Vignal *(Alice)*, Maurice Barrier *(Mercadot)*, Francois Perrot *(Perrin)*, Jean-Pol Dubois *(Andre)*, Daniel Russo *(Lt. Trevise)*, Michel Duchaussoy *(Gen. Villerieux)*, Arlette Gilbert *(Valentine)*, Louis Lyonnet *(Valentin)*, Charlotte Maury *(Cora Mabel)*, Francois Caron *(Julien)*, Thierry Gimenez *(Engineers' Adjutant)*, Frederique Meninger *(Mme. Lebegue)*, Pierre Trabaud *(Eugene Dilatoire)*, Jean-Roger Milo *(Mons. Lebegue)*, Catherine Verlor *(Nun on Beach)*, Jean-Christophe Lebert *(Amnesiac)*, Bruno Therasse

(Rougeaud), Philippe Uchan *(Legless Man)*, Marion Loran *(Solange de Boissancourt)*, Charlotte Kadi *(Nun in Hospital)*, Gabriel Cattand *(Prof. Mortier)*, Christophe Odent *(Poirleau)*, Jean Champion *(Lagrange)*, Philippe Deplanche *(Lecordier)*, Michel Cassagne *(Abel Mascle)*, Frederic Pierrot *(Marcel)*, Francois Domange *(Georges)*, Jean-Paul Comart *(Fagot)*, Patrick Massieu *(Cemetery Warden)*, Didier Harlmann *(One-armed Man)*, Pascal Elso *(Blind Man)*, Odile Cointepas *(Mme. Hannesson)*, Louba Guertchikoff *(Blue-eyed Woman)*, Jean-Claude Calon *(Sgt. Zele)*, Jean-Yves Gautier *(Corporal)*, Gilles Janeyrand *(NCO)*, Nicolas Tronc *(Soldier Lefevre)*, Jerome Frossard *(Messenger)*, Michele Gleizer *(Farmer)*, Daniel Langlet *(Mons. Ichac)*, Adrienne Bonnet *(Mme. Ichac)*, Marcel Zanini *(Leo)*, Marc Perrone *(Pochin)*, Geroges Staquet *(Priest)*, Alain Frerot *(Pelat)*, Francois Dyrek *(Vergnes)*, Oswald d'Andrea *(Cora Mabel, Pianist)*, Mickey Baker *(Banjo Player)*, Sangoma Everett *(Drummer)*, Stephen Potts *(Saxophonist)*, Mike Zwerin *(Jennings)*, Bruno Raffaelli *(Maginot)*, Eric Dufay *(Soldier Thain)*.

LIFE AND NOTHING BUT, the latest film from Bertrand Tavernier (ROUND MIDNIGHT [1986]; COUP DE TORCHON [1982]; A SUNDAY IN THE COUNTRY [1984]), is a compelling successor to such antiwar movies as Stanley Kubrick's PATHS OF GLORY (1957) and Lewis Milestone's ALL QUIET ON THE WESTERN FRONT (1930), focusing, like Kubrick's and Milestone's films, on WW I. Instead of detailing the ongoing carnage and cannon fire of life in the trenches, however, Tavernier paints a harrowing portrait of devastation after the fact. The year is 1920 (almost two years after the Armistice), and the massive task of counting corpses and identifying the missing among the French soldiers remains. Supervising these efforts is Major Dellaplane (Noiret), a career soldier obsessed with logic and detail who turns his responsibility into a personal crusade to justify the sacrifice made by the dead men, believing that by naming the unidentified and humanizing the grim statistics, he can somehow make sense of the horror that has occurred. Noiret's quest to tie up the loose ends of war in peacetime is interwoven with the story of another officer's mission to locate one suitable unknown soldier for ceremonial enshrinement in the Arc de Triomphe, and with vignettes concerning families seeking information about the fate of their relatives. Among those vying for Noiret's attention are Vignal, a young working-class woman looking for her fiance, and Azema, a senator's daughter-in-law traveling throughout Europe in search of her missing husband. Although he locks horns with the latter, a proud aristocrat who's tired of getting the bureaucratic run-around, Noiret also falls in love with her, and the fitful progress of their incongruous affair is played out on the former battlefields. In one scene, during a visit to a body identification center where family members sift through medals and personal belongings in the hope of locating loved ones, the travelers pause from their heartrending task to picnic on the grass, and an explosion rocks a tunnel where the dead are stored pending identification. It's as if the war's appetite can never be satisfied. When Noiret discovers that Vignal's fiance and Azema's husband are the same man, the knowledge frees each woman to go on with her life. The unknown soldier is interred and the war is officially laid to rest, but it will never be over for Noiret. Allowing Azema to slip out of his life, he can only proclaim his love in letters, after she's moved to America.

Cowritten by Tavernier and Jean Cosmos (a playwright and TV scenarist making his screenwriting debut), LIFE AND NOTHING BUT is a muted, carefully wrought drama about the emotionally shell-shocked survivors of WW I. Somber, handsome, exquisitely produced, and featuring a towering lead performance by Philippe Noiret in what is reportedly his 100th screen role, Tavernier's elegy strikes no false notes. With an extraordinary talent for conveying the bustle of life amidst the stasis of death, Tavernier employs his sweeping camera and his skill in relating characters to their widescreen environment to create an unforgettable *mise-en-scene*. Despite its brilliant technical accomplishment and its seamless blend of gallows humor and intriguing drama, however, Tavernier's examination of lives held in check by the fortunes of war lacks the full-throttle emotionalism that might have made it a classic pacifist epic. Visually, it couldn't be improved upon (Tavernier's cinematographer, once again, is the superb Bruno de Keyzer), but one does wish it were a little less calculated, a little more reckless. The *chagrin d'amour* of Noiret's unconsummated affair with Azema palls in comparison with Tavernier's moving depiction of war and loss on a larger scale. Somehow the intimate love story fails to move us as much as some of the vignettes, such as the darkly humorous scene in which town officials plead for re-zoning because they don't have any dead war heroes in their district. Even more haunting is the last shot, in which Noiret walks through a cemetery that appears to stretch on forever—remarking that the French victory parade lasted three hours, but a march by all the dead would have taken eleven days. (*Violence, adult situations, profanity.*)

p, Rene Cleitman and Albert Prevost; d, Bertrand Tavernier; w, Bertrand Tavernier and Jean Cosmos; ph, Bruno de Keyzer

(Eastmancolor); ed, Armand Psenny; m, Oswald d'Andrea; prod d, Guy-Claude Francois; set d, Pierre Fontaine; cos, Jacqueline Moreau; makeup, Eric Muller.

Drama   (PR:O   MPAA:PG)

LIMIT UP*½
89m Sterling/MCEG c

Nancy Allen (*Casey Falls*), Dean Stockwell (*Peter Oak*), Brad Hall (*Marty Callahan*), Danitra Vance (*Nike*), Ray Charles (*Julius*), Rance Howard (*Chuck Feeney*), Sandra Bogan (*Andy Lincoln*), William J. Wolf (*Rusty*), Ava Fabian (*Sasha*), Robbie Martini (*Assistant to Mr. Oak*), Teressa Ovetta Burrell (*Clerk*), Winifred Freedman (*Pit Recorder*), Luana Anders (*Teacher*), Richard Martini (*Student*), Kellie Joy Beals (*Reporter*), Nicky Blair (*Maitre D'*), Cal Gibson (*Truck Driver*), Charles Holman (*Parking Lot Kid*), Read Morgan (*Auctioneer*), Ray Rayner (*Announcer*), Steven Lundy, Antoine M. Lundy, Charles Nelson, Trisco Pearson (*Band Force MD's*), Sally Kellerman (*Nightclub Singer*), Daniel Deuble, Bill Evashwick, Richard Lavin, Victor Lespinasse, Robert Peters, Ken Truxal, Tim Ryan, Martin F. Schacker (*Traders*).

Nancy Allen plays an ambitious "runner" at the Chicago Board of Trade who hopes someday to break into the male-dominated world of trading. However, Allen's boss (Stockwell), a wealthy male chauvinist, refuses to give her the opportunity to become a trader. Into Allen's life comes a wildly dressed woman with bizarre hair and supernatural powers (Vance) who tells Allen that she can help her become a successful trader. There is a catch, though; Vance is the devil and Allen must sell her soul to become rich and famous. Allen reluctantly agrees, and after being fired by Stockwell (for giving a tip she received from Vance to another trader), she is hired by Howard as an assistant trader. She takes "trading classes," becomes successful, and falls in love with and eventually marries Hall, a trader who also works for Howard. Rich, married, and one of the most powerful grain traders in the country, Allen seems to have achieved the perfect life. But soon the time comes for Vance to collect on their bargain. One night, Vance appears and demands that Allen sign over her soul and corner the market in soybeans (thus bringing about world starvation). If she doesn't comply, Allen will lose everything—her house, her money, even Hall. Not only does Allen refuse to sign, but she also foils Vance's plan for global famine by selling herself into bankruptcy and evenly distributing her soybean wealth. Although Allen has seemingly lost everything, she gains self-respect and saves the world. What's more, when her house and possessions are auctioned off, a minor miracle

occurs involving the male traders. This isn't the film's last big surprise, however, as it is later revealed that Vance isn't who she appears to be and that God (played by Ray Charles) works in mysterious ways indeed.

LIMIT UP is too light and zany for its own good. Supernatural characters and silly slapstick are hardly what one expects to find in a movie concerned with greed, wealth, and famine. Had the whole "bargain with the devil" concept been replaced with a serious study of the moral turmoil of a market trader, this might have been a good movie. As it is, LIMIT UP is neither good nor funny. Moreover, some of the performances (especially Danitra Vance's) leave much to be desired, and the narrative is sloppy. (At one point Allen's Casey Falls is an embarrassed second-class trader; scant moments later, she is wildly successful, her face on the cover of *Time*!) Although Richard Martini's direction is sincere enough, he demonstrates no capacity for delving into serious or even seriocomic situations. He settles instead for hopelessly tacky montages (the Chicago skyline should get second billing) and unsuccessful sight gags. To his credit Martini does succeed in making the commodity-market scenes comprehensible for the layman. While it is difficult to follow the trading sequences in WALL STREET and TRADING PLACES, those in LIMIT UP are never confusing, and classes in trading are even presented in some interesting scenes. But for every interesting moment in LIMIT UP, there are at least two others that are dragged down by goofy costumes or cheap special effects. Martini's use of his Chicago setting is cheesy and synthetic, overloaded with stock shots of Wrigley Field, Michigan Avenue, Lincoln Park Zoo, and the Art Institute. After all of this nonsense, the movie ends with the mildly effective auction scene, carried by Dean Stockwell's performance and Allen's innocent, shining face. Tellingly, this scene only makes the weak elements of the movie stand out even more. Had the film been more serious, this ending could have been very moving. Although not as bad as Martini's last film—the horrible comedy YOU CAN'T HURRY LOVE—LIMIT UP is wholly forgettable. Songs include: "Mike Mercurie" (John Tesh), "Undress for Success" (Tesh, Michael Hanna, Diana DeWitt, performed by DeWitt), "Love Is a House" (Martin Lascelles, Geoff Gurd, G. Foster, performed by FORCE MDs), "Soybean Shuffle," "The River Charles" (Tesh, Hanna), "Black Coffee" (Paul Francis Webster, Sonny Burke), "Shout" (O. Kelly Isley, Ronald Isley, Rudolph Isley, performed by the Dynatones), "Making the Rules" (Hanna, DeWitt, performed by DeWitt). (*Profanity, adult situations.*)

p, Jonathan D. Krane; d, Richard Martini; w, Richard Martini and Lu Anders (based on a story by Martini); ph, Peter

Jami Gertz and Kirk Cameron in LISTEN TO ME (©Columbia).

Lyons Collister (Foto Kem Lab Color); ed, Sonny Baskin; m, John Tesh; prod d, R. Clifford Searcy; art d, Carol Bosselman; set d, Mark "Ma" Anderson; spec eff, Wizards, Inc.; cos, Reve Richards; chor, April Ortiz; makeup, Gigi Williams.

Comedy   (PR:C MPAA:PG-13)

🅥**LISTEN TO ME****
107m Weintraub Entertainment Group/COL c

Kirk Cameron *(Tucker Muldowney)*, Jami Gertz *(Monica Tomanski)*, Roy Scheider *(Charlie Nichols)*, Amanda Peterson *(Donna Lumis)*, Tim Quill *(Garson McKellar)*, George Wyner *(Dean Schwimmer)*, Anthony Zerbe *(Sen. McKellar)*, Christopher Atkins *(Bruce Arlington)*, Quinn Cummings *(Susan Hooper)*, Timothy Dang *(Bobby Chin)*, Peter De Luise *(Cameron Sweet)*, Jason Gould *(Hinkelstein)*, Jon Matthews *(Braithwaite)*, Christopher Rydell *(Tom Lloyd)*, Tom Schanley *(Stewart Shields)*, Dan Schneider *(Nathan Gore)*, Yeardley Smith *(Cootz)*, Moon Zappa *(Longnecker)*, Ron Masak *(Monica's Father)*, Dottie Archibald *(Monica's Mother)*, Jamie Kantrowitz *(Monica's Little Sister)*, Barbara Pilavin, Francene Selkirk *(Monica's Aunts)*, Rance Howard *(Tucker's Father)*, Sean Stewart *(Reform School Boy at Fence)*, Stephanie Copeland, Jodi Engelmann, Francine L. Julius, Alison Morgan, Traci L. Murray, Tammi Urner *(Kenmont Cheerleaders)*, Nancy

Valen *(Mia)*, Dorrie Krum *(Tasha)*, Dylan Stewart *(Chess Player)*, Julie Dretzin *(Sloan)*, Lynn Fischer *(Bobby Chin's Girl Friend)*, Mark Christopher Lawrence *("Attila")*, Robert A. Chumbook Jr. *("Horny")*, Lilyan Chauvin *(French Professor)*, Julie Simone, Annette Sinclair *(Fountain Girls)*, Dianne Turley Travis *(Garson's Mother)*, Anna Lee *(Garson's Grandmother)*, Kenneth G. Patterson *(Garson's Grandfather)*, Thomas Heinkel Miller *(Columbia Debate Official)*, Priscilla Kovary *(Charlie's Dancing Partner)*, Rick A. Lundin *(Hansom Cab Driver)*, Jon Lindstrom *(Television Newscaster)*, David Downing *(Officer of the Court)*, Dan Galloway *(Harvard Coach)*, Ed Wright *(Justice Patterson)*, Norwood Smith *(Justice Goodman)*, Dave Gilbert *(Justice Tarlton)*, Mary Gregory *(Justice Brooderworth)*, Martin West *(Justice Blyleven)*.

LISTEN TO ME—the title is more a plea than a command—revolves around three silver-tongued college debaters who desperately yearn to be understood, and for whom words are both weapons and protection. One is Cameron, a poor chicken farmer's son from Oklahoma who arrives at Kenmore College (a California school modeled after Stanford) on a full debating scholarship. His roommate, Quill, is the son of a prominent senator, one of the nation's top college debaters, and everything Cameron is not—specifically, rich and highly polished. Soon, Cameron

meets Gertz, a fellow food service worker who, it turns out, is *also* a debate scholarship winner. He's instantly smitten, but Gertz, a hardboiled type from working-class Chicago, rebuffs his overtures. Presiding over the debate club's first meeting is their charismatic coach cum guru, Scheider, who describes debate as the ultimate no-holds barred sport. The meeting is held in an indoor amphitheater, underscoring the gladiatorial overtones—further highlighted by the circling overhead photography. At another meeting, both Gertz and Cameron show their stuff when they must argue both sides of an issue chosen at random. Cameron, in contrast to Gertz's cool textbook presentation, wraps his arguments in a time-honored corn-pone style, concluding with a stirring rags-to-riches success story obviously based on his life—in what will not be the last time writer-director Douglas Day Stewart uses debate as a medium for personal revelation. The film heats up when the team enters a national tournament, with the final debate to take place before five members of the Supreme Court on television. The topic is abortion, an issue that sharply divides Gertz and Cameron. Naturally, Scheider pairs them as his freshman team and they tour the country, collecting an impressive array of awards; meanwhile, the seemingly charmed Quill writhes in private agony. A masterful debater, the senator's son views the activity as something his manipulative father has forced him into as a step in his preordained political career, though he wants to chart his own destiny and become a writer. He makes a deal with the coach: if Scheider likes the play he has written, Quill will give up debate; otherwise, he'll continue. The coach, though impressed by Quill's work, admits that he took the young man under his wing as part of a promise to his father, and much as he wants to encourage him, a promise is a promise. By the time the team reaches New York, a suicidal Quill is drowning his bitterness in alcohol. After he bumps into Gertz in a bar, they wind up together in Quill's room, where Gertz misinterprets Quill's confused attempts to reach out. She tries to leave, he accidentally strikes her, and she runs out of the hotel—only to be intercepted by Cameron, who grapples with the pursuing Quill, landing in the path of an oncoming car. Quill leaps to save his friend and is killed in the process. With the final debate looming, novices Cameron and Gertz must now lead the team. Overwhelmed and overmatched by the slick, arrogant Harvard team, they forgo legal argument in favor of the philosophical. In the all-too-tidy wrap-up, Gertz discusses abortion from the point of view of a woman who has been raped and suffered enduring emotional scars from a resultant abortion, a dramatic, sympathetic scenario that leaves the smug Harvard team reeling and defeated. Not surprisingly, her tale is a self-portrait, explaining and serving to exorcise her fear of men, and in the end she and Cameron embrace, walking in the closing overhead shot from the Supreme Court building toward the Capitol, presumably with much to discuss.

For a movie about the art of debate, LISTEN TO ME presents few striking or even artfully crafted arguments. Too often, we are told that a character has just delivered a clever rhetorical parry, despite all evidence to the contrary; arguments tend to be supported more by reactions (knowing smirks, bursts of appreciative applause) than by verbal dexterity. Stewart's view of debate as an extension of the psychiatrist's couch turns what should be fascinating intellectual play into an anti-intellectual, self-indulgent exercise. The crowning absurdity occurs when the wowed Supreme Court Justices (!) render their verdicts, one of them actually citing the Kenmore team's "fresh, new approach." Though LISTEN TO ME offers a lot of talk, it really has little to say (other than the not-so-subtle advancement of Stewart's "pro-life" agenda), and budding William F. Buckleys should seek inspiration elsewhere. Songs include "Listen to Me" (David Foster, Linda Thompson, Will Jennings, performed by Celine Dion and Warren Wiebe), "Love Dies in Slow Motion" (Judson Spence, M. Jones, performed by Spence), "Happy Every After" (Julia Fordham, performed by Fordham), "Tough Days Again" (J. Conrad, R. Bennett, performed by Todd Sharp), "Dark Light" (J. Raney, S. Marshall, performed by the Beat Farmers), "Invention No. 1 in C Major" (Johann Sebastian Bach), "Who's Gonna Love You Tonight" (David Foster, J. Bettis, K. Diamond, performed by Foster), "Teach Ya How Ta Rock" (M. Tanner, G. Rose, S. Rose, performed by Dominick Certo), "Tutti Frutti" (Richard Penniman, D. LaBostrie, Joe Lubin, performed by Little Richard [Penniman]), "Deck the Halls" (traditional, adapted by Richard Harvey), "Forever Young" (M. Gold, B. Lloyd, F. Mertens, performed by Alphaville), "Wanderlust" (M. Mueller, B. Gaitsch, performed by Donna Delorey), "Beautiful Dream" (M. Kershaw), "If We Can't Do It" (Cliff Magness, M. Mueller, performed by Magness). *(Adult situations.)*

p, Marykay Powell and Jerry A. Baerwitz; d, Douglas Day Stewart; w, Douglas Day Stewart; ph, Fred J. Koenekamp (CFI Color); ed, Anne V. Coates; m, David Foster; md, Tim Sexton; prod d, Gregory Pickrell; set d, Joe Hubbard; spec eff, Al Lannutti and Mike Wood; cos, Durinda Rice Wood; stunts, Mickey Gilbert; makeup, Jeremy Swan.

Drama   (PR:C MPAA:PG-13)

LITTLE MERMAID, THE***
82m Walt Disney-Silver Screen Partners
IV/BV c
VOICES OF: Rene Auberjonois *(Louis)*, Christopher Daniel Barnes *(Eric)*, Jodi Benson *(Ariel)*, Pat Carroll *(Ursula)*, Paddi Edwards *(Flotsam & Jetsam)*, Buddy Hackett *(Scuttle)*, Jason Marin *(Flounder)*, Kenneth Mars *(Triton)*, Edie McClurg *(Carlotta)*, Will Ryan *(Seahorse)*, Ben Wright *(Grimsby)*, Samuel E. Wright *(Sebastian)*, Hamilton Camp, Debbie Shapiro, Robert Weil, Ed Gilbert, Charlie Adler, Jack Angel, Susan Boyd, Steve Bulen, Nancy Cartwright, Philip Clarke, Jennifer Darling, Allan Davies, Gail Farrell, Donny Gerrard, Mitch Gordon, Willie Greene Jr., Linda Harmon, Walter S. Harrah, Phillip Ingram, Luana Jackman, William Kanady, Edie Lehmann, Anne Lockhart, Sherry Lynn, Melissa MacKay, Guy Maeda, Lynn Dolin Mann, Arne B. Markussen, Mickie T. McGowan, Gene J. Merlino, Lewis Morford, Kathleen O'Connor, Patrick Pinney, Marilyn Powell, Gloria G. Prosper, Michael Redman Jr., Sally Stevens, Robert Tebow, Rob Trow, Joe Turano, Jackie Ward, Bobbi White, Robert S. Zwirn.

THE LITTLE MERMAID is Walt Disney Studio's 28th full-length animated feature and its first animated fairy tale since SLEEPING BEAUTY (1958). Written and directed by John Musker and Ron Clements (THE GREAT MOUSE DETECTIVE), it is the story of Ariel, a mermaid with a beautiful voice who lives under the sea in a kingdom ruled by her father, Triton the Sea King. Ariel spends most of her time with her chubby fish companion, Flounder, scouring the surface for items left by humans to add to Ariel's collection. The teenaged mermaid, who longs to visit the world above the surface, is fascinated by these articles and keeps them in a secret place, dreaming of using them someday in the human world. Triton, meanwhile, is angry with his daughter for her fascination with humans, whom he hates for their love of seafood. He assigns his crab assistant Sebastian to keep an eye on Ariel and make sure she stays away from humans. Not surprisingly, Ariel swims to the surface again anyway and saves a prince from shipwreck and fire, falling in love with him in the process and longing to be with him. Upon regaining consciousness, Prince Eric hears Ariel singing (although he doesn't see her face clearly) and, mesmerized by the beauty of her voice, determines to make the possessor of that voice his princess. Triton learns what has happened and, in a fit of rage, destroys Ariel's collection of human artifacts, forbidding her ever to go to the surface again. Dejected and angry, Ariel seeks help from Ursula the Sea Witch, who secretly longs to rule the sea and uses this opportunity to trick Ariel in

the hope of destroying Triton. Ursula convinces Ariel to sign a contract stipulating that the little mermaid will trade her beautiful voice for a human body. If the prince kisses her in three days time, Ariel will remain human and live with the prince forever, but if the prince does not kiss her, she will be turned into a shriveled weed and added to the Witch's collection of lost mermaid souls. The prince finds Ariel on the beach and recognizes her, thinking that she is the one who had saved him until he discovers that Ariel can not speak. Now Ariel must make the prince fall in love with her. Ursula, however, has tricked Ariel and uses her voice (kept in a shell that hangs around the Sea Witch's neck) to lure the prince away from Ariel. Ursula takes on a human disguise, and upon hearing Ariel's voice coming from Ursula's new body, the prince is transfixed and immediately wants to marry her. After discovering that the mystery woman is really Ursula, Ariel and her friends disrupt the wedding, get Ariel's voice back, and prove to the prince that Ariel is his savior after all. But as the prince and Ariel are about to kiss, the sun sets on the third day and the little mermaid is whisked into the ocean where Ursula awaits. The film climaxes with a battle between Triton and Ursula for the possession of Ariel's soul and the sea itself. In the end, Ursula is destroyed, Triton grants Ariel's wish to be human, and she and the prince marry and live happily ever after.

Although neither as rich nor as memorable as Disney's earlier efforts, THE LITTLE MERMAID is still an impressive achievement. Its animation is exceptionally good (especially after the slapdash flatness of OLIVER AND COMPANY), with wonderful complex movements and smooth action. The film also contains some very strong characters, most notably Sebastian the crab. A wildly funny mixture of Caribbean persona and shellfish body, Sebastian is straight out of a Tex Avery cartoon. As a matter of fact, the finest moments in THE LITTLE MERMAID are the wacky, off-the-wall ones (the film's best sight gag involves the familiar jaw dropping bit). Nearly every character in the film is funny (even the evil Ursula has some big laughs), and cute creatures abound: in addition to Sebastian, a wacky sea gull, an adorable dog, a loony seahorse, and a loveable blowfish, not to mention the zany maid and crazy French chef. As entertaining and amusing as this all is (and it is very good family entertainment), some of the Disney magic seems to be missing. THE LITTLE MERMAID lacks the depth and emotional power of so many of the studio's classics. Instead of exploring the primal fears of childhood, in the brave but frightening way the best Disney films do, it skims the surface of its subject, and plays more like a weak John Hughes film than a strong Walt Disney one. The story, which is full of

THE LITTLE MERMAID (©Walt Disney).

potentially serious themes, is played strictly for bland emotionless laughs. The result is a movie that is fun to watch but that remains disappointing. Instead of the likes of Bambi and Dumbo, it presents characters with no emotional resonance. THE LITTLE MERMAID is great for kids, and some of it is quite funny, but when it's all over, it leaves you wanting more.

p, Howard Ashman and John Musker; d, John Musker and Ron Clements; w, John Musker and Ron Clements (based on the fairy tale by Hans Christian Andersen); ed, Mark Hester; m, Robby Merkin and Alan Menken; md, Howard Ashman; prod d, Maureen Donley; art d, Michael A. Peraza Jr. and Donald A. Towns; spec eff, Mark Dindal; anim, Mark Henn.

Animated/Children's

(PR:AA MPAA:G)

LITTLE THIEF, THE**½

(Fr.) 105m Orly-Renn-Cine Cinq-Les Films du Carrosse-Sedif/Miramax c Charlotte Gainsbourg *(Janine Castang)*, Didier Bezace *(Michel Davenne)*, Simon de la Brosse *(Raoul)*, Raoul Billerey *(Uncle Andre Rouleau)*, Chantal Banlier *(Aunt Lea)*, Nathalie Cardone *(Mauricette)*, Clotilde de Bayser *(Severine Longuet)*, Philippe Deplanche *(Jacques Longuet)*, Marion Grimault *(Kebadian)*, Erick Deshors *(Raymond)*, Remy Kirch *(Pascouette)*, Renee Faure *(Mother Busato)*, Claude Guyonnet *(Young Priest)*, Jacques Herlin *(Sexton)*, Gilbert Bahon *(Sergeant)*, Catherine Arditi *(Headmistress)*, Pierre Maguelon *(M. Fauvel)*, Marie-Therese Orain *(Mme. Pigier)*, Sherif Scouri *(Cohen)*, Joelle Bruyas *(Sr. Marie-Odile)*, Clothilde Baudon *(Bonnin)*, Jacky Nercessian *(M. Folies)*, Annie Legrand *(Hotel Reception-*

ist), Chantal Neuwirth *(Farmer's Wife)*, Denise Chiabaut *(Doctor)*, Florent Gibassier *(Carpenter)*.

THE LITTLE THIEF stars Gainsbourg as its title character, who, as the film opens, is a rebellious 15-year-old struggling against the provincial strictures of life in her small French village after WW II. Her penchant for petty thievery has aroused the wrath of her aunt and uncle, who have cared for her since her flighty mother, a Nazi collaborator, deserted them. Removed from school and put to work, first in a creamery and then as the maid of a rich young couple, Gainsbourg finds escape in the local cinemas, where she meets Bezace, a mild-mannered, married choirmaster for whom she conceives a convulsive passion. Bezace relieves Gainsbourg of her unwanted virginity and takes the reformation of her character in hand, subsidizing her entrance into secretarial school and teaching her the joys of reading. Things seem to go calmly, until Gainsbourg encounters de la Brosse, an itinerant motorcyclist with a similar bent for larceny. In an effort to start a life together and help out her uncle, who has fallen on hard times, they rob her employers. A romantic beach gambol is subsequently brought to an abrupt halt when Gainsbourg is captured by the local authorities, who haul her off to a women's reformatory. There, she befriends Cardone, a fellow inmate and amateur photographer who introduces her to the wonders of the camera. Together, they make their escape from the prison, then go their separate ways, Cardone giving Gainsbourg her camera as a symbol of their friendship. A pregnant Gainsbourg returns to her uncle's, but, finding herself unwelcome, steals for one last time and hits the road again, this time alone.

Francois Truffaut once said that the three most important elements of a film were the script, the script, and the script. THE LITTLE THIEF's main character was originally conceived as part of his THE 400 BLOWS, but cut to shorten the film. Truffaut never forgot her, however, and carried a 40-page treatment about her with him until he died of brain cancer in 1984. A few months before his death, he asked Claude Berri (JEAN DE FLORETTE) to direct the film, but when Berri proved too busy to do so, the task fell to Claude Miller, Truffaut's longtime production manager. With his wife, Annie Miller, and Luc Beraud, Miller wrote a full script, agreeing to film it on the condition that Charlotte Gainsbourg, with whom he had already worked in L'EFFRONTEE, be cast in the title role.

The spirit of Truffaut is very much in evidence in THE LITTLE THIEF: the affection for the past, the concern with adolescent angst, the abiding love of cinema. What's lacking is his radiantly omniscient sense of humanity, not to mention his sureness of control with both performances and film technique. Miller apes his style, going for a picaresque lyricism and using such self-consciously cinematic devices as irises and intercut newsreel footage. The difference is that when Truffaut employed such effects, they were usually uncannily, psychologically right for the moment, while with Miller they're merely static and rather immodest flourishes. The film is diverting and moves along briskly, but is never really moving or compelling. Too many of the scenes feel negligible, forced onto the screen rather than germane to the plot, and the script is particularly weak in its superficial treatment of Bezace's character, failing to convey the crucial nature of his role in Gainsbourg's life (and vice versa).

Other scenes, like that in which Gainsbourg robs a church, are flatly staged, and the film becomes very desultory in the beach idyll. (Particularly tiresome is the glaringly symbolic shot of Gainsbourg releasing a captured rabbit moments before she herself is arrested.) The prison scenes are similarly cliched—their ancestry can be traced to similar sequences in early Hollywood bad-girl films like Jean Harlow's HOLD YOUR MAN (1933)—and even include an unrequited lesbian-love suicide. Miller's interjection of newsreel footage (ladies' changing fashions, Rita Hayworth's marriage to Aly Khan, the Indochinese War) senselessly breaks off his story, as if to keep reminding us that this is all in the past—something milieu and detail should already have made clear. The use of photography to redeem Gainsbourg at the end is a salutary, Truffautesque gesture that also seems forced, since up until that moment the disaffected, restless girl has never shown the slightest interest in the arts.

Gangling Gainsbourg, with her hushed, sibilant voice, is as natural on screen as the young Jean-Pierre Leaud was in THE 400 BLOWS, and she's the best thing in the film. Whatever harrowing or wacky situation the script places her in, Gainsbourg maintains a matter-of-fact, stoic purity that is always authentic. Her sulky, Modigliani face takes to comic deadpan beautifully, and is also capable of breaking into a disarming, loopy grin, while her natural grace and emotional accuracy carry the film over many weak spots. Unfortunately, the actors chosen to portray Gainsbourg's lovers must be counted among these weaknesses. Didier Bezace gives an at-arm's-length performance as the over-idealized, kind, and gentle married man who introduces her to sex. His reactions—whether to Gainsbourg's physical aggression or to seeing his wife while in her company—have a facile, TV sitcom quality. Had Truffaut himself played the part (the character's surname is the same as that of the man Truffaut played in THE GREEN ROOM), he might have imbued it with a deeper melancholy—some yearning, frustrated passion. By contrast, when Bezace learns of Gainsbourg's unfaithfulness, it seems as if he might just as easily be expressing some slight displeasure over a dinner wine. Nor does his unprepossessing appearance—owlish little specs and an annoying fringe—help gain sympathy for the character.

De la Brosse is at least flamboyantly handsome as the hustler Raoul, but his performance also feels false as he vaults and leaps about like Fairbanks; does cigarette tricks and exclaims, "Zut!"; and gabs away nonsensically like a parody of (the grown) Leaud—all of which only serves to make one feel sorry for Gainsbourg for loving such a fool. (She cries only once in the film—while imagining that she sees de la Brosse in a newsreel.) Raoul Billerey and Chantal Banlier are more successful as her uncle and aunt, the former achieving poignancy when he hesitantly pays up the bill in a cafe, the latter showing a fierce, drunken embitteredness that pierces through some of the film's preciousness. Clotilde de Bayser, as Gainsbourg's yuppie employer, does her early scenes with the misguided animation of a Feydeau farce, but is touchingly direct when her character loses her baby; and Cardone has a dark, brutish sensuality that contrasts strikingly with Gainsbourg's pale, withdrawn quality. Dominique Chapuis' photography is quite lovely, subtly suggestive of the period and especially alive to the blue-greys of walls, Gainsbourg's first grown-up skirt, prison uniforms, and the beach's overcast sky and sea. Alain Jomy's music is nicely unstressed and makes effective use of traditional French folk chants, as well as pop-

ular songs of the era. *(Nudity, adult situations, sexual situations.)*

p, Alain Vannier and Claude Berri; d, Claude Miller; w, Claude Miller, Annie Miller, and Luc Beraud (based on the story by Francois Truffaut, Claude de Givray); ph, Dominique Chapuis (Fujicolor); ed, Albert Jurgenson; m, Alain Jomy; art d, Jean-Pierre Kohut-Svelko; spec eff, Jean-Francois Cousson and Guy Trielli; cos, Jacqueline Bouchard; stunts, Nella Barbier; makeup, Joel Lavau.

Drama   **(PR:O   MPAA:R)**

Ⓥ**LITTLE VERA***½
(USSR) 110m Gorky/International Film Exchange c
(MALENKAYA VERA)
Natalya Negoda *(Vera)*, Andrei Sokolov *(Sergei)*, Ludmila Zaitzeva *(Mother)*, Andrei Fomin *(Andrei)*, Alexander Alexeyev-Negreba *(Victor)*, Yuri Nazarov *(Father)*, Alexandra Tabakova *(Christyakova)*, Alexander Mironov *(Tolik)*, Alexander Linkov *(Mikhail Petrovich)*.

Set in a provincial industrial city, LITTLE VERA focuses on the plight of a rebellious teenager (Negoda), who, much to her parents' dismay, seems wholly uninterested in her future after she graduates from secondary school. Both her father, Nazarov, a heavy-drinking truck driver, and her mother, Zaitzeva, a controller at a sewing factory, are anxious for her to begin training as a telephonist. They would also like to see her eventually marry her devoted boy friend, who is off to join the navy. Negoda, however, isn't interested in either, and—almost always clad in a red-and-white striped jumper, black mini, fishnet stockings, and heels—is instead a good-time girl, hanging out in cafes, partying with friends, and toying with her lustful boy friend. When a rumble erupts at a local rock concert (with Armenians playing the Sharks to the Russian Jets) and police arrive on the scene, the fleeing Negoda ends up with Sokolov, a handsome metallurgy student whose cooler-than-cool demeanor sweeps her off her feet. Before long they are sleeping together, and her parents, convinced Negoda has become a slut, summon their doctor son (Negreba) from Moscow to straighten out his sister. When he learns that she has taken up with his old friend Sokolov, a legendary ladies' man, Negreba also hits the roof. Negoda refuses to break off the relationship, and when she says she is pregnant (though it's relatively clear that she isn't), Sokolov agrees to marry her and moves in with her family. The problem is that he can't stand them and they don't like him. One night, Nazarov, plastered as usual, takes his abuse of Sokolov too far, and the younger man locks him in a bathroom. When Nazarov is let out, he impulsively stabs Sokolov, sending the latter to the hospital. In the

days that follow, the family tries to persuade Negoda to lie to the police about the incident to protect her father, and, after much painful soul-searching, she does. Treated coolly by Sokolov during a hospital bedside visit, Negoda returns home and tries to kill herself. In a climax that is alternately emotionally high-pitched, capricious, and finally melancholy, Negreba happens upon his overdosed sister and saves her.

With an offbeat family-in-the-kitchen finale right out of MOONSTRUCK, LITTLE VERA is a far cry from the stridency of Soviet Realism, yet in its evocation of rank-and-file life it presents its own brand of kitchen-sink verisimilitude. Aided by marvelous performances and Maria Khmelik's well-crafted screenplay, director Vasily Pichul has fashioned an extraordinarily involving film that is as funny as it is poignant. Each of the principal actors establishes a clearly defined personality, transforming situations that are not inherently funny into scenes that are amusing and touching. In the film's most powerful scene, the family has taken Negoda to the beach for a picnic. There Negreba—back again from Moscow, where he is having problems with his own little family—is to make another plea to Negoda to protect her father by lying to the police. Knowing this, Negoda castigates the family, then runs off just before a thunderstorm strikes. Crying out for "his little girl," Nazarov searches for his daughter, and Pichul then presents an extremely expressive shot of Negoda cradled in her father's arms under an overhang as the rain pours down, stressing the pain of Negoda's internal conflict between her love for her family and her devotion to Sokolov.

Although his lighting is occasionally uneven, Pichul's handling of the camera is assured and inventive, and the moodily photographed shots of the industrial landscape (particularly a slow-motion rendering of the harbor at night) used as a bridge between the story's episodes are particularly evocative. His pacing is equally skilled and the film seems considerably shorter than its nearly two-hour length. Likewise, Pichul's direction of his actors is outstanding. When all is said and done, though, the most memorable thing about the film may be Little Vera herself, Natalya Negoda, whose captivating screen presence lingers long after the film has unspooled.

Containing a sex scene that is tame by Western standards but that reportedly caused something of a stir in the Soviet Union, LITTLE VERA did not receive an immediate release in the USSR. American film festival audiences were luckier (the film won awards at the Chicago Film Festival for Best Film and Best Actress). (In Russian; English subtitles.) *(Brief nudity, sexual situations, adult situations, violence, substance abuse.)*

d, Vasily Pichul; w, Maria Khmelik; ph, Yefim Reznikov; ed, Elena Zabolockaja; m, Vladimir Matetsky; cos, Natalya Polyakh; stunts, N. Sysoyev; makeup, Valentina Zakharchenko.

Drama   **(PR:O MPAA:NR)**

Ⓥ**LOCK UP***½
106m Gordon/Tri-Star c

Sylvester Stallone *(Frank Leone)*, Donald Sutherland *(Warden Drumgoole)*, John Amos *(Meissner, Captain of the Guards)*, Sonny Landham *(Chink)*, Frank McRae *(Eclipse)*, Darlanne Fluegel *(Melissa)*, Tom Sizemore *(Dallas)*, William Allen Young *(Braden)*, Larry Romano *(First Base)*, Jordan Lund *(Manly)*, John Lilla *(Wiley)*, Dean Duval *(Ernie)*, Jerry Strivelli *(Louis Munafo)*, David Anthony Marshall *(Mastrone)*, Kurek Ashley, Michael Petroni, Danny Trejo *(Chink's Gang)*, Frank D'Annibale, Tony Lip, Clarence Moore, Joe Pentangelo, Eli Rich, Bo Rucker, Randy Sandkuhl *(Guards)*, Robert Vazquez *(Officer Vazquez)*, Tony Munafo *(Prisoner)*, Frank Pesce *(Johnson)*, Troy Curvey Jr. *(Prison Receptionist)*.

Pity poor Sylvester Stallone, whose macho everyman must once again suffer the slings and arrows of a cruel and heartless society! In LOCK UP, the martyr played by Stallone is a basically decent guy who has been serving time in prison after putting a mean hurt on a group of thugs who roughed up his elderly mentor, a man who snatched young Sly from the streets and taught him to fix cars. When sadistic warden Sutherland refused to let Stallone out of jail on a weekend pass to visit his dying mentor, model-prisoner Stallone escaped and went to the media with tales of Sutherland's abuse of inmates. Sutherland was reprimanded and sent to preside over one of the worst prisons in the entire system, while noble escapee Stallone was forgiven and placed in a minimum-security prison—complete with weekend furloughs—to do the rest of his time. (All this information, of course, is backstory spelled out in brief passages of expository dialog sandwiched in between lengthy scenes of Stallone being tortured by the evil Sutherland and his sadistic prison guard.) The film opens as Stallone goes back to prison after spending an idyllic weekend furlough with his favorite girl, Fluegel. Back in prison, he is greeted like an old friend by the compassionate and trusting guards. That night, however, as the film's lighting scheme turns from glowing burnished orange to cold Fritz Langian expressionism, Sly is awakened in his bunk by hard-as-nails prison guard Amos and his storm troopers—who, without explanation, cuff Stallone, drag him from his comfy cell, and haul him to

the prehistoric prison run by Sutherland. It seems that the obviously psychotic warden, wanting revenge, had the model prisoner transferred to this hell-hole for the last six months of his sentence. While showing Sly the electric chair he has lovingly restored but isn't allowed to use, Sutherland vows to break Stallone one way or another. Tossed in with the regular prison population, Stallone soon must endure what seem like 1,000 Herculean trials, all the while repressing his temper in order to keep extra time from being added to his sentence. In addition to an amazing collection of sadistic guards, Sutherland employs the toughest con in the joint, Landham, to personally torment Stallone. Sutherland even goes so far as to order the destruction of the vintage '65 Mustang that Stallone and fellow inmate McRae earlier restored during a ROCKY-like montage (where they got the parts is anybody's guess). Frustrated because Stallone has yet to crack, Sutherland sends Landham to kill Sly's little buddy Romano, a naive young inmate who looks up to Sly. After Landham and his cohorts drop about 800 pounds of weights across the kid's chest in the prison gym, killing him, Sly finally goes nuts and womps on the goons. He's about to give Landham the same treatment the kid got, but Stallone's basic humanity bubbles to the surface and he spares the murderer's life—and gets a shiv in the kidneys in return. Recovering from his wound in the infirmary, Stallone learns that Sutherland has paid an inmate who is about to be released $1,000 to rape Fluegel. Determined to escape so that he can protect his girl, Sly makes his bid for freedom, but the whole thing is a setup and he is cornered in the boiler room by a detail of guards who work him over. The angry Sly, however, beats them all and captures Sutherland, locking him into his beloved electric chair. Standing before the fatal lever like Boris Karloff at the end of THE BRIDE OF FRANKENSTEIN (one waits for him to say, "We belong dead"), Stallone forces Sutherland to confess to his schemes in front of Amos and his heavily armed security detail. Sly then gives himself up, and Sutherland delights in the knowledge that his nemesis faces a lenghty extension of his sentence. In a surprise move, however, the law-abiding Amos has Sutherland arrested and grimly states that "a court of law" will sort out the warden's various crimes against humanity. In the end, Sly serves out his sentence without incident and is released into the loving arms of the long-suffering Fluegel.

Employing every prison-movie cliche in the book, the film becomes increasingly absurd with each scene. LOCK UP was coproduced by Stallone's fledgling production company, White Eagle, and the star's fingerprints are all over the film, although he did not write or direct it. Given Stal-

lone's penchant for drippy sentimentality and boneheaded simple-mindedness, however, one must assume that he had a hand in the screenplay by first-timer Richard Smith and veterans Jeb Stuart and Henry Rosenbaum. The script seems to have been stripped of anything resembling balance or ambiguity, and Sly's dialog—which alternates between impassioned speeches about the human spirit and passages in which his only lines are AARGGGHHH! and GRRRRRR!—has been pared down to the bare minimum, just the way the star likes it (he has stated in interviews that his idea of a perfect script would be one without dialog). This, of course, stacks the deck in his character's favor, making him completely good, while the beady-eyed Donald Sutherland is left to play pure evil. An excellent actor who can bring remarkable subtlety and nuance to even the smallest supporting appearance, poor Sutherland struggles mightily to wring something of value out of his woefully one-dimensional role. As for Stallone, he looks for every opportunity to remove his shirt and give the paying customer an eyeful of his rippling musculature.

With nothing in the way of performance to cling to, the audience is left to marvel at the mounting inanity of each scene. Sutherland's character is so obviously psychotic that the state probably wouldn't let him drive a car, let alone run a prison. How is it possible for a warden with a tainted reputation to have a model prisoner with six months left to serve transferred from a minimum-security prison to a maximum-security dungeon? Why doesn't Stallone's girl friend call the ACLU, or, if that fails, take his story to the media? Toward the end, after Stallone has been beaten, tortured, set up, and stabbed at Sutherland's command, why does he trust the warden enough to think that Sutherland would allow a conjugal visit from Fluegel to go uninterrupted? (Letting the action get hot and heavy for two minutes, two slobbering guards end the session and stand there ogling Fluegel while Sly suffers from a painful case of coitus interruptus). Most absurd of all is the fact that Amos, who has impassively watched Sutherland commit act after act of cruel and unconstitutional punishment, suddenly decides to nail his boss after Sutherland makes a confession under obvious duress (one can imagine the judge's face when he learns the confession was made only after an inmate forced the warden into the electric chair and threatened to throw the switch!).

It seems safe to say that Stallone has yet to learn that the public is growing weary of his cartoonish action heroes and are moving on toward more human and realistic protagonists, like Bruce Willis in DIE HARD (which, ironically, Jeb Stuart cowrote) or Robert De Niro in MIDNIGHT

RUN. Stallone would do well to reexamine his work in the very first "Rocky" movie and try to recapture it, for the successful action heroes of the 1990s will be more like Willis or De Niro and less like automatons. *(Violence, sexual situations, profanity.)*

p, Lawrence Gordon and Charles Gordon; d, John Flynn; w, Richard Smith, Jeb Stuart, and Henry Rosenbaum; ph, Donald E. Thorin (Technicolor); ed, Michael N. Knue and Donald Brochu; m, Bill Conti; prod d, Bill Kenney; art d, Wm. Ladd Skinner and Bill Groom; set d, Jerry Adams and George DeTitta Sr.; spec eff, Joe Digaetano, Dave Dohmeyer, Robert Wilson Sr., Robert Wilson Jr., and Edward Drohan; cos, Bernie Pollack; stunts, Frank Orsatti; makeup, Gary Liddiard.

Prison   **(PR:O MPAA:R)**

LOOK WHO'S TALKING***
93m Tri-Star c
John Travolta *(James)*, Kirstie Alley *(Mollie)*, Olympia Dukakis *(Rosie)*, George Segal *(Albert)*, Abe Vigoda *(Grandpa)*, Bruce Willis *(Voice of Mikey)*, Twink Caplan *(Rona)*, Jason Schaller, Jaryd Waterhouse, Jacob Haines, Christopher Aydon *(Mikey)*, Joy Boushel *(Melissa)*, Don S. Davis *(Dr. Fleisher)*, Louis Heckerling *(Lou)*, Brenda Crichlow *(Secretary)*, Andrea Mann *(Salesgirl)*, Douglas Tuck *(Cab Stealer)*, Alex Bruhanski *(Street Worker)*, B. Casey Grant *(Admitting Clerk)*, Oscar B. Ramos *(Hospital Worker)*, Aurelio DiNunzio *(Orderly)*, Jeff Irvine *(Admitting Doctor)*, Shirley Barclay *(Nurse)*, William B. Davis *(Drug Doctor)*, David Berner *(Mr. Impatience)*, Jerry Wasserman *(Mr. Anal)*, Daliah Novak *(Carrie)*, Zena Darawalla *(Lupe)*, Nicholas Rice *(Harry)*, Neal Israel *(Mr. Ross)*, Blu Mankuma *(Director)*, William Britos *(Home Orderly)*, Deejay Jackson *(Burly Orderly)*, Gerry Bean, Deryl Hayes *(Pilot Friends)*, Enid Saunders *(Ester)*.

LOOK WHO'S TALKING contains a different kind of explicit sex scene, one presenting an inside view of the action. After Alley and Segal fall to the floor in a fit of passion, the next thing on-screen is a school of sperm swimming upstream to the accompaniment of the Beach Boys' "I Get Around." Leading the charge is a sperm with a suspiciously familiar voice. It wins the race and succeeds in fertilizing the egg, all the while narrating its adventure. The familiar voice, of course, belongs to Willis, the *who* in LOOK WHO'S TALKING, a mildly amusing comedy buoyed by the voiceover gimmick. Alley stars as an accountant who has been having an affair with Segal, a married client. She repeatedly asks him to leave his wife, but he can't bring himself to do it because of his wife's emotional instability. Even Alley's pregnancy doesn't change his mind, so she decides to tell people she was artificially inseminated.

Although she is elated when Segal finally does leave his wife, Alley soon discovers that he has been unfaithful to her as well. After running out of a store where she has found Segal with a girl friend, Alley goes into labor on the street. The taxicab that picks her up is driven by Travolta, who accompanies her to the delivery room and shows up at her apartment a few days after the birth of her son to return the pocketbook she left in his cab. Alley hires him to baby-sit, and Travolta turns out to be a good companion for the child. She returns the favor by allowing Travolta, a New Jersey resident, to use her Manhattan address to get his grandfather (Vigoda) into a retirement home open only to New York City residents. Ignoring Travolta's attraction to her, Alley begins searching for a good father for her son. But she can barely stand to be with the men she dates, let alone invite them to raise her child. Eventually, she faces up to her feelings for Travolta and the two tumble onto her bed. While they undress, she envisions her future with Travolta—seeing herself stuck in the kitchen surrounded by a passel of noisy children, waiting for Travolta to come home with dinner he has picked out of the garbage. Taken aback by this nightmarish scenario, she brings their moment of passion to an abrupt end. At work, Alley is reassigned to Segal, who is now unattached and wants her back, but when she brings the baby to meet him, Segal shirks his responsibility, and Alley says goodbye to him for good. One day, she is called to the retirement home when Vigoda gets out of hand. While Travolta and Alley are calming the old man down, her son wanders off on his own, ending up in the middle of a traffic jam. His rescue brings Travolta and Alley together at last. Don't expect to be able to view babies naively again after seeing LOOK WHO'S TALKING. If you aren't already curious, the movie will awaken in you the same inquisitiveness that inspired Amy Heckerling to write the story on which it's based: "I used to look at my daughter in her baby seat and wonder what she was thinking about," Heckerling has said. "I assumed she thought the same way I did. You know, sort of cynical thoughts, not cute, adorable baby thoughts." Heckerling, who also directed the film, takes a clever idea and conveys it superbly. With his sarcastic delivery, Bruce Willis has the ideal voice for the baby, and his funny comments wonderfully complement the child's expressions. The voiceover also works well because the filmmakers use the device for all it's worth, with Willis providing a voice for the child when it's a sperm, a fetus, and a baby. Other babies in the movie have voices too. LOOK WHO'S TALKING is also clever in other respects, including its adept use of popular songs. In a marvelous inside joke, the baby cruises in his stroller to the Bee Gees' "Stayin' Alive,"

John Travolta and Jason Schaller in LOOK WHO'S TALKING (©Tri-Star).

the song to which Travolta strutted to fame in SATURDAY NIGHT FEVER; while Katrina and the Waves' peppy "Walking on Sunshine" helps Travolta teach the child how to dance. The soundtrack also features such baby-themed tunes as the Beach Boys'"When I Grow Up (To Be a Man)" and Shep and the Limelights' "Daddy's Home." Dream sequences further enliven the movie. When the doctor mentions Alley's ticking biological clock, she imagines herself clinging Harold Lloyd-like to a giant clock, and, while suffering through a date, she foresees how the man's bad habits would manifest themselves in his parenting. Regrettably, these lively additions provide LOOK WHO'S TALKING's only spark. Kirstie Alley's and John Travolta's characters are affable enough, but the story itself is ordinary and merely passes time until their inevitable coupling, the hastier occurrence of which could easily have been justified by the story. As a businesswoman, Alley worries about Travolta's carefree lifestyle, but his devotion to the baby surely might have won her over. Moreover, since she's so particular about Travolta's behavior, her infatuation with Segal isn't consistent with her character. We see hardly any of the tenderness or charm that may have attracted her to Segal; instead, he comes off mostly as selfish and devious. Travolta, on the other hand, is completely likable. LOOK WHO'S TALKING provides an excellent vehicle for rejuvenating his career, especially since he shows a new flair for romantic comedy. Alley, with a fine opportunity for a star turn, also gives an engaging performance. Unfortunately, the reliable Olympia Dukakis, who plays Alley's mother, is given too little screen time. What weakens LOOK WHO'S TALKING most are two car chases: the rush to the hospital early in the film and the baby's rescue at the end. In a movie with so original a premise, these routines stand out as markedly routine and unnecessary. The screeching stops, illegal U-turns, and near collisions they offer are uncalled for by the plot and belong in a second-rate cop comedy. But thanks to the ingenious voiceover, LOOK WHO'S TALKING rises above the second rate. It's a genial, entertaining film. Songs include: "I Love You So" (Morris Levy, Sonny Norton, performed by the Chantels), "I Get Around," "When I Grow Up (To Be a Man)" (Brian Wilson, performed by the Beach Boys), "And She Was" (David Byrne, performed by Talking Heads), "Dumb Things" (Paul Kelly, performed by Paul Kelly and the Messengers), "Cry Baby" (Norman Meade, Burt Russell, performed by Janis Joplin), "Walking on Sunshine" (Kimberly Rew, performed by Katrina and the Waves), "Stayin' Alive" (Barry Gibb, Maurice Gibb, Robin Gibb, performed by the Bee Gees), "Town Without Pity"(Dimitri Tiomkin, Ned Washington, performed by Gene Pitney), "Daddy's Home" (J. Sheppard, W.H. Miller, performed by Shep and the Limelights), "Let My Love Open the Door" (Pete Townshend, performed by Townshend), "You Need Hands" (Max Bygraves, performed by Dan Lennon), "(You're) Having My Baby" (Paul Anka). *(Profanity, sexual situations, adult situations.)*

p, Jonathan D. Krane; d, Amy Heckerling; w, Amy Heckerling; ph, Thomas Del Ruth (AlphaCine Color); ed, Debra Chiate; m, David Kitay; art d, Reuben Freed; set d, Barry W. Brolly; spec eff, Bill Orr; cos, Molly Maginnis; chor, Mary Ann Kellogg; tech, Brenda Johnston; stunts, Rick Avery; makeup, Todd McIntosh.

Comedy   (PR:C MPAA:PG-13)

⊙LOST ANGELS**
116m Orion c
Donald Sutherland *(Dr. Charles Loftis)*, Adam Horovitz *(Tim Doolan)*, Amy Locane *(Cheryl Anderson)*, Don Bloomfield *(Andy Doolan)*, Celia Weston *(Felicia Marks)*, Graham Beckel *(Richard Doolan)*, Patricia Richardson *(Mrs. Anderson)*, Ron Frazier *(Barton Marks)*, Joseph d'Angerio *(Sweeney)*, William O'Leary *(Link)*, Kevin Corrigan *(Gata)*, Gary Riley *(Spooky)*, Michael Cunningham *(D.A.B. Kid)*, Leonard Portar Salazar *(Paco)*, Jonathan Del Arco *(Angel)*, Eddie Hernandez II *(10th Street Boy)*, Cehlia Barnum Newman *(Paco's Girl)*, David Herman *(Carlo)*, Max Perlich *(Frankie)*, Gino De Mauro *(Barry)*, Nina Siemaszko *(Merilee)*, Shana O'Neil *(Jenny)*, Dana Behr *(Anita)*, Mary Greening *(Mary)*, Kevin Tighe *(Dr. Gaeyl)*, John C. McGinley *(Dr. Farmer)*, Jane Hallaren *(Grace Willig)*, Peter Maloney *(Dr. Peter*

Ames), Lee Wilkof *(Ted Bingham)*, James N. Harrell *(Shelby)*, Constance Shulman *(Beautician)*, Marjie Rynearson *(Receptionist)*, Frances Fisher *(Judith Loftis)*, Jack Gold *(Judge)*, Keone Young *(Victor Eng)*, Park Overall *(Richard Doolan's Girl Friend)*, Henry R. Harris *(Juvenile Hall Policeman)*, Fredric Arnold *(Mr. Shay)*, Sharmon Anciola *(Charles Loftis' Daughter)*, Gordon Michaels *(Bartender)*, John Dichter *(Policeman)*, Larry Gregory Nelson *(District Attorney)*.

LOST ANGELS is a would-be-cautionary tale dealing with the wayward offspring of the rich and vacuous in a Los Angeles depicted as a nihilistic playground-cum-battleground where unsupervised, pampered brats run riot. Beastie Boy Adam Horovitz makes his film debut as the central character, relating his story in an eerily detached voice-over. We first encounter him in the back seat of a luxury sedan, rolling his vacant eyes at the inanities lobbed by his mom and step-dad from the front seat. Ostensibly en route to Arizona, his mother explains they have to make a stop, and before he knows it, Horovitz is ushered into a white cafeteria where seemingly anesthetized teens docilely spoon lunch from their trays. When Horovitz looks up to see the door at the end of the room ominously shut and his mother apprehensively shrink from view, he realizes he's been deposited at an institute for troubled (and rich) youths. He rebels, is quickly subdued by a contingent of guards, and taken to a small room where he's bound to a table. As he tries to writhe free, he's visited by Sutherland, a sympathetic, if overburdened, psychiatrist who has little patience with the institute's profit-motivated rules. Horovitz's flashback narrative then re-creates the episodes leading to his institutionalization. At a Los Angeles nightclub dominated by gang leader Bloomfield, his sociopathic half-brother, Horovitz—a quiet, passive type—soon finds himself in the midst of a rumble. As sirens wail and the gang members disperse, Horovitz picks up the gun he finds and races to the house of his brother's girl friend (Locane), expecting to find him there. Instead Locane invites him into her mom's new sports car for a joint, and moments after casually reminding herself to wash the car, she drives it into the pool. Horovitz spends the night with Locane, but the next morning her irate mother has the police take them in (they're reunited at the institute, where they develop a romantic relationship). As Horovitz stands before a judge, his hothead father (Beckel), called in the absence of his mother (who is on a trip to China), produces the gun Horovitz stashed under his bed and a bag of amphetamines. More to get back at his ex-wife than as a means of disciplining his son, he insists on pressing charges. Once inside the institute, Horovitz attempts a couple of

escapes, but is quickly caught and reprimanded. Although he makes progress, he can't resist the influence of Bloomfield, who instigates a successful escape enabling Horovitz to meet a drugged and dissolute Locane. Horovitz drives her to Sutherland's home seeking help, but he has so abused the therapist's trust that he is turned away. Not surprisingly, Horovitz winds up back at the institute, but before long, again joins his brother. As Bloomfield drives his truck through revellers at a Latino street fair, he hands Horovitz a gun, instructing him to shoot at random to avenge an earlier near-fatal scrape. Horovitz is horrified, but at the last moment fires at the ground, scattering the crowd. In the ensuing madness, Bloomfield nudges Horovitz out of the car and drives off, leaving his brother to fend for himself. Racing to his father's house expecting to find Bloomfield, Horovitz instead confronts the irascible Beckel, who finally comes to understand his son's need for support. When Bloomfield arrives, Horovitz bolts from the house for a final showdown and parting of the ways. With nowhere to go, he calls on Sutherland, who is himself grappling with a personal crisis (the recent breakup of his marriage and a burgeoning drinking problem). Horovitz expresses concern for the psychiatrist's situation, and in an ironic twist, their roles are momentarily reversed. Finally realizing the emptiness and futility of his past, Horovitz returns home to his mother, resolved to clean up his act.

LOST ANGELS is crippled by an unresolved schizophrenia at every level, its depiction of a grim, amoral subculture undercut by lush photography and sinuous camerawork. British director Hugh Hudson (CHARIOTS OF FIRE), working from a script by playwright Michael Weller ("Moonchildren"), can't seem to figure out whom to hold accountable—at times he indicts the indifferent, self-absorbed authority figures, and at other times he points a finger at the incorrigible youth. Moreover, the film's uneven tone and languid rhythm are at odds with the subject it explores. At almost every opportunity, the film opts for the sensational at the expense of nuance and irony. Hudson has obviously made LOST ANGELS more out of sorrow than anger, and that's a large part of the problem. His sympathies are so diffuse, they become confused; LOST ANGELS is a film with as little sense of direction as the youth it depicts. Songs include: "Do It Better" (Paul Ryder, Shawn Ryder, Mark Day, Paul Davis, Garry Whelan, performed by Happy Mondays), "Self Preservation" (Oscar Cares, Doug King, performed by Raheem), "Yeah Yeah Yeah Yeah Yeah" (Shane MacGowan, performed by the Pogues), "Cat on the Snake" (Chris Cornell, Tim Thayil, Hiro Yamamoto, performed by Soundgarden), "Fascination

Street" (Robert Smith, Simon Gallup, Boris Williams, Roger O'Donnell, Paul Thompson, Laurence Tolhurst, performed by the Cure), "Let's Rock" (Miss Apollo Smile & The Groove Commander, performed by Smile), "Just Plain Evil" (David Pirner, performed by Soul Asylum), "Love Long Gone" (Joe Blanton, Chris Makow, performed by the Royal Court of China), "Many Rivers to Cross" (Jimmy Cliff, performed by Toni Childs), "San Fernando Valley" (George Jenkins, performed by Bing Crosby), "The Night They Invented Champagne" (Alan Jay Lerner, Frederick Loewe), "Mellow Yellow" (Donovan Leitch), "Mr. Tambourine Man" (Bob Dylan), "Anything Goes" (Cole Porter). *(Violence, nudity, profanity.)*

p, Howard Rosenman and Thomas Baer; d, Hugh Hudson; w, Michael Weller; ph, Juan Ruiz-Anchia (Deluxe Color); ed, David Gladwell; m, Philippe Sarde; prod d, Assheton Gorton; art d, Alex Tavoularis; set d, Robert Kensinger; spec eff, Dale L. Martin; cos, Judianna Makovsky; chor, B.H. Barry; stunts, Rick Barker; makeup, Karen Bradley.

Drama   **(PR:C MPAA:R)**

ⓥ**LOVERBOY****
98m Crecent/Tri-Star c
Patrick Dempsey *(Randy Bodek)*, Kate Jackson *(Diane Bodek)*, Robert Ginty *(Joe Bodek)*, Nancy Valen *(Jenny Gordon)*, Charles Hunter Walsh *(Jory Talbot)*, Barbara Carrera *(Alex Barnett)*, Bernie Coulson *(Sal)*, Ray Girardin *(Henry)*, Robert Camilletti *(Tony)*, Vic Tayback *(Harry Bruckner)*, Kim Miyori *(Kyoko Bruckner)*, Robert Picardo *(Reed Palmer)*, Kirstie Alley *(Joyce Palmer)*, Peter Koch *(Claude Delancy)*, Carrie Fisher *(Monica Delancy)*, E.G. Daily *(Linda)*, Christopher Cohill, Wayne Collins Jr. *(Little Leaguers)*, Kathy Spitz *(Blonde at Senor Pizza)*, Elizabeth Scherrer *(Brunette at Senor Pizza)*, Sandra Beall *(Robin)*, Faith Burton *(Champagne Woman)*, Laurie Brown *(Intellectual Woman)*, Anne Lavezzi *(Lion's Mane Woman)*, Alexandra More *(Fudge Sundae Woman)*, Marilou Miller *(Lovers Lane Woman)*, Rebecca Holden *(Anchovy Woman)*, Sir Lamont Rodeheaver *(Boy)*, Bonnie Rodeheaver *(Little Sister)*, Alisa Wilson *(Nurse Darlene)*, Bill Kalmenson *(Male Patient)*, Irene Olga Lopez *(Spanish Maid)*, H. Hunt Burdick *(Hotel Manager)*, Cheryl Rhoads *(Mom at Pool)*, Anne Silverman *(Little Girl at Pool)*, Tony Schwartz *(Guest at Tiki Joe's)*, Katie Regan *(Health Spa Woman)*, Roberto Martin Marquez *(Juan)*.

If you're looking for clearly defined motives or even a modicum of plausibility, this contemporary farce isn't the film for you. Patrick Dempsey (IN THE MOOD; CAN'T BUY ME LOVE) stars as a styl-

ishly "punked out" college sophomore who has managed to keep his on-campus cohabitation with his girl friend (Valen) a secret from his parents. As the film opens, however, Dempsey manages to alienate both Valen, who breaks off their relationship, and his father (Ginty), who, enraged by his son's poor grades, turns off the tuition spigot. Left to fend for himself in the "real world," Dempsey takes a delivery job with a Mexican/Italian fast food restaurant, hoping to collect enough tips to get back into school and reunite with Valen. While on one of his deliveries (dressed in a mariachi-like uniform, ensconced in a ridiculous sombrero-topped delivery truck), Dempsey spots a flirtatious older woman, follows her to a boutique, and asks her out. After she gives Dempsey the brush-off, an elegant woman (Carrera) approaches and, impressed with his moxie, outfits him with a snappy white blazer and Panama hat. All roads seem to lead to bed until Dempsey decides he'd better get back to work. But shortly thereafter, he receives an order from an unlikely address for pizza with "heavy anchovies." As he enters the tony hotel room, he's greeted by Carrera in a suggestive silk nightgown. More orders for pizzas with heavy anchovies follow until, toward the end of what will obviously be their final rendezvous, Carrera drops $100 bills onto Dempsey's pillow—this, however, won't be her last contribution to his college fund. Soon, Dempsey is delivering heavy anchovy pizzas to seemingly every bored, rich housewife in the area, including the Japanese spouse (Miyori) of a gruff toy importer (who happens to be a business associate of Dempsey's father's) and the photographer wife (Fisher) of a muscle-

Patrick Dempsey in LOVERBOY (©Tri-Star).

bound fitness consultant. Meanwhile, in the film's main subplot, Ginty begins to believe that his son is gay, while his wife (Jackson) suspects that her husband is fooling around with other women and shares her suspicions with her doctor (Alley, of TV's "Cheers"), who happens to be one of Dempsey's clients. Alley suggests that Jackson develop an appetite for pizza with anchovies, which she does, checking into a motel room and placing an order while Ginty waits unknowingly and impatiently at home for her return, so they can attend a party commemorating their 20th anniversary. When Dempsey discovers the identity of his newest client, he persuades one of his coworkers, an Italian exchange student/stud (Camilletti, onetime companion of Cher), to deliver the pie, but by the time Dempsey's replacement arrives, Jackson has gotten cold feet and tries desperately to flee his amorous advances. As she races to the party, Dempsey is pursued by three cuckolds who've just figured things out. Predictably, a melee ensues, as dips, jello molds, and a piano go flying, but by the happy ending everyone is reconciled, including Dempsey and Valen.

While LOVERBOY does have its comic moments, director Joan Micklin Silver (CROSSING DELANCEY; HESTER STREET) presides over what is, in the main, an utterly predictable, sophomoric romp. Although farce requires a willing suspension of disbelief, LOVERBOY makes a good many more demands than are ordinarily required. As was the case with IN THE MOOD, we are asked to believe that Dempsey, an engaging but physically unassuming actor, is a love machine older women can't resist. Here we must accept that the stunning and sophisticated Barbara Carrera is drawn to Dempsey like a magnet, and then that after some "coaching" he "performs" successfully for a bevy of jaded housewives . . . maybe. But wouldn't it all have been more believable—and funnier—if Dempsey had shown some signs of transformation? Yes, he develops a few increments of panache, but he never sheds quite enough of his youthful awkwardness to be even moderately credible as a lady-killer. LOVERBOY's "comedy" is a blend of genre cliches (the delivery truck, the pursuit of angry husbands, etc.) and slapstick, and, not surprisingly, the film delivers few laughs. Songs include: "Another Love" (Colin Campsie, George McFarlane, Gardner Cole, performed by Giant Steps), "Walkin' the Line" (Brian Wilson, Eugene Landy, Nick Laird-Clowes, Alexandra Morgan, performed by Wilson), "One for the Boys" (Wilson, performed by Wilson), "Melt Away" (Wilson, Landy, performed by Wilson), "What I Am" (Edie Brickell, Kenneth Withrow, John Houser, John Bush, Alan Aly, performed by Edie Brickell and New Bohemians), "Wild Wild West"

(Trevor Steel, John Holliday, John Christoforou, Milan Zekavica, performed by the Escape Club), "Anywhere's Better Than Here" (Paul Westerberg, performed by the Replacements), "I Wanna Be Around" (Sadie Vimmerstedt, Johnny Mercer, performed by Tony Bennett), "They Can't Take That Away from Me" (George Gershwin, Ira Gershwin, performed by Fred Astaire), "Blue Tango" (Mitchell Parish, Leroy Anderson, performed by the Claudius Alzner Orchestra), "Great Balls of Fire" (Otis Blackwell, Jack Hammer, performed by Jerry Lee Lewis), "Hawaiian War Chant" (Johnny Noble, Leleiohaku), "Tiger Rag" (Harry DeCosta, Edwin B. Edwards, D. James LaRocca, Anthony Sbarbaro, Larry Shields), "Blue Hawaii" (Leo Robin, Ralph Rainger), "Tell Me" (Joe Lynn Turner, Jack Conrad, performed by Bekka Bramlett). *(Adult situations.)*

p, Gary Foster and Willie Hunt; d, Joan Micklin Silver; w, Robin Schiff, Tom Ropelewski, and Leslie Dixon (based on a story by Robin Schiff); ph, John Hora (Technicolor); ed, Rick Shaine; m, Michel Colombier; prod d, Dan Leigh; art d, Ann Champion; set d, Ethel Robins Richards; spec eff, Howard Jensen and James Hart; cos, Rosanna Norton; stunts, James Arnett; makeup, Bruce Hutchinson.

Comedy   **(PR:C MPAA:PG-13)**

LUCKIEST MAN IN THE WORLD, THE***

82m Mclaughlin, Piven, Vogel Inc./Second Effort c

Philip Bosco *(Sam Posner)*, Doris Belack *(Mrs. Posner)*, Joanne Camp *(Laura)*, Matthew Gottlieb *(Sheldon)*, Arthur French *(Cleveland)*, Stan Lachow *(Schwartz)*, Yamil Borges *(Mrs. Gonzalez)*, J.D. Clarke *(Robert Whitley)*, Moses Gunn *(Voice)*, Joel Friedman, Teodorina Bella.

At one point in THE LUCKIEST MAN IN THE WORLD, Sam Posner says to his wife, "But I want to start over again," and she responds, "Who doesn't?" In this case, Sam, the "luckiest man in the world" because he was 10 minutes too late to catch a plane that crashed and left no survivors, is inspired to reform and reassess his life as a result of this miraculous near-miss. Philip Bosco is very convincing as Sam, the rich, hard-nosed garment factory owner of Posner Frocks, who, in the film's first five minutes, is shown trying to dodge a union representative and getting nasty with his wife (Belack), his mistress (Camp), a dressmaker, and his chauffeur (French). After eluding the crash, Bosco tries to calm down and figure out why he was spared in the airport men's room. He does so out loud, prompting the man in the next stall to tell him why he was saved: he's getting a second chance, an opportunity to turn over a new leaf. Not unlike Ebenezer Scrooge, Bosco then sets out to right all the wrongs he's committed. The people around him are not convinced, however, leading to some ironic reactions; even the newspaperman covering the crash (Clarke) tells Bosco his guilt is only temporary, noting that he's seen this kind of reaction before from people who have been saved from death.

Sam's need to express his "new self" makes for some very funny moments, as well as for some quite poignant ones. Writer-director Frank Gilroy's (FROM NOON TILL THREE; DESPERATE CHARACTERS; THE GIG) script is good; unfortunately, his direction is not. There just doesn't appear to be any direction for most of the film, as the lead actors, mostly theater people, just do what comes naturally—on stage. Joanne Camp's theatrical projections fail to draw the audience *into* her character; Doris Belack and Bosco often show the same tendency. All are very accomplished actors, but their performances are flawed by Gilroy's inability or unwillingness to rein them in, while the film as a whole also suffers from a sense of timing that is not quite cinematic and which proves distracting. (Gilroy, the Pulitzer Prize-winning playwright of "The Subject Was Roses," began his career as a writer for such live drama TV series as "Studio One" and "The U.S. Steel Hour.")

On the other hand, the actors in smaller roles shine. J.D. Clarke is very convincing as the cynical newspaperman, and Arthur French provides the funniest scene in the film. Matthew Gottlieb is excellent as Bosco's estranged, homosexual son, displaying a sense of timing that saves a difficult, confrontational scene between the two. Yamil Borges takes full advantage of her scenes as the widow of the man who got Bosco's seat on the plane, while Joel Friedman, as Bosco's hospitalized ex-partner, and Teodorina Bella, as his nurse, could take their show on the road. The film also boasts a great ending, leaving no loose ends, and a wonderful gospel number performed by 14 Karat Soul.

Though flawed, THE LUCKIEST MAN IN THE WORLD demonstrates a Capra-esque vision that merits recognition. The quintessential independent filmmaker—he does everything, including gathering investors, scouting locations, writing, and directing—Gilroy makes movies that shine by virtue of their optimism, simplicity, and the very fact that he manages to make them despite incredible financial constraints and distribution woes. His faith and talents deserve a wider audience. *(Adult situations.)*

p, Norman I. Cohen; d, Frank D. Gilroy; w, Frank D. Gilroy; ph, Jeri Sopanen (TVC Color); ed, John Gilroy; m, Warren Vache and Jack Gale; prod d, Nick Romanec.

Comedy   **(PR:A-C MPAA:NR)**

M

Ⓥ**MADE IN USA***
82m Nelson c
Christopher Penn, Lori Singer, Adrian Pasdar.

MADE IN USA is a film about several characters who have been affected by environmental pollution. Christopher Penn and Adrian Pasdar play the sons of miners who have been the victims of lung disease and alcoholism. Both characters are angry, lawless, and perverse. (Penn will remind some of Charles Manson.) The story takes the two young men throughout the US to various sites of industrial pollution. Along the way they hook up with Singer, who has been poisoned by dioxins. Later, they pick up a hitchhiker, a runaway Navajo girl who attended a school polluted by radon gas. At the beginning of the film, Penn lusts after a pin-up girl in a magazine; at the end, he finds her on a clean beach. But when the camera makes its final pan, it is revealed that industrial pollution lurks nearby. Since we haven't been made to care whether Penn ever finds the girl, this ending appears tacked on, an afterthought that has nothing to do with the film's central concern with the effect of pollution on humankind.

Ken Friedman, writer-director of MADE IN USA, is obviously concerned about the environment. The problem with his film is that he has failed to write a coherent script. His attempt to create new types of existential heroes and an ambience of despair is commendable, but good storytelling requires that characters interact and that their actions reveal something to the audience. The only feeling the viewer experiences watching MADE IN USA is detachment, the very thing Friedman is criticizing in our attitudes toward the environment.

It is nearly impossible to care about the characters in this film. Not only do they break the law, but they masturbate, salivate, and lust with the same intensity. Their repulsive actions are senseless, fueled by neither rage nor the desire for kicks. And because we don't care about the characters, we feel no indignation at the pollution-engendered atrocities they encounter. Moreover, MADE IN USA presents narrow-minded and, in some cases, downright degrading views of women. The male characters don't fare much better, but at least Friedman tries to make them buddies, and they behave decently toward one another (most of the time). On the other hand, the film's native Americans act like gang members, and anybody who isn't angry is portrayed as a nerd or a misfit.

The acting in MADE IN USA is so bad that it's embarrassing to watch. Pasdar and Penn sound so much alike that when they

are heard in voiceover it's impossible to tell which one is speaking; more important, we can't understand what they are saying anyway. As for the gorgeous Lori Singer, her posing is wholly appropriate for a film that often looks and sounds like a long Calvin Klein commercial. Written and performed by Sonic Youth, the film's loud, intrusive score should be of interest to fans of rock music with arcane lyrics; others may also find it a welcome relief from the film's uninspired dialog. The only positive aspects of MADE IN USA are its art direction and cinematography. Art director Tom Southwell demonstrates a strong sense of how color relates to subject matter, and cinematographer Curtis Clark is to be commended for his perfect deep focus shots. Friedman sometimes manages to do a good job of shot selection, too, especially for his carefully composed shots of polluted areas. However, the editing is sometimes choppy and contributes to the story's lack of cohesiveness.

In the final analysis, MADE IN USA is lifeless and nihilistic—a product of depression and detachment. *(Adult situations.)*

p, Charles Voren; d, Ken Friedman; w, Ken Friedman and Nick Wechsler; ph, Curtis Clark; ed, Curtis Clayton; m, Sonic Youth; md, Joe Regis; art d, Tom Southwell; cos, Katherine Morrison; stunts, Harry Wowchuk; makeup, Ronnie Spector.

Drama   **(PR:O MPAA:R)**

Ⓥ**MAJOR LEAGUE*****
106m PAR c
Tom Berenger *(Jake Taylor)*, Charlie Sheen *(Rickie Vaughn)*, Corbin Bernsen *(Roger Dorn)*, Margaret Whitton *(Rachel Phelps)*, James Gammon *(Lou Brown)*, Bob Uecker *(Harry Doyle)*, Rene Russo *(Lynn Wells)*, Wesley Snipes *(Willie Mays Hayes)*, Charles Cyphers *(Charlie Donovan)*, Chelcie Ross *(Eddie Harris)*, Dennis Haysbert *(Pedro Cerrano)*, Andy Romano *(Pepper Leach)*, Steve Yeager, Peter Vuckovich.

In 1949, Republic Pictures released THE KID FROM CLEVELAND, a movie about a juvenile delinquent whose life is turned around by the 1948 world champion Cleveland Indians. Four decades later, the Indians, after being clobbered by the New York Giants in the 1954 World Series, have yet to make a return appearance in the fall classic—but another kid from Cleveland, David Ward, the Academy Award-winning screenwriter of THE STING (1973), has changed all that with MAJOR LEAGUE, providing Indian fans with something to cheer about and moviegoers with a generally engaging baseball comedy.

Opening to the strains of "Burn On," Randy Newman's anthem to the city whose river once caught fire, the film intercuts between shots of Cleveland's smoke-

billowing industrial landscape and newspaper headlines chronicling the Indians' protracted lack of success. The story proper begins when Whitton, the former chorus-girl wife of the Tribe's recently deceased owner, takes over the club and sets in motion a plan to relocate the franchise in Miami. Her idea: field a team so abysmal it won't draw flies, thus allowing the club to break a stadium lease that can be terminated only if attendance falls below 800,000. To bring this about she hires Gammon, a longtime manager of mediocre minor league teams, to be the skipper, and assembles a motley collection of has-beens, never-weres, and assorted weirdos to make up the team. Among them are Sheen, a young pitcher with a blazing fastball but serious control problems—both on the mound and in life (his last hurling having occurred in the California Penitentiary League); Snipes, a base-stealing "run-on" whose biggest problem is getting to first base; Haysbert, a voodoo-practicing Cuban slugger who can't hit the curve; Ross, a born-again, over-the-hill hurler who applies a staggering variety of foreign substances to his pitches; and Bernsen, a legitimate, big-contract star who refuses to improve his inept fielding or expend any but the most perfunctory effort because he doesn't want to injure himself or his product endorsement career. At the center of the tale is Berenger, a onetime major league standout whose career has been sabotaged by bad knees. Reclaimed from boozing and the Mexican League, he tries to resurrect not only his career but also his relationship with brainy college librarian Russo, now engaged to a pompous lawyer. With Uecker providing alcohol-enhanced play-by-play, the rag-tag Indians follow Whitton's script, losing game after embarrassingly played game, while Berenger's attempts to rekindle his romance with Russo meet a similar fate. In time, however, Gammon learns of Whitton's plan, and, when he informs the players of her desire to get rid of them after the season, they pull together under Berenger's leadership and give their all to make their one season count. Outfitted with a pair of glasses, Sheen begins mowing down opposing batters, earning the rock'n'rolling admiration of adoring fans who christen him "Wild Thing." At the same time, Bernsen starts turning in defensive gems, Haysbert clobbers the ball, Snipes pilfers bases at a record rate, Berenger begins to weaken Russo's resolve, and the Indians climb in the standings despite Whitton's efforts to slow them down by forcing them to travel in antiquated planes and buses. By season's end the team has put all internal squabbling behind it, become baseball's hottest ticket, and wound up tied for first place in the Eastern Division, forcing a climactic playoff with the dreaded Yankees. Guess who wins, and guess who

Charlie Sheen, Dennis Haysbert, Rene Russo, Tom Berenger, Wesley Snipes, and Corbin Bernsen in MAJOR LEAGUE (©Paramount).

vaults from the box seats into Berenger's waiting arms when they do?

Touching all the well-worn bases, MAJOR LEAGUE doesn't offer much in the way of surprises, but it revels so unashamedly in its familiar fantasy that it's hard not to be swept along—even if you aren't an Indians fan—especially given the endearing performances of Charlie Sheen and Tom Berenger. Sheen, in particular, shines; refusing to allow a geometric punkish haircut and cut-off sleeves to substitute for character, he invests his 19-year-old fastballer with a well-tempered mixture of naivete, inarticulate rebelliousness, and intensity. Berenger is also impressive as the nice guy who refuses to finish last, bringing an understated edge to his actions both on and off the field (especially his encounter with Russo's fiance when the catcher follows her home one day). Though Corbin Bernsen ("L.A. Law") behaves more than he acts, he and the fine supporting cast (notably Wesley Snipes and James Gammon) bring the necessary conviction to their roles to make writer-director Ward's stock comic pieces work. Few of the gags and situations provided by the screenplay will be new to anyone who has seen more than a few sports films, but, well acted and directed, they still raise more than an occasional chuckle. Likewise, there are a number of similarities (as well as some very notable differences) between MAJOR LEAGUE and 1988's superior BULL DURHAM, but baseball movies will be baseball movies, and as Ward told *Boxoffice*, he did indeed set out to make a "baseball movie."

While MAJOR LEAGUE should appeal to baseball fans in general—its onfield action is believable, its uniforms authentic—as well as those who may respond more to the film's romantic subplot and goofy clubhouse goings-on, this underdog-makes-good story clearly holds special pleasures for long-suffering Indians fans such as Ward himself. Ward's career has been somewhat checkered since he won an Oscar for THE STING—his efforts including the screenplay for that film's awful sequel and the uneven CANNERY ROW, which he scripted and directed—but after successfully adapting John Nichols' *The Milagro Beanfield War* for Robert Redford's film of the same name, Ward again found himself in Hollywood's good graces. That the native Clevelander used this opportunity to make the ultimate fantasy about his favorite baseball team is proof enough that MAJOR LEAGUE is a labor of love, and Ward's affectionate opening sequence cements the point. It is all the more surprising, then, that he would allow Milwaukee County Stadium to stand in for the Indians' venerable lakefront home, Municipal Stadium, because of "cost efficiency." Most viewers probably won't notice the difference, but Indians fans' willing suspension of disbelief will be tested to the limit. On the other hand, how many perennially awful baseball teams get a film made about them . . . winning? *(Sexual situations, brief nudity, profanity.)*

p, Chris Chesser and Irby Smith; d, David Ward; w, David Ward; ph, Reynaldo Villalobos (Astro Color); ed, Dennis M. Hill; m, James Newton Howard; prod d, Jeffrey Howard; art d, John Krenz Reinhart Jr.; set d, Bill Rea; cos, Erica Edell Phillips.

Sports   (PR:O MPAA:R)

MALA NOCHE**
78m Northern/Frameline bw/c
(Trans: Bad Night)

Tim Strecter *(Walt Curtis)*, Doug Cooeyate *(Johnny)*, Ray Monge *(Roberto Pepper)*, Nyla McCarthy *(Betty)*.

The often maddening perversity of love and desire is captured most effectively in Gus Van Sant's MALA NOCHE, which received a theatrical release in late 1989 after Van Sant's DRUGSTORE COWBOY proved to be one of the year's biggest independent successes. Made in 1985 on a chicken-scratch budget of $25,000 and in 16-millimeter format, the gritty, poetic MALA NOCHE has had a lively existence on the international film festival circuit, and was named 1987's Best Independent/Experimental Film by the Los Angeles Critics Association. The story, which is really little more than an anecdote, concerns Streeter, an amiable skid-row liquor-store keeper in Portland, Oregon, who has fallen madly in love with Cooeyate, an illegal Mexican immigrant. Cooeyate is 18—although, as the infatuated Streeter happily notes, he looks 16—and is profoundly indifferent to his idolater's blandishments. He agrees to sleep with Streeter for $25; unfortunately, all Streeter has in his possession is $15. ("I'd give you $50 if I had it," Streeter tells Cooeyate, who helps himself to $10 instead.) Left to bleat his romantic woes into the sympathetic ear of his sister (McCarthy), Streeter extends a dinner invitation to Cooeyate, who insists on bringing a friend, Monge. When it turns out that Cooeyate much prefers McCarthy to Streeter, the rejected suitor settles for the more amenable, if less desirable, Monge. (The bedroom scene is shot with glancing, dangerously witty suggestiveness.) Streeter willingly becomes more and more involved in the boys' lives, lending them money, trying to speak with them in his God-awful Spanish, teaching them to drive (another lost cause), and nursing a sick Monge back to health. To them he is nothing but "a stupid faggot"; still, the ever-optimistic Streeter keeps coming back for more. Eventually, things take a violent turn and Monge is killed in a police fracas. Cooeyate disappears; Streeter is distraught ("We're so close and then it's all over . . . I really thought he was starting to like me"); McCarthy decides to move to Alaska to become a stripper. Later, on one sunny day, Streeter sees Cooeyate hanging out on a street corner. The smile with which he greets his erstwhile love object shows that Streeter has learned nothing—matters of the heart cannot be tidied up and put to rest for good.

The fluidly imaginative technique that Van Sant showed in DRUGSTORE COWBOY is clearly evident in this earlier, much lower budgeted effort. The highly graphic, grainy black-and-white camerawork makes ingenious use of partly blacked out frames, vertiginous angles, feverish, tight close-ups, and time-lapse photography. The savvy editing contributes greatly to the jokily laconic tone of the piece, as does the perfectly chosen music, which ranges from the twang of a solitary guitar to raucous, lewd Mexican bar tunes. And, as in DRUGSTORE COWBOY, Van Sant's script is frequently astonishing—funny and passionate. He celebrates the main character's love of Mexican boys here as freely and unapologetically as he portrayed the title character's addiction in DRUG-STORE COWBOY, wasting no time in getting down to basic emotions and experiences from the opening seconds of both films. This ultimate "outlaw" among American directors is able to discover and share the beauty of a boy's mindless face behind the wheel of a car as fully as he conveys a junkie's rush. Van Sant's work is a universe away from the up-market sterility of films like MAKING LOVE. As Van Sant himself has noted, the protagonists in his films are often villains or marginal characters in other movies. His point of view is that of an outsider; his empathic, painterly directoral sensibility is that of a Pacific Northwestern Cocteau.

MALA NOCHE's mostly nonprofessional cast effortlessly inhabit their seedy roles. Ray Monge and Doug Cooeyate (the latter is actually a Native American whose Spanish had to be dubbed in) have the brain-dead narcissism appropriate to youth, and Nyla McCarthy is wonderfully fresh in a role that could have made for a deadly stereotype. It is Tim Streeter, however, who really helps make MALA NOCHE the special experience that it is. Half-angel and half-yokel, he has a natural, aw-shucks quality reminiscent of Henry Fonda or Jimmy Stewart that is never overdone and that stamps him as a dramatist's ideal Everyman, despite his character's peculiar obsession and inability to develop. It's the kind of part that is virtually unplayable; the actor simply has to *be* this hopeless romantic, somehow. Streeter slyly suggests that his Walt even enjoys being duped, as evidenced by his dreamy, almost balletic walk the morning after his first night with Monge and his remark of the boys, "They don't have any imagination about sex, but I guess it's not their fault." (Van Sant's vision combines the mellow with the wry; the driving lessons, with radio blasting and the boys firing a gun out the windows, are high comedy.) Even MALA NOCHE's ending is a classic, an exquisitely rueful little flourish. *(Violence, profanity, nudity, substance abuse, sexual situations.)*

p, Gus Van Sant Jr.; d, Gus Van Sant Jr.; w, Gus Van Sant Jr. (based on the novella by Walt Curtis); ph, John Campbell; ed, Gus Van Sant Jr.; m, Creighton Lindsay, Karen Kitchen, and Peter Daamaan.

Drama   (PR:O MPAA:NR)

MAPANTSULA½**
(South Africa/Brit./Aus.) 105m Max Montocchio c

Thomas Mogotlane *(Panic)*, Marcel Van Heerden *(Stander)*, Thembi Mtshali *(Pat)*, Dolly Rathebe *(Ma Mobise)*, Peter Sephuma *(Duma)*, Eugene Majola *(Sam)*.

Judging by the fickle critical reaction to them, anti-apartheid movies would seem to have succumbed to a sort of flavor-of-the-month syndrome. First, critics were staggered by CRY FREEDOM; then they were touched by A WORLD APART. However, a critical backlash developed against both films because they emphasized the reaction of middle-class whites to the inhumanity of apartheid rather than focusing on black characters. With the appearance of A DRY WHITE SEASON—directed by a black woman (Euzhan Palcy) and starring Marlon Brando—critics felt free to resume their swooning. Upon the US release of MAPANTSULA, Sheila Benson of the *Los Angeles Times* could even say of the film, "A DRY WHITE SEASON can't touch it."

The lack of critical consensus that has accompanied the release of anti-apartheid films points to the fundamental drawback of these movies and social-issue dramas in general: they tend to be films that are good for you more often than they are good films. MAPANTSULA, like most of the recent dramas that attempt to deal in meaningful terms with South Africa's institutionalized oppression of its black majority, is afflicted with this well-intentioned failing. As a drama, it is unfocused and underdeveloped, and, as an expose, it fails to reveal much about South Africa that can be deemed newsworthy, despite its indisputable authenticity. Though a respectable effort—indeed, heroic, considering it was filmed under the very noses of strict South African censors—MAPANT-SULA ultimately demonstrates that any cinematic re-creation of the situation in South Africa is bound to pale next to the real-life horrors of apartheid. The film further exhibits a lack of dramatic resolution. MAPANTSULA (Zulu dialect for small-time crook) revolves around the political awakening of its title character, a petty thief nicknamed Panic, played effectively by Thomas Mogotlane, who also cowrote the script with director Oliver Schmitz. At the beginning of the film, Mogotlane's political rebellion is limited to robbing whites foolish enough to stray into his neighborhood. He arrogantly berates his girl friend (Mtshali) for working as a maid for a white couple, but he's willing to put his contempt aside to borrow money from her. As a thief, Mogotlane has shown even less honor, having once informed on a fellow criminal to gain an early prison parole. That's why, when Mogotlane is arrested again, the authorities feel confident they can coerce him into informing again—this time on an

anti-apartheid activist with whom Mogotlane's girl friend has become friendly.

Panic's story is told in flashback, with the film beginning when he's arrested. The police interrogation of him is intercut with the events that led to his arrest, but, regrettably, this structure only serves to further fragment and confuse the drama. Along the way, the film strives for journalistic comprehensiveness, touching on everything from Soweto rent strikes to police brutality, grassroots activism, and the black political appointees who serve as puppets for the white government. It's at once too much and not enough. As drama, MAPANTSULA might have been more compelling had it focused more on Panic himself and his slow transition from selfish lowlife to activist. But burdened with its cumbersome flashback structure and a surfeit of subplots, the drama becomes scattershot and ineffective. MAPANT-SULA spends too much time and energy telling us what we already know—that apartheid is a crushing, dehumanizing system—and doesn't tell us enough about the people who have been moved to action against the system despite overwhelming odds. As is the case with other anti-apartheid films, we expect MAPANTSULA's sad ending because we know going in that there can be no real ending—yet. So much about MAPANTSULA is so right, from its first-rate cast to its rich cinematography by Rod Stewart to the score by the Ouens. But, in the final analysis, this is a frustrating film that never quite makes an effective mix of its powerful ingredients. *(Adult situations, profanity, violence.)*

p, Max Montocchio; d, Oliver Schmitz; w, Oliver Schmitz and Thomas Mogotlane; ph, Rod Stewart (Irene Color); ed, Mark Baard; m, The Ouens; art d, Robyn Hofmmeyrr.

Political   (PR:C MPAA:NR)

MEET THE HOLLOWHEADS*½**
84m Linden/Moviestore c

John Glover *(Henry Hollowhead)*, Nancy Mette *(Miriam Hollowhead)*, Matt Shakman *(Billy Hollowhead)*, Richard Portnow *(Mr. Crabneck)*, Juliette Lewis *(Cindy Hollowhead)*, Lightfield Lewis *(Bud Hollowhead)*, Joshua Miller *(Joey)*, Logan Ramsey *(Top Drone)*, Anne Ramsey *(Babbleaxe)*, Chaz Conner *(Oliver)*, Shotgun Britton *(Grandpa)*.

Placing a warmhearted sitcom family into a truly nauseating future world, MEET THE HOLLOWHEADS is an advertising copywriter's dream. "Brazil: The Sitcom," the ads might have blared, or "The Jetsons on Acid." The shame is that MEET THE HOLLOWHEADS is anything but a sci-fi moviegoer's dream. Instead, special-effects expert Tom Burman, making his directing debut, has delivered the worst kind of science-fiction film, one in which the originality of the effects far outstrips the ingenuity of the plot or characters. Glover stars as Henry Hollowhead, a meter reader with United Umbilical, which supplies food and other domestic services through a network of tubes. Ambitious and overdue for a promotion, Glover jumps at a chance to ingratiate himself with his cretinous superior, Portnow, when the boss finally accepts an open invitation to join the Hollowhead family for dinner. While Glover's devoted wife, Mette, fusses over the meal—consisting of gooey, writhing goodies that dribble out of the tubes, and side dishes in a rainbow of unnatural colors—we meet the Hollowhead brood. The eldest son (Lightfield Lewis) is an aspiring rock musician whose instrument looks, and sounds, like a torture device for chickens (complete with its own chicken); pubescent daughter Juliette Lewis is eager to get out of the house and yield to her newly rampaging hormones; and the youngest son, Shakman, who also serves as the narrator, amuses himself and best pal Miller by pulling big, parasitic insects from the family's terminally mangy dog and squashing them against his bedroom wall. Upon Glover and Portnow's arrival *chez* Hollowhead, polite chatter quickly gives way to a battle for pride and dignity. Portnow humiliates both Shakman and Glover, then forces his lecherous attentions on the Hollowhead women. Driven too far, and certain that Glover's career has been jeopardized, the Hollowheads respond by frying and slashing Portnow into submission. Without the heart to finish off the boss, Glover instead locks Portnow in the basement and takes over his job, bringing about a happy ending.

Essentially a lunatic sitcom stretched to 90-minute length, MEET THE HOLLOWHEADS lacks comic energy and its characters are strictly cardboard creations. While the production design and special effects are both imaginative and meticulous, the script is hackneyed and the staging awkward. As the plot's linchpin, John Glover's Henry is the main casualty. His transformation from meek meter reader to ferocious defender of his homestead comes across as a case of schizophrenia rather than as a slow turning of the worm. With no character to latch onto, Glover's performance becomes a series of facial reactions. Like the rest of the cast, he tries hard, but it's a losing battle. From the outset, the humans in HOLLOWHEADS are strictly supporting players for Burman's wizardry with latex and the camera. The film also has incidental problems with its tone, mood, and point of view. Burman devotes a long sequence to parading the disturbingly youthful Juliette Lewis around in a series of provocative outfits in preparation for a night out with the boys, the camera

ogling her as Portnow's lascivious boss would. Still, Lewis (NATIONAL LAMPOON'S CHRISTMAS VACATION) takes the queasy edges off scenes like these with her bright, funny performance. Burman might benefit from some elementary courses in directing and screenwriting to go with his post-graduate special-effects expertise. Some may be interested to note a cameo appearance by the late Anne Ramsey (THROW MOMMA FROM THE TRAIN), to whom HOLLOWHEADS is dedicated. *(Violence, adult situations, profanity.)*

p, Joseph Grace and John Chavez; d, Tom Burman; w, Tom Burman, Lisa Morton, and Stanley Mieses; ph, Marvin Rush (Foto-Kem Color); ed, Carl Kress; m, Glenn Jordan; prod d, Edward C. Eyth; cos, Eduardo Castro.

Science Fiction   (PR:O MPAA:PG-13)

ⓥMIGHTY QUINN, THE***
98m A&M-MGM/MGM-UA c
Denzel Washington *(Xavier Quinn)*, Robert Townsend *(Maubee)*, James Fox *(Elgin)*, Mimi Rogers *(Hadley Elgin)*, M. Emmet Walsh *(Miller)*, Sheryl Lee Ralph *(Lola Quinn)*, Art Evans *(Jump)*, Esther Rolle *(Ubu Pearl)*, Norman Beaton *(Gov. Chalk)*, Alex Colon *(Patina)*, Keye Luke *(Dr. Raj)*, Tyra Ferrell *(Isola)*, Carl Bradshaw *(Cocodick)*, Maria McDonald *(Jax)*, Fitz Weir *(Athens)*, Baldwin Howe *(Bim)*, David McFarlane *(Henry)*, Bernie McInerney *(Dr. Stuhlberg)*, Ron Taylor *(McKeon)*, Oliver Samuels *(Rupert)*, David Ellis *(Jersey)*, Ronald Goshop *(Fudge)*, Kenneth Casey *(Phylo)*, Henry Judd Baker *(Nicotine)*, Fred Lloyd *(Pilot)*,

Cathi Levy *(Secretary)*, Renee Menzies McCallum *(Maid)*, Charles Hyatt *(Security Guard)*, Sharon Marley Prendergast *(Jody)*, Cedella Marley *(Eliza)*, Clive Walker *(Bartender)*, Dallas Anderson *(Francis)*, Calvin Mitchell *(Apollo)*, Rowan Byfield *(Blizzard)*, Nabbie Natural *(Turtle)*, Bob Andy *(Raisen)*, Dennis Titus *(Percy)*, Peter Lloyd *(Groom)*, Bobby Ghisays *(Donald Pater)*, Deon Silvera *(Beautician)*, Erica Aquart *(Bride)*, Michael London *(Preacher)*.

Making the most of its lush Caribbean setting, bouncy reggae soundtrack, and the charismatic presence of Denzel Washington (CRY FREEDOM), whom many have heralded as the next Sidney Poitier, THE MIGHTY QUINN is both a formula thriller and a buddy film with a twist. Washington plays Xavier Quinn, the dedicated police chief of a small island nation who isn't particularly popular with either the rich whites who dominate the local tourist industry or with his black countrymen, who believe their old friend, once the "Mighty Quinn" (after the Bob Dylan song), has become a toady. En route to investigate the murder of a prominent businessman, Washington nearly crashes into a wildly reckless motorcyclist, who turns out to be his boyhood buddy Maubee (Townsend), a local legend by virtue of his uncanny ability to avoid capture after breaking any number of laws. Despite the fact that they now stand on opposite sides of the law, the cop and dreadlocked rogue are still friends, and though Washington suspects that the suitcase Townsend is toting contains some ill-gotten gain, he is in too much of a hurry to pursue the matter. At the hotel murder scene, Washington finds the decapitated corpse of the busi-

Denzel Washington and Robert Townsend in THE MIGHTY QUINN (©MGM-UA).

nessman; however, the chief's investigation is hindered by Fox, the hotel's effete but powerful owner, who wants the murder hushed up (wouldn't want to scare off the tourists, you see), and Beaton, the island's black governor, a former poultry inspector who simply doesn't want to rock the boat. Moreover, Fox suggests that Townsend is the prime suspect. After Washington's questioning of Fox's attractive young wife (Rogers)—leading to the promise of a steamy sensual encounter that never happens but to no real clues—the chief goes in search of Townsend, accompanied by Walsh, a mysterious insurance investigator. In the meantime, Washington undergoes something of an identity crisis, trying to reconcile his old, carefree self with his new, more responsible existence and to lessen his estrangement from his wife (Ralph), the leader of a female reggae trio. But while Washington seems determined to return to his wife and son, women continually make themselves available to him —from Rogers to the sultry widow who makes an appearance early in the film. As the story progresses, it is revealed that Walsh is an operative for a Washington-based secret team that had targeted the stolen money in the murdered victim's hands for a contingent of "rebels," and that the cash is, in fact, now in Townsend's possession. As Walsh closes in on his prey, Washington begins to get to the heart of the matter, learning that the murdered businessman died of a snakebite engineered by a vengeful voodoo priestess (Rolle) whose daughter was impregnated and then shunned by the businessman. To conceal the real cause of death and protect the daughter, Townsend severed the dead man's head with a machete and swiped the suitcase full of $10,000 bills. Eventually, Washington catches up with Townsend at the remote location where the elusive one has stashed the cash, but just as Townsend puts all of his cards on the table, a helicopter containing Walsh swoops in. After a tense confrontation, Walsh takes off with the satchel containing the cash, while Townsend clings to one of the chopper's struts; however, the snake Townsend has put in the satchel bites the pilot and the copter crashes into the ocean. As the film winds down, Washington reconciles with his wife, and in the last scene strolls along the beach with his son, to whom he sings Townsend's praises. While the credits roll, the camera traces a set of footprints leading from the water—proof positive that against all odds the remarkable Maubee lives.

Based on the novel *Finding Maubee* by A.H.Z. Carr, Hampton Fancher's screenplay provides few surprises—at least none that depart from genre expectations—and merely scratches the surface of the sociopolitical dynamics underlying the postcolonial tensions that provide the

backdrop for the story. Further, while its villains are clearly involved in some sort of Contragate-like operation, THE MIGHTY QUINN only uses that provocative bit of recent history as a convenient plot device. Fancher and Swiss director Carl Schenkel have not set out to make a political statement, however; with THE MIGHTY QUINN they have made a film that is involving, often tension-filled, frequently leavened with humor, and, above all, fun. Drenched in warm tropical colors, Jacques Steyn's crisp photography and the film's energetic soundtrack "lively up" our journey through a mystery that occasionally defies logic and at other times is transparent—but that never loses our interest, primarily because of Washington's masterfully understated performance. He isn't asked to do a lot, but Washington makes the most of what he's given, even taking to the piano for his own version of "The Mighty Quinn." Far removed from his Oscar-nominated portrayal of Stephen Biko in CRY FREEDOM, Washington's work here, while failing to demonstrate the full range of his ability as an actor, certainly confirms his extraordinary screen presence. Hampered by limited screentime, HOLLYWOOD SHUFFLE's Robert Townsend, the film's other magnetic presence, is prevented from fully developing his character, but, though his role is less significant than his billing, Townsend still manages to convey his immense charm. He and Washington work well together, and the film also benefits from capable supporting performances by the reliable James Fox, M. Emmet Walsh, and Norman Beaton (PLAYING AWAY). Mimi Rogers' performance is more problematic and seems to have been truncated in the editing process, leaving one to wonder if the filmmakers felt Hollywood simply wasn't ready for the consummation of her seduction of Washington.

Nevertheless, THE MIGHTY QUINN, despite some minor flaws, achieves just what it sets out to do, offering 90 minutes of truly enjoyable entertainment. Its great (mostly) reggae soundtrack includes: "The Mighty Quinn" (Bob Dylan, performed by Sheryl Lee Ralph, Cedella Marley, Sharon Marley-Prendergast), "(I'm) Hurting Inside" (Bob Marley, performed by Ralph, C. Marley, S. Marley), "I Gotta Keep Moving On" (Curtis Mayfield, performed by UB40), "Groove Master" (A. Cassell, performed by Arrow), "Guess Who's Coming to Dinner" (Michael Rose, performed by Rose), "Giving/Sharing" (L. Roberts, performed by Half Pint), "La Habanera" (B. Blank, D. Mier, performed by Yello), "Yellow Moon" (A. Neville, J. Neville, performed by the Neville Bros.), "Send Fi Spanish Fly" (L. James, Little Twitch), "Mary Jane" (J. Engerman, S. Gumbs, J. Meyers, W. Michael, performed by Seventeen Plus). *(Violence, adult situations.)*

p, Sandy Lieberson, Marion Hunt, and Ed Elbert; d, Carl Schenkel; w, Hampton Fancher (based on the novel *Finding Maubee* by A.H.Z. Carr); ph, Jacques Steyn (Continental Color); ed, John Jympson; m, Anne Dudley; md, David Anderle; prod d, Roger Murray-Leach; art d, Gregory Keen; set d, Brian Read; spec eff, Giorgio Ferrari; cos, Dana Lyman; chor, Vincent Paterson; stunts, Dean Ferrandini; makeup, A. Medusah Aulenta.

Crime   (PR:C-O MPAA:R)

🅥MILLENNIUM*
106m Gladden Entertainment/FOX c
Kris Kristofferson *(Bill Smith)*, Cheryl Ladd *(Louise Baltimore)*, Daniel J. Travanti *(Dr. Arnold Mayer)*, Robert Joy *(Sherman the Robot)*, Lloyd Bochner *(Walters)*, Brent Carver *(Coventry)*, David McIlwraith *(Tom Stanley)*, Maury Chaykin *(Roger Keane)*, Al Waxman *(Dr. Brindle)*, Lawrence Dane *(Vern Rockwell)*, Thomas Hauff *(Ron Kennedy)*, Peter Dvorsky *(Janz)*, Raymond O'Neill *(Harold Davis)*, Philip Akin *(Briley)*, David Calderisi *(Leacock)*, Gary Reineke *(Carpenter)*, Eugene Clark *(Craig Ashby)*, Cedric Smith *(Eli Seibel)*, Michael J. Reynolds *(Jerry Bannister)*, Victoria Snow *(Pinky Djakarta)*, Susannah Hoffman *(Susan Melbourne)*, Claudette Roach *(Inez Manila)*, Barry Meier *(Helicopter Pilot)*, James Kirchner *(Foreman)*, Bill MacDonald *(FBI Agent Morgue)*, Jamie Shannon *(Young Bill Smith)*, Timothy Webber *(Audio Technician)*, Chapelle Jaffe, Christopher Britton, Gerry Quigley, Leonard Chow *(The Council Chamber)*, Scott Thompson *(Controller)*, John Kozak, James Mainprize, Bob Bainborough *(Investigators)*, Daryl Shuttleworth *(T.V. Reporter—Crash Site)*, Gerard Theoret *(Time Scan Operator)*, Edward Roy *(Gantry Controller)*, Debbie Kirby *(Stewardess)*, John Stoneham *(Hijacker)*, Linda Goranson *(Hostage)*, Syd Libman *(Passenger)*, Patrick Young, Paula Barrett, Richard Fitzpatrick, Reg Dreger, Cordelia Strube, Marvin Caron *(Reporters)*, Maida Rogerson *(Board Member)*, Mark Terene *(Waiter)*, Jank Azman *(Evacuation Worker)*, Kevin Fullam *(Tua Worker)*.

An underdeveloped script, anemic direction and pacing, uninspired production design, and miscasting of the two lead roles undermine some intriguing ideas and characters in MILLENNIUM. Despite its many deficiencies, however, this sci-fi brain teaser with love story elements is not entirely without interest. Directed by Michael Anderson (AROUND THE WORLD IN 80 DAYS; LOGAN'S RUN), one of the few active directors whose work dates back to the 1940s, the film stars Kristofferson as the chief investigator of a team looking into the mid-air collision of a 747 and a DC-10. While the accident seems attributable to computer error and a distracted air traffic controller, Kristofferson digs deeper when he happens upon what appears to be a futuristic weapon in the wreckage, and finds several passengers' watches are moving backwards in time. Adding to the mysterious doings is the presence at the crash site of a noted physics professor (Travanti). When the emotionally burned-out Kristofferson meets beautiful flight attendant Ladd in the investigation area, he uncharacteristically agrees to spend the night with her in his hotel room. In the morning, Ladd urges him to abandon the investigation, but he leaves for work anyway. Seconds later, deciding that he was too harsh, he returns to the room, only to find that it has been straightened up, the bed made, and Ladd gone. At this point the forward thrust of the narrative stops dead to accommodate some major exposition. It seems that Ladd is a time-traveling commando from a 1,000 years in the future, by which time the human race has grown infertile and is dying out. Ladd's team is responsible for going back into the past—by means of the "time gate"—rescuing passengers from about-to-crash airplanes and replacing them with look-alike corpses. The passengers are then projected through the gate to the far future, in hopes of repopulating the race. The greatest danger this presents is the risk of a "paradox,"an alteration imposed on the natural sequence of events that can trigger a "timequake" and destroy Ladd's civilization prematurely. Ladd is put in charge of correcting two paradoxes that threaten her people, both of which involve the loss of a weapon called a "stunner." One was lost by Ladd during a 1963 air rescue in which there was one survivor, a teenage boy. Found at the crash site by Travanti and in his possession for 26 years,

it has led the scientist to suspect the presence of time travelers. The second is the one found by Kristofferson. Ladd goes back to 1989 to retrieve the latter stunner, but fails to realize that Kristofferson has managed to hold onto its triggering device. He visits Travanti to compare information, which results in the two reassembling the stunner. Travanti is holding the weapon when Ladd crashes into his living room through the "gate." In the confusion, the stunner goes off, killing Travanti years before he is destined to die, and thereby causing a paradox and devastating timequake in Ladd's world. In the film's final moments, Kristofferson reveals that he was the teenage survivor of the 1963 air crash, and insists on accompanying Ladd back to the future. They arrive, the apocalyptic "quake" going full tilt, and assist the remaining air crash survivors back through the gate into an uncertain but hopeful future. Kristofferson and Ladd, who is pregnant, make it through the gate at the last possible second, leaving Ladd's robot sidekick, Joy, to announce that this is not the beginning of the end, merely the end of the beginning.

Like much science-fiction literature, MILLENNIUM is saddled with more expositional, scientific, and philosophical baggage than the filmmakers can handle, at the expense of suspenseful storytelling. What should have been the centerpiece of the film, the 1963 air crash and its profound effect on Kristofferson's life, gets lost in the shuffle of paradoxes and timequakes. What is fascinating, though barely explored in the film, is that while Kristofferson's Bill Smith is attempting to solve the mystery of the colliding aircraft, he is actually penetrating for the first time the mystery of his own life. He discovers not only his romantic destiny with Ladd but the reason for his obsession with investigating air disasters. This revelation moti-

vates his decision to step far into the future with Ladd and could have been the center of a compelling film.

Kristofferson, a naturally laconic screen actor, lacks the dynamism to make Smith's journey through time a moving one, and Ladd, whose performance is adequate, fails to radiate the mysterious presence and quicksilver intelligence called for by her role. Hampered by a leaden pace, the film could have been buoyed by eye-catching visuals, but the camerawork and special effects never rise above a TV-movie level.

One might wonder what director Peter Weir and stars like Harrison Ford and Ellen Barkin might have done with this material, but—as it stands—MILLENNIUM remains little more than a dull jumble of some interesting ideas.*(Adult situations, sexual situations, violence.)*

p, Douglas Leiterman and Robert Vince; d, Michael Anderson; w, John Varley (based on the story "Air Raid" by John Varley); ph, Rene Ohashi (Deluxe Color); ed, Ron Wisman; m, Eric N. Robertson; prod d, Gene Rudolf; art d, Charles Dunlop; set d, Jeffrey Ginn; spec eff, Nick Fischer; cos, Olga Dimitrov; stunts, Shane Cardwell; makeup, Barbara Palmer.

Science Fiction   (PR:A MPAA:PG)

Ⓥ**MINISTRY OF VENGEANCE****
95m MPCA/Concorde c
John Schneider *(David Miller)*, Ned Beatty *(Rev. Bloor)*, George Kennedy *(Rev. Hughes)*, James Tolkan *(Col. Freeman)*, Apollonia Kotero *(Zarah)*, Yaphet Kotto *(Mr. Whiteside)*, Robert Miano *(Ali Aboutd)*, Daniel Radell *(Al-Hassan)*, Maria Richwine *(Fatima)*, Meg Register *(Gail Miller)*, Joey Peters *(Kim Miller)*.

Drawing inspiration from the Book of Rambo, former "Dukes of Hazzard" star John Schneider dons a clerical collar and a glum expression to mow down bloodthirsty Arab terrorists in this tiresome macho revenge melodrama. Schneider plays a Vietnam vet who renounced violence and became a minister after he was forced to blow up a preteen Viet Cong in self-defense. As often happens in this kind of movie, however, violence finds Schneider anyway when his wife and daughter are killed by terrorists in a massacre at the Rome airport. Finding the State Department—represented by Kotto—to be impotent in the face of his pleas for justice, Schneider pockets his collar and picks up some heavy artillery to seek vengeance on his own. Helping him out is Tolkan, Schneider's old commander from Vietnam, who whips Schneider back into fighting shape. Tolkan also reserves a place for Schneider at a Lebanese safe house, where Schneider is joined by none other than Apollonia Kotero (better known to Prince and PURPLE RAIN fans as just "Apollonia"). Kotero is the ward of Beatty,

Brent Carver and Cheryl Ladd in MILLENIUM (©20th Century Fox).

an annoying minister whose flock seems to consist of beautiful Lebanese women who live with him at his rectory in the middle of the desert—which also happens to be the aforementioned safe house. Guided to the terrorists' headquarters by a dissident Lebanese woman, Schneider is spotted and pursued by the terrorists, then temporarily rescued by a fortuitously appearing Tolkan. It's not long before the pair are captured by the terrorists and tortured as a prelude to their execution, however, and the action climaxes after some politically paranoid, last-minute plot twists.

Under the direction of Peter Maris, MINISTRY OF VENGEANCE isn't terrible, just pointless. Even the acting isn't as bad as usual for this sort of film. Schneider is competent in the lead—making him a virtual Olivier of the genre compared to most hunky action heroes, from Chuck Norris to Sylvester Stallone himself. James Tolkan (best known as the carrier commander in TOP GUN) is better as Schneider's mentor, a kind of meat-and-potatoes Robert Duvall. Yaphet Kotto is typically first-rate as the duplicitous diplomat, conveying such a strong, sinister impression that one wonders once again why he can't seem to find roles in anything other than B-movies. Even Kotero, strong but tender as Beatty's orphan charge, doesn't look out of place wearing fatigues in the middle of Lebanon.

Nonetheless, MINISTRY OF VENGEANCE is strictly a case of deja vu. After three "Rambo" and three "Missing in Action" movies; UNCOMMON VALOR; and countless other clones and ripoffs in which one tough guy and a few of his buddies take on and defeat whole armies, even a fairly well-made film like MINISTRY OF VENGEANCE can't help but seem a tired reprise. The film only exposes its lack of originality in making its lead character a minister who takes up a gun, a potentially intriguing angle that falls flat because this vengeful killer and man of the cloth seems to undergo no moral crisis or internal conflict. In the end, the hero's ministry merely comes across as a gimmick. *(Violence, profanity.)*

p, Brad Krevoy and Steven Stabler; d, Peter Maris; w, Brian D. Jeffries, Mervyn Emryys, and Ann Narus (based on a story by Randal Patrick); ph, Mark Harris; ed, Michael Haight; m, Scott Roewe; prod d, Stephen Greenberg; set d, Troy Myers; cos, Terry Dresbach.

Action   **(PR:C MPAA:R)**

⊙MIRACLE MILE***½
87m Hemdale c
Anthony Edwards *(Harry Washello)*, Mare Winningham *(Julie Peters)*, John Agar *(Ivan Peters)*, Lou Hancock *(Lucy Peters)*, Mykel T. Williamson *(Wilson)*, Kelly Minter *(Charlotta)*, Kurt Fuller,

Danny de la Paz, Robert Doqui, Denise Crosby.

One of the most impressive B pictures in years, MIRACLE MILE is a taut, gripping, totally uncompromising apocalyptic thriller, written and directed with verve by Steve DeJarnatt, whose debut film, CHERRY 2000 (1988), went straight to home video. Somewhat reminiscent of the films American International Pictures targeted at the teen crowd in the late 1950s and early 60s (remember PANIC IN THE YEAR ZERO, starring and directed by Ray Milland?) or, perhaps, a forgotten Edgar Ulmer film, MIRACLE MILE begins harmlessly enough as Edwards, a shy young jazz musician, falls in love at first sight with Winningham while wandering through the Page Museum of Natural History, located near the La Brea Tar Pits (the title refers to a stretch of Wilshire Blvd. that links the prehistoric tar pits to the glittering office towers of modern LA). After meeting on a walkway above the tar pits, Edwards and Winningham spend the rest of the day together taking in the sights of Los Angeles. Before their "date" is over, Edwards is introduced to Winningham's cranky grandfather (Agar, in an excellent supporting performance) and grandmother (Hancock), who, he learns, much to Winningham's embarrassment, had a spat many years ago and haven't spoken to each other since. (Winningham shares an apartment with her grandmother, while her grandfather lives alone in a nearby building.) The day ends with Edwards and Winningham setting up a rendezvous to take place at midnight, when Winningham, who is a waitress at an all-night diner on Wilshire, gets off of work. Thrilled, Edwards returns to his hotel room to get a few hours of sleep before their date. Unfortunately, through a weird chain reaction of occurrences (Edwards flicks a lit cigarette, a bird picks it up and puts it in a nest resting on some electric cables, starting a fire) the hotel's power is knocked out while Edwards sleeps and he is several hours late for their meeting when his alarm doesn't go off. After waiting nearly an hour, the disappointed and angry Winningham goes home. By the time the desperate Edwards makes it to the restaurant it is 3 a.m. and one of Winningham's coworkers gives him her number. Using a phone booth outside, Edwards calls several times to apologize, but winds up talking to her answering machine. While he contemplates what to do next, the phone rings and Edwards impulsively answers it. On the other end of the line is a desperate young soldier who works at a missile silo in North Dakota. Thinking he is talking to his father (having misdialed the area code), the hysterical soldier announces that American nuclear missiles have been launched and only 70 minutes remain before the retaliatory strike hits. Edwards believes the call is a

joke until he hears gunfire on the other end and then an official-sounding voice saying, "Forget what you just heard and go back to bed." Convinced that what he has witnessed was the real thing, Edwards goes into the diner and tries to warn the motley collection of employees and patrons—none of whom believe him until a yuppie financier who once dated a government official makes a few phone calls and realizes that something is definitely up in Washington. Thinking quickly, the woman arranges for a helicopter to pick up the group from atop a nearby bank building and transport them to a plane to take them to Antarctica (the only safe place, apparently). Although he should go with the others, Edwards can only think of Winningham and is determined to find her and bring her along. While the others head for the airport, he searches frantically for Winningham (with only a vague idea of where she lives) as the clock ticks down to zero hour. Eventually finding his beloved (the impending holocaust also reunites her grandparents, who decide to spend their remaining moments together in a favorite spot), Edwards makes a desperate bid to get to the heliport on time. As dawn approaches, word gets out and the streets of Los Angeles go mad as crippling gridlock brings traffic to a standstill and the doomed populace goes on the rampage (murdering, looting, fornicating in the streets). By the time Edwards and Winningham get to the roof of the bank building, the helicopter has gone. As missiles whiz over the Hollywood Hills and explode somewhere in the desert, the lovers seek solace in each other. Unexpectedly, the helicopter pilot (who had promised to take them) returns and the couple jumps aboard. But it is too late, the concussion from an explosion sends the helicopter spinning out of control and it crashes, ironically, in the La Brea Tar Pits where Edwards and Winningham first met. As the chopper sinks into the quagmire—with fiberglass reproductions of prehistoric creatures stuck in tar and seemingly screaming in terror outside the window—the lovers kiss and the world ends in a white hot flash.

With a closing as grim and uncompromising as this, it is miraculous that MIRACLE MILE was made by an American studio considering Hollywood's recent obsession with upbeat endings. Indeed, in the final 15 minutes one waits for the missile strike to be called off, for Edwards to discover that he misinterpreted the phone call, for the lovers to somehow escape, or even for Edwards to wake up in his hotel room to discover that it was all a bad dream. But no. Nuclear annihilation is a reality, and we watch, stunned, as true love "burns" eternal. It is a tribute to the skills of director Steve DeJarnatt that he is able to keep the audience dangling on a string of hope throughout MIRACLE MILE's grim proceedings. The quirky combination of dizzy romance and apocalyptic horror works better than it has any right to due to DeJarnatt's skillful handling of the material, alternating between comedy, romance, and action-thriller, keeping the viewer breathless and off-balance throughout. Structured as a chain reaction—not unlike nuclear fission—the film introduces seemingly harmless actions that initiate a series of events that ultimately leads to the end of the world (Edwards' encounter with Winningham, the cigarette-caused power outage that makes him late for his date and puts him outside the phone booth when the call comes through from the soldier, etc.). Further, DeJarnatt concentrates on disturbing little details that serve to keep the viewer off-kilter, such as when Edwards, late for his date, pulls up to the diner and accidentally hits a palm tree while parking his car, causing several rats to fall onto his hood—an omen of things to come. The writer-director also enjoys toying with the audience's hope for a happy resolution by having Edwards' character begin to doubt himself and what he has heard on the telephone after events begin to snowball beyond his control. After all, he and he alone heard the desperate phone call and perhaps he misinterpreted the panicked message. Perhaps it was a joke. Perhaps Edwards overreacted and is personally responsible for the growing panic and resulting deaths. For most of its running time, MIRACLE MILE is a small-scale, claustrophobic little film that makes clever use of its offbeat locations. In this tiny environment there is room for the possibility that Edwards may be wrong about the impending nuclear attack, but as word of the attack spreads throughout Los Angeles, DeJarnatt's compositions begin to fill with frenzied extras and gridlocked cars, until the frame is jammed with scenes of mass chaos. The effect is startling, for the viewer is suddenly hurled into the madness and realizes the nuclear attack is for real and that there is no escape.

Despite the overwhelming grimness of MIRACLE MILE, DeJarnatt is a hopeless romantic at heart (a sensibility that also marks CHERRY 2000) and finds redemption and transcendence in true love. Yes, Edwards and Winningham are killed at the end, but there is some comfort in the fact that they have found each other before they die. Too much of a realist to resort to a Hollywood ending, DeJarnatt seems to be saying that yes, the world will end with a bang, but, if you're lucky, with a kiss too. *(Violence, profanity.)*

p, John Daly and Derek Gibson; d, Steve DeJarnatt; w, Steve DeJarnatt; ph, Theo Van de Sande; ed, Stephen Semel and Kathie Weaver; m, Tangerine Dream.

Romance/Science Fiction
                    (PR:C-O MPAA:R)

ⓥMISS FIRECRACKER**
102m Corsair c

Holly Hunter *(Carnelle Scott)*, Mary Steenburgen *(Elain Rutledge)*, Tim Robbins *(Delmount Williams)*, Alfre Woodard *(Popeye Jackson)*, Scott Glenn *(Mac Sam)*, Veanne Cox *(Tessy Mahoney)*, Ann Wedgeworth *(Miss Blue)*, Trey Wilson *(Benjamin Drapper)*, Amy Wright *(Missy Mahoney)*, Bert Remsen, Christine Lahti, Kathleen Chalfant, Robert Fieldsteel.

The town of Yazoo City, Mississippi, is agog over the annual Fourth of July Miss Firecracker Contest, and no one is more obsessed with winning this honor than Hunter. Known locally for her carnal exploits as "Miss Hot Tamale" and the recent recipient of a horrendous crimson dye-job, Hunter has more than a few obstacles to overcome if she is to win the title. Adding to the hubbub are the simultaneous arrivals of her cousins, Steenburgen and Robbins, with whom she was raised after being orphaned as a child. A former contest winner, Steenburgen has always been Hunter's idol, and now this wilted magnolia has returned to give the keynote speech, "My Life as a Beauty." Robbins, a poetic wild man, has had a less easy time of it: a recent stay at an insane asylum and a stint as a highway maintenance worker (specialty: scraping up dead dogs) have not tamed his manic exuberance. With the help of Woodard, a seamstress who designs for bullfrogs, and Glenn, her burnt-out, occasional lover, Hunter pursues her dream with relentless fervor. And by the end of the film she has discovered something about the nature of jealousy as well as hope.

Playwright Beth Henley specializes in this type of cloying Southern Gothic whimsy. Based on her play "The Miss Firecracker Contest," this is the fourth film to spring from her imagination (in descending order of quality, CRIMES OF THE HEART; TRUE STORIES; and NOBODY'S FOOL are the others), but what might have once seemed refreshingly quirky and a good actors' workout on the stage has become a desperate struggle for melodramatic laughs. Here Henley's use of language is only sporadically fresh; too often her references sound as if they've been lifted from a Tennessee Williams play. Moreover, director Thomas Schlamme's unsure handling of scenes and indiscriminate use of unappealing close-ups of actors emoting at full steam only emphasize the material's weakness. A Robert Altman, Jonathan Demme, or Preston Sturges might have been able to draw the audience into the idea of an entire town being caught up in the summery excitement of this event, offering characters to warm to and cheer on. Instead, two actresses are cruelly characterized as "dogs," Woodard is either directed or allowed to cartoon herself in a

way that might have given even Butterfly McQueen pause, and all the characters are offered up for detached observation like carnival show freaks.

Holly Hunter has amply demonstrated her comic talent in RAISING ARIZONA and BROADCAST NEWS. All she needs to learn now is restraint. Although she has no difficulty conveying her character's desperate insufficiency and is quite funny slamming about her ramshackle homestead in preparatory fury, her face is so often transformed by twitches, winces, and pouts that she frequently resembles a youthful Geraldine Page at her most unruly. Her over-eager apprehension of the camera works against the pathos that could more easily and effectively be hers. Compared to his wonderful Nuke Laloosh in BULL DURHAM, Tim Robbins' Delmount is an undeveloped sketch, though the actor brings what rangy energy he can to a role that largely consists of hurling objects and people about. Mary Steenburgen is the biggest letdown in a part that could have been ideal for her and a boon to those who adored her feathery charm in MELVIN AND HOWARD and TIME AFTER TIME. She retains her Jennifer Jones-Lonette McKee-plus-something-extra loveliness, but, from her wavering "honey-chile" accent and uncertain posturing, she appears not to have a clue as to what Elain should be. Her scenes with Robbins, in particular, are inappropriately romantic. Scott Glenn and Ann Wedgeworth are wasted in nothing roles, while Bert Remsen provides the funniest moment, as Delmount's dog-scraping boss, in this ultimately disappointing effort. *(Adult situations.)*

p, Fred Berner; d, Thomas Schlamme; w, Beth Henley (based on her play "The Miss Firecracker Contest"); ph, Arthur Albert (Duart color); ed, Peter C. Frank; m, David Mansfield and Homer Denison; prod d, Kristi Zea; art d, Maher Ahmad; set d, Debra Schutt; cos, Molly Maginnis.

Comedy/Romance   (PR:C MPAA:PG)

ⓥMOB WAR*½
96m Cinema Sciences/Shapiro Glickenhaus c

Johnny Stumper *(Todd Barrett)*, David Henry Keller *(John Falcone)*, Jake La Motta *(Don Ricci)*, Sven Nuvo *(Martin Spustein)*, John Rano *(Hectort)*, Oliver Daniels *(Juan)*, Adrianna Maxwell *(Whitney Barrett)*, Neave Benton *(Tommy Bradford)*, Dan Lutsky *(Vince Petracco)*, Angel Caban *(Felix)*, Nick Gomez *(Sal)*, Elizabeth Cuthrell *(Linda)*, Monica Helm *(Janice)*, Tony Kouk *(Tony)*, Buzzy Dannenfelser *(Joey)*, Rebecca Freeman *(Maria)*, Izzy Goldfarb *(Gary)*, Randolph Trojan *(Marco)*, Ernest Dansett *(Ernesto)*.

Despite its low budget and production values, MOB WAR is a sincere crime melodrama that aims for far more than it delivers. Filmed totally on location in New York City (with often unintelligible direct sound, presumably because the budget couldn't accommodate post-synchronization), this violent tale of internecine conflict within the Mafia is no mindless exploitation quickie. MOB WAR's ambitiousness is evident in the scale of its labyrinthine narrative and the number and variety of its locations, and viewers may well feel a grudging admiration for it even when it fails. Stumper, a public relations minimogul, is thrilled when he lands the wealthy and powerful Keller as a client. Although reputed to be a vicious Mafia mobster and drug overlord, Keller presents himself as a misunderstood legitimate businessman, and Stumper is hungry enough to believe him. Launching a media campaign (charitable contributions, photo opportunities, etc.) and an image makeover, Stumper ignores wife Maxwell's skepticism and the outright warnings of his friend Nuvo, an investigative reporter for a New York TV station who is intent on exposing Keller's mob activities. It's clear from the outset that Keller is at least as bad as his detractors think. Incurring the disfavor of his Mafia godfather (played by Jake La Motta, sometime actor and subject of Martin Scorsese's RAGING BULL) because, in flooding the city with drugs, he has drawn police and media heat to the "family," Keller is incensed when the don threatens to hand over the drug business to his arch-rival (Lutsky) if he doesn't softpedal his activities. Instead of falling into line, Keller hires a team of mercenaries to hijack Columbian drug shipments, has Lutsky and his lieutenants killed, and unsuccessfully tries to have La Motta assassinated, thus inciting the eponymous mob war. As Keller's true colors become apparent, PR man Stumper snorts more and more of the cocaine Keller has been giving him and pretends that all is well. Ordered by Keller to get Nuvo off the mobster's case, Stumper is nonplussed when Nuvo accuses him of having sold out and intensifies his campaign against Keller. After bumping off two Colombians who have come to New York to kill him, Keller silences Nuvo by having him murdered, after which Stumper finally acknowledges what he has gotten himself into and phones Keller to resign. Keller won't let him go that easily, however; he orders Maxwell's kidnaping, and has Maxwell and Stumper's apartment trashed—stashing one of the dead Colombians in the fridge for emphasis. Stumper goes for help to La Motta, who promises to kill Keller and loans Stumper his personal bodyguard (Benton) as backup. The two storm Keller's warehouse headquarters, where Maxwell is being held. Both Keller and Benton are killed after a raging gun battle, but Maxwell and the wounded Stumper

manage to escape. Relieved that his troubles are finally behind him, Stumper meets La Motta to express his thanks, only to be told in no uncertain terms that from now on he will be employing his public relations expertise exclusively on behalf of the Mafia. Like it or not, the chastened Stumper is now married to the mob.

J. Christian Ingvordsen, MOB WAR's director, coproducer, and cowriter, has apparently set out to make a mean streets of Manhattan movie, comparable to the early efforts of Martin Scorsese and Abel Ferrara. Although he has succeeded in terms of the film's tight plotting and effective structure, he is ultimately defeated by trying to do too much with too little. Steven Kaman's snappy editing can't compensate for the inept sound, stupefyingly intrusive music, lack of production design, and myriad other deficiencies the production is unable to properly address. While some of the film's dialog is suitably foul-mouthed and punchy, if writers Ingvordsen and John Weiner had been given five dollars every time they used the word "respect," there would have been no budget problem. The inconsistent performances range from adequate (Henry Keller and Johnny Stumper) to downright embarrassing (the wooden Adrianna Maxwell and the halfbaked Cheech and Chong routines of John Rano and Oliver Daniels). With a smaller role, La Motta might have contributed some grit and heft to the film, but his major part reveals too clearly his lack of range as an actor.

Ultimately, there is an underdog quality to MOB WAR that may make it more palatable to the viewer who is aware of the herculean task its makers faced in entering a marketplace filled with adequately budgeted, better-realized efforts. *(Violence, profanity, adult situations.)*

p, J. Christian Ingvordsen, Steven Kaman, and John Weiner; d, J. Christian Ingvordsen; w, J. Christian Ingvordsen and John Weiner; ph, Steven Kaman; ed, Steven Kaman; prod d, Chris Johnson; art d, Hope Weaver; spec eff, Willfred Caban; cos, Beatrice Monroe; stunts, John Christian; makeup, Isabelle Fritz-Cope.

Action/Crime **(PR:O MPAA:R)**

MONSIEUR HIRE

(See THE YEAR'S BEST)

MUSIC BOX**
124m Carolco/Tri-Star c
Jessica Lange *(Ann Talbot)*, Armin Mueller-Stahl *(Michael Laszlo)*, Frederic Forrest *(Jack Burke)*, Lukas Haas *(Michael "Mikey" Talbot)*, Donald Moffat *(Harry Talbot)*, Michael Rooker *(Karchy Laszlo)*, Cheryl Lynn Bruce *(Georgine Wheeler)*, Mari Torocsik *(Magda Zoldan)*, J.S. Block *(Judge Erwin Silver)*, Sol Frieder *(Istvan Boday)*, Elzbieta Czyzewska *(Melinda Kkalman)*, Magda Szekely Marburg *(Judit Hollo)*, Felix Shuman *(James Nathanson)*, Michael Shillo *(Geza Vamos)*, George Pusep *(Vladimir Kostav)*, Mitchell Litrofsky *(Sandy*

Jessica Lange and Armin Mueller-Stahl in MUSIC BOX (©Tri-Star).

Lehman), Albert Hall *(Mack Jones)*, Ned Schmidtke *(Dean Talbot)*, Joe Guzaldo *(Joe Dinofrio)*, Tibor Kenderesi *(Pal Horvath)*, Christiana Nicola *(Maria)*, Kevin White *(Clerk)*, Gyorgy Emod *(Andras Nagy)*, Ralph Foody *(Pawn Broker)*, Magda Sass, Agnes Gallwitz *(Translators)*, Owen Rice *(Courtroom Reporter)*, Margo Winkler *(Irma Kiss)*, Larry Brandenburg *(John Szalay)*, Pauline Kaner *(Reporter)*, Mark Steggerda, Leonard E. Boswell, Douglas Marcinek *(Courtroom Guards)*, Zoltan Gera *(Man in Budapest)*, Jane MacIver, Megan Warner *(Secretaries)*, Erica Heit MD *(Doctor)*, Tracy Grant *(Servant)*, Toni Fleming *(Housekeeper)*, Ed Blatchford *(Young Man)*, Andy Avalos, Tom Skilling *(Weathermen)*, Tom Stienke *(Sports Announcer)*, Donnez Harris *(Security Guard)*, Gabor Koncz *(Limo Driver)*.

As they did with BETRAYED (1988), critics have taken director Costa-Gavras to task for not approaching the subject of MUSIC BOX (the prosecution of WW II Nazi war criminals residing in the United States) in a more high-pitched, emotional manner. Yet, what MUSIC BOX arguably loses by keeping its emotions reined in is more than made up for by a deliberately detailed, deeply disturbing realism.

As he did with THE JAGGED EDGE (1985), writer Joe Eszterhas (who also wrote BETRAYED) starts with a sharp female defense lawyer facing a crisis of conscience when confronted with indisputable evidence of the guilt of a client with whom she has a deep emotional bond. Jessica Lange plays Ann Talbot, the troubled attorney who helps her father, Michael Laszlo, played by Armin Mueller-Stahl, with what she first assumes to be a case of mistaken identity. A Hungarian immigrant after the war, Mueller-Stahl claimed on his application for citizenship to have been a farmer. After decades of raising a family in America on a steelworker's pay, Mueller-Stahl is now faced with deportation on the nominal charge of having lied about his former occupation. In fact, he is being sent back to Hungary to be tried for wartime atrocities he is accused of committing as part of that country's Nazi collaborationist police force. He admits to having been with the police but claims innocence on the atrocity charges, saying he left the force in reaction to the very brutality of which he is accused. Up against badgering prosecutor Forrest, who is fueled by righteous rage, Lange is nevertheless able to puncture the testimony of key government witnesses. Masterfully she then builds her own case, presenting the deportation as a revenge-motivated sham orchestrated by the Hungarian communist government against Mueller-Stahl for his disruption of a cultural exchange with the US several years earlier (he threw garbage during a performance of a Hungarian dance company in Chicago, where the film

is set, and caused the company's nationwide tour to be cancelled in the wake of the ensuing publicity). While preparing her case, the only irregularity Lange is able to find in her father's life is a series of large payments—Mueller-Stahl dismisses them as loans—to a fellow immigrant subsequently killed in a hit-and-run accident. Only in her later investigation does she discover blackmail, at the heart of which lies the hideous truth about the man who raised her. At first, she is fierce and cunning in the defense of her father. Later, she's finally forced to see him as a man who, at one time, is said to have sadistically raped and tortured a 16-year-old girl while his friend, later to become his blackmailer, took photos. At this point Lange takes the only course of action open to her as a woman who has chosen the pursuit of justice as her life's work, but she does so at the cost of destroying her family. Similarly, the people from Mueller-Stahl's neighborhood, including nuns and priests, initially rally to his support, unable to conceive of a good, old patriotic family man like Laszlo and the brutal Nazi torturer "Mishka" as being the same man. Later, when Holocaust survivors terrorize Mueller-Stahl's family at home, throwing rocks through his window, the media get involved. Appearing on his front porch brandishing a baseball bat, Mueller-Stahl is photographed, the photos used this time to fuel the false image of Mike Laszlo, proud American, rather than Mishka, fugitive from justice. The manipulations, lies, and distortions extend to corporate suites, where Lange's ex-father-in-law, Moffat, a high-powered business attorney, perpetuates the "revisionist" view of the Holocaust, secretly teaching his grandson, Haas, to think of the murder of millions as nothing more than Semitic propaganda.

Throughout the film, Costa-Gavras chooses not to chastise or harangue. There is nothing shrill about his style here, nor about the performances he elicits from the uniformly excellent cast he has assembled. Rather, MUSIC BOX conveys a feeling of sadness and dread over American innocence, so easily turned to willful ignorance. Costa-Gavras defines Ann Talbot's dilemma as one shared by the nation. The main focus of MUSIC BOX is not on the trial itself, the outcome of which, to be honest, is never much in doubt. Rather, mirroring the ongoing debate in American politics, Costa-Gavras' real concern is showing the potential consequences of accepting easily digested images without examining the unsavory realities slick imagery is too often meant to conceal. Far from a hot-headed diatribe, MUSIC BOX is more a plaintive plea to America to leave its illusions behind even if it means, as it does in Ann Talbot's case, starting from scratch to build a braver new world. In the wake of films like MUSIC BOX and

BETRAYED, it's little wonder that so much of mainstream American culture has become obsessed with escapism. Costa-Gavras stubbornly insists on confronting us with those things we wish to escape, and it's not a pretty picture. *(Profanity, adult situations.)*

p, Irwin Winkler; d, Costa-Gavras; w, Joe Eszterhas; ph, Patrick Blossier; ed, Joele Van Effenterre; m, Philippe Sarde; md, Harry Rabinowitz; prod d, Jeannine Claudia Oppewall; art d, Bill Arnold; set d, Bill Fosser; spec eff, Sam Barkan; cos, Rita Salazar; chor, Eva Nemeth; makeup, Steve LaPorte.

Drama   **(PR:C MPAA:PG-13)**

Ⓥ**MUTANT ON THE BOUNTY***½
94m Canyon/Skouras c

John Roarke *(Carlson)*, Deborah Benson *(Justine)*, John Furey *(Dag)*, Victoria Catlin *(Babette)*, John Fleck *(Lizardo)*, Kyle T. Heffner *(Max)*, Scott Williamson *(Rick O'Shay)*, John Dubrin *(Manny the Weasel)*, Pepper Martin *(Capt. Lloydes)*.

It used to be that B movies looked to big-studio box-office hits for their inspiration. No more. It seems now that any movie with a reputation, no matter its budget, may be ripe for B-movie imitation. Never as funny as its advertising copy ("In space nobody weighs very much"), MUTANT ON THE BOUNTY is a science-fiction spoof that borrows heavily from John Carpenter's low-budget cult classic DARK STAR.

Kyle T. Heffner is the sax-playing title creature, who's been traveling through space as a beam of particle light for 23 years when he's intercepted by the crew of the spaceship *Bounty*. A little worse for the wear and tear, Heffner sports a sandblasted mug with accessories that could make even a mother blanch—mainly space junk acquired in his wanderings, including a phone receiver embedded in his head that rings whenever he gets excited. The *Bounty* has a motley crew, comprising perky blonde magazine writer Benson; laid-back ship's officer Furey; his uptight counterpart Roarke; indecipherable French doctor Catlin; and haywire, cross-dressing android Fleck. Pursuing Heffner through space in a broken-down replica of a space shuttle are two petty criminals (Williamson and Durbin), who dress like Las Vegas lounge lizards and who plan to use a vial of deadly virus in Max's possession to hold a planet hostage.

While establishing its characters and premise, MUTANT ON THE BOUNTY manages to be moderately amusing, making a humorous asset (as did DARK STAR) of its poverty-row production budget. The cast works well together—with Victoria Catlin delivering the most consistently funny work—and the script, written by coproducer Martin Lopez from a story by Lopez and coproducer-director Robert

Torrance, gives them a few zingy lines and some funny situations to work with. Unfortunately, once the plot proper kicks in MUTANT ON THE BOUNTY goes slack, lifeless, and predictable. What its makers apparently couldn't borrow from DARK STAR was the dark wit and originality Carpenter and writer Dan O'Bannon brought to their satire.

The film's biggest problem, however, is that it strives too self-consciously to be the type of movie that is almost never made on purpose—the midnight movie. With the producers' decision to release without an MPAA rating and its fondness, especially at the beginning, for gross-out humor (not to mention its "zany" title), MUTANT ON THE BOUNTY works hard to establish itself as a maverick feature. But a good midnight movie needs to have the courage of its corrosive convictions, and MUTANT ON THE BOUNTY does not. Instead of the take-no-prisoners sensibility of such late-night classics as ERASER-HEAD; THE ROCKY HORROR PICTURE SHOW; or DARK STAR; MUTANT ON THE BOUNTY only becomes more conventional as it goes along. A few sick jokes and a couple of delectable expletives uttered by its cast suggest this non-MPAA assessed film would probably just rate a borderline R. *(Profanity, violence, adult situations.)*

p, Robert Torrance and Martin Lopez; d, Robert Torrance; w, Martin Lopez (based on his story); ph, Randolph Sellars (Foto-Kem Color); ed, Craig A. Colton; m, Tim Torrance; prod d, Clark Hunter; art d, Hilja Keading.

Comedy/Science Fiction   (PR:C)

MY LEFT FOOT
(See THE YEAR'S BEST)

MYSTERY TRAIN***½
113m MTI/Orion c

Masatoshi Nagase *(Jun)*, Youki Kudoh *(Mitzuko)*, Screamin' Jay Hawkins *(Night Clerk)*, Cinque Lee *(Bellboy)*, Nicoletta Braschi *(Luisa)*, Elizabeth Bracco *(Dee Dee)*, Sy Richardson *(News Vendor)*, Tom Noonan *(Man in Diner)*, Stephen Jones *(The Ghost)*, Rufus Thomas *(Man in Station)*, Joe Strummer *(Johnny)*, Rick Aviles *(Will Robinson)*, Steve Buscemi *(Charlie)*, Vondie Curtis-Hall *(Ed)*, Jodie Markell *(Sun Studio Guide)*, William Hoch, Pat Hoch, Joshua Elvis Hoch *(Tourist Family)*, Reginald Freeman *(Conductor)*, Beverly Prye *(Streetwalker)*, Lowell Roberts *(Lester)*, Sara Driver *(Airport Clerk)*, Richard Boes *(Second Man in Diner)*.

Jim Jarmusch continues his deadpan Cook's Tour of America with MYSTERY TRAIN, a collection of three tangentially related stories set in Memphis, Tennessee, home of "the King of Rock 'n' Roll," Elvis Presley. As with STRANGER THAN PARADISE and DOWN BY LAW, Jarmusch focuses his offbeat sensibility on urban iconoclasts, small-town oddballs, and bewildered strangers in a strange land. No matter how placid America may look on the surface, the old melting pot is still on the boil.

All three of Jarmusch's tales center on the run-down Arcade Hotel, where each room is a shrine to Elvis, whose spirit somehow affects the lives of the film's principal characters. As MYSTERY TRAIN's first episode, "Far from Yokohama," opens, Nagase and Kudoh, two teenaged Japanese tourists on a pilgrimage to the Promised Land, "detrain" in Memphis. After checking into the Arcade, these devotees of American culture argue over rock 'n' roll favorites, make love, listen to Elvis on the hotel radio, and remain undisturbed by everything that occurs-even the gunshot they hear near checkout time. A candidate for the wrecking ball, the Arcade is staffed by two dedicated souls who seem to have no existence outside of the purgatorial night shift at this transient hotel. The older of these two black men (played by legendary rhythm & blues performer Screamin' Jay Hawkins) continually writes in the hotel logbook and remains unruffled by the weird patrons. His assistant (Lee), bedecked in a jaunty Philip Morris bellboy outfit, is a one-man hotel staff. On the unusually busy night during which MYSTERY TRAIN takes place, the Arcade also plays host to Braschi, an Italian woman visiting the States long enough to bring her dead husband back to Italy. The focus of the second episode, "A Ghost," Braschi is perpetually conned by the locals and harassed by a low-life who promises her she will be visited by visions of Elvis. At the hotel, she agrees to share her room with Bracco, an impoverished magpie who is skipping out on her British boy friend (nicknamed Elvis). Miraculously, all of Braschi's troubles evaporate when the ghost of Elvis appears to her. The third episode, "Lost in Space" (the most linear, but weakest, of the stories), involves Bracco's alcohol-crazed lover (Strummer), her nervous-wreck brother (Buscemi), and their fast-talking pal (Aviles), who is related to the Arcade's unflappable night manager. While trying to cheer up the heartbroken Strummer, his buddies are horrified when he shoots the racist proprietor of a liquor store. Terrified, the three hole up in the Arcade until morning, when Strummer accidentally shoots Buscemi. At checkout time, all the characters go their separate ways.

Jarmusch's mysteriously funny movie will work best for those who are attuned to his zonked-out sensibility. Jarmusch is a true original, but his originality lies in a quirky viewpoint that may leave some audience members cold. Others who abandon themselves to his deadpan drollery and Robby Muller's (DOWN BY LAW; THE AMERICAN FRIEND; PARIS, TEXAS) witty cinematography, which makes squalor look festive, will be rewarded with a cockeyed valentine to the cradle of rock 'n' roll. What is refreshing about Jarmusch's films is that they lack the smirky cynicism of many hip independent filmmakers' work. Tellingly, he is able to satirize the night clerks of a rundown hotel by finding humor in their situation, not by putting them down. The difference between this approach and that of other hip filmmakers becomes apparent when MYSTERY TRAIN is compared with a trendy satire like TRUE STORIES, which exploits American grotesques without ever plugging into their energy.

One wishes that the hometown characters in the third section of the film had been conceived and acted with as much grace as the tourists from Japan and Italy are in the first two episodes. Regrettably, as the comic crime caper grows more frenetic, Jarmusch's direction becomes less assured. These reservations notwithstanding, Jarmusch has created an irresistible vision of America in which even the natives seem cast adrift—lost in a benign Twilight Zone. It is refreshing to experience a character comedy that eschews belly laughs for the richness Jarmusch derives from exploring the essence of his characters as they sift through the pop culture junkyards of America.

As he has done before, Jarmusch again includes noted musicians among his cast. In addition to Hawkins and Joe Strummer (the latter a founding member of the Clash), Jarmusch calls on the acting talents of Tom Waits, who played one of the lead roles in DOWN BY LAW, and famed Memphis soul singer Rufus Thomas. Songs include: "Mystery Train" (Sam C. Phillips, Junior Parker, performed by Elvis Presley, Parker), "Blue Moon" (Richard Rodgers, Lorenz Hart, performed by Presley), "Pain in My Heart" (Naomi Neville, performed by Otis Redding), "Domino" (Phillips, performed by Roy Orbison), "The Memphis Train" (Mack Rice, Rufus Thomas, Willie Sparks, performed by Thomas), "Get Your Money Where You Spend Your Time" (Tommy Tate, James Palmer, performed by Bobby Blue Bland), "Soul Finger" (Jimmy King, James Alexander, Thalon Jones, Ben Cauley, Ronnie Caldwell, Carl Cunningham, performed by the Bar-Kays). *(Profanity, violence, nudity, sexual situations, substance abuse.)*

p, Jim Stark; d, Jim Jarmusch; w, Jim Jarmusch; ph, Robby Muller; ed, Melody London; m, John Lurie; prod d, Dan Bishop; set d, Dianna Freas; spec eff, Gary King; cos, Carol Wood; makeup, Meredith Soupios.

Comedy   (PR:O MPAA:R)

N

NATIONAL LAMPOON'S CHRISTMAS VACATION**½
97m Hughes/WB c

Chevy Chase (*Clark W. Griswold, Jr.*), Beverly D'Angelo (*Ellen Griswold*), Randy Quaid (*Cousin Eddie*), Miriam Flynn (*Catherine, Eddie's Wife*), Johnny Galecki (*Rusty Griswold*), Juliette Lewis (*Audrey Griswold*), John Randolph (*Clark W. Griswold, Sr.*), Diane Ladd (*Nora Griswold*), E.G. Marshall (*Art, Ellen's Father*), Doris Roberts (*Frances, Ellen's Mother*), Mae Questel (*Aunt Bethany*), William Hickey (*Uncle Lewis*), Cody Burger (*Rocky*), Ellen Hamilton Latzen (*Ruby Sue*), Julia Louis-Dreyfus (*Margo Chester*), Nicholas Guest (*Todd Chester*), Brian Doyle Murray (*Frank Shirley*), Nicolette Scorsese (*Mary*), Snots the Dog.

In 1983 the world was introduced to the Griswold family, a great American clan headed by the clumsy but well-meaning Clark (Chevy Chase). The Griswolds drove cross-country from Chicago to California in NATIONAL LAMPOON'S VACATION with mixed, though often hilarious, results. Two years later, they journeyed to the Continent in NATIONAL LAMPOON'S EUROPEAN VACATION, and the laughs were very minimal (thanks mainly to inept direction by Amy Heckerling). Now the Griswolds are back, and they are staying home for the holidays. Written by John Hughes and directed by Jeremiah S. Chechik, the latest installment in the Griswold saga chronicles an American family's wayward efforts to have an old-fashioned Christmas.

Chevy Chase in NATIONAL LAMPOON'S CHRISTMAS VACATION (©Warner Bros.)

Starting with a trek to the country to get the perfect Christmas tree, and concluding with a SWAT team breaking up the Griswold Christmas Eve party, NATIONAL LAMPOON'S CHRISTMAS VACATION is a loud and obnoxious satire of family life. Chase again plays the Griswolds' fearless leader, who frantically tries to pull off a successful Christmas gathering. After bringing home a huge 15-foot pine tree and jamming it into the living room, he wires up the house with thousands of Christmas lights, virtually destroying his home and the neighborhood in the process. Both sets of in-laws arrive (in typical Hughes fashion, one grandfather complains about a pint of fluid that was removed from his back, and a grandmother promises her kids a quarter if they massage the boil on her foot), Cousin Eddie (Quaid) and his wife (Flynn) pay a surprise visit, and the whole clan settles in for the holiday. For the remainder of the film, the normal Christmas traditions and celebrations are mangled into slapstick silliness. Chase falls off ladders, is hit in the face with boards, and flies across an interstate on a sled. Dogs chase rabid squirrels through the house, Christmas trees are torched, cats are gift-wrapped, and a sewer explodes, sending a plastic Santa sailing through the air. Lacking a standard plot (a scant idea involving Chase's Christmas bonus barely holds the narrative together), the film is instead a series of hit-and-miss sight gags. Some are funny (the rabid squirrel bit is surprisingly humorous); some aren't (the Christmas-light gag goes on forever). The film ends with the entire family (and half of the police force) standing on the lawn, gazing at the nighttime sky, in awe of the Christmas star. Chase is particularly moved; finally at peace, he is satisfied that he has given his family a real old-fashioned Christmas.

The first half-hour of NATIONAL LAMPOON'S CHRISTMAS VACATION is simply not funny. Full of tired sight gags and overblown stunts (an early car chase is particularly stupid), it quickly becomes tedious. Although Chase is very funny, the film doesn't come to life until the arrival of Randy Quaid, who steals the picture as the slimy Cousin Eddie. Quaid plays the character to the hilt, wearing ridiculous clothes (an outfit consisting of green polyester pants and a white shirt over a black dickie is especially funny) and spewing riotous lines about the metal plate in his head and his son's lip fungus. Also funny are E.G. Marshall and William Hickey as two of the stranger members of the family. CHRISTMAS VACATION is not entirely successful, but it's definitely the funniest thing Hughes has written in years. He continues to explore familiar territory (if he doesn't remake THE BREAKFAST CLUB, he remakes MR. MOM), but this time he leaves out the false sentiment that has sunk many of his other scripts. CHRISTMAS VACATION is a slapstick comedy with nothing else on its mind.

Although he's no worse than Hughes' usual directorial surrogate, Howard Deutsch (THE GREAT OUTDOORS; SOME KIND OF WONDERFUL), TV commercial veteran Chechik fails to demonstrate much of a flair for comedy. A lot of his sight gags could use more punch and his timing is a bit off. Still, CHRISTMAS VACATION remains an entertaining piece of lowbrow fluff, and though it is not as good as VACATION, it is infinitely better than EUROPEAN VACATION. With enough sight gags to please the fans of slapstick, and enough good-natured Christmas cheer to qualify as a good holiday film, NATIONAL LAMPOON'S CHRISTMAS VACATION should keep most viewers occupied and provide 97 minutes of goofy entertainment. (*Profanity, adult situations, brief nudity.*)

p, John Hughes and Tom Jacobson; d, Jeremiah S. Chechik; w, John Hughes; ph, Thomas Ackerman; ed, Jerry Greenberg; m, Angelo Badalamenti; prod d, Stephen Marsh.

Comedy   **(PR:C MPAA:PG-13)**

▼NAVIGATOR, THE**½
(Aus.) 92m Arenafilm-Film Investment Group of New Zealand/Circle bw-c

Bruce Lyons (*Connor*), Chris Haywood (*Arno*), Hamish McFarlane (*Griffin*), Marshall Napier (*Searle*), Noel Appleby (*Ulf*), Paul Livingston (*Martin*), Sarah Pierse (*Linnet*), Mark Wheatley (*Tog 1*), Tony Herbert (*Tog 2*), Jessica Cardiff-Smith (*Esme*), Roy Wesney (*Grandpa*), Kathleen-Elizabeth Kelly (*Grandma*), Jay Saussey (*Griffin's Girl Friend*), Charles Walker (*Old Chrissie*), Desmond Kelly (*Smithy*), Bill Le Marquand (*Tom*), Jay Lavea Laga'aia (*Jay*), Norman Fairley (*Submarine Captain*), Alister Babbage (*Grigor*).

THE NAVIGATOR is a singular experience, a time-warp, Chinese box-puzzle of a film that bespeaks the obsessed vision of its writer-director, Vincent Ward. It takes place in 1348 in Cumbria, New Zealand, where a psychic young boy (McFarlane) dreams of a way to save his village from the advancing black plague, later leading his brother (Lyons) and four other men on a quest that somehow transports them to the present time. Their mission is to place a tributary spire on a specified cathedral before dawn breaks and the village is lost forever. But, as McFarlane has envisioned, along the way one of their number will be betrayed and another will die. The six adventurers face everything on their journey from the suffocating, noxious confines of the tunnel they mine towards salvation to the terrifying technological wonders of the Antipodes, 1988. Each of them is an archetype in his own way. Besides the brothers there are Livingston the Philosopher, Napier the Realist, Appleby the Buffoon, and Haywood the Ferryman. All prophecies are fulfilled at the end, in a rather tortuous succession of plot twists.

With its simplistic parallels to the Christ story and the AIDS crisis, THE NAVIGATOR is compelling in a dumb kind of way. Ward obviously sees it as an extension of Spielbergian fantasy-adventure with heavy mystic and sociological overtones—not the most alluring of premises. In a strenuous effort to *not* tell his story as simply as possible, he engages a battery of film school cinematic effects—the mixed use of black and white with color, time lapse views of clouds scampering across ominous skies, superimpositions galore—and all of this in the first 10 minutes. The effect is brutalizing upon the audience; one yearns for the stirring straightforwardness of John Huston's work in THE MAN WHO WOULD BE KING or Alfred Hitchcock's canny timing in his use of extreme effects. Ward is the type of director who uses a close-up of a man pinned to the front of a thunderously onrushing train, screaming at the top of his lungs, and then overloads the moment even further by adding ear-splitting obvious music. It all becomes a bit wearing, like being seated at dinner next to a tirelessly loquacious guest, who proceeds to go on and on about his exploits, continually topping himself. Geoffrey Simpson's photography is admittedly breathtaking in spots, especially an extravagant pull-away view of the men digging their wormy way through the earth like nocturnal insects. As already mentioned, Davood A. Tabrizi's music underlines everything needlessly in a demeaning, Max Steiner-ish way.

To a man, the actors lay it on as thick as the Medieval mummers out of Breughel they're made up to resemble. Indeed, in the modern sequences, they often carry on like Snow White's dwarves. Hamish McFarlane has the screeching bossiness currently favored by many directors (most notably Spielberg) in their boy actors; a quiet visionary he is not. Bruce Lyons tries to impart a heroic gruff mellifluousness into his voice that rings especially phony. Moreover, all of the actors speak in a variant of the thickest Scotch burr since Katharine Hepburn's version of THE LITTLE MINISTER, rendering many lines unintelligible. *(Violence.)*

p, John Maynard and Gary Hannam; d, Vincent Ward; w, Vincent Ward, Kely Lyons, and Geoff Chapple; ph, Geoffrey Simpson; ed, John Scott; m, Davood A. Tabrizi; prod d, Sally Campbell; art d, Mike Becroft; spec eff, Paul Nichola; cos, Glenys Jackson; stunts, Timothy Lee; makeup, Marjory Hamlin.

Adventure/Fantasy   (PR:A MPAA:PG)

ⓥNECROMANCER*
88m Bonaire/Spectrum c
Elizabeth Kaitan *(Julie)*, Russ Tamblyn *(Prof. Charles DeLonge)*, John Tyler *(Eric)*, Rhonda Durton *(Freda)*, Stan Hurwitz *(Paul)*, Edward Wright *(Carl)*, Shawn Eisner *(Allan)*, Waide A. Riddle *(Ernest)*, Lois Masten *(Lisa, the Necromancer)*.

Who says revenge is sweet? According to NECROMANCER, it is anything but—and it's not very pretty to watch either.

Kaitan stars as Julie, a sweet blonde coed who is raped by a trio of low-lifes late one night in the school auditorium. In order to keep her quiet, the threesome threaten to tell her current beau (Tyler) about her past affair with drama professor Tamblyn, blackmailing her with the evidence of a letter she wrote Tamblyn that they discovered while looking for test answers in his office. The threat is enough to keep Kaitan away from the police, but she does confide in her best friend, Durton, and for some strange reason tells Tamblyn, too. Each party handles the situation in his or her own unique way: the sneaky professor holds Kaitan, comforting her, and gives her some "special" private coaching for her role as Juliet in the school's upcoming production of "Romeo and Juliet"; Durton, on the other hand, persuades her to respond to a classified ad offering professional revenge services. The ad leads the girls to a necromancer, Masten, who brings them into a tent in her backyard, instructs Kaitan to stand with her inside a circle, and announces that "Revenge is the only justice. I and others not of this world can help." Subsequently, all hell literally breaks loose as objects fly around, wind gusts, lights flash, Masten's voice changes, and Kaitan's eyes begin to glow. Kaitan and Durton flee, but strange things have just begun to happen and, one by one, the boys who raped Kaitan disappear. Masten's revengeful modus operandi, it turns out, is to take the form of Kaitan, dress in sexy lingerie, and approach her prey in a highly seductive manner. Then, before the not-so-innocent victim knows what is happening, the necromancer turns into a horrible monster that kills brutally and vanishes. Kaitan, of course, does not want this kind of revenge, but is powerless to stop it until the necromancer goes after Tyler, whereupon a showdown between woman and monster proves once again that good triumphs over evil.

NECROMANCER is a trite little horror film, borrowing heavily from better entries in the genre. Kaitan's voice deepens and distorts in EXORCIST style; blood spurts up from bodies a la NIGHTMARE ON ELM STREET, etc.; meanwhile, the premise is so silly and the main character so dumb that it's difficult to care about her plight. NECROMANCER is both duller and gorier than it is frightening. *(Violence, nudity, sexual situations.)*

p, Roy McAree; d, Dusty Nelson; w, Bill Naud; ph, Richard Clabaugh and Eric Cayla (Foto-Kem Color); ed, Carole A. Kenneally; m, Gary Stockdale, Kevin Klingler, and Bob Mamet; art d, Scott Harrison; makeup, William J. Males.

Horror   (PR:O MPAA:R)

NEW YEAR'S DAY**
89m Int'l. Rainbow c
Maggie Jakobson *(Lucy)*, Gwen Welles *(Annie)*, Melanie Winter *(Winona)*, Henry Jaglom *(Drew)*, David Duchovny *(Billy)*, Milos Forman *(Lazlo)*, Michael Emil *(Dr. Stadthagen)*, Donna Germain *(Dr. Stadthagen's Friend)*, Tracy Reiner *(Marjorie)*, Harvey Miller *(Lucy's Father)*, Irene Moore *(Lucy's Mother)*, James DePreist *(Lucy's Shrink)*.

Director Henry Jaglom's films are about as personal as any coming out of Hollywood these days. As such, they ask no quarter and give none. Either you wholeheartedly buy into his talking (and talking and talking) heads yuppie psycho-comedies, or you don't. Either you chuckle warmly for 90 minutes, or you keep checking your watch and looking for an exit. NEW YEAR'S DAY is part of what is essentially the continuing story that Jaglom began with 1985's ALWAYS, in which he fictionalized his breakup with his wife, actress Patrice Townsend. In 1988's SOMEONE TO LOVE, Jaglom went looking for a date, and in NEW YEAR'S DAY he comes, alone, to New York looking for a fresh start.

Although the name and occupation of Jaglom's character changes in each film, his screen persona remains more or less the same. In SOMEONE TO LOVE (best remembered for Orson Welles' last film appearance), Jaglom plays Danny, a filmmaker who stages a big singles party in an old movie theater and chases women with his camera, asking them embarrassing questions. In NEW YEAR'S DAY, he plays Drew, a writer who also asks people embarrassing questions at a party. Again Jaglom is an unmarried middle-aged man with the perpetually pained expression of a sad puppy that has been repeatedly kicked—really hard. All three Jaglom films revolve around parties (ALWAYS featured an Independence Day poolside bash) filled with boring, annoying people (one of whom, invariably, is played by Jaglom's brother, Michael Emil). The party guests talk endlessly about their neuroses, obsessions, and problems; then they receive quasi-profound advice from Jaglom or some sage-looking character actor. In this way, these three films can be seen as one lengthy cinematic record of the world's longest party from hell.

The dreary festivities of Jaglom's most recent installment begin as his Drew, newly arrived from the West Coast on New Year's Day, tries to reclaim his sublet apartment, only to find the sublessees still in residence. They are Jakobson, an animal behaviorist making ends meet by doing voices for Saturday morning cartoons; Gwen Welles, a gay public relations person for an art gallery who has a crush on Jakobson; and Winter, a blowsy blonde photographer contemplating an affair with one of her male models, solely for the purpose of having a baby. A misreading of the lease has led the women to believe that they have the apartment through January 1, while it is Jaglom's impression that he takes possession on that day. Failing to find a hotel room for the night, Jaglom decides to stay with the three offbeat women. Just when it looks as though a plot is about to rear its ugly head, the party guests start to arrive. Jakobson is about to relocate to Los Angeles to break free from her promiscuous boy friend (Duchovny), who shows up to swear his love for her, beg her not to leave, and put the make on every woman in sight. Everyone else in attendance also begs her not to leave, especially Welles, who hits the sheets with Duchovny because she thinks it will be like making love to Jakobson by proxy. Special guest stars drop in, like director Forman as Lazlo, the building janitor, who smokes cigars and talks about being impotent. Naturally, Emil makes his own obligatory appearance as a sex therapist who has a few Freudian observations about Forman's cigars, though Jaglom's camera doesn't hang around to catch Forman's reaction.

In fact, Jaglom's camera doesn't bother to hang around for much of anything. Of television, one character observes, "You have to know where the laughs are, then when things get emotional you know it's time for a commercial." As if he intended his work a reaction to this formula, Jaglom rarely knows where the laughs are in his films; just when something interesting is about to happen, he cuts away to yet another boring conversation. In short, Jaglom's fans will be delighted to know that NEW YEAR'S DAY is more of the same. Others may want to catch a good "Cheers" rerun instead. (Adult situations, profanity.)

p, Judith Wolinsky; d, Henry Jaglom; w, Henry Jaglom; ph, Joey Forsyte, Hanania Baer, and Nesya Blue (Technicolor).

Comedy   (PR:C MPAA:NR)

⊙NEW YORK STORIES: LIFE
LESSONS***1/2, LIFE WITHOUT
ZOE**, OEDIPUS WRECKS**1/2
130m Touchstone/BV c
LIFE LESSONS: Nick Nolte (Lionel Dobie), Rosanna Arquette (Paulette), Patrick O'Neal (Phillip Fowler), Jesse Borrego (Reuben Toro), Steve Buscemi (Gregory Stark), Peter Gabriel (Himself),

Illeana Douglas (Paulette's Friend), LIFE WITHOUT ZOE: Heather McComb (Zoe), Talia Shire (Charlotte), Giancarlo Giannini (Claudio), Paul Herman (Clifford, the Doorman), James Keane (Jimmy), Don Novello (Hector), Selim Tlili (Abu), Carmine Coppola (Street Musician), Carole Bouquet (Princess Soroya), OEDIPUS WRECKS: Woody Allen (Sheldon Mills), Mia Farrow (Lisa), Julie Kavner (Treva), Mae Questel (Mother), Marvin Chatinover (Psychiatrist), Jessie Keosian (Aunt Ceil), George Schindler (Shandu, the Magician), Bridgit Ryan (Rita), Mayor Edward I. Koch (Himself).

Like 1988's ARIA, NEW YORK STORIES is an omnibus film in the tradition of QUARTET (1949); TRIO (1950); and TALES OF MANHATTAN (1942). Here the connecting thread is locale, namely the New York City setting for three short films by three of America's preeminent (critically, if not popularly) filmmakers, Martin Scorsese, Francis Ford Coppola, and Woody Allen—all of whom also happen to be native New Yorkers, and in whose films the city, at one time or another, has served not only as a setting but as an indispensible character. While the films in NEW YORK STORIES have little besides their shared locale in common, all three are in very different ways concerned with how love affects their central characters, and all three are predictably stylish—each shot by a master cinematographer.

Most of the action in the first segment, Scorsese's "Life Lessons," takes place in the loft studio of Lionel Dobie (Nolte), a hulking abstract expressionist painter who is enjoying the fruits of critical and financial success that have come his way in middle age. With the opening of a show of his work rapidly approaching and far too many canvases still blank, Lionel's growing anxiety is brought to the boiling point when his beautiful, 22-year-old live-in assistant and lover, Paulette (Arquette), an aspiring painter, announces that their relationship is over. Although Lionel attempts to take this upheaval in stride—even allowing Paulette to continue to live in the studio and entertain boy friends there—he becomes increasingly jealous and obsessed with her. Notwithstanding all his best efforts to reconcile, however, the one thing Lionel will not do is deceive Paulette about her limited talents as an artist, while the conflict that arises from the breakdown of their relationship only seems to feed his own artistic drive, sending him back to the canvas, where he paints passionately to the varying strains of Procol Harum's "Whiter Shade of Pale," Bob Dylan's "Like a Rolling Stone," and Giacomo Puccini's "Turandot." Ultimately, Paulette moves out, Lionel's show is a success, and he finds another pretty young acolyte.

The inspiration for "Life Lessons," easily the best of the three segments, was provided by Fyodor Dostoyevski's short story "The Gambler." This, in turn, was based on the novelist's falling out with his mistress, aspiring writer Apollinaria Suslova, whose diaries also contributed to the screenplay by Scorsese's COLOR OF MONEY cowriter, Richard Price. Working with gifted cinematographer Nestor Almendros, Scorsese not only explores the creative impulse and presents a close-up study of the act of painting, but his constantly moving camera makes forever clear the connection between painting and filmmaking. Employing one of the cinema's oldest techniques, the iris shot (whereby the screen image expands from a central pinpoint or contracts down to one), a favorite of filmmaking pioneer D.W. Griffith, Scorsese forces the viewer momentarily to separate details from their context—be they a single brushstroke in one of Lionel's paintings or the bracelet on Paulette's ankle.

The brushstrokes on the screen were actually put there by New York artist Chuck Connelly, and the paintings that appear in the film are also his, though, as Scorsese told Premiere, he wanted "to show the seductiveness of art without inviting the audience to judge the merits of [Lionel's] work." Scorsese has succeeded brilliantly in demonstrating that seductiveness, not only with his trademark bravado camerawork but also by coaxing from Nick Nolte his finest, most nuanced film performance to date. Nolte's Lionel, if not a terribly complex character, is nonetheless possessed of a passion he is never quite able to express in words, a need that romance—with any woman—will only temporarily satisfy. Only in the act of painting is his true self expressed, and it is the painter and his art, not the man, that attract Paulette, engagingly portrayed by Rosanna Arquette.

The second segment, Coppola's "Life Without Zoe"—cowritten with his 17-year-old daughter, Sofia, and shot by legendary Italian cinematographer Vittorio Storaro—is even more of an exercise in style, though, unfortunately, it is style without much substance. Set in a benevolent New York that is unnervingly closer to the world of THE MIRACLE OF 34TH STREET than that of Howard Beach, this is the tale of wealthy 12-year-old Zoe (McComb), who lives in the Sherry-Netherland Hotel, watched over by a glib but caring butler (wonderfully played by Don Novello) while her not-quite-estranged parents, a world-renowned flautist father (Giannini) and fashion biz maven mother (Shire, Coppola's real-life sister), separately gallivant around the world. Much of the plot has to do with Zoe's attempt to return a fabulous earring, given to her father by a Middle Eastern princess, to its rightful place before the princess' gesture is misinterpreted by her countrymen. To do so, Zoe throws a lavish costume party for a classmate who happens both to be the "richest boy in the world" and to travel in the same circles as the princess in question. In the process Zoe also achieves her larger objective—reuniting her parents.

With "Life Without Zoe," Coppola has skillfully captured the look and sensibility of a "feel-good" 40s feature—but to what end? The film's production design, costumes (designed by Sofia), and photography all are nicely realized—and call out to be noticed—but this child's-eye view of how alternately fun and difficult (when one's parents are never around) it is to be rich never really goes anywhere emotionally, at least not in a way that will touch most viewers, save perhaps those whose lives the film mirrors. Furthermore, the idea that Zoe brings some kind of joy to the lives of street people (the film's only reminder of its 80s setting) by presenting them with chocolate kisses is reprehensible. Far less successful than THE OUTSIDERS and RUMBLEFISH, Coppola's other, far more assured and socially conscious, attempts to fuse stylistic experiment with adolescent themes, "Life Without Zoe" is without question NEW YORK STORIES' biggest disappointment, despite its fine cast.

More satisfying, though hardly on a par with its director's best work, is the film's final installment. Allen's return to the style of his "earlier, funnier" films, "Oedipus Wrecks," features Allen in the role of Sheldon, a 50-year-old Jewish lawyer in a super-WASPy firm, who is engaged to a gentile mother of three (Farrow). The bane of Sheldon's existence is his domineering mother (hilariously essayed by Mae Questel, onetime voice of Betty Boop and Olive Oyl). Mom doesn't think much of Sheldon's shiksa fiancee and, full of opinions and complaints, oblivious to her surroundings, she is a constant source of embarrassment for Sheldon. Not surprisingly, Sheldon wishes his mother would disappear, and when she does (during a magic show) his life takes a dramatic turn for the better. As in a number of Allen's films, "Oedipus Wrecks" includes sessions with a psychiatrist (Chatinover), but the switch this time is that when Sheldon starts "projecting," he really *projects*; and when his mother makes a dramatic return to the scene, she is literally larger than life, looking down on New York from the heavens, keeping a constant watch on her son's comings and goings, and offering a running commentary for the whole of the city to witness. Sheldon seeks help from Treva (Kavner), a mystic and breaker of spells, but it is only when he begins showing a romantic interest in the very Jewish Treva that his mother is happy and things get back to normal.

Although essentially based on a one-joke premise, "Oedipus Wrecks" manages to generate laughs through most of its approximately 40-minute running time, primarily because it's one joke, an over-the-top take on Jewish Motherhood, is a good one and well told. Fans of the lovable nebbish Allen has played so well in many of his films will be delighted by the opportunity to observe him (or at least another variation of this persona) at yet another stage in his life. But though there is much that is funny here, the insight into the human condition that distinguishes Allen's best work—be it his out-and-out comedies or his more serious, Bergman-esque efforts—is in short supply here. With the absence of Allen's reductive philosophical observations (his declaration in BROADWAY DANNY ROSE that he believes in "love, acceptance, and forgiveness," for example), there is more pressure on the film simply to be funny, and though the performances and the characters are amusing, they just aren't all *that* hilarious. Gorgeously photographed by longtime Bergman collaborator Sven Nykvist, "Oedipus Wrecks" is a pleasant but minor Woody Allen effort. *(Sexual situations, profanity, adult situations.)*

p, Barbara DeFina, Fred Roos, Fred Fuchs, and Robert Greenhut; d, Martin Scorsese, Francis Coppola, and Woody Allen; w, Richard Price, Francis Coppola, Sofia Coppola, and Woody Allen; ph, Nestor Almendros, Vittorio Storaro, and Sven Nykvist (Duart Color); ed, Thelma Schoonmaker, Barry Malkin, and Susan E. Morse; m, Carmine Coppola and Kid Creole and the Coconuts; prod d, Kristi Zea, Dean Tavoularis, and Santo Loquasto; art d, Wray Steven Graham and Speed Hopkins.

Comedy/Drama   (PR:C-O MPAA:PG)

NEXT OF KIN*½
105m Lorimar/WB c

Patrick Swayze *(Truman Gates)*, Liam Neeson *(Briar Gates)*, Adam Baldwin *(Joey Rosselini)*, Helen Hunt *(Jessie Gates)*, Andreas Katsulas *(John Isabella)*, Bill Paxton *(Gerald Gates)*, Ben Stiller *(Lawrence Isabella)*, Michael J. Pollard *(Harold)*, Ted Levine *(Willy)*, Del Close *(Frank)*, Valentino Cimo *(Rhino)*, Paul Greco *(Leo)*, Vincent Guastaferro *(Paulie)*, Paul Herman *(Antonelli)*, Don Herion *(Zimmer)*, Don James *(David)*, Brett Hadley *(De Witt)*, Rodney Hatfield *(Hollis)*, Richard Wharton *(Selkirk)*, Kelly Blair *(Tolbert)*, Charlie Williams *(Pierce)*, Michael Wise *(Snakeman)*, Joseph R. Ryan *(Grandpa)*, Anndrena Belcher *(Patsy-Ruth)*, Jean Ritchie *(Charlene)*, Nancy Jeffrey *(Aunt Peg)*, Tina Engle *(Rosalie)*, Kim Cole *(Hollis' Wife)*, Starla Fugate *(Gerald's Girl Friend)*, Michael Sassone *(Melvin)*, Neil Giuntoli *(Shorty)*, Fred Crowther *(Old Hillbilly)*, Billy Branch *(Preacher)*, Celene Evans *(Lady Bartender)*, Michael DiZonno *(Vinny)*, Tim Quill *(TV Reporter)*, Jack Kandel *(Hillbilly Bartender)*, Sally Murphy *(Hooker)*, Mark Roberts *(Furniture Mover)*, Patrick Balch *(Young Boy, Kentucky)*, Relioues Webb *(Young Boy, Chicago)*, Arlene Lencioni *(Mrs. Isabella)*, Lew Way Chin, Morgan Biscomb Melto *(Violin Students)*, Elizabeth Ruf *(Woman in Bar)*, Al Neal *(Man in Bar)*, Joelle Pasquale, Mia Ferro, Keela Gootee *(Daughters)*, Pamela Prater *(Selkirk's Wife)*, Mary Ann Berkhart *(De Witt's Wife)*.

Neither a buddy-buddy action-comedy nor a pyrotechnical showcase of explosions and stunts, NEXT OF KIN—an intelligently made and moodily atmospheric action melodrama—provides solid, satis-

Patrick Swayze in NEXT OF KIN (©Warner Bros.)

fying entertainment while demonstrating just how effective a fully realized genre film can be.

Chicago cop Swayze has alienated his rural Kentucky kinfolk by moving to the big city, where he acts as an unofficial liaison between the police department and the local hillbilly population and is happily married to Hunt, a violinist and music teacher. Back on the family spread, Swayze's older brother (Neeson), who has had to struggle ever since the local coal mine shut down, resents Swayze for abandoning the family and for having convinced their younger brother, Paxton, to do the same. Paxton, a truck driver for a vending machine company, feels torn between his two brothers. Meanwhile, a very different "family" dynamic operates within Chicago's Isabella Mafia organization, led by Katsulas. In an attempt to legitimize his enterprises, Katsulas is bringing his son, Stiller, a yuppified, recent business school graduate, into the family operation. This does not sit well with Baldwin, whose plans to succeed Katsulas are threatened by Stiller. Insulted by being forced to groom Stiller for a position he feels should be his, Baldwin reluctantly lets the young scion accompany him on an expedition to convince the owners of a local vending machine company to sell out to the Isabellas. Baldwin's method of achieving this goal is to hijack a company truck filled with merchandise, but its young driver—Paxton—leads the gangsters on a wildly perilous chase and nearly gets away before Baldwin shoots him dead. Over Swayze's protests, Neeson resolves to seek vengeance and heads for Chicago, where he checks into a sleazy flophouse run by the sympathetic Pollard and quickly zeroes in on the Isabellas as the killers. Conducting his own investigation, Swayze arrives at the same conclusion. The two brothers then forge an uneasy truce to bring them to justice, but the moment evidence is found naming Baldwin the murderer, Neeson goes after him and gets himself killed for his foolhardiness. After learning of his remaining brother's death and his own imminent fatherhood, Swayze decides that blood is thicker than water and hands in his badge. Meanwhile, Pollard phones Swayze's family in Kentucky. They gather their crossbows, hatchets, and a truckful of snakes and head for Chicago at once, arriving just in time to back up Swayze in his climactic nighttime battle against Baldwin and his hoods in a deserted cemetery.

While the plot mechanics of NEXT OF KIN are not appreciably better (or worse) than those of many other films of the same genre, the movie's meticulous execution makes it a particularly accomplished effort. Major themes, characters, and milieus are explored in fascinating detail; especially successful is the juxtaposition of the Gates and Isabella families, each of which is shown to comprise individuals of both light and dark natures, rather than simply pitting the good clan against the bad. The assured, painstaking direction of John Irvin (TURTLE DIARY [1985]; HAMBURGER HILL [1987]; RAW DEAL [1986]) fixes upon the parallel of the two families, lending their inner workings and rituals an almost epic quality that propels the film. Michael Jenning's screenplay provides well-motivated action, emotion, and humor; the contrasting worlds of Chicago and Kentucky are beautifully evoked by Steven Poster's subdued and painterly cinematography; and the production design and set decoration seem convincingly authentic (as does Jack Nitzsche's music).

In the leading role, Patrick Swayze offers a solid, low-key performance and renders a Kentucky accent quite believably—proving he doesn't *have* to dance or take off his shirt at every opportunity to maintain his star status. Adam Baldwin, Andreas Katsulas, Ben Stiller, Michael J. Pollard, and Helen Hunt also contribute fine characterizations, but Irish actor Liam Neeson (A PRAYER FOR THE DYING [1987]; THE GOOD MOTHER [1988]; THE DEAD POOL [1988]) impresses most with his intense portrayal of the brooding older brother, a performance that would seem right at home in a John Ford classic. Songs include: "Brothers" (Larry Gatlin, performed by Gatlin, Patrick Swayze), "Hillbilly Heart" (Troy Seals, Max D. Barnes, performed by Ricky Van Shelton), "Brother to Brother" (J. Fred Knoblock, performed by Gregg Allman, Lori Yates), "Hey, Backwoods" (Rodney Crowell, Steuart Smith, performed by Crowell), "The Yard Sale" (Terry Skinner, Billy R. Lawson, performed by Lawson), "Paralyzed" (Elvis Presley, Otis Blackwell, performed by Sweethearts of the Rodeo), "Straight and Narrow" (Don Schlitz, Paul Overstreet, performed by Ricky Skaggs), "Pyramid of Cans" (Buddy Cannon, Jimmy Darrell, Robert Corbin, performed by George Jones), "My Sweet Baby's Gone" (Charlie Daniels, performed by the Charlie Daniels Band), "Wailing Sax" (Michael Wells, performed by Duane Eddy), "My Sweet Understanding Lady" (B.B. King, performed by King), "Protect and Serve" (Stevie Salas, Pee Wee Jam, M.C. Jam, performed by Pee Wee Jam, M.C. Jam), "Serenade" (Sigmund Romberg, Dorothy Donnelly, performed by Mario Lanza). *(Violence, profanity, adult situations.)*

p, Les Alexander and Don Enright; d, John Irvin; w, Michael Jenning; ph, Steven Poster (Metrocolor); ed, Peter Honess; m, Jack Nitzsche; prod d, Jack T. Collis; set d, John Warnke; spec eff, Joe Lombardi; cos, Donfeld; stunts, Walter Scott; makeup, Art Anthony.

Action/Crime   (PR:C MPAA:R)

NIGHT GAME**½
95m Epic/Trans World c
Roy Scheider, Karen Young, Richard Bradford, Paul Gleason, Carlin Glynn, Lane Smith.

Call it the Hitchcock syndrome. Every so often, otherwise reasonable and humanistic film directors decide that a slasher movie could be genuinely exciting, if only it were done "right." It's easy to understand their temptation: Few genres are quite as purely visual as the white-knuckled killer-thriller, which allows filmmakers who have heretofore made a perfectly respectable living directing people exchanging dialog in rooms a chance to go outside, move their cameras around, and see if they can scare some people. However, despite such notable exceptions as Arthur Penn (DEAD OF WINTER), most name directors who've attempted the switch have foundered on the thriller, from Robert Benton (STILL OF THE NIGHT) to John Huston (PHOBIA).

Maybe it takes a really mean person to make a really mean movie—Hitch was never known for an excess of personal warmth. Whatever the directorial mentality necessary for success, Peter Masterson (who directed Geraldine Page to an Oscar in THE TRIP TO BOUNTIFUL) here becomes the latest victim of the Hitchcock syndrome. Masterson's NIGHT GAME will not erase memories of PSYCHO. Nevertheless, it's oddly agreeable—an amiably irreverent, low-key cop comedy that gets interrupted every so often by some rather nasty grappling-hook murders, linked obtusely to hometown wins by the Houston Astros baseball team. Roy Scheider (who seems of late to have developed a taste for roles in corrosive, hard-boiled melodramas like 52 PICKUP and COHEN AND TATE), stars here as an ex-ballplayer who's now a homicide detective with the Galveston police. About to marry a sassy blonde young enough to be his daughter (Young), Scheider at the same time is looking into the murders. The victims just happen to be sassy young blondes, who meet their grisly fates on the beach by the boardwalk where his fiancee works a concession with her mother (Glynn, Masterson's wife and the mother of actress Mary Stuart Masterson, herself a sassy—and talented—young blonde). Throughout the film, Scheider battles with Glynn over the wedding plans, which seem to be getting more epic by the minute. He also has to contend with a sleazy investigator from the Houston sheriff's office (Gleason) who may be working as a pimp in his spare time, and an insufferably officious aide to the governor, both of whom are determined to get their two cents worth of headlines from the case. The many distractions might explain why Scheider, an avid Astros fan, fails to see the connection between the murders and the team's fortunes until embarrassingly late in the movie. Unfortunately, they don't explain why there always seems to be an abundance of sassy blonde potential victims wandering alone at night in areas where sassy blondes have been biting the dust in sensational fashion. In case you haven't already guessed, the errant blondes come to include Young, who conveniently wanders off at night by herself to bring about the film's climax.

Suffice it so say that as tightly-knit thrillers go, NIGHT GAME drops more than a few stitches. But that doesn't mean it's without its compensations. The cast, from Scheider on, turn in good, solid performances portraying the array of colorful, offbeat characters in Spencer Eastman and Anthony Palmer's script. The dialog features a level of gallows wit uncommon to the slasher genre, and the climax, though it can be spotted from approximately six innings away, is nevertheless stylishly staged and sufficiently gripping.

It's only too bad that so many promising ingredients, with a director of Masterson's stature at the helm, have been put into the service of a suspense plot with more holes than a bad infield defense. NIGHT GAME's greatest single virtue may be that nobody involved seems to take the story very seriously. Still, parents and others with sensitive constitutions should be forewarned: When the going gets gruesome, it really gets gruesome. *(Graphic violence, adult situations, profanity.)*

p, George Litto; d, Peter Masterson; w, Spencer Eastman and Anthony Palmer (based on a story by Spencer Eastman); ph, Fred Murphy; ed, Robert Barrere; m, Pino Donaggio; prod d, Neil Spisak.

Thriller   (PR:O MPAA:R)

ⓥNIGHT OF THE DEMONS*½
89m Meridian-Paragon Arts/Intl. Film Marketing c
Lance Fenton *(Jay)*, Cathy Podewell *(Judy)*, Alvin Alexis *(Roger)*, Hal Havins *(Stooge)*, Mimi Kinkade *(Angela)*, Linnea Quigley *(Suzanne)*, Phillip Tanzini *(Max)*, Jill Terashita *(Fran)*, Allison Barron *(Helen)*, William Gallo *(Sal)*, Donnie Jeffcoat *(Billy)*.

This independently produced, low-budget film begins promisingly, with an effective opening credits sequence in which animated ghosts, goblins, full moons, and haunted houses swirl in and around the titles, making for some good spooky fun. Unfortunately, it's all downhill from there. Teenager Kinkade is throwing a Halloween party at an old, abandoned house for a few friends who like to "party down." But the party house is no ordinary house; it's a closed funeral home whose owner killed his whole family many years ago. The discovery of this gruesome fact gets the revelers in the mood for a seance, and as the group stares into a mirror, mumbling invo-

cations to the forces of the night, they release a demon from the basement crematory. The kids are possessed by the demon one by one, and as dawn approaches, the evil spirit has taken over (or caused the killing of) all but two of them—Podewell and Alexis, who, as the sun rises and Halloween ends, manage to avoid being devoured by the bloodthirsty hellspawn and scramble over the brick wall that surrounds the house. As the pair stumble home, an old man who was seen heckling the kids at the film's opening is served a razor-blade-laced pie by his wife. While her spouse bleeds to death, groping at his spurting throat, she smiles and nods approvingly.

NIGHT OF THE DEMONS is a disappointment. Notwithstanding its generic story line, the film has a nice sense of pace and dispatches its victims neatly. But, like many another HALLOWEEN-inspired epic, it fails to offer any interesting characters. Instead, writer-producer Joe Augustyn simply delivers the usual types, including the clown, the virgin (who survives, of course), and the bitch (Kinkade, the first to be possessed). If the audience doesn't care about these kids, it's not scared for them, which leaves viewers with nothing to do except wonder how the next victim will be killed and critique the special effects.

Director Kevin Tenney (who made the well-regarded WITCHBOARD, another Paragon Arts production) has a strong style that improves the script all it can. The sight of the possessed Kinkade floating down a dark, murky hallway as she stalks her prey is frightening yet visually captivating, an indispensable element of a good horror film. Unfortunately, good looks are not enough. In a common plight of horror filmmakers these days, Tenney needs to find a script that is as strong and as innovative as his direction. *(Graphic violence, profanity, nudity.)*

p, Joe Augustyn; d, Kevin S. Tenney; w, Joe Augustyn; ph, David Lewis; ed, Daniel Duncan; m, Dennis Michael Tenney; art d, Ken Aichele; set d, Sally Nicolav; cos, Donna Reynolds; stunts, John Stuart; makeup, Steve Johnson.

Horror   (PR:O MPAA:R)

ⓥNIGHTMARE ON ELM STREET 5: THE DREAM CHILD, A**½
90m New Line c
Robert Englund *(Freddy Krueger)*, Lisa Wilcox *(Alice)*, Danny Hassel *(Dan)*, Kelly Jo Minter *(Yvonne)*, Joe Seely *(Mark)*, Erika Anderson *(Greta)*, Whitby Hertford *(Jacob)*.

The latest installment of the never-ending saga of Freddy Krueger (Robert Englund)

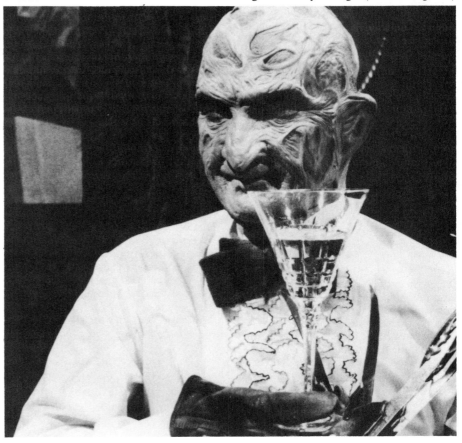

Robert Englund in A NIGHTMARE ON ELM STREET 5: THE DREAM CHILD (©New Line).

finds the heroine from the previous film, Wilcox, inexplicably suffering from Krueger-inspired nightmares again, despite the fact that she has apparently learned to control her subconscious and effectively block him from entering her dreams. One of her most frightening visions shows the evil Englund's conception—as the "bastard son of a 100 maniacs"—when a nun is accidentally locked in an asylum with the inmates. She is raped by the drooling psychos (actor Englund among them, sans makeup) and later gives birth to a grotesque child with a face just like the adult teen-killer. Unable to live with what she has wrought, the nun kills herself by jumping out of a church belltower. Back in reality-land, Wilcox, her boyfriend (Hassel), and their friends (Anderson, Seely, and Minter) graduate from high school. That night, however, Wilcox begins having horrible nightmares while still awake, and becomes certain that Englund has found some way to revenge himself on her and her friends. Sure enough, Hassel is killed in what appears to be a car wreck (he actually dreamed he was on a motorcycle that suddenly melded into his body, turning him into a gruesome H.R. Giger-like amalgam of man and machine), but Wilcox knows that Englund is responsible. Hysterical over her boy friend's death, a hospitalized Wilcox learns that she is pregnant with Hassel's child. Now she realizes how Englund has reentered the scene: through her unborn fetus' dreams. After considering abortion, Wilcox decides against it and grows determined to fight Englund and keep her baby; indeed, she even meets a little boy in her dreams who turns out to be her child and who helps her in her quest. Wilcox's friends, unfortunately, think she's still reeling from Hassel's death and refuse to believe her theory. Shortly thereafter, Wilcox's dreams show the rail-thin aspiring model Anderson being trapped by Englund at a dinner party and force-fed until she dies. Next on the list is graphic artist Seely, who is turned into a comic book character by Englund and propelled into a black-and-white world. Transformed into paper, he is ripped to shreds by Englund and his dreaded taloned glove. Now convinced that Wilcox was right, Minter helps her friend battle Englund by returning to the church where his mother committed suicide and summoning forth her spirit. It seems that Englund is afraid of his mother, and with the help of the ghostly nun and the dream child, Wilcox and Minter manage to defeat the fiend once again.

As with the last few entries in the series, A NIGHTMARE ON ELM STREET 5 is yet another collection of cleverly realized nightmare sequences strung together by the thinnest of plots. While the concept of an unborn child being able to channel its nightmares to its mother is interesting, and while the small army of writers (as many as five reportedly contributed to the screenplay, though only three were actually credited) did well in coming up with such a clever device to bring Freddy back after his seemingly final defeat in Part 4, the notion isn't really developed all that well and one wonders what direction the series will take in the inevitable Part 6. Director Stephen Hopkins, another talented newcomer, does an imaginative job in visualizing the bizarre, freely associative nightmares and produces some memorably surrealistic scenes, including a climactic chase on a maze of staircases straight out of M.C. Escher's art (a trick also used to good effect in the now-forgotten 1986 fantasy film LABYRINTH).

Gore fans will be disappointed to discover that the skittish MPAA forced the filmmakers to trim much of the bloodier special-effects work, a trend that has manifested itself during the last several "Friday the 13th" and "Nightmare" films. One promising note, however, is that the character of Freddy Krueger has recovered some of the evil edge he lost in the more recent installments. David Miller, the make-up artist who created Freddy's scarred visage for the original film (only to be replaced by Kevin Yagher for the sequels), is back for Part 5 and has returned Krueger's face to an older, darker, more menacing appearance. In addition, director Hopkins has pushed Freddy back into the shadows, making his appearances less frequent and, therefore, more frightening. Freddy's trademark wisecracks have also been cut back severely, again helping return the character to the stuff of nightmares rather than cult stardom. Englund turns in another solid performance as Krueger, and Lisa Wilcox, returning from Part 4, seems to have gained some confidence as an actress in the interim. The rest of the acting is predictably spotty, with Kelly Jo Minter the only standout in her role as the plucky friend who survives Freddy's onslaught. Though it seems that the series will be stuck in something of a narrative rut for quite some time, at least producers Robert Shaye and Rupert Harvey have the good sense to select strong young directors, keeping the series far more interesting than its chief rival, the moronic "Friday the 13th" films. *(Graphic violence, gore effects, sexual situations, profanity.)*

p, Robert Shaye and Rupert Harvey; d, Stephen Hopkins; w, John Skip, Craig Spector, and Leslie Bohem; ph, Peter Levy; ed, Chuck Weiss and Brent Schoenfeld; m, Jay Ferguson; prod d, C.J. Strawn.

Horror   **(PR:O MPAA:R)**

⊙976-EVIL*
93m Cinetel/New Line c
Stephen Geoffreys *(Hoax)*, Patrick O'Bryan *(Spike)*, Sandy Dennis *(Aunt Lucy)*, Jim Metzler *(Marty Palmer)*, Maria Rubell *(Angella Martinez)*, Robert Picardo *(Mark Dark)*, Lezlie Deane *(Suzie)*, J.J. Cohen *(Marcus)*, Paul Wilson *(Mr. Michaels)*, Greg Collins *(Mr. Selby)*, Darren Burrows *(Jeff)*, Joanna Keyes *(Suzie's Mother)*, Gunther Jensen *(Airhead)*, J.J. Johnston *(Virgil)*, Joe Slade *(John Doe)*, Demetre Phillips *(Sgt. Bell)*, Don Bajema *(Deputy)*, Jim Thiebaud *(Rags)*, Wendy Cooke *(Gang Girl)*, Thom McFadden *(Minister)*, Christopher Metas *(Cashier)*, Roxanne Rogers *(Waitress)*, Bert Hinchman *(Coroner)*.

976-EVIL marks the directorial debut of Robert Englund, better known as Freddy Krueger, the blood-lusting dream killer of the NIGHTMARE ON ELM STREET series. Regrettably, all that Englund manages to deliver here is 93 tedious minutes of uninspired storytelling, a horror film without horror or suspense. Geoffreys, a classic wimp, lives with his fanatically religious mother (veteran genre actress Dennis) and his slick cousin (O'Bryan). Late one evening, after satisfying yet another date, O'Bryan phones his "horrorscope," dialing the title number. What he hears is a brooding voice that instructs him on how to handle difficult situations that are surprisingly like those in which he is involved. Soon afterwards, Geoffreys finds a flier advertising the number, dials it himself, and begins acting on the advice of his horrorscope, eventually becoming addicted to the deadly recordings. Slowly, the messages begin to change Geoffreys. He stands up to his mother and the bullies at school; he even steals his cousin's girl. Reporter Metzler and high-school teacher Rubell become involved when they begin an investigation of the phone service and discover that it has long been disconnected. Transformed into a snarling, drooling demon, Geoffreys slaughters anyone who stands in his way. After more blood is spilled, Metzler and Rubell come face to face with the snarling beast, only to have the floor of his bedroom fall away at their feet, revealing Hell directly below them. After Metzler rescues Rubell, O'Bryan battles Geoffreys, pushing the monster into the abyss below. In the film's predictable coda, the owner of the phone service places Geoffreys' picture in a folder and mumbles evilly about his next victim.

Rambling on for 45 minutes, then coasting towards a climax that is neither exciting nor inventive, 976-EVIL generates little in the way of suspense. Virtually shockless, the first half of the film concentrates on O'Bryan's gambling habits and Geoffreys' attempts to transcend wimpdom. Not until the last reel are we introduced to the full power of the supernatural phoneline, and by that time we are too bored to care. We get the impression that director Englund doesn't care much either, and that he would be much happier making a straight drama. Not only does he fail to capitalize on his premise, but he also leaves many questions unanswered (in one scene in particular, a fish drops, without explanation, from the sky, bringing religious zealot Dennis to her knees). As for the acting, Stephen Geoffreys, playing the same character he portrayed in the much better FRIGHT NIGHT, whines throughout the film; while Patrick O'Bryan is considerably more likable as the tough biker cousin with a heart, though the script doesn't require him to do much more than wear leather and look cool. Even the technical credits are below standard; more than once the film loses its focus, literally. Clearly, Englund, whose storytelling skills are weak and visual sense is nonexistent, has much to learn about being a director. In short, he would be well-advised not to throw away his SAG card just yet. Songs include: "I'm a Wild One" (Steve Marston, Jill H. Roberts, Thomas Chase, Steve Rucker), "I Want You Tonight," "The Only Thing I Really Need" (Marston, Chase, Rucker). *(Violence, adult situations.)*

p, Lisa M. Hansen; d, Robert Englund; w, Rhet Topham and Brian Helgeland; ph, Paul Elliott (Foto-Kem Color); ed, Stephen Myers; m, Thomas Chase and Steve Rucker; art d, David Brian Miller; set d, Nancy Booth; spec eff, Kevin McCarthy and Sandra McCarthy; cos, Elizabeth Gower-Gruzinski; stunts, John Michael Stewart; makeup, Susan Reiner.

Horror   (PR:O MPAA:R)

Ⓥ**NO HOLDS BARRED****½
93m Shane/New Line c
Hulk Hogan *(Rip)*, Kurt Fuller *(Brell)*, Joan Severance *(Samantha Moore)*, Tom "Tiny" Lister *(Zeus)*, Mark Pellegrino *(Randy)*, Bill Henderson *(Charlie)*, Charles Levin *(Ordway)*, David Palmer *(Unger)*, Stan "The Lariat" Hansen *(Neanderthal)*, Armelia McQueen *(Sadie)*, Jesse "The Body" Ventura *(Himself)*, Gene Okerlund *(Announcer)*, Howard Finkel *(Ring Announcer)*.

Pro wrestling star Hulk Hogan portrays Rip Thomas, pro wrestling star, in this comic-book-style "drama." The slimy boss of the World Television Network (Fuller) wants Hogan to wrestle on his station to boost ratings. To this end, he offers Hogan a blank check to ditch the network for which he currently grapples, but Hogan is bound by word and contract to fulfill his obligation to Fuller's rival. Fuller throws a fit, but still doesn't manage to convince Hogan to change networks, so the TV exec instructs his goons to kidnap Hogan instead and take him to a warehouse. This provides an opportunity to show the

kidnapers' car careening wildly through the streets, bursting (in slow motion, naturally) through an empty news kiosk, terrorizing pedestrians, and narrowly missing other vehicles. Hogan, who pounds great dents in the roof in his effort to get out, finally explodes from the car, subdues his kidnapers, and escapes. Still, those visions of ad dollars and ratings points just won't let Fuller rest. When the WTN chief visits a filthy, rough local bar where patrons can indulge in drunken brawls and arguments in an actual ring set up for the purpose, Fuller gets the idea for a hit TV show, "The Battle of the Tough Guys." The show features a weekly contest in which challengers fight the current champ for fame (and lots of money) in an unregulated match. The fights go on the road, providing a welcome change of scenery, and the fierce Lister emerges as champ. In the meantime, Fuller sends lovely marketing exec Severance out to spy on Hogan, who is pointedly contrasted with the blood-thirsty wrestling fans from the bar. He's sophisticated, proving a perfect escort to Severance in a French restaurant. He's brave, foiling a restaurant hold-up (and reducing the place to a shambles). He's got a heart of gold, helping out at kids' wrestling matches on his days off. He's honorable and true, refusing either to take sexual advantage of Severance or to be coerced by Fuller. But he's also a loving brother, so when sibling Pellegrino must be hospitalized after a confrontation with Lister, the TV match is on. It will be the final installment of Fuller's show, with no rules (no holds barred) and the victor recognized as the world's champion Tough Guy. Lister prepares, Hogan helps his brother with his physical rehabilitation exercises, and things seem set for the big showdown when—in a typically diabolical move—Fuller has Severance

(now in love with Hogan) kidnaped and orders Hogan to throw the fight!

NO HOLDS BARRED is paced well, with broadly drawn good guys and bad guys. Two exceptions to this are Fuller's henchmen, played by Charles Levin and David Palmer, who seem too sensitive to do their boss' dirty work at the beginning of the film, though as the story progresses they become sufficiently brutalized to enjoy one of Hogan's violent tantrums before the big fight. More problematic is the murky status of the wrestling fans in the film. The "goodness" of Hulk Hogan's character is so markedly contrasted with the grossness of the wrestling-bar patrons that the film actually appears to be criticizing its star's fans—who are, after all, also the film's audience. Some may find the cartoonish violence excessive; the champion Tough Guy can't be anyone but a good guy, but that doesn't stop him from doling out to his enemies a very painful punishment. *(Violence.)*

p, Michael Rachmil; d, Thomas J. Wright; w, Dennis Hackin; ph, Frank Beascoechea (Metrocolor); ed, Tom Pryor and William Essary; m, Jim Johnston and Richard Stone; prod d, James Shanahan; set d, Lynn Wolverton; stunts, Buck McDancer.

Action/Sports   (PR:C MPAA:PG-13)

Ⓥ**NO RETREAT, NO SURRENDER II***½
(Hong Kong) 92m Seasonal/Shapiro Glickenhous Entertainment c
Loren Avedon *(Scott)*, Max Thayer *(Mac)*, Cynthia Rothrock *(Terri)*, Patra Wanthivanond *(Scott's Fiancee)*, Matthias Hues *(Yuri)*.

While visiting his fiancee (Wanthivanond) and best buddy (Thayer) in Thailand, Avedon is immediately challenged to an unfriendly kickboxing match that sets the

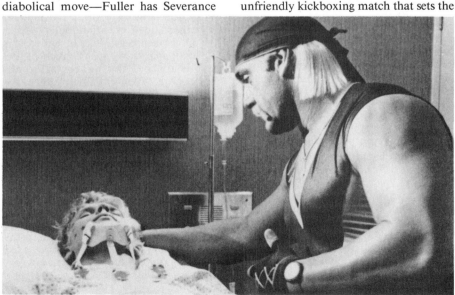

Mark Pellegrino and Hulk Hogan in NO HOLDS BARRED (©New Line).

precedent for much martial-arts wizardry to follow. When he and his girl friend are attacked by murderous thugs, he can't prevent her being kidnaped, but he does waste a few of the hoodlums and winds up on the local most-wanted list. Enlisting Thayer's aid after eluding the cops, Avedon discovers the plot behind the abduction. A longtime supporter of anti-communist movements, Avedon's would-be father-in-law has spent a fortune financing a Cambodian rebellion, an activity that's hardly popular with the Vietnamese, a group of whom have kidnaped Wanthivanond to flush her tycoon father out of hiding. Luckily, Thayer owns a booming black-market business in state-of-the-art artillery and can provide Avedon with firepower against the Reds. With the help of tomboyish, kickboxing Jill-of-all-trades Rothrock, the men are transported by helicopter into the area of jungle where Wanthivanond is held captive. Quicker than you can say "kung fu," the insurgent forces that have agreed to help our trio are totally decimated; next, a group of Buddhist monks turn out to be impostors with lethal feet. While Thayer and Avedon duck shrapnel, Rothrock is captured in the process of trying to steal a boat and escape. Meanwhile, back at the communist camp, Wanthivanond is being tortured by super-sadist Hues, an ultramuscular Soviet warrior who makes the Asian villains look like toy soldiers. Angry that his incarceration of Wanthivanond hasn't brought any response from her father, Hues demonstrates the latest Soviet-sponsored means of eliminating no longer useful prisoners —an alligator pit. The captured Rothrock is brought to camp, and it looks as if both women are doomed to become gator breakfast in the morning. Never fear, however, surveying the perilous situation, our heroes outwit the communist soldiers (who vastly outnumber them) by rigging carefully placed booby traps during the night. The next day, as the girls are dangled over the pit, the good guys swing into action with their ingenious barrage of weaponry. Though Rothrock is killed in the melee, Avedon treats the evil Hues to a fitting death, leaving Avedon, Thayer, and Wanthivanond free to head back to Thailand—presumably to await the screenplay for NO RETREAT, NO SURRENDER III.

Although it has little in common with its predecessor, the teen-oriented NO RETREAT, NO SURRENDER (1986), this adult action feature delivers a variety of bone-crunching, feet-flying thrills and spills. The choreographed chop-socky brutality enlivens the story like a good dance number in a bad musical, and ardent kickboxing fans may be able to overlook the abysmal acting, lapses in narrative logic, and threadbare, tongue-in-cheek dialog. More discriminating viewers will be pained by the screenplay. It's particu-

larly distressing to see the filmmakers trot out the old Red Menace once again as the story's arch-fiend—do we really need another movie that exploits Americans' disappointment over losing the Vietnam War by sending Yank characters back to Southeast Asia to wage victorious mini-wars against dirty Commies? True, the film isn't as blatant in this regard as some of Sylvester Stallone's or Chuck Norris' efforts, but its worn-out kidnaping plot and poor cast combine with the Red-bashing to produce staggeringly inept results. Nonetheless, the smash-or-be-smashed footwork is staged and filmed for maximum effectiveness (particularly Avedon's foot-and-fist duel to the death with the Soviet killing machine), and aficionados of self-defense, Oriental style, will get some kicks from NO RETREAT, NO SURRENDER II. All others are urged to stay away. *(Graphic violence, profanity, adult situations, nudity.)*

p, Roy Horan; d, Corey Yuen; w, Roy Horan, Keith W. Strandberg, and Maria Elene Cellino; ph, Nicholas Von Sternberg and Ma Kam Cheung (CFI Color); m, David Spear.

Action   **(PR:O MPAA:R)**

◉NO SAFE HAVEN*½
91m Vanguard-Soltar/Overseas Filmgroup c

Wings Hauser (*Clete Harris*), Robert Tessier (*Randy*), Robert Ahola (*Carlos*), Marina Rice (*Carol*), Branscombe Richmond (*Manuel*), Tom Campitelli (*Buddy Harris*), Harvey Martin (*Harvey Latham*), Evelyn Moore (*Mrs. Harris*), Chris Douridas (*J.J. Harris*), Nancy Locke (*Roberta*).

Veteran exploitation actor Wings Hauser turns up here in another revenge-driven actioner. At first glance, the poorly titled NO SAFE HAVEN looks a bit different from the standard genre fare, but soon after the plot machinery kicks in it becomes apparent that there wasn't much on the minds of the filmmakers after all. Although only tangentially related to the rest of the film, the opening sequence is actually quite exhilarating. Before the credits roll it is haphazardly established that a pro football player (Campitelli) is being pressured by drug dealers into throwing a game. Rather than give in to their demands, he breaks his arm so that he won't have to play, but when he stupidly goes home to his mother and younger brother, all of them are sadistically murdered. This well-done sequence grinds the rest of NO SAFE HAVEN into gear, as the family's third brother, Hauser, is recalled from Honduras, where he mans a US government listening post. Now that he's alone in the world, Hauser decides to go after the men responsible for killing his family. Calling in a favor from a friend at

headquarters, Hauser learns the whereabouts of the drug lords (conveniently displayed on a computer screen). This and other information with which he is provided make it so easy for Hauser, in fact, that the rest of NO SAFE HAVEN becomes a tedious waiting game. He hunts down and dispatches the evildoers one by one, stopping only to get involved with his brother's girl friend during his off hours. In an attempt to lend the proceedings a little more complexity, the plot requires Hauser to enlist the help of a sidekick (Tessier) for the final confrontation at the South American cocaine farm of the evil Ahola.

Perhaps because Hauser cowrote the screenplay (with his wife, actress Nancy Locke), his performance has the kind of casual, ad-lib quality usually found in productions more disorganized than this one appears to have been. In addition to occasionally meaningless dialog, the film suffers from continuity problems, since Ronnie Rondell's direction doesn't always keep the rather minimal story in focus. The film's three action sequences—the opening, a boat chase, and the climax—are at least coherent. NO SAFE HAVEN is not without a little blatant cruelty, however; in most instances, whenever anyone is about to die, their killer forces them to plead for mercy. On the plus side, the production values are exemplary for the genre, especially Steven McWilliams' photography and Joel Goldsmith's derivative but effective score. Notably, the closing song, "Dream Girl," is as appropriately vulgar as they come. Those videocassette viewers whose systems have stereo capability will also be treated to an outstanding sound mix. Unfortunately, the film's acting is not uniformly strong, with the best performances delivered by the doomed family in the pre-credit sequence. Tom Campitelli is a standout as the pro football player, and Branscombe Richmond also impresses with his earnestly portrayed criminal. NO SAFE HAVEN was held out of distribution for three years after it was made and then given a straight-to-video release. *(Violence, profanity, nudity, substance abuse, adult situations.)*

p, Gary Paul; d, Ronnie Rondell; w, Wings Hauser and Nancy Locke; ph, Steven McWilliams; ed, Drake Sullivan; m, Joel Goldsmith; stunts, Shane Dixon.

Action   **(PR:C MPAA:R)**

◉NOWHERE TO RUN**
85m Concorde c

David Carradine (*Harmon*), Jason Priestley (*Howard*), Jillian McWhirter (*Cynthia*), Kieran Mulroney (*Jerry Lee*), Henry Jones (*Judge Culbert*), Kelly Ashmore (*Saralynn*), Brenda Bakke (*Joanie*), Andy Wood (*Sheriff Tooley*), Sonny Carl Davis (*J.W.*).

NOWHERE TO RUN is such a crowded movie, so filled with subplots and characters, that it should have been called NO ROOM TO BREATHE. A would-be dramatic slice of small-town life, teen comedy, and action thriller all at once, the film has so many elements that it's virtually impossible to describe the story coherently. One can only relate some of the disjointed scenes comprising this mess.

The plot centers around two high-school seniors, Priestley and Mulroney, from the class of 1960 in a small town in Texas. The town is run by a corrupt judge (Jones) and an evil sheriff; the latter is up for re-election and may lose his job. His challenger, Wood, is the father of Priestley's girl friend (McWhirter) and will apparently do anything to make sure he wins. To that end, he releases convicted killer Carradine and frames the incumbent sheriff, making it appear as if his rival accepted money to release the criminal. This crime story is constantly interrupted by the concerns and general teenage high jinks of the class of 1960. Priestley and McWhirter have their first sexual experience, Mulroney (who narrates the movie) is chased by a lovesick girl, two kooky pranksters steal cars and turn garden hoses on people, and everyone worries about dates for the dance and what to put in the 1960 high-school time capsule. Meanwhile, Jones puts Carradine back in jail, Carradine's ex-wife has an affair with his lawyer, Wood makes incestuous moves on McWhirter, Carradine's secret box of money is stolen, a brothel is blown up, and Carradine escapes from custody to seek revenge—all within the film's first 50 minutes. Eventually, Carradine kills a couple of people, Priestley and McWhirter elope, Wood's villainy is exposed, Carradine drinks rat poison, Jones tries to cover up his death, and Mulroney and Priestley blackmail Jones. There's more, believe it or not, but after all of the subplots and characters go through their crowded and complex motions the whole thing leads to one event: the loss of Mulroney's virginity.

Carl Franklin seems to be attempting a stylistic combination of Walter Hill and Bob Clark in his direction here, and that mixture just doesn't work. Hill's action films SOUTHERN COMFORT and, especially, EXTREME PREJUDICE are obvious models for Franklin; Clark is responsible for PORKY'S and PORKY'S II, whose teenage shenanigans NOWHERE TO RUN often lapses into when it's not concerned with criminal doings. It's an odd combination, and the various subplots and many characters only add to the confusion. Franklin is a competent filmmaker, however, and some small, subtle moments (in particular, the very funny entrance of Carradine's ex-wife) raise the film above most exploitation pieces, as do the nice, smoky photography, fine use of deep focus and detail, and effective fade-to-blacks (all of which serve to make NOWHERE TO RUN the best thing Julie Corman has produced in years).

Unfortunately, the basics—like acting and script—are less than tolerable. Carradine sleepwalks through his role and none of the teenagers is memorable. Only Henry Jones seems lively (although, ironically, he plays an old, sickly character). NOWHERE TO RUN wants desperately to be taken seriously, and, schizophrenic as it is, sometimes it almost succeeds. But even the sum of its better parts can't raise the film above its failures. *(Violence, profanity, brief nudity, sexual situations, adult situations.)*

p, Julie Corman; d, Carl Franklin; w, Jack Canson and Nancy Barr (based on a story by Jack Canson); ph, Phedon Papamichael (Foto-Kem Color); ed, Carol Oblath; m, Barry Goldberg; prod d, Sherman Williams; cos, Darcee Olson.

Action   **(PR:O   MPAA:R)**

O

ⓥOFFERINGS*
96m Arista/Southgate c
Loretta Leigh Bowman *(Gretchen)*, Elizabeth Greene *(Kacy)*, G. Michael Smith *(Sheriff Chism)*, Jerry Brewer *(Jim Paxton)*, Richard A. Buswell *(John Radley)*, Rayette Potts *(Young John's Mother)*.

A typical grade Z slice-and-dicer, OFFERINGS replays for the umpteenth time the HALLOWEEN-FRIDAY THE 13TH plot of childhood cruelties that are violently avenged years later by a virtually unstoppable maniac. While this low-budget programmer, made entirely in Oklahoma, has little to recommend it, competent storytelling and a couple of amusing performances elevate it to an almost respectable position in a played-out genre that is saturated with regionally made, amateurish quickies targeted for the drive-in and video markets.

John, a seven-year-old near-genius, loses the ability to speak when his father deserts him and his mother. Having little sympathy for the boy's predicament, his caustic mother (Potts) is disgusted by her son's penchant for torturing his pet turtles, and she expresses her hostility by flicking cigarette ashes into the eggs she prepares for his breakfast. Of the neighborhood children in the Oklahoma suburb where John lives, only a pretty little girl named Gretchen wants to be his friend. The other kids are more than content to torment him at every opportunity. When the children dare the boy to walk the perimeter of a deep local well, he rises to the challenge, but plummets to the bottom when the meanest of the boys gives him a sudden scare. Gretchen, the only one who doesn't run away, tries to get him help. Ten years later, John (now played by Buswell) is a patient at a state mental institution, having murdered and cannibalized his mother after the fall into the well seemingly scrambled his brains. As the film kicks into gear, Buswell kills a nurse, escapes, and heads homeward to dispatch the former playmates responsible for his grotesquely unhappy circumstances. Now high-school seniors, the old neighborhood gang is not only still intact, but paired off into sexually active couples. Still pretty and blonde, Gretchen (Bowman) is the only "good girl" in the group. She seems remarkably unscarred by Buswell's tragedy, with the exception of occasional psychic "flash-forwards" that have afflicted her since the afternoon at the well. Although sheriff Smith is informed of Buswell's escape, the lawman has more pressing concerns, such as confiscating porno magazines from local youngsters so he can peruse them himself. Brewer, a psychologist specializing in violence, offers his expertise to Smith, and familiarizes himself with the details of the grisly case. One by one, Buswell's old nemeses are bludgeoned, shot, knifed, hanged, chain-sawed, or garroted. When he discovers the mutilated corpses hidden in the well, Brewer joins the burgeoning body count. Conveniently for Buswell, Bowman's parents are vacationing in Hawaii, so only she and her best friend (Greene), another alumna of the well incident, are occupying her sprawling house. After each murder, Buswell drops off a memento of the victim (the offerings of the title) at Bowman's front door. Among these souvenirs are a nose, an ear, and an unidentifiable object that Buswell places on a pizza the young women have ordered. When Buswell and Bowman finally confront each other, the ingenue manages to get hold of a gun and shoots the maniac several times, but it isn't until Smith shows up and blasts the killer with a powerful rifle that Buswell finally succumbs. Looking longingly at the appalled Bowman, with a tear falling from his eye, Buswell utters his first and last word, "love."

Boasting little that distinguishes it from the plethora of similar films, OFFERINGS at least progresses in logical sequence—which is more than can be said for most films of this genre. Nevertheless, the movie is flat and predictable. What's more, its lighting is poor, its pacing is flaccid, and Russell D. Allen's music is derivative of the HALLOWEEN score. Although some may find OFFERINGS' regional accents amusing, the performances in general are extremely overblown. However, G. Michael Smith does a respectable Ben Johnson-like turn as the sheriff, and Rayette Potts, who plays young John's mother in the film's opening scene, chews the scenery with relish. With a headful of curlers and a cigarette drooping from her mouth, Potts infuses her one scene with a sense of fun totally absent in the remainder of the film. Obviously operating on a shoestring, producer-director-screenwriter-editor Christopher Reynolds leaves few genre cliches unemployed. But while OFFERINGS doesn't have much to offer the viewer, it's not the worst of its ilk. *(Violence, adult situations.)*

p, Christopher Reynolds; d, Christopher Reynolds; w, Christopher Reynolds; ph, R.E. Braddock (Allied, WBS Color); ed, Christopher Braddock; m, Russell D. Allen.

Horror   (PR:O MPAA:R)

OLD GRINGO**
119m Fonda/COL c
Jane Fonda *(Harriet Winslow)*, Gregory Peck *(Ambrose Bierce)*, Jimmy Smits *(Arroyo)*, Patricio Contreras *(Col. Frutos Garcia)*, Jenny Gago *(La Garduna)*, Jim Metzler *(Ron)*, Gabriela Roel *(La Luna)*, Anne Pitoniak *(Mrs. Winslow)*, Pedro Armendariz Jr. *(Pancho Villa)*, Sergio Calderon *(Zacarias)*, Guillermo Rios *(Monsalvo)*, Samuel Valadez De La Torre *(Pedrito)*, Stanley Grover *(Consul Saunders)*, Josefina Echanove *(Clementina)*, Pedro Damian *(Capt. Ovando)*, Maya Zapata *(Dolores)*, Jose Olivares *(Trinidad)*, Alicia Del Lago *(His Wife)*, Carlos Cardan *(Matias Salazar)*, Evangelina Sosa Martinez *(Guadalupe)*, Hector Rivera *(Ataulfo)*, Victor Carpinteiro *(Hilario)*, Salvador Sanchez *(Floreal)*, Maria Victoria Mondragon *(Old Woman)*, Jose Juan Rodriguez *(Old Man)*, Mario Arevalo *(Casimiro)*, Laurel Lyle *(Librarian)*, Richardson Morse *(Editor)*, Jose Jorge Zepeda *(Administrator of Hacienda)*, Roberto Sosa Martinez *(Lucio)*, Maria Luisa Coronel *(Maria)*, Amelia Zapata *(Juana)*, Mark Kelty, John Williams *(Journalists)*, Arturo Rodriguez Doring *(Mexican Journalist)*, Fernando Moya *(Hotel Clerk)*, Juan Antonio Llanes *(Assistant Hotel Clerk)*, Abel Woolrich *(Tall Soldier)*, Rene Pereyra *(Short Soldier)*, Martin Palomares *(Wounded Man)*, Roberto Ortiz *(Federal Officer)*, Stewart Smith *(Journalist with Glasses)*, Paul Williams *(Cinematographer)*, Steven Spencer *(Assistant Consul)*.

The long-awaited film version of Carlos Fuentes' highly regarded novel, OLD GRINGO chronicles the adventures of an aging Washington, DC, schoolteacher (Fonda) as she ventures to Mexico during the revolution of 1913. Seeking to change her life (she lives with her domineering mother, who collects widow's compensation even though her husband is alive) and live up to her father's expectations, Fonda goes to Mexico intending to teach the children of the revolution. Arriving during the height of the upheaval, she becomes a pawn in the government's attempts to entrap revolutionaries. After witnessing several murders and being caught in the middle of a bloody battle, Fonda becomes involved with the leader of the local rebels (Smits). The film then settles into a love triangle of sorts with the appearance of an old man (Peck) who has arrived on the scene to gratify his romantic notions of life and death. Fonda is drawn to both men, and the fierce, strong Smits becomes her first lover, while the wise and mysterious Peck becomes a father figure. Battles rage, loyalties are tested, and Smits' growing resentment of Peck's beliefs and actions leads him to fulfill Peck's death wish. Shot in the back by Smits, Peck dies in Fonda's arms after she discovers that he is actually the famous writer Ambrose Bierce, whose work she greatly admires. After meeting Pancho Villa and claiming Peck's body, Fonda witnesses the execution of Smits (killed for murdering the American), then rides off into the sunset with Peck's casket.

She has indeed changed her life and affected the lives of Smits and Peck, who have also achieved their goals.

OLD GRINGO is a troubled film with a spotty history. With its release delayed a full year after its initial completion, the film was cut and recut, with voice-over narration added in an effort to make the story more comprehensible. The last-minute additions and changes do seem to have helped some, as the film's final hour moves along rather nicely and the narration helps make up for the lost footage. But the first half-hour of OLD GRINGO is absolutely incomprehensible. It opens with two meaningless sequences in Washington, DC, then, without explanation, moves to Mexico, where an expensive train-crash sequence is thrown in for no apparent reason. After the characters settle into the hacienda, the film starts to make sense, but not before the earlier confusion has already made the viewer very uncomfortable, if not angry.

The movie is lifeless, long, and full of less than stellar performances. Jane Fonda, in particular, is highly unconvincing as the virgin spinster—substituting wide eyes and an open mouth for a more developed performance. In order to show her age, Fonda uses less makeup than usual, but even this seems like a gimmick. A TV actor hopelessly lost on the big screen, Jimmy Smits plays his revolutionary with about as much passion as a wet sock (adding insult to injury, he also wears a ridiculously big moustache). Moreover, there is absolutely no chemistry between Smits and Fonda and their love scene is a big yawn. Gregory Peck, on the other hand, makes a valiant effort with his two-dimensional comic relief role (a part that was to have been played by Burt Lancaster, who was reportedly dropped from the project for insurance reasons). Peck even brings the film to life once or twice, and his scene with a Mexican hooker is especially funny.

Regrettably, Argentine director Luis Puenzo (whose THE OFFICIAL STORY won the Oscar for Best Foreign-Language Film of 1985) seems to be unaware of the importance of Peck's role, and the character's lack of depth takes much of the emotion out of the film. What's left is a nicely photographed, surprisingly trite look at the Mexican Revolution as seen through the wide eyes of a prude. The characters are reduced to meaningless symbols (Fonda wants to start a new life, Peck wants to end his, and Smits wants to change the world) and the situations range from awkward to downright boring (a seemingly endless ballroom dance sequence that contains the phoniest dusk backdrop used in a movie in years). Meanwhile, the film's most intriguing theme—Fonda's need to replace her father and find a lover—is given short shrift in favor of

slickly shot landscapes and cute dialog from Peck.

Although nicely photographed and filmed on a large scale, OLD GRINGO is never as visually impressive as an "epic" should be. Neither as bad as HEAVEN'S GATE nor as good as OUT OF AFRICA, OLD GRINGO is unquestionably beautiful to look at and sincere, but it remains a major disappointment. *(Brief nudity, violence, profanity, adult situations.)*

p, Lois Bonfiglio; d, Luis Puenzo; w, Aida Bortnik and Luis Puenzo (based on the novel *Gringo Viejo* by Carlos Fuentes); ph, Felix Monti (Deluxe Color); ed, Juan Carlos Macias, William Anderson, and Glenn Farr; m, Lee Holdridge; prod d, Stuart Wurtzel and Bruno Rubeo; art d, Scott Ritenour; set d, Steve Saklad and Tom Warren; spec eff, Jesus Duran Galvan; cos, Enrico Sabbatini; chor, Ana Merida; stunts, Mickey Gilbert; makeup, Lee Harman.

Historical   (PR:C MPAA:R)

Ⓥ**OPTIONS****
92m Lance Hool-Silver Lion/Vestron c
Matt Salinger *(Donald Anderson)*, Joanna Pacula *(Princess Nicole)*, John Kani *(Jonas)*, Danny Keogh *(Philippe)*, Tobie Cronje *(Rajid)*, James Keach *(Ed Sloan)*, Alan Pierce *(Raff)*, Siobhan Taylor *(Priscilla)*, Bobby Unser, Eric Roberts, Susan Anton.

In Hollywood, the word *option* refers to a producer's agreement to purchase the rights to a book, a play, or—increasingly—someone's life story for the purpose of turning it into a film. With the rise in made-for-TV moviemaking, a new trend has emerged among the noncreative personnel—known as the "suits"—manning the motion picture and television trade. These days, competition for optioning material based on real-life stories often resembles a feeding frenzy among sharks, and success is usually determined by how far a negotiator will go to achieve a "done deal." In OPTIONS, Salinger is a suit with a mission. Stuffy, parsimonious, and unusually naive, he is also tenacious and successful. Keach, his smarmy boss, has his eye on a prize life story and dispatches Salinger to option it for a TV film. Armed with only his trusty briefcase, a laptop computer, and a suit, Salinger flies to Africa to track down Pacula, a Belgian princess who has abandoned her sensational, tabloid-publicized lifestyle and failed marriage to serve and protect endangered elephants in the wilds of Zambia. Braving the threat of vampire bats and army ants is small stuff compared to the chilling reception Salinger receives when he attempts to get the princess to sell her tale for filming, however, and he returns home with no deal—only to learn that Pacula has been kidnaped and is being held

for ransom by poachers, an event that doubles the value of the rights to her story. Ordered back to Africa, Salinger finds that he now has to face stiff competition from a bevy of other deal-making clones. No one is anxious to rescue Pacula, however, so Salinger ventures to the princess' camp by himself and bribes Kani, Pacula's Zambian aide, to guide him to the poachers' hideout. After a botched escape attempt results in Salinger's being held along with Pacula, it is revealed that the leader of the kidnapers, Keogh, is none other than Pacula's ex-husband. In order to come up with the ransom money, Pacula signs Salinger's option agreement. Subsequently, the two are able to escape, but promptly fall into the hands of a local tribe that mistakes them for poachers, and are finally released only after Salinger manages to negotiate peace in a bitter intertribal quarrel. Salinger's new integrity kindles feelings of respect and affection in Pacula, but the couple must still deal with the pursuing Keogh. After several chase scenes and close shaves, the pair arrive safely at Lusaka airport, where they are greeted by the press and a gleeful Keach. Instead of handing over the signed contract, however, Salinger tears it up. He'll stay in Africa with his new life—and new wife.

OPTIONS has enough basis in truth—there *are* people in Hollywood who devour newspapers and magazines daily for real-life stories they can purchase the rights to—to make its premise potentially good material for satire. Unfortunately, this comedy-by-committee's better moments occur primarily in its opening scenes, leaving only the expansive African vistas, a clumsily developed love story, and repetitive chases to fill out the movie. Among the performers, James Keach provides the best moments as the hero's venal boss, Matt Salinger (REVENGE OF THE NERDS) brings enough quirks to his character to make him lovable as well as laughable, and former model Joanna Pacula (GORKY PARK) manages to do good work within the limitations of her poorly written role. Still, they can't quite save this picture—whose weaker stabs at comedy include a couple of inane cameos by Eric Roberts and Susan Anton that will be seen only by those who are hardy enough to stick with OPTIONS to the very end.

p, Lance Hool, Conrad Hool, and Edgar Bold; d, Camila Vila; w, Edward Decter and John J. Strauss (based on a story by Edward Decter, John J. Strauss, Stephen Doran, Paul Schneider); ph, Tony Imi, James Robb, and Leo Napolitano; ed, Christopher Greenbury; m, Roger Bellon; prod d, Hans Van Den Zanden.

Comedy   (PR:C MPAA:PG)

⊙OUT COLD*

91m Braunstein-Hamady/Hemdale c

John Lithgow *(Dave Geary)*, Teri Garr *(Sunny Cannald)*, Randy Quaid *(Lester Atlas)*, Bruce McGill *(Ernie Cannald)*, Lisa Blount *(Phyllis)*, Alan Blumenfeld *(Lew)*, Fran Ryan *(Atlas' Secretary)*, Morgan Paull, Barbara Rhoades, Tom Byrd, Frederick Coffin, Richard Embardo.

Movies don't come much sloppier than this alleged black comedy from British director Malcolm Mowbray (A PRIVATE FUNCTION). Lithgow stars as a thoroughly dull butcher who is used and abused by nearly everyone, including his business partner, McGill. Married to Garr, for whom he and Lithgow were once rivals, McGill's an old-fashioned kind of guy who constantly philanders and slaps the wife around if she questions him. Fed up with this brutality, Garr hires private detective Quaid to follow her husband and photograph his extramarital activities for use in divorce court. When McGill shows up one night at Lithgow's butcher shop to brag about his latest conquest and then begins taunting Lithgow about his lack of coordination, the situation leads to an impromptu football game between the two men and the violence escalates until Lithgow punches McGill, knocking him out on the floor of a walk-in freezer. Lithgow departs, and Garr (by virtue of a silly plot contrivance) shows up in a black wig. McGill revives and begins verbally abusing her, prompting her to remove the handle from the inside of the freezer door and slam it shut, trapping McGill. When Lithgow shows up for work the next day and finds his partner frozen to death, he believes he's responsible and conceals the body in the freezer, then visits Garr to confess his crime. Garr—who can't just let Lithgow take the rap, because Quaid photographed her entering the butcher shop the night before in the mistaken belief that she was one of McGill's lovers, and anybody less dumb would recognize her in the photos despite the black wig—conspires with Lithgow to get rid of the body. Since McGill was an avid hunter, they haul the body up to the woods and make it look as if McGill froze while stalking prey in the wilds. As Lithgow returns to his truck, however, Quaid (who's been tailing him) stumbles upon the scene. Garr shoots him to death with one of her husband's hunting rifles, tells Lithgow it was an accident, and then persuades him to get rid of Quaid's body. All seems well, with McGill's death ruled an accident a few weeks later and Quaid's corpse not yet discovered, until Garr tries to get Lithgow to sell the butcher shop, of which she is now part-owner. When he refuses, she locks him in the freezer as she did McGill. Quaid's body finally turns up in a surprising and inconvenient (for Garr) location, however, and she is arrested for murder, and Lithgow—who knows his freezer better than Garr—is seen happily alone in his beloved butcher shop at the fadeout.

In these days when dark humor is the norm, pulling off a black comedy is a difficult proposition. Merely giving a serious subject, such as murder, a light treatment isn't nearly enough to elicit laughs, yet OUT COLD settles for that and nothing more. A frozen body with a half-eaten ice cream bar stuck to its forehead is this film's primary comic device, and Mowbray milks it for all its worth—next to nothing. The dialog is humorless, leaving the cast with nothing to do but play it straight, which they do more than competently. In fact, John Lithgow is so convincing as the brooding dullard (he broods as well as anybody in movies today) that the revelation of his duplicity near the film's end is completely unbelievable. Couple the lack of humor with the very obvious plot devices (Garr's wig being just one of many) and failures of continuity (at one point, McGill emerges from the shower with nary a drop of water on him), and OUT COLD amounts to a truly abysmal and disappointing effort from the Hemdale company, which in recent years has produced such quality films as HOOSIERS; PLATOON; and RIVER'S EDGE. The film received a brief and very limited theatrical release on its way to collecting dust on the video shelves. *(Profanity, brief nudity, sexual situations.)*

p, George G. Braunstein and Ron Hamady; d, Malcolm Mowbray; w, Howard Glasser and George Malko (based on a story by Howard Glasser); ph, Tony Pierce-Roberts (CFI Color); ed, Dennis M. Hill; m, Michel Colombier; prod d, Linda Pearl; art d, Lisa Fischer; spec eff, Andy Schoneberg; stunts, Linda Bass.

Comedy   **(PR:O MPAA:R)**

PQ

ⓥPACKAGE, THE**
108m Orion c
Gene Hackman *(Sgt. Johnny Gallagher)*, Joanna Cassidy *(Lt. Col. Eileen Gallagher)*, Tommy Lee Jones *(Thomas Boyette)*, John Heard *(Col. Glen Whitacre)*, Kevin Crowley *(Walter Henke)*, Anatoly Davydov *(Col. Gregor Malekov)*, Chelcie Ross *(Gen. Thomas Hopkins)*, Joe Greco *(Gen. Robert Carlson)*, Dennis Franz *(Milan Delich)*, Pam Grier *(Ruth Butler)*, Ron Dean *(Karl Richards)*, Nathan Davis *(Soviet Press Secretary)*, Ike Pappas *(Himself)*, Marco St. John *(Marth)*, Reni Santoni *(Chicago Police Lieutenant)*, Michael Skewes, Johnny Lee Davenport *(MPs)*, Juan Ramirez, Miguel Nino, Mik Scriba *(Thugs)*, Thalmus Rasulala *(Secret Service Commmander)*, Joe Guzaldo *(Press Secretary Rogers)*, Michael Tomlinson, Cody Glenn, Harry Lennix, Carlos Sanz *(Johnny's Field Soldiers)*, Dianne Timmerman, Charles Mueller *(Backpackers)*, Wilhelm Von Homburg *(West Berlin Police Lieutenent)*, William Musyka, Gary Berkovich *(Soviet Generals)*, Allen Hamilton *(American General)*, Greg Noonan *(Command Post Commander)*, Harry Teinowitz, Don James, Gary Goldman *(Command Post Soldiers)*, Katherine Lynch *(Henke's Wife)*, Mary Seibel *(Henke's Mother)*, Joe D. Lauck *(Sen. Bruce)*, Dick Cusak *(Secretary of State)*, Boris Leskin *(Soviet Foreign Minister)*, Danny Goldring *(Undercover Bum)*, Gregory Alan-Williams *(Col. Woods)*, Jack Kandel *(Soldier with Orders)*, Nick Kusenko *(Gen. Carlson's Aide)*, Tina Gloschenko *(Henke's Girl Friend)*, John Hardy *(Sky Cap)*, Henry Godinez *(Lock-up Police Officer)*, Kathryn Joosten *(Waitress)*, Oksana Fedunszyn *(Eileen's Secretary)*, Ralph Foody *(Building Manager)*, Michael Bacarella *(Paramedic)*, Steve Barbo *(Hotel Police Officer)*, Eddie Bo Smith, Jr. *(Ft. Belvoir Duty MP)*, Greg Goossen *(Soldier in Provost Marshal's Office)*, Dennis Cockurm *(Computer Technician)*, Ivory Ocean *(Washington, DC, Police Officer)*, Metta Davis *(Washington, DC, Witness)*, Alex Ross *(Liquor Store Clerk)*, Will Zahrn, Michael Gaylord James *(Nazi Goons)*, Nancy Baird *(Milan's Wife)*, Gene Barge, Walter Markley *(Secret Service Agents)*, Otto Von Wernherr *(East German Army Lieutenant)*, Hilda McLean *(Old German Woman)*, Leon Samoilovich *(Soviet Security Agent)*, Dmitri Polytnsev, Lana Berkovich *(Translators)*, John D'Amico *(Soviet General Secretary)*, Ray Allen *(United States President)*, Dr. Christine Cassel *(Speaker at Governors Conference)*, Billy Bosco, Chad Smith *(Milan's Sons)*, Phillip Prerost *(Hospital Police Officer)*, Jack Gold *(Governor)*, Ray Starr.

For all its action, suspense, and slick, intricate plotting, THE PACKAGE comes across as a mostly leaden entry in the political-paranoia thriller category. Hackman stars as Sgt. Johnny Gallagher, who, as the film begins, is heading an American security team guarding a summit meeting in Germany between the US president and the Soviet premier. The superpower leaders are about to sign a nuclear disarmament treaty, and military heavyweights on both sides are in an uproar. American colonel Glen Whitacre (Heard) hatches an audacious plot with his Soviet counterparts to sabotage the treaty and keep the world safe for the international military-industrial complex, and Hackman is initially drawn into the conspiracy when he threatens, but fails, to prevent the assassination of an American general who opposes Heard's plans. His involvement deepens when Heard rigs an assignment for Hackman to escort a soldier (Jones), the title "package," back to the States to be court-martialed. As one might guess, Jones is not what he appears to be. Disappearing after Hackman is ambushed in an airport washroom, he resurfaces with a new identity in Chicago, where the American president and the Soviet leader will soon sign the final agreement. As Heard's plot advances, Hackman finds himself framed for murder and on the run while he tries to get to the bottom of the political skullduggery, helped only by his ex-wife (Cassidy) and a Chicago vice cop (Franz).

To give away much more of THE PACKAGE's plot would be to give away most of what little reason there is for seeing it—which is a shame, considering the high-caliber cast director Andrew Davis has assembled. In the past, Davis earned critical praise for not embarrassing himself in films starring marginal acting talents like Chuck Norris (CODE OF SILENCE) and Steven Seagal (ABOVE THE LAW). It would seem, on the evidence of THE PACKAGE, that Davis now finds himself at a loss with *real* actors to direct. Blindly following the pattern of his earlier films, Davis minimizes the movie's reliance on its stars and winds up wasting a good cast on a routine, if well-mounted, thriller.

THE PACKAGE is all plot, with neither a strong point of view behind the camera nor compelling characters in front of it. Lacking those, it's difficult to care much about what happens. Though favorably compared by some to THE MANCHURIAN CANDIDATE and THE DAY OF THE JACKAL, THE PACKAGE lacks the dark, bitter sense of humor in John Frankenheimer's film or Fred Zinnemann's moody, grim tone and artful building of tension in JACKAL. Gene Hackman fails to re-create the magic of his performances in past action films like THE FRENCH CONNECTION, mainly because John Bishop's mechanical script and Davis' workmanlike, undistinguished direction combine to make his character a bit of a bore, as action heroes go. Another, inescapable fact is that Hackman is simply getting too old to be busting his hump in genre exercises like this. Joanna Cassidy and Dennis Franz are similarly stranded in cookie-cutter roles that could have been played by virtually anybody with the same effect. John Heard and Tommy Lee Jones fare somewhat better as the villains, but even they pale badly compared to Edward Fox's title character in JACKAL, for instance, who becomes perversely compelling by virtue of his sheer, utter remorselessness and coldly professional determination. To put it another way, THE PACKAGE continually recalls other genre entries while making no impact on its own —a fatal flaw. Though handsomely wrapped, THE PACKAGE finally has little inside it except stale, hot air. Songs include: "Soul of the Land" (William Olvis, performed by Olvis), "I Don't Know" (Richard Davis, Tony Brown, Wayne Stewart, Steve Grisette, Mark Ohlsen), "God Rest Ye Merry Gentlemen" (Arcangelo Corelli). *(Violence, profanity.)*

p, Beverly J. Camhe and Tobie Haggerty; d, Andrew Davis; w, John Bishop (based on a story by Bishop, Dennis Haggerty); ph, Frank Tidy (Astro Color); ed, Don Zimmerman and Billy Weber; m, James Newton Howard; prod d, Michael Levesque; art d, Colleen Kennedy and Wynn Thomas; set d, William B. Fosser and Bundy Trinz; spec eff, Tom Ryba; cos, Marilyn Vance-Straker; tech, Rear Adm. Eugene Carroll; stunts, Terry Leonard; makeup, Rodger Jacobs.

Political/Thriller   (PR:C MPAA:R)

ⓥPAPERHOUSE**
(Brit.) 92m Working Title/Vestron c
Charlotte Burke *(Anna Madden)*, Elliott Spiers *(Marc)*, Glenne Headly *(Kate)*, Ben Cross *(Dad)*, Gemma Jones *(Dr. Sarah Nichols)*, Sarah Newbold *(Karen)*, Samantha Cahill *(Sharon)*, Jane Bertish *(Miss Vanstone)*, Gary Bleasdale *(Policeman)*, Steven O'Donnell *(Dustman)*, Barbara Keogh *(Hotel Receptionist)*, Karen Gledhill *(Nurse)*.

Horror films have always dealt with fears and feelings that we find too painful or threatening to allow ourselves to consider in a more realistic context. Like dreams, they confront the unthinkable with their own peculiar logic, teasing us into emotional states that may or may not promote self-awareness as they get our palms sweating and hearts pumping. Usually, however, the psychological or sociological insight provided by a horror film (if such insight exists) is below its surface, a symbolic subtext that the viewer pieces together after the fact. In PAPERHOUSE, the root psychological trauma is less veiled, as the pyrotechnics of the horror genre are used to explore the somewhat less fantastic, but no less horrific, dream life of a young girl whose subconscious is working overtime to sort out the confusion and emotional upset dominating her life.

The film opens on the 11th birthday of Burke, whose relationship with her mother (Headly) is strained and whose father (Cross) is away on business, as he often is. At school, Burke passes out and, dreaming, finds herself in the middle of large grassy field that leads to a house like one that she has drawn in her notebook. When Burke is revived, Headly arrives to take her to the doctor, but Burke claims that she faked the fainting spell and her mother makes her go back to school. Burke, however, runs off with a friend to play a game of hide-and-seek, during which she passes out in a boarded-up train tunnel. Again her dreams take her back to the strange house, until she is discovered by a search party of police, taken home, put to bed, and visited by the family physician (Jones), who diagnoses her glandular fever (mononucleosis). Confined to bed, Burke realizes that the house in her dream is the same as the one she has drawn, and when she adds the face of a young boy in the window, she finds Spiers waiting for her in her dream. He is unable to use his legs, but Burke awakens and draws a number of things she thinks will make his life happier—artificial legs, a bicycle, and an ice-cream maker. Burke also draws a picture of her absent father, thinking he will be able to help, but when the expression she gives his face seems too sad, she scratches him out. Cross appears in her dream world, however, blinded and menacing, stalking both his daughter and Spiers. As Burke's fever rages, she slips in and out of her dreams, comforted by Headly and Jones. The latter tells her about another young patient whose name, Marc, is the same as that of Spiers. As Spiers' plight worsens, so, too, does that of the real-life Marc, and Burke begins to believe that her dreams are determining his fate. While the unconscious Burke desperately flees Cross and tries to get Spiers to the sea, her flesh-and-blood father returns home. Eventually Burke recovers, but during a trip to the seaside with her parents she learns that Marc wasn't so lucky, and, falling into a kind of waking dream, she races to a lighthouse like the one in her dreams. Poised on the edge of a cliff, she imagines Spiers returning for her in a helicopter, dropping a rope down that she can't quite reach. Just as it appears as if Burke is about to fall into the sea below, Cross and Headly arrive and rescue her.

With PAPERHOUSE, producers Tim Bevan and Sarah Radclyffe, the founders of Working Title Productions (MY BEAUTIFUL LAUNDRETTE; PERSONAL SERVICES; SAMMY AND ROSIE GET LAID), and director Bernard Rose have arrived at an extremely inventive premise for what is essentially a horror film. Or is it that they have manipulated the genre conventions of horror to make a psychological drama? Both; unfortunately, their execution is not the equal of their conceptual inventiveness. Eschewing standard gore and violence, opting for less sensational situations, and refusing to round up the usual suspects, they have explored the troubled subconscious of a young girl through a horror film approach, attempting to exploit the genre's inherent tension and finding a frightening enough monster in a father whose absence has made him unfamiliar and threatening. Working from a screenplay by Matthew Jacobs based on Catherine Storr's book *Marianne Dreams*, Rose creates plenty of tension in the early going, but after the initial shock of his approach wears off the film becomes less frightening, without a commensurate gain in character development or psychological insight. Further, PAPERHOUSE is most effective when it suggests that its fantastic goings-on are merely the result of Burke's dream logic, and when the film begins to propose that somehow her dreams *have* spilled over into reality it compromises its psychological plausibility. Director Rose began his career making music videos (including "Relax" for Frankie Goes to Hollywood and "Red, Red Wine" for UB40), and while this film doesn't suffer from the glossiness that has marred the efforts of some video directors who have turned their hands to the big screen, its pacing does begin to fall apart about halfway into the film.

Although Charlotte Burke—chosen from 1,500 would-be Annas and making her acting debut—is convincingly innocent and confused, the other actors contribute less to the proceedings. Glenne Headly (MAKING MR. RIGHT; DIRTY ROTTEN SCOUNDRELS) of Chicago's famed Steppenwolf Theatre is hampered by a post-filming decision to make her erstwhile American character English and to have her loop her character's dialog in two days, and doesn't give the kind of performance she has shown to be capable of on the stage and in other film work; still, she is far more successful than Ben Cross (CHARIOTS OF FIRE), who appears to be sleepwalking even when he's not. In the final analysis, the makers of PAPERHOUSE deserve a great deal of credit for the risks they have taken in adopting an unconventional approach to subject matter that isn't particularly big box office to begin with. Unfortunately, the realization of PAPERHOUSE simply isn't as interesting as the idea of PAPERHOUSE. (Violence.)

p, Sarah Radclyffe and Tim Bevan; d, Bernard Rose; w, Mathew Jacobs (based on the novel *Marianne Dreams* by Catherine Storr); ph, Mike Southon (Technicolor); ed, Dan Rae; m, Hans Zimmer and Stanley Myers; prod d, Gemma Jackson; art d, Frank Walsh and Anne Tilby; spec eff, Alan Whibley; cos, Nic Ede; stunts, Gareth Milne; makeup, Jenny Shircore.

Horror   (PR:C   MPAA:PG-13)

ⓋPARENTHOOD*½**
124m Imagine Ent./UNIV c
Steve Martin *(Gil Buckman)*, Tom Hulce *(Larry Buckman)*, Rick Moranis *(Nathan)*, Jason Robards Jr. *(Frank Buckman)*, Martha Plimpton *(Julie)*, Mary Steenburgen *(Karen Buckman)*, Dianne Wiest *(Helen)*, Keanu Reeves *(Tod)*, Harley Kozak *(Susan)*, Leaf Phoenix *(Garry)*, Dennis Dugan *(David Brodsky)*, Eileen Ryan *(Marilyn)*, Helen Shaw *(Grandma)*, Jasen Fisher *(Kevin)*, Paul Linke *(George Bowman)*, Alisan Porter *(Taylor)*, Zachary Lavoy *(Justin)*, Ivyann Schwan *(Patty)*, Alex Burrall *(Cool)*, Lowell Ganz *(Stan)*, Rance Howard *(Dean at College)*, Max Elliott Slade *(Young Gil)*, Clint Howard *(Lou)*, Lamont Lofton *(Fotomat Clerk)*, Erika Rafuls *(Amy)*, Jordan Kessler *(Matt)*, Billy Cohen *(Eddie)*, Isabel Cooley *(Barbara Rice)*, Greg Gerard *(Doctor Lucas)*, Paul Keeley *(Kevin, age 21)*, Walter Von *(Opposing Coach)*, W. Bruce O'Donoghue *(Umpire)*, Claudio Jacobells, Hilary Mattews *(College Students)*, Sherry Ferguson *(Screaming Coed)*, Todd Hallowell *(Track Official)*, Maxie Pontius *(Safety Man at Track)*, Richard Kuhlman *(Young Frank)*, Brittany Bouck, Jonathan Bouck, Michael Mickens, Aspen Autrey *(Dwarfs)*, Lloyd Cleek *(Miles)*, Dana Mark *(Audrey)*, Louisa Marie, Cyndi Vicino *(Teachers)*, Steve Zurk *(Highway Policeman)*, Emil Felski *(Doctor at Hospital)*, Charmin Talbert *(Nurse at Hospital)*, Julie Lander *(Student in Hallway)*.

Occasionally corny, yet thoroughly entertaining, PARENTHOOD is a movie by, for, and about parents. Four generations are portrayed by an all-star cast, delivering a lesson in child-rearing worthy of Dr. Spock. Robards plays the father of Martin, Wiest, Kozak, and Hulce, all adults with children of their own. Still bothered by his father's inattentiveness to him during his childhood, Martin undertakes all activities involving his kids with zeal. Steenburgen, Martin's wife, understands her husband's determination to be a good father but tries to help him realize that it won't make their children perfect. Wanting to spend more time with his family, Martin finds himself under fire from his boss, who thinks overtime is the measure of one's value to the company. Also obsessed about his offspring is Moranis, Kozak's husband, who has their toddler daughter studying karate, Spanish, long division, and Kafka. Kozak, on the other hand, would like Moranis to devote his energy to restoring the romance in their marriage and eventually gets fed up and leaves him. Wiest, meanwhile, is a harried divorcee with two recalcitrant teenagers. Plimpton, Wiest's 16-year-old daughter, moves out after an argument over her boy friend (Reeves), then returns a short time later married to him. Despite persistent fighting between mother and newlywed husband and wife, Reeves turns out to be a helpful addition to the family, providing much-needed male companionship and sex education for 13-year-old Phoenix, who skulks silently around the house. Robards' youngest and favorite child is Hulce, an irresponsible drifter who shows up after a long absence with a son and a $21,000 gambling debt. When gamblers vow to kill Hulce, he takes off for good, leaving his son behind. But although the family loses a member, it soon gains several more, as by the movie's end, Steenburgen, Plimpton, and Wiest (who marries Phoenix's teacher) have had babies, and Kozak, reunited with Moranis, is pregnant.

PARENTHOOD's coscreenwriters, Ron Howard, Lowell Ganz, and Babaloo Mandell—the fathers of 14 children in all —have produced a funny, poignant script with very contemporary humor. It is the acting, though, that shines brightest in the movie. Rarely has such a formidable array of talent been assembled for one film, and theirs is truly an ensemble effort. While the Martin/Steenburgen household gets the most screen time, all the stories are well developed and interwoven. In an earnest performance, Steve Martin displays only glimpses of his formerly manic persona; Mary Steenburgen is a lovely combination of strength and tenderness; and Dianne Wiest's quirkiness works perfectly, as she evokes both laughs and tears. Even the usually nerdish Rick Moranis is endearingly cute. Jason Robards, who one would think had already brought all he could to patriarch roles, is as impressive as if this were new territory for him, while Keanu Reeves and Harley Kozak admirably hold their own among their better-known costars. The children are also all well cast, with Zachary Lavoy and Ivyann Schwan, the little blonds, especially adorable.

With SPLASH and COCOON—both of which had their touching moments—and now PARENTHOOD, director Howard has established himself as the king of heartwarming movies. PARENTHOOD does cross the border into schmaltz a number of times, such as when Martin's son (Jasen Fisher) makes a miraculous catch (in slow motion, of course) to win a Little League game and when Moranis woos back Kozak with an off-key rendition of "Close to You" while the high-school class she teaches looks on. Other incidents, like Wiest's pregnancy, teeter on improbability. Still,

the movie runs the gamut of realistic emotions as it depicts every stage in a parent-child relationship. One scene or another is bound to hit home with the parents who see the film. Moreover, there is much in PARENTHOOD that should reassure them. It is the quiet grandma (Helen Shaw) who offers the moral of the story: that the ups and downs of raising a family are not to be feared. A roller coaster may be more discomforting than a merry-go-round, she tells Martin, but you get more out of riding the roller coaster. Try as they might, parents—like those in the movie—can't control everything their kids do. All they can do is love them. Because of the movie's empathy with their experiences, most mothers and fathers will find something to love in PARENTHOOD. *(Profanity, adult situations.)*

p, Brian Grazer; d, Ron Howard; w, Lowell Ganz and Babaloo Mandel (from a story by Lowell Ganz, Babaloo Mandel, Ron Howard); ph, Donald McAlpine (Deluxe Color); ed, Michael Hill and Daniel Hanley; m, Randy Newman; prod d, Todd Hallowell; art d, Christopher Nowak; set d, Nina Ramsey; spec eff, Kevin Harris and Bob Cooper; cos, Ruth Morley; stunts, Artie Malesci; makeup, Fern Buchner.

Comedy   **(PR:C MPAA:PG-13)**

Steve Martin in PARENTHOOD (©Universal).

ⓥPARENTS***
82m Great American/Vestron c
Randy Quaid *(Nick Laemle)*, Mary Beth Hurt *(Lily Laemle)*, Sandy Dennis *(Millie Dew)*, Bryan Madorsky *(Michael Laemle)*, Juno Mills-Cockell *(Sheila Zellner)*, Kathryn Grody *(Miss Baxter)*, Deborah Rush *(Mrs. Zellner)*, Graham Jarvis *(Mr. Zellner)*, Helen Carscallen *(Grandmother)*, Warren Van Evera *(Grandfather)*, Wayne Robson *(Lab Attendant)*, Uriel Byfield *(Little Boy)*, Mariah Balaban *(Little Girl)*, Larry Palef *(Announcer)*.

Having settled into their home in the suburbs during the late 1950s, the Laemles (Quaid and Hurt) offer their young son (Madorsky) a continual display of their ravenous sexual appetites, but pay little attention to him, except to wonder why he won't eat his meat. Madorsky stumbles into a bizarre sexual interlude between his parents under a sunlamp and subsequently suffers a series of bloody nightmares, but when he tries to discuss them with his mother she dismisses them. Madorsky's disturbing dreams then surface in some drawings he makes at school, earning him a visit with ineffectual school psychiatrist Dennis. Back at home, he accuses his mother of always serving leftovers for dinner (rather than the entrees that would be their source), then surreptitiously follows his father to the company plant where he works, and after a frightening trip to the cellar of his own house concludes that his parents are slipping bodies out of the company morgue so they can carve them up into steaks and sausages and eventually serve them for dinner. He frantically relates these findings to a skeptical Dennis, who takes him on a tour of his cellar to dispel his fears. Instead, a corpse falls at their feet and Madorsky flees, leaving Dennis to fend for herself, and within moments she is stabbed by an unseen assailant. Later, when Madorsky confronts his parents with his discovery of their cannibalism, Quaid decides to do away with his son. Hurt's maternal instincts intervene, and in the subsequent eruption of violence and frenzied sexuality, Hurt is mortally wounded and Quaid stalks his son—who, at film's end, seems secure at the home of his kindly grandparents, but must still contend with a platter of steak sandwiches.

PARENTS, actor Bob Balaban's directorial debut, is a study of a repressed young boy who is exposed for the first time to his parents' sexuality. Balaban uses the fantastic plot metaphorically, both to convey the intricacies and untapped recesses of the child's mind and to give a sense of his larger predicament. While his passive, antisocial personality worries his teachers and alienates him from his peers, his parents ignore their son's problems, intent upon pursuing Middle American dreams and conforming to their new surroundings. Attempts to communicate with his mother are met with disinterest; his father is a remote, disconcerting threat; and the Oedipal dynamics are played out within a narrative that explicitly pits the child against his parents' all too carnal natures.

PARENTS concentrates on the child's Freudian pathology so heavily, however, that it loses sight of its story and becomes a confused collection of isolated vignettes. In adopting the boy's single-minded perspective, it prevents its characters from developing, so that Quaid hovers and glowers, Hurt giggles and flirts, and Madorsky lurks in dark recesses without variation from beginning to end. By the time the climactic confrontation between Quaid and Madorsky occurs, the father's constant threats have become so predictable that he no longer causes fear, either in his son or in the audience. Balaban clearly demonstrates a talent for visuals, however; his swooping, gliding camera indicates a sure and promising directorial hand. What he needs now is a script to match. *(Graphic violence, adult situations, sexual situations.)*

p, Bonnie Palef-Woolf; d, Bob Balaban; w, Christopher Hawthorne; ph, Ernest Day and Robin Vidgeon (Filmhouse Color); ed, Bill Pankow; m, Jonathan Elias, Angelo Badalamenti, and Sherman Foote; art d, Andris Hausmanis; set d, Michael Harris; spec eff, Gord Smith; cos, Arthur Rowsell; stunts, Rick Forsyth; makeup, Linda Gill.

Comedy/Horror   (PR:C MPAA:R)

PENN & TELLER GET KILLED**½
89m Lorimar/WB c
Penn Jillette *(Penn)*, Teller *(Teller)*, Caitlin Clarke *(Carlotta)*, David Patrick Kelly *(Fan)*, Leonardo Cimino *(Ernesto)*, Christopher Durang *(Jesus Freak)*, Alan North *(Old Cop)*, Jon Cryer.

PENN & TELLER GET KILLED left a bad taste in the mouths of many critics, whose negative reactions ranged from scratching their heads in befuddlement to expressing outrage that the director of BONNIE AND CLYDE, Arthur Penn, would lend his name and talents to an enterprise so supposedly beneath him. During an appearance on "Late Night with David Letterman," Penn Jillette—one-half of the popular comedy-magic team who cowrote the screenplay for the film in which they star—casually conceded that even the releasing studio hated PENN & TELLER GET KILLED. Warner Bros. seemed to prove his point by releasing the film, with almost no advertising, in a single theater in Los Angeles.

Still, it's hard to imagine a more fortunate conspiracy of creative talents than Penn, Penn, and Teller. At the very least, they deserve credit for refusing to compromise their approach for the sake of box-office success or critical laurels. More than that, they have made a deeply subversive film, a disillusionist work in an era when illusion permeates American culture. In our "kinder and gentler" times, PENN & TELLER GET KILLED is comedy that plays for keeps. Playing themselves, Penn & Teller start the film with an appearance on a TV program that's an insipid cross between "Saturday Night Live" and "Late Night with David Letterman." (Actually, the act the duo performs here is similar to one they performed on the Letterman show—a series of Grand Guignol gags in which the two bloodily assault each other with various sharp instruments, revealing the methods behind their madness as they go, as is their trademark). During the interview segment, Penn confesses that life has gotten a little dull lately and irresponsibly wishes that someone would liven things up by trying to kill him. In fact, things do get livelier as Penn and Teller each hatch elaborate plots against the other, with the gags that follow escalating in scale and potential violence. The action takes a darker turn when it seems that someone really is trying to kill Penn. The ending gets one of the film's biggest, bitterest laughs, not by any trick of Penn's or Teller's doing (they've already fulfilled the title's promise by this point), but by the presence of the Bee Gees' "I Started a Joke" on the soundtrack. In the end, PENN & TELLER GET KILLED becomes a joke that has gotten out of hand. Indeed, it may well have been out of hand from the start.

During its early sections, PENN & TELLER GET KILLED recalls the films of W.C. Fields and the Marx Brothers, acting as a showcase for the illusionist comedians, offering only the wispiest of plots to support them. But the film's covert subject—the way in which our culture has turned violence into entertainment—lends even the early passages an odd gravity. The jokes are cartoonish, but they hinge on everything from guns, scalpels, and knives to impalement by power tools and "psychic surgery" (literally performed by hand, without benefit of medical instruments or anesthesia). The film turns ominous by following its premise to its logical conclusion—that our cultural fascination with violence represents a kind of a national death wish.

In recent years, director Arthur Penn has turned more to what he has called "entertainments" and away from self-consciously serious subjects. But he has never made a frivolous film. In TARGET, within the context of an international spy thriller, he examined the complex roles families play; in DEAD OF WINTER, he turned a tricky, though conventional, lady-in-distress melodrama into a compelling study of the horror of loss of identity. In PENN & TELLER GET KILLED, he looks at entertainment as if it were a cultural Rorschach test, arriving at a suitably grim diagnosis. In this way PENN & TELLER GET KILLED connects with Penn's BONNIE AND CLYDE—a film, the director has always maintained, about how the culture of Depression-era America turned two bloodthirsty punks into media celebrities. The director could not have found a better vehicle for his cinematic ruminations than Penn & Teller, who, to promote their 1988 nationwide tour, used a TV commercial in which Penn teased potential ticket buyers with the possibility that he might screw up one night and actually kill Teller. Like Arthur Penn, Penn & Teller are loved by some and hated by others, but their power to provoke is undeniable. Their movie, like their act, is very serious fun, and most definitely not for all tastes. But those who have grown weary of saccharine, big-budget studio fantasies will find much to mull over in this strange, challenging, decidedly dark, but ultimately rewarding farce. And, lest we forget, it *is* funny—Penn's misadventures at an airport security checkpoint alone are worth the price of admission, and Teller has at least one golden moment when he shows a collection of journalists what he hates about most magic acts. *(Violence.)*

p, Arthur Penn and Timothy Marx; d, Arthur Penn; w, Penn Jillette and Teller; ph, Jan Weincke; ed, Jeffrey Wolf; m, Paul Chihara; prod d, John Arnone; cos, Rita Ryack.

Comedy   (PR:O MPAA:R)

PERFECT MODEL, THE**½
89m Chicago Cinema c
Stoney Jackson *(Stedman Austin)*, Anthony Norman McKay *(Mario Sims)*, Liza Cruzat *(Linda Johnson)*, Tatiana Tumbtzen *(Crystal Jennings)*, Catero Colbert *(David Johnson)*, Reggie Theus *(Dexter Sims)*, Morgan Proctor *(Howard Grey)*, Darryl Roberts *(Robert Darryls)*, Nadiera Bost *(Waitress)*, Barbara Falkenberg *(Director)*, Jim Zulevich *(Waiter)*, Tony Smith *(Gunman)*, Senuell Smith *(Kuda)*, Pat Bowie *(Aerobics Studio Owner)*, Denise Simon *(Cynthia)*, Dainese Gault *(Gail)*, Illeana Jordan *(Devin)*, Delia Inoue *(Movie Actress)*, Michael "King" Wood *(Pawn Shop Clerk)*, Karen Jones *(Girl at Party)*, Ray Thompson *(Alexis Abercrombie Fitzwater Dubois III)*, Pura Martinez *(Portia)*, Hildar Garrison *(Tanya Williams)*, Sylvia Mathis, Cia Richardson *(Girls in Bar)*, Kim Sheridan *(Exotic Dancer)*, Roxanne *(Herself)*, Paulette Tyler *(Edie)*, Twalla Jones *(Annette)*, Laura Cerone *(Cindy)*.

In the wake of the successes of Spike Lee and Robert Townsend comes Darryl Roberts, a 27-year-old independent filmmaker from Chicago making his feature debut with THE PERFECT MODEL. Working with a shoestring budget ($31,000) and a crew on deferred salaries, Roberts produced, directed, and wrote this heartfelt film, which he hoped would present a "more realistic portrait of blacks in the cinema," and, with neither Lee's militance nor Townsend's satire, delivered an honest and realistic look at a man and woman from very different sides of the tracks. One of them is McKay, a Hollywood actor who returns home to Chicago to act in a new project. Although he has had a taste of fame and runs with an elite crowd, he has not forgotten his roots in the ghetto, just chooses to ignore them. His childhood friend is Jackson, a wheeling and dealing beauty pageant promoter who uses his contest as a means to bed aspiring models, and whose upcoming "Perfect Model" contest McKay has agreed to host. When McKay catches 12-year-old Colbert breaking into his car, he drags the little thief home instead of calling the police. At the boy's home, one of a row of low- to middle-income brick bungalows, McKay learns that both of the youngster's parents have been killed, leaving his older sister, Cruzat, in charge and struggling to make ends meet. An aerobics instructor with dreams of opening her own dance studio, Cruzat is thrilled to meet the Hollywood star, and, after some cat-and-mouse games, goes out on a date with him. McKay genuinely seems to like Cruzat, but finds her an embarrassment around his high-powered friends. Ordering fried chicken and Riunite, Cruzat seems too much of a ghetto girl and an easy butt of the "elite's" jokes. Torn, McKay turns to his older brother (Orlando Magic guard Reggie Theus) for advice, and decides to follow his heart. He persuades Cruzat to enter Jackson's "Perfect Model" contest, but when Jackson fears that this low-class girl might win, he tries to force her to withdraw and, at the same time, to ruin her relationship with McKay. Before the finale, McKay sees the light and, although Cruzat drops out of the contest, he sticks with his girl. Realizing that she is a winner in her own right, he helps her get her start with her own dance studio.

THE PERFECT MODEL is all heart. Riddled with technical problems and showing only the most basic understanding of filmmaking skills, it's an imperfect film that manages to be a "perfect model" for those independent filmmakers who *must* make a feature film at all costs. Judged only on the basis of its maker's intentions and devotion, THE PERFECT MODEL rates far higher than most slapdash Hollywood product. Unfortunately, just about everything that could be wrong with a film is wrong here. Shooting with a non-union crew and assisted by a number of Chicago film school students, Roberts brought all the loose ends together for a two-week shoot—on only a portion of his eventual $31,000 budget. Unable to afford location permits, they shot the film "guerrilla" style, hoping to catch the needed shots before police or authorities arrived. Roberts, who majored in marketing rather than film, learned technique from film books and by viewing in theaters. Working as a producer of celebrity parties and events in Chicago, he met a number of local celebrities and secured the involvement of Theus (formerly of the Chicago Bulls); Dainese Gault (wife of former Chicago Bear wide receiver Willie Gault), who has a small role; and Tatiana Tumbtzen (the sexy star of Michael Jackson's video "The Way You Make Me Feel"), who plays a glamourous, snobby Hollywood actress. The rest of the cast performs nobly, though the script and direction are less than exciting. Only young Catero Colbert seems completely in control of his character, cracking jokes effortlessly and adding some humorous life to the proceedings.

Riding on hometown favoritism, THE PERFECT MODEL was released in nine theaters across Chicago in the hope that the film could reach the audience that flocked to see SHE'S GOTTA HAVE IT; SCHOOL DAZE; HOLLYWOOD SHUFFLE; and Keenan Ivory Wayans' I'M GONNA GIT YOU SUCKA! The spark never ignited, however, and THE PERFECT MODEL quickly disappeared from sight. *(Nudity, violence, profanity.)*

p, Darryl Roberts; d, Darryl Roberts; w, Darryl Roberts, Theresa McDade, and Ivory Ocean; ph, Sheldon Lane; ed, Tom Miller; m, Joe Thomas and Steve Grissette; prod d, Phillipe and Darryl Roberts; art d, Simmie Williams; set d, Phillipe; cos, Wilson Harris; chor, Rosemary Barnes; makeup, Phillipe.

Drama   **(PR:C MPAA:R)**

ⓥ**PET SEMATARY***½
103m PAR c

Dale Midkiff *(Dr. Louis Creed)*, Fred Gwynne *(Jud Crandall)*, Denise Crosby *(Rachel Creed)*, Blaze Berdahl *(Ellie Creed)*, Miko Hughes *(Gage Creed)*, Brad Greenquist *(Victor Pascow)*, Michael Lombard *(Irwin Goldman)*, Susan Blommaert *(Missy Dandridge)*, Stephen King *(Preacher)*, Mara Clark *(Marcy Charlton)*, Kavi Raz *(Steve Masterton)*, Mary Louise Wilson *(Dory Goldman)*, Andrew Hubatsek *(Zelda)*, Liz Davies *(Girl at Infirmary)*, Kara Dalke *(Candystriper)*, Matthew August Ferrell *(Jud as a Child)*, Lisa Stathoplos *(Jud's Mother)*, Elizabeth Ureneck *(Rachel as a Child)*, Chuck Courtney *(Bill Baterman)*, Peter Stader *(Timmy Baterman)*, Richard Collier *(Young Jud)*, Chuck Shaw *(Cop)*, Dorothy McCabe, Mary R. Hughes *(Seatmates)*, Eleanor Grace Courtemanche *(Logan Gate Agent)*, Donnie Greene *(Orinco Driver)*, Lila Duffy *(Budget Clerk)*, John David Moore *(Hitchhike Driver)*, Beau Berdahl *(Ellie Creed II)*.

A crushing disappointment for fans of the popular Stephen King novel on which it is based, PET SEMATARY takes a potentially rich and deeply disturbing premise—the collapse of the American family—and turns it into just another shock-a-minute horror show, with little in the way of character development, thematic exploration, or even simple suspense. Ineptly directed by Mary Lambert (SIESTA, several Madonna rock videos), the film begins as a young doctor, Midkiff; his wife, Crosby; and their two children, Berdahl and Hughes, move from Chicago to Maine. Although they are excited about the beautiful old home they are moving into, it turns out that the property faces a busy highway, where huge gasoline tanker-

Dale Midkiff in PET SEMATARY (©Paramount).

trucks zoom by at high speeds. Indeed, little Hughes, just a toddler, nearly gets splattered by one such vehicle even before the family steps into the house. Luckily, the boy is saved by friendly neighbor Gwynne, an elderly man who has lived across the street his entire life. The highway, it turns out, is so dangerous that hundreds of area pets have been killed on it, and Gwynne shows his new neighbors the pet cemetery behind their house where the local children have buried their beloved animals. All of this is a little too much for Midkiff and Crosby, both of whom have a great deal of trouble accepting death. Shortly thereafter, Midkiff sees a patient in the emergency room, a young jogger (Greenquist) who has been hit by a truck and gotten his skull split open. Despite Midkiff's valiant efforts to save him, the young man dies, only to come back as an increasingly decayed ghost-cum-guardian angel who warns the doctor not to meddle with the supernatural. Shaken, Midkiff tries to ignore his visions of Greenquist. When Crosby and the children go back to Chicago to visit her parents for Thanksgiving, Midkiff—who stays behind because he doesn't get along with his in-laws—is horrified to discover that his daughter's cat, named Church, has been hit by a truck. Sensing that little Berdahl would be terribly distraught by Church's death, Gwynne guides Midkiff *past* the pet cemetery and into an actual Indian burial ground that possesses magical qualities. Under Gwynne's supervision, Midkiff buries the cat there and, later that night, Church returns from the dead. Unfortunately, the feline has become vicious and smells bad, and his eyes glow in the dark; Gwynne later relates that as a child, he buried his beloved dog in the cemetery, only to have it, too, return as a frothing beast and die again the next day. While the cat is vicious around Midkiff, it seems to be the same old Church to his daughter—although she notices the cat's stench. Soon, predictably, little Hughes wanders onto the highway while the family picnics, and gets run over by a truck. After the funeral, Crosby and Berdahl go back to visit Chicago, leaving the distraught Midkiff behind. Unable to accept his son's death, Midkiff ignores the warnings of both Greenquist and Gwynne (who relates, in flashback, a rather nasty story from just after WW II, when an overwrought local father buried his son who was killed in the war in the Indian burial ground, only to have him return as a slobbering, murderous zombie), removes Hughes' body from its grave, and reburies him in the Indian burial ground. At the same time, in Chicago, Crosby is haunted by Greenquist, who tells her to return to Maine and stop her husband. She hops on the next plane and heads for home. Meanwhile, Hughes has indeed returned from the dead, but as a homicidal little tyke who

steals one of his father's scalpels to kill Gwynne and eventually his own mother before doing battle with Midkiff. Realizing he has made a mistake, Midkiff fills several syringes full of lethal doses of something-or-other and chases his boy around Gwynne's house, finally dispatching the kid with a shot to the neck and then setting the house on fire. However, having learned little from the awful experience, Midkiff takes his wife's corpse and buries *her* in the Indian burial ground; and yes, she too comes back as a nasty-looking zombie with pus oozing out of one eye. Driven mad by the whole thing, Midkiff passionately kisses his distinctly undead bride, who, during their embrace, reaches for a large knife and kills him.

While the King source material forcefully taps into some deep-seated fears—such as repressed feelings of professional, marital, and parental inadequacy and the inability to accept death as a fact of life—PET SEMATARY squanders its potential to be a deeply affecting and evocative horror film through the ham-handed direction of Lambert, who continually goes for visceral shocks at the expense of the more deeply disturbing psychological themes inherent in the material. Indeed, King fills his script with some truly frightening and taboo situations, but Lambert's obviousness is merely offensive and, at times, unintentionally laughable. Having been originally slated for George Romero, who then had to bow out of the project after being committed to it for years, PET SEMATARY was given to the relatively inexperienced Lambert. After SIESTA's critical and commercial failure, Lambert apparently was determined to put any doubts about her abilities to rest by delivering a truly frightening commercial horror film; unfortunately, she may have been a bit too enthusiastic, for many of PET SEMATARY's more grotesque gore effects wound up on the cutting room floor, further damaging an already poorly paced movie. As adapted by King and directed by Lambert, the motivations and development of the characters are simply too vague and perfunctory to be very effective. This is only aggravated by the bland performances of Dale Midkiff and Denise Crosby, who seem incapable of conveying the sort of nuance necessary to make the relationship between their characters involving. Because the viewer is not made to feel for the family or their loss as intensely as needed to make the story work, their subsequent actions, especially Midkiff's—considering the dire warnings of Greenquist and the vivid tales of terror from Gwynne (shown in poorly staged flashbacks)—seem distinctly stupid. Indeed, the characters become so unsympathetic that one almost eagerly anticipates their deaths.

Although the film is clumsily directed, some of the blame for its failure must also fall on King himself, whose script has too many holes in it to satisfy. One of the narrative's key flaws concerns Gwynne's seemingly ambiguous character: if he has had nothing but disastrous experiences with the burial ground and knows full well its potential for evil, why does he show Midkiff the place at all? A second nagging problem is the ghost played by Greenquist: beyond the wholly unconvincing reason cited by the ghost himself—that "you tried to help me"—why is he so determined to aid Midkiff and family? Who sent him and why? This is never sufficiently explained, although Brad Greenquist's nicely realized performance almost deflects such doubts. There are also several inadequately developed subplots: the extreme tension between Midkiff and his father-in-law is never explained; the suffering and subsequent suicide of a housekeeper is hastily introduced and then dismissed; and Crosby's grotesque flashbacks to her sister's being made a mad monster by crippling spinal meningitis are so overwrought and bluntly horrible (mostly due to Lambert's insensitive direction) as to be extremely offensive—but not at all frightening. In addition, as the film builds to its climax, King plunders Stanley Kubrick's adaptation of his own book *The Shining* by duplicating that film's sequence in which a character (Scatman Crothers in THE SHINING) receives a psychic message from far away, is motivated to make a hasty return entailing a long and difficult trip, and is killed in a matter of minutes after his arrival—this time using Crosby's character. There are similar (although certainly inadvertent) problems with the climax itself, in which the battle between father and son becomes MONKEY SHINES meets CHILD'S PLAY. (In MONKEY SHINES, a doctor with poison-filled syringes hunts a smaller creature wielding a sharp blade and hiding in a big, empty house; in CHILD'S PLAY, a doll resembling a small child is actually a homicidal knife-wielding maniac and a terrified mother must do battle with the highly mobile villain, who can hide just about anywhere). While the King source material was written before either of the aforementioned films was released, the similarities are unfortunately remarkable.

Perhaps the most frustrating thing about PET SEMATARY is that there *are* some isolated moments of effective terror in the film. A brief shot of Hughes' little hand, glimpsed as his coffin hits the ground and the lid pops open momentarily, and the zombie-boy's rather bitter accusation that it's "not fair" to his father after he is injected with a lethal dose of whatever at the climax are both chilling moments—but while they are memorable in and of themselves, they merely serve to remind one of just how botched the film is overall. (*Violence, gore effects, profanity.*)

p, Richard P. Rubinstein; d, Mary Lambert; w, Stephen King (based on his novel); ph, Peter Stein (Technicolor); ed, Michael Hill and Daniel Hanley; m, Elliot Goldenthal; prod d, Michael Z. Hanan; art d, Dina Danielsen; set d, Michael Reidy and Patricia Klawonn; spec eff, Lance Anderson; cos, Marlene Stewart; makeup, Hiram Ortiz.

Horror   (PR:O MPAA:R)

Ⓥ**PHANTOM OF THE MALL:
ERIC'S REVENGE***
88m Fries c
Kari Whitman (*Melody*), Morgan Fairchild (*Mayor Karen Wilton*), Derek Rydall, Jonathan Goldsmith, Rob Estes, Pauly Shore, Kimber Sissons, Tom Fridley, Gregory Scott Cummins, Ken Foree.

With all the renewed interest in "The Phantom of the Opera," it was only a matter of time before someone decided to modernize the story. PHANTOM OF THE MALL: ERIC'S REVENGE is a slasher update of the classic tale, set in that most modern of conveniences, the shopping mall. The film begins as a small town is celebrating the opening of its first mall. The mayor (Fairchild) is on hand to make a speech and kick off business, but lurking in the air ducts is a dark figure wearing a high-school letterman's jacket and mask, so you can bet the gala grand opening will not go smoothly. A variety of cute and stereotypical teenagers work or hang out in the mall, including Whitman, the former girl friend of Eric, a boy who was presumed killed when his house, which was situated on the site where the mall now stands, was destroyed in a fire. Mysteriously, Whitman starts receiving orchids (Eric's favorite flowers) and hearing "their song" on the jukebox (even when she doesn't play it). Moreover, she discovers with a journalist friend (Rydall) that the fire that destroyed Eric's house was set by people who wanted the mall built (even Fairchild helped out). Meanwhile, Eric creeps about and kills anyone who tries to bother Whitman—shooting a burglar with a crossbow, crushing a peeping-Tom security guard with a forklift, smashing an arsonist's head in a garbage compactor, and so on—when he's not ensconced in his lavishly furnished room beneath the mall, equipped with surveillance screens so he can monitor Whitman's actions and everything else that goes on in the mall. Eventually he takes Whitman, who is now in love with Rydall, to his lair and rigs a time bomb to explode the mall, destroy all his enemies, and unite him and Whitman forever. Rydall comes to the rescue and frees her, but Fairchild doesn't believe their story, pulls a gun on them and forces them into an office. Eric pops in, kills Fairchild in requisite grisly

fashion and chases Whitman. Rydall saves her again, and Eric now becomes the pursued party while the time bomb ticks away.

PHANTOM OF THE MALL is a good idea gone very, very bad. The script updates the story only in its location and the climactic battle scene, while the pathos and drama of the original gothic horror tale are replaced by slasher gimmicks and predictable characters that make one wonder why the filmmakers bothered with the phantom angle in the first place. With the central relationship between Eric and his lady love reduced to nothing but a couple of flashbacks of the pair making out and shots of Whitman holding orchids, the film must rely on style and suspense to carry it through; unfortunately Richard Friedman's flat-footed and visually dull direction is not up to the task. PHANTOM OF THE MALL even fails as a slasher film. While there are plenty of graphic murders and ghastly make-up effects, they are so matter-of-factly handled that the gross-out element is lost and gorehounds will be disappointed. The only lively moment occurs during a chase scene in which a speeding car hits a pedestrian, who then wildly flips a few feet backwards over the car, a knockout stunt that recalls some of the stuntwork in the action films from Hong Kong. (*Graphic violence, profanity, adult situations, sexual situations, nudity.*)

p, Tom Fries; d, Richard Friedman; w, Scott Schneid, Robert King, and Tony Michelman (based on a story by Fred Ulrich, Scott Schneid); ph, Harry Mathias (CFI Color); ed, Amy Tompkins and Gregg Plotz; m, Stacy Widelitz; stunts, David Zellitti; makeup, Matthew Mungle.

Horror   (PR:O MPAA:R)

Ⓥ**PHANTOM OF THE OPERA***
95m Menahem Golan/21st Film c
Robert Englund (*The Phantom*), Jill Schoelen (*Christine*), Alex Hyde-White (*Richard*), Bill Nighy (*Barton*), Stephanie Lawrence (*Carlotta*), Terence Harvey (*Hawking*), Nathan Lewis (*Davies*), Molly Shannon (*Meg, New York*), Emma Rawson (*Meg, London*).

Casting Robert Englund (Freddy Krueger of the NIGHTMARE ON ELM STREET series) as Gaston Leroux's venerable musical monster was probably a painful inevitability, like tax audits and termites. So it's probably better that veteran schlock producers Menahem Golan and Harry Alan Towers have gotten it out of the way rather than dragging out the agony. The results, as might be expected, are high on gross-out horror effects calculated to keep the coveted teen market awake and interested. However, despite some stylish bits of direction from Dwight H. Little (HALLOWEEN IV) and a few beguiling moments from Jill Schoelen (THE STEPFATHER) as the high-pitched heroine, Christine,

audiences generally are likely to spend much of the 95-minute running time battling boredom.

In streamlining THE PHANTOM for the MTV generation, executive producer Golan and producer Towers, with the help of two (count 'em, two) screenwriters, have pretty much jettisoned anything resembling a plot to concentrate on slice 'n' dice bloodletting. Schoelen is first seen as a modern, struggling New York singer who, during a search for attention-getting audition material, stumbles on a "lost" opera written by the Phantom. (In one of the film's more boneheaded lapses, it is revealed at the climax that this supposedly "lost" opera is also the one for which she is auditioning.) Getting beaned by a sandbag at the audition sends Schoelen reeling back in time, the distinctive crescendo from The Beatles' "A Day in the Life" swelling in the background, to find herself in Victorian London (rather than Paris, which was the setting of Leroux's novel). At this point the plot begins to crumble into massive confusion. As in past treatments, the Phantom lives in the sewer and lurks around the opera house during rehearsals, nurturing his obsession with the beautiful Christine. Unlike earlier versions, however, this retelling never really explains his unusual lifestyle. His work is respected and he seems to have money, leaving piles of gold coins wherever he goes. Why he can't live in a regular apartment is not clear. Apparently what makes the Phantom so ornery this time out is that he has made a bargain with the devil, trading his soul to be a composer on the order of Mozart or Bach, and has gotten the bum end of the deal. Not only is his music triumphantly (though unintentionally) mediocre, but an evil dwarf has touched his face, leaving it, of course, horribly scarred. For his trips to the outside world, the Phantom literally puts on the faces of his murder victims. He peels their dead faces and uses the human hide to fashion masks which he sews over his own rotting visage (all of which is shown in painful closeup). The results make him look like a dissipated cross between Robin Williams and Sean Penn. On his nocturnal jaunts, he sits in bars drinking and composing before going out to disembowel muggers, typically ending the evening by picking up a prostitute, who, under the Phantom's orders, becomes "Christine" for a night. Given the Phantom's busy social schedule and his periodic need to procure fresh flesh to keep himself looking dapper, there's scant screen time left for the police to investigate the corpses that pop up around the opera house. That's probably a good thing, since the chief detective's idea of investigative technique seems to consist of obliterating the crime scene and sending the witnesses home without interrogating them.

In short, Leroux's intricate, baroque tale of obsessive love, madness, and revenge has been reduced here to yet another sample of what critic Roger Ebert has called the "idiot plot"—one that would last no longer than 10 minutes if all the characters weren't such blathering idiots. By our calculations that makes this PHANTOM too long by 85 minutes. *(Excessive violence, brief nudity.)*

p, Harry Alan Towers; d, Dwight H. Little; w, Duke Sandefur (based on a screenplay by Gerry O'Hara and the novel by Gaston Leroux); ph, Elemer Ragalyi (Rank Color); ed, Charles Bornstein; m, Misha Segal; md, Misha Segal; art d, Tivadar Bertalan; makeup, Kevin Yagher.

Horror **(PR:O MPAA:R)**

Ⓥ**PHYSICAL EVIDENCE*****
99m Martin Ransohoff/COL c
Burt Reynolds *(Joe Paris)*, Theresa Russell *(Jenny Hudson)*, Ned Beatty *(James Nicks)*, Kay Lenz *(Deborah Quinn)*, Ted McGinley *(Kyle)*, Tom O'Brien *(Matt Farley)*, Kenneth Welsh *(Harry Norton)*, Ray Baker *(Strickler)*, Ken James *(Hank Carruth)*, Michael P. Moran *(Tony Reugger)*, Angelo Rizacos *(Tony Sklar)*, Lamar Jackson *(Delmar Fraser)*, Paul Hubbard *(Burt Knight)*, Larry Reynolds *(Trial Judge)*, Peter MacNeill *(Brannigan)*, Laurie Paton *(Mabel)*, Don Granbery *(Vincent Quinn)*, Barry Flatman *(Brody)*, Malcolm Stewart *(Ames)*, Richard Fitzpatrick *(Kravitz)*, J.W. Carroll *(Samson)*, Kathy Michael McGlynn *(Gladys)*, Djanet Sears *(Sheila)*, Claire Cellucci *(Tanya)*, Michael Donaghue *(Frank Stella)*, Anthony Sherwood *(Lou)*, Angie McNab *(Amy Farley)*, Laurie Holden *(Matt's Girl)*, David Clement *(Warden Debilis)*, Steve Whistance Smith *(Lee)*, Dave Efron *(Buddy)*, Stan Barrett *(Tiny)*, Ken Bates *(Jumper)*, Matt Cooke *(Arraignment Officer)*, Michael Rothery *(Doctor)*, Gene Mack *(Brawny Guard)*, Chris Thomas, Norm Henderson *(Nicks' Cops)*, Stewart Arnott *(Nick's Assistant)*, Eddie Driscoll *(Jenny's Assistant)*, David Ferry, Victor Ertmanis *(Cops)*, Michael Copeman *(Potential Juror)*, Diane Douglas *(Woman Juror)*, Allan Aarons *(Bastianelli)*, Steven Hunter *(Bailiff)*, Jennifer Inch *(Waitress)*, Francois Klanfner *(Louis)*, Terry Tweed *(Arraignemnt Judge)*, Louis Negin *(Jake Farley)*.

PHYSICAL EVIDENCE was reportedly developed as a sequel to JAGGED EDGE (1985) by the producer of both films, Martin Ransohoff. The idea was evidently abandoned, but the basic characterizations remained intact. Burt Reynolds' fallen cop, Joe Paris, bears a resemblance to Robert Loggia's seedy but likable detective from EDGE; Theresa Russell's careerist public defender, Jenny Hudson, roughly corresponds to Glenn Close's character

from the earlier film; and Ned Beatty's predatory prosecutor here echoes the character played by Peter Coyote in the 1985 film. Similarly, though promoted as a Reynolds vehicle, PHYSICAL EVIDENCE is actually much more about Russell's character (as JAGGED EDGE was about Close's) and how her contact with the Boston underworld forces her to see her complacent yuppie lifestyle in a harsh new light. As the film opens, Reynolds, suspended from the force for his hot temper, wakes up from a drinking binge to find himself accused of having killed a notorious, sleazy gangster and unable to account for his whereabouts at the time of the murder. Needing high-profile trial experience to bolster her resume, Russell takes Reynolds' case, although she will have to oppose the seasoned, conviction-hungry Beatty in court and combat the overwhelming evidence against her client (a police search of Reynolds' apartment has turned up the murder weapon and a blood-stained shirt). After some initial class-based bickering, the downwardly spiraling cop and yupwardly mobile lawyer team up to trap the real killer. But producer Ransohoff evidently paid attention to his market research this time around. Women bristled at the suggestion in EDGE that a respected female attorney like Close's character would risk dulling her professional edge by falling into bed with her client—even if he was played by Jeff Bridges—In PHYSICAL EVIDENCE, Russell comes close to succumbing to Reynolds, but refuses to fall, at least until after the final fadeout.

Indeed, both the mystery and romantic plots are virtually thrown away by director Michael Crichton in favor of developing the Russell character's feminist consciousness, which may explain why PHYSICAL EVIDENCE was undeservedly a flop in its theatrical release. Fans of hard-boiled police action were likely dismayed by Crichton's emphasis on Russell, while others probably stayed away from what they believed to be a formula action film. Crichton—who also centered his biggest hit, COMA, around the female lead played by Genevieve Bujold—hits hardest here in scenes dealing with rising male backlash in recent years against the feminist gains of the 1970s and 80s. When we first meet Russell, she's trying to make herself heard above a chorus of sexist raspberries from her male colleagues while pleading with her (male) boss to let her take Reynolds' case; later, under the strain of the case, she breaks up with her fiancee, a corrupt junk-bond trader, when he reveals his true condescension towards her and her career. Violence against women is also a recurring and resonant theme of PHYSICAL EVIDENCE's suspense plot.

In her offbeat collaborations with her director husband, Nicolas Roeg (TRACK

29), Russell has shown herself to be a true risk-taker among major actresses, a characteristic which makes her fascinating to watch here. Far from telegraphing the changes her character will undergo over the course of the film, Russell instead plays the lawyer initially as a sheltered, spoiled rich girl who takes the hard-won gains of the women's movement as a given. Russell is also unabashed about showing Jenny's starchy awkwardness in the courtroom, which is both plausibly consistent with the character's lack of trial experience and an effective means of showing her to be flawed and human, though undeniably intelligent. Russell's choices makes her character's metamorphosis all the more believable and compelling.

To give further credit where it's due, Reynolds' easy charm as a screen presence remains undiminished here, and in yielding many of the movie's best moments to Russell, he reinforces his career-long reputation for generosity as a performer. Sadly, Reynolds' reputation has also turned him into an underrated acting commodity in the 1980s, and PHYSICAL EVIDENCE, in turn, is one of the most underrated films of 1989. *(Violence, profanity.)*

p, Martin Ransohoff; d, Michael Crichton; w, Bill Phillips (based on a story by Steve Ransohoff, Bill Phillips); ph, John A. Alonzo (Medallion Color); ed, Glenn Farr; m, Henry Mancini; prod d, Dan Yarhi; art d, Dennis Davenport; set d, Jacques Bradette; spec eff, Al Griswald; cos, Betsy Cox; stunts, Stan Barrett; makeup, Katherine Southern.

Crime/Thriller **(PR:C MPAA:R)**

Ⓥ**PIN****½
(Can.) 102m Lance/NW c
David Hewlett *(Leon Linden)*, Cyndy Preston *(Ursula Linden)*, John Ferguson *(Sam Fraker)*, Terrance O'Quinn *(Dr. Linden)*, Bronwen Nantel *(Mrs. Linden)*, Jacob Tirney, Michelle Anderson, Steve Bernarski, Katie Shengler.

We've seen split personalities on the screen many times, in films from PSYCHO to SYBIL, but only in PIN has one of these personalities belonged to a plastic see-through medical teaching dummy.

Hewlett and Preston are the children of a well-to-do physician, O'Quinn (THE STEPFATHER). The doctor and his wife are neurotic, rigid, conservative people who cringe at the sight of dirt and treat their son and daughter much like army recruits. O'Quinn does much of his communicating with the children by throwing his voice into the aforementioned dummy, whose name is Pin. In fact, it is Pin who first "tells" Hewlett and Preston about the birds and the bees, after the siblings are caught stealing a look at a pornographic magazine, and it is Pin that the children go to with assorted problems while they are growing up. Hewlett feels closer to Pin than to anybody else. Then one night he sneaks away from home to "speak" with his special friend and accidentally witnesses a perverse nurse having her way with the dummy. The experience leaves Hewlett scarred for life and disgusted with the idea of sex. Thus as he and little sister Preston grow up, he feels it his duty to protect her from sex and men. Unfortunately for Hewlett, by the time Preston is 16, she is a real beauty and a hit with just about every guy at school. When she gets pregnant and has an abortion, this is enough to push Hewlett over the edge. Before long Hewlett's personality has split; he's begun throwing his own voice into Pin, believing that the dummy is actually speaking back to him. When his parents die tragically in an auto accident, Hewlett moves Pin into the house, dresses him up in his father's suits, and creates a human-looking head for him. Much to Preston's horror, Hewlett keeps Pin in a remote-controlled wheelchair, sits him at the dinner table with them, and becomes more and more intertwined with the dummy. Preston watches helplessly as her brother slips deeper and deeper into madness, but she doesn't have the heart to do anything about it. "And," she figures, "He's not hurting anyone." Not until he meets Ferguson, her boy friend, that is. Then jealousy incites Hewlett to attempt murder and ultimately to break down totally—until he and Pin finally become one.

PIN is an interesting, albeit macabre psychological thriller that adds an unusual twist to a fairly common theme. David Hewlett is intense enough to portray the crazy son, Leon, in a convincingly chilling manner. As sweet and innocent as Cyndy Preston is as the daughter, Ursula, it's a bit far-fetched to think that she would actually allow Hewlett to carry on his oddball behavior without consulting a professional. The parents, for as long as they are in the film, are stereotyped and flat, as is Preston's boy friend. Except for Leon/Pin, none of the characters are well-developed and this makes them considerably dull people. But all in all, PIN is a sometimes fascinating, different kind of film and painless enough to sit through, especially for fans of the weird. (Adult situations, violence.)

p, Rene Malo; d, Sandor Stern; w, Sandor Stern; ph, Guy Dufaux; ed, Patrick Dodd; m, Peter Manning Robinson; art d, Francois Seguin.

Horror   (PR:O MPAA:R)

♥PINK CADILLAC* **
122m Malpaso/WB c
Clint Eastwood *(Tommy Nowak)*, Bernadette Peters *(Lou Ann McGuinn)*, Timothy Carhart *(Roy McGuinn)*, John Dennis Johnston *(Waycross)*, Michael Des Barres

Clint Eastwood and Bernadette Peters in PINK CADILLAC (©Warner Bros.)

(Alex), Geoffrey Lewis *(Ricky Z)*, William Hickey, Bill McKinney, Paul Benjamin, Frances Fisher, Jim Carrey, Mara Corday, Tiffany Gail Robinson, Angela Louise Robinson, Jimmie F. Skaggs, Bill Moseley, Michael Champion.

It seems every time Clint Eastwood steps out of his familiar Man with No Name/Dirty Harry persona to attempt something different, his effort is rejected by critics and public alike. Eastwood is caught in an unfortunate catch-22, damned if he does and damned if he doesn't. When he does give the public what it wants (starring in another "Dirty Harry" movie) the majority of critics moan that he is incapable of doing anything else. But when he tries to expand his range and explore new territory (BRONCO BILLY; HONKY TONK MAN), the public is overwhelmingly indifferent and critics claim he's out of his depth. This is extremely unfortunate, because Eastwood is one of the few contemporary American filmmakers who understands how to make extremely satisfying, entertaining movies and at the same time use the form to explore themes important to him—themes that regularly occur in his work, such as the conflict between the individual and the community, the notion of a personal code of conduct versus the code of law, the nature of identity, and the problem of finding a satisfying niche for oneself in the world. While Eastwood's action films contain plenty to please the paying customer, his more offbeat work is infused with genuine warmth, compassion, humor, and an insight into the human condition worthy of John Ford or Howard Hawks.

Although directed by longtime Eastwood associate Buddy Van Horn (THE DEAD POOL), PINK CADILLAC is very much another personal project for Eastwood, and continues his exploration of the screen persona he began with his directorial debut, PLAY MISTY FOR ME (1971). Here Eastwood plays a "skip tracer," a bounty hunter hired by a bail bondsman to track and capture people who have skipped out on bail. Eastwood is one of the best in the business, often fooling his quarry by adopting a variety of identities and disguises (a loud disc jockey, a chauffeur, a rodeo clown, a gold-lame-clad Las Vegas huckster, a greasy redneck with a speech impediment). His latest assignment is to retrieve Peters, a young mother whose bumbling, no-good husband, Carhart, has involved her with a counterfeiting ring run by a white supremacist group called "The Birthright"—a rather ineffectual bunch of alienated rednecks who get together deep in the woods to swap racist propaganda and shoot automatic weapons at wooden targets. Caught passing the phony bills, Peters is arrested by federal agents and hauled off to jail, where, fed up with her husband and his friends, she refuses to accept their offer to post bail and instead turns to the bail bondsmen for whom Eastwood works. Once free, Peters skips bail, taking her baby and her husband's beloved vintage pink Cadillac and heading for her sister's home in Reno. She soon discovers that Carhart has stashed $250,000 in the car, and although she initially thinks it's just more counterfeit currency, she eventually discovers that the cash is genuine and that the Birthright is desperate to get it back. Leaving her baby with her sister,

Peters decides to hide out in Las Vegas for a while. Eastwood is dispatched to find her, and does so without much difficulty, catching up with Peters in a casino. Fully intending to march her right back to jail, he instead finds himself attracted to the spunky, willful woman, and is soon caught up in her problems. When Eastwood takes Peters back to her sister's to retrieve the baby, they are confronted by Carhart and a vicious Birthright warrior. A skirmish ensues, leaving Carhart's friend mortally wounded by Eastwood, but the supremacist pair make off with Peters' baby and hold it hostage until the money—and Peters—are delivered to them. Eastwood decides to help Peters rescue her child, and, posing as a tobacco-chewing redneck with a goofy lisp, infiltrates the Birthright compound and finds the baby. With Peters helping every step of the way, Eastwood outfoxes the inept Birthrighters and escapes with Peters, the baby, the money, and the Cadillac. As they drive down a lonely country road together, Peters makes plans to go into the skip tracer business, with Eastwood as her partner.

The plot isn't much (some critics described it as an unsuccessful combination of last year's MIDNIGHT RUN and BETRAYED), but PINK CADILLAC is rich in character, containing some of the most heartfelt and engaging moments in an Eastwood film since his unjustly neglected BRONCO BILLY. Midway through the film, Eastwood asks the fugitive Peters whether she's heard the maxim that a woman should never "mess with a man's vehicle," in reference to her stealing her husband's beloved pink Cadillac. While the line initially appears to be a new macho catch-phrase, PINK CADILLAC is actually a call for women to do exactly that—to mess with men's vehicles. Tired of being dominated by males, Peters breaks free, taking her baby, her husband's car, and (inadvertently) the money, and becomes determined to cut her own path in life. When Eastwood tracks her down, it looks as if she will once again find herself "taking shit from men"; instead, it's Eastwood who adapts and changes his routine to accommodate her, perhaps because his own life is so stagnant—and because, as he states, "I'm through taking shit from men too."

Indeed, he appears only to come to life when he takes on another identity to fool bail-jumpers, a trick he tackles with hammy relish, and the entire film concerns such role-playing. Thus, when Eastwood catches up with Peters, she pretends to be much dumber and more helpless than she really is, hoping to con him into letting her go. He, however, is too experienced to fall for such a trick, and a frustrated Peters mocks Eastwood by mimicking his macho stoicism; he responds in kind by imitating her little-girl voice and fluttering his eye-

lids (a hilarious must-see for any Eastwood fan), an acknowledgement of her game-playing. The motto of the film, spoken by a wacked-out character (Geoffrey Lewis) expert at creating new identities by faking birth certificates, credit cards, passports, and other official papers, is that "People want to change their identity, to drop in and drop out. It's all part of the game." As a movie star and director, Eastwood has made that same notion the driving force in much of his oeuvre. From THE OUTLAW JOSEY WALES, in which he reinvents the traditional western hero, to FIREFOX, in which his character literally becomes one with a machine, Eastwood has always been fascinated by his "star" persona and with how he can explore it by giving his role a new and unexpected spin.

While the public will accept such tinkering if it is subtle and delivers the crowd-pleasing action goods (SUDDEN IMPACT; TIGHTROPE; HEARTBREAK RIDGE), audience expectations seem to prohibit Eastwood from making a more radical change in his image through more playful or offbeat films like BRONCO BILLY; HONKY TONK MAN; or PINK CADILLAC. If there simply isn't enough action in a film like PINK CADILLAC to satisfy fans of the "Dirty Harry" movies, however, what concessions Eastwood has made to the audience in this film have found disfavor with some critics (most notably Roger Ebert) who have fixated on the film's subplot, expressing dismay at the portrayal of violent white supremacists as comic buffoons (Ebert called this "thoughtless"). One might concur, but PINK CADILLAC's approach isn't that simple. The film shows the group to be dangerous, but denies them any moments that could possibly be considered brave or heroic. Instead, by portraying the racists as fools, the filmmakers deprive anyone who might sympathize with the Birthright's message or methods of any opportunity for heroic identification. None of the racists goes out in a blaze of glorious martyrdom; rather, they are shown to be dim-witted and incompetent —not an appealing image for potential recruits. Nor are they evil-incarnate, all-powerful bad guys—their humanity is all too evident in its misguided ignorance.

The "action" in PINK CADILLAC seems to have satisfied no one, but while the plot may not rush headlong to its conclusion and the climax is more of a letdown than a catharsis, the film is filled with wonderful little character touches, such as the vision of Peters tooling down the highway in the pink Cadillac with the top down and her foot on the dashboard, happily blowing bubbles from a huge chaw of pink gum, the perfect picture of joyous liberation. As with Eastwood's best work, PINK CADILLAC contains much more than meets the eye. His error here may have been one of cranky

individualism, of daring to make such a leisurely work, viewer expectations be damned. With the dark view of his audience presented in THE DEAD POOL, uncompromising approach in BIRD, and now the low-key PINK CADILLAC, Eastwood seems more determined than ever to throw off the shackles of audience expectations and to do what *he* wants as an artist. *(Violence, sexual situations, profanity.)*

p, David Valdes; d, Buddy Van Horn; w, John Eskow; ph, Jack N. Green (Technicolor); ed, Joel Cox; m, Steve Dorff; prod d, Edward C. Carfagno; set d, Thomas L. Roysden.

Comedy/Drama (PR:C MPAA:PG-13)

Ⓥ**POLICE ACADEMY 6: CITY UNDER SIEGE***
83m Maslansky/WB c
Bubba Smith *(Hightower)*, David Graf *(Tackleberry)*, Michael Winslow *(Jones)*, Leslie Easterbrook *(Callahan)*, Marion Ramsey *(Hooks)*, Lance Kinsey *(Proctor)*, Matt McCoy *(Nick)*, Bruce Mahler *(Fackler)*, G.W. Bailey *(Capt. Harris)*, George Gaynes *(Commandant Lassard)*, Kenneth Mars *(Mayor)*, Gerrit Graham *(Ace)*, George R. Robertson *(Police Commissioner Hurst)*, Brian Seeman *(Flash)*, Darwyn Swalve *(Ox)*, Billie Bird *(Mrs. Stanwyck)*, Arthur Batanides *(Mr. Kirkland)*, Beans Morocco *(Bank President)*.

POLICE ACADEMY 6: CITY UNDER SIEGE stars (yes, stars) Bubba Smith as one of a number of bumbling Los Angeles police officers trying to catch the Wilson Heights Gang, a band of thieves on a robbery spree. As the film opens, police captain Bailey and another officer are in the process of staking out a bank. While the two cops talk, the thieves escape right under their noses. After this setback, Bailey enlists the aid of the town's mayor (Mars), who seems to be as inept as Bailey. After Mars decides to assign a special police squad—the usual gang, including Smith, Winslow, Graf, Ramsey, Easterbrook, Mahler, and Kinsey—to the case, the crack forces are briefed on the robberies at the station house, where an atmosphere similar to that in a junior-high classroom prevails. At the Wilson Heights Gang's hideout, meanwhile, a mysterious figure turns out to be the mastermind behind the recent thefts. Next, our brilliant heroes in blue set a trap for the gang by baiting them with a fake diamond, a scheme that fails, of course, allowing the crooks to get away with the loot once again. But all is not lost, since one cop (Gaynes) actually manages to put the pieces of the puzzling crime spree together. After the mandatory chase scene and an anticlimactic confrontation in the office of the police commissioner (Robertson) near the movie's end, the mastermind and master plot are uncovered.

Like its series predecessors, POLICE ACADEMY 6 (directed by Peter Bonerz, best known as Jerry the dentist on TV's "Bob Newhart Show") offers only a few funny moments of sophomoric humor. Such lame bits of slapstick as people slipping on pencils and putting glue on chair seats run through the entire movie; Bruce Mahler's character, especially, was obviously added to the script for the sole purpose of creating sight gags. Again, Michael Winslow is on hand only to do his usual impersonations and sound effects, while Leslie Easterbrook and Marion Ramsey present offensive bimbo caricatures. On the plus side, POLICE ACADEMY 6 is skillfully photographed by Charles Rosher, Jr., and has a very good soundtrack, supplied by Robert Folk. Unfortunately, high production values are wasted on films this slow-paced and silly. Perhaps the next sequel should be called POLICE ACADEMY 7: AUDIENCE UNDER SIEGE. Songs include: "What's the Matter with Your World" (Melle Mel, R.C. Vansilk, Ron Dean Miller, performed by Mel and Vansilk); "Tutti Frutti" (Richard Penniman, Dorothy La Bostrie, Joe Lubin, performed by Little Richard [Penniman]).*(Profanity.)*

p, Paul Maslansky; d, Peter Bonerz; w, Stephen J. Curwick (based on characters created by Neal Israel, Pat Proft); ph, Charles Rosher Jr. (Technicolor); ed, Hubert de la Bouillerie; m, Robert Folk; prod d, Tho E. Azzari; set d, Richard Fernandez and Eric Orbom; spec eff, Gene Grigg; cos, Peter Flaherty; makeup, Bernadine Anderson.

Comedy   (PR:A-C MPAA:PG)

PRANCER***½
103m Raffaella-Nelson-Cineplex Odeon/Orion c
Sam Elliott *(John Riggs)*, Rebecca Harrell *(Jessica Riggs)*, Cloris Leachman *(Mrs. McFarland)*, Rutanya Alda *(Aunt Sarah)*, John Joseph Duda *(Steve Riggs)*, Abe Vigoda *(Dr. Orel Benton, Veterinarian)*, Michael Constantine *(Mr. Stewart/ Santa)*, Ariana Richards *(Carol Wetherby)*, Mark Rolston *(Herb Drier)*, Johnny Galecki *(Billy Quinn)*, Walter Charles *(Minister)*, Victor Truro *(Mr. Young)*, Marcia Porter *(Mrs. Fairburn)*, Loren Janes *(Mr. Soot)*, Robert Zimmerman *(Wagnall)*, Shirley Starnes *(Mrs. Hofsetter)*, Michael Luciano *(Bert)*, Jesse Bradford, Eric Sardeson *(Boys)*, Joseph Morano *(Boy with Santa)*, Belinda Bremner *(Miss Bedelia)*, Terry Jayjack *(Mrs. Wetherby)*, Steven Pressler *(Hank)*, Dale Balsbaugh *(Mr. Wood)*, Sandra Olson *(Town Woman)*, Dan Atherton *(Town Man)*, Boo the Reindeer *(Prancer)*, Frank Welker *(Prancer's Voice)*.

Unafraid to be herself, plucky nine-year-old Harrell confidently sings off-key at

school, gets into her father's hair at the family orchard, and resolutely believes in Santa Claus even though her schoolmates think she's a baby. Like Pollyanna, Anne of Green Gables, and other proponents of "keeping your sunny side up," she has the courage of her convictions. Fascinated with Christmas legends, which she accepts as reality, Harrell spots a reindeer in a nearby forest (far from regular reindeer stomping grounds) and recognizes him as Prancer, a member of Saint Nick's trustworthy sleigh team. Her father, Elliott, a taciturn, hardworking widower, has little patience with his daughter's overactive imagination. Burdened by a failing farm and crushed by the death of his wife, he decides pragmatically that Harrell must go to live with her aunt. One frosty evening, while Elliott and Harrell argue about her future after he catches her hiking through the dark woods alone, they come across a wounded reindeer in the middle of the road. Before the no-nonsense Elliott can put the animal out of its misery, Prancer vanishes from view. When the little girl next encounters the reindeer, she leads him to the barn and vows to nurse him back to health so he can rendezvous with Santa in time for the big night. She badgers Vigoda, an elderly doctor, into a veterinary mission of mercy. She also does chores for eccentric recluse Leachman to pay for Prancer's oats, and makes a long-term dish-washing agreement to appease her cynical older brother, Duda. Desperate to get word to the real Santa about her plans, Harrell visits shopping-mall Santa Constantine and urges him to transmit her message to the North Pole. Instead, he spills the beans to a local newspaper editor, who splashes Prancer's story all over the human interest page. While Harrell's pastor is singing her praises at church, Prancer wanders from the barn and wrecks the inside of her house. Rather than shoot the reindeer in full view of the neighbors who've come to gawk at the celebrated animal, Elliott sells him to a merchant for use as part of a promotional stunt. More determined than ever to return her reindeer pal to his annual holiday duties, Harrell sneaks out of the house and plots his escape with the help of her brother, who's really not such a bad guy after all. But while trying to free Prancer, the little girl falls out of a tree. Bitterly disappointed when Prancer stays by her side rather than fly away to freedom, Harrell temporarily loses her faith in miracles. Reconciled with her father, she agrees to accompany him and the reindeer into the deep woods. Magically, Prancer bounds away and disappears, taking his place in Santa's flying caravan.

When children's films are released for the holidays, one's heart sinks at the memory of such seasonal "gems" as SANTA CONQUERS THE MARTIANS; SANTA CLAUS: THE MOVIE, and TV's "It Came

upon a Midnight Clear" and "The Little Match Girl." These alleged family entertainments are cute, sticky, and artificial—like so many stale candy canes languishing on the branches of a Christmas tree. PRANCER marches to the beat of a different little drummer boy, however. It deals with fleshed-out characters who behave as if they live in the real world (not some area of Sitcomland on the outskirts of the North Pole). Harsh economic realities and recognizable domestic conflicts keep the fanciful story line refreshingly down to earth. Nothing magical happens for almost the entire film; it's even possible for Scrooges to consider the film's fantastic ending to be metaphorical. Even so, miracles of an emotional nature do take place, for everyone in town is changed by the innocence of the little girl's mission. Leachman's Mrs. McFarland, the village's version of Miss Haversham, rejoins the community; Harrell's emotionally exhausted father is able to express his love for his family again; and the townspeople bask in the glow of the child's shining belief in the impossible.

Sensitively directed by John Hancock and filmed in the Indiana area where he grew up, PRANCER benefits from its authentic atmosphere; the film's one-horse, one-cow farm looks like the real thing, not a Hollywood art director's approximation of a struggling farm. There's no condescension toward small towns, no glorification of cherubic child actors, and few false notes. Both Abe Vigoda and Cloris Leachman overplay their first scenes, but, ultimately, they, too, lay off the Christmas ham. At some points the pacing drags, particularly in the scenes with Prancer; of course, it may be difficult to get an inspired performance out of a reindeer. Despite her furry costar's limitations, Rebecca Harrell sparks the film's storybook spirit with her unaffected charm. Because of her radiance and the screenplay's insight into family dynamics, PRANCER is indeed a holiday miracle. Good family films are as rare as flying reindeer, but PRANCER deserves to join the select ranks of those Christmas movies we return to again and again.

p, Raffaella De Laurentiis, Greg Taylor, and Mike Petzold; d, John Hancock; w, Greg Taylor (based on his story); ph, Misha Suslov; ed, Dennis O'Connor; m, Maurice Jarre; md, Maurice Jarre; prod d, Chester Kaczenski; art d, Marc Dabe; set d, Thomas Wilkins; spec eff, Mike Menzel; cos, Denny Burt; stunts, Bobby Porter; makeup, Lance Anderson.

Drama   (PR:AA MPAA:G)

QUEEN OF HEARTS
(See THE YEAR'S BEST)

R

RABID GRANNIES***
83m Stardust/Troma c

Catherine Aymerie (Helen), Caroline Braekman (Suzie), Richard Cotica (Gilbert), Danielle Daven (Elisabeth Remington), Patricia Davia (Alice), Robert Du Bois (Fr. Percival), Florine Elslande (Bertha), Raymond Lescot (Reverend Father), Elliot Lison (John), Michel Lombet (Roger), Anne Marie Fox (Victoria Remington), F.S. Granvel II (Publicity Executive), Paule Herreman (Miss Barnstable), Bobette Jouret (Erika), Francoise Lamoureux (Jessica), Le Pepe (Taxi Driver), Jack Mayar (Harvey), Francoise Moens (Rachel), Joelle Morante (Elisabeth, the Monster), Sebastien Radovitch (Radu), Cindy Rimoe (Woman at the Gate), Suzanne Vanina (Victoria, the Monster), Guy Van Riet (Fred), Jonathan Rambert (Police Officer), Jan De Ketelaere (Gardener), James Desert (Peasant), Jill the Dog.

As RABID GRANNIES opens, the slightly dotty, extremely old, and very wealthy Daven and Fox prepare a sumptuous banquet to celebrate their upcoming birthdays. What they don't realize is that the beloved relatives they've invited to their party can't wait for them to expire. Among the greedy celebrants are condom manufacturer Van Riet and his young wife, Lamoureux; playboy Lombet; munitions tycoon Mayar; repressed virgin Elslande; worldly priest Du Bois; lesbian writer Jouret and her "collaborator," Moens: bourgeois in-law Lison and his stuck-up wife, Aymerie; and the last's two kids, Cotica and Braekman. While the servants put the final flourishes on the feast and bad-mouth the guests, the rapacious relatives bend the old ladies' ears with insidious gossip about one another. The back-biting celebration is proceeding like some outtake from a Bunuel film when a mysterious stranger delivers a gift from an absent nephew, who has been disinherited because of his devil-worshiping proclivities. When the nonagenarians open their surprise package, the black sheep nephew extracts a terrible revenge. Transformed magically into the slobbering harpies of the title, the birthday girls begin adding their nasty dinner guests to the menu. Jouret becomes the first appetizer, prompting the rest to run for cover without regard to the unwritten maxim "Women and children first." After making mincemeat out of two servants, the ravenous Daven and Fox start eliminating their potential heirs—it's no longer the relatives who bite the hand that feeds them.

Huddled in one room, Aymerie, Lison, Moens, and little Cotica grudgingly grant sanctuary to Du Bois; elsewhere, Van Riet, Mayar, and Elslande discuss their options. Sneaking out through an underground cavern, Lombet and Lamoureux escape from the death house and make it to a car. Unfortunately, they have a hungry backseat driver in one rabid granny, who polishes them both off by knifing Lombet and crushing Lamoureux with the car. Meanwhile, Braekman, Aymerie's eight-year-old daughter, who had previously wandered off to the bathroom, encounters one of her cunning great aunts. By the time the child's distraught mother realizes she's missing, she's gastronomic history. One by one, the assembled invitees are terrorized, toyed with, and treated like so many hors d'oeuvres by the carnivorous senior citizens. Du Bois is taunted into committing suicide, choosing to face eternal damnation rather than his aunties' sharp teeth. When portly Van Riet gets stuck inside an attic window, his ample backside proves a tasty addition to the old ladies' bill of fare. Only after the spinster Elslande destroys the devil worshiper's Pandora's Box are the old women released from their torment. Unfortunately, though Moens and Cotica survive relatively unharmed, Aymerie has gone mad and poor Elslande is infected with the rabid curse, continuing in the grand chomp-and-chew tradition of her aunts.

A surprisingly witty black comedy from Troma, the company that brought us the "Toxic Avenger" series, RABID GRANNIES is a biting attack on greed and a yummy parody of haunted-house movies. Although this Belgian import has been dubbed, the match between images and voices is exceptionally good, and the bitchy repartee is high-grade camp. Working on the satisfying premise by which the sweet old ladies turn the tables on their money-grubbing heirs, RABID GRANNIES is a twisted relative of the "Sleeping Beauty" fairy tale (in which a fairy godmother is so upset at not being invited to a christening that she puts a curse on the baby princess). However, the film defeats itself somewhat in its savagery—no matter how unsympathetic the relatives are, we don't enjoy seeing them ripped to shreds. By laying on the ultragory special effects (by Steven Fernandez) with such zeal—perhaps for an intended audience of young gorehounds—the film diminishes the audience's pleasure in the avaricious relatives' comeuppance, since the graphic nature of its depiction dilutes the comedy and does not push the movie into the realm of full-fledged horror. It's not a fatal flaw, but it's a miscalculation, mainly because the movie is edited too indifferently to truly terrify us.

When it's not laying on the gore, RABID GRANNIES is a snarlingly good comedy with its share of cruelly funny moments. Continuity problems mar the film (as when, after racing through the caverns, Lombet and Lamoureux are suddenly outside the house), but viewers who can overlook this occasional choppiness and can accept the gore, as well as the predictability of the "Ten Little Indians" formula, can sit back and enjoy watching as each successive house guest becomes a tasty treat. For all its lapses in "taste," RABID GRANNIES sinks its teeth into juicy material, especially when it keeps its fairy tale parallels strong. This black comedy about gray power is a gutsy movie spoof, its avenging title characters finally discovering what their worthless relatives are good for—once they eat them. (Graphic violence, gore effects, nudity, profanity, sexual situations.)

p, James Desert and Jonathan Rambert; d, Emmanuel Kervyn; w, Emmanuel Kervyn; ph, Hugh Labye (Eastmancolor); ed, Philippe Ravoet; m, Peter Castelain and J.B. Castelain; prod d, Luke Bertrand; spec eff, Steven Fernandez; makeup, Jean Pierre Finoto.

Comedy/Horror   (PR:O MPAA:NR)

RACE FOR GLORY**
104m BPS/New Century-Vista c

Alex McArthur (Cody Gifford), Peter Berg (Chris Washburn), Pamela Ludwig (Jenny Eastman), Ray Wise (Jack Davis), Oliver Stritzel (Klaus Kroeter), Burt Kwouk (Yoshiro Tanaka), Jerome Dempsey (Ray Crowley), Lane Smith (Joe Gifford).

Take the basic "young athlete shooting for an impossible dream" formula, plug it into Grand Prix motorcycle racing, and you have this standard sports film directed by Rocky Lang. McArthur is a small-town motorcycle racer with a big-time ambition: he wants to take his American-built bike, and his mechanic and best friend (Berg), to Europe, to compete with the Japanese "rice burners" on the Grand Prix circuit. He begins his quest by entering a local race that features the Samurai-riding Stritzel, the greatest racer in the world. After getting off to a poor start, McArthur is about to be lapped by Stritzel but refuses to yield to the European champ, causing the two riders to crash. Impressed by McArthur's gutsy riding, the manager of the Samurai racing team (Wise) offers the young American the opportunity to race with his team for a season. Not only will McArthur be able to earn enough money to rebuild his battered bike for next year, but Berg will be permitted to come along as his friend's mechanic. The two accept the offer (though Berg does so reluctantly), but it isn't long before political infighting begins. When McArthur becomes so good that he threatens to steal golden boy Stritzel's thunder, a plan is hatched. Seduced by success, McArthur is persuaded to sign a new contract that calls for him to ride an experimental bike. Berg is violently opposed to these new conditions and goes home in a huff. Soon, McArthur is humbled when he is blamed for a wreck caused by Stritzel. Returning to the States, McArthur patches things up with Berg, who, it just so happens, has been reconstructing their original bike, hoping to prove the superiority of American workmanship. Can they enter it in the Grand Prix finals? Can McArthur finally beat Stritzel head-to-head? Is the director's first name Rocky? Quicker than you can say "kick start," American honor is restored.

RACE FOR GLORY isn't a terrible movie; it's just not a very good one. Replete with hackneyed situations, two-dimensional characters, and some wild stretching of credibility, it is a hodgepodge of events that serve only to lead the viewer to a payoff that can be seen long before the victory flag is waved. RACE FOR GLORY's appeal is purely visceral. Moreover, each of the film's strengths is outweighed by a greater weakness. The race sequences are exciting, but they are stripped of all suspense. Peter Berg gives a convincingly impassioned performance as the betrayed mechanic, but much of the time it's hard to tell what his big gripe is: he gets mad when they go to Europe, he throws a tantrum when asked to work with a Japanese partner who knows the Samurai bike inside and out, and he becomes enraged when McArthur is asked to sign the new contract. One begins to believe that if he were asked about the weather, Berg's Chris would explode. Yet his Big Scene—in which he pleads, "This was supposed to be *our* chance!"—is moving.

The film's major weakness is its unsympathetic main character. Alex McArthur's Cody has everything going for him—good looks, talent, a devoted girl friend, and a proud father. What he loses in the movie is lost because Cody cares more about himself than anyone else. Significantly, little is provided that gives a sense of Cody's friendship with his mechanic, so it's difficult to care when Chris sells out. RACE FOR GLORY does have slick production values, but in the vast world of sports movies, this film isn't much more than a pit stop. *(Profanity, sexual situations.)*

p, Jon Gordon and Daniel A. Sherkow; d, Rocky Lang; w, Scott Swanton; ph, Jack N. Green (Technicolor); ed, Maryann Brandon; m, Jay Ferguson; prod d, Cynthia Charette; art d, Kurt Gauger and J.M. Hugon; set d, Donna Casey and Annie Seneghal; cos, Leslie Peters Ballard; stunts, Bill Anagnos.

Sports   (PR:C MPAA:R)

❶RACHEL PAPERS, THE***
(Brit.) 95m Initial-Longfellow/UA c
Dexter Fletcher *(Charles Highway)*, Ione Skye *(Rachel Seth-Smith)*, Jonathan Pryce *(Norman)*, James Spader *(DeForest)*, Bill Paterson *(Gordon Highway)*, Shirley Anne Field *(Mrs. Seth-Smith)*, Jared Harris *(Geoff)*, Aubrey Morris *(Sir Herbert)*, Claire Skinner *(Gloria)*, Nicola Kimber *(Vanessa)*, Lesley Sharp *(Jenny)*, Michael Gambon *(Dr. Knowd)*, Pat Keen *(Mrs. Tauber)*, Gina McKee *(Kathy)*, Daniel John *(Chris Minor)*, Shirley King *(Tauber Academy Assistant)*, Siri Neal *(Suki)*, Di Langford *(Charlotte Highway)*, Hepburn Graham *(Andy)*, Amanda Dickinson *(Peppermint Park Waitress)*, Joe Wreddon *(Valentine Minor)*, Amy Fleetwood *(Rachel's Friend)*, Jimmy Buchanan *(Mr. Greenchurch)*, Amanda de Cadenet *(Yvonne)*, Willie Ross *(Busker)*.

Though based on Martin Amis' 1973 novel, THE RACHEL PAPERS is of a piece with other recent British films, from MY BEAUTIFUL LAUNDRETTE to DISTANT VOICES, STILL LIVES, with its bleak undercurrents of vaguely diminished expectations. What makes this film different is that it buries its sour notes in what first appears to be a bright, hip coming-of-age comedy.

Dexter Fletcher, the striking star of CARAVAGGIO and THE RAGGEDY RAWNEY, plays Charles Highway, who has turned swinging in London into a science—literally. On his home computer he has created a program, "Conquests and Techniques," into which he has poured the accumulated data of his love life and constructed from it the technique he uses to plot future seductions. But when Fletcher meets the Rachel of the title (Skye), his system seems to break down. He's suddenly forced to think on his feet to keep up with this sleek American, who's living in London with her mother while contemplating a modeling career in New York. Fletcher begins to think he's in love when Skye drops her snobbish American boy friend (Spader) to spend a passionate weekend with him. Yet, there's more to Skye than meets the eye. Showing up at the house Fletcher shares with his blowsy sister and boozy brother-in-law (Pryce), Skye coolly declares, "I can only make one of you happy." Gradually, it emerges that Fletcher has met his match in the art of seduction, yet it would seem that Skye, too, thinks she's in love. Over the weekend, however, a rift appears as they get to know each other better. The difference between them is embodied in their bathroom habits—she leaves the door open; he keeps it locked. When British fastidiousness meets American earthiness, both Fletcher and Skye come away nonplussed.

After the onset of that disillusionment, writer-director Damian Harris (son of actor Richard Harris) utilizes the conventions of the teen romantic comedy only to give them an acerbic twist. Instead of the boy getting, losing, and getting the girl back, in THE RACHEL PAPERS the boy loses the girl and both go their separate ways. In the long run, Fletcher has a more meaningful relationship with his computer than with the women it helps him conquer.

THE RACHEL PAPERS contrasts well with another 1989 release, the American-produced SAY ANYTHING, by virtue of Ione Skye's presence in both films in essentially the same role. In SAY ANYTHING, Skye is a creature of ethereal fantasy as she beguiles John Cusack (she also made a good many male critics wish they were 16 again on the evidence of the raves she and the film received), but she was never quite real. Even her struggle to break free of her felonious father's influence amounted to a flight from reality into Cusack's poor-but-honest arms. In THE RACHEL PAPERS, Skye looks and sounds the same, but she has a gravity and dark complexity. In short, she is too real. As a result, it is Fletcher's Charles who flees. Significantly, the film never reveals whether Rachel and Charles are more miserable for having broken up. Indeed, love doesn't even seem to be an issue, except by virtue of its absence. Both characters use deception to gain their emotional objects, and, in the end, each becomes just another exit on the other's emotionally transitory road of life.

Like its two principals, THE RACHEL PAPERS is never quite what it seems to be, which is both its strength and weakness. While its ambiguity may have the resonance of reality, it's never clear whether Harris intends to be ambiguous or if he simply can't decide how he wants to leave matters. Although he seems to want us to like Charles, Harris persistently shows us the character's swinishness and shallowness. Also a little hard to buy is Charles attractiveness to women. An entertaining enough actor, Fletcher looks like he could be Mick Jagger's scrawny little brother, and Skye's dropping of Spader to be with him calls for a maximum suspension of disbelief.

Still, whatever THE RACHEL PAPERS is, it is not a conventional dewy-eyed romance. It is, instead, genuinely challenging and frankly erotic. Skye may again have male viewers wishing they were in their teens, but she also proves that she's a fine actress. Providing solid support are Jonathan Pryce, in an amusing, raucous turnabout from the wan dreamer he played in BRAZIL, and Michael Gambon (of TV's "The Singing Detective"), who has a short, but pungent, scene as an Oxford don. THE RACHEL PAPERS may not be quite the film it could have been, but it remains intriguing nonetheless for what it attempts and the distance it goes towards succeeding. *(Adult situations, nudity.)*

p, Andrew S. Karsch and Paul Raphael; d, Damian Harris; w, Damian Harris (based on the novel by Martin Amis); ph, Alex Thomson (AgfaColor); ed, David Martin; m, Chaz Jankel and David Storrs; md, Debbie Mason; prod d, Andrew McAlpine; art d, Lia Cramer; cos, Marit Allen; stunts, Stuart St. Paul; makeup, Sally Sutton.

Comedy   (PR:C MPAA:R)

RACHEL RIVER***
90m Taurus c

Zeljko Ivanek *(Momo)*, Pamela Reed *(Mary Graving)*, Craig T. Nelson *(Marlyn Huutula)*, James Olson *(Jack Canon)*, Alan North *(Beske)*, Viveca Lindfors *(Harriet White)*, Jo Henderson *(Estona)*, Jon De Vries *(Baker)*, Ailene Cole *(Svea)*, Courtney Kjos *(Annie)*, Ollie Osterberg *(Arne)*, Wellington Nelson *(Einar)*, Richard Jenkins *(Cordell)*, Michael Gallagher *(Will)*, Richard Riehle *(Merv)*, Ron Duffy *(Duane)*, Don Cosgrove *(Bud)*, Stephen Yoakum *(Larry)*, Cliff Rakerd *(Tommy)*, Patricia Mary Van Oss *(Lil)*.

The death of Cole, an eccentric old woman, has the entire town of Rachel River, Minnesota, abuzz. Although assumed to have been an absolute recluse, it appears that she touched several lives, including those of Nelson, her boorish nephew; Henderson, his shrew of a sister; Lindfors, a contemporary, now herself facing the rigors of old age; Ivanek, the village simpleton; Olson, the undertaker; and Reed, a lonely, divorced mother of two and local disc jockey. Reed commands nearly as much interest herself, being the wary recipient of the attentions of Nelson and Olson, as well as a few others. Adding to the general excitement is the rumor of a buried fortune on Cole's property. In the week that follows her death, the money is located and each person comes to learn a little something about himself and his neighbors.

RACHEL RIVER is as slight as its synopsis, really nothing more than a cinematic short story. So muted in tone and leisurely paced is it that an impatient viewer not in the proper mood could well miss its special qualities, including some wonderful, albeit small-scaled performances. Tiny, cherubic comedienne Pamela Reed brings a quiet radiance to her part. One senses the pride she takes in her work as a broadcaster, struggling over her copy; moreover, she projects just enough of the panic she feels at her life's emptiness. Craig T. Nelson obviously enjoys his slob of a character and provides earthy comic relief whether endlessly bickering with his hatchet-faced sister over the cost of coffins or coming on to Reed's drunken Mary in a funny bar scene that has a charmingly spontaneous feel. James Olson, too, is perfect as the type of well-meaning bore that complex women like Mary always seem to attract. One of director Sandy Smolan's major achievements here is toning down the usually monstrously over-scaled Viveca Lindfors. She actually behaves like a recognizable human being and gains a dignified sympathy in scenes that could have resulted in bravura hysterics; her conversations with Reed have an unforced sincerity (due also in great part to Reed's lambent talent for listening). The smaller roles are aptly filled as well.

Judith Guest's script has a novelist's attention to detail and behavioral humor. Certain scenes—Reed's humanities class being cancelled by an unfeeling Henderson; Olson receiving a coffee shop lesson in casket-selling; the endless gossip in the town's one bar—have a real vividness. There are few recent films that have been about so little yet manage to convey as much emotional impact. While there may be too many shots of Zeljko Ivanek's Momo wandering ecstatically through field and forest, the ending rewards with its simple, droll statement of at least one human's (Mary's) condition.

Technically, the production is a knockout in two areas: photography and music. The northern Minnesota locale is bleakly commanding and Paul Elliott's Nykvist-rich lenswork is a celebration of beautifully graded color: in the late autumnal foliage and wintry skies, the light streaming through a bedroom window or reflected in Reed's eyes, and some of the most exquisite, becalmed snow ever captured on film. Moreover, Arvo Part's piercingly evocative European-flavored music is entirely appropriate to the material and the mood, always a welcome rarity for movie-goers. This film had a June showing on the PBS television network. *(Adult situations.)*

p, Timothy Marx and Nan Simons; d, Sandy Smolan; w, Judith Guest (based on the stories of Carol Bly); ph, Paul Elliott; ed, Susan Crutcher; m, Arvo Part; prod d, David Wasco; cos, Linda Fisher.

Comedy/Drama   (PR:A MPAA:PG-13)

⊙RAINBOW, THE***
110m Vestron c

Sammi Davis *(Ursula Brangwen)*, Paul McGann *(Anton Skrebensky)*, Amanda Donohue *(Winifred Inger)*, Christopher Gable *(Will Brangwen)*, David Hemmings *(Uncle Henry)*, Glenda Jackson *(Anna Brangwen)*, Dudley Sutton *(MacAllister)*, Jim Carter *(Mr. Harby)*, Judith Paris *(Miss Harby)*, Ken Colley *(Mr. Brunt)*, Glenda McKay *(Gudrun Brangwen)*, Molly Russell *(Molly)*, Rupert Russell *(Rupert)*, Mark Owen *(Jim Richards)*.

Except for a few characteristic visual flourishes it would be difficult to identify this filming of D.H. Lawrence's novel *The Rainbow* as the work of aging maverick moviemaker Ken Russell. Russell's second trip into Lawrence territory is nowhere near as outrageous as his earlier outing, WOMEN IN LOVE. This time there is no wild imagery and no Oliver Reed to devour the scenery. Compared to, say, CRIMES OF PASSION, THE RAINBOW seems almost pitched at the "Masterpiece Theater" crowd, with only a few funky moments reminding us that Russell is in charge. Sammi Davis (HOPE AND GLORY) takes the lead as Lawrence's her-

oine, Ursula Brangwen, who pursues the ephemeral title object both literally and figuratively. In a precredit sequence, Ursula is first seen as a little girl chasing the rainbow that follows a spring rain. Scooped up by her indulgent father (Gable), she petulantly rejects the rainbow jelly sandwich he offers her and gazes out the window, wondering why she can't have the real thing.

Next seen as the blossoming Davis, Ursula proves early on to be a woman who wants to have it all, starting with a liaison with her bisexual gym teacher, Winnie (Donohoe). Her adolescent crush begins to sour, however, when Donohoe passes Davis on to an artist friend, MacAllister (Sutton), who disgusts the young woman by suggesting some mild discipline in addition to the nude modeling she does for him. Davis' infatuation with Donohoe threatens to turn to hatred when the teacher takes a fancy to Davis' Uncle Henry (Hemmings), falls in love with him, and marries him. Hemmings has earned the scorn of Davis by having made a fortune in mining—some of which has trickled down to Davis' family. Davis hates the way men and women are beaten, then broken by a lifetime in the mines. When Donohoe protests that the miners have adapted themselves to their lot, Davis capsulizes her philosophy of life with the retort that people should be able to adapt the world to suit them. (Ironically, mining, by providing a cheap heating fuel without decimating the forests, is, in fact, a case of man altering his environment to make life more comfortable—as the Industrial Revolution, during which the action of THE RAINBOW is set, did in general.)

The pain of Davis' breakup with Donohoe is soothed somewhat by the attentions of Anton (Paul McGann—WITHNAIL AND I; DEALERS), a strapping soldier-engineer. When McGann departs to fight the Boers in South Africa, Davis leaves for London to become a teacher. Much taken with the idea of helping young minds to appreciate the finer things in life, Davis finds herself defeated by the brutal ignorance of her charges, the first children of the Industrial Revolution. She also must match wits with her lecherous headmaster, Mr. Harby (Carter), who vows to destroy her when she rejects him. Her final victory is a bitter one, since she becomes what she has most despised by breaking a cane over the back of a youngster who has been tormenting her since her arrival. Her class becomes quiet and obedient, and even Carter shrinks from tangling with her after the classroom outburst. Nevertheless, Davis quits and returns home, defeated by her failure to live up to her own unrealistically high standards. Still another blow comes her way after she expresses doubts about entering into the enslavement of marriage. This idea is clearly too radical for McGann, and he dissolves the engagement and marries another. Davis is left much as she was at the beginning, with her indulgent father, though not so defeated that she can't pack her bags and continue to chase rainbows.

During the production of CRIMES OF PASSION, Russell and his wife, Vivian (with whom he cowrote THE RAINBOW), were married by "Reverend" Tony Perkins, and it appears as if marriage and age have mellowed the daring director. The only Russell "touches" to be seen in THE RAINBOW include the frank treatment of Ursula's sexuality and an occasional baroque flourish—such as when MacAllister, Ursula's rejected suitor, flings his paintbrush, leaving a bright, crimson streak over the bare buttocks of a female statue. Whatever Lawrence intended, Ursula's radicalism is viewed here with a more skeptical eye than Russell might once have brought to the project. Rather than being characterized by the world-shaking rumblings of a budding intellectual, Ursula is depicted as something of a middle-class brat, whose views are tolerated by a family that has pampered and indulged her throughout her life.

Russell is obviously sympathetic to Ursula, but her enemies are not the monsters they might have been if Russell had made THE RAINBOW only a few years ago. David Hemmings' exploitative Henry is downright likable, while Dudley Sutton and Jim Carter are more sad than evil as the lecherous MacAllister and Mr. Harby, respectively. Despite the fact that Amanda Donohoe's Winnie has taught Ursula to regard Henry as an enemy, the teacher sees no contradiction in marrying him; indeed, Winnie is portrayed almost as heroically as Ursula is. While Ursula refuses to compromise her ideals, Winnie bends rather than break. Like the others who betray Ursula, Winnie is portrayed as anything but a monster—in contrast to the comically campy villainess Donohoe played in Russell's self-parodic THE LAIR OF THE WHITE WORM, which was filmed back-to-back with THE RAINBOW, employing several of the same cast members, including Davis.

More than ever before, Russell seems to regard the world as a place with room enough and need for the Ursulas, Winifreds, and even Uncle Henrys. Whether Russell's mellowing has made him a better filmmaker is less clear. By virtue of its "Masterpiece Theater" style—not quite pompous but decidedly stuffier than Russell's past work—THE RAINBOW is more accessible than most of the director's earlier films. But Russell is, and always has been, a director of ideas rather than emotions, which tends to make THE RAIN-

BOW intermittently heavy going. Tellingly, the film's most distasteful characters, MacAllister and Mr. Harby, are also the most vividly rendered because they are the only two in the film driven almost solely by their emotions, specifically by their lust for Ursula. However, while it's possible to be captivated by Ursula, it's never quite possible to be touched by her. Like many of Russell's other characters, and for all her passion, Ursula talks more like a newspaper editorial than an emotionally complex young woman who is discovering the world and her relationship to it. As a result, though THE RAINBOW is certainly a very good film, and Russell's best in recent memory, it nonetheless remains doggedly earthbound when it should be soaring. *(Nudity, sexual situations, profanity.)*

p, Ken Russell; d, Ken Russell; w, Ken Russell and Vivian Russell (based on the novel by D.H. Lawrence); ph, Billy Williams (Technicolor); ed, Peter Davies; m, Carl Davis; prod d, Luciana Arrighi; art d, Ian Whittaker; cos, Luciana Arrighi.

Drama   **(PR:O MPAA:R)**

⊘RED SCORPION**
102m Shapiro Glickenhaus c
Dolph Lundgren *(Lt. Nikolai)*, M. Emmet Walsh *(Dewey Ferguson)*, Al White *(Kallunda)*, T.P. McKenna *(Gen. Vortek)*, Ruben Nthodi *(Sundata)*, Carmen Argenziano *(Zayas)*, Alex Colon *(Mendez)*, Brion James *(Krasnov)*, Regopstaan *(Gao, bushman)*.

Drought-ridden Africa is the setting for this actioner starring Dolph Lundgren, best known as Sylvester Stallone's Soviet nemesis in ROCKY IV. Here he again plays a Russian, this time a Soviet special forces "killing machine" sent by his sadistic boss (McKenna) to an unnamed African nation (obviously modeled on Angola), where he is to assassinate a rebel leader who's causing problems for Cuban forces occupying the country. White, the leader's second-in-command, has been jailed and Lundgren's plan is to get himself locked up with White and gain his trust. After starting a tavern brawl, Lundgren is thrown into jail, not only with White, but also with Walsh, a vulgar American newspaperman who absolutely hates communists. The three pull off an escape, then head for a rebel camp in a truck, with Little Richard blaring from Walsh's cassette player.

At the camp, Lundgren is introduced to Nthodi, the man he has been sent to eliminate. But he later botches his assassination attempt, and when he returns to his Soviet comrades, he pays for his failure by being tortured by Cubans who stick long needles into his body. Eventually, Lundgren escapes and makes his way into the desert where he is stung by a scorpion, and nursed back to health by a native (Regopstaan)

who tattoos the image of a scorpion on the Soviet's chest. These experiences lead to Lundgren's political conversion, and when he returns to the rebels' camp, this time he's on their side. "Let's kick some ass," he tells his new comrades as they attack a Soviet garrison. Lundgren destroys tanks, lifts a truck out of a ditch, and downs a Russian gunship in which McKenna is a passenger, as he leads the rebels to a stirring victory over their oppressors.

As commie-bashing action films go, RED SCORPION is slightly better than most. Of course, Lundgren is an even less-accomplished thespian than Stallone, Chuck Norris, or Arnold Schwarzenegger, but the film actually offers some character development, thanks largely to the skill of veteran actor M. Emmet Walsh, who injects a lot of humor into his foul-mouthed character, and Al White, who lends credibility to his role as a committed rebel. Director Joseph Zito does a nice job in handling the battle scenes, and even takes a stab at depicting the plight of the beleaguered natives as mere pawns in super power games in a couple of evocative, albeit brief, scenes. Naturally, Lundgren's Soviet and Cuban cohorts are all ludicrously evil, as communists must be in this kind of film. Indeed, RED SCORPION offers little that hasn't been seen in countless films of its ilk, and the twist of making the hero a Russian is hardly enough to breathe life into a film with only limited appeal for those other than hardcore action fans.

A long-troubled project, RED SCORPION was originally to be shot in Swaziland, but that nation's government objected to some of the content in the script and refused to allow cameras to roll. Production was then moved to South Africa-controlled Namibia, and the film was scheduled for a summer of 1988 release; however, controversy arose when the film's South Africa connection was made public in stories noting that the project was bankrolled by South African investors, shot in Namibia, and used equipment and soldiers from South African army. Warner Bros. quickly backed out of its deal to distribute the film, and when it was finally released in the spring of this year, RED SCORPION disappeared from the theatres within a few weeks. *(Violence, excessive profanity.)*

p, Jack Abramoff; d, Joseph Zito; w, Arne Olsen (based on a story by Robert Abramoff, Jack Abramoff, Arne Olsen); ph, Joao Fernandes (Deluxe Color); ed, Daniel Loewenthal; m, Jay Chattaway; prod d, Ladislav Wilheim; spec eff, John Evans; stunts, Eddie Stacey; makeup, Tom Savini.

Action   **(PR:C-O MPAA:R)**

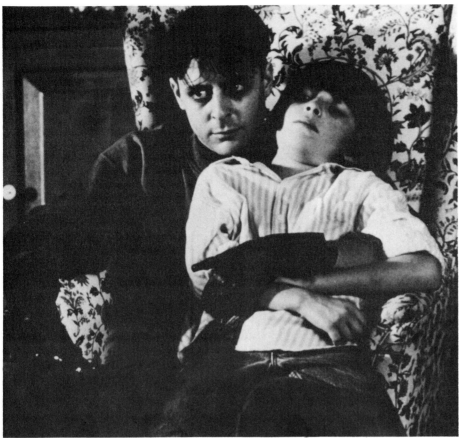

Judd Nelson and Brendan Ryan in RELENTLESS (©New Line).

ⓋRELENTLESS*
92m Cinetel/New Line c
Judd Nelson *(Buck Taylor)*, Robert Loggia *(Bill Malloy)*, Leo Rossi *(Sam Dietz)*, Meg Foster *(Carol Dietz)*, Patrick O'Bryan *(Todd Arthur)*, Mindy Seger *(Francine)*, Ron Taylor *(Capt. Blakely)*, Beau Starr *(Ike Taylor)*, Angel Tompkins *(Carmen)*, Harriet Hall *(Angela Taylor)*, Ken Lerner, Frank Pesce, George "Buck" Flower, Armand Mastroianni.

In RELENTLESS, Judd Nelson plays the son of a crazed Los Angeles super cop who has been trained as a child to be as tough as his dear old dad. When Nelson, now grown, is rejected by the police department, he goes round the bend, beginning a series of murders committed solely so that he will be caught. First he calls his victims and tells them they are about to be killed; then he breaks into their houses and murders them (with various weapons, the most creative of which is piano wire), "aided" by the victims' own hands. The one connecting thread among his victims is the similarity of their names to his. At each murder scene he leaves a page from the telephone book with a written message and the victim's name circled, hoping these clues will bring the police closer to him. Assigned to the case are two detectives: a newly promoted plainclothesman from

New York (Rossi) and a crusty Los Angeles veteran (Loggia), who must overcome their differences in approach (Loggia loafs, Rossi doesn't) to find the murderer (now dubbed "The Sunset Killer"). As the case wears on (and the bodies pile up), the detectives arrive at a loose comradery and both men's domestic lives are changed. Rossi and his wife (Foster) learn to adjust to the laid-back LA lifestyle, and Loggia begins to care about his police work. When Nelson discovers that the cops might be on to him, he circles Loggia's name in the phone book and puts Rossi's wife and child on top of his list of potential victims. The climax takes place in Rossi's house as the insane Nelson, who holds Foster at gunpoint, is surprised by Rossi, who breaks in and blows Nelson away.

Although RELENTLESS is a prime example of poor B-grade filmmaking, it is nonetheless a step up for William Lustig (MANIAC; MANIAC COP), a director of limited ability whose strength lies in his ability to turn viewers' stomachs. Gratuitous violence, needless exploitation of women, and a surfeit of foul language are commonplace in Lustig's films (check out MANIAC for heavy doses of all three.), but RELENTLESS is virtually free of these excesses, and though violent, is tame in comparison with his other movies. Unfor-

tunately, violence is the only thing that holds the film together—its story is predictable (how many times can one suffer the "young cop-old cop" routine), the stalking scenes are suspenseless, and the dialog is laughable.

Lustig is not helped at all by Nelson (probably the least talented Brat Packer), whose performance consists of rolling his eyes, sweating, and lurching at the camera —creating a simple two-dimensional villain the audience doesn't even dislike enough to care whether he is caught. As for Robert Loggia and Leo Rossi, they do the best they can with the little they are given. Loggia, who is more or less re-creating his character from THE JAGGED EDGE, has one or two moments that stand out, but the film's finest performance belongs to Rossi, who lends some much-needed depth to the shallow dialog. An underrated character actor, Rossi has played villains for most of his career (most memorably in THE ACCUSED) and it is nice, for once, to see him play a likable, heroic character. Lacking pretension, RELENTLESS aspires to be nothing more than a grade B thriller; unfortunately, it is a very bad grade B thriller. *(Violence, profanity, adult situations.)*

p, Howard Smith; d, William Lustig; w, Jack T.D. Robinson; ph, James Lemmo (Foto-Kem Color); ed, David Kern; m, Jay Chattaway; prod d, Gene Abel; set d, Ann Job; stunts, Spiro Razatos.

Thriller   (PR:O MPAA:R)

REMBRANDT LAUGHING½**
100m Jon Jost c
Jon A. English, Barbara Hammes, Jennifer Johanson, Ed Green, Nathaniel Dorsky, Jerry Barrish.

Another of Jon Jost's very independent films, REMBRANDT LAUGHING is an experimental narrative feature shot in San Francisco with the director's friends serving as actors. The story involves a man (English) who pays a surprise visit to his former live-in girl friend (Hammes) on the fifth anniversary of their breakup and presents her with a token of his affection—a photocopy of an etching of Rembrandt laughing. He wonders if they made a mistake when they split, though Hammes is sure they did the right thing. We then see both of them in their daily routines: English is a composer who earns money however he can, first as a framemaker's assistant and later as a museum guide in a children's science exhibit; Hammes is an assistant at a small architectural firm. Much of the film depicts their relatively mundane (by Hollywood standards) existence, with Jost devoting much screen time to poetic images of a bicycle being peddled, miso soup being stirred, and sand blowing in the wind. Eventually, English meets with an advertising executive friend who, it is later revealed, was once Hammes' lover. The ad exec, who is something of an eccentric and collects sand samples from beaches all over the globe, asks English to be executor of his will. Only at the film's end, when the story resumes some months later, are we able to connect all of the narrative's loose ends: English's friend has recently died, and, according to his wishes, English delivers his sand collection to Hammes. Mixed among the samples are his ashes—his final attempt to be near her forever.

Filmed on almost no budget at all, as are all of Jost's features, REMBRANDT LAUGHING goes against the grain of standard filmmaking practices. Not only is the picture pieced together with very little concern for narrative structure, but its experimentation and nonconformity extend to the production process as well. In the notes that accompany the film, Jost (who acted as director, screenwriter, cinematographer, and editor) makes special mention of his attempt to "deindustrialize" filmmaking, to reduce the overwhelming technical and financial demands and replace them with human and poetic concerns. Instead of making the picture on a strict schedule, for example, Jost and his collaborators filmed for only one or two hours a day, thereby making the process of filmmaking as enjoyable as the film itself.

A filmmaking maverick with no intention of surrendering to Hollywood, Jost is more concerned with capturing real people and their everyday situations than with providing Hollywood-style escapism. For this reason he casts real people in the lead roles. While his previous fiction film, BELL DIAMOND (1987), was acted by citizens of Butte, Montana, whom he had not known before the production began, REMBRANDT LAUGHING is cast with many of the director's friends and filmmaking collaborators. Jon English, who composed the scores for this film and BELL DIAMOND, plays the male lead; Barbara Hammes, the lead actress, previously appeared in Jost's SLOW MOVES (1983); and costar Nathaniel Dorsky is a Bay area filmmaker whose abstract films of blowing sand are integrated into REMBRANDT LAUGHING. As a result, the film has a strong informal feeling that, combined with a certain lack of technical polish, reminds the audience that the images on-screen are of real life, the conversations are real conversations, and the people are real people—and, as might be expected of real people, these representations of their behavior are somewhat banal. This is exactly Jost's point: that real people, no matter how trivial their daily routine, belong on the big screen just as much as Dustin Hoffman or Meryl Streep do. REMBRANDT LAUGHING is filled not just with the commonplace, however, but with the poetry of the quotidian (the

mysteries that a bowl of miso soup holds, for example), and this is where Jost succeeds as a filmmaker. REMBRANDT LAUGHING is not a masterpiece of American independent cinema, nor is Jost a cinematic genius, but his films have a certain integrity and honesty that one cannot help but respect.

p, Jon Jost and Henry Rosenthal; d, Jon Jost; w, Jon Jost and den Darstellern; ph, Jon Jost; m, Jon A. English.

Drama (PR:A MPAA:NR)

ⓥRENEGADES**
105m Morgan Creek-Interscope/ UNIV c

Kiefer Sutherland (*Buster McHenry*), Lou Diamond Phillips (*Hank*), Jami Gertz (*Barbara*), Rob Knepper (*Marino*), Bill Smitrovich (*Finch*), Floyd Westerman (*Red Crow*), Joe Griffin (*Matt*), Clark Johnson (*JJ*), Peter MacNeill (*Denny Ransom*), John Di Benedetto (*Corvo*), Gary Farmer (*George*), Kyra Harper (*Nema*), Joseph Hieu (*Gang Leader*), Dee McCafferty (*Cop Outside Bar*), Heide Von Palleske (*Hooker in Bar*), Tom Butler (*Det. Geddies*), Jack Blum (*Keith Weinstock*), Paul Butler (*Capt. Blalock*), Big Yank (*Dealer*), Robert La Sardo (*Skinhead*), Alar Aedma (*Big Ponytail*), Michael Rhoades (*Small Ponytail*), Joyce Gordon (*Receptionist*), Kay Tremblay (*Old Woman*), Justin Louis (*Rookie Cop*), Steve Whistance-Smith (*Store Detective*), Jackie Samuda (*Woman Cop*), Andy Knott (*Hotel Clerk*), Zoey Adams (*Saleswoman*), Jack Newman (*Bookkeeper*), Marcelle Griffith (*Hooker in Motel*), Thom Christopher (*Hooker's John*), Dick Callahan (*Bartender*), Janelle Hutchison (*Annette*), Steve Wayne Lederman (*Detective*), Garfield Andrews (*Thug Knife*), Gene Mack (*Cop in Alley*), Martin Neufeld, Rick Barabia, Dave Mucci, Al Greene (*Marino's Gang*), Richard Gira (*Cullen*), Richard Sali (*Cop by Salon*), Von Flores, David Lee, Gaston Poon (*Gangbangers*), Paul Hill, Kyle Anderson (*Nema's Kids*), Richard Acheampong (*Teen on Train*), Matt Birman (*Yuppie with Corvette*), Robert Latimer (*Chauffeur*), Real Andrews (*Cop*).

RENEGADES is a crash 'n burn actioner of such numbskull intensity that, while consistently inane, is nonetheless never boring. Undercover cop Sutherland involves himself in a diamond heist that gets ferociously out of hand due to the sadism of its criminal mastermind, Knepper, a slight, foppish type, given to horse breeding and polka-dot ascots, more resembling a snotty maitre d' than a brutal thug. The theft is accomplished only after innumerable vehicles are trashed, innocent bystanders slaughtered, a gallery showing of native American art disrupted, and a prized, mystical lance from the

Lakota tribe stolen. This weapon is the McGuffin upon which the silly FRENCH CONNECTION meets A MAN CALLED HORSE plot turns, as a young tribesman (Phillips) vows to retrieve it and avenge the death of his brother. More incendiary chases ensue, Knepper's gang is systematically decimated, Phillips's wise old daddy chief (Westerman) is murdered and a wary alliance is forged between Sutherland and Phillips before all is put right in the fiery, ear-shattering finale.

Director Jack Sholder's job appears to be largely one of directing traffic in the innumerable catch-me-if-you-can-or-explode sequences. Luckily, he's a fervid wiz at this and is abetted by an army of stuntmen, editors, and second unit personnel. Nothing new, of course, but the sight of all that orange flame mushrooming over charred cars and the sound of metal crashing into plate glass windows (obligatory for the genre) have a visceral thrill appealing to the six-year-old in everyone. This is definitely a check-your-brain-at-the-box-office experience, as the script is as lame as can be, and replete with offensive stereotypes (Chinese cop-killing gangs, Italian mafiosi scarfing up piles of pasta, drug-dealing blacks, and noble, put-upon native Americans). Gratuitous violence abounds, offering such cruel divertissements as a woman's curlers being shot off the top of her head and a man being shoved by the heroes, alive and kicking, into a car trunk (we never do find out what happens to him).

Kiefer Sutherland shares his father Donald's hangdog mien and somewhat leaden air of deliberation. His tired, misunderstood-but-upright role affords him no opportunity for the sleazy gleam he showed in THE LOST BOYS or BRIGHT LIGHTS, BIG CITY. Lou Diamond Phillips overdoes the poker-faced stoicism, trudging through the film like an angry totem pole, with the stringiest hair since Anna Magnani. The mystical aspects of his character are so shabbily hinted at that when he goes into a clairvoyant seizure in a department store it merely looks like a bad reaction to Clinique products. Both actors are so physically slight that belief must take a walk as they pulverize men three times their size. Jami Gertz, an actress capable of hilarious, Isabel Jewell ineptitude, has a meaningless gun-moll bit that provides no chance for her to be as baroquely bad as she was playing her gypsy-vampire-groupie in THE LOST BOYS or coke-crazed princess in LESS THAN ZERO. Screenwriter David Rich doesn't even permit her to have a relationship with either hero, but her overly contorted face in a slo-mo death fall does provide a giggle. (*Graphic violence, profanity.*)

p, David Madden and Paul Schiff; d, Jack Sholder; w, David Rich; ph, Phil Meheux; ed, Caroline Biggerstaff; m, Michael

Kamen; prod d, Carol Spier; art d, James McAteer; set d, Elinor Rose Galbraith; spec eff, Tim Fisher; cos, Gina Kiellerman; stunts, Mickey Gilbert; makeup, Christine Hart.

Action   (PR:O MPAA:R)

ⓥRETURN OF SWAMP THING, THE**

88m Lightyear Entertainment/ Miramax c

Louis Jourdan *(Dr. Anton Arcane)*, Heather Locklear *(Abby Arcane)*, Sarah Douglas *(Dr. Lana Zurrell)*, Dick Durock *(Swamp Thing)*, Ace Mask *(Dr. Rochelle)*, Joey Sagal *(Gunn)*.

In a southern bayou, mad scientist Jourdan is performing macabre genetic experiments in which he turns human specimens into partial animals and insects. When Jourdan's stepdaughter (Locklear), a flighty Valley Girl type, visits his estate to resolve the mysterious circumstances under which her mother died years earlier, Jourdan decides to use Locklear to rejuvenate himself. Like her mother, she has the correct gene code for the process (which is

Dick Durock in RETURN OF THE SWAMP THING (©Miramax).

why her mother died, of course). One evening in the swamp, Locklear stumbles upon two moonshiners, who attack her. Luckily, Swamp Thing (Durock) appears just in time to save the day, as he so often does. Durock tells Locklear that he was once a scientist who developed a regenerative gene formula that Jourdan wanted. Jourdan's men therefore blew up Durock's lab, causing him to spill the formula on himself and covering him in flames. When he jumped into the swamp to put out the fire, the water slime regenerated with his tissue, transforming him into a walking plant. Now Jourdan is intent on capturing Durock and obtaining a sample of the ex-scientist's highly regenerative tissue, needing the sample along with Locklear's gene code to carry out his plan. Knowing she will lead them to Durock, Jourdan's goons follow Locklear. Durock is shot, disappears into Jourdan's mansion through a drain pipe as liquid slime, and rescues Locklear, fleeing with her into the swamp. (Some of his tissue remains behind for use in Jourdan's project, however.) Later, Locklear is nabbed by Jourdan and crew again, but this time Durock does not arrive in time to save her and instead finds her dead in the laboratory. In a rage, he attacks Jourdan, destroys the lab, and kills the doctor's chief henchman. Durock then takes Locklear's lifeless body to the swamp and rejuvenates her. He explains that there may be side effects from the process, but he's not sure what they'll be—and the camera focuses on her foot, from which a small flower is sprouting.

For a definition of camp, see THE RETURN OF SWAMP THING, with its endless string of good-naturedly cheap jokes and comic-book style. Louis Jourdan, as the hokey scientist obsessed with rejuvenation, even manages a few comical references to his most famous film, GIGI. (Significantly, his estate is guarded by a legion of female soldiers in tight outfits.) Unfortunately, the film is burdened with a needless subplot about two young boys who are determined to photograph Swamp Thing and collect a fee for the picture from a local newspaper, and who are apparently intended to provide "comic relief" in what is already a spoof. Still, THE RETURN OF SWAMP THING is more fun than the original SWAMP THING (1982), which— perhaps because it was directed by horror *auteur* Wes Craven—was a lot less funny. *(Violence.)*

p, Ben Melniker and Michael Uslan; d, Jim Wynorski; w, Derek Spencer and Grant Morris (based on the D.C. Comics character); ph, Zoran Hochstatter (Deluxe Color); ed, Leslie Rosenthal; m, Chuck Cirino; prod d, Robb Wilson King; set d, Frank Galline; spec eff, Len Wein and Berni Wrightson; cos, Vicki Graef; makeup, Steve Neill.

Science Fiction   (PR:C MPAA:PG-13)

ⓥROAD HOUSE**

114m Silver Pictures-UA/MGM-UA c

Patrick Swayze *(Dalton)*, Kelly Lynch *(Dr. Elizabeth "Doc" Clay)*, Sam Elliott *(Wade Garrett)*, Ben Gazzara *(Brad Wesley)*, Marshall Teague *(Jimmy)*, Julie Michaels *(Denise)*, Red West *(Red Webster)*, Sunshine Parker *(Emmet)*, Jeff Healey *(Cody)*, Kevin Tighe *(Tilghman)*, John Doe *(Pat McGurn)*, Kathleen Wilhoite *(Carrie)*, Travis McKenna *(Jack)*, Roger Hewlett *(Younger)*, Kurt James Stefka *(Hank)*, Gary Hudson *(Steve)*, Terry Funk *(Morgan)*, Michael Rider *(O'Connor)*, John Young *(Tinker)*, Anthony DeLongis *(Ketchum)*, Joe Unger *(Karpis)*, Tiny Ron *(Mountain)*, Sheila Caan *(Judy)*, Jon Paul Jones *(Stroudenmire)*, Lauri Crossman *(Stella)*, Keith David *(Ernie Bass)*, Ed DeFusco *(Oscar)*, Humberto Larriva, Anthony Marisco, Gonzalo Quintana III, Marshall Rohner *(Cruzados)*, John Oldach, Joey Plewa *(Bandstand Tough Guys)*, Susan Lentini, Patricia Tallman *(Bandstand Babes)*, Mike Fisher, Bob A. Jennings *(Bandstand Bouncers)*, Dawn Ciccone, Julie Royer *(Steve's Girls)*, Frank Noon *(Barfly)*, Cristopher Collins *(Sharing Husband)*, Cheryl Baker *(Well-Endowed Wife)*, Michael Wise *(Gawker)*, Charles Hawke *(Heckler)*, Tom Finnegan *(Chief of Police)*, Christine Anderson, Lisa Axelrod, Debra Chase, Lisa Westman, Kymberly Herrin, Kym Malin, Heidi Paine, Jacklyn Palmer, Marta Rinchusiuso, Meg Thayer *(Party Girls)*, Laura Albert, Christina Veronica Jasae, Michele Burger, Pamela Jackson *(Strip Joint Girls)*, Daryl Sandy Marsh *(Strip Joint Bartender)*, Laura Lee Kasten *(Nurse)*, Bill Dunnam *(Car Salesman)*, Terrance Scott *(Loudmouth)*, Sylvia Baker *(Table Dancer)*, Dennis Ott *(Bar Character)*, Ancel Cook *(Grillman)*, Chino "Fats" Williams *(Derelict)*.

The oldest of western plots gets updated in ROAD HOUSE, starring Patrick Swayze as Dalton, the man with one name who rides into town to restore law and order to seedy saloons. This is quite a guy. He's got a degree in philosophy from New York University, he's amazingly skilled in the martial arts, and he's a mystic who feels no pain. Oh yeah, and he killed a man in Memphis. Ripped his throat clean out. Of course, it was justified (the guy pulled a gun on him), but our hero still feels troubled by it because—well, that's just the kind of guy he is. As the movie opens, a call has gone out to super-bouncer Swayze asking him to saddle up his Mercedes and ride to the Double Deuce bar in Jasper, Missouri, and clean up the place. Tighe, the owner of the Double Deuce, is tired of brawling louts making a shambles of his place, especially since he's planning major renovations that will transform the joint into the Studio 54 of Jasper. Swayze arrives, takes a room in a dilapidated ranch owned by the kindly Parker, and quickly takes control of the tavern situation. He fires a few of the staff members, gives the survivors a crash course in proper bar management, cracks the heads of some rowdy patrons, and in no time the Double Deuce is a model of decorum. But there's more than a bar to clean up in Jasper. It seems the whole town is under the thumb of the vicious Gazzara, who's been extorting money from local businessmen for more than 30 years. It doesn't take long for the town tyrant to feel threatened by Swayze and he sends some of his boys down to the Double Deuce to let him know who's boss. Swayze and his employees knock the emissaries senseless, which makes Gazzara very mad, and he gets madder still when Swayze starts dating the town's pretty doctor (Lynch), whom Gazzara adores. He escalates his attacks on the Double Deuce, but help arrives when Swayze's old friend and mentor (Elliott) rides into town just in time to shatter a few kneecaps. While Elliott and Swayze renew their friendship, Gazzara decides to vent his spleen against the rest of the town, destroying an auto parts store and a car dealership. Then he has his top goon (Teague) blow up Parker's house. Swayze catches Teague leaving the scene of the crime, setting up the long-awaited dual of the titans, a fierce battle until Swayze finally gets the upper hand and Teague pulls a gun. Guess he never heard about that guy in Memphis. Teague is soon a throatless corpse and when Gazzara learns he's lost his favorite thug, he gets hopping mad. To extract his revenge, he has Elliott killed, which pushes Swayze over the edge. He attacks Gazzara's estate, quickly dispatches four heavily armed men, then faces Gazzara one on one. They fight, Gazzara pulls a gun, Swayze gets ready to go for the throat—and then stops, suddenly overwhelmed with the senselessness of it all. He begins to walk away, just asking for a bullet in the back, but luckily several citizens appear out of nowhere to kill Gazzara with a volley of gunfire. When the police arrive (their first appearance in the film), the killers all slyly say they don't know what happened. In the film's final scene, a whole bunch of locals are enjoying an outing in the woods while Swayze and Lynch skinny dip in a nearby river.

What might have been mindless fun is merely mindless under the direction of the appropriately named Rowdy Herrington (JACK'S BACK). Once he's seen to it that all the conventions of the western are firmly in place, Herrington presents an all-out brawl on the average of about every 12 minutes or so. Naturally, one would expect a picture called ROAD HOUSE to feature drinking and fighting, but the battles are so frequent and so brutal that they quickly grow tiresome. Swayze's muscles and dancer's dexterity are on frequent display in the fight scenes, and since that's all the

part requires of him he's more than equal to it. Trapped in a hopelessly evil caricature, Ben Gazzara seems unable to rise above the material, while Kelly Lynch (COCKTAIL) continues to prove that acting ability is not necessary for a career in Hollywood. Sam Elliott, looking thoroughly dissipated, provides the only respite from the film's earnestness, imbuing his grizzled veteran of the bar wars with an easy charm and a welcome sense of humor. Unfortunately he shows up too late and dies too quickly to be of much help. Veteran cinematographer Dean Cundey does provide some handsome visuals, and there's a nice bluesy score by Michael Kamen. But ROAD HOUSE is recommended only to those who really appreciate broken bones. *(Violence, profanity, nudity, sexual situations, substance abuse.)*

p, Joel Silver; d, Rowdy Herrington; w, David Lee Henry and Hilary Henkin (based on a story by David Lee Henry); ph, Dean Cundey (Deluxe Color); ed, Frank J. Urioste and John F. Link; m, Michael Kamen; md, Michael Kamen; art d, William J. Durrell Jr.; set d, Mark Fabus; spec eff, Al di Sarro; cos, Marilyn Vance-Straker; stunts, Charles Picerni; makeup, Scott Eddo.

Action   **(PR:O   MPAA:R)**

ⓥROMERO***
94m Paulist Pictures/Four Seasons c
Raul Julia *(Archbishop Oscar Romero)*, Richard Jordan *(Fr. Rutilio Grande)*, Ana Alicia *(Arista Zalads)*, Tony Plana *(Fr. Morantes)*, Harold Gould *(Francisco Galedo)*, Alejandro Bracho.

In March 1980, the liberal archbishop Oscar Arnulfo Romero of El Salvador was assassinated while performing mass for a group of nuns and patients in a hospital chapel, becoming a victim of the ongoing civil war that has devastated his country and claimed more than 60,000 lives. His killer, never apprehended, is believed to have been a member of a military right-wing death squad. ROMERO is an account of the last three years of the life of this man who has been called a modern-day saint in action, and whose death shocked the world into awareness of El Salvador's tragedy.

The film follows the initially mild, theologically traditional Fr. Romero (Julia) as he gradually becomes conscious of the gross injustices and horrific violence rampant in his country, forcing him to renounce his apolitical stance and become a heroic advocate of human rights and liberation theology. Director John Duigan and screenwriter John Sacret Young (creator of TV's "China Beach") take a simple, economical approach to the story that delivers emotionally. The obscenities of civil war are unflinchingly depicted; scenes

of a brutal soldier's destruction of the Eucharist or the executions of priests and civilians have a numbing, mounting intensity. (A beneficent moment of relief occurs when Romero relaxes with a group of nuns, singing the traditional "De Colores" in a convent kitchen.) The film, shot in Mexico City for its resemblance to San Salvador and the willing cooperation of the local clergy, benefits from adroit photography and a simple yet moving score. To his credit, Duigan rarely overplays his dramatic hand. (An exception is his too obvious lingering over the murder of a child.)

Of crucial importance in a film such as ROMERO is a convincing central performance, and Raul Julia delivers just that, giving what is easily his finest screen portrayal to date. Playing a virtuous man of faith is always problematic, a task too easily leading to pompous grandstanding or mere boredom. Max Von Sydow did an admirably objective, complex job with his inflexible minister in HAWAII, but Julia's work comes closer to Pierre Fresnay's transcendent Vincent de Paul in the Maurice Cloche-Jean Anouilh MONSIEUR VINCENT. Looking strappingly handsome, Julia gives a calm, thoughtful portrayal. Romero's growing awareness of the need for committed action is carefully implanted by the actor. He overdoes nothing, whether in the early scenes depicting him as the bookish, "safe" compromise choice as archbishop or in later instances of defiant courage. When, imprisoned, he overhears the sounds of torture, his anguish is deeply memorable; while in the pivotal moment that represents Romero's turning point of conscience—a deadly trap for any actor—he achieves a brilliance worthy of Renee Falconetti in THE PASSION OF JOAN OF ARC. Kneeling before the grave of a slain priest, his stricken, terrified, exalted face conveys everything there is to know. Julia is backed by strong supporting work from Alejandro Bracho as a doubting priest and Ana Alicia as a willfully uncomprehending matriarch; Richard Jordan is, unfortunately, an embarrassment as another activist priest, and introduces the only jarringly false note in the film.

ROMERO is the first film from Paulist Pictures, the media wing of that order. Fr. Ellwood E. Kieser, the producer (who also created and produced for 23 years the Emmy-winning educational TV series "Insight"), originally envisioned Romero's story as a television movie, but when all three major American networks as well as the Hollywood film studios rejected his proposal, he went ahead with the project himself, raising the funds for his $3.5 million budget from the Paulists and various Catholic bishops. Both Kieser's efforts and his results are to be commended. *(Violence, adult situations.)*

p, Ellwood E. Kieser; d, John Duigan; w, John Sacret Young; ph, Geoff Burton; m, Gabriel Yared.

Biography/Political

(PR:O MPAA:NR)

ⓥ**ROOFTOPS***

95m Koch-Mark/Jett/New Visions c
Jason Gedrick *(T)*, Troy Beyer *(Elana)*, Eddie Velez *(Lobo)*, Alexis Cruz *(Squeak)*, Tisha Campbell *(Amber)*, Allen Payne *(Kadim)*, Steve Love *(Jackie-Sky)*, Rafael Baez *(Raphael)*, Jaime Tirelli *(Rivera)*, Luis Guzman *(Martinez)*, Millie Tirelli *(Squeak's Mom)*, Robert La Sardo *(Blade)*, Jay M. Boryea *(Willie)*, Rockets Redglare *(Carlos)*, Edouard De Soto *(Angelo)*, John Canada Terrell *(Junkie Cop)*, Bruce Smolanoff *(Bones)*, Edythe Jason *(Lois)*, Paul Herman *(Jimmy)*, Lauren Tom *(Audry)*, Stuart Rudin *(Wino)*, Robert Weil *(Hotel Clerk)*, Coley Wallace *(Lester)*, Jose Ynoa *(Young Cook)*, Danny O'Shea *(Rookie Narc)*, Herb Kerr III *(Jorge)*, Kurt Lott *(Zit)*, Peter Lopez *(Burn)*, Jed James *(X)*, Woodrow Asai *(Yard Foreman)*, Angelo Florio *(Cop at Dance)*, Diane Lozada *(Older Sister)*, Imani Parks *(Young Sister)*.

The characters in ROOFTOPS, who live atop abandoned tenement buildings on New York's Lower East Side, may have found the solution to Manhattan's housing crunch. "Great view, low rent, plenty of light—just what everybody in the city wants," explains one rooftop denizen. But the film itself exemplifies another modern-day problem: long music videos passing themselves off as movies. In fact, ROOFTOPS is among the worst of these to date. Gedrick is a loner who has set up house in a rooftop water tower; Cruz is the young graffiti artist who moves in with him after being kicked out of the house by his mother's boy friend. Their makeshift home is threatened by Velez, a crack dealer who has moved his operation into their building. When Gedrick refuses to work for Velez or to move out, the battle for turf is on. Velez and his gang ransack Gedrick's place, then, after they are arrested on drug charges, burn down the water tower and beat up Gedrick, convinced that he turned them in. Meanwhile, Gedrick falls in love with Beyer, who works for Velez (her cousin) in order to support her ailing father and younger sisters. When she visits Gedrick in a neighboring rooftop home where he is nursing his wounds, he tells her his sad story (his mother was accidentally electrocuted during a fight with his father, who later committed suicide) and they make love. The next day, Cruz is killed as the fight with Velez resumes. A vengeful Gedrick trashes the crackhouse, leading to another battle in which Velez is killed. Gedrick, Beyer, and their friends celebrate

their victory with some "combat dancing," their special brand of footwork.

The saddest thing about ROOFTOPS is that it was directed by Robert Wise, the former editor of CITIZEN KANE and THE MAGNIFICENT AMBERSONS who has directed nearly 40 films in several genres, including THE BODY SNATCHER (1945); THE SET-UP (1949); WEST SIDE STORY (1961); and many movies incomparably better than than ROOFTOPS. With its urban setting and lovers from rival camps, ROOFTOPS inevitably recalls WEST SIDE STORY, but even to include the two films in the same sentence is almost to insult the latter, and one is tempted to assume that Wise ceded most of the filmmaking responsibilities in ROOFTOPS to the producer, writer, and choreographers. Apart from its attempt to combine music and urban drama in the WEST SIDE STORY vein, ROOFTOPS (which is not technically a musical, since the characters don't sing and the songs don't advance the story) has other failed ambitions—to start a dance craze a la DIRTY DANCING; FLASHDANCE; or SATURDAY NIGHT FEVER, for example. However, the combat dancing (a mixture of breakdancing, acrobatics, and kickboxing) is neither well-performed nor entertaining enough to inspire such a trend. The film also means to present a sizzling love story, but—like the story as a whole—the romance falls flat. Jason Gedrick and Troy Beyer lack the chemistry and individual sex appeal that would make them a memorable screen couple, and Gedrick is especially miscast. He looks much more like a suburban high-school football star than a street tough, and (what with all the dancing, fighting, and motorcycling his character indulges in) his stunt doubles probably log more screen time than he does. Also annoying is the fact that a white character is the film's hero. Anyone disturbed by Hollywood's tendency to cast African-American and Latino actors primarily as vagabonds, drug dealers, prostitutes, and the like will not be pleased with ROOFTOPS. Having a white knight save the day only makes the stereotyping more offensive and comes across as a weak attempt to sweeten the inner-city characters' plight, a recurring fault in ROOFTOPS. As shown in this movie, living on a roof is not necessarily the last resort of displaced youths; it's something they choose to do. (Gedrick's water tower is furnished like a college dorm room, complete with decorator milk crates and hot pot.) ROOFTOPS was the first film to be produced by the independent New Visions Entertainment, chaired by producer-director Taylor Hackford (AGAINST ALL ODDS; AN OFFICER AND A GENTLEMAN). Made on a budget of $8 million without the benefit of a "name" cast, it flopped at the box office.

But ROOFTOPS is an inauspicious feature debut dramatically as well as financially; ultimately, the rooftop life and characters it presents seem merely absurd. Songs include: "Avenue D" (David A. Stewart, Etta James, Richard Feldman, performed by James and Stewart), "Drop" (George Chandler, Jimmy Chambers, Jimmy Helms, Liam Hensall, performed by London Beat), "Freedom" (Pat Seymour, performed by Seymour), "Rooftops" (Stewart, Seymour, Feldman, performed by Jeffrey Osborne), "Keep Runnin'" (Robert Reed, James Avery, performed by Trouble Funk), "Loving Number One" (Vince Hudson, Jude Hudson, performed by Kisses from the Kremlin), "Revenge (Part II)" (Stewart, Annie Lennox, performed by Eurythmics), "Stretch" (Charlie Wilson, Stewart, performed by Wilson), "Meltdown" (Stewart, Michael Kamen, performed by Joniece Jamison), "Bullet Proof Heart" (Grace Jones, Chris Stanley, performed by Jones). *(Violence, profanity, substance abuse, adult situations, sexual situations.)*

p, Howard W. Koch Jr.; d, Robert Wise; w, Terence Brennan (based on a story by Allan Goldstein, Tony Mark); ph, Theo Van de Sande (Deluxe Color); ed, William Reynolds; m, David A. Stewart and Michael Kamen; prod d, Jeannine Claudia Oppewall; art d, John Wright Stevens; set d, Gretchen Rau; spec eff, Candy Flanagin and Steve Kirshoff; cos, Kathleen Detoro; chor, Jelon Vieira; stunts, Gary Baxley; makeup, Anne Pattison.

Drama   (PR:C MPAA:R)

ROSE GARDEN, THE**
(W. Ger./US) 112m CCC Film Kunst-Golan-Globus/Cannon c
Liv Ullmann *(Gabriele Schlueter-Freund)*, Maximilian Schell *(Aaron Reichenbach)*, Peter Fonda *(Herbert Schlueter)*, Jan Niklas *(George Paessler)*, Kurt Hubner *(Arnold Krenn)*, Hanns Zischler *(Prof. Eckert, the Prosecutor)*, Gila Almagor *(Ruth Levi)*, Katarina Lena Muller *(Tina Schulueter-Freund)*, Mareike Carriere *(Ms. Moerbler)*, Georg Marischka *(Brinkmann)*, Nicolaus Sombart *(Judge)*, Ozay Fecht *(Mrs. Marques)*, Achim Ruppel *(Klaus)*, Friedhelm Lehmann *(Prof. Stauffer)*, Lutz Weidlich *(Schubert)*, Peter Kortenbach *(Emminger)*, Marco Kroger *(Harald)*, Hans Jurgen Schatz *(Hrudek)*, Dagmar Cassens *(Dr. Kurth)*, Horst Scheel *(Ward Physician)*, Roland Schafer *(SS Doctor)*, Uwe Schawz *(SS Unterscharfueher)*, Rolf Mautz *(SS Rottenfuehrer)*, Martin Hoppe *(Young Krenn)*, Helga Sloop *(Old Lady)*, Helmut Kraus *(Taxi Driver)*, Hans-Martin Stier *(Patient)*, Barbara Werz *(Frau Hasold)*, Sylvia Martin *(Frau Stulp)*, Andreas Schmidt *(Vladimir)*, Dierdre Fitzpatrick *(Helga)*, Ines Fridman *(Rachel*

Reichenbach), Evelyn Kussmann *(Ruth Reichenbach)*, Ute Brankatsch *(Journalist)*, Jean-Theo Jost *(Court Officer)*.

Early in this contemporary courtroom drama inspired by a particularly repugnant incident that took place during the Holocaust, the heroine, a divorced Frankfurt public defender (Ullmann), speaks to her young daughter (Muller) of the child's father (Fonda) having left them. When Muller corrects her, saying that Fonda has said that it was Ullmann who broke up their marriage, Ullmann does not argue, but tells Muller that she must decide for herself whom and what to believe. THE ROSE GARDEN poses a similar dilemma in asking audiences to believe its dramatic premise that Nazi war criminals not only remain free from prosecution and punishment, but do so with impunity if not outright arrogance, flaunting their ability to evade justice for a new generation of Nazi true believers. Dutch director Fons Rademakers and screenwriter Paul Hengge present a story that freely mixes fact and fiction, challenging audiences to think and reflect. At the end of the film, an epilog outlining THE ROSE GARDEN's factual basis reveals that the story's most outrageous, implausible, and disturbing elements are precisely those drawn directly from historical record.

Rademakers, who directed the Best Foreign-Language Film Oscar-winner THE ASSAULT (1987), works in English this time out, though the story is set in West Germany. At the Hamburg airport, while Ullmann and Muller wait to meet Fonda (who is to have custody of Muller for the weekend), a dishevelled old man (Schell) abruptly attacks the dapperly dressed, elderly Hubner just as Hubner is about to board a flight out of the country. Badly injured, Hubner presses charges against Schell. Urged on by her daughter (who feels sorry for Schell), Ullmann takes Schell's case, despite the fact that it seems sure to lose, being prosecuted by one of Hamburg's top lawyers. Seeking a connection between Schell and Hubner, she uncovers an abhorrent incident from the Holocaust, when a group of children were infected with tuberculosis as part of a bizarre experiment late in WW II, then injected with morphine and hanged, one by one, while the British closed in. (The eponymous garden was subsequently planted as a memorial to the murdered children.) Ullmann discovers that one of Schell's sisters was among the children, and that Hubner was the SS commander who ordered her murder. Through a series of legal manuevers, Hubner has avoided being tried for his crimes, and was about to leave West Germany for the same reason when Schell confronted him at the airport. Now, while Hubner continues to avoid prosecution, it becomes increasingly likely that Schell will be convicted and imprisoned at

lightning speed due to the testimony of Hubner, whose own trials have been postponed due to his supposed ill health.

THE ROSE GARDEN is overly complicated at times by its instant changes of setting, which hinder dramatic tension. Because she lives in Frankfurt and tries the case in Hamburg, Ullmann's character seems to spend most of the film in transit. It seems likely, however, that Rademakers has intentionally dampened the suspense in order to keep his characters and theme to the fore, an unwieldy strategy that works nonetheless. One of Rademakers' chief concerns here (as in THE ASSAULT) is to show the Holocaust's continuing human toll. In this he is helped by Hengge's thoughtful, well-crafted script, which keeps a sharp focus on ideas without reducing the characters to mouthpieces.

But THE ROSE GARDEN's cast is its major attraction. Liv Ullmann, still one of the screen's most exciting actresses, gives a performance of rare passion and intelligence, showing the subtlety and precision that made her one of Ingmar Bergman's favorite actresses. Maximilian Schell has rarely been better than he is here, and gives dimension to his difficult character, a man who has lost virtually all contact with the world because of his obsessive rage. The supporting players are no less persuasive; even the strangely cast Peter Fonda, playing Ullmann's sophisticated ex-husband, appears credibly German. Well-directed, well-scripted, and well-acted, THE ROSE GARDEN ultimately proves a rare example of a "message" film with enough drama

to match its good intentions. *(Violence, adult situations.)*

p, Artur Brauner; d, Fons Rademakers; w, Paul Hengge; ph, Gernot Roll (Eastmancolor); ed, Kees Linthorst; m, Egisto Macchi; art d, Jan Schlubach; spec eff, Adolf Woytinek; cos, Monika Jacobs; stunts, Gerd Gzrezcak; makeup, Karin Bauer-Hurst.

Drama   **(PR:C MPAA:NR)**

⊙RUDE AWAKENING*
101m Aaron Russo/Orion c
Eric Roberts *(Fred)*, Cheech Marin *(Hesus)*, Julie Hagerty *(Petra)*, Robert Carradine *(Sammy)*, Louise Lasser *(Ronnie)*, Cliff DeYoung *(Brubaker)*, Dion Anderson *(Dr. Binibon)*, Peter Boyden *(Dr. Childs)*, Nicholas Wyman *(Dr. Albert)*, Michael Luciano *(Merlin)*, Amy Glass, Becky Glass *(Twins)*, Ed Fry *(Agent Drome)*, Aaron Russo *(Voice of Fish)*, Patrick John Hurley, Daniel Chapman *(Agents in Jungle)*, William C. Carraro *(Agent on Street)*, David Peel, Greg Rex *(Hippy Singers)*, Dr. Timothy Leary, Jerry Rubin, Bobby Seale *(Diners at Ronnie's)*, Rosanna Iversen, Michael Louden, Charlie Gates, Darrick Harris, Janet Harper *(La Fleck Models)*, Peter Nevargic *(Julian)*, Elzbieta Czyzewska *(Eema)*, William C. Paulson *(Phil)*, Larry Attile *(Agent Blandish)*, Tom Sizemore *(Ian)*, Frederikke Borge *(Mona)*, Deena Levy *(Wanda)*, Kevin Dornan *(Jay)*, Davidson Thomson *(Amos)*, Cindy Williams *(June)*, Timothy L. Halpern *(Lance)*, Rodney Clark *(Cowboy)*, Andrea Martin *(April)*,

Eric Roberts and Cheech Marin in RUDE AWAKENING (©Orion).

Buck Henry *(Lloyd)*, B.J. Jefferson *(Newscaster)*.

A promising premise—60s hippies confronting 80s yuppies—goes badly awry in this comedy from directors Aaron Russo and David Greenwalt. The film opens in New York in 1969, introducing us to a quartet of hippies (the idealistic Roberts, his lover, Hagerty, the perpetually stoned Marin, and aspiring writer Carradine) who hang out at the apartment of earth mother Lasser. Roberts and Marin are being hounded by a nearly psychotic Justice Department agent (DeYoung) for crimes ranging from draft evasion to inciting a riot, and are forced to go underground. The film then flashes forward 20 years, to the jungles of the Central American country "Managuador," where Roberts and Marin have been living in a commune, completely isolated from the rest of the world, for nearly two decades. The jungle silence is broken by gunfire, and commune members discover a mortally wounded US government agent carrying top secret documents. He dies, and Roberts finds that his papers include plans for the US to start a war in Managuador, then invade it. Roberts decides that he and Marin should return to New York to tell the world about the heinous plot, but the two are being watched by yet more government agents (why these agents don't just take the documents away from them is a mystery) and are kept under surveillance once they arrive in New York. The two head off to find Lasser, who now operates a successful restaurant frequented by yuppies (among those playing her patrons are 60s icons Jerry Rubin, Timothy Leary, and Bobby Seale). She directs them to Hagerty, now a neurotic millionaire fashion designer. Hagerty's not at all happy to see her long-lost friends, but a little marijuana mellows her out and she spends the night with Roberts, awakening more anxious than ever to be rid of these two blasts from the past. In the meantime, DeYoung (still a fed and more demented than ever) is back on the trail of his quarry, and he bursts into Hagerty's apartment to arrest the pair. They subdue the lawman and escape with Hagerty, though she insists she wants no part of their activities. Next comes a visit to Carradine, who lives in a New York apartment with his shrewish wife (Williams) and teenage son (Halpern). A successful owner of a chain of tanning salons, Carradine has caved into Williams' demands that they move into a very expensive co-op, and are in the process of being screened by the co-op president (Henry) and his wife (Martin) when Carradine's three old friends show up. Predictably, the hippies make a shambles of the affair, forcing an angry Carradine to demand they leave. He quickly regrets his actions, however, and physically throws the snobbish Henry out of his apartment before going

out to find his friends. By now, Hagerty has gotten over her anxiety and is enjoying the company of Roberts and Marin, and when Carradine finds them at Lasser's place, the reunited friends set out to radicalize the 80s, taking over a building on the campus of New York University, though Roberts' attempts to bestir the students there with fiery rhetoric are met with apathy. DeYoung and his minions arrive, capture the protestors, and demand that Roberts reveal the location of the secret papers. Roberts, however, has already given the papers to Carradine's son, who has delivered them to the *New York Times*, and soon the invasion plans are revealed in publications across the nation. Ironically, polls show a majority of Americans think it's a good idea, so the president sends troops into Managuador and war breaks out. Believing he is the cause of the war, a despondent Roberts bids farewell to his friends and heads down the street without knowing where he's going. Suddenly, he is surrounded by a group of students who heard him at the university and want his help in organizing protest groups. Roberts agrees and the film ends.

Just after Roberts and friends take over the university building, he asks Carradine and Hagerty to fill him in on the major issues of the 80s. In a rather matter-of-fact way, they tick off such modern-day horrors as holes in the ozone layer, acid rain, nuclear waste, AIDS, and farm foreclosures, then get into a very passionate argument over the relatively mundane issue of film colorization. The scene neatly makes this film's point about commitment (or lack thereof) in the 80s, but it's buried under the rubble of so many bad gags, lapses in logic, and aimless scenes that any viewer who's still around at that point isn't likely to care. RUDE AWAKENING's codirectors have one previous directing credit between then—Greenwalt helmed the forgettable SECRET ADMIRER in 1985. Russo made a bunch of money in the music business before entering films as a producer (THE ROSE; TRADING PLACES), leading to the formation of Aaron Russo Enterprises, and RUDE AWAKENING is the company's first film project. It's impossible to tell who directed what here, but virtually none of it works. In their maniacal pursuit of laughs, the filmmakers offer us wildly overdrawn caricatures (DeYoung's being the worst), acid flashbacks (Marin's hallucinations include a talking fish and a Sergio Leone-style gunfighter), dopey names (Henry and Martin are "the Stooles"), and satirical *New York Post* headlines (haven't we had enough of them?). Food also serves as a "comic" inspiration; Lasser, Hagerty, and Martin all must endure scenes requiring them to eat in a manner one guesses is supposed to be funny. It all plays like a series of bad "Saturday Night Live" skits—which isn't too

surprising, since coscripter Neil Levy got his start as an "SNL" writer.

As the sincerely committed hippie who is completely in touch with emotions, Eric Roberts for once plays a character who isn't destroyed by his bizarre intensity. Julie Hagerty, a strange actress who never seems to connect with the cast around her, is fine as a hippie and a neurotic, but less effective when she tries for some sort of normalcy in the last third of the movie, while the previously anonymous Robert Carradine remains so in this film (he's around mainly just to fill out the foursome). This is a step backwards for Cheech Marin, however, who had put some distance between himself and his Cheech and Chong days with 1987's BORN IN EAST L.A., a rather gentle comedy which he starred in, wrote, and directed. In RUDE AWAKENING, Marin returns to his roots with a vengeance, playing a character who smokes zeppelin-sized joints and who'll ingest anything on the chance of getting high. Marin plays this character as well as anyone can, but we've seen it too many times before; it just isn't all that funny any more. Songs include: "Rainy Day Women #12 & 35" (Bob Dylan, performed by Dylan), "Star Spangled Banner" (Francis Scott Key, performed by Pat Boone, Jimi Hendrix), "Somebody to Love" (Darby Slick, performed by the Jefferson Airplane), "Paper Doll" (Johnny Black), "Uncle John's Band" (Robbie Hunter, Jerry Garcia, performed by the Grateful Dead), "Run Through the Jungle" (John C. Fogerty, performed by the Georgia Satellites), "We the People" (Franke Previte, performed by Franke & the Knockouts), "I Like Marijuana" (David Peel, performed by David Peel and the Lower East Side), "Roadhouse Blues" (the Doors, performed by the Doors), "Comin' Home" (Previte, Jim Nuzzo, performed by Kim Carnes), "Success" (Degville, James, Whitmore, performed by Sigue Sigue Sputnik), "Darling Be Home Soon" (John Sebastian, performed by Phoebe Snow), "Conga" (Enrique Garcia, performed by Miami Sound Machine), "Raga Multani" (performed by Dr. Lalmani Misra), "Rude Awakening" (Rick Rose, performed by Bill Medley), "Revolution" (John Lennon, Paul McCartney, performed by Mike and the Mechanics). *(Brief nudity, profanity, sexual situations, substance abuse.)*

p, Aaron Russo; d, Aaron Russo and David Greenwalt; w, Neil Levy and Richard LaGravenese (based on a story by Neil Levy); ph, Tim Sigel (Technicolor); ed, Paul Fried; m, Jonathan Elias; prod d, Mel Bourne; art d, Dan Davis; set d, Carol Nast; spec eff, Barnaby Jackson and Gary Zeller; cos, Peggy Farrell; stunts, Jery Hewitt; makeup, Leslie Fuller.

Comedy   (PR:O   MPAA:R)

S

SAND AND BLOOD**½

(Fr.) 101m Septembre-Films A2-La Sept-Images Investissements-Centre National de la Cinematographie/ New Yorker c

(DE SABLE ET DE SANG; AKA: BLOOD AND SAND)

Sami Frey (Manuel Vasquez), Andre Dussollier (Emilio), Clementine Celarie (Marion Vasquez), Patrick Catalifo (Francisco Jimenez), Maria Casares (Dolores, Manuel's Mother), Catherine Rouvel (Carmina, Francisco's Mother), Stephane Albouy (Mario Jimenez), Camille Grandville (Annie), Pierre Forget (Francisco's Father).

Slow-moving but richly atmospheric, this competently made French production tells the story of a young matador, of his eventual disdain for his profession, and of the friendship that brings about his conversion. Set in the south of France, it stars Patrick Catalifo as a French bullfighter, and Sami Frey as a Spanish expatriate doctor and musician. Frey is on hand when Catalifo is injured in a traffic accident, and treats the young matador. A friendship quickly develops between the two, and Catalifo invites Frey to a bullfight. Despite his abhorrence of the sport, Frey attends the fight but ends up leaving in disgust. When the two meet later, Frey explains that his aversion to bullfighting is an outgrowth of his painful memories of life in Spain under the repressive Franco regime. This prompts Catalifo to reconsider his choice of profession, which until this point he has seen simply as a way out of poverty. To complicate matters further, Catalifo's younger brother, Albouy, becomes interested in the sport; however, his father talks Albouy into taking Catalifo's old job in a slaughterhouse. In the meantime, Catalifo attends Frey's concerts, and the doctor continues to drag himself to bullfights. Eventually, the two travel to Spain, where Frey confronts his past and Catalifo retires his red cape.

With the help of cinematographer Andre Neau, writer-director Jeanne Labrune has created a film that is suffused in the atmosphere of the bull ring. Labrune's graphic re-creation of the bullfights is often spectacular, but, like the director's careful rendering of the matadors' preparations, these sequences retain a documentary-like quality that illustrates both the glamour and the ritual of a matador's life. Moreover, Labrune's pursuit of realism is nicely augmented by convincing performances from Frey, Catalifo, Stephane Albouy, Clementine Celarie, and Andre Dussollier. (Violence, profanity, nudity, sexual situations.)

p, Jean Nainchrik; d, Jeanne Labrune; w, Jeanne Labrune; ph, Andre Neau; ed, Nadine Fischer; m, Anne-Marie Fijal and Nina Corti; set d, Patrice Mercier.

Drama   (PR:O MPAA:NR)

ⓥSATURDAY THE 14TH STRIKES BACK*

78m Concorde c

Jason Presson (Eddie Baxter), Ray Walston (Gramps), Avery Schreiber (Frank), Patty McCormack (Kate), Julianne McNamara (Linda), Rhonda Aldrich (Alice), Daniel Will-Harris (Bert), Pamela Stonebrook (Charlene), Joseph Ruskin, Riad, Leo V. Gordon, Michael Berryman, Phil Leeds, Tommy Hall.

In 1981 the horror spoof SATURDAY THE 14TH—in which Paula Prentiss and Richard Benjamin spent 90 minutes telling tremendously unfunny jokes in a haunted house—was released to little notice. Now comes a sequel, SATURDAY THE 14TH STRIKES BACK. The bad news is that it's just as stupid as the original, the good news is, it's shorter.

The story of Presson and his kooky family is related by Presson himself in flashback. Standing on a beach, Presson remembers the summer when he turned 16 and saved the world. It all started when a convict uncle was electrocuted and left his house to Presson's family, namely Presson, parents Schreiber and McCormack, grandpa Walston, and loud-mouth sister McNamara. Presson's meddling aunt (Aldrich) and stupid uncle (Will-Harris) eventually move in with the family, hoping to change the will and inherit the house themselves. Soon strange things begin happening: the whole family begins sleepwalking and building objects out of chocolate pudding, while Presson finds a sexy vampire (Stonebrook) in his bedroom and talks to an evil Egyptian in his basement. Eventually, he learns that the house was built over a crack in the earth that lets in all the evil of the afterworld, and he must seal the fissure to prevent an apocalypse. As the house fills up with spirits, Presson is seduced by an Egyptian slave girl and also acquires a magic power that nearly corrupts him: If he chooses to use this power for malevolent purposes (like making his sister shut up or forcing his mom to cook him cheeseburgers) he will become Prince of Darkness and rule the evil world himself. As the ultimate evil force gets set to arrive at the stroke of midnight on Saturday the 14th and take over the world, Presson finds out Walston is really not his grandfather, but a wizard who gives him a magic bell and a lucky coin to conquer the darkness. Presson and the evil force do battle amidst avalanches, hurricanes, and explosions (all throwaway footage from other movies) and he emerges victorious when he decides not to abuse his power.

The film ends with Presson back on the beach, wondering if it was all real; when the Egyptian girl appears, he smiles, and they walk off into the sunset.

SATURDAY THE 14TH STRIKES BACK is among the worst films of this or any year. The jokes fall completely flat, the story (for lack of a better word) is ridiculously muddled, and the performances are embarrassing. Jason Presson is a stiff, Ray Walston hams it up pathetically, and Avery Schreiber is his usual overbearing self. The film has no comic point of view; it doesn't know whether it's a farce or a satire. One uninspired running gag has the family hooked on the media coverage of a little girl trapped in a cardboard box while rescue teams try to free her. Produced by Julie Corman for her father Roger's Concorde Pictures, SATURDAY THE 14TH STRIKES BACK is a very sad example of low-budget filmmaking. Once Roger Corman was a pioneer in the film industry who would spot talented young filmmakers (like Joe Dante, Paul Bartel, or, earlier, Francis Ford Coppola) and give them a very small budget to make a movie. The results were usually positive and sometimes astounding, with the raw talent and energy of the directors shining through the constraints of the budget. Sadly, Corman has lost his touch—director-writer Howard Cohen, who helmed the similarly inept TIME TRACKERS, appears completely talentless —and seems to be stuck with much smaller budgets and even smaller imaginations these days. (Adult situations, violence.)

p, Julie Corman; d, Howard R. Cohen; w, Howard R. Cohen; ph, Levie Isaacks (Foto-Kem Color); ed, Bernard Caputo; m, Parmer Fuller; prod d, Stephen Greenberg.

Comedy/Horror   (PR:A MPAA:PG)

SAY ANYTHING

(See THE YEAR'S BEST)

ⓥSCANDAL***

(Brit.) 114m Palace-British Screen-Miramax/Miramax c

John Hurt (Stephen Ward), Joanne Whalley-Kilmer (Christine Keeler), Bridget Fonda (Mandy Rice-Davies), Ian McKellen (John Profumo), Leslie Phillips (Lord Astor), Britt Ekland (Mariella Novotny), Roland Gift (Johnnie Edgecombe), Jeroen Krabbe (Eugene Ivanov).

In 1988, the British film WHITE MISCHIEF took a swipe at the decadence of the aristocracy in colonized Nairobi in 1941, a group of wealthy whites who drank scotch, took heroin, and had wild orgies while their countrymen back home were at war. Into this licentiousness stepped playboy Josslyn Hay, the Earl of Erroll, who was murdered after openly cuckolding an

Joanne Whalley and John Hurt in SCANDAL (©Miramax).

aging nobleman with the latter's pretty young wife. The mystery of his murder was never solved, but the scandal rocked the aristocracy at home and in the colonies. In 1989, another British film (costarring WHITE MISCHIEF's John Hurt), Michael Caton-Jones' SCANDAL, peeks under the bedsheets of Britain's ruling class. This time the target is the British government and the infamous "Profumo Affair," the sex scandal that eventually caused Conservative Party Prime Minister Harold Macmillan to resign and brought about an electoral victory for Labour.

In the early 1960s, Minister of War John "Jack" Profumo, a Conservative and the husband of former film star Valerie Hobson (THE BRIDE OF FRANKENSTEIN; GREAT EXPECTATIONS; SPY IN BLACK; KIND HEARTS AND CORONETS), was romantically linked to accused prostitute Christine Keeler, who, as it happened, was also involved with Soviet attache Eugene Ivanov, an alleged spy. Keeler met both men through Dr. Stephen Ward, a high-society osteopath (his clients included Winston Churchill, Elizabeth Taylor, Paul Getty, and members of the royal family), portraitist of the rich and famous, and aspiring James Bond. Ward had been living with Keeler and, working with the tacit approval of the British intelligence agency MI5, got Keeler to sleep with Ivanov in order to gain information on the Soviet's movements. (Ivanov presumably was privy to secrets regarding the deployment of atomic weaponry in

Europe during the Cuban missile crisis. During his stay in England, he attempted to negotiate an agreement between the Soviet Union and the United States, using Great Britain as an unofficial intermediary and approaching Ward as a potential go-between with government figures.) To make matters even more risque, Ward and his circle, which included the teenage beauty Mandy Rice-Davies and infamous slumlord Peter Rachman, were frequent participants in extravagant orgies thrown by Mariella Novotny, an alleged lover of John F. Kennedy. Meanwhile, Rice-Davies was bedding the highly respected Lord Astor and, according to some reports, Douglas Fairbanks, Jr. If that weren't enough to offend the prim and proper Brits of 1963, there were also reports that film director Anthony Asquith (son of the prime minister) had attended these parties, hiding his face behind a mask and wearing a sign around his neck that read, "Please beat me if I fail to satisfy."

The problem with SCANDAL is that all of this seems much less shocking today then it did in the 1960s. As scandals go, the Profumo Affair is pretty tame. After all, who should be surprised that a few stuffy government types were carrying on with young ladies? In WHITE MISCHIEF we were at least treated to a murder and even a hint of necrophilia; SCANDAL merely presents us with events that *were* a scandal in 1963, but even then only because the press made them so. By now—after Chappaquiddick; Iran-Contra; Prince Andrew

and Koo Stark; JFK and Marilyn; Gary Hart, Donna Rice, and *Monkey Business* —scandals have become pretty routine; sex, power, and corruption seem rather commonplace. It's no wonder SCANDAL seems innocuous.

Instead of sleaze, director Caton-Jones and screenwriter Michael Thomas deliver a vindication of the affair's chief scapegoats—Ward and Keeler—in the form of a two-hour nostalgia trip (complete with Beatle hits, or rather, obvious imitations of the Beatles doing their songs) with some complex and powerful performances. For those who remember it, the film plays like a greatest hits album featuring everybody's favorite lines and characters from the Profumo Affair. All the characters and all the scenes are here—the nude swim by Christine (played by dead-ringer Joanne Whalley-Kilmer), after which she accidentally winds up in the arms of Profumo; her involvement with a lovesick, pistol-wielding West Indian, Johnnie Edgecombe (played by Roland Gift, part-time actor [SAMMY AND ROSIE GET LAID] and part-time singer with Fine Young Cannibals); Mandy's supposed involvement with Douglas Fairbanks, Jr. (who threatened a libel suit if he were named in the film, though Rice-Davies had already named him in her autobiography, *My Life and Lovers*); Mandy's infamous response— "Well, he would, wouldn't he?"—to Lord Astor's denial of having had intercourse with her; the mysterious "man in the mask" who begs to be disciplined (allegedly Asquith, but not named here); Profumo's gifts to Christine: a 20-pound note for her mother, an expensive cigarette lighter, and a love letter written on War Ministry stationery; the orgies of Novotny and a casual JFK reference; Peter Rachman's brief involvement with Ward and Keeler; and, last but not least, Ward's suicide, complete with a verbatim reading of the suicide note ("I do hope I haven't let people down too much . . . The car needs oil in the gearbox") and a closeup on the bottle of Nembutal. Of course, the screen is filled with various other sights you'd expect in a film set in early 1960s London: miniskirts, smoke-filled dens filled with West Indians, rows of tenements, opportunistic newsmen from tabloids, and a solid round of pop music.

The atmosphere is effective and the performances excellent (especially that of Hurt as a pathetic, sad Ward, and Bridget Fonda as the spunky Rice-Davies, taking the role Emily Lloyd dropped), but overall the direction is uninspired—competent, but uninspired. More than anything, the film exists to show that Ward (who killed himself before he was pronounced guilty of "living on immoral earnings") was not a pimp who procured women for high officials, but a likable, if rather pathetic, creature who simply wanted to fit in among the elite class with which he allied himself. Because he was essentially a powerless hanger-on, Ward was made the scapegoat, as was Keeler, who, while living a generally amoral existence, was never the call-girl the press and prosecution made her out to be. As with so many scandals, the little guy got buggered—Ward was put through the ringer and driven to suicide, while Keeler now lives on the dole in a council flat, but Profumo, after years of community service in London's East End, was made a CBE (Commander of the British Empire) by the Queen in 1975.

Unfortunately, director Caton-Jones (who previously made THE MAKING OF *ABSOLUTE BEGINNERS*, a documentary about Julien Temple's 1986 film, which, incidentally, costarred Mandy Rice-Davies) is at once too literal and not literal enough in his depiction of events in SCANDAL. Factually, the film is right on the money, although considerations of length excluded many of the details, such as the Cuban missile crisis angle. (Originally, the film was planned as a seven-hour miniseries for British TV.) Oddly, however, considering its story of sex and power games behind the scenes of British government, SCANDAL is far more delicate than it should be. Not that one wants CALIGULA circa 1963, but SCANDAL is no naughtier than a grade-school game of spin-the-bottle. The greatest scandal of all is that this relatively tame picture (there is much more sex and nudity in THE UNBEARABLE LIGHTNESS OF BEING, not to mention any number of excessively violent films) initially received an "X" from the MPAA. The rating was revised to "R," but reportedly all that was necessary for this change was the excision of a shot of a penis during the orgy scene. Thus, although SCANDAL (and countless other films) contains both topless and full-frontal female nudity, the hypocritical MPAA took exception only to a shot of full-frontal *male* nudity, while, for all the cultural stereotypes about British propriety, SCANDAL was released uncut in England.

If it's a poke at England's Conservatives you're looking for, the honest fiction of Mike Leigh's HIGH HOPES has done more to make them bleed than the pointless fact of SCANDAL. In addition to the numerous background songs, Dusty Springfield performs the Pet Shop Boys' "Nothing Has Been Proved." *(Nudity, sexual situations, substance abuse, profanity, violence.)*

p, Stephen Woolley; d, Michael Caton-Jones; w, Michael Thomas; ph, Micke Molloy (Technicolor); ed, Angus Newton; m, Carl Davis; prod d, Simon Holland; art d, Chris Townsend.

Biography/Political   (PR:O MPAA:R)

⊙SCENES FROM THE CLASS STRUGGLE IN BEVERLY HILLS**½
102m North Street/Cinecom c
Jacqueline Bisset *(Clare Lipkin)*, Ray Sharkey *(Frank)*, Robert Beltran *(Juan)*, Mary Woronov *(Lisabeth Hepburn-Saravian)*, Ed Begley Jr. *(Peter Hepburn)*, Wallace Shawn *(Howard Saravian)*, Arnetia Walker *(To-bel Hepburn)*, Rebecca Schaeffer *(Zandra Lipkin)*, Barret Oliver *(Willie Saravian)*, Edith Diaz *(Rosa)*, Paul Bartel *(Dr. Mo Van De Kamp)*, Paul Mazursky *(Sidney Lipkin)*, Jerry Tendo *(June-bug)*, Susan Saiger *(Kelly)*, Michael Feinstein *(Himself)*.

Asked to come up with a free-associative label for independent filmmaker Paul Bartel, moviegoers familiar with his work would most likely offer "bad taste." While the actor-director isn't quite in the same league with shock master John Waters—in terms of both talent and vulgarity—and while his satirical barbs haven't always been especially insightful or funny, Bartel has raised plenty of eyebrows himself with movies like EATING RAOUL; LUST IN THE DUST; and LONGSHOT. With SCENES FROM THE CLASS STRUGGLE IN BEVERLY HILLS, Bartel continues his assault on decorum and refuses to pull any punches, but again his film is a hit-and-miss affair.

The scene is set for this modern-day bedroom farce when Woronov, a wealthy recent divorcee, moves in with her Beverly Hills neighbor, Bisset, while her own house is fumigated—presumably to remove any traces of Woronov's weaselish ex-husband, gynecologist Shawn. Bisset, an aging but beautiful onetime sitcom star, has recently been widowed—though her philandering husband's ghost (played by movie director Paul Mazursky) turns up periodically to taunt her—and is now determined to revive her acting career. Joining Woronov among Bisset's houseguests are Woronov's invalid son, Oliver; her brother, Begley, a talentless playwright; and Walker, the African-American Las Vegas showgirl Begley married after a five-day acquaintance. Woronov's sleazy but worldly houseman, Sharkey, also takes up residence, and in short order makes a $5,000 bet with Bisset's live-in servant, Beltran, that he'll be able to bed Bisset before Beltran can do the same with Woronov. Facing the wrath of gangsters unless he pays off a big gambling debt, Beltran has little choice but to accept Sharkey's wager, even though losing means that he'll have to go to bed with the pansexual Sharkey. An upstairs-downstairs game of musical mattresses follows, as the help pursue the ladies of the house (who are anything but oblivious to the physical charms of their employees); newlywed Begley woos Bisset; and Walker hops in the sack with Sharkey, initiates young Oliver into the world of sex, and bedevils Shawn, who turns out to be her former lover and

who tries pathetically to rekindle his relationship with Woronov. Drifting emotionlessly through the whole proceedings are Bisset's campy "thinologist" (Bartel) and blase daughter (Schaeffer, in her penultimate film role before her much-publicized murder; see Obituaries). Meanwhile, Diaz, the Hispanic housekeeper, serves up bizarre mystical aphorisms. Propositions are made (Beltran's are endearingly ineffectual), clothes are shed, accusations fly, and honor even raises its unlikely head before the bedsheets are all back in place.

While there is something to offend most sensibilities in SCENES FROM THE CLASS STRUGGLE IN BEVERLY HILLS, Bartel's film isn't nearly as shocking as he appears to intend it to be. Sex of all kinds is spicily discussed (and discussed, and discussed), social mores are flaunted, and libidos lampooned, but once the no-holds-barred tenor of the film is established, its pithy prurience loses its sting. Moreover, Bartel and screenwriter Bruce Wagner provide next to nothing in the way of insight (class-based or otherwise) into their characters' motivations, and anyone who takes the title at its word and expects anything like social analysis will be sorely disappointed. If Bartel intended his film as satire, he has failed to infuse it with deeper truths that would resonate after the laughter stops.

If, on the other hand, he intended SCENES as nothing more than farce, he has for the most part succeeded. Bartel and Wagner offer a number of interesting and funny caricatures, most of them well played, and the director's pacing keeps the bedroom doors revolving quickly and unexpectedly enough to keep the partner-switches amusing. Not all of the performances from the strong cast are as effective as that of the pneumatic Arnetia Walker in the role of hot-to-trot social climber To-bel, but in general the cast does a good job of selling the uneven script. Ed Begley, Jr., has some very funny moments as the pitiful playwright, Ray Sharkey is suitably slimy as the Machiavellian seducer, Jacqueline Bisset demonstrates a surprising deftness with comedy, Robert Beltran is convincingly sincere as the film's most sympathetic character, Mary Woronov (a frequent Bartel collaborator) vacillates effectively between ice queen and sex kitten, Bartel himself is amusingly droll as the "thinologist," and Wallace Shawn is Wallace Shawn.

Not everyone will find a lot to laugh at in SCENES. Few will find it hilarious; most, depending on their temperament, will find it either pretty funny or not so funny at all. It's that kind of movie. To be sure, it has some great moments, but occasionally the wait between them becomes a little tiring. Whatever it is, however, SCENES FROM THE CLASS STRUGGLE IN BEVERLY

HILLS is Bartel's film. After two years of shopping the script around to the studios, who liked it but found it too outrageous, Bartel considered toning down the screenplay. Then Cinecom Entertainment Group offered him hands-off financing to the tune of $4.5 million, and Bartel was able to make his film the way he wanted to.(*Excessive profanity, nudity, sexual situations.*)

p, James C. Katz; d, Paul Bartel; w, Bruce Wagner (based on a story by Paul Bartel, Wagner); ph, Steven Fierberg (CFI Color); ed, Alan Toomayan; m, Stanley Myers; prod d, Alex Tavoularis; art d, Bob Kensinger; cos, Dona Granata.

Comedy   (PR:O MPAA:R)

ⓥ**SCREWBALL HOTEL** zero
101m Maurice Smith-Avatar/UNIV c
Michael C. Bendetti *(Mike)*, Andrew Zeller *(Herbie)*, Jeff Greenman *(Norman)*, Kelly Monteith *(Mr. Ebbel)*, Corinne Alphen *(Cherry Amour)*, Charles Ballinger *(Stoner)*, Laurah Guillen *(Miss Walsh)*, Lori Deann Pallet *(Candy)*.

It took four credited writers, plus a fifth who provided "additional material," to take a situation ripe with opportunity and come up with a script completely devoid of laughs. After a military academy expels three young men—two interchangeable girl chasers (Bendetti and Zeller) and a John Candy clone (the rotund Greenman) —their parents kick them out of their homes, telling them to find jobs. After spotting a want ad for a Florida hotel offering fun in the sun, room and board, and tips, the trio heads south. They arrive at the Rochester Hotel only to find that its owner (Monteith) must come up with $300,000 in five weeks or turn the place over to creditors. However, he is too distracted to be worried. In a running gag that elicits the film's only snickers, Monteith and his voluptuous secretary (Guillen) act out sexual fantasy scenes from classic movies, costumed as Snow White and Sneezy, Bogart and Bergman, the Tin Man and Dorothy, or a struggling swimmer and Jaws. Unbeknownst to Monteith, his general manager (Ballinger) has not only made a deal to take control of the hotel, but also has booked the Miss Purity Beauty Pageant and plans to keep all the profits for himself. However, the resourceful new employees enact a plan to save the hotel, opening a casino in the basement and offering entertainment. When the sweet, innocent contestants arrive for the pageant, one of the boys dresses as a nun (Sister Blister) and another as Moses (with a fake beard that covers his mouth and makes most of his dialog unintelligible); together they convince the girls that they are taking part in a religious ritual, when, in fact, they are performing an oil-wrestling show for casino guests. Mean-

while, Ballinger has made a drug deal with some Mafia men, lost the five kilos of coke, and is now the target of a hired killer. Ultimately, the beauty pageant takes place at night around the huge and beautifully lit hotel pool, with predictable results.

SCREWBALL HOTEL's climactic action makes good use of the real star of the film, the hotel itself; however, the antics are so sophomoric that the old architectural beauty seems to be blushing at having ever allowed the movie crew on the premises. There isn't really anything to laugh at here, unless, of course, you are amused by lines like: "Get lost, hemorrhoid" or "Virginity is like a traveler's check . . . it's okay to lose it." And if you think that's funny, SCREWBALL HOTEL's has even more hilarity in store for you as it provides the opportunity to watch a dog get killed in a clothes dryer, hotel dining room guests inadvertently lap up pudding laced with cocaine, a Crocodile Dundee-like hotel guest overcome with jealousy when another man crawls in bed with his sheep, and beauty contestants make fools of themselves on TV after being secretly drugged. Incidentally, if anyone cares, the boys save the hotel by selling videocassette rights to the pool-side debacle. (*Nudity, adult situations, substance abuse.*)

p, Maurice Smith; d, Rafal Zielinski; w, B.K. Roderick, Phil Kueber, Charles Wiener, Nick Holeris, and Sam Kaufman; ph, Thomas F. Denove (Continental & Foto-Kem Color); ed, Joseph Tornatore; m, Nathan Wang; prod d, Naomi Shohan.

Comedy   (PR:O MPAA:R)

SEA OF LOVE****½
113m Martin Bregman/UNIV c
Al Pacino *(Frank Keller)*, Ellen Barkin *(Helen)*, John Goodman *(Sherman)*, Michael Rooker *(Terry)*, William Hickey *(Frank Keller, Sr.)*, Richard Jenkins *(Gruber)*, Paul Calderon *(Serafino)*, Gene Canfield *(Struk)*, Larry Joshua *(Dargan)*, John Spencer *(Lieutenant)*, Christine Estabrook *(Gina Gallagher)*, Barbara Baxley *(Miss Allen)*, Patricia Barry *(Older Woman)*, Mark Phelan, Gerald Lenton *(Murdered Men)*, Michael O'Neill *(Raymond Brown)*, Michael Fischetti *(Doorman)*, Luis Ramos *(Omar Maldonado)*, Rafael Baez *(Efram Maldonado)*, Samuel L. Jackson *(Black Guy)*, Damien Leake *(Ernest Lee)*, Zachary Michael Simmons *(Ernest's Son)*, John Thaddeus *(Tommy)*, Joshua Nelson *(Willie)*, Christofer De Oni *(Supermarket Manager)*, Dwayne McClary *(Supermarket Cashier)*, Thom Curley *(Toastmaster)*, Fred Sanders *(Cable Supervisor)*, Thomas Wagner *(Bartender)*, Manny Alfaro *(Doorman)*, Brian Paul *(Mackey)*, Deborah Taylor *(Tense Woman)*, Ferne Downey *(Sasha)*, Nancy Beatty *(Raymond Brown's Wife)*, Jackie Laidlaw, Paul Hubbard *(Yuppie Detec-*

tives), Bill Haslett, James Kidnie *(Surveillance Team)*, Bridget O'Sullivan *(Sherman's Wife)*, Delaney Moore-Wickham *(Helen's Daughter)*, Franz Fridal *(Criminal Type)*, Philip Ho *(Karate Cop)*, Igor Stern *(Violinist)*, Miranda de Pencier *(Bride)*, Ty Templeton *(Groom)*.

A thriller featuring a mysterious femme fatale, an involving plot, believable characters, and some nice off-beat twists, SEA OF LOVE owes a good deal to Hitchcock, including a McGuffin (the clue that isn't), and such recent efforts as FATAL ATTRACTION and JAGGED EDGE, though it can claim plenty of originality as well. A serial killer is on the loose in the New York singles scene; several men who have responded to the personals in a popular urban magazine have been found murdered in their beds. Enter 20-year veteran cop Pacino, a stressed-out borderline alcoholic. The force is all that's left for Pacino, whose wife has left him for another detective and whose boozy father, Hickey, is his sole remaining family tie. Pacino teams up with Goodman, a jolly family man, to track the serial killer and, in the process, they achieve a gentle camaraderie. The clues in the case—the men all wrote their ads in verse, a 45 rpm single of "Sea of Love" is always on the phonograph at the crime scene, all the victims were found naked and shot in the head as they slept— point to a female stalker who answers poetic ads. To flush out the killer, the cops plant a verse ad and "date" the respondents. Posing as a waiter and man-on-the-make in a busy singles bar, the detectives check out a long line of ladies with a drink and some chit-chat, then hustle away their wine glasses to inspect their fingerprints. One respondent, single mother Barkin, is sexy, aggressive, and direct, a tough and savvy player in the dating game. She rejects Pacino as not sufficiently poetic and doesn't touch her glass of wine; later, however, the two accidentally meet again and sparks fly. Breaking the first rule of investigation—never get involved with a suspect —Pacino takes Barkin home, where she makes aggressive love to him. During this episode, he discovers a gun in her purse and almost goes berserk before finding out that the gun is a starter's pistol. Caught in a web of infatuation and rough, steamy sex, Pacino becomes more deeply involved with Barkin, despite signs that she might be the killer. When she discovers he's a cop and investigating her, Barkin furiously ends the affair. Pacino, overcome with loss, goes to her apartment and suggests she and her daughter live with him—then notices some personal ads tacked to the refrigerator door, with circles drawn around the names of the three dead men. He retreats in shock to his apartment, Barkin shows up for another confrontation and leaves, and shortly afterwards some suspicious noises outside Pacino's door set the stage for the cop's final battle with the killer.

Working to SEA OF LOVE's advantage more than its slight (if satisfying) plot is the realism of its characterizations. Even the smaller roles are played in such a way as to establish the characters as individuals, and the dialog sounds natural, spoken rather than written. The sad string of single women looking for love includes some especially compelling portrayals. Writer Richard Price—who scripted Martin Scorsese's "Life Lessons" in NEW YORK STORIES, the strongest of that film's segments—is a master at contriving characters who are messed up enough to be believable and believable enough in their fight for survival to deserve our encouragement. His dialog, here the skewed, elliptical jargon of urban social maneuvering, rings true and weaves the rough fabric of this film to near perfection. Director Harold Becker (THE ONION FIELD; TAPS) skillfully frames, paces, and controls the tension, subtly selecting just the right lighting, details, and mood to unobtrusively but solidly support the drama.

As the sloppy, weary, bourbon-slugging veteran cop, Al Pacino is a stray dog that craves affection but retains the instinct to turn and bite when threatened. Shuffling through the purgatory of his cop's life, Pacino gives his character just enough sense of hope to survive. In the scene in which he discovers Barkin's gun, Pacino virtually bounces off the wall in terror, confusion, and panic, suggesting a range of conflicting feelings so tellingly that he verifies his stature as one of America's best actors in this brief scene alone. Pacino gives perhaps his best film performance since DOG DAY AFTERNOON; Ellen Barkin matches him well as the hard-bitten, voraciously carnal suspect whose emotional vulnerability is concealed beneath all of her big-city single woman's armor. Pacino and Barkin make a realistically uncertain romantic team: two lonely people whose adolescent behavior is both infuriating and humane enough to elicit our sympathy. SEA OF LOVE captures the urban singles scene, showing the emotional risk, calculation, and usually false hope of its players—particularly the women—so accurately it's almost painful to watch.

The film has some flaws, including a plethora of characters early in the investigation that makes for some confusion and some plot twists that prove less than unexpected. There are also a number of real surprises, though, and the identity of the killer (if not the killer's motive) should come as a reasonably good jolt to most. Songs include: "Sea of Love" (George Khoury, Phillip Baptiste, performed by Phil Phillips with the Twilights), "Lament" (J.J. Johnson, performed by Branford Marsalis), "Siempre Hay Esperanza" (Stu-

Ellen Barkin and Al Pacino in SEA OF LOVE (©Universal).

art Matthewman, Sade Adu, Leroy Osbourne, performed by Sade), "Beyond the Sea" (Charles Trenet, Jack Lawrence, performed by Bobby Darin). *(Violence, profanity, nudity, alcohol abuse, sexual situations, adult situations.)*

p, Martin Bregman and Louis A. Stroller; d, Harold Becker; w, Richard Price; ph, Ronnie Taylor (Deluxe Color); ed, David Bretherton; m, Trevor Jones; prod d, John Jay Moore; set d, Gordon Sim; cos, Betsy Cox; stunts, Dick Ziker; makeup, Irene Kent.

Mystery/Thriller   (PR:O MPAA:R)

ⓥSEASON OF FEAR***
89m Filmstar./MGM-UA c
Michael Bowen *(Mick Drummond)*, Ray Wise *(Fred Drummond)*, Clancy Brown *(Ward St. Clair)*, Clara Wren *(Sarah Drummond)*, Michael J. Pollard *(Bob)*, Heather Jane McDonald *(Penny)*, Dean Fortunato *(David)*, Gregory Wolf *(Bartender)*, Susan Cherones *(Cindy)*, Janice Clare Dorsey *(Ranch Woman)*, Gannon McClaskey Wise *(Young Mick)*, Chrissy McCarthy, Heino C. Moller *(Bar Patrons)*, Henry Harris *(Hank)*, Rocky Capella *(Precision Driver)*.

A young man discovers that he has some really scary family ties in this enjoyable, surprisingly taut thriller. When Bowen receives a letter from his estranged father (Wise) asking him to come to his California

ranch for a reunion, Bowen doesn't know that Wise has a new wife, beguiling blonde Wren. As Bowen drives into the town, he's stopped by the sheriff (Brown) and instructed to fix his car. Bowen pulls into a gas station, but its owner (Pollard) runs like hell when he learns that Bowen is Wise's son. Finally arriving at his father's ranch, Bowen is greeted by Wren, who introduces herself as Wise's "housesitter." As darkness falls and the wind starts to howl, Bowen and Wren enjoy a night of lovemaking. The next day Bowen gets the shock of his life when he learns that Wren is his father's new bride.

To reveal any more of the story would spoil the fun, but be assured that SEASON OF FEAR will scare the devil out of you before the many twists and turns of its plot have been resolved. From Clancy Brown's down-home sheriff to Michael Bowen's prodigal son, the acting is excellent. In fact, Michael J. Pollard's gas station owner and Ray Wise's Fred Drummond are among the creepiest characters to emerge in the cinema since BLUE VELVET, while Clair Wren sizzles as the sexy stepmother who drives men crazy. To put it simply, writer-director Doug Campbell has made one of the most entertaining B movies in recent years. The real mystery here is why MGM-United Artists decided to release SEASON OF FEAR on so limited a basis. Don't watch this one alone. *(Violence, sexual situations, profanity.)*

p, Scott J. Mulvaney; d, Doug Campbell; w, Doug Campbell (based on a story by

Doug Campbell, Scott J. Mulvaney); ph, Chuy Elizondo (Monaco Color); ed, Dan Selakovich; m, David Wolinski; prod d, Phillip Michael Brandes.

Thriller   (PR:O MPAA:R)

SEDUCTION: THE CRUEL WOMAN*
90m First Run Features c
Mechthild Grossmann *(Wanda)*, Carola Regnier *(Caren)*, Udo Kier *(Gregor)*, Sheila McLaughlin *(Justine)*, Georgette Dee *(Friederike)*, Peter Weibel *(Herr Marsch)*.

Inspired by Sacher-Masoch's "Venus in Furs," the German SEDUCTION: THE CRUEL WOMAN is an attempt at a stylish exploration into sado-masochism. Grossmann is an authoritative, smokey-voiced woman who runs a sex gallery in which her various friends and lovers enact scenes of sadism upon each other for the entertainment of audiences and for the occasional private client. Grossmann is having romantic problems of her own, as she finds herself torn between her wimpy husband Kier, a failing artist, and Regnier, a repressed woman who owns a shoe boutique, where she can often be found lasciviously stroking the merchandise and fantasizing about seducing her well-heeled customers. The gallery group is joined by McLaughlin, a young American woman who seems ambivalent about being part of the S&M scene. Meanwhile, Grossmann takes a break from the toils of her complicated career and personal life for an interview with a journalist who, it turns out, is more than professionally eager for this assignment. The reporter gets to act out all his innermost longings as he is given a demonstration of Grossmann's work. By the end of the interview, the man is groveling for Grossmann to let him be her toilet. As the film ends, Kier tries one last, desperate attempt to win back Grossmann; he shoots her in the middle of a performance. The bullet hits her hand, and Grossmann is driven to laughter at her husband's incompetence. The door to the gallery forever closes on Kier, and the performance continues.

SEDUCTION: THE CRUEL WOMAN is filled with images of the tunnel of waste underneath the city, an obvious metaphor for the proclivities of the gallery performers. In the locations, photography, and performances, the film tries to reach a kind of stylized decadence which keeps emotional resonance at bay. Unfortunately, too many of these elements are simply muddled, not too mention laughably cliched (as for instance the shoe-fetishist boutique owner). While the film contains some graphic sex (only between women), it is devoid of eroticism. In one sense this is in keeping with the overt intention of separating sensuality and kinkiness, but in

another it feeds into a lack of completeness, a feeling of things not being fully thought through, that weakens the whole production. Although the sillier, more obvious cliches may provoke some giggles, the film doesn't reach the level of camp that might make it a midnight classic; nor does it provoke any intellectual ruminations on its subject matter. *(Violence, profanity, nudity, sexual situations.)*

p, Elfi Mikesch and Monika Treut; d, Elfi Mikesch and Monika Treut; w, Elfi Mikesch and Monika Treut.

Drama   (PR:O MPAA:NR)

ⓥSEE NO EVIL, HEAR NO EVIL*½
103m Tri-Star c
Gene Wilder *(Dave Lyons)*, Richard Pryor *(Wally Karew)*, Joan Severance *(Eve)*, Kevin Spacey *(Kirgo)*, Alan North *(Braddock)*, Anthony Zerbe *(Sutherland)*, Louis Giambalvo *(Gatlin)*, Kirsten Childs *(Adele)*, Hardy Rawls *(Beefy Tourist)*, Audrie Neenan *(Policewoman/Marilyn)*, Lauren Tom *(Mitzie)*, John C. Capodice *(Scotto)*, George Bartenieff *(Huddelston)*, Alexandra Neil *(Sally)*, Tonya Pinkins *(Leslie)*, Bernie McInerney *(Dr. Cornfield)*, Keith Langsdale *(Male Doctor)*, Jamie De Roy *(Female Doctor)*, Mary Kay Adams *(Dr. Bennett)*, Alan Pottinger *(Parking Attendant)*, Bill Luhrs *(Herman)*, Lisby Larson *(Reporter)*, Mark Smaltz, Rico Elias *(Policemen)*, Doug Yasuda *(Prof. Kasuda)*, James Pyduck *(Businessman)*, Michael John McGann *(Salesman)*, Edward Hyland *(Cabbie)*, Thom Curley *(Laundry Van Driver)*, John Ring *(Teller)*, George Buck *(Security Guard)*, Phil Goodbody *(Blind Man)*, George Harris *(Bartender)*, Zach Grenier *(Jerk)*, Joe Viviani *(Fingerprint Cop)*, Alice Spivak *(Dispatcher)*, Shiek Mahmud-Bey *(Walkie-Talkie Cop)*, Joel Swetow *(Cabbie)*, Jane Connell *(Woman)*, Pirie MacDonald *(Lodge Tourist)*, Manuel Santiago *(Raoul)*, Harry Madsen *(Cop with Bullhorn)*, Tom Kubiak *(Plainclothes Cop)*, Cynthia Lopez *(Puerto Rican Woman)*.

SEE NO EVIL, HEAR NO EVIL is the third film to costar Richard Pryor and Gene Wilder (SILVER STREAK and STIR CRAZY preceded it). In this one, Wilder plays the deaf owner of a newsstand who hires Pryor, a blind gambler, to work for him. Together, they "witness" a murder: when Pryor's bookie comes to the newsstand to collect a debt, he is shot by a mysterious woman (played sexily by Severance), but, before dying, he drops a priceless coin into Wilder's cigar box till. Pryor hears the shot; Wilder sees only Severance's legs as she leaves. The police arrive, and Pryor and Wilder are mistaken for the killers and arrested. Hoping to get their hands on the coin, which has since

found its way into Pryor's pocket, Severance and her English partner (Spacey) pose as Wilder's lawyers and offer to post bail for him and Pryor. Realizing that Severance is the killer (Wilder recognizes her legs) but that all the evidence points to them, Wilder and Pryor escape from police custody. A series of coincidences and plot twists (including the kidnaping of Pryor's sister, and the stealing and restealing of the coin) comes to a head at the mansion of Zerbe, a tyrannical crime lord, who also happens to be blind. After rescuing Pryor's sister, our heroes are captured and brought to Zerbe's office. Zerbe shoots Spacey, plays blind games with Pryor and Wilder, and threatens Severance, who kills the crime lord and escapes, pursued by Pryor and Wilder. Ultimately, the two bring Severance to justice and are reunited with Pryor's sister. With their names cleared, Pryor and Wilder sit in the park once again, dealing with their handicaps by smashing ice cream cones on each other's head.

SEE NO EVIL, HEAR NO EVIL is a complete waste of talent, reducing its two gifted stars to pawns who wander through a script full of cheap disability jokes. How many times can one laugh at Pryor bumping into walls or Wilder misreading someone's lips? Director Arthur Hiller (who has directed some funny movies, including SILVER STREAK) has no shame, and keeps the cheap sight gags and profanity-laced one liners flowing steadily, until the viewer's head is ready to explode. The plot is a recycled mishmash of countless comedy thrillers and Hiller's own "buddy" films—THE IN-LAWS and OUTRAGEOUS FORTUNE—all hobbled by the gimmick of deaf and blind humor. Lowbrow comedy at its worst, SEE NO EVIL, HEAR NO EVIL is full of stupid car chases and boring shootouts, and none of it is very entertaining.

Wilder and Pryor struggle mightily to pull it off, and, to their credit, they make some of this nonsense watchable (even wringing a few laughs from the tired comic device of masquerading as a kooky-accented foreign doctor). Unfortunately, their efforts are undermined by the weak script (written by five writers, including Wilder) and humorless "comic" situations. Although slightly misogynist in tone, the strongest character in the film is Joan Severance's Eve. Stunningly beautiful and full of mysterious charm, Severance steals every scene she's in. With the help of Victor Kemper's crisp photography, she almost makes SEE NO EVIL, HEAR NO EVIL a pleasure to watch, personally redeeming several sequences (her nude scene results in the film's most subtle and amusing sight gag). But even a gorgeous woman can't save this picture. Wilder and Pryor (who have yet to make a movie equal to their talents) deserve better and are capable of much more than this

Richard Pryor and Gene Wilder in SEE NO EVIL, HEAR NO EVIL (©Tri-Star).

gimmick-filled comedy allows. With simpleminded setups and loud sitcom payoffs, SEE NO EVIL, HEAR NO EVIL suffocates its stars, and the result is one of the unfunniest movies in a long time. Songs include: "Anything Can Happen" (Don Was, David Was, Aaron Zigman, performed by Was Not Was), "Twilight Zone" Theme (Marius Constant). *(Profanity, violence, brief nudity, adult situations.)*

p, Marvin Worth; d, Arthur Hiller; w, Earl Barret, Arne Sultan, Eliot Wald, Andrew Kurtzman, and Gene Wilder (based on a story by Earl Barret, Arne Sultan, Marvin Worth); ph, Victor J. Kemper (Technicolor); ed, Robert C. Jones; m, Stewart Copeland; prod d, Robert Gundlach; art d, James T. Singelis; set d, George DeTitta Jr.; spec eff, Al Griswold; cos, Ruth Morley; stunts, Conrad E. Palmisano; makeup, Toy Russell-Van Lierop.

Comedy   **(PR:C-O   MPAA:R)**

Ⓥ**SEE YOU IN THE MORNING****½
115m Lorimar/WB c
Jeff Bridges *(Larry Livingston)*, Alice Krige *(Beth Goodwin)*, Farrah Fawcett *(Jo Livingston)*, Drew Barrymore *(Cathy Goodwin)*, Lukas Haas *(Petey Goodwin)*, David Dukes *(Peter Goodwin)*, Frances Sternhagen *(Neenie)*, Heather Lilly *(Robin Livingston)*, George Hearn *(Martin)*, Theodore Bikel *(Bronie)*, Linda Lavin *(Sidney)*.

Watching SEE YOU IN THE MORNING is apt to evoke feelings of sympathy, compassion, and hope. Unfortunately, these emotions are not exactly a response to the film's story and characters so much as they are expressions of support for the good intentions of its writer-director, Alan Pakula. SEE YOU IN THE MORNING stars Bridges as a psychiatrist whose marriage to Fawcett, a successful television model, is long on looks and short on substance. The film's opening establishes their sorry state, intercutting the parallel story of Krige and Dukes. Krige, a potential world-class photographer, subordinates her career to her role as the wife of concert pianist Dukes and the mother of his two children. Bridges and Fawcett (who have two kids themselves) divorce amicably; meanwhile, Krige is more tragically made single when Dukes dies prematurely. Disappointed and feeling helpless over the divorce, Bridges reluctantly allows his academic, upscale friends to coax him back into the dating pool, and, of course, meets Krige. The two seem to enjoy the adolescent giddiness of their attraction, but—despite the matchmaking moves of mutual friend Lavin and given their demographic status as newly single parents—their courtship is not an easy one. However, where love has a will, it finds a way—though happiness ever after is another matter. Bridges and Krige wed, but find they still have to overcome the demons of their marital pasts, including dealing with their children and step-children. The fact that they are bright, attractive, accomplished people only adds to their frustrations. Bridges is clearly aware that he is living in another man's home and that he appears as something of a pretender to the throne in the eyes of Krige, her kids, and even the family dog. At the same time, he feels the burden of being an absentee father to his own children. Surprisingly, his greatest support at this time turns out to be his former mother-in-law (Sternhagen), whose death adds to Bridges' emotional baggage later in the story. Still, the film is determined to heal all wounds between spouses and ex-spouses, parents and children, and not surprisingly achieves its goal by the end.

As the writer and/or director of such works as SOPHIE'S CHOICE; ALL THE PRESIDENT'S MEN; and KLUTE, Pakula has earned high marks for sensitivity and intelligence in commercial filmmaking over the years. Unfortunately, his autobiographical SEE YOU IN THE MORNING remains a disappointment. The subject (love the second time around) is not original, but that's not the problem, and neither is the basic scenario. It's what the characters reveal—or don't reveal, in the case of Bridges' role—that undermines this distended tale.

For all its sensitivity to the real problems of transplanted partnerships and the pressures they put on the partners' children, SEE YOU IN THE MORNING is badly in need of a wake-up call. Television has been trafficking in this material for years (admittedly, mostly through sophomoric sitcoms), and Pakula fails to deepen our understanding of the tangled relationships that result when families break up to re-form in new units. Pakula's seriousness is a given, but his dramatic choices in exploring and resolving the downside of second-chance love are sadly inadequate to the task. The film is full of intimate details and fine strokes that prove curiously unenlightening—closing the gaps in character development, rather than simply presenting it in detailed layers, could have generated far more interest. (For example, what difference does it make that Bridges' character is a psychiatrist, other than suggesting a certain irony in his own arrested emotions?)

Still, one can take genuine pleasure in many of Bridges' scenes with his children and step-children, even in some of the more contrived moments (particularly a sequence involving one child's shoplifting). The cast performs earnestly and well as an ensemble, and Pakula has provided the principals with some rich little scenes to shine in individually as well. But the film as a whole is far too talky and plodding. It's full of grace notes that fail to combine in a truly compelling piece. *(Sexual situations, adult situations.)*

p, Alan J. Pakula; d, Alan J. Pakula; w, Alan J. Pakula; ph, Donald McAlpine (Metrocolor); ed, Evan Lottman; prod d, George Jenkins; art d, Robert Guerra; cos, John Boxer.

Drama   **(PR:C   MPAA:PG-13)**

SEX, LIES AND VIDEOTAPE***½
101m Outlaw c

James Spader (Graham Dalton), Andie MacDowell (Ann Millaney), Peter Gallagher (John Millaney), Laura San Giacomo (Cynthia Bishop), Ron Vawter (Therapist), Steven Brill (Barfly), David Foil (John's Colleague), Earl Taylor (Landlord), Alexandra Root (Girl on Tape).

Most film titles—big, blocky, and loud—announce; SEX, LIES AND VIDEO-TAPE, which appears on the screen entirely in lower case letters, insinuates. The title, like the film, sneaks by quietly, in subtle increments, gradually accumulating force. The film opens as the sexually repressed, emotionally blocked MacDowell speaks to her therapist, discussing, among other things, the imminent arrival of her husband's old college friend Spader, whom we see on the road, en route. Spader arrives at the couple's upscale suburban home in Baton Rouge and is greeted by MacDowell. An awkward conversation ensues, during the course of which it's revealed that he has not been in contact with MacDowell's husband (Gallagher) since they both graduated from college nine years ago. Although they were very much alike then, it is immediately apparent that the similarity no longer holds: Spader is jobless, directionless, and conspicuously alienated; Gallagher is an aggressive yuppie attorney who is having an affair with his wife's sister, San Giacomo. San Giacomo is animated by competition with her (by Baton Rouge standards) prettier and more successful sister, and uses sex to beat her sister by bedding her husband; but her general promiscuity also frees her from the other characters' hang-ups. In contrast to Gallagher and San Giacomo's secret sexual rendezvous, Spader and MacDowell's friendship develops openly, through conversation. MacDowell is surprised by Spader's frankly personal questions and a bit mystified by his revelation that he has been impotent for some time, but is also flattered by his attentions and charmed by his eccentricities, and as protective of their private relationship as San Giacomo is mum about her trysts with Gallagher. MacDowell is jarred, however, when she discovers Spader's collection of videotapes at the apartment he's taken. Spader gingerly explains that they contain conversations—confessions, actually—with women who've consented to speak intimately about sex before his camera. Disillusioned and disgusted, MacDowell flees. Earlier, her reluctance to have San Giacomo and Spader meet aroused the former's curiosity and yen for mischief; now, when MacDowell intimates they've had a falling out, San Giacomo pays Spader a visit and finds out about his videotapes. All too eager to upset MacDowell

Andie MacDowell in SEX, LIES AND VIDEOTAPE (©Miramax).

by sating Spader's voyeuristic appetite and genuinely turned on by the idea, she makes a tape. MacDowell is accordingly repulsed, but, finding out about her sister and her husband's affair (ironically, just as San Giacomo ends it), she eventually arrives at Spader's place and insists on being taped herself. Before we see the full interview, the story flashes several hours forward, as MacDowell informs Gallagher that their marriage is over and revealing that she made a tape. Gallagher rushes over to Spader's, fights him, and locks Spader out before viewing his wife's tape. She begins to speak of her marriage, then turns the tables and the camera at Spader, the eye of the lens probing mercilessly as she asks him why he's made such a mess of his life. Spader confesses the cause of his impotency, sexual and otherwise—a revelation that causes the shaken Gallagher, in turn, to confront Spader with more uncomfortable truths that eventually lead to Spader's psychological liberation—and as the film ends Spader and McDowell are able to continue their relationship in greater freedom.

An unusually self-assured debut from a young filmmaker with a refreshingly mature sensibility, SEX, LIES AND VIDEOTAPE was the winner of the Cannes Film Festival's top prize, the Palme d'Or, scoring a rare double win when James Spader was named Best Actor as well. (MacDowell's work was also highly regarded at Cannes, where she was Meryl Streep's main competition for the Best Actress prize.) The first fiction feature

from Baton Rouge native Steven Soderbergh (he previously directed a feature-length concert film for the rock group Yes), the film was made on a $1.2 million budget and initially written in eight days while Soderbergh was on the road from Baton Rouge to Los Angeles. Its premiere (in an unfinished version) at the US Film Festival in Park City, Utah, was the first in a string of "surprise" successes for SEX, LIES AND VIDEOTAPE, which beat out both Denys Arcand's JESUS OF MONTREAL and Spike Lee's DO THE RIGHT THING for the Cannes Palme d'Or, then went on to an amazingly strong US box-office business for an independent film of such spareness and seriousness.

Notwithstanding the fervency of its reception, SEX, LIES AND VIDEOTAPE is a quiet film whose charm lies in its resonances. It has the understated interplay of a sharply etched minimalist novel. Though the title is not a misnomer, the film relies on talk rather than scenes of sex or nudity to make its points, and in the process establishes a far more intimate tone than many more explicit pictures. Soderbergh has an unerring eye for subtle but telling mood shifts—his talent resting on more than ability to move a camera, story, or scene—and his unusually sensitive direction of his actors coaxes remarkably well-nuanced performances from the four principals. Beautifully edited by Soderbergh, the film is evenly paced, its subtleties accreting slowly and inexorably. The story seems to progress casually, to drift almost, but by the end it has gathered an emotionally powerful momentum. (Adult situations, sexual situations, brief nudity, profanity.)

p, Robert Newmyer and John Hardy; d, Steven Soderbergh; w, Steven Soderbergh; ph, Walt Lloyd (CFI Color); m, Cliff Martinez; art d, Joanne Schmidt; set d, Victoria Spader; cos, James Ryder.

Drama   (PR:C MPAA:R)

SHAG**½
(Brit.) 100m Palace-Hemdale/Tri Star c

Phoebe Cates (Carson McBride), Scott Coffey (Chip Guillyard), Bridget Fonda (Melaina Buller), Annabeth Gish (Pudge Carmichael), Page Hannah (Luanne Clatterbuck), Robert Rusler (Buzz Ravenel), Tyrone Power III (Harley Ralston), Jeff Yagher (Jimmy Valentine).

Remember WHERE THE BOYS ARE? Basic premise: four swinging bachelorettes looking for guys and giggles at the beach. SHAG is a fluffy variant on that time-honored formula (stretching back to Betty Grable and beyond). Each one of its characters fits her feminine stereotype snugly, sans any Yvette Mimieux tragedy. Cates is Princess Perfection, out for one last fling before she marries her upright hunk; Fonda is the group's daredevil sexpot, obsessed with winning the Miss Sun

Queen contest. Hannah, a prim, bespectacled nerdette and a self-appointed duenna to her more frivolous friends, announces, "We're going to have a good time, but we *cannot* be wild," and expresses horror at the absurdity of Fonda's fantasy of having an affair with President Kennedy. Gish, as her name, Pudge, would indicate, is overweight but game. During their busy weekend at Myrtle Beach, the four find romance, dance up a storm, make serious career connections, and lose every inhibition in time to primly assemble for a last, plaintively sung rendition of their school anthem.

It's all as inconsequential as cherry pop and goes down just as easily. Director Zelda Barron has a real affection for her characters, enabling them to retain a sweet dignity even under the most excessive circumstances (dictated by an unimaginative, slight script): Fonda's shaving cream/toilet paper humiliation at the hands of jealous rivals, for instance, or the obligatory "Let's trash the house" party. Barron also has a killer eye for succinct period detail circa 1963: girls practicing the latest dance crazes in their bedrooms, using a rope for a partner; the gabby, congested communing at drive-ins with roller-skating service; Peter Pan collars on gingham frocks; and big hairdo controversies like the flip vs. the upsweep. Kenny Ortega's re-creations of the demurely syncopated dances of the era are a great asset, as is the music, which includes such melodic memory-joggers as "Up on the Roof," "Stay," "Alley Oop," and "Under the Boardwalk." Even the photography has an appropriate, cheesy Kodachrome look to it.

The cast is uniformly attractive and energetic, and boasts three movie star offspring. Patrician-faced Bridget Fonda (Peter's daughter) once more proves herself to be the dazzling find she was in ARIA and SCANDAL with her vivacious performance here. Her body is one for the ages and she flaunts it superbly whether doing a lewd solo dance with a Confederate flag or striking poses like some figurative hood ornament. Tyrone Power, Jr., has some of his father's liquid black Irish good looks and is properly uptight as Cates' stuffy fiance. Carrie Hamilton steals every scene she's in with the same fierce comic aplomb of her mother, Carol Burnett, playing a backwoods bitch out to give our girls a bad time. Her long-limbed, Olive Oyl gyrations, aping the posturings of the Sun Queen contestants, are the film's comic highlight. Freckled Page Hannah makes Luanne's hoary metamorphosis from clenched cocoon to love-crazed butterfly both slapstick and touching. (She's especially droll coaching Fonda in Scarlett O'Hara's big "Tara" monolog—performed much more effectively here than in MISS FIRECRACKER.) Annabeth Gish is likably vulnerable as insecure, dance-mad

Pudge, and Scott Coffey, who reveals an Astaire-like way with the "Shag," is the perfect, bumbling partner for her. Doe-eyed Phoebe Cates has improved her diction and acquits herself more ably in this than in anything since her Valley Girl in FAST TIMES AT RIDGEMONT HIGH. However, it's a shame her character is the most underwritten, as your mind may begin to wander during her scenes to speculation over whether her Eurasian beauty makes her more resemble Merle Oberon or Ralph Macchio. *(Substance abuse, sexual situations.)*

p, Stephen Woolley and Julia Chasman; d, Zelda Barron; w, Robin Swicord, Lanier Laney, and Terry Sweeney (based on a story by Laney, Sweeney); ph, Peter MacDonald; ed, Laurence Mery Clark; prod d, Buddy Cone; set d, Kara Lindstrom; cos, Mary E. Vogt; chor, Kenny Ortega.

Comedy/Romance   (PR:C MPAA:PG)

SHE-DEVIL*½
99m Seidelman-Brett/Orion c
Meryl Streep *(Mary Fisher)*, Roseanne Barr *(Ruth Patchett)*, Ed Begley Jr. *(Bob Patchett)*, Linda Hunt *(Hooper)*, Sylvia Miles *(Mrs. Fisher)*, Elisebeth Peters *(Nicolette Patchett)*, Bryan Larkin *(Andy Patchett)*, A. Martinez *(Garcia, the Butler)*, Maria Pitillo *(Olivia Honey)*, Mary Louise Wilson *(Mrs. Trumper)*, Susan Willis *(Ute)*, Jack Gilpin *(Larry)*, Robin Leach *(Himself)*, Nitchie Barrett *(Bob's Secretary)*, June Gable *(Realtor)*, Jeanine Joyce *(Flower Lady)*, Deborah Rush *("People" Reporter)*, Sally Jessy Raphael *(Herself)*, Doris Belack *(Paula)*, Max *(Fuzzy)*, Cerius & Cinderella *(Juliette)*, Herbie *(Himself)*, Lori Tan Chinn *(Vesta Rose Woman)*, Joe Pentangelo *(Detective)*, Mark Steiner *(Valet)*, Rosanna Carter *(Judge Brown)*, George Kodisch *(Court Officer)*, Manny Olmo *(Cook)*, Alain Jarry *(Alain)*, John Richard Reynolds *(Bookstore Customer)*, George Trow *(Douglas)*, Cynthia Adler *(Vesta Rose Commercial Voice)*, Sandra Fine, Christopher Collins Lee, Julie Signizter, Scott Wyatt Rawls *(Roslyn Artists String Quartet)*, Mack Brandon, Will Ford *(The Mack Brandon Duo)*, Sally Sockwell, Larry Marshall *(Guggenheim Party Guests)*, Mary Marshall, R. Patrick Sullivan, Anna Marie Winds, Steven Prince, Martin Snaric *(Mary's Party Guests)*.

One of the biggest moviegoing disappointments of the year, Susan Seidelman's screen adaptation of Fay Weldon's wonderfully macabre novel *The Life and Loves of a She-Devil* transforms a black-comic masterpiece about a woman's bizarre revenge on her straying spouse into a watered-down, dim-witted vehicle for TV sitcom star Roseanne Barr. Although presented with humorous intent, SHE-DEVIL delivers few laughs, and most of these come

from a surprising source—Meryl Streep, who demonstrates a heretofore little-seen flair for comedy. Indeed, the film is worth watching just to witness her broad vamping in the role of an over-the-top glamor puss. Still, SHE-DEVIL provides ample fodder for critics of Hollywood's propensity for capitalizing on TV ratings; striking while an actor is "hot," producers tailor roles for new sensations that don't always fit. If nothing else, this misguided approach reveals the larger-than-life Barr to be something of a lightweight on the big screen. On the other hand, Streep, playing against her usual dramatic persona, shows again that she is arguably the best actress of her generation.

Playing a hack romance novelist, Streep is rich, phenomenally successful, and lives a fairy-tale existence in a dream house overlooking the sea. Her chauffeur-driven limousine has vanity license plates that read AMOUR, and her lavish lifestyle has been immortalized by Robin Leach. At a swank cocktail party, she sets her sights on Begley, an accountant who's moving into "creative management." Although married, Begley has a roving eye, and falls easily for Streep. Barr, his fat, clumsy wife, spills a drink on Streep's dress, then idiotically wanders the party blithely announcing, "I just spilled my wine on Mary Fisher, the famous writer." Barr's trust in her husband proves to be misplaced when he agrees to give Streep a lift to her home—75 miles away—and then spends the night with her. Begley becomes Streep's business manager and lover, eventually leaving Barr and moving in with the writer. Who could blame him? Sloppily obese, with an ugly mole the size of a quarter on her lip, Barr is grossly unattractive, and when he leaves her, Begley accuses her of being a she-devil, a bad cook, a bad wife, and a bad mother. (From what we're shown, he's not altogether wrong.) This, of course, means war. Barr itemizes Begley's assets—"Home, Family, Career, Freedom"—and through the rest of the film, she systematically attacks each of them. She burns down their house, leaves their bratty kids with Streep (much to the writer's horror and inconvenience), and disappears. Assuming an alias, Barr becomes an orderly at the Golden Twilight Rest Home, where she befriends nurse Hunt (underutilized in an all-too-brief role). All the patients, including Streep's octogenarian mother, Miles (practically unrecognizable until she opens her mouth), are kept sedated to make life easier for the staff. Barr shakes things up a little when she replaces Miles' valium with vitamins, and persuades the patient to visit her estranged daughter. While Miles is away, Barr pours a bucket of urine on her bed. Since the rest-home administrator won't tolerate incontinence, Miles isn't allowed to return, and Streep is aghast. (Advised to try some TLC on her

Roseanne Barr, Ed Begley Jr., and Meryl Streep in SHE-DEVIL (©Orion).

mother, Streep asks, "What's that, a new drug?") The combination of ill-bred kids and Miles (typecast as a gratuitously vulgar, loud-mouthed harridan) turns Begley and Streep's idyllic love nest into a nightmare. (Barr crosses "Family" off her list.) Except for butler Martinez, her onetime lover, Streep's staff deserts her, and she is forced to do the cleaning, washing, and baby-sitting for two generations of slovens. When reporters from *People* magazine come to the estate to do a feature story on the famous novelist, Miles airs the family's dirty laundry, revealing that her daughter is 41, not 34, that the elegant background Streep claims is a lie, and that the novelist was a "teenage tramp." Needless to say, Streep finds herself on the cover of the next issue of *People*. The novelist's career receives another setback when her new book, *Love in the Rinse Cycle*, strays from her usual formula and is rejected. Thoroughly demoralized, Streep, like Barr before her, becomes a slattern. Ever the cad, Begley uses his new sports car to spend nights in the city with other women. In the meantime, Barr and Hunt leave the nursing home, and, with Hunt's savings, open Vista Rose, an employment agency "for the unloved and unwanted." Among the housewives and hookers they place is sexy Pitillo, who takes a job as Begley's secretary, then informs Barr of Begley's embezzling when he fires Pitillo after a brief affair. Sneaking into Begley's office at night, Barr and Pitillo use a computer to transfer thousands of dollars into Begley's secret Swiss bank account. After they tip off the IRS about Begley's misdeeds, he is arrested. (Barr crosses "Career" off her list.) Streep learns that some of the money Begley has embezzled was hers, and she leaves him. When a judge who goes easy on white-collar criminals is assigned to Begley's case,

Barr sees to it that an unsympathetic African-American female judge replaces him, and Begley receives an 18-month prison sentence and a $250,000 fine. In attendance at the trial, Barr crosses out "Freedom," and, in voiceover, says, "Poor Bob. I almost felt sorry for him. Almost." The film ends with a newly conservative Streep at a book promotion, unwittingly signing a copy of her new nonfiction best-seller, *Trust and Betrayal*, for Barr, who leaves with a smug smile on her face.

With seemingly everything going for it, SHE-DEVIL should work. Yet in spite of a big budget and an ingenious story with a history of success (in print and on TV), director Seidelman (SMITHEREENS; DESPERATELY SEEKING SUSAN) has succeeded in making a sow's ear out of a silk purse. A sardonic feminist rallying cry for women who don't quite measure up to a pin-up image, Weldon's novel has been perverted into meaningless nonsense. Understandably, SHE-DEVIL failed with the critics and at the box office. It needn't have. Seidelman could have followed the stunning example set by Ted Whitehead's 1986 television adaptation of the novel for the BBC. So good was Whitehead's version that it beat out "The Singing Detective" for a BAFTA (the British equivalent of an Emmy) award as Best Dramatic Television Series. When it first aired, the bewitching four-part series became the highest-rated program since the wedding of Prince Charles to Lady Diana. Faithful to Weldon's book and featuring a particularly intelligent performance by Julie T. Wallace as the grossly oversized *hausfrau*, this production has become a cult favorite.

In Weldon's novel and Whitehead's adaptation, the revenge that Ruth so artfully exacts is perfectly fitting, offering catharsis for anyone who has been dumped

by an insensitive lover. Not only does Ruth cleverly destroy the relationship between her husband and his novelist-lover, but in the process she transforms herself into an almost merciless wielder of power, a She-Devil. Regrettably, many of the devilishly wicked romantic fable's bizarre plot twists are missing from the movie, including Ruth's seduction of a Catholic priest and a sadistic judge, and the years of plastic surgery she undergoes so that by the end of the novel she physically resembles her rival. Weldon's novel is witty, wacky, and wonderfully way out; the film is none of those things. The problem lies with Seidelman's miscasting of Barr in the pivotal role of Ruth. Once the part was hers, the whole script had to be rewritten around her drearily monotonous delivery and limited acting ability, much to the detriment of the plot. Instead of eliciting sympathy, Barr only invites ridicule. Skip SHE-DEVIL to see the TV series in reruns and read the book. They're both unforgettable.

Songs include: "I Will Survive" (Dino Fekaris, Frederick Perren, performed by Sa-Fire), "Party Up" (Frank Buonadonna, Denya Versailles, Chubby Checker, performed by Checker, the Fat Boys), "Tied Up" (Boris Blank, performed by Yello), "C'mon and Get My Love" (D. Poku, performed by D. Mob), "It's Getting Hot" (Albert Cabrera, Mark Morales, Damon Wimbley, Darren Robinson, performed by the Fat Boys), "Always" (Tom Kimmel, Doug Sisemore, performed by Kimmel), "Tren D'Amor" (Jermaine Stewart, Curnow, Harding, performed by Stewart), "You're the Devil in Disguise" (Bernie Baum, Bill Giant, Florence Kaye, performed by Elvis Presley), "You Can Have Him" (Bill Cook, performed by Carmel), "That's What I Call Love" (Kate Ceberano, Ashley Cadell, performed by Ceberano). *(Nudity, profanity.)*

p, Jonathan Brett and Susan Seidelman; d, Susan Seidelman; w, Barry Strugatz and Mark R. Burns (based on the novel *The Life and Loves of a She-Devil* by Fay Weldon); ph, Oliver Stapleton (DuArt Color); ed, Craig McKay; m, Howard Shore; prod d, Santo Loquasto; art d, Tom Warren; set d, George DeTitta Jr.; spec eff, Efex Specialists; cos, Albert Wolsky; makeup, Joseph Campayno.

Comedy   **(PR:A MPAA:PG-13)**

⊘SHE'S OUT OF CONTROL**
97m Weintraub/COL c

Tony Danza *(Doug Simpson)*, Catherine Hicks *(Janet Pearson)*, Wallace Shawn *(Dr. Fishbinder)*, Dick O'Neill *(Mr. Pearson)*, Ami Dolenz *(Katie Simpson)*, Laura Mooney *(Bonnie Simpson)*, Derek McGrath *(Jeff)*, Dana Ashbrook *(Joey)*, Matthew L. Perry *(Timothy)*, Lance Wilson-White *(Richard)*, Michael Alaimo *(Baggage Handler)*, Marcie Barkin

(Doug's Secretary), Diana Barrows *(Lisa)*, Jan Bina *(Harpist)*, Michael Bower *(Kid at Beach)*, Mitch Braiman *(Joey's Friend)*, Todd Bridges *(Water Man)*, Robert Casper *(Maitre'd)*, Dustin Diamond *(Kid on the Beach)*, Marc Gilpin *(Parking Attendant)*, John Hendrickson *(Beach Boy)*, Kenneth Hoyt *(Disheveled Kid)*, Susan Isaacs *(Receptionist)*, Brad Kesten *(Andy)*, Mina Kolb *(Mrs. Pearson)*, Rusdi Lane *(Doctor)*, Peter Linari *(Security Guard)*, Tony Max *(Patient)*, Jeff Maynard *(Boy Friend)*, Bess Meyer *(Cheryl)*, Scott Morris *(Corvette Kid)*, Oliver Muirhead *(Nigel)*, Kate Murtagh *(Chaperone)*, Kevin O'Keefe *(Beach Boy)*, Ron Pace *(Security Officer)*, Ria Pavla *(Robin)*, Robbie Rist *(Corvette Kid's Friend)*, Philip Arthur Ross, Steven Robert Ross *(Dates)*, Gary Schwartz *(Optometrist)*, Michael Shepard *(Dr. Feldman)*, Scooter Stevens *(Bonnie's Date)*, Laura Summer *(Receptionist)*, Brad Tanner *(Boy Friend No. 2)*, Dylan Tucker *(Tommy)*, Joshua Waggoner *(12-year-old Kid)*, Terry Wills *(Flight Captain)*, Thomas R. Zak *(Lifeguard)*, Jim Ladd *(Voice of KHEY-FM 97.5)*.

The dynamics of a father's relationship with his teenage daughter certainly seem a subject worthy of cinematic exploration, but SHE'S OUT OF CONTROL is not the way to do it. This family movie in thriller style opens as a shadowy figure charges up the stairs of Los Angeles radio station KHEY, races into the control room, throttles a guest at the microphone, and then crashes out of a window to the street below. In the hospital, the assailant turns out to be Danza, who, incredibly, has suffered only a sprain. Questioned by police, he begins to explain the motivation for the attack, launching into the flashback that forms SHE'S OUT OF CONTROL's story proper. Danza is the 37-year-old general manager of the beleaguered KHEY, an FM oldies station that's steadily plummeting in the ratings. A widower, Danza's bigger concerns are his two preteen daughters, Dolenz and Mooney. Dolenz, a school brain with Coke-bottle eyeglasses, braces, a gangly body, and an innocent charm, is turning 15. Danza takes her, Mooney, and nerdy Wilson-White—the boy next door and Dolenz's longtime steady—to a disco for a birthday party, where they are joined by Hicks, a successful fashion designer and Danza's girl friend. During the celebration, Dolenz breaks up with Wilson-White, then, when Danza leaves town to attend a radio convention, Hicks takes her on an all-out makeover spree. When Danza returns, his home has turned into "dating central," with phones and doorbells constantly ringing. The now nubile Dolenz drifts downstairs in slow motion while Danza speechlessly gapes at her, and soon Daddy is the one who goes out of control. Angry with Hicks for pushing Dolenz into womanhood, he vows to screen every

suitor who comes near his daughter, remaining obsessed with her while his radio station's numbers continue to slide. It's time to see therapist Shawn, a statistics-spewing expert and author of the best-selling *Daddy's Little Girl: A Guide to Raising Your Teenage Daughter*, who instructs Danza to follow his book to the letter as Danza consults him in an attempt to deal with his daughter's many suitors, who include punker Ashbrook and super-rich Perry. When Danza spies Perry womanizing, he grounds Dolenz, but relents at her request to attend Perry's prom. Hearing this, Shawn hits the roof and predicts Dolenz will lose her virginity on prom night. Danza insists he can "control" Dolenz, assuaging Shawn's tantrum by promising the therapist a shot on the air at KHEY; next, Hicks' parents come to town and take Hicks and Danza to dinner at the club where the prom is being held. Danza continues to monitor his daughter's doings, following Dolenz and Perry to a motel. Perry corners Dolenz, she rebuffs him, and Danza bursts into the room, much to his daughter's embarrassment. Driving home, an ashamed Danza tunes in KHEY, only to hear Shawn on the air, freely admitting he is not a father and has never had a teenage daughter. As the story comes full circle to the film's beginning, Danza races to the station, storms into the control room, assaults Shawn, and tumbles out of the window. After Danza finishes his confession, Hicks tells him Dolenz is about to head for Europe, but a police escort gets him to the airport just in time to make things up.

Why does Hollywood make TV movies and palm them off as theatrical releases? SHE'S OUT OF CONTROL would have done far better in the TV ratings than it has at the box office. It features some perfectly good television talent—namely Tony Danza ("Taxi," "Who's the Boss?"), Ami Dolenz ("General Hospital"), and director Stan Dragoti (the "I Love New York" ad campaign)—but these folks are simply not up to theatrical snuff. Despite Dragoti's success with LOVE AT FIRST BITE and MR. MOM, he's still making very long commercials. SHE'S OUT OF CONTROL has all the production pluses of national ad campaigns: smart art direction, lighting, and costume design, plus a catchy mix of old and new rock'n'roll on the soundtrack. Unfortunately, SHE'S OUT OF CONTROL also resembles commercials in that it hopes to appeal to everyone and basically endears itself to no one. Writers Seth Winston and Michael J. Nathanson cloud a worthwhile subject with dozens of late 80s musical, ethnic, and social cliches (without, amazingly, a single reference to safe sex or AIDS). As a result, SHE'S OUT OF CONTROL fails to examine its father-daughter dilemma with the depth it deserves, in striking contrast to

the far more successful SAY ANYTHING. All the characters are cartoons: the boys are stupid and unlikable, Dolenz regresses from brain to flake, Hicks coos over her diamond ring, and Danza just turns yo-yo, pulled between memories of his own puberty and the reality of fatherhood. Danza is, however, to be commended for his dumbstruck reactions to the dating mayhem around him, a comic touch that is genuinely funny and that speaks for all fathers who must helplessly watch their daughters' passage into womanhood. Wallace Shawn also gets points for doing what he does best: a madman in a lisping nerd's body who's certain he's sane and everyone else is crazy. Shawn is worth the price of a video rental . . . or at least an evening in front of the television. Songs include "California Dreamin'"(John Phillips, Michelle Phillips, performed by the Mamas and the Papas), "You Really Got Me" (Ray Davies, performed by the Kinks), "16 Candles" (Luther Dixon, Allyson R. Khent, performed by the Crests), "Rock Me" (John Kay, performed by David Morgan, Gary Falcone), "Maniac" (Michael Sembello, Dennis Matkosky, performed by Sembello), "Concentration" (Phil Thornalley, performed by Thornalley), "You Should Be Loving Me" (Lotti Golden, Tommy Faragher, performed by Brenda K. Starr), "Venus" (Ed Marshall, performed by Frankie Avalon), "Feel the Shake" (Mickey Finn, Fernie Rod, performed by Jetboy), "Oh Yeah" (Boris Blank, Deiter Meier, performed by Yello), "Rocky Mountain Way" (Joe Walsh, Joe Vitale, Ken Passarelli, Rocke Grace, performed by Gary Falcone), "Mona" (E. McDaniel, performed by Bo Diddley [McDaniel]), "Angel Baby" (Rose Hamlim, performed by Beth Anderson), "Incense & Peppermints" (Timothy Gilbert, John Carter, performed by the Strawberry Alarm Clock), "Baby Please Don't Go" (Joe Williams, performed by David Morgan), "Make Some Noise" (Finn, Rod, Billy Rowe, Ron Tostenson, Sam Yaffa, performed by Jetboy), "Our Day Will Come" (Bob Hilliard, Mort Garson, performed by Ruby and the Romantics), "Secret Agent Man" (Phil F. Sloan, Steve Barri, performed by Johnny Rivers), "The Loneliest Heart" (Michael Jeffries, Jay Logan, performed by Boys Club), "Happy to Be Alive" (N. Ingman), "Lover's Serenade" (A. Morehouse), "Winning Side" (Danny Elfman, performed by Oingo Boingo), "La Bamba" (Ritchie Valens, performed by Valens), "Hunger of Love" (Harold Faltermeyer, Keith Forsey, performed by Faltermeyer), "Daddy's Little Girl" (Brian Wilson, Alexandra Morgan, Eugene E. Landy, performed by Wilson). *(Sexual situations, adult situations, violence.)*

p, Stephen Deutsch and John G. Wilson; d, Stan Dragoti; w, Seth Winston and

Michael J. Nathanson; ph, Donald Peterman (CFI Color); ed, Dov Hoenig; m, Alan Silvestri; md, Tim Sexton; prod d, David L. Snyder; art d, Joe Wood; set d, Bruce Gibeson; spec eff, Clay Pinney; cos, Marie France; stunts, Willy Crowder; makeup, Frank Griffin.

Comedy   (PR:A MPAA:PG)

SHIRLEY VALENTINE***
(Brit.) 108m PAR c
Pauline Collins (Shirley Valentine-Bradshaw), Tom Conti (Costas Caldes), Alison Steadman (Jane), Julia McKenzie (Gillian), Joanna Lumley (Marjorie), Bernard Hill (Joe Bradshaw), Sylvia Syms (Headmistress), Gillian Kearney (Young Shirley), Catherine Duncan (Young Marjorie), Tracie Bennett (Milandra Bradshaw), Gareth Jefferson (Brian Bradshaw), George Costigan (Dougie), Anna Keaveney (Jeanette), Tracie Bennett (Millandra), Ken Sharrock (Sydney), Karen Craig (Thelma), Cardew Robinson (Londoner), Honora Burke (Londoner's Wife), Marc Zuber (Renos), Deborah Yhip (Sharon-Louise), Ray Armstrong (Executive Type), John Hartley, Marlene Morley (German Tourists), Annee Blott (Chambermaid), Matthew Long (Teacher), Ruth Russell (Veronica), Sarah Nolan (Maureen), Diane Whitley (Liz), Joanne Zorian (Carol), Geraldine Griffiths (Sally), Elaine Boisseau (Woman in Taverna), Giorgos Xidakis (Spiro), Sheila Aza (Cooking Teacher), Alex Wright (Kid in Car), Ged McKenna (Van Driver).

While some may object to the story-telling techniques employed by playwright and screenwriter Willy Russell to depict his title character, others will find themselves enchanted by SHIRLEY VALENTINE, in which Pauline Collins (the superb British actress, re-creating her role in the Broadway and London hit) cocks an eyebrow and saucily addresses the camera to explain the actions, reactions, characters, and events of her daily existence from her own point of view. Shirley's sly asides will not seem contrived to viewers who accept them in the spirit in which they are delivered. Born and raised in Liverpool, she doesn't hesitate to confide her innermost thoughts to her unseen audience or even to speak her mind to the kitchen wall, as if it, too, were human. Shirley is an original, a dreamer who, over the years, has lost sight of her dreams by letting herself get sidetracked. Through brief flashbacks, we learn that Shirley was a rebellious girl who feared nothing, ready to taste life to its fullest without regrets. Alas, her adolescent ambitions were interrupted by matrimony and at least one child, who turned out to be an incorrigible brat. Shirley's hard-working but insensitive husband, Joe (played splendidly by Bernard Hill), can't understand his wife's old dreams, nor does he grasp her

basic needs or yearnings. He's a strictly meat-and-potatoes man, for whom a wife's primary functions are to provide him with hot meals, rear his children, and attend to his physical needs. There seems to be no end to Shirley's humdrum existence in sight, until her friend Jane (Steadman) invites her to come along on an all-expense-paid, two-week holiday in Greece won in a contest. Reflecting on who she was and what she has become, Shirley decides to go with Jane to Greece, where she indulges in a seaside romance with smooth-talking Costas (Conti). It isn't long before she's disillusioned, but it really doesn't matter, for by then Shirley has regained her self-respect and natural independence. Rediscovering herself, she decides to stay in Greece. Now it's Joe's turn to come to grips with reality, and to decide just how badly he wants his wife to come home.

It's easy to see why Collins won a Tony Award for her stage role in "Shirley Valentine." She is wonderful in the part, and seems born to play Shirley—just as Julie Walters seemed born to play Rita in the play and 1983 film version of EDUCATING RITA, which marked the first cinematic collaboration between writer Russell and producer-director Lewis Gilbert. Gilbert helms SHIRLEY VALENTINE with a sure hand and, best of all, does justice to the author's insightful delineation of his characters' relationships, with all the play's clever dialog intact. SHIRLEY VALENTINE is a movie in its own right, however, and not merely a photographed stageplay. Though hardly a masterpiece, the film is solidly entertaining, enhanced not only by Collins' memorable performance, but by uniformly excellent production values as well. (Adult situations, profanity, brief nudity.)

p, Lewis Gilbert; d, Lewis Gilbert; w, Willy Russell (based on his play); ph, Alan Hume (Technicolor); ed, Lesley Walker; m, George Hadjinassios and Willy Russell; md, Harry Rabinowitz; prod d, John Stoll; set d, Amanda Ackland-Snow; cos, Candice Paterson; makeup, Basil Newall.

Comedy/Drama/Romance
                          (PR:C MPAA:R)

SHOCKER**½
110m Alive/UNIV c
Mitch Pileggi (Horace Pinker), John Tesh (TV Newscaster), Heather Langenkamp (Victim), Peter Berg (Jonathan Parker), Jessica Craven (Counterperson), Cami Cooper (Alison), Richard Brooks (Rhino), Sam Scarber (Cooper), Theodore Raimi (Pac Man), Keith Anthony Lubow-Bellamy (Football Player), Virginia Morris (Diane), Emily Samuel (Sally), Michael Murphy (Lt. Don Parker), Peter Tilden (Reporter), Bingham Ray (Bartender), Sue Ann Harris (Waitress), Eugene

Chadbourne (Man in Bar), Jack Hoar (Rookie), Richard J. Gasparian, Joyce Guy (Cops), Joseph Roy O'Flynn, Bobby Lee Swain (Priests), Michael Matthews (Evil Mouth), Linda Kaye (Woman at Stairs), Vincent Guastaferro (Pastori), Janne K. Peters (Doctor), Bruce Wagner (Executioner), Marvin Elkins, Christopher Kriesa (Guards), Richardo Gutierrez (Guard Sergeant), Ernie Lively (Warden), John Mueller (Fireman), Jonathan Christian Craven (Jogger), Lindsay Parker (Little Girl), Dendrie Allyn Taylor (Young Mother), Kane Roberts (Road Worker), Stephen R. Hudis (Officer Robinson), Gary Michael Davies (Cameraman), Christopher Keyes (Bruno), Dr. Timothy Leary (TV Evangelist), Marji Martin (Woman Couch Potato), Ray Bickel (Man Couch Potato), Mark Slama (Kid with Crow Bar), Karl Vincent (Kid with Mask), Wes Craven, Holly Kaplan (Neighbors).

Wes Craven has directed such horror classics as LAST HOUSE ON THE LEFT (1972); THE HILLS HAVE EYES (1978); the brilliant THE SERPENT AND THE RAINBOW (1988); and the original NIGHTMARE ON ELM STREET (1984). He has also directed such failures as THE HILLS HAVE EYES II (1985); THE SWAMP THING (1982); and the terrible DEADLY FRIEND (1986). SHOCKER, the latest film from the talented but erratic Craven, seems to be something he had to get out of his system. A sloppy and often goofy chiller, the film is full of references to and outright rip-offs from other movies, especially those of New Line Cinema. Craven has had a rocky, litigious past with New Line, the producer of the "Nightmare on Elm Street" series, and apparently wants to show them that he can do their films one better. New Line's bread and butter is Freddy Krueger, a character Craven created as a terrifying monster in the first NIGHTMARE, whom they have since turned into a kind of cartoon, reducing the series to a mindless show of special effects and eliminating the subversive impact of Craven's original conception. In SHOCKER, Craven gets revenge: not only has he created a villain without any redeeming qualities, he has also cribbed scenes from the later "Nightmare" installments and re-directed them with tongue in cheek, as if to prove they can be made effective in the hands of a good filmmaker. Moreover, Craven virtually remakes New Line's only non-"Nightmare" genre success, THE HIDDEN, when SHOCKER reaches its third reel.

The story concerns limping, psychotic TV repairman Pileggi, a killer who wipes out entire families with a swipe of his hunting knife. After murdering the girl friend and most of the foster family of college football star Berg, Pileggi is arrested and sentenced to death in the electric chair, an event that Berg, his police-detective foster father (played with wonderful hamminess by Michael Murphy), and several others gather to witness. When Pileggi is brought in and strapped to the chair, he reveals that he is Berg's real father ("I used to beat you good, boy," he screams) and that Berg is responsible for his limp (as a boy, he shot Pileggi in the knee after he saw Pileggi beat his mother). When the switch is pulled, Pileggi—a dabbler in black magic who previously was shown making a weird electronic pact with the devil in his cell—becomes a burst of energy and disappears. In a plot device that will be familiar to fans of THE HIDDEN, he now becomes a video spirit who can possess anyone and turn them into limping psychotics intent on murdering Berg. Pileggi's spirit initially escapes the prison in the body of a female doctor, then jumps from person to person, until he finds a way to enter TV sets and live in their transmissions. Eventually, after several confrontations, Berg and Pileggi have their final showdown in the TV world, crashing through "Leave It to Beaver" and battling with remote controls (at one point, Berg catches Pileggi in a freeze frame, then rewinds him). Berg's plan is to trap Pileggi in transmission and blow the power in the city, causing his menacing father to disappear. With help from his football teammates and the spirit of his dead girl friend, he puts the scheme into action.

As silly as it sounds (and is), SHOCKER has moments of brilliance. Craven knows how to manipulate his audience, and combines elements of horror and satire perfectly. Especially impressive and assured is the extended scene in which Pileggi goes through five bodies while chasing Berg through a park (when possession by the mad killer turns a five-year-old girl into a spitting, swearing, limping psychotic, the effect is riotously funny). Unfortunately, Craven's repeated raids of other films (besides New Line's movies, he steals from EVIL DEAD; POLTERGEIST; NIGHT OF THE LIVING DEAD; and PRISON; while the bare bones of the plot even bear a striking resemblance to the recent, subpar HORROR SHOW, in which another electrocuted killer lives on as a ball of energy) cannot substitute for the originality that has made his best films so influential. Although technically sharp, wonderfully performed, and interestingly photographed (by Jacques Haitkin), SHOCKER is a disappointment, especially since it comes on the heels of Craven's sharpest, most serious, and most complex work yet, THE SERPENT AND THE RAINBOW. SHOCKER, by contrast, is little more than a silly swipe at New Line Cinema that will have most horror fans counting (on both hands) the number of shameless ripoffs from other movies it contains. But it's still a Wes Craven film (and undeniably entertaining), and as such

Charles Lane and Nicole Alysia in SIDEWALK STORIES (©Island).

it's worth seeing. *(Graphic violence, adult situations, profanity.)*

p, Marianne Maddalena, Barin Kumar, Peter Foster, and Bob Engelman; d, Wes Craven; w, Wes Craven; ph, Jacques Haitkin (Foto-Kem Color); ed, Andy Blumenthal; m, William Goldstein; prod d, Cynthia Kay Charette; art d, Randy Moore; set d, Keith B. Burns; spec eff, Larry Fioritto; cos, Isis Mussenden; stunts, Tony Cecere; makeup, Suzanne Parker Sanders.

Horror   (PR:O   MPAA:R)

SIDEWALK STORIES***
97m Palm/Island bw
Charles Lane *(Artist)*, Nicole Alysia *(Child)*, Sandye Wilson *(Young Woman)*, Darnell Williams *(Father)*, Trula Hoosier *(Mother)*, George Riddick *(Street Partner)*, Tom Hoover *(Portrait Artist)*, Michael Baskin *(Doorman)*, Luis Ramos, Frank John Trezza *(Kidnapers)*, Olivia Sklar *(Librarian)*, Michael Luciano *(Detective Grasso)*, Ed Kershen *(Detective Brooks)*, Joseph Verhaus *(Cab Driver)*, Ian Klapper *(Juggler)*, Herb Reynolds *(Ventriloquist)*, Jomo Wilson *(Magician)*, Jody O'Neil *(Customer No. 1)*, Michael Baskin *(Street Cop No. 1)*, Angel Cappellino *(Bully's Mother)*, Paul James Levin *(Bully)*, Robert Tuftee *(Carriage Driver)*, Bill Sage, Edie Falco *(Carriage Couple)*, Robin McWilliams *(Breakdancer)*, Ellia English *(Bag Lady)*, Edwin Anthony, Lewis Anthony Jordan, Eric Payne *(Penny Pitchers)*, Goma Sellman *(Fine Woman)*, Gerald Lane *(Shelter Director)*, Robert Clohessy, Franklin Gordon, Bobby How-

ard *(Alley Toughs)*, Henry Steen *(Three-Card Monte Man)*, Chris Kapp *(Homeless Mother)*, Elizabeth Lesser *(Pregnant Park Mother)*, Deena Engle, Mary Ann Orbe, Nell Gutman, Pier Robinson *(Park Mothers)*, Jeffrey Carpentier *(Homeless Native American)*, Bobby Johnson *(Homeless Youth)*, Ben Schneeberg *(Homeless Raver)*, Luis Garcia *(Homeless Spanish Speaker)*, Michael Baskin, Tom Wallace, Jimmy Clohessy, Raymond Jenkins *(Precinct Cops)*, Jan Leder, Ronald Jackson, Marcel Smith, Joe Solomon *(Jazz Quartet)*.

This self-consciously winsome, black-and-white, almost completely silent comedy focuses on homelessness through the Chaplinesque figure of the Artist (Lane), a homeless African-American street portraitist in Greenwich Village who stumbles upon a foundling (Alysia) in an alley after her father is killed, then takes the adorable little girl to his squat lodgings in an abandoned church, attempting to care for her and to find her mother. He also develops a friendship with the Young Woman (Wilson), the middle-class proprietor of a baby boutique who magnanimously overlooks the proxy father's shoplifting and, taking both man and child into her heart, treats them to dinner at her comfortable apartment. When Lane returns "home" one night, only to discover that the empty building has been demolished, he and Alysia are forced to sleep in a shelter, and they eventually wind up on the cold winter streets. Further complicating matters are a couple of thugs who almost kidnap the infant (whose money-making potential they have witnessed earlier, in a comic scene in which Alysia's child "art" sells like hotcakes to the passers-by who ignore Lane's street artistry). However, the would-be kidnapers scheme is foiled after a slapstick chase that is one of the film's least successful moments. Eventually, Lane finds Alysia's distraught, beautiful mother and somewhat regretfully hands over his charge, to whom he has become very attached. Wilson searches for her friend and, in the film's last scene, finds him with a number of other homeless people in a park. As Wilson and Lane sit on a bench, sharing the sandwich she has brought him, the park inhabitants' requests for change, crazed mutterings, and conversations—SIDEWALK STORIES' only lines of dialog—are heard on the soundtrack, continuing as the film fades to black.

Charles Lane, SIDEWALK STORIES' producer-writer-director-star, is nothing if not audacious in his feature debut. Working in silence and in black-and-white, with an unknown cast of mainly African-American actors and less-than-upbeat subject matter, Lane asks a mighty concession of modern audiences used to dialog, Spielbergian narratives, and high-tech effects. Moreover, in adopting a naive, impoverished comic persona that pointedly recalls Chaplin's Little Tramp, and in employing a plot that clearly borrows from Chaplin's THE KID, Lane forces comparisons between his own work and that of one of cinema's greatest artists—comparisons by which SIDEWALK STORIES must be judged wanting, a flawed *hommage* performed by actors whose pantomime skills are only adequate to the task, directed with more conviction than genius.

SIDEWALK STORIES is more than just a Chaplin imitation, however, and Lane's decision to film his tale in the style of early cinema for the most part works surprisingly well. It is doubtful, for instance, whether Lane's sentimental characterization of his naif main character, the sweetness of the relationships between Lane and Wilson and between Lane and Alysia, or the somewhat glossy, idealized look of the film (both the squat and the homeless shelter look quite comfortable in comparison to their real-life models) could have worked in sound and in color. But because modern-day audiences view silent films as "unrealistic" to begin with, Lane's stylizations are for the most part neither distracting nor offensive, and his emphasis on homeless people's humanity and essential decency comes through more strongly as a result. On the other hand, Lane relies on having a sensitive—if not already converted—audience. As in the work of Chaplin, whose comedies contain some of the most devastating portraits of poverty put on film, SIDEWALK STORIES is often most telling by implication. The real existence of homelessness, poverty, and racism are implied in small moments and urban-

ite details: the difference between Lane's attire and women's fur coats; the subtle variations among pedestrians' responses to Lane and Alysia, which usually end in the same uncharitable outcome; the homeless black hero's immoderate fear of the police; the contrast between Lane's squat and the nearby high-rent gallery district of SoHo; the disapproving looks Lane gets from Wilson's buppie friends.

A more dubious advantage of Lane's use of the silent medium is that it masks certain typical low-budget flaws—notably, amateurish acting. It's regrettable that movie audiences have lost some of their ability to determine what is good silent-screen pantomime, but this ignorance aids in the suspension of disbelief when watching the actors in SIDEWALK STORIES, whose miming seems credible if not expert. (By contrast, the introduction of the homeless people's voices at the end, in a scene which already verges on overkill, proves ineffective because the actors' voices sound inauthentic—these are clearly *actors*, and not the best actors.) Lane carries the biggest acting burden, and for the most part does so well, although he has given himself some particularly Chaplinesque bits of physical business that fall flat—his initial difficulty, and later facility, in maneuvering Alysia's stroller; a kind of shuffling movement he occasionally affects, in the style of the Little Tramp's waddle, which ultimately proves pointless. Nicole Alysia, however, is completely natural; it's a pleasure to see a movie baby who is thoroughly charming without being the slightest bit movie-cute. Sandye Wilson, as Lane's unlikely love interest, is also compelling, effectively suggesting both a strong will and a soft heart.

The film is marred by some superfluous sequences, including the ill-mimed, unconvincing scene in which Alysia's father (Darnell Williams, of "All My Children" fame) is killed; the foiled kidnaping, with its clumsy slapstick; and a brief, comic sexual fantasy that not only blows SIDEWALK STORIES' chances for a G rating but also borrows too much from Spike Lee's SHE'S GOTTA HAVE IT. On the other hand Lane's film, like Lee's, boasts polished black-and-white photography (by Bill Dill) and a particularly effective score (by Marc Marder).

SIDEWALK STORIES has more heart than art—it is not the aesthetic equal of SHE'S GOTTA HAVE IT or Jim Jarmusch's STRANGER THAN PARADISE, the decade's two most auspicious black-and-white films by young New York independent directors focusing on inner-city characters—but it provides further evidence that a viable black independent filmmaking movement may at last be under way, and signals the advent of an ambitious, impassioned filmmaker. Shot on a $200,000 budget in just over two

weeks on New York locations, SIDEWALK STORIES met with enough critical and audience favor to gain Lane a contract with Island Pictures, apparently ensuring the release of his next film, a contemporary romantic drama in color and sound that was in production at the time of this writing. On the evidence of SIDEWALK STORIES, Lane's career is worth watching. *(Nudity, sexual situations, adult situations.)*

p, Charles Lane; d, Charles Lane; w, Charles Lane; ph, Bill Dill; ed, Anne Stein and Charles Lane; m, Marc Marder; prod d, Lyn Pinezich; art d, Ina Mayhew; cos, Jane Tabachnick; makeup, Lisa A. Johnson.

Comedy (PR:C MPAA:R)

⊙**SIGNS OF LIFE****½
91m American Playhouse
Theatrical/Avenue c
(AKA: ONE FOR SORROW, TWO FOR JOY)
Arthur Kennedy *(Owen Coughlin)*, Kevin J. O'Connor *(Eddie Johnson)*, Vincent Philip D'Onofrio *(Daryl Monahan)*, Michael Lewis *(Joey Monahan)*, Beau Bridges *(John Alder)*, Kate Reid *(Mrs. Wrangway)*, Mary Louise Parker *(Charlotte)*, Georgia Engel *(Betty)*, Will Patton *(Mr. Coughlin, Sr.)*, Kathy Bates *(Mary Beth)*, Anna Besaud *(Dee Dee)*, Brooke Lawsing *(Carrie)*, Wellington Santos *(Carlos Castanho)*, Martin Shakar *(Mr. Castanho)*, Paul Cunha *(Jamie Castanho)*, Lazaro Perez *(Uncle Reynaldo)*, Alex Goulart Jr., Manuel Januaro *(Castanhos)*, Graciella Lecube *(Mrs. Castanho)*, Ralph Williams *(Ernie)*, Keith Reddin *(Dr. Pound)*, Matthew Cowles *(Pierre)*, Mary Joy *(Cranberry Woman)*, Brad Sullivan *(Lobsterman)*.

Although it's an obviously heartfelt attempt to expose movie audiences to the lives of America's not-so-rich and famous, SIGNS OF LIFE, which was coproduced by PBS' American Playhouse, suffers from the usual PBS-sponsored symptoms: it's too bland and contrived to be very rewarding. Saved only by its excellent ensemble acting, the film proposes to show us a day in the life of a dying seaside town somewhere in Maine. The action revolves around the last day of business at an ancient boatyard owned by crotchety old shipbuilder Kennedy. Although the yard has been building beautiful wood boats for several generations, business has collapsed in the 1980s because of competition from Kennedy's nemesis, fiberglass. Having built their last boat for a proud family of Portuguese fishermen, Kennedy and his employees (Bridges, O'Connor, D'Onofrio, and Lewis, D'Onofrio's retarded brother) must close down the shop and look for new work—a prospect about which none of them is enthusiastic. The oldest of the employees, Bridges, has four young daughters and a wife (Bates) in labor with their fifth. Although he would like to move to Maryland in search of another shipbuilding job, he must stay to face the reality of begging his smug brother-in-law for a sales position at the local hardware franchise (where a ridiculous tri-cornered hat will be part of his uniform). O'Connor and D'Onofrio have made plans to move to Miami and get jobs as salvage divers, but both must divest themselves of some emotional baggage first, O'Connor having to break off his relationship with his waitress girl friend (Parker) and D'Onofrio forced to put his retarded brother in a special school. While O'Connor has fulfilled his part of the bargain (only to be rewarded by a punch in the head from Parker), the compassionate D'Onofrio procrastinates. Even worse off is Kennedy, who has recently found himself haunted by the spirit of his shipbuilding father (Patton)—a constant reminder of his failure. Determined to save the shipyard, Kennedy at first tries to pitch one of his oldest customers, but in his desperation doesn't even realize that the man has had a stroke and doesn't even recognize him. Crushed and defeated, the angry Kennedy grabs his Rolodex and starts phoning his former customers to vent his rage: "Your grandfather bought a boat from my grandfather, your father bought a boat from my father, and you bought a boat from someone in California! You ruined my business, you bastard!" Kennedy seems determined to call everyone in town and is stopped only when his faithful housekeeper, Reid, discreetly disconnects the phone. Meanwhile, Bridges, looking for work at the hardware store, is seized by a momentary panic and steals $200 from the cash register. Another crisis arises when D'Onofrio accompanies O'Connor to the local diner, leaving his brother in Kennedy's care. While O'Connor does battle with Parker—who is determined to make him stay with her no matter what— Kennedy becomes so distracted in his bitterness that he loses sight of Lewis, who hides in a rowboat and winds up adrift far from shore. The humiliated Bridges drives to a remote location and lies on a rock, staring at the sky as his loot blows away in the wind, while the search for Lewis lasts well into the night. Just as they are about to find him, the retarded boy panics and falls into the water, sinking like a stone (during this crisis it is revealed that O'Connor can't swim). D'Onofrio is shattered by his brother's apparent drowning and Kennedy begs the ghost of his father to exchange his life for that of the boy. Miraculously, however, Lewis turns up alive in the net of the Portuguese fishermen. During a bittersweet party to commemorate the closing of the shipyard and celebrate the rescue of Lewis, O'Connor, who finally admits to himself that he can't be a deep-

sea diver if he can't swim, decides to stay in Maine and marry Parker; Bridges finally comes to his senses and enlists his daughters to find the scattered money so that he can make things right with his brother-in-law; and D'Onofrio decides to go to Miami by himself. After the party, Kennedy is visited by his father's spirit and is compelled to fulfill his part of the bargain for Lewis' life by hanging himself. The attempt is botched, however, and Kennedy realizes he can make amends by caring for the retarded boy while D'Onofrio makes a new life for himself in Florida.

While SIGNS OF LIFE is certainly a decent alternative to the many violent, mindless, and emotionless movies released each year, it still doesn't manage to avoid the seemingly inevitable pitfalls that accompany this kind of material, namely an almost grating earnestness that compels the filmmakers to fall back on cliches (the retarded boy) and predictable devices (the ghost of the past) to generate some sort of "magical" quality. As scripted by Mark Malone (coauthor of 1987's DEAD OF WINTER), SIGNS OF LIFE veers between the subtle and the cloying, the genuine and the contrived, the unusual and the typical. His script is so overloaded with obvious symbolism and death/life, man/woman motifs that at times it plays like the opening to "Ben Casey." But it is Malone's deployment of simplistic screenwriter's devices to move his story along that really disappoints. The retarded or otherwise impaired supporting character is an age-old narrative ploy, usually used to generate easy sympathy and to force other characters to learn more about them-

selves through him or her. Last year's RAIN MAN rose above this contrived concept by turning the autistic savant Raymond into a complex and compelling character with a life of his own, elevating him beyond a mere plot device; SIGNS OF LIFE, despite a nicely nuanced performance from Michael Lewis, never makes that step and the character remains clearly labeled as either "burden" or "salvation" at various points in the movie. The other, even more annoying, contrivance is that of the ghost character. While such a part may work well in a Dickensian tale, this is an original screenplay and on the screen the character is nothing more than an obvious scriptwriter's crutch—an easy and convenient way to plumb the emotional depths of a taciturn and introverted character by giving him someone he can talk aloud to. In SIGNS OF LIFE, this device is so inconsistently employed that the character seems imposed on the material instead of derived from it.

Luckily, director John David Coles skirts some of these problems by creating a vivid visual milieu for his characters (the dying town is as much a character as any human being in the film) and guiding his excellent cast to downplay the material's easy sentimentality. The ensemble cast brings weight and authenticity to their roles (despite frequently slipping in and out of their Maine accents), convincing the viewer that they have known each other all of their lives. Veteran Hollywood actor Arthur Kennedy came out of retirement to play his role, and does so with zest, presenting a fairly complex portrait of an old man who feels he's a failure. Kevin J. O'Connor, last seen in

Michael Lewis and Vincent Philip D'Onofrio in SIGNS OF LIFE (©Avenue).

THE MODERNS and CANDY MOUNTAIN, is wonderful as the naive and somewhat confused young man who really doesn't want to leave his girl, but thinks it's the right thing to do. Vincent Phillip D'Onofrio does a fine job of underplaying his role as the conflicted and compassionate brother, and Beau Bridges is heartwrenching as the heavily burdened father and husband forced to swallow his pride to beg for work he considers beneath him. The women—especially Kate Reid and Mary Louise Parker—are the true standouts, however, triumphing over their stereotyped roles and bringing something fresh and compelling to their parts, underscripted as they are. Despite such writing flaws, however, SIGNS OF LIFE deserves kudos for acknowledging the economic depression of areas of the American landscape and painting a vivid picture of the noble citizens who inhabit them. *(Sexual situations, profanity.)*

p, Marcus Viscidi and Andrew Reichman; d, John David Coles; w, Mark Malone; ph, Elliot Davis (Technicolor); ed, William Anderson and Angelo Corrao; m, Howard Stone; prod d, Howard Cummings; art d, Beth Rubino; set d, Jeanette Scott.

Drama   **(PR:C MPAA:PG-13)**

Ⓥ**SILENT NIGHT, DEADLY NIGHT 3: BETTER WATCH OUT!***
91m Arthur H. Gorson/Quiet c
Richard Beymer *(Dr. Newbury)*, Bill Moseley *(Ricky)*, Samantha Scully *(Laura)*, Eric Da Re *(Chris)*, Laura Herring *(Jerri)*, Elizabeth Hoffman *(Granny)*, Robert Culp *(Lt. Connely)*, Isabel Cooley *(Receptionist)*, Leonard Mann *(Psychiatrist)*, Carlos Palomino *(Truck Driver)*.

There was hardly any need for another sequel to SILENT NIGHT, DEADLY NIGHT, but director Monte Hellman has bravely brought this third installment to the screen anyway. Picking up a few months after Part II (a sorry rehash of the original, with more old footage than new) left off, the story opens as Moseley, "The Santa Claus Killer," lies in a deep coma. After being shot several times, Moseley required brain reconstruction and was left with half a skull (the top of his head is now a glass dome, displaying his new brain). Moseley is part of an experiment conducted by Beymer, who is investigating a young blind girl's dreams and their weird relation to Moseley's past. The girl (Scully) has sighted dreams in which Moseley and a knife-wielding Santa stalk her through white hallways. After several such psychic connections Scully definitely needs a vacation, so she, her brother (Da Re), and his girl friend (Herring) go to Scully's grandmother's house for the holidays. It's not long, however, before Moseley comes out of his coma, kills a drunken Santa Claus (a compassionate fellow who refers

to Moseley as a "vegetable" and asks him if his favorite singer is "Perry Coma"), and escapes to pursue Scully—who, according to Beymer, has touched Moseley's soul. After killing a truck driver and beheading a gas station attendant, Moseley arrives at the house of Scully's grandmother (Hoffman) before Scully does. Kindly Hoffman feeds him and offers him a gift, and he thanks her by killing her. While Beymer and police lieutenant Culp follow Moseley's trail, Scully and company arrive at Hoffman's house, only to find that Granny is strangely absent (Da Re and Herring are so upset by this fact that they immediately have sex in the bathtub). Eventually—as he must—Moseley attacks, killing Herring and Beymer before Scully is able to impale him on a wooden stake and Culp finally comes to her rescue. As the film ends, Moseley's body is being taken away in an ambulance. "Hurry; with a little luck we can save this guy," a paramedic says. "Merry Christmas," Scully says—sarcastically, while she rides away from the scene in a police car. "And a happy New Year," adds a tuxedo-clad Moseley in the film's final shot.

Though the straight-to-video SILENT NIGHT, DEADLY NIGHT III is certainly better than its two predecessors, that's not saying much. It's still very bad. Hellman has a flair for effectively chaotic camera angles, and handles the film's inside cinematic references (including shots inspired by the original NIGHTMARE ON ELM STREET and direct clips from THE RAVEN) quite nicely. But the whole thing is still a laughably misguided mess. Scully's blindness and psychic powers—which might have given the film some interesting psychological angles—are never explored, and the shocks are cheap and lack suspense. In fact, the film is so slowly paced that one "frantic" chase plays more like a funeral march, with some strange chit chat (about the convenience of cellular phones!) thrown in.

The performances are uniformly bad, though Robert Culp is worst as the cop who says "It's time to relieve the reptile" before urinating on the side of the road. Thankfully, he's only in the final third of the film. It's also to the film's credit that the Killer-Santa angle is virtually absent this time out and the gore is relatively restrained. SILENT NIGHT, DEADLY NIGHT III isn't offensive, it's just a badly paced slasher movie that's sometimes so stupid it's funny. The vision of the hospital-gown-clad, dome-headed Moseley hitchhiking on the roadside is supremely silly, and Beymer's dialog is so overwritten it slips into hilarity. It's possible that SILENT NIGHT, DEADLY NIGHT III might have worked as a flat-out parody. As it is, it's just another unnecessary sequel to another unnecessary splatter-film series. *(Violence,*

nudity, profanity, adult situations, substance abuse.)

p, Arthur H. Gorson; d, Monte Hellman; w, Carlos Laszlo (based on a story by Laszlo, Monte Hellman, Richard N. Gladstein); ph, Josep M. Civit (Foto-Kem Color); ed, Ed Rothkowitz; m, Steven Soles; prod d, Philip Thomas; art d, Laurie Post; spec eff, Nina Kraft; cos, Pia Dominguez; stunts, Rawn Hutchinson.

Horror   **(PR:O MPAA:R)**

SKELETON COAST*
98m Walanar-Breton/Silvertree c
Ernest Borgnine *(Col. Smith)*, Robert Vaughn *(Col. Schneider)*, Oliver Reed *(Capt. Simpson)*, Herbert Lom *(Elia)*, Daniel Greene *(Rick Weston)*, Leon Isaac Kennedy *(Chuck)*, Simon Sabela *(Gen. Sekatri)*, Nancy Mulford *(Sam)*, Peter Kwong, Robin Townsend, Arnold Vosloo, Larry Taylor.

SKELETON COAST suffers from a skeletal script, an obviously low budget, and an unusually flagrant disregard for anything approaching plot logic. What it doesn't suffer from is a shortage of second-level character stars. Leading the mayhem, set in southwest Africa, is a fit-looking Borgnine, playing a retired US Marine colonel whose CIA agent son has been taken prisoner by the Angolan army after aiding a rebel uprising led by general Sabela. With the help of Greene, Borgnine assembles a semimagnificent seven—one of them (Kwong) is even named Toshiro in case we fail to get the point—to storm the fortress where Borgnine's son is being held by a sadistic East German colonel (Vaughn, who seems barely able to muster the energy to maintain his accent). Also among the seven are Kennedy and the magnificently endowed Mulford, who deserves some sort of special prize for making it through the entire movie in a succession of outrageously revealing tops without once coming undone amid the film's ferocious action sequences. Along the way, Borgnine runs afoul of low-life wheeler-dealer Lom, from whom he buys information on his son's whereabouts (using counterfeit money), and diamond mine security officer Reed (after Greene snaps the neck of one of his men like a big pretzel). Lom confines his expression of outrage to hurling his cordless phone against the wall, but Reed stages a jolly ambush in the desert, first commanding his men to kill Borgnine's band then leaving the scene—and the film—after destroying their truck convoy and pinning them down. Lom also vanishes, after committing phone-icide. Stealing a plane to continue their journey—and making us wonder why they didn't just use a plane in the first place—Borgnine, the boys, and the girl are shot down just short of their goal by none other than Sabela and his guerrillas, who make up for this indiscretion by joining Borgnine on his mission. The ensuing two-fisted attack on Vaughn's fortress contains all the expected scenes, from the tearful reunion between father and son to Vaughn ripping open Mulford's T-shirt in an eye-popping closeup (but still managing to reveal less than an average *Sports Illustrated* swimsuit issue spread).

Along with the passably staged, big, noisy action sequences; the bewildering parade of truncated semistar cameos; and Mulford's amazing decolletage, SKELETON COAST does contain some good, if probably unintentional, humor. A scene that might not have looked out of place on an episode of "McHale's Navy" features Borgnine passing off himself and his seven, including Toshiro, as Cubans in an encounter with *real* Cubans. But mostly the movie just lumbers along from one pitched battle to the next, on the shoulders of a shaky script as noteworthy for what it lacks as for what it contains.

Like dialog. Not the least of SKELETON COAST's oddities is that somebody seems to have forgotten to write more than a handful of lines for the supporting players, although there is a strong indication that they may also have fallen prey to the editor's scissors. (Some evidence of this can be seen in odd continuity errors, such as Borgnine's crisp, white tropical suit in one scene appearing smudged and dirty in the next, without explanation.) Despite the almost unending array of cinematic spoonerisms that add to its general air of poverty-row absurdity, however, SKELETON COAST is finally just too dull and routine even to be entertainingly bad. As was the probable intention, it's finally a film strictly for those who just can't get enough of watching things get blown up. *(Violence, profanity.)*

p, Harry Alan Towers; d, John "Bud" Cardos; w, Nadia Calliou (based on a story by Peter Welbeck [Harry Alan Towers]); ph, Hanro Mohr; ed, Allan Morrison and Mac Errington; m, Colin Shapiro and Barry Bekker; prod d, Leonardo Coen Cagli; stunts, Reo Ruiters.

Action **(PR:C MPAA:R)**

⊙SKIN DEEP*½
102m BECO-Morgan Creek/FOX c
John Ritter *(Zach Hutton)*, Vincent Gardenia *(Barney)*, Alyson Reed *(Alex Hutton)*, Joel Brooks *(Jake)*, Julianne Phillips *(Molly)*, Chelsea Field *(Amy)*, Peter Donat *(Sparky)*, Don Gordon *(Curt)*, Nina Foch *(Alex's Mother)*, Denise Crosby *(Angie)*, Michael Kidd *(Dr. Westford)*, Dee Dee Rescher *(Bernice)*, Bryan Genesse *(Rick)*, Bo Foxworth *(Greg)*, Raye Hollit *(Lonnie)*, Jean Marie McKee *(Rebecca)*, Brenda Swanson *(Emily)*, Heidi Paine *(Tina)*, Diana Barton *(Helena)*, Bobb Hopkins *(Jonas)*,

Robert Burleigh *(Martin Dunn)*, Sol Vang Tanney *(Hotel Concierge)*, Karen Haber *(Leah)*, Judy Toll *(Dixie)*, Sheryl Lee Ralph *(Receptionist)*, Arsenio "Sonny" Trinidad *(Danny the Butler)*, Toni Attell *(Waitress)*, Ben Hartigan *(Blind Man)*, Robert Arthur *(Wedding Minister)*, Deryl Carroll *(Funeral Minister)*, Robert Dowdell *(Traffic Judge)*, Harlan Arnold *(Divorce Judge)*, John McCann *(Howard Simon)*, William Hubbard Knight *(Adam White)*, Mark Goldstein *(TV Director)*, Sati Jamal *(Floor Director)*, Don Maxwell *(Fire Chief)*, John Curran *(Jasper)*, Scott Kraft *(Lucas)*, Steven Majewicz *(Romeo)*, Diane Dickson *(Juliet)*.

Blake Edwards could learn something from Zach Hutton, the main character in his movie SKIN DEEP: When your writing starts to go bad, take a break. Hutton is an award-winning writer who has fallen into a creative void and, consequently, hasn't written a word in years. Edwards (THE PINK PANTHER and its sequels; 10; VICTOR/VICTORIA; S.O.B.) also appears to be stuck in a formidable rut, but unlike Hutton, he keeps on working, forcing moviegoers to suffer through the drought with him. Edwards last effort was the insipid SUNSET; this year, he brings us SKIN DEEP, the dull story of a man who must give up alcohol and women, his two favorite pastimes, to win back his estranged wife.

Ritter plays Hutton, whose marriage to news anchorwoman Reed ends the day she returns home to find Crosby, his mistress, holding him at gunpoint after finding him in bed with his hairdresser (Paine). Already jobless because of his prolonged case of writer's block, Ritter ends up homeless as well when Reed divorces him and is awarded their house in court. He spends his days shuttling between a barstool and a

psychiatrist's couch, and his despair worsens when he is impotent during a one-night stand. He soon resumes his skirt-chasing activities, however, and shacks up with Phillips for some time until she ends the relationship by burning down their house. Ritter then gets involved with Hollit, a bodybuilder and aerobics instructor whose prowess in bed overwhelms him. Next, Ritter attempts to woo Field away from her violently jealous rock-star boy friend (Genesse). This leads to a fight with Genesse, which takes place in the dark with the men wearing only glow-in-the-dark condoms, and lands Ritter in the police station, troubles that worsen when he is later arrested for reckless driving. The post-divorce mayhem convinces Ritter that Reed, who is about to remarry, is his only salvation. He crashes her wedding, which she subsequently calls off, although she still refuses to take Ritter back. He then moves into a friend's house and, one day, is swept away by a giant wave while meditating on the sand. Ritter comes out of the flood with the inspiration for a new book: an account of his recent experiences. It becomes a best-seller, and Ritter, cured at last of his alcoholism and womanizing, reunites with Reed.

Midlife angst in wealthy Southern California is familiar ground for writer-director Edwards, but SKIN DEEP is a far cry from 10, possibly his best treatise on the subject. SKIN DEEP not only fails to be funny, it's not even interesting. Part of the problem is the casting of John Ritter, who has neither the looks nor the charisma for his role. He performs adequately, but is neither actor nor star enough to carry the film, as the part requires him to do. Worse, the slapstick shtick familiar from Ritter's role on TV's "Three's Company" again rears its tiresome head in a number of scenes here,

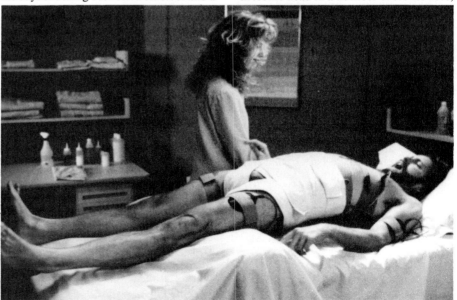

Julianne Phillips and John Ritter in SKIN DEEP (© 20th Century Fox).

in which his character joins an aerobics class, tries to walk after "electrostimulation" therapy, and shows up at a black-tie affair dressed for a masquerade party.

The Edwards who created the role of Zach Hutton is as much at fault as the Edwards who cast Ritter to play it, however. Even with a more appealing star, SKIN DEEP would elicit little sympathy for its protagonist. All that is revealed about Ritter's character is his weakness for booze and young women; since we see him only in the bar or in the bedroom, we learn nothing about what makes him tick. Deep down, is he loving? Insecure? Selfish? What attracted his wife and girl friends to him in the first place? The film's character development is weak generally: Reed seems like a decent, hard-working woman, but we don't see any side of her except that she is fed up with Ritter; a bartender (Gardenia) and an attorney (Brooks) listen to Ritter's problems and offer advice but have no personalities of their own. One can't like or dislike the characters in SKIN DEEP, because they're not characters in the first place—they're caricatures or stick figures.

But the film's biggest fault is that it just isn't funny, and parts of it don't even make sense. One example: Brooks tells Ritter that a model Ritter wants to meet will be at a party thrown by her magazine that night. In the next scene, Brooks and his wife are dressing for a party, but after Brooks gets into a cowboy costume, his wife reminds him that tonight's party is a black-tie affair for *Shape* magazine; not the costume party they plan to attend next week. Uh-oh. Brooks tells his wife he misinformed Ritter, and sure enough, Ritter shows up at the formal affair in a costume. But two scenes earlier, Brooks gave Ritter the correct invitation (to *Shape*'s party). What happened?

The flourescent condom fight does live up to its billing as the most memorable scene of SKIN DEEP, although that's faint praise considering the movie's sluggishness. But at least it's an original joke, and somewhat amusing. It's surprising, though, that it required the extraordinary talents of Industrial Light and Magic (George Lucas' company), which is credited with SKIN DEEP's visual effects, to provide the sight gag. Condoms that glow in the dark are hardly the caliber of spectacle one has come to expect from that crew. Songs include: "Falling out of Love" (Ivan Neville, performed by Neville), "Just to Keep You Satisfied" (Marvin Gaye, Anna Gaye, Elgie Stover, performed by Gaye), "I Can't Go Home" (Robert Cray, performed by the Robert Cray Band), "It's Just a Matter of Time" (Brook Benton, Belford Hendricks, Clyde Otis, performed by Benton), "Skin Deep" (Debra Holland, Ted Jacobs, performed by Holland), "Songbird" (Kenny G., performed by Kenny G.), "Dreamin'" (L. Montgomary, G. Paschal,

performed by Vanessa Williams), *Eine Kleine Nachtmusik* (Wolfgang Amadeus Mozart, performed by the Falla Trio). *(Nudity, substance abuse, excessive profanity, sexual situations.)*

p, Tony Adams; d, Blake Edwards; w, Blake Edwards; ph, Isidore Mankofsky (Technicolor); ed, Robert Pergament; md, Tom Bocci; prod d, Rodger Maus; set d, Bob Beall; spec eff, Danny Cangemi, Industrial Light & Magic, Michael Owens, Jim Morris, and Charlie Bailey; cos, Nolan Miller; chor, John Clifford; stunts, Joe Dunne; makeup, Brad Wilder.

Comedy   **(PR:O MPAA:R)**

ⓥSLASH DANCE zero
83m Double Helix/Glencoe Ent. c
Cindy Maranne *(Tori Raines)*, James Carroll Jordan *(Logan)*, Joel Von Ornsteiner *(Amos)*, Jay Richardson *(Edison)*, Queen Kong *(Repo)*, William Kerr *(Oliver)*, John Bluto *(Rupert)*, Jackson Daniel *(Jeff)*, Kelle Favar *(Mavis)*, Vinece Lee *(Cleo)*, Janice Patterson *(Maxine)*, Shari Blums *(Anni)*, Susan Kay Deemer *(Holly)*, Lanell Henson *(Susie)*, Cynthia Cheston *(Alice)*, Joleen Troop *(Misty)*, Richard Scalata *(Trope)*, Daniel Friedman *(Sling)*.

Despite the fact that the major Hollywood studios seem to be doing better than ever—raking in hundreds of millions of dollars with mega-hit sequels and sales of ancillary products—ultra-low budget filmmakers have managed to hang on by producing small genre efforts for theatrical release overseas and for the US home video market. Unfortunately, the vast majority of these efforts are incredibly amateurish, not just due to budgetary restrictions, but because the filmmakers do not seem to understand that making movies requires much more than simply getting a properly exposed image back from the processor. A perfect example of this lack of awareness is SLASH DANCE, a particularly uninspired bargain basement thriller shot mostly in a Hollywood Boulevard tourist attraction known as "The Haunted Theater."

It seems that a number of young, beautiful dancers have been murdered in the dilapidated Van Slake Theater, and it is up to crusading female police detective Tori Raines (played by Cindy Maranne, a one-time professional wrestler on the syndicated television show "GLOW: The Gorgeous Ladies of Wrestling") to crack the case. Posing as a dancer, Maranne shows up at the theater to audition for the director, Jordan; the theater owner, Kerr; and Kerr's retarded brother, Von Ornsteiner. Of course, Maranne makes the final call and winds up in the chorus line. During rehearsals she comes to believe that the sometimes violent and definitely weird Von Ornsteiner is the killer, but when he stabs himself to death with what he thinks

was a rubber prop knife (the killer has replaced it with a real one), her main suspect winds up in the morgue and Maranne is taken off the case. Before leaving the theater, however, Maranne is stalked by the masked killer; then she and Kerr are confronted by him, as he reveals his identity and explains the motivation for the murders before another killing and a wild chase bring the film to its violent, ambiguous conclusion.

While SLASH DANCE is less odious than most films of its ilk—its sex and violence quotient low (no frontal nudity, very little blood)—this restraint is of little consequence when filmmaking is as rudimentary as this is. Incompetent on nearly every level, the movie suffers from a variety of ills, not the least of which are a bad script and lethargic direction from James Shyman. Drawing its inspiration from innumerable TV cop shows and formula action thrillers, SLASH DANCE at times is reminiscent of relatively superior exploitation efforts such as ANGEL (1984) and STRIPPED TO KILL (1987), with its emphasis on a gun-wielding female investigator's exploration of Hollywood's seedy underside. But while those films had some memorable characters and succeeded in creating a vivid atmosphere while spinning fairly engaging yarns, SLASH DANCE fails on all counts. Its incredibly thin story is padded out by monotonous scenes of chorus girls rehearsing a stupefyingly lame production number over and over again (if any of these women are actually dancers, they keep their talent well hidden), seemingly endless shots of Maranne walking alone while voice-over flashbacks inform us of the drug-overdose death of her sister and suicide of her mother, some pointless romantic banter between Maranne and her married superior, and, worst of all, scenes of comic relief involving her precinct's preening, politically ambitious captain (who provides one of the film's "comic" highlights by clipping his nose hair with great vigor). None of this is especially interesting or has much to do with character development; instead it feels like the editor is stalling in a vain effort to lengthen this short feature, failing to realize that he isn't improving the film but only prolonging the agony. By the time SLASH DANCE does stumble to its ineptly staged climax, one doesn't really care who the killer is or why he murders.

All that a fan of bad cinema can cling to in SLASH DANCE are the grotesquely bad performances from a decidedly amateur cast. Top honors in this department go to female wrestler Queen Kong for her loud, grating performance as a black market steroid salesman. One can't help but be amused as this six-foot-four-inch behemoth gropes for her inane dialog, then delivers it with the utmost sincerity, as if

Robert Towne had written the screenplay! William Kerr is a close second as the theater owner. With his southern accent and perpetually confused countenance, Kerr brings the same degree of bewilderment to each line he spouts, be he angry, exasperated, or frightened. Joel Von Ornsteiner, on the other hand, contributes the film's most offensive performance with his portrayal of the imbecilic Amos. Working furiously through all the anguished cliches associated with cinematic depictions of the mentally handicapped, Von Ornsteiner delivers a cartoonish portrayal that merely reenforces the magnificence of Dustin Hoffman's delicately nuanced performance in RAIN MAN. Director Shyman must, however, share the blame for his actors' lackluster work, because ultimately it is the director who is responsible for shaping the performances, and obviously Shyman was not up to the task. SLASH DANCE is yet another forgettable little film that will fade into well-deserved obscurity, and one only hopes that those who participated in it will either learn from the experience or give a less demanding career some serious thought. *(Violence, sexual situations, profanity.)*

p, Andrew Maisner; d, James Shyman; w, James Shyman; ph, Geza Sinkovics; ed, Larry Rosen; m, Emilio Kauderer; art d, Wayne Lehrer; cos, Nancy Bassett; makeup, LaDina Kay.

Thriller   (PR:C   MPAA:NR)

Ⓥ**SLAVES OF NEW YORK****
125m Gary Hendler-Merchant Ivory/Tri-Star c
Bernadette Peters *(Eleanor)*, Chris Sarandon *(Victor Okrent)*, Mary Beth Hurt *(Ginger Booth)*, Madeleine Potter *(Daria)*, Adam Coleman Howard *(Stash Stotz)*, Nick Corri *(Marley Mantello)*, Mercedes Ruehl *(Samantha)*, Betty Comden *(Mrs. Wheeler)*, Steve Buscemi *(Wilfredo)*, Tama Janowitz *(Abby)*, Bruce Peter Young *(Mikell)*, Tammy Grimes *(Georgette)*, Charles McCaughan *(Sherman McVittie)*, John Harkins *(Chuck Dade Dolger)*, Anna Katarina *(Mooshka)*, Michael Schoeffling *(Jan)*, Christine Dunford *("B")*, Joe Leeway *(Jonny Jalouse)*, Michael Butler, Johann Carlo *(Performance Artists)*, Philip Lenkowsky *(Fritz)*, Harsh Nayyar *(Dr. Pandiya)*, Stanley Tucci *(Darryl)*, Louis Guss *(Vardig)*, Maura Moynihan *(Mona)*, Ken Kensei *(Kiochi)*, Kevin John Gee *(Kyoshi)*, Rick Hara *(Tetsu)*, Francine Hunter, Anthony Crivello *(Hairdressers)*, Jonas Abry *(Mickey)*, Stephen Bastone *(Chauffeur)*, Mark Boone Jr. *(Mitch)*, Dianne Brill *(Jogger)*, Richy Canatta *(Saxophonist)*, Raye Dowell *(Cheerleader)*, Stash Franklin, Aaron Goodstone *(Graffiti Artists)*, Adam Green *(Max)*, George Harris *(Super)*, Sakina Jaffrey *(Wilfredo's Recep-

Bernadette Peters and Mercedes Ruehl in SLAVES OF NEW YORK (©Tri-Star).

tionist)*, Anthony La Paglia *(Henry)*, Jennifer Lee *(Polly)*, Suzanne O'Neill *(Victor's Receptionist)*, Lazaro Perez *(Bill)*, Paul Potter *(Simon St. Simon)*.

The New York East Village art scene of the early 1980s was a flamboyant one, where low-budget but imaginative worlds of fashion, music, and painting came together in a mini-fete reminiscent of the creativity of the 1960s. Tama Janowitz's short-story collection *Slaves of New York*, a major literary "brat pack" success, caught some of that time's ambience—and while the book's studied air of depressive whimsy would be a tricky prospect for any filmmaker, it's hard to think of a director as ill-suited to it as James Ivory, whose films with Ismail Merchant are distinguished both by their attention to decor and their fatal neglect of the rudiments of film pacing. (A ROOM WITH A VIEW is the sole exception, the Merchant-Ivory vision holding together in that film mainly because of E.M. Forster's succinct plot and a perfect cast). Ivory's lack of structure and timing has never been more apparent than in SLAVES OF NEW YORK. Forsaking Victorian drawing rooms to wander the mean streets of Manhattan, he gets it wrong from the decorative first shot: of his heroine ambling along with dog and groceries to a noodling Muzak theme. Involvement with the characters and their dilemmas is eminently resistible in SLAVES OF NEW YORK; Ivory seems to view them all as sociological oddities to be ogled in this Cook's tour of bohemia, and leaves them sadly underdeveloped.

The script—by Janowitz—centers on the destructive relationship between Peters, an aspiring milliner, and Howard, a churlish young painter. Howard is rotten to

Peters, who, to quote Woody Allen, has the self-esteem of Kafka and keeps coming back for more, her "slave" status reinforced by the fact that *he* owns the loft they inhabit in real estate-obsessed Manhattan. Circling around them like dilettante buzzards are an assortment of dealers, designers, Japanese photographers, and hangers-on who create more problems for the pair. Peters is humiliated, betrayed, and enshrined as a chic 15-minute success before she finally breaks free of the demeaning Howard, and is last seen careening over the Brooklyn Bridge on the back of her new lover's motorcycle.

Casting Bernadette Peters as Janowitz's Eleanor makes about as much sense as having Madonna play Pollyanna. With her kewpie-doll face, Pre-Raphaelite curls and quavering voice and persona, she suggests the retro, whereas the part calls for up-to-the-minute modernism. Granted, the character is an emotional victim, but she's a survivor as well, and one doubts whether Peters, with her now-patented vulnerability, could make it through one day in Manhattan's Alphabet City. Even Audrey Hepburn's gamine Holly Golightly, in BREAKFAST AT TIFFANY'S, had a flinty materialism to counteract and support her flights of fancy. Peters can be stunning in the right role (PENNIES FROM HEAVEN), but here, her eternal suffering and penchant for tears, fainting at parties, and professional mousiness tend to irritate rather than charm. Adam Coleman Howard, as her opposite number, has a thanklessly chauvinistic role, but brings a raw force to it anyway; his absolute humorlessness is rather funny. Madeleine Potter is momentarily effective as a desperate femme fatale, especially as she piggishly opens birthday presents in the full, spotlighted view of her guests, but, like Peters, she too seems to have strayed out of a cartoon by Burne-Jones. The rest of Ivory's cast is typically eclectic, but consigned to little more than cameo roles in which the men are uniformly callow and self-centered and the women are bitchy, hard-edged groupies.

With most of its episodes left undeveloped and flat, the film's remaining high points are strictly incidental, including the savvy music with some effective use of various pop artists, Peters' staggeringly tacky ashtray hat, and a psychedelically filmed Stephen Sprouse fashion show. Three Supremes-impersonating transvestites pop up at one point for no reason, but provide the single most diverting moment in the movie. The director lingers over their cavorting, as if even he were bored by his main characters' problems. Songs include "Mother Dearest" (Joe Leeway, performed by Leeway), "Say Hi to Your Guy" (Johann Carlo, Michael Butler, performed by Carlo and Butler), "Some Guys Have All the Luck" (Jeff Fortgang, performed by Maxi Priest), "Tumblin' Down" (Ziggy Marley, Tyrone Downie, performed by Ziggy Marley and the Melody Makers), "Admit It," "Love Overlap" (Arto Lindsay, Peter Scherer, performed by Ambitious Lovers), "Buffalo Stance" (Neneh Cherry, Cameron McVey, Phil Ramacon, Jamie Morgan, performed by Cherry), "Girlfriend" (George O'Dowd, Vlad Naslas, performed by Boy George), "Change Your Mind" (Camper Van Beethoven, performed by Camper Van Beethoven), "Good Life" (Kevin Saunderson, Paris Grey, Roy Holman, performed by Inner City), "Fall in Love with Me" (Iggy Pop, David Bowie, Hunt B. Sales, Tony Sales, performed by Pop), "Tongue Dance" (Catherine Ringier, Frederic Chichin, performed by Rita Les Mitsouko), "Warrior" (Allan Dias, Lu Edmonds, John Lydon, John McGeogh, Bruce Smith, performed by Public Image, Ltd.), "Am I Blue?" (Grante Clarke, Harry Akst, performed by Billie Holiday), "Dad, I'm in Jail" (David Was, Don Was, performed by Was (Not Was)), "Grand Tour" (Carmol Taylor, George Richey, Norris Wilson, performed by George Jones), "Gluck, das mir verlieb" (Erich Wolfgang Korngold, performed by Carol Neblett), "Love Is Like an Itching in My Heart" (Brian Holland, Lamont Dozier, Edward Holland, performed by Diana Ross and the Supremes), "I Need a Man" (Annie Lennox, Dave Stewart, performed by the Eurythmics), "O Ruddier Than the Cherry" (George Frederick Handel, performed by John Ostendorf). *(Profanity, nudity, adult situations, sexual situations.)*

p, Ismail Merchant and Gary Hendler; d, James Ivory; w, Tama Janowitz (based on her stories); ph, Tony Pierce-Roberts (Technicolor); ed, Katherine Wenning; m,

Richard Robbins; prod d, David Gropman; art d, Karen Schultz; set d, Carol Nast; spec eff, Steve Kirshoff; cos, Carol Ramsey; stunts, Phil Neilson; makeup, Marilyn Carbone.

Comedy/Romance   (PR:O MPAA:R)

ⓥSLEEPAWAY CAMP 3: TEENAGE WASTELAND**
79m Double Helix c
Pamela Springsteen *(Angela)*, Tracy Griffith *(Marcia)*, Michael J. Pollard *(Herman)*, Mark Oliver *(Tony)*, Kim Wall *(Cindy)*, Kyle Holman, Daryl Wilcher, Haynes Brooke, Stacie Lambert, Kashina Kessler, Cliff Brand, Randi Layne, Jill Terashita.

A made-for-video production, SLEEPAWAY CAMP 3: TEENAGE WASTELAND is also a made-for-money formula teen movie in which scenes of sex, gore, and "camp" humor race along to a rock beat. For campers and counselors at Camp New Horizons (formerly Camp Rolling Hills), it's no summer vacation in the woods when Angela (Pamela Springsteen, Bruce's sister, reprising her role from SLEEPAWAY CAMP 2) returns to wage her gruesome crusade against "bad" kids. This time, Springsteen slips into New Horizons by assuming the identity of a camper whom she ran over with a garbage truck while her victim was en route to meet the camp bus. In light of the murders Springsteen committed in the previous series installment, New Horizons' opening day generates considerable interest in the news media. Owner and counselor Pollard tries to cover up last year's massacre by publicizing his camp's experimental new sharing program, designed to promote a bond of warmth among the teenage campers by socially integrating wealthy valedictorian types and underprivileged urban delinquents. While Pollard blathers to a newscaster about the anticipated harmony between the groups, the kids are visible in the background, spray-painting the trees with graffiti, polishing switchblades, or turning up their noses in snubs. The teens are divided into three groups, one of which is led by a cop counselor who lost his son to Springsteen the previous year. He's the most dedicated to the youths; Pollard, on the other hand, just lusts after the girls under his charge, while his lazy counselor wife sits by her tent and barks orders. Pseudo-camper Springsteen makes her way through the three groups faster than poison ivy, although she does take some time off to enjoy the great outdoors, roasting marshmallows over the dead or helping her next victim hook fishing bait. (When suspicion concerning her adult looks arises, she deflects it by maintaining that a lack of fluoride in her hometown's water has aged her appearance.) With no two murders alike, she shoots, axes, mutilates, and tortures the campers, although the

whimsical murderess never slays without a justifying quip regarding each victim's offense against wholesomeness, be it promiscuity, arrogance, or bad rap music. Only two sincere lovers—an urban gang leader and a rich princess—are spared, after the gang leader is given 30 seconds to find his girl friend among the corpses in cabins 1, 2, and 3. The couple defeats Springsteen . . . for the time being, of course. It's more than likely that the wretch will return and continue to "take care of business" in SLEEPAWAY CAMP 4.

Like a gorehound John Waters, coproducer-director Michael Simpson continues in the satirical, shock-value vein of the previous "Sleepaway Camp" films—which lack taste, but do acknowledge adolescent frustrations. Springsteen's character represents the rebel yell, her murders more symbolic than convincing acts of violence, and the special effects and makeup, while suitably gory, don't overwhelm the plot. Among the actors, Springsteen manages to lend her killer a benevolent aura that effectively contrasts with the character's sadism, and Michael J. Pollard is his usual wacky, animated self. *(Nudity, substance abuse, graphic violence, sexual situations.)*

p, Jerry Silva and Michael A. Simpson; d, Michael A. Simpson; w, Fritz Gordon (based on a story idea by Robert Hiltzik); ph, Bill Mills (Cinefilm Color); ed, Amy Carey and John David Allen; m, James Oliverio; stunts, Lonnie Smith; makeup, Bill Johnson.

Horror   (PR:O MPAA:R)

ⓥSLIPPING INTO DARKNESS*
87m MCEG c
Michelle Johnson *(Carlyle)*, John DiAquino *(Fritz)*, Neill Barry *(Ebin)*, Anastasia Fielding *(Genevieve)*, Cristen Kauffman *(Alex)*, Vyto Ruginis *(Otis)*, David Sherrill, Terrence Markovich, Adam Roarke.

Three thrill-seeking college girls (Johnson, Fielding, and Kauffman) cruise a small town looking for trouble and find it in this RIVER'S EDGE-inspired film. For excitement, they follow and flirt with a group of bikers. When the bikers get rough with Johnson, DiAquino, an ex-biker turned student, intercedes on her behalf. Unknown to DiAquino, Johnson has been secretly seeing his retarded brother, Barry. Later the girls accidentally hit Barry's dog with their car. Fielding and Kauffman are surprised to see that Barry seems to know Johnson, although she denies it. In the next scene, Johnson eats ice cream as Barry runs onto some railroad tracks to retrieve a ball and is hit by a train. A distraught DiAquino is convinced that the girls seduced and murdered his brother and asks his biker buddies to help him avenge the death. Ruginis and another member of the gang known only as T-Bone shave their beards and shed their biker garb so they won't be recognized. Then, DiAquino, Ruginis, and T-Bone lure the girls to a deserted factory. After revealing his identity, DiAquino accuses the girls of the killing, insisting that "someone's got to pay." Johnson attempts to calm DiAquino by telling him she was at the vet with Barry's dog at the time the boy was killed, leading DiAquino to believe that Fielding and Kauffman are responsible for his brother's death. Meanwhile, Fielding seduces Ruginis in the cemetery behind the factory. The next morning, the group discovers that Ruginis has killed Fielding to avenge Barry. In a RIVER'S EDGE-like scene, they coldly gawk at her seminude body displayed on a stone monument, before Ruginis buries her in an old grave. While driving Ruginis out of town, the little group runs out of gas and stops at a farm house. Ruginis, who has been degenerating steadily since the murder, goes crazy and tries to slice up the other four with a scythe. After a struggle with DiAquino, he is killed. T-bone and Kauffman decide to leave town; DiAquino wants to call the police, but Johnson persuades him to sell out the other two. In short order, Johnson returns home to find the police and Kauffman talking to her parents. It seems that Kauffman and T-Bone have been arrested. However, Johnson and her father claim that she was at her uncle's house all weekend. The true, sordid story of the death then unfolds after Kauffman confronts DiAquino.

SLIPPING INTO DARKNESS borrows unashamedly from Tim Hunter's excellent RIVER'S EDGE but offers a shoddy script and unconvincing, inconsistent characters. Notably, DiAquino's Fritz demands that someone pay for his brother's death, but later halfheartedly decides to let the girls go. Ruginis' Otis goes insane and, for no particular reason, tries to kill Fritz and T-Bone. Not surprisingly, the script is also a bit confused. Most important, it is difficult to determine just who actually does kill the retarded Ebin (though it's clear it's one of two people) because several versions of the night in question are presented. In addition, it is never certain whether Fritz is responsible for the arrest of Alex and T-Bone. The muddled or nonexistent motivations of the detached characters make it difficult for the viewer to sympathize with them, especially after Fielding's Genevieve is killed. In RIVER'S EDGE, the characters at least displayed a morbid curiosity about their dead friend. With SLIPPING INTO DARKNESS, one is left thinking only about the better-than-average photography. *(Nudity, excessive profanity, violence.)*

p, Jonathan D. Krane; d, Eleanor Gaver; w, Eleanor Gaver; ph, Loren Bivens (Foto-Kem Color); ed, Barbara Pokras; m, Joey Rand; prod d, Patricia Woodbridge.

Thriller   (PR:O MPAA:R)

⊙SOME GIRLS***
97m MGM-Oxford/MGM-UA c
(AKA: SISTERS)
Patrick Dempsey *(Michael)*, Jennifer Connelly *(Gabby)*, Sheila Kelley *(Irenka)*, Andre Gregory *(Father)*, Ashley Greenfield *(Simone)*, Florinda Bolkan *(Mother)*, Lila Kedrova *(Grandmother)*, Lance Edwards *(Nick)*, Jean-Louis Millette, Sanna Vraa, Cedric Noel, John Cuthbert, Harry Hill, Renee Girard, Claude Prefontaine, Fanny.

The most recent collaboration of director Michael Hoffman and producer Rick Stevenson (PROMISED LAND), SOME GIRLS might have been another entry on the list of forgettable and self-indulgent coming-of-age memoirs, but instead turns out to be a refreshing, original, and gently persuasive comedy that rises quickly above the schmaltzy SUMMER OF '42 mode of initiation. The story opens as Dempsey arrives in Quebec City to spend what he hopes will be a romantic Christmas holiday with Connelly, an exotic beauty he regards as his college sweetheart. Connelly's attractive yet spooky family and family home enchant the eager and callow American student. Connelly is intelligent and aloof; her sisters, Kelley and Greenfield, are also beautiful and beguiling. Patriarch Gregory, by contrast, is an amusingly eccentric scholar (and nudist) obsessed with writing a massive treatment of the life and works of Pascal. Connelly's mother (Bolkan) is the moral arbitrator in the family, much concerned with propriety and sexually paranoid. Dempsey is willing to go with the flow as long as he can enjoy the favors of Connelly, but when she admits she no longer loves him, he's forced to gather his wits to survive as a stranger in this most strange and bewitching household. Even Beowulf, the family's sheepdog, shows little mercy. Dempsey's only source of perspective clarity is provided by Edwards, a lusty hunk of a handyman who favors Kelley and who manages to bypass locked doors whenever passion's opportunity knocks. The story takes a seriocomic turn when Kedrova, Connelly's hospitalized grandmother who has "kangaroos in the top hat" and lives in the past, makes one of her periodic escape attempts and mistakes Dempsey for her long dead husband, which only adds to the American's consternation. Meanwhile, the baroque, sex-farce complications of the story multiply. Dempsey is frustrated when each of the three sisters teases him, in a series of look-but-don't-touch comical and musical bed-hopping episodes. This is clearly not the triumphant coming-of-age Dempsey had in mind: Connelly is coquettishly contrary; Kelley, a fetching beauty, presents a formidable distraction; and youngest sister Greenfield, though apparently willing, is prohibitively young. Dempsey is able to develop a real emotional bond only with

Kedrova, who finally escapes the hospital and manages to make it to the snowbound St. Emilion country home she once shared with her late husband. Dempsey, Connelly, Kelley, and Edwards arrive in pursuit, and fan out through the snowy woods to look for the old woman. When the hapless Dempsey falls into a deep crevice, Kedrova arrives to save him. Afterward, he builds a fire for her inside the long-vacant house and Kedrova, still believing that Dempsey is her dead spouse, speaks to him of their early love and life together. Later, the sisters return to the house and hail the young man as a hero; the next morning, Gregory and Greenfield arrive for a day of cross-country skiing. Dempsey and Kedrova are left free to explore their relationship further. When Dempsey retrieves the summer shoes Kedrova left in a tree long ago and presents them to her, she tells him she no longer needs them—foreshadowing her imminent death. Though Edwards and Dempsey drive her back to the hospital, she doesn't make it. After Kedrova's burial, Kelley seduces Dempsey, who subsequently tells Connelly that he's slept with her sister. She knows already and doesn't mind. Dempsey then wanders out, buys a bouquet of flowers, and takes them to the family's mausoleum, where he encounters a mysterious woman who is apparently the youthful Kedrova incarnate. After Dempsey tells her that he really loved Kedrova, she kisses him and disappears. Back at the house, Dempsey sees a portrait of Kedrova as a young beauty and recognizes her as the specter at the mausoleum. Dazed and confused, Dempsey is drawn into a man-to-man talk with Gregory over the ineffable feminine mystique, and the men commiserate with each other about the frustration of never really knowing what women want. But Gregory has little to teach Dempsey, who has learned, through Kedrova, what real love is. He returns to school alone, without Connelly but with greater confidence and maturity.

Narrated by Dempsey's character, SOME GIRLS might easily have degenerated into a locker-room, PORKY'S-style anecdote, especially given Dempsey's resume of sexually hopped-up characters (IN THE MOOD; CAN'T BUY ME LOVE). Instead, writer Rupert Walters and director Hoffman have wisely balanced this farce cum fantasy with the utmost sympathy for the would-be lover and the object(s) of his ardor, whose devastating beauty wreaks havoc on the boy's soul. Dempsey makes a most sympathetic Everyman—neither handsome nor homely, neither too bright nor a total clod, neither too puerile nor too wise. He's sensitive, inquisitive, and well-meaning, but still ruled by his hormones. In SOME GIRLS, Dempsey's coming-of-age is not so much a sexual initiation as it is an acquisition of knowledge, an awakening to the fact that women will remain a life-long mystery. The closely bonded three sisters are all mysteriously beautiful, sensuous, and quite capable of manipulation, an indication of what the young protagonist will continue to face in the vain pursuit of the ineffable and ethereal. His relationship with Kedrova suggests that real love can only be understood when viewed from the long perspective, after long romantic questing.

Nowhere is it suggested that physical beauty guarantees love or happiness. Does it matter that SOME GIRLS is populated by beautiful and intelligent (if quirky) folk? Perhaps, but only to show that even refined, witty, and articulate people can be rendered foolish, confused, and uncertain by passion. Moreover, SOME GIRLS manages to remain highly entertaining through all its bizarre and improbable turns of events. The performances are all delivered with gentle affection, even if the characters' amorous teasing sometimes seems cruel. SOME GIRLS is not so much about sexual conquest as it is about the discovery of real love (surely not a proprietary right of the young) and all its confounding permutations—passion, frustration, manipulation, embarrassment, loss, and the pursuit of wistful desires. (Sexual situations, nudity, adult situations, profanity.)

p, Rick Stevenson; d, Michael Hoffman; w, Rupert Walters; ph, Ueli Steiger; ed, David Spiers; m, James Newton Howard; prod d, Eugenio Zanetti.

Comedy/Drama   (PR:C MPAA:R)

SPEAKING PARTS**

(Can.) 92m Ego Film Arts/Cinephile c
Michael McManus (Lance), Arsinee Khanjian (Lisa), Gabrielle Rose (Clara), Tony Nardi (Eddy), David Hemblen (Producer), Patricia Collins (Housekeeper), Gerard Parkes (The Father), Jackie Samuda (The Bride), Peter Krantz (The Groom).

In 1988, Atom Egoyan's FAMILY VIEWING garnered a number of awards and established the director as one of Canada's hottest young filmmakers. Now comes SPEAKING PARTS, in which Khanjian plays a maid in a big Toronto hotel whose days are filled with dirty linen and the fruitless pursuit of fellow employee McManus, an ambitious actor with whom she appears to have had some kind of an affair. Now, however, McManus—who, in addition to his housekeeping duties, has sex with some hotel guests at the behest of the establishment's manager—literally refuses to say a word to Khanjian. She contents herself with renting and re-renting videotapes of films in which McManus appears as an extra—for he's yet to land a "speaking part." The only person with whom Khanjian has any kind of rapport is

Nardi, the video store manager, who moonlights as a video filmmaker himself, taping weddings and orgies for his clients. When McManus discovers a film script in the room of Rose, a novice screenplay writer, he assumes that she's casting the film and leaves his picture and resume for her. Rose's script, it turns out, is a fictionalized retelling of how her own life was saved by an organ donation from her brother, who later died, and whom McManus physically resembles. (In fact, all the main characters in SPEAKING PARTS look like one another.) After meeting (and making love with) McManus, Rose helps get him the lead in the film, but she herself is on the verge of being fired, and therefore instructs McManus to try to prevent the producer (Hemblen) from altering her screenplay. The dour Khanjian, meanwhile, suffers stoically over McManus—especially after a hotel guest apparently kills herself in frustrated desire for the actor/prostitute—but manages to find some diversion in becoming a colossally inept assistant to Nardi. Things come to a head after McManus finds that taking Rose's side in her artistic conflict means forfeiting his big break, resulting in a crisis on the first day of shooting. In the end, McManus and Khanjian are united, and he speaks to her for the first time in the film.

SPEAKING PARTS' subject matter has inevitably led to comparisons between writer-director Egoyan and Steven Soderbergh, the director of SEX, LIES AND VIDEOTAPE, but Egoyan is also mentioned in connection with Wim Wenders, who became a fan and financial backer of Egoyan's after seeing FAMILY VIEWING and who is thanked in SPEAKING PARTS' credits; and with David Cronenberg, another Canadian filmmaker deeply interested in the psychological effects of video culture (addressed most emphatically in Cronenberg's VIDEODROME). In SPEAKING PARTS, Egoyan clearly means to provide some insight into the nature of image, (mis)communication, and ego in contemporary relations. Regrettably, however, his film is mainly a pretentious collection of Orwellian Big Brother imagery, of attempts to convey a fancy anomie a la Resnais or Antonioni, and of endless tricks converting film into video and back. Egoyan's hyperstyle is both alienating and confusing (he's especially fond of meaningless flashbacks) and his use of video screens as a vehicle for his estranged characters to communicate is badly cliched. A scene in which McManus and Rose masturbate together via a video conference hook-up is unintentionally amusing, while a disastrous wedding that was probably *meant* to seem amusing only results in a feeling of discomfort for the actors.

Among the players, Arsinee Khanjian does all too well as the obsessed-yet-catatonic Lisa; it's as if she had seen Isabelle Adjani's devastating last scenes of romantic obsession in THE STORY OF ADELE H. and determined to outdo that performance in every frame of SPEAKING PARTS. A more irritatingly mannered heroine would be hard to imagine. Michael McManus, as the object of desire, conveys his character's facility and ability to gauge the moods of those he exploits, while Gabrielle Rose does the best she can as Clara, a snuffling, self-righteous drag of a part. Tony Nardi is overly sincere as the only selfless character in the film, and David Hemblen hams it up as the self-deified producer, a character we've seen far too many times before. (Adult situations, nudity, sexual situations.)

d, Atom Egoyan; w, Atom Egoyan; ph, Paul Sarossy; ed, Bruce McDonald; m, Mychael Danna; art d, Linda Del Rosario.

Drama   (PR:O MPAA: NR)

ⓥSPEED ZONE*

95m Entcorp/Orion c
John Candy (Charlie Cronyn), Donna Dixon (Tiffany), Matt Frewer (Alec), Joe Flaherty (Vic), Tim Matheson (Jack), Mimi Kuzyk (Heather), Melody Anderson (Lee), Shari Belafonte (Margaret), Brian George (Valentino), Art Hindle (Flash), Dick Smothers (Nelson Van Sloan), Tom Smothers (Randolph Van Sloan), Peter Boyle (Chief Spiro T. Edsel), Don Lake (Whitman), John Schneider, Jamie Farr (Cannonballers), Lee Van Cleef (Grandfather), Harvey Atkin (Gus Gold), Eugene Levy (Leo Ross), Michael Spinks (Bachelor), Brooke Shields (Stewardess), Alyssa Milano (Truck Driver), Louis Del Grande (Salesman), Carl Lewis (Jogger).

Somewhere on the East Coast, an array of oddballs and high-performance cars convene for the start of a supposedly clandestine Cannonball Run across the United States to the Santa Monica Pier in California. The race is threatened from the start, however, when Boyle, the megalomanic head of the Fraternal Order of Police Chiefs, rounds up all the professional drivers slated for the run. With oodles of sponsors' promotional dollars at stake, the hasty devising of unlikely rookie driving teams puts the race back on track. Oafish Candy and starlet Dixon take the BMW; loan shark Flaherty and English deadbeat Frewer pilot the Jaguar XJ-12; Belafonte and Anderson finagle their way into the Ferrari Daytona Spyder; macho cop Hindle and skittish Italian George take off in a Lamborghini Countach; TV reporters Matheson and Kuzyk enter in their station's mobile unit van; and the spoiled silly Smothers Brothers, comfortably ensconced in their Bentley Corniche convertible, round out the field. Predictably, Boyle's determination to abort the race isn't the only obstacle along the way. The real drama is derived from the greed-fueled dirty tricks employed by the rag-tag cannonballers against the other cars, which, along with the bickering between the driving duos, contribute to the leap-frog changes in the lead. Sustaining the comic action are a series of campy celebrity cameos from the likes of Shields, Spinks, Lewis, and other familiar faces who preferred to remain creditless, until—with enough wrecked vehicles left in their wake to give a State Farm agent cardiac arrest—the convoy of cannonballers finally converges on the Santa Monica Pier for the anticlimactic finish.

Several shopworn formulas have gone into the premise, writing, acting, and directing of SPEED ZONE, and despite its comically well-endowed cast, the gags are disappointingly dull. Even the presence of such "SCTV" stalwarts as Joe Flaherty, John Candy, and Eugene Levy can't save this low-lead cross between IT'S A MAD, MAD, MAD, MAD, WORLD and CANNONBALL RUN. Screenwriter Michael Short and director Jim Drake (themselves Second City and "SCTV" alumni) rely heavily on the star personae and familiar TV incarnations of their actors, while showcasing the spills and thrills (and the ubiquitous product plugs) to provide transitions between the sputtering jokes.

Certainly the most candid moment in this self-mocking film comes when Brooke Shields (in a cameo as a stewardess) tells the Smothers Brothers that she doesn't want to spend the rest of her life doing bit parts in movies. They respond by telling her that "it's not that bad"—but it is. Songs include: "Drivin'" (Robbie Stevens, Richie Havens, performed by Havens), "Perfect Crime" (Ross Vannelli, Ed Grenga, performed by Billy Burnette), "Born to Race" (Vannelli, Grenga, performed by Vannelli), "Roll Away" (Michael Mugrage, John Scott Sherrill, Bob DiPiero, performed by Felix Cavaliere), "Dizzy Miss Lizzy" (Larry Williams, performed by Splash), "Tiffany's Theme" (David Wheatley, performed by Wheatley). *(Profanity.)*

p, Murray Shostak and Vivienne Leebosh; d, Jim Drake; w, Michael Short; ph, Francois Protat and Robert Saad (Filmhouse Color); ed, Mike Economou; m, David Wheatley; prod d, Richard Hudolin; set d, Gilles Aird and Patti Hall; spec eff, John Thomas; cos, Paul Andre Guerin; stunts, Betty Thomas; makeup, Jocelyne Bellemare.

Comedy   (PR:C MPAA:PG)

⊘STAR TREK V: THE FINAL FRONTIER**½
108m PAR c
William Shatner *(Adm. James T. Kirk),* Leonard Nimoy *(Mr. Spock),* DeForest

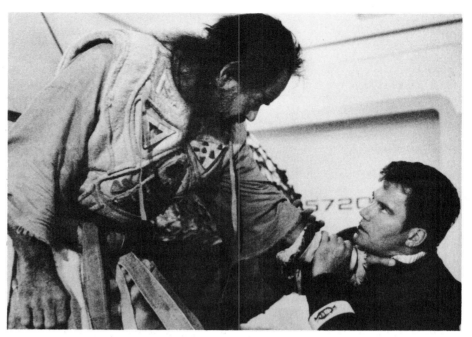

Laurence Luckinbill and William Shatner in STAR TREK V: THE FINAL FRONTIER (©Paramount).

Kelley *(Dr. Leonard "Bones" McCoy),* James Doohan *("Scotty" Scott),* Walter Koenig *(Navigator Pavel Chekov),* Nichelle Nichols *(Comdr. Uhura),* George Takei *(Helmsman Sulu),* Laurence Luckinbill *(Sybok),* David Warner *(St. John Talbot),* Charles Cooper *(Klingon Consul General Korrd),* Cynthia Gouw *(Romulan Representative Caithlin Dar),* Todd Bryant *(Klingon Captain Klaa),* Spice Williams *(Klingon Warrior Vixis),* Rex Holman *(J'onn),* George Murdock *("God," Alien Being),* Cynthia Blaise *(Amanda),* Bill Quinn *(McCoy's Father),* Melanie Shatner *(Enterprise Yeoman).*

Despite a $32 million budget that was recouped within its first month, STAR TREK V isn't much more than an expanded TV episode, and not a particularly memorable one at that. Yet, even with its many shortcomings, including less-than-exciting action scenes and cartoonlike special effects used to hardly any effect at all, this sequel's popularity reaffirms the enduring appeal of the once and future king of TV reruns.

Star William Shatner, in an undistinguished directorial debut, is hampered by a largely uneventful plot that deals with such highly metaphysical pursuits as the search for God and the mysteries of the cosmos, both allegedly to be found on the legendary planet Shakaree. In an interview, Shatner (who also shares the writing credit) explained that Shakaree is simply the name *Sean Connery* spoke quickly. But in the film, Shatner's antagonist, Luckinbill, a messianic Vulcan, defines it as both "a place from which creation sprang" and "the source" of heaven and evil. Although this ontological approach may be intri-

guing, it fails to generate the kind of thoughtful, exciting adventure that made the Gene Roddenberry TV series so compelling. In part, the plot here is derivative of prior TV episodes from the series' first season in 1967 ("The Alternative Factor," "This Side of Paradise," "The Return of the Archons"), with what seem to be obvious steals from STAR WARS (the Cantina scene) and SUPERMAN (the stalagmites surfacing in the Cave of Solitude).

Luckinbill, emerging from the desert (at first, looking every bit like Darth Vader as Lawrence of Arabia), appears on the barren, squalid planet Nimbus III with a divine mission: to hijack a starship, cross the Great Barrier, and find God. In a throwback to the touchy-feely encounter group methods of the late 60s, Luckinbill quickly gains converts to his cause by a literal hands-on approach. (Grasping them, staring intently into their eyes, and intoning, "Your pain runs deep; share your pain," he separates them from their pain—whatever that's supposed to mean.) With help from his new disciples, he holds three high-level Starfleet Federation members hostage—a ruse to lure and hijack one of their starships to take him to the final frontier of the film's title, the Garden of Eden. To the rescue, and into this trap, come Shatner, Nimoy, and Kelley, who were on temporary shore leave on Earth. Along with all the old familiar Star Trek crew aboard the *Enterprise,* they're commandeered by the crazed Luckinbill, who turns out to be Vulcan Nimoy's half-brother.

En route to the final frontier, there's a subplot involving Klingon warrior Williams, Shatner's old adversary, who, just for old times sake, tries (but fails, of course) to kill him. In conversation, the Klingons (highly effective with fishbone foreheads and guttural alien speech that's translated by subtitles) provide some welcome serio-comic relief in this almost humorless film that tends to take itself too seriously. In another of the too few stabs at humor, when Luckinbill does find "God," it's as a malevolent apparition more closely resembling Olivier's ghost of Hamlet than the Father of our Judeo-Christian ethic. Shatner, unconvinced that it's the Supreme Being, demands proof, only to have Kelley testily counter, "Jim, you don't ask the Almighty for his I.D." Eventually, the bad guys are destroyed, and Shatner, Nimoy, and Kelley, staunch friends for almost a quarter century, resume their shore leave around a campfire, singing a reprise of "Row, Row, Row Your Boat," and no doubt contemplating their next appearance in STAR TREK VI.

But if so, Paramount had better hurry. Sad to say, Star Trek's days may be numbered. It's part of the phenomenon of creator Roddenberry's brainchild that, unlike the James Bond movies with their interchangeable leads, Star Trek really can't exist without its original cast. (Just ask any loyal Trekkie.) None of them are expendable. Nostalgia plays an extraordinary part in the film's appeal. Though the familiar, reassuring banter between the crew and its captain remains, the truth is the cast has all gotten formidably, uncomfortably old. (In fact, as a bit of Trekkie trivia, Shatner's real-life daughter, Melanie, has a small role as an *Enterprise* yeoman.) Unfortunately with this uninspired sequel, Star Trek's fine actors, now decidedly middle-aged, haven't been allowed to age gracefully. It's hard to take them seriously as they cavort in unflattering costumes, or perform feats of derring-do that border on the absurd and undignified. Never once, for example in the 79 TV episodes or four prior films, did Capt. Kirk ever show any interest in mountain climbing. Yet there he is, in the prolog to STAR TREK V, climbing the perilous peaks of Yosemite with a skill that pretenders to Mt. Everest could envy. Not until he's on safe ground, the stuntman out of view, does the camera reveal the out-of-shape Shatner's earnest-but-jowly face and obvious paunch. So much for realism—or the lack of it. The macho-man image just doesn't wash.

Released in a summer season of blockbuster movies, STAR TREK V raked in a then-record $17 million plus in its opening weekend, temporarily out-grossing all rivals at the box office. In an earlier day, this B movie (produced at Grade A expense) might have been the second half of a double bill. But like its four predecessors, which cumulatively surpassed the $200 million mark, in the most basic law of sequels, STAR TREK: THE FINAL FRONTIER is devised to preserve the sentiment-and-science-fiction formula that has proved so successful in the past.

STAR TREK V was filmed at Paramount Studios, and on location in the California desert and Yosemite National Park, where the opening and closing camping scenes were shot. *(Violence.)*

p, Harve Bennett; d, William Shatner; w, David Loughery (based on a story by Shatner, Bennett, Loughery, and characters created by Gene Roddenberry); ph, Andrew Laszlo (Panavision, Technicolor); ed, Peter Berger; m, Jerry Goldsmith; prod d, Herman Zimmerman; art d, Nilo Rodis-Jamero; set d, Ronald R. Wilkinson, Richard Frank McKenzie, Andrew Neskoromny, and Antoinette Gordon; spec eff, Bran Ferren; cos, Nilo Rodis-Jamero; makeup, Wes Dawn.

Science Fiction   (PR:A MPAA:PG)

STAYING TOGETHER*½
91m Joseph Feury/Hemdale c
Sean Astin *(Duncan McDermott)*, Stockard Channing *(Nancy Trainer)*, Melinda Dillon *(Eileen McDermott)*, Jim Haynie *(Jake McDermott)*, Levon Helm *(Denny Stockton)*, Dinah Manoff *(Lois Cook)*, Dermot Mulroney *(Kit McDermott)*, Tim Quill *(Brian McDermott)*, Keith Szarabajka *(Kevin Burley)*, Daphne Zuniga *(Beverly Young)*, Sheila Kelley *(Beth Harper)*, Ryan Hill *(Demetri Harper)*, Rick Marshall *(Charlie)*, Michael Burgess *(Workman)*, Leon Joseph Pinner *(Newsman)*, Ed Carter, Susan Aude Fisher, Jim Gandy *(Announcers)*, Steve Jackson *(Contestant)*, Bonnie Cook *(Waitress)*, Robby Sedgwick *(Doctor)*, Ann Pierce *(Nurse)*, Nathan LeGrand *(Husband)*, Paul Branin, Jim Weider, Frank Campbell, Randy Ciarlante, Stan Szelest *(Band)*, Wayne Coleman *(Wedding Photographer)*, Thelma McNinch, James R. Barrow *(Customers)*, Frances Arndt *(Mrs. Crawford)*.

There's no question of the sincere intent of this mawkish little film. Certainly, it means well and aspires to a universal message, but given its simplistic characterizations, this story of a small-town family undergoing radical change is more akin to the pat TV sitcoms of the 1960s and 70s (with a little sex thrown in), and might better be titled "Not-So-Happy Days for My Three Sons."

The scene: Ridgeway, USA, where the advances of the late 20th century are just beginning to encroach upon the little community. The McDermotts—father Haynie (COUNTRY), mother Dillon (CLOSE ENCOUNTERS), and three sons ranging in age from 17 to the early 20s—operate a fried chicken business that the boys expect to inherit one day. Life for the boys is relatively uneventful and predictable. Quill (HAMBURGER HILL), the oldest and most intense, is having a quiet, no-strings-attached affair with mayoral candidate Channing. Too-good-to-be-true middle brother Mulroney is in love with beautiful bimbo Zuniga (GROSS ANATOMY), who loves him as well, but is engaged to marry a building contractor (Szarabajka) because she needs "someone to lean on." And Astin (GOONIES) is the goony, smart-aleck kid brother whose every other word is a wisecrack and whose main concern is how to bed Manoff, the sexy older waitress who works in the family restaurant.

Abruptly, the family bubble bursts, and the boys' Great American Dream of eventually going nationwide with McDermotts' Famous Chicken dissolves—along with any sense of security about their future. Without consulting his sons, Haynie accepts the archetypal *unrefusable* offer and sells the restaurant to a condominium developer. It seems he never even liked chicken, and only became involved with the business to support his family. Frankly, he tells his stunned offspring, he'd much rather be fishing or climbing a mountain when he dies, and proceeds to take off with Dillon in a camper for two weeks in Yosemite, leaving the boys to fend for themselves. Each brother reacts differently. Bitterly resentful of both parents, Quill leaves home and lands a job as a laborer with Szarabajka's construction outfit, then hustles his way to a position as foreman. Mulroney finds work at a local store, and Astin, still in high school, has yet to figure out what he'll do when he graduates.

Bit by bit, life as the boys have known it is disrupted. The family restaurant is bulldozed out of existence, replaced by Clucky's fast food drive-in; Channing breaks off her affair with Quill when she wins the election in an upset ("We both knew this wouldn't last," she says; "I didn't," he replies); and Quill reacts by creating an "instant family" when he becomes involved with a widow (with a young son) who sells pot to make ends meet. Meanwhile, Mulroney sneaks away with Zuniga to a cabin for a night of lovemaking, still hoping he can persuade her not to marry Szarabajka. Instead, she invites him to the ceremony: "I want you there. The modern woman always has her lovers at her wedding." Since the sale, Quill has avoided the homestead, but he returns after Haynie dies of a sudden heart attack. Severely shaken by her husband's death, the unassertive Dillon (who sang in a bar before she was married but hasn't done much since), tries to piece her life together. Finally, she goes on a date with Mulroney's bachelor boss, and when Mulroney later falsely accuses her of sleeping with him, Dillon uncharacteristically responds by dumping a whole pot of spaghetti on her son's plate and saying, "That's the last food I'll ever make for you, so eat it." Unable to handle rejection from both Dillon and

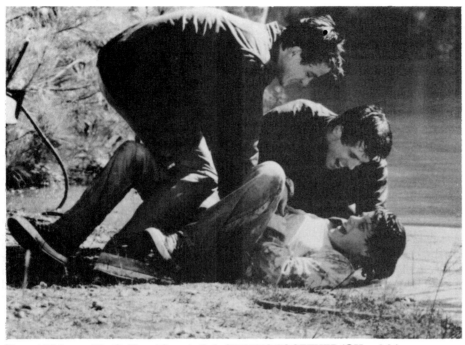

Dermot Mulroney, Tim Quill, and Sean Astin in STAYING TOGETHER (©Hemdale).

Zuniga, Mulroney runs away from home—actually only down the road a piece. His loyal brothers follow him in their pickup, however, and all of them end up splashing in a local pond as the film ends, with the three, as the title suggests, destined to stay together happily for the rest of their cinematic lives.

No doubt first-time screenwriter Monte Merrick hoped to show us the world in a grain of sand—using Ridgeway as a microcosm, and the sale of the family store as a metaphor for the passing of old values. But under Lee Grant's direction, Merrick's characters become caricatures, painted in such broad strokes and framed in such unlikely situations that they are never convincing. Notably, it's "instant warmth" time when Dillon's tentative matriarch, who hasn't sung in public in years, is persuaded to get up before a crowd at the local bistro to offer a less-than-compelling rendition of a Peggy Lee ballad ("While We're Young"). Within seconds, all the customers put down their beer and, with arms around each other, sway nostalgically to her thoroughly amateurish delivery. The only performers who come out ahead in STAYING TOGETHER are Stockard Channing (GREASE) and Grant's real-life daughter, Dinah Manoff, two wonderful, underrated talents who light up the screen every time they appear. Unfortunately, they're not around long enough to make a difference. *(Sexual situations.)*

p, Joseph Feury; d, Lee Grant; w, Monte Merrick; ph, Dick Bush (CFI Color); ed, Katherine Wenning; m, Miles Goodman; md, Miles Goodman; prod d, Stuart Wurtzel; art d, W. Steven Graham; set d, Elaine O'Donnell; spec eff, Cliff Wenger;

cos, Carol Oditz; stunts, Gil Combs; makeup, Christa Reusch.

Comedy/Drama   (PR:C MPAA:R)

STEALING HEAVEN*½
(Brit./Yugo.) 108m Amy-Jadran/Film Dallas c
Derek de Lint *(Abelard)*, Kim Thomson *(Heloise)*, Denholm Elliott *(Fulbert)*, Bernard Hepton *(Bishop)*, Kenneth Cranham *(Suger)*, Patsy Byrne *(Agnes)*, Mark Jax *(Jourdain)*, Tim Watson *(Francois)*, Rachel Kempson *(Prioress)*, Angela Pleasence *(Sister Cecilia)*, Cassie Stuart *(Petronilla)*, Philip Locke *(Poussin)*, Victoria Burgoyne *(Prostitute)*, Antonia Cutic, Andrew McLean *(Gerard)*, Thomas Lockyer *(Thomas)*, Mark Audley *(Luke)*, Kai Dominic *(Paul)*, Slavica Maras *(Marie Duroc)*, Miki Hewitt *(Sister Claire)*, Yvonne Bryceland *(Baroness Lamarck)*, Vjenceslav Kapural *(Baron Lamarck)*, Ivo Husnjak *(Gaston Lamarck)*, Jeremy Hawk *(Ancient Priest)*, Moniek Kramer *(Jeanne)*, Drago Mitrovic *(Priest)*, Eugen Marcelic *(Astralabe)*, Lela Simecki *(Sister Therese)*, Diana Belinic *(Girl in Street)*, Davor Fejzagic *(Boy in Street)*, Zvonimir Ferencic *(Bishop)*.

Adapted by Chris Bryant from Marion Meade's historical novel of the same name, STEALING HEAVEN retells the true story of the ill-fated romance between the French religious philosopher Abelard (de Lint) and Heloise (Thomson), niece of a church canon, in 12th-century Paris. The most brilliant and charismatic teacher at the cathedral school of Notre Dame, de Lint is a rational humanist and a lover of

earthly delights except one: because of his vocation, he is required to practice celibacy. To remove him from the questionable influence of his lusty students, the bishop of Paris (Hepton) orders de Lint to move from his rooming house into the home of the canon, Fulbert (Elliott), just as Thomson returns from convent school to be bartered in marriage by Elliott, who is her uncle and also a minor nobleman with a booming business in phony religious relics. Thomson has developed a reputation as an intellectual firebrand herself, and chafes at being treated as merchandise to be traded into an unloving marriage for acres of land and heads of cattle by Elliott. Though Thomson has been smitten with the handsome de Lint from the moment she first laid eyes on him, the real trouble starts when he volunteers to oversee the continuation of her education at home. De Lint soon finds himself as stimulated by Thomson's sharp mind as he is aroused by her ravishing, red-haired beauty, and the two finally yield to their forbidden emotions on Christmas Eve, when the customary exchange of a holiday kiss escalates into a night of passion. Contrary to what one might expect, de Lint's employer, bishop Hepton, proves more broad-minded about the affair than Elliott, though not for unselfish reasons. To lose de Lint's services as a teacher, even as the result of a scandal, would endanger the welfare of the cathedral school. However, Elliott—whose concern for his niece, the film implies, is not without its own tinge of unhealthy desire—becomes obsessed with avenging himself on de Lint, ostensibly for turning Thomson into "damaged goods" in the marriage marketplace. The stage is thus set for a confrontation not only between Elliott and de Lint, but also between Elliott and Hepton, who is becoming increasingly irritated by Elliott's embarrassingly public campaign against the bishop's prized teacher.

As told from Heloise's point of view, STEALING HEAVEN plays with the pulpy fervor of a classic bodice-ripping romance. But it's an uncommonly well-crafted one. Veteran director Clive Donner, who has lately become something of a telemovie romance specialist (he directed the well-received 1982 TV remake of THE SCARLET PIMPERNEL), displays a sure hand with Bryant's complex script, making evocative use of the Yugoslavian locations where the movie was filmed, as well as a first-rate cast. Derek de Lint, star of the Oscar-winning THE ASSAULT, is both believably charismatic and emotionally compelling in conveying Abelard's interior struggle between the spirit and the flesh, and Kim Thomson is equally effective as the provocative Heloise, bringing balanced measures of spirited intelligence and fiery sensuality to her part. Veteran British players Denholm Elliott and Bernard Hepton are likewise outstanding in their supporting roles.

And, yes, that is the same Susan George, credited as executive producer, who once played Dustin Hoffman's nubile child-bride in Sam Peckinpah's STRAW DOGS. Along with her husband, actor and STEALING HEAVEN coproducer Simon MacCorkindale, George has in recent years become a respected figure on the international filmmaking scene. On the strength of STEALING HEAVEN, it's easy to see why. One reservation: In its very limited May 1989 theatrical release, HEAVEN played a reported 116 minutes, while the video version reviewed here runs only 108. As a result, unless you were one of the dozen or so who actually saw HEAVEN in a theater, you're likely never to see the full picture. *(Nudity, sexual situations.)*

p, Simon MacCorkindale and Andros Epaminondas; d, Clive Donner; w, Chris Bryant (based on the novel by Marion Meade); ph, Mikael Salomon; ed, Michael Ellis; m, Nick Bicat; prod d, Voytek Roman; art d, Dusko Jericevic; set d, Maria Djurkovic; spec eff, Willy Neuner; cos, Phyllis Dalton; stunts, Petar Buntac; makeup, Paul Engelen.

Historical/Romance (PR:C MPAA:NR)

STEEL MAGNOLIAS***
118m Rastar/Tri-Star c

Sally Field *(M'Lynn Eatenton)*, Dolly Parton *(Truvy Jones)*, Shirley MacLaine *(Ouiser Boudreaux)*, Daryl Hannah *(Annelle Dupuy Desoto)*, Olympia Dukakis *(Clairee Belcher)*, Julia Roberts *(Shelby Eatenton Latcherie)*, Tom Skerritt *(Drum Eatenton)*, Dylan McDermott *(Jackson Latcherie)*, Kevin J. O'Connor *(Sammy Desoto)*, Sam Shepard *(Spud Jones)*, Bill McCutcheon *(Owen Jenkins)*,

Ann Wedgeworth *(Aunt Fern)*, Knowl Johnson *(Tommy Eatenton)*, Jonathan Ward *(Jonathan Eatenton)*, Bibi Besch *(Belle Marmillion)*, Janine Turner *(Nancy Beth Marmillion)*, James Wlcek *(Marshall Marmillion)*, Ronald Young *(Drew Marmillion)*, Nancy Parsons *(Janice Van Meter)*, Robert Ginnaven *(Mayor Van Meter)*, Tom Hodges *(Louie Jones)*, Rick Hurst *(Bark Boone)*, Robert Harling *(Minister)*, C. Houser *(Jack, Jr., Age 1)*, Daniel Camp *(Jack, Jr., Age 3)*, Norman Fletcher *(Mr. Latcherie, Sr.)*, Lori Tate *(Mrs. Latcherie, Sr.)*, Robert Adams *(Dr. Judd)*, Carol Sutton *(Nurse Pam)*, Aja Sansone *(Monique)*, Rodney Alan Fulton *(Bobby Ray Ross)*, Spencer Henderson, Sandra Asbury-Johnson *(Dancing Couple)*, Gale J. Odom *(Church Singer)*, Betsy Widhalm *(Church Organist)*, Oscar J. Bienvenu Jr. *(Doctor)*, Teresa Beaudion *(Receptionist)*, Gladys Mallard, Betty J. Dove *(Nurses)*, Travis Harrison *(Delivery Boy)*, James Shapkoff III *(Delivery Man)*, Walker May *(Newspaper Boy)*, Robert R. Morgan *(Cook)*, Roger D. McCann, Debbie McCann *(Cook's Helpers)*.

With the rise of the women's buddy genre (OUTRAGEOUS FORTUNE; BEACHES, etc.) in 1980s Hollywood, the old-fashioned "klatsch" film has all but disappeared. Klatsch films involve women relating to women in gender-exclusive domestic groupings, and it's this gender exclusiveness that makes the klatsch ensemble a prefeminist relic. Where buddy heroines act out their destinies in the public world of men (and generally according to men's competitive rules), klatschers opt for the community of the coffee table. Theirs is a sealed-in world, inferior to men's in terms of power but superior to it in emotion, understanding, and insight into the things that "really matter." Separate but more than equal, so goes the

klatscher myth. Not surprisingly, it's a myth concocted largely by males (consider, for example, Ingmar Bergman's SECRETS OF WOMEN and BRINK OF LIFE or the 1930s and 40s films of George Cukor).

STEEL MAGNOLIAS follows the conventional klatsch formula to a T. Based on screenwriter Robert Harling's own award-winning off-Broadway play, it tells the story of six southern women whose lives interconnect in a beauty parlor in their small Louisiana town. Field, a middle-aged wife and mother with years of domestic frustration etched in her face, worries over the upcoming marriage of headstrong daughter Roberts, who is determined to live life free of her mother's doting concern. Together, they've come to Truvy's, the beauty parlor run by Parton with the help of newly hired assistant Hannah, for the obligatory wedding makeover. Around to comment and gossip are Dukakis, an aristocratic local widow, and MacLaine, the town scold. As the group chatters on, the source of Field's maternal anxiety suddenly rears its head when Roberts has a diabetic seizure. With a firmness (and suppressed resentment) born of long and painful necessity, Field works both with and against her daughter to get the seizure under control. The other women (save newcomer Hannah) have long been familiar with Roberts' condition and offer their understanding and support, but Field continues to fret. She believes her daughter's marriage is a mistake and fears for the children Roberts promises to bring into the world. Still, the marriage goes on as planned, and after a few months it's clear that Field's worst fear will soon be realized: Roberts is going to have a baby. Meanwhile, the women continue to meet and gossip and cope with a variety of problems, among them a failing marriage for Parton and some chameleonlike changes for Hannah. The baby is born healthy, Roberts' condition stabilizes with treatment, and suddenly everything seems possible for the town's youngest family. But again the calender leaves fall and life takes another turn. Roberts lapses into a diabetic coma, and this time neither medical nor family care can pull her through. Field is devastated by her daughter's death. In an emotional graveside outburst, she rages against the fates that have taken her child from her and made a mockery of her years of care and worry. At first she spurns all consolation, but soon the circle of friends closes around her—warm, sympathetic, supportive— and the ability of women to endure, to renew life and nurture it, is once again affirmed. Men should have it so good.

But, in fact, they do, since the production muscle behind these gender affirmations is largely male. Harling and director Herbert Ross even fill out the story with superfluous male characters—husbands and boy friends that hang around like the

Sally Field and Julia Roberts in STEEL MAGNOLIAS (©Tri-Star).

angels in Wim Wender's WINGS OF DESIRE, vague and ungrounded, out of touch with female tangibility (they're more elusive here than in the original one-set play, where they never appear at all). On the other hand, the self-effacing Ross (FUNNY LADY; THE TURNING POINT) isn't one to ride roughshod over a script. He gives the performers plenty of room to work and contents himself mainly with bridging gaps brought about by the transition from stage to screen and deftly redistributing the dialog in time and space. He's methodical, gracious, cinematically impersonal—the perfect escort for a star vehicle like this. Of the women's ensemble, Sally Field frequently astonishes in a role that really doesn't suit her. She's not always successful at staying inside her character, and the nice-girl straining takes its customary toll, but her best moments—during Roberts' seizure, when her face swiftly tightens into a Louise Fletcher mask, and at the graveyard—are superb. She's so good she's terrifying. Dolly Parton is also good, though she breezes through her part as if she's stepped in from another film—too cloudless and airy to connect effectively with Field. Julia Roberts "southernizes" herself a bit too much, while Olympia Dukakis holds on to her New Jersey roots, coming across as a genial Bea Arthur in regional disguise. Shirley MacLaine seems always to be fussing with her attitude, though once in a while an honest bit of feeling manages to push through.

Made on a $17-million budget, STEEL MAGNOLIAS was shot on location in Natchitoches, Louisiana, hometown of actor-turned-writer Harling, who based his play on the experiences of his own mother and sister. (In 1985, Harling's sister Susan died of diabetic complications after giving birth.) The film is unapologetically old-fashioned. There's hardly an ounce of invention in it, and its matriarchal comforts and sorority assumptions have a moldy, regressive taint (beware these men bearing pacifying gifts). Nonetheless, it goes down easily, like the after-dinner morsel it's intended to be. And there's always Field to wait for and enjoy. Songs include: "I Got Mine" (Ry Cooder, performed by Cooder), "Gypsy Blood" (Mason Ruffner, performed by Ruffner), "Two Step Mamou" (Wayne Toups, Jay Miller, Jean Arceneaux, performed by Wayne Toups and Zydecajun), "Les Grands Bois" (performed by Jo-el Sonnier), "Ma Louisianne" (Zachary Richard, performed by Richard), "Cajun Christmas," "Would You Fly" (Marsha Brown, performed by Monty Brown, Marsha Brown), "Lookin' for You" (Holly Dunn, performed by Dunn), "Old Time Rock and Roll" (George Jackson, Tom Jones III, performed by Tommy Funderburk), "Jambalaya" (Hank Williams, performed by Funderburk), "Yankee Doodle Dandy" (George M. Cohan), "Winter Wonderland" (Felix Bernard, Dick Smith). (Adult situations.)

p, Ray Stark; d, Herbert Ross; w, Robert Harling (based on his play); ph, John A. Alonzo; ed, Paul Hirsch; m, Georges Delerue; prod d, Gene Callahan and Edward Pisoni; art d, Hub Braden and Michael Okowita; set d, Steven Wolff; spec eff, Kevin Harris; cos, Julie Weiss; chor, Spencer Henderson; makeup, Christina Smith.

Comedy/Drama   (PR:C   MPAA:PG)

STEPFATHER 2: MAKE ROOM FOR DADDY**½
86m ITC/Millimeter c

Terry O'Quinn (Dr. Gene Clifford), Meg Foster (Carol Grayland), Caroline Williams (Matty Crimmins), Jonathan Brandis (Todd Grayland), Henry Brown (Dr. Joseph Danvers), Mitchell Laurance (Phil Grayland), Leon Martell, Renata Scott, John O'Leary, Eric Brown.

When last we saw the Stepfather, he had been fatally shot and stabbed. Well, like HALLOWEEN's Michael Myers, Jerry Blake is back again although this sequel to Joseph Ruben's well-received THE STEPFATHER (1987) is far more welcome than the umpteenth installment of the "Friday the Thirteenth" or "Halloween" series.

Directed by Jeff Burr, STEPFATHER 2 opens with O'Quinn (whose lead performance was so riveting in the original) biding his time at the Puget Sound Psychiatric Hospital. This is no place for an All-American family man, of course, and he soon finds a way to use his renowned woodworking skills to engineer an escape. He enters the office of a trusting shrink, carrying a model home that comes complete with a daddy figurine concealing a deadly weapon. Quicker than you can say, "Father knows best!" the predatory patriarch is loose, and the body count includes the psychiatrist, a guard, and an unlucky traveler whose car strikes stepfather O'Quinn's fancy. While watching a rerun of "Dream House," O'Quinn hears about the idyllic Palm Meadows community. There, he encounters divorced realtor Foster, who has a teenage son, and a nearby house for rent. Drawing on his years of psychoanalysis, O'Quinn becomes a family counselor and spends his spare time checking out videos from a dating service. Sensing that Foster is Mrs. Right, O'Quinn courts her successfully until two roadblocks to matrimony appear. First, Foster's ex-husband, Laurance, realizes the error of his philandering ways and wants his family back. Second, Foster's feisty postal worker buddy, Williams, begins questioning O'Quinn's psychological expertise. O'Quinn "counsels" Foster's repentant husband by beaning him with a wine bottle and taking him and his car to a junkyard,

where both are flattened. When Williams snoops through the Stepfather's mail and discovers his true identity, she seals her own doom. Never one to waste time, O'Quinn strangles Williams, slyly rearranges the crime scene to resemble a suicide, and steals a bottle of the victim's best wine as a gift for Foster. (His only slip-up is that a blind neighbor has heard him whistling "De Camptown Races," the Stepfather's signature tune.) Despite Williams' tragic death, O'Quinn moves in for the marital kill on Foster, and the happy wedding day arrives. Before she can say "I do," Foster receives a wedding present from her late girl friend's parents—special wine exactly like the bottle O'Quinn mysteriously gave her in the middle of the night. When she overhears her son whistling "De Camptown Races," Foster realizes that her wedding march may end up a dance of death.

Dazzlingly directed by Ruben, THE STEPFATHER was a bracingly original, bone-chilling horror film loosely based on the infamous List case. Tautly written, it also poked fun at marriage and our own sitcom-warped search for perfect family bliss. All STEPFATHER 2 does (though often skillfully) is cover familiar slasher territory. Still, unlike other horror film sequels, it's not an offensive rip-off; rather it offers variations on the bogey man theme. Instead of investigating the Stepfather's bloody origins or taking him in a new direction, this movie delivers the scary goods without packing any unexpected wallop. The opening crosscutting is cleverly handled, detailing each step in the Stepfather's ingenious escape plan, and the suspense builds nicely as he plays cat and mouse with the overly curious postal worker before permanently withdrawing her wedding invitation. More than its predecessor, STEPFATHER 2 delights in one-liners that sustain the blackly comic tone even when the suspense falters. Basically, however, it is a workable, assembly-line remake of the original thriller.

Led by Terry O'Quinn's brilliant chameleonlike performance as the hard-to-please family man(iac), the cast is uniformly excellent, although Meg Foster has some trouble submerging her natural gutsiness in a victim role. Nonetheless, most reservations about this sequel are swept aside by the crowd-pleasing Grand Guignol climax, which hacks to pieces every cliched wedding scene in Hollywood history. For this sequence alone, one can overlook the film's cannibalism of its superior predecessor; husband and wife start battling even before the knot is tied—wrecking wedding presents, destroying decorations, and exhibiting severe premarital jitters by trying to kill each other. Smoothly directed, tightly edited, and crisply acted, the film is savvy enough not to emasculate the Stepfather character by turning him into the kind of camp creation

Norman Bates or Freddy Krueger have become. Although a bit too derivative, STEPFATHER 2 remains a cut above most slasher sequels. *(Graphic violence, profanity, nudity.)*

p, Darin Scott and William Burr; d, Jeff Burr; w, John Auerbach (based on characters created by Carolyn Lefcourt, Brian Garfield, Donald E. Westlake); ph, Jacek Laskus (Foto-Kem Color); ed, Pasquale A. Buba; m, Jim Manzie and Pat Regan; prod d, Bernadette Disanto; art d, Aram Allen; set d, Johnna Butler; cos, Julie Carnahan; makeup, Michelle Burke.

Horror   (PR:O MPAA:R)

Ⓥ**STORM****
(Can.) 110m Groundstar/Cannon c
David Palfy *(Lowell)*, Stan Kane *(Jim)*, Tom Schioler *(Booker)*, Harry Freedman *(Stan)*, Lawrence Elion, Stacy Christensen.

Though a promising debut for its producer-writer-director, David Winning, STORM, by most standards, takes a lively premise and fritters it away. Reportedly made in Canada for a mere $72,000, this hybrid of crime thriller and DELIVER-ANCE-style suspense adventure is long on atmosphere but short on solid plotting and storyline.

The action starts with two sets of players. Nerdish student Palfy idolizes his macho best friend, Schioler. Both are also accomplished players in the game of assassination, a fad from the early 80s in which college students stalked each other around campuses trying to score "kills" using toy weapons. As the film begins, Palfy and Schioler are planning a weekend camping trip to test their survival skills in the real wilderness. Meanwhile, an aging trio of bankrobbers (Kane, Freedman, and Elion) has loaded up a camper, and headed for the same wilderness to recover $750,000 in loot from a robbery that took place in 1946. Not averse to bloodshed, the three are shown, in a prolog and flashbacks, to have killed a hostage taken during the robbery, along with a backwoods dweller who objected to the theft of his truck. When Schioler's pickup truck gets stalled in a puddle, Palfy takes a stroll through the woods, only to come upon the three robbers digging for their buried money. As Palfy watches, an argument develops that leaves one of the trio dead. At that inopportune moment, Palfy's watch alarm sounds, giving away his presence and leading the other robbers to chase him. Following Palfy back to Schioler's truck, the criminal duo kills Schioler, leaving Palfy alone to match wits with the hardened killers, having only his gaming experience to rely on to survive.

Unfortunately, the film itself is not nearly as suspenseful as its synopsis. Triple-threat Winning succumbs to a mixture of contrivance and self-indulgence, deflating all but the most obvious opportunities for suspense. Palfy's stumbling alone upon the killer trio, for example, depends on the rugged Schioler's being too afraid of getting wet in the puddle where his truck has stalled to step out of the cab. In order to allow the conflict among the robbers to develop (which itself depends upon an implausible contrivance that becomes the plot's key), Winning resorts to padding the action with Palfy's forest wanderings. Also slackening the pace are flashbacks and nightmares that are probably intended to deepen our understanding of the characters. Much of the time they wind up belaboring the obvious, especially in the case of Palfy, whose character only becomes pointlessly confusing as time goes on. Especially implausible are the gang leader's fantasies of the dead bank robber coming back to haunt him. In the prolog we've seen him kill two people in cold blood; it's less than likely that a third killing is suddenly going to send him into spasms of paralyzing guilt. The climax seems to come out of left field, relying on the possibility of Palfy's dragging a rather large corpse a long distance through the woods to bring about a macabre, but wholly unlikely, final confrontation.

STORM has all the earmarks of a story that might have filled an hour of network television and that has been padded out to feature length. It also has all the earmarks of a novice screenwriting effort, with its over-reliance on dreams, nightmares, and flashbacks to flesh out characters who aren't all that interesting to begin with. The performances are serviceable, but there are no standouts. Winning shows most promise as a visual storyteller; working with cinematographer Tim Hollings, he gets good mileage out of lighting in the dreams and flashbacks and the cold, modernist architecture of the Calgary university where the campus sequences were filmed. All Winning needs on his next effort is a visual story worth telling. With a decent budget—and a no-nonsense, veteran story editor on board—STORM itself might even be worth remaking. *(Violence, profanity, adult situations.)*

p, David Winning; d, David Winning; w, David Winning; ph, Tim Hollings (Kodak Color); ed, Bill Campbell; m, Amin Bhaatia.

Thriller   (PR:C MPAA:PG-13)

STORY OF WOMEN***
(Fr.) 110m MK2-Films A2-Films Du Camelia-La Sept-La Sofica Sofinergie/ New Yorker c
Isabelle Huppert *(Marie)*, Francois Cluzet *(Paul)*, Niels Tavernier *(Lucien)*, Marie Trintignant *(Lulu/Lucie)*, Louis Ducreux, Michel Beaune, Dominique Blanc, Marie Bunel.

In a German-occupied French village in 1941, Marie Latour (Huppert) struggles to eke out an existence for herself and two children. Taking in knitting barely pays for the food on the table, but another, more lucrative profession becomes a possibility when she performs an amateur abortion on a desperate neighbor. As word of her ability as a "maker of angels" spreads, she becomes successful enough to move her family from their squalid flat to a spacious new apartment. Huppert's newfound affluence increases after she befriends a prostitute (Trintignant) and offers to rent out her spare rooms for assignations; meanwhile, her husband (Cluzet) returns from the war in an emotionally and physically shattered state. Huppert, who feels only repugnance and contempt for the weakened Cluzet, continues to enjoy the luxuries her industry can provide, buying black-market treats, hiring a housekeeper, and taking a lover in the form of an attractive young collaborator (Tavernier). Though single-minded in her self-interest, she experiences a small moment of doubt when, for the first time, one of her clients dies after a botched abortion, and she's even more affected (and displays a naive bewilderment) when her best friend, a Jew, is deported. To satisfy Cluzet, with whom she is no longer intimate, she bribes her housekeeper to seduce him and becomes even bolder in her affair with Tavernier. Cluzet discovers the two in the apartment, and—like so many citizens of the time—turns informer, getting his own wife arrested for performing illegal abortions. Taken to Paris to stand trial for her "crime against the state," the strong-willed woman finally breaks down and confesses to everything, expecting to be pardoned. Her reprieve is not to be, however, for the Vichy government, intent on maintaining a high birth rate to compensate for war casualties, has decided to make an example of her. In June 1943, she is condemned to death on the guillotine, one of the last women to be executed in France.

A semifactual version of the life of Marie-Louise Giraud, an actual abortionist who was executed by the Vichy government, STORY OF WOMEN is technically impressive on every level. Adapted by director Claude Chabrol and Colo Tavernier O'Hagan (BEATRICE [1988]) from Francis Szpiner's nonfiction account of Giraud's case, *Une Affaire de Femmes*, the film is an absorbing and well-crafted account of a dark period in French history. Chabrol's economical control of cinematic narrative, as usual, stands him in good stead, lending his depiction of the nightmare of the Occupation the kind of melodramatic tension that has characterized his tales of minor crimes among the provincial bourgeoisie—such films as LA FEMME INFIDELE (1968); LE BOUCHER (1969); and JUSTE AVANT LA NUIT

(1971)—a genre of which he is French cinema's foremost practitioner.

Although one doesn't quibble as its engrossing story unfolds with such inexorable, clinically tasteful logic, STORY OF WOMEN fails to achieve tragic power. It's too schematic and almost cursory in its conception, distancing the viewer. One can appreciate the main character's instinct for survival, but she is made such an amoral cipher that any real interest in her is subverted. Is it Chabrol's rigorous faithfulness to the text, and refusal to show her in any sympathetic light that prevents emotional involvement on the viewer's part, or is it Isabelle Huppert's lack of star magnetism? Both are obviously trying to do something different here: Marie is shown to be an Occupation version of a yuppie who does whatever she can to thrive, and Chabrol's refusal to soften her story is also an attempt to record a past national shame. But it's all too thin and treatiselike to work really well, to the point that one almost feels voyeuristic watching the icy machinations on the screen.

Huppert took the best actress award at the 1988 Venice Film Festival for her performance here, and it's undeniably an accomplishment. She remains stoically in character throughout, almost daring viewers to sympathize with her as the film shows her cold-bloodedness; her lack of affection for her rather cliched, suffering cuckold of a husband (he seems to be always clad in pajamas); her undisguised favoring of her daughter over her grave, wide-eyed son. It only repels us. Why is this woman such a bitch? There is no exposition to explain her contempt for men; some undeveloped sequences fail to explain her motivations when she takes up with the collaborators; and her subservience to her loutish, enigmatic lover seems out of character. Her ignorance of what has happened to the Jews also plays flatly—it's too schematically pat and ironic. (And shouldn't Marie, who has aspirations to be a grand chanteuse, at least have a decent voice? Huppert's game but off-putting caterwauling only adds to the sense of alienation.) For the film to really work, Chabrol needed an actress capable of the kind of electrifying, magnetic bitchery a young Bette Davis or Jeanne Moreau could provide, a woman who attracted while she repelled. Huppert is too purposely opaque—though she comes through brilliantly in the final moments, when Marie recites a tearfully obscene Hail Mary in her jail cell, a scene that was condemned by the French Catholic hierarchy and that was protested with a tear-gas attack on a Montparnasse cinema in which one audience member died in the rush to escape.

Although the camera focuses squarely on Huppert throughout to the effacement of the rest of a huge cast, it should be mentioned that Marie Trintignant is the most captivatingly exquisite whore since Vivien Leigh sauntered through a train station in WATERLOO BRIDGE. *(Adult situations, sexual situations, profanity.)*

p, Marin Karmitz; d, Claude Chabrol; w, Colo Tavernier O'Hagan and Claude Chabrol (based on *Une Affaire de Femmes* by Francis Szpiner); ph, Jean Rabier; ed, Monique Fardoulis; m, Matthieu Chabrol.

Drama   **(PR:O)**

ⓥ**STREET JUSTICE***
94m Lorimar-Sandy Howard c
Michael Ontkean *(Curt Flynn)*, Joanna Kerns *(Katharine Watson)*, Catherine Bach *(Tamarra)*, J.D. Cannon *(Arthur Dante)*, Jeanette Nolan *(Edith Chandler)*, Richard Cox *(Sam Chandler)*, William Windom *(Fr. Burke)*, Sandra Currie *(Mandy)*, Richard C. Sarafian *(Taxi Driver)*.

In STREET JUSTICE, a CIA agent who was believed dead returns to his hometown to find his wife and daughter, then becomes embroiled in a political conspiracy. Michael Ontkean portrays Maj. Curt Flynn, who was sent to Leningrad 12 years earlier to escort a defecting Russian scientist into the United States. The CIA doubted the scientist's loyalties and blew up the plane carrying both men. Miraculously, Flynn survived the crash, but was incarcerated in a Russian prison for years until he escaped to the US embassy in West Germany. In the opening sequence, the CIA accuses Ontkean of spying for the Soviets and imprisons him at a military installation. Again he escapes, and heads for New Jersey to find his wife (Kerns) and his daughter. When his former CIA boss dispatches several agents to track him down and kill him, Ontkean decides not to reveal his presence in town to his wife. In a bar in Hoboken he befriends a hooker (Currie) who lets him stay at her apartment. From her, he learns that a corrupt, wealthy family headed by matriarch Nolan runs the city council and the police, and that his wife has married one of their main adversaries. Ontkean acts as guardian angel to his wife's new family while he tries to find evidence to expose Nolan and her family. Meanwhile, Ontkean is being stalked by CIA hit men. At one point, he and Currie return to her apartment to find the door rigged with explosives, but he manages to kill the operatives with their own booby trap. Eventually, Kerns hears about Ontkean's return from her pastor, who reports that a man came looking for her days before. Having already observed someone watching her, she starts to suspect it's Ontkean. Next, Nolan's men run Ontkean's daughter and her boy friend off the road as a scare tactic; Ontkean breaks into the home of Nolan's son, Cox, to pilfer records; and Cox's mistress, eager to dupe her abusive lover, gives Ontkean a stack of incriminating financial documents. To escape from Cox's house, Ontkean has to kill Cox and a couple of others, including his old CIA boss, who was waiting outside the estate to shoot him. In the end, Kerns catches a glimpse of Ontkean outside the hospital on the day their daughter is being released. She follows him and asks him to stay, but he tells her it is too late.

STREET JUSTICE's clumsy script pursues too many tangents. For one thing, Ontkean has an overabundance of adversaries—Cox and his mother, the ex-boss and the CIA goon squad, Cox's henchmen, a corrupt police chief (Cannon)—none of whom is developed into a formidable challenge. Each can be categorized as a stock character—the villainous ex-boss who, like a James Bond villain, never underestimates his enemy; the power-hungry crime family; the corrupt cops. Futhermore, it is nearly impossible to differentiate the thugs and henchmen from one another, especially when they appear in so many short scenes, some without dialog. In addition to the stereotyped villains, the film is filled with other routine characters: the hooker with a heart of gold; the double-crossing mistress who sells out her lover because he's been slapping her around; and the virtuous wife who is placed in serene settings like a schoolyard full of children, by her husband's side, or talking with her pastor. Ontkean himself perfects a sullen, stupefied look throughout the film, adding another two-dimensional characterization to the list. The incidental subplot in which CIA operatives hunt Ontkean's character doesn't further the story or have any relevance to the misadventure in Hoboken. A lot of the dialog is also filler, or is cryptic and misleading. At the end, after Ontkean's wife finally catches up with him, he says, "Where I am going, you and Nancy cannot follow." Such writing, besides being outdated and trite, is a bit enigmatic for the end of a below-standard action film. That is, unless STREET JUSTICE was intended to be the pilot for a television series about a mysterious drifter who appears in the nick of time to defend the oppressed and rescue cats from trees. *(Violence, profanity, adult situations.)*

p, David Witz and Michael Masciarelli; d, Richard C. Sarafian; w, James J. Docherty; ph, Roland "Ozzie" Smith and Roger Olkowski (Medallion Color); ed, Mark Goldberg; m, Jamii Szmadzinski and Paul Hertzog; art d, Joanne Chorney.

Action   **(PR:C MPAA:R)**

ⓥ**STRIPPED TO KILL II:
LIVE GIRLS***
82m Concorde c
Maria Ford *(Shady)*, Eb Lottimer *(Sgt. Decker)*, Karen Mayo Chandler *(Cassandra)*, Birke Tan *(Dazzle)*, Marjean

Holden *(Something Else)*, Debra Lamb *(Montra)*, Lisa Glaser *(Victoria)*, Tom Ruben *(Ike)*, Virginia Peters *(Shirl)*.

STRIPPED TO KILL II: LIVE GIRLS delivers on its lurid title for B-movie thrill-seekers, but it also offers something more: an uncommonly sympathetic look at a world to which the baby- and family-obsessed mainstream cinema rarely devotes serious screen time nowadays. The film is set in the Paragon Club, located in an unnamed city—if, indeed, it's located in a city at all. (The film's sole daytime scene set outside the club appears to take place out in the middle of nowhere, with nothing in sight but a few trees and a free-way in the distance.) As the film opens, one of the Paragon strippers, Ford, is suffering from a disturbing dream in which one of her fellow strippers, Glaser, gets brutally murdered at the climax of her club act by a masked woman with a razor blade in her mouth. Ford wakes up—with blood on her own mouth—in the loft she shares with another Paragon stripper (Chandler), and rushes to the club, where she is relieved to find that Glaser is safe. Later, however, when Ford returns to the club after closing time for a late date with Glaser, she finds her dead after all, just as in her dream. As the dreams, dancing, and death continue, Ford becomes involved with the investigating detective on the case, Lottimer, who fears that his feelings for Ford are clouding his judgment. He doesn't want to believe she is a killer, but the evidence is getting a little hard to dismiss.

LIVE GIRLS really isn't much of a mystery thriller. Though the film is overrun with red herrings—virtually every character who isn't an obvious victim-to-be is an obvious suspect—the real killer's identity is none too subtly tipped early on. The film does deliver heady doses of steamy strip-tease eroticism, since the husband-wife team of producer Andy Ruben and writer-director Katt Shea Ruben cast real-life exotic dancers as some of the Paragon strippers. But the film complicates our feelings about the dances and the dancers, and not just by cutting away to reveal that the dances are often part of the Ford character's deathly dreams. (Bad dreams have become a leading B-movie horror cliche, inspired by the "Nightmare on Elm Street" series, in movies ranging from BLOODY POM POMS to, uh, BAD DREAMS.) Instead, LIVE GIRLS adopts the riskier ploy of introducing the dancers as complex and not necessarily enticing, but realistic personalities, whose acts reveal and comment on their characters with varying degrees of subtlety.

Just as the Paragon is not an average striptease club, neither are Ford and Lottimer's characters an average couple. No good girl unwillingly caught in a tawdry life, Ford is aggressively sexual as she drives the initially standoffish Lottimer into a lustful frenzy before making love to him, standing up, in the alley behind the club as thunder rumbles overhead. Neither, however, is she merely some hot-blooded male sex fantasy. In the past, it's revealed, she assaulted an ex-lover with a can opener and had a nervous breakdown, while Lottimer lost a leg and his marriage after he was unable to shoot a 12-year-old boy robbing a convenience store. Together, they are wounded, lonely, unsentimentalized people groping for each other in the dark.

LIVE GIRLS' predecessor, also a Ruben production, had a more original premise, toplining Kay Lenz as a police detective who goes undercover to solve a series of stripper murders, only to find she gets a charge out of stripping herself. The sequel improves on the first film with its more polished direction and script, but has a major flaw in its cast. Maria Ford, a drop-dead knockout offstage and a sizzler onstage, is no match for Lenz in the acting department, and the rest of the cast is similarly spotty—the movie paying the price of realism, perhaps, for the casting of dancers in key acting roles. An exception is the decidedly unglamorous Virginia Peters, who, as Lottimer's dispatcher, practically steals the film with wry, funny, and very welcome comic relief. In spite of its flaws, however, LIVE GIRLS is a rarity among low-budget exploitation flicks, an absorbing diversion for truly adult audiences. *(Violence, profanity, nudity, sexual situations.)*

p, Andy Ruben; d, Katt Shea Ruben; w, Katt Shea Ruben; ph, Phedon Papamichael (Foto-Kem Color); ed, Stephen Mark; m, Gary Stockdale; prod d, Virginia Lee; art d, Greg Maher; set d, John Shipiro; cos, Ellen Gross; chor, Ted Lin.

Mystery/Thriller   (PR:O MPAA:R)

Ⓥ**SWEET LIES****
96m Goldeneye/Island c
Treat Williams *(Peter Nicholl)*, Joanna Pacula *(Joelle)*, Julianne Phillips *(Dixie)*, Laura Manszky *(Lisa)*, Norbert Weisser *(Bill)*, Marilyn Dodds Frank *(Maggie)*, Aina Walle *(Isabelle)*, Gisele Casadesus *(Nemo)*, Bernard Fresson *(Mr. Leguard)*, Lucy Morgan *(Bradshaw)*.

Oh, the games people play. Both men and women do it, but the fun often leads to someone getting hurt, which Treat Williams discovers in SWEET LIES. An American investigating insurance fraud in Paris, Williams becomes the willing but unknowing victim of a bet between two beauties (Phillips and Pacula) who compete to see which of them can get him into bed first. The daughter of the owner of the small hotel where Williams is staying tries to turn the delivery of fresh towels into a romantic rendezvous with the handsome Yank. Alas, she is far too young for him, but her two friends are the perfect age.

Pacula, a French radio announcer, attracts Williams' attention by running into him with her car. He's fine, but she insists on nursing him back to health at her home. Before he leaves, she steals the tape recorder from his coat pocket, certain that he will be back for it. Of course, she's right, and their second meeting is not so innocent. So begins romance No. 1. Phillips employs an equally creative method to meet Williams; posing as a strolling clarinetist, she flings herself into the Seine in a phony suicide attempt as soon as she spots him. Gallant Williams proceeds to "save" Phillips and returns her to the coziness of her houseboat. Life starts looking better once they've dried off, and Williams is swept off his feet for the second time that week. Charmed by both women, Williams apparently has no intention of choosing between them; that is, until he discovers that the two are friends and that he is merely the object of their contest. By that time, of course, the plan has backfired and both Phillips and Pacula have fallen in love with him, creating hard feelings all around, especially when Williams seeks his revenge.

SWEET LIES' silly premise might have been sufficient for a half-hour television episode, but it lacks the necessary *oomph* to get a full-length feature off the ground. We keep waiting for something at least slightly exciting to happen; instead we spend a lot of time watching three undeniably attractive people cavort around Paris. Low-key, simple, and occasionally funny, SWEET LIES would be a much better film had its female leads offered more in the way of performance than their pretty faces. Harmless enough, but unresolved, SWEET LIES is ultimately unfulfilling. Songs include: "Sweet Lies" (performed by Robert Palmer). *(Brief nudity, sexual situations.)*

p, Serge Touboul; d, Nathalie Delon; w, R. Dunn (based on a story by Nathalie Delon); ph, Dominique Chapuis (LTC-Franay Color, Metrocolor); ed, Marie-Sophie Dubus; m, Trevor Jones; art d, Bruno Held; set d, Laurent Barbat.

Comedy   (PR:C MPAA:R)

SWEETIE****½
(Aus.) 97m Arenafilm/UGC c
Genevieve Lemon *(Dawn, Sweetie)*, Karen Colston *(Kay)*, Tom Lycos *(Louis)*, Jon Darling *(Gordon)*, Dorothy Barry *(Flo)*, Michael Lake *(Bob)*, Andre Pataczek *(Clayton)*, Jean Hadgraft *(Mrs. Schneller)*, Paul Livingston *(Teddy Schneller)*, Louise Fox *(Cheryl)*, Ann Merchant *(Cheryl)*, Robyn Frank *(Ruth)*, Bronwyn Morgan *(Sue)*, Sean Fennell *(Boy Clerk)*, Sean Callinan *(Simboo)*, Norm Galton *(Notary)*, Charles Abbott *(Meditation Teacher)*, Diana Armer *(Melony)*, Barbara Middleton *(Clayton's*

Mum), Emma Fowler *(Little Sweetie)*, Irene Curtis *(Mandy)*, Ken Porter *(Lead Jakaroo)*, John Negroponte, John E. Hughes, Gerard Lee, Alan Close, Marco Colombani, Geoff Shera, Andrew Traucki *(Jackaroos)*, Norman Phillips, Shirley Sheppard *(Nosy Neighbors)*, Ben Cochrane, Kristoffer Pershouse *(Boys in Tree)*, Larry Brand, Cedric McLaughlan, Bruce Currie *(Man with Saw)*, Warren Hensley, Doug Ramsey.

Despite its title, which ironically conjures up benign images, SWEETIE is not an optimistic fable about a good-natured heroine, but a harrowing look at the destruction a mentally ill woman's behavior wreaks on her family. To appreciate its complexity and uniqueness, try to imagine Polanski's REPULSION reworked as a comedy, or De Palma's SISTERS reshaped as a farce. It's as if Shirley Temple and Jane Withers had grown up and starred in a sequel to BRIGHT EYES, in which Jane was diagnosed as schizophrenic and Shirley became a near-catatonic trying to cope with Jane's now-deranged mischief.

As SWEETIE opens, we're introduced to Colston, a gaunt, withdrawn young Australian woman whose life is ruled by superstition. A control freak, she fervidly believes every word of a fortune teller's prediction that she'll meet a man with a question mark on his forehead (this turns out to be a curl of hair drooping over a beauty mark). Determined to make this vague vision a reality, Colston steals a coworker's fiance (Lycos) who fits the seer's description. For a while, the uptight woman relaxes into her new relationship, but her phobic behavior is never completely overcome. When Lycos plants a tree to symbolize the growth of their love, she responds coldly. Why do trees terrify her? Why does she uproot this sapling and hide it? In her own way, she cannot let anything grow normally. When her fun-loving sister, Lemon ("Sweetie"), arrives, we begin to understand why Colston is a paranoid bundle of repression. Fat and sassy, Lemon gobbles up life voraciously— eating food like Jack Sprat's wife and sampling men like an Australian Mae West. To Lycos' disgust, Colston immediately starts considering ways to throw her sister out. Accompanied by her perpetually stoned "manager" Lake, Lemon clings to the dreams of show-biz glory her parents drummed into her when she was a sweet, attention-getting youngster. Yet, behavior that's adorable in a child can be unseemly in an adult. Wily enough to manipulate her family, she has always gotten her own way, but her family is at the end of its collective rope. When Colston's dad, Darling, arrives to drive Colston and her boy friend to a family outing, they have to scheme in order to leave the disruptive Lemon behind. Finally fooling her, Colston takes a temporary breather from her sibling's psycholog-

Genevieve Lemon and Karen Colston in SWEETIE (©UGC).

ical tyranny and visits her mother, Barry, at the outback ranch where Barry works as a cook. When Colston returns from this interlude, Lemon has regressed and demands to be treated like a puppy. Then, at the family home, Lemon climbs into her childhood treehouse and refuses to come down. Violently spoiled, she demands that Colston bring back a neighbor's child so she'll have company. Ruling the roost from her home in the clouds, Lemon begins stomping up and down on the treehouse floor to terrify her parents. The supporting boughs break, and Lemon is killed in the fall. After her funeral, we see an eerie flashback of the young Lemon singing, an image of youthful promise and expectation, a lost moment of hope cruelly frozen in time.

In this darkly comic case study, her feature debut, Australian director Jane Campion has fashioned a domestic slapstick tragedy. The laughter she mines from mental illness only deepens the pain felt by each of the characters. While she has been compared to both Jim Jarmusch and David Lynch, Campion is a unique artist who has created an idiosyncratic and fearfully unnerving comedy about suffering. Working elliptically rather than through overt dramatic flourishes, the director reveals the chaos mental illness inflicts on the victim's entire family—the disorder attacks everyone, from the parents, who waste their lives foolishly pretending nothing is wrong, to the siblings shunted into the background because attention must be paid to the neediest.

In addition to being a remarkable visual stylist (brilliantly aided by cinematographer Sally Bongers), Campion elicits miracles of acting from her cast. In this comically heightened version of reality, the

actors might all too easily have overplayed the laughs and forced the tears. But these players make you feel as if they live down the block in your hometown—they're colorful enough to make you spy over your backyard fence on their problems, but disquieting enough to make you glad the fence is there. Campion also uses symbols effectively, integrating them organically with the events and not letting them become portentous restatements of the theme. When we finally see Sweetie squatting maliciously in her treehouse, we understand her sister's terror of trees, usually symbols of shelter and strength. The family has been trying to coax Sweetie out of that treehouse, and out of her arrested development, all her life. In the end, not only does the treehouse rot and collapse— no one can cling to childhood forever—but Sweetie won't rest peacefully because treeroots growing across her grave prevent her coffin from being lowered into the ground. Her illness, and the memory of what she might have been, will haunt her family forever.

A remarkable debut feature, cruelly honest and pitilessly funny, SWEETIE is about forgiveness forged in a terrible self-awareness. This sad study of a distaff Peter Pan straitjacketed in a little girl's frilly party dress is one of the nakedest explorations of familial love and desperation ever recorded on film. *(Violence, nudity, profanity, sexual situations.)*

p, John Maynard; d, Jane Campion; w, Jane Campion and Gerard Lee (based on an idea by Jane Campion); ph, Sally Bongers; ed, Veronika Heussler; m, Martin Armiger; prod d, Peter Harris; cos, Amanda Lovejoy; stunts, Bernie Ledger; makeup, Wendy Freeman.

Comedy   (PR:O MPAA:NR)

T

TALVISOTA****

(Fin.) 195m National-Filmi Oy/
Finnkino Oy c
(AKA: THE WINTER WAR)
Taneli Makela *(Martti Hakala)*, Konsta Makela *(Paavo)*, Vesa Vierikko *(Jussi Kantola)*, Timo Torikka *(Pentti Saari)*, Heikki Paavilainen *(Vilho Errkila)*, Antti Raivio *(Erkki Somppi)*, Esko Kovero *(Juho Pernaa)*, Martti Suosalo *(Arvi Huhtala)*, Tomi Salmela *(Matti Ylinen)*, Samuli Edelman *(Maari Haapasalo)*, Vesa Makela *(Yrjo Haavisto)*, Aarno Sulkanen *(Battalion Commander)*, Pirkko Hamalainen *(Marjatta Hakala)*, Kari Kihlstrom, Esko Salminen, Kari Sorvali, Ari-Kyosti Seppo, Esko Nikkari, Ville Virtanen, Eero Melasnieme, Pertti Sveholm.

TALVISOTA, Finland's 1989 entry into Oscar competition, is a deeply moving, epic drama commemorating the 50th anniversary of the country's heroic border stand against a massive Russian invading force during the Russo-Finnish War. Outmanned 50 to 1, the Finnish forces suffered 25,000 casualties and gave up important territory, including the strategic Karelian Isthmus, the "dagger pointed at Leningrad," only 20 miles away and within artillery range of the Soviet city. But Finland remained independent and exacted staggering losses from the inept and underprepared invaders, who lost 200,000 lives, 700 planes, and 1,600 tanks.

One need not be a student of history to be thoroughly engrossed by TALVISOTA, which follows a single platoon into combat. These are not John Wayne- or Rambo-style supersoldiers charging the barricades, only farmers doing their patriotic duty with widely varying degrees of zeal. The platoon leader, though level-headed and capable, seems a type who would be more at home helping children through their lessons than guiding men into grueling combat; the men matter-of-factly interrupt their journey toward the front to help a village of women (left behind by war) turn the town's fields. The film's realism makes the men's occasional heroism seem all the more spontaneous, and therefore genuinely exciting. In the end, it's only their unquestioning resilience that keeps them going from one skirmish to the next, and the skirmishes grow bigger and bloodier as the men approach the Finnish frontier. Thrown together by chance, the platoon members are just beginning to become friends as, one by one, they are cut down in combat. Martti (Taneli Makela) becomes the central figure by default: by film's end he's the only one of the group left standing, unable to save his own brother (blown in two during an artillery

barrage), though successful in helping to save his country. The film ends with a freeze-frame closeup of his haunted, weary face, which seems to have aged 50 years since the audience first saw it, and which says more about the human price of war than any number of noble speeches.

TALVISOTA succeeds by balancing the epic with the intimate. Rather than presenting a panoramic, detached view of history, it works through an accumulation of small details—ranging from incidents in the men's private lives to particulars of military strategy—that gradually draw viewers into the drama. Pekka Parikka's direction and Kari Sohlberg's richly textured cinematography consistently keep the camera at soldier's-eye level, bringing us into the trenches during harrowing hand-to-hand combat, into the crowded bunker and command center, into the midst of the smoke and confusion of bombing raids, and even (in a particularly Scandinavian touch) into the makeshift sauna where the men find fleeting respite from combat. The cast is uniformly excellent, giving rich, understated portrayals of the platoon soldiers, allowing us to become involved with history because we have become involved with its unwilling players. Even the film's 195-minute length works in its favor, since the filmmakers use the time to develop a realistic sense of day-to-day life, meticulously presented against the backdrop of awesome history. The resulting impression of what real warfare is like is as strong as any presented on the screen.

TALVISOTA has moments—both eerily haunting and wrenchingly violent—that recall Akira Kurosawa at his best. The battle scenes have an almost poetic grandeur and fearsome intensity, and the sequences showing artillery shelling and bombing raids are nightmarish in their brutal thoroughness. Lingering longest in the memory, however, are the odd, small moments that continually put the war into personal perspective: Martti and Paavo's home leave, during which the tension around the dinner table approaches the intensity of combat because relatives, desperate for news from the front, clash with the brothers, who are just as desperate to forget the horrors they have seen; the scene in which a horse pulling a sled laden with corpses through a serene, snow-covered field is frightened by a sudden artillery attack, and almost spills the sled's awful cargo; a tense argument between platoon leaders that threatens to turn into a showdown. Poignant and true in such small moments, rousing in its big scenes, TALVISOTA emerges as both a fitting, heartfelt tribute to a proud nation and an exceptionally well-crafted war drama. *(Violence, profanity, adult situations.)*

p, Marko Rohr; d, Pekka Parikka; w, Antii Tuurin and Pekka Parikka (based on the novel by Antii Tuurin); ph, Kari Sohlberg

(Eastmancolor); ed, Keijo Virtanen; m, Juha Tikka and Jukka Haavisto; prod d, Pertti Hilkamo; spec eff, Esa Parkatti; cos, Tuula Hilkamo; stunts, Aldo Tamsaar.

War   (PR:O MPAA:NR)

TANGO AND CASH***

98m Guber-Peters/WB c
Sylvester Stallone *(Ray Tango)*, Kurt Russell *(Gabe Cash)*, Teri Hatcher *(Kiki)*, Jack Palance *(Yves Perret)*, Brion James *(Courier/Requin)*, James Hong *(Quan)*, Mark Alaimo *(Lopez)*, Phillip Tan *(Gunman/Chinese Guy)*, Michael J. Pollard *(Owen)*, Robert Z'Dar *(Face)*, Lewis Arquette *(Wyler)*, Edward Bunker *(Capt. Holmes)*, Leslie Morris *(Hendricks)*, Roy Brocksmith *(Federal Agent Davis)*, Susan Krebs *(Prosecutor)*, David Byrd *(Judge)*, Richard Fancy *(Nolan)*, Jerry Martinez *(Santos)*, Michael Jeter *(Skinner)*, Bing Russell *(Van Driver)*, Alphonse V. Walter *(Station Cop)*, Peter Stensland *(Kagan)*, Phil Rubenstein *(Sokowski)*, Elizabeth Sung *(Interpreter)*, Clint Howard *(Slinky)*, Ed DeFusco, Jack Goode Jr., Geoff Vanderstock, Larry Humberger *(Federal Agents)*, Mark Wood *(Desk Cop)*, Andre Rosey Brown *(Cash's Cellmate)*, Savely Kramarov *(Car Owner)*, Michael Francis Clarke, Anne Marie Gillis, Tammy Richardson, Patricia Davis *(Reporters)*, Richard Duran, Doug Ford, Kenneth Pruitt, Ronald Moss, Ricky Dominguez *(Prisoners)*, Kristen Hocking *(Lynn)*, Tamara Landry, Anna Joyner *(Girls in Bar)*, Christie Mucciante, Lucia Neal, Roxanne Kernahan, Dori Courtney *(Dressing Room Girls)*, Dale Swann *(Captain)*, John Walter Davis *(Slobber)*, Shabba-Doo *(Dancer)*, David Lea *(Sonny)*, Glenn Morshower *(Coworker)*, Salvador Espinoza *(Weasel)*, Christopher Wolf *(State Trooper)*, Larry White *(Cop)*, Richard J. Larson, Fred Trombley, Matt Tufo *(Detectives)*, David Phillips, Lewis Guido, James Reilley, Gilbert Esparza *(Inmates)*, Martin Valinsky *(Bailiff)*, Donald Zinn, Duane Allen *(Guards)*, Robert David Armstrong *(Club Doorman)*, Philip Wyland, Paul Lewis, Ron Cummins *(Customers)*.

TANGO AND CASH has got to be seen to be believed. It has the ingredients to be a typical buddy-cop picture in the tradition of LETHAL WEAPON; ALIEN NATION; and 48 HRS., but under the direction of Andrei Konchalovsky, TANGO AND CASH is a wild and weird exercise in excess that also works as a satire of its genre. Stallone plays Tango, a sophisticated, wealthy detective lionized by the press and public as the best cop in Los Angeles. Russell is Cash, a sloppy, scruffy type who is himself a celebrated LA detective, and who competes with Stallone in making big busts. Their fierce rivalry is put to the test when they are thrown together in an effort to end the activities of California's biggest drug dealer (Jack Palance, playing his character with wild glee). Exchanging insults and wisecracks (most of them painfully unfunny), the two gunslingers are set up by Palance and arrested for a murder they didn't commit, victims of a conspiracy in which Palance has colluded with members of the FBI, policemen, and a sound expert whose phony tape eventually sends Stallone and Russell up the river. In jail, the detectives' problems *really* mount. After being beaten up by Palance and his cohorts and nearly electrocuted, Stallone and Russell come up with a plan to escape. On a stormy night, they successfully break out of the penitentiary, eluding the law and Palance's henchmen to resurface on the streets. Russell visits the crooked soundman and retrieves the real tape that can clear their names; meanwhile, Stallone shakes down an FBI man for information on the frame-up. Also involved is Stallone's sister (Teri Hatcher, who was so good in THE BIG PICTURE), who, of course, falls for Russell—though Stallone (of course) disapproves. After getting a high-powered, fully armed RV from a strange little weapons expert (the delightfully insane Michael J. Pollard), Stallone and Russell storm Palance's fortress, shooting wildly and destroying a lot of property in the process. The final confrontation takes place in a hall of mirrors, where Palance holds Hatcher at gunpoint. Stallone and Russell shoot Palance, rescue Hatcher, and escape from Palance's place before it explodes. They have cleared their names and stopped the drug lord, becoming friends in the process.

Clearly, this is all nonsense. The plot is a recycled mess, the dialog is embarrassingly bad, and the character motivation is nil. Thanks to Konchalovsky, however, TANGO AND CASH is not only bearable, it's likable. The Soviet-born Konchalovsky (one of the film's jokes involves a car stolen from a Russian and destroyed by a big, dumb American, providing a strong and funny statement within an otherwise typical chase scene) is responsible for some of the finest films of the 80s, including MARIA'S LOVERS; RUNAWAY TRAIN; and SHY PEOPLE; he is a bold, strong artist (and an odd choice to direct here) whose work has a unique intensity. Although he was just a hired gun on this project and did not have a hand in the script, making this his least personal film, TANGO AND CASH still has enough Konchalovsky in it to make it worth a look. The picture has an insane, kinetic energy that makes for both effective action sequences (the chase scenes are competently handled, and the fistfights are strongly edited) and potent satire. Konchalovsky skewers the silly, Hollywood buddy genre by pumping up its basic elements to hysterical proportions (the

usual homophobic subtext and male bonding is so over the top that at times it's barely watchable), while the photography lends it all an incongruous beauty.

The sets are ominously large, the atmosphere incredibly thick, and the special effects blatantly excessive. After a while, TANGO AND CASH becomes so loud and numbing that it goes beyond satire and into surrealism. Stallone seems completely out of his element in such an environment, delivering his idiotic lines with as much finesse as a chainsaw and going through his motions like a robot, but Russell—whose Cash is the closest thing to a true Konchalovsky character in the film—fares much better, and has the energy to complement TANGO AND CASH's wild tone. Action fans should find the shoot-outs and violence enough to keep them occupied, while half-naked dancers and exploding hand grenades fulfill the rest of the genre requirements.

Despite its ample violence, however, TANGO AND CASH is not a film meant to be taken seriously. Instead, it's a very funny movie (if not because of its screenplay) that will have some viewers laughing while others shake their heads in confusion. Konchalovsky, who reportedly left or was fired from this Guber-Peters production before its completion because of a dispute over how the film should end, has successfully created a typically large-scale American action film while satirizing the form, an achievement that deserves praise for sheer audacity, if nothing else. Beautiful to look at and professionally put together, original in its wild, dizzying excessiveness, TANGO AND CASH is a disappointment coming from a talent like Konchalovsky but a winner compared to such films as the overrated LETHAL WEAPON. Strange that it took a Russian to do it right—and wrong. This is a very smart "dumb movie." Songs include: "Best of What I Got" (John Waite, Jonathan Cain, Neal Schon, performed by Bad English), "Let the Day Begin" (Michael Been, performed by the Call), "Don't Go" (Vince Clarke, performed by Yaz), "Poison" (Alice Cooper, Desmond Child, John McCurry, performed by Cooper), "It's No Crime" (L.A. Reid, D. Simmons, performed by Baby Face), "Harlem Nocturne" (Earle Hagen, performed by Darktown Strutters). *(Graphic violence, profanity, adult situations, brief nudity.)*

p, Jon Peters and Peter Guber; d, Andrei Konchalovsky; w, Randy Feldman; ph, Donald E. Thorin (Panavision, Technicolor); ed, Stuart Baird; m, Harold Faltermeyer; prod d, J. Michael Riva; art d, David Klassen and Richard Berger; set d, Alan Kaye and Louis Mann; spec eff, Jon G. Belyeu; cos, Bernie Pollack; chor, Jeff Hornaday; stunts, James Arnett; makeup, Gary Liddiard.

Action   (PR:O MPAA:R)

⊙TANGO BAR***

90m Zaga-Beco/Manley bw

Raul Julia *(Ricardo)*, Valeria Lynch *(Elena)*, Ruben Juarez *(Antonio)*.

The tango, in all its splendor, shimmering sensuality, beguiling innocence, and high-voltage energy, takes center stage in this well-executed cinematic anthology of the Argentine dance form. Highlighted by several brilliantly choreographed tango-ballet sequences and featuring generous film clips that illustrate the tango's evolution, TANGO BAR is straightforward in its presentation and concept, skillful performances (acting as well as dancing), screenplay, and deft direction by Marcos Zurinaga (helming his second theatrical feature). TANGO BAR is both a fascinating musical—close to one-half of its fast-paced 90 minutes is devoted to dance numbers performed by world-renowned exponents of the art form, including dancers from the stage production "Tango Argentino"—and a documentary employing historical narration and vintage film clips to illustrate how the tango evolved among Argentina's lower classes, then broadened its popularity throughout Europe and America. (Clips range from Gene Kelly dancing a familiar tango in "Anchors Aweigh" to Rudolph Valentino's fancy footwork in the silent masterpiece THE FOUR HORSEMEN OF THE APOCALYPSE.)

The story skeleton upon which the whole hangs concerns the reunion of Antonio (Ruben Juarez, said to be the foremost tango singer and bandoneon player in Argentina) with fellow cabaret entertainers Ricardo (Raul Julia) and Elena (Valeria Lynch, who has been hailed as the number one female pop singer in Latin America) following Juarez's 10 years of self-imposed exile from his native Buenos Aires in protest of the military takeover of his country. These three stars of the Tango Bar jointly founded the unique nightspot. Juarez and Lynch were once lovers, but she chose to remain behind in Buenos Aires with Julia when Juarez departed, and the questions of how Juarez will react to the new relationship between his former lover and his best friend and whether Lynch will go back to Juarez thicken the bare-bones plot. The leads acquit themselves well within the confines of this tale told in flashback, which pleasantly surprises in its inherent gentleness and sweetness (though there is some implied violence in a few of the dance numbers). The three friends eventually have a poignant encounter and, together again, delve into nostalgia as they perform before an appreciative cabaret audience in what becomes a truly memorable reunion. The film is for the most part acceptable viewing for the entire family, although the adult romantic complications that arise briefly among the three principals, along with some of the more sensual gyrations performed by the dancers, may disqualify it for very young children. *(Adult situations.)*

p, Roberto Gandara and Juan Carlos Codazzi; d, Marcos Zurinaga; w, Jose Pablo Feinman, Juan Carlos Codazzi, and Marcos Zurinaga; ph, Marcos Zurinaga; ed, Pablo Mari; m, Atilio Stampone; prod d, Maria Julia Bertotto.

Docu-drama/Musical

(PR:C MPAA:NR)

Ⓥ**TAP****½
110m Tri-Star c
Gregory Hines *(Max Washington)*, Suzzanne Douglas *(Amy)*, Sammy Davis Jr. *(Little Mo)*, Savion Glover *(Louis)*, Joe Morton *(Nicky)*, Dick Anthony Williams *(Francis)*, Sandman Sims *(Sandman)*, Bunny Briggs *(Bunny)*, Steve Condos *(Steve)*, Jimmy Slyde *(Slim)*, Pat Rico *(Spats)*, Arthur Duncan *(Arthur)*, Harold Nicholas *(Harold)*, Jane Goldberg, Frances E. Nealy, Dianne Walker, Dorothy Wasserman *(Shim Sham Dancers)*, Louis Castle *(Anthony)*, Barbara Perry *(Milly)*, Lloyd Kino *(Party Hood)*, Kevin Guillaume *(Piano Player)*, Randy Brenner *(Brian)*, Joel Weiss *(Limo Driver)*, Garner "Skip" Thomas, King Errisson, Elmira Collins, Alvino Bennett, David Abravanel, Lanny Cordolla, Chris Tedesco *(Harry's Band)*, Mike Anthony Perna, Pat Zicari *(Street Musicians)*, Bill Anagnos, Cheryl Baxter, Frederick Boothe, Paul Delvecchio, Sharie Dietz, Linda Sohl Donnell, Carla Earle, Ruddy L. Garner, Owen Johnston II, Shaun Jones, Stephenie Lawton, Bernie Lenoff, Terry Lindholm, Jamie Pisano, Van Porter, Karen Prunczik, Nikki Rene, Kelly Shenefiel, Wynonna Smith, Chance Taylor, Catherine Wilkinson, Damon Winmon, Steve Zimmerman *(Dancers)*.

As every aficionado knows, the final curtain came down on the golden era musicals several decades ago; however, this film, a boon for lovers of tap dancing, is helping to bring back that special magic that's been missing so long from Hollywood. After doing time in Sing-Sing for burglary, Hines, the son of a legendary hoofer, returns to his late father's seedy Harlem dance studio. Haunted by memories of his youth as a tap-dancing child prodigy, he feels again rhythmic stirrings he thought had died within him. In the studio's private third-floor practice room, he bares his soul through his dancing and quickly attracts the attention of former Apollo Theater headliners-in-residence Sims, Briggs, Condos, Slyde, Rico, Duncan and Nicholas (of the Nicholas Brothers), as well as an ailing Davis, Hines' mentor and his father's best friend. A "challenge" dance ensues that highlights the high-stepping of each of the veteran hoofers, and speaks to Hines' condition. In his heart he yearns to interpret the complex rhythms of the streets, but he rationalizes that a return to a life of crime will be more profitable than the dancer's dream that brought him little more than abject poverty. Meanwhile, Hines attempts to rekindle a romance with Douglas, Davis' beautiful daughter, a dance instructor he deserted in favor of life as a second-story man. He also attempts to renew his relationship with Glover, Douglas' 14-year-old son, whom Hines tried to raise as his own. Encouraged by Douglas, Hines auditions unsuccessfully for the solo tap spot in a Broadway musical hit. Feeling thwarted and not yet convinced of the promise of Davis' plan to merge tap dancing with rock (with Tap-Tronics, an innovation that connects a dancer's shoes to a synthesizer to create thrilling rhythmic musical effects), Hines decides to commit another burglary at the urging of Morton, his former partner in crime. Fortunately, Hines changes his mind, returns to Douglas, and helps realize Davis' dream of combining tap and rock.

TAP is the first film to attempt not only to update tap dancing from the days of Bill Robinson, Fred Astaire, and Gene Kelly, but also to consider the darker side of this truly American art form. A tough jazz tap is brilliantly rendered during the film's opening sequence when Hines, in prison, hears the irritating rhythm of a dripping water pipe and taps out his anger, frustration, and despair. Although too subdued in mood at times (TAP has a tendency to remain earthbound when it should soar), and despite some obvious plot contrivances, the picture still manages to be a very special one—thanks largely to the wonderful hoofing by Gregory Hines and the seven veteran tappers. The film's unabashed highlight is that dazzling "challenge" dance in which everyone plies his talents with astonishing proficiency. Writer-director Nick Castle, Jr. (whose father collaborated with Astaire and Kelly) also pays homage to vintage musicals by incorporating a charming Hines-Douglas rooftop rendition of an Astaire-Rogers classic, "Cheek to Cheek." Another unique moment is a street dance that utilizes various urban sounds to inspire an electrifying group ensemble routine. Finally, Hines dazzles with an incredible display of fancy footwork in the film's Tap-Tronics finale. Ultimately, TAP becomes an interesting blend of contemporary and old-fashioned musical styles, offering enough tapping, romancing, pathos, and suspense to be genuinely appealing to all ages. Songs include: "All I Want Is Forever" (Diane Warren, performed by Regina Belle, James "J.T." Taylor), "Max's Theme" (Stanley Clarke, performed by Clarke), "Lover's Intuition" (Joe Ericksen, Barbara Rothstein, Dorothy Gazeley, performed by Amy Keys), "Strong as Steel" (Warren, performed by Gregory Abbott), "Baby What You Want Me to Do" (Jimmy Reed, performed by Etta James), "Bad Boy" (Dennis Matkosky, Matthew Wilder, performed by

Sandman Sims, Henry LeTang, Gregory Hines and Sammy Davis Jr. in TAP (©Tri-Star).

Teena Marie), "Forget the Girl" (Everton DeLuke McCalla, Jeffrey Calvert, performed by Tony Terry), "Somebody Like You" (Gerard Mansis, Tony Valor, Michel Mansis, performed by Melissa Rowan), "Can't Escape the Rhythm" (James Newton Howard, Glen Ballard, performed by Gregory Hines), "Free" (Matkosky, Wilder, performed by Russ Titelman, Gwen Guthrie), "On the Sunny Side of the Street" (Dorothy Fields, Jimmy McHugh, performed by Bunny Briggs), "Stormy Monday" (Aaron T. Walker, performed by T. Bone Walker), "Cheek to Cheek" (Irving Berlin). *(Brief nudity, profanity, adult situations, violence.)*

p, Gary Adelson and Richard Vane; d, Nick Castle Jr.; w, Nick Castle Jr.; ph, David Gribble (CFI color); ed, Patrick Kennedy; m, James Newton Howard; md, Joe Sill; prod d, Patricia Norris; set d, Leslie Morales; spec eff, Phil Cory; cos, Patricia Norris; chor, Henry Le Tang; stunts, Greg Elam; makeup, Michelle Buhler.

Dance/Drama   (PR:C MPAA:PG-13)

Ⓥ**TEEN WITCH***
105m Trans World c
Robyn Lively *(Louise)*, Dan Gauthier *(Brad)*, Joshua Miller *(Richie)*, Caren Kaye *(Margaret)*, Dick Sargent *(Frank)*, Lisa Fuller *(Randa)*, Mandy Ingber *(Polly)*, Zelda Rubinstein *(Serena)*, Noah Blake *(Ahet)*, Tina-Marie Caspary *(Shawn)*, Megan Gallivan *(Kiki)*, Alsari Al-Shehali *(Vincent)*, Shelly Berman *(Mr. Weaver)*.

Lively, a bright but shy high-school girl, has a crush on Gauthier, the handsome star of the football team. As things stand, her chances of winning his affections are nonexistent. Not only is Lively unpopular, but Gauthier already has a gorgeous cheerleader girl friend (Fuller). All this changes, however, when Lively visits the home of Rubinstein, a local fortune teller. Rubinstein explains to Lively that some of the girl's ancestors were witches and that she will "come into her powers" in one week, on her 16th birthday. In this way the teen witch is born, and Lively proceeds to use her new powers both to exact revenge on those who have done her wrong—most notably, English teacher Berman—and to win popularity and Gauthier.

One keeps waiting for something interesting to happen in TEEN WITCH, but it never does. Notwithstanding its supernatural elements, the film is basically a standard teenage love story, and a squeaky clean one at that. Lively is a good witch; Rubinstein's attempts to corrupt her are all good-natured; and even Fuller, the blonde you love to hate, is too vapid to be a bad girl. What's more, the film is full of clean-cut, cheery teenagers who attend an array of school dances, plays, and football

games. TEEN WITCH also offers several musical numbers, the strangest of which, an extravaganza in the girls' locker-room, is reminiscent of "Beach Party" movies. Most of the film's percussive songs are unmemorable, though the music-videolike opening credit sequence is, perhaps, the best part of the film.

As the teen witch, the adorable Robyn Lively rises above an awful script and a total lack of direction. A natural, she never overacts, and, against all odds, she manages to convey just the right blend of youthful beauty and awkwardness. Regrettably, the best thing that can be said about costar Dan Gauthier's performance is that he looks good. If teenage girls still watch this kind of movie in search of heartthrobs, it may not matter that Gauthier can't act. But, unlike "Beach Party" pretty boys Fabian and Frankie Avalon, Gauthier doesn't even sing! Still, TEEN WITCH does offer some wonderful cameos; however, because director Dorian Walker has no idea where to aim his camera, and because the writers have no feel for comedy, the contributions of Shelly Berman and Dick Sargent (TV's "Bewitched") are wasted.

The film also has its share of technical problems. In particular, the lighting is badly handled. Using the same lighting intensity for both interior and exterior scenes, the film is blinding. Only the scenes in the fortune teller's house appear anything like normal. The editing also works against the film's success, and destroys what might otherwise have been a wonderful scene, in which a home-economics teacher has to give her first talk on sex.

Pleasant but bland, TEEN WITCH is the cinematic equivalent of vanilla ice cream.

p, Alana Lambros and Rafael Eisenman; d, Dorian Walker; w, Vernon Zimmerman and Robin Menken; ph, Marc Reshovsky (CFI Color); ed, Natan Zahavi; m, Richard Elliot; prod d, Stephen Rice; art d, Dana Torrey; set d, Anna Rita Raineri; spec eff, Eddie Surkin; stunts, Willie Chowder; makeup, Jenny Brown.

Fantasy   (PR:A MPAA:PG-13)

Ⓥ**TERROR WITHIN, THE***
86m Concorde c
George Kennedy *(Hal)*, Andrew Stevens *(David)*, Starr Andreeff *(Sue)*, Terri Treas *(Linda)*, John LaFayette *(Andre)*, Tommy Hinchley *(Neil)*, Yvonne Saa *(Karen)*, Roren Sumner *(Gargoyle)*.

THE TERROR WITHIN, produced by Roger Corman's Concorde Pictures, is a completely unoriginal, uninspired mess—one that freely borrows from Ridley Scott's ALIEN and James Cameron's ALIENS, and does so shamelessly. The end result is a montage of stock scenes strung loosely together by a thread of a story, a movie that

plays more like a made-for-television film than the major theatrical release it means to be.

Kennedy stars as the leader of a small group of soldiers living beneath the ground in the Mojave Desert. It's the early 21st century and the Earth is now a desolate planet, its millions of inhabitants having been killed off by a plague, the result of a major lab accident. While searching for food above ground, two soldiers are killed, prompting Kennedy to send his number one man, Stevens, to investigate. After an extensive search, Stevens stumbles upon a cave full of slaughtered men, and has only a moment to ponder the horror before a terrified woman runs past. He catches her and takes her back to the base, where the team doctor examines the woman and announces that she is pregnant. Meanwhile, noises can be heard from above— the inhuman growls of the terrifying gargoyle-like creatures that now populate the surface world. Next, the pregnant woman, who the day before was judged a mere three months pregnant, is literally full to bursting—giving birth to a monster (exploding, of course, from her abdomen in the usual geyser of red) that escapes into the air vent system. The soldiers break into groups to hunt the mutant, which, as expected, is growing rapidly. One by one, all are killed, with Kennedy being one of the first to go (most likely because the production couldn't afford his services for more than a few days), until Stevens and the medical officer are the only ones left to battle the beast. Eventually, they kill it by driving it into a large air duct (with the help of a dog whistle, wouldn't you know) and chop it to pieces with the machine's fan blades. Relieved, they explode the base and set out on foot for the nearest settlement, in the Rocky Mountains.

THE TERROR WITHIN is a prime example of the thinking that plagues Hollywood today, the idea that "if it worked once, it can work again, and again, and so on," leaving the moviegoing public stupified with boredom. It's sad to watch a film like this. Granted, Roger Corman, the king of the Bs, was never one to offer the public completely original material, but this film stoops lower than usual. Everything is borrowed, even down to the sets, and the performances are mediocre at best. George Kennedy sleepwalks through his role; Andrew Stevens gives it his best shot but quickly becomes a victim of the terrible production. Director Thierry Notz's style is nonexistent and the monster, the real star in this type of film, is a special-effects joke—not much scarier that a Halloween costume bought at the local five-and-dime. They say that imitation is the truest form of flattery. If that is so, Scott and Cameron can rest assured that they are truly loved at Concorde Pictures. *(Violence, gore effects, profanity.)*

p, Roger Corman, Rodman Flender, and Reid Shane; d, Thierry Notz; w, Thomas M. Cleaver; ph, Ronn Schmidt (Foto-Kem Color); ed, Brent Schoenfeld; m, Rick Conrad; prod d, Kathleen B. Cooper; spec eff, Dean Jones.

Horror   (PR:O MPAA:R)

ⓥTHREE FUGITIVES**

96m Touchstone-Silver Screen Partners IV/BV c

Nick Nolte *(Daniel Lucas)*, Martin Short *(Ned Perry)*, Sarah Rowland Doroff *(Meg Perry)*, James Earl Jones *(Detective Dugan)*, Alan Ruck *(Tener)*, Kenneth McMillan *(Horvath)*, David Arnott *(Bank Teller)*, Bruce McGill *(Charlie)*, Lee Garlington *(Woman Cop)*, Sy Richardson *(Tucker)*, Rocky Giordani *(Bowles)*, Rick Hall *(Dog Handler)*, Bill Cross *(Guard at Prison)*, Stanley Brock *(Release Sergeant)*, John Procaccino *(Highway Patrolman)*, Kathy Kinney *(Receptionist)*, Way Ching Yu *(Girl in Children's Home)*, Jack McGee *(Fisherman)*, Albert Henderson *(Man in Raincoat)*, Larry Cox, Jeff Perry *(Orderlies)*, Rhoda Gemignani *(Radio Operator)*, Clive Rosengren *(Desk Sergeant)*, Maryssa Larose *(Woman at Bank)*, Scott Lincoln *(Passenger Cop)*, John C. Cooke, Yahoots Magoondi *(Thugs)*, Mike MacDonald *(Sergeant)*, Bruno Acalinas, Lance August *(Motorcycle Cops)*, Charles Noland *(Bartender)*, Anthony Frederick *(Cop with Phone)*, Terence Hollingsworth *(Money Quick Customer)*, Dean Smith *(Playboy)*, Richard E. Butler, R.L. Tolbert *(Watchmen)*.

While film distributors have virtually halted the release of foreign-language movies because of American unwillingness to read subtitles, Hollywood has discovered a way to exploit overseas product, taking successful French comedies and remaking them in English with American directors and popular American actors—in other words, extracting their *foreignness*. This practice has spawned such forgettable fare as the 1981 Billy Wilder-directed comedy BUDDY BUDDY, starring Jack Lemmon and Walter Matthau (based on L'EMMERDEUR, 1973); the 1982 Richard Pryor comedy THE TOY (based on LE JOUET, 1976); the 1984 Gene Wilder-Gilda Radner comedy THE WOMAN IN RED (based on PARDON MON AFFAIRE, 1977); the 1985 Tom Hanks film THE MAN WITH ONE RED SHOE (based on THE TALL BLOND MAN WITH ONE RED SHOE, 1972); 1986's DOWN AND OUT IN BEVERLY HILLS (atrociously reinterpreting Jean Renior's 1932 classic BOUDU SAVED FROM DROWNING); the monster hit of 1987, THREE MEN AND A BABY (based on TROIS HOMMES ET UN COUFFIN, 1985); and, in 1989, the double-header of COUSINS (based on COUSIN,

COUSINE, 1975) and THREE FUGITIVES (based on LES FUGITIFS, 1986). The formula has only spawned one runaway success, but no matter, one $200 million hit will justify a whole string of flops in Hollywood. Now, with the advent of THREE FUGITIVES, we are treated to the spectacle of a French director remaking *his own* film for American audiences. Francis Veber (who wrote or directed an inordinate amount of the pictures mentioned above) actually struck the deal with Touchstone executives *before shooting a frame* of LES FUGITIFS, which starred Gerard Depardieu and Pierre Richard. In the American version, Nick Nolte and Martin Short are cast in the Depardieu and Richard roles (a nice piece of casting, actually) and the action is set in Portland, Oregon.

Paroled from prison after serving a five-year sentence for armed robbery, Nolte, a veteran thief, is met by police detectives Jones and Ruck, a pair of cops who have arrested him several times and wouldn't trust him as far as they can throw him. They escort him to their car and take him for a ride, warning him to stay out of trouble. When they offer to drop him someplace, Nolte suggests a bank, and though he merely wants to open an account, the paranoid detectives begin to wonder if he isn't flagrantly resuming his life of crime. While Nolte stands in line, a nervous little man with a stocking mask over his head (Short) bursts into the bank and announces a hold-up. Brandishing a pistol and a grenade, Short demands that the large sack he carries be filled with cash. He tosses the bag to a teller, and when the teller fills it and tosses it back, it gets caught in a chandelier high above Short's head. Seeing that Nolte is the biggest man in the room, Short forces the ex-robber to help him retrieve the money. By this time, a silent alarm has gone off and the cops—including Jones and Ruck, now convinced that Nolte has robbed the bank—have the place surrounded. Short—whose face was revealed when he attempted to pull the pin from the grenade with his teeth, thus tearing his stocking mask—makes the incredulous Nolte his hostage and forces him outside. Knowing that the cops think that he's the robber, Nolte attempts to capture the much-smaller Short himself by thrashing him about like a rag-doll; however, the police think it's all a ruse and, sensing a no-win situation, Nolte makes a getaway with Short. Totally dominating the little thief, Nolte tries to turn Short in by dragging him into the police station, but again the cops think Nolte the fugitive and attempt to arrest him. Nolte and Short escape again, but during the chaotic chase, Short accidentally shoots Nolte in the leg. Feeling responsible, he takes Nolte to McMillan, a senile veterinarian who mistakes Nolte for a big dog. We soon learn

that the criminally inexperienced Short is an unemployed man desperate to raise money to send his young daughter, Doroff, to a special school. The child has not spoken a word since the death of her mother, but when she and Nolte meet, the girl begins to open up to the big man and even says, "Don't go," when they are about to part ways. This, of course, melts the heart of softy Nolte, who forgives Short for dragging him into this mess and helps them evade the police—but with the stipulation that Short sign a confession clearing Nolte of the robbery. Nolte takes the document to the cops, who accept it and drop the charges, but Jones and Ruck keep an eye on the ex-con. Fulfilling his part of the bargain, Nolte helps Short and Doroff escape into Canada by dressing Doroff up like a little boy and Short like a pregnant woman. Posing as a typical American family on vacation, the trio make a run for the border, with the cops in hot pursuit. After several slapstick misadventures—including Short's faking labor for the benefit of a patrolman and a subsequent trip to the emergency room—our heroes make it into Canada for the happy ending.

An obvious attempt to tap into the same audience that flocked to THREE MEN AND A BABY (indeed, this could have been titled "Two Men and a Toddler"), THREE FUGITIVES is as about as lifeless as they come. Part of Veber's deal with Touchstone Pictures required that the French version of THREE FUGITIVES, LES FUGITIFS, not be released in the US until after the American version had come and gone. Those who have seen the original version report that not only is the American version a scene-for-scene remake of the French, it is actually *shot for shot* the same film. Veber's rather uninspired approach to directing the American version goes a long way toward explaining why THREE FUGITIVES seems so formulaic, mechanical, and tedious, despite a pair of engaging performances from Short and Nolte. While the opening 20 minutes or so are fairly amusing, the picture quickly disintegrates into an uneasy combination of extremely violent slapstick and incredibly treacly sentiment, with Nolte alternating between beating the snot out of Short, et al., and getting all maudlin over the fate of the little girl. At times the film veers toward exploring more than just the variety of ways Nolte can throttle people for Three Stooges-type laughs, as in the scene in which Nolte and Short pose as husband and wife, but Veber is either blissfully ignorant of the implications of his narrative (men make the best women?) or simply chooses to ignore them. What the viewer is left with, then, is the sight of two talented actors struggling to inject a modicum of spontaneity into this listless project, and a nice character turn from the late Kenneth McMillan, in his final role, as the addled

Martin Short and Nick Nolte in THREE FUGITIVES (©Buena Vista).

vet who thinks Nolte is a dog and Doroff a kitten (the wordless scene wherein he enters Nolte's recovery room and quietly puts down a bowl of dog food for the dumfounded ex-con is the biggest laugh in the film). Although THREE FUGITIVES was far from a major hit for Touchstone, it certainly made enough money to encourage the studio to continue plundering product from overseas in the hopes of assembling another megahit like THREE MEN AND A BABY. *(Violence.)*

p, Lauren Shuler Donner; d, Francis Veber; w, Francis Veber; ph, Haskell Wexler (Metrocolor); ed, Bruce Green; m, David McHugh; prod d, Rick Carter; art d, Margie Stone McShirley; set d, Lauren Cory; spec eff, Roland Tantin; cos, April Ferry; stunts, Joe Dunne; makeup, Edouard F. Henriques III.

Comedy/Crime

(PR:A-C   MPAA:PG-13)

⊙TIME TRACKERS*
87m Concorde c
Ned Beatty *(Harry)*, Wil Shriner *(Charles)*, Kathleen Beller *(R.J.)*, Bridget Hoffman *(Madeline)*, Alex Hyde-White *(Edgar)*, Lee Bergere *(Zandor)*.

It takes a certain flair to pull off a time-travel movie, and unfortunately there is little flair in TIME TRACKERS. Produced by Roger Corman on an ultra-low budget, TIME TRACKERS follows the adventures of three scientists as they chase

a madman through the ages. The film begins in 2033, when Shriner and Beller are experimenting with a time machine. Keeping an eye on the experiments is the evil Bergere, who, after witnessing a successful time jaunt, steals the machine's computer chip and uses a prototype of the device to escape into the past. Once there, he plans to murder one of Beller's ancestors (thus negating the future existence of Beller and her scientist father) and claim the invention as his own. Shriner and Beller, joined by weapons expert Hoffman, chase Bergere to the year 1991, where they encounter undercover detective Beatty and foil Bergere's first assassination attempt. Bergere flees his pursuers by heading further into the past, while Beatty follows the suspicious looking trio on Bergere's tail and ends up traveling back to 1146 England with them. The film now turns into your basic medieval adventure, complete with knights and kings. It seems that Bergere has taken on the role of King and is about to marry the sister of the Red Duke (Alex Hyde-White), whom Bergere has been trying to capture, because Hyde-White is also an ancestor of Beller's and his death would wipe her family line out. Shriner and Hoffman are caught, while Beller and Beatty find appropriate clothing and search for Bergere. Beatty teams up with a monk and Beller meets Hyde-White in the forest, falling in love with him (Shriner, meanwhile falls for Hoffman). Together, with help from Beatty, the time

travelers foil Bergere's plans, bring him back to the year 2033 for trial, and send him off careening through time endlessly. Beller then returns to 1146 to be with her true love, Hyde-White.

It all sounds very stupid, but even a plot this ridiculous can be made to work in the right hands. TIME TRACKERS, however, fails miserably, and is one of the most ineptly made films in recent memory. While borrowing heavily from other films, especially THE TERMINATOR and TIME AFTER TIME, it takes on none of the quality of its progenitors. Shots are badly lit, the photography is dull, and the stock footage from other films is clumsily employed (at one point, a scene using 25 extras magically changes into a scene with what looks like a *thousand* extras, and brighter photography). The dialog is so badly looped that the actors might as well be appearing in a bad kung-fu movie, and the editing may have well been done with bush shears. The actors seem sadly unaware of their predicament, however, save Ned Beatty, who plays his undercover cop with about as much subtlety as a sledgehammer. Complete with a bad suit and a seemingly endless supply of dumb jokes, he seems to be having fun. Near the end of TIME TRACKERS, Beatty is dropped off in the year 1991, steps out of the time machine (still in his medieval garb), and walks through the park, commenting, "I feel like such an idiot." He couldn't have summed it up better. *(Adult situations, violence.)*

p, Roger Corman; d, Howard R. Cohen; w, Howard R. Cohen; ph, Ronn Schmidt (Foto-Kem Color); ed, Brent Schoenfeld; m, Parmer Fuller; art d, Peter Flynn; spec eff, Gregory Landerer; cos, Twenty-First Century; makeup, Roy Knyrim.

Science Fiction   (PR:A   MPAA:PG)

⊙TO DIE FOR*½
90m Skouras c
Brendan Hughes *(Vlad Tepish)*, Scott Jacoby *(Martin Planting)*, Sydney Walsh *(Kate Wooten)*, Amanda Wyss *(Celia Kett)*, Steve Bond *(Tom)*.

Vampires are alive and well and living in modern-day Los Angeles in TO DIE FOR, which in its opening scene shows a young couple, Walsh and Jacoby, at a party. During the evening, Walsh becomes mysteriously drawn to a strange man; meanwhile, a hideous monster murders someone in the parking lot. When Walsh leaves the party, she is followed home by the monster but not attacked. The next day, real-estate agent Walsh is instructed to show a house (actually a castle) at night. Sure enough, the client turns out to be the mystery man from the party, Hughes, who falls in love with the place and with Walsh. Walsh's roommate, Wyss, goes to work for Hughes and also falls under his spell, leading to the inevitable peck on the neck. Once bitten, Wyss shocks her fiance and Walsh with her strange behavior. The following week, Hughes and his friend Bond—the beast from the parking lot—throw a big party at the castle. Determined to woo Walsh away from Hughes, Bond begins telling her about his and Hughes' dark past, only to be interrupted by the very nervous Hughes. Downstairs, one of the guests discovers a coffin, and Jacoby finds an old book about vampires. (In fact, as is later revealed, Hughes is not just your everyday run-of-the-mill vampire, but the infamous Vlad the Impaler, the real-life, 15th-century original of Bram Stoker's Dracula.) When Wyss is attacked and then taken to the hospital later that evening, Jacoby and Wyss' fiance visit her sickbed and drive a stake through her heart, since Wyss has been transformed into a blood-sucker herself. Finally, Walsh confronts Hughes, and they somehow end up in bed. Bond then shows up out of the blue and starts a fight with Hughes. Things get pretty ugly—especially after Hughes and Bond are transformed into monsters—and Bond ends up dead, impaled on a bedpost. Meanwhile, worried that Walsh might become one of the undead, the guys rush from the hospital to Hughes' castle. They manage to rescue Walsh, and Hughes is exposed to daylight—spelling death for the vampire.

With very high production values (especially the art direction), decent acting, and commendable direction (by Deran Sarafian), TO DIE FOR is better than the average horror film on the market these days. Unfortunately, it remains run-of-the-mill in its overemphasis on graphic violence and gory special effects. Had the filmmakers spent more time developing a sophisticated story, TO DIE FOR might have been a more engaging movie. *(Graphic violence, profanity, nudity, sexual situations.)*

p, Barin Kumar and Greg Sims; d, Deran Sarafian; w, Leslie King; ph, David Boyd; ed, Dennis Dolan; m, Cliff Eidelman; prod d, Maxine Shepard; art d, Greg Oehler; spec eff, John Carl Buechler; cos, Cynthia Bergstrom; makeup, Jerrie Werkman.

Horror   **(PR:O MPAA:R)**

TO KILL A PRIEST**
(Fr.) 117m J.P. Prods-FR3 Films/COL c
(LE COMPLOT)
Christopher Lambert *(Fr. Alek)*, Ed Harris *(Stefan)*, Joanne Whalley *(Anna)*, Joss Ackland *(Colonel)*, David Suchet *(Bishop)*, Tim Roth *(Feliks)*, Timothy Spall *(Igor)*, Pete Postlethwaite *(Joseph)*, Cherie Lunghi *(Halina)*, Tom Radcliffe *(Young Soldier)*, Gregor Fisher *(Fr. Irek)*, Charles Condou *(Mirek)*, Andre Chaumeau *(Wacek)*, Vincent Grass *(Volak)*, Matyelok Gibbs *(Colonel's Wife)*,

Nicolas Serreau *(Staszek)*, Brian Glover *(Minister)*, Paul Crauchet *(Alek's Father)*, Janine Darcey *(Alek's Mother)*, Wojciech Pszoniak *(Bridge Player)*, Anne-Marie Pisani, Jerome Flynn, Eugeniusz Priwieziencew, Georges Birt, Huguette Faget.

With the American media filled with earthshaking news from Eastern Europe, 1989 seemed like a perfect year for the US release of TO KILL A PRIEST (which came to European screens in 1988). Based on the 1984 murder of Solidarity supporter Fr. Jerzy Popieluszko, this powerful English-language film has all the marks of a huge hit. To begin with it was directed by renowned Polish expatriate Agnieszka Holland—known for her Oscar-nominated film ANGRY HARVEST, her script for the critically acclaimed ANNA, and her collaboration with Andrzej Wajda. It also features a fine cast that includes French heartthrob Christopher Lambert and the highly-respected Ed Harris (THE ABYSS), and it revolves around an explosive story of power and politics. Unlike Jerzy Skolimowski's brilliant and subtle MOONLIGHTING (1982), which appeared at the dawn of Poland's Solidarity movement, TO KILL A PRIEST treats its subject matter on a grand Hollywood scale. Overflowing with emotional intensity, Holland's film is also highly symbolic; yet the characters are so burdened with movie contrivances that, despite its noble motives, the film becomes laughable.

It opens in Warsaw, on a snowy Christmas Eve, 1981, as martial law is instituted and tanks roll menacingly down the streets. At one end of the political spectrum is Lambert's heroic priest. Standing up to the military might of the Communist Party, he holds vigils in his church, prays for peace, and gives sanctuary to the politically persecuted. At the other end of the spectrum is militia captain Harris, a devoted cog in the Party machine, who would like nothing more than to rid Poland of this powerful cleric. Posing as a parishioner, Harris infiltrates Lambert's church and witnesses the chilling spectacle of one of the priest's sermons. Haunted by the specter of this charismatic leader, Harris eagerly accepts the opportunity to head a secret death squad; with the priest dead, the Solidarity movement will theoretically unravel, and the Communist Party will once again hold the political reins of a country that is careening out of control. Faced with the reality of his mission, Harris is so tormented by inner demons that he furtively warns the priest of his impending assassination. Instead of heeding Harris' warning, the priest bravely proceeds with his daily schedule. On a lonely stretch of road, Lambert is kidnaped by Harris and two lackeys (Roth and Spall). Obviously frightened and inexperienced, Harris and his men beat the priest to death over the course of the evening. Later, the captain's

superiors in the Party treat him not as a hero but as a scapegoat, leaving him to bear the blame in the official investigation that follows.

Everything that exists around the edges of TO KILL A PRIEST is worthy of praise: the supporting performances of British actors Joss Ackland (WHITE MISCHIEF), Joanne Whalley (SCANDAL), Tim Roth (THE HIT), and Peter Postlethwaite (DISTANT VOICES, STILL LIVES); the crisp cinematography of Adam Holender; Georges Delerue's score; and the set design that effectively transforms French locations into the Warsaw of the early 1980s. Much more problematic is the center of the film, which is undone by the filmmakers' attempt to arrive at an easily exportable commercial property. Working in English, Holland lacks the deftness and sincerity that helped her achieve success with her earlier pictures. Dialog that should deeply unnerve the audience merely induces squirms of embarrassment.

Unfortunately, Holland receives no help from her two leads. Lambert (who was also miscast in HIGHLANDER and THE SICILIAN) looks perpetually sleepy and lacks the charisma to be believable as a political firebrand; the very American-looking Harris, while interestingly cast, recklessly hams up an already hammy part. However, what is most disappointing about TO KILL A PRIEST is its failure to live up to its potential. Although it raises a number of very important issues—the Polish Catholic church's role as both spiritual and political guide; the waning power of the Communist Party in Poland and, by extension, in all of Eastern Europe; and the implied collaboration between the Church and the Communist Party in maintaining the status quo—the film is content to waste time on every plot contrivance imaginable. A story of this nature always offers the opportunity to tempt the priest with the ways of the flesh, and, of course, Holland doesn't miss her chance. Moreover, every time Harris' assassin is driven to do or say something evil, Holland balances his character with humane attributes—the most absurd example being the captain's relationship with his young son and Pope, the puppy he gives him. Worst of all is the weak psychological connection Holland makes between Harris' bungled but ultimately successful act of murder and his virility as a lover. It should come as no surprise that TO KILL A PRIEST (like so many other releases from Columbia Pictures, including 1989's THE ADVENTURES OF BARON MUNCHAUSEN and THE BIG PICTURE, and a slew of pictures from 1988) was dumped into a handful of theaters with little or no publicity. Hoping to find some sort of built-in audience, Columbia opened the picture in Chicago —the city with the largest concentration of

Poles outside of Warsaw. Their strategy failed, however, and TO KILL A PRIEST disappeared almost immediately—just weeks before the prayers of the Solidarity movement were answered and the Communist Party's stranglehold on Poland was loosened. Songs include: "The Many Crimes of Cain" (Joan Baez), "Church Song" (Zbigniew Preisner). *(Violence, profanity, sexual situations, adult situations.)*

p, Jean-Pierre Alessandri; d, Agnieszka Holland; w, Agnieszka Holland and Jean-Yves Pitoun; ph, Adam Holender; ed, Herve de Luze; m, Georges Delerue, Zbigniew Preisner, and Giuseppe Verdi; prod d, Emile Ghigo; spec eff, Jean-Charles Drevel; cos, Anna Sheppard; stunts, Daniel Breton; makeup, Didier Lavergne.

Drama   **(PR:O MPAA:R)**

TOO BEAUTIFUL FOR YOU***
(Fr.) 91m Cine
Valse-D.D.-Orly-S.E.D.I.F.-T.F.1/Orion Classics c
(TROP BELLE POUR TOI)
Gerard Depardieu *(Bernard Barthelemy)*, Josiane Balasko *(Colette Chevassu)*, Carole Bouquet *(Florence Barthelemy/ Neighbor)*, Roland Blanche *(Marcello)*, Francois Cluzet *(Pascal Chevassu)*, Didier Benureau *(Leonce)*, Philippe Loffredo *(Tanguy)*, Sylvie Orcier *(Marie-Catherine)*, Myriam Boyer *(Genevieve)*, Flavien Lebarbe *(The Son)*, Juana Marques *(The Daughter)*, Denise Chalem *(Lorene)*, Jean-Louis Cordina *(Gaby)*, Stephane Auberghen *(Paula)*, Philippe Faure *(Colette's Husband)*, Jean-Paul Farre *(Pianist)*, Richard Martin *(Man on the Tram)*, Sylvie Simon *(Receptionist)*.

Bertrand Blier's wry serio-comedy TOO BEAUTIFUL FOR YOU is a love triangle with some unexpected angles. Depardieu, a stolid bourgeois, has made a success of his life, with a thriving business, two bright children, and a surpassingly beautiful, upper-class wife (Bouquet). Into this life comes a stout and no longer young secretary (Balasko) with whom he falls recklessly in love. Electrified with passion, he finds himself in a continual state of sexual excitement in which the woman who should be his wife is his mistress and vice versa. Starting from this topsy-turvy turn of events, Blier (director of GOING PLACES; GET OUT YOUR HANDKERCHIEFS; and the irresistibly wacky MENAGE) fashions a droll and often surreal comedy of manners. TOO BEAUTIFUL FOR YOU is a bedroom farce played in slow motion, however; there is a melancholy undertone to the ironic adultery taking place beneath the bedsheets.

The early scenes, establishing the growing attraction between the beefy boss and his plump secretary-seductress, are the film's most successful. Although Depardieu and his stunning spouse are the

envy of their friends, the picture-perfect Bouquet senses trouble in paradise. Dropping by Depardieu's office unexpectedly, Bouquet is relieved to discover that her husband's office temp is a nonthreatening frump. Depardieu, however, is unable to curb his animal lust and begins absenting himself from hearth and home often enough to reawaken Bouquet's suspicion, a reversal that is also the impetus of a fantasy sequence in which Bouquet appears as Balasko's bedraggled neighbor, who has been abandoned by her husband. In another comic high point, Balasko wanders around a subway station full of men, sharing the afterglow of her love-making with these strangers as if she were the town crier of sexual satisfaction. When presenting such slyly exaggerated versions of reality, director-writer Blier sends our spirits soaring. Unfortunately, as the affair unravels, so does the film—though not before a brilliant set-piece that foreshadows the unhappy ending: through subtle camera movement and costume changes, a dinner party is transformed from a feast for the long-married couple into their wedding celebration, then into yet another party that is crashed by Balasko. By the time Depardieu comes to his senses, his wife has lost all but proprietary interest in him, while Balasko (in flash forwards) settles into a comfortable domestic life with another man. Depardieu is no longer torn between wife and mistress, but abandoned by both.

Since the conceptual interest of Blier's wife-mistress role reversal can only energize his film partially, TOO BEAUTIFUL FOR YOU derives much of its energy from such cinematic devices as flash forwards and internal monologs that express the characters' thoughts. But Blier's narrative freedom and fluid camera cannot provide enough *elan* to preserve the farcically upbeat tone. With no rapprochement in the battle of the sexes, the comedy turns sour as Blier explores his theme, apparently concluding that sexual passion and marital love cannot exist in the same relationship. Blier fails, however, to bring much depth to his observations of how people make their own beds but refuse to lie in them, relying on his considerable technical skills to take the place of insight. Having been led to expect a comedy, one feels betrayed when the film's message turns out to be not only bleak but unedifying. Though TOO BEAUTIFUL FOR YOU remains prodigiously clever, and individual sequences continue to impress, this film about the impossibility of sustaining love is a failure of sustentation in itself. Instead of informing our sadness, Blier's comedic sequences only make it more painful. Musical selections include: Impromptus, Op. 90, Nos. 2 and 3; Andantino, Sonata in D Major, D.959 (performed by Odette Garentlaub);

"Rosamunde," D.797, Entr'acte No. 2 (performed by Elly Ameling, Kurt Masur); String Quartet in D Minor, D.810, No. 14 ("Death and the Maiden") (performed by the Melos Quartet); "Wiegenlied," D.498 (performed by Ameling, Dalton Baldwin); Sonata for Piano and Arpeggione, D.821 (performed by Mstislav Rostropovitch, Benjamin Britten); "Fierabras," D.796, Overture (performed by Paul Angerer); Serenade (performed by Doris Soffel, Roland Keller, Marinus Voorberg); "Deutsche Messe," D.872 ("The Lord's Prayer") (performed by the Tolzer Knabenchor, Gerhard Schmidt-Gaden); "German Dance," D.90, No. 1 (performed by Horst Stein, the Bamberger Symphony); "Zwischenaktmusik," Op. 26, No. 3 (performed by Stein, the Bamberger Symphony); Mass in E-flat Major, D.950 ("Sanctus") (performed by Sawallisch, Donath, Popp, Fassbaender, Schreier, Araiza, Dallapozza, Fischer-Dieskau); Waltz, D.779, No. 18 (performed by Alice Ader), all by Franz Schubert; "Love Story" (Francis Lai). *(Adult situations, profanity, nudity, sexual situations.)*

d, Bertrand Blier; w, Bertrand Blier; ph, Philippe Rousselot (Eastmancolor); ed, Claudine Merlin; m, Franz Schubert; prod d, Theobald Meurisse; cos, Michele Mermande-Cerf; makeup, Joel Lavau.

Comedy   **(PR:O MPAA:R)**

TORA-SAN GOES TO VIENNA***
(Jap.) 111m Shochiku/Kino c
(OTOKOWA TSURAIYOO TORAIJIRO KOKORO NO TABIJI)
Kiyoshi Atsumi *(Torajiro Kuruma, "Tora-San")*, Chieko Baisho *(Sakura Suwa)*, Gin

Kiyoshi Atsumi in TORA SAN GOES TO VIENNA (©Kino International).

Meada *(Hiroshi Suwa)*, Masami Shimojo *(Ryozo Kuruma)*, Chieko Misaki *(Tsune Kuruma)*, Hisao Dazai *(President of Printing Company)*, Chisu Ryu *(Gozen-Sama, Priest)*, Hayato Nakamura *(Mitsuo)*, Keiko Takeshita *(Kumiko)*, Keiko Awaji *(Madam)*, Martin Loschberger *(Hermann)*, Vivien Dybal *(Therese)*, Akira Emoto *(Hyoma Sakaguchi)*.

Tora-San, played by Kiyoshi Atsumi, is a strolling peddler and bumbling dreamer, the Japanese equivalent of Charlie Chaplin's Little Tramp. In Japan, he is a folk hero who has proven his popularity in more than 40 films; to Western audiences, he is of a piece with the comedic tradition of Chaplin and Jacques Tati, the simpleton who allows us to laugh at ourselves and the ridiculous complexity of our lives.

In TORA-SAN GOES TO VIENNA, Tora-San uses some money his sister sent him to take a train trip. The journey is interrupted when his train stops to avoid hitting Sakaguchi (Akira Emoto), a businessman who has thrown himself on the tracks in a suicide attempt. Tora-San suggests to the train conductor that it might not be a good idea to leave the suicidal man alone and, accordingly, begins to help Sakaguchi recover from his depression simply by accepting him. When Sakaguchi tells Tora-San that it has always been his dream to go to Vienna, Tora-San not only urges him to follow that dream, but also—without the foggiest idea where or what Vienna is—agrees to accompany his new friend on the journey. Once the pair arrive in the Austrian capital, the provincial Tora-San is dismayed to discover he can't speak the language, dislikes the cuisine, and has no interest in sightseeing. It's only after he meets and falls in love with Kumiko (Keiko Takeshita), a Japanese working as a tour guide, that he begins to enjoy himself in Vienna, eating Japanese home cooking and meeting Kumiko's remarkable friend, the Madam (who displays several pictures of a man she claims is her husband and a spy, but is actually Orson Welles). Tora-San is destined to be unlucky in love, however, and the film ends as he returns to his native land alone.

Like all great comedy, TORA-SAN GOES TO VIENNA is social commentary. The pressure to succeed in the Japanese business world becomes the undoing of both Sakaguchi and Mitsuo (Hayato Nakamura), Tora-San's nephew, who has failed his college entrance exams and who dreams of following in his uncle's wayward footsteps. Tora-San's family upholds the businessman's ethic, insisting that Tora-San should not take the trip to Vienna on Sakaguchi's tab, because everyone will think he is a bum.

Tora-San, by contrast, is free because he lacks such worldliness. He's bored in Vienna—can't understand all the fuss. Yearning for a Japanese breakfast and for

home, he takes no interest in Viennese cultural monuments, and surmises that Mozart must have been a great man only because of the impressive size of his statue. Although such provincial, old-world ways make us laugh, they strike home, too, just as the Little Tramp's naive mishaps do.

This is the 41st film in the "Tora-San" series, but the first to be released in the US. Yoji Yamada, who directed all but two of Tora-San's previous outings, does so again here (and shares screenwriting credit with Yoshitaka Asama). Yamada's long acquaintance with Tora-San—perennially played by Atsumi—pays off here in his seamless direction and flair for staging comedy, while the wonderful acting engages our sympathies immediately. Atsumi (who professes to be much like Tora-San in real life) displays great timing in the role Yamada created for him, while Emoto's physical precision tells us everything we need to know about the stressed-out businessman Sakaguchi. The stock characters—including the skeptical, wise-cracking elders and Takeshita's pretty young ingenue—will all be recognizable for Western audiences, too. There's no language barrier here.

There are few films to which the overused adjective "poignant" may be more justly applied than this funny and moving tale. Director Yamada has a touch of Frank Capra in him, and his film isn't just a "Japanese movie" but a film that should play everywhere. The themes are universal, and the characters are as old as comedy itself. East doesn't meet West in TORA-SAN GOES TO VIENNA—they already know each other.

p, Kiyoshi Shimazu and Kiyo Kurosu; d, Yoji Yamada; w, Yoji Yamada and Yoshitaka Asama; ph, Tetsuo Takaba; ed, Iwao Ishii; m, Naozumi Yamamoto; art d, Mitsuo Degawa.

Comedy   (PR:A MPAA:NR)

⊙TOXIC AVENGER, PART II, THE*½
95m Lloyd Kaufman-Michael Herz/Troma c

Ron Fazio, John Altamura *(The Toxic Avenger)*, Phoebe Legere *(Claire)*, Rick Collins *(Apocalypse Inc. Chairman)*, Rikiya Yasuoka *(Big Mac)*, Tsutomu Sekine *(Announcer)*, Mayako Katsuragi *(Masami)*, Shinoburyu *(Shockikuyama)*, Lisa Gaye *(Malfaire)*, Jessica Dublin *(Mrs. Junko)*, Jack Cooper *(Mr. Junko)*, Erika Schickel *(Psychiatrist)*.

The sequel to Troma Pictures' most successful film to date is, like the original TOXIC AVENGER, a bizarre mixture of *Mad* magazine-style humor and FRIDAY THE 13TH gore involving a superhero who drinks Drano for lunch and runs around in a shredded pink tutu. This is no ordinary good guy, nor is this an ordinary

film. On occasion this strange mix of ingredients cohere into something that works, but, as with the first installment, TOXIC AVENGER, PART II eventually runs out of ideas and surprises, despite its ambition and good intentions.

Fazio plays Melvin, who, at the beginning of the first film, was pushed into a barrel of toxic waste by a bunch of high-school bullies. When Melvin fished himself out of the bubbling, green liquid he was shocked to find himself transformed into a mop-wielding, tutu-wearing blob of a muscle man—the Toxic Avenger. As TOXIC AVENGER 2 unfolds, we find the Avenger working at a home for the blind in the small, peaceful town of Tromaville. He has found true love with one of the school's many blonde, busty students, and all is well in his world, until Collins, the evil chairman of Apocalypse Inc., decides that Tromaville is the perfect place to dump his company's toxic waste. First, however, he proclaims, the Toxic Avenger will have to be got rid of. One sunny afternoon, Toxic

cially at the beginning and end) that it may entertain die-hard cult film fans. In most cases, however, the best cult films are those that don't appear to have been made as cult films. More than aware that he is a cult film star, Toxie acknowledges his status in practically every frame (to the point of admitting he's just a character in a bad movie). After a while it is simply no longer amusing. *(Graphic violence, nudity, adult situations, sexual situations, profanity.)*

p, Lloyd Kaufman and Michael Herz; d, Michael Herz and Lloyd Kaufman; w, Gay Partington Terry and Lloyd Kaufman (based on a story by Lloyd Kaufman); ph, James London (TVC Color); ed, Joseph McGirr; m, Christopher Demarco and Antonin Dvorak; art d, Alexis Grey; cos, Susan Douglas; stunts, Scott Leva.

Comedy/Science Fiction

(PR:O MPAA:R)

TOXIC AVENGER PART III, THE: THE LAST TEMPTATION OF TOXIE*½
89m Lloyd Kaufman-Michael Herz/Troma c

Ron Fazio, John Altamura *(Toxic Avenger)*, Phoebe Legere *(Claire)*, Rick Collins *(Apocalypse Chairman/The Devil)*, Lisa Gaye *(Malfaire)*, Jessica Dublin *(Mrs. Junko)*, Tsutomu Sekine *(Announcer)*, Michael J. Kaplan *(Little Melvin)*, Traci Mann *(Snake Lady)*.

Based in New Jersey, the Troma Team has gained a reputation as the maker of bizarrely funny low-budget films that have become cult favorites. Humorously violent, badly acted, and full of strange sight gags, films like THE CLASS OF NUKE 'EM HIGH; RABID GRANNIES; and SURF NAZIS MUST DIE have become midnight movie standards. The best of the bunch is THE TOXIC AVENGER, an ultralow-budget science-fiction comedy about a 98-pound nerd who accidentally falls into a barrel of toxic waste and becomes the title superhero, saving Tromaville from corrupt villains. A surprise hit, THE TOXIC AVENGER provided cult movie fans with an abundance of wild violence and big laughs. Fans of the original found the sequel, THE TOXIC AVENGER PART II, a major disappointment, however. Played strictly for laughs (but without much wit), it lacked the dark attitude and willful nastiness of the original.

THE TOXIC AVENGER PART III: THE LAST TEMPTATION OF TOXIE is better than the first sequel, but it, too, fails to capture the spirit of the original. Beginning with a terrific sequence in a video store—in which Toxie (played by Fazio and Altamura) disposes of a group of lunatics in various violent ways—the film once again seems to have found the right balance of comedy, ineptitude, and violence that have been Troma's hallmark. But once the film flashes back to explain Toxie's flirtation with evil, it begins to take itself too seriously. After being brainwashed and given money to pay for an eye operation for his girl friend (played broadly and amusingly by Legere), Toxie begins working for Apocalypse, Inc., an evil company whose sole purpose is to destroy Tromaville. Transformed into a yuppie (complete with Evian water and a Rolex), Toxie loses the love and admiration of the citizens of Tromaville. Finally, he wakes up and starts to fight crime again.

The entire middle section of the movie, involving Toxie's temptation and domestic life, doesn't work. It's not until the film's final reel—which ends with a hilarious showdown between Toxie and the devil—that THE TOXIC AVENGER PART III returns to the approach that cult audiences have found so satisfying. Packed with gross sight gags and bad jokes, the final minutes work wonderfully. The climactic battle includes Toxie changing back to his 98-pound alter ego (Kaplan, who steals the show) and his poor girl friend again losing her eyesight. Ultimately, Toxie destroys the devil (with help from God), and he and Legere marry and live happily ever after.

THE TOXIC AVENGER worked well because directors Michael Herz and Lloyd Kaufman knew they had a bad film on their hands, and they had fun with it. Herz and Kaufman now seem to believe they have become talented filmmakers and biting wits. Regrettably, they are neither. By taking themselves too seriously, Herz and Kaufman have undercut the charm of their "Toxic Avenger" movies and actually made them (if you can believe it) pretentious. Nevertheless, TOXIC AVENGER PART III: LAST TEMPTATION OF TOXIE contains enough goofiness (espe-

Ron Fazio in THE TOXIC AVENGER, PART III: THE LAST TEMPTATION OF TOXIE (©Troma).

receives a letter from his father—who, to the surprise of our hero, is now living in Japan and is in great danger—asking his son to travel to that country and help him out of his predicament. Off goes Toxic, sailing to Japan, only to find out that (1) his father is not there, and (2) this must be some sort of crazy plot. Spilling over with anger, the Toxic Avenger storms back to Tromaville to find the town torn apart by waste, greed, and politics. The TA gets PO'd, kicks some serious corporate butt, and all is well again in Tromaville.

Directors Michael Herz and Lloyd Kaufman, who also helmed the original film, bring back all the elements that made the first movie a worldwide hit in THE TOXIC AVENGER, PART II, which, for all its toilet humor and shocking makeup effects, is an off-the-wall example of tasteless filmmaking with a heart—a sort of Marvel Comics version of John Waters. With a bigger budget and longer shooting schedule, this sequel is more ambitious (the production actually shot in Japan for a few weeks) and better-looking than the first installment, and the humor, while probably too far-fetched for most audiences, will appeal to the reliable college and midnight-movie crowd. But despite its wit and soul, THE TOXIC AVENGER, PART II eventually bogs down in a series of gags and car chases that quickly become monotonous. About halfway through the film, after a few dozen fight scenes with our hero ripping off the arms and crushing the skulls of the bad guys, the movie stalls and never rises above its comic-book influences. As the mutant superman, Ron Fazio (John Altamura is also cocredited in the role) is obviously enjoying himself, and his performance—combined with the film's general goofiness—provides TOXIC AVENGER II's best moments. Unfortunately, this spirit is not sustained, and the movie quickly disintegrates from sight and mind. Better luck next time, Toxy. *(Graphic violence, nudity, profanity.)*

p, Lloyd Kaufman and Michael Herz; d, Lloyd Kaufman and Michael Herz; w, Gay Partington Terry (based on a story by Lloyd Kaufman); ph, James London (TVC Color); ed, Michael Schweitzer; m, Barrie Guard; art d, Alex Grey; spec eff, Pericles Lewnes.

Comedy/Science Fiction

(PR:O MPAA:R)

TRIUMPH OF THE SPIRIT*
120m Nova-Shimon Arama-Arnold Kopelson-Robert M. Young/Triumph c Willem Dafoe *(Salamo Arouch)*, Wendy Gazelle *(Allegra)*, Robert Loggia *(Father Arouch)*, Kario Salem *(Jacko Levy)*, Kelly Wolf *(Elena)*, Edward James Olmos *(Gypsy)*, Costas Mandylor *(Avram Arouch)*, Edward Zentara *(Janush)*, Hartmut Becker *(Maj. Rauscher)*, Burkhard Heyl *(Aide to Rauscher)*, Sofia Saretok *(Momma)*, Grazyna Kruk-Schejbal *(Julie)*, Karolina Twardowska *(Benuta)*, Juranda Krol *(Sarah)*, Wiktor Mlynarczyk *(Beppo)*, Jerzy Gralek *(Kapo Kyr)*, Jack Messinger, Tuvia Tavi, Danny Segev, Avi Keidar *(Greek Prisoners)*, Andrzej Wojaczek *(Kapo Otto)*, Sebastian Spandel *(Lud)*, Ewa Lesniak *(Kapo Hilda)*, Anna Chitro *(Naomi)*, Halina Chrobak *(Clog Thief)*, Ireneusz Tomczak *(Fratelli)*, Teddy Atlas *(Silber)*, Andrzej Leszczynski *(Referee)*, Lew Rywin *(Announcer)*, Arthur Coburn *(Rabbi)*, Maria Probosz *(Rauscher's Girl Friend)*, Stefania Zubrowna *(Dying Woman)*, Hanna Pater *(Prisoner Nurse)*, Dorota Bialy-Wieczorek *(SS Woman)*, Michal Juszczakiewicz *(Sonderkammando)*, Zenon Kostrzewski, Sigal Cohen, Toni Bark, Maria Stokowska, Izabela Wandzel, Jerzy Szaniawski, Marian Skorupa, Wociech Gorniak, Marek Slosarski, Marzena Urbanska *(Greeks)*, Magda Nodzio, Maciej Gruszczynski, Marek Wudkowski, Edward Skarga, Anna Toronczyk, Irena Romanska, Piotr Sielka, Jerzy Krol, Tomasz Piasecki, Czeslawa

Willem Dafoe and Wendy Gazelle in TRIUMPH OF THE SPIRIT (©Nova International).

Pszczolinska, Boguslawa Fraczek, Anna Nowak, Zofia Jaronczyk, Tomasz Lulek, Krzysztof Baumann, Yagoda Nowak-Nowinski, Elzbieta Trojanowska, Arkadiusz Bazak, Antoni Gryzik *(Prisoners)*, Jacek Domanski, Jadwiga Grygierczyk, Jan Kiemens, Jolanta Gladeczek-Nowak, Mieczyslaw Janowski *(Kapos)*, Benard Krawczyk, Jacek Brzostynski, Marek David, Igor Kujawski, Barbara Pohorecka-Bogdol, Anna Wesolowska, Jan Bogdol, Roman Kuossowsky, Yossi Graber, Yehonadav Pearlman, Tadeusz Sobolewicz, Olek Wolejko, Janusz Ostrowski, Andrezej Bryg, Artur Reszke, Zbigniew Wrobel, Malgorzata Kozlowska, Adam Baumann, Marek Frackowiak, Edward Kusztal, Janusz Dziubinski, Andrzej Dopierala, Zenia Korczarowski *(SS Officers)*, Josef Lis, Evan Kopelson, Mieczyslaw Budzynski, Krzysztof Tadak *(Boxers)*.

Systematically stripped of human dignity, the prisoners of Auschwitz waged a minute-to-minute struggle for mere existence. Like caged animals governed by sadistic overseers, they were left to fight for their food, shoes, and space; those who refused to scheme and scrap suffered and died. TRIUMPH OF THE SPIRIT focuses on a fight within the larger fight, the travails of real-life Greek boxer Salamo Arouch (Dafoe), forced to battle for his life against other inmates for the off-hours diversion of the camp's SS hierarchy, who wagered on the outcome of these boxing matches.

The film opens in Dafoe's Greek hometown, where he begins a successful boxing career, fighting his way to the Balkan middleweight title. His rise is intercut with scenes of his warm, exuberant, close-knit Mediterranean family. The outbreak of WW II and the German invasion drastically disrupt their lives; occupying troops herd the area's Jews and Gypsies into a ghetto, from which Dafoe, his father (Loggia), and his brother, Avram (Mandylor), are taken daily and impressed into forced labor, yellow stars of David pinned to their chests. As the family tries to retain a semblance of its past life, Dafoe arranges a clandestine rendezvous outside the ghetto with his fiancee, Allegra (Gazelle), whose family has managed to elude the SS. One afternoon, word spreads that the ghetto-dwellers are to be relocated to Poland. A cautious optimism buoys their spirits. Dafoe's family gathers its most valued possessions in preparation for the journey, only to be herded onto cattle cars in which they travel for six days to their final destination, Auschwitz. In the film's most harrowing scene, those prisoners who are fortunate enough to have survived the trip stagger from the train cars, clutching their loved ones for dear life. While the furnace chimney roars in the background, the prisoners are divided along gender lines, and the weak are separated from the strong, then marched to the showers (gas chambers) for "delousing." Dafoe, Loggia, and Mandylor are quickly indoctrinated in the ferociously dehumanizing rituals of the camp. They are confined to unheated, overcrowded barracks to which they repair in the evening after a full day of backbreaking labor. The barracks are tyrannized by a Gypsy inmate (Olmos), who keeps the others in line in exchange for an assortment of perks. One morning, as the prisoners toil in the field, Dafoe is confronted by a thuggish enforcer; they fight and Dafoe knocks him out. The prostrate enforcer is casually shot by an SS officer and Dafoe is summoned by the camp's commandant, who learns both of the incident and of Dafoe's boxing past. The commandant enlists him as "his" fighter and the Greek engages in an unending series of fights to the finish. Each victory earns him a bonus of bread, which he takes back to his father and brother. Soon, Dafoe learns that each fellow inmate he beats is summarily shot, but the camp's survivalist mentality prevents him from dwelling on this moral dilemma. Mandylor is forced to join a group charged with the task of hauling gassed bodies to and from the incinerator. The chore is too enormous to contemplate; he and the others refuse and are shot. Interspersed with Dafoe's ongoing existential struggle are scenes concerning Gazelle, who toils in another, segregated part of the far-flung death camp. One day, she spots Dafoe from afar, and they exchange longing, meaningful looks—each knowing that the other is alive, they have some slim hope. The strong Loggia falters under the strain and, despite Dafoe's connections, is deemed unfit and executed. Although his toil continues virtually unabated, Dafoe continues to "enjoy" his relatively privileged position—until he is suspected of taking part in the bombing of the crematoria. Facing almost certain death, he is given a reprieve. As the Russians continue their advance, the SS resign themselves to certain defeat and begin to collapse. Finally, the camp is liberated, and as the film closes, Dafoe is pictured wandering outside the periphery of the camp like the Ancient Mariner, doomed, yet forever hopeful. (The written postscript informs us that Arouch was subsequently reunited with his wife and that they presently reside in Israel.)

TRIUMPH OF THE SPIRIT was the first film of its kind to be shot on the grounds of Auschwitz. Director Robert M. Young (SHORT EYES; DOMINICK AND EUGENE) makes judicious use of his setting—neither shrine nor stage set, it gives the film a firm grounding in history, and thus a commitment to truth. This earnestness, however, is undermined by a manipulative, obvious soundtrack that aspires to the operatic but instead bathes the entire film in cloying sentimentality, only serving to undermine the historical bedrock upon which the film is built. Willem Dafoe as Arouch gives another intelligent, well-chiselled performance; Robert Loggia is a slowly crumbling tower of patriarchal strength; and Edward James Olmos as the brutal, conniving Gypsy and Wendy Gazelle as Arouch's long-suffering girl friend also contribute fine work. But although interesting and competently made, this graphic re-creation of a singularly horrifying period offers few if any new insights into the evil machinations of

Hitler's efficient killers. Musical selections include: "Schatzilein" (Alexander Courage, Annemarie North, performed by Sandig Muth and His Orchestra) and "Colossus" (Courage, performed by Sandig Muth and His Orchestra). *(Adult situations.)*

p, Arnold Kopelson and Shimon Arama; d, Robert M. Young; w, Andrzej Krakowski, Laurence Heath, Robert M. Young, Arthur Coburn, and Millard Lampell (based on a story by Shimon Arama, Zion Haen); ph, Curtis Clark (Rank Color); ed, Arthur Coburn; m, Cliff Eidelman; md, Cliff Eidelman; art d, Krystyna Maslowska; set d, Izabela Paprocka; spec eff, Eddie Surkin; cos, Hilary Rosenfeld; chor, Teddy Atlas; makeup, Pier Antonio Mecacci.

Biography   **(PR:C MPAA:R)**

Ⓥ**TROOP BEVERLY HILLS***
105m Fries-Avanti-Weintraub/COL c
Shelley Long *(Phyllis Nefler)*, Craig T. Nelson *(Freddy Nefler)*, Betty Thomas *(Velda Plendor)*, Mary Gross *(Annie Herman)*, Stephanie Beacham *(Vicki Sprantz)*, Audra Lindley *(Frances Temple)*, Edd Byrnes *(Ross Coleman)*, Jenny Lewis *(Hannah Nefler)*, Kellie Martin *(Emily Coleman)*, Emily Schulman *(Tiffany Honigman)*, Tasha Scott *(Jasmine Shakar)*, Ami Foster *(Claire Sprantz)*, Carla Gugino *(Chica Barnfell)*, Heather Hopper *(Tessa DiBlasio)*, Aquilina Soriano *(Lily Marcigan)*, David Gautreaux *(DiBlasio)*, Karen Kopins *(Lisa)*, Dinah Lacey *(Cleo)*, Shelley Morrison *(Rosa)*, David Wohl *(Dr. Jerry Honigman)*, Tori Spelling *(Jamie)*, Daniel Ziskie *(Arthur Barnfell)*, Kareem Abdul-Jabbar, Frankie Avalon, Dr. Joyce Brothers, George Christy, Annette Funicello, Robin Leach, Cheech Marin, Ted McGinley, Pia Zadora *(Themselves)*, Brinda Andrews *(Redondo Troop Leader)*, Monty Ash *(Old Duffer)*, Jan Bina *(Freida)*, Kathleen Bradley *(Mrs. Shakar)*, Eloise Broady *(Starlet at Party)*, Mercy Bubalo *(Troop Photographer)*, Patrika Darbo *(Mar Vista Troop Leader)*, Flo Di Re, Claudia Robinson, Karin Woodward *(Wilderness Officials)*, Nancy Fish *(Mrs. Grundman)*, Pamela Galloway *(Mrs. Honigman)*, Willie Garson *(Bruce)*, Mary Pat Gleason *(Kindly Troop Leader)*, Bitsy Gorman *(Pomona Troop Leader)*, Mary Gregory *(Judge)*, James "Gypsy" Haake *(Henri)*, Alvin Ing *(Ho)*, Deborah Rose *(Beauty Salon Attendant)*, Ann Ryerson *(Bitsy Barnfell)*, Christophe Schatteman *(Beauty Salon Owner)*, Hilary Shepard *(Salesgirl)*, Ramon Sison *(Bong Bong)*, Bob Snead *(Phyllis Nefler's Lawyer)*, J.J. Wall *(Jack Sprantz)*.

A slow-moving comedy with few laughs, TROOP BEVERLY HILLS stars Long as a spoiled Beverly Hills resident who tries to change her ways. As the film opens, Long arrives home after another expensive shopping spree, prompting her husband (Nelson) to complain about her mindless spending. It's clear their marriage is on the rocks when Nelson tells Long that she's spoiled, selfish, and living a wasted life. To prove him wrong, Long decides to become the leader of Wilderness Girls Troop Beverly Hills (a sort of Girl Scout group). Unfortunately, Troop Beverly Hills is composed of local brats who fail at every rugged task and have become the laughing stock of the scouting community. However—despite the lack of encouragement from Wilderness Council members Thomas, Lindley, and Gross—Long is bound and determined to succeed. Her formula for whipping the troop into wilderness shape includes a round of outrageous shopping sprees, dancing lessons, and so on. While Long and her small cohorts are busy wearing their credit cards and shoe soles thin, Thomas dispatches Gross to spy on these activities, then uses the information in an attempt to get Long kicked out of the Wilderness Girls organization. When this plan fails, Thomas, tough cookie that she is, takes one last shot at humiliating Troop Beverly Hills at the big Wilderness Jamboree, a somewhat paramilitary event at which the various scout troops compete in an obstacle course. After a few initial setbacks, Troop Beverly Hills manages to come out on top, of course. And—assuming anyone cares—Long and Nelson get back together, too.

The premise of TROOP BEVERLY HILLS might have worked as a comedy skit, but could hardly sustain a feature-length film. Unfortunately, the premise is virtually all that the film's screenplay supplies. There is no character development, even by today's comedy film standards. Mary Gross, for instance, seems to have no other function in the film than to grimace, though this is a less serious flaw than the film's failure to make Shelley Long's character anything more than a cartoon. Where Goldie Hawn's Judy Benjamin, in the similarly plotted PRIVATE BENJAMIN, underwent a transformation from pampered socialite to capable adult that was at least superficially credible, Long's reformation is never convincing. The movie's spirit can be summed up in the victory cheer that Troop Beverly Hills sings at the end: "We come from Beverly Hills. Shopping is our greatest skill. We will fight and try real hard, leave behind our credit cards. Beverly Hills what a thrill!"

The direction (by Jeff Kanew) and performances are about as good as can be expected in this kind of Hollywood fluff. The Girl Scouts are definitely owed an apology. *(Profanity.)*

p, Ava Ostern Fries; d, Jeff Kanew; w, Pamela Norris and Margaret Grieco Oberman (based on a story by Ava Ostern Fries); ph, Donald E. Thorin (Metrocolor); ed, Mark Melnick; m, Randy Edelman; prod d, Robert F. Boyle; art d, Jack G. Taylor Jr.; set d, Anne McCulley-Reynolds; spec eff, Fred Z. Gebler; cos, Theadora Van Runkle; chor, Dorain Grusman; stunts, Conrad E. Palmisano; makeup, Del Acevedo.

Comedy   **(PR:A-C MPAA:PG)**

Ⓥ**TRUE BELIEVER*****
103m Lasker-Parkes/COL c
James Woods *(Eddie Dodd)*, Robert Downey Jr. *(Roger Baron)*, Margaret Colin *(Kitty Greer)*, Yuji Okumoto *(Shu Kai Kim)*, Kurtwood Smith *(Robert Reynard)*, Tom Bower *(Cecil Skell)*, Miguel Fernandes *(Art Esparza)*, Charles Hallahan *(Vincent Dennehy)*, Sully Diaz *(Maraquilla Esparza)*, Misan Kim *(Mrs. Kim)*, John Snyder *(Chucky Loeder)*, Luis Guzman *(Ortega)*, Graham Beckel *(Sklaroff)*, Tony Haney *(Montell)*, Joel Polis *(Dean Rabin)*, Will Marchetti *(Judge Quealy)*, Maureen McVerry *(Billy)*, Abigail Van Alyn *(Connie Dennehy)*, Deborah Offner *(Laura Gayley)*, Thomas Wagner *(Tommy)*, Richard Fancy *(Ballistics Expert)*, Kurt Fuller *(George)*, Ginger Chung *(Translator)*, Thelton E. Henderson *(Judge Baum)*, Gerry Bamman *(Brian Nevins)*, Charles Dean, Gustave Johnson *(Detectives)*, Cab Covay *(Teardrop)*, Tony Abatemarco *(Glen Fulton)*, Kenneth Grantham *(Cecil's Judge)*, Ralph Peduto *(Court Officer)*, Margot Rose *(Ms. Jessum)*, Jan Schultz *(Lindeman)*, George Maguire *(Maitre d')*, David Espinoza *(Corrections Officer)*, George Jenesky *(Slim Jim)*, Sean O'Brien *(Clyde Gruner)*, Cully Fredricksen *(Scarecrow)*, Taylor Gilbert *(Reynard's Receptionist)*, Peter Anthony Jacobs *(Reporter)*, Stu Klitsher *(Magnate)*, David Booth *(Minister)*, Peter Fitzsimmons *(Court Clerk)*, Jarrett Sullivan *(Boy)*, Michael Stone *(Client)*.

Fresh out of law school, Roger Baron (Downey), an idealistic midwesterner, journeys to New York to serve as a clerk for his idol, Edward Dodd (Woods). Woods' inventive tactics in civil rights cases in the 1960s and 70s made him one of the country's most respected and well-known attorneys, but Downey is saddened to find he is now a dope-smoking shyster, plying his trade in the service of sleazy drug dealers. When a Korean woman shows up at Woods' office and begs him to defend her son, Woods wants nothing to do with the case; however, he is brow-beaten into taking it on by Downey. An inmate at Sing Sing, the woman's son (Okumoto) is awaiting trial for slaying another prisoner, a member of a white supremacist gang called the Aryan Army. Clearly the killing was in self defense, but as Woods investigates, he grows more interested in the eight-year-old case that sent Okumoto to prison.

James Woods, Robert Downey Jr., and Yuji Okumoto in TRUE BELIEVER (©Columbia).

Okumoto was convicted of shooting a man to death in Chinatown, with the police contending the act was part of Okumoto's initiation into a gang. Woods, Downey, and a private investigator (Colin) find that two eye witnesses identified Okumoto as the killer, but a third, never called during the trial, swore the police had the wrong man. Woods locates the dissenter (Bower) in a mental hospital but learns that in addition to believing Okumoto is innocent, Bower is also certain the phone company was behind the assassination of John F. Kennedy. However, Bower's testimony is enough to get the Chinatown murder trial reopened, and Woods is quickly summoned to the office of the self-righteous district attorney (Smith), who says that if the case goes back to trial he will personally prosecute. Woods is then attacked and beaten by a thug (Snyder) who says he's a soldier in the Aryan Army and warns that Woods will be killed if he persists in defending Okumoto. After learning that Snyder is not a member of the Aryan Army, Woods has Colin track him down. She finds him working for a plumbing manufacturer (Fernandes), but when Woods tries to talk to him, Snyder escapes, and that night dies from a drug overdose. The new trial of Okumoto on the Chinatown murder charge doesn't begin well for the defendant, as Woods, who had hoped to undermine the credibility of one of the policeman involved with the original investigation (Hallahan), drops that strategy when the officer shows up in court in a wheelchair and in obvious pain. After one court session, Downey notices Fernandes' wife (Diaz) leaving the courtroom and fol-

lows her to her husband's factory, where he witnesses a shouting match between the two. Confronting Diaz, Downey learns she was having an affair with the man who was murdered in Chinatown. Later, while studying old police files, Downey and Woods determine that Fernandes was the killer; then Woods goes to Hallahan's home and the cop fills in the blanks for him: most notably that Fernandes had been the key source of information in a three-year investigation that resulted in the smashing of a huge Columbian drug ring and on which Smith built his career. When Fernandes begged for help after murdering his wife's lover, Smith had Hallahan and his partners (Beckel and Haney) engineer a cover-up to protect their prized informant. Finding Okumoto, who bore a strong resemblance to Fernandes, in a mug book, the cops framed the young Korean for the murder. As Woods is leaving Hallahan's apartment building with his new witness, he is confronted by Beckel, Haney, and Fernandes, the last of whom pulls a gun and threatens to shoot Woods. Before Fernandes is able to do so, Haney instead shoots and kills Fernandes, saying, "I should have done that eight years ago." Back in court, Woods puts Smith on the witness stand and challenges him with the information he has gathered. Eventually Smith concedes that Woods allegations are true, insisting that it was all for the greater good, and adding that he'd do it again. Of course, Okumoto's innocence is now clearly established and he goes free.

Though the story contains not one shred of plausibility, TRUE BELIEVER is nevertheless an intriguing and entertaining

mystery thanks to James Woods' performance and the direction of Joseph Ruben. In his 1987 feature THE STEPFATHER, Ruben took what was potentially just another mad slasher film and turned it into a fascinating character study that also worked as a compelling thriller. Here he's given one of the most time-worn of all plots (crusading lawyer frees innocent man), and revitalizes it with an exhilarating pace and inventive action. Nowhere is this more apparent than in Woods' chase of Snyder through the plumbing supply factory. Chases have been done to death in recent years, yet this is a harrowing scene, as Ruben manages to capture not just the urgency of the pursuit, but to convey a chilling sense of danger presented by the factory environment. The director also makes effective use of flashbacks, using elegant black-and-white scenes to depict the Chinatown murder and events surrounding it.

If the pace is swift, Ruben has a lead actor who is equal to it in Woods, one of Hollywood's most riveting performers. This role gives him a chance to display a wide range of emotions—depression, excitement, rage, cynicism, compassion— and it's a chance he obviously relishes. His destruction of a hostile witness' testimony in the Okumoto trial is done in the most filmically stereotypical fashion, but it's done with such glee it has to be appreciated. There is no one better than Woods at playing an iconoclast, though there is a danger that he may be working that side of the street too often. In the past few years he has played a maverick journalist (SALVADOR), a maverick criminal (BEST

SELLER), a maverick cop (COP), and now a maverick lawyer. This is not to suggest he consider playing the lead in a remake of GOODBYE MR. CHIPS, but his decision to undertake a sympathetic mainstream character in IMMEDIATE FAMILY seems to be a good career move.

Robert Downey, Jr., who has himself proved to be a mercurial performer in films such as LESS THAN ZERO and THE PICKUP ARTIST, here settles into a more traditional role, much as he did in his other 1989 film, CHANCES ARE. Downey's part here isn't a very challenging one and doesn't allow him much room to use his talents, but he does all right with it, even managing to milk some humor from the character—as when he engages mental patient Bower in a pointless debate about the phone company's role in the Kennedy assassination. Margaret Colin, in the cliched role of the dogged investigator, is appealing, but would have benefited from more screen time. As the arrogant prosecutor, Kurtwood Smith is smug in the exaggerated way only movie villains are, which does little to enhance the film's credibility, and that's the area in which TRUE BELIEVER fails most glaringly. Upon closer scrutiny, almost none of the action makes any sense, with the cover-up plot being particularly absurd. Fortunately the Ruben-Woods combination simply overwhelms the flaws in the script. Songs include: "Busload of Faith" (Lou Reed, performed by Reed), "All Along the Watchtower" (Bob Dylan, performed by Jimi Hendrix), "Freedom Rider" (Steve Winwood, Jim Capaldi, performed by Traffic), "Crystal Ship" (Jim Morrison, Ray Manzarek, John Densmore, Robby Krieger, performed by The Doors), "La Marea" (Ruben Blades, performed by Blades). (Profanity, violence, substance abuse.)

p, Walter F. Parkes and Lawrence Lasker; d, Joseph Ruben; w, Wesley Strick; ph, John W. Lindley (Deluxe Color); ed, George Bowers; m, Brad Fiedel; prod d, Lawrence Miller; art d, Jim Pohl; set d, Jim Poynter; spec eff, John McLeod; cos, Erica Edell Phillips; stunts, Rocky Capella; makeup, Deborah Figuly.

Crime/Mystery   (PR:O MPAA:R)

Ⓥ TRUE BLOOD**
97m Maris/Fries c
Jeff Fahey (Ray Trueblood), Chad Lowe (Donny Trueblood), Sherilyn Fenn (Jennifer), James Tolkan (Lt. Joe Hanley), Billy Drago (Spider Masters), Ken Foree (Charlie).

This low-budget action film tells the story of a pair of brothers who try desperately to leave the mean streets of New York for the quiet beauty of Wyoming. Older brother Ray Trueblood (Fahey) is the leader of the Shadows, a tough street gang that is at war with Drago and his cohorts. So fierce is the rivalry between Fahey and Drago that it leads the latter to murder a cop. When he is framed for that murder, Fahey makes his getaway on a train, leaving his little brother (Lowe) behind. Ten years later, Fahey returns from the Marine Corps to the streets of New York, searching for his brother. Greeted coldly by his old neighbors, he soon discovers that Lowe is now in Drago's gang. Fahey confronts Drago, they fight, and Lowe appears, apparently a drugged-out maniac, faithful to Drago. Fahey escapes and vows to rescue Lowe from the streets. Taking a job at a diner, he meets waitress Fenn, who helps him in his efforts to save Lowe and to get Drago. But Fahey is still considered a fugitive, and the murdered policeman's partner (Tolkan) is bent on revenge. One night, after a robbery, Lowe is shot by the cops and ends up at Fahey's door. Fahey brings Lowe to Fenn's place to remove the bullet, and in the morning, Fahey and Lowe have it out over their past differences and decide to work together to clear Fahey's name. After a few chases and fights, Fahey makes a deal with the cops: he will give them information that will lead them to Drago in exchange for Lowe's continued freedom. Meanwhile, Lowe and Fenn strike up a reluctant friendship. When Drago attacks Fenn in her home, Lowe is the first to find her; Drago, in the meantime, has gone off to kill Fahey. The two longtime foes confront each other on a rooftop, where Drago gives Fahey a gun and challenges him to draw. Of course, Fahey's gun is empty, and Drago shoots him in the stomach, only to be shot himself by the just-arrived Lowe. Drago dies and Fahey is brought to a hospital. The film ends with the brothers meeting at the train; finally able to put the ugliness of the city behind them, they are free to start life anew in Wyoming.

More ambitious than most films of this type, but still of only marginal interest, TRUE BLOOD is a truly strange movie. The cast comprises an interesting combination of B-movie performers of limited talent (Sherilyn Fenn, Chad Lowe, and Ken Foree) and capable character actors (Jeff Fahey, James Tolkan, and the terrific Billy Drago), and the combination provides TRUE BLOOD with an oddly compelling charm. Although Frank Kerr's weak script and unfocused direction ultimately undermine the film, TRUE BLOOD does have its moments. Fahey (who was terrific in 1988's SPLIT DECISIONS) is such a strong screen presence that his performance nearly saves the film. Eyes burning with intensity, he tries valiantly to lend sincerity to the terrible dialog. Tolkan (TOP GUN; BACK TO THE FUTURE I and II) also gives an enjoyable performance as a vengeful cop, especially in the early scenes. But the movie's finest moments belong to Drago (Frank Nitti in

THE UNTOUCHABLES), whose weird presence and strange physical appearance help create a memorable villain. One of TRUE BLOOD's major flaws, however, is Lowe's performance. Where Fahey is believable and passionate, Lowe is shrill and fake, and as result their relationship, so crucial to the success of the film, falls flat.

Kerr's often embarrassing dialog— including such gems as, "You're a disgusting barbarian and an insufferable lout!"—doesn't help matters much. Neither do TRUE BLOOD's uninspired action sequences—horribly cliched car chases and fight scenes that are totally lacking in visceral impact. What's more, the screenplay is full of predictable, derivative situations (BLOODBROTHERS and THE WARRIORS stand out as obvious role models). But with all of its problems (and there are plenty of them), TRUE BLOOD is a sincere work that is acted with more energy than it deserves. There are worse films than this, and Billy Drago has to be seen to be believed. (Violence, profanity, brief nudity, adult situations.)

p, Peter Maris; d, Frank Kerr; w, Frank Kerr; ph, Mark H.L. Morris (CFI Color); ed, Mac Haight; m, Scott Roewe; art d, Katherine Terr; stunts, James Lovelett.

Action   (PR:C-O MPAA:R)

TRUE LOVE***
104m Forward/MGM-UA c
Annabella Sciorra (Donna), Ron Eldard (Michael), Star Jasper (J.C.), Aida Turturro (Grace), Roger Rignack (Dom), Michael J. Wolfe (Brian), Kelly Cinnante (Yvonne), Rick Shapiro (Kevin), Suzanne Costallos (Fran), Vinny Pastore (Angelo), Marianne Leone (Carmella), John Nacco (Benny), Ann Tucker (Barbara), Marie Michaels (Chickie).

The top prize-winner at the 1989 US Film festival in Park City, Utah, TRUE LOVE is a low-budget first feature that, while no masterpiece, is an entertaining comedy filled to the brim with likable characters. Reminiscent in some ways of Barry Levinson's superb 1982 debut, DINER (with its pre-wedding scene that hinges on the bride's being able to pass an exam about football), TRUE LOVE is about young couples, family friendship, the onslaught of adulthood, and neighborhood life. Directing her first feature, New York University alum Nancy Savoca (along with her coproducer-husband, Richard Guay) has, like previous NYU alum Martin Scorsese, turned for inspiration to the working-class Italian-American neighborhood in which she was raised. At the center of the story is a young couple in their early 20s—Sciorra, playing a strong but somewhat empty-headed young woman who is determined to get her man to the altar, and Eldard, the groom-to-be, who doesn't mind giving out an engagement ring and exchanging an occasional "I love you," but isn't so generous when it comes to actually exchanging marriage vows. Instead, Eldard would rather pal around with his neighborhood buddies (Rignack, Wolfe, and Shapiro). He's trying to hang on to his youth as long as he can, and the prospect of a wife and a go-nowhere job in his uncle's liquor store hangs over his head like a storm cloud. Although Sciorra, her best friends (Turturro and Jasper), and her little sister (Cinnante) are well aware that none of the neighborhood guys could be called a prize, they also know the social uproar that will ensue if the wedding is called off.

What makes TRUE LOVE such an entertaining picture isn't the story itself (it's as old as the movies), but the uncanny resemblance the characters and situations bear to real life. Each of the characters is created with care and a flair for individuality, every scene brought to life with humor and poignancy. Although there is very little "love" evident in the film, clearly everything about it is "true," and truth is a rare commodity in today's sitcom-influenced motion pictures. What is even more promising is the fact that TRUE LOVE was directed by a newcomer to the film scene and stars a cast full of unknowns, the most pleasant surprise being Annabella Sciorra, appearing in her first feature. Grossing less than a million dollars at the box office, this very low-budget entry, with no marquee names to speak of, unfortunately never reached its full potential—a sad comment on the nature of motion picture distribution in America. (Profanity, adult situations, sexual situations.)

p, Richard Guay and Shelley Houis; d, Nancy Savoca; w, Nancy Savoca and Richard Guay; ph, Lisa Rinzler (Duart Color); ed, John Tintori; prod d, Lester W. Cohen; art d, Pamela Woodbridge; cos, Deborah Anderko.

Comedy   (PR:O MPAA:R)

⊙TRUST ME**

85m Clein Feldman White/Cinecom c

Adam Ant *(James Callendar)*, David Packer *(Sam Brown)*, Talia Balsam *(Catherine Walker)*, William DeAcutis *(Billy Brawthwaite)*, Joyce Van Patten *(Nettie Brown)*, Barbara Bain *(Mary Casal)*, Brooke Da Vida *(Denise Tipton)*, Simon McQueen *(Holly Windsor)*, Alma Beltran *(Imelda)*, Marilyn Tokuda *(Chic Girl)*, Barbara Petty *(Severe Woman)*, Virgil Frye *(Thug)*, Morri Beers *(Man in Sandals)*, Anna Cray Carduno *(Woman in Sandals)*, Bill Satto *(Scowling Man)*, Kenia *(Latin Girl)*, Rance Howard *(Vern)*, Tony Payne *(Mac)*, Kimmy Robertson *(Party Gal)*, Brigitte Burdine *(Valette)*, Ken Olfson *(Benjamin Greenberg)*, Adam Gregor, Nick Conti *(Hit Men)*.

Beginning with the premise that an artist is worth more dead than alive, director Bobby Houston razzes the razzle-dazzle, sleazy side of the southern California art scene, focusing on a trendy Los Angeles art dealer played by Adam Ant. With his gallery on the verge of bankruptcy and his treasured model 911 Porsche convertible about to be repossessed for non-payment, Ant is ready to resort to anything, even murder, to build up his bank balance and get back on the fast track. After learning that rival gallery-owner Bain has made a fortune from the posthumous sale of paintings by a young artist whose work quadrupled in value following his very suspicious demise, Ant, interested in the possibility of showing work by his own dead artist, latches on to Packer, a young painter and Yale graduate (temporarily moonlighting as a messenger). Art is more important than money, however, to the slightly nerdy Ivy Leaguer, who lives in a huge loft (where rats "use the rafters as a freeway") above a Japanese funeral supply shop, employs a sock as coffee filter, and goes to a Japanese bath house because his home is without hot water. As suitable as Victorian gift wrap as they are for lining the walls of a contemporary art emporium, Packer's canvases, filled with floating cherubs, might best be described as neo-Caravaggio. But with enough hype anything is possible. Ant wages a publicity campaign, mounts a show, and Packer nets rave reviews from the critics. Once Packer's reputation is established, Ant bungles an attempt to permanently dispose of his protege, and is last heard from as an advertising executive with Merrill Lynch in their Commercial Accounts department—the inferred logical end for a slimy mercenary of his ilk.

Both David Packer and his love interest, Talia Balsam (who plays Ant's honorable gallery manager), are personable and attractive, and give creditable performances considering the trivial script. For Balsam, daughter of actor Martin, TRUST ME became a family affair, with her real-life mother, Joyce Van Patten, a fine character actress best known for her work on Broadway, playing Packer's dipsomaniac mother. (Balsam and Van Patten were cast independently, and their relationship came as a total surprise to the producers.) English rock star-turned-film actor Ant is suitably superficial and unsavory, but Barbara Bain (TV's "Mission Impossible"), in what amounts to a cameo, struts her few moments upon this filmic stage as a caricature of a duplicitous art dealer who'll stoop to anything to make a profit.

Unfortunately, this would-be cynical spoof of the art world (far better handled in the Martin Scorsese segment of NEW YORK STORIES) places a higher premium on camp than on more straightforward humor or character development. Moreover, in the end, there are just too

many loose ends and inconsistencies. Houston, who also cowrote the screenplay, seems to have an axe to grind about some of the less appealing aspects of the art economy, where taste falls victim to greed and out-and-out skulduggery. Although he won't say whether the film was based on actual events, Houston has admitted that in the last five years, as in his plot, several LA dealers have gotten into trouble for stealing artists' work, selling the same piece of art twice, and otherwise committing fraud.

For a low-budget picture—a 21-day wonder that was brought in three days ahead of schedule—TRUST ME's sets come off best. Packer's loft (created from an attic atop a Hollywood prop rental company) is itself a work of art. The cherubic canvases, specially commissioned from LA artist Michael Reinman, may not win any awards, but they're wonderfully ridiculous. As for the rest of the paintings shown throughout the movie, they're all authentic. TRUST ME may be forgettable fluff, but if art's your thing, the visual delight of seeing paintings by Robert Motherwell, Andy Warhol, Keith Haring, and a slew of fine contemporary painters might be worth the price of admission.

p, George Edwards; d, Bobby Houston; w, Bobby Houston and Gary Rigdon; ph, Thomas Jewett (United Color Lab); ed, Barry Zetlin; m, Pray For Rain and Max Vague; md, Larry K. Smith; set d, Richard Dearborn; cos, Debbie Shine; stunts, Bobby Bragg; makeup, Cheryl Markowitz.

Comedy   (PR:A MPAA:R)

⊙TURNER & HOOCH**

98m Touchstone-Silver Screen Partners IV/BV c

Tom Hanks *(Scott Turner)*, Mare Winningham *(Emily Carson)*, Craig T. Nelson *(Police Chief Hyde)*, Reginald VelJohnson *(Detective David Sutton)*, Scott Paulin *(Zack Gregory)*, J.C. Quinn *(Walter Boyett)*, John McIntire *(Amos Reed)*, David Knell *(Ernie)*, Ebbe Roe Smith *(Harley McCabe)*, Kevin Scannell *(Jeff Foster)*, Joel Bailey *(Ferraday)*, Mary McCusker *(Katie)*, Ernie Lively *(Motel Clerk)*, Clyde Kusatsu *(Kevin Jenkins)*, Elaine Renee Bush *(Store Clerk)*, Eda Reiss Merin *(Mrs. Remington)*, Victor DiMattia *(Sean Boyett)*, Elden Ratliff *(Eric Boyett)*, Cheryl Anderson *(Mrs. Boyett)*, Ursula Lentine *(Bride)*, Sharon Madden *(Mrs. Kathy Harper)*, Daniel Ben Wilson *(Mike Harper)*, Jenny Drugan *(Christine Harper)*, Madeleine Cowie Klein *(Animal Control Woman)*, Julian Sylvester *(Animal Control Man)*, Nick Dimitri *(Casey)*, Scott Stevens *(Cop)*, Terry Israel, Andrew Walker, Frederick Ponzlov *(Police Officers)*, Linda Eve

Miller *(Mrs. Pine)*, Jim Beaver *(Plant Manager)*, Beasley *(Hooch the Dog)*.

Like Jim Belushi with K9, Tom Hanks, in TURNER & HOOCH, has chosen to ignore the old actor's adage about never costarring with animals. But unlike Belushi, Hanks doesn't fare particularly well, though it's neither his fault nor that of his canine costar. Another old adage, especially applicable here, warns filmgoers to beware of movies written by five people, the number credited for cowriting TURNER's script. Although some of them are among Hollywood's top word-smiths, rarely have so many labored to so little effect. Indeed, there's barely enough meat on TURNER's bones for an agree-able made-for-TV movie, and much of what's here seems to have been pasted in from other, better films.

Hanks plays Turner, a detective improb-ably employed by the police department in a sleepy California seaside town where bicycle thieves are considered big-time criminals. Not surprisingly, he looks for-ward to an upcoming move to the "big city" of Sacramento, where he hopes to investigate real crimes. Since there wouldn't be much of a movie otherwise, it isn't too long before real crimes come to him instead. When a cranky but lovable old salt (McIntire) who lives on a barge in the harbor is murdered, the only eyewit-ness is Hooch (Beasley the Dog), McIntire's equally cranky mutt. After ani-mal control officers threaten to send Hooch to that big dog house in the sky, Hanks adopts Hooch with the notion of using him to finger the killer. A little like Belushi and his German shepherd costar, Jerry Lee . . . oh heck, *exactly* like Belushi and Jerry Lee . . . Hanks and Beasley are at each other's throats, literally, at first. But in movies like this, only a rock could resist a filthy, ill-tempered mongrel that flings phlegm all over the living room walls. Before you can say fetch, cop and dog are frolicking all over the furniture like an overgrown boy and his big sloppy puppy. The film's crime plot, on the other hand, is barely worth mentioning. Having some-thing to do with a fish-processing plant used as a front for money laundering, it's simply an excuse to stage some random violence and a few nighttime gunfights, though all well within the borders of the film's PG rating.

For those keeping score of TURNER & HOOCH's movie borrowings, a fish-pro-cessing facility also figures prominently in LICENCE TO KILL's Bond-ed mayhem, while money laundering is the crime of choice in LETHAL WEAPON 2. More-over, reaching for a twist ending, the filmmakers more or less update the close of OLD YELLER (this is, after all, a Touchstone—read Disney—production), but, like so much else in TURNER & HOOCH, the idea backfires.

Tom Hanks and Beasley in TURNER AND HOOCH (©Buena Vista).

Another, more basic, problem with TURNER & HOOCH, however, is the miscasting of Hanks himself. Unlike Belushi, who looks a little like a dog to begin with, Hanks is too urbane to be very believable as the admirer of an oversized, disagreeable mutt. Beasley has the edge over Jerry Lee when it comes to screen presence, but Hanks seems barely able to hide his embarrassment when he's called upon to show bearish, unbridled affection for a dog that bears a disturbing resem-blance to Ernest Borgnine from certain camera angles. Hanks looks more relaxed, and is far more amusing in his scenes with Mare Winningham, playing the pretty vet-erinarian who hooks up with the detective as result of Hooch's slobbering lust for her pretty female collie. But Winningham, who gives a typically warm, appealing per-formance, is finally shunted aside by the center-screen romance between man and dog.

It would be tempting to conclude that TURNER & HOOCH might have been more entertaining if K9 hadn't been released several months before it. However, with its derivative, mishmash script under Roger Spottiswoode's plodding, routine direction, it's hard to imagine TURNER

being very entertaining under any circum-stances. *(Violence, adult situations.)*

p, Raymond Wagner and Michele Ader; d, Roger Spottiswoode; w, Dennis Shryack, Michael Blodgett, Daniel Petrie Jr., Jim Cash, and Jack Epps Jr. (based on a story by Shryack, Blodgett, Petrie); ph, Adam Greenberg (Metrocolor); ed, Garth Cra-ven, Paul Seydor, Mark Conte, Kenneth Morrisey, and Lois Freeman-Fox; m, Charles Gross; prod d, John DeCuir Jr.; art d, Sig Tinglof; set d, Cloudia; spec eff, Alan E. Lorimer; cos, Jeane Rosone; stunts, Conrad E. Palmisano; makeup, Dan Striepeke.

Comedy/Crime/Thriller

(PR:C MPAA:PG)

TWICE DEAD*½
85m Concorde/Nelson c

Tom Breznahan *(Scott)*, Jill Whitlow *(Robin/Myrna)*, Jonathan Chapin *(Crip/Tyler Walker)*, Christopher Burgard *(Silk)*, Sam Melville *(Harry)*, Brooke Bundy *(Sylvia)*, Joleen Lutz *(Candy)*, Todd Bridges *(Petie)*, Ray Garcia, Travis McKenna, Shawn Player.

A cheapo, updated haunted-house thriller, TWICE DEAD was unable to scare up much interest as a video release from new, hip distributor Nelson Entertainment. Combining rinky-dink production values and an old-fashioned plot with a little APRIL FOOL'S DAY trickery thrown in, TWICE DEAD follows the exploits of a family that moves into a decaying (but potentially valuable) property left them by a mysterious relative. First, however, the film provides a flashback prolog telling us what the main characters will discover later—it always helps if the audience is one step ahead, right? Set in the 1930s, the prolog concerns movie star Tyler Walker (Chapin), who inhabits a fashionable Tinseltown mansion with Myrna (Whitlow), the love of his life. In typical Grand Guignol style, the two end up dead (presumably for the first time) as a result of their passion. Jump forward to the 1980s and some exposition explaining why high schoolers Scott (Breznahan) and Robin (Whitlow again), their parents (Melville and Bundy), and their black cat, Meow, are now moving into Walker's mansion. Before they are even past their new front porch, however, the family encounters a gang of thugs led by a fellow named Silk (Burgard). It seems that Silk and his boys have been using the place as a hangout and are none too happy with the idea of having to pick up and establish residence elsewhere. After some prolonged sequences in which adversarial positions are established, with a number of run-ins between teenagers Silk and Scott at school, the story's supernatural forces finally grow impatient enough to unleash themselves for good. Scott is nearly strangled by an unseen force, Meow starts behaving a little more spookily than usual, and other strange occurrences become routine. Are all these bizarre happenings being caused by the terrorizing street gang, or is the house really possessed by a hammy actor from beyond the grave? In light of the prolog, the answer seems more than obvious. Still, screenwriters Bert Dragin (who also directed) and Robert McDonnell (who coproduced) generously provide an additional twist in the revenge tactics Scott and Robin put into play after their parents conveniently leave town for a time. Apparently, the spirit of Tyler Walker has been killing off obnoxious gang members one by one in fun and interesting ways that have to do with the house and/or Walker's legacy: a dumbwaiter smashes someone's skull, someone else's head is found spinning on an antique victrola, an electric blanket turns one love/death scene into a real eye-opener, and so on. But—ha, ha; fooled ya!—it's actually Scott and Robin, just trying to scare the punks off. Or is it?

Either way, it hardly matters. Notwithstanding its rather tidy twist ending, TWICE DEAD is more than twice dull, and almost bewilderingly formulaic. Tom

Breznahan and Jill Whitlow play the teen brother and sister with a near-incestuous chemistry—it's as if they'd seen (or acted in) so many stalk-and-slash teen films in which the leads were boy friend and girl friend (as is usually the case in this genre) that they just automatically followed suit here, purring their dialog like lovers-to-be when they should be indulging in realistic sibling bickering. The lack of effects is also fatal: after a quick dose of the heavy metal favored by the gang members, the soundtrack music is virtually nonexistent, and there's a conspicuous absence of extras or activity in the street scenes. And does anyone remember the last time the sound of thumping heartbeats was used to generate suspense? *(Profanity, violence, adult situations.)*

p, Guy J. Louthan and Robert McDonnell; d, Bert Dragin; w, Bert Dragin and Robert McDonnell; ph, Zoran Hochstatter (Foto-Kem Color); ed, Patrick Rand; m, David Bergeaud; spec eff, Michael Burnett; stunts, John Branagan.

Thriller   (PR:C MPAA:R)

❼TWO TO TANGO zero
(US/Arg.) 87m New
Horizons-Aries/Concorde c
Don Stroud *(James Conrad)*, Adrienne Sachs *(Cecilia Lorca)*, Duilio Marzio *(Paulino Velasco)*, Michael Cavanaugh *(Dean Boyle)*, Alberto Segado *(Lorenzo "Lucky" Lara)*, Francisco Cocuzza *(Carlos Pino)*.

After producing LOS ULTIMOS DIAS DE LA VICTIMA (1982), Adolfo Aristarain's adaptation of Jose Pablo Feinman's novel *Last Days of the Victim*, Argentine filmmaker Hector Olivera (A FUNNY, DIRTY LITTLE WAR; BARBARIAN QUEEN) has now directed an English-language remake of the film. TWO TO TANGO has enough grist for the thriller mill, but when the viewer is asked to empathize with its cardboard antihero's newfound morality, the film's foundation collapses like a house of cards. Veteran professional assassin Stroud, fresh from a business-as-usual execution in Miami, travels to Buenos Aires for his next assignment. After 15 years of faithful employment for a faceless organization known only as "The Company," it dawns on him that he might have chosen the wrong line of work. Maybe there's a more righteous path to follow. But his tendering two weeks' notice is hardly sufficient for the likes of The Company, and Stroud wisely elects to make his South American hit before retiring in Nepal. Posing as a Boston newspaper reporter, he secures lodging in a little hotel conveniently located across the street from the secured compound of his quarry, the dangerous Segado. Although he has the firepower and skill to drop his man at any time, from any distance, Stroud must

remain content to take target practice with his Nikon until the official word comes down. While clicking off snapshots one night, he manages to capture a sizzling lovemaking session between Segado and Sachs, his leggy mistress. Stroud has also managed to plant bugging devices throughout the compound so that he hears as well as sees their passionate encounter. On his night off, Stroud wanders into a local watering hole where he runs into Cavanaugh, an associate from his mysterious past and coincidentally the owner of the bar. Their camaraderie evolves into a reverie of regret for their past wicked ways, but the picture brightens for Stroud when he learns that Sachs is employed as a tango dancer in that very bar. Disregarding the dangers of a possible liaison, he presses her for a date, which amounts to coffee and sex in her apartment the next day. Both admit the fatigue of faking it through life and love, so Stroud suggests she follow him to "the top of the world" for a new view of existence. After Cavanaugh asks him to act as his bodyguard on a dangerous drug deal, during which the two are nearly killed, Stroud can't wait to complete the job and clear out. He reveals his true identity to Sachs, but before they can advance their plans, they are ambushed. With the girl dead, Stroud must go it alone. Storming into Segado's now unguarded house, he is startled to learn that it is he who has been under surveillance the whole time, and that the last murder he will be involved with is his own.

When a character occupies virtually every scene in a movie, it's not unreasonable for the audience to expect to find him likable, admirable, or at least interesting; Don Stroud's character posts zeros in all of these categories and a few more. His weak attempt at a moral transformation is belated and wholly contrived. While the introduction of the lusty Adrienne Sachs adds an erotic touch to the exotic locale, her dramatic contribution falls woefully short. TWO TO TANGO's air of mystery is derived more from its clouded exposition than through any well-crafted writing or directing. Valuable information is presented as if it were incidental. Moreover, the characterization is flimsy, the tango dancing is so-so, and the last line of the movie, "You forgot that it takes two to tango," sums up the trite dialog. Even Raul Garello's whiny score only adds another layer of annoyance to this puerile attempt at intrigue. *(Sexual situations, adult situations, nudity, violence, profanity.)*

p, Roger Corman and Alex Sessa; d, Hector Olivera; w, Yolande Finch and Jose Pablo Feinman (based on Feinman's novel *Last Days of the Victim*); ph, Leo Solis; ed, Ed Lowe; m, Cardozo Ocampo and Raul Garello; art d, Al Guglielmoni.

Crime   (PR:O MPAA:R)

UV

⊙UHF✱✱½
97m Cinecorp/Orion c

Al Yankovic (George Newman), Victoria Jackson (Teri), Kevin McCarthy (R.J. Fletcher), Michael Richards (Stanley Spadowski), David Bowe (Bob), Stanley Brock (Uncle Harvey), Anthony Geary (Philo), Trinidad Silva (Raul Hernandez), Gedde Watanabe (Kuni), Billy Barty (Noodles), John Paragon (Richard Fletcher), Fran Drescher (Pamela Finklestein), Sue Ane Langdon (Aunt Esther), David Proval (Head Thug), Grant James (Killer Thug), Emo Philips (Joe Earley), Jay Levey (Gandhi), Harry Kipper, Harry Kipper (Kipper Kids), Lou B. Washington (Cameraman), Vance Colvig (Bum), Nik Hagler (FCC Man), Robert K. Weiss (Bartender), Eldon G. Hallum (Spatula Husband), Sherry Engstrom (Spatula Wife), Sara Allen (Spatula Neighbor), Bob Hungerford (Sy Greenblum), John Cadenhead (Crazy Ernie), Francis M. Carlson (Blind Man), Ivan Green (Earl Ramsey), Adam Maras (Joel Miller), Travis Knight (Billy), Joseph Witt (Little Weasel), Tony Frank (Teri's Father), Billie Lee Thrash (Teri's Mother), Barry Friedman, Kevin Roden (Fletcher Cronies), Lisa R. Stefanic (Phyllis Weaver), Nancy Johnson (Big Edna), Debbie Mathieu (Betty), Wilma Jeanne Cummins (Little Old Lady), Cliff Stephens (Animal Deliveryman), Dr. Demento (Whipped Cream Eater), Bob Maras, George Fisher (Thugs), Tony Salome, Joe Restivo (Guides), Charles Marsh (Yodeler), Belinda Bauer, Lori Wagner (Mud Wrestlers), Patrick O'Brian (Satan), Roger Callard (Conan the Librarian), Robert Frank (Timid Man), Jeff Maynard (Boy with Books), M.G. Kelly, Jay Gardner, John Harlan, Jim Rose (Promo Announcers).

The satire is strictly hit and miss and the plot is by the numbers in UHF, musical parodist "Weird Al" Yankovic's film debut. Yankovic plays George, a daydreaming misfit who's unable to hold a steady job until his uncle (Brock) puts him in charge of U-62, a rundown UHF TV station Brock won in a poker game. With the station facing bankruptcy, a despairing Yankovic walks out on hosting chores midway through a lame kiddie show, leaving dimwitted janitor Richards to finish the program. Not surprisingly, Richards is an instant hit. Taking a cue from this success, Yankovic fills U-62 with similarly moronic offerings, knocking out competition all over the dial. Of course, it isn't long before his triumph has evil crosstown rival McCarthy sputtering with rage. Striking a bargain with the debt-ridden Brock, McCarthy plans to buy the station and turn

it into a parking lot unless Yankovic can raise the bucks to counter his offer. A telethon to save the station is staged, with late complications arising when McCarthy has U-62 superstar Richards kidnapped.

UHF's slob-outsiders-versus-uptight-establishment plot has become a B-movie comedy staple in recent years, in films ranging from ANIMAL HOUSE to POLICE ACADEMY and its too-frequent sequels. Coscripting with his manager, Jay Levey, who also directed, Yankovic fails to come up with anything new to freshen the stock storyline, and is content instead to let it serve as a creaky showcase for his true forte, media parodies. But the quality is inconsistent even here. The movie and music parodies suffer from being obvious and out of date: despite the fact that it has already spawned two sequels, RAIDERS OF THE LOST ARK gets sent up in the movie's fade-in, and the joke runs on long after it has run out of gas. A later parody of RAMBO is also long-winded and stale, and though the two-fisted GANDHI take-off (featuring director Levey as the title pacifist-turned-street vigilante) provokes a few chuckles, the use of this 1982 movie as a target again makes one wonder how long UHF's script sat on the shelf before it went in front of the cameras. The funniest thing about a similarly dated parody of Dire Straits' "Money for Nothing" music video (in which the lyrics are replaced with those of the "Beverly Hillbillies" theme) is the presence of Straits guitarist Mark Knopfler spoofing his own hit.

The TV parodies fare better, mainly because of hilarious guest-starring turns. Wiry comedian Emo Philips enlivens the early going as a "butterfingered" high-school teacher whose shop class demonstration quickly, and hilariously, deteriorates into table-saw grand guignol. Gedde Watanabe also gets sidesplittingly into the action as the unusually strict karate teacher recruited to host U-62's "Wheel of Fortune" ripoff, "Wheel of Fish." Nearly stealing the movie is the late Trinidad Silva (to whom UHF is dedicated), hosting "Raul's Wild Kingdom," the funniest—though easily the most tasteless—parody in the film. Dashing maniacally around his pet-cluttered apartment, Silva reveals a rarely seen gift for comedy while demonstrating the qualities of turtles as "nature's suction cups." And watch out for those flying poodles.

On the down side, virtually none of the principals is as funny as any of the guest stars. When not doing his parodies, Yankovic is likable but unexceptional as the daydreaming George. Kevin McCarthy has his moments as the odious rival, but he's finally hobbled by his cliched character, and Victoria Jackson (of "Saturday Night Live") is wasted in a nothing role as George's on-again, off-again girl friend.

Michael Richards fares better, but his character ultimately wears as well.

Weird Al's core of devoted admirers will probably get the most pleasure from UHF. Others may want to catch it later, when it makes its way to the title's TV netherworld. (Violence.)

p, Gene Kirkwood, John Hyde, Kevin Breslin, and Deren Getz; d, Jay Levey; w, Al Yankovic and Jay Levey; ph, David Lewis (Deluxe Color); ed, Dennis O'Connor; m, John Du Prez; prod d, Ward Preston; set d, Robert Zilliox; spec eff, Mike Menzel; cos, Tom McKinley; stunts, George Fisher; makeup, Lynne Eagan.

Comedy   (PR:C MPAA:PG-13)

⊙UNCLE BUCK✱✱½
100m UNIV c

John Candy (Uncle Buck Russell), Jean Kelly (Tia Russell), Gaby Hoffman (Maizy Russell), Macaulay Culkin (Miles Russell), Amy Madigan (Chanice Kobolowski), Elaine Bromka (Cindy Russell), Garrett M. Brown (Bob Russell), Laurie Metcalf (Marcie Dahlgren-Frost), Jay Underwood (Bug), Brian Tarantina (Rog), Mike Starr (Pooter-the-Clown), Suzanne Shepherd (Mrs. Hogarth), Dennis Cockrum (Pal), Matt Craven (Walt Bernstein), Jerry E. Postt (Marko the Mechanic), Zak Spector (Mechanic), Joel Robinson, Colin Baumgartner, Eric Whiple (Miles' Friends), Mark Rosenthal, Doug Van Nessen, Wayne Kneeland (Party Boys), Gigi Casler (Party Girl in Bedroom), Gina Doctor, Rachel Thompson Perrine (Party Girls), Ron Payne (Maizy's Teacher), Jane Vickerilla (Teacher).

Like the character he plays in the film, John Candy matures in UNCLE BUCK, downplaying his usual slapstick humor and fat jokes in the role of an estranged uncle with an unexpected knack for taking care of children. Kelly, Hoffman and Culkin play the nieces and nephew entrusted to Candy when their parents must visit a sick relative out of town. Eight-year-old Culkin and six-year-old Hoffman take a liking to Candy, but the teenage Kelly resents him—just as she resents her parents, who moved the family from Indianapolis to Chicago for no apparent reason. Despite Kelly's hostility, Candy soon becomes concerned about her and her boy friend (Underwood). His efforts to keep them apart annoy Kelly, who exacts revenge by telling Candy's girl friend (Madigan) that he is dating another woman. When Madigan catches Candy dancing with a neighbor (Metcalf), she gives up on him—after having waited eight years for him to commit to their relationship. Meanwhile, Candy amuses Culkin and Hoffman with giant pancakes, bowling outings, and other treats. After Kelly

John Candy and Mike Starr in UNCLE BUCK (©Universal).

goes out on the town, leaving the little children without a baby-sitter, Candy, who plans to cash in big at the racetrack, packs the kids into the car for another field trip, but cancels the outing when he learns that Kelly has left to spend the weekend with Underwood. Determined to rescue Kelly from the unworthy youth, Candy leaves the younger kids in Madigan's care and crashes a party where Underwood is luring a girl to bed in an upstairs room. Candy breaks into the room, only to discover that the girl with Underwood is not Kelly, whom he finally finds walking through the dark streets alone. She tearfully confesses that Candy's suspicions about her boy friend were true, and, to cheer her up, Candy opens the trunk of his car, revealing a bound and gagged Underwood. They chase him away, then return home so that Candy can patch things up with Madigan. But when her parents return home the next day, it's Kelly's turn to patch things up.

The supposed twist of UNCLE BUCK is that Candy is initially the last person you'd want to watch the children, yet both he and the kids benefit from the experience. The film falters on this premise, however, since Candy never seems as bad as he is made out to be. Yes, he drives a noisy old car, has never held a steady job, and, after eight years, still can't say, "I love you," to Madigan. But he's a decent person, likable from the start, who immediately agrees to take care of the kids, tries to make do without the parents' money, and shows no interest in Metcalf's lustful advances. Ironically, however, UNCLE BUCK succeeds as a whole because it fails in this respect. Had Uncle Buck been the crass, inconsiderate oaf that his brother and sister-in-law think he is, Candy merely would have provided his usual obnoxious antics instead of the

more thoughtful performance he gives here. The film is corny, but at least it's not just a succession of gags along the fish-out-of-water theme (although there are a few of them).

In addition to featuring Candy's most appealing film work to date, UNCLE BUCK is also one of writer-director John Hughes' more pleasant efforts. While the film features Hughes' usual parent- and teacher-bashing, there's more to it than the whiny teenage rebellion in his previous THE BREAKFAST CLUB; PRETTY IN PINK; and FERRIS BUELLER'S DAY OFF. (One can only wonder about the indignities Hughes suffered as a child at the hands of authority figures, considering the massive chip he still carries on his shoulder.) Jean Kelly's character, however, is unmistakably Hughes: a self-centered and antagonistic teen. Although an explanation is provided for her attitude toward her parents, she's nasty to Candy and her siblings for no reason. It's also hard to determine whether the parents' indifference is in character or the result of Elaine Bromka and Garrett M. Brown's wooden acting.

The movie's script and editing could stand improvement, too. A few scenes are thrown in just to get the audience to see what a good guy Uncle Buck is—as, for example, when a principal tells Candy she plans to discipline Hoffman because the little girl is not serious enough and Candy reprimands the principal, in turn, for her insensitivity to children. The scene seems contrived; nothing before or after relates even remotely to it. Likewise, the scene in which Candy shares a bed with the two little children is merely an effort to tug at our heart strings. There's no denying that Gaby Hoffman and Macaulay Culkin are cute, though, and their interplay with

Candy provides the highlights in UNCLE BUCK. *(Mild profanity, adult situations.)*

p, John Hughes and Tom Jacobson; d, John Hughes; w, John Hughes; ph, Ralf D. Bode (Deluxe Color); ed, Lou Lombardo, Tony Lombardo, and Peck Prior; m, Ira Newborn; prod d, John W. Corso; set d, Dan May; spec eff, Jeff Jarvis; cos, Marilyn Vance-Straker; chor, Miranda Garrison; stunts, James Arnett; makeup, Ben Nye Jr.

Comedy   **(PR:A MPAA:PG)**

Ⓥ**UNDER THE GUN***
89m Marquis c
Sam Jones *(Mike Braxton)*, Vanessa Williams *(Samantha Richards)*, John Russell *(Simon Stone)*, Michael Halsey *(Frank)*, Nick Cassavetes *(Tony Braxton)*, Steven Williams *(Gallagher)*, Bill McKinney *(Miller)*, Rockne Tarkington, Don Stark, Chris Mulkey, Michelle Russell, Steve Geray.

Appropriately enough in a film about arms dealers, UNDER THE GUN features weaponry that is sophisticated, deadly, and inclined toward overkill, accounting for more of the production budget than such niceties as proper lighting and sound dubbing. The action begins when St. Louis cop Jones receives a terrified last phone call from his brother (Cassavetes) in Los Angeles, just before the young bartender is crushed and killed in a phone booth, then pushed off a bridge, by a truck. Cassavetes' last words accuse his employer, a restaurateur, of having gotten him into great trouble. Jones journeys to LA and initiates a nasty confrontation with this man (played by former TV western star John Russell) at the latter's restaurant, then escapes the wrath of Russell's thugs by hiding in the car driven by the beautiful woman (Williams) who has been making eyes at him. Williams, it turns out, is an attorney working for Russell's lawyer, who is in Maui. Jones goes home with her, and she foolishly calls her boss' henchman (Halsey). The couple soon find themselves under fire and escape in Williams' Mercedes, only to be chased by a truck equipped with a rocket launcher. Jones employs some crafty moves to wipe out the opposition, but during the ensuing freeway battle Williams is taken prisoner by two sadists in a limousine. Meanwhile, radioactive material is being smuggled out of a high-tech laboratory nearby in a Robotech lunchbox. Arms dealer Russell, uncomfortable because the plutonium is being stored in his wine room and the police are watching his restaurant, decides to move the dangerous stuff—along with the movie's principal action—to his secluded ranch, where he plans to meet and deal with McKinney, a zillionaire gun nut said to "want his own country, and his own nuke power." In a shoot-out at the ranch, Jones rescues Williams. Doing their best to thwart Russell's attempt to sell the plutonium, they manage to stall things until the police arrive to clean up "this theme park for mercenaries," whereupon Jones walks off down a country road with Williams, in search of a hot shower and a back rub.

All the cliches of the low-budget action film are in place: cars blowing up in billows of orange flame, slow-motion karate moves, death scenes with bloody wounds from spraying automatic weapons. Only great vitality in the actors' performances can redeem such low-budget thrillers, but here the dramatic efforts are badly guided, and the total effect is one of stupefying dullness. *(Graphic violence.)*

p, Warren Stein; d, James Sbardellati; w, Almer John Davis, James Devney, and James Sbardellati (based on a story by Devney); ph, Gary Thieltges (United Color); ed, George Copanas; m, John Sterling; prod d, James Shumaker; set d, Dian Perryman; stunts, Harry Wowchuk.

Action   **(PR:O MPAA:R)**

UNREMARKABLE LIFE, AN***
98m Continental Filmgroup/SVS c
Patricia Neal *(Frances McEllany)*, Shelley Winters *(Evelyn McEllany)*, Mako *(Max Chin)*, Rochelle Oliver, Charles Dutton, Lily Knight, Jenny Chrisinger, Michael O'Neill, Madeleine Sherwood.

Competently directed by Amin Q. Chaudhri, with a sensitive but derivative script by Marcia Dinneen, AN UNREMARKABLE LIFE might also be termed an unremarkable film, were it not for its lead performances by Patricia Neal and Shelley Winters as aging sisters whose comfortably interdependent lifestyle is permanently disrupted when romance intrudes into their cloister. Neal, forever apologizing and unsure of herself, is a retired spinster schoolteacher whom Winters fusses over as if she were a child. The two maintain their domestic regimen religiously, their lives consumed by daily rituals, an arrangement made sadder in that Neal has never had a life of her own. Her dream of flying with other women pilots in WW II ended when she had to care for her ailing, domineering father; now, never-married and childless, she spends her twilight years with Winters—who, by contrast, has been married and has a daughter, granddaughter, and great-grand-children. A bossy, churchgoing do-gooder, Winters is most motivated by fear—of burglars, of integration, of being tossed out into the street, of spontaneity and change. When a Caucasian couple with an adopted Korean child moves across the street, Neal graciously welcomes them, but Winters is upset by their integrated family. Later, Neal develops a relationship with Asian garage mechanic Mako, but Winters (whose husband was captured by the Japanese during

WW II) hates her sister's suitor sight unseen. Neal, meanwhile, blossoms under the mechanic's liberating, life-affirming influence (one of the joys of the actress' performance is the way she appears to grow lovelier as the romance deepens). Mako even rents a plane, allowing her to revisit the wild blue yonder she was forced to abandon. Once she has tasted this freedom, she is reluctant to come down to earth. But after standing Winters up for a planned girl's night out at the mall—whereupon the distraught Winters runs away to a bus station like a frightened child—Neal temporarily relinquishes her last chance at love. In the bittersweet ending, while the reunited lovers are vacationing in Greece, Winters moves out of the family home, which Neal has sold. Apparently softened (she is shown embracing the Korean child), she mentions that Mako and Neal have promised to take her along on their next trip.

Neal and Winters transform a heartfelt but conventional domestic drama into something memorable here. Neal's face beautifully registers her character's regret, loneliness, and eventual joy, while Winters—after years of hamming it up in tripe like WITCHFIRE (1986)—is a revelation. The terror in her eyes when she hears that a friend was forced into a nursing home and the despairing resignation with which she slumps into a chair when she realizes that Neal has forgotten their date are but two of the most memorable moments in a beautifully detailed performance. Neal and Winters are so good at bringing these sisters to life that the film's climactic confrontation, in which Neal gives vent to years of resentment while Winters pours out her pathetic longings, has a devastating impact despite its formulaic inevitability. If nothing else, AN UNREMARKABLE LIFE proves that one can still derive pleasure and emotion from an old-fashioned, well-made movie in which seasoned professionals give performances of great power. *(Adult situations.)*

p, Amin Q. Chaudhri; d, Amin Q. Chaudhri; w, Marcia Dinneen; ph, Alan Hall; ed, Sandi Gerling; m, Avery Sharpe; md, Avery Sharpe; prod d, Norman B. Dodge Jr..

Drama   **(PR:C MPAA:PG)**

♥**VALENTINO RETURNS****
88m Owl/Skouras c
Barry Tubb *(Wayne Gibbs)*, Frederic Forrest *(Sonny Gibbs)*, Veronica Cartwright *(Patricia Gibbs)*, Jenny Wright *(Sylvia)*, David Packer, Seth Isler, Miguel Ferrer, Kit McDonough, Macon McCalman, Jenny Gago, Leonard Gardner, William Frankfather, Jerry Hardin.

Low-budget coming-of-age dramas with comedic overtones seem to be as much a staple of movies today as was the B western

of a bygone era. VALENTINO RETURNS is yet another stale example of what happens when filmmakers, in effect, run out of fresh material and original ideas. Not that this film, directed by Peter Hoffman from a screenplay by *Fat City* author Leonard Gardner (basing his script on his own short story "Christ Has Returned to Earth and Preaches Here Nightly"), doesn't have a few effective moments, but the film overall doesn't have much impact. Frederic Forrest and Veronica Cartwright give fine performances, but even these impressive players are overshadowed by the film's generally lackluster direction; choppy, irritating editing; and often ill-defined subplot characters, whose clarity and development might have been enhanced by another rewrite. In short, the film lacks focus and style. It is difficult to become involved with the characters most of the time; just when one scene begins to grip the viewer, the film elects to veer from that action to some unrelated situation of much less pith and moment.

It is as if the filmmakers couldn't decide where to put the emphasis—upon the relationship between the estranged spouses played by Forrest and Cartwright, or upon the couple's teenage, naive son (Tubb) and his frustrating romance with local tart Wright, the adolescent daughter of a Bible-spouting fanatic farmer (a stereotypical character if there ever was one). Set in northern California during the late 1950s, VALENTINO RETURNS does capture a certain tone and mood of bleak and dreary small-town Americana, complete with crude language, barroom brawls, beer-guzzling in honky-tonks, and sexual intrigue. In an attempt to relieve his boredom, young Tubb marches into an automobile showroom and purchases a flamingo pink 1958 Cadillac. For any movie patron who has seen more than one or two features of this genre before, it is not difficult to guess that, before the final reel unspools, the beautifully sleek Caddy is going to end up worse for wear. Tubb hopes his new car will get him his chance for a roll in the hay with Wright, who's had every other young stud and farmhand in town but him. Meanwhile, Forrest does his darnedest to win back his fussing wife. It's a long and bumpy road, but by the fadeout, Forrest, Cartwright, and Tubb finally manage to pull together as a family toward what just might be some form of mutual understanding.

Everything in VALENTINO RETURNS has been done better before. The film is predictable, obvious, contrived, and tedious. Forrest and Cartwright acquit themselves well, but the same cannot be said for Tubb, who delivers a bland, colorless performance as their sexual-fulfillment-seeking son. Wright does what she can as the town whore, but labors in yet another stereotypical role in a story filled to overflowing with cliched characters and events. *(Violence, excessive profanity, substance abuse, brief nudity, adult situations, sexual situations.)*

p, Peter Hoffman and David Wisnievitz; d, Peter Hoffman; w, Leonard Gardner (based on the story "Christ Has Returned to Earth and Preaches Here Nightly" by Leonard Gardner); ph, Jerzy Zielinski (Alpha Cine Color); ed, Denine Rowan; art d, Woody Romine.

Comedy/Drama   (PR:O MPAA:R)

VALMONT**
137m Claude Berri-Renn/Orion c
Colin Firth *(Vicomte de Valmont)*, Annette Bening *(Marquise de Merteuil)*, Meg Tilly *(Mme. de Tourvel)*, Fairuza Balk *(Cecile de Volanges)*, Sian Phillips *(Mme. de Volanges)*, Jeffery Jones *(Mons. Gercourt)*, Henry Thomas *(Chevalier Danceny)*, Fabia Drake *(Mme. de Rosemonde)*, T.P. McKenna *(Baron)*, Isla Blair *(Baroness)*, Ian McNeice *(Azolan)*, Aleta Mitchell *(Victoire)*, Ronald Lacey *(Jose)*, Vincent Schiavelli *(Jean)*, Sandrine Dumas *(Martine)*, Sebastien Floche *(Priest)*, Anthony Carrick *(President de Tourvel)*, Murray Gronwall *(Flea Market Salesman)*, Alain Frerot, Daniel Laloux, Christian Bouillette *(Thugs)*, John Arnold, Niels Tavernier *(Knights of the Maltese Order)*, Yvette Petit *(Mother Superior)*, Richard De Burnchurch *(Volanges' Majordomo)*, Jose Licenziato *(Blind Guitar Player)*, Ivan Palec *(Servant)*.

VALMONT is the third film adaptation of Choderlos de Laclos' epistolary masterpiece *Les Liaisons Dangereuses*. In 1957, Roger Vadim did a modern-dress version chiefly memorable for its orgies, Jeanne Moreau's magnificently leonine Juliette de Merteuil, and Vadim's own hysterically funny, overripe introductory narration. In 1988 came Stephen Frears' hit DANGEROUS LIAISONS, a credible, if snail-paced, adaptation of Christopher Hampton's popular stage version of Laclos' novel. Milos Forman's latest attempt to film the novel is the weakest by far, suffering from willfully wrongheaded casting, a comic-strip "free" adaptation by Bunuel's frequent collaborator Jean-Claude Carriere, and Forman's heavy-handed direction of material that requires the most sophisticated glancing touch. (The ideal production would have been directed by Josef von Sternberg.)

Forman and Carriere focus primarily on the eponymous Valmont (Firth), ending the film after his death in a duel and omitting both the demise of his amorous victim, Mme. de Tourvel (Tilly), and Laclos' audience-gratifying comeuppance for the scheming Marquise de Merteuil (Bening). The filmmakers' choice throws the whole ornately devised mechanism of Laclos' story—an unrelenting battle of wit and

seduction between Valmont and Merteuil —completely off. With its ineffectual performers uttering Carriere's slovenly dialog, VALMONT plays like some period sex romp, its concerns reduced to the level of who sleeps with whom and who gets dumped. Forman hypes the action, opening things up at every opportunity with picnic scenes, an archery lesson, noisome marketplaces, antics in a tavern, and even a near-royal wedding. Though Laclos' background of stultifying formality and intricate, 18th-century mores are vital to the movement of his story, Forman blithely does away with all that in the interests of immediacy (as in his hugely overrated AMADEUS), underestimating his audience's ability to understand and sympathize with the passions of another time and place. Other infelicitous touches include the tacky love den operated by Merteuil, Merteuil's costuming of the young Cecile (Balk) in a Folies Bergeres get-up before an assignation, Valmont's slapstick fall into a river while wooing Tourvel, and an enigmatic blackmail scheme. Expectations lowered, one begins to look forward to a wildly Gothic treatment of Merteuil's disfigurement by smallpox, but Forman has somehow overlooked this lurid possibility. It's impossible not to feel, as VALMONT progresses, that the subtle brilliance of the original material is simply beyond Forman's scope.

As Valmont, Colin Firth is more conventionally handsome and dashing than John Malkovich in Frears' film, but Malkovich remains the better seducer. Firth is effective in introspective roles (as in ANOTHER COUNTRY or A MONTH IN THE COUNTRY), but lacks the charismatic bravado and sexual menace necessary for Valmont. He's too boyish, and not all that different from his rival, the young music teacher Danceny (played by Henry Thomas, ET's Elliott grown up). Malkovich managed to heat up Glenn Close's formidably chilly Merteuil and faced Keanu Reeves' Danceny down with ambiguous intensity in DANGEROUS LIAISONS; when Firth and Thomas meet in VALMONT, you almost expect them to join forces and cruise babes at the mall. Where Malkovich was maddeningly perverse in his treatment of Tourvel, Firth makes Valmont's actions seem mere, meaningless narcissism.

Annette Bening (THE GREAT OUTDOORS) is also lightweight in her role, delivering a facile and annoyingly arch performance as Merteuil, a problem compounded by Forman and Carriere's characterization, in which Merteuil is graceless and lascivious. (Her celebrated declaration of war is staged with TV-sitcom crassness—Valmont overturns the bathtub in which she has immodestly received him.) As Tourvel, Meg Tilly (AGNES OF GOD; THE GIRL IN A

SWING) once again exhibits the weirdly enervated acting style that probably made her seem perfect for the role in Forman's mind, but her tentative mousiness is boring and predictable here. Even her scene of degradation, in which she stands bedraggled in the rain outside Valmont's residence, is an unaffecting cliche (cadged from Truffaut's STORY OF ADELE H.) Thomas gives a more successful performance (once you adjust to his American tones), making Danceny affecting in his woebegone sincerity and boyish ambitions, but Fairuza Balk, as his love interest, is irritatingly whiny in a style more suited to John Hughes' film universe. Among the other supporting players, Fabia Drake makes Mme. de Rosemonde a tiresomely dear old lady, forever winking at Valmont's naughtiness or falling asleep and querulously inquiring as to the identities of familiars. Sian Phillips, as Mme. de Volanges, is the one performer who really seems at home; her astringent elegance would have made her an ideal Merteuil earlier in her career.

The production is adequate but unexciting. The setting has been backdated 50 years from DANGEROUS LIAISONS' period to a less photogenic time, though it would have been hard to compete with James Acheson's glorious Boucher/Fragonard-inspired costumes for the Frears film in any case (Acheson's period wardrobe was one of the greatest ever seen on-screen). Forman provides a nice image at the beginning, as the camera picks Cecile out of a choir in a hazily lit convent, and there's an impressive shot of a vast duelling gallery; otherwise the film is not particularly memorable in its visuals. The score— filled with the requisite harpsichord flourishes and noodlings that complement the various nocturnal pairings in a sort of rococo version of "The Love Boat"—is similarly undistinguished. Musical selections include: "Le Sorcier," "Tom Jones" Overture and Finale (Francois-Andre Danican Philidor), "Richard Coeur de Lion" Overture (Andre-Ernest-Modeste Gretry), "Te Deum" (Marc-Antoine Charpentier), Minuet from Quartet in F, Op. 50, No. 5 (Joseph Haydn), Divertimento for Winds in B, K. 240 (Wolfgang Amadeus Mozart), "Les Oiseaux Elegants," "L'Apotheose de Lulli" (Francois Couperin), "Les Songes de Dardanus" (Jean-Philippe Rameau), "A Knight Riding Through the Glade," "Love, If You Will Come" (Baldassari Galuppi, Anne Gyory, Hope Newman), "Pity the Fate" (Philidor, Gyory, Newman). *(Nudity, sexual situations, adult situations.)*

p, Paul Rassam and Michael Hausman; d, Milos Forman; w, Jean-Claude Carriere (based on the novel *Les Liaisons Dangereuses* by Choderlos de Laclos); ph, Miroslav Ondricek; ed, Alan Heim and Nena Danevic; m, Christopher Palmer;

md, Sir Neville Marriner; prod d, Pierre Guffroy; art d, Albert Rajau and Loula Morin; spec eff, Garth Inns and Michel Norman; cos, Theodor Pistek; chor, Ann Jacoby; makeup, Paul LeBlanc.

Drama   **(PR:O MPAA:R)**

Ⓥ**VICE ACADEMY***
90m c

Linnea Quigley *(Didi)*, Ginger Lynn Allen *(Holly)*, Karen Russell *(Shawnee)*, Jayne Hamil *(Devonshire)*, Ken Abraham *(Dwayne)*, Stephen Steward *(Chucky)*, Jeannie Carol, Tami Bakke, Jo Brewer.

It is not the least bit surprising that VICE ACADEMY went straight to video without so much as a single matinee showing in any major market. Beneath contempt and unprofessional in every respect, this exercise in borderline soft-core pornography is wholly without credibility despite the presence of B-movie queen Linnea Quigley. Ostensibly about the training of a group of police cadets, the film is primarily concerned with exhibiting its largely female cast in as many stages of undress as possible in 90 minutes. Few movies provide their casts with as many opportunities to bend over, bare their breasts, and engage in sex as VICE ACADEMY does. The film can be divided into two parts, though there are few differences between them. The first part deals with a training mission that calls for the cadets to go undercover to break up a pornography operation that employs underage girls; the second concerns an assignment involving a prostitution ring. Allen, a captain's daughter, and fellow cadet Quigley are engaged in a vicious game of one-upmanship, as each tries to win the favor of Hamil, the director of the training program. The token male among the bevy of curvaceous beauties aspiring to vice squad membership is Abraham (whose attempts at comic relief are neither comic nor relieving). Sparks begin to fly when Hamil assigns Quigley, Abraham, and their friend Russell to arrest 10 members of an infamous prostitution ring—a task Hamil knows they will never be able complete. The catch is that the trio's graduation hinges on the fulfillment of this assignment. When the threesome ingeniously infiltrates the ring by posing as prostitutes and a john, it looks like they've beaten the odds. However, the cadets manage to lose the ringleader, a customer, and several prostitutes and have to pursue them through various storerooms that all look suspiciously similar, as if the same room has been filmed repeatedly without so much as altering the camera angle.

Judging from the production values, writer-director-producer-editor Rick Sloane must have had a budget in the $50 to $60 range. Set design is all but nonexistent, as the majority of the action transpires in storerooms, public parks, and private residences. While the cadets are put through their paces on a field, a major highway can be seen in the background. Mercifully, the highway is close enough that when the insipidity of VICE ACADEMY becomes too unbearable, one's attention can be turned to the cars caught in rush hour traffic. Alan der Marderosian's synthesized score isn't any more interesting than the set, and more than invites comparison with the familiar themes from TV's "Jeopardy" and the "James Bond" and "Psycho" films. Not even the coronation music from the Imperial Margarine television commercials is safe. The acting in VICE ACADEMY ranges from barely acceptable (Ginger Lynn Allen and Linnea Quigley are capable of more) to horrendous, due partly to the fact that many of the performers are newcomers. As one character says to another when she is handcuffed in the warehouse hideout of the prostitution ring, "Scream all you want, no one can help you now!" Fortunately, viewers of VICE ACADEMY will find themselves in the same predicament only if their VCRs become stuck on *play. (Nudity, sexual situations.)*

p, Rick Sloane; d, Rick Sloane; w, Rick Sloane; ph, Stephen Ashley Blake; ed, Rick Sloane; m, Alan der Marderosian.

Comedy   **(PR:C MPAA:R)**

W

ⓥWAR BIRDS zero
88m Hess Kallberg-Skyhawk/Vidmark c
Jim Eldert *(Billy Hawkins)*, Timothy
Hicks *(Jim Harris)*, Bill Brinsfield *(Lt.
Col. Ronson)*, Cully Holland *(Vince Costello)*, David Schroeder *(Van Dam)*, Stephen Quadros *(Jeff Rinks)*, Joanne
Watkins *(Carolyn)*, Rick Anthony Monroe *(Salim)*.

Give director Ulli Lommel credit for sheer
gumption. There aren't many filmmakers
around who would attempt a TOP GUN
ripoff on a thrift-shop budget. But gumption is not enough to make Lommel's
WAR BIRDS worth more than a fly-by.

Imagine TOP GUN without the aerial
dogfights, without Tom Cruise and Kelly
McGillis, and without a script (not that
TOP GUN's script was any work of genius
in the first place), and you'll have a relatively good idea of what WAR BIRDS is
like. What's a little harder to convey is the
slow numbing of the brain and glazing over
of the eyes you'll experience while sitting
through this 88 minutes of militaristic bargain-basement baloney. Minus the big-studio budget and cast, what you get in WAR
BIRDS is endless views of guys getting into
and out of plane cockpits, closeups of
cheesy-looking prop instrument panels,
guys in rented off-the-rack uniforms standing around and shouting into prop telephones (describing battles that Lommel
evidently didn't have the money to film),
stock footage of F-16s (*lots* of it), and that
perennial staple of all low-budget action
movies, plenty of things getting blown up.
What you also get is a plot from hunger,
conceived almost solely to stretch the
film's approximately two minutes of original action footage into some 30 minutes
of "battle" scenes.

For those who care, WAR BIRDS takes
place in one of those mythical Middle Eastern countries, El Ala-something-or-other,
governed by a diminutive sheik who looks
like he might be Libyan leader Muammar
Qaddafi's stunted little brother. As the film
begins, the sheik's sheikdom is being overrun by a bunch of exotic-looking, bad character actors playing rebels in red berets. A
frantic call for help is made to Washington
(represented in the film by a minimally
furnished war room that looks like a television news set doing double time), and the
bureaucrats who take the call—referred to
later in the film as "those pencil-pushing
pansies"—bring in beefy lieutenant colonel Brinsfield to take command of a covert
mission to bomb the red-beret bunch back
to the Stone Age. This is immediately followed by scenes of Brinsfield standing
around in suburban backyards, saying
things like, "He used to be one of the best,
but we hear he's got a girl friend now who's

clipped his wings," as he sets about recruiting a group of generic-looking, bad American character actors (alleged grads of the
"Top Gun" school, natch) to pretend
they're flying F-16 planes. After a lot of
high-fives and talk about "kicking butt," it
takes not one, but *three*, essentially identical bombing missions (four, if you count
the flashback that WAR BIRDS couldn't
be a truly bad movie without) before the
job is completed. That's because one of the
sheik's military commanders has gotten
into the disagreeable habit of driving over
to the red-beret camp in his jeep after work
to tell the rebels exactly when the attacks
will occur. The American bombing runs,
it's worth noting, are directed by Vietnam
vet Brinsfield via marine telephone from
the cabin of his yacht, which looks like it's
docked in Long Beach, suggesting yet
another intriguing theory as to how we lost
the war.

Taken on its own terms, WAR BIRDS is
better than average in the things-blowing-up department—they used lots of napalm
on this one. Otherwise, covert military
action isn't the only activity of dubious
legality going on here. There's also the
criminal waste of perfectly good film stock
to consider. Do we really need to say it?
WAR BIRDS is a turkey. *(Profanity, violence.)*

p, Kurt Eggert and Joanne Watkins; d,
Ulli Lommel; w, Clifford B. Wellman and
Ulli Lommel; ph, Deland Nuse (Foto-Kem Color); ed, Joe Negron; m, Jerry
Lambert; prod d, Angela Allaire and Lou
Ann Quast.

War   **(PR:C MPAA:R)**

WAR OF THE ROSES, THE
(See THE YEAR'S BEST)

WAR PARTY**½
99m Hemdale/Tri-Star c
Billy Wirth *(Sonny Crowkiller)*, Kevin
Dillon *(Skitty Harris)*, Tim Sampson
(Warren Cutfoot), Jimmy Ray Weeks *(Jay
Stivic)*, Kevin M. Howard *(Calvin)*, M.
Emmet Walsh *(Detweiler)*, Cameron Thor
(Lindquist), Jerry Hardin *(Sheriff)*, Kevin
Major Boyd *(Calvin Morrisey)*.

It's just about time for a moratorium on
European directors coming to the US to
make films about racial injustice.
Although filmmakers have long examined
social problems in countries other than
their own, in the 1980s the US became an
easy target. In ALAMO BAY (1985),
French director Louis Malle depicts the
abysmal treatment Vietnamese "boat people" received at the hands of white Texans.
In 1988 Costa-Gavras (who has repeatedly
cast a reproving eye on repression and
scandal in foreign cultures, though Z, set
in his Greek homeland, remains his best
film) focused on white supremacists in

BETRAYED. That same year, British
director Alan Parker offered MISSISSIPPI
BURNING, his tale of the Civil Rights
struggle in the American South in the
1960s. With WAR PARTY, another British
filmmaker, Franc Roddam, takes his shot
at depicting the racial insensitivity of white
Americans. However, those familiar with
Roddam's rocky career will recognize this
film as little more than a reworking of
QUADROPHENIA, the director's masterful 1979 screen adaptation of The Who's
rock 'n' roll album of the same name.
QUADROPHENIA centered on the clash
between teenage tribes (the Mods and
Rockers) in 1960s England; WAR PARTY
re-creates the dynamics of that violent
confrontation in an American setting with
only limited success. Indeed, Roddam
might have done better to confine his social
criticism to his own back yard, as fellow
British director Stephen Frears (SAMMY
AND ROSIE GET LAID; MY BEAUTIFUL LAUNDRETTE) has done so brilliantly.

WAR PARTY opens in 1889 in Binger,
Montana, during a massacre of Blackfoot
Indians by whites. The camera pans away
from the bloody battle to modern Binger,
100 years later, where things haven't
changed much: the town is populated by
many Native Americans, but there are still
plenty of white racists on hand. Binger's
white mayor decides to stage a reenactment of the massacre for the entertainment of the tourists arriving for the town's
Labor Day festivities (the sort of thing that
only a screenwriter could dream up). Obviously, the situation is not without potential
for conflict. Sure enough, a deranged,
drunken white guy dressed in a soldier's
outfit pumps real lead into one of the
Native Americans. Although the killing
occurs in front of hundreds of witnesses,
they all assume it is part of the show. Sonny
Crowkiller (Wirth) soon becomes Sonny
Drunkenwhiteguykiller when he and some
friends retaliate for the murder. Mayhem
breaks out and the five Native American
friends are forced to take refuge in the
wilderness. Two of the group fall victim to
a posse of angry whites. Pursed by the posse
and the National Guard, the surviving
trio—Wirth, Dillon (IMMEDIATE FAMILY), and Sampson (son of Will Sampson)—struggle to survive, but events take
their toll on them, especially on Wirth,
who was to have been married on the day
of the slaying (more fanciful invention
from the filmmakers). Just when it seems
as if the fugitives have gotten the best of the
law, a bounty hunter (Walsh) comes onto
the scene. The film closes on a highly
moral note, but many viewers may not
make it through enough of this hateful,
bloody film to get to Roddam's didactic
message. *(Profanity, graphic violence.)*

p, John Daly, Derek Gibson, and Bernard
Williams; d, Franc Roddam; w, Spencer

Eastman; ph, Brian Tufano (CFI Color); ed, Sean Barton; m, Chaz Jankel; prod d, Michael Bingham.

Action   (PR:O MPAA:R)

ⓥWE THINK THE WORLD OF YOU***

(Brit.) 94m Gold Screen/Cinecom c

Alan Bates *(Frank Meadows)*, Gary Oldman *(Johnny Burney)*, Max Wall *(Tom Burney)*, Liz Smith *(Millie Burney)*, Frances Barber *(Megan)*, Sheila Ballantine *(Margaret)*, Kerry Wise *(Rita)*, Betsy the Alsatian Dog *(Evie)*, Ryan Batt *(Dickie)*, David Swift *(Bill)*, Pat Keen *(Miss Sweeting)*, Ivor Roberts *(Harry)*, Paula Jacobs *(Deidre)*, Edward Jewesbury *(Judge)*, Nick Stringer *(Butcher)*, Danny MacDonald *(Boy)*, Nicola Wright *(Post Girl)*, Ian Hastings *(RSPCA Inspector)*, Barbara New *(Mrs. Grant)*, Stewart Harwood *(Stallholder)*, Barbara Hicks, Irene Sutcliffe *(Residents' Association Ladies)*, David Trevena *(Meter Man)*.

At first glance, WE THINK THE WORLD OF YOU looks depressingly like what many Americans regard as a typical British film: period setting, literary source, and lots of "acting." Before one consigns it to the "tasteful classics" bin, however, it's well worth noting that the film not only contains social commentary and allegory, but is also a scalding comedy of manners and a full-blooded, if perverse, love story. Set in the 1950s, WE THINK THE WORLD OF YOU stars Bates as a middle-aged civil servant who is intelligent, comfortably wealthy, and in love. Unfortunately, the object of his affections is Oldman: young, working-class, and married. In the opening scenes, Bates is visiting Oldman, who is in jail after being arrested for breaking into a house. Bates readily offers Oldman money, but balks at his former lover's request that he take in Oldman's pet Alsatian, Evie. When Oldman is sentenced to a year's imprisonment, Bates visits Oldman's mother (Smith) and stepfather (Wall), who are looking after Evie and their young grandson in a cramped council house while Barber—Oldman's pregnant wife—copes as best she can with her daughter. Bates continues to visit Smith, his only connection with Oldman, and begins to grow fond of Evie. He identifies with the dog, viewing her as another lover spurned by Oldman, and deplores the way she is cooped up without exercise. Unable to see or write to Oldman—visiting rights are all taken up by the hated Barber—Bates becomes obsessed with Evie, and tries to buy her when he learns that the dog has been kicked and beaten. Oldman refuses to sell, however, and his insulted parents insist that Bates end his relationship with the dog. Once Oldman is released from jail, he and Bates see each other occasionally.

Bates is allowed to bring Evie back to his flat on weekends, but it becomes impossible to continue his friendship with Oldman; too much divides them. When they meet by chance in a pub, Oldman tells Bates that he cannot afford to keep Evie any longer, and bitterly accepts Bates' offer to buy her. Later, their paths cross in a park —Bates is with Evie, Oldman with his family. Oldman confides that Bates got the better deal.

J.R. Ackerley's novel *We Think the World of You* is very much a product of the repressive society it studies, as is director Colin Gregg's film adaptation. Just as Bates' love for Evie is a perversion of his natural feeling for Oldman, so this story is an extraordinary transposition of the love that dare not speak its name, in the 1950s or today. As an allegorical response to censorship of homosexual literature and social intolerance, WE THINK THE WORLD OF YOU is fairly compelling—and relevant in contemporary Britain, where legislation has been passed against art that may "promote" homosexuality (Thatcher's notorious Section 28). Although Bates' relationship with Oldman dictates the action, it is never more than implicit— there are no sex scenes, not even a kiss. The film's color scheme emphasizes grays and muted browns, suggesting that the society it depicts is only half-alive. The characters are all trapped in one way or another, each in his or her own cage: Smith and Wall never venture out of their crowded council house; Barber is seen only in her own home or within the even more restricting confines of a telephone booth; Oldman is in prison for most of the movie, as well as trapped in a loveless marriage. Bates' character, by virtue of his affluence and education, is able to traverse these boundaries, but he is still a prisoner of his own impossible desires, both for Oldman and for Evie. The dog is the symbolic embodiment of all these captives: kept in a tiny stone yard and deprived of exercise, sick and mad as a result. The only relief from the claustrophobic mise-en-scene comes in the bright exterior sequences, when Bates walks (or runs) Evie.

The film's real strength, however, is the bizarre love story itself. Alan Bates' carefully modulated performance makes his identification with Evie quite credible; rooted in compassion and love, his obsessional behavior is impossible to dismiss simply as madness. Unlike Hollywood's recent buddy-doggie movies, K-9 and TURNER AND HOOCH, WE THINK THE WORLD OF YOU never anthropomorphizes. Director Gregg allows no trace of Disneyfied cuteness (or Gallic romanticism, as in THE BEAR) to creep into his movie: the dog is only a dog. This restraint gives the film a realistic grounding that serves it well, tingeing its humor with sadness, as when Bates attempts to take his

recalcitrant pet to the office, for example, or when Evie joins Bates in bed.

Around this central, absurd-but-real "relationship" of man and dog, an excellent cast delineates a slightly caricatured picture of British prejudice, snobbery, and repression. Frances Barber (Rosie of SAMMY AND ROSIE GET LAID) stands out in her stillness, Gary Oldman (SID AND NANCY; TRACK 29) does another virtuoso variation on his boyish charmer, and Liz Smith (APARTMENT ZERO; HIGH SPIRITS) does her batty turn as wittily as ever. None of these characters is very likable (the film is especially vulnerable to charges of misogyny), but none is completely without dignity; rather, they are simply products of a class-ridden, hypocritical society. In this regard, perhaps the most tragic characters in the film are Oldman and Barber's unwanted, unloved kids, for whom the future will be bleak. *(Adult situations.)*

p, Tommaso Jandelli and Paul Cowan; d, Colin Gregg; w, Hugh Stoddart (based on the novel by Joseph R. Ackerley); ph, Mike Garfath (Technicolor); ed, Peter Delfgou; m, Julian Jacobson; md, Julian Jacobson; prod d, Jamie Leonard; art d, Chris Edwards; cos, Doreen Watkinson; makeup, Jennifer Boost.

Comedy/Drama   (PR:A-C MPAA:PG)

ⓥWEEKEND AT BERNIE'S**½

99m Gladden/FOX c

(AKA: HOT AND COLD)

Andrew McCarthy *(Larry Wilson)*, Jonathan Silverman *(Richard Parker)*, Catherine Mary Stewart *(Gwen Saunders)*, Terry Kiser *(Bernie Lomax)*, Don Calfa *(Paulie)*, Catherine Parks *(Tina)*, Eloise Broady *(Tawny)*, Gregory Salata *(Marty)*, Louis Giambalvo *(Vito)*, Ted Kotcheff *(Jack Parker)*, Margaret Hall *(Secretary)*, Timothy Perez *(Mugger)*, Mark Kenneth Smaltz *(Security Officer)*, Anthony Mannino *(Superintendent)*, Polly Segal *(Woman in Elevator)*, Bob Horen *(Maitre D')*, Bruce Barbour *(Beach Bum)*, Jason Woliner *(Bratty Kid)*, Dan Cox *(Handsome Guy)*, Steve Howard *(Plastic Surgeon)*, Lorri Lindberg *(Aukthoress)*, Jack Hallett *(Tennis Pro)*, John Bennes *(Harvey)*, Augustina Berlings *(Larry's Pick-Up)*, Mert Hatfield *(Cop)*, Jack Canon *(Murray Rose)*, Nello Tare *(Party Man)*, Joyce Bowden *(Fashion Designer)*, Stefanos Miltsakakis *(Body Builder)*, Dan Preston *(Exercise Trainer)*, Jean Liles *(Girl on Dock)*, Lisa Sherrill Gannon, Rachel Lewis *(Beach Girls)*, Dan Wargo *(Party Guest)*, Patricia Roseman *(Female Model)*, David Arey *(Male Model)*, Ronald Ross *(Man at Table)*, George Cheung *(Gardener)*, Lou Criscuolo *(First Islander)*, Edwin Little Dean *(Water Taxi Driver)*, Stephen Fischer *(Man on Elevator)*, Cindy Foster Jones *(Girl at Ambu-*

lance), Richard W. Boucher (*Handsome Man No. 2*), Leslie Sternchak, Tina Diane King (*Girls at Party*), Michelle Vincent (*Girl on Boat*).

WEEKEND AT BERNIE'S is a one-joke movie—and what you think of the joke will basically determine what you think of the movie. McCarthy and Silverman play two rookie accountants at a big insurance company run by the title character (Kiser), as oily and venal a CEO as they come. While putting in weekend overtime, McCarthy and Silverman uncover a series of fraudulent claims that have cost the company $2 million. Flushed with pride and braced for big promotions, they bring the scam to the attention of Kiser, who appears accordingly impressed, to the point that he invites the boys out for a weekend fling at his sprawling beach house. What the accountants don't know is that the scammer is none other than Kiser himself, who, it further turns out, has mob connections. Unbeknownst to the boys, Kiser asks mobster Giambalvo to kill them in order to keep the larceny quiet. Unbeknownst to Kiser, Giambalvo orders hitman Calfa to bump off Kiser instead. Calfa gets the job done before McCarthy and Silverman arrive at the beach house, where they find the dead Kiser but are forced to delay the discovery of his demise, fearful that they will be framed for his murder. The film's sole joke is that, with a little help from McCarthy and Silverman, Kiser subsequently becomes more of a party animal dead than alive. Among other things, he becomes a tougher bargainer when it comes to "selling" a car and he even becomes a better lover to his girl friend, who also happens to be Giambalvo's mistress—a major factor in his decision to do away with Kiser. Further complicating matters is Silverman's attempted romance with a pretty company summer intern (Stewart) and Calfa's return to the beach house to finish what he thinks is a botched hit.

WEEKEND AT BERNIE'S will never erase memories of Alfred Hitchcock's similar—and inspired—THE TROUBLE WITH HARRY. Robert Klane's script is never as funny as it wants to be; though individual scenes have comic spark, the dialog is spotty and the overall plotting lacks focus. Andrew McCarthy and Jonathan Silverman are competent in their roles, but don't quite click as a comic team. Individually, they're easily outshone by the reclining Terry Kiser, who's truly hilarious as Bernie, both dead and alive.

Ted Kotcheff's direction, however, keeps the film afloat, getting the most out of the good scenes and skimming through the weaker moments. The early scenes, sending up corporate life and setting up the scrappy mavericks played by McCarthy and Silverman, have hints of the sharp satire and comic energy Kotcheff brought

to THE APPRENTICESHIP OF DUDDY KRAVITZ and NORTH DALLAS FORTY, with their similar outsider-versus-establishment themes. Later in the film, Kotcheff, who has also never let good taste get in the way of a joke, gets indecently potent comic mileage out of the endless gags revolving around the abuse of a corpse. The comic pacing is impeccable, with the effect of convincing you that you're watching a much better film than you actually are.

Needless to say, even at its best, WEEKEND AT BERNIE'S is not a film for all tastes. It is not decent, wholesome, or uplifting and does nothing to reinforce family values. It's bawdy, irreverent humor pushes the envelope of its MPAA PG-13 rating. But adults in the mood for something a little different could do worse than to spend a 99-minute weekend with Bernie, the stiff who winds up stealing the film. Songs include: "Hot and Cold" (Andy Summers, Winston "Pipe" Matthews, performed by Jermaine Stewart), "Vissi D'arte, Vissi D'amore" (Giacomo Puccini), "Night on Bald Mountain" (Modest Mussorgsky). (*Adult situations, profanity.*)

p, Victor Drai; d, Ted Kotcheff; w, Robert Klane; ph, Francois Protat (Duart Color); ed, Joan E. Chapman; m, Andy Summers; prod d, Peter Jamison; art d, Michael Novotny; set d, Jerie Kelter; spec eff, Phil Cory and Joe DiGaetano; cos, Dana Campbell; stunts, Conrad E. Palmisano; makeup, Barbara Palmer.

Comedy   (PR:O   MPAA:PG-13)

WELCOME HOME***
87m COL-RANK c
Kris Kristofferson (*Lt. Jake Robbins*), JoBeth Williams (*Sarah*), Brian Keith (*Jake's Father*), Sam Waterston (*Woody*), Trey Wilson (*Col. Barnes*), J.J. "John Marshal" Jones Jr. (*Dwayne*), Thomas Wilson Brown (*Tyler*), Kieu Chinh (*Leang*), Lela Ivey, Jamie Jones, Jeremy Ratchford, Norah Grant, Bill Lynn.

Recent Hollywood movies are beginning to show the strain of having to have the last word on the Vietnam War. For that reason, it's refreshing to see WELCOME HOME strive to be a movie about Vietnam, rather than "the" movie about Vietnam. If anything, WELCOME HOME may be too modestly scaled for its own good insofar as its major weakness is that its script raises more complex issues than the film is able to meaningfully address.

WELCOME HOME begins as Air Force pilot Jake Robbins (Kris Kristofferson), declared a war casualty in 1970, resurfaces in 1987 with a Cambodian wife and two children. After being shot down over Cambodia and held prisoner by the Khmer Rouge, Kristofferson escaped into the jungle, where he met his wife and lived happily for the next decade and a half. ("We had a

hammock out back," Kristofferson tells his father. "Hell, it was like living in Syracuse.") But when Kristofferson becomes too sick to be cared for by his wife, she brings him to Thailand for hospitalization. She is then taken away, with her children, to a border refugee camp, while Kristofferson winds up in an Army hospital. There, Col. Barnes (Trey Wilson) does his best to keep Kristofferson and his story under wraps. As Wilson and the Army see it, renewed public speculation on the possibility of other missing GIs like Kristofferson could endanger the rapprochement being undertaken by the US and Vietnam. The film's real concern, however, is with the effect Kristofferson's return has on his father (Brian Keith) and, especially, on his American wife (JoBeth Williams) and son, Tyler (Thomas Wilson Brown). Williams has since made a new life with Woody (Sam Waterston), a decent man in the lumber business who uses wood-siding metaphors to interpret life. Kristofferson's return causes a crisis for Williams—who had pledged never to stop loving him—and for his son, who first takes Kristofferson to be his mother's adulterous lover, then believes him to be a deserter. While trying to make peace with his past at home and move ahead with his life, Kristofferson also wages a running battle with Wilson and the military bureaucracy, as he tries to reunite with his Cambodian family.

As a homefront Vietnam film, WELCOME HOME recalls Francis Coppola's equally understated (and underrated) GARDENS OF STONE in its attempt to show how a war fought half a world away had an impact on average Americans. Also like Coppola's film, it admirably refrains from making sweeping, definitive statements in favor of an intimate, human exploration of how ordinary people cope with an extraordinary situation. In this endeavour, veteran director Franklin J. Schaffner, who died before WELCOME HOME's release, is greatly helped by his cast, especially Kristofferson and Williams, who hold the film together with intelligence, sensitivity, and quiet dignity. Though Williams is (as usual) outstanding throughout the movie, there have been few moments in recent films more unexpectedly moving than the simple yet powerful shock of recognition her character undergoes when seeing Kristofferson's Jake for the first time after his return. Kristofferson, meanwhile, brings a similarly compelling, low-key conviction to every scene he's in.

WELCOME HOME's only real fault is that its dual plots finally prove too much for its modest scale. While its family drama ends with a satisfying note of reconciliation, the resolution of Jake's battle with the military is too pat and contrived. The easy disposal of the added complications raised by Jake's Cambodian family provides an especially convenient means by which to shift the film's focus to Jake's problems back home. Nevertheless, as a result of Kristofferson's and Williams' performances and Schaffner's assured, effective direction, WELCOME HOME is a worthwhile addition to Hollywood's cinematic explorations of the Vietnam conflict. *(Adult situations, profanity.)*

p, Martin Ransohoff; d, Franklin J. Schaffner; w, Maggie Kleinman; ph, Fred J. Koenekamp (Eastmancolor); ed, Bob Swink; prod d, Dan Yarhi and Dennis Davenport.

Drama   **(PR:C   MPAA:R)**

WE'RE NO ANGELS*
105m Art Linson/PAR c
Robert De Niro *(Ned/Fr. Reilly)*, Sean Penn *(Jim/Fr. Brown)*, Demi Moore *(Molly)*, Hoyt Axton *(Fr. Levesque)*, Bruno Kirby *(Deputy)*, Ray McAnally *(Warden)*, James Russo *(Bobby)*, Wallace Shawn *(Translator)*, Jay Brazeau *(Sheriff)*, Elizabeth Lawrence *(Mrs. Blair)*, John Reilly *(Young Monk)*, Ken Buhay *(Bishop Nogulich)*, Jessica Jickels *(Rosie)*.

Irish director Neil Jordan's films to date have been genre efforts—THE COMPANY OF WOLVES (horror), MONA LISA (crime), HIGH SPIRITS (supernatural comedy)—but they've also been something more: literate, visually stunning, and unexpectedly moving. After being mightily disappointed by his first Hollywood experience (HIGH SPIRITS), Jordan was ready to head back home. Recut into a more "commercial" product, HIGH SPIRITS flopped with both critics and audiences. However, Jordan was lured back to Tinseltown to direct WE'RE NO ANGELS, undoubtedly by the chance to work with producer Art Linson (THE UNTOUCHABLES) and playwright-screenwriter-director David Mamet, not to mention stars Robert DeNiro (who is credited as the film's executive producer) and Sean Penn. This time around both Hollywood and Jordan come out winners; WE'RE NO ANGELS is one of the year's most intriguing and enchanting films.

Jordan once again brings his fresh, personal perspective to a genre formula—here in a film only superficially based on the 1955 Bogart comedy of the same title, in which hardened convicts are softened by charity and good works. Set near the Canadian border during the Depression, Jordan's film deals with two prisoners (DeNiro and Penn) who reluctantly become involved in a prison break staged by a condemned convict (Russo) as he is literally being strapped into the electric chair. Separated from their "leader," the two wind up in a ramshackle border town. Straight out of Steinbeck, complete with its own bogus "miracle" shrine and caustic

five-dollar hooker (Demi Moore), the town is filmed with a rich mixture of gritty realism and storybook splendor by Philippe Rousselot. Cold and desperate, the two escapees are picked up at the edge of town by an old woman who has hit a deer with her truck and who mistakes the convicts for priests. In town, DeNiro and Penn find themselves in the middle of a throng of monks and priests who have come for the annual ceremony honoring the shrine that houses a weeping statue of the Virgin Mary. Everybody knows that the statue is actually a sham (its "tears" come from a leak in the roof), yet it is honored for the faith it inspires. While evading the vengeful prison warden (the late Ray McAnally, to whom WE'RE NO ANGELS is dedicated), Penn and DeNiro masquerade as theologians who have written an influential book about the significance of the shrine. They also cross paths with Moore, whose deaf daughter's participation is necessary in the ceremony they hope to use to get across the Canadian border. Further complications arise when the "priests" are unwillingly reunited with Russo, who makes his reappearance at the worst possible time, bringing about the film's hair-raising climax.

Though it has its share of humorous moments, on the whole WE'RE NO ANGELS doesn't work as well as a comedy as it does as a study of how people bring meaning to their lives by believing in some kind of heavenly design. It's also about how belief can sometimes give rise to miracles not from heaven, but from within—the human equivalent of the leak in the roof.

Confidence games are at the center of Mamet's HOUSE OF GAMES (his first film as a director) and his play "Glengarry Glen Ross." But WE'RE NO ANGELS, as might be expected, is closer to the gentle spirit of Mamet's THINGS CHANGE, though without that film's treacly whimsicality. Jordan is no stranger to confidence schemes himself; HIGH SPIRITS deals with a hotel owner (Peter O'Toole) who tries to con tourists into believing his hotel is haunted, only to find himself with a gaggle of real ghosts on his hands. Deceit also plays a major role in MONA LISA and THE COMPANY OF WOLVES: the characters in the former allow love to cloud reality, while in the latter, fairy tales mask grim, ugly truths. But, like Jordan's other works, WE'RE NO ANGELS is ultimately a resolute little film, and it is its hard-headedness that makes it work. Even its old-fashioned climax works because its emotions are earned. Released at the end of 1989, WE'RE NO ANGELS is a Christmas film in the best sense: it leads us to contemplate the good in humankind without ignoring human imperfection. That a movie with so much generosity of heart and toughness of spirit was made and released in Hollywood in 1989 is no small miracle. *(Brief nudity, profanity, violence.)*

p, Art Linson; d, Neil Jordan; w, David Mamet; ph, Philippe Rousselot (Panavision); ed, Mick Audsley and Joke Van Wijk; m, George Fenton; prod d, Wolf Kroeger; cos, Theoni V. Aldredge.

Comedy   **(PR:C   MPAA:PG-13)**

Sean Penn and Robert De Niro in WE'RE NO ANGELS (©Paramount).

Meg Ryan and Billy Crystal in WHEN HARRY MET SALLY...(©Columbia).

ⓥWHEN HARRY MET
SALLY. . .***
96m Castle Rock-Nelson Ent./COL c
Billy Crystal *(Harry Burns)*, Meg Ryan
(Sally Albright), Carrie Fisher *(Marie)*,
Bruno Kirby *(Jess)*, Steven Ford *(Joe)*,
Lisa Jane Persky *(Alice)*, Michelle
Nicastro *(Amanda)*, Gretchen Palmer
(Stewardess), Robert Alan Beuth *(Man on
Aisle)*, David Burdick *(9-year-old Boy)*,
Joe Viviani *(Judge)*, Harley Kozak
(Helen), Joseph Hunt *(Waiter at Wed-
ding)*, Kevin Rooney *(Ira)*, Franc Luz
(Julian), Tracy Reiner *(Emily)*, Kyle T.
Heffner *(Gary)*, Kimberley Lamarque
(Waitress), Stacey Katzin *(Hostess)*,
Estelle Reiner *(Older Woman Customer)*,
John Arceri *(Christmas Tree Salesman)*,
Peter Day *(Joke Teller at Wedding)*, Kuno
Sponholz, Charles Dugan, Connie Saw-
yer, Katherine Squire, Al Christy, Bernie
Hern, Frances Chaney, Rose Wright, Aldo
Rossi, Peter Pan, Donna Hardy, Jane
Chung *(Documentary Couples)*.

Set in Manhattan and dealing with the
problems of friendship between the sexes,
WHEN HARRY MET SALLY is Rob
Reiner's attempt at a grown-up romance a
la Leo McCarey or Woody Allen. Harry
(Crystal) meets Sally (Ryan) on a post-
graduation drive from the University of
Chicago to New York. He is attracted to
her, but she rebuffs his flip come-on, and
instant antipathy is born. Over the next 10
years, the two bump into each other at
various crucial points in their emotional
lives—most notably after Crystal is
knocked for a loop by a divorce and Ryan
is dumped by her long-standing boyfriend—and eventually manage to effect a
friendship. However, sex rears its insistent
head once more, and following a period of
readjustment, commitment-shy Crystal
learns that staying an entire night with
one's object of lust is actually possible.
Fade-out on marital bliss.

Although this plot may appear to be anything but fresh, director Reiner has a killer,
sitcom instinct for setting up jokes and
punchlines, helped to a certain extent by
Nora Ephron's sometimes spiky script and
vastly by the performing skills and chemistry of Billy Crystal and Meg Ryan. Some
of the drollest moments in the film —
including Crystal's spitting grape seeds
directly into a closed car window—were
improvised by the actor, and he manages to
goose up nearly every scene he's in with
fine-honed timing. This, in spite of the fact
that Reiner and Ephron have lazily
endowed him with a surfeit of Woody
Allen baggage that seems purely imitative
(his obsessions with death and CASA-
BLANCA, for example). Indeed, these der-
ivations, along with the facile use of
holiday cliches and pop ballads like "It
Had to Be You" to underline every romantic development, New York locations that
are like a yuppie's gleamingly upscale tour
of the city, and the too-calculated use of
cutesy interviews with happily married
couples, are the only major obstacles to
complete, unquestioned enjoyment. One
would also, however, like to see Crystal and
Ryan *occasionally* working at the supposedly dazzling careers (political consultant
and journalist, respectively) that have
vouchsafed the expansive dream apart-
ments both enjoy. Even Allen, in MAN-
HATTAN, took time off from his urban
gambols to depict his character's travails as
a TV comedy writer and to berate Diane
Keaton's Mary Wilke for demeaning her
talent by doing film novelizations. Such
inclusions would surely have provided a
weight and sounder base for Reiner's
comic riffs.

With her sumptuous grin, Ryan proves
herself a comic find here. Although her
role is often little more than a straight person for Crystal's noodling, she literally
sparkles with a pragmatic winsomeness,
and makes the most of Sally's compulsive

habits of exasperatingly ordering everything "on the side" in restaurants and dou-
ble-checking every piece of mail before
dropping it in the box. Her climactic,
rather forced crying jag is something no
actress could pull off (it's hard to believe
that someone so beautiful and successful
could be so unlucky in romance), but she
is effortlessly convincing in her abiding
need for Harry, a somewhat questionable
love object, and her touted orgasm scene *is*
a riot (if a tad out of character). Bruno
Kirby and Carrie Fisher are delightful as
the leads' best friends and the story's play-
by-play commentators. Fisher, in particular, has a savvy tartness reminiscent of the
gal pal of all time, Eve Arden; it's a shame
both she and Kirby lose their bite when
they link up in happily-ever-after-land.

The entire production has a polished
look, like the toniest boutique interiors,
and one would have to be made of stone
not to respond (on cue) to the nicely
arranged soundtrack standards by Harry
Connick, Jr. Undoubtedly, Reiner has concocted a surefire audience pleaser. Only a
real sourpuss would dare to call it rather
bland. Songs include: "It Had to Be You"
(Isham Jones, Gus Kahn, performed by
the Harry Connick, Jr., Trio), "Our Love Is
Here to Stay," "Let's Call the Whole Thing
Off," "But Not for Me" (George Gershwin,
Ira Gershwin, performed by the Harry
Connick, Jr., Trio), "Don't Pull Your Love"
(Brian Potter, Dennis Lambert, performed
by Hamilton, Joe Frank & Reynolds),
"Ramblin' Man" (Forrest Richard Betts,
performed by the Allman Brothers),
"Right Time of the Night" (Peter McCan,
performed by Jennifer Warnes), "Where or
When" (Lorenz Hart, Richard Rodgers,
performed by Ella Fitzgerald), "I Could
Write a Book" (Hart, Rodgers, performed
by Harry Connick, Jr.), "Lady's Lunch"
(Marc Shaiman), "The Tables Have
Turned" (Laura Kenyon, Shaiman, Scott
Wittman), "Plane Cue" and "La
Marseillaise" from CASABLANCA (Max
Steiner), "Autumn in New York" (Vernon
Duke, performed by the Harry Connick,
Jr., Trio), "Winter Wonderland" (Felix
Bernard, Dick Smith, performed by Ray
Charles), "Say It Isn't So" (Irving Berlin),
"The Surrey with the Fringe on Top" (Rod-
gers, Oscar Hammerstein II), "Stompin' at
the Savoy" (Benny Goodman, Chick
Webb, Edgar Sampson, Andy Razaf, per-
formed by the Harry Connick, Jr., Trio),
"String Quintet in E-Flat Major" (Wolf-
gang Amadeus Mozart), "Don't Be That
Way" (Sampson, Goodman, Mitchell Par-
ish), "Have Yourself a Merry Little Christ-
mas" (Ralph Blane, Hugh Martin,
performed by Bing Crosby), "Call Me"
(Tony Hatch), "Don't Get Around Much
Anymore" (Duke Ellington, Bob Russell,
performed by Harry Connick, Jr.), "Isn't It
Romantic" (Lorenz Hart, Richard Rodgers). *(Adult situations, sexual situations.)*

p, Rob Reiner, Andrew Scheinman, Jeffrey Stott, and Steve Nicolaides; d, Rob Reiner; w, Nora Ephron; ph, Barry Sonnenfeld (Duart Color, CFI Color); ed, Robert Leighton; m, Marc Shaiman and Harry Connick Jr.; prod d, Jane Musky; set d, George R. Nelson and Sabrina Wright-Basile; cos, Gloria Gresham; makeup, Stephen Abrums.

Comedy/Romance   (PR:C MPAA:R)

WHEN THE WHALES CAME**

(Brit.) 99m Golden Swan/FOX c

Irene Wilson (Molly Woodcock), Fergus Rees (The Birdman as a Boy), Paul Scofield (The Birdman), Helen Pearce (Gracie Jenkins), Max Rennie (Daniel Pender), Frederick Warder, Keith Low (Fishermen), Nicholas Jones (Vicar), Kerra Spowart (Margaret Pender), Barbara Ewing (Mary Pender), John Hallam (Treve Pender), David Suchet (Will), Barbara Jefford (Auntie Mildred), Dexter Fletcher (Big Tim), Blue Philpott (Albert Pender), David Threlfall (Jack Jenkins), Helen Mirren (Clemmie Jenkins), Penny Rogers (Maisie), Derek Pearce (Fiddle player), Susan Curnow (Fisherwoman), James Stedeford, Paul Thomas, David Sherris (Big Tim's Gang), Jeremy Kemp (Mr. Wellbeloved), Joanna Bartholomew (Miss Tregarthen), Stephen Dan (Watchboy), David Quilter (Mr. Bullhead).

A cinematic work with its heart in the right place, WHEN THE WHALES CAME tells a cautionary tale about human disharmonies—with nature, and with eccentrics, those who don't conform to social norms. The screenplay by Michael Morpurgo, based on his own best-selling children's novel Why the Whales Came and set in the Scilly Isles at the beginning of WW I, tells of a mysterious curse incurred by an island populace who abused a group of whales, of friendship between two children and an eccentric outcast, and of the outcast's humane mission to prevent the curse from being perpetuated.

In the opening prolog, a young boy tells us of the terrible luck that befell the inhabitants of Samson Isle after they had slaughtered the narwhals (rare, tusked mammals) that were beached on the island in 1844. Ultimately, the island became uninhabitable, and the residents were forced to move to the neighboring Isle of Bryher. Two children, Pearce and Rennie, meet an old recluse, "the Birdman" (Scofield), on the beach and befriend him, despite warnings from the other islanders, who superstitiously regard him as a warlock. Deaf and eccentric, the gentle, kindly old man turns out to be the last of the people who moved from Samson. He tutors the children in natural lore, and enchants them with his beautiful carvings of birds. When war breaks out, Threlfall, Pearce's father, volunteers for service, leaving her mother (Mirren) to manage alone on this barren island that affords at best a hard, marginal living. Word comes that Threlfall is missing, believed dead. Meanwhile, Rennie's life at home is marred by a drunken, abusive father, who beats the boy. When one of a school of narwhals beaches itself on Bryher, Scofield, the only person who remembers the events on Samson, is afraid that the curse will be repeated. Although a group of vicious teens has set fire to his house, the old man refuses to be distracted from his mission. He pleads with the islanders not to kill the whale and, with the help of the children, tells the assembled crowd of the curse on Samson. He succeeds in persuading the crowd to help the stranded creature back into the sea and to scare the rest of the school away from the land. Pearce's father returns from war, safe after all, and the film ends on a note of harmony.

The problems with this visually striking film are of two kinds. It is constructed around a set of ideas that overwhelm image, action, character, and drama. The filmmakers seem more interested in promoting a Greenpeace, small-planet philosophy of life than in setting a group of dramatic entities in motion and letting the sparks fly. Scofield's character is given some undiluted sermons to deliver, material which threatens to topple his otherwise creditable performance as the impossibly sweet old man. The other performances are polished and craftsmanlike, but the players cannot quite surmount the film's insistently reverential tone. In addition there are problems of plotting. The interaction of humans and nature that forms the basic plot is bolstered by a couple of subplots—Threlfall's going to war, Rennie's unhappy home. But these subplots are never integrated with the main action. Instead of expanding or clarifying the old man's mission to rescue the whales, these elements feel like filler, a way to mark time until the whales arrive. Even World War I is incidental, rather than woven into motivations and plot.

The film's primary strength is Robert Paynter's photography of the marvelous land and seascapes around the Scillies. But, alas, beautiful scenery and a laudable moral don't constitute good cinema. The youngsters at whom the film is aimed are likely to find it tough slogging—its pace too slow and ponderous to capture and retain most kids' attention. (Profanity.)

p, Simon Channing-Williams; d, Clive Rees; w, Michael Morpurgo (based on the novel Why the Whales Came by Michael Morpurgo); ph, Robert Paynter; ed, Andrew Boulton; m, Christopher Gunning and Ruth Rennie; prod d, Bruce Grimes; art d, Colin Grimes; spec eff, Peter Hutchinson; cos, Lindy Hemming; makeup, Norma Webb.

Drama   (PR:AA MPAA:PG)

Ⓥ WHO'S HARRY CRUMB?*

87m Tri-Star-NBC/Tri-Star c

John Candy (Harry Crumb), Jeffrey Jones (Eliot Draisen), Annie Potts (Helen Downing), Tim Thomerson (Vince Barnes), Barry Corbin (P.J. Downing), Shawnee Smith (Nikki Downing), Valri Bromfield (Det. Casey), Doug Steckler (Dwayne), Renee Coleman (Jennifer Downing), Wesley Mann (Tim, the Butler), Tamsin Kelsey (Marie), Joe Flaherty (Doorman), Fiona Roeske (Crumb Receptionist), Lori O'Byrne (Karen), Michele Goodger (Mrs. MacIntyre), Beverley Elliott (Joanne), P. Lynn Johnson (Kelly), Peter Yunker (Jeffrey Brandt), Brenda Crichlow (Suki's Salon Receptionist), Garwin Sanford (Dennis Kimball), Tony Dakota (Freddy), Rob Morton (Airport Cop), Marcel Maillard (Chauffeur), Leslie Ewen (Airport X-ray Guard), Manny Perry (Cop in Car), Gary Heatherington (Lover), Patrick McKenna (TV Man), Daliah Bache (TV Woman), Eve Smith (Elderly Woman), Tino Insana (Smokey), Frank T. Hernandez, Frank Casado (Salesmen), Cyndi Lee Rice (Stewardess), Lyle Alzado (Man in Apartment), Deanna Oliver (Woman in Apartment), Ira Miller (Accountant), Stephen Young (Interior Decorator), James Belushi.

It's hard to imagine just who would care enough to pose the title question of this occasionally funny, but mostly boring, detective farce. As the film opens, spectacularly inept private eye Crumb (Candy) has been exiled to the Tulsa office of his own family's nationwide detective firm, founded by his grandfather and now run by the weaselish Jones. When the daughter of one of the firm's wealthy clients is kidnaped, Jones inexplicably (at first) summons Candy back to the home office in Los Angeles to take the case. After the expected blundering, the usual car chases, the donning of a variety of disguises, and the standard big-scale, destructive sight gags, Candy stumbles onto the "solution" and almost accidentally brings the villains to justice.

If this sounds familiar, it should. The bumbling detective has been a staple of movie comedies from Buster Keaton's Sherlock, Jr., to Peter Sellers' Inspector Clouseau. Unfortunately, even the dullest of Sellers' PINK PANTHER entries has more laughs in a single reel than HARRY CRUMB has in its entire length, which at times seems endless. The humor is crude and obvious, and while John Candy manages to squeeze a few laughs from the shopworn, cliche-ridden script (by Robert Conte and Peter Martin Wortmann), he still has a long way to go before he'll erase memories of the inspired zaniness of the similarly dimwitted Clouseau. HARRY CRUMB is even more dispiriting for the failure of its reunion of Second City comedy talents, including executive producer

**John Candy in WHO'S HARRY CRUMB?
(©Tri-Star).**

Candy. Veteran Second City writer-director Paul Flaherty (who made his equally undistinguished feature debut with 18 AGAIN) directs broadly and obviously, with little feeling for comic pacing. His brother, Joe Flaherty, familiar for his side-splitting Count Floyd and Guy Caballero characters on SCTV, shows up in an all-too-brief cameo, as does Second City stage alumnus Jim Belushi.

On the plus side, Candy remains a likable screen presence with a flair for the outrageous, seen to best advantage in SPLASH and PLANES, TRAINS AND AUTOMOBILES. But he'll fast wear out his welcome if he keeps making films like WHO'S HARRY CRUMB?, easily his weakest big-screen outing since ARMED AND DANGEROUS. Among the supporting cast, Shawnee Smith is bright and appealing as the kidnaped girl's younger sister who teams up with Crumb to assist his sleuthing, and Barry Corbin lends solid support as the distraught, good-hearted father. Wesley Mann steals a few funny moments as Corbin's boorish, lazy butler. The other star performers, including Jeffrey Jones (AMADEUS; FERRIS BUELLER'S DAY OFF) and Annie Potts (GHOSTBUSTERS; TV's "Designing Women"), the latter as the conniving, man- and money-hungry stepmother of the kidnaped girl, have generally been much funnier elsewhere.

Though kids would normally be the best audience for the broad, buffoonish jokes of WHO'S HARRY CRUMB?, parents may not care for the film's occasional forays into crude sexual humor and profanity. Teens, evidently meant to be drawn by Smith (who played the feisty heroine of the teen-hit remake of THE BLOB), will most likely be turned off by the film's slow pac-

ing and uninspired plot. Adults, meanwhile, may find themselves wondering why the same folks who kept them in stitches on the Second City stage and TV show can barely manage to provoke a chuckle here. Trying to include something for everyone, the makers of WHO'S HARRY CRUMB? wound up with a film guaranteed to entertain virtually no one. Songs include: "On Your Side Tonight" (Michel Colombier, Kathy Wakefield, performed by Richard Martin Ross), "Big Fun (Harry Crumb)" (Jon Lind, Phil Gladston, David Was, performed by the Temptations), "Holding out for a Hero" (Jim Steinman, Dean Pitchford, performed by Bonnie Tyler), "I Got You Babe" (Sonny Bono), "I Got You (I Feel Good)" (James Brown, performed by Brown). *(Profanity, adult situations.)*

p, Arnon Milchan and George W. Perkins; d, Paul Flaherty; w, Robert Conte and Peter Martin Wortmann; ph, Stephen M. Katz (Alpha Cine Service Color); ed, Danford B. Greene; m, Michel Colombier; prod d, Trevor Williams; art d, Stephen Geaghan; set d, Elizabeth Wilcox; spec eff, Dewey Gene Grigg; cos, Jerry R. Allen; stunts, Bill Ferguson; makeup, Jan Newman.

Comedy   (PR:C MPAA:PG-13)

◉WICKED STEPMOTHER½
92m MGM/MGM-UA c

Bette Davis (*Miranda*), Barbara Carrera (*Priscilla*), Colleen Camp (*Jenny*), David Rasche (*Steve*), Lionel Stander (*Sam*), Tom Bosley (*Lt. MacIntosh*), Shawn Donahue (*Mike*), Richard Moll (*Nat*), Evelyn Keyes (*Witch Mistriss*), Susie Garrett (*Nandy*), Laurene Landon (*Vanilla*).

WICKED STEPMOTHER is not the high-caliber swan song that screen legend Bette Davis deserved, but at least it's not an abject failure. In fact, one wonders why MGM/UA dumped this carefree comedy onto the video market without any theatrical release to speak of.

When policeman Bosley investigates a family's disappearance, he's horrified to discover that the missing persons have been shrunk to Lilliputian proportions. If witchcraft is afoot, whose beleaguered family will be next? Meanwhile, Camp and Rasche return from vacation, and are shocked to find that Camp's father (Stander) has fallen under the spell of Davis, a chain-smoking, carnivorous sorceress. Married to Davis, and happy to the point of stupor, the balding Stander does nothing but watch TV game shows and wait for his hair to grow in. Resentful of Davis' influence and allergic to cats, Camp is determined to prove that Davis has a feline stashed away somewhere, but doesn't realize that the cat houses the spirit of Davis' fellow witch, Carrera. While Camp puzzles over her inexplicable allergy attacks, sultry Carrera visits Rasche's

courtroom and, by blowing his opponent's legal briefs into disarray, enables him to win a difficult case; then she transforms his son, Donahue, into a star volleyball player and beach hero. Sensing that her family is in trouble, Camp visits private eye Moll in hopes of discrediting Davis. Turning up mysteriously on their doorstep one night, Carrera claims to be Davis' daughter and moves in as if she owned the place. (At this point, Davis' small role in the movie is finished, since she and Carrera share a common "physical manifestation." In a few shots sprinkled through the rest of the film, however, a sleek black cat puffs on a cigarette, mimicking Davis.) Carrera soon exercises more control over the household, and Moll and Camp worry about a snapshot Moll took of Carrera that develops as a photo of Davis. While Camp scours the shelves of an occult bookstore, Carrera kicks her plan into high gear—after Stander wins a fortune on the quiz show "Winners and Losers," she will shrink the family and use his winnings to live in witchly luxury. But Camp attends a witchcraft workshop, where she becomes a fledgling spell-caster and meets Bosley. The two compare notes and vow to foil the Davis/Carrera Incredible Shrinking Family crime spree. Cleverly, Camp convinces Carrera she's leaving Rasche, thus giving the witch a free hand; then, with Moll's assistance, Camp further tricks Carrera into believing Davis is scheming to gain sole custody of the physical body they share. Although Stander does make game-show history, the witches' take-over plot goes haywire. After nearly destroying her own home with mixed-up curses, Camp learns the correct spell from Stander (who assures her he's "the man who knows everything") and zaps Carrera/Davis into kitty-cat submission. Stander's knowledge of spells isn't available to Bosley, however; as he drives the mischievous cat containing the spirits of Davis and Carrera to police headquarters, the witches start shrinking him right on the freeway!

The movie's troubled production history helps to account in some degree for its disjointed structure. As originally conceived, the movie starred Davis, not Carrera. But Davis, once the consummate professional, was already terminally ill when shooting began and, unhappy with the way she was being photographed, walked out during filming. It is doubtful that WICKED STEPMOTHER would have been a truly distinguished comedy even with Davis' full participation, however; although obviously disrupted by script changes necessitated by the star's departure, the film is basically a silly, good-natured spookshow. Occasionally hilarious and graced with some ingenious (and some indifferent) special effects, WICKED STEPMOTHER isn't sophisticated enough to qualify as a stylish black comedy, and is better appreciated as a fractured fairy tale.

Faced with salvaging his screenplay, writer-director Larry Cohen (IT'S ALIVE; Q) might have added more spice to this too-tame witches' brew. Instead of including so many repetitive scenes of witchly mayhem, which give the film a padded-out feeling, more screen time could have been spent detailing Colleen Camp and Barbara Carrera's rivalry—these two actresses have the style to make WICKED STEPMOTHER an all-out camp spectacular. (On the plus side, the sassy supporting cast never wear out their welcome; one wishes veterans Evelyn Keyes and Lionel Stander had even more footage.) Dynamo Camp is irresistibly funny as the one-woman suburban witch patrol, and Carrera's smashing rendition of a hell-on-wheels spellbinder reveals her as one of those rare beauties with true comic spirit. Despite her ravaged appearance, Davis goes out in style, giving a gleefully nasty performance worthy of a sorceress in her last film. Racked with pain from terminal illness, she exited Hollywood on her own terms—with her name billed above the title. While short on witty dialog, WICKED STEPMOTHER is breezy, bewitching fun, full of in-jokes (a photo of Joan Crawford serves as a picture of Camp's mother) and tongue-in-cheek zaniness. (Violence, sexual situations.)

p, Robert Littman; d, Larry Cohen; w, Larry Cohen; ph, Bryan England (Deluxe Color); ed, David Kern; m, Robert Folk; art d, Gene Abel.

Comedy/Horror   (PR:A MPAA:PG-13)

Ⓥ**WINTER PEOPLE, THE****½
110m Nelson/COL c
Kurt Russell (Wayland Jackson), Kelly McGillis (Collie Wright), Lloyd Bridges (William Wright), Mitchell Ryan (Drury Campbell), Amelia Burnette (Paula Jackson), Eileen Ryan (Annie Wright), Lanny Flaherty (Gudger Wright), Don Michael Paul (Young Wright), David Dwyer (Milton Wright), Jeffrey Meek (Cole Campbell), Bill Gribble (Skeet Campbell), Wallace Merck (Harmon Campbell), Walker Averitt (Margaret Campbell), Dashiell Coleman (Jonathan Wright), Barbara Freeman (Mavis McGregor), Gary Bullock (Mr. McGregor), Ivan Green (Mr. Crawford), Lucile Dew McIntyre (Mrs. Crawford), Judy Simpson Cook (Gudger's Wife), James Eric (Bartering Man), Rebecca Koon (Bartering Woman), Dick Parkinson, Stacy Moore (Campbell Men).

A distinctly old-fashioned tale of moral accountability, family, community, tradition, honor, and romance set against a harsh but beautiful American landscape, WINTER PEOPLE is an admirable attempt to recapture the look and feel of the melodramatic wide-screen, Techni-

color epics of the 50s. Regrettably, while the film boasts some impressive visuals, it ultimately fails due to an underdeveloped script and some wildly inconsistent acting styles. Set during the Depression, it opens as widowed clockmaker Russell and his precocious 10-year-old daughter, Burnette, pack up their belongings and leave their small town for Philadelphia. Somewhere in the Appalachians their truck breaks down in the middle of a stream, forcing father and daughter to seek shelter in the remote cabin of McGillis, a strong-willed single mother who would rather live alone, isolated from her family, than reveal the identity of her infant son's father. After spending the night, Russell discovers that his truck has been looted and destroyed by the Campbells, the most feared mountain clan in the area, led by patriarch Ryan. With the onset of winter, Russell decides to stay in town and live with McGillis, with whom he has fallen in love. Striking a deal with McGillis' father, Bridges, a kindly but powerful man who practically owns the town and runs it with his three sons (Flaherty, Paul, and Dwyer), Russell agrees to build a clock tower for the local church in exchange for a new truck. While McGillis' kinfolks are slow to accept the quiet, pacifist Russell, the clockmaker eventually earns her family's grudging respect. Trouble looms, however, in the form of Meek, a particularly brutal and dangerous member of Ryan's clan who just happens to be the father of McGillis' baby. Because their families are locked in a perpetual feud, McGillis and Meek have kept their affair a secret, with Meek dropping in to visit his "family" whenever it suits him. The presence of the baby, however, has led McGillis to a greater sense of independence, and as a result of her gentle, loving relationship with Russell, she decides that she wants no more of Meek's brutal attentions. This brings about a vicious fight between the monstrous Meek and the much smaller Russell—a battle that spills into the chilly river near McGillis' cabin and nearly results in Meek's drowning. Russell puts the still-alive Meek astride his horse and sends him home, but the nearly frozen man falls from his mount and is dragged through the stream. When Meek is found dead the next day, Ryan demands revenge and declares an all-out war on Bridges and his family unless restitution is made. Bridges knows that aside from the life of one of his own sons, the only deal Ryan will accept is for Russell to forgo his impending marriage to McGillis and leave the area forever. Russell nobly accepts blame for the death (although everyone agrees he didn't kill Meek) and agrees to leave, but McGillis, unwilling to let him take full responsibility for a situation she helped create, goes to Ryan herself and reveals that her baby is his grandson. To atone for her sins, she offers Ryan and his

clan her baby—exchanging a "new life" for that of Meek. Struck by McGillis' passion and sincerity, Ryan agrees to this arrangement and Russell is allowed to stay; however, McGillis is so devastated by the bargain that she nearly dies of grief. Eventually she recovers, and on the day she is to marry Russell, Ryan appears alone on a horse with his grandson in his arms. In a surprising act of compassion and charity, Ryan returns the baby to McGillis, beginning what may be a truce between the two families.

WINTER PEOPLE contains all the elements of a classic film: love, loss, and renewal; questions of moral responsibility; the conflict between the individual and the community; man's struggle against his environment; and the family as both a positive and negative force. Unfortunately, the script by Carol Sobieski, based on a novel by John Ehle, is merely a series of broadly drawn episodes that never tap into the essence of the tale. The characters are merely ciphers, the relationships sketchy, the romance between McGillis and Russell perfunctory and unengaging, the sense of community more spoken about than felt, and the struggle between families lacks development. Director Ted Kotcheff never really breathes life into the characters, and seems so disinterested in his performers that he allows Paul to throw the entire film out of whack with his overacting.

But although Kotcheff fails with his performers, he succeeds impressively with his visuals. Employing the wide-screen frame and remarkable landscape with a skill reminiscent of the westerns of Anthony Mann (tellingly, the Campbell family is similar in behavior and appearance to the Tobin clan in Mann's classic MAN OF THE WEST, 1958), Kotcheff delivers some breathtaking and unforgettable images. As in the Kotcheff-directed FIRST BLOOD (1982), WINTER PEOPLE is set in a beautiful, rugged, and varied landscape that becomes just as much a character as the human beings who inhabit it. Like Mann, Kotcheff uses his setting to define his characters and themes, at times expressionistically conveying the internal turmoil of his characters through it, lending the material an almost biblical feel. Mann is not the only great filmmaker whose visual style is reflected in Kotcheff's work; D.W. Griffith's influence is also present, most notably during the winter scenes—especially in the sequence wherein McGillis carries her baby across the icy river that separates her clan from the Campbells. This beautiful series of shots could almost have come from Griffith's similarly plotted silent classic WAY DOWN EAST (1919).

Regrettably, WINTER PEOPLE's exciting and evocative visuals simply don't compensate for its lack of narrative cohesion and unfocused performances. Even the physical production falters occasionally, with the all-important snow looking badly faked at times. If only more care had been taken with the script and more attention paid to the actors, WINTER PEOPLE, a brave and unusual project in these days of comic-book action heroes and mindless joy-rides, could have been a classic, instead of an interesting failure. *(Violence, sexual situations.)*

p, Robert H. Solo; d, Ted Kotcheff; w, Carol Sobieski (based on the novel by John Ehle); ph, Francois Protat (Deluxe Color); ed, Thom Noble; m, John Scott; prod d, Ron Foreman; art d, Charles Butcher; set d, Leslie Morales; spec eff, John Stirber; cos, Ruth Morley; stunts, Eddy Donno; makeup, Richard Arrington.

Romance   **(PR:C MPAA:PG-13)**

Ⓥ**WIRED****½
110m F/M-Lion Screen/Taurus c
Michael Chiklis *(John Belushi)*, Ray Sharkey *(Angel Velasquez)*, J.T. Walsh *(Bob Woodward)*, Patti D'Arbanville *(Cathy Smith)*, Lucinda Jenney *(Judy Belushi)*, Gary Groomes *(Dan Aykroyd)*, Alex Rocco *(Arnie Fromson)*, Jerre Burns *(Lou)*, Clyde Kusatsu *(Coroner)*, Tom Bower, Earl Billings *(Detectives)*, Billy Preston *(Himself)*, Dakin Matthews *(Washington Post Editor)*, J.C. Quinn *(Comedy Coach)*, Steve Vinovich *(Studio Executive)*, Matthew Faison *(Doctor Robbins)*, Jon Snyder *(Film Director)*, Finis Henderson III *(Morgue Attendant)*, Amy Michelson *(Photographer)*, Blake Clark *(Jenkins)*, Scott Plank *(Herb Axelson)*, Brooke McCarter *(Punk Rocker)*, Paul Ben-Victor *(Perino)*, Richard Feldman *(Studio Page)*, Ned Bellamy *(Forrest)*, John Apicella *(Loading Supervisor)*, Joe Urla *(Stage Manager)*, Diane Behrens *(Typist)*, Roger Rook *(Coroner's Assistant)*, Ron Perkins *(Record Producer)*, Drew Pillsbury *(Morgue Nurse)*, Charles Holman *(SNL Cast Member)*, Nancy DeCarl *(Hotel Manager)*, Keith Joe Dick *(Man in Club)*, Pete Willcox *(Elvis Impersonator)*, A.C. Meadows *(Colonel Impersonator)*, Neil Portnow *(Band Leader, King Bee)*, Michael Ruff, Cliff Hugo, David Williams, Bruce Wallenstein, Marc Caz Macino, Ralph Humphrey, Jimmy Haslip, Buzzy Feiten, Richard Elliott, Keith Joe Dick, Allan Thomas *(Blues Brothers and SNL Bands)*.

Based on Bob Woodward's book of the same name about the death of comedian John Belushi, WIRED is the movie Hollywood supposedly didn't want made or shown, which for some will be reason enough to make it a must-see. In one sense, however, Hollywood's fear proved unwarranted. WIRED was booed at Cannes, where it had its world premiere, and critical reaction Stateside was largely negative. As a result, it did a nosedive at the box office. Still, the very fact that WIRED played at all in multiplexes next to such Hollywood-wholesome summer 1989 hits as PARENTHOOD can't have done much to comfort the perpetually nervous moviemaking community, who, in the summer of family values, would just as soon forget that mainstream Hollywood has, or ever had, anything whatsoever to do with recreational drugs.

In the face of so much anti-hype, it hardly comes as a surprise that WIRED is not the embarrassment it was widely reported to be. But that doesn't mean it's very good, either. Rather than being inept, WIRED simply succumbs to the problems inherent in any anti-drug drama, the chief difficulty being that there can be no drama, no conflict, where the dramatic arc is a downward spiral. Compounding the problem is the movie's fragmented format, which works against the emergence of Belushi as a compelling character while confusing all but those who already knew his life story going in.

WIRED starts at the end, as Belushi's body is being wheeled into the morgue, only to have Belushi (Chiklis) come back to life and be escorted through key scenes in his past by Angel (Sharkey), a Puerto Rican cab driver. Besides occasional tender moments between Belushi and either his wife, Judy (Jenney), or Dan Aykroyd (Groomes, who gives a good performance, though he's actually a dead ringer not for Aykroyd, but for current "Saturday Night Live" trooper Kevin Nealon), the mood is strictly sour. Belushi's professional triumphs are shown to be hollow here; scenes on the "Saturday Night Live" set are dominated by tension and falsity, with Belushi stopping in mid-rehearsal in one instance to argue about his contract. In other "SNL" scenes, director Larry Peerce's camera keeps tilting up to emphasize the oppressive glare of the spotlights, or dollies back to reveal the "Applause" signs prompting the audience. A well-staged live performance by Belushi and Aykroyd as the Blues Brothers (too well-staged; it's more polished than any of the real Blues Brothers shows ever were) is deflated when audience members are shown pelting Belushi with packets of cocaine. Belushi's hit movie debut in NATIONAL LAMPOON'S ANIMAL HOUSE is reduced here to a re-enactment of the filming of Belushi's famous scene in which the actor, playing Bluto, made his way down a cafeteria serving line gobbling everything in his path. What's never shown is the offscreen Belushi enjoying his successes. Instead, WIRED cuts almost directly to the troubled production of THE BLUES BROTHERS, during which Belushi's drug habit (by Woodward's account) was already well out of control. Throughout the film, Peerce and screenwriter Earl Mac Rauch keep cutting away to scenes of Woodward (Walsh) gathering material for the book, or flashing forward ominously to Cathy Smith (D'Arbanville) and that last, fateful night at Hollywood's Chateau Marmont hotel—at which, in this version at least, Woodward is present, albeit only in spirit. Belushi died at the Marmont from an overdose while attempting a last, desperate rewrite on what was to have been his next film, all too appropriately titled "Nobel Rot."

WIRED is most commendable for what it doesn't do. It doesn't preach and it doesn't try to supply glib, pat explanations for Belushi's decline and fall. Its depiction of the pressures of show business have an ugly-accurate, insider's feel, as if the film were directed towards the very people it's most likely to infuriate, and the performances are uniformly excellent, from Michael Chiklis' uncanny re-creation of Belushi to Patti D'Arbanville's quietly effective, low-key portrayal of Smith. But, in the end, WIRED succeeds best only in re-creating that sad, empty feeling many of us had when we read the news the morning after Belushi's death in March 1982. *(Drug abuse, profanity.)*

p, Edward S. Feldman and Charles R. Meeker; d, Larry Peerce; w, Earl Mac Rauch (based on the book by Bob Woodward); ph, Tony Imi; ed, Eric Sears; m, Basil Poledouris; md, Michael Ruff; prod d, Brian Eatwell; art d, Richard F. Mays; set d, Sally Thornton; cos, Shari Feldman; chor, Joanne DiVito; stunts, Scott Wilder; makeup, Robin Beauchesne.

Biography   **(PR:C MPAA:R)**

WIZARD, THE*
97m Finnegan-Pinchuk/UNIV c
Fred Savage *(Corey Woods)*, Luke Edwards *(Jimmy Woods)*, Christian Slater *(Nick Woods)*, Beau Bridges *(Sam Woods)*, Vincent Leahr *(Tate)*, Wendy Phillips *(Christine)*, Dea McAllister *(Counselor)*, Sam McMurray *(Bateman)*, Will Seltzer *(Putnam)*, Roy Conrad *(Bus Clerk)*, Jenny Lewis *(Haley)*, Roderick Dexter, Ray Bickel *(Truckers)*, Chuck Skinner *(Grease Monkey)*, W.K. Cowan, William C. Thompson *(Salesmen)*, Sonny Dukes *(Biker)*, T. Dan Hopkins *(Old Navajo)*, Jason Oliver, Rowdy Metzger, Preston Scott Lee *(Tough Teens)*, Beth Grant *(Diner Manager)*, Gregor Hesse *(Younger Boy)*, Jackey Vinson *(Lucas)*, Tom Kerley *(Pinball Teen)*, Frank McRae *(Spanky)*, Gene Skillen *(Stickman)*, Blair Anthony *(Hotel Security)*, Thomas Stanczyk *(Rick, the Video Counselor)*, Jacqueline Lear *(Bubblegum Girl)*, Valana C. Hatter *(Diner Waitress)*, Roderick Dexter *(Wrecking Yard Man)*, Terri Lynn Neish *(Poolside Waitress)*, Lee Arenberg *(Armageddon Registrar)*, Steven Grives *(Armageddon Announcer)*, Marisa DeSimone *(Mora Grissom)*, Zed James

Frizzelle *(Lucas' Buddy)*, Jim Pirri *(Studio Tour Guide)*, David D'Ovidio *(Armageddon Official)*.

In THE WIZARD, Fred Savage and Luke Edwards play brothers who travel from Utah to California to play in a video-game championship. Edwards is a slow, deeply traumatized young boy who says only one word, "California." After he is institutionalized, his older brother (Savage) kidnaps him from the children's home, and together they set off on a cross-country trek (shades of RAINMAN), pursued by their father (Bridges), an older brother (Slater), and a goofy but sadistic tracker of runaways (Seltzer). Slater and Bridges desperately want to find the boys before the Seltzer does; if he gets to Edwards first, the unfortunate lad will be forced to return to the children's home. On the road, Savage and Edwards meet a tough but cute girl (Lewis) who helps them along their way. Lewis and Savage soon discover that Edwards is a "wizard" at video games, and immediately put his gift to use in conning older, less experienced players. After swindling their way into some big money (not to mention stopping off in Reno to shoot some craps), our young heroes head for California. Meanwhile, Bridges and Slater have a number of run-ins with the tracker —most of which involve the destruction of their respective cars—before they get to California themselves. Finally, Savage and company arrive at the site of the video game championships (Universal Studios, conveniently enough). Having suffered many hardships (including run-ins with street punks and thieves, and countless arguments), they are now ready for Edwards to give the contest a shot. After a final chase scene involving the boys and Seltzer, Edwards takes the stage for the finals. With "everyone" (Bridges and Slater, as well as various friends and relatives) in the audience rooting for him, Edwards wins the contest. On the way home, he makes the family stop at a tourist attraction that they once visited, and there the true nature of his trauma—paralyzing guilt over the death of his twin sister— becomes apparent. Edwards is now free to live happily with his family. Savage has succeeded in making his brother's dream come true.

Essentially a 90-minute commercial for Nintendo, THE WIZARD is unforgivably trite and shallow. When the film isn't flashing various Nintendo games across the screen, it's depicting idiotic, disturbing behavior (like the boys flying down the middle of the highway on a skateboard or wandering through Reno in the middle of the night) that provides anything but a responsible model for the film's target audience of children. Also upsetting is THE WIZARD's exploitation of both its juvenile leads (especially the film's use of its central character's condition for cheap

Luke Edwards and Fred Savage in THE WIZARD (©Universal).

laughs) and its youthful audience. With a cast of young heartthrobs and a teeny-bopper soundtrack (including songs from Bobby Brown and the New Kids on the Block), THE WIZARD is clearly aimed at the pre-pubescent crowd, but the situations it depicts are so utterly predictable and the plot so blatantly thin that after 30 minutes even Nintendo junkies are bound to lose interest. The cast is likable enough, but the players quickly become lost in the rampant idiocy and commercialism. Saddled with ridiculous dialog, Christian Slater and Beau Bridges are reduced to slapstick robots. (It is especially painful to see this display so soon after Bridges' assured performance in THE FABULOUS BAKER BOYS and Slater's strong turn in HEATHERS.) Savage (TV's "The Wonder Years," VICE VERSA) delivers an oh-so-cute performance that may satisfy his fans; however, he makes no progress as an actor with this nonsense, and continues to exude naive smugness (it's a perverse pleasure to see him get beaten up in this movie).

Director Todd Holland is clueless when it comes to action sequences (a chase staged at a drive-in theater, possibly inspired by a similar scene from BLUE THUNDER, is absolutely wretched). Seemingly more concerned with selling video games than with his movie, he brings no dramatic depth to any of the film's serious moments. With THE WIZARD, the transformation of children's entertainment into gross commercialism reaches its dubious zenith. In the end the film comes down to one disturbing message: "Nintendo solves all problems and brings a family closer together." Skip this one.

Songs include: "Nowhere to Run" (Lamont Dozier, Brian Holland, Eddie Holland, performed by Martha and the Vandellas), "My Way" (Paul Anka, performed by Anka), "Send Me an Angel" (Richard Zatorski, David Sterry, performed by Real Life), "I Live by the Groove" (Paul Carrack, Eddie Schwartz, performed by Carrack), "(You've Got It) The Right Stuff," "Hangin' Tough" (Maurice Starr, performed by the New Kids on the Block), "Don't Be Cruel" (Bobby Brown, performed by Brown), "Leavin' on Your Mind" (Wayne Walker, performed by Patsy Cline), "Red River," "You Don't Get Much" (Kurt Neumann, Sam Lianas, performed by the Bo Deans), "I Found My Way" (Stacy Widelitz, Lara Cody, performed by Sally Dworsky). *(Violence, profanity, adult situations.)*

p, David Chisholm and Ken Topolsky; d, Todd Holland; w, David Chisholm; ph, Robert Yeoman (Deluxe Color); ed, Tom Finan; m, J. Peter Robinson; prod d, Michael Mayer; art d, Rob Sissman; set d, Claire J. Bowin; spec eff, Eddie Surkin; cos, Scilla Andreen-Hernandez; stunts, James Halty; makeup, Lynne Eagan.

Children's/Comedy   (PR:A   MPAA:PG)

Ⓥ**WOMAN OBSESSED, A***½
105m Platinum c
Ruth Raymond *(Arlene Bellings)*, Linda Blair *(Evie Barnes)*, Gregory Patrick *(Ted Barnes)*, Troy Donahue *(Jack Barnes)*, Carolyn Van Bellighen *(Wanda Barnes)*, Frank Stewart *(Bobby Trumbal)*, Christina Veronica *(Crystal the Maid)*, Miriam Zucker *(Betsy)*.

While doing his daily jogging, yuppie New York City lawyer Patrick is dragged off the street into an art exhibition by an insistent gallery manager. Prominently displayed within is his portrait—one he never posed for. Later, while speculating about the painting origin's at a gallery soiree, Patrick and his wife (Blair) meet the mystery artist, Raymond, a wealthy, high-strung dilettante. Over dinner, Raymond reveals that she is Patrick's mother, and that the model for the lookalike portrait was none other than Patrick's late, ne'er-do-well father. Out in the Hamptons, Van Bellinghen, Patrick's adoptive mother, admits that (1) Patrick is adopted, (2) his father was a social climber willing to sell his own baby for cash and sex, and (3) she stole Junior after his unsavory papa failed to show up for one of their pay-as-you-go adoption-plan sessions. Eager to become acquainted with his real mom after having heard all this, Patrick goes out to spend the weekend at Raymond's fabulous Long Island estate. There, she fusses over him possessively, promises to leave him everything in her will, and pretends to tolerate Blair. Raymond is not a model of mental stability, however, and Mad Mama begins poisoning Blair as the first step in her scheme to have Patrick all to herself. After craftily providing Blair with a daily dose of lethal Alka-Seltzer, Raymond beats to death her bimbo maid (Veronica) for having the nerve to proposition Patrick. En route to Manhattan to obtain medical care for his wife, Patrick drives over Veronica's corpse (dumped in the road by Raymond), forcing him to return with Blair to the nightmare mansion. The incestuousness really kicks into high gear when, having discovered that a pussycat has croaked after eating some tasty Brie, Blair crawls downstairs and finds the drunken Raymond seducing her own son! After Blair is stabbed to death (in slow motion), Patrick succumbs to a Mickey Finn and awakens to find himself tied to a bed. Before you can say "Oedipus Rex," Maniacal Mommy is regaling him with news of their upcoming nuptials. Confusing her son with his deceased father, Raymond now goes completely bananas, but calms down long enough to get rid of a cop investigating Veronica's death and to alleviate the suspicions of Patrick's adoptive parents, Van Bellinghen and Donahue, who turn up unannounced. Relishing her power over the captive Patrick, Raymond tries to starve him into submission, breaks his toes, and puts the finishing touches on her upcoming re-wedding ceremony. When Van Bellinghen sneaks back in the house and sees her son attired in tuxedo and formal noose around his neck, however, a Battle of Mothers ensues. (Donahue gets into the act, too, but gets pushed down a staircase.) Cornered in the attic, Van Bellinghen is apparently saved when the butchering bride's veil gets

caught in a jumbo fan and chokes her—but no, Raymond survives even that, only to be shot by Donahue. In the end, adoptive parents and battered son pick themselves up, dust themselves off, and go home to the Hamptons.

Maniacs follow their own peculiar logic, no doubt, but A WOMAN OBSESSED suffers from credibility problems that even the title character's psychosis can't explain away. In fact, this fright-nighter so blatantly pursues cheap thrills that its above-average production values and the admirable restraint of its early expository sequences ultimately fail to recommend it. While the plot grows wilder and wilder, character motivation and caution are thrown to the wind, until neither the director (Larry Vincent) nor the cast are up to the challenge of making us feel caught up in the psychological labyrinth the characters inhabit. Linda Blair performs capably, but seems more at home bouncing her way through women's prison pictures; Gregory Patrick is attractive but comes off as too narcissistic to command sympathy; and Ruth Raymond, as the nutcase, doesn't just chew the scenery—she masticates 50 times per bite and swallows it.

This increasingly whacked-out psycho thriller possesses an uncommon ability to steamroller over the gaping holes in its plot that easily places it in the so-bad-it's-good category. If you want finesse, you're in for a bumpy ride. If you want a shallow haunted-house remake crossing THE STORY OF ADELE H. with HUSH... HUSH, SWEET CHARLOTTE, you might enjoy yourself. Unfortunately, lapses in good taste abound. Why would the filmmakers cast the *Playboy* Playmate-ish Christina Veronica as the maid when they have some pretensions toward making A WOMAN OBSESSED a serious psychological chiller? Why does the crazed mother who claims she wants Patrick all to herself decide to invite the entire neighborhood to a ceremony in which the reluctant groom will be marched down the aisle attached to a rope, like an organ grinder's monkey? Why does the film never come to grips with the central issue of incest? Screenwriter Craig Horrall's memory seems as full of holes as the title character's. Raymond sometimes realizes that Patrick is her stolen son; at other times she's ready to pounce on him sexually. When this loony movie stoops to showing the crazed woman raping her own son, it's clear the filmmakers intend nothing but exploitation.

Still, the unbelievably bizarre denouement, in which Mommy Craziest tries to polish off her rivals for Junior's love while attending to the details of the wedding reception, is sick fun raised to spectacularly campy heights. You've never seen so many people you thought were dead get up again. Nondiscriminating horror buffs will

rank the battle of the Two Mommies on a par with Godzilla vs. King Kong, or at least a better-than-average episode of TV's "Glamorous Ladies of Wrestling." In the end, though, A WOMAN OBSESSED may serve best as a warning to adopted children to think twice about looking for their natural parents. *(Graphic violence, profanity, nudity, sexual situations, adult situations.)*

d, Larry Vincent; w, Craig Horrall; ph, Larry Revene; ed, James Davalos; m, Joey Mennonna; art d, Hilary Wright; cos, Jeffrey Wallach.

Thriller (PR:O MPAA:R)

WORTH WINNING*
102m A&M/FOX c

Mark Harmon *(Taylor Worth)*, Madeleine Stowe *(Veronica Briskow)*, Lesley Ann Warren *(Eleanor Larimore)*, Maria Holvoe *(Erin Cooper)*, Mark Blum *(Ned Braudy)*, Andrea Martin *(Claire Braudy)*, Tony Longo *(Terry Childs)*, Alan Blumenfeld *(Howard Larimore)*, Devin Ratray *(Howard Larimore, Jr.)*, David Brenner *(Celebrity Auctioneer)*, Jon Korkes *(Sam)*, Brad Hall *(Eric)*, Shannon Lawrence *(Chloe Braudy)*, Todd Cameron Brown *(Owen Braudy)*, Russ Bolinger *(Gus)*, Joan Severance *(Lizbette)*, Emily Kuroda *(Cory Chu)*, Karen Newman *(Amy)*, John Walcutt *(Chip)*, Rick Hurst *(Big Bouncin' Bob)*, Meg Wyllie *(Granny)*, Arthur Malet *(Ticket Taker)*, John Carter *(Mr. Cooper)*, Nancy Glass *(Channel 8 Newscaster)*, Thomas Bellin *(Minister)*, Ben Kronen, Sanford Jensen, Ian Bruce *(Bidding Men at Auction)*, Catherine M. Cummings *(Box Office Woman)*, Phillip Simon *(Maitre'd)*, Micah Rowe *(Bryan)*, Francis J. D'Imperio, Raymond J. Mullen, Samuel Shipman, Dustin Perez, William P. McManus *(Kids in Volvo)*, Paul M. Basta, Richard G. Price, Irv Waitsman *(Camera Operators)*, Andrew McCullough *(Stage Manager)*, Robert Mayon *(Sportscaster)*, Marcy Shelton *(Track Cashier)*, Cari Lightfoot *(Ticket Seller)*, Dan Clark, John Page, Robert Gus Blue, Jeff Benson, Reggie Doss, Linden King, John Sciarra *(Football Players at Party)*, Julie Merrill, Linda Dona *(Ladies at the Paddock)*, Gerald J. Wilson *(Video Tech)*.

Mark Harmon hits another brick wall in his quest for big-screen success with this slack and uninvolving quasi-romantic comedy. As Harmon vehicles go, WORTH WINNING may make viewers nostalgic for the anemic SUMMER SCHOOL. Harmon plays Taylor Worth, a vain, insipid stud plying his trade of TV weatherman and leaving a trail of broken hearts throughout the quainter sections of Philadelphia. Harmon makes a wager with his best friend, psychiatrist Blum, that he can get three women of Blum's choice to accept his proposal of marriage (on videotape) within three months. The selected trio includes bitchy concert pianist Stowe; virginal blonde knockout Holvoe, a receptionist for the Philadelphia Eagles football team; and wealthy, oversexed housewife Warren. Of course, Harmon gets each to succumb before his sneaky camera, and, of course, the three women eventually discover his deception and join forces to exact their revenge. Finally (of course), Harmon learns the meaning of true love and resolves to give up his philandering.

We won't give away which of the three contenders gets the wedding ring—but it's not too hard, given the conservative climate of current Hollywood cinema, to figure out that the woman who commits adultery with Harmon and the woman who impulsively beds down with a football player to see what sex is like before her wedding night are both out. OK, so we did give it away. Does anyone care? Harmon never really gets a handle on his character, and director Will Mackenzie doesn't seem to know what to make of him either. As scripted by Josann McGibbon and Sara Parriott from Dan Lewandowski's novel, Harmon's Taylor Worth is simply a creep, a cool and sly manipulator. First seen as he callously dumps one woman (the beautiful Joan Severance) in order to date her roommate, he never convinces us of his eventual

redemption, and he remains completely detached throughout the film, continually breaking out of character (in one of WORTH WINNING's many serious mistakes) to comment on the action. Though the ending is meant to leave audiences with the warm, moist feeling that Stowe was actually after Harmon all along (rather than the other way around), the real effect is to baffle the viewer. WORTH WINNING has been so convincing in establishing its main character's vapid egotism that it's hard to imagine any intelligent woman wanting him around for more than one night, if that long. Further confusing the film's message are its three main actresses functioning mostly as set (or is that sex?) decoration, despite the fact that both Stowe (STAKEOUT) and Warren (CHOOSE ME) have proven their acting talents in other films, while newcomer Holvoe shows potential.

Many movies set in American cities are actually filmed in Toronto and Vancouver, so it's probably worth noting that WORTH WINNING was actually filmed partly in Philly, although that's surely faint praise for this catatonic comedy. WORTH WINNING might possibly have worked if Harmon's character had been either much warmer or much colder, but the point is hardly worth debating. Ultimately, this

thoroughly botched film accomplishes little beyond adding to the depressingly growing body of evidence that Hollywood has forgotten how to make what was once its stock-in-trade: the sharp, sexy, well-crafted romantic comedy. Musical selections include: "Girls" (Dwight Twilley, performed by Twilley), "All of My Days" (Angie Rugin, Shelley Speck, performed by N'Dea), "Forgiveness," "Worth Winning" (Liz Story, performed by Story), "The Fashion Show" (Bruce Wooley, Simon Darlow, Trevor Horn, Steve Lipson, performed by Grace Jones), "We've Only Just Begun" (Paul Williams, Roger Nichols, performed by the Carpenters), Etude, Op. 25, No. 2 (Frederic Chopin, performed by Vlado Perlemuter). *(Adult situations, profanity.)*

p, Gil Friesen and Dale Pollock; d, Will Mackenzie; w, Josann McGibbon and Sara Parriott (based on the novel by Dan Lewandowski); ph, Adam Greenberg (Deluxe Color); ed, Sidney Wolinsky; m, Patrick Williams; md, David Anderle; prod d, Lilly Kilvert; art d, Jon Hutman; set d, David Klassen; spec eff, King Hernandez; cos, Robert Blackman; stunts, Norman Howell; makeup, Lona Jeffers.

Comedy   **(PR:O MPAA:PG-13)**

XYZ

YAABA****

(Burkina Faso) 90m Arcadia-Les Films de L'Avenir-Thelma-Television Suisse Romande-ZDF-La Sept-Centre National de la Cinemagraphic-Department Federal des Affaires Etrangeres-COE/New Yorker c
(Trans: Grandmother)
Fatimata Sanga (Yaaba), Noufou Ouedraogo (Bila), Roukietou Barry (Nopoko), Adama Ouedraogo (Kougri), Amade Toure (Tibo), Sibidou Ouedraogo (Poko), Adama Sidibe (Razougou), Rasmane Ouedraogo (Noaga), Kinda Moumouni (Finse), Assita Ouedraogo (Koudi), Zenabou Ouedraogo (Pegda), Ousmane Sawadogo (Taryam).

Set in a village in Burkina Faso, YAABA begins as young cousins Bila (Noufou Ouedraogo) and Nopoko (Barry) playfully sprint across a sparse, beautifully serene savannah, where they encounter the mysterious Sana (Sanga), an old woman who has been branded a witch and ostracized by the adults in their village. In the next scene, a group of villagers tries to put out a fire in the hut that has served as their grocery, which was set ablaze under suspicious circumstances. Already, director Idrissa Ouedraogo has set up the poles of his story, pitting the innocence of Bila and Nopoko against the intrigue and superstition among the elders. The social codes and work habits in the village are also established quickly: although the men, as providers, are clearly dominant, the women are strong, sly, and more than capable of holding their own. Relationships in the community are intricate; the village seems almost to be one extended, quarrelsome family. The curious and sensitive Bila becomes something of a "problem child" in this family, however, when he develops a relationship with the outcast Sana—who, far from being a witch, is a benign, contemplative sort given to dispensing small nuggets of wisdom. Bila savors these nuggets and respectfully calls her "Yaaba" ("Grandmother"), touching the old woman, who has never been addressed in that way before. A few subplots are developed alongside Bila and Sana's relationship, one involving a woman whose husband is a good man, but alcoholic and impotent, leading her to begin a secret affair with a man who lives outside the village. Eventually, Nopoko suffers an injury that leads to a tetanus infection, which is misdiagnosed as malaria. Her case becomes increasingly grave, and a shaman is summoned to prescribe a cure. When he insists that the "witch" has stolen the child's soul and must be banished, the villagers hunt for Sana. She, however, has been warned by Bila and leaves her hut, which one villager sets afire (suggesting that he may have been responsible for the earlier blaze, which was also blamed on Sana's black magic), then journeys across a river to meet the healer Taryam (Ousmane Sawadogo). The old man concocts a remedy for Nopoko and travels with Sana back to the village, where the child is near death. Although the (male) elders turn them away, Bila's mother, who has been tending the motherless Nopoko, secretly instructs Bila to run after the old people and bring back the healer's antidote. The medicine works, and Nopoko is soon back on her feet—though the elders insist her recovery had nothing to do with Sana, who remains a pariah. As the film nears its conclusion, Bila and Nopoko find Sana leaning lifelessly against one of the walls of what remains of her home, and summon one of the men (the drunken husband) to help them give her a dignified burial. We now learn the origin of Sana's sinister reputation—her mother died while giving birth to her and her father died a short time later. In a touching act of faith and memory that testifies to his love for both Sana and Nopoko, Bila presents his cousin with a bracelet Sana gave him, and the film ends as it began, with Bila chasing Nopoko across the gracefully photographed sweep of plain.

The winner of the International Critics Prize at the 1989 Cannes Film Festival, YAABA is a visually striking, poignant film that communicates much through refreshingly economical means. Director Ouedraogo (YAM DAABO [The Choice]) filmed this elegant work in his own village, using a nonprofessional cast that includes several Ouedraogo family members and that renders uniformly convincing and natural performances. (Noufou Ouedraogo and Roukietou Barry, the two young leads, are especially winning and spirited.) Relying on deft mise-en-scene, Quedraogo captures the village's unique rhythms with precision and wrests great emotional power from the simple story, paralleling the love between the two children—of whom Bila is more of a loner than the easy-going Nopoko—with that between Bila and the outcast Sana. Painting from a palette of rich earth tones, he conveys the texture of a day-to-day world that seems hardly mundane, wholly catching viewers up in a world whose reality is both particular and transcendant. (Brief nudity.)

p, Freddy Denaes, Michel David, Pierre-Alain Meier, and Idressa Ouedraogo; d, Idressa Ouedraogo; w, Idressa Ouedraogo; ph, Matthias Kalin; ed, Loredana Cristelli; m, Francis Bebey; tech, Sekou Ouedraogo; makeup, Nathalie Tanner.

Drama (PR:A)

⊙YOUNG EINSTEIN***

(Aus.) 91m Serious/WB c
Yahoo Serious (Albert Einstein), Odile le Clezio (Marie Curie), John Howard (Preston Preston), Pee Wee Wilson (Mr. Einstein), Su Cruickshank (Mrs. Einstein), Lulu Pinkus (The Blonde), Kaarin Fairfax (The Brunette), Michael Lake (Manager), Jonathan Coleman (Wolfgang Bavarian), Johnny McCall (Rudy Bavarian), Michael Blaxland (Desk Clerk), Ray Fogo (Bright Clerk), Terry Pead, Alice Pead (Inventor Couple), Frank McDonald (Nihilist), Tony Harvey (Bursar), Tim Elliot (Lecturer), Ray Winslade (Droving Student), Ian "Danno" Rogerson (Randy Student), Wendy De Waal (Prudish Student), P.J. Voeten (Chinese Student), Peter Zakrzewski, Sally Zakrzewski, Zanzi Mann, Conky Heygate, Shannen De Villermont, Mark Bell (The Kids), Albert Heygate, Wombat (Dogs), Warren Coleman (Lunatic Professor), Glenn Butcher (Ernest Rutherford), Steve Abbott (Brian Asprin), Russell Cheek (Nurse), Warwick Irwin (Gate Guard), Keith Heygate (Scientist's Guard), Roger Ward (Cat Pie Cook), Michael Matou, Ted Reid (Asylum Guards), Martin Raphael (Crazed Lunatic), The Film Crew (Dangerous Lunatics), Max Meldrum (Mr. Curie), Rose Jackson (Mrs. Curie), Basil Clarke (Charles Darwin), Adam Bowen (Guglielmo Marconi), Esben Storm (Wilbur Wright), Tim McKew (Sigmund Freud), Phillipa Baker (Freud's Mother), Geoff Aldridge, Hugh Wayland (Lumiere Brothers), Ian James Tait (Thomas Edison), Aku Kadogo (African Lady), Margot Ross (Emotional Mother), Madeleine Ross (Baby Scientist), Nick Conroy (Clark Gable), Michael Shirley (Admiral Shackleton), Ollie Hall, Christian Manon (Darwin's Bodyguards), John Even Hughes (Drunk), Sylvester's Sextet (Bavarian Band), Rhonvic Brolga Dancers (Polka Dancers), Pepper Soudakoff (Darwin's Beagle), Johnny McCall (Tasmanian Devil), Megan Shapcott, Inge Burke, Georgie Parker (Country Girl Fans), David Ngoom (Aborignial Dancer), Wick Wilson (News Cameraman), David Roach, Colin Gibson (Country Yokels), Michael Lake (Lonely Street Hotel Manager).

To say that Yahoo Serious (formerly known as Greg Pead), the Australian writer, director, coproducer, editor, and star of YOUNG EINSTEIN, takes a few liberties with the title physicist's life in this off-the-wall "mockudrama" is like saying that Ingmar Bergman is "concerned with major themes." Serious couldn't overtly be further from seriousness himself, but it's hard to imagine Einstein minding YOUNG EINSTEIN too much. As the film notes in its closing credits, the genius of Princeton was not without his own wry sense of humor regarding his history-making discoveries.

A box-office record breaker in its country of origin, YOUNG EINSTEIN offers more smiles than knee-slapping laughs. As the title character, Serious sports a younger version of Einstein's familiar fright-wig haircut, but there the resemblance ends. Serious' Einstein, dressed in knee pants and suspenders, is the son of humble Tasmanian apple farmers Wilson and Cruickshank. Happening upon the theory of relativity early in life, he uses his discovery to split the beer atom, adding bubbles to what had hitherto been a rather flat brew. Later in life, Serious invents both the electric guitar and the surfboard, leading to the discovery of rock'n'roll as well as a new recreational use for gnarly waves. Meanwhile, he finds time to court young Marie Curie (le Clezio), who is using her Nobel Prize to study at Sydney University. Serious, who has arrived in Sydney to make his fortune, lives at a cheap, though chaste, hotel/bordello where he conducts science classes for the resident ladies of the evening, who threaten to turn into budding physicists themselves. His rival for the beautiful le Clezio's hand is Howard, an evil beer brewer who steals Serious' formula without realizing its potential for destruction. When Howard's perfidy is discovered, Serious and his high-IQ lady love set out in a hot air balloon for the Science Academy Awards, racing to stop the brewer from unleashing the awesome power of the beer atom and causing a nuclear disaster.

EINSTEIN's satire tends toward Monty Python territory, though without the Brits' vicious bite. Serious' sendup of Einstein is rather warmly affectionate, if not downright respectful; if anything, EINSTEIN plays like screwball comedy filtered through an oddball, science buff's sensibility, managing to be at once broad and subtle, raucous and gentle, crude and sophisticated, scattershot and utterly precise. Lanky and loose-limbed, yet unexpectedly low-key and graceful as a physical comic, Serious himself is a pleasantly cartoonish screen presence, but he conveys an underlying, offhand intelligence that hints at an extreme familiarity with his subject.

Indeed, Serious may finally be more serious than he lets on. Children and scientists will probably be the best audiences for YOUNG EINSTEIN, and the film is in part a meditation on how little distance there is between the two. For children, YOUNG EINSTEIN could plant seeds of curiosity about the real-life genius; for scientists, the film is crammed with witty inside jokes as it lightly skewers history and some of its most famous minds. It's civilian adults who may find themselves feeling uncomfortable—for, though not a work of genius itself, this reasonably entertaining, off-the-wall story has just enough grains of recognizable biographical truth to cause us to reflect, perhaps with a little embarrassment, on how little we really know about one of this century's towering figures.

p, Yahoo Serious, Warwick Ross, and David Roach; d, Yahoo Serious; w, Yahoo Serious and David Roach; ph, Jeff Darling; ed, David Roach, Neil Thumpston, Peter Whitmore, and Amanda Robson; m, William Motzing, Martin Armiger, and Tommy Tycho; art d, Steve Marr, Laurie Faen, Colin Gibson, and Ron Highfield; cos, Susan Bowden; chor, Aku Kadogo; anim, Flicks Animation; stunts, Yahoo Serious; makeup, Sherry Hubbard.

Comedy **(PR:AA MPAA:PG)**

●**YOUNG NURSES IN LOVE zero**
76m Platinum c

Jeanne Marie *(Nurse Ellis)*, Alan Fisler *(Dr. Reilly)*, Jane Hamilton *(Francesca)*, Jamie Gillis *(Dr. Spencer)*, Harv Siegel *(Dr. Young)*, James Davies, Barbra Robb, Jennifer Delora, Beth Broderick, Annie Sprinkle, Sharon Moran, John Altamura, Daniel Chapman.

Before all the giddiness of *Glasnost*, intense Soviet-American rivalry fostered many a movie premise. There have been pseudoserious, flag-waving warnings of the Red Menace and semirealistic spy thrillers. More often what is offered in today's Yakov Smirnoff age of comedy are silly burlesques like YOUNG NURSES IN LOVE, another titillating tidbit from Platinum Pictures and filmmaker Chuck Vincent (NEW YORK'S FINEST). Posing as an American nurse, Soviet agent Marie infiltrates Hoover Hospital in order to break into its world famous sperm bank. Stored there is the frozen issue of such geniuses as Einstein, FDR, and Duke Ellington, which she is to steal so that Mother Russia can breed a generation of masterminds. The hospital's most eligible bachelor doctor, Fisler, who also happens to be a CIA operative, is hip to the plan, but allows himself to fall in love with Marie. Without letting on that he knows about her mission, Fisler raises Marie's political consciousness, rhapsodizing about a world without subversive politics—a world where humankind will be served by science. Meanwhile, the rest of the hospital (and movie) is literally up for grabs, with a host of philandering physicians, pathetic patients, and predictable pratfalls introduced to showcase the antics and anatomies of such adult film stars as Annie Sprinkle, James Gillis, and Jane Hamilton (aka Veronica Hart.) In a typical gag, the already overly endowed Sprinkle (portraying actress Twin Falls) is scheduled for breast enhancement; however, it is a mobster-on-the-lam who winds up under the knife and with a new identity. To get the plot back into the picture, Marie's Soviet superior shows up for a showdown against the newly enlightened defector.

They say laughter is the best medicine, but the prescription followed by YOUNG NURSES IN LOVE has gone stale. Though the film, a very unofficial sequel to Fox's 1982 YOUNG DOCTORS IN LOVE, was originally made in 1986, it wasn't released until this year. The cast of lowbrow Vincent regulars appear to enjoy working with one another, but they are never quite able to involve the audience in their shared good times. Since YOUNG NURSES IN LOVE went directly to video, viewers might want to try playing with the fast forward on their VCRs to invest the action with a Benny Hill look. Otherwise there's not much here of interest. *(Nudity, profanity, sexual situations.)*

p, Chuck Vincent; d, Chuck Vincent; w, Chuck Vincent and Craig Horrall; ph, Larry Revene; ed, Chuck Vincent and James Davalos; m, Bill Heller; art d, D. Gary Phelps.

Comedy **(PR:O MPAA:R)**

THE MOTION PICTURE ANNUAL

1990

People to Watch

PEOPLE TO WATCH

Jon Amiel

A director who has worked until now primarily in television in his native Britain, Jon Amiel made his theatrical film debut with the magical QUEEN OF HEARTS, which drew critical kudos on both sides of the Atlantic. Amiel's television work has been seen by American audiences in Dennis Potter's acclaimed mini-series, "The Singing Detective"; from this, and from QUEEN OF HEARTS, just two samples of his work, his distinctive strengths as a director begin to emerge. "Detective" takes a slew of negatives, from the heartbreak of psoriasis to marital hostility, and presents them in a darkly comic, fantastic light, without in the least diminishing their painfulness. QUEEN OF HEARTS is more gently comic, but tells of an Italian immigrant family's struggles with real and serious adversity, the story presented through the eyes of an optimistic, fantasizing 11-year-old boy. In both cases, Amiel's direction uses tonal discrepancies to produce subtle and satisfying irony. In his hands, amazing events are treated with a serene acceptance that carries audiences along, but results at the same time in comedy-drama that is filled with surprises. Amiel's gift is to sustain this delicate balance. His whimsical, ironic style is a most welcome addition to the world of feature film, and audiences can look forward to seeing a lot more of it. His next movie project is the forthcoming AUNT JULIA AND THE DETECTIVE.

Kenneth Branagh

Following in the gigantic footsteps of Orson Welles and Laurence Olivier, Kenneth Branagh has given us a film version of Shakespeare's "Henry V" that, despite less than unanimous critical acclaim, establishes Branagh as a force to be reckoned with. Branagh both directed and stars in this dark but inspiring version of the Bard's great history play, giving us battle scenes mired in blood and muck and a Henry who develops in the course of the drama from a young, untried monarch to a self-assured, seasoned leader of men and nations. Branagh's rendering of Henry is fresh and powerful, communicating the contradictions, the moral and intellectual conflicts, at the heart of leadership. His performance has garnered overwhelmingly positive commentary on both sides of the Atlantic, and his presentation of the play as a complex, brutal representation of war has provoked considerable critical interest. Branagh is no newcomer to the character of Henry, nor to theater generally. He played Henry in a Royal Shakespeare Company production, and in 1987 he founded his own company, producing, writing, and playing the

Kenneth Brannagh

lead in his own creation, "Public Enemy." The company—and Branagh—subsequently toured Britain with productions of "Twelfth Night," "Hamlet," "Much Ado About Nothing," and "As You Like It." Born in Belfast but raised in England, Branagh attended the prestigious Royal Academy of Dramatic Art. He has been seen by American audiences in the TV mini-series "Fortunes of War," and his movie credits include a highly praised performance in the 1988 film HIGH SEASON. During the 1990 theater season, he planned to bring productions of "King Lear" and "A Midsummer Night's Dream" to the US, playing supporting roles in both. And he will surely be a presence on American movie screens in the future, given his great talent as an actor and his desire to "keep [his] horizons open."

Steve DeJarnatt

A decade of tenacity paid off for writer-director Steve DeJarnatt when the screenplay he wrote for MIRACLE MILE in 1978 finally came to the screen under his direction this year. Part offbeat love story, part apocalyptic thriller, DeJarnatt's tightly woven B-movie marvel concentrates on the final 70 minutes in the life of a young saxophonist (wonderfully played by Anthony Edwards) as he traverses LA's "Miracle Mile" in search of the woman he's just fallen for, while the clock ticks toward imminent nuclear annihilation. Loaded with meticulously crafted details, deft foreshadowing, and skillfully composed shots, MIRACLE MILE unfolds at a carefully escalated pace that inexorably

involves the viewer in the fate of the film's doomed lovers. Yet MIRACLE MILE was almost never filmed. American Film Institute graduate DeJarnatt sold his screenplay to Warner Bros., who wanted to produce it as a big-budget feature, but were unwilling to allow the untried DeJarnatt to direct so major a project. For years the script languished on Warners' shelves, and in 1983 *American Film* magazine named it one of the 10 best unmade scripts. Luckily, using money he made for writing STRANGE BREW, DeJarnatt bought back the rights to his screenplay for some $25,000. Determined to make the film himself, he refused a $400,000 offer to sell his rewrite back to Warner Bros. Eventually Hemdale bankrolled the $3.7 million production and permitted DeJarnatt to make the film his way. Much less successful than this engrossing movie was DeJarnatt's previous directorial effort, CHERRY 2000, an odd science-fiction film starring Melanie Griffith that was made in 1985 but released straight to video in 1988. DeJarnatt also had a hand in the script for GREMLINS, and is reportedly at work on a screenplay about firemen. If his next project is as accomplished as MIRACLE MILE, there will be little doubt that the gifted filmmaker has arrived.

Bridget Fonda

With two sharp and witty performances in recent British productions under her belt, Bridget Fonda can very soon cease to worry that she's known first as a scion of the famous family (she's Peter Fonda's daughter), and stand on the merits of her own work. In SCANDAL (starring Joanne Whalley, another Person to Watch), Fonda turned her supporting role into a memorable screen triumph. Playing the irrepressible, gutsy Mandy Rice-Davies, Christine Keeler's teenaged party-girl buddy, Fonda is sassy, seductive, and sharply comic. Like her real-life character, Fonda makes the most of her material; her portrayal of Rice-Davies' day in court accomplishes a sly comic richness in a relatively brief scene. Wide-eyed and demure, she wields her youthful sexuality like a goad, exploding the conventional hypocrisies of the British upper classes. Before SCANDAL, Fonda worked in SHAG for the same production team, bringing a mixture of cool blond innocence and red-hot knowingness to her role as a star-struck southern belle in Myrtle Beach, South Carolina. Fonda, who studied acting at New York University, is a great admirer of her late grandfather, Henry Fonda, whom she has called a "very professional and giving actor." She made her screen debut in 1988, playing

Joanne Whalley and Bridget Fonda

one of the young lovers (opposite James Mathers) in Franc Roddam's "Liebestod" segment of ARIA, giving a transcendent performance that communicated high tragic emotion in a brief sequence without dialog. ("I died on screen in seven minutes," Fonda remarked of the part.) Given the brevity of her exposure to date, she has made a resounding impact. In the lead roles that seem sure to follow, expect her to convey further shadings of the emotion, humor, and sexual allure that have distinguished her work to date.

Charlotte Gainsbourg
The daughter of English actress Jane Birkin (who lives and works in France) and singer-songwriter Serge Gainsbourg, Charlotte Gainsbourg has an indisputable performer's pedigree, and her work in a number of recent French films gives evidence of a major talent. With her captivating, whispery voice and brooding, expressive face, Gainsbourg has a natural screen presence, enhanced by a lucid command of her craft. Two of her feature films have been widely seen during the past year by American audiences: KUNG

FU MASTER, in which she persuasively communicates the complex emotions of an adolescent, and THE LITTLE THIEF, in which she has a starring role that promises to bring her international acclaim. THE LITTLE THIEF is a kind of posthumous spin-off from Francois Truffaut's THE 400 BLOWS, and while the film ultimately succumbs to a box-office-oriented cheeriness, Gainsbourg in many ways embodies Truffaut's darker vision to perfection. As the disaffected, unloved delinquent teen, she projects a variety of nasty traits—she's callous, spiteful, and calculating, her conscience stunted by self-protective toughness. Like Bernadette Lafont's murderous character in SUCH A GORGEOUS KID LIKE ME (1973), Gainsbourg's Janine is irredeemably shifty, a moral and emotional quicksand. But unlike Lafont's character, Janine is neither very bad nor intensely appealing. Within that narrower range, Gainsbourg's performance reverberates powerfully, never slipping out of her adolescent anti-social nastiness, yet commanding our sympathy for her

vulnerability and need for love. Before directing her in THE LITTLE THIEF, Claude Miller had previously worked with Gainsbourg in L'EFFRONTEE, and insisted she be cast in the THIEF title role as a condition of his direction. She has the kind of talent we can expect to see more of—working perhaps again with Miller, or with other prominent directors.

Steve Kloves
Suffused in the atmosphere of the Seattle cocktail lounges in which its eponymous pianist protagonists—played by Jeff and Beau Bridges—perform, THE FABULOUS BAKER BOYS is the uneven but promising directorial debut of 29-year-old Steve Kloves. Reworking the familiar Hollywood story about a partnership that is threatened when a member of the opposite sex joins the act (in this case Michelle Pfeiffer, whose sultry performance garnered much critical praise), Kloves' character study is not without its weaknesses. But while its plot and focus falter, the film offers many electric moments and fine performances from the leads; moreover, with the expert help of cinematographer Michael Ballhaus (THE LAST TEMPTATION OF CHRIST), Kloves deftly evokes the smoky, late-night milieu of piano bars and the harsh clarity of mornings after. After writing the screenplay for RACING WITH THE MOON (1984)—Richard Benjamin's gentle, offbeat tale of two friends preparing to go off to fight in WW II—the then-23-year-old UCLA dropout Kloves wrote the script for THE FABULOUS BAKER BOYS. During the five years it took to bring the story to the screen, he turned down other writing offers, including an opportunity to adapt *A Confederacy of Dunces*. As his screenplay made the rounds (a Warner Bros.' property at one point, nearly directed by George Roy Hill at another), Kloves balked at the suggestion that it become a vehicle for the likes of Dan Aykroyd. When producers Paula Weinstein and Mark Rosenberg finally decided that Kloves' passion for the project was qualification enough for him to direct the film, he persuaded the Bridges brothers to come aboard, and 20th Century Fox eventually backed the $11.5 million production. While Kloves is clearly still learning his craft, THE FABULOUS BAKER BOYS shows him to be a quick study and a writer-director of great promise.

Charles Lane
Although it made a lesser splash than SEX, LIES AND VIDEOTAPE or DRUGSTORE COWBOY, Charles Lane's SIDEWALK STORIES is in some respects the most daring of these three acclaimed independent features. As a silent film shot in black and white with-

Charles Lane with Sandye Wilson in SIDEWALK STORIES.

out star performers, and as a self-consciously Chaplinesque comedy with a very serious subject (homelessness), SIDEWALK STORIES is an audacious project indeed. That Lane was able to get it made was already a feat; that the film gained the Prix du Publique at Cannes, met with general critical favor upon release, and garnered Lane—its director, producer, writer, and star—distribution and a three-film contract with Island is truly remarkable. A Bronx-born African-American, Lane was unknown before SIDEWALK STORIES, with only a black-and-white, silent student short called A PLACE IN TIME to his credit. That film was the basis for SIDEWALK STORIES, but its concept was amended after Lane had a long conversation with a homeless man on the street, an exchange that caused Lane to re-examine his perception of homeless people's humanity. This feeling for the homeless as individuals rather than as a stereotyped mass is SIDEWALK STORIES' strongest quality, informing its sentimentality. Shot on location in New York City over two weeks, the film was made on $200,000 provided by Lane's lawyer, executive producer Howard Brickner. Brickner originally offered the sum to Lane as financing for SKINS, Lane's pet project of many years; and though Lane needed more money for SKINS, SIDEWALK STORIES' success appears to have guaranteed the former film's realization at last. Currently in production, SKINS (a sound and color film) concerns an interracial couple's struggles to stay together. If SKINS manages to make good the promise of SIDEWALK STORIES, Lane could emerge as a significant independent voice.

Andie MacDowell
Although her acting career began inauspiciously, supermodel Andie MacDowell proved she was not just another world-famous pretty face in Stephen Soderbergh's SEX, LIES AND VIDEOTAPE, giving a performance so good that she nearly beat Meryl Streep for Best Actress honors at Cannes. As Ann Millaney, the sexually repressed wife who leaves her adulterous husband at the end of Soderbergh's surprise hit, MacDowell provides a nuanced, compelling portrait of conflicted Southern womanhood. Beautiful, self-effacing Ann, the "perfect" housewife who wants everything to be nice—but who would prefer that her husband not touch her—eventually proves the film's strongest character, and MacDowell makes the transition seamlessly, conveying the intelligence and warmth behind Ann's prudish self-censorship. As a South Carolina native and the youngest of four sisters, MacDowell knows something about Southern female stereotypes,

Andie MacDowell

and as a top model whose face has been seen in hundreds of magazines and TV ads, she knows something about stereotypes in general. Critics panned her as yet another model-turned-bad-actress after her film debut as Jane in GREYSTOKE: THE LEGEND OF TARZAN, LORD OF THE APES (1984), a performance marred by director Hugh Hudson's decision to dub her character's voice with a British accent (provided by Glenn Close). Appearances on Italian TV and in the Brat Pack showcase ST. ELMO'S FIRE (1985) did little to improve her reputation, but with SEX, LIES AND VIDEOTAPE, MacDowell was finally hailed as a natural presence on the big screen. With her income guaranteed by modeling—she's L'Oreal's highly paid exclusive model—MacDowell is reportedly selecting her future projects carefully. After SEX, LIES AND VIDEOTAPE, she should have ample choice.

John McNaughton
Writer-producer-director John McNaughton waited nearly three years for his chillingly realistic slasher film HENRY: PORTRAIT OF A SERIAL KILLER to transform him into an "overnight" success. Shot entirely in Chicago in 1986 with a cast of local actors, this dark, disturbing low-budget ($120,000) film became a midnight-movie favorite in the Windy City before garnering critical praise and a limited national release this year. Few films are as unnerving as HENRY, which, in a detached, nonjudgmental manner, follows an outwardly normal but psychically scarred young man (brilliantly played by Michael Rooker, before his success in such films as EIGHT MEN OUT and SEA OF LOVE) as he matter-of-factly kills not only strangers but also those who are closest to him. McNaughton's daring, no-holds-barred screenplay was created in collaboration with playwright Richard Fire ("E/R Emergency Room"), and inspired in part by a "20/20" segment dealing with convicted serial killer Henry Lee Lucas. Working in 16 mm, Chicago native McNaughton drenches his film in moody atmosphere, making especially effective use of camera movement to slowly draw the viewer into Henry's out-of-kilter world. While the gore that McNaughton chooses to show is graphic, most of the film's violence occurs offscreen. Still, the MPAA assigned the film an X rating (refused by the distributors, who released HENRY unrated), not for any particular scene, for violence, or for nudity, but because of the film's general tone and approach. The straightforward realism of HENRY may prove too much for some, but this stylish film's undeniable power signals the arrival of a filmmaker with a big future. McNaughton's next project, THE BORROWER, was awaiting distri-

bution at the time of this writing. A one-time carnival pitchman, McNaughton also has a screenplay about carnival life in the offing.

Euzhan Palcy

Even were it not the fine film it is, Euzhan Palcy's A DRY WHITE SEASON would still represent a breakthrough, being the first feature directed by a black woman for a major US studio. Moreover, this $9-million "gamble" proved a sure bet: contradicting Hollywood wisdom as to what kind of films women can and cannot make, the 32-year-old Palcy handles her large international cast, "big" theme, and brutal subject matter with complete assurance, while retaining the shrewd characterizations and insider's perspective that distinguished her low-budget feature debut, SUGAR CANE ALLEY. The Martinique-born Palcy's youthful ambitions were fueled by a kind of negative inspiration: growing up in a third-world colony, she was exposed to the demeaning, stereotyped depictions of blacks in the American and French cultural product that flooded local markets, and became determined to challenge such images by creating her own. After apprenticing in local television, Palcy studied at the Vaugirard film school in Paris, then returned to Martinique with a budget of less than $1 million and made SUGAR CANE ALLEY, which won widespread critical praise and a Best Foreign Film Cesar in 1984. She then became interested in making a film about South African apartheid, but her "uncommercial" story ideas, focusing exclusively on black

characters, failed to gain much producer interest. After meeting Paula Weinstein —an independent producer charged by Warner Bros. with finding someone to film the novel *A Dry White Season*, the rights to which the studio owned—Palcy adapted Andre Brink's book herself, shifting its focus to concentrate equally on blacks and whites and emphasizing its white lead's function as a participant initiated into resisting apartheid, rather than a heroic leader in the struggle. Warners subsequently passed on the film (feeling that CRY FREEDOM had exhausted the audience for South African stories), but Palcy and Weinstein got MGM's backing, scoring a casting coup when Marlon Brando agreed to make his first film appearance in nine years for minimum wage (all the actors agreed to pay cuts). The result—a large-scale, Hollywood "message" film that retains a distinctive viewpoint and a feeling for its characters' everyday lives—bodes well for the future of Palcy, an impassioned and confident filmmaker.

Winona Ryder

Although this fetching young actress has demonstrated considerable promise from her first film appearance, in LUCAS (1986), through her work in SQUARE DANCE (1987), 1969 (1988), and BEETLEJUICE (1988), it was her knock-out performances in this year's HEATHERS and GREAT BALLS OF FIRE that cemented her reputation as one of Hollywood's most exciting new performers. In GREAT BALLS OF FIRE, Jim McBride's disappointing biography of controversial rock 'n' roller Jerry Lee

Lewis, Ryder conveys an innocent sensuality that is perfectly suited to her role as Myra, the "Killer's" 13-year-old cousin-cum-wife. The scene in which Myra moves out of her parents' house, toting her belongings in a doll's house, lingers long after the rest of the film has faded from memory. Even more memorable is Ryder's portrayal of Veronica Sawyer, the soulful, reluctant teenage social climber whose rise to the pantheon of high-school popularity and whose complicity in the murderous scheming of rebellious newcomer J.D. (Christian Slater, see People to Watch) are so essential to the success of HEATHERS (see Daniel Waters, People to Watch). Born Winona Horowitz, the product of an "alternative" upbringing, Ryder was exposed to the likes of Allen Ginsberg and Timothy Leary (her godfather) by her hippie intellectual parents, who worked as editors. After living in Haight Ashbury and on an upscale commune, the family moved to suburban Petaluma, and junior high schooler Ryder began taking classes at San Francisco's American Conservatory Theatre. There "Noni" was spotted by a talent scout and auditioned unsuccessfully for DESERT BLOOM; however, her role in LUCAS followed. Expanding her horizons, Ryder has collaborated with BEETLEJUICE screenwriter Michael McDowell on a romantic script about a girl who works in a bobby-pin factory. She is also slated to star in Jim Abrahams' WELCOME HOME, ROXY CARMICHAEL. Surely only bigger and better things await this skyrocketing 17-year-old.

Christian Slater

Aping the mannerisms and speech of his idol Jack Nicholson, 19-year-old actor Christian Slater set himself up to become a star in his own right with memorable performances in two films this year. In Graeme Clifford's unexpectedly entertaining GLEAMING THE CUBE, Slater undergoes a convincing transformation from a disaffected, skateboarding punk into a mensch who solves the mystery of his stepbrother's murder. However, it was his wonderfully over-the-top interpretation of the vengeful and manipulative J.D. in Michael Lehmann's extraordinary black comedy HEATHERS (see Daniel Waters, People to Watch) that finally thrust Slater into the limelight. Punctuating his nasal drollness with arched eyebrows, Slater's motorcycle-riding new kid is part Nicholson, part James Dean, and all attitude—the warped embodiment of the cynical underbelly of adolescent mall culture, a latter-day rebel with a morbid cause (killing his high-school classmates and staging the affair to look like a mass suicide). HEATHERS' director, Lehmann, was determined to cast the film's teenage roles with teenagers, and the terrific

Winona Ryder with Dennis Quaid in GREAT BALLS OF FIRE.

Christian Slater

chemistry between Slater and costar Winona Ryder (see People to Watch) more than proved the wisdom of that decision. (During filming, Slater broke up with real-life girl friend Kim Walker, who plays one of the Heathers, and began dating Ryder, though only for a few weeks.) Coming from a show business family—dad Michael Hawkins is a stage actor, mom Mary Jo Slater a casting director—young Slater first appeared onstage, at age nine, with Dick Van Dyke in "The Music Man." After Broadway roles in "Macbeth" and "David Copperfield," Slater moved on to television and films, appearing in THE INVISIBLE BOY and the as-yet-unreleased TWISTED, then quietly distinguishing himself as Sean Connery's apprentice in THE NAME OF THE ROSE and as Jeff Bridges' eldest son in TUCKER. If Slater's career continues its upward trend, it may not be long before young actors are borrowing their attitudes from him.

Stephen Soderbergh
Even before his film became the summer of 1989's sleeper hit, Stephen Soderbergh, the director-writer-editor of SEX, LIES AND VIDEOTAPE, was already one of the film world's "people to watch."

Soderbergh's independent feature debut first stirred interest in January 1989, when it was shown as an in-process work at the US Film Festival at Park City, Utah, and won the Audience Award, as well as critical acclaim and widespread industry interest. At Cannes later that year, the finished film scored an even bigger coup when it beat out such festival hits as DO THE RIGHT THING and JESUS OF MONTREAL for the Palme d'Or. (Soderbergh, at 26, is the youngest filmmaker to have won the prize.) The story behind the $1.2-million movie subsequently became well publicized: Soderbergh was a typically anonymous young filmmaker with some short films, TV editing credits, and a Grammy-nominated concert movie (for the rock group Yes) on his resume when he wrote SEX, LIES AND VIDEOTAPE within eight days, half of them spent on the road to Los Angeles. ("It wasn't an act of creation —it was an act of expulsion," Soderbergh later said about writing the film, a confessional work whose four characters represent aspects of Soderbergh's own personality.) Slightly more than a year later, Soderbergh's first feature was ready to make its big splash at Park City. Set in Baton Rouge, Soderbergh's hometown, the film is a study of sexual repression, manipulation, and revelation among a husband and wife, her sister, and the husband's college friend, an impotent loner who videotapes women's sexual confessions. Despite this racy premise, the film is a psychological chamber piece without explicit sex scenes, distinguished by Soderbergh's assured direction of actors; controlled, languid camerawork; authorial integrity; and flair for editing shots and dialog, which gives this talky film its subtly ineluctable rhythms. Next up for Soderbergh: an adaptation of William Brinkley's *The Last Ship*, a tale about survivors of WW III to be produced by Sydney Pollack for Universal— which, along with other Hollywood powers, declined to finance SEX, LIES AND VIDEOTAPE.

Gus Van Sant
Following up MALA NOCHE, his little-seen but acclaimed first feature (made for $25,000, it won the Los Angeles Film Critics Award for best independent film of 1987 and was re-released at the end of 1989), Gus Van Sant delivered another superb indie effort with DRUGSTORE COWBOY, and this time found the audience he deserves. Adapted by Van Sant and Dan Yost from an unpublished novel by prison inmate James Fogle, DRUGSTORE COWBOY conveys its characters' junkie lifestyle with an insider's realism and sympathy, though with enough detachment to lend the film its bizarrely comic tone. Adding to this deadpan, drugged-out quality are Van

Sant's abrupt changes in rhythm and focus, dark, slightly queasy color scheme, and matter-of-fact transference of the story's unglamorous milieu. Like MALA NOCHE, DRUGSTORE COWBOY is set and was filmed in the seedier districts of Portland, Oregon (Van Sant's adopted hometown), and displays an almost beatnik sensibility—a view that neither romanticizes nor condemns its fringe characters, but seeks to portray their world honestly. (Van Sant has called himself a "student" of beatnik novelist William Burroughs, who appears in DRUGSTORE COWBOY and who previously worked with Van Sant on a short-film adaptation of a Burroughs story.) Given that its main character is a "shameless dope fiend," DRUGSTORE COWBOY is all the more noteworthy in our days of wars on drugs. In fact, Van Sant told *Variety* that some 50 or 60 potential producers passed on DRUGSTORE COWBOY, scared off by its non-judgmental approach, before Avenue commendably took a chance on the $5 million film. Van Sant's next project, reportedly concerning the relationship between two male prostitutes, may engender similar risks for producers. It's to be fervently hoped that DRUGSTORE COWBOY's enthusiastic popular and critical reception—it won the National Society of Film Critics' Best Film, Best Director, *and* Best Screenplay awards— will override such concerns.

Daniel Waters
It would be difficult to overestimate the importance of 26-year-old screenwriter Daniel Waters' contribution to HEATHERS, the wildly inventive black comedy that was among the year's most surprisingly satisfying films. Working closely with Waters, 31-year-old first-time director Michael Lehmann fashioned a cynical but hilarious film that is less a satire of adolescent suicide than it is a take on the treatment teenagers and teenage suicide receive in the media and in "serious" films. Drawing on his own experiences at Riley High School in South Bend, Indiana, Waters crafted a script that deftly conveys the backbiting insensitivity, adolescent angst, and desperate need for approval that underlie high-school caste systems. Yet he has given the whole affair a surreal, morbid spin reflective of his avowed intention to write the sort of teen film Stanley Kubrick would make. Laced with uproariously funny slang, Waters' brilliant dialog hits its mark again and again, and his portrait of contemporary teenage culture is ultimately as telling as it is humorous. A graduate of Montreal's McGill University, Waters worked on HEATHERS' script for two years while managing a video store in Los Angeles. Although the studios took notice of his considerable talents, they were unwilling

to gamble on the young screenwriter's off-beat script. But when it was brought to Lehmann's attention by friends from the USC film school (where he made the highly regarded "Beaver Gets a Boner"), the director was anything but reluctant to film it, and HEATHERS was made for New World Pictures on a budget of $3 million. In the wake of the film's success, Waters was hired to rewrite a screenplay for producer Joel Silver (DIE HARD); he also began work on a script concerning the world of high-fashion modeling. It's a good bet that Waters' fertile imagination holds even more surprises for filmgoers.

Joanne Whalley

With an extensive background in quality television, many stage appearances, and roles in several acclaimed British films, Joanne Whalley has achieved widespread recognition in her native England, where she has been heralded by the press as one of Britain's most promising young actresses. Now, her starring role in SCANDAL appears likely to garner her the same kind of applause and recognition on this side of the Atlantic. In this sober, stylish reconstruction of the events surrounding the 1963 Profumo affair, Whalley takes the part of Christine Keeler, the ex-showgirl whose bed-hopping helped to topple the Conservatives from power. What Whalley brings to the role is an impressive, detailed command of her craft that results in a thoroughly convincing portrait of good-time-girl Keeler. She gets under the skin of the naively calculating, shallowly sophisticated character and gives her a faintly sad, ambiguous quality, augmented by powerful, doe-eyed sexuality. Although she is known to American audiences chiefly for "The Singing Detective" and "Reilly, Ace of Spies," Whalley has appeared in many other television productions, among them the award-winning serial "The Edge of Darkness" and the Granada TV series "A Kind of Loving." On the British stage, she took the female lead in a 1988 National Theatre dramatization of William Faulkner's "As I Lay Dying," and has appeared in numerous productions at the Royal Court, Greenwich, Bush, and Crucible theatres. In addition to SCANDAL, her film credits include DANCE WITH A STRANGER (1985); NO SURRENDER (1986); THE GOOD FATHER (1986); and George Lucas' WILLOW (1988). Born in Stockport, Manchester, Whalley began her acting career at age 12, in the Granada TV play "Life and Soul." In 1988 she married American actor Val Kilmer.

THE MOTION PICTURE ANNUAL

1990

Obituaries

OBITUARIES

Ailey, Alvin
Born 5 Jan. 1931, Rogers, Tex.; died 1 Dec. 1989, New York, N.Y.
Dancer-Choreographer
Ailey began dancing professionally during the 1940s, when he joined Lester Horton's company in LA. In 1954 he moved to New York City, where he danced in Broadway productions and studied with Martha Graham, Hanya Holm, and Charles Weidman before forming his own company, the Alvin Ailey American Dance Theater, in 1958. Incorporating African-American musical forms and themes within a mainstream modern dance idiom, Ailey's company became a showcase for black performers and choreographers—including Ailey himself, who danced with the troupe until 1968 and choreographed nearly 80 ballets. Ailey's work has been performed by many leading companies, including the American Ballet Theater and the Joffrey, Paris Opera, and Royal Danish ballet companies. Leslie Browne performs his "Vortex" in THE TURNING POINT (1977), Herbert Ross' balletic soap opera starring Anne Bancroft, Shirley MacLaine, Browne, and Mikhail Baryshnikov in his movie debut.

Backus, Jim [James Gilmore Backus]
Born 25 Feb. 1913, Cleveland, Ohio; died 3 July 1989, Santa Monica, Calif.
Actor
Backus started out in summer stock and vaudeville, then turned to radio as a more lucrative medium in the mid-1930s. He performed on numerous shows (debuting on Broadway during this period as well), gaining fame in the 40s on Alan Young's

show, as Hubert Updyke III—a prototype for millionaire Thurston Howell III on TV's "Gilligan's Island," for whom, along with the nearsighted cartoon figure Mr. Magoo, Backus is best remembered. After making his screen debut in 1949's EASY LIVING, starring Victor Mature (a boyhood friend of Backus') and Lucille Ball, Backus appeared in scores of films—often playing fools or bumblers in both comedies and dramas, including James Dean's ineffectual father in REBEL WITHOUT A CAUSE (1955). He won two Oscars for his work in "Mr. Magoo" shorts, screened in theaters in the mid-50s and subsequently a hit on TV, where Backus' many credits include his role as the husband on "I Married Joan," "Blondie," "What's My Line?" and, of course, "Gilligan's Island." Often in collaboration with his wife, Backus wrote several autobiographical books, including *Rocks on the Roof, What Are You Doing After the Orgy?, Backus Strikes Back,* and *Forgive Us Our Digressions,* the last two humorously detailing his life with Parkinson's disease. His films include: A DANGEROUS PROFESSION; EASY LIVING; FATHER WAS A FULLBACK; THE GREAT LOVER; ONE LAST FLING (1949); CUSTOMS AGENT; EMERGENCY WEDDING; THE KILLER THAT STALKED NEW YORK; MA AND PA KETTLE GO TO TOWN (1950); BRIGHT VICTORY; HALF ANGEL; HIS KIND OF WOMAN; HOLLYWOOD STORY; I WANT YOU; I'LL SEE YOU IN MY DREAMS; THE IRON MAN; M; THE MAN WITH A CLOAK (1951); ANDROCLES AND THE LION; DEADLINE—U.S.A; DON'T BOTHER TO KNOCK; HERE COME THE NELSONS; PAT AND MIKE (1952); ANGEL FACE; GERALDINE; ABOVE AND BEYOND; I LOVE MELVIN (1953); DEEP IN MY HEART (1954); FRANCIS IN THE NAVY; REBEL WITHOUT A CAUSE; THE SQUARE JUNGLE (1955); THE GIRL HE LEFT BEHIND; MEET ME IN LAS VEGAS; THE NAKED HILLS; THE OPPOSITE SEX; YOU CAN'T RUN AWAY FROM IT (1956); EIGHTEEN AND ANXIOUS; THE GREAT MAN; MAN OF A THOUSAND FACES; TOP SECRET AFFAIR (1957); THE HIGH COST OF LOVING; MACABRE (1958); ASK ANY GIRL; THE BIG OPERATOR; 1001 ARABIAN NIGHTS; A PRIVATE'S AFFAIR; THE WILD AND THE INNOCENT (1959); ICE PALACE (1960); BOYS' NIGHT OUT; THE HORIZONTAL LIEUTENANT; THE WONDERFUL WORLD OF THE BROTHERS GRIMM; ZOTZ! (1962); CRITIC'S CHOICE; IT'S A MAD, MAD, MAD, MAD WORLD; JOHNNY COOL;

MY SIX LOVES; OPERATION BIKINI; SUNDAY IN NEW YORK; THE WHEELER DEALERS (1963); ADVANCE TO THE REAR; JOHN GOLDFARB, PLEASE COME HOME (1964); BILLIE; FLUFFY (1965); DON'T MAKE WAVES; HURRY SUNDOWN (1967); WHERE WERE YOU WHEN THE LIGHTS WENT OUT? (1968); HELLO DOWN THERE (1969); THE COCKEYED COWBOYS OF CALICO COUNTY; MR. MAGOO'S HOLIDAY FESTIVAL; MYRA BRECKINRIDGE (1970); NOW YOU SEE HIM, NOW YOU DON'T (1972); CRAZY MAMA; FRIDAY FOSTER (1975); PETE'S DRAGON (1977); GOOD GUYS WEAR BLACK (1978); C.H.O.M.P.S.; SEVEN FROM HEAVEN (1979); ANGELS BRIGADE; THERE GOES THE BRIDE (1980); SLAPSTICK OF ANOTHER KIND (1984); PRINCE JACK (1985).

Ball, Lucille
Born 6 Aug. 1911, Celeron, N.Y.; died 26 April 1989, Los Angeles, Calif.
Actress-Comedienne
Although Ball, the First Lady of Television, became the best-known female face in the world through that medium, she appeared in dozens of films before establishing her immortal "Lucy" persona on TV in the 1950s. At first her career was set back by illness and others' lack of faith in her talents; after some success as a model in New York, however, she got her big break in 1933 when she replaced another chorine to become one of the "Goldwyn Girls" in ROMAN SCANDALS, her first film. Several bit parts followed until, in 1935, RKO signed Ball to a seven-year contract. Sprinkled among the many forgettable RKO films she appeared in were a few major features: STAGE DOOR; THE AFFAIRS OF ANNABEL; FIVE CAME BACK; DANCE, GIRL, DANCE; and TOO MANY GIRLS, the last bringing together Ball and Desi Arnaz, her future husband and partner. In the early 40s, beginning with DU BARRY WAS A LADY, MGM groomed her for musical stardom with indifferent success; in 1948, Ball found her comedic niche with CBS radio's "My Favorite Husband," the show that was the prototype for "I Love Lucy," employing several of the TV show's future key creative personnel. In 1951, it was brought to TV with its new name and new costar (Arnaz, as Ricky Ricardo) under the banner of Desilu, Arnaz and Ball's production company. Desilu eventually became one of TV's top production companies and made Ball, who took the company over from Arnaz after their divorce, one of the most powerful women in TV. "I Love Lucy" ran from 1951 to 1957 (and is still syndicated all over the world), setting technical and

thematic precedents (filming before a live audience, introducing Lucy's pregnancy into the story line), and establishing Ball as TV's queen of comedy. Her reign continued with "The Lucy Show" and "Here's Lucy" in the 1960s and 70s. "Life with Lucy" in 1986 was her only series failure. After moving to TV Ball made few films; her last big-screen vehicle was 1974's ill-received MAME. Her films include: BLOOD MONEY; BROADWAY THROUGH A KEYHOLE; ROMAN SCANDALS (1933); THE AFFAIRS OF CELLINI; BOTTOMS UP; BROADWAY BILL; BULLDOG DRUMMOND STRIKES BACK; FUGITIVE LADY; HOLD THAT GIRL; JEALOUSY; KID MILLIONS; MEN OF THE NIGHT; MOULIN ROUGE; NANA (1934); CARNIVAL; I DREAM TOO MUCH; OLD MAN RHYTHM; ROBERTA; TOP HAT; THE WHOLE TOWN'S TALKING (1935); BUNKER BEAN; CHATTERBOX; THE FARMER IN THE DELL; FOLLOW THE FLEET; WINTERSET (1936); DON'T TELL THE WIFE; STAGE DOOR; THAT GIRL FROM PARIS (1937); AFFAIRS OF ANNABEL; ANNABEL TAKES A TOUR; GO CHASE YOURSELF; HAVING WONDERFUL TIME; JOY OF LIVING; NEXT TIME I MARRY; ROOM SERVICE (1938); BEAUTY FOR THE ASKING; FIVE CAME BACK; PANAMA LADY; THAT'S RIGHT—YOU'RE WRONG; TWELVE CROWDED HOURS (1939); DANCE, GIRL, DANCE; THE MARINES FLY HIGH; TOO MANY GIRLS; YOU CAN'T

FOOL YOUR WIFE (1940); A GIRL, A GUY, AND A GOB; LOOK WHO'S LAUGHING (1941); THE BIG STREET; SEVEN DAYS' LEAVE; VALLEY OF THE SUN (1942); BEST FOOT FORWARD; DU BARRY WAS A LADY; THOUSANDS CHEER (1943); MEET THE PEOPLE (1944); ABBOTT AND COSTELLO IN HOLLYWOOD; WITHOUT LOVE; ZIEGFELD FOLLIES (1945); THE DARK CORNER; EASY TO WED; LOVER COME BACK; TWO SMART PEOPLE (1946); HER HUSBAND'S AFFAIRS; LURED (1947); EASY LIVING; MISS GRANT TAKES RICHMOND; SORROWFUL JONES (1948); FANCY PANTS; THE FULLER BRUSH GIRL; A WOMAN OF DISTINCTION (1950); THE MAGIC CARPET (1951); THE LONG, LONG TRAILER (1954); FOREVER DARLING (1956); THE FACTS OF LIFE (1960); CRITIC'S CHOICE (1963); A GUIDE FOR THE MARRIED MAN (1967); YOURS, MINE AND OURS (1968); MAME (1974).

Bari, Lynn [Marjorie Schuyler Fisher]

Born 18 Dec. 1913, Roanoke, Va.; died 20 Nov. 1989, Goleta, Calif.

Actress

Bari broke into films as a dancer in the 1933 MGM musical DANCING LADY, which was also Fred Astaire's debut film. After working as a showgirl or extra in several films, she became a contract player with Fox in 1933, and over the next 10 years rose from the status of stock performer to become the studio's "Queen of the Bs"—a label that was apt in light of Bari's many second-feature leads, but belied her frustration over Fox's unwillingness to star her in major productions. Called "The Girl with the Million-Dollar Figure" during the period when she was among the most popular WW II pinups, Bari was often typecast as the "other

woman" in A movies. Her most prominent roles came in the early 40s, when she appeared in THE MAGNIFICENT DOPE; ORCHESTRA WIVES; SUN VALLEY SERENADE; and CHINA GIRL. Increasingly disappointed with her films after the failure of THE BRIDGE OF SAN LUIS REY, Bari asked to be released from her Fox contract in 1946, after which she appeared in only 14 more films. She continued to perform on stage until the mid-1970s, however, and starred in the TV series "Detective's Wife" and "Boss Lady" in 1949 and 1951. Her films include: DANCING LADY (1933); STAND UP AND CHEER (1934); DOUBTING THOMAS; GEORGE WHITE'S 1935 SCANDALS; THE MAN WHO BROKE THE BANK AT MONTE CARLO; MUSIC IS MAGIC (1935); GIRLS' DORMITORY; LADIES IN LOVE; MY MARRIAGE; PIGSKIN PARADE; SING, BABY, SING (1936); LANCER SPY; LOVE IS NEWS; ON THE AVENUE; SING AND BE HAPPY; THIS IS MY AFFAIR; WEE WILLIE WINKIE; WIFE, DOCTOR AND NURSE (1937); ALWAYS GOODBYE; THE BARONESS AND THE BUTLER; BATTLE OF BROADWAY; CITY GIRL; I'LL GIVE A MILLION; JOSETTE; MEET THE GIRLS; MR. MOTO'S GAMBLE; SHARPSHOOTERS; SPEED TO BURN; WALKING DOWN BROADWAY (1938); CHARLIE CHAN IN THE CITY OF DARKNESS; CHASING DANGER; HOLLYWOOD CAVALCADE; HOTEL FOR WOMEN; NEWS IS MADE AT NIGHT; PACK UP YOUR TROUBLES; PARDON OUR NERVE; RETURN OF THE CISCO KID (1939); CHARTER PILOT; CITY OF CHANCE; EARTHBOUND; FREE, BLONDE AND 21; KIT CARSON; LILLIAN RUSSELL; PIER 13 (1940); BLOOD AND SAND; MOON OVER HER SHOULDER; THE PERFECT SNOB; SLEEPERS WEST; SUN VALLEY SERENADE; WE GO FAST (1941); CHINA GIRL; THE FALCON TAKES OVER; THE MAGNIFICENT DOPE; THE NIGHT BEFORE THE DIVORCE; ORCHESTRA WIVES; SECRET AGENT OF JAPAN (1942); HELLO, FRISCO, HELLO (1943); THE BRIDGE OF SAN LUIS REY; SWEET AND LOWDOWN; TAMPICO (1944); CAPTAIN EDDIE (1945); HOME SWEET HOMICIDE; MARGIE; NOCTURNE; SHOCK (1946); THE MAN FROM TEXAS; THE SPIRITUALIST (1948); THE KID FROM CLEVELAND (1949); I'D CLIMB THE HIGHEST MOUNTAIN; ON THE LOOSE; SUNNY SIDE OF THE STREET (1951); HAS ANYBODY SEEN MY GAL?; I DREAM OF JEANIE (1952); FRANCIS JOINS THE WACS (1954); ABBOTT AND COSTELLO MEET THE KEYSTONE KOPS (1955); THE WOMEN OF

PITCAIRN ISLAND (1957); DAMN CITIZEN (1958); TRAUMA (1962); THE YOUNG RUNAWAYS (1968).

Beckman, John
Born Astoria, Ore.; died 26 Oct. 1989, Sherman Oaks, Calif., age 91
Film/TV Art Director-Set Designer
Although he did not receive his first screen credit until 1947, when he served as art director on Chaplin's MONSIEUR VERDOUX, Beckman had worked in Hollywood since the 1920s—when, with no formal training, he began a career as an architect and helped design the interiors of Grauman's Chinese and Egyptian theaters. After working on the set design of NANA in 1934, Beckman created sets on dozens of films, including CASABLANCA; MR. DEEDS GOES TO TOWN; THE ADVENTURES OF ROBIN HOOD; LOST HORIZON; MILDRED PIERCE; and THE MALTESE FALCON, to name only a few—although only the art directors of these films received screen credit. After becoming an art director-production designer himself, Beckman worked primarily for Warner Bros. until 1970, and later took on design chores for a number of television shows, including "Designing Women," for which he was set designer at the time of his death. His films (as art director only) include: MONSIEUR VERDOUX (1947); THE IRON MISTRESS; SPRINGFIELD RIFLE (1952); SO BIG; THE SYSTEM (1953); LUCKY ME (1954); THE McCONNELL STORY; YOUNG AT HEART (1955); HELL ON FRISCO BAY; TOWARD THE UNKNOWN (1956); LAFAYETTE ESCADRILLE; TOO MUCH, TOO SOON (1958); THE FBI STORY; THE HELEN MORGAN STORY (1959); GUNS OF THE TIMBERLAND; WAKE ME WHEN IT'S OVER (1960); THE DEVIL AT FOUR O'CLOCK; A MAJORITY OF ONE (1961); GYPSY (1962); MARY, MARY (1963); THE TROUBLE WITH ANGELS (1966); WHO'S MINDING THE MINT? (1967); ASSIGNMENT TO KILL; IN ENEMY COUNTRY (1968); HOOK, LINE AND SINKER (1969); WHICH WAY TO THE FRONT? (1970).

Berlin, Irving [Israel Baline]
Born 11 May 1888, Tyumen [USSR]; died 22 Sept. 1989, New York, N.Y.
Composer-Lyricist
The son of emigree Russian Jews, Berlin had only two years of schooling and no formal musical training, yet by 1924 he was already such a well-established composer and lyricist that Jerome Kern was able to make the famous assertion, "Irving Berlin has no place in American music—he *is* American music." The man who contributed "White Christmas," "God Bless America," "Cheek to Cheek," "Always," "There's No Business Like Show Busi-

ness," and hundreds more to the lexicon of American popular music began his career when he was still a boy, serving as the "eyes" and occasional accompanist of a blind busker on the streets of New York City's Bowery. He soon became a street and cafe performer himself, learned a rather rudimentary piano (throughout his life, Berlin could only compose in the key of F sharp), and cowrote (with Nick Nicholson) his first song, "Marie from Sunny Italy," at age 18. A printer's error caused his name to appear on the sheet music as "I. Berlin," and "Izzy" Baline kept the pseudonym. After gaining his first Tin Pan Alley hit with "Alexander's Ragtime Band" (first performed by George M. Cohan in 1911), Berlin began writing for the stage, composing his first complete Broadway score, the Vernon and Irene Castle review "Watch Your Step," in 1914. During the next five decades, Berlin racked up Broadway success after Broadway success; his 23 scores include the tunes for the Marx Brothers' "Cocoanuts," "As Thousands Cheer," the WW II revue "This Is the Army," and the Ethel Merman showcases "Call Me Madam" and "Annie Get Your Gun." His songs and scores also graced many classic Hollywood films—including the first talkie, THE JAZZ SINGER (1927), which included an early version of "Blue Skies." Among Berlin's most popular screen musicals were the Astaire-Rogers TOP HAT and FOLLOW THE FLEET; EASTER PARADE (costarring Astaire and Judy Garland); WHITE CHRISTMAS (featuring Bing Crosby singing the title classic, which he also performed in HOLIDAY INN); THIS IS THE ARMY (in which the composer sang "Oh, How I Hate to Get Up in the Morning," and which raised millions for war relief in both its stage and screen forms); ALEXANDER'S RAGTIME BAND; and ANNIE GET YOUR

GUN. A two-time Oscar winner in the Best Song category (for "White Christmas" and "Cheek to Cheek"), Berlin was also the recipient of a Congressional gold medal (for "God Bless America") and the Army's Medal of Merit (for "This is the Army"). Berlin was also a fierce champion of songwriters' legal rights, cofounding ASCAP with Victor Herbert, Kern, and John Philip Sousa (among others) in 1914, and, after 1919, publishing his own work through the Irving Berlin Music Corp. By the time Berlin retired—writing his last published tune, "An Old-Fashioned Wedding," for a Broadway revival of "Annie Get Your Gun" in 1966—his catalog listed some 1,500 songs. When he died at the age of 101, obituary notices hailed him as "America's Songwriter." Major films featuring Berlin songs include: THE JAZZ SINGER (1926); THE AWAKENING (1928); THE COCOANUTS; COQUETTE; HALLELUJAH (1929); GLORIFYING THE AMERICAN GIRL; MAMMY; PUTTIN' ON THE RITZ (1930); REACHING FOR THE MOON (1931); KID MILLIONS (1934); TOP HAT (1935); FOLLOW THE FLEET; THE GREAT ZIEGFELD (1936); ON THE AVENUE (1937); ALEXANDER'S RAGTIME BAND; CAREFREE (1938); THE STORY OF VERNON AND IRENE CASTLE; SECOND FIDDLE (1939); HOLIDAY INN; LOUISIANA PURCHASE (1942); HOW'S ABOUT IT; HELLO, FRISCO, HELLO; THE POWERS GIRL; THIS IS THE ARMY (1943); BLUE SKIES; THE JOLSON STORY (1946); THE FABULOUS DORSEYS (1947); EASTER PARADE; BIG CITY (1948); JOLSON SINGS AGAIN (1949); ANNIE GET YOUR GUN (1950); MEET DANNY WILSON (1952); CALL ME MADAM (1953); THERE'S NO BUSINESS LIKE SHOW BUSINESS; WHITE CHRISTMAS (1954); LOVE ME OR LEAVE ME (1955); SAYONARA (1957).

Blake, Amanda [Beverly Louise Neill]
Born 20 Feb. 1929, Buffalo, N.Y.; died 16 Aug. 1989, Los Angeles, Calif.
Actress
After getting her start in stock theater and radio, Blake played primarily supporting roles in films during the early 1950s, then landed the role for which she will be remembered: Miss Kitty, proprietress of the Long Ranch Saloon and love interest of Matt Dillon on "Gunsmoke." Blake stayed with the show from its premiere in 1955 until 1974 (it left the air the following year). Later, she appeared occasionally as a guest star on TV shows and movies, and in her last years returned to the big screen with roles in THE BOOST and B.O.R.N. Her films include: BATTLEGROUND; COUNTERSPY MEETS SCOTLAND YARD; THE DUCHESS OF IDAHO;

Amanda Blake with James Arness and Milburn Stone on the set of "Gunsmoke."

STARS IN MY CROWN (1950); SMUGGLER'S GOLD; SUNNY SIDE OF THE STREET (1951); CATTLE TOWN; SCARLET ANGEL (1952); LILI; SABRE JET (1953); ABOUT MRS. LESLIE; ADVENTURES OF HAJJI BABA; MISS ROBIN CRUSOE; A STAR IS BORN (1954); THE GLASS SLIPPER; HIGH SOCIETY (1955); THE BOOST (1988); B.O.R.N. (1989).

Blanc, Mel

Born 30 May 1908, San Francisco, Calif.; died 10 July 1989, Los Angeles, Calif.
Voice Actor-Musician-Composer
"The Man of a Thousand Voices" started out as a musician, playing in bands throughout the Northwest and making his radio debut in 1927. In 1933, Blanc and his wife created "Cobwebs and Nuts," a weekly radio show in which the couple performed the parts of an entire "company." Working in regional radio in LA in the mid-1930s, he finally landed his break with the company that became Warner Bros. Looney Toons, debuting as a drunken bull in a Porky Pig short in 1937, and taking over the role of Porky—his first major character in a repertoire that grew to include Bugs Bunny, Yosemite Sam, Daffy Duck, Sylvester, Tweety Pie, the Road Runner, and hundreds more—shortly thereafter. In 1938 Blanc took on another character, Happy Rabbit, who was renamed Bugs Bunny and given the tag line, "What's up, Doc?" at his suggestion. Eventually, Blanc voiced more than 850 Warners cartoons—becoming the first actor to receive screen credit for cartoon voicing—and some 3,000 animated films (including several features) in all. In the 30s, 40s, and 50s, he appeared on many

radio shows, most notably his own and Jack Benny's, playing Benny's car, parrot, violin teacher, gardener, and polar bear and staying with the show when it moved to television. Among numerous TV credits, Blanc was the coproducer-star of ABC's "Bugs Bunny Show," and resumed work with Hanna-Barbera to give voice to Barney Rubble on "The Flintstones" and Mr. Spacely (George's boss) on "The Jetsons." He also made more than 60 records, including the million-selling "Woody Woodpecker" (Blanc voiced the Walter Lanz character until 1950) and "I Tawt I Taw a Puddy Tat," Tweety Pie's anthem. It has been estimated that more than 20 million people currently hear Blanc's voice daily. His films include: NEPTUNE'S DAUGHTER (1949); CHAMPAGNE FOR CAESAR (1950); GAY PURREE (1962); HEY THERE, IT'S YOGI BEAR; KISS ME, STUPID (1964); THE MAN CALLED FLINTSTONE (1966); THE PHANTOM TOLLBOOTH (1970); SCALAWAG (1973); JOURNEY BACK TO OZ (1974); BUGS BUNNY, SUPERSTAR (1975); BUCK ROGERS IN THE 25TH CENTURY; GREAT AMERICAN BUGS BUNNY-ROAD RUNNER CHASE (1979); THE LOONEY, LOONEY, LOONEY BUGS BUNNY MOVIE (1981); BUGS BUNNY'S THIRD MOVIE—1,001 RABBIT TALES (1982); DAFFY DUCK'S MOVIE: FANTASTIC ISLAND; STRANGE BREW (1983); HEATHCLIFF: THE MOVIE (1985); WHO FRAMED ROGER RABBIT (1988); JETSONS: THE MOVIE (forthcoming).

Blier, Bernard

Born 11 Jan. 1916, Buenos Aires, Argentina; died 29 March 1989, Paris, France
Actor

Mel Blanc and friends.

One of France's most versatile, consistently employed actors, Blier debuted in Paris theater in the mid-1930s, and by 1937 had begun his long film career with a part in Raymond Rouleau's TROIS-SIX-NEUF. During the next decade he had roles in more than 30 films, including Marcel Carne's HOTEL DU NORD; after WW II his career really took off, with the portly, balding Blier appearing in scores of French and Italian films in all manner of genres, including Clouzot's QUAI DES ORFEVRES (US title: JENNY LAMOUR), Cayatte's AVANT LE DELUGE, and Allegret's DEDEE D'ANVERS (US: DEDEE). From the 50s through the 80s he acted under the direction of Visconti, Tavernier, Yves Robert (THE TALL BLOND MAN WITH ONE BLACK SHOE), Scola, and his son, filmmaker Bertrand Blier (CALMOS; BUFFET FROID). In 1988 he made his last film, Moshe Mizrahi's MANGECLOUS, and was awarded a Cesar for career achievement. His films include: GRIBOUILLE; LA DAME DE MALACCA; L'HABIT VERT; LES MESSAGER; TROIS-SIX-NEUF (1937); ALTITUDE 3200; DOUBLE CRIME SUR LA LIGNE MAGINOT; ENTREE DES ARTISTES; GRISOU; HOTEL DU NORD; PLACE DE LA CONCORDE (1938); DAYBREAK; L'ENFER DES ANGES; NUIT DE DECEMBRE; QUARTIER LATIN (1939); CAPRICES; L'ASSASSINAT DU PERE NOEL; LE PAVILLON BRULE; PREMIER BAL (1941); LA FEMME QUE J'AI LE PLUS AIMEE; LA NUIT FANTASTIQUE; LE JOURNAL TOMBE A CINQ HEURES; MARIE-MARTINE; ROMANCE A TROIS (1942); DOMINO; LES PETITES DU QUAI AUX FLEURS; JE SUIS AVEC TOI (1943); FARANDOLE (1944); MONSIEUR GREGOIRE S'EVADE; SEUL DAN LA NUIT (1945); CARMEN; LE CAFE DU CADRAN; MESSIEURS LUDOVIC (1946); SYMPHONIE FANTASTIQUE (1947); D'HOMME A HOMMES; JENNY LAMOUR (1948); DEDEE (1949); THE CHEAT; LA SOURICIERE; LES ANCIENS DE SAINT-LOUP; L'INVITE DU MARDI; MONSEIGNEUR (1950); AGENCE MATIMONIALE; JE L'AI ETE TROIS FOIS; LA MAISON BONNADIEU; PASSION FOR LIFE; SAN LAISSER D'ADRESSE; SOUVENIRS PERDUS (1951); AVANT LE DELUGE; SUIVEZ CET HOMME (1953); SCENES DE MENAGE; SECRETS D'ALCOVE; SPICE OF LIFE (1954); LE DOSSIER NOIR; LES HUSSARDS (1955); RIVELAZIONE; CRIME ET CHATIMENT (1956); L'ECOLE DE COCOTTES; LES MISERABLES; QUAND LA FEMME S'EN MELE; RETOUR DE MANIVELLE; SANS FAMILLE (1957); EN LEGITIME DEFENSE; THE GAMBLER; LES GRANDES FAMILLES; MARIE-OCTOBRE (1958); THE CAT; HISTOIRES D'AMOUR DEFENDUES; LE SECRET DU CHEVALIER D'EON; LES YEUX DE L'AMOUR; MARCHE OU CREVE (1959); VIVE HENRI IV, VIVE L'AMOUR (1960); THE GREAT WAR; I BRIGANTI ITALIANI; LE MONOCLE NOIR; LE PRESIDENT; LES PETITS MATINS (1961); THE COUNTERFEITERS OF PARIS; LE JEUNE FILLES DE BONNES FAMILLES; THE MAGNIFICENT TRAMP; POURQUOI PARIS? (1962); GERMINAL; THE HUNCHBACK OF ROME; LES TONTONS FLINGUEURS; MATHIAS SANDORF (1963); AND SUDDENLY IT'S MURDER!; LA BONNE SOUPE; LA CHANCE ET L'AMOUR; LES BARBOUZES; THE ORGANIZER; THE SEVENTH JUROR (1964); CASANOVA '70; GREED IN THE SUN; HIGH INFIDELITY; LES BONS VIVANTS; THE MAGNIFICENT CUCKOLD; MALE HUNT; WOMEN AND WAR (1965); DELITTO QUASI PERFETTO; DUELLO NEL MONDO; LE GRAND RESTAURANT; QUAND PASSENT LES FAISANS; UN IDIOT A PARIS; UNA QUESTIONE D'ONORE (1966); DU MOU DANS LA GACHETTE; SI J'ETAIS UN ESPION; THE MADMAN OF LAB 4; THE STRANGER (1967); CAROLINE CHERIE; COPLAN SAUVE SA PEAU; HOW TO SEDUCE A PLAYBOY (1968); FAUT PAS PRENDRE LES ENFANTS DU BON DIEU POUR DE CANARDS SAUVAGES; MON ONCLE BENJAMIN; RIUSCIRANNE I NOSTRI EROI A RITROVARE L'AMICO MISTERIOSAMENTE SCOMPARSO IN AFRICA? (1969); APPELES-MOI MATHILDE; BIRIBI; LE CRI DU CORMORAN LE SOIR AU-DESSUS DES JONQUES; LE DISTRAIT; TO COMMIT A MURDER (1970); CATCH ME A SPY; HOMO EROTICUS; JO; LAISSE ALLER, C'EST UNE VALSE (a&w) (1971); ELLE CAUSE PLUS... ELLE FLINGUE; TOUT LE MONDE IL EST BEAU, TOUT LE MONDE IL EST GENTIL (1972); LE MAIN A COUPER; MOI Y EN A VOULOIR DES SOUS; PAR LE SANG DES AUTRES; THE TALL BLOND MAN WITH ONE BLACK SHOE (1973); BONS BAISERS A LUNDI; C'EST DUR POUR TOUT LE MONDE; C'EST PAS PARCE QU'ON A RIEN A DIRE QU'IL FAUT FERMER SA GUEULE; LES CHINOIS A PARIS (1974); CE CHER VICTOR; THE DAYDREAMER; LE FAUX-CUL; AMICI MIEI (1975); CALMOS; LE CORPS DE MON ENNEMI; NUIT D'OR (1976); LE COMPROMIS (1978); BUFFET FROID; SERIE NOIRE (1979); IL MALATO IMMAGINARIO (1980); PASSION OF LOVE (1982); AMICI MIEI ATTO III; BILLY ZE KICK; CA N'ARRIVE QU'A MOI; SCEMO DI GUERRA; THE TWO LIVES OF MATTIA PASCAL (1985); JE HAIS LES ACTEURS; LET'S HOPE IT'S A GIRL; TWIST AGAIN A MOSCOU (1986); THE FAMILY; I PICARI; SOTTO IL RISTORANTE CINESE (1987); ADA DAN LA JUNGLE; MANGECLOUS; UNA BOTTA DI VITA (1988).

Bright, John

Died 14 Sept. 1989, Panorama City, Calif., age 81
Screenwriter
As a teenager Bright was Ben Hecht's copy boy at the *Chicago Daily News*, then became a reporter himself. At age 19, he wrote the book *Hizzoner Big Bill Thompson*, and was subsequently sued by the eponymous Chicago mayor. After moving to Hollywood in 1929, Bright and his partner, Kubec Glasmon, were hired to adapt their own material for what became THE PUBLIC ENEMY (reportedly, the writers also urged director William Wellman to star erstwhile second lead James Cagney in the film). They next scripted BLONDE CRAZY; SMART MONEY; and THE CROWD ROARS, and in 1933 they were among the 10 founders of the Screen Writers Guild. A leftist whose political activism began with the Sacco and Vanzetti trial, Bright was fired by MGM for his involvement with the Conference of Studio Unions in 1945, and later blacklisted after being denounced before the HUAC. His last scripting credit was THE BRAVE BULLS (1951), directed by Robert Rossen, who testified to Bright's membership in the Communist Party before the HUAC. Bright eventually returned to films as a reader, story editor, and literary advisor in Hollywood. His films include: BLONDE CRAZY; THE PUBLIC ENEMY; SMART MONEY (1931); THE CROWD ROARS; IF I HAD A MILLION; TAXI!; THREE ON A MATCH; UNION DEPOT (1932); SHE DONE HIM WRONG (1933); THE ACCUSING FINGER; GIRL OF THE OZARKS; HERE COMES TROUBLE (1936); JOHN MEADE'S WOMAN; SAN QUENTIN (1937); BACK DOOR TO HEAVEN (1939); GLAMOR FOR SALE (1940); BROADWAY; SHERLOCK HOLMES AND THE VOICE OF TERROR (1942); CLOSE-UP; FIGHTING MAD; I WALK ALONE; OPEN SECRET (1948); THE KID FROM CLEVELAND (1949); THE BRAVE BULLS (1951).

Cassavetes, John

Born 9 Dec. 1929, New York, N.Y.; died 3 Feb. 1989, Los Angeles, Calif.
Director-Actor-Screenwriter-Playwright
The young Cassavetes studied at the American Academy of Dramatic Arts, where he met his future wife, muse, collaborator, and star, Gena Rowlands. Beginning his

acting career in summer stock, he landed his first film work as an extra in 14 HOURS in 1951, and by mid-decade found further roles in movies and on TV, with substantial parts on "Studio One," "Playhouse 90," and similar programs. During this period he also led a class in Method acting, an improvisational exercise that provided the basis for SHADOWS, his first film as a director. Shot over two years on 16 mm (later blown up to 35 mm); using actors from the class, handheld cameras, and an improvised structure and script; and made on Cassavetes' savings from his starring role in TV's "Johnny Staccato" series, SHADOWS set the pattern for most of his work as one of the US' most personal independent filmmakers. On the strength of its resounding critical success, Hollywood financed his next two films, TOO LATE BLUES and A CHILD IS WAITING, both commercial failures. Angered by studio tampering with these films, Cassavetes returned to independent projects—gaining, perhaps inevitably, his career-long reputation for self-indulgent filmmaking—financing, writing, directing, and often promoting and distributing his own work with the help of his close-knit regular ensemble of actors (himself, Rowlands, Peter Falk, Seymour Cassel, and Ben Gazzara among them). FACES, his next directorial effort, was one of his rare commercial *and* critical successes (A WOMAN UNDER THE INFLUENCE was another). Throughout, he continued to act in other director's films and on TV, most memorably as Mia Farrow's evil husband in ROSEMARY'S BABY; as one of THE DIRTY DOZEN; and in THE TEMPEST. A filmmaker who can truly be called controversial—in that audiences either loved or hated his films and in that their critical reputation in some circles was equaled only by their obscurity in the mainstream—Cassavetes' numerous honors included Oscar nominations for writing, directing, *and* acting, a rare feat. His films include: 14 HOURS (1951); TAXI (1953); THE NIGHT HOLDS TERROR (1955); CRIME IN THE STREETS (1956); AFFAIR IN HAVANA; EDGE OF THE CITY (1957); SADDLE THE WIND (1958); SHADOWS (d); VIRGIN ISLAND (1960); TOO LATE BLUES (p,d&w); THE WEBSTER BOY (1962); A CHILD IS WAITING (d) (1963); THE KILLERS (1964); BANDITS IN ROME; DEVIL'S ANGELS; THE DIRTY DOZEN (1967); FACES (d,w&ed); ROSEMARY'S BABY (1968); IF IT'S TUESDAY, THIS MUST BE BELGIUM (1969); HUSBANDS (a,d&w); MACHINE GUN McCAIN (1970); MINNIE AND MOSKOWITZ (a,d&w) (1971); A WOMAN UNDER THE INFLUENCE (d&w) (1974); CAPONE (1975); THE KILLING OF A CHINESE BOOKIE (d&w); MIKEY AND NICKY; TWO-MINUTE WARNING (1976); HEROES; OPENING NIGHT (a,d&w) (1977); BRASS TARGET; THE FURY (1978); GLORIA (p,d&w) (1980); WHOSE LIFE IS IT ANYWAY? (1981); THE INCUBUS; THE TEMPEST (1982); MARVIN AND TIGE (1983); LOVE STREAMS (a,d&w) (1984); BIG TROUBLE (d) (1986).

Cayatte, Andre

Born 3 Feb. 1909, Carcassonne, France; died 6 Feb. 1989, Paris, France
Director-Screenwriter
In the mid-1930s, Cayatte abandoned his law practice for filmmaking, convinced that this medium could be the most powerful force for the dissemination of ideas on moral and social questions of his time. He began as a scriptwriter, debuting in this capacity with Allegret's ENTREE DES ARTISTES in 1938, and within four years began directing as well as writing (or cowriting, often with Charles Spaak) his own films, which frequently dealt with failures of French justice, tackling such issues as capital punishment and euthanasia. Such Cayatte films as JUSTICE EST FAITE; WE ARE ALL MURDERERS (NOU SOMMES TOUS DES ASSASSINS); AVANT LE DELUGE; and LE DOSSIER NOIR were both popular and critically acclaimed, although his characteristic stress on theme and content at the expense of form gained him some detractors among the French New Wave. His films include: ENTREE DES ARTISTES (w) (1938); TEMPETE SUR PARIS (w) (1939); CAPRICES (w); LE CLUB DES SOUPIRANTS (w); MONTMARTRE SUR SEINE (w) (1941); LA FAUSSE MAITRESSE (d&w); LE CAMION BLANC (w) (1942); AU BONHEUR DES DAMES (d&w); PIERRE ET JEAN (d&w) (1943); FARANDOLE (w) (1945); LA REVANCHE DE ROGER-LA-HONTE (d&w); LE DERNIER SOU (d&w); ROGER-LA-HONTE (d&w); SERENADE AUX NUAGES (d&w); STORMY WATERS (w) (1946); LE CHANTEUR INCONNU (d&w) (1947); LE DESSOUS DES CARTES (1948); RETOUR A LA VIE (d&w, "Tante Emma") (1949); JUSTICE EST FAITE (d&w) (1950); THE LOVERS OF VERONA (d&w) (1951); AVANT LE DELUGE (d&w) (1954); LE DOSSIER NOIR (d&w) (1955); OEIL POUR OEIL (d&w); WE ARE ALL MURDERERS (d&w) (1957); THE MIRROR HAS TWO FACES (d&w) (1959); LE GLAIVE ET LA BALANCE (d&w) (1963); LA VIE CONJUGALE (d&w, comprising two films, FRANCOISE and JEAN MARC); TOMORROW IS MY TURN (d&w) (1964); PIEGE POUR CENDRILLON (d&w) (1965); LES RISQUES DU METIER (d&w) (1967); LES CHEMINS DE KATMANDOU (d&w) (1969); MOURIR D'AIMER (d&w) (1970); IL N'Y A PAS DE FUMEE SANS FEU (d&w) (1973); THE VERDICT (d&w) (1975); A CHACUN SON ENFER (d&w) (1977); LA RAISON D'ETAT (d&w); JUSTICES (d&w); L'AMOUR EN QUESTION (d&w) (1978).

Chapman, Graham

Died 4 Oct. 1989, Maidstone, England, age 48
TV/Film Writer-Actor-Comedian
A founding member of the Monty Python comedy troupe, Chapman was educated at Cambridge, where he met his longtime collaborator John Cleese. Chapman and Cleese wrote for the British TV series "Marty" and "At Last the 1948 Show" before debuting the surrealistically silly "Monty Python's Flying Circus" in 1969. Cowritten and coperformed by Chapman, Cleese, Terry Jones, Eric Idle, Michael Palin, and Terry Gilliam, "Monty Python" ran on the BBC until 1974. It was then picked up by American public television, providing exposure that gained the Python gang international stardom and led to such big-screen hits as MONTY PYTHON AND THE HOLY GRAIL and MONTY PYTHON'S LIFE OF BRIAN, both of which featured Chapman in the "lead" role. During the original "Python" BBC run, Cleese and Chapman continued to collaborate as writers on other projects, including THE MAGIC CHRISTIAN; THE RISE AND RISE OF MICHAEL RIMMER; and RENTADICK. Later, Chapman would prove less successful individually than the other Python alumni— neither THE ODD JOB nor YELLOWBEARD was a critical or popular hit, and a 1985 Cleese-Chapman screenplay for what was to be Chapman's directorial debut was never produced. Chapman published *A Liar's Autobiography* in 1981. His films include: DOCTOR IN TROUBLE; THE MAGIC CHRISTIAN (a&co-w); THE RISE AND RISE

OF MICHAEL RIMMER (a&co-w) (1970); THE MAGNIFICENT SEVEN DEADLY SINS (w); THE STATUE (1971); AND NOW FOR SOMETHING COMPLETELY DIFFERENT (a&co-w); RENTADICK (co-w) (1972); MONTY PYTHON AND THE HOLY GRAIL (a&co-w) (1975); THE ODD JOB (a,co-p&co-w) (1978); MONTY PYTHON'S LIFE OF BRIAN (a&w) (1979); MONTY PYTHON LIVE AT THE HOLLY-WOOD BOWL (docu); THE SECRET POLICEMAN'S OTHER BALL (docu) (1982); MONTY PYTHON'S THE MEANING OF LIFE (a&co-w); YELLOWBEARD (a&co-w) (1983).

Chiari, Mario
Born 14 July 1909, Florence, Italy; died 9 April 1989, Rome, Italy
Art Director-Costume Designer
Trained as an architect, Chiari switched to set design in the 1930s, first with Florence's Guf theater and later for operatic productions. He began in films as an assistant director, and also collaborated on the scripts of Alessandro Blasetti's LA CORONA DI FERRO and FABIOLA (1941 and 1948; during this period, Chiari also directed short documentaries). His first film as an art director was William Dieterle's VOLCANO in 1951; that same year, he designed the costumes for Vittorio De Sica's MIRACLE IN MILAN. Chiari thereafter became one of film's most respected art directors, contributing to works by Renoir, Vidor, Visconti, Fellini, Huston, Ritt, and others. His films include: MIRACLE IN MILAN (cos); VOLCANO (1951); BELLISSIMA; LA CARROZZA D'ORO: LA NEMICA (1952); THE LOVES OF THREE QUEENS; TOO BAD SHE'S BAD (1954); I VITELLONI; WAR AND PEACE (1956); TEMPEST; THIS ANGRY AGE (1958); IL DOLCI INGANNI; FIVE

BRANDED WOMEN (1960); NEAPOL-ITAN CAROUSEL; WHITE NIGHTS (1961); BARABBAS; THE RELUCTANT SAINT (1962); THE HUNCHBACK OF ROME; SON OF THE RED CORSAIR (1963); THE BIBLE; CONQUERED CITY (1966); DOCTOR DOLITTLE; WEEKEND, ITALIAN STYLE (1967); THE QUEENS; UN TRANQUILO POSTO DI CAMPAGNA (1968); FRAU-LEIN DOKTOR (1969); THE DESERTER (1971); LUDWIG (1973); KING KONG (1976); WOMANLIGHT (1979); CLAIR DE FEMME (1980).

Clarke, T.E.B. [Thomas Ernest Bennett Clarke]
Screenwriter-Author
Having worked in advertising and journalism, and for the London police, Clarke turned to screenwriting in the mid-1940s, and in that capacity scripted some of the best of the hugely popular comedies made by London's Ealing Studios, most notably PASSPORT TO PIMLICO; THE TITFIELD THUNDERBOLT; and THE LAVENDER HILL MOB, the last of which won him an Oscar. His range extended beyond comedy as well, comprising film adaptations of *Sons and Lovers* and *A Tale of Two Cities;* he also scripted John Ford's only film shot in Britain, GIDEON'S DAY (GB: GIDEON OF SCOTLAND YARD). In addition, Clarke wrote novels, travel books, and an autobiography, *This Is Where I Came In.* His films include: FOR THOSE IN PERIL (1944); DEAD OF NIGHT; JOHNNY FRENCHMAN (1946); AGAINST THE WIND (1948); PASSPORT TO PIMLICO (1949); THE BLUE LAMP; HUE AND CRY; THE MAGNET (1950); ENCORE; THE LAVENDER HILL MOB (1951); TRAIN OF EVENTS (1952); THE TITFIELD THUNDERBOLT (1953); THE RAINBOW JACKET (1954); WHO DONE IT? (1956); LAW AND DISOR-DER; A TALE OF TWO CITIES (1958); GIDEON OF SCOTLAND YARD (1959); SONS AND LOVERS (1960); A MAN COULD GET KILLED (1966); A HITCH IN TIME (1978).

Coulouris, George
Born 1 Oct. 1903, Manchester, England; died 25 April 1989, London, England
Actor
Defying his parents, Coulouris ran away from home to become an actor, debuting on the British stage in 1926, on Broadway in 1929, and in films in 1933 (in CHRIS-TOPHER BEAN). In 1937 he joined Orson Welles' Mercury Theater, taking his first Mercury role as Marc Antony in their modern-dress "Julius Caesar" and later appearing in CITIZEN KANE, playing Charles Foster Kane's (Welles') guardian, Walter Parks Thatcher. Steady movie roles followed, often villainous or eccentric parts, in such British and American films

as FOR WHOM THE BELL TOLLS; Carol Reed's AN OUTCAST OF THE ISLANDS; KING OF KINGS; PAPIL-LON; MURDER ON THE ORIENT EXPRESS; and THE LONG GOOD FRI-DAY. Coulouris received a Best Supporting Actor Oscar nomination for his traitorous role in WATCH ON THE RHINE; he had already appeared in the original Broadway and touring versions of the play. His films include: CHRISTOPHER BEAN (1933); ALL THIS AND HEAVEN TOO; THE LADY IN QUESTION (1940); CITIZEN KANE (1941); ASSIGNMENT IN BRITTANY; FOR WHOM THE BELL TOLLS; THIS LAND IS MINE; WATCH ON THE RHINE (1943); BETWEEN TWO WORLDS; THE CONSPIRA-TORS; THE MASTER RACE; MR.

SKEFFINGTON; NONE BUT THE LONELY HEART (1944); CONFIDEN-TIAL AGENT; HOTEL BERLIN; LADY ON A TRAIN; A SONG TO REMEM-BER (1945); CALIFORNIA; MR. DIS-TRICT ATTORNEY; NOBODY LIVES FOREVER; THE VERDICT (1946); WHERE THERE'S LIFE (1947); BEYOND GLORY; JOAN OF ARC; SLEEP, MY LOVE; A SOUTHERN YANKEE (1948); KILL OR BE KILLED (1950); ISLAND RESCUE; AN OUT-CAST OF THE ISLANDS (1952); THE ASSASSIN; A DAY TO REMEMBER (1953); DOCTOR IN THE HOUSE; DUEL IN THE JUNGLE; THE HEART OF THE MATTER; THE RUNAWAY BUS (1954); DOCTOR AT SEA; A RACE FOR LIFE; THE TECKMAN MYS-TERY (1955); PRIVATE'S PROGRESS (1956); DOCTOR AT LARGE; THE MAN WITHOUT A BODY; TARZAN AND THE LOST SAFARI (1957); I

ACCUSE; KILL ME TOMORROW; LAW AND DISORDER; SPY IN THE SKY; TANK FORCE (1958); THE BEASTS OF MARSEILLES; SON OF ROBIN HOOD; THE WOMAN EATER (1959); BLUEBEARD'S TEN HONEYMOONS; THE BOY WHO STOLE A MILLION; CONSPIRACY OF HEARTS; SURPRISE PACKAGE (1960); KING OF KINGS (1961); THE BIG MONEY; THE DOG AND THE DIAMONDS (1962); FURY AT SMUGGLER'S BAY; IN THE COOL OF THE DAY (1963); THE CROOKED ROAD (1964); THE SKULL (1965); ARABESQUE (1966); TOO MANY THIEVES (1968); THE ASSASSINATION BUREAU; LAND RAIDERS (1969); NO BLADE OF GRASS (1970); BLOOD FROM THE MUMMY'S TOMB; HORROR OF SNAPE ISLAND (1972); PAPILLON (1973); MAHLER; MURDER ON THE ORIENT EXPRESS; PERCY'S PROGRESS (1974); THE LAST DAYS OF MAN ON EARTH (1975); THE RITZ; SHOUT AT THE DEVIL (1976); THE TEMPTER (1978); IT'S NOT THE SIZE THAT COUNTS (1979); BEYOND THE FOG (1981); THE LONG GOOD FRIDAY (1982).

Dali, Salvador
Born 11 May 1904, Figueras, Spain; died 23 Jan. 1989, Figueras, Spain
Surrealist Painter
A pioneer of the Surrealist movement and the foremost exponent of the form in strictly commercial terms, Dali was educated in Madrid, where he became close friends with Luis Bunuel. The two collaborated on the surrealist landmark films UN CHIEN ANDALOU and L'AGE D'OR in 1929 and 1930, although Dali's contribution is generally acknowledged to have been the lesser and fairly slight in the latter, with which he claimed to have been "frightfully disappointed." By this time Dali was already a prominent and popular member of the Surrealist enclave in Paris whose first show there had drawn considerable attention, his paintings already exhibiting Dali's distinctive combination of extreme technical command in a traditional medium (oil) and thoroughly subversive, frequently blasphemous, hallucinatory images detailed in a highly realistic manner. This unlikely mix of anarchy and super-stylization was also a hallmark of Dali's famously outrageous persona, which, like his art, he cultivated and marketed with stunning energy and success (prompting Andre Breton, in a famous anagram, to nickname his colleague "Avida Dollars"). After 1940 (when Dali moved to the US, though he later returned to the Spanish town of his birth, Figueras), it became accepted wisdom in avant-garde circles that Dali's work had lost the power and will to disturb so essential to its aesthetic significance—he

became personally more conservative as well—but his fall from grace with the general public came decades later, when it was alleged that he had signed thousands of blank sheets of paper that were regenerated as Dali "originals," and the controversy for which he was so famous increasingly tended to generate *around* rather than from him. Although Dali had early proclaimed his disenchantment with the cinematic medium, he did design the surrealistic dream sequence for Hitchcock's psychoanalytic mystery SPELLBOUND (1945), and later did the sets and costumes for the Spanish film DON JUAN TENORIO (1951) and directed some short films.

Dalrymple, Ian
Born 26 Aug. 1903, Johannesburg, South Africa; died 28 April 1989, London, England
Screenwriter-Producer-Director-Editor
A South African native, Dalrymple began in British films as an editor in the late 1920s. He soon began scriptwriting, first for documentaries and later for features, his screenplays including PYGMALION; SOUTH RIDING; and THE GOOD COMPANIONS. During WW II he branched further into directing and producing, and continued the patriotic vein of films like LONDON CAN TAKE IT and LISTEN TO BRITAIN in such postwar features as THE WOODEN HORSE and HELL IN KOREA. Though in later years Dalrymple devoted himself primarily to producing with his own Wessex Films, he did direct ESTHER WATERS (Dirk Bogarde's debut) in 1948. His films include: TAXI FOR TWO (w) (1929); HOUND OF THE BASKERVILLES (ed); MICHAEL AND MARY (ed); THE OFFICE GIRL (ed) (1932); THE CUCKOO IN THE NEST (p); THE GOOD COMPANIONS (w); THE MAN THEY COULDN'T ARREST (ed); NIGHT AND DAY (ed) (1933); CHANNEL CROSSING (p); EVERGREEN (ed); THE GHOUL (ed); THE WOMAN IN COMMAND (ed) (1934); HER LAST AFFAIRE (w) (1935); THE BROWN WALLET (w); JURY'S EVIDENCE (w); RADIO LOVER (w) (1936); STORM IN A TEACUP (d&w) (1937); THE CITADEL (w); THE DIVORCE OF LADY X (w); PYGMALION (w); SOUTH RIDING (w) (1938); CHEER BOYS CHEER (w); CLOUDS OVER EUROPE (w); FRENCH WITHOUT TEARS (w) (1939); THE LION HAS WINGS (w); LONDON CAN TAKE IT (p); OLD BILL AND SON (d&w) (1940); LISTEN TO BRITAIN (p) (1941); COASTAL COMMAND (p); LADY IN DISTRESS (w); PIMPERNEL SMITH (w) (1942); CLOSE QUARTERS (p) (1943); PERFECT STRANGERS (p) (1945); ESTHER WATERS (p&d) (1948); ALL OVER THE TOWN (p); DEAR MR. PROHACK

(p&w); THE WOMAN IN THE HALL (p&w) (1949); MANIACS ON WHEELS (p); THE WOODEN HORSE (p) (1951); THE HEART OF THE MATTER (p&w) (1954); THREE CASES OF MURDER (p&w) (1955); HELL IN KOREA (w) (1956); THE ADMIRABLE CRICHTON (p); RAISING A RIOT (p&w) (1957); A CRY FROM THE STREET (p) (1959); HUNTED IN HOLLAND (p&w) (1961); MIX ME A PERSON (w) (1962); CALAMITY THE COW (p) (1967).

Davis, Bette [Ruth Elizabeth Davis]
Born 5 April 1908, Lowell, Mass.; died 6 Oct. 1989, Paris, France
Actress
Although many critics would later consider her Hollywood's greatest actress, Davis was hardly an overnight sensation. After being rejected as a student by Eva La Galliene, she enrolled in John Murray Anderson's school in 1928, and soon did her first professional acting with a stock troupe in Rochester, N.Y., but was fired by its director, George Cukor. She followed her New York City stage debut in a 1929 production of "The Earth Between" with a Broadway bow in "Broken Dishes," but failed her first screen test (for Goldwyn) shortly thereafter. Eventually she tested successfully for Universal, however, and made her first film appearance in BAD SISTER (1931). While making movies for Universal and on loan-out, she caught the eye of George Arliss, who suggested her as his costar in THE MAN WHO PLAYED GOD. It was her first film for Warner Bros., the studio with which she constantly battled and with which she remained until 1949—earning the nickname "the fourth Warner brother." Initially cast in a succession of mediocre films by Warners, Davis nevertheless managed to impress the critics, especially after she fought Warners to be allowed to play Mildred in RKO's OF HUMAN BONDAGE (1934). The role made her a star, and began to establish the famous Davis mannerisms and persona—that of an aggressive, sexy if unglamorous, independent, and sometimes downright mean modern woman (though she gave many classic portrayals of "good" women, too, as in NOW, VOYAGER). Warners continued to pitch her in poor, low-budget films, however, even though her performance in the otherwise negligible DANGEROUS (1935) was good enough to win her a Best Actress Oscar. (She won again for JEZEBEL [1938], and was nominated 10 times in all, a record in the category.) Tired of being wasted in such material, Davis refused some roles and either demanded or amended others, leading Warners to suspend her without pay in 1936. Prevented from acting in Europe when Warners issued an injunction, she sued the studio. She lost in court, but apparently proved her point: Warners (which paid her legal expenses) subse-

quently gave Davis some of the best roles of her career. Over the next 10 years, she gave performances of astounding range and quality in MARKED WOMAN; JEZEBEL; DARK VICTORY; THE OLD MAID; THE PRIVATE LIVES OF ELIZABETH AND ESSEX; THE LETTER; THE GREAT LIE; THE LITTLE FOXES (for Goldwyn); NOW, VOYAGER; THE CORN IS GREEN; and A STOLEN LIFE, to name only a few. Nonetheless Davis—Hollywood's top female box-office draw by 1940—found her stardom waning by the end of the decade, and the now-middle-aged actress seemed headed for has-been status when, in 1951, she gave what many consider her greatest performance as Margo Channing, the Broadway queen whom Anne Baxter's Eve schemes to overthrow in ALL ABOUT EVE. (Gary Merrill, Davis' EVE costar, was her fourth husband, from 1950 to 1960.) EVE was only a temporary triumph, however, and by the mid-50s Davis was supplementing scarce film roles with TV and stage appearances, including the Davis-Merrill touring show "An Evening with Carl Sandburg." After POCKETFUL OF MIRACLES failed to strike box-office gold in 1961, she resorted (presumably with tongue half in cheek) to soliciting work through ads in *Variety*. But she made yet another comeback soon thereafter, costarring opposite her former rival Joan Crawford in Robert Aldrich's WHATEVER HAPPENED TO BABY JANE? After her no-stops-pulled performance as the demented, eponymous ex-child star of BABY JANE and her work in its horror follow-up, HUSH . . . HUSH, SWEET CHARLOTTE (appearing with Olivia de Havilland and Joseph Cotten under Aldrich's direction), Davis ended her career in a series of film and television character roles, often in horror movies (THE NANNY; BURNT OFFERINGS; TV's "Dark Secret of Harvest Home"), all-star vehicles (DEATH ON THE NILE), and TV melodramas ("Little Gloria . . . Happy At Last"). In 1987 she starred with Lillian Gish in THE WHALES OF AUGUST, then made her last feature film appearance in Larry Cohen's WICKED STEPMOTHER (1989). (Her performance, interrupted when she departed horror maverick Cohen's production midway, survived the film's final cut.) The fifth recipient and the first woman to be given the American Film Institute's Life Achievement Award, Davis is the author of *The Lonely Life, Mother Goddamn: The Story of the Career of Bette Davis* (with Whitney Stine), and 1987's *This 'N That*. The last was a reply to daughter B.D. Hyman's damaging portrait of Davis in the 1985 book *My Mother's Keeper*; what cannot be damaged is Davis' stature as the actress who paved the way for a legion of strong female American film stars to follow, and as the "First Lady of the American

Bette Davis (right) with Lillian Gish in THE WHALES OF AUGUST.

Screen." Her films include: BAD SISTER; SEED; WATERLOO BRIDGE (1931); CABIN IN THE COTTON; THE DARK HORSE; HELL'S HOUSE; THE MAN WHO PLAYED GOD; THE MENACE; THE RICH ARE ALWAYS WITH US; SO BIG; THREE ON A MATCH; WAY BACK HOME (1932); BUREAU OF MISSING PERSONS; EX-LADY; PARACHUTE JUMPER; THE WORKING MAN; 20,000 YEARS IN SING SING (1933); THE BIG SHAKEDOWN; FASHIONS OF 1934; FOG OVER FRISCO; HOUSEWIFE; JIMMY THE GENT; OF HUMAN BONDAGE (1934); BORDERTOWN; FRONT PAGE WOMAN; THE GIRL FROM TENTH AVENUE; SPECIAL AGENT (1935); DANGEROUS; THE GOLDEN ARROW; THE PETRIFIED FOREST; SATAN MET A LADY (1936); IT'S LOVE I'M AFTER; KID GALAHAD; MARKED WOMAN; THAT CERTAIN WOMAN (1937); JEZEBEL; THE SISTERS (1938); DARK VICTORY; JUAREZ; THE OLD MAID; THE PRIVATE LIVES OF ELIZABETH AND ESSEX (1939); ALL THIS AND HEAVEN TOO; THE LETTER (1940); THE BRIDE CAME C.O.D.; THE GREAT LIE; THE LITTLE FOXES (1941); IN THIS OUR LIFE; THE MAN WHO CAME TO DINNER; NOW, VOYAGER (1942); OLD ACQUAINTANCE; THANK YOUR LUCKY STARS; WATCH ON THE RHINE (1943); HOLLYWOOD CANTEEN; MR. SKEFFINGTON (1944); THE CORN IS GREEN (1945); DECEPTION; A STOLEN LIFE (a&p) (1946); JUNE BRIDE; WINTER MEETING (1948); BEYOND THE FOREST (1949); ALL

ABOUT EVE (1950); PAYMENT ON DEMAND (1951); ANOTHER MAN'S POISON; PHONE CALL FROM A STRANGER (1952); THE STAR (1953); THE VIRGIN QUEEN (1955); THE CATERED AFFAIR; STORM CENTER (1956); JOHN PAUL JONES; THE SCAPEGOAT (1959); POCKETFUL OF MIRACLES (1961); WHATEVER HAPPENED TO BABY JANE? (1962); DEAD RINGER; THE EMPTY CANVAS; HUSH . . . HUSH, SWEET CHARLOTTE; WHERE LOVE HAS GONE (1964); THE NANNY (1965); THE ANNIVERSARY (1968); BUNNY O'HARE; CONNECTING ROOMS (1971); THE SCIENTIFIC CARDPLAYER (1972); BURNT OFFERINGS (1976); DEATH ON THE NILE; RETURN FROM WITCH MOUNTAIN (1978); THE WATCHER IN THE WOODS (1980); THE WHALES OF AUGUST (1987); THE WICKED STEPMOTHER (1989).

Diffring, Anton
Born 20 Oct. 1918, Koblenz, [West] Germany; died 20 May 1989, Chateauneuf-de-Grasse, France
Actor
Character actor Diffring fled Nazi Germany and emigrated to North America in 1939, acting on Canadian and American stages before entering films in Britain after WW II. Ironically, his Aryan features caused his frequent typecasting as a Nazi, former Nazi, or German officer in primarily British and European films that ranged from I AM A CAMERA; THE SEA SHALL NOT HAVE THEM; and THE BLUE MAX to 1988's French horror

Anton Diffring with Julie Harris in I AM A CAMERA.

thriller LES PREDATEURS DE LA NUIT, in which Diffring essayed the role of an ex-brownshirt for the last time. His films include: HIGHLY DANGEROUS (1950); THE GREAT MANHUNT; HOTEL SAHARA (1951); ISLAND RESCUE (1952); ALBERT, R.N.; NEVER LET ME GO; NORMAN CONQUEST; OPERATION DIPLOMAT (1953); BETRAYED; PARATROOPER; THE WOMAN'S ANGLE (1954); THE COLDITZ STORY; I AM A CAMERA; THE SEA SHALL NOT HAVE THEM (1955); THE BLACK TENT; DOUBLE CROSS (1956); THE CROOKED SKY; LADY OF VENGEANCE; REACH FOR THE SKY; TRIPLE DECEPTION (1957); THE ACCURSED; MARK OF THE PHOENIX (1958); THE BEASTS OF MARSEILLES; THE MAN WHO COULD CHEAT DEATH; A QUESTION OF ADULTERY (1959); CIRCUS OF HORRORS (1960); ENTER INSPECTOR DUVAL (1961); THE HEROES OF TELEMARK (1965); THE BLUE MAX; FAHRENHEIT 451; INCIDENT AT MIDNIGHT (1966); COUNTERPOINT; THE DOUBLE MAN (1967); WHERE EAGLES DARE (1968); ZEPPELIN (1971); DEAD PIGEON ON BEETHOVEN STREET (1972); LITTLE MOTHER (1973); THE BEAST MUST DIE (1974); MARK OF THE DEVIL II; NO WAY OUT (1975); CALL HIM MR. SHATTER; OPERATION DAYBREAK; POTATO FRITZ; THE SWISS CONSPIRACY (1976); LES INDIENS SONT ENCORE LOIN; L'IMPRECATEUR; VALENTINO; VANESSA (1977); TUSK (1980); VICTORY (1981); MARIE WARD—ZWISCHEN GALGEN UND GLORIE (1985); DER SOMMER DES SAMURAI (1986); LES PREDATEURS DE LA NUIT (1988).

du Maurier, Daphne [Lady Browning]
Born 13 May 1907, London, England; died 19 April 1989, Par, England
Novelist-Short Story Writer
The daughter of actor Sir Gerald du Maurier and the granddaughter of novelist George du Maurier, Daphne du Maurier wrote some of this century's best and most popular Gothic novels, most famously *Rebecca*, upon which Alfred Hitchcock's film of the same name is based. Her romantic, eerily suspenseful fiction also provided the inspiration for Hitchcock's JAMAICA INN and THE BIRDS and for Nicholas Roeg's DON'T LOOK NOW, among others. Du Maurier, who published her first novel in 1931, also wrote plays ("The Years Between" was adapted for the screen) and nonfiction, including biographies of Patrick Branwell Bronte and of her famous father, as well as the autobiographical *Not After Midnight* and *Growing Pains*. Films based on her work include: JAMAICA INN (1939); REBECCA (1940); FRENCHMAN'S CREEK (1944); HUNGRY HILL; THE YEARS BETWEEN (1947); MY COUSIN RACHEL (1952); THE SCAPEGOAT (1959); THE BIRDS (1963); DON'T LOOK NOW (1973).

Evans, Maurice
Born 3 June 1901, Dorchester, England; died 12 March 1989, Rottingdean, England
Actor-Stage Producer-Director
One of the century's best-known Shakespeareans, Evans made his professional debut in 1926, and in three years was a stage success in London. He first appeared on Broadway opposite Katherine Cornell in "Romeo and Juliet" in 1935, and in 1937 starred in a long-running "Richard II," a Broadway success surpassed the next

year when Evans (with director Margaret Webster, with whom he worked often) produced and starred in the first full-length "Hamlet" presented on the modern-day US stage. In WW II, his abridged "GI Hamlet" was among the shows Evans, by then a US citizen, staged as a major in charge of entertainment in the Central Pacific. Later, his many acclaimed Broadway performances included the role of the murderous husband in "Dial M for Murder"; he also produced such plays as "The Teahouse of the August Moon." Evans' TV appearances ranged from his familiar Shakespearean roles to a stint on "Bewitched"; his infrequent film work comprised movies as disparate as ANDROCLES AND THE LION; ROSEMARY'S BABY; and PLANET OF THE APES. His films include: RAISE THE ROOF; WHITE CARGO (1930); SHOULD A DOCTOR TELL? (1931); MARRY ME; WEDDING REHEARSAL (1932); THE EMPRESS AND I; HEART SONG (1933); BYPASS TO HAPPINESS; THE PATH OF GLORY (1934); CHECKMATE; SCROOGE (1935); KIND LADY (1951); ANDROCLES AND THE LION (1952); THE GREAT GILBERT AND SULLIVAN (1953); MACBETH (1963); THE WAR LORD (1965); ONE OF OUR SPIES IS MISSING (1966); JACK OF DIAMONDS (1967); PLANET OF THE APES; ROSEMARY'S BABY (1968); THE BODY STEALERS; OUT OF THIN AIR (1969); BENEATH THE PLANET OF THE APES (1970); TERROR IN THE WAX MUSEUM (1973); THE JERK (1979).

Fain, Sammy [Samuel Feinberg]
Born 17 June 1902, New York, N.Y.; died 6 Dec. 1989, Los Angeles, Calif.
Composer-Lyricist
A 12-time Academy Award nominee, Fain started out as an employee of a music publishing company and as a pianist-singer. In the mid-1920s, he began composing songs, often collaborating with lyricist Irving Kahal. The two produced such hits as "Let a Smile Be Your Umbrella on a Rainy (Rainy) Day" and "Wedding Bells Are Breaking Up That Old Gang of Mine," then were enlisted by Hollywood to write songs for films, including THE BIG POND (1930), in which Maurice Chevalier introduced "You Brought a New Kind of Love to Me," and FOOTLIGHT PARADE (1933), in which Dick Powell sang "That Old Feeling." In the late 1930s, Fain contributed music to Broadway's "Hellzapoppin'" and "Right This Way"—the latter including the Fain-Kahal classics "I Can Dream Can't I" and "I'll Be Seeing You." After the 1940s Fain—working mainly with Paul Francis Webster, but also with Sammy Cahn, E.Y. Harburg, Bob Hilliard, and others—again wrote primarily for films, and won Best Song Oscars for CALAMITY JANE's "Secret Love"

(1953) and LOVE IS A MANY-SPLENDORED THING's title song (1955). Films featuring Cain's songs include: IT'S A GREAT LIFE (1929); THE BIG POND (1930); COLLEGE COACH; FOOTLIGHT PARADE; MOONLIGHT AND PRETZELS (1933); DAMES (a&m); FASHIONS OF 1934; HAPPINESS AHEAD; HAROLD TEEN; HERE COMES THE NAVY; MANDALAY (1934); GOIN' TO TOWN; SWEET MUSIC (1935); NEW FACES OF 1937; VOGUES OF 1938 (1937); HELLZAPOPPIN' (1941); I DOOD IT; SWING FEVER (1943); I'LL BE SEEING YOU; TWO GIRLS AND A SAILOR (1944); ANCHORS AWEIGH; THRILL OF A ROMANCE; WEEKEND AT THE WALDORF (1945); NO LEAVE, NO LOVE; TWO SISTERS FROM BOSTON (1946); THE UNFINISHED DANCE; THIS TIME FOR KEEPS (1947); THREE DARING DAUGHTERS (1948); CALL ME MISTER (1951); ALICE IN WONDERLAND (1952); CALAMITY JANE; THE JAZZ SINGER; PETER PAN; THREE SAILORS AND A GIRL (1953); LUCKY ME (1954); LOVE IS A MANY-SPLENDORED THING (1955); HOLLYWOOD OR BUST (1956); APRIL LOVE (1957); A CERTAIN SMILE; MARDI GRAS; MARJORIE MORNINGSTAR (1958); THE BIG CIRCUS (1959); TENDER IS THE NIGHT (1962); MADE IN PARIS (1965); MYRA BRECKINRIDGE (1970); THE STEPMOTHER (1973); THE TEACHER (1974); THE SPECIALIST (1975); THE RESCUERS (1977).

Forrest, William H.
Died 26 Jan. 1989, Santa Monica, Calif., age 86
Actor

Although his best-known role was that of Maj. Swanson on television's "The Adventures of Rin Tin Tin," character actor Forrest also graced scores of films. A former football star at Princeton, Forrest began acting in 1938 with the Pasadena Playhouse, and made his screen debut two years later. The distinguished-looking Forrest often played authority figures, such as military men or judges, over his 30-year film and TV career. His films include: THE LONE WOLF MEETS A LADY; THE MAN WHO TALKED TOO MUCH; NOBODY'S CHILDREN; THE SECRET SEVEN (1940); BARNACLE BILL; DIVE BOMBER; DOWN IN SAN DIEGO; FLIGHT FROM DESTINY; HERE COMES MR. JORDAN; HOLD THAT GHOST; INTERNATIONAL LADY; KEEP 'EM FLYING; LIFE BEGINS FOR ANDY HARDY; THE

LONE WOLF TAKES A CHANCE; LUCKY DEVILS; MEET JOHN DOE; MILLION DOLLAR BABY; THE PHANTOM SUBMARINE; SUN VALLEY SERENADE (1941); FLIGHT LIEUTENANT; HITLER'S CHILDREN; IN THIS OUR LIFE; JOE SMITH, AMERICAN; LUCKY JORDAN; MY FAVORITE BLONDE; MY FAVORITE SPY; PRIORITIES ON PARADE; SLEEPYTIME GAL; SPY SHIP; THEY DIED WITH THEIR BOOTS ON; WAKE ISLAND; YANKEE DOODLE DANDY (1942); AIR FORCE; DU BARRY WAS A LADY; FLIGHT FOR FREEDOM; THE IRON MAJOR; IT AIN'T HAY; MISSION TO MOSCOW; MUG TOWN; SO PROUDLY WE HAIL (1943); ABROAD WITH TWO YANKS; THE FIGHTING SEABEES; FOLLOW THE BOYS; HERE COME THE WAVES; LAURA; MARINE RAIDERS; MR. SKEFFINGTON; MR. WINKLE GOES TO WAR; WILSON (1944); ANCHORS AWEIGH; BEHIND CITY LIGHTS; THE CARIBBEAN MYSTERY; GANGS OF THE WATERFRONT; GIRLS OF THE BIG HOUSE; GOD IS MY CO-PILOT; ROAD TO ALCATRAZ; ROUGH, TOUGH AND READY; SALTY O'ROURKE; WITHOUT LOVE; YOUTH ON TRIAL (1945); DANGEROUS BUSINESS; THE JOLSON STORY; THE KID FROM BROOKLYN; MEET ME ON BROADWAY; NOBODY LIVES FOREVER; TILL THE CLOUDS ROLL BY; TILL THE END OF TIME; THE WELL-GROOMED BRIDE (1946); THE CORPSE CAME C.O.D.; DEAD RECKONING; DEVIL ON WHEELS; DEVIL SHIP; THE GUILT OF JANET AMES; THE MIRACLE ON 34TH STREET;

MOTHER WORE TIGHTS; SARGE GOES TO COLLEGE; THE SENATOR WAS INDISCREET; THE SPIRIT OF WEST POINT (1947); ALIAS A GENTLEMAN; FORT APACHE; THE GENTLEMAN FROM NOWHERE; HOMECOMING; RACE STREET; THREE DARING DAUGHTERS; TRAPPED BY BOSTON BLACKIE (1948); ANGELS IN DISGUISE; ARSON, INC.; THE DEVIL'S HENCHMEN; THE GIRL FROM JONES BEACH; THE STORY OF SEABISCUIT; TRAIL OF THE YUKON; THE YOUNGER BROTHERS (1949); EMERGENCY WEDDING; SQUARE DANCE KATY (1950); FLIGHT TO MARS; FOLLOW THE SUN; FORT DODGE STAMPEDE; GASOLINE ALLEY; THE HARLEM GLOBETROTTERS; I WAS A COMMUNIST FOR THE F.B.I.; I'LL SEE YOU IN MY DREAMS; MISSING WOMEN; SMUGGLER'S GOLD; SPOILERS OF THE PLAINS (1951); DEADLINE—U.S.A.; JET JOB; NIGHT WITHOUT SLEEP; ONE MINUTE TO ZERO; THE ROSE BOWL STORY; THE STORY OF WILL ROGERS (1952); THE BANDITS OF CORSICA; DESTINATION GOBI (1953); EDDIE DEMETRIUS AND THE GLADIATORS; THE FRENCH LINE (1954); THE COURT MARTIAL OF BILLY MITCHELL; FRANCIS IN THE NAVY; THE GIRL IN THE RED VELVET SWING; THE MAN CALLED PETER; NEW YORK CONFIDENTIAL; ONE DESIRE; RAGE AT DAWN (1955); BEHIND THE HIGH WALL; THE FIRST TRAVELING SALESLADY; PARDNERS; THESE WILDER YEARS; YOU CAN'T RUN AWAY FROM IT (1956); BAND OF ANGELS; JAILHOUSE ROCK; LOVING YOU (1957); THE LAST HURRAH; TOUGHEST GUN IN TOMBSTONE (1958); THE HORSE SOLDIERS (1959); ONE-EYED JACKS (1961); PARADISE ALLEY; SWEET BIRD OF YOUTH (1962); GOOD NEIGHBOR SAM (1964); BILLY THE KID VS. DRACULA (1966); THE MARRIAGE OF A YOUNG STOCKBROKER (1971).

Frome, Milton
Died 21 March 1989, Woodland Hills, Calif., age 78
Actor-Vaudevillian
Beginning his career in vaudeville and burlesque, veteran straightman Frome went on to appear in numerous films, including several Jerry Lewis comedies. On stage, he toured with the USO and in "Sugar Babies" and was a popular musical comedy performer; on television, his credits ranged from regular roles on "The Red Skelton Show" and "The Beverly Hillbil-

lies" to "Texaco Star Theater," "The Milton Berle Show," "Police Story," "Love American Style," "Superior Court," and a variety of commercials. His film's include: RIDE 'EM COWGIRL; SMASHING THE MONEY RING (1939); THE SEVEN LITTLE FOYS; YOU'RE NEVER TOO YOUNG (1955); THE MAN WHO KNEW TOO MUCH; PARDNERS (1956); THE DELICATE DELINQUENT; THE FUZZY PINK NIGHTGOWN; HEAR ME GOOD; THE LONELY MAN; PUBLIC PIGEON NO. 1; SHORT CUT TO HELL (1957); THE YOUNG LIONS (1958); GO, JOHNNY, GO! (1959); PLEASE DON'T EAT THE DAISIES (1960); THE ERRAND BOY; THE POLICE DOG STORY (1961); IT'S ONLY MONEY (1962); BYE BYE BIRDIE; THE NUTTY PROFESSOR; A TICKLISH AFFAIR; WHO'S MINDING THE STORE? (1963); THE DISORDERLY ORDERLY; I'D RATHER BE RICH; JOHN GOLDFARB, PLEASE COME HOME (1964); THE BIRDS AND THE BEES; DR. GOLDFOOT AND THE BIKINI MACHINE; THE FAMILY JEWELS; FLUFFY (1965); BATMAN; THE SWINGER; WAY . . . WAY OUT (1966); ENTER LAUGHING; THE ST. VALENTINE'S DAY MASSACRE (1967); CHUBASCO; WITH SIX YOU GET EGGROLL (1968); WHICH WAY TO THE FRONT? (1970); THE SHAGGY D.A. (1976).

Geronimi, Clyde
Died 24 April 1989, Newport Beach, Calif., age 87
Animator-Animation Director
After launching his career as an animator with New York's Hearst studios, Geronimi joined Disney in 1931. He worked on many of Disney's early cartoons, then made his directorial debut in 1938 with the short "Beach Picnic." Other Geronimi-directed shorts include "Tugboat Mickey" and the Oscar-winning "Ugly Duckling" and "Lend a Paw." After the studio moved into feature-length animation, Geronimi codirected many of their most popular films, including THE THREE CABALLEROS; CINDERELLA; and SLEEPING BEAUTY; later, he helmed many Disney TV presentations. His films include: THE THREE CABALLEROS (1944); MAKE MINE MUSIC (1946); MELODY TIME (1948); THE ADVENTURES OF ICHABOD AND MR. TOAD (1949); CINDERELLA (1950); ALICE IN WONDERLAND (1951); PETER PAN (1953); THE LADY AND THE TRAMP (1955); SLEEPING BEAUTY (1959); ONE HUNDRED AND ONE DALMATIANS (1961).

Green, Johnny
Born 10 Oct. 1908, New York, N.Y.; died 15 May 1989, Beverly Hills, Calif.

Composer-Conductor-Music Director
Green graduated Harvard with a degree in economics, but soon began his lifelong career in music, working as an arranger for Guy Lombardo and Paul Whiteman and composing his first hit, "Coquette," by 1928. The next year he entered the film world as a rehearsal pianist (later composer-conductor) at the Paramount Astoria studios on Long Island. Throughout the 30s and 40s, Green was popular as a bandleader and composer of songs (his titles include "I Cover the Waterfront," "I Wanna Be Loved," "Easy Come, Easy Go," and "Body and Soul") recorded and performed in various media. Moving to Hollywood in 1942, he became MGM's staff conductor and composer, and from 1949 to 1958 served as the studio's general music director, overseeing such musicals as SUMMER STOCK; AN AMERICAN IN PARIS; ROYAL WEDDING; and BRIGADOON before leaving to work as a free lance in films and with TV's Desilu Productions. A 14-time Academy Award nominee, Green (who produced two Oscar shows and was music director-conductor on 10 others) won Oscars for his arrangements and adaptations of the scores of EASTER PARADE; AN AMERICAN IN PARIS; WEST SIDE STORY; and OLIVER!, and for producing a segment in the "MGM Concert Hall" short film series (he also won a Grammy for the WEST SIDE STORY soundtrack album). Green was, moreover, associate conductor of the Los Angeles Philharmonic for two years, and a guest conductor with groups ranging from the Chicago and Cleveland orchestras to the Boston Pops. His films include: THE SAP FROM SYRACUSE (m) (1930); HONOR AMONG LOVERS (m) (1931); LITTLE TOUGH GUY (m); START CHEERING (m) (1938); STAGE DOOR CANTEEN (m) (1943); BATHING BEAUTY (m); LOST IN A HAREM (m) (1944); WEEKEND AT THE WALDORF (m&md) (1945); EASY TO WED (m); THE SAILOR TAKES A WIFE (m) (1946); CYNTHIA (md); FIESTA (m); IT HAPPENED IN BROOKLYN (m); SOMETHING IN THE WIND (m&md); EASTER PARADE (md); UP IN CENTRAL PARK (md) (1948); THE INSPECTOR GENERAL (m&md) (1949); A LIFE OF HER OWN (md); SUMMER STOCK (md); THE TOAST OF NEW ORLEANS (md) (1950); AN AMERICAN IN PARIS (md); THE GREAT CARUSO (m); IT'S A BIG COUNTRY (md); MR. IMPERIUM (md); ROYAL WEDDING (md); TOO YOUNG TO KISS (md) (1951); BECAUSE YOU'RE MINE (m) (1952); BRIGADOON (md); RHAPSODY (md) (1954); HIGH SOCIETY (m&md); INVI-

TATION TO THE DANCE (md) (1956); RAINTREE COUNTY (m) (1957); PEPE (m) (1960); WEST SIDE STORY (md) (1961); BYE BYE BIRDIE (m); TWILIGHT OF HONOR (m&md) (1963); ALVAREZ KELLY (m); JOHNNY TIGER (m) (1966); OLIVER! (md) (1968); THEY SHOOT HORSES, DON'T THEY? (m&md) (1969).

Gunn, Bill
Born Philadelphia, Pa.; died 5 April 1989, New York, N.Y., age 59

Playwright-Actor-Screenwriter-Film Director
Gunn began his career as an actor, debuting on Broadway in the mid-1950s. His first play, "Murder in the High Grass," premiered in 1960.; Gunn later won the admiration of New York theater maven Joseph Papp, who called him "one the of great black writers" and whose staging of his "The Forbidden City" opened one day after Gunn's death. Gunn, who also wrote screen- and teleplays and the novels *All the Rest Have Died* and *Rhinestone Share-cropping*, is best-known among film buffs for his GANJA AND HESS, a vampire tale written, directed, and acted in by Gunn that gained cult status (although it was severely edited for re-release) for its serious exploration of African-American culture and subculture within a Hollywood blaxploitation format. His films include: THE INTERNS (1962); PENELOPE; THE SPY WITH MY FACE (1966); THE ANGEL LEVINE (w) (1970); GANJA AND HESS (a,d&w) (1973); LOSING GROUND (1982).

Halliwell, Leslie
Born Bolton, England; died 21 Jan. 1989, Surrey, England, age 59
Author
Halliwell's encyclopedic *Filmgoer's Companion* (first published in 1965), *Film Guide*, and, most recently, *Television Companion* were among the most popular and useful film reference books, notwithstanding his self-confessed strong preference for the films of Hollywood's "golden age" over those of latter decades. The author also served as a film buyer-researcher for British television (with Granada, ITV, and Channel 4), and was film critic for *Sight and Sound* and *Picturegoer*. His other works include ghost stories, two plays, a novel, and the autobiography *Seats in All Parts*.

Hoffman, Abbie
Born 30 Nov. 1936, Worchester, Mass.; died 12 April 1989, New Hope, Pa.
Writer-Activist
Hoffman became involved with activist

politics in 1960 as a student at Berkeley, then with the Student Non-Violent Coordinating Committee in Mississippi. As the 60s progressed, he began to formulate his distinct personal philosophy and protest style within the context of the radical Left's opposition to the Vietnam War. A "semi-freak among the love children" who "held [his] flower in a clenched fist," he wedded political commitment to satire, absurdist theater, and a flair for publicity, forming the Youth International Party (Yippies) and leading demonstration-stunts, such as the 1967 march to levitate/exorcise the Pentagon. His position as a countercultural leader was secure after the student protests during the 1968 Democratic Convention in Chicago, when an obstreperous Hoffman stood trial, as one of the Chicago Seven, for conspiring to disrupt the convention (acquitted) and crossing state lines with intent to riot (conviction overturned). In 1974, Hoffman went underground to evade arrest on a drug charge, resurfacing to serve a minor term in 1980. Throughout the Reagan years, he continued to protest various leftist causes—though his impact was blunted by public apathy and, ironically, by his media status as an "American legend" (as Timothy Leary noted, comparing Hoffman to Babe Ruth and Huck Finn) and 60s artifact. His books include *Steal This Book*, the autobiography *Soon to Be a Major Motion Picture*, *The Best of Abbie Hoffman*, and *The Faking of the President: Politics in the Age of Illusion* (with Jonathan Silvers). Hoffman appears, as himself, in the films BRAND X (1970); PROLOGUE (1970); and Oliver Stone's BORN ON THE FOURTH OF JULY (1989).

Ivens, Joris [Goerg Henri Anton Ivens]

Born 18 Nov. 1898, Nijmegen, the Netherlands; died 28 June 1989, Paris France
Documentary Filmmaker

Although he was often called "one of the world's leading avant-garde documentary filmmakers," there was nothing avant-garde about the subject matter and concerns of Ivens' mature work, which consistently focused on popular struggles against adverse social, political, or natural conditions and which he termed "dramatizations of daily life." The son of a Dutch camera equipment supplier, Ivens made his first film (FLAMING ARROW or WIGWAM), a cowboys-and-Indians story, at age 13. As a young man he cofounded Filmliga, one of the first film societies, and soon thereafter made a name for himself with THE BRIDGE (1928), an impressionistic view of a Rotterdam drawbridge that, along with the similar BREAKERS and RAIN, won Ivens acclaim in European avant-garde circles. A 1929 visit to the Soviet Union confirmed a turn towards a more realistic—though still stylized—approach in his work, evidenced in such films as SONG OF HEROES (shot in the USSR); BORINAGE, made in sympathy with striking Belgian miners; NEW EARTH; and the film many consider his masterpiece, THIS SPANISH EARTH. Made in 1936 under the banner of a production company Ivens formed with Lillian Hellman, Ernest Hemingway, John Dos Passos, and others in order to record contemporary events, the film detailed the plight of villagers and the problems of irrigation during the Spanish Civil War, with narration by Hemingway. Proceeds were contributed to the Republicans, for whom Ivens himself fought. Moving to the US in 1936, Ivens was commissioned to make THE POWER AND THE LAND (on rural electrification), OUR RUSSIAN FRONT (with Lewis Milestone), and others, but was stymied in his attempts to get Hollywood funding for feature projects and left the US permanently after he was denounced at HUAC hearings in the 1950s. Another exile began after Ivens was named the Dutch Film Commisioner for the Netherlands East Indies in 1944. He resigned his post in solidarity with the Indonesian independence movement, making the pro-revolution INDONESIA CALLING in 1946, and did not see Holland again until 20 years later, when the Dutch government formally sanctioned his return to make ROTTERDAM—EUROPOORT. Establishing a base in Prague and, later, Paris, Ivens—latterly codirecting with his wife, Marceline Loridan—focused on revolutionary movements throughout the world, especially in Cuba, Vietnam, and China; and made two features, LES AVENTURES DE TILL L'ESPIEGLE, a collaboration with actor-director Gerard Philipe, and UN HISTOIRE DU VENT, a fantasy concerning the efforts of a director (played by Ivens) to make a film about the wind in China. UNE HISTOIRE DU VENT was Ivens' last work, capping a long life in which the documentarist was a continual and outspoken witness to history. Ivens wrote two autobiographical works, *The Camera and I* (1969) and *Joris Ivens ou la memoire d'un regard* (1982). His films include: FLAMING ARROW (amateur) (1911); ZEEDYK FILM STUDY (amateur) (1927); THE BRIDGE (1928); BREAKERS; RAIN; "I" FILM; SKATING (1929); CAISSON BORNN ROTTERDAM; PILE DRIVING; NIEUWE ARCHITECTUUR; WE ARE BUILDING; ZUID LIMBURG; ZUIDERZEE (1930); PHILIPS RADIO; CREOSOTE (1931); SONG OF HEROES (1932); BORINAGE (1933); NEW EARTH (1934); THE SPANISH EARTH (1937); THE 400 MILLION (1938); THE POWER AND THE LAND (1940); OUR RUSSIAN FRONT (1941); OIL FOR ALADDIN'S LAMP (1942); ACTION STATIONS! (1943); INDONESIA CALLING (1946); THE FIRST YEARS (1949); PEACE WILL WIN (1951); FRIENDSHIP TRIUMPHS; FRIEDENSFAHRT (1952); LIED DER STROME (1954); DIE WINDROSE; LES AVENTURES DE TILL L'ESPIEGLE (feature, co-d with Gerard Philipe) (1956); LA SEINE A RENCONTRE PARIS (1957); EARLY SPRING; 600 MILLION PEOPLE ARE WITH YOU (1958); L'ITALIA NONE UN PAESE POVER; DEMAIN A NANGUILA (1960); CARNET DE VIAJE; CUBA, PUEBLO ARMADO (1961); A VALPARAISO; LE PETIT CHAPITEAU (1963); THE VICTORY TRAIN (1964); LE MISTRAL; LE CIEL LA TERRE (1965); ROTTERDAM—EUROPOORT (1966); LOIN DU VIETNAM (1967); LE 17E PARALLELE: LE VIETNAM EN GUERRE (1968); LE PEUPLE ET SES FUSILS; LE GUERRE POPULAIRE AU LAOS; RECONTRE AVEC LE PRESIDENT HO CHI MINH (1969); CHINE (1973); THE RETURN OF THE FLYING DUTCHMAN (1974); COMMENT YUKONG DEPLACE LES MONTAGNES (1976); UN HISTOIRE DU VENT (feature) (1988).

Johnston, Julanne

Born 1906, Indianapolis, Ind.; died 30 Dec. 1989, Grosse Pointe, Mich.
Actress

Originally a dancer, Johnston broke into silent films in 1917's YOUTH and found her greatest screen fame as the exotic object of Douglas Fairbanks' desire in THE THIEF OF BAGDAD (1924). She

appeared in a number of silents (several starring her friend Colleen Moore) and early talkies, retiring in the 1930s after her marriage to a Michigan electrical engineer. Her films include: YOUTH (1917); BETTER TIMES (1919); FICKLE WOMEN; SEEING IT THROUGH; SITTING ON THE WORLD; MISS HOBBS (1920); THE BRASS BOTTLE; MADNESS OF YOUTH (1923); THE THIEF OF BAGDAD (1924); BIG PAL (1925); ALOMA OF THE SOUTH SEAS; DAME CHANCE; DANGEROUS VIRTUE; PLEASURES OF THE RICH; TWINKLETOES (1926); CAPTAIN FEARLESS; GARRANGOLE; GOOD TIME CHARLEY; HER WILD OAT; PRIDE'S FALL; VENUS OF VENICE (1927); BLACK ACE; NAME THE WOMAN; OH, KAY!; THE OLYMPIC HERO; THE WHIP WOMAN (1928); CITY OF TEMPTATION; GENERAL CRACK; PRISONERS; SMILING IRISH EYES; SYNTHETIC SIN; THE YOUNGER GENERATION (1929); GOLDEN DAWN; MADAME SATAN; STRICTLY MODERN; WAY OF ALL MEN (1930); STEPPING SISTERS (1932); THE SCARLET EMPRESS (1934).

La Shelle, Joseph
Born 9 July 1900, Los Angeles, Calif.; died Aug. 20 1989, La Jolla, Calif.
Cinematographer
Trained as an electrical engineer, La Shelle became involved in films when he went to work for the Famous Players-Lasky film lab in 1923. By 1925 he was head of the lab, and shortly thereafter he became a camera operator at Metropolitan Studios. In 1932, La Shelle became the assistant to Fox cinematographer Arthur Miller, and continued to work with Miller until 1943, when he took his first director of photography credit for HAPPY LAND. The following year, La Shelle won an Academy Award for his contribution to Otto Preminger's atmospheric LAURA; he was later to gain Oscar nominations for his cinematography in COME TO THE STABLE; MY COUSIN RACHEL; MARTY; CAREER; HOW THE WEST WAS WON (of which La Shelle shot two episodes, including John Ford's Civil War sequence); THE APARTMENT; IRMA LA DOUCE; and THE FORTUNE COOKIE. The last three films were directed by Billy Wilder, with whom La Shelle worked frequently, as he did with Preminger, whose THE RIVER OF NO RETURN was La Shelle's first film in color and Cinemascope. His films include: HAPPY LAND (1943); BERMUDA MYSTERY; THE EVE OF ST. MARK; LAURA; TAKE IT OR LEAVE IT (1944); A BELL FOR ADANO; DOLL FACE; FALLEN ANGEL; HANGOVER SQUARE (1945); CLUNY BROWN (1946); THE FOXES OF HARROW; THE LATE GEORGE APLEY (1947); DEEP WATERS; IN THIS CORNER; LUCK OF THE IRISH; ROAD HOUSE (1948); COME TO THE STABLE; EVERYBODY DOES IT; THE FAN (1949); THE JACKPOT; MISTER 880; MOTHER DIDN'T TELL ME; UNDER MY SKIN; WHERE THE SIDEWALK ENDS (1950); ELOPEMENT; THE GUY WHO CAME BACK; MR. BELVEDERE RINGS THE BELL; THE THIRTEENTH LETTER (1951); LES MISERABLES; MY COUSIN RACHEL; THE OUTCASTS OF POKER FLAT; SOMETHING FOR THE BIRDS (1952); DANGEROUS CROSSING; MR. SCOUTMASTER (1953); RIVER OF NO RETURN (1954); MARTY (1955); THE CONQUEROR; OUR MISS BROOKS; RUN FOR THE SUN; STORM FEAR (1956); THE ABDUCTORS; THE BACHELOR PARTY; CRIME OF PASSION; FURY AT SHOWDOWN; THE FUZZY PINK NIGHTGOWN; I WAS A TEENAGE WEREWOLF; NO DOWN PAYMENT (1957); THE LONG, HOT SUMMER; THE NAKED AND THE DEAD (1958); CAREER (1959); THE APARTMENT (1960); ALL IN A NIGHTS'S WORK; THE HONEYMOON MACHINE (1961); HOW THE WEST WAS WON; THE OUTSIDER (1962); A CHILD IS WAITING; IRMA LA DOUCE (1963); KISS ME, STUPID; WILD AND WONDERFUL (1964); THE CHASE; THE FORTUNE COOKIE; SEVEN WOMEN (1966); BAREFOOT IN THE PARK (1967); KONA COAST (1968); 80 STEPS TO JONAH (1969).

LeBorg, Reginald
Born 11 Dec. 1902, Vienna, Austria; died 25 March 1989, Los Angeles, Calif.
Stage/Film Director
LeBorg apprenticed with the Max Reinhardt School in his native Vienna before moving on as a writer-director of operas and operettas in Europe, then arrived in Hollywood in the 1930s, entering films as an extra and establishing himself as a director of musical sequences and MGM shorts. He wrote the Academy Award-winning, 1943 two-reeler HEAVENLY MUSIC, and thereafter graduated to feature direction, primarily of B pictures, including the majority of Monogram's "Joe Palooka" films and such horror cheapies as THE MUMMY'S GHOST; WEIRD WOMAN; and VOODOO ISLAND. His films include: ONE NIGHT OF LOVE (ch) (1934); LOVE ME FOREVER (ch); THE MELODY LINGERS ON (ch) (1935); SWING IT SOLDIER (ch) (1941); CALLING DR. DEATH; HEAVENLY MUSIC (w, short); SHE'S FOR ME (1943); ADVENTURE IN MUSIC; DEAD MAN'S EYES; DESTINY; JUNGLE WOMAN; THE MUMMY'S GHOST; SAN DIEGO, I LOVE YOU (p&d); WEIRD WOMAN (1944); HONEYMOON AHEAD (1945); JOE PAL-OOKA, CHAMP; LITTLE IODINE; SUSIE STEPS OUT (d&w) (1946); ADVENTURES OF DON COYOTE; FALL GUY; JOE PALOOKA IN THE KNOCKOUT; PHILO VANCE'S SECRET MISSION (1947); FIGHTING MAD; JOE PALOOKA IN WINNER TAKE ALL; PORT SAID; TROUBLE MAKERS (1948); FIGHTING FOOLS; HOLD THAT BABY!; JOE PALOOKA IN THE COUNTERPUNCH (1949); JOE PALOOKA IN THE SQUARED CIRCLE; WYOMING MAIL; YOUNG DANIEL BOONE (d&w) (1950); G.I. JANE; JOE PALOOKA IN TRIPLE CROSS (1951); MODELS, INC. (1952); BAD BLONDE; THE FLANAGAN BOY; THE GREAT JESSE JAMES RAID; SINS OF JEZEBEL (1953); THE WHITE ORCHID (p,d&w) (1954); THE BLACK SHEEP (1956); THE DALTON GIRLS; VOODOO ISLAND; WAR DRUMS (1957); THE FLIGHT THAT DISAPPEARED (1961); DEADLY DUO (1962); DIARY OF A MADMAN; THE EYES OF ANNIE JONES (1963); SO EVIL MY SISTER (1973).

Leone, Sergio
Born 23 Jan. 1929, Rome, Italy; died 30 April 1989, Rome, Italy
Director-Screenwriter-Producer
The son of Italian silent filmmaker Vincenzo Leone and actress Francesca Bertini, Sergio Leone entered the film world at age 18, serving as an assistant director on more than 50 features, both Italian and visiting US productions (such as William Wyler's BEN-HUR, whose famous chariot race Leone is credited with helping to stage). In the late 1950s he collaborated on several screenplays, chiefly of the "sword and sandal" variety, although several films officially credited to other directors are said to have benefitted heavily from Leone's directorial hand, THE DAYS

OF POMPEII and SODOM AND GOMORRAH among them. Officially, his directorial debut was 1961's THE COLOSSUS OF RHODES, but it was Leone's next film, A FISTFUL OF DOLLARS (1964), that established him as one of the decade's most influential and distinctive directors. That film revived the declining "spaghetti western" subgenre; launched TV star Clint Eastwood to superstardom; and established Leone's unmistakable mix of hyperstyle (extreme closeups alternating with panoramic vistas, intense colors and expressive composition, sparse dialog and complex flashback narratives, and the ever-present evocative Ennio Morricone score) and simple themes (chiefly the notion of an individual code of justice in a violent universe), combining to create a distinctly European, mythic reinterpretation of the American West and the Hollywood western. FOR A FEW DOLLARS MORE; THE GOOD, THE BAD, AND THE UGLY; ONCE UPON A TIME IN THE WEST; and DUCK, YOU SUCKER came next and solidified Leone's following, although his work failed to gain widespread respect until years later. In the 70s, Leone set up his own production company, Rafran Cinematografica, sponsoring films ranging from the spaghetti western parodies of Terence Hill to the comedies of Italian actor-director Carlo Verdone, and occasionally provided cameo appearances in other directors' works. In 1984 he finished filming his dream project, ONCE UPON A TIME IN AMERICA, a nearly four-hour epic that paid homage to and re-imagined the American gangster film. Though hailed—along with ONCE UPON A TIME IN THE WEST—as a Leone masterpiece in this long version, the film was released in the US in a drastically cut form that Leone termed as "barbarously massacred." At the time of his death, Leone was preparing to film what would have been his biggest production yet, a $70-million tale of Leningrad under siege in WW II, set to star Robert De Niro and to be coproduced by the USSR. His films include: THE BICYCLE THIEF (a) (1947); SIGN OF THE GLADIATOR (w) (1959); DUEL OF THE TITANS (w); THE LAST DAYS OF POMPEII (w); THE SEVEN REVENGES (w) (1960); THE COLOSSUS OF RHODES (d&w) (1961); SODOM AND GOMORRAH (second-unit direction, uncredited codirection according to some sources) (1962); DUEL OF THE TITANS (w) (1963); A FISTFUL OF DOLLARS (d&w) (1964); FOR A FEW DOLLARS MORE (d&w); THE GOOD, THE BAD, AND THE UGLY (d&w); THE SEVEN REVENGES (w) (1967); UN CORDE . . . UN COLT (a) (1968); ONCE UPON A TIME IN THE WEST (d&w) (1969); DUCK, YOU SUCKER (d&w) (1972); MY NAME IS NOBODY (p) (1974); UN GENIO DUE COMPARI E UN POLLO (d) (1975); IL GATTO (p) (1978); AN ALMOST PERFECT AFFAIR (a); FUN IS BEAUTIFUL (p) (1979); RED, WHITE, & VERDONE GREEN (p) (1980); ONCE UPON A TIME IN AMERICA (a,d&w) (1984).

Levine, Nat
Died 6 Aug. 1989, Woodland Hills, Calif., age 90
Film Producer-Studio Head
A former office boy and later private secretary to New York theater owner Marcus Loew, Levine began distributing films independently in 1920, handling product rejected by studios. In 1926, he produced the serial THE SILENT FLYER and sold it to Universal; the next year, he formed Mascot Pictures, which merged with Liberty, Majestic, and Monogram in 1935 to become Republic Pictures. As president and production head at Mascot and Republic, Levine became known as the "King of the Serials," casting Gene Autry (who made his film debut in a Levine feature, IN OLD SANTA FE), Boris Karloff, Harry Carey, Red Grange, Clyde Beatty, and Tom Mix in the weekly installments and producing many feature films as well. In 1937 he sold his interest in Republic to his partner Herbert J. Yates; later, Levine managed a California TV studio and joined California Sterling Theaters, with whom he built and managed theaters until his retirement in 1972. His films include: THE SILENT FLYER (serial) (1926); KING OF THE CONGO (serial) (1929); THE GALLOPING GHOST (serial); THE VANISHING LEGION (serial) (1931); THE LAST OF THE MOHICANS (serial) (1932); CRIMSON ROMANCE; THE LOST JUNGLE (serial); THE PHANTOM EMPIRE (serial) (1934); BEHIND GREEN LIGHTS; HARMONY LANE; IN OLD SANTA FE; LADIES CRAVE EXCITEMENT; THE MIRACLE RIDER (serial); THE MARINES ARE COMING; MELODY TRAIL; ONE FRIGHTENED NIGHT; SAGEBRUSH TROUBADOUR; TUMBLING TUMBLEWEEDS; WATERFRONT LADY; $1,000 A MINUTE (1935); BOLD CABALLERO; BULLDOG EDITION; COMIN' ROUND THE MOUNTAIN; DOUGHNUTS AND SOCIETY; DOWN TO THE SEA; FOLLOW YOUR HEART; GENTLEMAN FROM LOUISIANA; GIRL FROM MANDALAY; GUNS AND GUITARS; THE HARVESTER; HEARTS IN BONDAGE; HITCH HIKE LADY; THE HOUSE OF A THOUSAND CANDLES; THE LONELY TRAIL; NAVY BORN; THE PRESIDENT'S MYSTERY; RIDE, RANGER, RIDE; THE SINGING COWBOY; SITTING ON THE MOON; THE THREE MESQUITEERS; TICKET TO PARADISE; WINDS OF THE WASTELAND (1936); BEWARE OF LADIES; THE BIG SHOW; CIRCUS GIRL; COUNTRY GENTLEMEN; GHOST TOWN GOLD; HAPPY-GO-LUCKY; HIT THE SADDLE; JOIN THE MARINES; LARCENY IN THE AIR; THE MANDARIN MYSTERY; OH, SUSANNAH; PARADISE EXPRESS; RIDERS OF THE WHISTLING SKULL; ROARIN' LEAD; ROUNDUP TIME IN TEXAS; TWO WISE MAIDS (1937); FOUR GIRLS IN WHITE (1939).

Lillie, Beatrice [Lady Peel]
Born 29 May 1894, Toronto, Canada; died 20 Jan. 1989, Henley-on-Thames, England
Actress-Comedienne
The comedienne who became "the toast of two continents" began her stage career as part of the Lillie Trio along with her

mother and sister. She debuted in London in 1914, when she began appearing in Andre Charlot's popular revues, one of which brought her to Broadway in 1924. Four years later, she appeared in the long-running "This Year of Grace," written by her close friend and frequent collaborator Noel Coward (whose "Mad Dogs and Englishmen" was one of her signature numbers). By the 1930s she was an established star—her persona defined by her long cigarette holder, short black hair and cap, and inimitable delivery—appearing on Broadway and in the West End, in films, and on her own radio program; after WW II she toured the world in such shows as "An Evening with Beatrice Lillie." Her autobiography, *Every Other Inch a Lady*, puns on her official title as the widow of Sir Robert Peel. Her films include: STAGE STARS OFF STAGE (1925); EXIT SMILING (1926); BLACK WATERS; THE SHOW OF SHOWS (1929); ARE YOU THERE? (1930); DR. RHYTHM (1938);

WELCOME TO BRITAIN (1943); ON APPROVAL (1944); SCRAPBOOK FOR 1933 (1949); AROUND THE WORLD IN 80 DAYS (1956); THOROUGHLY MODERN MILLIE (1967).

Mack, Marion [Joey Marion McCreery]

Born Mammoth, Utah; died 1 May 1989, Costa Mesa, Calif., age 87
Actress-Screenwriter

Arriving in Hollywood in 1920, Joey Marion McCreery became one of Mack Sennett's bathing beauties, eventually changing her name to Marion Mack. Having performed in numerous shorts and some features, she wrote and starred in the semiautobiographical MARY OF THE MOVIES in 1923, following with appearances in ONE OF THE BRAVEST (1925); ALICE IN MOVIELAND (1926); and THE CARNIVAL GIRL (1926) before landing her most important role as Annabelle Lee, Buster Keaton's estranged, kidnapped love interest, in Keaton's Civil War comedy THE GENERAL (1927). Ill-received upon its release, THE GENERAL is now recognized as one of the silent screen's classics, and Mack frequently spoke at festival screenings of the film in the 1970s. She was married to producer Louis Lewyn, for whom she wrote short-subject scripts after her retirement from acting.

Mahoney, Jock [Jacques O'Mahoney, Jack Mahoney]

Born 7 Feb. 1919, Chicago, Ill; died 14 Dec. 1989, Bremerton, Wash.
Actor-Stuntman

After serving in WW II, Mahoney entered films as a stuntman in 1945. He soon found bad-guy roles in B westerns, and in 1951 was contracted to star in the TV series "Range Rider" by Gene Autry (for whom he had previously doubled). He then signed with Universal, starring in several of their films (SHOWDOWN AT ABILENE) and lending support in others (Douglas Sirk's A TIME TO LOVE AND A TIME TO DIE), before landing the role with which he is most identified, that of the dandyish gunman Yancey Derringer in the late-50s TV show of the same name. Mahoney continued to act in the 60s and 70s, primarily in exploitation and Tarzan films (he was the 13th actor to star as the vine-swinging elephant-caller, and also played supporting roles in TARZAN THE MAGNIFICENT and TARZAN'S DEADLY SILENCE). The former stepfather of Sally Field (with whom he appeared in THE END), Mahoney effectively retired in 1981, when he acted on TV's "B.J. and the Bear" and coordinated stunts on John and Bo Derek's TARZAN, THE APE MAN. His films include: THE FIGHTING FRONTIERSMAN (1946); SOUTH OF THE CHISHOLM TRAIL (1947); THE DOOLINS OF OKLA-

HOMA; JOLSON SINGS AGAIN; SMOKY MOUNTAIN MELODY (1949); THE NEVADAN (1950); PECOS RIVER; SANTA FE (1951); THE HAWK OF WILD RIVER; JUNCTION CITY; THE KID FROM BROKEN GUN; LARAMIE MOUNTAINS; THE ROUGH, TOUGH WEST; SMOKY CANYON (1952); OVERLAND PACIFIC (1954); AWAY ALL BOATS; A DAY OF FURY; I'VE LIVED BEFORE; SHOWDOWN AT ABILENE (1956); BATTLE HYMN; JOE DAKOTA; THE LAND UNKNOWN; SLIM CARTER (1957); THE LAST OF THE FAST GUNS; MONEY, WOMEN AND GUNS; A TIME TO LOVE AND A TIME TO DIE (1958); TARZAN THE MAGNIFICENT (1960); THREE BLONDES IN HIS LIFE (1961); TARZAN GOES TO INDIA (1962); CALIFORNIA; TARZAN'S THREE CHALLENGES (1963); MORO WITCH DOCTOR; THE WALLS OF HELL (1964); MARINE BATTLEGROUND; RUNAWAY GIRL (1966); THE GLORY STOMPERS (1967); BANDOLERO!; THE LOVE BUG (1968); TARZAN'S DEADLY SILENCE (1970); TOM (1973); THE BAD BUNCH (1976); THE END; THEIR ONLY CHANCE (1978); TARZAN THE APE MAN (stunt coordinator) (1981).

Manes, Gina [Blanche Moulin]

Born 7 April 1895, Paris, France; died 6 Sept. 1989, Toulouse, France
Actress

Debuting on-screen in Louis Feuillade's L'HOMME SAN VISAGE in 1919, Manes became one of Europe's bigger female stars, often playing femme fatales and starring under the direction of Jean Epstein, Marcel L'Herbier, Julien Duvivier, and other major directors. Her greatest roles

were that of Josephine in Abel Gance's NAPOLEON (1927) and the title character in Jacques Feyder's THERESE RAQUIN (1928). Manes' popularity declined in the mid-1930s, but she returned to French screens 20 years later in a number of films, and acted with a theater company in Toulouse until 1972. Her films include: L'HOMME SANS VISAGE (1919); COEUR FIDELE; L'AUBERGE ROUGE (1923); AMES D'ARTISTES (1925); LE TRAIN SANS YEUX (1926); NAPOLEON (1927); LOOPING THE LOOP; SABLES; SIN; THERESE RAQUIN (1928); NUITS DE PRINCES (1930); SALTO MORTALE (1931); LA TETE D'UN HOMME (1933); BARCAROLE; DIVINE (1935); MAYERLING (1937); MOLLENARD; NOSTALGIE (1939); LA LOI DES RUES (1956); RAFLES SUR LA VILLE (1958); LES AMANTS DE DEMAIN (1959); NIGHTS OF SHAME; PALACE OF NUDES (1961); PAS DE PANIQUE (1965).

Mangano, Silvana

Born 21 April 1930, Rome, Italy; died 16 Dec. 1989, Madrid, Spain
Actress

Mangano debuted in films after winning the Miss Rome beauty contest in 1946. Three years later she won her first movie lead as Silvana, the romantic dreamer who falls for a petty crook in Giuseppe De Santis' erotic Neo-Realist story BITTER RICE. The role won her international fame—more for her "statuesque" physique than for her acting, which showed talent—and many lead roles followed (as did marriage to BITTER RICE's producer, Dino De Laurentiis, whom she divorced some 35 years later). Like Sophia Loren,

who was to eclipse her as Italian cinema's top female star, she eventually gained credibility as a serious actress, winning notable roles in Mario Camerini's ULYSSES (as Penelope and Circe); Pier Paolo Pasolini's TEORAMA; IL DECAMERONE; and EDIPO RE; and Luchino Visconti's DEATH IN VENICE; LUDWIG; and CONVERSATION PIECE. Among Mangano's last films were DUNE (produced by her daughter, Raffaella De Laurentiis) and Nikita Mikhalkov's DARK EYES, which starred her childhood sweetheart Marcello Mastroianni. Her films include: L'ELISIR D'AMORE (1946); IL DELITTO DI GIOVANNI EPISCOPO (1947); GLI UOMINI SONO NEMICI (1948); BLACK MAGIC (1949); BITTER RICE; IL BRIGANTE MUSOLINO; IL LUPO DELLA SILA (1950); ANNA (1951); MAMBO; ULYSSES (1955); UOMINI E LUPI (1956); GOLD OF NAPLES (1957); TEMPEST; THIS ANGRY AGE (1958); FIVE BRANDED WOMEN (1960); THE GREAT WAR; IL GUIDIZIO UNIVERSALE; UN VITA DIFFICILE (1961); BARABBAS (1962); THE VERONA TRIAL (1963); AND SUDDENLY IT'S MURDER!; LA MIA SIGNORA; THE FLYING SAUCER (1964); IO, IO, IO . . . E GLI ALTRI (1966); EDIPO RE; SCUSI, LEI E FAVOREVOLE O CONTRARIO? (1967); CAPRICCIO ALL'ITALIANA (1968); TEORAMA; THE WITCHES (1969); DEATH IN VENICE; IL DECAMERONE; SCIPIONE DETTO ANCHE L'AFRICANO (1971); THE SCIENTIFIC CARDPLAYER (1972); D'AMOR SI MUORE; LUDWIG (1973); CONVERSATION PIECE (1976); DUNE (1986); DARK EYES (1987).

Marsh, Tiger Joe [Joseph Marusich]
Born Chicago, Ill.; died 9 May 1989, Chicago, Ill.
Actor-Wrestler
The former Joe Marusich won the world heavyweight wrestling title under the name "Tiger Joe" in 1937, then gave up the canvas in 1954, when he debuted onstage in "Teahouse of the August Moon" with Burgess Meredith in Chicago. That same year he appeared as the union "muscle" in Elia Kazan's ON THE WATERFRONT, having already appeared in bit roles for Kazan in PINKY; PANIC IN THE STREETS; and VIVA ZAPATA!, as well as in THE JOE LOUIS STORY. Marsh continued acting in theater and films for many years, last appearing on screen in 1979's LOVE AT FIRST BITE. His films include: PINKY (1949); PANIC IN THE STREETS (1950); VIVA ZAPATA! (1952); THE JOE LOUIS STORY (1953); THE EGYPTIAN; ON THE WATERFRONT (1954); THE TALL MEN (1955); THE TEAHOUSE OF THE AUGUST MOON (1956); THE BLOB (1958); HERE COME THE JETS; THE REBEL SET (1959);

John Matuszak with Anjelica Huston in THE ICE PIRATES.

VENGEANCE (1964); C'MON, LET'S LIVE A LITTLE (1967); CACTUS IN THE SNOW; TOP OF THE HEAP (1972); ESCAPE TO WITCH MOUNTAIN (1975); THE CAT FROM OUTER SPACE (1978); LOVE AT FIRST BITE (1979).

Matuszak, John
Born Oak Creek, Wis.; died 17 June 1989, Los Angeles, Calif., age 38
Football Player-Actor
Houston's No. 1 pick in the NFL draft in 1973, Matuszak played for the Oilers, the Chiefs, and the Redskins before signing on as a defensive lineman with the Oakland (later LA) Raiders early in their 1976 Super Bowl season. The unruly Matuszak's play made him one of the team's key players and helped lead them to another Super Bowl victory (1980 season) before he retired from football to pursue acting full time in 1982. In films, his best role came in the football expose NORTH DALLAS FORTY, his screen debut, but he also had many TV appearances to his credit, both as a guest star on various shows and as a regular on "Hollywood Beat" and HBO's football comedy "First and Ten." His films include: NORTH DALLAS FORTY (1979); CAVEMAN (1981); THE ICE PIRATES (1984); THE GOONIES (1985); ONE CRAZY SUMMER (1986).

McAnally, Ray
Born in County Donegal, Ireland; died 15 June 1989, County Wicklow, Ireland, age 63
Actor
Debuting onstage at the age of 18, McAnally was a leading player with Dublin's famed Abbey Theater from 1947 to 1963. In London, his stage credits ranged from appearances with the Royal Shakespeare

Co. to his 1988 role (as George Bernard Shaw) opposite Sir John Gielgud in "The Best of Friends." He entered films in the late 1950s, with early roles in SHAKE HANDS WITH THE DEVIL and BILLY BUDD, but drew attention as a film actor in the 80s, when he demonstrated his versatility in such disparate films as CAL; THE MISSION; NO SURRENDER; and THE FOURTH PROTOCOL. Best-known in the US for his acclaimed lead performances in "A Very British Coup" and "A Perfect Spy," both shown on PBS in 1988, McAnally had just completed work in Neil Jordan's WE'RE NO ANGELS at the time of his death. His films include: SHAKE HANDS WITH THE DEVIL (1959); THE NAKED EDGE

(1961); BILLY BUDD; DESERT PATROL; MURDER IN EDEN; SHE DIDN'T SAY NO! (1962); SHE WHO RIDES A TIGER (1966); THE LOOKING GLASS WAR (1970); FEAR IS THE KEY (1973); CAL (1984); THE MISSION; NO SURRENDER (1986); EMPIRE STATE; THE FOURTH PROTOCOL; THE SICILIAN; WHITE MISCHIEF (1987); WE'RE NO ANGELS (1989).

McCarthy, Mary
Born 21 June 1921, Seattle, Wash.; died 25 Oct. 1989, New York, N.Y.
Author-Critic
The product of a rigorous upbringing detailed in her memoirs, *Memories of a Catholic Girlhood* and *How I Grew*, McCarthy built her fictions out of well-observed, sometimes thinly disguised autobiographical details—as in her best-known novel, *The Group* (1963), a best-seller chronicling the lives of eight Vassar graduates in the 1930s. The book was filmed in 1966, with Joan Hackett, Shirley Knight, and Jessica Walter among an ensemble cast directed by Sidney Lumet. *The Group*, like most of McCarthy's work, chronicles the intellectual, social, and sexual life of her generation, observed through the decades from McCarthy's vantage point as America's "first lady of letters" (to quote Norman Mailer). Known for the ferocity and occasional cruelty of her political and literary judgments, McCarthy was a theater critic for *The Nation*, *The New Republic*, and *Partisan Review*; her experiences as a member of the last journal's set in the late 30s and the 40s formed the basis of *The Oasis* and *The Charmed Life*, *romans a clef* containing withering portraits of two literary lions: her ex-lover Philip Rahv and her second husband, Edmund Wilson. Most recently, she was embroiled in a well-publicized dispute with Lillian Hellman—ended by the playwright's death in 1984—reviving the anti-Stalinist/anti-McCarthy (Joe) debate among the American Left in the 1950s. She was the sister of actor Kevin McCarthy.

McMillan, Kenneth
Born Brooklyn, N.Y., 1932; died 8 Jan. 1989, Santa Monica, Calif.
Actor
McMillan studied at New York's High School for the Performing Arts, but his acting talent didn't bear fruit until he was 30, when he toured in "Sweet Bird of Youth." Hollywood employed him in the 1970s, when he entered films in SERPICO and played Valerie Harper's boss on TV's "Rhoda," and many character roles followed, with McMillan memorably portraying such tough guys with a hollow core as the bigoted fire chief in RAGTIME and Robert Duvall's corrupt partner in TRUE CONFESSIONS. He was best known, however, for his work on the New York

stage, where he appeared in many New York Shakespeare Festival plays, the original "American Buffalo" and "Streamers," and numerous Off-Broadway works, giving an Obie-winning performance in "Weekends and Other People." His films include: SERPICO (1973); THE TAKING OF PELHAM ONE, TWO, THREE (1974); THE STEPFORD WIVES (1975); BLOODBROTHERS; OLIVER'S STORY (1978); BORDERLINE; CARNY; HIDE IN PLAIN SIGHT; LITTLE MISS MARKER (1980); EYEWITNESS; HEARTBEEPS; RAGTIME; TRUE CONFESSIONS; WHOSE LIFE IS IT ANYWAY? (1981); CHILLY SCENES OF WINTER; PARTNERS; THE KILLING HOUR (1982); BLUE SKIES AGAIN (1983); DUNE; THE POPE OF GREENWICH VILLAGE; PROTOCOL; RECKLESS (1984); CAT'S EYE; RUNAWAY TRAIN (1985); ARMED AND DANGEROUS (1986); MALONE (1987); THREE FUGITIVES (1989).

Meillon, John
Died 11 Aug. 1989, Sydney, Australia, age 55
Actor
Meillon began acting professionally on Australian radio at age 11 and made his stage debut the following year. After entering films in 1959 as a sailor in ON THE BEACH, Meillon moved to Britain, where his film credits included BILLY BUDD and THE LONGEST DAY. He returned to Australia in the mid-1960s to gain fame in the TV series "My Name's McGooley, What's Yours?" and with the Australian cinema's revival in the 1970s starred in such films as Peter Weir's THE CARS THAT ATE PARIS. In the 1980s, Meillon gained worldwide exposure as Paul

Hogan's tour guide partner in "CROCODILE DUNDEE" and its sequel. His films include: ON THE BEACH (1959); THE SUNDOWNERS (1960); THE LONG AND THE SHORT AND THE TALL; OFFBEAT; WATCH IT, SAILOR! (1961); BILLY BUDD; DEATH TRAP; THE LONGEST DAY; OPERATION SNATCH; THE VALIANT (1962); CAIRO; THE RUNNING MAN (1963); GUNS AT BATASI; SQUADRON 633 (1964); DEAD MAN'S CHEST (1965); THEY'RE A WEIRD MOB (1966); OUTBACK; WALKABOUT (1971); SUNSTRUCK (1973); THE CARS THAT ATE PARIS; THE DOVE; INN OF THE DAMNED (1974); SIDECAR RACERS (1975); RIDE A WILD PONY (1976); THE PICTURE SHOW MAN (1980); HEATWAVE; THE WILD DUCK (1983); THE CAMEL BOY (1984), BULLSEYE; "CROCODILE" DUNDEE (1986); FRENCHMAN'S FARM (1987); "CROCODILE" DUNDEE II; THE EVERLASTING SECRET FAMILY (1988).

Morrison, Ernie [Sunshine Sammy Morrison]
Born New Orleans, La.; died 24 July 1989, Lynwood, Calif., age 76
Actor-Vaudevillian
Morrison's father worked as a chef in Beverly Hills, where the father of child actress Baby Marie Osborne discovered young Morrison and brought him to Pathe studios in 1917. At Pathe, he appeared in 14 Baby Marie films and acquired his nickname, "Sunshine Sammy." Margaret Roach noticed him and brought him to the attention of her husband, producer Hal Roach, who signed Morrison to an initial two-year contract—said by some to be the first between a black performer and a

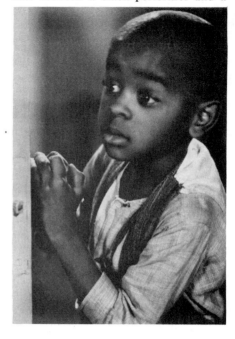

major studio; Morrison then starred in Roach Studios' "Sunshine Sammy" comedy shorts of 1921 and 1922, which eventually developed into the long-running "Our Gang" series. He appeared in 28 of the "Our Gang" shorts of 1922-24, then forsook movies (with the exception of one short, for MGM, in 1929) to perform in vaudeville, primarily in New York. He returned to the screen in the 1940s as Scruno, a member of the East Side Kids (later the Bowery Boys), and appeared in a few more features before retiring from films permanently after WW II and pursuing a career in the aerospace industry. In later years Morrison occasionally put in cameo appearances on TV's "Good Times" and "The Jeffersons"; in 1987 he was inducted into the Black Filmmakers Hall of Fame. His films include: *Features*—PENROD (1922); BOYS OF THE CITY; FUGITIVE FROM A PRISON CAMP; THAT GANG OF MINE (1940); BOWERY BLITZKRIEG; FLYING WILD; PRIDE OF THE BOWERY; SPOOKS RUN WILD (1941); IN THIS OUR LIFE; LET'S GET TOUGH; MR. WISE GUY; 'NEATH BROOKLYN BRIDGE; SMART ALECKS (1942); CLANCY STREET BOYS; GHOSTS ON THE LOOSE; KID DYNAMITE (1943); FOLLOW THE LEADER; GREENWICH VILLAGE; SHINE ON, HARVEST MOON (1944). *"Our Gang" Shorts*—ONE TERRIBLE DAY; OUR GANG; A QUIET STREET; SATURDAY MORNING; YOUNG SHERLOCKS (1922); BACK STAGE; THE BIG SHOW; BOYS TO BOARD; THE CHAMPEEN; THE COBBLER; DERBY DAY; DOGS OF WAR; GIANTS VS. YANKS; JULY DAYS; LODGE NIGHT; NO NOISE; A PLEASANT JOURNEY; STAGE FRIGHT; SUNDAY CALM (1923); BIG BUSINESS; THE BUCCANEERS; COMMENCEMENT DAY; CRADLE ROBBERS; FAST COMPANY; IT'S A BEAR; SEEIN' THINGS; TIRE TROUBLE (1924).

Newman, Lionel

Born 4 Jan 1916, New Haven, Conn.; died 3 Feb. 1989, Los Angeles, Calif. Music Director-Composer-Conductor Newman came to Hollywood as a teenager, and got a job conducting for the Earl Carroll Vanities. Later, he became Mae West's piano player, and performed with the star until 1943, when he joined Fox as a rehearsal pianist. He remained with the studio through 1985, composing, conducting, and/or supervising the scores of more than 250 films, garnering 11 Academy Award nominations along the way and winning a Best Musical Adaptation Oscar for 1969's HELLO, DOLLY! Newman, who also worked briefly for MGM near the end of his life, was one of five brothers who worked in the film industry, and was the uncle of singer-songwriter Randy Newman. His films include: SON OF FRANKENSTEIN (1939); JOHNNY APOLLO (m) (1940); BILL AND COO; KISS OF DEATH; NIGHTMARE ALLEY (1947); APARTMENT FOR PEGGY; CRY OF THE CITY; DEEP WATERS; GIVE MY REGARDS TO BROADWAY; GREEN GRASS OF WYOMING; LUCK OF THE IRISH; ROAD HOUSE; SCUDDA-HOO! SCUDDA-HAY!; THE STREET WITH NO NAME; THAT WONDERFUL URGE; WALLS OF JERICHO; YOU WERE MEANT FOR ME (1948); COME TO THE STABLE; FATHER WAS A FULLBACK; I WAS A MALE WAR BRIDE; IT HAPPENS EVERY SPRING; SLATTERY'S HURRICANE; THIEVES' HIGHWAY (1949); CHEAPER BY THE DOZEN; I'LL GET BY; THE JACKPOT (m); LOVE THAT BRUTE; MISTER 880; MOTHER DIDN'T TELL ME; STELLA; THREE CAME HOME; TICKET TO TOMAHAWK; WABASH AVENUE; WHEN WILLIE COMES MARCHING HOME; WHERE THE SIDEWALK ENDS (1950); AS YOUNG AS YOU FEEL; ELOPEMENT; FIXED BAYONETS; FOLLOW THE SUN; THE FROGMEN; GOLDEN GIRL; THE GUY WHO CAME BACK; HALLS OF MONTEZUMA; I CAN GET IT FOR YOU WHOLESALE; I'D CLIMB THE HIGHEST MOUNTAIN; LET'S MAKE IT LEGAL; LOVE NEST; MEET ME AFTER THE SHOW; THE MODEL AND THE MARRIAGE BROKER; MR. BELVEDERE RINGS THE BELL; RAWHIDE (m&md); THE SECRET OF CONVICT LAKE; THE THIRTEENTH LETTER; YOU'RE IN THE NAVY NOW (1951); BELLS ON THEIR TOES; BLOODHOUNDS OF BROADWAY (m); DEADLINE—U.S.A.; DIPLOMATIC COURIER; DON'T BOTHER TO KNOCK (m); DREAMBOAT; THE I DON'T CARE GIRL; LES MISERABLES; LYDIA BAILEY; MONKEY BUSINESS; MY PAL GUS; MY WIFE'S BEST FRIEND; NIGHT WITHOUT SLEEP; THE OUTCASTS OF POKER FLAT; THE PRIDE OF ST. LOUIS; RED SKIES OF MONTANA; RETURN OF THE TEXAN; SOMETHING FOR THE BIRDS; WE'RE NOT MARRIED (1952); A BLUEPRINT FOR MURDER; CITY OF BAD MEN (m); DANGEROUS CROSSING (m); DOWN AMONG THE SHELTERING PALMS; GENTLEMEN PREFER BLONDES; THE GIRL NEXT DOOR; INFERNO; THE KID FROM LEFT FIELD (m); MAN IN THE ATTIC; MR. SCOUTMASTER; NIAGARA; PICKUP ON SOUTH STREET; POWDER RIVER; THE SILVER WHIP; TAXI; TITANIC; VICKI (1953); BROKEN LANCE; THE GAMBLER FROM NATCHEZ (m); GORILLA AT LARGE; NIGHT PEOPLE; PRINCESS OF THE NILE (m); RIVER OF NO RETURN; THE ROCKET MAN (m); THE SIEGE AT RED RIVER (m); THERE'S NO BUSINESS LIKE SHOW BUSINESS; THREE YOUNG TEXANS (1954); THE GIRL IN THE RED VELVET SWING; GOOD MORNING, MISS DOVE; HOUSE OF BAMBOO; HOW TO BE VERY, VERY POPULAR; THE RACERS; THE RAINS OF RANCHIPUR; SEVEN CITIES OF GOLD; SOLDIER OF FORTUNE; THE VIEW FROM POMPEY'S HEAD; VIOLENT SATURDAY; WHITE FEATHER (1955); THE BEST THINGS IN LIFE ARE FREE (m); D-DAY, THE SIXTH OF JUNE; THE GIRL CAN'T HELP IT; THE HARDER THEY FALL; HILDA CRANE; THE KILLER IS LOOSE (m); A KISS BEFORE DYING (m); THE LAST WAGON (m); THE LIEUTENANT WORE SKIRTS; LOVE ME TENDER (m); ON THE THRESHOLD OF SPACE; THE PROUD ONES (m); THE REVOLT OF MAMIE STOVER; THE SOLID GOLD CADILLAC; TEENAGE REBEL; 23 PACES TO BAKER STREET (1956); AN AFFAIR TO REMEMBER; BERNARDINE (m); DESK SET; THE ENEMY BELOW; KISS THEM FOR ME (m); NO DOWN PAYMENT; THE SUN ALSO RISES; THE TRUE STORY OF JESSE JAMES; THE WAY TO THE GOLD (m); THE WAYWARD BUS; WILL SUCCESS SPOIL ROCK HUNTER? (1957); THE BRAVADOS (m); THE GIFT OF LOVE; IN LOVE AND WAR; THE LONG, HOT SUMMER; MARDI GRAS (m&md); A NICE LITTLE BANK THAT SHOULD BE ROBBED (m); RALLY 'ROUND THE FLAG, BOYS!; SING, BOY, SING (m); THE YOUNG LIONS; 10 NORTH FREDERICK (1958); COMPULSION (m); HOUND-DOG MAN; JOURNEY TO THE CENTER OF THE EARTH; A PRIVATE'S AFFAIR; THE REMARKABLE MR. PENNYPACKER; SAY ONE FOR ME; THE SOUND AND THE FURY; WARLOCK; WOMAN OBSESSED (1959); LET'S MAKE LOVE (m&md); NORTH TO ALASKA (m&md); WAKE ME WHEN IT'S OVER (1960); MOVE OVER, DARLING (m) (1963); THE PLEASURE SEEKERS (m) (1964); DO NOT DISTURB (m) (1965); THE SAND PEBBLES (1966); DOCTOR DOLITTLE; THE ST. VALENTINE'S DAY MASSACRE (1967); A FLEA IN HER EAR; THE BOSTON STRANGLER (m) (1968); HELLO, DOLLY! (m&md) (1969); THE GREAT WHITE HOPE (m) (1970); THE SALZBURG CONNECTION (m&md); WHEN THE LEGENDS DIE (1972); THE BLUE BIRD (m) (1976); UNFAITHFULLY YOURS (1984).

O'Hanlon, George

Born 1912; died 11 Feb. 1989, Burbank, Calif.

Actor-TV Writer

Though he essayed character roles in films ranging from JEZEBEL to ROCKY, played William Bendix's neighbor Dudley on TV's "Life of Riley" and the husband on radio's "Me and Janie," wrote for Jackie Gleason and appeared in the Warner Bros. "Behind the 8-Ball" shorts, O'Hanlon will be best remembered as the voice of George Jetson, leader of the 1960s' prime-time cartoon clan "The Jetsons." O'Hanlon won the part of Hanna-Barbera's futuristic family man in 1962, after being turned down for the role of Fred Flintstone. He reprises the role in JETSONS: THE MOVIE, scheduled for a Christmas 1989 release. His films include: JEZEBEL (1938); HELL'S KITCHEN; WOMEN IN THE WIND (1939); A CHILD IS BORN; THE FIGHTING 69TH; SAILOR'S LADY (1940); NAVY BLUES; NEW WINE (1941); MAN FROM HEAD-QUARTERS (1942); CORVETTE K-225; HERS TO HOLD; LADIES' DAY; NEARLY EIGHTEEN (1943); HEAD-ING FOR HEAVEN; THE HUCK-STERS; THE SPIRIT OF WEST POINT (1947); ARE YOU WITH IT?; THE COUNTERFEITERS; JUNE BRIDE (1948); JOE PALOOKA IN THE BIG FIGHT; ZAMBA (1949); THE TANKS ARE COMING (1951); CATTLE TOWN; THE LION AND THE HORSE; PARK ROW (1952); BATTLE STATIONS (1956); KRONOS (1957); $1,000,000 DUCK (1971); NOW YOU SEE HIM, NOW YOU DON'T (1972); CHARLEY AND THE ANGEL (1973); ROCKY (1976); JETSONS: THE MOVIE (forth-coming).

Olivier, Laurence [Sir Laurence Olivier, Lord Olivier]

Born 22 May 1907, Dorking, England; died 11 July 1989, Ashurst, England

Film/Stage Actor-Director-Producer

The man generally considered the greatest English-speaking actor of his generation made his stage debut at age nine, playing Brutus in a school version of "Julius Caesar." In the audience was Sybil Thorndike, who reportedly told Olivier's clergyman father that his son was "absolutely an actor. Born to it." By age 15 he had appeared (in another school production) at Stratford-on-Avon, as Katherine in "The Taming of the Shrew." He made his professional debut soon thereafter, and in 1926 joined the Birmingham Repertory. A West End regular by 1930, he gained acclaim that year in Noel Coward's "Private Lives"—meeting his first wife, actress Jill Esmond, when the production moved to Broadway in 1931—and made his screen debut in THE TEMPORARY WIDOW. After being fired from his role as Greta Garbo's

Laurence Olivier (center) with Eileen Herlie and Basil Sydney in HAMLET.

lover in QUEEN CHRISTINA (1933), Olivier made a "comeback" onstage in Coward's "Theatre Royal," but the production in which he may be said to have "arrived" as a great actor was the famous West End "Romeo and Juliet" of 1935, in which he and John Gielgud alternated the roles of Romeo and Mercutio over the course of 155 shows. By 1939, Olivier had established himself, mainly through a series of Shakespearean *tours de force*, as a star of British theater and films (the latter including FIRE OVER ENGLAND, in which he acted with his future wife Vivien Leigh) and was ready to conquer Hollywood as Heathcliff in WUTHERING HEIGHTS. (Olivier credited director William Wyler, who initially found his style overblown, with teaching him how to act onscreen.) The role won him the first of nine Oscar nominations and international stardom as a screen heartthrob—a status reinforced by his performances in 1940's REBECCA and PRIDE AND PREJU-DICE. Olivier's greatest years were yet to come, however. After serving in WW II, he was codirector (with Ralph Richardson) of the Old Vic for a brief but memorable time, and in 1945 performed his famous "Oedipuff" double bill—leaving audi-ences exhausted by his turn in the tragic title role of "Oedipus Rex," only to return later in the evening as the fop Mr. Puff in Sheridan's "The Critic." While at the Old Vic, Olivier began work on HENRY V (1944), serving as director, producer, and star. He repeated the feat in HAMLET (1948) and RICHARD III (1955)—together, the three films established Olivier as Shakespeare's definitive English-lan-guage screen interpreter, both behind and before the cameras, and at the same time did much to popularize the Bard with hith-erto culture-shy audiences. (His planned film of "Macbeth," costarring Leigh, was

never brought to the screen.) By the mid-50s, however, Olivier suffered professional setbacks (his THE PRINCE AND THE SHOWGIRL, with Marilyn Monroe, was ill-received) and personal tragedy: Leigh was suffering increasingly from mental ill-ness, and their marriage was failing even as they reigned as British theater's Royal Cou-ple. Never one to balk at risks, Olivier switched gears drastically in 1956, when he starred at the Royal Court Theatre in John Osborne's Angry Young Man classic "The Entertainer." As that play's seedy title char-acter, the vaudevillian Archie Rice, Olivier bucked not only his own establishment-sanctioned cultural eminence but also the establishment itself. His performance was so powerful that he won accolades, both on stage and in Tony Richardson's 1960 screen version. Having divorced Leigh, Olivier married Joan Plowright, who also appeared in "The Entertainer," in 1961. Two years later he was named the first artistic director of Britain's National The-atre. During his 10-year stint there, he directed and/or starred in (despite a now-famous, five-year bout with stage fright) a series of acclaimed productions, among them "Long Day's Journey into Night," "The Dance of Death" (filmed in 1971), "Othello" (filmed in 1965), and "The Mer-chant of Venice." In 1974 he was struck with the first of several illnesses that crip-pled him in his last years, and gave his last public performance in London (in Trevor Griffith's "The Party"). Olivier subse-quently took on more film and television roles, character parts that allowed him to continue his lifelong preoccupation with technique—building his character from the outside in, as he said, rather than from the inside out (as favored by Method-influ-enced actors). Giving performances of varying seriousness in works ranging from the excellent SLEUTH; MARATHON

MAN; "Brideshead Revisited"; and 1983's televised "King Lear" to the awful THE BETSY or THE JAZZ SINGER (1980), the ailing actor continued to display the characteristics that had distinguished him throughout his career: versatility, technical assurance and audacity, physical courage and stamina, and sheer power of presence. Knighted in 1947 and made a baron in 1970, Olivier was the author of *Confessions of an Actor* and *On Acting*. His last professional appearance was in a cameo role in Derek Jarman's film adaptation of Britten's "War Requiem." His films include: THE TEMPORARY WIDOW (1930); FRIENDS AND LOVERS; HER STRANGE DESIRE; THE YELLOW TICKET (1931); WESTWARD PASSAGE (1932); PERFECT UNDERSTANDING (1933); NO FUNNY BUSINESS (1934); AS YOU LIKE IT; CONQUEST OF THE AIR (docudrama); I STAND CONDEMNED (1936); FIRE OVER ENGLAND (1937); THE DIVORCE OF LADY X (1938); CLOUDS OVER EUROPE; WUTHERING HEIGHTS (1939); CONQUEST OF THE AIR; PRIDE AND PREJUDICE; REBECCA; TWENTY-ONE DAYS TOGETHER (1940); THE INVADERS; THAT HAMILTON WOMAN; WORDS FOR BATTLE (docu; voice only) (1941); HENRY V (a,d&p); THIS HAPPY BREED (1944); ADVENTURE FOR TWO (1945); HAMLET (a,d,w&p) (1948); CARRIE; THE MAGIC BOX (1952); THE BEGGAR'S OPERA (a&p); A QUEEN IS CROWNED (docu; voice only) (1953); RICHARD III (a,d&p) (1956); THE PRINCE AND THE SHOWGIRL (a,d&p) (1957); THE DEVIL'S DISCIPLE (1959); THE ENTERTAINER; SPARTACUS (1960); TERM OF TRIAL (1962); BUNNY LAKE IS MISSING; OTHELLO (1965); KHARTOUM (1966); ROMEO AND JULIET (narration); THE SHOES OF THE FISHERMAN (1968); THE BATTLE OF BRITAIN; OH! WHAT A LOVELY WAR (1969); DAVID COPPERFIELD (1970); THE DANCE OF DEATH; NICHOLAS AND ALEXANDRA (1971); LADY CAROLINE LAMB; SLEUTH (1972); THREE SISTERS (a&d) (1974); MARATHON MAN (1976); A BRIDGE TOO FAR; THE SEVEN-PER-CENT SOLUTION; UNCLE VANYA (1977); THE BETSY; THE BOYS FROM BRAZIL (1978); DRACULA; A LITTLE ROMANCE (1979); THE JAZZ SINGER (1980); CLASH OF THE TITANS; INCHON (1981); WAGNER (1983); THE BOUNTY; THE JIGSAW MAN (1984); WILD GEESE II (1985); WAR REQUIEM (1988).

Ondine [Bob Olivo]
Born 1937; died 27 April 1989, New York, N.Y.
Actor

Born Bob Olivo, Ondine adopted his pseudonym as a member of New York's gay subculture in the early 1960s. One of Andy Warhol's underground "superstars" during his Factory's prolific period of experimental filmmaking, Ondine appeared in VINYL; THE CHELSEA GIRLS; and FOUR STARS, the last of which was edited into THE LOVES OF ONDINE. He was also active in New York's "ridiculous" theater fringe, appearing in Theater of the Ridiculous productions at the La Mama theater and performing in plays by Charles Ludlam, Michael Smith, and Ron Tavel. His films include: RAW WEEKEND (1964); VINYL (1965); THE CHELSEA GIRLS; FOUR STARS (1967); THE LOVES OF ONDINE (1968); THE TELEPHONE BOOK (1971); SUGAR COOKIES (1973); SILENT NIGHT, BLOODY NIGHT (1974).

Oswald, Gerd
Born 9 June 1916, Berlin, Germany; died 22 May 1989, Los Angeles, Calif.
Actor Director-Screenwriter-Producer
Oswald entered show business as an actor, appearing in the films of his father, Austrian producer-director-impresario Richard Oswald, and also on the stage. He became his father's assistant, accompanying him to the US in 1938, where the younger Oswald became an assistant director in Hollywood in the 1940s, taking on producing chores with Fox in the 50s. His first and best-known film as a director, A KISS BEFORE DYING, starring Robert Wagner, was released in 1956. Oswald later directed Wagner on TV's "It Takes a Thief," one of the director's many TV credits (ranging from "Bonanza" and "Perry Mason" to the 1980s "Twilight Zone"). His films include: THE BRASS LEGEND; A KISS BEFORE DYING (1956); CRIME OF PASSION; FURY AT SHOWDOWN; VALERIE (1957); PARIS HOLIDAY; SCREAMING MIMI (1958); AM TAG ALS DER REGEN KAM (1959); THREE MOVES TO FREEDOM (d&w) (1960); BRAINWASHED (1961); THE LONGEST DAY (one sequence) (1962); TEMPESTA SU CEYLON (1963); AGENT FOR H.A.R.M. (1966); 80 STEPS TO JONAH (w) (1969); BUNNY O'HARE (p&d) (1971); BIS ZUR BITTEREN NEIGE (1975).

Payne, John
Born 23 May 1912, Roanoke, Va.; died 6 Dec. 1989, Malibu, Calif.
Actor
The son of a gentleman farmer and an amateur singer, Payne studied singing at Juilliard and acting at Columbia. He started out as a professional wrestler and performer in stock, then moved to Hollywood after a scout saw him perform (as an understudy) in a 1935 Beatrice Lillie revue. After making his screen debut in

DODSWORTH, Payne signed with Warner Bros. (for whom he made five films), then moved to Fox, where he rose to stardom as a leading man opposite Betty Grable, Alice Faye, June Haver, and others in films like TIN PAN ALLEY; HELLO, FRISCO, HELLO; and THE DOLLY SISTERS. Reportedly tired of musicals, Payne bought the rights to the soap opera SENTIMENTAL JOURNEY and convinced Darryl Zanuck to film it in 1946; in another shrewd move the next year, he bought the story for and ensured the making of what is now his best-known film, the Christmas classic MIRACLE ON 34TH STREET. In the 1950s, he switched to western and action roles, then left movies to produce and star in his own TV series, "The Restless Gun," in 1957. He returned briefly to films as the director-star of THEY RAN FOR THEIR LIVES (1968) and in THE SAVAGE WILD (1970), and reunited with Faye in a touring revival of the revue "Good News" in 1973. Formerly married to Anne Shirley and Gloria de Haven, he was the father of actress Julie Payne. His films include: DODSWORTH (1936); FAIR WARNING; HATS OFF; LOVE ON TOAST (1937); COLLEGE SWING; GARDEN OF THE MOON (1938); INDIANAPOLIS SPEEDWAY; KID NIGHTINGALE; WINGS OF THE NAVY (1939); THE GREAT PROFILE; KING OF THE LUMBERJACKS; MARYLAND; STAR DUST; TEAR GAS SQUAD; TIN PAN ALLEY (1940); THE GREAT AMERICAN BROADCAST; REMEMBER THE DAY; SUN VALLEY SERENADE; WEEKEND IN HAVANA (1941); FOOTLIGHT SERENADE; ICELAND; SPRINGTIME IN THE ROCKIES; TO THE SHORES OF TRIPOLI (1942); HELLO, FRISCO, HELLO (1943); THE DOLLY SISTERS (1945);

THE RAZOR'S EDGE; SENTIMENTAL JOURNEY; WAKE UP AND DREAM (1946); MIRACLE ON 34TH STREET (1947); LARCENY; THE SAXON CHARM (1948); CAPTAIN CHINA; THE CROOKED WAY; EL PASO (1949); THE EAGLE AND THE HAWK; TRIPOLI (1950); CROSSWINDS; PASSAGE WEST (1951); THE BLAZING FOREST; CARIBBEAN; KANSAS CITY CONFIDENTIAL (1952); RAIDERS OF THE SEVEN SEAS; THE VANQUISHED; 99 RIVER STREET (1953); RAILS INTO LARAMIE; SILVER LODE (1954); HELL'S ISLAND; THE ROAD TO DENVER; SANTA FE PASSAGE; TENNESSEE'S PARTNER (1955); THE BOSS (a,p&co-w); HOLD BACK THE NIGHT; REBEL IN TOWN; SLIGHTLY SCARLET (1956); BAILOUT AT 43,000; HIDDEN FEAR (1957); THEY RAN FOR THEIR LIVES (a&d) (1968); THE SAVAGE WILD (1970).

Pringle, Aileen [Aileen Bisbee]
Born 23 July 1895, San Francisco, Calif.; died 16 Dec. 1989, New York, N.Y.
Actress
The daughter of well-to-do businessman George Bisbee, Pringle was educated abroad, and made her acting debut on the London stage in 1915. Returning Stateside, she appeared on Broadway and in her first film, REDHEAD, before reaching her 20s. She soon became a familiar face in silent films, frequently playing opposite Lew Cody, and joined Colleen Moore as one of the screen's leading liberated sirens when she starred in THREE WEEKS and HIS HOUR (both 1924), scripted by "flapper" popularizer Elinor Glyn (who also wrote Clara Bow's IT [1927]). In 1929, she successfully segued into talkie leads, but demand for her talents soon lessened and she officially retired from films in 1939, although she continued to appear occasionally as an extra and bit player. Pringle's second husband was novelist James M. Cain. Her films include: REDHEAD (1919); EARTH-BOUND (1920); OATHBOUND; STRANGER'S BANQUET (1922); THE CHRISTIAN; DON'T MARRY FOR MONEY; IN THE PALACE OF THE KING; MY AMERICAN WIFE; SOULS FOR SALE; THE TIGER'S CLAW (1923); HIS HOUR; MARRIED FLIRTS; NAME THE MAN; ROMANCE OF A QUEEN; THREE WEEKS; TRUE AS STEEL; WIFE OF THE CENTAUR (1924); A KISS IN THE DARK; THE MYSTIC; ONE YEAR TO LIVE; SOUL MATES; A THIEF IN PARADISE; WILDFIRE (1925); THE GREAT DECEPTION; TIN GODS; THE WILDERNESS WOMAN (1926); ADAM AND EVIL; BODY AND SOUL; TEA FOR THREE (1927); THE BABY CYCLONE; BEAU BROADWAY; DREAM OF LOVE; MAN ABOUT TOWN; SHOW PEOPLE; WICKED-NESS PREFERRED (1928); NIGHT PARADE; A SINGLE MAN; WALL STREET (1929); PRINCE OF DIAMONDS; PUTTIN' ON THE RITZ; SOLDIERS AND WOMEN (1930); ARE THESE OUR CHILDREN?; CONVICTED; MURDER AT MIDNIGHT; SON OF MINE; SUBWAY EXPRESS (1931); AGE OF CONSENT; FAME STREET; THE PHANTOM OF CRESTWOOD (1932); BY APPOINTMENT ONLY (1933); LOVE PAST THIRTY; ONCE TO EVERY BACHELOR (1934); JANE EYRE; SONS OF STEEL (1935); PICCADILLY JIM; THE UNGUARDED HOUR; WIFE VERSUS SECRETARY (1936); JOHN MEADE'S WOMAN; THE LAST OF MRS. CHEYNEY; NOTHING SACRED; SHE'S NO LADY; THANKS FOR LISTENING (1937); MANPROOF; TOO HOT TO HANDLE (1938); CALLING DR. KILDARE; THE HARDYS RIDE HIGH; THE NIGHT OF NIGHTS; SHOULD A GIRL MARRY? (1939); THEY DIED WITH THEIR BOOTS ON (1942); DR. GILLESPIE'S CRIMINAL CASE; THE YOUNGEST PROFESSION (1943); LAURA; SINCE YOU WENT AWAY (1944).

Quayle, Anthony [Sir Anthony Quayle]
Born 7 Sept. 1913, Ainsdale, England; died 20 Oct. 1989, London, England
Actor-Stage Director
Quayle made his professional acting debut in London vaudeville in 1931. He subsequently joined the Old Vic, took his first Broadway bow in "The Country Wife" in 1936, and gained his first film role in Anthony Asquith's PGYMALION in 1938. By this time a West End veteran who excelled in Shakespeare, Quayle interrupted his acting career to serve in WW II, an experience he fictionalized in two nov-

els, *Eight Hours from England* (1945) and *On Such a Night* (1947). Afterwards, he made his directing debut with a 1946 London version of "Crime and Punishment" starring John Gielgud, Peter Ustinov, and Edith Evans, and was named head of the Shakespeare Memorial Theatre at Stratford-on-Avon in 1948. During his eight-year tenure at Stratford, Quayle performed in and/or directed many productions, and persuaded Britain's top actors to perform with the company for nominal pay. He also continued to act in films (and later on TV) as a way of making ends meet, finding his best roles in DESERT ATTACK; WOMAN IN A DRESSING GOWN; THE GUNS OF NAVARONE; LAWRENCE OF ARABIA; and ANNE OF THE THOUSAND DAYS (and gaining a Best Supporting Actor Oscar nomination for his Cardinal Wolsey in the last). But he remained best known as the stage actor who starred in "Galileo," "Up the Tree," and "Tamburlaine the Great" on Broadway, and who scored his first real smash hit in the London and New York productions of "Sleuth" in 1970. Quayle joined the Round Table of British acting knights in 1985. His films include: PYGMALION (1938); HAMLET (1948); SARABAND (1949); OH ROSALINDA; THE WRONG MAN (1956); NO TIME FOR TEARS; PURSUIT OF GRAF SPEE; WOMAN IN A DRESSING GOWN (1957); DESERT ATTACK; THE MAN WHO WOULDN'T TALK (1958); TARZAN'S GREATEST ADVENTURE (1959); IT TAKES A THIEF (1960); THE GUNS OF NAVARONE (1961); DAMN THE DEFIANT!; IMMORAL CHARGE; LAWRENCE OF ARABIA (1962); EAST OF SUDAN; THE FALL OF THE ROMAN EMPIRE (1964); OPERATION CROSSBOW (1965); THE POPPY IS ALSO A FLOWER; A STUDY IN TERROR (1966); ANNE OF THE THOUSAND DAYS; BEFORE WINTER COMES; MacKENNA'S GOLD (1969); EVERYTHING YOU ALWAYS WANTED TO KNOW ABOUT SEX, BUT WERE AFRAID TO ASK (1972); THE NELSON AFFAIR (1973); THE TAMARIND SEED (1974); GREAT EXPECTATIONS (1975); THE EAGLE HAS LANDED; MOSES (1976); THE CHOSEN (1978); MURDER BY DECREE (1979); BUSTER; LA LEGGENDA DEL SANTO BEVITORE; SILENT NIGHT (1988).

Quine, Richard
Born 12 Nov. 1920, Detroit, Mich.; died 10 June 1989, Los Angeles, Calif.
Actor-Director-Screenwriter
Quine started out in vaudeville as a child, then moved on to radio and films, debuting on-screen at age 13 in COUNSELLOR-AT-LAW. In the late 1930s, the singer-dancer-actor appeared on Broadway in "My Sister Eileen," leading in turn

to his casting in the 1942 film adaptation of the play and in such MGM musicals BABES ON BROADWAY and FOR ME AND MY GAL. Two years after his lead performance in WE'VE NEVER BEEN LICKED, Quine debuted as a film director, in collaboration with William Asher, with LEATHER GLOVES in 1948. In the next decade, he made B musicals and thrillers (several scripted by Blake Edwards) and the second remake of MY SISTER EILEEN (a musical) before moving on to the increasingly dark comedies, often starring Jack Lemmon, for which he was best known, including BELL, BOOK, AND CANDLE and HOW TO MURDER YOUR WIFE. His films include: COUN-SELLOR-AT-LAW; THE WORLD CHANGES (1933); DAMES; DINKY; A DOG OF FLANDERS; JANE EYRE; LITTLE MEN (1935); KING OF THE UNDERWORLD; LIFE RETURNS (1939); BABES ON BROADWAY (1941); DR. GILLESPIE'S NEW ASSISTANT; FOR ME AND MY GAL; MY SISTER EILEEN; STAND BY FOR ACTION; TISH (1942); WE'VE NEVER BEEN LICKED (1943); THE COCKEYED MIRACLE (1946); COMMAND DECI-SION; LEATHER GLOVES (p&d); WORDS AND MUSIC (1948); THE CLAY PIGEON (1949); FLYING MIS-SILE; NO SAD SONGS FOR ME; ROOKIE FIREMAN (1950); PURPLE HEART DIARY (d); SUNNY SIDE OF THE STREET (d) (1951); RAINBOW 'ROUND MY SHOULDER (d&w); SOUND OFF (d&w) (1952); ALL ASHORE (d&w); CRUISIN' DOWN THE RIVER (d&w); SIREN OF BAGDAD (d) (1953); DRIVE A CROOKED ROAD (d&w); PUSHOVER (d); SO THIS IS PARIS (d) (1954); BRING YOUR SMILE ALONG (w); MY SISTER EILEEN (d&w) (1955); HE LAUGHED LAST (w); THE SOLID GOLD CADIL-LAC (d); FULL OF LIFE (d) (1956); OPERATION MAD BALL (d) (1957); BELL, BOOK AND CANDLE (d) (1958); IT HAPPENED TO JANE (p&d) (1959); STRANGERS WHEN WE MEET (p&d); THE WORLD OF SUZIE WONG (d) (1960); THE NOTORIOUS LANDLADY (d) (1962); PARIS WHEN IT SIZZLES (p&d); SEX AND THE SINGLE GIRL (d) (1964); HOW TO MURDER YOUR WIFE (d); SYNANON (p&d) (1965); HOTEL (d); OH DAD, POOR DAD, MAMA'S HUNG YOU IN THE CLOSET AND I'M FEELIN' SO SAD (d); HOTEL (d) (1967); A TALENT FOR LOVING (d) (1969); THE MOONSHINE WAR (d) (1970); W (d) (1974); THE PRISONER OF ZENDA (d) (1979).

Radner, Gilda
Born in Michigan; died 20 May 1989, Los Angeles, Calif., age 42
Comedienne-Actress

After starting out as a member of the Toronto "Second City" troupe, Radner moved to New York and joined the "National Lampoon Radio Hour" and "National Lampoon Show," several of whose alumni became, along with Radner, the original writers and stars of TV's "Saturday Night Live." The show gained Radner fame in the guise of such comic characters as Emily Litella, Roseanne Roseannadanna, and Lisa Lupner, work that won her an Emmy in 1978. After leaving the show in 1980, she appeared on Broadway in "Lunch Hour" and in several films, meeting her future husband, Gene Wilder, while working on HANKY PANKY in 1982. *It's Always Something*, Radner's book describing life with cancer, was released shortly after her death. Her films include: THE LAST DETAIL (1973); FIRST FAMILY; GILDA LIVE (1980); HANKY PANKY (1982); THE WOMAN IN RED (1984); MOVERS AND SHAKERS (1985); HAUNTED HONEYMOON (1986).

Robinson, Sugar Ray [Walker Smith, Jr.]
Born 3 May 1921, Detroit, Mich.; died 12 April 1989, Culver City, Calif.
Boxer
A five-time middleweight and two-time welterweight boxing champion, the original "Sugar Ray" inspired the "pound for pound" assessment of boxing greatness through his mastery in different divisions. Born Walker Smith, Jr., Robinson (who became known as Ray Robinson as a teen,

after he borrowed a fellow amateur's union card) made his pro debut in 1940, eventually compiling a record of 179 victories and 19 losses (none by knockout). Known for his flashy style in and out of the ring (he spent 22 months between titles in the 50s performing as a tap dancer), Robinson, despite negotiating his own contracts, boxed past his prime to keep financially afloat and retired in December 1965. He subsequently appeared in THE DETEC-TIVE; the all-star debacle CANDY; and the film adaptation of George Plimpton's PAPER LION, all in 1968; and in THE TODD KILLINGS in 1971.

Roud, Richard
Born 6 July 1929, Boston, Mass.; died 13 Feb. 1989, Nimes, France
Film Historian-Critic-Festival Director
The founder (with Amos Vogel) and long-time director of the New York Film Festival, Roud began writing on film as the London correspondent for *Cahiers du Cinema* in the 1950s. He later became film critic for the *Manchester Guardian*, and

contributed to *Sight and Sound* and *Films and Filming*. Through the British Film Institute, Roud became program director of the BFI-sponsored London Film Festival in 1959, his success there leading the Lincoln Center to invite him to organize and direct the first New York Film Festival in 1963. Roud remained the festival's program director and program committee chairman (becoming festival director as well in 1969) until 1987, when he was removed from the post, prompting several committee members to resign in protest. During his term as director, he built the festival into an influential force in bringing foreign films to the attention of American programmers, introducing to US screens many of the most important new directors in the Italian, German, Swiss, US, and French cinemas, especially the filmmakers of the French New Wave. Roud, who received France's Legion of Honor for his "contribution to the prestige of the French cinematographic art and its commercial progress in the United States" in 1979, was the author of influential monographs on Jean-Luc Godard, Jean-Marie Straub, and Max Ophuls; *A Passion for Films: Henri Langlois and the Cinemateque Francaise*; and a study of Francois Truffaut completed shortly before Roud's death.

Schaeffer, Rebecca
Born Eugene, Ore.; died 18 July 1989, Los Angeles, Calif., age 21
Actress
A professional model by the age of 14, Schaeffer worked in Japan, then returned to the States in 1984, landing a role in the TV soap opera "One Life to Live." Roles in Woody Allen's RADIO DAYS (1987), made-for-TV movies, and the TV series "My Sister Sam" (costarring Schaeffer with Pam Dawber) followed. In 1989, Schaeffer appeared as the daughter of Jacqueline Bisset's character in SCENES

FROM THE CLASS STRUGGLE IN BEVERLY HILLS, released just before she was murdered by an "obsessive fan," attaining a tragic posthumous stardom in the aftermath. She had just wrapped filming on Dyan Cannon's feature directorial debut, ONE POINT OF VIEW; a TV miniseries on the *Achille Lauro* hijacking that costarred Schaeffer is also forthcoming.

Schaffner, Franklin
Born 30 May 1920, Tokyo, Japan; died 2 July 1989, Santa Monica, Calif.
Film/TV/Stage Director

Born in Japan to American missionaries, Schaffner returned to the US and studied law, but after WW II service became an assistant director with the "The March of Time." He next joined CBS-TV's news and public affairs department, and eventually directed programs ranging from the documentary "Tour of the White House" with Jackie Kennedy to dramatic programs, including "Playhouse 90," "Studio One," and the original TV broadcasts of "Twelve Angry Men" and "The Caine Mutiny Court-Martial," both of which won him Emmys. Schaffner staged "Advise and Consent" on Broadway in 1960, and in 1963 made his film debut with THE STRIPPER, an adaptation of a William Inge play starring Joanne Woodward. His subsequent films, varying widely in subject but often informed by a sense of history, include the Gore Vidal story THE BEST MAN; PLANET OF THE APES; PATTON, which won Schaffner an Academy Award; NICHOLAS AND ALEXANDRA; and THE BOYS FROM BRAZIL. LIONHEART, made in 1987, and WELCOME HOME, filmed in 1989, were unreleased at the time of his death. His films include: THE STRIPPER (1963); THE BEST MAN (1964); THE WAR

LORD (1965); THE DOUBLE MAN (a&d) (1967); PLANET OF THE APES (1968); PATTON (1970); NICHOLAS AND ALEXANDRA (1971); PAPILLON (p&d) (1973); ISLANDS IN THE STREAM (1977); THE BOYS FROM BRAZIL (1978); SPHINX (1981); YES, GIORGIO (1982); WELCOME HOME (1989); LIONHEART (forthcoming).

Scott, Walter
Born Cleveland, Ohio; died 2 Feb. 1989, Los Angeles, Calif., age 82
Set Decorator
Hired by Fox's set decoration department in 1931, Scott became a set decorator two years later and was supervising set decorator from 1952 to 1972, remaining with Fox throughout his career and working on many of the studio's best-known films. A 21-time Academy Award nominee, Scott won Oscars for his set decoration on THE ROBE; THE KING AND I; THE DIARY OF ANNE FRANK; FANTASTIC VOYAGE; HELLO, DOLLY!; and CLEOPATRA. His films include: HEAVEN CAN WAIT; THE MOON IS DOWN (1943); THE LODGER; THE PURPLE HEART (1944); NOB HILL (1945); FOREVER AMBER; THE HOMESTRETCH (1947); APARTMENT FOR PEGGY; CALL NORTHSIDE 777; A LETTER TO THREE WIVES; THAT LADY IN ERMINE; THAT WONDERFUL URGE (1948); HOUSE OF STRANGERS; I WAS A MALE WAR BRIDE; WHIRLPOOL (1949); UNDER MY SKIN; WHERE THE SIDEWALK ENDS (1950); PEOPLE WILL TALK; THE THIRTEENTH LETTER (1951); DEADLINE—U.S.A.; LES MISERABLES; MONKEY BUSINESS; MY COUSIN RACHEL; WITH A SONG IN MY HEART (1952); KING OF THE KHYBER RIFLES (1953); THE EGYPTIAN; HELL AND HIGH WATER; RIVER OF NO RETURN (1954); GOOD MORNING, MISS DOVE; HOUSE OF BAMBOO; THE LEFT HAND OF GOD; THE RAINS OF RANCHIPUR; THE SEVEN YEAR ITCH; SOLDIER OF FORTUNE; THE TALL MEN; UNTAMED; THE VIEW FROM POMPEY'S HEAD (1955); THE KING AND I; THE MAN IN THE GREY FLANNEL SUIT; TEENAGE REBEL; 23 PACES TO BAKER STREET (1956); AN AFFAIR TO REMEMBER; DESK SET; FORTY GUNS; KISS THEM FOR ME; KRONOS; OH MEN! OH WOMEN!; PEYTON PLACE; THE SUN ALSO RISES; THE THREE FACES OF EVE; THE TRUE STORY OF JESSE JAMES (1957); GANG WAR; IN LOVE AND WAR; THE LONG, HOT SUMMER; SHOWDOWN AT BOOT HILL; SOUTH PACIFIC (1958); JOURNEY TO THE CENTER OF THE EARTH; THE MAN WHO UNDERSTOOD WOMEN; A PRIVATE'S AFFAIR; RETURN OF THE FLY; SAY ONE FOR ME; THE STORY

ON PAGE ONE; WARLOCK; WOMAN OBSESSED (1959); FLAMING STAR; FROM THE TERRACE; THE LOST WORLD; NORTH TO ALASKA; SEVEN THIEVES; WILD RIVER (1960); THE COMANCHEROS; THE FIERCEST HEART; FRANCIS OF ASSISI; MISTY; PIRATES OF TORTUGA; RETURN TO PEYTON PLACE; THE RIGHT APPROACH; SANCTUARY; THE SECOND TIME AROUND; SNOW WHITE AND THE THREE STOOGES; TENDER IS THE NIGHT; VOYAGE TO THE BOTTOM OF THE SEA; WILD IN THE COUNTRY (1961); ADVENTURES OF A YOUNG MAN; FIVE WEEKS IN A BALLOON; MADISON AVENUE; MR. HOBBS TAKES A VACATION; STATE FAIR; SWINGIN' ALONG (1962); CLEOPATRA; MOVE OVER, DARLING; THE STRIPPER; TAKE HER, SHE'S MINE (1963); FATE IS THE HUNTER; GOODBYE CHARLIE; JOHN GOLDFARB, PLEASE COME HOME; THE PLEASURE SEEKERS; RIO CONCHOS; SHOCK TREATMENT; WHAT A WAY TO GO (1964); DEAR BRIGETTE; DO NOT DISTURB; MORITURI; THE REWARD; THE SOUND OF MUSIC (1965); I DEAL IN DANGER; OUR MAN FLINT; THE SAND PEBBLES; STAGECOACH; WAY . . . WAY OUT (1966); DOCTOR DOLITTLE; THE FLIM-FLAM MAN; A GUIDE FOR THE MARRIED MAN; HOMBRE; IN LIKE FLINT; THE ST. VALENTINE'S DAY MASSACRE; TONY ROME; VALLEY OF THE DOLLS (1967); THE DETECTIVE; LADY IN CEMENT; PLANET OF THE APES; THE SECRET LIFE OF AN AMERICAN WIFE; STAR!; THE SWEET RIDE; THE BOSTON STRANGLER (1968); BUTCH CASSIDY AND THE SUNDANCE KID; CHE!; HELLO, DOLLY!; JUSTINE; THE UNDEFEATED (1969); BENEATH THE PLANET OF THE APES; COVER ME BABE; THE GREAT WHITE HOPE; M; MOVE; THE ONLY GAME IN TOWN; TORA! TORA! TORA!; TRIBES (1970); ESCAPE FROM THE PLANET OF THE APES; THE MARRIAGE OF A YOUNG STOCKBROKER; THE MEPHISTO WALTZ; THE SEVEN MINUTES (1971); THE CULPEPPER CATTLE COMPANY (1972); HEX (1973).

Simenon, Georges
Born 13 Feb. 1903, Liege, Belgium; died 4 Sept. 1989, Lausanne, Switzerland
Novelist
As a teenager, Simenon worked as a newspaper reporter, but this cannot account for the incredible speed with which the creator of Inspector Maigret turned out his hundreds of books. He had already written his first novel when, at age 19, he began writing pulp stories for French weeklies. He quickly moved on to sensational dime nov-els—it is estimated that he wrote some 200 of these under 17 pseudonyms between the years of 1924 and 1933, making a comfortable living thereby. In 1931 he wrote the first of his 84 *romans policiers* featuring Maigret, a rather ordinary sort more notable for his love of creature comforts than for Mike Hammer machismo or for arcane erudition of the sort Holmes and Poirot display. Instead, the French sleuth relies on basic psychological insight to solve his cases, while Simenon relies on well-observed detail and psychological subtlety to sustain suspense. The formula worked smashingly: in 1932, one year after his birth, Maigret was already on the French screen in films by Duvivier, Renoir, and Tarride. The detective was subsequently portrayed by Michel Simon, Charles Laughton (THE MAN ON THE EIFFEL TOWER), Jean Gabin (MAIGRET LAYS A TRAP; MAIGRET ET L'AFFAIRE SAINT-FAICRE; MAIGRET VOIT ROUGE), and many others, especially during the period of escapist French filmmaking during the Occupation. In addition, Simenon wrote 136 novels under his own name that he called his "non-Maigrets," and these books—which include some of his most critically acclaimed and philosophically speculative work—proved equally popular as cinematic subjects. Gabin starred in Carne's LA MARIE DU PORT; Autant-Lara's LOVE IS MY PROFESSION; and THE CAT; among others, while Duvivier (PANIQUE), Tavernier (THE CLOCKMAKER), and Clouzot (who scripted STRANGERS IN THE HOUSE) were three of the more notable filmmakers to do non-Maigret adaptations. (Most recently, Patrice Leconte released the well-received MONSIEUR HIRE [1989].) Simenon—who retired in 1973 to work on his memoirs, which appeared in the US in 1981 as *Intimate Memoirs*—died the world's most widely published author, with 600 million copies of his books sold in 40 countries and 47 languages. Films based on his books include: LA NUIT DU CARREFOUR; LA TETE D'UN HOMME; LE CHIEN JAUNE (1932); LES CAVES DU MAJESTIC (1945); PANIQUE (1947); THE MAN ON THE EIFFEL TOWER; STRANGERS IN THE HOUSE; TEMPTATION HARBOR (1949); LA MARIE DU PORT; MIDNIGHT EPISODE (1951); BRELAN D'AS; LA VERITE SUR BEBE DONGE (1952); THE PARIS EXPRESS (1953); A LIFE IN THE BALANCE (1955); THE BOTTOM OF THE BOTTLE; LE SANG A LA TETE (1956); THE BROTHERS RICO (1957); LE PASSAGER CLANDESTIN; MAIGRET LAYS A TRAP (1958); FORBIDDEN FRUIT; LE BARON DE L'ECLUSE; LOVE IS MY PROFESSION; MAIGRET ET L'AFFAIRE ST. FIACRE (1959); LE PRESIDENT (1961); LE BATEAU D'EMILE; THE PASSION OF SLOW FIRE (1962); L'AINE DES FERCHAUX; MAIGRET VOIT ROUGE (1963); TROIS CHAMBRES A MANHATTAN (1965); MAIGRET UND SEIN GROSSTER FALL (1966); COP-OUT; MAIGRET A PIGALLE (1967); LE TRAIN (1973); THE CAT (1975); THE CLOCKMAKER (1976); THE HATTER'S GHOST (1982); L'ETOILE DU NORD (1983); MONSIEUR HIRE (1989).

Spinell, Joe [Joseph J. Spagnuolo]
Born New York, N.Y.; died 13 Jan. 1989, New York, N.Y., age 51
Actor
Spinell entered films in the role of gangster Willy Cicci in THE GODFATHER (playing the part again in the 1974 sequel THE GODFATHER, PART II), and was soon in demand for gangster and other character roles suited to his tough-guy build and face, working with Sylvester Stallone (PARADISE ALLEY; ROCKY; ROCKY II), Martin Scorsese (TAXI DRIVER); and Jonathan Demme (MELVIN AND HOWARD; MARRIED TO THE MOB), among others. In addition to his acting credits, Spinell cowrote, executive produced, and starred in the gore cult film MANIAC. His films include: THE GODFATHER (1972); COPS AND ROBBERS; THE SEVEN UPS (1973); THE GODFATHER, PART II (1974); FAREWELL, MY LOVELY; 92 IN THE SHADE; RANCHO DELUXE (1975); ROCKY; STAY HUNGRY; TAXI DRIVER (1976); SORCERER (1977); NUNZIO; ONE MAN JURY; PARADISE ALLEY (1978); LAST EMBRACE; ROCKY II; STARCRASH; TILT; WINTER KILLS (1979); BRUBAKER; CRUISING; THE FIRST

Joe Spinell with Caroline Munro in THE LAST HORROR FILM.

DEADLY SIN; FORBIDDEN ZONE; THE LITTLE DRAGONS; MANIAC (a&w); THE NINTH CONFIGURATION; MELVIN AND HOWARD (1980); NATIONAL LAMPOON GOES TO THE MOVIES; NIGHTHAWKS (1981); MONSIGNOR; NIGHT SHIFT; ONE DOWN TWO TO GO (1982); THE BIG SCORE; EUREKA; THE LAST FIGHT; LOSIN' IT; VIGILANTE (1983); THE LAST HORROR FILM (1984); HOLLYWOOD HARRY; WALKING THE EDGE (1985); THE WHOOPEE BOYS (1986); DEADLY ILLUSION; THE MESSENGER; THE PICK-UP ARTIST (1987); MARRIED TO THE MOB (1988).

Stone, Irving [Irving Tennenbaum]
Born 14 July 1903, San Francisco, Calif.; died 26 Aug. 1989, Los Angeles, Calif. Novelist

Stone may have invented and was certainly the best-known exponent of the contemporary biographical novel, but his success did not come immediately. After studying political science and economics on teaching fellowships at USC and Berkeley, Stone abandoned academia to focus on his writing. He had already written many short stories and at least 17 unpublished plays when, in 1926, he traveled to Paris and saw an exhibition of the works of Van Gogh. This event—which Stone later described as "the most compelling emotional experience of [his] life"—led to the conception of *Lust for Life*, an omniscient re-creation of the artist's life that was rejected by more than 17 publishers until Stone, with the help of his future wife and lifelong editor, Jean Factor, managed to get it into print in 1934. (Meanwhile, he had published his first book, *Pageant of Youth*, in 1933.) An immediate best-seller and critical hit, *Lust for Life* set the pattern for most of Stone's subsequent work—heavily researched, very popular, often revisionist fictionalized biographies of historical figures, including Jack London, Andrew and Rachel Jackson, Mary Todd Lincoln, Sigmund Freud, Charles Darwin, and Eugene Debs. (Stone also wrote "straight" biographies of Clarence Darrow and Earl Warren, and edited Van Gogh's letters to his brother in *Dear Theo*.) Along with LUST FOR LIFE (1956), Vincente Minnelli's film starring Kirk Douglas (as Van Gogh) and Anthony Quinn (as Gauguin), other film adaptations of Stone's books include ARKANSAS JUDGE (1941); MAGNIFICENT DOLL (1946); THE PRESIDENT'S LADY (1953); and THE AGONY AND THE ECSTASY (1965). The last, after LUST FOR LIFE, was the most popular; based on Stone's 1961 novel of the same name, it starred Charlton Heston (as Michelangelo) and Rex Harrison (as Pope Julius II) under Carol Reed's direction. Delivering history in an entertaining form to many who might otherwise have remained unexposed to his subjects, Stone wrote more than 25 books and sold at least 30 million copies worldwide.

Thomson, Virgil
Born 25 Nov. 1896, Kansas City, Mo.; died 30 Sept. 1989, New York, N.Y. Composer-Critic

One of the most influential figures in modern American music, both as critic and composer, Thomson wrote symphonies, ballets, and chamber pieces, but is best known for his operas and film scores. With Gertrude Stein (whom he met, after graduating from Harvard, while he was studying with Nadia Boulanger in Paris), he wrote the pioneering operas *Four Saints in Three Acts* (1928) and *The Mother of Us All* (1947). The former premiered in 1934 under the direction of John Houseman (whose 1964 documentary JOURNEY TO AMERICA featured a Thomson score), and immediately established Thomson's reputation and style—that of a collagist mixing American folk, popular, and traditional idioms within a relatively simple melodic structure. From 1940 to 1954, as the music critic for the *New York Herald*, Thomson consistently reviewed avant-garde, innovative, or otherwise ignored work with a passion that made him something of an *enfant terrible* even among musical fellow travelers. Less controversial was the acclaim for his LOUISIANA STORY (1948) score, which won the only Pulitzer Prize awarded for film music. In addition to this Robert Flaherty docudrama and JOURNEY TO AMERICA, Thomson scored the documentaries THE PLOW THAT BROKE THE PLAINS (1936) and THE RIVER (1937), films suited to the composer's invocations of his Midwestern musical heritage. His books include the autobiography *Virgil Thomson on Virgil Thomson* (1966), *The State of Music* (1939), *American Music Since 1910* (1971), and *A Virgil Thomson Reader* (1981).

Treen, Mary
Born 1907, St. Louis, Mo.; died 20 July 1989, Newport Beach, Calif., age 82 Actress

Before she became a much-employed character actress, Treen began a career as a dancer in vaudeville revues and stage musicals. After performing in some early Bryan Foy short subjects, she was signed by Warner Bros. and made her feature-film debut in 1934, when she appeared in BABBITT; HAPPINESS AHEAD; and THE ST. LOUIS KID. Thereafter, she was often cast in "plain" secondary parts—as the heroine's friend, as an office girl, or as an otherwise supportive type (Cousin Tilly in IT'S A WONDERFUL LIFE, for instance)—usually in comedies. Treen's film career spanned more than 30 years and more than 100 movies. Her films include: BABBITT; HAPPINESS

AHEAD; THE ST. LOUIS KID (1934); BROADWAY GONDOLIER; THE CASE OF THE LUCKY LEGS; DON'T BET ON BLONDES; FRONT PAGE WOMAN; G-MEN; THE GIRL FROM TENTH AVENUE; I FOUND STELLA PARISH; I LIVE FOR LOVE; A NIGHT AT THE RITZ; PAGE MISS GLORY; RED HOT TIRES; SHIPMATES FOREVER; SWEET ADELINE; SWEET MUSIC; THE TRAVELING SALESLADY (1935); BRIDES ARE LIKE THAT; COLLEEN; DANGEROUS; DOWN THE STRETCH; FRESHMAN LOVE; THE GOLDEN ARROW; JAILBREAK; LOVE BEGINS AT TWENTY; MURDER BY AN ARISTOCRAT; THE MURDER OF DR. HARRIGAN; SNOWED UNDER; STAGE STRUCK (1936); THE CAPTAIN'S KID; DANCE, CHARLIE, DANCE; EVER SINCE EVE; FUGITIVE IN THE SKY; THE GOGETTER; GOD'S COUNTRY AND THE WOMAN; MAID OF SALEM; SECOND HONEYMOON; SWING IT SAILOR; TALENT SCOUT; THEY GAVE HIM A GUN (1937); KENTUCKY MOONSHINE; SALLY, IRENE AND MARY; STRANGE FACES; YOUNG FUGITIVES (1938); FIRST LOVE; FOR LOVE OR MONEY; WHEN TOMORROW COMES (1939); BLACK DIAMONDS; DANGER ON WHEELS; DOUBLE ALIBI; GIRL IN 313; KITTY FOYLE; QUEEN OF THE MOB; TOO MANY HUSBANDS (1940); FATHER TAKES A WIFE; THE FLAME OF NEW ORLEANS; MIDNIGHT ANGEL; TALL, DARK AND HANDSOME; YOU BELONG TO ME (1941); BETWEEN US GIRLS; THE GREAT MAN'S LADY; LADY BODYGUARD; THE NIGHT BEFORE THE DIVORCE; PACIFIC BLACKOUT; THE POWERS GIRL; RINGS ON HER FINGERS; ROXIE

HART; SHIP AHOY; THEY ALL KISSED THE BRIDE; TURN TO THE ARMY (1942); FLIGHT FOR FREEDOM; HANDS ACROSS THE BORDER; HIT PARADE OF 1943; THE MORE THE MERRIER; MYSTERY BROADCAST; SO PROUDLY WE HAIL; THANK YOUR LUCKY STARS; THEY GOT ME COVERED (1943); CASANOVA BROWN; I LOVE A SOLDIER; THE NAVY WAY; SWING IN THE SADDLE (1944); BLONDE FROM BROOKLYN; DON JUAN QUILLIGAN; HIGH POWERED; TAHITI NIGHTS (1945); FROM THIS DAY FORWARD; A GUY COULD CHANGE; IT'S A WONDERFUL LIFE; ONE EXCITING WEEK; STRANGE IMPERSONATION; SWING PARADE OF 1946 (1946); A LIKELY STORY (1947); LET'S LIVE A LITTLE; THE SNAKE PIT; TEXAS, BROOKLYN AND HEAVEN (1948); YOUNG DANIEL BOONE (1950); SAILOR BEWARE (1951); DREAMBOAT; ROOM FOR ONE MORE (1952); CLIPPED WINGS; THE GREAT JESSE JAMES RAID; LET'S DO IT AGAIN (1953); BUNDLE OF JOY; WHEN GANGLAND STRIKES (1956); GUN DUEL IN DURANGO; THE JOKER IS WILD; THE SAD SACK (1957); I MARRIED A MONSTER FROM OUTER SPACE (1958); CAREER (1959); ADA; ALL IN A NIGHT'S WORK; THE ERRAND BOY (1961); WHO'S MINDING THE STORE? (1963); THE BIRDS AND THE BEES (1965); PARADISE, HAWAIIAN STYLE (1966).

Tugend, Harry
Born 17 Feb. 1898, Brooklyn, N.Y.; died 11 Sept. 1989, Los Angeles, Calif.
Film/TV/Stage/Radio Writer-Film/TV Producer
After trying his hand at a variety of professions, Tugend began a career in show business, first as a vaudeville performer and then as a Ziegfeld Follies sketch-writer. He also provided material for the Washington Square Players, starring Fanny Brice and Fred Allen, and continued with Allen as the writer-director of many of the comedian's radio shows. After following Allen to Hollywood to work on THANKS A MILLION, Tugend became one of the founding members of the Screen Writers Guild in 1933, and signed a contract with Fox that led to the filming of CAPTAIN JANUARY and THE LITTLEST REBEL (two of four Tugend-scripted Shirley Temple movies) in 1935. In 1941 he moved to Paramount, for whom he wrote Bob Hope's CAUGHT IN THE DRAFT and STAR SPANGLED RHYTHM; Bing Crosby's BIRTH OF THE BLUES; and the Hope-Crosby ROAD TO BALI, which Tugend also produced (the studio made him a production executive in 1945, when he was one of seven screenwriters named

among the 200 best-paid people in Hollywood). After leaving Paramount in the late 40s to work as a free lance, Tugend worked mainly in TV (producing "The Ray Milland Show" and "General Electric Theater"), but also cowrote Frank Capra's POCKETFUL OF MIRACLES and Jerry Lewis' WHO'S MINDING THE STORE?, the latter with Frank Tashlin. His films include: CAPTAIN JANUARY; THE LITTLEST REBEL; THANKS A MILLION (1935); KING OF BURLESQUE; PIGSKIN PARADE; POOR LITTLE RICH GIRL; SING, BABY, SING (1936); ALI BABA GOES TO TOWN; LOVE IS NEWS; WAKE UP AND LIVE; YOU CAN'T HAVE EVERYTHING (1937); LITTLE MISS BROADWAY; MY LUCKY STAR; SALLY, IRENE AND MARY; THANKS FOR EVERYTHING (1938); SECOND FIDDLE (1939); LITTLE OLD NEW YORK; SEVEN SINNERS (1940); BIRTH OF THE BLUES; CAUGHT IN THE DRAFT; KISS THE BOYS GOODBYE; POT O' GOLD (1941); THE LADY HAS PLANS; STAR SPANGLED RHYTHM (1942); LET'S FACE IT; TRUE TO LIFE (1943); CROSS MY HEART (p&w) (1946); GOLDEN EARRINGS (p); THE TROUBLE WITH WOMEN (p) (1947); A SONG IS BORN; A SOUTHERN YANKEE (1948); TAKE ME OUT TO THE BALL GAME (1949); WABASH AVENUE (1950); DARLING, HOW COULD YOU! (p) (1951); ROAD TO BALI (p&w) (1952); OFF LIMITS (p) (1953); PUBLIC PIGEON NO. 1 (p&w) (1957); POCKETFUL OF MIRACLES (1961); WHO'S MINDING THE STORE? (1963).

Van Cleef, Lee
Born 9 Jan. 1925, Somerville, N.J.; died 16 Dec. 1989, Oxnard, Calif.
Actor
After WW II service in the Navy, Van Cleef tried his hand at various jobs—including accountancy, though it's hard to imagine this classic movie villain punching numbers. After acting in amateur theater in his native New Jersey, Van Cleef landed a role in the "Mr. Roberts" road company in 1951, and was spotted by Stanley Kramer, who was then producing the great western HIGH NOON. Kramer cast Van Cleef as one of the four gunfighters who shoot it out with Gary Cooper, and the role set the pattern for Van Cleef's career of bad-guy portrayals—usually in character roles, until he became an international star in the 1960s films of Sergio Leone. (Van Cleef's second movie, the gangster story KANSAS CITY CONFIDENTIAL, is said to have influenced Leone.) Although he won his first lead in a science-fiction film, playing a nice-guy dupe in Roger Corman's IT CONQUERED THE WORLD (1956), the sharp-faced, narrow-eyed Van Cleef is best remembered for his work in several outstanding American westerns, including

THE BRAVADOS; HOW THE WEST WAS WON; RIDE LONESOME; and THE MAN WHO SHOT LIBERTY VALANCE, as well as in the violent, surreal European revival of the genre epitomized by Leone's "spaghetti westerns." Cast opposite Clint Eastwood in Leone's FOR A FEW DOLLARS MORE and in THE GOOD, THE BAD, AND THE UGLY (as The Bad), Van Cleef became a top star of westerns and action movies filmed in Europe, and also became a bigger name in Hollywood, though he remained primarily a supporting player there. In the 80s, Van Cleef was most often seen in action films like ARMED RESPONSE or 1989's SPEED ZONE. His films include: HIGH NOON; KANSAS CITY CONFIDENTIAL; THE LAWLESS BREED; UNTAMED FRONTIER (1952); ARENA; THE BANDITS OF CORSICA; THE BEAST FROM 20,000 PHANTOMS; JACK SLADE; THE NEBRASKAN; PRIVATE EYES; TUMBLEWEED; VICE SQUAD; WHITE LIGHTNING (1953); ARROW IN THE DUST; DAWN AT SOCORRO; THE DESPERADO; GYPSY COLT; PRINCESS OF THE NILE; RAILS INTO LARAMIE; THE YELLOW TOMAHAWK (1954); THE BIG COMBO; I COVER THE UNDERWORLD; A MAN ALONE; THE ROAD TO DENVER; TEN WANTED MEN; TREASURE OF RUBY HILLS; THE VANISHING AMERICAN (1955); ACCUSED OF MURDER; THE CONQUEROR; IT CONQUERED THE WORLD; PARDNERS; TRIBUTE TO A BADMAN (1956); THE BADGE OF MARSHALL BRENNAN; CHINA GATE; GUN BATTLE AT MONTEREY; GUNFIGHT AT THE O.K. CORRAL; JOE DAKOTA; THE LAST STAGECOACH WEST; THE LONELY MAN; THE QUIET GUN;

RAIDERS OF OLD CALIFORNIA (1957); GUNS, GIRLS AND GANGSTERS; MACHETE; THE YOUNG LIONS (1958); RIDE LONESOME (1959); POSSE FROM HELL (1961); HOW THE WEST WAS WON; THE MAN WHO SHOT LIBERTY VALANCE (1962); BEYOND THE LAW; FOR A FEW DOLLARS MORE; THE GOOD, THE BAD, AND THE UGLY (1967); THE BIG GUNDOWN (1968); DEATH RIDES A HORSE; SABATA (1969); BARQUERO; DAY OF ANGER; EL CONDOR (1970); CAPTAIN APACHE (1971); BAD MAN'S RIVER; THE GRAND DUEL; THE MAGNIFICENT SEVEN RIDE; RETURN OF SABATA (1972); BLOOD MONEY (1974); TAKE A HARD RIDE (1975); CRIME BOSS; MEAN FRANK AND CRAZY TONY (1976); GOD'S GUN; KID VENGEANCE; THE PERFECT KILLER (1977); THE HARD WAY; THE OCTAGON; THE SQUEEZE (1980); ESCAPE FROM NEW YORK (1981); CODENAME WILDGEESE; JUNGLE RAIDERS (1985); ARMED RESPONSE; KILLER MACHINE (1986); SPEED ZONE (1989).

Vanel, Charles [Marie-Charles Vanel]

Born 21 Aug. 1892, Rennes, France; died 15 April 1989, Cannes, France

Actor-Director

With a screen career ranging from a 1912 silent to a 1987 sex farce, Vanel was perhaps the century's leading French character actor, appearing in some 200 films. Debuting on the Parisian stage in "Hamlet" at age 16 and on the screen in JIM CROW (1912), Vanel landed his first screen contract in the early 1920s, appearing in such popular silent features as the serial LA MAISON DE MYSTERE; TEMPETES; Rene Clair's LA PROIE DU VENT; and PECHEUR D'ISLAND (by Jacques de Baroncelli, who cast Vanel in six of his films). After writing, directing, and starring in his own DANS LE NUIT (1929), Vanel made the transition to sound with stunning success in the 1930s, appearing in more than 40 films in a variety of parts, excelling particularly in tragic roles and working with the era's major directors (and directing one more film himself, 1935's LE COUP DE MINUIT). His career faded somewhat during the Occupation and postwar years, until he made a significant comeback in Henri-Georges Clouzot's THE WAGES OF FEAR, winning a Cannes Best Actor award and subsequently appearing in films by Clouzot (LES DIABOLIQUES; LA VERITE), Sacha Guitry, Julien Duvivier, Luis Bunuel (LA MORT EN CE JARDIN, US title GINA), Pierre Chenal, and Alfred Hitchcock—whose TO CATCH A THIEF was Vanel's only Hollywood film. With the advent of the French New Wave his career

again waned, though he occasionally acted in such major films as Francesco Rosi's CADAVERI EXCELLENTI and appeared with some frequency on French TV. Apparently retiring after making Rosi's THREE BROTHERS (1982), Vanel returned to the screen shortly before his death in features by popular filmmakers Claude Goretta and Jean-Pierre Mocky. His films include: JIM CROW (1912); DE CRESPUSCULE A L'AUBE (1919); CRESPUSCULE D'EPOUVANTE; LA FILLE DE LA CARMARGUE (1921); GYPSY PASSION; LA MAISON DU MYSTERE; PHROSE; TEMPETES (1922); CALVAIRE D'AMOUR; L'ATRE; LA MENDIANTE DE SAINT-SULPICE; LE VOL (1923); IN THE SPIDER'S WEB; L'AUTRE AILE; LA FLAMBEE DES REVES; LA NUIT DE LA REVANCHE; PECHEUR D'ISLANDE (1924); AIME L'ARTISTE; BAROCCO; LA FLAMME; LA PROIE DU VENT; LE REVEIL; L'ORPHELIN DU CIRQUE; 600,000 FRANCS PAR MOIS (1925); MARTYRE; NITCHEVO (1926); CHANTE; FEU!; MAQUILLAGE; PANANE N'EST PAS PARIS (1927); LE PASSAGER; WATERLOO (1928); DANS LE NUIT (a,d&w); FEUX FOLLETS; LA FEMME REVEE; LA PLONGEE TRAGIQUE; LES FOURCHAMBAULT; THE WHITE SLAVE (1929); ACCUSED—STAND UP; CHIQUE; LA MAISON JAUNE DU RIO; LE CAPITAINE JAUNE; LES 50 ANS DE DON JUAN; L'OBSESSION; MAISON DE DANSE (1930); L'ARLESIENNE (1931); AU NOM DE LA LOI; FAUBOURG MONTMARTRE; GITANES; LES CROIX DE BOIS (1932); LE ROI DE CAMARGUE (1933); AU BOUT DU MONDE; L'ENFANT DU CARNEVAL; LE GRANDE JEU (1934); DOMINO VERT; L'EQUIPAGE; LE COUP DE MINUIT (a&d); L'IMPOSSIBLE AVEU (1935); L'ASSAUT; LA FLAMME; LA PEUR; LES GRANDS; LES MISERABLES; JENNY; MICHEL STROGOFF; POLICE MONDAINE; PORT ARTHUR; S.O.S. SAHARA; VERTIGE D'UN SOIR (1936); COURRIER SUD; LES PIRATES DU RAIL; L'OCCIDENT; TROIKA SUR LA PISTE BLANCHE; YAMILE SOUS LES CEDRES (1937); ABUSED CONFIDENCE; BAR DE SUD; CROSSROADS; LA FEMME DU BOUT DU MONDE; LA SONATE A KREUTZER; LEGIONS D'HONNEUR; LES BATALIERS DE LA VOLGA; THEY WERE FIVE (1938); LA LOI DU NORD; L'OR DU CRISTOBAL (1939); LA NUIT MERVEILLEUSE; LE DIAMANT NOIR (1940); LE SOLEIL A TOUJOURS RAISON (1941); HAUT-LE-VENT; LES AFFAIRES SONT LES AFFAIRES; PROMESSE A L'INCONNUE (1942); LES ROQUEVILLARD (1943); GRINGOLET; LA CABANE A SOUVENIRS;

LA FERME DU PENDU; LE BATEAU A SOUPE (1946); LE DIABLE SOUFFLE (1947); LA FEMME QUE J'AI ASSASSINEE; LE PAIN DE PAUVRES; SAVAGE BRIGADE (1948); LA BRIGADE VOLANTE; LE SECRET DES MENDOVIC; LES MAUVENTS; JEUNESSE SUR LA MER; UN NOMMA DELLA LEGGE; THE WOMAN WHO DARED (1949); GLI INESORABILI (1950); IL BIVIO; OLIVIA; PLUS FORT QUE LA HAINE; ULTIMA SENTENZIA (1951); CUORI SUL MARC; MADDELENA (1953); L'AFFAIRE MAURIZIUS; LES GAITES DE L'ESCADRON (1954); DIABOLIQUE; LA FEMME SCANDELEUSE; LE MISSIONAIRE; TAM-TAM; TO CATCH A THIEF; THE WAGES OF FEAR (1955); DEFEND MY LOVE (1956); LE CIEL EST A VOUS; LE FEU AUX POUDRES; LES SUSPECTS; ROYAL AFFAIRS IN VERSAILLES (1957); THE GORILLA GREETS YOU; LE PIEGE; RAFLES SUR LA VILLE (1958); LA VALSE DU GORILLE; LE NAUFRAGEURS; PECHEUR D'ISLANDE (1959); MARIA, MATRICULA DE BILBOA; PRISONER OF THE VOLGA (1960); GINA; TINTIN ET LE MYSTERE DE LA TOISON D'OR; THE TRUTH (1961); LO SGARRO (1962); L'AINE DES FERCHAUX; LA POURSUITE; RIFIFI IN TOKYO; THE STEPPE (1963); LE CHANT DU MONDE; LES TRIBULATIONS D'UN CHINOIS EN CHINE; SYMPHONY FOR A MASSACRE (1965); BALLADE PAR UN CHIEN; SHOCK TROOPS (1968); LA PRISONNIER (1969); COMPTES A REBOURS; ILS; LA NUIT BULGARE (1970); IL CONTESTO; L'AVENTURE C'EST L'AVENTURE; THE MOST WONDERFUL EVENING OF MY LIFE (1972); 7 MORTS SUR ORDANNANCE (1975); CADAVERI ECCELENTI; ES HERRSCHT RUHE IM LAND; NUIT D'OR (1976); ALICE, OR THE LAST ESCAPADE; DEATH IN THE GARDEN (1977); NE PLEURE PAS (1978); THREE BROTHERS (1982); SI LE SOLEIL NE REVENAIT PAS; LES SAISONS DU PLAISIR (1987).

Varden, Norma

Born 1898 in England; died 19 Jan. 1989, Santa Barbara, Calif., age 90

Actress

Trained as a concert pianist, Varden found acting success as a foil for Britain's Aldwych Theater group, entering films with other the Aldwych cut-ups in 1932's A NIGHT LIKE THIS. After appearing in a score of British movies, Varden moved to Hollywood in 1939, acting in many American films, including CASABLANCA; NATIONAL VELVET; THE SOUND OF MUSIC; RANDOM HARVEST; and GENTLEMEN PREFER BLONDES,

Norma Varden (left) with Marilyn Monroe in GENTLEMEN PREFER BLONDES.

before retiring in 1968. Varden, who frequently played snooty upper-crust types, was also seen as Jack Benny's mother on the "Jack Benny Show" in the 1950s. Her films include: A NIGHT LIKE THIS (1932); TURKEY TIME (1933); HAPPY (1934); FOREIGN AFFAIRS; GET OFF MY FOOT; THE IRON DUKE; MUSIC HATH CHARMS (1935); BOYS WILL BE BOYS; EAST MEETS WEST; THE STUDENT'S ROMANCE; WHERE THERE'S A WILL (1936); MAKE-UP; RHYTHM RACKETEER; THE STRANGE ADVENTURES OF MR. SMITH; WANTED; WINDBAG THE SAILOR (1937); EVERYTHING HAPPENS TO ME; FOOLS FOR SCANDAL; YOU'RE THE DOCTOR (1938); HOME FROM HOME (1939); THE EARL OF CHICAGO; SHIPYARD SALLY; WATERLOO BRIDGE (1940); GLAMOUR BOY; ROAD TO ZANZIBAR; SCOTLAND YARD (1941); CASABLANCA; FLYING WITH MUSIC; THE GLASS KEY; THE MAJOR AND THE MINOR; RANDOM HARVEST; WE WERE DANCING (1942); DIXIE; THE GOOD FELLOWS; SHERLOCK HOLMES FACES DEATH; SLIGHTLY DANGEROUS; WHAT A WOMAN! (1943); MADEMOISELLE FIFI; NATIONAL VELVET; THE WHITE CLIFFS OF DOVER (1944); BRING ON THE GIRLS; THE CHEATERS; GIRLS OF THE BIG HOUSE; HOLD THAT BLONDE; THOSE ENDEARING YOUNG CHARMS (1945); THE GREEN YEARS; THE SEARCHING WIND (1946); FOREVER AMBER; IVY; MILLIE'S DAUGHTER; THE SENATOR WAS INDISCREET; THE TROUBLE WITH WOMEN; WHERE THERE'S LIFE (1947); HOLLOW TRIUMPH; LET'S LIVE A LITTLE; MY OWN TRUE LOVE (1948); ADVEN-TURE IN BALTIMORE; THE SECRET GARDEN (1949); FANCY PANTS (1950); STRANGERS ON A TRAIN; THUNDER ON THE HILL (1951); LES MISERABLES; SOMETHING FOR THE BIRDS (1952); GENTLEMEN PREFER BLONDES; LOOSE IN LONDON; YOUNG BESS (1953); ELEPHANT WALK; THREE COINS IN THE FOUNTAIN (1954); JUPITER'S DARLING (1955); THE BIRDS AND THE BEES (1956); WITNESS FOR THE PROSECUTION (1957); THE BUCCANEER; IN THE MONEY (1958); FIVE MINUTES TO LIVE (1961); ISLAND OF LOVE; THIRTEEN FRIGHTENED GIRLS (1963); THE SOUND OF MUSIC; A VERY SPECIAL FAVOR (1965); DOCTOR DOLITTLE (1967).

Von Karajan, Herbert

Born 5 April 1908, Salzburg, Austria; died 16 July 1989, Anif, Austria
Conductor

Dubbed "the general music director of Europe" during the late 1950s and early 60s—when he led the Berlin Philharmonic, La Scala, the Philharmonia Orchestra in London, the Vienna State Opera, and the Salzburg Festival—von Karajan was one of the leading conductors of his age, an heir to Toscanini and Furtwangler. Having made his conducting debut in Austria in 1929, von Karajan established himself in Berlin in 1937, becoming Furtwangler's rival for pre-eminence in German music. After WW II, the nature of his former allegiance to the Nazi party (which he joined in 1933 and 1934 in Austria and then Germany), became an issue, one that was never cleared up to the satisfaction of many patrons and performers who boycotted his concerts long after the war. His talent, however, was never in dispute, and his reputation was shored by his more than 800 recordings, the most by any conductor; comprehensive repertoire of about 140 symphonies and operas; high personal profile and flamboyant lifestyle; and position as "conductor for life" of the Berlin Philharmonic, ranked as one of the world's top three orchestras. Von Karajan's actual residence with the Philharmonic, from 1955 to April 1989, was marked by many disputes between the imperious conductor and the self-governing orchestra, most notably the famous 1982 dispute after von Karajan, who was known for championing young talent, attempted to hire a young female clarinetist against the wishes of the all-male orchestra. Von Karajan conducts La Scala to provide the Puccini score of director Franco Zefferelli's LA BOHEME (1965), considered one of the best filmed operas ever made; he also produced the picture.

Warren, Robert Penn

Born 24 April 1905, Guthrie, Ky.; died 15 Sept. 1989, Stratton, Vt.
Poet-Novelist-Critic

Warren's oeuvre, with its unusual range, influence, popularity, and beauty, ranks him among this century's most eminent American men of letters. While studying at Vanderbilt in the 1920s, he joined the group known as the Fugitives or the Agrarians, including poet-scholar John Crowe Ransom. Ransom proved an especially great influence on Warren, whose writing, like Ransom's, drew inspiration from the Southern past. However, Warren eventually rejected the "agrarian," reactionary stance espoused by Ransom and his other co-essayists in *I'll Take My Stand* (1930) for an approach that took history and local legend as both narrative subject and as a point from which to explore moral and metaphysical themes. This practice provided the gripping plots of his novels, the best known of which is 1946's *All the King's Men*. Based on the life of Huey Long, it won Warren the first of his three Pulitzer Prizes (the others were for poetry) and was originally intended as a play, but though Warren tried to bring the work to the stage for years, it was most memorably adapted for the movies by Robert Rossen, who produced, directed, and scripted ALL THE KING'S MEN in 1949. The film won Best Picture and Best Actor (Broderick Crawford) Oscars; in 1957, Warren's *Band of Angels* was less well filmed under Raoul Walsh's direction. Warren's poetry was less widely read than his fiction, but proved the better forum for his mix of philosophy and history, and his stature as one of the US' greatest poets was recognized when he was made the country's first Poet Laureate in 1986. No less important were Warren and Cleanth Brooks' college textbooks *Understanding Poetry* and *Understanding Fiction*, which helped make New Criticism the standard approach to literature after WW II. (Ransom and the Vanderbilt circle were also influential here.) Among Warren's many other achievements were the cofounding and coeditorship (1935-42) of the still-extant *Southern Review*. He taught at Vanderbilt, LSU, Yale, and the University of Minnesota.

Webber, Robert
Born 1 Oct. 1924, Santa Ana, Calif.; died 17 May 1989, Malibu, Calif.
Actor
After serving in WW II, Webber left his native California for New York and an acting career. He worked in summer stock, then made his Broadway debut in a bit part in 1948. In the next decade he entered films as a gangster in HIGHWAY 301 (1950), appeared several times on Broadway, and performed often on both live and filmed TV—catching the eye of Martin Ritt, who recommended him to Sidney Lumet for the role of Juror No. 12 in 12 ANGRY MEN, a breakthrough part for the actor. Webber's career proceeded apace in the 60s—he said he had done more than

400 TV roles when he stopped counting early in the decade—and he was increasingly popular in films as a character actor who could play both sympathetic and villainous types, but often combined them by playing handsome, smooth-talking rats. His range further expanded in the 70s, when he appeared in some foreign films and began working with Blake Edwards, who cast him against type in 10 and S.O.B. Webber's familiar face was last seen on TV's "Moonlighting" (as Maddie's father) and in Ritt's 1987 film NUTS (as the prosecutor). His films include: HIGHWAY 301 (1950); 12 ANGRY MEN (1957); THE NUN AND THE SERGEANT (1962); THE STRIPPER (1963); HYSTERIA; THE SANDPIPER; THE THIRD DAY (1965); DEAD HEAT ON A MERRY-GO-ROUND; HARPER; THE SILENCERS (1966); THE DIRTY DOZEN; DON'T MAKE WAVES; THE HIRED

KILLER (1967); MANON 70 (1968); THE BIG BOUNCE (1969); THE GREAT WHITE HOPE (1970); $ (1971); BRING ME THE HEAD OF ALFREDO GARCIA (1974); MIDWAY; PASSI DI MORTE PERDUTI NEL BUIO (1976); THE CHOIRBOYS; L'IMPRECATEUR; MADAME CLAUDE (1977); CASEY'S SHADOW; REVENGE OF THE PINK PANTHER (1978); GARDENIA; 10 (1979); PRIVATE BENJAMIN; SUNDAY LOVERS (1980); S.O.B. (1981); WRONG IS RIGHT (1982); THE FINAL OPTION (1983); WILD GEESE II (1985); NUTS (1987).

White, Chrissie [Ada White, Chrissie Edwards]
Born 23 May 1894, London, England; died 18 Aug. 1989, in England
Actress
Young Ada White entered films as a substitute for her sister Gwen, an actress, at Britain's Cecil M. Hepworth studios in the early 1900s. Renamed "Chrissie," she quickly became one of the first British film stars, appearing in scores of silent shorts (often under the direction of Lewin Fitzhamon). After WW I she made the transition to feature-film acting and leading-lady status, marrying her frequent costar and director, Henry Edwards, in the 1920s. White retired in 1924—after having acted in more than 160 shorts and features—but returned to the screen briefly to make her talkie debut in THE CALL OF THE SEA (1930) and to star in GENERAL JOHN REGAN (1933), which Edwards directed. Her films include: FOR THE LITTLE LADY'S SAKE (1908); TILLY THE TOMBOY GOES BOATING (1910); THE MERMAID (1912); THE CLOISTER AND THE HEARTH; DAVID GARRICK; KISSING CUP; THE VICAR OF WAKEFIELD (1913); AS THE SUN WENT DOWN; BARNABY RUDGE; HER BOY; THE NIGHTBIRDS OF LONDON; SWEET LAVENDER (1915); A BUNCH OF VIOLETS; MOLLY BAWN (1916); BROKEN THREADS; CARROTS; DAUGHTER OF THE WILDS; DICK CARSON WINS THROUGH; THE ETERNAL TRIANGLE; HER MARRIAGE LINES; THE MAN BEHIND "THE TIMES" (1917); THE HANGING JUDGE; TOWARDS THE LIGHT (1918); THE AMAZING QUEST OF MR. ERNEST BLISS; THE CITY OF BEAUTIFUL NONSENSE; HIS DEAREST POSSESSION; THE KINSMAN; POSSESSION (1919); AYLWIN; JOHN FORREST FINDS HIMSELF; A TEMPORARY VAGABOND (1920); THE BARGAIN; THE LUNATIC AT LARGE; WILD HEATHER (1921); SIMPLE SIMON; TIT FOR TAT (1922); BODEN'S BOY; LILY OF THE ALLEY (1923); THE WORLD OF WONDERFUL REALITY (1924); THE CALL OF THE SEA (1930);

GENERAL JOHN REGAN (1933).

Wilde, Cornel [Cornelius Louis Wilde]
Born 13 Oct. 1915, New York, N.Y.; died 15 Oct. 1989, Los Angeles, Calif.
Actor-Film Director-Producer
As the son of a Hungarian cosmetics industry representative based in New York, the young Wilde traveled extensively in Europe, learning several languages. After his family moved to the US permanently in 1932, he won a scholarship to Columbia's College of Physicians and Surgeons and was named to the US Olympic fencing team, but quit both (passing up the 1936 Berlin Olympics) to continue acting on Broadway and in stock. Wilde's way with a sword landed him his first big break in 1940, when he played Tybalt and was the fencing instructor in the Olivier-Leigh Broadway production of "Romeo and Juliet." While rehearsing for the play in Hollywood, he signed a contract with

Warner Bros. (making his screen debut in LADY WITH RED HAIR [1940]), but soon moved to Fox, which cast the tall, dark, and handsome actor in his first lead roles. Ironically, the athletic Wilde gained stardom (and a Best Actor Oscar nomination) after playing the consumptive Chopin in A SONG TO REMEMBER; major roles in LEAVE HER TO HEAVEN; A THOUSAND AND ONE NIGHTS; FOREVER AMBER; and ROAD HOUSE followed. Nonetheless, by the 1950s Wilde found himself remanded to swashbuckler B films, prompting him to form his own Theodora Productions in 1955. He subsequently divided his time between directing and producing Theodora projects—sometimes starring in them opposite his wife and business partner, Jean Wallace—and acting in other films. Most notable among Wilde's solo efforts were the macho NAKED PREY and the pacifist BEACH RED. His films include: LADY WITH RED HAIR (1940); HIGH SIERRA; KISSES FOR BREAKFAST; KNOCKOUT; THE PERFECT SNOB (1941); LIFE BEGINS AT 8:30; MANILA CALLING; RIGHT TO THE HEART (1942); WINTERTIME (1943); A SONG TO REMEMBER; A THOUSAND AND ONE NIGHTS (1945); THE BANDIT OF SHERWOOD FOREST; CENTENNIAL SUMMER; LEAVE HER TO HEAVEN (1946); FOREVER AMBER; THE HOMESTRETCH; IT HAD TO BE YOU; STAIRWAY FOR A STAR (1947); ROAD HOUSE; WALLS OF JERICHO (1948); SHOCKPROOF (1949); FOUR DAYS LEAVE; TWO FLAGS WEST (1950); AT SWORD'S POINT (1951); CALIFORNIA CONQUEST; THE GREATEST SHOW ON EARTH; OPERATION SECRET (1952); MAIN STREET TO BROADWAY; SAADIA; TREASURE OF THE GOLDEN CONDOR (1953); PASSION; WOMAN'S WORLD (1954); THE BIG COMBO; THE SCARLET COAT (1955); HOT BLOOD; STAR OF INDIA; STORM FEAR (a,p&d) (1956); BEYOND MOMBASA; THE DEVIL'S HAIRPIN (a,p,d&w); OMAR KHAYYAM (1957); MARACAIBO (a,p&d) (1958); EDGE OF ETERNITY (1959); CONSTANTINE AND THE CROSS (1962); SWORD OF LANCELOT (a,p&d) (1963); THE NAKED PREY (a,p&d) (1966); BEACH RED (a,p&d) (1967); THE COMIC (1969); NO BLADE OF GRASS (p&d) (1970); SHARK'S TREASURE (a,p,d&w) (1975); BEHIND THE IRON MASK (1977); THE NORSEMAN (1978).

Williams, Guy

Died 6 May 1989, Buenos Aires, Argentina, age 65

Actor

Williams had worked as a model and an actor, with a few film appearances to his credit, before he was chosen by Disney in 1957 to star as the masked hero of their "Zorro" series, a role he reprised on movie screens in THE SIGN OF ZORRO three years later. Among various other film and TV credits, Williams' second-best remembered part was probably that of the head of the marooned family in the 1960s TV show "Lost in Space." His films include: BONZO GOES TO COLLEGE (1952); ALL I DESIRE; THE GOLDEN BLADE; THE MAN FROM THE ALAMO; THE MISSISSIPPI GAMBLER (1953); THE LAST FRONTIER; SEVEN ANGRY MEN; SINCERELY YOURS (1955); I WAS A TEENAGE WEREWOLF (1957); THE SIGN OF ZORRO (1960); DAMON

AND PYTHIAS (1962); CAPTAIN SINDBAD (1963); GENERAL MASSACRE (1973).

Wilson, Trey [Donald Yearnsley Wilson III]

Born Houston, Tex.; died 16 Jan. 1989, New York, N.Y., age 40

Actor

After working in regional theater in California, Wilson moved to New York in the 1970s, his numerous appearances on and off Broadway comprising roles in "Tintypes," "The First," "Foxfire," "Peter Pan," "The Front Page," and "Personals." In the 1980s he established himself as an equally versatile film actor, winning much praise in supporting roles, such as the father of the kidnaped baby in RAISING ARIZONA, the manager in BULL DUR-

HAM, the head of the FBI in MARRIED TO THE MOB, and Sun Records owner Sam Phillips in GREAT BALLS OF FIRE, and making guest appearances on several TV series. His films include: DRIVE-IN (1976); THE VAMPIRE HOOKERS (1979); PLACES IN THE HEART; A SOLDIER'S STORY (1984); MARIE (1985); F/X (1986); RAISING ARIZONA (1987); BULL DURHAM; THE HOUSE ON CARROLL STREET; MARRIED TO THE MOB; TWINS (1988) MISS FIRECRACKER; GREAT BALLS OF FIRE; WELCOME HOME (1989).

Woodbury, Joan

Born 17 Dec. 1915, Los Angeles, Calif.; died 22 Feb. 1989, Desert Hot Springs, Calif.

Actress-Stage Producer-Director

In Depression-era Los Angeles, Woodbury began a career as a dancer before entering films in the mid-1930s, appearing in such features as ANTHONY ADVERSE and THE EAGLE'S BROOD. She went on to act in dozens of films over the next 30 years, often playing sexy, cynical fallen women in B pictures, and starred in the 13-part BRENDA STARR—REPORTER serial in 1945. Previously married to British actor Henry Wilcoxon, Woodbury retired from movies in the 60s to found Palm Springs' Valley Players Guild theater, where she produced and directed scores of productions in collaboration with her second husband, actor-radio star Ray Mitchell. Her films include: EIGHT GIRLS IN A BOAT (1934); BULLDOG COURAGE; FOLIES BERGERE; ONE EXCITING ADVENTURE (1935); ANTHONY ADVERSE; THE EAGLE'S BROOD; THE LAST ASSIGNMENT; THE LION'S DEN; THE ROGUES' TAVERN; SONG OF THE GRINGO (1936);

Trey Wilson in BULL DURHAM.

CHARLIE CHAN ON BROADWAY; CRASHING HOLLYWOOD; FORTY NAUGHTY GIRLS; GOD'S COUNTRY AND THE WOMAN; LIVING ON LOVE; THE LUCK OF ROARING CAMP; MIDNIGHT COURT; SUPER SLEUTH; THERE GOES MY GIRL; THEY GAVE HIM A GUN (1937); ALGIERS; ALWAYS IN TROUBLE; CIPHER BUREAU; NIGHT SPOT; PASSPORT HUSBAND; WHILE NEW YORK SLEEPS (1938); CHASING DANGER; MYSTERY OF THE WHITE ROOM (1939); BARNYARD FOLLIES (1940); CONFESSIONS OF BOSTON BLACKIE; I'LL SELL MY LIFE; IN OLD CHEYENNE; KING OF THE ZOMBIES; PAPER BULLETS; RIDE ON VAQUERO; TWO LATINS FROM MANHATTAN (1941); DR. BROADWAY; THE HARD WAY; I KILLED THAT MAN; THE LIVING GHOST; MAN FROM HEADQUARTERS; PHANTOM KILLER; SHUT MY BIG MOUTH; SUNSET SERENADE; SWEETHEART OF THE FLEET; A YANK IN LIBYA (1942); THE DESPERADOES; HERE COMES KELLY (1943); THE CHINESE CAT; THE WHISTLER (1944); BRENDA STARR—REPORTER (serial); BRING ON THE GIRLS; FLAME OF THE WEST; NORTHWEST TRAIL; TEN CENTS A DANCE (1945); THE ARNELO AFFAIR; YANKEE FLAIR (1947); HERE COMES TROUBLE (1948); BOSTON BLACKIE'S CHINESE VENTURE (1949); THE TEN COMMANDMENTS (1956); THE TIME TRAVELERS (1964).

Zavattini, Cesare
Born 29 Sept. 1902, Luzzara, Italy; died 13 Oct. 1989, Rome, Italy
Screenwriter-Theoretician-Novelist
An instrumental figure in the Neo-Realist movement, Zavattini collaborated with director Vittorio De Sica to produce some of Italian cinema's greatest works. Embarking on a literary career in the 1920s, he wrote fiction and became an editor of the *Parma Gazette*, then moved to Milan, where he contributed to several magazines. In 1931 he published his first book (*Parliamo Tanto Di Me*); four years later he wrote his first film script, for Mario Camerini's DARO UN MILIONE (remade in the US as I'LL GIVE A MILLION in 1938). For the next few years he worked mainly in the escapist genre known as "white telephone" films, but in 1941 he collaborated with De Sica for the first time as the cowriter of TERESA VENERDI, and his 1942 script for Alessandro Blassetti's QUATTRO PASSI FRA LE NUVOLE was an early attempt to address social concerns within a cinematic form. Zavattini continued in this vein with De Sica in 1943's THE LITTLE MARTYR (US release 1947; also known as THE CHILDREN ARE WATCHING US), whose natural locations and anti-Fascist subtext set the tone for the pair's post-WW II masterpieces, SHOE SHINE and THE BICYCLE THIEF. With their nonprofessional casts, stripped-down narrative and dialog, location shooting, and unsparing view of the era's deplorable social conditions, these films represented Neo-Realist ethic and art at their height, as did the later MIRACLE IN MILAN (an adaptation of Zavattini's children's book *Toto Il Buono*) and UMBERTO D, which is often called the last true Neo-Realist movie. While continuing to formulate cinematic strategies, including *Italia Mia*, a type of *cinema verite* realized chiefly in the form of "survey films" like AMORE IN CITTA, Zavattini worked with most of the major Italian directors of the 40s, 50s, and 60s, including Visconti (BELISSIMA), Lattuada, Germi, and Zampa. As the popularity and impact of Neo-Realism waned, he worked increasingly in lighter formats—mainly with De Sica, with whom he made nearly 25 films—while retaining his stature in Italian letters as the author of some 14 books, including *Diary of Cinema and Life*, an autobiography, and a collection of poetry. By the time he made his directorial debut with 1982's surreal LA VERITA-A-A-A-A, Zavattini's last great work was behind him, in the form of De Sica's "comeback films" THE GARDEN OF THE FINZI-CONTINIS and A BRIEF VACATION. His films include: DARO UN MILIONE (1935); I'LL GIVE A MILLION (1938); TERESA VENERDI (1941); QUATTRO PASSI FRA LE NUVOLE (1942); LA PORTA DEL CIELO (1945); UN GIORNO NELLA VITA (1946); THE LITTLE MARTYR; SHOE SHINE (1947); CACCIA TRAGICA (1948); THE BICYCLE THIEF (1949); DOMENICA D'AGOSTO; E PRIMAVERA; THE WALLS OF MALAPAGA (1950); MIRACLE IN MILAN (1951); BELISSIMA; FATHER'S DILEMMA; IL CAPPOTTO; ROME ORE 11; THE SKY IS RED (1952); AMORE IN CITTA; HIS LAST TWELVE HOURS; SIAMO DONNE; UN MARITO PER ANNA ZACCHEO (1953); ALI BABA; INDISCRETION OF AN AMERICAN WIFE (1954); THE SIGN OF VENUS; UMBERTO D (1955); ANGELS OF DARKNESS; IL TETTO (1956); ERA DI VENERDI 17; GOLD OF NAPLES (1957); THE AWAKENING (1958); RAT (1960); IL GIUDIZIO UNIVERSALE; TWO WOMEN (1961); BOCCACCIO '70 (1962); ARTURO'S ISLAND; IL BOOM; THE CONDEMNED OF ALTONA (1963); YESTERDAY, TODAY, AND TOMORROW (1964); THE DOLL THAT TOOK THE TOWN; LIPSTICK (1965); AFTER THE FOX; A YOUNG WORLD (1966); WOMAN TIMES SEVEN (1967); A PLACE FOR LOVERS; THE WITCHES (1969); SUNFLOWER (1970); LO CHIAMEREMO ANDREA (1972); A BRIEF VACATION (1975); THE GARDEN OF THE FINZI-CONTINIS (1976); THE CHILDREN OF SANCHEZ; UN CUORE SEMPLICE; LIGABUE (1978); LA VERITA-A-A-A-A-A (d,w&a) (1982).

THE MOTION PICTURE ANNUAL

1990

Awards

AWARDS

This section covers the major film industry awards given to films released in 1989. Included are honors given by: the Academy of Motion Picture Arts and Sciences (Oscars), American Society of Cinematographers, British Academy of Film and Television Awards, Directors Guild of America Awards, Academy of Canadian Cinema and Television (Genies), the Hollywood Foreign Press Association (Golden Globes), Los Angeles Film Critics Association, National Board of Review (D.W. Griffith Awards), National Society of Film Critics, the New York Film Critics Circle Awards, and the Writers Guild of America. Where appropriate an asterisk (*) denotes the winning film.

62ND AWARDS OF THE ACADEMY OF MOTION PICTURE ARTS AND SCIENCES
Best Picture
BORN ON THE FOURTH OF JULY
DEAD POETS SOCIETY
DRIVING MISS DAISY*
FIELD OF DREAMS
MY LEFT FOOT
Best Actor
Kenneth Branagh for HENRY V
Tom Cruise for BORN ON THE FOURTH OF JULY
Daniel Day-Lewis for MY LEFT FOOT*
Morgan Freeman for DRIVING MISS DAISY
Robin Williams for DEAD POETS SOCIETY
Best Actress
Isabelle Adjani for CAMILLE CLAUDEL
Pauline Collins for SHIRLEY VALENTINE
Jessica Lange for MUSIC BOX
Michelle Pfeiffer for THE FABULOUS BAKER BOYS
Jessica Tandy for DRIVING MISS DAISY*
Best Supporting Actor
Danny Aiello for DO THE RIGHT THING
Dan Aykroyd for DRIVING MISS DAISY
Marlon Brando for A DRY WHITE SEASON
Martin Landau for CRIMES AND MISDEMEANORS
Denzel Washington for GLORY*
Best Supporting Actress
Brenda Fricker for MY LEFT FOOT*
Anjelica Huston for ENEMIES, A LOVE STORY
Lena Olin for ENEMIES, A LOVE STORY
Julia Roberts for STEEL MAGNOLIAS
Dianne Wiest for PARENTHOOD
Best Director
Oliver Stone for BORN ON THE FOURTH OF JULY*
Woody Allen for CRIMES AND MISDEMEANORS
Peter Weir for DEAD POETS SOCIETY
Kenneth Branagh for HENRY V
Jim Sheridan for MY LEFT FOOT
Best Original Screenplay
Woody Allen for CRIMES AND MISDEMEANORS
Tom Schulman for DEAD POETS SOCIETY*
Spike Lee for DO THE RIGHT THING
Steven Soderbergh for SEX, LIES AND VIDEOTAPE
Nora Ephron for WHEN HARRY MET SALLY . . .
Best Adapted Screenplay
Oliver Stone, Ron Kovic for BORN ON THE FOURTH OF JULY
Alfred Uhry for DRIVING MISS DAISY*
Roger L. Simon, Paul Mazursky for ENEMIES, A LOVE STORY
Phil Alden Robinson for FIELD OF DREAMS
Jim Sheridan, Shane Connaughton for MY LEFT FOOT
Best Foreign Film
CAMILLE CLAUDEL (Fr.)
CINEMA PARADISO (It.)*
JESUS OF MONTREAL (Can.)
SANTIAGO, THE STORY OF HIS NEW LIFE (Puerto Rico)
WALTZING REGITZE (Den.)
Best Art Direction
THE ABYSS
THE ADVENTURES OF BARON MUNCHAUSEN
BATMAN*
DRIVING MISS DAISY
GLORY
Best Cinematography
THE ABYSS
BLAZE
BORN ON THE FOURTH OF JULY
THE FABULOUS BAKER BOYS
GLORY*
Best Costume Design
THE ADVENTURES OF BARON MUNCHAUSEN
DRIVING MISS DAISY
HARLEM NIGHTS
HENRY V*
VALMONT
Best Documentary Feature
ADAM CLAYTON POWELL
COMMON THREADS: STORIES FROM THE QUILT*
CRACK U.S.A.: COUNTRY UNDER SIEGE
FOR ALL MANKIND
SUPER CHIEF: THE LIFE AND LEGACY OF EARL WARREN
Best Documentary Short Subject
FINE FOOD, FINE PASTRIES, OPEN 6 TO 9
THE JOHNSTOWN FLOOD*
YAD VASHEM: PRESERVING THE PAST TO INSURE THE FUTURE
Best Film Editing
THE BEAR
BORN ON THE FOURTH OF JULY*
DRIVING MISS DAISY
THE FABULOUS BAKER BOYS
GLORY
Best Makeup
THE ADVENTURES OF BARON MUNCHAUSEN
DAD
DRIVING MISS DAISY*
Best Original Score
John Williams for BORN ON THE FOURTH OF JULY
David Grusin for THE FABULOUS BAKER BOYS
James Horner for FIELD OF DREAMS
John Williams for INDIANA JONES AND THE LAST CRUSADE
Alan Menken for THE LITTLE MERMAID*
Best Original Song
"After All" from CHANCES ARE
"The Girl Who Used to Be Me" from SHIRLEY VALENTINE
"I Love to See You Smile" from PARENTHOOD
"Kiss the Girl" from THE LITTLE MERMAID
"Under the Sea" from THE LITTLE MERMAID*

Best Animated Short Film
BALANCE*
COW
THE HILL FARM
Best Live Action Short Film
AMAZON DIARY
THE CHILD EATER
WORK EXPERIENCE*
Best Sound
THE ABYSS
BLACK RAIN
BORN ON THE FOURTH OF JULY
GLORY*
INDIANA JONES AND THE LAST CRUSADE
Best Sound Effects Editing
BLACK RAIN
INDIANA JONES AND THE LAST CRUSADE*
LETHAL WEAPON 2
Best Visual Effects
THE ABYSS*
THE ADVENTURES OF BARON MUNCHAUSEN
BACK TO THE FUTURE, PART II

4TH AMERICAN SOCIETY OF CINEMATOGRAPHERS AWARDS
Stephen H. Burum for THE WAR OF THE ROSES
Robert Richardson for BORN ON THE FOURTH OF JULY
Philippe Rousselot for THE BEAR
Mikael Salomon for THE ABYSS
Haskell Wexler for BLAZE*

BRITISH ACADEMY OF FILM AND TELEVISION AWARDS
Best Film
THE LAST EMPEROR
Best Direction
Louis Malle for AU REVOIR, LES ENFANTS
Best Actor
John Cleese for A FISH CALLED WANDA
Best Actress
Maggie Smith for THE LONELY PASSION OF JUDITH HEARNE
Best Supporting Actor
Michael Palin for A FISH CALLED WANDA
Best Supporting Actress
Judi Dench for A HANDFUL OF DUST
Best Original Screenplay
Shawn Slovo for A WORLD APART
Best Adapted Screenplay
Jean-Claude Carriere, Philip Kaufman for THE UNBEARABLE
LIGHTNESS OF BEING
Best Score
John Williams for EMPIRE OF THE SUN
Best Foreign Language Film
BABETTE'S FEAST (Den.)

41ST DIRECTORS GUILD OF AMERICA AWARDS
Woody Allen for CRIMES AND MISDEMEANORS
Rob Reiner for WHEN HARRY MET SALLY . . .
Phil Alden Robinson for FIELD OF DREAMS
Oliver Stone for BORN ON THE FOURTH OF JULY*
Peter Weir for DEAD POETS SOCIETY

16TH GENIE AWARDS OF THE ACADEMY OF CANADIAN CINEMA AND
TELEVISION
Best Motion Picture
BYE BYE BLUES

COLD COMFORT
JESUS OF MONTREAL*
TERMINI STATION
Best Actor
Lothaire Bluteau for JESUS OF MONTREAL*
Maury Chaykin for COLD COMFORT
Michel Cote for CRUSING BAR
Michael McManus for SPEAKING PARTS
Stephen Ouimette for THE TOP OF HIS HEAD
Best Actress
Colleen Dewhurst for TERMINI STATION
Megan Follows for TERMINI STATION
Rebecca Jenkins for BYE BYE BLUES*
Margaret Langrick for COLD COMFORT
Gabrielle Rose for SPEAKING PARTS
Catherine Wilkening for JESUS OF MONTREAL*
Best Supporting Actor
Remy Girard for JESUS OF MONTREAL
Don McKellar for ROADKILL
Michael Ontkean for BYE BYE BLUES*
Gilles Pelletier for JESUS OF MONTREAL
Wayne Robson for BYE BYE BLUES
Best Supporting Actress
Pauline Martin for JESUS OF MONTREAL
Robyn Stevan for BYE BYE BLUES*
Johanne-Marie Tremblay for JESUS OF MONTREAL
Best Director
Denys Arcand for JESUS OF MONTREAL*
Jean Beaudry, Francois Bouvier for LES MATINS INFIDELES
Atom Egoyan for SPEAKING PARTS
John N. Smith for WELCOME TO CANADA
Anne Wheeler for BYE BYE BLUES
Best Cinematography
Guy Dufaux for JESUS OF MONTREAL*
Richard Leiterman for THE FIRST SEASON
Pierre Mignot for CRUISING BAR
Rene Ohashi for MILLENNIUM
Best Original Screenplay
Denys Arcand for JESUS OF MONTREAL*
Atom Egoyan for SPEAKING PARTS
Don McKellar for ROADKILL
Peter Mettler for THE TOP OF HIS HEAD
Colleen Murphy for TERMINI STATION
Anne Wheeler for BYE BYE BLUES
Best Adapted Screenplay
Richard Beattie, L. Elliott Simms for COLD COMFORT*
Dany LaFerriere, Richard Sadler for COMMENT FAIRE L'AMOUR AVEC
UN NEGRE SANS SE FATIGUER
John Varley for MILLENIUM
Best Art Direction-Production Design
John Blackie for BYE BYE BLUES
Reuben Freed for PALAIS ROYALE
Francois Seguin for JESUS OF MONTREAL*
Best Film Editing
Isabelle Dedieu for JESUS OF MONTREAL*
Frank Irvine for THE FIRST SEASON
Christopher Tate for BYE BYE BLUES
Best Costume Design
Olga Dimitrov for MILLENNIUM
Louise Jobin for JESUS OF MONTREAL*
Maureen Hiscox for BYE BYE BLUES
Louise Labrecque for CRUISING BAR
Martha Snetsinger for THE LAST WINTER@TI4 =
Katherine Vieira for PALAIS ROYALE
Best Music Score
Jeff Danna, Mychael Danna for COLD COMFORT
Mychael Danna for SPEAKING PARTS

Milan Kymlicka for BABAR: THE MOVIE
Yves LaFerriere for JESUS OF MONTREAL*
Lawrence Shragge for PALAIS ROYALE
Best Original Song
"Restless Dreamer" from AMERICAN BOYFRIENDS
"On Vit de Femmes" from COMMENT FAIRE L'AMOUR
   AVEC UN NEGRE
SANS SE FATIGUER
"When I Sing" from BYE BYE BLUES*
"This Old Earth" from THE TOP OF HIS HEAD
"Elephant March" from BABAR: THE MOVIE
"The Best We Both Can Be" from BABAR: THE MOVIE
Best Documentary Feature
LE TROU DU DIABLE
STRAND, UNDER THE DARK CLOTH*
WHITE LAKE
Best Documentary Short
READING BETWEEN THE LINES
STUNT PEOPLE*
WHO GETS IN?
Best Live Action Short
IN SEARCH OF THE LAST GOOD MAN*
THE JOURNEY HOME
MIKE
MONSTER IN THE COAL BIN
MULTIPLE CHOICE
ODYSSEY IN AUGUST
Best Animated Short
IN AND OUT
JUKE BAR*
THE DINGLES

47TH GOLDEN GLOBE AWARDS
Best Drama
BORN ON THE FOURTH OF JULY, Oliver Stone
Best Director (Drama)
Oliver Stone for BORN ON THE FOURTH OF JULY
Best Actor (Drama)
Tom Cruise for BORN ON THE FOURTH OF JULY
Best Actress (Drama)
Michelle Pfeiffer for THE FABULOUS BAKER BOYS
Best Comedy or Musical Feature
DRIVING MISS DAISY, Bruce Beresford
Best Actor (Comedy)
Forman Freeman for DRIVING MISS DAISY
Best Actress (Comedy)
Jessica Tandy for DRIVING MISS DAISY
Best Supporting Actor
Denzel Washington For GLORY
Best Supporting Actress
Julia Roberts for STEEL MAGNOLIAS
Best Original Score
THE LITTLE MERMAID, Alan Menken
Best Original Song
"Under the Sea," Alan Menken, Howard Ashman
Best Foreign Film
CINEMA PARADISO (It.), Giuseppe Tornatore

LOS ANGELES FILM CRITICS ASSOCIATION AWARDS
Best Film
DO THE RIGHT THING, Spike Lee
Best Director
Spike Lee for DO THE RIGHT THING
Best Actor
Daniel Day-Lewis for MY LEFT FOOT (Brit.)
Best Actress (shared)
Andie MacDowell for SEX, LIES AND VIDEOTAPE
Michelle Pfeiffer for THE FABULOUS BAKER BOYS

Best Supporting Actor
Danny Aiello for DO THE RIGHT THING
Best Supporting Actress
Brenda Fricker for MY LEFT FOOT (Brit.)
Best Screenplay
Gus Van Sant, Jr., and Daniel Yost for DRUGSTORE
   COWBOY
Best Foreign Film (shared)
DISTANT VOICES, STILL LIVES (Brit.), Jim Sheridan
STORY OF WOMEN (Fr.), Claude Chabrol
Best Documentary
ROGER AND ME, Michael Moore
Best Animation
THE LITTLE MERMAID, John Musker and Ron Clements

NATIONAL BOARD OF REVIEW D.W. GRIFFITH AWARDS
Best Film
DRIVING MISS DAISY, Bruce Beresford
Best Actor
Morgan Freeman for DRIVING MISS DAISY
Best Actress
Michelle Pfeiffer for THE FABULOUS BAKER BOYS
Best Supporting Actor
Alan Alda for CRIMES AND MISDEMEANORS
Best Supporting Actress
Mary Stuart Masterson for IMMEDIATE FAMILY
Best Director
Kenneth Branagh for HENRY V
Best Documentary
ROGER AND ME, Michael Moore
Best Foreign Film
STORY OF WOMEN (Fr.), Claude Chabrol
Honorary Career Award
Richard Widmark

24TH NATIONAL SOCIETY OF FILM CRITICS AWARDS
Best Film
DRUGSTORE COWBOY, Gus Van Sant, Jr.
Best Director
Gus Van Sant, Jr. for DRUGSTORE COWBOY
Best Actor
Daniel Day-Lewis for MY LEFT FOOT (Brit.)
Best Actress
Michelle Pfeiffer for THE FABULOUS BAKER BOYS
Best Supporting Actor
Beau Bridges for THE FABULOUS BAKER BOYS
Best Supporting Actress
Anjelica Huston for ENEMIES, A LOVE STORY
Best Screenplay
DRUGSTORE COWBOY, Gus Van Sant, Jr., Daniel Yost
Best Cinematography
Michael Ballhaus for THE FABULOUS BAKER BOYS
Best Documentary
ROGER AND ME, Michael Moore

55TH NEW YORK FILM CRITICS CIRCLE AWARDS
Best Film
MY LEFT FOOT (Brit.), Jim Sheridan
Best Director
Paul Mazursky for ENEMIES, A LOVE STORY
Best Actor
Daniel Day-Lewis for MY LEFT FOOT (Brit.)
Best Actress
Michelle Pfeiffer for THE FABULOUS BAKER BOYS
Best Supporting Actor
Alan Alda for CRIMES AND MISDEMEANORS

Best Supporting Actress
Lena Olin for ENEMIES, A LOVE STORY
Best Screenplay
Gus Van Sant, Jr., Daniel Yost for DRUGSTORE COWBOY
Best Cinematographer
Ernest Dickerson for DO THE RIGHT THING
Best Foreign Film
STORY OF WOMEN (Fr.), Claude Chabrol
Best Documentary
ROGER AND ME, Michael Moore
Best New Director
Kenneth Branagh for HENRY V (Brit.)

42ND WRITERS GUILD OF AMERICA AWARDS
Best Original Screenplay
Woody Allen for CRIMES AND MISDEMEANORS*
Nora Ephron for WHEN HARRY MET SALLY . . .
Steve Kloves for THE FABULOUS BAKER BOYS
Tom Schulman for DEAD POETS SOCIETY
Steven Soderbergh for SEX, LIES AND VIDEOTAPE
Best Adapted Screenplay
Shane Connaughton, Jim Sheridan for MY LEFT FOOT
Kevin Jarre for GLORY
Phil Alden Robinson for FIELD OF DREAMS
Oliver Stone, Ron Kovic for BORN ON THE FOURTH OF
    JULY
Alfred Uhry for DRIVING MISS DAISY*

FILMS BY STAR RATING

All films in this annual are listed below by their star ratings: The ratings indicate:
****: excellent; ***: good; **: fair; *: poor; zero: without merit

****
BEAR, THE
DO THE RIGHT THING
DRIVING MISS DAISY
DRUGSTORE COWBOY
GLORY
HENRY: PORTRAIT OF A SERIAL
 KILLER
HIGH HOPES
MALA NOCHE
MONSIEUR HIRE
MUSIC BOX
MY LEFT FOOT
QUEEN OF HEARTS
SAY ANYTHING
TALVISOTA
WAR OF THE ROSES, THE
YAABA

***1/2
BACK TO THE FUTURE PART II
CASUALTIES OF WAR
COHEN AND TATE
DEAD CALM
DEAD POETS SOCIETY
DISTANT VOICES, STILL LIVES
84 CHARLIE MOPIC
FEW DAYS WITH ME, A
FIELD OF DREAMS
HEATHERS
HUNGARIAN FAIRY TALE, A
I, MADMAN
LETHAL WEAPON 2
LICENCE TO KILL
LIFE AND NOTHING BUT
LITTLE VERA
MIRACLE MILE
MYSTERY TRAIN
NEW YORK STORIES: LIFE
 LESSONS
NEXT OF KIN
PARENTHOOD
PENN & TELLER GET KILLED
PRANCER
SEA OF LOVE
SEX, LIES AND VIDEOTAPE
STEALING HEAVEN
TAP

***
ADVENTURES OF BARON
 MUNCHAUSEN, THE
ADVENTURES OF MILO AND OTIS,
 THE
ALL DOGS GO TO HEAVEN
APARTMENT ZERO
BORN ON THE FOURTH OF JULY
CHANCES ARE
CHEETAH

CHORUS OF DISAPPROVAL, A
COUSINS
CRIMES AND MISDEMEANORS
CRIMINAL LAW
DEAD-BANG
DREAM TEAM, THE
DRY WHITE SEASON, A
GANG OF FOUR, THE
GETTING IT RIGHT
GLEAMING THE CUBE
HELL HIGH
HIGH STAKES
HONEY, I SHRUNK THE KIDS
IMMEDIATE FAMILY
INNOCENT MAN, AN
JACKNIFE
LITTLE MERMAID, THE
LOOK WHO'S TALKING
LUCKIEST MAN IN THE WORLD,
 THE
MAJOR LEAGUE
MIGHTY QUINN, THE
PARENTS
PHYSICAL EVIDENCE
PINK CADILLAC
RABID GRANNIES
RACHEL PAPERS, THE
RACHEL RIVER
RAINBOW, THE
ROMERO
ROSE GARDEN, THE
SCANDAL
SEASON OF FEAR
SHIRLEY VALENTINE
SIDEWALK STORIES
SOME GIRLS
STEEL MAGNOLIAS
STORY OF WOMEN
STRIPPED TO KILL II: LIVE GIRLS
TANGO AND CASH
TANGO BAR
TOO BEAUTIFUL FOR YOU
TORA-SAN GOES TO VIENNA
TRIUMPH OF THE SPIRIT
TRUE BELIEVER
TRUE LOVE
UNREMARKABLE LIFE, AN
WE THINK THE WORLD OF YOU
WELCOME HOME
WE'RE NO ANGELS
WHEN HARRY MET SALLY. . .
YOUNG EINSTEIN

**1/2
ALWAYS
BABAR: THE MOVIE
BATMAN
BILL & TED'S EXCELLENT
 ADVENTURE

BLACK RAIN
BLAZE
BREAKING IN
'BURBS, THE
CAMILLE CLAUDEL
EARTH GIRLS ARE EASY
ENEMIES, A LOVE STORY
FABULOUS BAKER BOYS, THE
FROM HOLLYWOOD TO
 DEADWOOD
HARDCASE AND FIST
HEART OF DIXIE
IN COUNTRY
INDIANA JONES AND THE LAST
 CRUSADE
IRON TRIANGLE, THE
JOHNNY HANDSOME
K-9
KICKBOXER
L.A. HEAT
LA LECTRICE
LEAN ON ME
LEVIATHAN
LITTLE THIEF, THE
MAPANTSULA
NATIONAL LAMPOON'S
 CHRISTMAS VACATION
NAVIGATOR, THE
NEW YORK STORIES: OEDIPUS
 WRECKS
NIGHT GAME
NIGHTMARE ON ELM STREET 5:
 THE DREAM CHILD, A
NO HOLDS BARRED
PIN
REMBRANDT LAUGHING
SAND AND BLOOD
SCENES FROM THE CLASS
 STRUGGLE IN BEVERLY HILLS
SEE YOU IN THE MORNING
SHAG
SHOCKER
SIGNS OF LIFE
STAR TREK V: THE FINAL
 FRONTIER
STEPFATHER 2: MAKE ROOM FOR
 DADDY
UHF
UNCLE BUCK
WAR PARTY
WEEKEND AT BERNIE'S
WICKED STEPMOTHER
WINTER PEOPLE, THE
WIRED

**
ABYSS, THE
BACKFIRE
BEST OF THE BEST

BLOODHOUNDS OF BROADWAY
CHECKING OUT
COOKIE
CRIME ZONE
CRUSOE
DEEPSTAR SIX
DOIN' TIME ON PLANET EARTH
DREAM A LITTLE DREAM
ECHOES IN PARADISE
EDDIE AND THE CRUISERS II:
   EDDIE LIVES!
ERIK THE VIKING
FAR FROM HOME
FAREWELL TO THE KING
FAT MAN AND LITTLE BOY
FEAR, ANXIETY AND DEPRESSION
FLETCH LIVES
FOR QUEEN AND COUNTRY
FRIGHT NIGHT—PART 2
GHETTOBLASTER
GNAW: FOOD OF THE GODS II
GREAT BALLS OF FIRE
GROSS ANATOMY
HARLEM NIGHTS
HEART OF MIDNIGHT
HOMEBOY
HOW I GOT INTO COLLEGE
HOW TO GET AHEAD IN
   ADVERTISING
JANUARY MAN, THE
KINJITE: FORBIDDEN SUBJECTS
KUNG FU MASTER
LAST WARRIOR, THE
LISTEN TO ME
LOST ANGELS
LOVERBOY
MINISTRY OF VENGEANCE
MISS FIRECRACKER
NEW YEAR'S DAY
NEW YORK STORIES: LIFE WITH
   ZOE
NOWHERE TO RUN
OLD GRINGO
OPTIONS
PACKAGE, THE
PAPERHOUSE
RACE FOR GLORY
RED SCORPION
RENEGADES
RETURN OF SWAMP THING, THE
ROAD HOUSE
SHE'S OUT OF CONTROL
SLAVES OF NEW YORK
SLEEPAWAY CAMP 3: TEENAGE
   WASTELAND
SPEAKING PARTS
STORM
SWEET LIES
THREE FUGITIVES
TO KILL A PRIEST
TRUE BLOOD
TRUST ME
TURNER & HOOCH
VALENTINO RETURNS
VALMONT
WHEN THE WHALES CAME

*1/2
ALEXA

CODE NAME VENGEANCE
COMMUNION
CUTTING CLASS
DEATHSTALKER AND THE
   WARRIORS FROM HELL
DISORGANIZED CRIME
DR. HACKENSTEIN
DOWN TWISTED
FAMILY BUSINESS
FLY II, THE
FORBIDDEN SUN
FRIENDS, LOVERS AND LUNATICS
GHOSTBUSTERS II
GIRL IN A SWING, THE
GOING UNDERCOVER
GOR
GUNRUNNER, THE
HOWLING 5: THE REBIRTH, THE
KARATE KID PART III, THE
L.A. BOUNTY
LET IT RIDE
LIMIT UP
LOCK UP
MEET THE HOLLOWHEADS
MOB WAR
MUTANT ON THE BOUNTY
NIGHT OF THE DEMONS
NO RETREAT, NO SURRENDER II
NO SAFE HAVEN
PERFECT MODEL, THE
PET SEMATARY
SEE NO EVIL, HEAR NO EVIL
SHE-DEVIL
SKIN DEEP
STAYING TOGETHER
TO DIE FOR
TOXIC AVENGER PART III, THE:
   THE LAST TEMPTATION OF
   TOXIE
TOXIC AVENGER, PART II, THE
TWICE DEAD
WOMAN OBSESSED, A

*
AFTER MIDNIGHT
AFTER SCHOOL
AMERICAN NINJA 3: BLOOD HUNT
BERT RIGBY, YOU'RE A FOOL
BEVERLY HILLS BRATS
BIG BLUE, THE
BIG PICTURE, THE
BLACK ROSES
BLOODFIST
B.O.R.N.
BUY & CELL
CAGE
CAMERON'S CLOSET
CARPENTER, THE
CHAIR, THE
C.H.U.D. II: BUD THE C.H.U.D.
CURFEW
CYBORG
DAD
DANCE OF THE DAMNED
DANGER ZONE II: REAPER'S
   REVENGE
DARK TOWER
DEADLY OBSESSION
DEALERS

EASY WHEELS
EDGE OF SANITY
EXPERTS, THE
FAST FOOD
FEAR
FIST FIGHTER
GRANDMOTHER'S HOUSE
HER ALIBI
HORROR SHOW, THE
MADE IN USA
MILLENNIUM
NECROMANCER
976-EVIL
OFFERINGS
OUT COLD
PHANTOM OF THE MALL: ERIC'S
   REVENGE
PHANTOM OF THE OPERA
POLICE ACADEMY 6: CITY UNDER
   SIEGE
RELENTLESS
ROOFTOPS
RUDE AWAKENING
SATURDAY THE 14TH STRIKES
   BACK
SEDUCTION: THE CRUEL WOMAN
SILENT NIGHT, DEADLY NIGHT 3:
   BETTER WATCH OUT!
SKELETON COAST
SLIPPING INTO DARKNESS
SPEED ZONE
STREET JUSTICE
TEEN WITCH
TERROR WITHIN, THE
TIME TRACKERS
TROOP BEVERLY HILLS
UNDER THE GUN
VICE ACADEMY
WHO'S HARRY CRUMB?
WIZARD, THE
WORTH WINNING

Zero
CHASING DREAMS
CRACK HOUSE
DEADLY POSSESSION
DR. ALIEN
FREEWAY MANIAC, THE
FRIDAY THE 13TH PART
   VIII—JASON TAKES
   MANHATTAN
GATOR BAIT II: CAJUN JUSTICE
GLITCH
HALLOWEEN 5: THE REVENGE OF
   MICHAEL MYERS
SCREWBALL HOTEL
SLASH DANCE
TWO TO TANGO
WAR BIRDS
YOUNG NURSES IN LOVE

FILMS BY GENRE

All films included in this annual are listed below by the genre best suited to the film. Those films which can be classified in more than one genre are listed under each of the category in which they fit.

Action
AMERICAN NINJA 3: BLOOD HUNT
BEST OF THE BEST
BLOODFIST
CAGE
CODE NAME VENGEANCE
COHEN AND TATE
CRIME ZONE
CYBORG
DANGER ZONE II: REAPER'S
   REVENGE
DOWN TWISTED
EASY WHEELS
FEAR
FIST FIGHTER
GATOR BAIT II: CAJUN JUSTICE
GHETTOBLASTER
GLEAMING THE CUBE
GOR
GUNRUNNER, THE
HARDCASE AND FIST
HARLEM NIGHTS
JOHNNY HANDSOME
KICKBOXER
L.A. BOUNTY
LAST WARRIOR, THE
MINISTRY OF VENGEANCE
MOB WAR
NEXT OF KIN
NO HOLDS BARRED
NO RETREAT, NO SURRENDER II
NO SAFE HAVEN
NOWHERE TO RUN
RED SCORPION
RENEGADES
ROAD HOUSE
SKELETON COAST
STREET JUSTICE
TANGO AND CASH
TOXIC AVENGER, PART II, THE
TRUE BLOOD
UNDER THE GUN
WAR PARTY

Adventure
BACK TO THE FUTURE PART II
BEAR, THE
CHEETAH
CODE NAME VENGEANCE
DANGER ZONE II: REAPER'S
   REVENGE
DEATHSTALKER AND THE
   WARRIORS FROM HELL
GLEAMING THE CUBE
INDIANA JONES AND THE LAST
   CRUSADE
NAVIGATOR, THE

Animated
ALL DOGS GO TO HEAVEN
BABAR: THE MOVIE
LITTLE MERMAID, THE

Biography
BLAZE
CAMILLE CLAUDEL
GREAT BALLS OF FIRE
MY LEFT FOOT
ROMERO
SCANDAL
TRIUMPH OF THE SPIRIT
WIRED

Children's
ADVENTURES OF MILO AND OTIS,
   THE
ALL DOGS GO TO HEAVEN
BABAR: THE MOVIE
CHEETAH
HONEY, I SHRUNK THE KIDS
LITTLE MERMAID, THE
WIZARD, THE

Comedy
BERT RIGBY, YOU'RE A FOOL
BEVERLY HILLS BRATS
BIG PICTURE, THE
BILL & TED'S EXCELLENT
   ADVENTURE
BLOODHOUNDS OF BROADWAY
BREAKING IN
'BURBS, THE
BUY & CELL
CARPENTER, THE
CHANCES ARE
CHECKING OUT
CHORUS OF DISAPPROVAL, A
C.H.U.D. II: BUD THE C.H.U.D.
COOKIE
COUSINS
CUTTING CLASS
DISORGANIZED CRIME
DO THE RIGHT THING
DR. ALIEN
DR. HACKENSTEIN
DOIN' TIME ON PLANET EARTH
DREAM A LITTLE DREAM
DREAM TEAM, THE
DRIVING MISS DAISY
EARTH GIRLS ARE EASY
EASY WHEELS
ENEMIES, A LOVE STORY
EXPERTS, THE
FABULOUS BAKER BOYS, THE
FAMILY BUSINESS
FAST FOOD

FEAR, ANXIETY AND DEPRESSION
FLETCH LIVES
FREEWAY MANIAC, THE
FRIENDS, LOVERS AND LUNATICS
FRIGHT NIGHT—PART 2
GETTING IT RIGHT
GHOSTBUSTERS II
GLITCH
GOING UNDERCOVER
GROSS ANATOMY
HARLEM NIGHTS
HEATHERS
HER ALIBI
HIGH HOPES
HOW I GOT INTO COLLEGE
HOW TO GET AHEAD IN
   ADVERTISING
JANUARY MAN, THE
K-9
LA LECTRICE
LET IT RIDE
LIMIT UP
LOOK WHO'S TALKING
LOVERBOY
LUCKIEST MAN IN THE WORLD,
   THE
MISS FIRECRACKER
MUTANT ON THE BOUNTY
MYSTERY TRAIN
NATIONAL LAMPOON'S
   CHRISTMAS VACATION
NEW YEAR'S DAY
NEW YORK STORIES
OPTIONS
OUT COLD
PARENTHOOD
PARENTS
PENN & TELLER GET KILLED
PINK CADILLAC
POLICE ACADEMY 6: CITY UNDER
   SIEGE
QUEEN OF HEARTS
RABID GRANNIES
RACHEL PAPERS, THE
RACHEL RIVER
RUDE AWAKENING
SATURDAY THE 14TH STRIKES
   BACK
SAY ANYTHING
SCENES FROM THE CLASS
   STRUGGLE IN BEVERLY HILLS
SCREWBALL HOTEL
SEE NO EVIL, HEAR NO EVIL
SHAG
SHE-DEVIL
SHE'S OUT OF CONTROL
SHIRLEY VALENTINE
SIDEWALK STORIES

SKIN DEEP
SLAVES OF NEW YORK
SOME GIRLS
SPEED ZONE
STAYING TOGETHER
STEEL MAGNOLIAS
SWEET LIES
SWEETIE
THREE FUGITIVES
TOO BEAUTIFUL FOR YOU
TORA-SAN GOES TO VIENNA
TOXIC AVENGER PART III, THE:
  THE LAST TEMPTATION OF
  TOXIE
TOXIC AVENGER, PART II, THE
TROOP BEVERLY HILLS
TRUE LOVE
TRUST ME
TURNER & HOOCH
UHF
UNCLE BUCK
VALENTINO RETURNS
VICE ACADEMY
WAR OF THE ROSES, THE
WE THINK THE WORLD OF YOU
WEEKEND AT BERNIE'S
WE'RE NO ANGELS
WHEN HARRY MET SALLY. . .
WHO'S HARRY CRUMB?
WICKED STEPMOTHER
WIZARD, THE
WORTH WINNING
YOUNG EINSTEIN
YOUNG NURSES IN LOVE

Crime
BIG BLUE, THE
BLACK RAIN
COOKIE
CRACK HOUSE
DEAD-BANG
DISORGANIZED CRIME
HENRY: PORTRAIT OF A SERIAL
  KILLER
INNOCENT MAN, AN
JANUARY MAN, THE
JOHNNY HANDSOME
K-9
KINJITE: FORBIDDEN SUBJECTS
L.A. HEAT
LETHAL WEAPON 2
MIGHTY QUINN, THE
MOB WAR
NEXT OF KIN
PHYSICAL EVIDENCE
THREE FUGITIVES
TRUE BELIEVER
TURNER & HOOCH
TWO TO TANGO

Dance
TAP

Docu-drama
TANGO BAR

Drama
AFTER SCHOOL
ALEXA

BLOODHOUNDS OF BROADWAY
BORN ON THE FOURTH OF JULY
CHASING DREAMS
CHORUS OF DISAPPROVAL, A
CRIMES AND MISDEMEANORS
CRUSOE
DAD
DEAD POETS SOCIETY
DEALERS
DISTANT VOICES, STILL LIVES
DO THE RIGHT THING
DRIVING MISS DAISY
DRUGSTORE COWBOY
DRY WHITE SEASON, A
EDDIE AND THE CRUISERS II:
  EDDIE LIVES!
ENEMIES, A LOVE STORY
FABULOUS BAKER BOYS, THE
FAMILY BUSINESS
FEW DAYS WITH ME, A
FOR QUEEN AND COUNTRY
FORBIDDEN SUN
GANG OF FOUR, THE
GETTING IT RIGHT
GROSS ANATOMY
HEART OF DIXIE
HENRY V
HIGH HOPES
IMMEDIATE FAMILY
IN COUNTRY
JACKNIFE
KARATE KID PART III, THE
LA LECTRICE
LEAN ON ME
LIFE AND NOTHING BUT
LISTEN TO ME
LITTLE THIEF, THE
LITTLE VERA
LOST ANGELS
MADE IN USA
MALA NOCHE
MUSIC BOX
NEW YORK STORIES
PERFECT MODEL, THE
PINK CADILLAC
PRANCER
RACHEL RIVER
RAINBOW, THE
REMBRANDT LAUGHING
ROOFTOPS
ROSE GARDEN, THE
SAND AND BLOOD
SAY ANYTHING
SEDUCTION: THE CRUEL WOMAN
SEE YOU IN THE MORNING
SEX, LIES AND VIDEOTAPE
SHIRLEY VALENTINE
SIGNS OF LIFE
SOME GIRLS
SPEAKING PARTS
STAYING TOGETHER
STEEL MAGNOLIAS
STORY OF WOMEN
TAP
TO KILL A PRIEST
UNREMARKABLE LIFE, AN
VALENTINO RETURNS
VALMONT
WE THINK THE WORLD OF YOU

WELCOME HOME
WHEN THE WHALES CAME
YAABA

Fantasy
ADVENTURES OF BARON
  MUNCHAUSEN, THE
ALWAYS
BACK TO THE FUTURE PART II
BATMAN
CHANCES ARE
DEATHSTALKER AND THE
  WARRIORS FROM HELL
ERIK THE VIKING
GOR
HEATHERS
HUNGARIAN FAIRY TALE, A
NAVIGATOR, THE
TEEN WITCH

Historical
FAT MAN AND LITTLE BOY
GLORY
HENRY V
INDIANA JONES AND THE LAST
  CRUSADE
OLD GRINGO
STEALING HEAVEN

Horror
AFTER MIDNIGHT
BLACK ROSES
B.O.R.N.
BRAIN, THE
CAMERON'S CLOSET
CARPENTER, THE
C.H.U.D. II: BUD THE C.H.U.D.
CUTTING CLASS
DANCE OF THE DAMNED
DARK TOWER
DEAD CALM
DEEPSTAR SIX
DR. HACKENSTEIN
EDGE OF SANITY
FAR FROM HOME
FLY II, THE
FREEWAY MANIAC, THE
FRIDAY THE 13TH PART
  VIII—JASON TAKES
  MANHATTAN
FRIGHT NIGHT—PART 2
GHOSTBUSTERS II
GNAW: FOOD OF THE GODS II
GRANDMOTHER'S HOUSE
HALLOWEEN 5: THE REVENGE OF
  MICHAEL MYERS
HELL HIGH
HENRY: PORTRAIT OF A SERIAL
  KILLER
HORROR SHOW, THE
HOWLING 5: THE REBIRTH, THE
I, MADMAN
NECROMANCER
NIGHT OF THE DEMONS
NIGHTMARE ON ELM STREET 5:
  THE DREAM CHILD, A
976-EVIL
OFFERINGS
PAPERHOUSE

PARENTS
PET SEMATARY
PHANTOM OF THE MALL: ERIC'S
    REVENGE
PHANTOM OF THE OPERA
PIN
RABID GRANNIES
SATURDAY THE 14TH STRIKES
    BACK
SHOCKER
SILENT NIGHT, DEADLY NIGHT 3:
    BETTER WATCH OUT!
SLEEPAWAY CAMP 3: TEENAGE
    WASTELAND
STEPFATHER 2: MAKE ROOM FOR
    DADDY
TERROR WITHIN, THE
TO DIE FOR
WICKED STEPMOTHER

Musical
BERT RIGBY, YOU'RE A FOOL
GREAT BALLS OF FIRE
TANGO BAR

Mystery
BACKFIRE
BIG BLUE, THE
FROM HOLLYWOOD TO
    DEADWOOD
HER ALIBI
SEA OF LOVE
STRIPPED TO KILL II: LIVE GIRLS
TRUE BELIEVER

Political
HUNGARIAN FAIRY TALE, A
MAPANTSULA
PACKAGE, THE
ROMERO
SCANDAL

Prison
CHAIR, THE
LOCK UP

Romance
ALWAYS
CHANCES ARE
COUSINS
ECHOES IN PARADISE
FRIENDS, LOVERS AND LUNATICS
HIGH STAKES
KUNG FU MASTER
MIRACLE MILE
MISS FIRECRACKER
QUEEN OF HEARTS
SHAG
SHIRLEY VALENTINE
SLAVES OF NEW YORK
STEALING HEAVEN
WHEN HARRY MET SALLY. . .
WINTER PEOPLE, THE

Science Fiction
ABYSS, THE
COMMUNION
CRIME ZONE
DEEPSTAR SIX

DR. ALIEN
EARTH GIRLS ARE EASY
FLY II, THE
HONEY, I SHRUNK THE KIDS
LEVIATHAN
MEET THE HOLLOWHEADS
MILLENNIUM
MIRACLE MILE
MUTANT ON THE BOUNTY
RETURN OF SWAMP THING, THE
STAR TREK V: THE FINAL
    FRONTIER
TIME TRACKERS
TOXIC AVENGER PART III, THE:
    THE LAST TEMPTATION OF
    TOXIE

Sports
FIELD OF DREAMS
HOMEBOY
MAJOR LEAGUE
NO HOLDS BARRED
RACE FOR GLORY

Spy
LICENCE TO KILL

Thriller
APARTMENT ZERO
BACKFIRE
BLACK RAIN
COHEN AND TATE
CRIMINAL LAW
CURFEW
DEAD CALM
DEADLY OBSESSION
DEADLY POSSESSION
DOWN TWISTED
GIRL IN A SWING, THE
GOING UNDERCOVER
HEART OF MIDNIGHT
HIGH STAKES
KINJITE: FORBIDDEN SUBJECTS
LETHAL WEAPON 2
MONSIEUR HIRE
NIGHT GAME
PACKAGE, THE
PHYSICAL EVIDENCE
RELENTLESS
SEA OF LOVE
SEASON OF FEAR
SLASH DANCE
SLIPPING INTO DARKNESS
STORM
STRIPPED TO KILL II: LIVE GIRLS
TURNER & HOOCH
TWICE DEAD
WOMAN OBSESSED, A

War
BORN ON THE FOURTH OF JULY
CASUALTIES OF WAR
84 CHARLIE MOPIC
FAREWELL TO THE KING
GLORY
IRON TRIANGLE, THE
LAST WARRIOR, THE

TALVISOTA
WAR BIRDS
WAR REQUIEM

FILMS BY PARENTAL RECOMMENDATION (PR)

All films in this volume are listed below by the parental recommendation given to the film. The PR ratings indicate the following:

AA: Good for children; A: Acceptable for children; C: Cautionary; O: Objectionable for children.

AA
ADVENTURES OF MILO AND OTIS, THE
CHEETAH
ERIK THE VIKING
LITTLE MERMAID, THE
PRANCER
WHEN THE WHALES CAME
YOUNG EINSTEIN

A
ALL DOGS GO TO HEAVEN
BABAR: THE MOVIE
BACK TO THE FUTURE PART II
BILL & TED'S EXCELLENT ADVENTURE
CHANCES ARE
CHASING DREAMS
COUSINS
DEAD POETS SOCIETY
DRIVING MISS DAISY
EDDIE AND THE CRUISERS II: EDDIE LIVES!
FIELD OF DREAMS
GHOSTBUSTERS II
HENRY V
HONEY, I SHRUNK THE KIDS
HUNGARIAN FAIRY TALE, A
MILLENNIUM
MY LEFT FOOT
NAVIGATOR, THE
QUEEN OF HEARTS
RACHEL RIVER
REMBRANDT LAUGHING
SATURDAY THE 14TH STRIKES BACK
SHE-DEVIL
SHE'S OUT OF CONTROL
STAR TREK V: THE FINAL FRONTIER
TEEN WITCH
TIME TRACKERS
TORA-SAN GOES TO VIENNA
TRUST ME
UNCLE BUCK
WICKED STEPMOTHER
WIZARD, THE
YAABA

A-C
ADVENTURES OF BARON MUNCHAUSEN, THE
ALWAYS
BATMAN
BEAR, THE
'BURBS, THE
CHORUS OF DISAPPROVAL, A
CRIMES AND MISDEMEANORS
INDIANA JONES AND THE LAST CRUSADE
KARATE KID PART III, THE
LUCKIEST MAN IN THE WORLD, THE
POLICE ACADEMY 6: CITY UNDER SIEGE
SAY ANYTHING
THREE FUGITIVES
TROOP BEVERLY HILLS
WE THINK THE WORLD OF YOU

C
ABYSS, THE
AMERICAN NINJA 3: BLOOD HUNT
BEST OF THE BEST
BEVERLY HILLS BRATS
BIG BLUE, THE
BIG PICTURE, THE
BLACK RAIN
BLOODHOUNDS OF BROADWAY
BREAKING IN
BUY & CELL
CASUALTIES OF WAR
C.H.U.D. II: BUD THE C.H.U.D.
CODE NAME VENGEANCE
COMMUNION
COOKIE
CRUSOE
DAD
DARK TOWER
DEATHSTALKER AND THE WARRIORS FROM HELL
DEEPSTAR SIX
DISORGANIZED CRIME
DISTANT VOICES, STILL LIVES
DR. HACKENSTEIN
DOIN' TIME ON PLANET EARTH
DREAM A LITTLE DREAM
DREAM TEAM, THE
DRY WHITE SEASON, A
EARTH GIRLS ARE EASY
ECHOES IN PARADISE
ENEMIES, A LOVE STORY
EXPERTS, THE
FAMILY BUSINESS
FAREWELL TO THE KING
FAST FOOD
FAT MAN AND LITTLE BOY
FEAR, ANXIETY AND DEPRESSION
FEW DAYS WITH ME, A
FLETCH LIVES
FORBIDDEN SUN
FREEWAY MANIAC, THE
FRIENDS, LOVERS AND LUNATICS
FROM HOLLYWOOD TO DEADWOOD
GANG OF FOUR, THE
GLEAMING THE CUBE
GLORY
GOING UNDERCOVER
GOR
GREAT BALLS OF FIRE
GROSS ANATOMY
GUNRUNNER, THE
HARDCASE AND FIST
HEART OF DIXIE
HER ALIBI
HIGH HOPES
HOMEBOY
HOW I GOT INTO COLLEGE
HOW TO GET AHEAD IN ADVERTISING
HOWLING 5: THE REBIRTH, THE
IMMEDIATE FAMILY
IN COUNTRY
INNOCENT MAN, AN
JACKNIFE
K-9
KICKBOXER
L.A. HEAT
LEAN ON ME
LET IT RIDE
LEVIATHAN
LIMIT UP
LISTEN TO ME
LOOK WHO'S TALKING
LOST ANGELS
LOVERBOY
MAPANTSULA
MINISTRY OF VENGEANCE
MISS FIRECRACKER
MUSIC BOX
MUTANT ON THE BOUNTY
NATIONAL LAMPOON'S CHRISTMAS VACATION
NEW YEAR'S DAY
NEXT OF KIN
NO HOLDS BARRED
NO SAFE HAVEN
OLD GRINGO
OPTIONS
PACKAGE, THE
PAPERHOUSE
PARENTHOOD
PARENTS
PERFECT MODEL, THE
PHYSICAL EVIDENCE
PINK CADILLAC
RACE FOR GLORY
RACHEL PAPERS, THE
RETURN OF SWAMP THING, THE
ROOFTOPS
ROSE GARDEN, THE
SEE YOU IN THE MORNING
SEX, LIES AND VIDEOTAPE
SHAG
SHIRLEY VALENTINE
SIDEWALK STORIES
SIGNS OF LIFE
SKELETON COAST

SLASH DANCE
SOME GIRLS
SPEED ZONE
STAYING TOGETHER
STEALING HEAVEN
STEEL MAGNOLIAS
STORM
STREET JUSTICE
SWEET LIES
TANGO BAR
TAP
TRIUMPH OF THE SPIRIT
TURNER & HOOCH
TWICE DEAD
UHF
UNREMARKABLE LIFE, AN
VICE ACADEMY
WAR BIRDS
WELCOME HOME
WE'RE NO ANGELS
WHEN HARRY MET SALLY. . .
WHO'S HARRY CRUMB?
WINTER PEOPLE, THE
WIRED

C-O

FABULOUS BAKER BOYS, THE
I, MADMAN
LAST WARRIOR, THE
LICENCE TO KILL
MIGHTY QUINN, THE
MIRACLE MILE
NEW YORK STORIES
RED SCORPION
SEE NO EVIL, HEAR NO EVIL
TRUE BLOOD

O

AFTER MIDNIGHT
AFTER SCHOOL
ALEXA
APARTMENT ZERO
BACKFIRE
BERT RIGBY, YOU'RE A FOOL
BLACK ROSES
BLAZE
BLOODFIST
B.O.R.N.
BORN ON THE FOURTH OF JULY
CAGE
CAMERON'S CLOSET
CAMILLE CLAUDEL
CARPENTER, THE
CHAIR, THE
CHECKING OUT
COHEN AND TATE
CRACK HOUSE
CRIME ZONE
CRIMINAL LAW
CURFEW
CUTTING CLASS
CYBORG
DANCE OF THE DAMNED
DANGER ZONE II: REAPER'S
    REVENGE
DEAD-BANG
DEAD CALM
DEADLY OBSESSION
DEADLY POSSESSION

DEALERS
DO THE RIGHT THING
DR. ALIEN
DOWN TWISTED
DRUGSTORE COWBOY
EASY WHEELS
EDGE OF SANITY
84 CHARLIE MOPIC
FAR FROM HOME
FEAR
FIST FIGHTER
FLY II, THE
FOR QUEEN AND COUNTRY
FRIDAY THE 13TH PART
    VIII—JASON TAKES
    MANHATTAN
FRIGHT NIGHT—PART 2
GATOR BAIT II: CAJUN JUSTICE
GETTING IT RIGHT
GHETTOBLASTER
GIRL IN A SWING, THE
GLITCH
GNAW: FOOD OF THE GODS II
GRANDMOTHER'S HOUSE
HALLOWEEN 5: THE REVENGE OF
    MICHAEL MYERS
HARLEM NIGHTS
HEART OF MIDNIGHT
HEATHERS
HELL HIGH
HENRY: PORTRAIT OF A SERIAL
    KILLER
HIGH STAKES
HORROR SHOW, THE
IRON TRIANGLE, THE
JANUARY MAN, THE
JOHNNY HANDSOME
KINJITE: FORBIDDEN SUBJECTS
KUNG FU MASTER
L.A. BOUNTY
LA LECTRICE
LETHAL WEAPON 2
LIFE AND NOTHING BUT
LITTLE THIEF, THE
LITTLE VERA
LOCK UP
MADE IN USA
MAJOR LEAGUE
MALA NOCHE
MEET THE HOLLOWHEADS
MEMORIES OF PRISON
MIDNIGHT COP
MOB WAR
MONSIEUR HIRE
MYSTERY TRAIN
NECROMANCER
NIGHT GAME
NIGHT OF THE DEMONS
NIGHTMARE ON ELM STREET 5:
    THE DREAM CHILD, A
976-EVIL
NO RETREAT, NO SURRENDER II
NOWHERE TO RUN
OFFERINGS
OUT COLD
PENN & TELLER GET KILLED
PET SEMATARY

PHANTOM OF THE MALL: ERIC'S
    REVENGE
PHANTOM OF THE OPERA
PIN
RABID GRANNIES
RAINBOW, THE
RELENTLESS
RENEGADES
ROAD HOUSE
ROMERO
RUDE AWAKENING
SAND AND BLOOD
SCANDAL
SCENES FROM THE CLASS
    STRUGGLE IN BEVERLY HILLS
SCREWBALL HOTEL
SEA OF LOVE
SEASON OF FEAR
SEDUCTION: THE CRUEL WOMAN
SHOCKER
SILENT NIGHT, DEADLY NIGHT 3:
    BETTER WATCH OUT!
SKIN DEEP
SLAVES OF NEW YORK
SLEEPAWAY CAMP 3: TEENAGE
    WASTELAND
SLIPPING INTO DARKNESS
SPEAKING PARTS
STEPFATHER 2: MAKE ROOM FOR
    DADDY
STORY OF WOMEN
STRIPPED TO KILL II: LIVE GIRLS
SWEETIE
TALVISOTA
TANGO AND CASH
TERROR WITHIN, THE
TIMES TO COME
TO DIE FOR
TO KILL A PRIEST
TOO BEAUTIFUL FOR YOU
TOXIC AVENGER PART III, THE:
    THE LAST TEMPTATION OF
    TOXIE
TOXIC AVENGER, PART II, THE
TRUE BELIEVER
TRUE LOVE
TWO TO TANGO
UNDER THE GUN
VALENTINO RETURNS
VALMONT
WAR OF THE ROSES, THE
WAR PARTY
WEEKEND AT BERNIE'S
WOMAN OBSESSED, A
WORTH WINNING
YOUNG NURSES IN LOVE

REVIEW ATTRIBTUION

Listed below are the contribuotrs to the 1990 MOTION PICTURE ANNUAL and the reviews they wrote.

Bertelsen, John
FAST FOOD
FROM HOLLYWOOD TO
   DEADWOOD
GUNRUNNER
LICENSE TO DRIVE
NO SAFE HAVEN
TWICE DEAD
VICE ACADEMY

Besch, Drea
SHE'S OUT OF CONTROL

Blocker, Judith
CRIMINAL LAW
LORDS OF THE DEEP
SLEEPAWAY CAMP III

Brucker, Meredith Babeaux
CURFEW
FEAR
GRANDMOTHER'S HOUSE
SCREWBALL HOTEL
UNDER THE GUN

Buckley, Constance R.
ERNEST SAVES CHRISTMAS
HER ALIBI
KUNG FU MASTER
NO HOLDS BARRED

Charity, Tom
WE THINK THE WORLD OF YOU

Cordes, James
CHECKING OUT
EARTH GIRLS ARE EASY
GLORY
HIGH STAKES
KINJITE
SEA OF LOVE

Cramer, Barbara
ABYSS, THE
BIG PICTURE, THE
DISTANT VOICES, STILL LIVES
DRY WHITE SEASON, A
EDGE OF SANITY
HENRY V
MY LEFT FOOT
QUEEN OF HEARTS
SHE-DEVIL
STAR TREK V: THE FINAL
   FRONTIER
STAYING TOGETHER
TRUST ME

Curran, Daniel
BEAR, THE
CHANCES ARE
CRIMES AND MISDEMEANORS
EDDIE AND THE CRUISERS II:
   EDDIE LIVES!
KARATE KID PART III, THE
LA LECTRICE
LITTLE VERA
REMBRANDT LAUGHING
SCANDAL
TO KILL A PRIEST
TRUE LOVE
WAR PARTY

Digilio, Nick
AFTER MIDNIGHT
AFTER SCHOOL
ALL DOGS GO TO HEAVEN
BEST OF THE BEST, THE
BLACK ROSES
BLOODFIST
BORN ON THE FOURTH OF JULY
CAGE
COHEN AND TATE
CRIMINAL LAW
FAMILY BUSINESS
GATOR BAIT II: CAJUN JUSTICE
HALLOWEEN 5: THE REVENGE OF
   MICHEAL MYERS
HENRY: PORTRAIT OF A SERIAL
   KILLER
I, MADMAN
L.A. BOUNTY
LIMIT UP
LITTLE MERMAID, THE
NATIONAL LAMPOON'S
   CHRISTMAS VACATION
NOWHERE TO RUN
OLD GRINGO
PHANTOM OF THE MALL: ERIC'S
   REVENGE
RELENTLESS
SATURDAY THE 14TH STRIKES
   BACK
SEE NO EVIL, HEAR NO EVIL
SHOCKER
SILENT NIGHT, DEADLY NIGHT 3:
   BETTER WATCH OUT!
TANGO AND CASH
TIME TRACKERS
TOXIC AVENGER PART III, THE:
   THE LAST TEMPTATION OF
   TOXIE
TRUE BLOOD
WIZARD, THE

Epstein, Charles
CASUALTIES OF WAR
COUSINS
HOMEBOY
LEAN ON ME
LISTEN TO ME

LOST ANGELS
LOVERBOY
MIGHTY QUINN, THE
SEX, LIES AND VIDEOTAPE
TRIUMPH OF THE SPIRIT
YAABA

Garcia, Maria
CHAIR, THE
DEADLY POSSESSION
ERIK THE VIKING
LEVIATHAN
LUCKIEST MAN IN THE WORLD,
   THE
MADE IN USA
TEEN WITCH
TORA-SAN GOES TO VIENNA

Gillogly, Kevin
BACK TO THE FUTURE PART II
BUY AND CELL
DREAM TEAM
EXPERTS, THE
FLETCH LIVES
OPTIONS
SEE YOU IN THE MORNING
SOME GIRLS
SPEED ZONE
TWO TO TANGO
YOUNG NURSES IN LOVE

Graham, J. Patrick
ALWAYS
DAD
GROSS ANATOMY
HARLEM NIGHTS
HUNGARIAN FAIRY TALE, A
JOHNNY HANDSOME
STEEL MAGNOLIAS

Hinckley, Tom
BEVERLY HILLS BRATS
BLACK RAIN
BLAZE
BREAKING IN
CRACK HOUSE
CRIME ZONE
C.H.U.D. II: BUD THE C.H.U.D.
DANCE OF THE DAMNED
DANGER ZONE II: REAPER'S
   REVENGE
DARK TOWER
DOIN' TIME ON PLANET EARTH
ENEMIES, A LOVE STORY
FABULOUS BAKER BOYS, THE
FAR FROM HOME
FAT MAN AND LITTLE BOY
FRIENDS, LOVERS AND LUNATICS
GIRL IN THE SWING, THE
GLITCH
HEART OF MIDNIGHT
HEART OF DIXIE
IMMEDIATE FAMILY

IN COUNTRY
INNOCENT MAN, AN
JACKNIFE
K-9
KICKBOXER
L.A. HEAT
LET IT RIDE
LETHAL WEAPON 2
MACHO DANCER
MAPANTSULA
MEET THE HOLLOWHEADS
MINISTRY OF VENGEANCE
MUSIC BOX
MUTANT ON THE BOUNTY
NEW YEAR'S DAY
NIGHT GAME
PACKAGE, THE
PENN & TELLER GET KILLED
PHANTOM OF THE OPERA
PHYSICAL EVIDENCE
RACHEL PAPERS, THE
RAINBOW, THE
ROSE GARDEN, THE
SEVENTH SIGN, THE
SKELETON COAST
STEALING HEAVEN
STORM
STRIPPED TO KILL II: LIVE GIRLS
TALVISOTA
TURNER AND HOOCH
WAR BIRDS
WAR OF THE ROSES
WEEKEND AT BERNIE'S
WELCOME HOME
WE'RE NO ANGELS
WIRED
WHO'S HARRY CRUMB?
UHF
YOUNG EINSTEIN

Hoffman, Christina
RETURN OF SWAMP THING, THE
STREET JUSTICE

Ike, Jane
CYBORG

Johnson, Mark R.
GLEAMING THE CUBE

Jonas, Larry
DEAD POETS SOCIETY
HOW TO GET AHEAD IN
    ADVERTISING

Kerwin, Jeff
SEASON OF FEAR

Krusling, Chuck
CODENAME VENGEANCE
FREEWAY MANIAC
HARDCASE AND FIST
PARENTS

Mueller, Jenny
ADVENTURES OF BARON
    MUNCHAUSEN, THE

BATMAN
DO THE RIGHT THING
SCENES FROM THE CLASS
    STRUGGLE IN BEVERLY HILLS

Mulay, James J.
BILL & TED'S EXCELLENT
    ADVENTURE
'BURBS, THE
CRUSOE
DISORGANIZED CRIME
84 CHARLIE MOPIC
FAREWELL TO THE KING
FLY II, THE
FRIDAY THE 13TH PART
    VIII—JASON TAKES
    MANHATTAN
GHOSTBUSTERS II
GREAT BALLS OF FIRE
HONEY, I SHRUNK THE KIDS
HORROR SHOW, THE
INDIANA JONES AND THE LAST
    CRUSADE
JANUARY MAN, THE
LICENCE TO KILL
LOCK UP
MIRACLE MILE
NIGHTMARE ON ELM STREET 5:
    THE DREAM CHILD, A
PERFECT MODEL, THE
PET SEMATARY
PINK CADILLAC
SIGNS OF LIFE
SLASH DANCE
THREE FUGITIVES
WINTER PEOPLE

Munroe, Dale
BERT RIGBY, YOU'RE A FOOL
BLOODHOUNDS OF BROADWAY
COOKIE
DEAD CALM
DRIVING MISS DAISY
EASY WHEELS
FEW DAYS WITH ME, A
FRIGHT NIGHT—PART 2
HOW I GOT INTO COLLEGE
SHIRLEY VALENTINE
TANGO BAR
TAP
VALENTINO RETURNS

Nabhan, Martin W.
AMERICAN NINJA 3: BLOOD HUNT
RACE FOR GLORY

Nickelberg, Diane L.
B.O.R.N.
DR. ALIEN
NECROMANCER
PIN
SWEET LIES

Noh, David
BIG BLUE, THE
CHASING DREAMS
DEALERS

GROUND ZERO
HEATHERS
IRON TRIANGLE, THE
LITTLE THIEF, THE
MISS FIRECRACKER
NAVIGATOR, THE
RACHEL RIVER
RENEGADES
ROMERO
SHAG
SIDEWALK STORIES
SLAVES OF NEW YORK
VALMONT
WHEN HARRY MET SALLY

Onofri, Adrienne
DR. HACKENSTEIN
DREAM A LITTLE DREAM
LOOK WHO'S TALKING
PARENTHOOD
ROOFTOPS
SKIN DEEP
UNCLE BUCK

Pardi, Robert
APARTMENT ZERO
ALEXA
COMMUNION
CUTTING CLASS
DEATHSTALKER AND THE
    WARRIORS FROM HELL
DOWN TWISTED
ECHOES IN PARADISE
FORBIDDEN SUN
GHETTOBLASTER
GOING UNDERCOVER
GOR
HOWLING 5: THE REBIRTH, THE
LIFE AND NOTHING BUT
MONSIEUR HIRE
MYSTERY TRAIN
NO RETREAT, NO SURRENDER
PRANCER
RABID GRANNIES
STEPFATHER 2: MAKE ROOM FOR
    DADDY
SWEETIE
TOO BEAUTIFUL FOR YOU
UNREMARKABLE LIFE, AN
WICKED STEPMOTHER

Pavia, Mark
GNAW: FOOD OF THE GODS II
NIGHT OF THE DEMONS
976-EVIL
TERROR WITHIN, THE
TOXIC AVENGER, PART II, THE

Satuloff, Bob
BACKFIRE
DEAD BANG
DEEPSTAR SIX

LAST WARRIOR, THE
MILLENIUM
MOB WAR
NEXT OF KIN
OFFERINGS

Schackman, Daniel
SEDUCTION: THE CRUEL WOMAN

Stewart, Linda
ADVENTURES OF MILO AND OTIS,
  THE
CARPENTER, THE
CHEETAH
CHORUS OF DISAPPROVAL, A
FEAR, ANXIETY AND DEPRESSION
FIST FIGHTER
POLICE ACADEMY 6: CITY UNDER
  SIEGE
SAND AND BLOOD
TO DIE FOR
TROOP BEVERLY HILLS

Wallenfeldt, Jeff
FIELD OF DREAMS
FOR QUEEN AND COUNTRY
HIGH HOPES
MAJOR LEAGUE
NEW YORK STORIES
SAY ANYTHING